T0234571

Lecture Notes in Computer Science 8947

Commenced Publication in 1973
Founding and Former Series Editors:
Gerhard Goos, Juris Hartmanis, and Jan van Leeuwen

Editorial Board

More information about this series at http://www.springer.com/series/7407

Bijaya Ketan Panigrahi
Ponnuthurai Nagaratnam Suganthan
Swagatam Das (Eds.)

Swarm, Evolutionary, and Memetic Computing

5th International Conference, SEMCCO 2014
Bhubaneswar, India, December 18–20, 2014
Revised Selected Papers

 Springer

Editors
Bijaya Ketan Panigrahi
Department of Electrical Engineering
IIT
New Delhi
India

Ponnuthurai Nagaratnam Suganthan
School of Electrical and Electronic
    Engineering
Nanyang Technological University
Singapore
Singapore

Swagatam Das
Electronics and Communication Sciences
    Unit
Indian Statistical Institute
Kolkata
India

ISSN 0302-9743   ISSN 1611-3349   (electronic)
Lecture Notes in Computer Science
ISBN 978-3-319-20293-8   ISBN 978-3-319-20294-5   (eBook)
DOI 10.1007/978-3-319-20294-5

Library of Congress Control Number: 2015942555

LNCS Sublibrary: SL1 – Theoretical Computer Science and General Issues

Springer Cham Heidelberg New York Dordrecht London

Printed on acid-free paper

Springer International Publishing AG Switzerland is part of Springer Science+Business Media
(www.springer.com)

Preface

This LNCS volume contains the papers presented at the 5th Swarm, Evolutionary and Memetic Computing Conference (SEMCCO-2014) held during December 18–20, 2014, at the Institute of Technical Education and Research, Siksha 'O' Anusandhan University, Bhubaneswar, Odisha, India. SEMCCO is regarded as one of the most prestigious international conference series that aims at bringing together researchers from academia and industry to report and review the latest progress in cutting-edge research on swarm, evolutionary, memetic computing, and other novel computing techniques such as neural and fuzzy computing, to explore new application areas, to design new bio-inspired algorithms for solving specific hard optimization problems, and finally to create awareness of these domains to a wider audience of practitioners.

SEMCCO-2014 received 250 paper submissions from 18 countries across the globe. After a rigorous peer-review process involving 800 reviews, 96 full-length articles were accepted for oral presentation at the conference. This corresponds to an acceptance rate of 38.4 % and is intended for maintaining the high standards of the conference proceedings. The papers included in this LNCS volume cover a wide range of topics in swarm, evolutionary, memetic, and other intelligent computing algorithms and their real-world applications in problems selected from diverse domains of science and engineering.

The conference featured four distinguished keynote speakers: Prof. Kalyanmoy Deb, Michigan State University, USA; Prof. Bidyut Baran Chaudhuri, Indian Statistical Institute, Kolkata, India; Prof. Yaochu Jin, University of Surrey, UK; and Dr. P.N. Suganthan, NTU, Singapore.

We take this opportunity to thank the authors of all submitted papers for their hard work, adherence to the deadlines, and patience with the review process. The quality of a reviewed volume depends mainly on the expertise and dedication of the reviewers. We are indebted to the Program Committee/Technical Committee members, who not only produced excellent reviews but also did these in the short time frames that they were given.

We would also like to thank our sponsors for providing all the logistic support and financial assistance. First, we are indebted to ITER Management and Administrations (faculty colleagues and administrative personnel of the School of Computer Science, School of Electronics Engineering, and School of Electrical Engineering) for supporting our cause and encouraging us to organize the conference at ITER, SOA University, Bhubaneswar, Odisha, for the second time. In particular, we would like to express our heartfelt thanks to Prof. (Dr.) Manojranjan Nayak, President, Siksha O Anusandhan Trust for providing us with the necessary financial support and infrastructural assistance to hold the conference. Our sincere thanks are due to Prof. R.P. Mohanty, Vice Chancellor, SOA University, Prof. P.K. Sahoo, Dean, ITER, Prof. M.K. Mallick, Director Administration, Prof. P.K. Nanda, Dean, Research, and Prof. P.K. Dash, Director, Research, for their continuous support. We thank Prof. Carlos A. Coello Coello and Prof Nikhil R. Pal, the general chairs, for providing valuable guidelines and inspiration to overcome various difficulties in the process of organizing this conference. We would also like to thank the participants of this conference, who have considered the conference above all hardships. Finally, we would like to thank all the volunteers for their tireless effort in meeting the deadlines and arranging every detail to make sure that the conference could run smoothly. We hope the readers of these proceedings find the papers inspiring and enjoyable.

December 2014

Bijaya Ketan Panigrahi
Ponnuthurai Nagaratnam Suganthan
Swagatam Das

Organization

Chief Patrons

Manojranjan Nayak, India

Patrons

R.P. Mohanty, India

Honorary Chair

P.K. Dash

General Chairs

Nikhil R. Pal, India
Carlos A. Coello Coello, Mexico

General Co-chairs

Swagatam Das, India
B.K. Panigrahi, India

Program Chair

P.K. Nanda, India

Finance Chair

Manas Kumar Mallick, India

Steering Committee Chair

P.N. Suganthan, Singapore

Publicity Chairs

S.S. Dash, India
S.C. Satpathy, India
N.C. Sahoo, Malaysia

Special Session Chairs

Sanjoy Das, USA
Zhihua Cui, China
Samuelson Hong, Taiwan

Tutorial Chair

G. Panda, India

Organizing Secretariat

Debahuti Mishra
A.K. Jagadev, India

International Advisory Committee/Technical Review Committee

Almoataz Youssef Abdelaziz, Egypt
Athanasios V. Vasilakos, Athens
Alex K. Qin, France
Amit Konar, India
Anupam Shukla, India
Ashish Anand, India
Boyang Qu, China
Carlos A. Coello Coello, Mexico
Chilukuri K. Mohan, USA
Delin Luo, China
Dipankar Dasgupta, USA
D.K. Chaturvedi, India
Dipti Srinivasan, Singapore
Fatih M. Tasgetiren, Turkey
Ferrante Neri, Finland
Frank Neumann, Australia
Fayzur Rahman, Portugal,
G.K. Venayagamoorthy, USA
Gerardo Beni, USA
Hai Bin Duan, China
Heitor Silvério Lopes, Brazil
Halina Kwasnicka, Poland
Hong Yan, Hong Kong
Javier Del Ser, Spain
Jane J. Liang, China
Janez Brest, Slovenia
Jeng-Shyang Pan, Taiwan

Juan Luis Fernández Martínez, Spain
Jeng-Shyang Pan, Taiwan
Kalyanmoy Deb, India
K. Parsopoulos, Greece
Kay Chen Tan, Singapore
Ke Tang, China
K. Shanti Swarup, India
Lakhmi Jain, Australia
Leandro Dos Santos Coelho, Brazil
Ling Wang, China
Lingfeng Wang, China
M.A. Abido, Saudi Arabia
M.K. Tiwari, India
Maurice Clerc, France
Meng Joo Er, Singapore
Meng-Hiot Lim, Singapore
M.F. Tasgetiren, Turkey
Namrata Khemka, USA
N. Puhan, India
Oscar Castillo, Mexcico
Pei-Chann Chang, Taiwan
Peng Shi, UK
Qingfu Zhang, UK
Quanke Pan, China
Rafael Stubs Parpinelli, Brazil
Rammohan Mallipeddi, Singapore
Roderich Gross, England

Ruhul Sarker, Australia
Richa Sing, India
Robert Kozma, USA
Suresh Sundaram, Singapore
S. Baskar, India
S.K. Udgata. India
S.S. Dash, India
S.S. Pattanaik, India
S.G. Ponnambalam, Malaysia
Saeid Nahavandi, Australia

Saman Halgamuge, Australia
Shizheng Zhao, Singapore
Sachidananda Dehuri, Korea
Samuelson W. Hong, Taiwan
Vincenzo Piuri, Italy
X.Z. Gao, Finland
Yew Soon Ong, Singapore
Ying Tan, China
Yucheng Dong, China

Organizing Committee

Niva Das
Guru Prasad Mishra
Renu Sharma
Bibhu Prasad Mohanty
Badri Narayan Sahoo
Kabri Das
Biswa Mohan Acharya
Priyabrata Pattnaik
Sharmista Kar
Tapas Kumar Mohapatra

Sajia Hassan
Anuja Nanda
Sandeep Kumar Satapathy
Ambika Prasad Mishra
Manas Kumar Nanda
Sikha Mishra
Nibedan Panda
Shruti Mishra
Soumendra Mohanty

Contents

Differential Evolution with Two Subpopulations

Nandar Lynn[1], Rammohan Mallipeddi[2],
and Ponnuthurai Nagaratnam Suganthan[1(✉)]

[1] School of Electrical and Electronics Engineering, Nanyang Technological
University, Singapore, Singapore
{nandar001, epnsugan}@ntu.edu.sg
[2] School of Electronics Engineering, Kyungpook National University,
Daegu, South Korea
mallipeddi.ram@gmail.com

Abstract. In this paper, differential evolution with two subpopulations is proposed for balancing exploration and exploitation capabilities. The first population is responsible for exploring over the search space to find good regions using only its own subpopulation. The second subpopulation is responsible for exploiting good regions. The exploitation-oriented sub-population is permitted to make use of the whole population to select best solution candidates to generate offspring. Hence, this heterogeneous one-way information transfer allows the exploration subpopulation to maintain diversity even when exploitation group converges. This is an efficient realization of population based algorithm enabling simultaneous use of highly exploitative and explorative characteristics simultaneously. Hence, this approach can be an effective substitute for memetic algorithms in the real-parameter optimization domain. The performance of the algorithm is evaluated using the shifted and rotated benchmark problems. To verify the performance of the proposed algorithm, it is also applied to solve the unit commitment problem by considering 10 and 20 unit power systems over 24 h scheduling period.

Keywords: Differential evolution · Subpopulations · Exploration · Exploitation · Memetic algorithms · Power systems · Unit commitment problem · Scheduling

1 Introduction

Differential Evolution (DE) is a population–based optimization algorithm, proposed by Storn and Price [1, 2]. The DE algorithm is one of the popular evolutionary algorithms due to its simplicity and efficiency. It had been used to solve numerical optimization problems [3–5] and real-world applications from different fields [6–9] and showed remarkable performance.

In standard DE algorithm, there are three main evolutionary operations (mutation, crossover and selection operations) and they are employed in each generation to search the optimum over the problem search space. The objective function to be minimized can be expressed as:

© Springer International Publishing Switzerland 2015
B.K. Panigrahi et al. (Eds.): SEMCCO 2014, LNCS 8947, pp. 1–13, 2015.
DOI: 10.1007/978-3-319-20294-5_1

$$\min f(x), x = [x_1, x_2, \ldots, x_D]$$
$$x \in (X_{min}, X_{max}) \tag{1}$$

where, D is the dimensionality of the search space and X_{min} and X_{max} are the upper and lower bounds of the search space. Similar to other population-based evolutionary algorithms, the DE algorithm starts the search with a set of initial population $\{X_i = (x_i^1, x_i^2, \ldots, x_i^D), i = 1,2, \ldots, NP\}$, where, NP is the population size. In generation $g = 0$, the individuals are randomly generated from uniform distribution and initialized within the search space as follows:

$$x_i^j = x_{min}^j + rand_i^j(0, 1) * \left(x_{max}^j - x_{min}^j\right) \tag{2}$$

where, $rand_i^j(0, 1)$ is a uniformly distributed random number in the range of $(0, 1)$ and is instantiated independently for each jth dimension of the ith individual member. x_{max}^j and x_{min}^j are the lower and upper bounds on each jth dimension. After initialization, DE performs the evolutionary process which includes mutation, crossover and selection operations.

Mutation: Mutation operation is applied to each individual target vector $X_{i,g}$ in each generation g to create its corresponding mutant vector $V_{i,g}$. There are different mutation strategies and the notation "*DE/a/b*" is used to distinguish the DE mutation strategies, where "*a*" represents the vector to be mutated and "*b*" is the number of difference vectors used. The most frequently used five mutation strategies are:

(1) "DE/rand/1"

$$V_{i,g} = X_{r1,g} + F * \left(X_{r2,g} - X_{r3,g}\right) \tag{3}$$

(2) "DE/best/1"

$$V_{i,g} = X_{best,g} + F * \left(X_{r1,g} - X_{r2,g}\right) \tag{4}$$

(3) "DE/current-to-best/1"

$$V_{i,g} = X_{i,g} + F * \left(X_{best,g} - X_{i,g}\right) + F * \left(X_{r2,g} - X_{r3,g}\right) \tag{5}$$

(4) "DE/best/2"

$$V_{i,g} = X_{best,g} + F * \left(X_{r1,g} - X_{r2,g}\right) + F * \left(X_{r3,g} - X_{r4,g}\right) \tag{6}$$

(5) "DE/rand/2"

$$V_{i,g} = X_{r1,g} + F * \left(X_{r2,g} - X_{r3,g}\right) + F * \left(X_{r4,g} - X_{r5,g}\right) \tag{7}$$

where, the indices r_1, r_2, r_3, r_4 and r_5 are distinct integers randomly selected from the population $\{1, 2, \ldots, NP\}$ excluding the index i. $X_{best,g}$ is the best individual of the current population. F is the mutation scale factor that amplifies the difference vector.

Crossover: After mutation operation, DE performs crossover operation in which some components of mutant vector $V_{i,g}$ are exchanged with target vector $X_{i,g}$ to generate the trial vector $U_{i,g}$ and enhances population diversity. There are two kinds of crossover operators in DE, exponential (or two point modulo) and binomial (or uniform). In exponential crossover operator, the integer n and L are randomly selected from the numbers [1, D]. The first integer n acts as starting point where the target vector is exchanged components with mutant vector. L represents the numbers of components that mutant vector contributes to target vector to obtain trail vector. With the exponential crossover operator, trial vector $U_{i,g}$ is generated as below:

$$u_{i,g}^{j} = \begin{cases} v_{i,g}^{j}, for\, j = \langle n \rangle_D, \langle n \rangle_{D+1}, \ldots, \langle n+L-1 \rangle_D \\ x_{i,g}^{j}\, for\, all\, other\, j \in [1,D] \end{cases} \tag{8}$$

where, the angular brackets $\langle \rangle_d$ denotes a modulo function with modulus D. C_r is a control parameter and called the crossover rate. Probability $(L = v) = (C_r)\, v - 1$ for any positive integer v lying in the interval $[1, D]$. With the binomial crossover operator, trail vector $U_{i,g}$ is created as below:

$$u_{i,g}^{j} = \begin{cases} v_{i,g}^{j}\, if\, rand_i^{j}(0,1) \le C_r or\, j = j_{rand} \\ x_{i,g}^{j}\, other\, wise \end{cases} \tag{9}$$

where, $rand_i^{j}(0,1) \in [0,1]$ is a uniformly distributed random number generated for each jth dimension of the ith vector. The crossover rate C_r is in the range of [0, 1]. j_{rand} is a randomly chosen index and belong to (1,2, ..., D). j_{rand} ensures that $U_{i,g}$ gets at least one component from $V_{i,g}$. If trail vector $U_{i,g}$ is beyond the search space boundary, it will be reinitialized within the range of lower and upper boundary $[X_{min}, X_{max}]$.

Selection: selection operation determines whether the target $X_{i,g}$ or the trial $U_{i,g}$ vector enters to the next generation, $g = g + 1$. For minimization problem, the selected vector is given by:

$$X_{i,g+1} = \begin{cases} U_{i,g}\, if\, f(U_{i,g}) \le f(X_{i,g}) \\ X_{i,g}\, if\, f(U_{i,g}) > f(X_{i,g}) \end{cases} \tag{10}$$

where, $f(X)$ is the objective function to be minimized. Between trail and target vector, the vector with the better fitness will survive to the next generation as shown in (10).

When employing evolutionary algorithms such as DE algorithm for finding the global optimum, the issue is to balance the exploration and the exploitation capabilities of the algorithm and to obtain the trade-off between them. The excessive exploration can find the global optima with high probability. However it slows down the convergence of the algorithm. Excessive exploitation can lead the solution to a local optimum. In order to balance the exploration and exploitation capabilities of DE algorithm, many researchers had been proposed various mutation strategies and different control parameter settings of scaling factor F, crossover rate C_r and population size.

Besides the most frequently used mutation strategies mentioned above, Price proposed DE/current-to-rand/1 mutation strategy in which binomial crossover operator is replaced with the rotationally invariant arithmetic recombination operator [10]. With the main objective of balancing exploring and exploiting capabilities of DE, Das proposed a hybrid mutation scheme that combines explorative (local neighborhood mutation) and exploitative (global neighborhood mutation) mutation operators [11]. Both neighborhood mutation operators use the "current-to-best/1" strategy. In local neighborhood mutation, the best solution is selected from the small neighborhood for mutating the target vector. In global neighborhood mutation, it is selected from the entire population. Later the two local and global neighborhood mutation operators are combined with a weight factor.

Using the information of multiple good solutions, the greedy mutation strategy DE/current- to-$p$best/1 is introduced in JADE [12]. Rather than using the best solution from the entire population, the $p$best is selected from the top $p\%$ solutions of the whole population and the control parameters for the individual are adjusted based on their previous success experience. Islam also proposed a variant of DE/current-to-best/1 [13]. For mutation operation in [13], the best solution is chosen from a group formed by the randomly selected number and its group size is $q\%$ of the whole population size. In Gaussian bare-bones DE (GBDE) [14], a Gaussian mutation strategy is proposed where Gaussian sampling method is used to mutate each individual target vector. Modified GBDE is also presented in [14] by hybridizing GBDE with DE/best/1 to speed up the convergence rate of GBDE.

For parameter control in DE, Liu and Lampinen proposed a fuzzy logic controller to adapt the control parameters for mutation and crossover operations [15]. Self-adaptive control parameters of F and C_r are introduced in jDE [16]. In each generation, new F_i and C_{ri} for each individual member are randomly generated. In [17], Qin and Suganthan presented a self-adaptive DE (SaDE) where mutation strategies and their associated control parameters are selected adaptively by learning from their previous experience. Wang proposed *composite* DE (CoDE) with three mutation strategies and three control parameter settings of F and C_r [18]. In each generation, three mutation strategies are randomly combined with the control parameter settings to generate the trial vector for each target vector. In [19], Mallipeddi and Suganthan proposed an ensemble of mutation strategies and control parameters with DE (EPSDE). In EPSDE, a pool of mutation strategies along with a pool of F and C_r values competes to obtain the successful offspring vector. In [20], a new mutation strategy DE/*lbest*/1 with two-level control parameter adaption scheme is proposed in which the population is divided into a predefined number of non over lapping group and multiple locally best solutions are selected to guide its respective groups.

In this paper, we propose DE algorithm with two subpopulations in order to obtain the balance between exploration and exploitation capabilities of DE algorithm. The proposed DE algorithm is described in detail in Sect. 2 and its numerical experiment results are presented in Sect. 3. The proposed DE algorithm is applied to unit commitment problem and its experiment results are shown in Sect. 4. Finally, the paper is concluded in Sect. 5.

2   DE with Two Subpopulations

In this section, DE algorithm with two subpopulations is proposed. The population is divided into two subpopulation groups. The two subpopulation group sizes are kept unchanged throughout the evolution process. The first subpopulation is responsible for exploration. The following mutation strategies are used for mutating subpopulation group1 members:

(1) "DE/current-to-rand/1"

$$V_{i,g} = X_{i,g} + rand * (X_{r1,g} - X_{i,g}) + F * (X_{r2,g} - X_{r3,g}) \qquad (11)$$

(2) "DE/rand/2"

$$V_{i,g} = X_{r1,g} + F * (X_{r2,g} - X_{r3,g}) + F * (X_{r4,g} - X_{r5,g}) \qquad (12)$$

For the first subpopulation exploration group, a two difference vector strategy, DE/rand/2 mutation strategy [1] and DE/current-to-rand/ mutation strategy [10] are proposed and randomly selected from uniform distribution to generate the mutant vector for each target vector. The DE/rand/2 has good exploration ability due to its Gaussian-like perturbation and DE/current-to-rand/1 is a rotation invariant operator and has the ability to solve the rotated problems more effectively than other mutation strategies. For (11) and (12), the scaling factor $F = 0.8$ and crossover rate $C_r = 0.9$ are used to encourage strong exploration ability as recommended in [10, 16], respectively. The exploration population is responsible for exploring over the search space to find good regions using only its own subpopulation.

The second subpopulation group is responsible for exploitation. Among mutation strategies, DE/current-to-best/1 mutation strategy [2] has strong exploitation ability. However, by following only the best solution X_{best} from the entire population for generating the mutant vector, the population may lose exploration ability within the small number of generations and premature convergence can be occurred. Thus, in this paper, the following JADE mutation strategy (DE/current-to-$p$best with archive) [12] is proposed for the second subpopulation exploitation group:

$$V_{i,g} = X_{i,g} + F_i * (X_{pbest,g} - X_{i,g}) + F_i * (X_{r1,g} - \tilde{X}_{r2,g}) \qquad (13)$$

where, $X_{i,g}$, $X_{r1,g}$ and $X_{pbest,g}$ are selected from the current population. $X_{pbest,g}$ is randomly selected as one of the top 100 $p\%$ individuals in both subpopulation with p in the range of (0,1). $\tilde{X}_{r2,g}$ is randomly chosen from the union $(P \cup A)$ of the current combined population P and the archive A (a set of archived inferior solutions). By using X_{pbest} rather than X_{best}, the population diversity can be maintained while avoiding getting trapped into local optimum. The control parameters F_i and $C_{r,i}$ are generated for each individual X_i using the adaptive parameter control scheme as used in JADE [12]. The exploitation-oriented sub-population is permitted to make use of the whole population to select best solution candidates to generate offspring.

For (11) and (13), the exponential crossover operator is used to generate the trail/offspring vector $U_{i,g}$. For (12), the trail vector $U_{i,g}$ is created using the following arithmetic crossover operator [18]:

$$U_{i,g} = X_{i,g} + rand * \left(V_{i,g} - X_{i,g} \right) \qquad (14)$$

As described above, in the proposed DE algorithm, exploration is performed by the first subpopulation group using (11) and (12) and exploitation is done by the second subpopulation group using (13). By using two subpopulations to perform exploration and exploitation, the exploration group can prevent from occurring premature convergence and maintain population diversity while the exploitation group is fine-tuning and converging to the global optimum. Hence, this heterogeneous one-way information transfer allows the exploration subpopulation to maintain diversity even when exploitation group converges. This is an efficient realization of population based algorithm enabling simultaneous use of highly exploitative and explorative characteristics simultaneously. Hence, it can be an effective substitute for memetic algorithms [22] in the real-parameter optimization domain as a trade-off between exploration and exploitation is obtained within the proposed single DE algorithm framework without hybridization and without using a separate local search algorithm. The performance of the proposed algorithm is evaluated on the shifted and rotated problems and compared with recent state-of-art DE algorithm in the next section.

3 Numerical Experiment and Results

The first 14 functions from CEC 2005 special session in real parameter optimization [21] are used as test functions in this paper and the proposed DE algorithm is compared with recent state-of-art DE algorithms. Before comparing with other DE algorithms, firstly the proposed algorithm is tuned with different subpopulation group sizes. In this paper, g_1 is referred to as the first subpopulation exploration group size and g_2 is referred to as the second subpopulation exploitation group size. The experiment is conducted for population size 30 and run times 25 for each problem. The number of function evaluation (FES) is set at 300,000 for each run.

The subpopulation group size is tuned for different number of combinations of g_1 and g_2 sizes. The best results obtained from different combinations are highlighted in bold and the second best results are highlighted in line in Table 1. As described in Table 1, the combination of $g_1 = 5$ and $g_2 = 25$ provides best results for most problems. However, this combination fails to offer best results for function F_4 and F_6 and other combinations performs better on those two problems. On the other hand, the proposed algorithm with the combination of $g_1 = 10$ and $g_2 = 20$ performs second best on most of test problems and offers satisfactory and consistent performance throughout all 14 problems. Thus, the combination of $g_1 = 10$ and $g_2 = 20$ is selected for further performance evaluation of the proposed DE algorithm.

In this paper, the performance of the proposed DE algorithm is compared with other state-of-art DE algorithms such as JADE [12], CoDE [18] and SaDE [17] in terms of mean error value and standard deviation. The parameter setting of F and C_r for JADE,

Table 1. Calibration of subpopulation group size

F	$g_1 = 5,$ $g_2 = 25$	$g_1 = 10,$ $g_2 = 20$	$g_1 = 15,$ $g_2 = 15$	$g_1 = 20,$ $g_2 = 10$	$g_1 = 25,$ $g_2 = 5$
	Error means $(F(x) - F(x^*))$				
F_1	0	0	0	0	0
F_2	**7.97E-28**	3.36E-27	1.76E-12	3.38E-16	1.53E-09
F_3	**6.86E+03**	2.01E±04	3.66E+04	1.02E+05	1.82E+05
F_4	11.24	4.57E-03	**9.85E-05**	4.32E-04	1.23E-03
F_5	4.93E+02	4.75E±02	5.77E+02	5.44E+02	**4.58E+02**
F_6	3.91	2.96	1.12	**0.48**	**0.48**
F_7	1.73E-02	1.63E-02	1.71E-02	1.53E-02	**1.35E-02**
F_8	2.09E+01	2.09E+01	2.09E+01	2.09E+01	2.09E+01
F_9	0	0	0	0	0
F_{10}	**3.87E+01**	4.05E±01	4.38E+01	4.29E+01	4.34E+01
F_{11}	**2.67E+01**	2.75E+01	2.72E+01	2.69E±01	2.72E+01
F_{12}	7.49E+03	**6.77E+03**	8.49E+03	6.94E+03	1.17E+04
F_{13}	**1.27**	1.30	1.35	1.57	1.65
F_{14}	1.25E+01	**1.23E+01**	1.24E+01	**1.23E+01**	1.25E+01

CoDE and SaDE are used as same as in their original papers. All experiments are run with population size 30, FES 300000 and 30 trials. The experimental results are in Table 2 and the best experimental results are highlighted in bold.

Table 2. Comparison of JADE, CoDE, SaDE and proposed DE algorithm

Function type	F	JADE	CoDE	SaDE	$g_1 = 10, g_2 = 20$
		Error means $(F(x) - F(x^*))$ ± standard deviation			
Uni-modal test functions	F_1	0	0	0	0
		0	0	0	0
	F_2	**2.39E-27** ± 1.96E-27	1.69E-15 ± 3.95E-15	8.26E-06 ± 1.65E-05	3.36E-27 ± 2.03E-27
	F_3	**8.00E+03** ± 7.94E +03	1.05E+05 ± 6.25E +04	4.27E+05 ± 2.08E +05	2.01E+04 ± 1.49E +04
	F_4	3.29 ± 9.66	5.81E-03 ± 1.38E-02	1.77E+02 ± 2.67E +02	**4.57E-03** ± 2.26E-02
	F_5	**2.96E+02** ± 2.90E +02	3.31E+02 ± 3.44E +02	3.25E+03 ± 5.90E +02	4.75E+02 ± 2.93E +02
Multi-modal test functions	F_6	1.27E+01 ± 2.89E +01	**1.60E-01** ± 7.85E-01	5.31E+01 ± 3.25E +01	2.96 ± 6.03
	F_7	**1.56E-02** ± 1.37E-02	7.64E-03 ± 8.55E-03	1.57E-02 ± 1.38E-02	1.63E-02 ± 1.13E-02
	F_8	2.09E+01 ± 6.49E-02	2.01E+01 ± 1.41E-01	2.09E +01 ± 4.95E-02	2.09E+01 ± 1.63E-01
	F_9	**0**	**0**	0.24	**0**
		0	0	±0.43	0
	F_{10}	4.28E+01 ± 1.07E +01	4.15E+01 ± 1.16E +01	4.72E+01 ± 1.01E +01	**4.05E+01** ± 1.05E +01
	F_{11}	2.68E+01 ± 2.19	**1.18E+01** ± 3.40	1.65E+01 ± 2.42	2.75E+01 ± 1.76
	F_{12}	6.97E+03 ± 8.37E +03	3.05E+03 ± 3.80E +03	**3.02E+03** ± 2.33E +03	6.77E+03 ± 6.66E +03
	F_{13}	**1.22** ± 1.52E-01	1.57 ± 3.27E-01	3.94 ± 2.81E-01	1.30 ± 1.57E-01
	F_{14}	1.25E+01 ± 3.10E-01	**1.23E** **+01** ± 4.81E-01	1.26E **+01** ± 2.83E-01	**1.23E** **+01** ± 3.47E-01

Compared to JADE algorithm, the proposed DE algorithm outperforms on the functions F_4, F_6, F_{10}, F_{12} and F_{14} and performs approximately equal on the functions F_1, F_8, and F_9. JADE outperforms the proposed algorithm for the rest functions F_2, F_3, F_5, F_7, F_{11} and F_{13}. Compared to CoDE algorithm, the proposed DE performs better on the functions F_2, F_3, F_4, F_{10} and F_{13} and approximately equal on the functions F_1, F_8, F_9 and F_{14}. For the rest functions, CoDE provides better performance.

Compared to SaDE algorithm, the proposed DE provides better performance on 9 out of 14 functions; F_2 to F_6, F_9, F_{10}, F_{13} and F_{14}. The two algorithms perform approximately equal on function F_1 and F_8. SaDE outperforms the proposed algorithm on function F_7, F_{11} and F_{12}. For overall performance, the proposed DE algorithm outperforms CoDE and SaDE on unimodal functions and performs well consistently on multimodal functions.

4   Unit Commitment Problem

Unit commitment problem (UCP) is a constrained optimization problem for determining optimal schedule of power generating units over a scheduling period while meeting the system demand and reserve requirement at the minimum operating cost. The problem is subject to equipment and environmental constraints. UCP includes two sub-optimization problems: to determine on/off or 0/1 schedule of power generating units over a given period of time and optimal output power amounts to be produced by those committed units at the minimum cost. The first problem is known as unit scheduling problem and the latter is called economic dispatch (ED) problem.

4.1   Problem Formulation

The UC problem can be formulated mathematically as production cost minimization problem, subject to system and unit constraints as follows [5]:

Objective: Minimize Production Cost (*PC*)

$$PC = \sum_{i=1}^{N} \sum_{t=1}^{T} [F_i(P(i,t)) + ST(i,t)(1 - I(i,t-1)]I(i,t) \qquad (15)$$

where, N = number of generators, T = number of time steps in scheduling period, $P(i,t)$ = generation of unit i at time t, $I(i,t)$ is on/off status of unit i at time t (on = 1 and off = 0). $F(P(i,t))$ is fuel cost of unit I at time t which is a function of output power generation of a unit with operating cost coefficients of unit i, $a(i)$, $b(i)$ and $c(i)$ as:

$$F(P(i,t)) = a(i) + b(i)P(i,t) + c(i)P(i,t)^2 \qquad (16)$$

$ST(i,t)$ is start up cost of unit i at time t. The start up cost depends on minimum down time $T_{down}(i)$, cold start-up time $T_{cold}(i)$ and the time the unit has been off before start up $T_{off}(i,t)$ of each unit i.

$$ST(i,t) = \begin{cases} ST_h(i) \text{ if } T_{off}(i,t) \leq T_{down}(i) + T_{cold}(i) \\ ST_c(i) \text{ if } T_{off}(i,t) > T_{down}(i) + T_{cold}(i) \end{cases} \tag{17}$$

where, $ST_h(i)$ and $ST_c(i)$ are hot and cold start up cost of unit i respectively. Subject to the following system and unit constraints:

System Constraints

1. System power balance: Generated power from the committed units must be balanced with the system power load demand $P_{LD}(t)$ at time t.

$$\sum_{i=1}^{N} I(i,t)P(i,t) = P_{LD}(t) \tag{18}$$

2. System spinning reserve requirement: To prevent load interruption from certain equipment outages, spinning reserve requirement $P_{RS}(t)$ are required in the operation of a power system. The reserve is usually considered to be 5 or 10 % of the forecasted load demand.

$$\sum_{i=1}^{N} I(i,t)P_{\max}(i) \geq P_{LD}(t) + P_{RS}(t) \tag{19}$$

Unit Constraints

3. Generation power limits: Generation power of each unit is limited by the minimum $P_{min}(i, t)$ and maximum $P_{max}(i, t)$ power values as follows:

$$P_{min}(i,t) \leq P(i,t) \leq P_{max}(i,t) \tag{20}$$

4. Unit minimum up T_{up} and down T_{down} time: Each unit must be on/off for a certain number of hours before it can be shut down/brought online.

$$T_{on}(i,t) \geq T_{up}(i,t) \tag{21}$$

$$T_{off}(i,t) \geq T_{down}(i,t) \tag{22}$$

5. Unit initial status: The initial status at the start of the scheduling period must be taken into account into optimization.

4.2 Experiment Results of 10 and 20 Unit Power Systems

In this paper, 10 and 20 unit power systems of unit commitment problems are considered to evaluate the performance of the proposed DE algorithm. The priority method based on maximum power generation of each unit is used to solve the first unit scheduling problem. The unit with highest maximum power generation will have highest priority to commit and for units of equal maximum power generation, the one with lower heat rate (average fuel piece rate per output power generation) will have higher priority. The heat rate is formulated as follows:

$$hr = \frac{F_i(P_i(t))}{P_i(t)} \qquad (23)$$

The data specifications of 10 unit system are given in Table 3 with load demand over 24 h scheduling period in Table 4. For 20 unit power system, 10 unit system and load demand are doubled. The minimum production cost obtained by the proposed DE algorithm is compared with simple DE algorithm. For both algorithms, population size 30 is used for 10 unit power system and population size 50 is used for 20 unit power system. Both algorithms run for 30 trails to achieve minimum production cost. The minimum production costs of simple DE and proposed DE algorithm are in Table 5. The proposed DE algorithm outperforms DE algorithm on both case studies.

Table 3. Data specifications of 10 unit power systems

	Unit 1	Unit 2	Unit 3	Unit 4	Unit 5
P_{max}	455	455	130	130	162
P_{min}	150	150	20	20	25
a	1000	970	700	680	450
b	16.19	17.26	16.60	16.50	19.70
c	0.00048	0.00031	0.002	0.00211	0.00398
T_{up}	8	8	5	5	6
T_{down}	8	8	5	5	6
ST_h	4500	5000	550	560	900
ST_c	9000	10000	1100	1120	1800
CSH	5	5	4	4	4
Initial status	8	8	−5	−5	−6
	Unit 6	Unit 7	Unit 8	Unit 9	Unit 10
P_{max}	80	85	55	55	55
P_{min}	20	25	10	10	10
a	370	480	660	665	670
b	22.26	27.74	25.92	27.27	27.79
c	0.00712	0.00079	0.00413	0.00222	0.00173
T_{up}	3	3	1	1	1
T_{down}	3	3	1	1	1
ST_h	170	260	30	30	30
ST_c	340	520	60	60	60
CSH	2	2	0	0	0
Initial status	−3	−3	−1	−1	−1

Table 4. Load demand

Hr	Demand	Hr	Demand	Hr	Demand
1	700	9	1300	17	1000
2	750	10	1400	18	1100
3	850	11	1450	19	1200
4	950	12	1500	20	1400
5	1000	13	1400	21	1300
6	1100	14	1300	22	1100
7	1150	15	1200	23	900
8	1200	16	1050	24	800

Table 5. Comparison of minimum production cost

	Proposed DE	DE
10 unit system	5.16E+05	5.20E+05
20 unit system	1.11E+06	1.12E+06

5   Conclusion

In this paper, we present DE with two subpopulations for balancing exploration and exploitation capabilities of DE algorithm. Instead of using one population, the proposed DE algorithm uses two subpopulation groups to explore over the problem search space and to fine-tune the good region and converge to the global optimum. In order to prevent loss of population diversity, the information from exploitation group is not shared with the exploration group. Thus, the population diversity is maintained throughout the evolutionary process and the population may avoid getting trapped into a local optimum. This is an efficient realization of population based algorithm enabling simultaneous use of highly exploitative and explorative characteristics simultaneously. Hence, this approach can be an effective single search method-based substitute for hybridized memetic algorithms in the real-parameter optimization domain. Perfor-mance evaluation of the proposed DE algorithm is conducted using CEC 2005 special session real parameter optimization problems and unit commitment problem. The experiment results showed that the proposed DE algorithm performs well on shifted and rotated unimodal and multimodal problems and also on 10 and 20 unit power systems of unit commitment problem.

Acknowledgement. The authors are pleased to acknowledge the Cambridge Centre for Carbon Reduction in Chemical Technology (C4T) project for financial support.

References

1. Storn, R., Price, K.: Differential evolution: a simple and efficient heuristic for global optimization over continuous spaces. J. Glob. Optim. **11**(4), 341–359 (1997)
2. Storn, R., Price, K.V., Lampinen, J.: Differential Evolution–A Practical Approach to Global Optimization. Springer, Berlin (2005)
3. Das, S., Suganthan, P.N.: Differential evolution: a survey of the state-of-the-art. IEEE Trans. Evol. Comput. **15**(1), 4–31 (2011)
4. Wang, Y., Cai, Z.X.: Combining multi-objective optimization with differential evolution to solve constrained optimization problems. IEEE Trans. Evol. Comput. **16**(1), 117–134 (2012)
5. Halder, U., Das, S., Maity, D.: A cluster-based differential evolution algorithm with external archive for optimization in dynamic environments. IEEE Trans. Syst. Man Cybern. **43**(3), 881–897 (2013)
6. Rogalsky, T., Derksen, R.W., Kocabiyik, S.: Differential evolution in aerodynamic optimization. In: Proceedings of 46th Conference of Canadian Aeronautics and Space Institute, pp. 29–36 (1999)
7. Joshi, R., Sanderson, A.C.: Minimal representation multi-sensor fusion using differential evolution. IEEE Trans. Syst. Man Cybern. Part – A **29**(1), 63–76 (1999)
8. Das, S., Konar, A.: Design of two dimensional IIR filters with modern search heuristics: a comparative study. Int. J. Comput. Intell. Appl. **6**(3), 329–355 (2006)
9. Sengupta, S., Das, S., Nasir, M., Vasilakos, A.V., Pedrycz, W.: An evolutionary multi-objective sleep scheduling scheme for differentiated coverage in wireless sensor networks. IEEE Trans. Syst. Man Cybern. Part – C **42**(6), 1093–1102 (2012)
10. Price, K.V.: An introduction to differential evolution. In: Corne, D., Dorigo, M., Glover, V. (eds.) New Ideas in Optimization, pp. 79–108. McGraw-Hill, London (1999)
11. Das, S., Abraham, A., Chakraborty, U.K., Konar, A.: Differential evolution using a neighborhood-based mutation operator. IEEE Trans. Syst. Man Cybern. **13**(3), 526–553 (2009)
12. Zhang, J.Q., Sanderson, A.C.: JADE: adaptive differential evolution with optional external archive. IEEE Trans. Evol. Comput. **13**(5), 945–958 (2009)
13. Islam, S.M., Das, S., Ghosh, S., Roy, S., Suganthan, P.N.: An adaptive differential evolution algorithm with novel mutation and crossover strategies for global numerical optimization. IEEE Trans. Syst. Man Cybern. Part – B **42**(2), 397–413 (2012)
14. Wang, H., Rahnamayan, S., Sun, H., Omran, M.G.H.: Gaussian bare-bones differential evolution. IEEE Trans. Cybern. **43**(2), 634–647 (2013)
15. Liu, J., Lampinen, J.: A fuzzy adaptive differential evolution algorithm, soft computing – a fusion found. Methodol. Appl. **9**(6), 448–462 (2005)
16. Brest, J., Greiner, S., Bošković, B., Mernik, M., Žumer, V.: Self adapting control parameters in differential evolution: a comparative study on numerical benchmark problems. IEEE Trans. Evol. Comput. **10**(6), 646–657 (2006)
17. Qin, A.K., Huang, V.L., Suganthan, P.N.: Differential evolution algorithm with strategy adaptation for global numerical optimization. IEEE Trans. Evol. Comput. **13**(2), 398–417 (2009)
18. Wang, Y., Cai, Z.X., Zhang, Q.F.: Differential evolution with composite trial vector generation strategies and control parameters. IEEE Trans. Evol. Comput. **15**(1), 55–66 (2011)
19. Mallipeddi, R., Mallipeddi, S., Suganthan, P.N., Tasgetiren, M.F.: Differential evolution algorithm with ensemble of parameters and mutation strategies. Appl. Soft Comput. **11**, 1679–1696 (2011)

20. Yu, W.-J., Shen, M., Chen, W.-N., Zhan, Z.-H., Gong, Y.-J., Lin, Y., Lin, O., Zhang, J.: Differential evolution with two-level parameter adaptation. IEEE Trans. Cybern. **44**(7), 1080–1099 (2014)
21. Suganthan, P.N., Hansen, N., Liang, J.J., Deb, K., Chen, Y.-P., Auger, A., Tiwari, S.: Problem definitions and evaluation criteria for the CEC 2005 special session on real-parameter optimization. Technical report, pp. 1–50 (2005)
22. Neri, F.: Memetic algorithms and memetic computing optimization: a literature review. Swarm Evol. Comput. **2**, 1–12 (2012)

Intelligent Water Drops Algorithm
for Multimodal Spaces

Harish Y., Venkateshwarlu B.$^{(\boxtimes)}$, Chakravarthi Jada,
Kranthi Kumar Rachavarapu, and Irfan Feroz Gramoni Mohammed

Rajiv Gandhi University of Knowledge Technologies, Basara 504107, India
{yharish.586,boddupally.venkatesh,chakravarthij,
rkkr.2100,irfan2497}@gmail.com

Abstract. This paper presents a new nature inspired Intelligent Water
Drops (IWD) based algorithm for finding peaks in continuous multimodal optimization problems. Initially various conceptual similarities
were identified between IWD algorithm and Genetic Algorithm(GA).
Simultaneously applying IWD-Continuous Optimization(IWD-CO) algorithm and GA on a function in finding the global optima and found IWD-
CO having faster convergence qualities. By taking this as basis, GA has
been replaced with IWD-CO in a recently developed Modified Roaming
Optimization(MRO) algorithm and applied to various benchmark functions and found drastic variation in convergence. Results are proving that
replacing GA with IWD-CO can be a novel step in evolutionary based
multimodal search algorithms.

Keywords: Genetic algorithm · Intelligent water drops algorithm ·
Roaming optimization · Modified roaming optimization · Evolutionary
computation

1 Introduction

The nature besides the fact that it evolved a highly sophisticated life form of
human being from an ape houses a wide range of life forms. Since the dawn of
time, the whole of flora and fauna has gradually evolved and developed intelligent techniques for attracting the mates, finding food and all the basic needs.
For many years researchers inspired from natural phenomenon and started imitating its processes to create meta-models. Nature inspired problem solving methods
such as Evolutionary algorithms, Swarm based optimization algorithms etc., have
been contributing much innovation in major areas like Robotics, Signal Processing etc. Most of them mainly contribute to optimization algorithms which can be
defined as the process to make a system or design as effective or functional as possible by satisfying the given constraints. In these cases having secondary/multiple
optimal solutions in hand may allow us to perform the required task. This has led
to the development of multimodal optimization methodologies. In principle multimodal optimization is defined as finding multiple local optima(not necessarily

© Springer International Publishing Switzerland 2015
B.K. Panigrahi et al. (Eds.): SEMCCO 2014, LNCS 8947, pp. 14–26, 2015.
DOI: 10.1007/978-3-319-20294-5_2

equal). The major advantages of having all multiple optima are obtaining insight into the multimodal function landscape and alternative solutions can be chosen if the behavior of the constraints in the search space makes previous optimum solution unfeasible to implement. Some of the major areas where multimodal function optimization arises are localization, classification etc.

The Evolutionary Computation (EC) encompasses Genetic Algorithms (GAs), Differential Evolution (DE) etc. Traditional GAs are successfully identified the optima in the domain but they are incapable of maintaining rules of secondary importance. Attempts have been made to solve multimodal function optimization problems using a wide range of new approaches including Goldberg and Richardson's *sharing* [1], divides population using similarity of the individuals into possible solution spaces. DeJong's *crowding* [2], creates separate niches by replacing existing strings according to their similarity with other strings in an overlapping population. Rodica Lung and D. Dumitrescu's Roaming Optimization(RO) [3], divides the population into groups called sub-populations in a quest for multiple solutions. Besides sub-population concept, *Archive Test* plays major role in deciding the optimal solutions. RO has been successfully applied for detecting Nash equilibrium in multi-player games [4] and later Modified Roaming Optimization(MRO) [5] proposed by Chakravarthi J et al. added *Density based cluster removal step* for drastic decrements in running time of algorithm. This solved Inverse Kinematics(IK) problems of SCARA and PUMA robots as well. As there are ample of techniques for multimodal optimization, fastness became predominant factor of algorithms. In Genetic Algorithms, *mutation* helps to achieve the speed by having comparisons with previous results. Recently a novel evolutionary Intelligent Water Drops (IWD) algorithm [6], developed by Hamed Shah Hosseini, behaves similar to GA. Nagalakshmi et al. used IWD - Continuous Optimization(IWD-CO) algorithm [8] to solve Combined Economic and Emission Dispatch (CEED) [7] to find optimal cost values for 3, 6 plant power generating stations. Their work illustratively proving that IWD-CO has faster convergence compare to GA. In this paper, we have identified various similarities between IWD-CO and GA, simultaneously both have been applied to a continuous function in capturing it's global peak and various comparisons were made and later we replaced GA with IWD-CO in MRO [5] for finding peaks in multimodal benchmark test functions.

Rest of the paper has arranged in this way. Chapter-II explains IWD-CO algorithm and compares IWD-CO with GA, Chapter-III gives the proposed IWD algorithm for Multimodal Spaces, simulations and results are presented in Chapter-IV. Finally concluding remarks are given in chapter-V.

2   Intelligent Water Drops Continuous Optimization Algorithm

2.1   Basic IWD-CO Algorithm

In nature, water flow occurs in rivers and canals. Natural river paths have been created by swarm of water drops. Natural water drops have the tendency to flow from high terrain to low terrain. In order to reach an ideal path, water drops always try to change the real path which is having many twists and turns [8]. After observing natural phenomena of water flow and to mimic this process Hamed-Shah Hosseini [6] has created Intelligent Water Drops algorithm. The Intelligent Water Drops are given some properties of natural water drops such as,

– Water drop transfers some amount of soil when it moves from one place to another.
– While moving, soil of water drop increases and soil on the path will be decreased.

This nature-inspired evolution based Intelligent Water Drops are used to solve discrete and continuous optimization problems as well. The steps of Intelligent Water Drops-Continuous Optimization (IWD-CO) algorithm are as follows.

Problem Representation: Consider our problem is either to maximize or minimize an objective function $F(x_1, x_2, x_3, ..., x_M)$ where $x_1, x_2, x_3, ..., x_M$ are input parameters to the function. Mathematically, we can represent it as

$$max \ (or) \ min(F(x_1, x_2, x_3, ..., x_M)) \tag{1}$$

A directed graph with $(M \times P)$ nodes and $(2 \times M \times P)$ directed edges will be created. Between every adjacent nodes there will be two edges named 0 and 1. Here, M represents M-variable function and P represents the Precision which is the number of binary digits required to represent each variable. Initially same amount of soil is deposited on all the edges. Each IWD will carry some amount of soil with it and initially this value is kept zero and increases as it is passing through the nodes.

$soil(e_{i,i+1}(k))$ represents amount of soil present on k^{th} edge between i^{th} and $i+1^{th}$ node. k is an edge that can be either 0 or 1 and i is a node that ranges from 1 to $M \times P$. $soil_j^{IWD}$ represents soil possessed by j^{th} IWD. According to [6], various steps in IWD-CO algorithm are Edge Selection, Local soil updation, Mutation based local search and Global soil updation. Throughout this paper we used $P = 32$ and initial soil on the edges is 10000.

Edge Selection: Every IWD starts its journey from node 1 and finishes it by visiting the last node through edge selection process. Edge Selection for IWD is to choose an edge that is connected to next node. If the IWD is at node i then it selects the next edge $(e_{i,i+1})$ by choosing either 0 or 1 string between i and $i+1$ nodes. The probability $P^{IWD}(e_{i,i+1}(k))$ for selecting an edge is given by

$$P^{IWD}(e_{i,i+1}(k)) = \frac{f(soil(e_{i,i+1}(k)))}{\sum\limits_{l=0}^{1} f(soil(e_{i,i+1}(l)))} \tag{2}$$

where,

$$f(soil(e_{i,i+1}(k))) = \frac{1}{0.0001 + g(soil(e_{i,i+1}(k)))} \tag{3}$$

and

$$g(soil(e_{i,i+1}(k))) = \begin{cases} soil(e_{i,i+1}(k)); \; if \; min_{l=0,1}(soil(e_{i,i+1}(l))) \geq 0 \\ soil(e_{i,i+1}(k)) - min_{l=0,1}(soil(e_{i,i+1}(l))); \; \; else \end{cases} \quad (4)$$

Local Soil Updation: During visiting the nodes and selecting edges, the IWD updates the soil carrying by itself and removing some soil from the currently used edge. The soil of the IWD, $soil^{IWD}$ and soil of the visited edge, $soil(e_{i,i+1}(k))$ are updated by

$$soil(e_{i,i+1}(k)) = 1.1 * soil(e_{i,i+1}(k)) - 0.01 * \Delta soil(e_{i,i+1}(k)) \quad (5)$$

$$soil^{IWD} = soil^{IWD} + \Delta soil(e_{i,i+1}(k)) \quad (6)$$

where,

$$\Delta soil(e_{i,i+1}(k)) = 0.001 \quad (7)$$

Mutation Based Local Search: In IWD-CO mutations are nothing but changing the IWD position randomly in the search space by switching an edge in its path to avoid *premature* convergence. These mutations change the behavior of IWD path probabilistically. To improve the efficacy strong mutations have been introduced. Strong mutations accept the mutated fitness only if it is greater than previous fitness otherwise it remains unchanged.

Global Soil Updation: The Iteration best solution T^{IB}, among all IWDs is found at the end of current iteration by considering the best fitness value. In order to increase the probability for other IWDs to follow the best IWD's tour, soil on the respective edges are modified. This updation is given by

$$soil(e_{i,i+1}(k)) = min(max(TempSoil(e_{i,i+1}(k)), MinSoil), MaxSoil) \quad (8)$$

$$\forall \; e_{i,i+1}(k) \in T^{IB}$$

where,

$$TempSoil(e_{i,i+1}(k)) = 1.1*soil(e_{i,i+1}(k)) - 0.01*\frac{soil_{IB}^{IWD}}{(M*P)}; \quad \forall \; e_{i,i+1}(k) \in T^{IB}$$

$$(9)$$

$soil_{IB}^{IWD}$ represents the soil of best IWD. Here, Global soil updation is bounded by [MinSoil, MaxSoil]. Global soil updation will be done to the soil profile of the best IWD tour. This updation helps other IWDs to follow the best tour. In previous work [7], It is identified that IWD-CO has faster in convergence compare to GA and to check this, experiments have been done along with identification of various similarities between IWD-CO and GA explained in next section.

2.2   Comparison of IWD-CO with GA

The main aim of this section is to show the similar behavior of the major steps in both GA and IWD-CO and to reasonably prove the faster convergence capacity of IWD-CO over GA which led us to replace GA part in Modified Roaming Optimization(MRO) algorithm with IWD-CO to improve the efficacy of the results by proposing a new hybridized algorithm called Intelligent Water Drops algorithm for Multimodal Spaces (IWD-MS).

Major Steps of GA and IWD-CO: Genetic Algorithm is a stochastic approach based on genetic parameters such as selection, crossover and mutation. In GA, the selection process means pairing of parent chromosomes and crossover means exchanging of information of chromosomes i.e. generating child chromosomes(Child population) from parent chromosomes. Mutations are nothing but switching the genes(binary bits), which helps in random exploration of search space. After completing above steps we use best half part of parent population and best half part of Child Population to create New population to persist the present best solution further. IWD-CO is based on Evolution parameters such as Global soil updation, Local soil updation and Mutations. In each iteration Global soil updation is carried out on the path of best IWD tour by decreasing the soil on the edges of that tour to increase the probability of next iteration IWDs to follow this path. Local soil updation is helpful in selecting the best edge i.e. to generate the best solution. Mutations in IWD-CO are called strong mutations for it's capacity of always increasing or maintaining the best fitness value. From these depictions we observe the similarities in the evolution parameters of IWD-CO and GA explained in next section.

Similarities in Evolutionary Parameters of IWD-CO and GA:

Global Soil updation - Selection: Global soil updation in IWD-CO behaves similar to the Selection process in GA. Global soil updation is done to sustain the best path by making new IWDs to follow it. Similarly GA uses Best chromosomes(parents having high fitness) in Selection process to sustain the best parental information for upcoming children population.

Local Soil updation - Crossover: Local soil updation in IWD-CO functions similar to Crossover in GA. Crossover is mating of parent chromosomes resulting the child population (New solutions). Similarly Local Soil updation in combination with Edge-Selection process produces the new solutions. Selected edge (New Solution) will have the cumulative effect of all the previously flown IWDs which changes the soil amount through Local soil updation. Here mating process among all previous IWDs is internally happening in their journey. So this internally mating process(Local soil updation and Edge selection) in IWD-CO is imitating the function of *crossover* as in GA.

Mutations in IWD-CO - Mutations in GA: Mutation step is same in both the algorithms but IWD-CO uses strong mutations. The mutations help in both GA and IWD-CO, to push the solution from the local optima towards the global optima. By the above observations, IWD-CO can be thought of analogous to GA.

Efficacy of IWD-CO over GA: To check the difference between the convergence capabilities of both algorithms, we considered peaks function f_2 in Table 1,

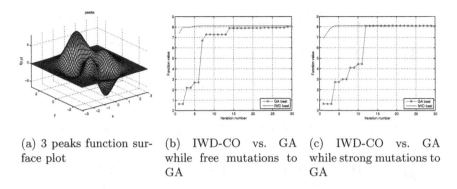

(a) 3 peaks function sur-
face plot

(b) IWD-CO vs. GA
while free mutations to
GA

(c) IWD-CO vs. GA
while strong mutations to
GA

Fig. 1. (a) 3 peaks function surface plot (b) IWD-CO vs. GA while free mutations to
GA (c) IWD-CO vs. GA while strong mutations to GA

shown in Fig. 1(a), which has its global optima value 8.1062 at (-0.0087,1.5813).
We applied both GA and IWD-CO for that function by considering 6 initial solutions (also known as chromosomes in GA and IWDs in IWD-CO). Figure 1(b)
shows the convergence in both algorithms. From this we can observe that IWD-
CO has faster convergence and it is taking less number of iterations to capture
global optima, whereas GA is taking relatively more number of iterations. Here
the differences are considered as Strong mutations in IWD-CO and Free mutations in GA. But even if we apply strong mutations in GA, we can see the same
response as shown in Fig. 1(c). Even in this case, IWD-CO is showing faster
convergence. But there is an improvement in faster convergence of GA compare
to free mutations in GA case but still relatively it is slower than IWD-CO. The
reason for this effect is, in case of GA, the new chromosomes will be generated
based on previous two parent chromosomes only. So the solution provided by
new chromosomes will not have the effect of other chromosomes i.e. some of
the new solutions may miss the effect of best parent too. Due to this reason
the solution of present chromosomes may or may not support in updating the
global solution for next iteration. If this happens so for all the chromosomes, the
solution improvement may get delay in GA, even if we apply strong mutations
as well. Whereas due to the Global soil updation on the best IWD tour (edges
travelled by best IWD) will have effect in generating next best solution. So we
can guarantee the improvement or consistency of best solution to next iteration.

   Figure 2 shows the convergence of individual IWDs and chromosomes.
Figure 3(a) shows parent and child best populations for all iterations in GA
and Fig. 3(b) shows the IWD parent and child best solutions. From this, we can
observe that next iteration best in IWD-CO has the cumulative effect of all the
previously flown IWDs and best IWD from previous iteration. For instance we
can observe this behavior from Fig. 2 which shows the individual IWD convergence where behavior of IWD4 is the evolved behavior of IWD-1, IWD-2, IWD-3.
Similarly IWD-6 behavior is the evolved behavior of IWD-1 to IWD-5. New IWD
always tries to follow the best IWD path, which can be observed from Fig. 4,

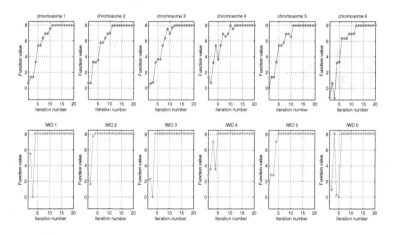

Fig. 2. IWD-CO vs. GA comparison of individual agents plot

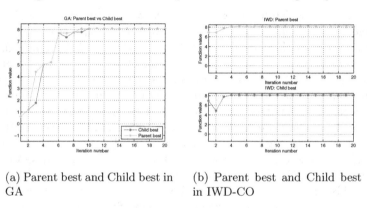

(a) Parent best and Child best in GA

(b) Parent best and Child best in IWD-CO

Fig. 3. (a) Parent best and Child best in GA (b) Parent best and Child best in IWD-CO

which shows convergence of global best solution and particular IWD solution. Whereas GA has random effect in generating new (child) population. Strong mutations are making IWD-CO to find the solution with very less number of iterations because of it's ability to make the solution better or constant each time. From the above, we observe the analogy between GA and IWD-CO and also the efficacy of IWD-CO with respect to the convergence. We expect better results if we replace GA with IWD-CO in any of the evolutionary based parameters like *sharing* [1], *crowding* [2] and *sub-population* [3] for finding multiple peaks of a multimodal optimization problems. For this we considered recently developed MRO [5] and we come up with new hybridized algorithm Intelligent Water Drops algorithm for Multimodal Spaces (IWD-MS) explained in next section.

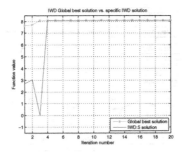

Fig. 4. Covergence plot of global best solution and specified IWD solution

3 Intelligent Water Drops Algorithm for Multimodal Spaces

This paper uses the concept of sub-population bound search for capturing multimodal peaks in a multimodal search space. It uses the concept proposed in Modified Roaming Optimization [5] by replacing GA with IWD-CO because of its fast converging capability seen in the Fig. 1, which is key for MRO algorithm. Figure 5, shows the block diagram of MRO algorithm [5]. IWD-MS algorithms has been created by including IWD-CO in place of GA in the MRO algorithm. Figure 6, shows the flowchart of IWD-MS algorithm. The steps in this algorithm are: Stability Measure, Roaming, Density based cluster removal and Archive test. These are explained below.

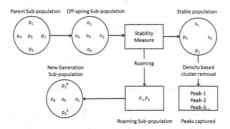

Fig. 5. Block diagram representation of MRO algorithm

Stability Measure: Best agent in each sub-population is regarded as potential optima. High stable potential optima contributes a near-optima point to the stable population. Stability measure determines, how better present sub-population compare to its off-spring sub-population. If a sub-population's stability exceeds a predefined threshold then it is considered as high stable population [3]. Let P_i and P_i^1 are i^{th} parent subpopulation and off-spring subpopulation respectively and x_i^* is potential optima of ith subpopulation. Then we define a set 'B', containing the off-springs of P_i which are better than x^*.

$$B(x_i^*) = \left\{ x \in P_i^1 : x > x_i^* \right\} \qquad (10)$$

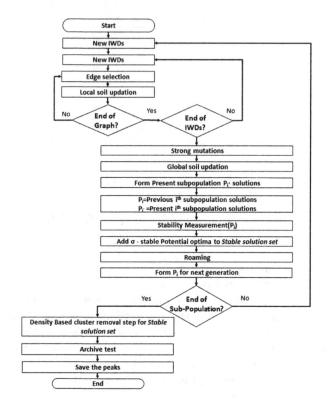

Fig. 6. Flow chart representation of IWD-MS

The stability measure of ith subpopulation is defined as,

$$SM(P_i) = 1 - \{B(x_i^*)/|P_i|\} \tag{11}$$

In each iteration potential optima from the high stable populations will be saved.

Roaming: Roaming is necessary to search in the unexplored areas of the search space. The sub-populations having greater stability will contribute a potential optima and move to new areas in quest for other optima and mutation is used in roaming for the purpose of exploring new areas [3].

Density Based Cluster Removal Step: This step is applied on the *Stable Solution Set* which contains the points that are near to peaks. Plot of the *Stable Solution Set* depicts dense points around all the peaks as shown in Fig. 8. *Density based cluster removal step* identifies and saves a peak and removes all the points around that peak and it repeats the same procedure till the *Stable Solution Set* becomes empty. In the process of identifying the cluster, it uses the concept of density. Here, density is defined as,

$$density(x, \delta) = N/\delta \tag{12}$$

where δ is a small constant and N is no.of points in the range.

Archive Test: Archive test is applied on the final solutions obtained from Density based cluster removal step. It finds existence of a valley between every two solutions. If there is no valley between any two solutions then it's an indication that those two points belong to the same peak. Best solution among them is saved and the other one will be deleted. This step results final solutions(peaks) of the given multimodal function.

It has been proved that the MRO is more efficient with inclusion of *Density based cluster removal* step in reducing the total convergence time as compared to Roaming Optimization(RO) [3]. This paper focused on checking the capability of IWD-CO in capturing multiple peaks in a multimodal search space.

4   Simulations and Results

The proposed "Intelligent Water Drops Algorithm for Multimodal Spaces"(IWD-MS) has been tested on various benchmark test functions shown in Table 1, for its capability and efficacy in capturing multimodal peaks. Simulations conclusively show the better convergence times for all benchmark test functions compared to RO and MRO. Here, for illustrative purpose the Rastrigin benchmark function f_1 with 64 peaks in the range of [-4, 4] has been considered. Figure 7 shows the surface plot of Rastrigin function and Fig. 8 shows the surface plot with all stable points. Here, the proposed algorithm took 2.8216 sec. MRO and RO took 6.3165 and 96.434 sec respectively. Figure 9 shows 2-D plot of stable points after applying the step *Density based cluster removal* proposed in MRO. Figure 10 shows the Rastrigin function with final solutions of captured 64 peaks after application of *archive test*.

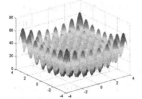

Fig. 7. Surface plot of Rastrigin function

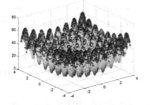

Fig. 8. Rastrigin function with all Stable points

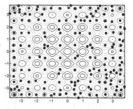

Fig. 9. 2-D plot of stable points after Density step

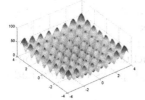

Fig. 10. Final plot with all peaks captured

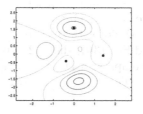

Fig. 11. 2-D plot of 3 peaks function

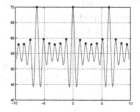

Fig. 12. 2-D plot of 19 peaks function

Table 1. Multimodal benchmark functions

Function	Profile	Range	Peaks
Rastrigin(2D)	$f_1(x,y) = 20 + \sum\limits_{i=1}^{2} x_i^2 + (-1)^i * 10\cos(2\pi x_i)$	$[-5,5]^2$	100
Peaks	$f_2(x,y) = 3(1-x)^2 e^{-x^2-y^2} - 10((x/5) - x^3 - y^5)e^{-x^2-y^2} - (1/3)e^{-(x+1)^2-y^2}$	$[-3,3]^2$	3
Shubert(1D)	$f_3(x) = \sum\limits_{j=1}^{5} j\cos((j+1)x+j)$	$[-10,10]^2$	19
Shubert(2D)	$f_4(x,y) = (\sum\limits_{i=1}^{5} i\cos((i+1)x)+i)*(\sum\limits_{j=1}^{5} j\cos((j+1)y)+j)$	$[-10,10]^2$	361
$f_5(x,y)(2D)$	$f_5(x,y) = \cos^2(x) + \cos^2(y)$	$[-4,4]^2$	9
Griewangk(2D)	$f_6(x,y) = \dfrac{1}{4000}\sum\limits_{i=1}^{2} x_i^2 - \prod\limits_{i=1}^{2} \cos(\dfrac{x_i}{\sqrt{i}}) + 1$	$[-4.8,4.8]^2$	4

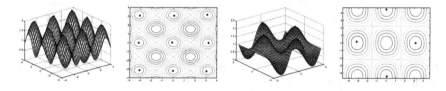

(a) 3-D plot of f_5 (b) 2-D plot of f_5 (c) 3-D plot of f_6 (d) 2-D plot of f_6

Fig. 13. (a) 3-D plot of f_5 (b) 2-D plot of f_5 (c) 3-D plot of f_6 (d) 2-D plot of f_6

Comparison of Proposed algorithm with MRO and RO: It is already proved in the MRO [5] that it is taking less convergence time as compared to RO because of density step. After having conclusions with respect to IWD-CO vs GA, from chapter-II and from the above example on the Rastrigin function, it is showing even less convergence time with same number of peaks captured as compared to MRO and RO. To check the efficacy of the algorithm, it has been applied to Rastrigin function with various ranges for which the number of peaks also varies. Table 2 shows the comparison of proposed algorithm with MRO and RO in terms of their captured peaks and total convergence time. To validate the proposed algorithm for different characterized multimodal spaces, it has been applied to three more multimodal space functions which have larger variation in the number of peaks and search ranges. Figs. 11 and 12 show the 2-D plots of 3-peaks and 19-peaks functions at final iteration. Figure 13(a) shows the 3-D plot of f_5 and Fig. 13(b) shows 2-D plot with the captured peaks of f_5 and Fig. 13(c) shows the 3-D plot of f_6 and Fig. 13(d) shows 2-D plot with the captured peaks of f_6. Table 3 shows the comparison chart for all benchmark functions considered for testing and the efficacy of the algorithm with peaks captured and convergence time.

Table 2. Comparison of IWD-MS, MRO and RO for different ranges of Rastrigin function

Method	Range	Total Peaks	Detected Peaks	Time (sec)
IWD-MS	$[-1,1]^2$	4	4	0.1796
MRO			4	0.6513
RO			4	1.322
IWD-MS	$[-2,2]^2$	16	16	0.3136
MRO			16	1.8449
RO			16	8.513
IWD-MS	$[-3,3]^2$	36	36	0.8108
MRO			36	2.7393
RO			36	24.623
IWD-MS	$[-4,4]^2$	64	64	2.8216
MRO			64	6.3165
RO			64	96.434
IWD-MS	$[-5,5]^2$	100	100	9.0472
MRO			100	16.1865
RO			100	368.217

Table 3. Comparison of IWD-MS, MRO and RO for different test functions

Function	Method	Detected Peaks	Total Peaks	Time (sec)
f_1	IWD-MS	100	100	9.0472
	MRO	100		16.1865
	RO	100		368.217
f_2	IWD-MS	3	3	0.1470
	MRO	3		0.3382
	RO	3		0.3891
f_3	IWD-MS	19	19	0.1083
	MRO	19		0.7295
	RO	19		3.189
f_4	IWD-MS	361	361	31.1359
	MRO	361		53.6204
	RO	361		732.5
f_5	IWD-MS	9	9	0.15
	MRO	9		2.71
	RO	9		4.42
f_6	IWD-MS	4	4	0.11
	MRO	4		1.12
	RO	4		1.62

5   Conclusions and Future Works

This paper has made its trails to show the possibility of using the Intelligent Water Drops algorithm, a nature inspired algorithm for multimodal spaces to capture peaks. The process of comparing IWD-CO with GA, shows slow convergence in GA in each iteration for both free and strong mutations and fastness as basis, later by replacing IWD-CO with GA in MRO algorithm for different test functions to capture multimodal peaks depicting that the convergence time with IWD-MS is very less compared to GA in MRO and RO. These results creating a new path in the evolutionary algorithms that GA can be replaced with IWD-CO in other themes like sharing, crowding which are also other techniques in multimodal optimization problems.

References

1. Goldberg, D., Richardson, J.: Genetic algorithms with sharing for multimodal function optimization. In: Proceedings of the 2nd International Conference on Genetic Algorithms, pp. 41–49 (1987)
2. de Jong, K.A.: An Analysis of the Behavior of a Class of Genetic Adaptive Systems, Ph.D thesis, department of Computer and Communication Sciences, University of Michigan, Ann Arbor, MI (1975)
3. Lung, R.I., Dumitrescu, D.: Roaming optimization: a new evolutionary technique for multimodal optimization. Studia Univ. Babes-Bolyai, Informatica **49**(1), 99–109 (2004)

4. Lung, R.I., Mihoc, T.D., Dumitrescu, D.: Nash equilibria detection for multi-player games, In: IEEE Congress on Evolutionary Computation, pp. 1–5 (2010)
5. Chakravarthi, J., Harish, Y., Kranthi Kumar, R., Chittipolu, N., Omkar, S.N.: Modified roaming optimization for multi-modal optima. In: IEEE Third International Conference of Emerging Applications of Information Technology, pp. 56–61, CSI, Kolkatta, December 2012
6. Shah-Hosseini, H.: Problem solving by intelligent water drops. In: Proceedings of IEEE Congress on Evolutionary Computation, Swissotel the Stamford, pp. 3226–3231, Singapore (2007)
7. Nagalakshmi, P., Harish, Y., Kranthi Kumar, R., Jada, C.: Combined economic and emission dispatch using intelligent water drops-continuous optimization algorithm. In: IEEE International Conference on Recent Advancements in Electrical, Electronics and Control Engineering(IConRAEeCE 2011), pp. 168–173, Sivakashi, India, December 2011
8. Shah-Hosseini, H.: An approach to continuous optimization by the intelligent water drops algorithm. Procedia - Soc. Behav. Sci. **32**, 224–229 (2012)

Glowworm Swarm Based Informative Attribute Selection Using Support Vector Machines for Simultaneous Feature Selection and Classification

Aniket Gurav[1], Vinay Nair[1], Utkarsh Gupta[1,2], and Jayaraman Valadi[1,3](✉)

[1] Evolutionary Computing and Image Processing Group,
Centre for Development of Advanced Computing, Pune 411007, India
vinayn@cdac.in
[2] Department of Information Technology, NITK, Surathkal, Mangalore 575025, India
[3] Centre for Informatics, Shiv Nadar University, Dadri 203207, Uttar Pradesh, India
jayaraman.valadi@snu.edu.in

Abstract. In this paper, we propose a hybrid filter-wrapper algorithm, *GSO-Infogain*, for simultaneous feature selection for improved classification accuracy. *GSO-Infogain* employs Glowworm-Swarm Optimization(GSO) algorithm with Support Vector Machine(SVM) as its internal learning algorithm and utilizes feature ranking based on information gain as a heuristic. The GSO algorithm randomly generates a population of worms, each of which is a candidate subset of features. The fitness of each candidate solution, which is evaluated using Support Vector Machine, is encoded within its luciferin value. Each worm probabilistically moves towards the worm with the highest luciferin value in its neighbourhood. In the process, they explore the feature space and eventually converge to the global optimum. We have evaluated the performance of the hybrid algorithm for feature selection on a set of cancer datasets. We obtain a classification accuracy in the range 94-98 % for these datasets, which is comparable to the best results from other classification algorithms. We further tested the robustness of *GSO-Infogain* by evaluating its performance on the CoEPrA training and test datasets. *GSO-Infogain* performs well in this experiment too by giving similar prediction accuracies on the training and test datasets thus indicating its robustness.

1 Introduction

The accuracy of classification tasks involving large datasets is affected by many factors, prominent among which are problems arising due to the high-dimensional nature of large datasets, viz., the sparseness of large datasets [1],

V.N. gratefully acknowledges Council of Scientific and Industrial Research, New Delhi for awarding a Junior Research Fellowship.
V.K.J. gratefully acknowledges financial support from Department of Science and Technology, New Delhi.

© Springer International Publishing Switzerland 2015
B.K. Panigrahi et al. (Eds.): SEMCCO 2014, LNCS 8947, pp. 27–37, 2015.
DOI: 10.1007/978-3-319-20294-5_3

noise and redundancy in the datasets [2] and large computational resources required to process these datasets. As the number of dimensions/features in a dataset increases, the sampling space increases exponentially in volume as a function of dimensionality. However, the exponential increase in sampling space is not accompanied by an exponential increase in the number of samples, which remain constant [1]. This sparseness of data in high-dimensional datasets leads to reduced performance while analyzing the data using statistical methods, as the number of samples may be too less for accurate estimation [3]. Additionally, the features within these large high-dimensional datasets tend to be noisy and/or redundant and subsequently reduce the learning accuracy of the various machine learning algorithms used for classification tasks [2]. The large size of the datasets also impose additional restraints on the computational resources required for processing them. To resolve these aforementioned problems, it often becomes necessary to reduce the number of dimensions of the dataset keeping only those features that contribute towards the final output.

Feature selection is a commonly utilized strategy for dimensionality reduction of high-dimensional datasets. As defined by Webb [4], for a given dataset of size p dimensions, feature selection involves the process of optimization of all possible subsets X_d, each of size d dimensions, where $d < p$, over some evaluative function J, with the objective of determining the subset X_d for which,

$$J(X_d) = \max_{X \in X_d} J(X)$$

Various strategies have been developed for the efficient selection of an optimal subset of features from the original dataset and can be broadly categorized into filter, wrapper and embedded strategies. In the filter model, the individual contribution of each dimension towards the final output is determined by analyzing the general characteristics of the data [5]. In the wrapper model, various strategies are employed wherein a learning algorithm is used to evaluate subsets of features and determine a subset relevant to the final output of the dataset [6]. The embedded model is a combination of the previous two models wherein a learning algorithm is used to evaluate the individual contribution of each dimension towards the final output [7].

Support Vector Machine(SVM) is a commonly utilized supervised-learning algorithm [8]. SVM functions by projecting the data into a n-dimensional hyperspace (where n is the number of features) and fitting a hyperplane that separates the data. The hyperplane aims to separate the data into its respective classes and maximize the margin between the data and the hyperplane in the hyperspace. Further, SVMs employ kernel functions that let them deal with the problem of intractabiliy by performing all the computations in the input space itself. SVMs have gained immense popularity in recent times due to their efficiency with handling large data and robustness. SVMs have been utilized for wide purposes in various fields ranging from biological prediction [9–11] and image recognition [12,13] to web-content filtering [14,15] for both classification as well as regression tasks.

In this work, we propose *GSO-Infogain*, a hybrid wrapper-filter algorithm, for dimensionality reduction of high-dimensional data. The Glowworm Swarm Optimization Algorithm (GSO) algorithm, originally proposed by Krishnanand *et al.*[16], is a swarm optimization algorithm based on the Ant-Colony Optimization (ACO)[17] family of algorithms. It is inspired from the behaviour of glowworms in which a glowworm uses the phenomenon of bioluminescence to attract other glowworms to itself during mating. GSO was originally implemented by Krishnand and Ghose as a wrapper algorithm for optimization of unimodal and multimodal functions. We propose to use GSO, with Support Vector Machine as the learning algorithm, as a wrapper to determine the optimal subset from a high-dimensional dataset for a classification problem. In order to increase the quality of the optimal solution, we propose to add a filter, viz., Information Gain based on Kullback-Leibler divergence values [18]. We propose to rank the dimensions using the filter and incorporate the ranking of the dimensions within the wrapper algorithm to improve the solution.

2   Methodology

2.1   Support Vector Machine and Cross-Validation Statistics

Support Vector Machine, developed by Cortes and Vapnik [8], is one of the most widely used supervised learning algorithms for classification and regression purposes. SVM builds a prediction model for a dataset by projecting the data into a high-dimensional space and generating a hyperplane or set of hyperplanes that maximizes the distance (in each dimension) between the hyperplane/s and the different classes within the data. The prediction model learned from the data can be used to predict the class or values of unknown samples. In this study, LIBSVM, an implementation of SVM in C++ is utilized [19].

In order to ensure the robustness of the features selected using *GSO-Infogain*, 10-fold cross-validation accuracy(CVA) is utilized as the fitness function in *GSO-Infogain*. To obtain the k-fold CVA (k=10 in this study), the dataset is randomly divided into k folds, each consisting of a/k samples, where a is the number of samples in the dataset. A learning algorithm then develops a prediction model using $k-1$ folds as the training dataset and the prediction accuracy of the model is determined using the remaining fold as the test dataset. This process is repeated k times and the mean classification accuracy of the k iterations is determined. This approach prevents the learning algorithm from overfitting to the training data and increasing the robustness of the model generated. In *GSO-Infogain*, SVM is used as the learning algorithm for the 10-fold cross-validation.

2.2   GSO Algorithm

The objective of the GSO algorithm proposed by Krishnanand *et al.* [16] was function optimization. In order to extend the algorithm for feature selection, numerous modifications were made to the original algorithm. The modified GSO algorithm is described below.

The GSO algorithm considers a set of n glowworms over t generations. Each glowworm i consists of m features randomly selected from the entire set of features, where m is the number of features to be selected. The search radius for the glowworms, $R(t)$ is set as the mean of the individual euclidean distances between all the glowworms.

$$R(t) = \frac{1}{n} \sum_{i=1}^{n} \sum_{j=1}^{n} d(i, j) \tag{1}$$

where n is the number of glowworms and $d(i, j)$ is the Euclidean distance between glowworms i & j.

The 10-fold CVA, i.e. the fitness, of each glowworm i is then evaluated using SVM and encoded in the luciferin intensity $L_i(t)$ of the glowworm.

For each glowworm i, a list (neighborhood list) $N_i(t)$ containing all the glowworms j, within the search radius $R_i(t)$, with a luciferin value higher than itself is generated.

$$N_i(t) = \{j : d(i, j) < R(t) \,\&\, L_j(t) > L_i(t)\} \tag{2}$$

where $L_i(t)$ & $L_j(t)$ are luciferin values of glowworm i & j respectively.

Since the volume of the feature space being evaluated is often very large, worms with empty neighborhoods are frequently observed. For such worms, it has been observed that the neighborhood remains empty through several successive iterations. This leads to reduced efficiency of the algorithm, in terms of convergence to the optimal solution. To overcome this problem, a probabilistic movement of the worm towards a new position by changing one of its features with a new feature is employed

$$\text{new\_dim} = \begin{cases} ceil(\text{orig\_dim} - (rand \times 5)), & \text{if probability} < 0.75 \\ ceil(\text{orig\_dim} + (rand \times 5)), & \text{if probability} > 0.75 \end{cases} \tag{3}$$

where, new_dim & orig_dim are the new and original dimensions respectively, $rand$ is a random number and $rand \in (0,1)$. The values 5 and 0.75 utilized for scaling and the probabilistic switch have been selected after extensive evaluation with respect to time and number of steps required for convergence.

If the neighbourhood list is not empty then the glowworm i selects a glowworm j from the neighbourhood list, with a probability $P_{ij}(t)$.

$$P_{ij}(t) = \frac{L_j(t) - L_i(t)}{\sum_{k \in t} L_k(t) - L_i(t)} \tag{4}$$

where $j \in N_i(t)$ and $L_k(t)$ is the luciferin value of glowworm k from the set of all glowworms. The glowworm i then moves towards glowworm j by reducing the individual distance between each feature.

$$X_i(t + 1) = X_i(t) + s \tag{5}$$

Algorithm 1. Pseudocode for *GSO-Infogain*:

```
1: Initialization
2: Set number of dimensions = m
3: Set number of glowworms = n
4: Set maximum number of iterations = iter_m
5: for each glowworm i do
6:        Choose m dimensions randomly from the entire domain.
7: end for
8: while t< iter_m or optimal solution reached do
9:        Calculate search radius R(t)
10:       for each glowworm i do
11:           evaluate cross-validation accuracy L(i) using SVM
12:           generate the neighborhood list
13:           if N_i(t) is empty then
14:               generate random number
15:               if random number > 0.5 then
16:                   if random number < 0.75 then
17:                       replace random dimension with dimension using Eqn. 3
18:                   else
19:                       replace random dimension with dimension using Eqn. 3
20:                   end if
21:               end if
22:           else
23:               generate random number
24:               if random number > 0.5 then
25:                   randomly replace random dimension with Infogain ranked dimen-
                       sion
26:               else
27:                   for each glowworm j∈ N_i(t) do
28:                       calculate probability P_i(t)
29:                   end for
30:                   select glowworm_j with probability P_{ij}(t)
31:                   move glowworm_i towards glowworm_j
32:               end if
33:           end if
34:       end for
35:       t = t+1
36: end while
```

where s is the step size, which is calculated dynamically for each feature.

$$s = \frac{d(X_i, X_j)}{2} \tag{6}$$

where, X_i and X_j are the individual features of worms i and j respectively.

At the end of each generation, the fitness of the glowworms are calculated and the luciferin values are updated. The search radius $R(t)$ is also updated at the end of each generation. The entire process is repeated until the maximum number of generations or the desired optimal value is reached.

2.3   GSO-Infogain Algorithm

In order to increase the performance of our algorithm in terms of accuracy and convergence time, we use heuristic information to bias the algorithm towards the optimal solution. We use Information gain as the heuristic filter for ranking the dimensions in the order of their contribution to the accuracy of the classification problem. Infogain denoted as $IG(Y|X)$, is a measure of the information gained when trying to approximate a distribution Y in the presence or absence of a distribution X [20].

$$IG(Y|X) = H(Y) - H(Y|X) \tag{7}$$

where $H(Y|X)$ is the conditional entropy of Y, where X is known and $H(Y)$ is the entropy of Y. Based on the Infogain values, the dimensions were ranked in decreasing order of their contribution to accuracy of the classification problem. The infogain ranking was performed using Weka, a popular machine-learning software suite [21].

2.4   Datasets

We have tested *GSO-Infogain* on three microarray datasets, viz., colon-cancer [22], leukemia [23] and breast-cancer [24], containing mainly gene expression profiles from various biological samples. The colon dataset contains gene expression levels of 2000 probes for 40 tumour and 22 normal colon tissues. The leukemia dataset obtained from the Kent Ridge Bio-medical Data Set Repository [22] consists of gene expression profiles from bone marrow samples to study 7129 probes from 6817 human genes for 38 bone marrow samples (27 class I and 11 class II) [23]. The breast-cancer dataset is similar to the leukemia dataset and consists of gene expression profiles of 7129 probes for 49 bone marrow samples (22 class I and 22 class II) [24].

Further, to test the robustenss of *GSO-Infogain*, the classification datasets from the 'Comparative Evaluation of Predictive Algorithms' (CoEPrA) competition held in 2006 (accessible online at: http://www.coepra.org) were used. These datasets were obtained from a large number of different domains, such as

Table 1. Dimensions of Datasets

Dataset	No. of Features	No. of Samples	
Colon Cancer	2000	62	
Leukemia	7129	38	
Breast Cancer	7129	44	
		Train	Test
CoEPrA-I	5787	89	88
CoEPrA-II	5144	76	76
CoEPrA-III	5787	133	133

Table 2. 10-fold Cross-Validation Accuracies for GSO and *GSO-Infogain* on various Datasets

Dataset	No. of Features	10-fold CVA	
		GSO	*GSO-Infogain*
Colon	20	91.93	95.16
Breast	20	93.18	97.72
Leukemia	20	92.11	94.73

cheminformatics, drug design, etc. Each CoEPrA dataset consists of a training dataset and a test dataset consisting of unseen samples. The dimensions of each dataset are given in Table 1.

3 Results and Discussion

The performance of *GSO-Infogain* was tested with respect to the quality of the features selected and the convergence to optimal solutions. Towards this, *GSO-Infogain*, was tested on various standard classification datasets. 25 runs were performed for each simulation, with each simulation comprising 50-100 worms for 20-100 generations. The evolution of the algorithm towards the optimal solution for a representative simulation, for the cancer datasets, is depicted in Fig. 1(a). It is observed that, for each dataset, the algorithm converges to optimal or sub-optimal solutions within 30-35 generations with minute improvements in the later generations. The convergence to the optima in a reduced number steps is indicative of the sampling efficiency of *GSO-Infogain* and its ability to identify the relevant features in an effective manner.

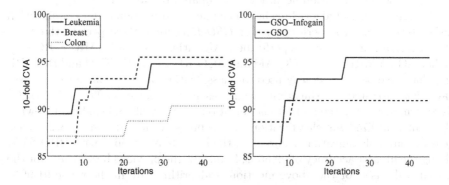

Fig. 1. (a) 10-fold CVA values for fittest worm in each generation from a representative simulation demonstrating convergence to optimal/sub-optimal solution (b) Comparison of rate of convergence for *GSO-Infogain* and GSO for breast-cancer dataset

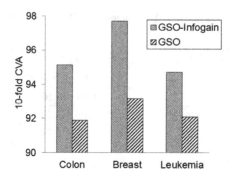

Fig. 2. Comparison of 10-fold cross validation accuracies for the optimal subsets selected by *GSO-Infogain* and GSO.

In order to determine the improvement in performance on incorporation of heuristic information, the convergence rates of *GSO-Infogain* and traditional *GSO* were compared (Fig. 1(b)). The initial higher performance of traditional *GSO* over *GSO-Infogain* as seen in Fig. 1(b) can be explained by the random selection of features for generating the glowworms for the simulations. In the simulation depicted in Fig. 1(b), the fittest glowworm seems to have selected a fitter set of features as compared to the fittest glowworm in *GSO-Infogain*. This is purely a chance event and doesnt affect the simulation in any manner. Further, it can be seen that *GSO-Infogain* converged faster to optimal/ sub-optimal solutions as compared to *GSO*. It is believed the probabilistic bias towards the infogain-ranked features leads to an increased accuracy due to incorporation of the higher-ranked features by the worms. Further, the classification accuracies of the final optimal subsets selected by *GSO-Infogain* and GSO were also compared and is depicted in Fig. 2. It is observed that for all the datasets, *GSO-Infogain* gives a higher classification accuracy as compared to GSO (Table 2).

A large number of algorithms have been designed previously for classification tasks. To evaluate the performance of *GSO-Infogain* with respect to the other algorithms, a comparison was performed. Algorithms such as SVMRFE-RG [25], Fisher-RG-SVMRFE [26], ACO-AM and ACO-RF [27], BBO-SVM and BBO-RF [28] that have been previously used for classification of the colon cancer dataset have demonstrated classification accuracies in the range 93-99 % with BBO-SVM demonstrating the highest classification accuracy of 98.39 % [28]. Likewise, algorithms utilized for classification of the breast cancer dataset [28,29] have demonstrated classification accuracy in the range 91.9 -99.56 % with BBO-SVM giving the highest accuracy of 99.56 %. Similarly, the previous best results for the leukemia dataset for the above mentioned algorithms are in the range 91-99 % with the highest classification accuracy being demonstrated by combined dissimilarity based classifiers. The highest classification accuracies obtained utilizing *GSO-Infogain* are given in Table 3. It is observed that although, *GSO-Infogain* does not give the best results, the results obtained are comparable to the results obtained from other algorithms. An additional note in this regard may be made

Table 3. Classification accuracies of various algorithms on Colon, Breast and Leukemia Datasets

Algorithm	Colon	Breast	Leukemia
BBO-SVM	**98.39**	**99.56**	-
BBO-RF	92.34	94.38	-
SVMRFE-RG	93.3	-	-
FisherRG-SVMRFE	94.7	-	-
ACO-AM	95.47	-	-
ACO-RF	96.77	-	-
Dissimilarity-Based	-	91.9	**98.62**
RCBT	-	-	91.18

to the performance of BBO-SVM, which gives the highest classification accuracy for the Colon and Breast Cancer datasets. The number of optimal features selected by BBO-SVM from each dataset is believed to be quite low (in the range 9-19). Subsequently, it is believed that the high-results obtained by BBO-SVM may be a result of overfitting to the training data. The problem of overfitting to training data is analyzed for *GSO-infogain* as described below.

As mentioned previously, feature selection algorithms have a tendency to overfit to the training data. This reduces the performance of the algorithm when it is exposed to previously unseen data. To determine if overfitting is involved in the high classification accuracy demonstrated by *GSO-Infogain* on the cancer datasets, the algorithm is tested on the CoEPrA classification datasets. The CoEPrA data consists of three datasets from three different experiments. Each dataset consists of a set of training data and test data. For each dataset, a classification model is generated using the features from the training dat selected utilizing *GSO-Infogain* and the model is used to classify the test data. The prediction accuracy for the three datasets obtained thus is given in Table 4. It is observed that the difference between the 10-fold CVA obtained during training and the prediction accuracy obtained on the test datasets is relatively small. This indicates that *GSO-Infogain* is a robust algorithm and is not prone to overfitting to the dataset.

Table 4. 10-fold Cross-Validation Accuracies and Prediction Accuracy for GSO-Infogain on CoEPrA datasets

Dataset	10-fold CVA	Prediction Accuracy	
		GSO	*GSO-Infogain*
CoEPrA-I	88.76 %	84.09 %	86.36 %
CoEPrA-II	89.47 %	84.21 %	85.52 %
CoEPrA-III	67.67 %	62.41 %	67.66 %

4   Conclusion

In this study, the GSO algorithm has been extended for feature selection for improving the prediction of classification tasks involving large datasets. Heuristic information has been incorporated into the traditional GSO algorithm and has been shown to improve the performance of the algorithm by reducing number of iterations required for convergence to the optimal solution. The *GSO-Infogain* algorithm demonstrates good performance in terms of classification accuracy and is at par with other algorithms previously reported in literature. Additionally, the robustness of the algorithm has been tested and it is demonstrated that the algorithm identifies the relevant features efficiently without overfitting to the dataset and functions effectively on previously unseen data.

References

1. Bellman, R.E.: Adaptive control processes - A guided tour. Princeton University Press, Princeton (1961)
2. Ng, A.Y.: On feature selection: learning with exponentially many irrelevant features as training examples. In: Proceedings of the Fifteenth International Conference on Machine Learning, pp. 404–412, Morgan Kaufmann (1998)
3. Hughes, G.: On the mean accuracy of statistical pattern recognizers. IEEE Trans. Inf. Theor. **14**(1), 55–63 (1968)
4. Webb, A.R.: Statistical Pattern Recognition, 2nd edn. John Wiley & Sons, NJ (2002)
5. Kira, K., Rendell, L.A.: The feature selection problem: traditional methods and a new algorithm. In: Proceedings of the Tenth National Conference on Artificial intelligence, AAAI 1992, pp. 129–134. AAAI Press (1992)
6. Kohavi, R., John, G.H.: Wrappers for feature subset selection. Artif. Intell. **97**(1–2), 273–324 (1997)
7. Breiman, L., Friedman, J., Stone, C.J., Olshen, R.A.: Classification and Regression Trees, 1st edn. Chapman and Hall/CRC, London (1984)
8. Cortes, C., Vapnik, V.: Support-vector networks. Mach. Learn. **20**(3), 273–297 (1995)
9. Nair, V., Dutta, M., Manian, S.S., Kumari, R., Jayaraman, V.K.: Identification of penicillin-binding proteins employing support vector machines and random forest. Bioinformation **9**(9), 481 (2013)
10. Brown, M.P., Grundy, W.N., Lin, D., Cristianini, N., Sugnet, C.W., Furey, T.S., Ares, M., Haussler, D.: Knowledge-based analysis of microarray gene expression data by using support vector machines. Proc. Natl. Acad. Sci. **97**(1), 262–267 (2000)
11. Furey, T.S., Cristianini, N., Duffy, N., Bednarski, D.W., Schummer, M., Haussler, D.: Support vector machine classification and validation of cancer tissue samples using microarray expression data. Bioinformatics **16**(10), 906–914 (2000)
12. Guo, G., Li, S.Z., Chan, K.L.: Face recognition by support vector machines. In: Proceedings of the Fourth IEEE International Conference on Automatic Face and Gesture Recognition, pp. 196–201, IEEE (2000)
13. Pontil, M., Verri, A.: Support vector machines for 3d object recognition. IEEE Trans. Pattern Anal. Mach. Intell. **20**(6), 637–646 (1998)

14. Rowley, H.A., Jing, Y., Baluja, S.: Large scale image-based adult-content filtering. In: VISAPP (1), pp. 290–296, Citeseer (2006)
15. Sculley, D., Wachman, G.M.: Relaxed online svms for spam filtering. In: Proceedings of the 30th Annual International ACM SIGIR Conference on Research and Development in Information Retrieval, pp. 415–422. ACM (2007)
16. Krishnanand, K.N., Ghose, D.: Detection of multiple source locations using a glowworm metaphor with applications to collective robotics. In: Proceedings 2005 IEEE Swarm Intelligence Symposium, SIS 2005, pp. 84–91 (2005)
17. Colorni, A., Dorigo, M., Maniezzo, V., et al.: Distributed optimization by ant colonies. In: Proceedings of the First European Conference on Artificial Life. vol. 142, pp. 134–142, Paris, France (1991)
18. Kullback, S., Leibler, R.A.: On information and sufficiency. Ann. Math. Statist. $22(1)$, 79–86 (1951)
19. Chang, C.C., Lin, C.J.: Libsvm: a library for support vector machines. ACM Trans. Intel. Syst. Technol. (TIST) $2(3)$, 27 (2011)
20. Kent, J.T.: Information gain and a general measure of correlation. Biometrika $70(1)$, 163–173 (1983)
21. Hall, M., Frank, E., Holmes, G., Pfahringer, B., Reutemann, P., Witten, I.H.: The weka data mining software: an update. SIGKDD Explor. Newsl. $11(1)$, 10–18 (2009)
22. Alon, U., Barkai, N., Notterman, D., Gish, K., Ybarra, S., Mack, D., Levine, A.: Broad patterns of gene expression revealed by clustering analysis of tumor and normal colon tissues probed by oligonucleotide arrays. Proc. Natl. Acad. Sci. $96(12)$, 6745–6750 (1999)
23. Golub, T.R., Slonim, D.K., Tamayo, P., Huard, C., Gaasenbeek, M., Mesirov, J.P., Coller, H., Loh, M.L., Downing, J.R., Caligiuri, M.A., Bloomfield, C.D., Lander, E.S.: Molecular classification of cancer: class discovery and class prediction by gene expression monitoring. Science $286(5439)$, 531–537 (1999)
24. West, M., Blanchette, C., Dressman, H., Huang, E., Ishida, S., Spang, R., Zuzan, H., Olson, J.A., Marks, J.R., Nevins, J.R.: Predicting the clinical status of human breast cancer by using gene expression profiles. Proc. Natl. Acad. Sci. $98(20)$, 11462–11467 (2001)
25. Guyon, I., Weston, J., Barnhill, S., Vapnik, V.: Gene selection for cancer classification using support vector machines. Mach. Learn. $46(1–3)$, 389–422 (2002)
26. Mohammadi, A., Saraee, M.H., Salehi, M.: Identification of disease-causing genes using microarray data mining and gene ontology. BMC Med. Genomics $4(1)$, 12 (2011)
27. Sharma, S., Ghosh, S., Anantharaman, N., Jayaraman, V.K.: Simultaneous informative gene extraction and cancer classification using aco-antminer and aco-random forests. In: Proceedings of the International Conference on Information Systems Design and Intelligent Applications 2012 (INDIA 2012) held in Visakhapatnam, India, pp. 755–761.Springer, January 2012
28. Nikumbh, S., Ghosh, S., Jayaraman, V.K.: Biogeography-based informative gene selection and cancer classification using svm and random forests. In: 2012 IEEE Congress on Evolutionary Computation (CEC), pp. 1–6. IEEE (2012)
29. Blanco, Á., Martín-Merino, M., De Las Rivas, J.: Combining dissimilarity based classifiers for cancer prediction using gene expression profiles. BMC Bioinform. 8(Suppl 8), S3 (2007)

TLBO Based Hybrid Forecasting Model for Prediction of Exchange Rates

Anindita Dutta[1]([✉]), Minakhi Rout[2], and Babita Majhi[3]

[1] ITER, Siksha O Anusandhan University, Bhubaneswar, India
aninditadtt9@gmail.com
[2] Department of CSE, ITER, Siksha O Anusandhan University,
Bhubaneswar, India
minakhi.rout@gmail.com
[3] Department of CSIT, G.G. Vishwavidyalaya, Central University,
Bilaspur, India
babita.majhi@gmail.com

Abstract. The teacher-learning based optimization (TLBO) algorithm is a new meta-heuristic approach, having the ability to solve non-linear problem and free from algorithm parameters. This paper proposes an efficient prediction model for forecasting currency exchange rate in term of 1 US Dollar to Indian Rupees, Singapore Dollar and Canadian Dollar using FLANN (Functional Link Artificial Neural Network). The teaching and learning algorithm has been used to optimize the weights of the forecasting models. The mean absolute percentage error (MAPE) is used to find out the performance of the model. The performance of the model is evaluated through simulation study and the results have been compared with FLANN-PSO and FLANN-DE forecasting models. It is observed that the model gives better performance result.

Keywords: Exchange rates forecasting · Functional Link Artificial Neural Network (FLANN) · Teaching-learning based optimization (TLBO) · Particle swarm optimization (PSO) and Differential evolution (DE)

1   Introduction

Forecasting exchange rate is a very challenging task as it is one of the most important financial markets for investors. Since exchange rates are highly volatile in nature and changes rapidly over short period of time, the investors are very anxious to determine the future trend of the exchange rates in the markets to reduce the risk. Many financial models have been used to analyze the behavior of the exchange rate because of the fact that exchange rates are dynamic, non-linear, non-stationary, chaotic and complex in nature. Thus conventional methodology can hardly forecast the exchange rate. Hence financial industry is depending upon advance computer technologies in order to maintain competitiveness in the global economy [1].

© Springer International Publishing Switzerland 2015
B.K. Panigrahi et al. (Eds.): SEMCCO 2014, LNCS 8947, pp. 38–48, 2015.
DOI: 10.1007/978-3-319-20294-5_4

A particle swarm optimization back propagation network (PSOBPN) model where PSO is used to select the optimal input layer neuron for prediction of exchange rates by back propagation network (BPN) has been proposed in [2]. In [3] a hybrid model is used to forecast the future trend of the exchange rates that combines both fundamental and technical analysis. Three ANN based forecasting model are investigated to predict the six exchange rates Australian dollar [4]. Reference [5] proposed a forecasting model based on neural network with weighted fuzzy membership functions (NEWFM) to predict the GBP/USD and Indian rupee/USD exchange rate using the Haar wavelet transforms (WT). A model based on multilayer perceptron (MLP) neural network using Bayesian learning and markov chain montecarlo (MCMC) method for forecasting exchange rates has been reported in [6]. The study in [7] proposed a generalized auto regressive conditional heteroskedasticity (GARCH) model to predict the future changes in exchange rates and ant colony algorithm was used for optimization. The paper in [8] indicated the use of functional link artificial neural network which is a single layer feed forward network for task classification because of its simple architectural design and less computational complexity. An integrated functional link interval type-2 fuzzy neural system (FLIT2FNS) for predicting the stock market indices has been proposed recently in [9]. The hybrid model uses a TSK (Takagi-Sugano-Kang) type fuzzy rule base that employs type-2 fuzzy sets in the antecedent parts and the outputs from the functional link artificial neural network (FLANN) in the consequent parts. Back propagation and particle swarm optimization (PSO) learning algorithms have been used independently to optimize the parameters of all the forecasting models. An adaptive model for the forecast of exchange rates has proposed in [10], in which the weights of the network are updated based on differential evolution (DE) algorithm. In the recent past teaching-learning based optimization (TLBO) [11–13] has been used for mechanical design optimization problems due to its less computational complexity and high consistency. It has no algorithm-specific parameters unlike other evolutionary optimization techniques. TLBO requires only common controlling parameters like population size and number of generations for its working.

In this paper we have proposed a simple model for forecasting, using functional link artificial neural network (FLANN) as the basic model and teaching-learning based optimization algorithm as the learning tool to accurately and efficiently predict the exchange rate of US Dollar in terms of Indian Rupees, Singapore Dollar and Canadian Dollar. The organization of the paper is as follows: Sect. 1 deals with literature review, problem formulation and motivation behind the problem selection. Section 2 describes the detail of teaching-learning based optimization. Section 3 outlines the process of feature extraction from raw data set. The development and algorithm of the proposed model and the weight optimization of the network based on TLBO is described in Sect. 4. The simulation study and result analysis is discussed in Sect. 5. Finally the conclusion is discussed in Sect. 6.

2   Teaching-Learning Based Optimization

TLBO was introduced by Rao, Savsani and Vakharia in [11] as a meta-heuristic, population based optimization algorithm. Recently this technique was used for the optimization of mechanical design problem. TLBO have been used to obtain approximate global solution for non-linear problem with less computational complexity. It is a simple algorithm because no algorithm parameters are required for the working of the algorithm. It is inspired by passing of knowledge within a classroom environment, where a learner acquires knowledge from its teacher and other classmates. The teacher is considered as a highly learned person. As TLBO is a population based approach, it uses a population of solution to reach the global or optimal solution. In this technique the population is considered as a group of learners. Every optimization algorithm has design variables. In TLBO different design variables are considered as different subjects and the result obtained by each learner is taken as fitness values. The learner with best fitness value is considered as teacher. The teacher tries to disseminate knowledge among learners, which will in turn increase the knowledge level of the whole class and help learners to get good marks or grades. The quality of the students is judged from the mean value of the population. The teacher tries to move the mean of the class to its own level thus increasing the learners' level to a new mean. As the mean increases to a new level, a new teacher is obtained of better quality than the students. The algorithm has the following steps:

A. Initialization Phase: A population of size P_n each having number of design variables (D), of variables is initialized such that, $(x_i = 1, 2, . . , P_n)$ and $(x_{ij}, j = 1, 2, .., D)$. Each variable has to be optimized so that the objective function is minimized.

population =

$$\begin{bmatrix} a_{1,1} & a_{1,2} & \cdots & a_{1,n} \\ a_{2,1} & a_{2,2} & \cdots & a_{2,n} \\ \vdots & \vdots & \ddots & \vdots \\ a_{m,1} & a_{m,2} & \cdots & a_{m,n} \end{bmatrix}$$

B. Teacher Phase: The mean of the population is calculated column-wise, which gives the mean of each subject (variable)

$$M_{new,D} = [m_1, m_2, ..., m_D] \tag{1}$$

The learner with minimum objective function is considered as the teacher for that iteration. Hence,

$$X_{teacher} = X_{f(X)=min}$$

The teacher will try to shift the mean from M_D towards $X_{teacher}$ which will act as a new mean

$$M_D = X_{teacher,D}$$

The difference between two means is given as

$$Differencemean_i = r(M_{new} - T_F M_i) \tag{2}$$

Where r is a random number within the range [0,1] and T_f can either be 1 or 2 which is decided accordingly The obtained difference is added to the current solution to update its values using $T_f = \text{round}[1+\text{rand}(0,1)2-1]$
The current solution is updated by using the Eq. (3),

$$X'_{new,D} = X_{old,D} + DifferenceMean_D \tag{3}$$

Accept $X'_{new,D}$ if it gives better function value.

C. Learner Phase: In this phase the learners enhance their knowledge through mutual interaction. Two learners are randomly chosen p and q such that $X'_{new-p,D} \neq X'_{new-q,D}$ (where $X'_{new-p,D}$ and $X'_{new-q,D}$ are the updated values of $X_{old-p,D}$ and $X_{old-q,D}$ at the end of the teacher phase)

$$X''_{new-p,D} = X'_{new-p,D} + r(X'_{new-p,D} - X'_{new-q,D}) If X'_{new-p,D} < X'_{new-q,D} \tag{4}$$

$$X''_{new-p,D} = X'_{new-p,D} + r(X'_{new-q,D} - X'_{new-p,D}) If X'_{new-p,D} > X'_{new-q,D} \tag{5}$$

$X''_{new-p,D}$ is accepted if it gives a better function value.

3 Feature Extraction from Raw Data

The past exchange rate data which consists of one currency value for each month is collected for the period January 1973 to October 2013, January 1981 to March 2014 and January 1999 to March 2014 for Indian Rupees, Singapore Dollar and Canadian Dollar respectively with respect to US Dollar. Then the values were normalized so that the values lie between 0 and +1 by dividing each value by the maximum value in the entire data set. A sliding window of size 12 containing past 11 months normalized values and the present value is used to extract three features for each i.e. 12th month value, mean and variance of each group are given as input to the model. In this way 488, 399 and 183 set of features of Indian Rupees, Singapore Dollar and Canadian Dollar respectively were extracted. Out of the total obtained set of features 80 % of the features set are used for training and remaining 20 % of the features are used for testing the performance of the model.

4 Development of FLANN Based Prediction Model

The hybrid model consists of a FLANN as shown in Fig. 1. The weights of the prediction model are updated by the principle of TLBO. FLANN is a single layer neural network in which each input pattern undergoes functional expansion and

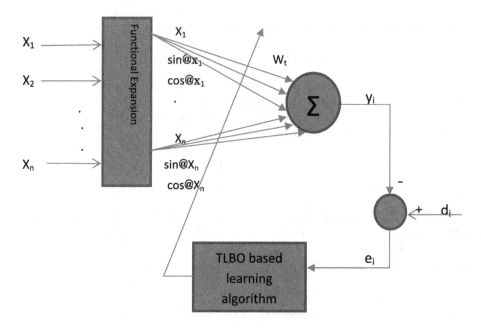

Fig. 1. A FLANN-TLBO based prediction model

increases in the input vector dimensionality. Each member of the population in TLBO represents a possible weight vector of the model which is updated to progressively minimize the mean square error(MSE).

The development of the prediction model proceeds as follows:

Step-1. Features are extracted from the raw data and are given as input to the FLANN.

Step-2. The weights of the model are initialized randomly and these weights act as the member of the initial population having P individual. Each member of the population constitutes D number of parameters which represent the weight values of the FLANN.

Step-3. Out of total K set of features, L sets (80 % of K approximately) are used for training and rest (K-L) sets are used for testing the performance of the model.

Step-4. The first feature set is applied to the model and the corresponding desired output is obtained. The output of the model corresponding to the ith set of feature is estimated as

$$y_i = \sum_{d=1}^{D} w_{i,d} x_{i,d} \tag{6}$$

Step-5. After the application of L number of training sets, L errors is produced. The mean square error(MSE) for a set of parameters corresponding to the ith individual is determined by

$$MSE(i) = \frac{\sum_{l=1}^{L} e^2(l)}{L} \tag{7}$$

where the error is calculated as

$$e_i = d_i - y_i \tag{8}$$

This is repeated for P times.

Step-6. The weight(each individual) is updated in two phases. In teacher phase the weight is updated using (3). The fitness value of the new population is computed. Comparison is done between the two fitness values, the one with minimum fitness value is selected for the learner phase. In the learner phase the weight is updated using (4) or (5). The fitness value of the new population is again computed. Comparison is done between the two fitness values; the one with minimum fitness value is selected for the next generation. The entire process is repeated for certain generations.

Step-7. At each generation minimum MSE is obtained and plotted against the number of generation to show the learning characteristics of the model.

Step-8. The learning process is stopped when MMSE reaches to a minimum possible floor level.

Step-9. The potential ability of the model is tested with the known feature of some previous months.

5   Simulation Study and Result Analysis

The simulation study is carried out to signify and estimate the prediction performance of the proposed model (FLANN-TLBO) and is compared with the result obtained from DE and PSO based models. The data set has been taken from the website www.forecasts.org. Simulation has been done for the prediction of three different exchange rates (Indian Rupees, Singapore Dollar and Canadian Dollar with respect to US Dollar). The prediction efficiency of the model is assessed for 1 month, 3 months and 6 months ahead. The entire data set is divided into training set and testing set. All the inputs are normalized by using (9)

$$y_i = \frac{x_i}{x_{max}} \tag{9}$$

where y_i, x_i and x_{max} represent the normalized, actual value and maximum value in the entire data set respectively.

The input pattern are extracted from the data set by grouping the data using a shifting window of size 12 and the 12th value, mean and variance of each group is taken as input to the FLANN. These three extracted features are first functionally expanded using trigonometric function. Then the expanded input are weighted and summed to obtain the output. After all the patterns are applied to each individual weight vector and the minimum MSE (MMSE) is obtained then weights of the model are updated using teaching-learning based optimization technique. The performance of the model is determined by calculating the mean absolute percentage of error (MAPE) as given in (10).

$$MAPE(k) = \frac{1}{M} \sum_{m=1}^{M} \frac{y(m) - \hat{y}(m)}{y(m)} \tag{10}$$

where y(m), $\hat{y}(m)$ and M represents actual exchange price, predicted exchange price and total number of test samples respectively.

The convergence characteristics of FLANN-TLBO of US Dollar to Indian Rupees for 1 month, 3 months and 6 months ahead is obtained and shown in the Fig. 2. From these figures it is contemplated that TLBO has faster convergence rate. The comparison of convergence characteristics of FLANN-TLBO along FLANN-DE and FLANN-PSO has been shown in the Fig. 3. The comparison of actual and predicted values of US Dollar to Indian Rupees for 1 month ahead prediction are shown in Fig. 4 during testing period. In Fig. 5 the comparison of actual and predicted values of US Dollar to Singapore Dollar for 6 months ahead prediction during training period is depicted. Similarly Fig. 6 represents the actual and predicted values of US Dollar to Canadian Dollar for 3 months ahead prediction during training period. The MAPE values obtained for the three data sets by using FLANN-TLBO, FLANN-DE and FLANN-PSO are given in Tables 1, 2 and 3. From the following tables it is revealed that FLANN-TLBO based model gives better prediction performance than the other two models.

Table 1. Comparison of MAPE obtained by different prediction models for Indian Rupees

Months ahead	FLANN-TLBO	FLANN-DE	FLANN-PSO
1	0.5422	0.6010	0.7460
3	0.5251	0.8021	1.1207
6	1.3900	1.5293	1.7692

Table 2. Comparison of MAPE obtained by different prediction models for Singapore Dollar

Months ahead	FLANN-TLBO	FLANN-DE	FLANN-PSO
1	1.5885	1.7287	1.8782
3	1.5243	2.1928	2.7999
6	1.7109	2.0547	2.7072

Table 3. Comparison of MAPE obtained by different prediction models for Canadian Dollar

Months ahead	FLANN-TLBO	FLANN-DE	FLANN-PSO
1	0.3894	0.5147	1.5210
3	0.9544	1.1398	1.9541
6	1.0845	1.4866	2.5592

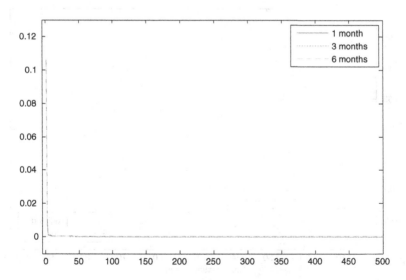

Fig. 2. Comparison of convergence characteristics for different months ahead prediction for Indian Rupees using FLANN-TLBO model

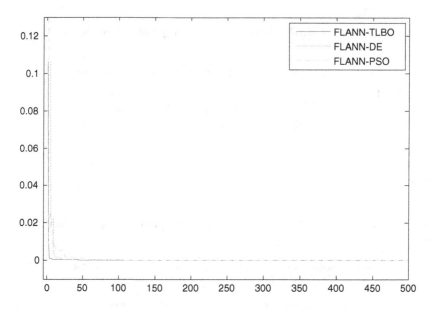

Fig. 3. Comparison of convergence characteristics for one month ahead prediction for Indian rupees of different prediction models

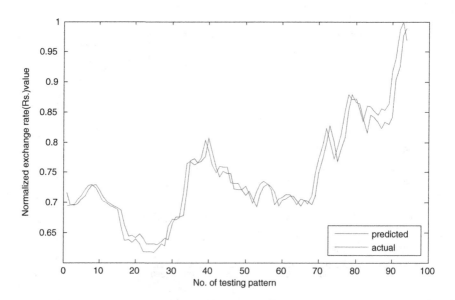

Fig. 4. Comparison of actual and predicted value of Indian Rupees for 1 month ahead prediction using FLANN-TLBO model during testing

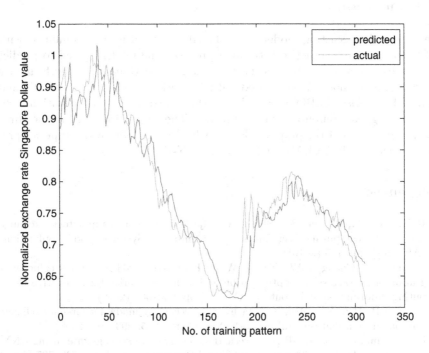

Fig. 5. Comparison of actual and predicted value of Singapore Dollar for 6 months ahead prediction using FLANN-TLBO model during training

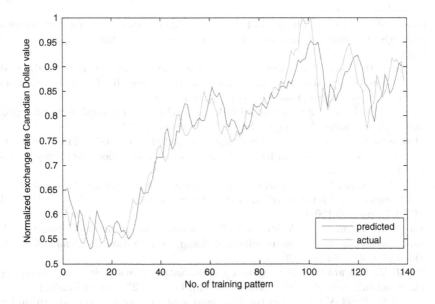

Fig. 6. Comparison of actual and predicted value of Canadian Dollar for 3 months ahead prediction using FLANN-TLBO model during training

6 Conclusion

The proposed forecasting model is developed first, and is then combined with TLBO to optimize the network training process. The model is used to predict different exchange rates fromthe past exchange rate values. The performance of the proposed model is compared with two other models, FLANN-DE and FLANN-PSO. Also, TLBO perform better than the other two optimization technique, having less computational complexity. The comparison among the three models indicates that the proposed FLANN-TLBO model provides superior prediction accuracy than FLANN-DE and FLANN-PSO.

References

1. Rahamneh, Z., Reyalat, M., Sheta, A., Aljahdali, S.: Forecasting stock exchange using soft computing techniques. In: Computer Systems and Applications (AICCSA), pp. 1–5 (2010)
2. Chang, J.F., Chang, C.W., Tzeng, W.Y.: Forecasting exchange rates using integration of particle swarm optimization and neural networks. In: Innovative Computing, Information and Control (ICICIC), pp. 660–663 (2009)
3. Chen, A.P., Hsu, Y.C., Hu, K.F.: A hybrid forecasting model for foreign exchange rate based on a multi-neural network. Nat. Comput. **5**, 293–298 (2008)
4. Kamrwzaman, J., Sarker, R.A.: Forecasting of currency exchange rates using ANN: a case study. In: Neural Network and Signal Processing, vol. 1, pp. 793–797 (2003)
5. Lee, S.H., Lim, J.S.: Extracting input features and fuzzy rules for forecasting exchange rate using NEWFM. In: Management of Innovation and Technology, pp. 542–547 (2008)
6. Huang, W., Lai, K.K., Zhang, J., Bao, Y.: Foreign exchange rates forecasting with multilayer perceptron neural network by bayesian learning. Nat. Comput. **7**, 28–32 (2008)
7. Xiaofeng, H., Junjian, W., Jingshu, C.: Research on the GARCH model optimized by the ant colony algorithm of forecast exchange rate. In: Computer Science-Technology and Applications vol. 1, pp. 380–383 (2009)
8. Misra, B.B., Dehuri, S.: Functional link artificial neural networkfor classification task in data mining. J. Comput. Sci. **3**(12), 948–955 (2007)
9. Chakravarty, S., Dash, P.K.: A PSO based integrated functional link net and interval type-2 fuzzy logic system for predicting stock market indices. Appl. Soft Comput. **12**, 931–941 (2012)
10. Rout, M., Majhi, B., Mohapatra, U.M.: Development and performance evaluation of DE based time series prediction model. In: Energy, Automation, and Signal (ICEAS), pp. 1–5 (2011)
11. Rao, R.V., Savsani, V.J., Vakharia, D.P.: Teaching-learning-based optimization: A novel method for constrainedmechanical design optimization problems. Comput. Aided Des. **43**, 303–315 (2011)
12. Rao, R.V., Kalyankar, V.D.: Parameter optimization of machining processes using a new optimization algorithm. Mater. Manuf. Process. **27**, 978–985 (2012)
13. Rao, R.V., Patel, V.: An elitist teaching-learning-based optimization algorithm for solving complex constrained optimization problems. Int. J. Ind. Eng. Comput. **3**, 535–560 (2012)

A Comparative Study of Two Types of Fuzzy Logic Controllers for Shunt Active Power Filters

D.A. Gadanayak and Irani Majumder[(✉)]

Department of Electrical and Electronics Engineering, Institute of Technical
Education and Research, SOA University, Bhubaneswar, India
debadattagadanayak@soauniversity.ac.in,
majumder.irani@yahoo.com

Abstract. In this work, two types of fuzzy logic controllers have been designed for a shunt active power filter and their steady state as well as transient performance has been compared to a conventional PI-controller. The performance of the various controllers has been judged on the basis of their ability to reduce Total Harmonic Distortion and their ability to reduce DC-link capacitor voltage settling time during load change. The second factor is important since it signifies controller's usefulness in rapid load changing industrial environment. Also, DC-link capacitor voltage rise at the time of decrease in load is taken as another factor for comparison as it might affect the voltage ratings of the power electronic devices used in the filter.

Keywords: Shunt active power filter · Mamdani type FLC · TSK type FLC · Indirect current control technique · Harmonics · Total harmonic distortion · Point of common coupling · MATLAB SimPowerSystems toolbox

1 Introduction

Advances in control techniques of solid state power converters has resulted in extensive use of them in a wide range of applications such as adjustable speed drives, uninterruptable power supplies, HVDC systems, renewable energy systems etc. However, due to their non-linear characteristics these loads draw harmonic currents which in turn distort the voltage waveforms at the point of common coupling (PCC). Such harmonics not only create more voltage or current stress but also are responsible for electromagnetic interference, more losses, capacitor failure due to overloading, harmonic resonance etc. [1] Use of active power filters for harmonic current compensation and hence making the voltage of PCC unaffected has been so far proposed and verified [2, 3]. Active power filter (APF) has gained much attention because of excellent harmonic and reactive power compensation in two-wire (single phase), three-wire (three phase without neutral) and four-wire (three phase with neutral) ac power networks with non-linear loads [4].

The shunt active power filter eliminates harmonics by injecting a current at the PCC that is equal to the load harmonic current. However, load harmonics to be compensated is very complex in nature and changes with change in load. Hence the shunt active

© Springer International Publishing Switzerland 2015
B.K. Panigrahi et al. (Eds.): SEMCCO 2014, LNCS 8947, pp. 49–61, 2015.
DOI: 10.1007/978-3-319-20294-5_5

power filter need to be accurate in current tracking and should respond quickly to any change in loading conditions. Two most popular control strategies, namely direct and indirect current control techniques, which are based on reference current estimations by regulating the DC side capacitor voltage of PWM converter has been discussed in [5]. The difference between these two types of current control techniques is in the number of current sensors used. In direct current control technique both load and filter currents are sensed, where as indirect current control technique is based on sensing source current only. For both the schemes a conventional PI-controller was used in [5] to obtain reference current templates.

It is well known that a PI controller fails to perform satisfactorily when the system is complex because of either non-linearity or parameter variation issues. But an intelligent or self-organizing control system can identify the model, if necessary, and give the predicted performance even with a wide range of parameter variation [6]. Fuzzy logic based controllers are not new. These have been used in numerous applications and have proved to be superior to conventional controllers.

The design of a Mamdani type fuzzy logic controller is mainly based on a mixture of logical reasoning and intuitiveness arising out of the experience of the system. The Mamdani type fuzzy controller used for control of shunt active power filters gives better performance than conventional PI-controller both in terms of steady state and transient response [7]. But it has drawback of a large number of fuzzy sets, rules and coefficients to be optimized. This increases the complexity of controller and demands large computation time. As a result it may not be useful for real time applications with small sampling time [8].

In this work, both Mamdani type and TSK type fuzzy logic controllers have been implemented using MATLAB Fuzzy Logic toolbox, alongside a conventional PI-controller to a three phase shunt active power filter, modeled using MATLAB SimPowerSystems toolbox and their steady state as well as transient performance has been studied in detail. The performance of the various controllers has been judged on the basis of two factors. First, their ability in reducing Total Harmonic Distortion (THD) and secondly, their ability to reduce DC-link capacitor voltage settling time during load change. The second factor is important since it implies time taken for real power balance. Hence reduction in it signifies its usefulness in rapid load changing industrial environment.

2 Basic Indirect Current Control Scheme

A simpler control scheme which involves sensing load current only was proposed in [9]. It was suitably modified for real time implementation and given the name 'indirect current control technique in [5]. The basic indirect current control scheme is given in Figs. 1 and 2. The scheme is based on reference current estimations by regulating the DC side capacitor voltage of PWM converter. Under steady state conditions the real power supplied by the source must be equal to summation of real power consumed by the non-linear load and negligible loss in the filter circuit. But however, when there is a change in loading, the power balance between the source and the load is disturbed and the difference is compensated by the DC-link capacitor. This compensation process

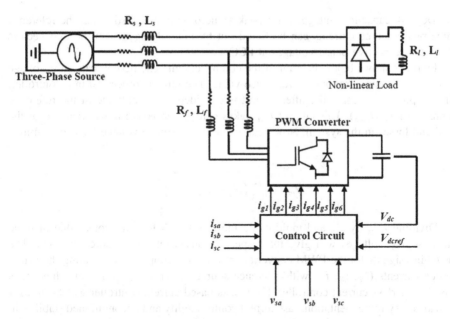

Fig. 1. Basic indirect current control scheme

charges or discharges the capacitor depending upon whether extra requirement of real power at the time of increase in load is drawn from it or surplus real power at the time of decrease in load is consumed by it. Charging or discharging changes the capacitor voltage away from the reference value. Hence the value of capacitor voltage is an indication of whether real power supplied by the source and hence the peak value of source current should be increased or decreased and by what amount. So, we can conclude that the peak value of reference source current can be estimated by regulating

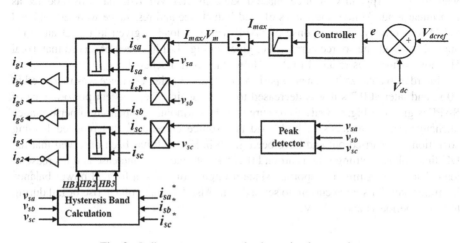

Fig. 2. Indirect current control scheme implementation

the DC-link capacitor voltage. Once peak value of current is estimated, the reference three phase source currents can be found out by multiplying it with the unit vectors along the respective phase voltages at PCC.

Figure 2 shows block diagram of the control circuit. The dc-link capacitor voltage is sensed and compared with a reference value. The error is processed in a controller. The output of the controller after a limit is considered as amplitude of the reference source current (I_{max}). This current I_{max} takes care of the active power demand of the load and losses in the system. Now peak value of the source voltage V_m is determined as

$$V_m = \sqrt{\frac{2}{3}\left(v_{sa}^2 + v_{sb}^2 + v_{sc}^2\right)}$$

Dividing I_{max} by V_m and multiplying the result with instantaneous value of three phase source voltages will give the respective phase reference source currents. The switching signals for the PWM converter are obtained simply by comparing the actual source currents (i_{sa}, i_{sb}, i_{sc}) with reference source currents (i_{sa}^*, i_{sb}^*, i_{sc}^*) in a hysteresis based carrierless current controller. Hysteresis based current controller was taken as it provides easy implementation, fast current controllability and unconditioned stability in comparison to other methods. It creates an environment for fastest control with minimum hardware and has excellent dynamics [10].

In this work, for comparison purpose, primarily a PI-controller was designed and its steady states as well as dynamic performances were analyzed. Later, after implementation of proposed fuzzy controllers, their performances were compared with this conventional controller.

2.1   Performance of a Conventional PI-controller

The system parameters taken for simulation in MATLAB-SIMULINK environment were given in Appendix. A three phase diode converter with R-L load was modeled as non-linear load. At first, the values of load inductance and resistance were 20 mH and 6.7 Ω respectively. The response of SAPF with this load is given in Fig. 3 and FFT analysis of load and source currents are given in Fig. 4. It has been observed that Total Harmonic Current is reduced to 2.41 % by this control scheme.

In order to analyze its transient performance, at 0.3 s the resistance was increased to 10 Ω and later at 0.7 s it was decreased to 6.7 Ω again. The transient performance of SAPF is given in Fig. 5. Only to be sure that the harmonic compensation performance unchanged, THD analysis of both load and source currents at this reduced loading condition was carried out and have been given in Fig. 6. It has been observed that the DC-link voltage settling time is around 0.225 s both incase of increase and decrease in load. This settling time is important since it implies time taken for real power balance i.e. time taken for source current to settle down. Also DC-link voltage rise or fall during transient period is about 23 V.

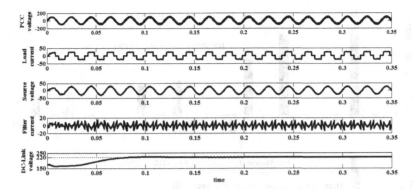

Fig. 3. Steady state performance with PI-controller

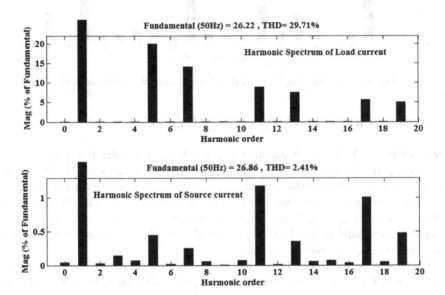

Fig. 4. Harmonic analysis of load and source currents

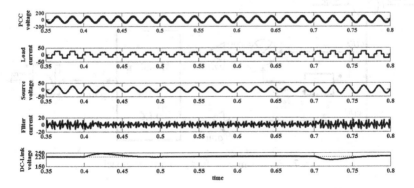

Fig. 5. Transient performance with PI-controller

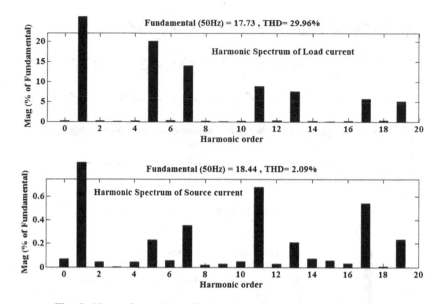

Fig. 6. Harmonic analysis of load and source currents at reduced load

3   Design of a Mamdani Type Fuzzy Logic Controller

Fuzzy control is basically an adaptive and non-linear controller that gives robust performance for a linear or non-linear plant with parameter variations [11]. Any given linear control can be achieved with a fuzzy controller for a given accuracy [12]. A Mamdani type fuzzy logic controller has been designed to replace the PI-controller. The error $e(k) = V_{dcref} - V_{dc}(k)$ and the change in error $\Delta e(k) = e(k) - e(k-1)$ are used as inputs to the Mamdani type Fuzzy logic controller (FLC) and the maximum value of source current (I_{max}) is taken as output.

The Mamdani type FLC scheme implemented in this work is given in Fig. 7. To construct a rule base, the inputs and output are partitioned into seven primary fuzzy

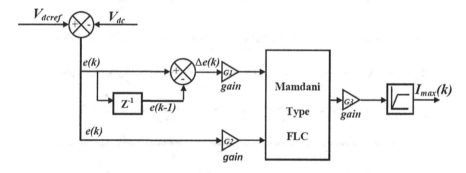

Fig. 7. Mamdani type fuzzy controller model

sets labeled as {NB, NM, NS, ZE, PS, PM, PB}. The determination of the membership functions depends on the designer experiences and expert knowledge [13]. In our case, triangular membership functions are taken only for the sake of simplicity in implementation. The normalized input and output membership functions are given in Fig. 8. The gain values G_1, G_2 and G_3 depends up on the maximum values of error, change in error and change in output in each iteration. The maximum values of error, change in error and change in output in each iteration from the PI-control model were taken as initial values for G_1, G_1 and G_3 and then modified using Simulink Design Optimization toolbox. The rules are expressed in the form **IF** (antecedent) **THEN** (consequence). The FLC rule-base constitutes of the form **IF** e is A_1 **AND** Δe is B_1 **THEN** I_{max} is C_1. A rough rule base was constructed using the simple logic that large error and large change in error requires large change in output and smaller error and change in error requires smaller change in output. The final rule base was constructed by modifying this rough one based on simulation performance. The rule base is given in Table 1.

The same SAPF model was simulated using Mamdani type fuzzy logic controller replacing the PI-controller. The steady state and dynamic responses are given in Figs. 9 and 11. The FFT analysis of the source current is shown in Fig. 10.

We can see that THD in source current is 2.35 %. It is better than THD with PI-controller which is 2.41 %. It should be noted that the result for the load 20 mH and 6.7 Ω is compared. However, if for the reduced load THD is compared; in that case also Mamdani type FLC gives better performance. The DC-link voltage settling time is around 0.1 s. both incase of increase and decrease in load. DC-link voltage rise or fall during transient period is about 7 V.

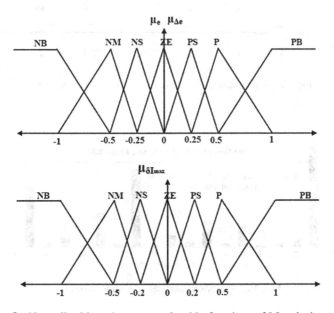

Fig. 8. Normalized input/output membership functions of Mamdani model

Table 1. Control rule table for Mamdani model

e Δe	NB	NM	NS	ZE	PS	PM	PB
NB	NB	NB	NB	NB	NM	NS	ZE
NM	NB	NB	NB	NM	NS	ZE	PS
NS	NB	NB	NM	NS	ZE	PS	PM
ZE	NB	NM	NS	ZE	PS	PM	PB
PS	NM	NS	ZE	PS	PM	PB	PB
PM	NS	ZE	PS	PM	PB	PB	PB
PB	ZE	PS	PM	PB	PB	PB	PB

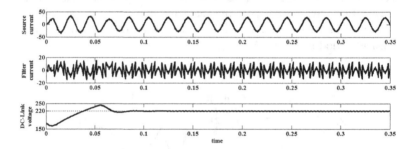

Fig. 9. Steady state performance with Mamdani type FLC

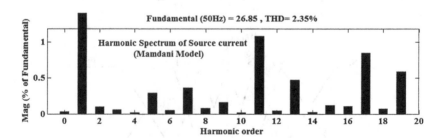

Fig. 10. Harmonic analysis of source current

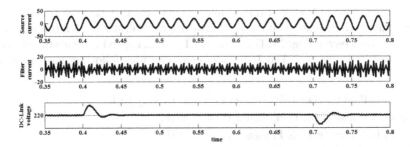

Fig. 11. Transient performance with Mamdani type FLC

4 Design of TSK-Type Fuzzy Logic Controller

Among various kinds of fuzzy methods, the Takagi–Sugeno-Kang (TSK) fuzzy model is widely accepted as a tool for design and analysis of fuzzy control systems [14]. Takagi, Sugeno and Kang proposed the popular TSK fuzzy model as a result of their effort to develop a systematic method for generation of fuzzy rule base out of a given input-output training data set. A typical fuzzy rule in TSK fuzzy model has the form: If inputs x is "A" and y is "B" then output z = f(x, y), where "A" and "B" are fuzzy sets in antecedent and z = f(x, y) is a crisp function in the consequent. The order of the TSK-fuzzy model is given by the order of the polynomial f(x, y). A TSK-type fuzzy controller can provide a wide range of control gain variation and can use both linear and non-linear rules in the consequent expression of the fuzzy rule base [15]. The Mamdani type of fuzzy controller used for the control of SAPF has the drawback of larger number of fuzzy sets and rules. Also there are a larger number of coefficients have to be optimized to get better performance. Increase in such type of complexity of controller demands larger computational time for control execution; hence it may not be useful for real time applications with small sampling time [8]. On the other hand TSK controller is less complex and computationally efficient. Also it has guaranteed continuity of output surface. Design of a novel variable gain PI-controller using TSK fuzzy model is given in [8, 15]. Application of similar controller to SAPF is given in Fig. 12.

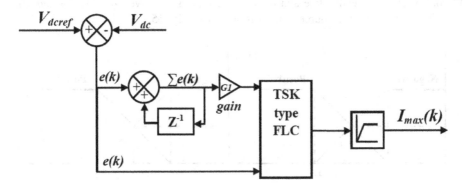

Fig. 12. TSK-type fuzzy controller model

The input to the FLC is error (e) and integration of error ($\int$e taken as Σe). The error and integration of error are partitioned into two trapezoidal fuzzy sets P (positive) and N (negative) as given in Fig. 13. The value of L1 and L2 depend upon maximum value of error and its integration. The TSK fuzzy controller uses following four simplified rules:

1. If $e(k)$ is P and $\int e(k)$ is P, then $u_1(k) = a_1.e(k) + a_2.\int e(k)$
2. If $e(k)$ is P and $\int e(k)$ is N, then $u_2(k) = K_2 u_1(k)$
3. If $e(k)$ is N and $\int e(k)$ is P, then $u_3(k) = K_3 u_1(k)$
4. If $e(k)$ is N and $\int e(k)$ is N, then $u_4(k) = K_4 u_1(k)$

In the above rule u_1, u_2, u_3, u_4 represent the consequent of TSK fuzzy controller. Using AND operation and general defuzzifier, the output u(k) is given by:

$$u(k) = \frac{\sum_{j=1}^{4} (\mu_j)^{\gamma} u_j(k)}{\sum_{j=1}^{4} (\mu_j)^{\gamma}}$$

For centroid method of de-fuzzification, $\gamma = 1$; hence output u(k) will be:

$$u(k) = a.e(k) + b. \int e(k)$$

Where a = a_1K and b = a_2K
And

$$K = \frac{(\mu_1 + K_2\mu_2 + K_3\mu_3 + K_4\mu_4)}{(\mu_1 + \mu_2 + \mu_3 + \mu_4)}$$

Hence the above controller is basically a variable gain PI-controller. The K operator is condition dependent; hence the effective value of control gain varies widely during the control process. The above TSK fuzzy controller is a highly non-linear variable gain controller and the coefficients a_1, a_2 produce wide variations of controller gain [8].

Again our SAPF model was simulated using this TSK type variable gain PI-controller. The steady state and dynamic responses are given in Figs. 14 and 16. The FFT analysis of the source current is shown in Fig. 15.

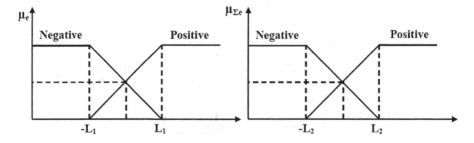

Fig. 13. Input membership functions for TSK model

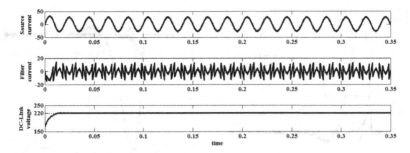

Fig. 14. Steady state performance with TSK-type FLC

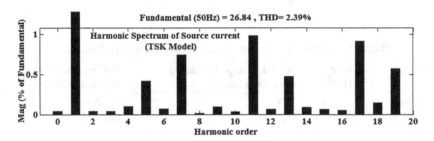

Fig. 15. Harmonic analysis of source current

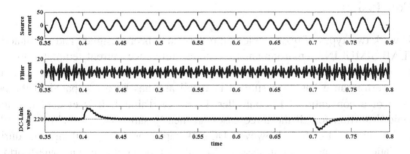

Fig. 16. Transient performance with TSK-type FLC

We have observed that THD of source current in case of TSK-type FLC is 2.39 %. It is a little bit more than THD with Mamdani type FLC. However, the DC-link voltage settling time is drastically decreased. It is around 0.055 s only both in case of increase and decrease in load. DC-link voltage rise or fall during transient period is also reduced to a very negligible amount. It is about 4 V only.

The performance of DC link capacitor voltage regulation during increase and decrease in load for the above three control schemes, considering one control scheme at a time is shown in Fig. 17. Also a comparative analysis of the performance of all three controllers is given in Table 2.

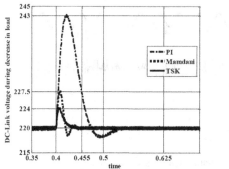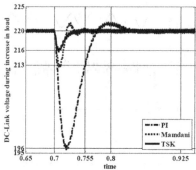

Fig. 17. DC-link capacitor voltage comparison during transient conditions

Table 2. Comparison between three types of controller performance

Controllers	% of THD	DC-link voltage rise during decrease in load	Settling time during change in load
PI-controller	2.41 %	23 V	0.225 s
Mamdani-type FLC	2.35 %	7 V	0.1 s
TSK-type FLC	2.39 %	4 V	0.055 s

5 Conclusion

In this work two types of fuzzy logic controllers have been designed and simulated in MATLAB-SIMULINK environment to generate reference current templates in indirect current control mode of shunt active power filter control. Their steady state and transient performance has been studied in detail and has been compared to the performance of a conventional PI-controller. From the Table 1, it is evident that total harmonic distortion for all the three cases are nearly same and are below the IEEE standard requirement of 5 %. However, DC-link capacitor voltage settling time during load variations is nearly half in case of Mamdani type controller and one-fourth in case of TSK-type controller as compared to the conventional controller. This settling time is important since it implies the settling time of source current as well, which is an immensely useful quality for a controller in a rapid load changing environment. Also it has been observed that DC-link voltage rise at the time of decrease in load in case of PI-controller is 23 volt which is more than 10 % of its steady state value of 220 V. It definitely affects the voltage ratings of the power electronic switches used in the filter. The fact that the performance of the TSK controller is excellent in all respect and keeping in mind that it demands less computation time than the other fuzzy variant, we can conclude that the TSK-type controller is immensely useful for control of SAPF.

References

1. Bhattacharya, A., Chakraborty, C., Bhattacharya, S.: Parallel-connected shunt hybrid active power filters operating at different switching frequencies for improved performance. IEEE Trans. Ind. Electron. **59**(11), 4007–4019 (2012)
2. Akagi, H.: Trends in active power line conditioners. IEEE Trans. Power Electron. **9**(3), 263–268 (1994)
3. Singh, B., Al-Haddad, K., Chandra, A.: A review of active filters for power quality improvement. IEEE Trans. Ind. Electron. **46**(5), 960–971 (1999)
4. Mikkili, S., Panda, A.K.: Type-1 and type-2 fuzzy logic controller based shunt active filter Id-Iq control strategy for mitigation of harmonics with triangular membership function. In: 2012 IEEE International Conference on Power Electronics, Drives and Energy Systems (PEDES), pp. 1–6, 16–19 Dec 2012
5. Singh, B.N., Chandra, A., Al-Haddad, K.: Performance comparison of two current control techniques applied to an active filter. In: 8th International Conference on Harmonics and Quality of Power Proceedings, 1998, vol. 1, pp. 133–138. 14–18 Oct 1998
6. Kumar, P., Mahajan, A.: Soft computing techniques for the control of an active power filter. IEEE Trans. Power Deliv. **24**(1), 452–461 (2009)
7. Jain, S.K., Agrawal, P., Gupta, H.O.: Fuzzy logic controlled shunt active power filter for power quality improvement. IEE Proc. Electr. Power Appl. **149**(5), 317–328 (2002)
8. Bhende, C.N., Mishra, S., Jain, S.K.: TS-fuzzy-controlled active power filter for load compensation. IEEE Trans. Power Deliv. **21**(3), 1459–1465 (2006)
9. Duke, R.M., Round, S.D.: The steady-state performance of a controlled current active filter. IEEE Trans. Power Electron. **8**(2), 140–146 (1993)
10. Ray, P.K., Panda, G., Puhan, P.S.: Fuzzy logic based intelligent shunt hybrid filter applied to single phase system. In: India Conference (INDICON), 2013 Annual IEEE, pp. 1–6, 13–15 Dec 2013
11. Suresh, Y., Panda, A.K., Suresh, M.: Real-time implementation of adaptive fuzzy hysteresis-band current control technique for shunt active power filter. Power Electron. IET **5**(7), 1188–1195 (2012)
12. Galichet, S., Foulloy, L.: Fuzzy controllers: synthesis and equivalences. IEEE Trans. Fuzzy Syst. **3**(2), 140–148 (1995)
13. Belaidi, R., Haddouche, A., Guendouz, H.: Fuzzy logic controller based three-phase shunt active power filter for compensating harmonics and reactive power under unbalanced mains voltages. Energy Proc. **18**, 560–570 (2012)
14. Wu, Z.-G., Shi, P., Su, H., Chu, J.: Sampled-data fuzzy control of chaotic systems based on a T-S fuzzy model. IEEE Trans. Fuzzy Syst. **22**(1), 153–163 (2014)
15. Mishra, S., Dash, P.K., Panda, G.: TS-fuzzy controller for UPFC in a multimachine power system. IEE Proc. Gener. Transm. Distrib. **147**(1), 15–22 (2000)

A Quantum Behaved Particle Swarm Approach for Multi-response Optimization of WEDM Process

Bijaya Bijeta Nayak[(✉)] and Siba Sankar Mahapatra

Department of Mechanical Engineering, National Institute of Technology,
Rourkela 769008, India
{bijeta.mechanical,mahapatrass2003}@gmail.com

Abstract. The present study highlights a quantum behaved particle swarm optimization approach combined with maximum deviation theory to determine the optimal process parameters in wire electrical discharge machining process during taper cutting operation. Experiments have been conducted using six process parameters such as part thickness, taper angle, pulse duration, discharge current, wire speed and wire tension each at three levels for obtaining the responses like angular error, surface roughness, and cutting speed. Taguchi's L_{27} orthogonal array is used to gather information regarding the process with less number of experimental runs. Traditional Taguchi approach is insufficient to solve a multi response optimization problem. In order to overcome this limitation, maximum deviation method has been implemented, to convert multiple responses into equivalent single response called composite score. A process model has been developed by using non-linear regression analysis. Finally, optimal parameter setting is obtained by quantum behaved particle swarm optimization technique.

Keywords: Quantum behaved particle swarm optimization · Taper cutting · Wire electrical discharge machining · Maximum deviation method

1 Introduction

Wire electrical discharge machining (WEDM) is a highly potential non-traditional machining process because it provides an effective solution for many complex, difficult-to-machine parts involving tight corners, deep slots and features at multiple angles especially in the aerospace and defense industry applications. In WEDM the conductive materials are machined with a series of electrical discharges that are produced between an accurately positioned moving wire and the workpiece. High frequency pulses of alternating or direct current is discharged from the wire to the workpiece with a very small spark gap through an insulated dielectric fluid. The movement of the wire is precisely monitored by a computer numerically controlled system [1]. In today's manufacturing scenario, the development of precision and die industries not only requires more productivity, tolerances and dimensional accuracy but also demands complicated profiles

© Springer International Publishing Switzerland 2015
B.K. Panigrahi et al. (Eds.): SEMCCO 2014, LNCS 8947, pp. 62–73, 2015.
DOI: 10.1007/978-3-319-20294-5_6

with inclined or curved surfaces. Hence, tapering process is one of the most important applications of WEDM process. During taper cutting operation in wire-EDM, the wire is subjected to deformation resulting deviations in the inclination angle of machined parts. As a result, the machined part losses its precision. Hence, selection of the process parameters is a major issue in the field of taper cutting operation in WEDM.

Several researches related to optimization aspects of WEDM process by using various traditional and evolutionary optimization techniques were observed in the past. However most of them focused on straight path cutting using WEDM. Kuraiakose and Shunmugam [2] have developed a multiple regression model to represent the relationship between input and output variables and a multi-objective optimization method based on a Non-Dominated Sorting Genetic Algorithm (NSGA) to optimize WEDM process. Mahapatra and Patnaik [3] have established the relationship between control factors and responses like MRR, surface finish and kerf by means of non-linear regression analysis resulting in valid mathematical models. Finally, genetic algorithm is employed to optimize the WEDM process with multiple objectives. Back propagation neural network combined with simulated annealing algorithm (SAA) was used by Chen et al. [4]. Kondayya and Gopal Krishna [5] have proposed the prediction models for material removal rate and surface roughness using a potential evolutionary modelling algorithm genetic programming (GP). Mukherjee et al. [6] have applied six different non-traditional optimization algorithms such as genetic algorithm, particle swarm optimization, sheep flock algorithm, ant colony optimization, artificial bee colony and biogeography based optimization for single and multi-objective optimization of WEDM process. It is suggested that all the six algorithms have potential to achieve optimal parameter settings but the biogeography based algorithm performs better amongst all. Teaching learning based optimization algorithm was also employed by Rao and Kalyankar [7]. Majumder [8] describes an application of a hybrid approach using fuzzy logic and particle swarm optimization (PSO) for optimizing the process parameters in the electrical discharge machining process. Aich and Banerjee [9] have developed a process model for EDM process by support vector machine regression and obtained the best parametric combination using particle swarm optimization. However the application of optimization techniques and evolutionary algorithms in the field of taper cutting operation using WEDM process is very limited.

The problem of taper cutting is proposed first time by Kinoshita et al. [10]. They have developed a linear model for wire deformation neglecting the forces produced during the process. Chiu et al. [11] have carried out an on-line adjustment of the axial force imposed by the machine on the wire in taper cutting. Sanchez et al. [12] presented a approach for the prediction of angular error in wire-EDM taper cutting. They analysed the factors that influence angular error in taper cutting that leads to the development of experimental and numerical methods for the prediction of the error. Plaza et al. [13] developed two models for the prediction of angular error in WEDM taper cutting and found that part thickness and taper angle are most influencing variables. However a few researchers discussed about the problem of simultaneous optimization of various response during taper cutting operation in WEDM process. The information is also not readily available to select proper input parameters for taper cutting in WEDM process. With a view to alleviate this difficulty, a simple but reliable method based on Taguchi's design of experiment is used in the present work for investigating the effect of various process parameters on angular error, surface roughness and cutting speed. However, Taguchi method fails to solve multi objective optimization problems. To overcome this shortcoming, in the present work, maximum deviation theory is implemented to determine objective weight of each response. The composite score of the responses is then calculated which is considered as the equivalent single response. The relationship between the process parameters and composite score of the responses is expressed mathematically using non-linear regression analysis. Finally a quantum behaved particle swarm optimization approach is employed to obtain best parametric combination that maximizes composite score during taper cutting process in WEDM.

2 Proposed Methodology

The present work proposes an approach for optimization of process parameters of WEDM process during taper cutting operation for simultaneously minimizing the angular error, surface roughness and maximizing the cutting speed. The procedure of the proposed approach consists of three parts. In the first part maximum deviation method is applied to convert multi responses into single equivalent response known as composite score. The functional relationship between input factors and composite score has been developed by non-linear regression analysis. Finally the fitness function is optimized by using quantum behaved particle swarm optimization.

Maximum Deviation Method. Usually the weights assigned in the multi attribute decision making (MADM) are quite subjective in nature and affect the decision of ranking the alternative solutions. Therefore to avoid the embedded uncertainty and due to the subjective assigning of weights from the experts and to extract the accurate information from the available numerical data, maximum deviation method was proposed by Wang [14]. The little difference in the performance value of each alternative under an attribute shows the significance of that attribute in the priority ranking of alternatives. Contrariwise, higher difference in the performance value of alternatives in an attribute dictates the higher significance of that attribute in selection of best alternative. Therefore, the attribute having similar values across all alternatives should be assigned a smaller weight in comparison to the attribute having larger deviations. Especially, if the attribute values of all alternatives are equal with respect to a given attribute will be judged unimportant by most decision makers. In other word, such an attribute should be assigned a very small weight. Wang [14] suggests that zero weight should be assigned to the corresponding attribute. Hence to obtain the response weight for the given problem the following steps are suggested.

Step-1: Normalization of the response variables

The normalization process is needed to transform different scales and units among various attributes into common measurable units to allow the comparisons of different attributes. The decision matrix $[x_{ij}]$ is obtained from the experimental results. Each element of the decision matrix $[x_{ij}]$ represents the value of jth attribute of ith alternative, where $i = 1, 2 \ldots n$ and $j = 1, 2 \ldots m$. To normalize the evaluation matrix following equations are used.

$$x_{ij} = \frac{max\{x_{ij}\} - x_{ij}}{max\{x_{ij}\} - min\{x_{ij}\}} \quad \text{For non - beneficial attributes} \tag{1}$$

$$x_{ij} = \frac{x_{ij} - min\{x_{ij}\}}{max\{x_{ij}\} - min\{x_{ij}\}} \quad \text{For beneficial attributes} \tag{2}$$

Step-2: Weights determination through maximum deviation method

In the present work, maximum deviation method is considered to compute the differences of performance values of each alternative. For the attribute $\{A_j | j = 1, 2, \ldots, m\}$, the deviation value of the alternative $\{S_i | i = 1, 2, \ldots n\}$ from all the other alternatives can be computed as follows

$$D_{ij}(w_j) = \sum_{l=1}^{N} d(\tilde{r}_{ij}, \tilde{r}_{ij}) w_j \tag{3}$$

Then the total deviation values of all alternatives with respect to other alternatives for the attribute $\{A_j | j = 1, 2, \ldots, m\}$, can be defined

$$D_j(w_j) = \sum_{j=1}^{M} D_{ij}(w_j) = \sum_{i=1}^{N} \sum_{l=1}^{N} d(\tilde{r}_{ij}, \tilde{r}_{ij}) w_j \tag{4}$$

The deviation of all the attributes along all the alternatives can be represented as

$$D(w_j) = \sum_{j=1}^{M} D_j(w_j) = \sum_{j=1}^{M} \sum_{i=1}^{N} \sum_{l=1}^{N} d(\tilde{r}_{ij}, \tilde{r}_{ij}) w_j \tag{5}$$

Based on the above analysis, we have to choose the weight vector w to maximize all deviation values for all the attributes, for which we can construct a linear model as follows

$$\begin{cases} D(w_j) = \sum_{j=1}^{M} \sum_{i=1}^{N} \sum_{l=1}^{N} d(\tilde{r}_{ij}, \tilde{r}_{ij}) w_j \\ s.t \ \sum_{j=1}^{M} w_j^2 = 1, w_j \geq 0, \ j = 1, 2, \ldots, M \end{cases} \tag{6}$$

To solve the above model, we construct the Lagrange function:

$$L(w_j, \lambda) = \sum_{j=1}^{M} \sum_{i=1}^{N} \sum_{l=1}^{N} d(\tilde{r}_{ij}, \tilde{r}_{ij}) w_j + \lambda \left(\sum_{j=1}^{M} w_j^2 - 1 \right) \tag{7}$$

where λ is the Lagrange multiplier. The partial derivative of $L(w_j, \lambda)$ with respect to w_j and λ are:

$$\begin{cases} \frac{\partial L}{\partial w_j} = \sum_{i=1}^{N} \sum_{l=1}^{N} d(\tilde{r}_{ij}, \tilde{r}_{ij}) w_j + 2\lambda w_j = 0 \\ \frac{\partial L}{\partial \lambda} = \sum_{j=1}^{M} w_j^2 - 1 = 0 \end{cases} \tag{8}$$

Thus from Eq. (19) and (20) w_j and λ can be determined as

$$\begin{cases} 2\lambda = \sqrt{\sum_{j=1}^{M}\left(\sum_{i=1}^{N}\sum_{l=1}^{N} d\left(\tilde{r}_{ij},\tilde{r}_{ij}\right)\right)^2} \\ w_j = \dfrac{\sum_{i=1}^{N}\sum_{l=1}^{N} d\left(\tilde{r}_{ij},\tilde{r}_{ij}\right)}{\sqrt{\sum_{j=1}^{M}\left(\sum_{i=1}^{N}\sum_{l=1}^{N} d\left(\tilde{r}_{ij},\tilde{r}_{ij}\right)\right)^2}} \end{cases} \qquad (9)$$

Further the normalized attribute weights from the above can be determined as follows:

$$w_j = \frac{\sum_{i=1}^{N}\sum_{l=1}^{N} d\left(\tilde{r}_{ij},\tilde{r}_{ij}\right)}{\sum_{j=1}^{M}\sum_{i=1}^{N}\sum_{l=1}^{N} d\left(\tilde{r}_{ij},\tilde{r}_{ij}\right)} \qquad (10)$$

Step-3: Calculation of composite score

Finally the multi-responses are converted into single equivalent response by determining the composite score of each experiment by summing the weighted performance in all the attributes.

Quantum Behaved Particle Swarm Optimization. Particle swarm optimization (PSO) is an evolutionary computation technique inspired by the flocking behaviour of the birds. It was first developed by Kennedy and Eberhart [15]. PSO is a population based heuristic where the population of the potential solutions is called a swarm and each individual solution within the swarm is called a particle. Each particle moves around in the search space with a velocity which is continuously updated by the particle's individual contribution and the contribution of the particle's neighbours or the contribution of the whole swarm. The members of the whole population are maintained during the search procedure so that information is socially shared among all individuals to direct the search towards the best position in the search space. Each particle has a fitness value and the optimization process involves finding the minimum fitness value for each particle. Hence PSO is very easy to be understood and implemented. PSO has already been tried and tested in various standard optimization problems with excellent results [16–18]. However the main disadvantage of the classical PSO algorithm is that it does not assure global convergence because it is trapped into local optimal though it converges fast. The reason being that the velocity vectors assume very small values as iterations proceed. Hence, classical PSO algorithm has a risk to trap in local minima and loose its exploration and exploitation ability. To deal with this problem, including the concept of global convergence, a modified PSO technique known as quantum behaved particle swarm optimization (QPSO) was developed by Sun et al. [19].

In the QPSO the, the state of a particle is described by wave function ψ (X, t) instead of position and velocity of PSO. The dynamic behaviour of the particle is widely divergent form that of the particle in the PSO systems in that the exact values of X_i and V_i cannot be determined simultaneously. We can only run the probability of the particle's appearing in position X_i from probability density function $|\psi(X,t)|^2$. The particles move according to the following equation [20].

$$X^j_{i,(t+1)} = P^j_{i,(t+1)} - \beta * \left(M_{Best^j_t} - X^j_{i,t}\right) * \ln\left(1/u\right) \ if \ k \geq 0.5 \tag{11}$$

$$X^j_{i,(t+1)} = P^j_{i,(t+1)} - \beta * \left(M_{Best^j_t} - X^j_{i,t}\right) * \ln\left(1/u\right) \ if \ k < 0.5 \tag{12}$$

$$P^j_{i,(t+1)} = \theta * P_{Best^j_{i,t}} + (1-\theta) * g_{Best^j_t} \tag{13}$$

$$M_{Best^j_t} = \frac{1}{N}\sum_{l=1}^{N} P_{Best^j_{i,t}} \tag{14}$$

In Eqs. (11–14), M_{Best} is the mean best position defined as the mean of all the best positions of the population and g represents the index of the best particle among all the particles in the population. $k, u,$ and θ are random numbers distributed uniformly in [0, 1]. β, called contraction –expansion co-efficient, is the only parameter in the QPSO algorithm, which can be tuned to control the convergence speed of the algorithms. The value of β is allocated as per the Eq. (15).

$$\beta = \beta_{max} - (\beta_{max} - \beta_{min})^t/t_{max} \tag{15}$$

Where β_{max} is the initial contraction-expansion factor, β_{min} is the final contraction-expansion factor value, t is the current generation number and t_{max} is the maximum no. of generations.

3 Experimental Design

Experiments were conducted on AC Progress V2 high precision CNC WEDM, which is manufactured by Agie-Charmilles Technologies Corporation. A wire commonly used nowadays for taper cutting, the coated Broncocut-W (by Bedra), diameter 0.2 mm, has been used for the experiment. This wire is used due to its low yield strength and high elongation property. Deionized water is used as di-electric medium. AISI D2 tool steel [Carbon 1.55 %, Manganese 0.6 %, Silicon 0.6 %, Chromium 11.8 %, Molybdenum 0.8 %, Vanadium 0.8 % and rest is iron] of diameter 25 mm and thickness of 20 mm, 30 mm and 40 mm respectively has been chosen as work piece material. The input and fixed parameters used in the present study are listed in Table 1. These were chosen through review of literature, experience, and some preliminary investigations. Their limits were set on the basis of capacity and limiting conditions of the WEDM, ensuring continuous cutting by avoiding the breakage of the wire.

Angular error (AE), surface roughness (SR) and cutting speed (CS) were considered the three important output performance measures for optimizing machining parameters of WEDM taper cutting process. The surface roughness value (in μm) has been obtained by measuring the mean absolute deviation, Ra (surface roughness) from

Table 1. Input parameters with their levels

Input variables	Unit	Symbol	Levels		
			Level I	Level II	Level III
Part thickness	mm	A	20	30	40
Taper angle	Degree	B	5	6	7
Pulse duration	μs	C	24	28	32
Discharge current	Amp	D	14	16	18
Wire speed	mm/s	E	90	120	150
Wire tension	N	F	12	14	16

the average surface level using SURFCOM 130A. The angular error can be expressed in minute and calculated by the following formula:

$$\text{Angular error} = \Phi - \theta$$

where θ is the programmed angle or the angle expected in the machined part.

Φ is the actual angle obtained in the machined part due to the wire deformation as shown in Fig. 1.

After machining, the angle of the inclined surface (Φ) is measured with respect to the top surfaces using a Zeiss 850 CNC coordinate measuring machine.

For WEDM cutting speed is also a desirable characteristic and it should be as high as possible to give least machine cycle time leading to increased productivity. In the present study cutting rate is a measure of job cutting which is digitally displayed on the screen of the machine and is given in mm/min.

In the present work, Taguchi's L_{27} orthogonal array is used to gather maximum information regarding the process with less number of experimental run. The factors and their interaction are assigned to the columns by using the standard linear graph as [21] (Table 2).

4 Results and Discussion

The experiments are conducted using Taguchi's L_{27} orthogonal array design of experiment and the response values are calculated as described in Sect. 3. Initially all the response variables are normalized by using Eqs. (1–2) to avoid the scaling effect. The objective weights are determined for the normalized values of responses by applying maximum deviation method using Eqs. (3–10). The weights obtained through the maximum deviation method are 0.4047, 0.3584 and 0.2368 for angular error, surface error and cutting speed respectively. The weighted normalized objective values are calculated by multiplying the normalized objective values and the objective weights. The solutions are ranked based upon the composite scores obtained by summing all the weighted objective function values for each alternative as shown in Table 3.

Table 2. Experimental results using L_{27} orthogonal array

Exp. No	A	B	C	D	E	F	Angular error (min)	Surface roughness (μm)	Cutting speed (mm/min)
1	1	1	1	1	1	1	29.81	2.406	0.7644
2	1	1	2	2	2	2	44.36	2.219	0.8951
3	1	1	3	3	3	3	42.11	2.897	1.5764
4	1	2	1	2	2	3	45.15	2.968	0.8616
5	1	2	2	3	3	1	47.33	2.866	0.9515
6	1	2	3	1	1	2	48.79	3.008	0.9986
7	1	3	1	3	3	2	52.65	2.994	0.9412
8	1	3	2	1	1	3	49.63	2.706	0.8664
9	1	3	3	2	2	1	50.86	3.219	1.1892
10	2	1	1	2	3	2	54.63	2.841	0.7828
11	2	1	2	3	1	3	57.25	2.912	0.9508
12	2	1	3	1	2	1	41.99	3.205	0.9768
13	2	2	1	3	1	1	52.61	3.451	0.7489
14	2	2	2	1	2	2	54.56	3.527	0.8808
15	2	2	3	2	3	3	50.25	3.661	1.1932
16	2	3	1	1	2	3	25.86	2.824	0.7644
17	2	3	2	2	3	1	34.21	3.004	0.8648
18	2	3	3	3	1	2	26.25	3.678	0.9673
19	3	1	1	3	2	3	30.99	2.433	0.8164
20	3	1	2	1	3	1	22.14	2.182	0.919
21	3	1	3	2	1	2	24.24	2.339	1.0156
22	3	2	1	1	3	2	43.01	2.515	0.8952
23	3	2	2	2	1	3	52.29	2.608	0.9518
24	3	2	3	3	2	1	35.32	2.963	1.3104
25	3	3	1	2	1	1	42.23	2.845	0.5616
26	3	3	2	3	2	2	39.94	2.971	0.9812
27	3	3	3	1	3	3	31.71	3.156	1.1156

Due to the complexity involved in the tapering process of WEDM, in the present work, an attempt is made to develop a non-linear regression model by multi-variable regression analysis. The relationship between the composite score of response variables and input factors is present in Eq. 16 and the higher correlation coefficients ($r^2 = 0.987$) value confirm the suitability of the proposed model.

$$CS = 0.566x_1^{0.430}x_2^{-0.943}x_3^{0.318}x_4^{-0.441}x_5^{0.135}x_6^{-0.0186} \tag{16}$$

Present work aims at simultaneously minimizing the angular error and surface roughness as well as maximizing the cutting speed during taper cutting in WEDM process. To achieve the above goal, composite score of the responses are calculated

Table 3. Calculation of composite score of responses

Exp. No	Normalized response values			Weighted normalized response values			Composite score
	Angular error	Surface roughness	Cutting speed	Angular error	Surface roughness	Cutting speed	
1	0.782	0.850	0.200	0.316	0.305	0.047	0.668
2	0.367	0.975	0.329	0.149	0.350	0.078	0.576
3	0.431	0.522	1.000	0.175	0.187	0.237	0.598
4	0.345	0.475	0.296	0.139	0.170	0.070	0.380
5	0.283	0.543	0.384	0.114	0.195	0.091	0.400
6	0.241	0.448	0.431	0.098	0.161	0.102	0.360
7	0.131	0.457	0.374	0.053	0.164	0.089	0.305
8	0.217	0.650	0.300	0.088	0.233	0.071	0.392
9	0.182	0.307	0.618	0.074	0.110	0.146	0.330
10	0.075	0.559	0.218	0.030	0.201	0.052	0.282
11	0.000	0.512	0.384	0.000	0.184	0.091	0.274
12	0.435	0.316	0.409	0.176	0.113	0.097	0.386
13	0.132	0.152	0.185	0.053	0.054	0.044	0.152
14	0.077	0.101	0.315	0.031	0.036	0.074	0.142
15	0.199	0.011	0.622	0.081	0.004	0.147	0.232
16	0.894	0.571	0.200	0.362	0.205	0.047	0.614
17	0.656	0.451	0.299	0.266	0.161	0.071	0.498
18	0.883	0.000	0.400	0.357	0.000	0.095	0.452
19	0.748	0.832	0.251	0.303	0.298	0.059	0.660
20	1.000	1.000	0.352	0.405	0.358	0.083	0.847
21	0.940	0.895	0.447	0.381	0.321	0.106	0.807
22	0.406	0.777	0.329	0.164	0.279	0.078	0.521
23	0.141	0.715	0.385	0.057	0.256	0.091	0.405
24	0.625	0.478	0.738	0.253	0.171	0.175	0.599
25	0.428	0.557	0.000	0.173	0.200	0.000	0.373
26	0.493	0.473	0.413	0.200	0.169	0.098	0.467
27	0.727	0.349	0.546	0.294	0.125	0.129	0.549

Table 4. Optimum parameter setting

Control factors and performance measure	Optimum machining conditions
Part thickness (A)	33.3362 ≈ 34
Taper angle (B)	5.384 ≈ 5
Pulse duration (C)	30.781 ≈ 31
Discharge current (D)	16.804 ≈ 17
Wire speed (E)	138.3804 ≈ 139
Wire tension (F)	12.679 ≈ 13
Composite score	0.9875

which is treated as equivalent single response for the above problem. Then the best parametric combination has been obtained by QPSO technique. QPSO algorithm is coded using MATLAB 13.0. The algorithm considers a swarm size of 20 and maximum number of iterations 100. The other parameters are selected suitably to achieve

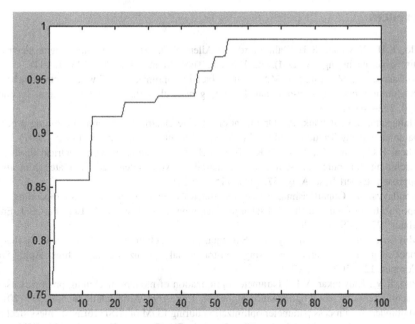

Fig. 1. Convergence plot

the convergence. A number of trials were conducted to optimize the parameters during taper cutting process of WEDM. Finally, the maximum value of composite score and the statistical values of the best solution obtained by QPSO algorithm is present in Table 4.

Figure 1 illustrates that QPSO algorithm converges towards global optimum. From the above result we can conclude that the QPSO method can make the convergence speed for WEDM parameters optimization problems faster with good global searching capability.

5   Conclusions

The proposed approach can effectively assist engineers in determining the optimal process parameter setting for simultaneously minimizing the angular error, surface roughness and maximizing cutting speed during taper cutting operation using WEDM.

The suggested process model can be used in any taper cutting operation for prediction of angular error, surface roughness and cutting speed before experimentation because a high degree of correlation is obtained. Optimization of multiple responses is demonstrated through a latest, simple, and efficient meta-heuristic like QPSO algorithm. In terms of convergence, the simulation result shows that the QPSO converges to obtain solutions closer to the good solution.

References

1. Ho, K.H., Newman, S.T., Rahimifard, S., Allen, R.D.: State of the art in wire electrical discharge machining (WEDM). Int. J. Mach. Tools Manuf. **44**, 1247–1259 (2004)
2. Kuriakose, S., Shunmugam, M.S.: Multi-objective optimization of wire-electro discharge machining process by non-dominated sorting genetic algorithm. J. Mater. Process. Technol. **170**, 133–141 (2005)
3. Mahapatra, S.S., Patnaik, A.: Optimization of wire electrical discharge machining process parameters using Taguchi method. Int. J. Adv. Manuf. Technol. **34**, 911–925 (2007)
4. Chen, H.C., Lin, J.C., Yang, Y.K., Tsai, C.H.: Optimization of wire electrical discharge machining for pure tungsten using a neural network integrated simulated annealing approach. Expert Syst. Appl. **37**, 7147–7153 (2010)
5. Kondayya, D., GopalKrishna, A.: An integrated evolutionary approach for modelling and optimization of wire electrical discharge machining. Proc. Inst. Mech. Eng. Part B J. Eng. Manuf. **225**, 549–567 (2011)
6. Mukherjee, R., Charkraborty, S., Samanta, S.: Selection of wire electrical discharge machining process parameters using non-traditional optimization algorithms. Appl. Soft Comput. **12**, 2506–2516 (2012)
7. Rao, R.V., Kalyankar, V.D.: Parameter optimization of modern machining processes using teaching-learning based optimization algorithm. Eng. Appl. Artif. Intell. **26**, 524–531 (2013)
8. Majumder, A.: Process parameter optimization during EDM of AISI316LN stainless steel by using fuzzy based multi-objective PSO. J. Mech. Sci. Technol. **27**, 2143–2151 (2013)
9. Aich, U., Banerjee, S.: Modelling of EDM responses by support vector machine regression with parameters selected by particle swarm optimization. Appl. Math. Model. **38**, 2800–2818 (2014)
10. Kinoshita, N., Fukui, M., Fujii, T.: Study on wire-EDM: accuracy in taper cut. CIRP Ann. Manuf. Technol. **36**, 119–122 (1987)
11. Chiu, Y.Y., Liao, Y.S., Li, H.C., Sue, P.C.: Study of taper cut machining of WEDM machine. In: Proceedings of the 2nd Manufacturing Engineering Society International Conference, MESIC 2007, Madrid, 9–11 July 2007
12. Sanchez, J.A., Plaza, S., Ortega, N., Marcos, M., Albizuri, J.: Experimental and numerical study of angular error in wire-EDM taper cutting. Int. J. Mach. Tools Manuf. **48**, 1420–1428 (2008)
13. Plaza, S., Ortega, N., Sanchez, J.A., Pombo, I., Mendikute, A.: Original models for the prediction of angular error in wire-EDM taper- cutting. Int. J. Adv. Manufact. Technol. **44**, 529–538 (2009)
14. Wang, Y.M.: Using the method of maximizing deviations to make decision for multi-indices. Syst. Eng. Electron. **7**, 24–26 (1998)
15. Kennedy, J., Eberhart, R.: Particle swarm optimization. Proc. IEEE Int. Conf. Neural Netw. **4**, 1942–1948 (1995)
16. Ghosh, S., Das, S., Kundu, D., Suresh, K., Panigrahi, B.K., Cui, Z.: An inertia-adaptive particle swarm system with particle mobility factor for improved global optimization. Neural Comput. Appl. **21**(2), 237–250 (2012)
17. Agrawal, S., Panigrahi, B.K., Tiwari, M.K.: Multiobjective particle swarm algorithm with fuzzy clustering for electrical power dispatch. IEEE Trans. Evol. Comput. **12**(5), 529–541 (2008)
18. Panigrahi, B.K., Pandi, V.R., Das, S.: An adaptive particle swarm optimization approach for static and dynamic economic load dispatch. Int. J. Energy Convers. Manag. **49**, 1407–1415 (2008)

19. Sun, J., Feng, B., Xu, W.B.: Particle swarm optimization with particles having quantum behaviour. In: IEEE Proceedings of Congress on Evolutionary computation, pp. 325–331 (2004)
20. Zou, H., Liang, D., Zeng, J., Feng, L.: Quantum behaved particle swarm optimization algorithm for the reconstruction of fiber Bragg grating sensor strain profiles. Opt. Commun. **285**, 539–545 (2012)
21. Peace, S.G.: Taguchi Methods: a Hands on Approach. Addison-Wesley, New York (1993)

A Particle Swarm Approach Embedded with Numerical Analysis for Multi-response Optimization in Electrical Discharge Machining

Chinmaya P. Mohanty[✉], Manas Ranjan Singh,
Siba Sankar Mahapatra, and Suman Chatterjee

Department of Mechanical Engineering, National Institute of Technology,
Rourkela, Rourkela 769008, India
{chinmaymohantymech,manasranjan.singh,
mahapatrass2003,mrsumanmech}@gmail.com

Abstract. Present work proposes a thermo-numerical model for accurate prediction of material removal and tool erosion for electrical discharge machining (EDM) process. The data collected for the numerical analysis is based on Box-Behnken's experimental design, a popular response surface methodology (RSM) approach. The numerical model is validated by comparing experimental results on a die sinking EDM machine. A sequentially coupled thermo-structural model has also been proposed to estimate the residual stress distribution on the work piece. Analysis of variance is conducted to identify significant parameters. Regression analysis is conducted on the model to develop valid mathematical models relating responses with process parameters. Finally, a multi objective particle swam (MOPSO) algorithm has been adopted for simultaneous optimization of responses. The proposed model can be employed for selecting ideal process states to improve process productivity and finishing capabilities.

Keywords: Electrical discharge machine · Finite element method · Multi-objective particle swarm optimization

1 Introduction

In order to produce components having complex shapes made of high strength to weight ratio materials at less machining time, electrical discharge machining (EDM) process is found to be suitable and is extensively used in broad variety of industries such as mold and die making, aerospace, critical parts used in automobile and other manufacturing industries. The machining process deals with controlled erosion of electrically conductive materials by virtue of continuous spark discharges between the tool and the work piece separated by dielectric fluid which reduces premature discharge until a constricted spark gap is maintained between the tool and the work piece. Occurrence of spark discharges results vaporization and melting of material from both the electrodes. There is no mechanical contact between tool and work piece during the whole process but small volumes of work material is continuously removed by vaporization through a

© Springer International Publishing Switzerland 2015
B.K. Panigrahi et al. (Eds.): SEMCCO 2014, LNCS 8947, pp. 74–87, 2015.
DOI: 10.1007/978-3-319-20294-5_7

series of electric spark discharges between tool and work piece. The complex nature of the process involving the physics of spark discharges makes the process difficult to analyze the process experimentally and estimate the process responses viz., crater morphology and tool erosion. Joshi and Pande [1] have suggested a finite element method (FEM) based numeral model for EDM for accurate prediction of process responses. Yadav et al. [2] have concluded that compressive and tensile stresses develop near the spark locality where the thermal stress is higher than the maximum stress of the work piece. The model was validated through experimental data. Helmi et al. [3] have considered surface roughness and material removal rate as responses on electro discharge grinding process employing Taguchi method where tool steel is employed as the work piece with brass and copper as the tool material. Chen and Allen [4] have suggested a thermo-numerical model which simulates a single spark discharge for the process. The numerical model was authenticated by comparing with experimental work by means of scanning electron microscopy (SEM) and optical evaluation technique. A residual stress distribution on the molybdenum work piece with a tungsten tool was also presented by the same authors.

EDM literature reveals plenty of experimental, statistical and technological investigations for enhancement of accuracy, productivity and versatility of the process. It also indicates that only a few studies reported until now to analyze the EDM process numerically. To address this issue, present study reports a numerical model for precise and accurate prediction of material removal and tool erosion on work and tool material. A thermo-structural model has been presented to estimate the induced residual stress distribution on work surface. Finally, a multi objective particle swarm optimization (MOPSO) algorithm has been proposed for the multi objective optimization of the predicted responses.

2 Simulation of EDM Process

2.1 Thermal Modeling of the Process

- It is assumed that both work and tool material are homogeneous and isotropic.
- The material properties of the work and tool material together depend on temperature.
- The only mode of heat transfer is conduction, other heat losses are ignored.
- It is assumed that spark radius is a function of discharge current and time.
- Single spark analysis is considered for the process.
- There is no accumulation of recast layers on the machined surfaces, as 100 % flushing efficiency is considered for the analysis.
- Ambient temperature is assumed to be considered as room temperature i.e. 298 K.

2.2 Governing Equation Required for the Analysis

Fourier heat conduction equation is employed as governing equation for the single spark analysis of the EDM process. ANSYS solves the heat conduction differential equation for the heat transfer of the two dimensional axisymmetric model. The equation is given by

$$\rho c \frac{\partial T}{\partial t} = \frac{1}{r}\frac{\partial}{\partial r}\left(kr\frac{\partial T}{\partial r}\right) + \frac{\partial}{\partial z}\left(k\frac{\partial T}{\partial z}\right) \qquad (1)$$

where, r and z denote cylindrical coordinates of the work and tool material. ρ is the density, c is the specific heat and k is the thermal conductivity of the work and tool material.

2.3   Boundary Condition for the Analysis

Figure 1 shows the boundary conditions allied for the electrical discharge machining (EDM) process for the single spark analysis. AD is an axisymmetric boundary. It is assumed that, boundaries of the domain away from the spark radius are insulated. Heat flux is applied to the top boundary (AB) where the spark occurs.

2.4   Heat Input Required for Analysis

Heat input, material properties and radius of spark are the important parameters which affects significantly to the precise calculation of responses in single spark EDM analysis. In this model, Gaussian distribution of heat flux is assumed with quantity of heat flux flowing into the two-dimensional work material is given by relation

$$q_w(r) = \frac{4.56PVI}{\pi R_s^2}\exp\left\{-4.5\left(\frac{r}{R_s}\right)^2\right\} \qquad (2)$$

2.5   Spark Radius Calculation

The spark radius for the analysis is calculated by the relation

$$R_s = (2.04\exp-3)I_p^{0.43}T_{on}^{0.44} \qquad (3)$$

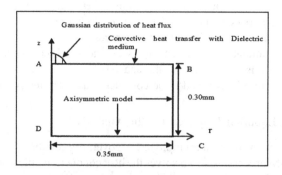

Fig. 1. An axi-symmetric two dimensional model for the EDM process analysis

Where I_p is the discharge current, T_{on} is the pulse-on-time and R_s is the spark radius.

2.6 Solution Methodology of Thermal-Structral Analysis Using ANSYS

ANSYS 10.0 solves the governing Eq. 1 with boundary conditions as shown in Fig. 1 by Finite Element Method to predict the temperature distribution. The 2-Dimensional, axisymmetric, thermal solid element of (PLANE 55), of size (0.35×0.3) mm was employed for the thermal analysis. Model geometry is formed and meshing is done with element size of 1 μm. Material property viz. density, specific heat and thermal conductivity were employed along with initial work piece temperature is set at 298 K. The heat flux equation is introduced Eq. 2 and applied to the spark locality on the center of the two dimensional continuum. Temperature distribution is calculated and nodes having temperature higher than melting point temperature were identified and eliminated from the model. The MRR and TWR were calculated from coordinate data of the craters of work and tool material respectively.

A coupled thermal-structural analysis has been employed to estimate the induced residual stress distribution on the work piece, in sequence to predict the residual stresses with ANSYS 10 as the FEM solver employing planes PLANE 55 for thermal analysis and PLANE 42 for structural analysis. The residual stress distribution was calculated by solving the previously achieved temperature profiles within structural surroundings with application of structural boundary conditions after the elements above the melting temperature of the work piece were killed. The relation in between the thermal stress analysis and thermal loading is given by

$$\{\sigma\} = [D]\{e\} - \{m\}, \tag{4}$$

where,

$$\{\sigma\} = \left\{\sigma_{rr}, \sigma_{\theta\theta}, \sigma_{yy}, \sigma_{ry}\right\}^T \tag{5}$$

$$[D] = \frac{E}{(1+v)(1-1v)} \begin{bmatrix} 1-v & v & v & 0 \\ v & 1-v & v & 0 \\ v & v & 1-v & 0 \\ 0 & 0 & 0 & \frac{1-2v}{2} \end{bmatrix}, \tag{6}$$

$$\{e\} = \left\{e_{rr}, e_{\theta\theta}, e_{yy}, e_{ry}\right\}^T \tag{7}$$

$$\{m\} = \frac{E\alpha\Delta T}{1-2v}\{1\ 1\ 1\ 0\}^T, \tag{8}$$

At this point, σ is the thermal stress, σ is the strain, E is the Young's modulus, V the Poisson's ratio, α the coefficient of thermal expansion, ΔT the thermal loading because of temperature change and m is the latent heat of fusion.

The structural boundary conditions (as shown in Fig. 1) are given by

$$u_r = 0 \quad t_y = 0 \qquad \text{on boundary AD;}$$
$$u_y = 0 \quad t_r = 0 \qquad \text{on boundary CD;}$$
$$t_r = 0 \quad t_y = 0 \quad \text{on boundaries AB and BC.}$$

3 Particle Swarm Optimization

Particle swarm optimization (PSO) algorithm, originally introduced by Kennedy and Eberhart [5] is a population based evolutionary computation technique. It is motivated by the behavior of organisms such as bird flocking and fish schooling. In PSO, each member is called particle and each particle moves around in the multidimensional search space with a velocity which is constantly. Two variants of the PSO algorithm have been developed, namely PSO with a local neighborhood and PSO with a global neighborhood. According to the global neighborhood, each particle moves towards its best previous position and towards the best particle in the whole swarm, called the gbest model in the literature. On the other hand, based on the local variant so called the pbest model, each particle moves towards its best previous position and towards the best particle in its restricted neighborhood. PSO is basically characterized as a simple heuristic of well-balanced mechanism with flexibility to progress and adjust to both global and local exploration capabilities. PSO, the initial population is generated randomly and parameters are initialized. After evaluation of the fitness function, the PSO algorithm repeats the following steps iteratively:

- Personal best (best value of each individual so far) is updated if a better value is discovered.
- Then, the velocities of all the particles are updated based on the experiences of personal best and the global best in order to update the position of each particle with the velocities currently updated.
- Permutation is determined through an encoding scheme so that evaluation is again performed to compute the fitness of the particles in the swarm.

After finding the personal best and global best values, velocities and positions of each particle are updated using Eqs. 9 and 10 respectively.

$$v_{ij}^t = w^{t-1} v_{ij}^{t-1} + c_1 r_1 \left(p_{ij}^{t-1} - x_{ij}^{t-1} \right) + c_2 r_2 \left(g_{ij}^{t-1} - x_{ij}^{t-1} \right) \qquad (9)$$

$$x_{ij}^t = x_{ij}^{t-1} + v_{ij}^t \qquad (10)$$

Where v_{ij}^t represents velocity of particle i at iteration t with respect to j^{th} dimension (j = 1,2,...n). p_{ij}^t represents the position value of the ith personal best with respect to the jth dimension. x_{ij}^t is the position value of the ith particle with respect to j^{th} dimension. c_1 and c_2 are positive acceleration parameters which provide the correct balance between exploration and exploitation, and are called the cognitive parameter and the social parameter, respectively. r_1 and r_2 are the random numbers provide a stochastic characteristic for the particles velocities in order to simulate the real behaviour of the birds in a flock. The inertia weight parameter w is a control parameter which is used to control the impact of the previous history of velocities on the current velocity of each particle. Hence, the parameter w regulates the trade-off between global and local exploration ability of the swarm. The recommended value of the inertia weight w is to set it to a large value for the initial stages, in order to enhance the global exploration of the search space, and gradually decrease it to get more refined solutions facilitating the local exploration in the last stages. In general, the inertia weight factor is set according to the following Eq. 11.

$$w = w_{max} - \frac{w_{max} - w_{min}}{iter_{max}} \times iter \tag{11}$$

Where w_{min}, w_{max} are initial and final weights, $iter_{max}$ is the maximum number of iterations and $iter$ is the current iteration number.

3.1 Multi-objective Particle Swarm Optimization (MOPSO)

Multi-objective optimization (MOO) has been an active area of research in last two decades. Such problems arise in many applications where two or more objective functions have to be optimized simultaneously. PSO has been extended for solving the MOO problems, which is generally known as the multi-objective particle swarm optimization (MOPSO). The main difference between a basic PSO (single-objective) and MOPSO is the distribution of g_{best}. In MOPSO algorithm, g_{best} must be redefined in order to obtain a set of non-dominated solutions (Pareto front). In single-objective problems, there is only one g_{best} exists. In MOO problems, more than one conflicting objectives will be optimized simultaneously. There are multiple numbers of non-dominated solutions which are located on or near the Pareto front. Therefore, each non-dominated solution can be the g_{best}. Extending PSO to handle multi-objectives have been proposed by researches [6]. The Pareto approach on the other hand provides an alternative approach for multi-objective optimization. In Pareto approach, the solutions are compared based on the Pareto dominance relation. Solution 'A' dominates solution 'B', if 'A' is not worse than 'B' for all objectives or is better than 'B' for at least one objective. Solution 'A' is Pareto optimal if it is not dominated by any other solution [7]. The Pareto approach produces a set of Pareto optimal solutions which represent the trade-off between objectives through the distribution of obtained solutions. The user can select the favorite solution directly from the number of Pareto optimal solutions.

To summarize, the main difference between a basic PSO (single-objective) and MOPSO is the distribution of g_{best}. In single-objective problems, there is only one g_{best} exists. In MOPSO algorithm, g_{best} must be redefined in order to obtain a set of non-dominated solutions (Pareto front). Therefore, multiple numbers of non-dominated solutions are located on or near the Pareto front. Each non-dominated solution can be a g_{best}. The important feature of MOPSO is that the individuals also maintain a personal archive which is known as p_{best} archive with a maximum size. The p_{best} archive contains the most recent non-dominated positions a particle has encountered in the past. In every iteration t, each particle i is allocated with two guides p_{best} and g_{best} from its p_{best} archive and swarms global archive 'A_t'. After the guide selection, positions and velocities of particles are updated according to the Eqs. 12 and 13 where v_{ij}^t represents velocity and x_{ij}^t is the position value of the ith particle with respect to j^{th} dimension. Maximum number of generations is set as termination criterion. The complete algorithm for MOPSO is shown as follows:

Proposed MOPSO algorithm
MOPSO Algorithm

1. For i = 1 to M (M is the population size)
   a. Initialize position of the particles randomly
   b. Initialize $v_{ij}^t = 0$ (v is the velocity of each particle)
   c. Evaluate each particle's fitness
   d. Compare each particle's fitness with the particle's p_{best}. Compare the fitness with the population's overall previous best
   e. Find out the personal best (p_{best}) and global best (g_{best}).
2. End For
3. Initialize the iteration counter t = 0
4. Store the nondominated vectors found into archive 'A_t' ('A_t' is the external archive that stores non-dominated solutions found)
5. Repeat
   a. Compute the crowding distance values of each nondominated solution in the archive 'A_t'
   b. Sort the nondominated solutions in 'A_t' in descending crowding distance values
   c. For i = 1 to M
      i. Randomly select the global best guide from a specified top 10 % of the sorted archive 'A_t' and store its position to g_{best}.
      ii. Compute the new velocity:

$$v_{ij}^t = w^{t-1}v_{ij}^{t-1} + c_1r_1\left(p_{ij}^{t-1} - x_{ij}^{t-1}\right) + c_2r_2\left((A_t)_{ij}^{t-1} - x_{ij}^{t-1}\right) \qquad (12)$$

$((A_t)_{ij}^{t-1}$ is the global best guide for each nondominated solution)
      iii. Calculate the new position of

$$x_{ij}^t = x_{ij}^{t-1} + v_{ij}^t \qquad (13)$$

      iv. Evaluate x_{ij}^t
   d. End For
   e. Insert all new nondominated solution into archive 'A_t' if they are not dominated by any of the stored solutions. All dominated solutions in the archive are removed by the new solution from the archive. If the archive is reached its maximum, the solution to be substituted is determined by the following steps:

   i. Compute the crowding distance values of each non-dominated solution in the archive 'A_t'

   ii. Sort the non-dominated solutions in archive 'A_t' in descending crowding distance values

   iii. Randomly select a particle from a specified bottom 10 % of the sorted archive 'A_t' and replace it with the new solution

  f. Update the personal best solution of each particle. If the current p_{best} dominates the position in memory.

  g. Increment iteration counter t

6. Until maximum number of iterations is reached.

4 Experimental Details and Model Validation

To validate the above proposed numerical model experiments are conducted as per response surface methodology (RSM) on a die sinking EDM machine (ELECTRON-ICA- ELECTRAPULS PS 50ZNC) with servo-head (constant gap). Commercial grade EDM oil of specific gravity = 0.763, freezing point = 94° C) was used as dielectric fluid. DOE is basically a scientific approach to effectively plan and perform experiments using statistics and is commonly used to improve the quality of a products or processes with less experimental runs. Table 1 shows the coding of the process parameters and Table 2 shows the experimental strategy along with the obtained responses for the EDM process analysis. AISI D2 steel with a diameter of 25 mm is chosen as the work material for electrical discharge machining, which is basically an air-hardened high carbon, high chromium tool steel alloyed with molybdenum and vanadium characterized by high wear resistance, good compressive strength, high stability in hardening and finds extensive application in manufacturing of space crafts, forming dies, punches, forming rolls, knives, shear blades etc. Commercially available brass is chosen as the electrode material owing to excellent thermal properties. Table 3 shows the material properties of AISI D2 steel and brass. Based on initial trials and extensive literature review three parameters viz. discharge current (I_p), pulse-on-time (T_{on}) and duty factor (τ) are identified as important factors and are selected to study their consequences on process responses such as material removal rate (MRR), tool wear rate (TWR) and residual stress (RS) developed on work piece. The experimental residual stresses are determined through X-ray diffraction measurement method [8]. The model of XRD equipment used was XRD-PHILIPS Analytical Ltd. PW 3040.

Table 1. Process parameters and their codes

Process parameters	Symbols	Codes		
		−1	0	1
Discharge current (I_p) in Amp	A	5	7	9
Pulse-on- time(T_{on}) in µs	B	100	200	300
Duty factor (τ) in %	C	70	80	90

Table 2. Box-Behnkein design experimental strategy along with obtained responses

Runs	A	B	C	Num. MRR mm^3/ min	Expt. MRR mm^3/ min	Num. TWR mm^3/ min	Expt. TWR mm^3/ min	Num. residual stress M Pa.	Expt. residual stress M Pa.
1	−1	−1	0	2.69	2.52	2.85	2.78	13.92	13.5
2	1	−1	0	4.48	4.32	4.53	4.48	16.91	16.5
3	−1	1	0	2.78	2.69	2.29	2.25	12.93	12.7
4	1	1	0	8.39	8.3	4.28	4.25	18.42	18.35
5	−1	0	−1	2.56	2.49	2.34	2.29	13.83	13.5
6	1	0	−1	6.48	6.39	3.89	3.78	17.65	17.4
7	−1	0	1	3.13	3.03	2.94	2.89	13.95	13.6
8	1	0	1	7.57	7.42	5.55	5.45	17.94	17.5
9	0	−1	−1	3.08	3.06	3.02	2.99	13.53	13.3
10	0	1	−1	4.29	4.15	2.74	2.68	16.75	16.45
11	0	−1	1	3.69	3.65	4.19	4.11	13.66	13.42
12	0	1	1	5.42	5.37	3.71	3.68	14.74	14.65
13	0	0	0	4.71	4.55	3.82	3.67	15.56	15.37
14	0	0	0	4.71	4.65	3.82	3.85	15.67	15.62
15	0	0	0	4.71	4.85	3.82	3.68	15.51	15.45
16	0	0	0	4.71	4.81	3.82	3.91	15.59	15.55
17	0	0	0	4.71	4.77	3.82	3.71	15.52	15.48

Table 3. Material properties of AISI D2 steel and brass

Properties	AISI D2 steel	Brass
Density (ρ)	7,710 kg/m^3	8565 kg/m^3
Specific heat (C_p)	460 J/kgK	377 J/kgK
Thermal conductivity (K)	20 W/mK	115 W/mK
Poission's ratio (υ)	0.29	
Young's modulus (E)	200 GPa	
Thermal expansion (α)	$11.2 \times 10e^{-6}$	
Melting temperature (Tm)	1657 K	1203 K

Table 2 shows the comparison predicted results of the numerical analysis of MRR, TWR and residual stress with experimental results. From the comparisons it is clear that the values of the responses predicted by numerical model are closer to the experimental results. Thus, it can be concluded that the numerical model would give equal or better prediction of process responses compared to the previously reported models. Figures 2, 3 and 4 shows the predicted crater, tool wear on brass tool and residual stress distribution on the work piece respectively at current 9 A, pulse-on-time

Fig. 2. Predicted crater of 8.4 mm³/min at current 9 A, pulse-on-time 300 μs, duty factor 80 % and voltage 45 V

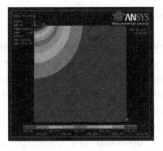

Fig. 3. Tool erosion of 4.28 mm³/min at current 9 A, pulse-on-time 300 μs, duty factor 80 % and voltage 45 V

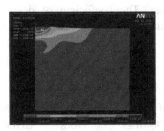

Fig. 4. Residual stress distribution of 18.4 MPa at current 9 A, pulse-on-time 300 μs, duty factor 80 % and voltage 45 V radial direction

300 μs, duty factor 80 % and voltage 45 V. Figure 5 shows the thermal stress distribution in radial direction. It is observed that the stresses developed beneath the spark locality are compressive whereas the stresses away from the spark location are tensile. A similar trend of thermal stress distribution has been also reported in the numerical model of previous researchers [4].

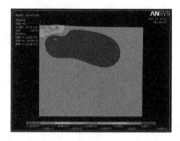

Fig. 5. Thermal stress distribution showing compressive stress developing near crater beneath in radial direction at current 9 A, pulse-on-time 300 µs, duty factor 80 % and voltage 45 V

5   Results and Discussions

Analysis of variance (ANOVA) is carried out for the responses obtained through numerical analysis. Table 4 shows the ANOVA table for MRR after elimination of insignificant parameters. From the ANOVA table it clearly visible that discharge current, pulse-on-time, interaction term discharge current × pulse-on-time and square term pulse-on-time × pulse-on-time are the most dominant parameters. Effect of duty factor is not significant as comparison with other two parameters. Similarly, form the ANOVA table of TWR it is observed that discharge current and pulse-on-time, interaction term discharge current × duty factor and square term discharge current × discharge current are important parameters. Similarly, form the ANOVA table of residual stress it is observed that discharge current and pulse-on-time, interaction term discharge current × pulse-on-time and square term discharge current × discharge current are important parameters. The coefficient of determination is quite large as R-square and adjacent R-square values for MRR 95.03 % and 91.16 % for TWR

Table 4.   ANOVA for MRR

Source	Sum of squares	df	Mean square	F Value	p-value prob > F	
Model	43.58	7	6.23	62.8	<0.0001	Significant
A	31.05	1	31.05	31.3	<0.0001	
B	6.02	1	6.02	60.7	<0.0001	
C	1.45	1	1.45	14.6	0.0041	
AB	3.65	1	3.65	36.8	0.0002	
AC	0.068	1	0.068	0.68	0.4303	
A^2	0.55	1	0.55	5.58	0.0425	
B^2	0.87	1	0.87	8.75	0.016	
Residual	0.89	9	0.099			
Lack of fit	0.36	5	0.073	0.55	0.7356	Not significant
Pure error	0.53	4	0.13			
Cor total	44.47	16				

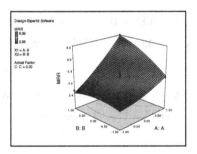

Fig. 6. Surface plot of MRR with discharge current and pulse- on-time

98.2 % and 96.9 % and for residual stress 95.03 and 91.1 respectively. The lack of fit is not significant for all the responses.

Figure 6 shows the surface plot of MRR with discharge current and pulse-on-time. It is clearly visible that MRR increases monotonically with increase in discharge current from 5 A to 9 A. The figure also indicates that MRR shows an increasing trend with increase in pulse-on-time but shows a slight decreasing trend further beyond a pulse-on-time of 200 μs. Even though effect of duty factor on MRR is not significant as compared to other two parameters its observed that MRR increases very slowly with increase in pulse on time.

Figure 7 shows the surface plot of TWR discharge current and duty factor. The figure shows that tool erodes heavily with increase in discharge current and duty factor. Similarly, from the surface plot of residual stress discharge current and duty factor it is observed that residual stress increases heavily with increase in discharge current from 5 A to 9 A. The plot also indicates that residual stress shows a decreasing trend with increase in pulse-on-time before reaching a maximum value. Effect of duty factor on residual stress is minimal.

The process model of three responses obtained through regression analysis is given in terms of equation below.

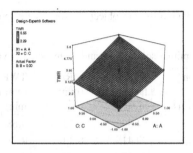

Fig. 7. Surface plot of TWR with discharge current and duty factor

$$MRR = +4.62 + 1.97 \times A + 0.87 \times B + 0.42 \times C + 0.95 \times A \times B + 0.13 \times A$$
$$\times C + 0.36 \times A^2 - 0.45 \times B^2 \quad \text{(Coded form)}$$

$$(14)$$

$$TWR = +3.75 + 0.98 \times A - 0.20 \times B + 0.55 \times C + 0.078 \times A \times B + 0.27 * A$$
$$* C - 0.27 * B^2 - 0.073 \times C^2 \quad \text{(Coded form)}$$

$$(15)$$

$$\text{Residual Stress} = +15.38 + 1.93 \times A + 0.70 \times B - 0.18 \times C + 0.82 \times A \times B - 0.52$$
$$\times B \times C + 0.52 \times A^2 - 0.67 \times B^2 \quad \text{(Coded form)}$$

$$(16)$$

The empirical relation between the process parameters and process responses established from the RSM analysis is used as objective function for solving the multi-objective particle swarm optimization (MOPSO) problem. The optimization model was run on MATLAB 13 platform in a Pentium IV desktop. Simulation study is carried out to demonstrate the potentiality of MOPSO algorithm. Figure 8 shows the Pareto-front for MRR, TWR and Residual stress. A Sample set of the optimal solution has been given in Table 5.

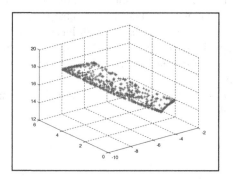

Fig. 8. Pareto frontier objectives for three responses

Table 5. Pareto optimal solution set and corresponding variable settings

No.	Current (Ip) in Amp.	Pulse on time (ton) in μs	Duty factor (τ) in %	MRR (mm³/ min)	TWR (mm³/ min)	Residual stress of work piece (MPa)
1	8.942	300	84.80	8.48	4.68	18.18
2	9	300	79.41	8.29	4.28	18.67
3	9	300	88.37	8.78	4.97	18.04
4	9	300	86.98	8.70	4.87	18.14
5	8.887	300	85.68	8.42	4.71	18.01

6 Conclusions

A thermo-numerical approach of modeling of electrical discharge machining on AISI tool steel has been presented in this work. The numerical model is validated through experimentation. A sequentially coupled thermo-structural model has been also proposed to estimate the induced residual stress distribution on the work piece. Finally, a multi objective particle swarm optimization algorithm (MOPSO) implemented to obtain Pareto optimal solution for multi objective optimization of responses. The proposed model can be employed for selection of best process parameters to improve process efficiency and finishing capabilities.

References

1. Joshi, S.N., Pande, S.S.: Development of an intelligent process model for EDM. Int. J. Adv. Manuf. Technol. **45**(3-4), 300–317 (2009)
2. Yadav, V., Jain, V.K., Dixit, P.M.: Thermal stresses due to electrical discharge machining. Int. J. Mach. Tools Manuf. **42**(8), 877–888 (2002)
3. Helmi, M., Hafiz, MH., Azuddin, M., Abdullah, W.: Investigation of surface roughness and material removal rate (MRR) on tool steel using brass and copper electrode for electrical discharge grinding (EDG) process. Int. J. Integr. Eng. **1**(1), (2011)
4. Allen, P., Chen, X.: Process simulation of micro electro-discharge machining on molybdenum. J. Mater. Process. Technol. **186**(1), 346–355 (2007)
5. Kennedy, J., Eberhart, R.: Particle swarm optimization. In: Proceedings of IEEE International Conference on Neural Network, Washington, USA, 4 Nov/Dec 1942–1948 (1995)
6. Agrawal, S., Panigrahi, B.K., Tiwari, M.K.: Multiobjective particle swarm algorithm with fuzzy clustering for electrical power dispatch. IEEE Trans. Evol. Comput. **12**(5), 529–541 (2008)
7. Panigrahi, B.K., Pandi, V.R., Das, S., Das, S.: Multiobjective fuzzy dominance based bacterial foraging algorithm to solve economic emission dispatch problem. Energy **35**(12), 4761–4770 (2010)
8. Anderoglu, O.: Residual stress measurement using X-ray diffraction. Ph.D. dissertation., A&M University, Texas (2004)

Biological Data Analysis Using Hybrid Functional Link Artificial Neural Network

Manaswini Jena[1]([✉]), Rasmita Dash[1], and Bijan Bihari Misra[2]

[1] Department of Computer Science and Information Technology,
Institute of Technical Education and Research, Siksha o Anusandhan
University, Khandagiri Square, Bhubaneswar, India
manaswini.jena88@gmail.com,
rasmitadash@soauniversity.ac.in
[2] Department of Computer Science and Engineering,
Silicon Institute of Technology, Bhubaneswar 751024, Odisha, India
misrabijan@gmail.com

Abstract. With rapid growth in field of medical sciences; biologists have stepped up and had discovered many biological characteristics for different diseases. There are many issues involved in knowledge discovery from these huge biomedical data for useful medical application. Traditional algorithms for neural network such as multi-layer perceptron model have proven to be inefficient for the classification of different biological data, as in many cases to get a better classifier we have to increase number of layers in simple artificial neural network which increases the complexity of the network. In contrast to multiple layer perceptron networks, Functional Link Artificial Neural Network (FLANN) can be implemented for the task of data classification with reduced complexity. In this proposed paper work an experimental study has been presented where a simple FLANN based classification model is compared with Hybrid FLANN models. In the first hybrid model an optimization technique i.e. Particle Swarm Optimization (PSO) is applied along with FLANN for weight updation. Then in the second hybrid FLANN model a feature selection technique i.e. Signal to Noise Ratio (SNR) is applied. Finally the classification accuracies are compared for the estimation of good performances.

Keywords: Data mining · Classification · Functional link artificial neural network · Particle swarm optimization · Signal to noise ratio

1 Introduction

With evolution in medical field the discovery of different biological characteristic like gene sequence, DNA microarray, protein interaction, diseases pathways have been discovered for different maladies. Many computational and mathematical approaches have been discovered to precisely analyze the complexities arising in fields like biology, medicine, humanities, management sciences etc. Reference [1] Data mining has some of its underlying difficulties that restrict the proper discovery of knowledge which can be used for clinical application. But the mathematical models have a strict

© Springer International Publishing Switzerland 2015
B.K. Panigrahi et al. (Eds.): SEMCCO 2014, LNCS 8947, pp. 88–97, 2015.
DOI: 10.1007/978-3-319-20294-5_8

boundary which could not be applied to solve problems those are uncertain, unpredictable or lies between 0 and 1. But soft computing can also it works fine on the problems having uncertainty and partial truth. The principal component of soft computing techniques includes artificial neural network, Fuzzy logic and Genetic algorithms.

For the classification of biological data traditional algorithms for neural network such as multi-layer perceptron network can be used. But to make it a better classifier the number of layers has to be increased in simple artificial neural network and hence the complexity of the network becomes more. Comparing to multiple layer perceptron networks, FLANN can be a reasonable approach as for its simple architecture which makes this neural network more suitable.

Further a combination of multiple techniques creates a hybrid model which leads to a significant improvement in its performance. For the purpose of classification, techniques like optimization and feature selection can be fused. Optimization selects the best element with regard to some criteria from a set of available alternatives. Feature selection chooses a subset of input variables by eliminating features, which are irrelevant or do not have predictive information.

Here FLANN has been incorporated with optimization technique (PSO) and feature selection technique (SNR) over biological data for classification and has been elaborated in the following sections.

2 Related Works

Data mining is a process of extracting useful knowledge from a huge collection of day to day data. During last two decades neural network has found its significant role in the evolution of data mining classification techniques for current trends of data processing and used as a prominent tool by researchers for achieving greater performance [4–6]. The complexity of the MLP due to the presence of hidden layer can be minimized and an approximated curve fitting can be done by FLANN [7]. The architecture of FLANN is designed to get the accuracy of highly complex and computationally intensive multi layer neural network with ease of linearity of single layer neural network. Many other single layer neural networks like Polynomial Perceptron Network (PPN) and Legendre Neural Network (LeNN) can also be considered but among these; FLANN is found to give better accuracy and take less time for convergence with reduced complexity of network [3]. A savvy combination of multiple classifiers may lead to a significant improvement in performance of classification which is marked to be better than a simple classifier. Here in this study swarm optimization algorithm and a feature selection technique is used for coalition of techniques to give a better FLANN model. A broad study has shown that ISO-FLANN (Improved Swarm Optimization - FLANN) performs better as for the comparison between the classifier using ISO-FLANN, MLP and Simple FLANN [9]. The optimization through PSO is generally accepted as a better approach than other algorithms in terms of success rate and solution quality with fairly satisfactory processing time among many evolutionary based optimization algorithms [16]. Feature selection has proved its magnificence in loads of research area like pattern recognition, machine learning, statistics and data mining communities [21].

3 Background Studies

3.1 Functional Link Artificial Neural Network

The FLANN architecture was originally proposed by Pao et al. It uses a single layer feed forward neural network as hidden layers of the simple artificial neural network is replaced by functional expansion of input vector which reduces the computational cost and complexity of learning algorithm as compared to the MLP structure. It has been successfully used in many applications such as system identification, channel equalization, classification, pattern recognition and prediction [23]. Many experiments have demonstrated that this architecture is very effective for classification task [15]. Different functional expansions can be used for the FLANN such as trigonometric, power series or Chebyshev expansion etc. Based on some experiments trigonometric function is found to be better compared to other expansions [2, 3] for which here trigonometric expansion is implemented for the functional expansion of the input vector.

A simple FLANN architecture [8]-

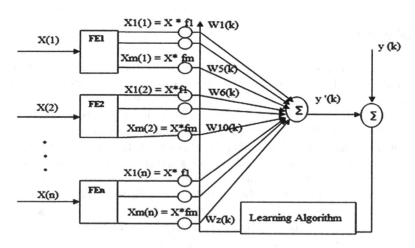

Fig. 1. FLANN architecture

In Fig. 1 Xf_m is the functionally expanded input at k_{th} iteration and $W_m(k)$ is the m_{th} weight at the k_{th} iteration and $W_m(0)$ is initialized with some random value from the range.

The functional expansion of a single input element is as follows (Fig. 2).

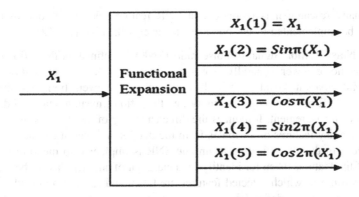

Fig. 2. Functional expansion of the first element

3.2 Particle Swarm Optimization

Particle Swarm Optimization (PSO) proposed by Kennedy and Eberhart in 1995, is a meta-heuristic optimization technique based on a concept called social metamorphosis and simulates the behavior of bird flocks searching for targets. During searching, each individual continuously adjusts its position/movement according to its own experience i.e. its best position so far and the best position its neighborhood has experienced. This meta-heuristic simulates a society where all individuals contribute their knowledge to obtain a better solution [17].

In this meta-heuristic each individual is called particle and moves through a multidimensional space that represents the social space or search space. The dimension of space depends on the variables used to represent the problem. In the search space, the position of each particle is updated by using its current location and its velocity vector; this vector tells how fast the particle will move. There are two models of PSO, one with a global neighborhood and another with a local neighborhood. In the global model, a particle has information of its own and of the entire population, whereas in the local model, a particle has information of its own and of its nearest neighbors. And the global model has been proved to be faster than the local model.

In global model the particle updates its velocity according to the global best solution and its own best solution. By this it tries to explorer the unevaluated area of the search space. This approach has shown to give a reasonably better solution.

3.3 Feature Selection: Signal to Noise Ratio Approach

Many times the dataset contains some attributes that are not necessary and contains no useful information for classification; this is where feature selection plays important role [14]. Feature selection distinguishes and extracts those unwanted features and reduces the dataset for ease of classification. Generally, feature extraction for classification refers to searching all possible combinations of the feature set for the best one that preserves class separability as much as possible with the lowest possible dimensionality

[20]. In many research it is reported that SNR feature selection is one of the best method to be implemented to get good result for classification [11, 12].

Signal to Noise Ratio. Signal-to-noise ratio (SNR) is defined as the ratio of signal power to the noise power, generally expressed in decibels. It can be referred as the ratio of useful information to false or irrelevant data in a conversation. An alternative definition of SNR has derived accordingly i.e., the ratio of mean to standard deviation of a signal or measurement. It reduces the dimensionality of the datasets by extracting some of the noisy features or attributes from the dataset and then it can be applied for classification. In this classification technique SNR is implanted to measure the effectiveness of the features taken for identifying a class out of another class or between two classes according to which selected features are taken and rest are removed.

Mathematically it is defined as,

$$SNR = \frac{\mu_1 - \mu_2}{\delta_1 + \delta_2} \tag{1}$$

Where μ_1 and μ_2 are the mean expression level for samples in class1 and class2 respectively

And δ_1 and δ_1 are the standard deviations for the sample in each class [13].

4   Experimental Results

Two datasets i.e. pima diabetes dataset and breast cancer datasets are taken here. The pima diabetes datasets have 8 attributes with 786 samples and is a 2 class label dataset. Similarly the cancer dataset contains 9 attributes with 286 samples and also a 2 class label dataset (Table 1).

Table 1. Following are the data description of the taken data

Data sets	Attributes of the datasets
Pima Indian diabetes dataset (9*768)	No of times pregnant Plasma glucose concentration Diastolic blood pressure Triceps skin fold thickness 2-h serum insulin Body mass index Diabetes pedigree function Age
Breast cancer dataset (9*286)	Age Menopause Tumor-size Inv-nodes Node caps Deg-malig Breast Breast-quad Irradiates (class label-yes/no)

4.1 Results

At first the datasets are applied to the simple FLANN and the error is calculated. The following graph in Fig. 3(a) and (b) describes the error rate with increasing iteration.

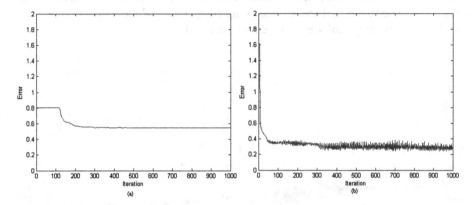

Fig. 3. (a) Graph shows the error rate for the diabetes dataset taken with increasing iteration in FLANN; (b) graph shows the calculated error rate for the breast-cancer dataset taken with increasing iteration in FLANN

From the above Fig. 3(a) and (b) it can be seen that the error level becomes constant after a certain iterations and the error is not minimized enough to be acceptable. So this result motivates for a better solution procedure. In the second phase the optimization algorithm i.e. the PSO is applied along with FLANN and the error is calculated again. Following graph as in Fig. 4(a) and (b) describes the decrease in error rate with increasing iteration due to the optimization of weight.

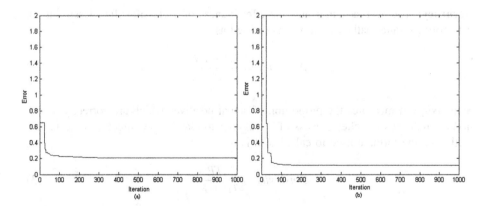

Fig. 4. (a) Graph shows the error rate for the diabetes dataset taken with increasing iteration in PSO-FLANN; (b) Graph shows the error rate for the breast-cancer dataset taken with increasing iteration using PSO-FLANN

Form the Fig. 4(a) and (b) it can be observed that PSO improves the result with decrease in error. But still the error is not minimized enough so it leads to finding of a better algorithm. In the final step feature selection is done using SNR technique to differentiate and extract the redundant features from the original given feature with the help of signal to noise ratio (SNR). After some unwanted features are extracted the error is calculated again and the accuracies are compared. And the following Fig. 5(a) and (b) gives the graphical view how error is reduced.

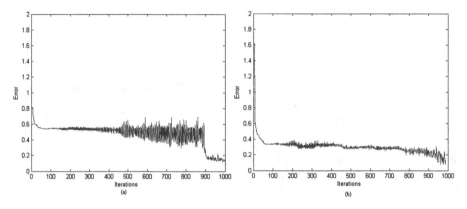

Fig. 5. (a) Graph shows the error rate for the diabetes dataset taken with increasing iteration after the feature selection; (b) graph shows the error rate for the breast-cancer dataset taken with increasing iteration after the feature selection

In Fig. 5(a) and (b); it can be clearly seen that the reduction of error is not saturated and still decreasing even more than the previous methods. So the sufficient number of iteration leads to a minimized acceptable error in FLANN.

The output is analyzed using the parameters as follows:

Accuracy: The accuracy indicates the effectiveness of a classifier for classifying all data correctly and mathematically it is defined as -

$$Accuracy = \frac{TP + TN}{N} \tag{2}$$

Sensitivity: It measures the proportion of actual positives which are correctly identified i.e. indicates the effectiveness of a classifier to classify the affected subjects correctly and the formula used to calculate it is –

$$Sensitivity = \frac{TP}{TP + FN} \tag{3}$$

Specificity: It measures the proportion of negatives which are correctly identified i.e. indicates the effectiveness of a classifier for classifying normal subjects correctly and is calculated as –

$$Specificity = \frac{TN}{TN + FP} \qquad (4)$$

Precision: It is the positive predictive value or PPV and is defines as –

$$Precision = \frac{TP}{TP + FP} \qquad (5)$$

Negative predictive value (NPV): It is known as the negative precision and is defined as –

$$NPV = \frac{TN}{TN + FN} \qquad (6)$$

Here TP is True Positive, TN is True Negative, FP is False Positive, FN is False Negative and N is the total number of class levels.

Table 2. Performance analysis of pima indian diabetes dataset.

Different FLANN models	Simple FLANN	PSO-FLANN	FLANN with SNR
Accuracy	0.70	0.79	0.98
Sensitivity	0.61	0.62	0.96
Specificity	0.74	0.88	0.99
Precision	0.56	0.74	0.99
NPV	0.78	0.81	0.98

Table 3. Performance analysis of breast cancer dataset.

Different FLANN models	Simple FLANN	PSO-FLANN	FLANN with SNR
Accuracy	0.97	0.97	1.00
Sensitivity	0.98	0.98	1.00
Specificity	0.97	0.95	1.00
Precision	0.95	0.97	1.00
NPV	0.99	0.96	1.00

By analyzing the result shown in Tables 2 and 3 it is clearly visible that the performance of the FLANN model increases with feature selection and hybridization techniques. Different performance metrics are calculated by taking two biological datasets. First in the simple FLANN model the accuracy and other metrics are not satisfactory, but after using the PSO-FLANN it increases and finally the FLANN with

SNR gives a better outcome compared to other two models due to the removal of noisy attributes. And hence form the above analysis we can say hybridization of classification model gives better performance result.

5 Conclusion

In this research work three FLANN based classification models have been compared. First a simple FLANN model is taken, followed by a hybrid FLANN model where the Particle Swarm Optimization is applied to optimize the weights of FLANN. At last a feature selection technique i.e. Signal to noise ratio is applied to reduce the attributes and FLANN is used as the classifier for the newly formed dataset. From the analysis it is clearly visible that an improved classifier can be formulated with the combination of one or more techniques i.e. better performance of a hybrid classifier is justified here. With the addition of PSO to FLANN the accuracy has improved and further amelioration has been done by applying feature selection method. Though FLANN is a better classifier compared to simple ANN or MLP and other types of neural networks in terms of complexity reduction, convergence speed etc., it works better with the addition of optimization and feature reduction technique like SNR.

References

1. Mitra, S., Mitra, P.: Data mining in soft computing framework: a survey. IEEE Trans. Neural Netw. **13**(1), 3–14 (2002)
2. Mili, F., Hamdi, M.: A hybrid evolutionary functional link artificial neural network for data mining and classification. In: 6th International Conference on Sciences of Electronics, Technologies of Information and Telecommunications (2012)
3. Mili, F., Hamdi M.: A comparative study of expansion functions for evolutionary hybrid functional link artificial neural networks for data mining and classification. In: 2013 International Conference on Computer Applications Technology (ICCAT). IEEE (2013)
4. Nanda, S.K., Tripathy, D.P.: Application of functional link artificial neural network for prediction of machinery noise in opencast mines. Adv. Fuzzy Syst. **2011**, 4 (2011). (Hindawi Publishing Corporation)
5. Liao, S.H., Chu, P.H., Hsiao, P.Y.: Data mining techniques and applications – a decade review from 2000 to 2011. Expert Syst. Appl. **39**(12), 11303–11311 (2012)
6. Zhang, G.P.: Neural networks for classification: a survey. IEEE Trans. Syst. **30**(4), 451–462 (2000)
7. Kumar, K., Thakur, G.S.M.: Advanced applications of neural networks and artificial intelligence: a review. Int. J. Inf. Technol. Comput. Sci. **4**(6), 57–68 (2012)
8. Pradhan, G., Korimilli, V., Satapathy, S.C., Pattnaik, S., Mitra, B.: Design of simple ANN (SANN) model for data classification and its performance comparison with FLANN (functional link ANN). Int. J. Comput. Sci. Netw. Secur. **9**(10), 105–115 (2009)
9. Misra, B.B., Dehuri, S.: Functional link artificial neural network for classification task in data mining. J. Comput. Sci. **3**(12), 948 (2007)

10. Dehuri, S., Roy, R., Cho, S.B., Ghosh, A.: An improved swarm optimized functional link artificial neural network (ISO-FLANN) for classification. J. Syst. Softw. **85**(6), 1333–1345 (2012)
11. Minaei-Bidgoli, B., Kortemeyer, G., Punch, W.F.: Optimizing classification ensembles via a genetic algorithm for a web-based educational system. In: Fred, A., Caelli, T.M., Duin, R.P. W., Campilho, A.C., de Ridder, D. (eds.) SSPR 2004 and SPR 2004. LNCS, vol. 3138, pp. 397–406. Springer, Heidelberg (2004)
12. Huang, C.J., Liao, W.C.: A comparative study of feature selection methods for probabilistic neural networks in cancer classification: In: Proceedings of the 15th IEEE International Conference on Tools with Artificial Intelligence (2003)
13. Ryu, J., Cho, S.B.: Gene expression classification using optimal feature/classifier ensemble with negative correlation. In: Proceedings of the 2002 International Joint Conference on Neural Network, pp. 198–203, (2002)
14. Mishra, D., Sahu, B.: Feature selection for cancer classification: a signal-to-noise ratio approach. Int. J. Sci. Eng. Res. **2**(4), 1–7 (2011)
15. Hengpraprohm, S., Chongstitvatana, P.: Feature selection by weighted-SNR for cancer microarray data classification. Int. J. Innovative Comput. Inf. Control (2008)
16. Hassim, Y.M.M., Ghazali, R.: Training a functional link neural network using an artificial bee colony for solving a classification problem (2012). arXiv:1212.6922
17. Emad, E., Hegazy, T., Grierson, D.: Comparison among five evolutionary-based optimization algorithms. Adv. Eng. Inform. **19**(1), 43–53 (2005)
18. Vu, T.V.: A comparison of particle swarm optimization and differential evolution. Int. J. Soft Comput. (IJSC) **3**(3), (2012)
19. Sierra, A., Macías, J.A., Corbacho, F.: Evolution of functional link networks. IEEE Trans. Evol. Comput. **5**(1), 54–65 (2001)
20. Dehuri, S., Sung, B.C.: Evolutionarily optimized features in functional link neural network for classification. Expert Syst. Appl. **37**(6), 4379–4391 (2010)
21. Pechenizkiy, M., Puuronen, S., Tsymbal, A.: Feature extraction for classification in the data mining process. Int. J. Inf. Theor. Appl. **10**, 271 (2003)
22. Ramaswami, M., Bhaskaran, R.: A study on feature selection techniques in educational data mining. J. Comput. **1**(1), 7–11 (2009)
23. Huan, L., Motoda, H., Setiono, R., Zhao, Z.: Feature selection: an ever evolving frontier in data mining. J. Mach. Learn. Res. Proc. **10**, 4–13 (2010)
24. Mohmad Hassim, Y.M., Ghazali, R.: Functional link neural network – artificial bee colony for time series temperature prediction. In: Murgante, B., Misra, S., Carlini, M., Torre, C.M., Nguyen, H.-Q., Taniar, D., Apduhan, B.O., Gervasi, O. (eds.) ICCSA 2013, Part I. LNCS, vol. 7971, pp. 427–437. Springer, Heidelberg (2013)
25. Ma, H., Simon, D., Fei, M., Chen, Z.: On the equivalences and differences of evolutionary algorithms. Eng. Appl. Artif. Intell. **26**(10), 2397–2407 (2013)
26. UCI Repository of Machine Learning Databases. http://www.ics.uci.edu/~mlearn/MLRepository.html
27. Rajasekharan, S., Vijayalaxmi Pai, G.A.: Neural Networks, Fuzzy Logic, and Genetic Algorithms, Synthesis and Applications. PHI Publications, Delhi (2010)

R-HV: A Metric for Computing Hyper-volume for Reference Point Based EMOs

Kalyanmoy Deb[1]([⊠]), Florian Siegmund[2], and Amos H.C. Ng[2]

[1] Computational Optimization and Innovation (COIN) Laboratory,
Michigan State University, East Lansing, MI 48824, USA
kdeb@egr.msu.edu
http://www.egr.msu.edu

[2] Virtual Systems Research Center, University of Skövde,
Högskolevägen, 54128 Skövde, Sweden
{Florian.Siegmund,Amos.Ng}@his.se

Abstract. For evaluating performance of a multi-objective optimization for finding the entire efficient front, a number of metrics, such as hyper-volume, inverse generational distance, etc. exists. However, for evaluating an EMO algorithm for finding a subset of the efficient frontier, the existing metrics are inadequate. There does not exist many performance metrics for evaluating a partial preferred efficient set. In this paper, we suggest a metric which can be used for such purposes for both attainable and unattainable reference points. Results on a number of two-objective problems reveal its working principle and its importance in assessing different algorithms. The results are promising and encouraging for its further use.

Keywords: Evolutionary multi-objective optimization · Performance metric · Hyper-volume · Reference point

1 Introduction

In multi-objective optimization, there are two goals: (i) convergence to the efficient front and (ii) diversity of the obtained set of points in representing the entire efficient front [7]. When different multi-objective optimization algorithms were developed (mainly using evolutionary algorithms) [6,8,17,19], the resulting evolutionary multi-objective optimization (EMO) algorithms needed to be evaluated for both aspects of convergence and diversity maintenance. Despite the existence of performance metrics for evaluating convergence and diversity independently, the metrics that evaluated both aspects of EMO had gained popularity. The hyper-volume metric [3,5,18], μ-distributed hyper-volume indicator [1], inverse generational distance metric [7] and others [14] are some common measures used for this purpose. Despite some idiosyncrasies with each of these metrics, they were mainly suitable for evaluating a set of representative points on the entire efficient front.

Unfortunately, the existing performance metrics are not suitable for evaluating a set of preferred points on a specific part of the efficient front. In preference

© Springer International Publishing Switzerland 2015
B.K. Panigrahi et al. (Eds.): SEMCCO 2014, LNCS 8947, pp. 98–110, 2015.
DOI: 10.1007/978-3-319-20294-5_9

based EMO applications, it is desired to find a preferred part of the Pareto-optimal set, instead of a set covering the entire efficient front. Reference point based NSGA-II (R-NSGA-II) [12], light beam search based EMO [10], reference direction based EMO [9], epsilon-dominance based MOEA [11] are some such examples for EMO-based algorithms. Since the focus in these EMO methods is to find a partial front focused on a specific part of the efficient front, the hyper-volume metric or IGD value may not be optimum for a desired preferred set. Additional but unwanted points may provide a better metric value, thereby making these metrics unsuitable for the purpose.

In this paper, we propose a hyper-volume based R-metric (R-HV) in Sect. 2 that performs the following operations: (i) it filters the entire set of points to keep relevant solutions *close* to the supplied reference point, (ii) it translates the filtered points so as to make the points meaningful according to a multi-criteria decision making (MCDM) approach, and (iii) it computes the hyper-volume value for the translated points. The pre-processing approach of computing the R-HV gives importance for *convergence* to the desired part of the efficient front and also to maintain a relevant *diversity* among them. The proposed R-HV metric can be used with attainable or unattainable reference points without any change in the procedure. The proposed R-HV is then applied to several two-objective optimization problems in Sect. 3 to illustrate its working principle. The metric is ready to applied in evaluating EMO algorithm's performance for solving three and higher objective test and applied problems. Conclusions are drawn in Sect. 4.

2   Proposed R-Metric Computation Principle

The R-metric computation procedure uses hyper-volume metric but uses a pre-processing procedure based on the preference information used in the respective EMO procedure. We assume that the following entities are known before computing the R-metric:

Number of objectives:	M
Reference point:	$\mathbf{Z}^r$
Worst point for computing R-metric:	$\mathbf{Z}^w$ (assume $\mathbf{Z}^r$ dominates $\mathbf{Z}^w$)
Size of trade-off set:	N
Trade-off set:	$S = (\mathbf{f}^{(j)}, \ j = 1, 2, \ldots, N)$

The idea uses a multi-criteria decision-making (MCDM) concept for ranking different solutions, given a reference point and a weight vector. We illustrate the procedure using Fig. 1. In this hypothetical problem, let us imagine that an EMO used the information of a reference point $\mathbf{Z}^r$ and found a set of eight solutions as shown in the figure as S. The performance of the algorithm in solving the problem with above information now needs to be evaluated using a performance metric. First, it is evident from the figure that the set S is not quite close to the efficient front. An appropriate performance metric should evaluate this set

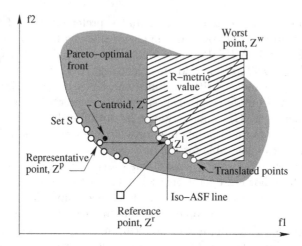

Fig. 1. R-metric computation for a set S for a reference point $\mathbf{Z}^r$.

of solutions to be not as good as another set (say, 'ideal set') which would have been closer to the reference point.

If the usual hyper-volume is computed for this set of eight solutions with the worst point $\mathbf{Z}^w$ (shown in the figure), the resulting hyper-volume value may be larger or equivalent to the hyper-volume computed for the ideal set mentioned above. This indicates that the usual hyper-volume metric may not be suitable for preference based EMO algorithms for which the target is to find a biased set of preferred solutions and not the whole efficient front. We now describe the procedure for computing our proposed R-HV metric.

In order for any reference point $\mathbf{Z}^r$ to be used, we bring in the achievement scalarizing function (ASF) concept [16] for computing the R-HV metric, but we also take into consideration the desired spread of solution set S. First, we identify a representative point from the set S. In the figure, we use the centroid of S in the objective space as a representative point, but any other ideas of arriving at a representative point may also be used. Then, other solutions from set S that can be considered as meaningful for the R-metric computation are filtered. Thereafter, the representative point and the filtered set of points are evaluated using ASF and a corresponding iso-ASF point ($\mathbf{Z}^l$) on the line joining $\mathbf{Z}^r$ and $\mathbf{Z}^w$ is located. This iso-ASF point will provide us with an information about the *closeness* of the representative point to the desired preferred point on the efficient front due to the specification of the supplied reference point $\mathbf{Z}^r$. Thereafter, all members of the set S are translated towards the weight vector and the hyper-volume is computed as usual using the supplied worst point $\mathbf{Z}^w$. The step-by-step procedure is presented below:

Step 1: Identify a Representative Point: Identify a representative point ($\mathbf{Z}^p$) of the set S. A typical way to identify such a point may be to first find the centroid point, as follows:

$$z_i^c = \frac{1}{N} \sum_{j=1}^{N} f_i^{(j)}, \quad \forall i = 1, 2, \ldots, M, \tag{1}$$

and then identify the point which is closest to the centroid as $\mathbf{Z}^p$.

Step 2: Filter the Set S**:** Keep points that are close to $\mathbf{Z}^p$ for R-metric computation. One way to filter the points would be to keep points that are within an Euclidean distance Δ from $\mathbf{Z}^p$.

Step 3: Translate Filtered Points to the Reference Line: This operation requires a few sub-steps:
Find joining $\mathbf{Z}^r$ to $\mathbf{Z}^w$ using the following steps.
1. Construct a reference line joining $\mathbf{Z}^r$ to $\mathbf{Z}^w$.
2. Identify the intersection point ($\mathbf{Z}^l$) of the ASF contour line with the reference line. This requires to identify the objective (k) that contributes to the ASF contour value:

$$k = \mathrm{argmax}_{i=1}^{M} \left(\frac{z_i^p - z_i^r}{z_i^w - z_i^r} \right). \tag{2}$$

and then compute $\mathbf{Z}^l$ as follows:

$$z_i^l = z_i^r + \frac{z_k^p - z_k^r}{z_k^w - z_k^r}(z_i^w - z_i^r). \tag{3}$$

3. Shift all members of S by the vector $(\mathbf{Z}^l - \mathbf{Z}^p)$.

Step 4: Compute Hyper-volume: Compute hyper-volume using the translated solutions and by using $\mathbf{Z}^w$ as the worst point and declare the hyper-volume as the R-metric.

Larger the value of the R-metric, the better is the set *close* to the reference point $\mathbf{Z}^r$.

Interestingly, two sets of trade-off points S_1 and S_2, as shown in Fig. 2, have different R-HV metric values. Here, in Step 2, we do not filter any of the solutions; instead consider all points to compute the R-HV metric. The one (S_2) *closer* to the reference point $\mathbf{Z}^r$ has a larger R-HV metric value (shown as the white space). Since, the representative point of S_2 has a better (smaller in this case) ASF value, the translation effect of these points is smaller than that for S_1 (shown as a shaded region). This cases the R-HV metric value of S_2 to be larger than that of S_1.

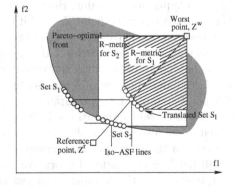

Fig. 2. R-HV metric value of set S_2 is better than that of set S_1. In this case, set S_2 does not get translated.

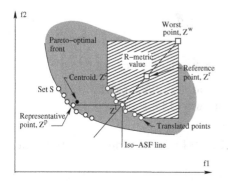 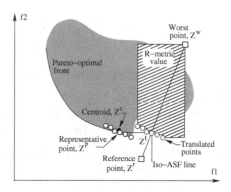

Fig. 3. R-HV metric computation for an attainable reference point $\mathbf{Z}^r$.

Fig. 4. R-HV metric computation for an arbitrary reference point $\mathbf{Z}^r$.

The above R-HV metric can also be used for reference points that lie on the feasible objective space or for cases where the reference point is supplied outside the region bounded by the ideal and nadir point of the Pareto-optimal front, as illustrated in Figs. 3 and 4.

It is also intuitive to realize that if an EMO fails to find a good distribution of points, the resulting R-HV metric value will be smaller, meaning a worse performance compared to a widely-distributed set of points. However, the modification suggested in the next subsection ensures that a limited distribution is preferred over an overly large distribution for certain special EMO algorithms.

Another interesting fact is that the R-HV metric becomes equal to the usual hyper-volume metric, if following procedures are used in Steps 1 and 2. In Step 1, the representative point $\mathbf{Z}^p$ can be chosen as the point closest point to the reference line, or the point having the smallest ASF value (point A shown in Fig. 5). In Step 2, no filtering is performed. If there exists a Pareto-optimal point in the set S on the reference line, it will be chosen as $\mathbf{Z}^p$, and Step 3 reduces to no translation process. Thus, in Step 4, the hyper-volume computation will result in the usual hyper-volume value. However, if the ideal point of the obtained front is chosen as the reference point $\mathbf{Z}^r$ and if in Step 2 no filtering is performed, for a set S covering the entire Pareto-optimal front, the representative point $\mathbf{Z}^p$ make a slight shift of the set for the R-HV metric computation, as shown in Fig. 5.

We now compute a complexity estimate of implementing the R-HV metric. In Step 1, the identification of a representative point $\mathbf{Z}^p$ from a non-dominated set of N points requires $O(N)$ computations. The filtering of points in Step 2 can be achieved in $O(N)$ computations. In Step 3, translating at most N points on the reference line also requires $O(N)$ computations. The hyper-volume computation in Step 4 is the only time-consuming effort and governs the complexity of the overall R-HV computational effort. Although calculation of exact hyper-volume is exponential to the number of objectives [13], faster sample-based methods exist [2,4,5,15] and can also be used in computing R-HV metric value.

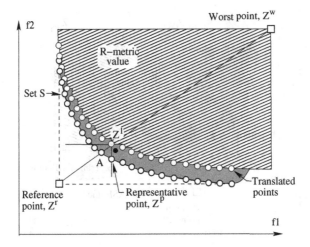

Fig. 5. If the reference point $\mathbf{Z}^r$ is considered to be the ideal point, the resulting R-HV metric value may closely represent the hyper-volume measure.

2.1   R-HV Metric for ϵ-dominance Based EMOs

If the R-HV metric is to be computed for an ϵ-dominance based EMO algorithm, the above procedure can be modified slightly to take into account the extent of desired spread in solution set S. Assuming that a maximum of N points are to be found at the end and there is a minimum difference of ϵ is desired between two consecutive solutions in the objective space, we expect all solutions S to lie within $\Delta = \pm(N/2)\epsilon$ around the centroid $\mathbf{Z}^p$. One way to restrict this is to eliminate all points that lie outside $(z_i^p \pm (N/2)\epsilon_i)$ and compute the R-HV metric for all the solutions that are inside the hyper-box. Thereafter the procedure is identical to the generic procedure given earlier. Figure 6 illustrates the idea.

Again, the larger the value of the R-HV metric, the *closer* is the set to the reference point $\mathbf{Z}^r$. Like the generic case, the above ϵ-based R-HV metric can also be used for attainable reference points and for other cases. Also, both the above R-HV metrics can be used for any number of objectives.

3   Results

We now present results of the above R-HV metric on a number of two-objective test problems.

3.1   Problem ZDT1

First, we consider two-objective ZDT1 problem and show the change of R-HV metric for different sets of Pareto-optimal solutions. A total of $N = 41$ points are created along the front $(f_2 = \sqrt{1 - f_1})$ and centered around a point

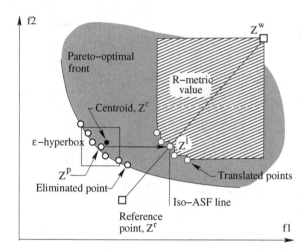

Fig. 6. R-HV metric computation for ϵ-dominance based EMO algorithms.

$\mathbf{Z}^p = (z_1^p, z_2^p)^T$. The extent of $N/2$ points on either direction of $\mathbf{Z}^p$ is a specified quantity: Δ. We vary z_1^p from zero to one with an interval of 0.01 and create a total of N points around $\mathbf{Z}^p$. Then, remove all solutions outside $[0,1]$ on both f_1 and f_2 axes and apply the above step-by-step R-HV computing procedure.

Unattainable Reference Points: The R-HV metric is computed using $\mathbf{Z}^w = (1.1, 1.1)^T$. Figure 7 shows the change in R-HV metric value with z_1^p for a supplied reference point $\mathbf{Z}^r = (0.25, 0.25)^T$. It can be seen that the R-HV metric

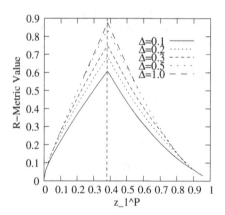

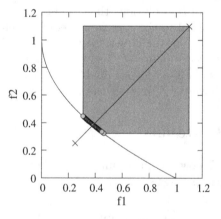

Fig. 7. Variation of R-HV metric value with z_1^p.

Fig. 8. R-HV metric reaches its maximum for a set which is closest to the supplied reference point $\mathbf{Z}^r = (0, 25, 0.25)^T$.

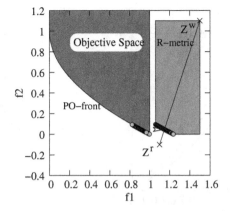
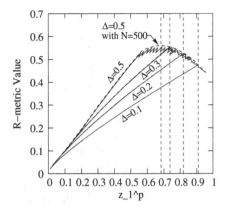

Fig. 9. Variation of R-HV metric value with z_1^p for different values of Δ. A large population makes the variation more smooth.

Fig. 10. R-HV metric reaches its maximum for a set which is closest to the supplied reference point $\mathbf{Z}^r = (1.1, -0.1)^T$.

value is largest ($= 0.606$) for a set centered around $z_1^p = 0.38$. As shown in Fig. 8, at this z_1^p, the line joining $\mathbf{Z}^r$ and $\mathbf{Z}^w$ intersects the Pareto-optimal front. In this scenario, the representative point $\mathbf{Z}^p$ is 'closest' to the the reference point $\mathbf{Z}^r$, which makes the R-HV metric to achieve its maximum.

Extreme Reference Points: Next, we consider a reference point that is outside the range of Pareto-optimal front: $\mathbf{Z}^r = (1.1, -0.1)^T$. We also change the worst point as $\mathbf{Z}^w = (1.5, 1.1)^T$. Figure 9 shows the variation of R-HV metric with z_1^p. It can be seen that the R-HV metric value is now maximum when $z_1^p = 0.91$. Figure 10 shows the distribution of points for ZDT1 problem for other parameter values identical to that in the previous case. Since $\mathbf{Z}^r$ lies on one extreme, it is expected that for a set of Pareto-optimal points at the respective extreme boundary is desired and our R-HV metric is able to capture this fact. For larger Δ values, $N = 40$ population points are too sparsed and introduce a fluctuation in the R-HV metric value, but as shown in Fig. 9 the fluctuation reduces with a larger population size ($N = 500$). For $\Delta = 0.2$, 0.3 and 0.5, the maximum R-HV occurs at $z_1^p = 0.820$, 0.738, and 0.682, respectively.

Attainable Reference Points: Figure 11 shows the variation of R-HV metric for an attainable reference point: $\mathbf{Z}^r = (0.75, 0.75)^T$. Since this point lies on a 45° line from the worst point, for ZDT1 problem we should expect to have an identical R-HV value as that obtained for $\mathbf{Z}^r = (0.25, 0.25)^T$ in Fig. 7. Notice that these two figures are identical. This illustrates that the proposed R-HV metric also works with reference points that lie in the feasible objective space.

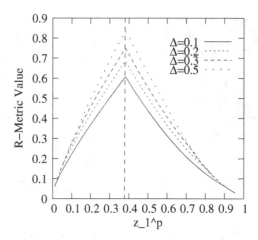

Fig. 11. R-HV metric variation for an attainable reference point.

3.2   Problem ZDT2

We now compute the R-HV metric for the ZDT2 problem, having a Pareto-optimal front $f_2 = 1 - f_1^2$. Figure 12 shows the variation of R-HV metric for different z_1^p values for $\mathbf{Z}^r = (0.25, 0.25)^T$, $\mathbf{Z}^w = (1.1, 1.1)^t$ and $N = 41$. For different Δ values, the maximum R-HV value occurs at $z_1^p = 0.62$, which happens to be the 'closest' point from the chosen reference point to the efficient front. Figure 13 shows 41 points on the Pareto-optimal front and the measured R-HV metric value.

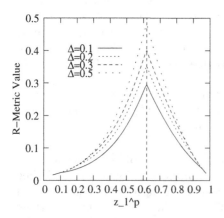

Fig. 12. Variation of R-HV metric value with z_1^p on ZDT2 problem.

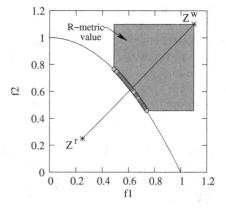

Fig. 13. R-HV metric reaches its maximum for a set with $z_1^p = 0.62$ which is closest to the supplied reference point $\mathbf{Z}^r = (0, 25, 0.25)^T$.

3.3   R-HV Metric Computation for ϵ-Dominated Points

To show the effect of ϵ, we consider a problem with linear Pareto-optimal front: $f_2 = 1 - f_1$. We also consider $\mathbf{Z}^r = (0.4, 0.4)^T$ and $\mathbf{Z}^w = (0.6, 0.6)^T$. It is then expected that a set centered around $\mathbf{Z}^p = (0.5, 0.5)^T$ will produce the highest R-HV value. Let us say different sets of solutions around $\mathbf{Z}^p$ but having a spread of $\pm\Gamma$ on each objective axis are obtained by an algorithm, but we filter solutions around $\pm\Delta$ of $\mathbf{Z}^p$ on both objectives for computing the R-HV metric value. Since we shall consider points within $\pm\Delta$ ($\Delta_1 = \Delta_2 = 0.707$ is fixed here) around $\mathbf{Z}^p$, if too sparse a set of solutions (meaning $\Gamma > \Delta$) is found by an algorithm, fewer points will be used to compute the R-HV metric and hence the R-HV metric will be calculated to be small. Figure 14 shows R-HV metric values for different sets of trade-off solutions having different Γ/Δ ratios from 0.25 to 3.0 with $N = 21$ points. It is clear from the figure that, when all 21 points are found covering the entire Δ-box, the R-HV metric becomes large. For other cases (when a more-densed ($\Gamma < \Delta$) or less-densed ($\Gamma > \Delta$) set of points), the R-HV metric value is small. Figures 15 and 16 show two distributions (with $\Gamma/\Delta = 1$ and 3, respectively) and their R-HV metric values. It is clear that the first distribution having a distribution matching the desired Δ-box has a better R-HV metric value, compared to the second one which is unnecessarily more sparse. It is interesting also to note that the difference in R-HV metric values between these two cases is much smaller than if a similar range of distribution was found in another location on the Pareto-optimal front.

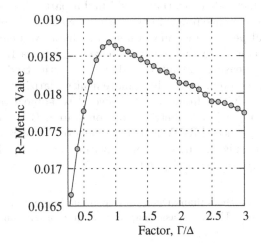

Fig. 14. R-HV metric variation with differently sparsed points. $\Gamma/\Delta \approx 1$ means a desired distribution of points obtained and evaluates to have the near-largest R-HV metric value.

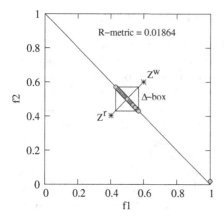

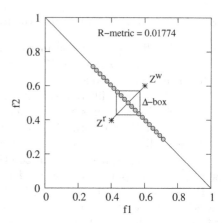

Fig. 15. Distribution of points within the entire Δ-box makes a large R-HV metric value.

Fig. 16. Distribution of a unnecessary sparse set of points does not make a large R-HV metric value.

4   Conclusions

Performance metrics for evaluating the convergence and diversity aspects of a set of trade-off optimized solutions obtained by an evolutionary multi-objective optimization (EMO) algorithm has been an important matter of study. Besides finding the entire efficient front, EMO researchers have also worked on developing MCDM-based methodologies that would find a part of the efficient frontier often dictated by a reference point. In evaluating such a set of preferred trade-off solutions, the usual performance metrics, such as hyper-volume and IGD metrics, do not work as well. In this paper we have suggested a R-HV metric that uses hyper-volume measure but filters and translates the trade-off points near the supplied reference point using the achievement scalarizing function concept borrowed from the MCDM literature. On several two-objective problems, the efficacy of the proposed R-HV metric is demonstrated. Based on the achievement of desired properties of R-HV metric, we believe that it is now ready to be applied to three and higher objective optimization algorithms for their ability to find a preferred set of trade-off points.

Acknowledgment. Authors thank Debayan Deb, an undergraduate student of Michigan State of University, USA, for assisting in computer programming of the R-HV metric concept.

References

1. Auger, A., Bader, J., Brockhoff, D.: Theoretically investigating optimal μ-distributions for the hypervolume indicator: first results for three objectives. In: Schaefer, R., Cotta, C., Kołodziej, J., Rudolph, G. (eds.) PPSN XI. LNCS, vol. 6238, pp. 586–596. Springer, Heidelberg (2010)

2. Bader, J., Deb, K., Zitzler, E.: Faster hypervolume-based search using Monte Carlo sampling. In: Proceedings of Multiple Criteria Decision Making (MCDM 2008), LNEMS, vol. 634, pp. 313–326. Springer, Heidelberg 2010
3. Bader, J., Zitzler, E.: Hype: an algorithm for fast hypervolume-based many-objective optimization. Evol. Comput. J. **19**(1), 45–76 (2011)
4. Beume, N., Fonseca, C.M., López-Ibáñez, M., Paquete, L., Vahrenhold, J.: On the complexity of computing the hypervolume indicator. IEEE Trans. Evol. Comput. **13**(5), 1075–1082 (2009)
5. Bradstreet, L., While, L., Barone, L.: A fast incremental hypervolume algorithm. IEEE Trans. Evol. Comput. **12**(6), 714–723 (2008)
6. Corne, D. W., Knowles, J. D., Oates, M.: The Pareto envelope-based selection algorithm for multiobjective optimization. In: Proceedings of the Sixth International Conference on Parallel Problem Solving from Nature VI (PPSN-VI), pp. 839–848 (2000)
7. Deb, K.: Multi-Objective Optimization Using Evolutionary Algorithms. Wiley, Chichester (2001)
8. Deb, K., Agrawal, S., Pratap, A., Meyarivan, T.: A fast and elitist multi-objective genetic algorithm: NSGA-II. IEEE Trans. Evol. Comput. **6**(2), 182–197 (2002)
9. Deb, K., Kumar, A.: Interactive evolutionary multi-objective optimization and decision-making using reference direction method. In: Proceedings of the Genetic and Evolutionary Computation Conference (GECCO-2007), pp. 781–788. The Association of Computing Machinery (ACM), New York (2007)
10. Deb, K., Kumar, A.: Light beam search based multi-objective optimization using evolutionary algorithms. In: Proceedings of the Congress on Evolutionary Computation (CEC 2007), pp. 2125–2132 (2007)
11. Deb, K., Mohan, M., Mishra, S.: Evaluating the ϵ-domination based multi-objective evolutionary algorithm for a quick computation of Pareto-optimal solutions. Evol. Comput. J. **13**(4), 501–525 (2005)
12. Deb, K., Sundar, J., Uday, N., Chaudhuri, S.: Reference point based multi-objective optimization using evolutionary algorithms. Int. J. Comput. Intell. Res. (IJCIR) **2**(6), 273–286 (2006)
13. Fonseca, C. M., Paquete, L., López-Ibáñez, M.: An improved dimension sweep algorithm for the hypervolume indicator. In: Proceedings of the 2006 Congress on Evolutionary Computation (CEC 2006), pp. 1157–1163. IEEE Press, Piscataway, NJ (2006)
14. Knowles, J. D., Corne, D. W.: On metrics for comparing nondominated sets. In: Congress on Evolutionary Computation (CEC-2002), pp. 711–716. IEEE Press, Piscataway, NJ (2002)
15. While, L., Hingston, P., Barone, L., Huband, S.: A faster algorithm for calculating hypervolume. IEEE Trans. Evol. Comput. **10**(1), 29–38 (2006)
16. Wierzbicki, A.P.: The use of reference objectives in multiobjective optimization. In: Fandel, G., Gal, T. (eds.) Multiple Criteria Decision Making Theory and Applications, pp. 468–486. Springer-Verlag, Berlin (1980)
17. Zitzler, E., Laumanns, M., Thiele, L.: SPEA2: improving the strength Pareto evolutionary algorithm for multiobjective optimization. In: Giannakoglou, K. C., Tsahalis, D. T., Périaux, J., Papailiou, K. D., Fogarty, T.(eds.) Evolutionary Methods for Design Optimization and Control with Applications to Industrial Problems, International Center for Numerical Methods in Engineering (CIMNE), pp. 95–100. Athens (2001)

18. Zitzler, E., Thiele, L.: Multiobjective optimization using evolutionary algorithms - a comparative case study. In: Eiben, A.E., Bäck, T., Schoenauer, M., Schwefel, H.-P. (eds.) PPSN 1998. LNCS, vol. 1498, pp. 292–301. Springer, Heidelberg (1998)
19. Zitzler, E., Thiele, L.: Multiobjective evolutionary algorithms: a comparative case study and the strength Pareto approach. IEEE Trans. Evol. Comput. 3(4), 257–271 (1999)

Performance Comparison of Supervised Machine Learning Algorithms for Multiclass Transient Classification in a Nuclear Power Plant

Manas Ranjan Prusty[1(✉)], Jaideep Chakraborty[1], T. Jayanthi[1], and K. Velusamy[2]

[1] Computer Division, Indira Gandhi Centre for Atomic Research,
Kalpakkam, India
manas.iter144@gmail.com,
{jaideep,jayanthi}@igcar.gov.in
[2] Mechanics and Hydraulics Division, Indira Gandhi Centre for Atomic
Research, Kalpakkam, India
kvelu@igcar.gov.in

Abstract. For safety critical systems in nuclear power plant (NPP), accurate classification of multiclass transient leads to safer operation of the plant. Supervised machine learning is a key technique which solves multiclass classification related problems. The most widely used multiclass supervised machine learning methods for this purpose are k-nearest neighbor algorithm, support vector machine algorithm and artificial neural network (ANN) algorithm. This paper describes a comparative study on the performance of these algorithms towards classifying some of the transients in NPP. The performance analysis is mostly based on the prediction accuracy in classifying the correct transient occurred. Along with prediction accuracy, total number of epochs, training time and root mean square error was also observed as a characteristic feature for determining the performance of any backpropagation ANN. A 10-fold cross validation was carried on all these algorithms for ten times and the best among them was finally concluded for multiclass transient classification in NPP.

Keywords: Nuclear power plant · Supervised machine learning · k-Nearest neighbor · Support vector machine · Artificial neural network · k-Fold cross validation

1 Introduction

A nuclear power plant (NPP) contains many safety critical systems. For an operator sitting in the main control room in a NPP, decision making becomes very difficult when he is overloaded with too much of information during an adverse situation. This information comes from the big displays, small displays, control panels, consoles,

© Springer International Publishing Switzerland 2015
B.K. Panigrahi et al. (Eds.): SEMCCO 2014, LNCS 8947, pp. 111–122, 2015.
DOI: 10.1007/978-3-319-20294-5_10

annunciators, flash lights, LEDs, hooters, etc. At this moment, the operator should be provided with only the most important information related to that adverse situation. An occurrence of a transient is accounted as an adverse condition where the plant deviates from it steady or normal state to an abnormal condition. During this time, the operator action holds a very key role in bringing back the plant to a stable state. In order to achieve this, the operator has to identify properly the transient which lead to this abnormal state. There are cases where indentifying the transient during a post-mortem process is also an important task based on the history of the data collected during that time. These are some of the instances where classification of transients is vital. In NPP, there could be a number of transients which may occur during the running state of a plant which makes this a multiclass classification problem. A multiclass classification problem can be dealt with using supervised learning [1].

Supervised learning is a machine learning methodology where a training set of data with known input and output labels, is used to train a system for unknown or test data. The output label of the test data is found by mapping a test data on to a function inferred from the training data. Out of the various supervised learning algorithms for multiclass classification, k-nearest neighbor (kNN), support vector machine (SVM) and artificial neural network (ANN) are popularly used [2–8]. Fuzzy logic can also be used for online transient identification in NPP [9]. There are number of modifications being done to these algorithms for classification of power quality disturbances [10, 11]. The performance of these algorithms is measured based on the prediction accuracy, training speed, computational cost and root mean square error. As this paper is based on transient classification of a NPP, the prediction accuracy is the major performance parameter which is considered. Other performance parameters are also looked upon with keen interest. In this paper, Sect. 2 explains briefly about the different supervised machine learning algorithms that have been considered for multiclass classification of transients. Section 3 explains the methodology adapted for the execution of the code for these algorithms. Section 4 explains the results and discussions on the performance of each algorithm. Section 5 concludes the paper inferring the best supervised machine learning algorithm for multiclass transient classification from the analyzed algorithms.

2 Training Algorithms

The various supervised machine learning algorithms which has been considered in this paper are kNN algorithm, SVM and backpropagation algorithms for ANN. A brief summary of these algorithms have been highlighted in this section.

2.1 Overview of kNN Algorithm

The kNN algorithm is a supervised machine learning algorithm which classifies a query or a test data based on the k-nearest training data taken as reference. It is a very simple and robust algorithm. No extra computation time as the training set samples are used during execution time. This algorithm proves to be very effective, in terms of reducing the misclassification error, when the number of samples in training dataset is large [12]. Another advantage of the kNN method over many other supervised machine learning methods like SVM, decision tree, neural network, etc., is that it can easily deal with problems in which the class size is three and higher [13]. So it can be easily used in incremental learning environments (adding new train data during execution) but its execution time is usually longer than other algorithms (which have training phase).

2.2   Overview of SVM Algorithm

SVM is a supervised machine learning algorithm which is mostly used for classification or regression analysis. A SVM constructs an optimal hyper plane (OHP) with the largest distance between the nearest training data of opposite class called as support vectors. This distance is called functional margin which is inversely proportional to the generalization error of the classifier [14]. DirectSVM follows a iterative update scheme that is based on a few intuitively-simple heuristics [15]. Another way of getting the maximum margin hyperplane is by creating non linear classifiers using kernel trick. Some commonly used kernels are polynomial kernel, Gaussian radial basis function (rbf) kernel and hyperbolic tangent kernel [16]. Multi kernels SVM are also used with high accuracy and great generalization [17]. In this paper, various single kernel functions are used for classification and the prediction accuracy was found.

2.3   Overview of ANN Algorithm

ANN is a supervised learning algorithm where a network is established between neurons in the input, output and one or more hidden layers. These layers consist of interconnected neurons and their corresponding optimized weights yields the final output. The performance of the network is calculated by the prediction accuracy, the number of epochs, the training time and the mean square error (MSE). ANN is used in classification and regression related problems. Backpropagation is an optimization process where the aim is to get minimum error in least number of epochs and lesser training time. This improves the performance of the network. There are many ways of carrying out the backpropagation process. There are basically six various categories of backpropagation algorithm [18]. In this paper, these six classes of the back propagation algorithm have been considered. MATLAB is used for the execution using their training functions.

1. Additive Momentum

   • Gradient Descent with momentum backpropagation (GDM)

2. Self adaptive learning rate

   • Gradient Descent with adaptive learning rate backpropagation (GDA)
   • Gradient Descent with momentum and adaptive learning rate backpropagation (GDMA)

3. Resilient Backpropagation (RB)
4. Conjugate Gradient Backpropagation

- Scaled conjugate gradient back propagation (SCG)
- Conjugate gradient backpropagation with Powell-Beale restarts (CGB)
- Conjugate gradient backpropagation with Fletcher-Reeves updates (CGF)
- Conjugate gradient backpropagation with Polak-Ribiére updates (CFP)

5. Quasi-Newton

- Levenberg-Marquardt backpropagation (LM)
- BFGS quasi-Newton backpropagation (QN)
- One-step secant backpropagation (OSS)

6. Bayesian Regularization (BR).

3   Task and Methodology

Transient classification in NPP during crisis situation is a confusing operation. Supervised machine learning could be used in order to make life simpler for the operators in the main control room. This necessarily may not act as an expert system but could certainly guide the operator and avoid information overloading. This could also be used as a post-mortem tool after any accident has happened. Out of the huge varieties of supervised machine learning algorithms, some very widely used multiclass classification algorithms have been chosen for this purpose. In this section, we have compared the performance of kNN, SVM and ANN for classification of some of the steam water side transients. The dataset collected consists of five classes. These five classes represent five transients in the steam water side of Prototype Fast Breeder Reactor (PFBR) operator training simulator [19]. This dataset was divided into training dataset and test data set. The training dataset consisted 746 rows and each row had 2 columns. The number of rows represents the total number of training data and the number of column represent the attribute value corresponding to each training data. The training dataset had a training dataset label representing the class to which each row belongs to i.e. 746 rows and one column in this training dataset label. These two datasets are used for training purpose. The test dataset consisted on 32 rows and each row had 2 columns. The test dataset was used for testing purpose. Three datasets, training dataset, training dataset label and the test dataset was fed to the code. The test dataset label was not fed to the code as it was used only for personal verification purpose.

3.1   Classification Using kNN Algorithm

A training dataset was prepared containing two attributes and a multiclass label. MATLAB was used as the medium for execution of the code. The code was made to run for various values of k from 3 to 51. This was done in order to check the performance of the kNN algorithm for different values of k and find the best from it. The performance was also checked using 10-fold cross validation method for ten times.

3.2   Classification Using SVM Algorithm

The same training dataset was used to check the performance of SVM algorithm. The code was executed in MATLAB using its inbuilt function. For SVM algorithm, different kernels were used such as linear, quadratic, polynomial and radial basis function kernels. The percentage accuracy on each kernel was noted. The average prediction accuracy of 10-fold cross validation for ten times on the SVM algorithm was also noted.

3.3   Classification Using Back Propagation ANN Algorithm

The same training dataset was used to check the performance of a number of back propagation ANN algorithms on a two layered network. This two layered network consisted of two inputs to the input layer, one hidden layer and one output from the output layer. The number of neurons in the hidden layer varied from 5 to 20 in each execution. This was done in order to observe the importance of the number of neurons in the hidden layer of a two layered neural network. The code was executed in MATLAB using the inbuilt functions for specific back propagation ANN algorithms. Before executing the program, the training dataset label was modified according to the MATLAB format for executing ANN algorithms. The performance of each algorithm was noted based on the prediction accuracy, number of epochs, training time and root mean square error. A 10-fold cross validation was done on each algorithm for ten times. Performance parameters such as average prediction accuracy, average root mean square error, total number of epochs, total training time and the best prediction accuracy from the cross validation process were also observed.

4   Result and Discussions

Figure 1 shows the performance of a kNN algorithm based transient classification system with different k-values. Figure 1(a) shows the prediction accuracy which varied from 71 % to 75 % for k-values ranging from 3 to 51. This accuracy did not follow any specific pattern for subsequent changes in the k-values. Figure 1(b) shows the average prediction accuracy for 10-fold cross validation of kNN algorithm done for ten times for transient classification. This varied from 72 % to 76 %. As a rule of thumb, the k-value is taken to be square root of the number of training sample i.e. 27, to get the maximum prediction accuracy. But here, the prediction accuracy was found to be 74 %. The average prediction accuracy after cross validation was around 76 % which is also not a considerable change from the rest of the accuracies for different k-value. This shows that there is no significant change in the prediction accuracy of the model if the k-value varies from 3 to 51 for kNN algorithm.

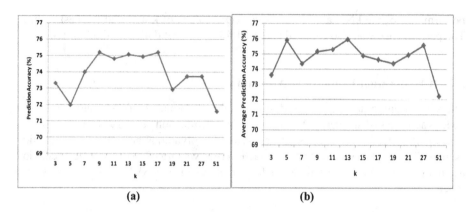

Fig. 1. (a) Prediction accuracy of kNN algorithm for different k-values (b) average prediction accuracy for 10-fold cross validation of kNN algorithm for different k-values

Figure 2 shows the performance of a SVM algorithm based transient classification system for different kernel functions. From Fig. 2(a), the prediction accuracy of a linear kernel was found to be 41.5 %. For all the other types of kernels those were taken into consideration produced a prediction accuracy ranging from around 90 % to 94 %. The rbf kernel and the polynomial kernel with order 3, 6, 8 and 9 produced the maximum prediction accuracy of 93.75 %. Figure 2(b) shows the average prediction accuracy for 10-fold cross validation of SVM algorithm done for ten times for transient classification. The maximum average prediction accuracy was found to be around 94 % for the rbf kernel function and for almost all polynomial kernel functions except the polynomial function with degree 10 which had an average accuracy of around 90 %.

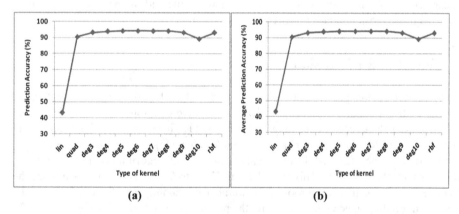

Fig. 2. (a) Prediction accuracy of SVM algorithm for different kernels (b) average prediction accuracy for 10-fold cross validation of SVM algorithm for different kernels

The performance parameters which were considered in this paper for the analysis of the back propagation ANN algorithms were prediction accuracy, root mean square error, number of epochs and training time. In a NPP, the most important performance parameter which should be considered is the prediction accuracy of the transient classification system. Figure 3 shows the performance of different back propagation ANN algorithms with different number of neurons in the single hidden layer. This shows that BR back propagation ANN algorithm with 5 neurons in the hidden layer was able to achieve best prediction accuracy with least root mean square error as shown in Fig. 3(a) and (b). The number of epochs taken is also less compared to others as shown in Fig. 3(c). The training time increases for BR backpropagation as the number of neurons increases in the hidden layer as shown in Fig. 3(d). This is acceptable for safety critical systems in NPP where the prediction accuracy has a major importance than any other performance parameters. This is the best performance achieved among all the other supervised machine learning algorithms analyzed in this paper. None of the other algorithms were able to produce this prediction accuracy even with higher number of neurons using backpropagation ANN. With 5 neurons in the hidden layer, other back propagation ANN algorithms which has produced appreciable prediction accuracy are RP, SCG, GDA and GDAM back propagation ANN algorithms. These algorithms could be used for systems which are comparatively less critical and where the processing load is limited. Again, there is no real pattern on any of the performance parameters in any of the back propagation ANN algorithms when the number of neurons is increased.

Figure 4 shows the average of the performance parameters of the 10-fold cross validation of these backpropagation ANN training algorithms done for ten times. Figure 4(a) shows that for BR back propagation ANN algorithm, 8 neuron hidden layer produces a slightly better average prediction accuracy than 5 neuron hidden layer. Figure 4(b) shows that the average root mean square error of BR back propagation ANN algorithm increases slightly. These changes happen because the cross validation method is the average of all the performance captured for the specified number of iterations or folds. These characteristic features are data dependent. Depending on the nature of the training dataset, the performance of the test dataset from these machine learning algorithms could be determined. The total number of epochs and the total training time is within acceptable range for BR back propagation ANN algorithm as shown in Fig. 4(c) and (d) for safety critical systems. Figure 4(e) shows that the best prediction accuracy to be around 99 % irrespective of the number of neurons in the hidden layer for BR backpropagation ANN algorithm. Finally, from Table 1 it is evident that BR back propagation ANN algorithm is found to be computationally low in cost and produces a much acceptable performance among the above analyzed supervised machine learning algorithms for safety critical systems in NPP.

From Table 1, the best two classifiers based on the cross validation accuracy are RB-ANN and BR-ANN. For better understanding and clarity, ROC of these two algorithms is shown in Fig. 5. It shows that BR-ANN performs better than RB-ANN

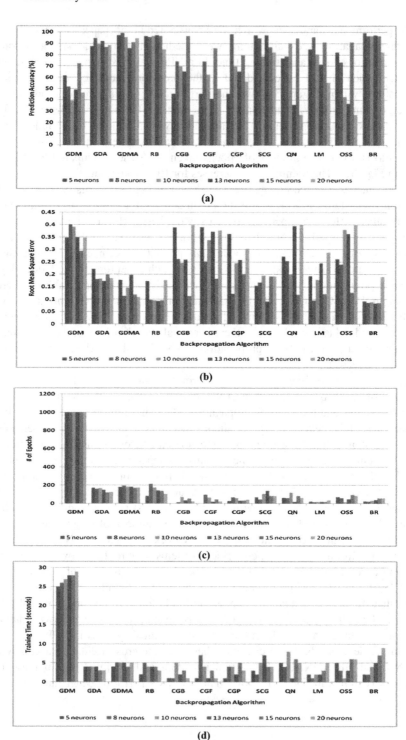

Fig. 3. (a) Predictive accuracy (b) root mean square error (c) number of epochs (d) training time for backpropagation ANN algorithms

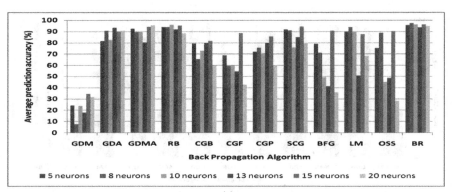

(a)

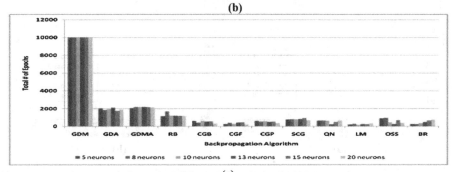

(b)

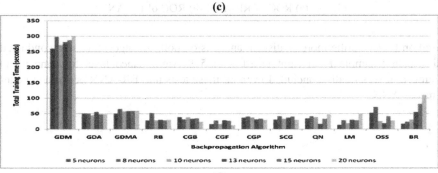

(c)

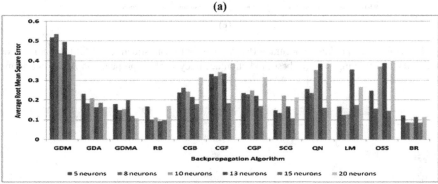

(d)

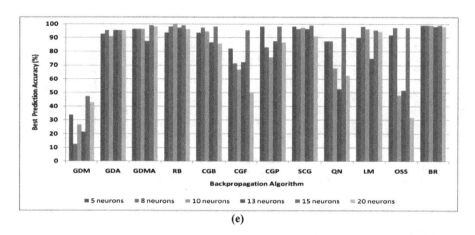

(e)

Fig. 4. (a) Average prediction accuracy (b) average root mean square error (c) total number of epochs (d) total training time (e) best prediction accuracy for backpropagation ANN algorithms

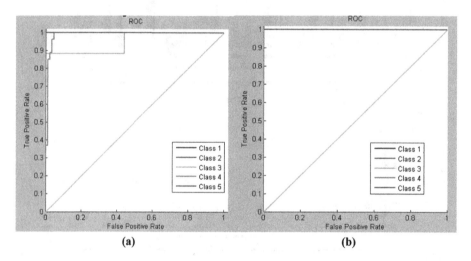

Fig. 5. (a) ROC of RB-ANN (b) ROC of BR-ANN

based on ROC. Furthermore, statistical analysis on both the algorithms was conducted using paired sample t-test right tailed with 5 % significance level to come to an inference. It was finally concluded from all these tests that BR-ANN performed better than RB-ANN.

Table 1. Comparison of kNN, SVM and ANN algorithms

Algorithm	Best prediction accuracy (%)	Respective parameter	Respective average prediction accuracy after 10-times 10-fold cross validation (%)
kNN	75.20	k = 13	75.96
SVM	93.75	rbf kernel	93.17
GDM-ANN	61.60	5 neurons	24.1
GDA-ANN	94.60	8 neurons	90.66
GDMA-ANN	99.10	8 neurons	89.5
RB-ANN	97.30	13 neurons	95.29
CGB-ANN	96.40	15 neurons	81.67
CGF-ANN	85.70	15 neurons	88.57
CGP-ANN	98.20	8 neurons	75.6
SCG-ANN	97.30	5 neurons	91.8
QN-ANN	94.60	15 neurons	90.62
LM-ANN	95.50	8 neurons	93.84
OSS-ANN	91.10	15 neurons	90.25
BR-ANN	99.10	5 neurons	95.68

5 Conclusion

In this paper, it is concluded that the Bayesian Regularization backpropagation ANN is the best among the above considered supervised machine learning algorithms for transient classification in safety critical systems in NPP. This paper also says that high prediction accuracy can be achieved with less number of neurons in a two layered neural network containing a single hidden layer. This prediction accuracy is better than kNN and SVM too. The root mean square error was also found within limit. The training time is less and the number of epochs is small for this algorithm compared to any other backpropagation ANN algorithm. But for comparatively less critical systems with limited processing load, Resilient backpropagation, Gradient descent with adaptive learning backpropagation and Scaled conjugate gradient backpropagation performs well with better prediction accuracy and lower training time.

Acknowledgement. The authors express their sincere thanks to the PFBR Operator Training simulator (KALBR-SIM) team members and Shri S.A.V. Satya Murty, Director, EIRSG, IGCAR for providing constant guidance and support in completing this research. The authors are greatly indebted to the constant support and motivation provided by Dr. P.R. Vasudeva Rao, Director, IGCAR.

References

1. Waegeman, W., Verwaeren, J., Slabbinck, B., Baets, B.D.: Supervised learning algorithms for multi-class classification problems with partial class memberships. Fuzzy Sets Syst. **184**, 106–125 (2011)
2. Ventouras, E.M., Asvestas, P., Karanasiou, I., Matsopoulos, G.K.: Classification of error-related negativity (ERN) and positivity (Pe) potentials using kNN and support vector machines. Comput. Biol. Med. **41**, 98–109 (2011)
3. Chen, J., Wang, C., Wang, R.: Adaptive binary tree for fast SVM multiclass classification. Neurocomputing **72**, 3370–3375 (2009)
4. Kumar, M.A., Gopal, M.: Reduced one-against-all method for multiclass SVM classification. Expert Syst. Appl. **38**, 14238–14248 (2011)
5. Li, Y.: A novel statistical algorithm for multiclass EEG signal classification. Eng. Appl. Artif. Intell. **34**, 154–167 (2014)
6. Oong, T.H., MatIsa, N.A.: One-against-all ensemble for multiclass pattern classification. Appl. Soft Comput. **12**, 1303–1308 (2012)
7. Chena, K., Xu, L., Chi, H.: Improved learning algorithms for mixture of experts in multiclass classification. Neural Netw. **12**, 1229–1252 (1999)
8. Ahmed, S.S., Rao, B.P.C., Jayakumar, T.: A framework for multidimensional learning using multilabel ranking. Int. J. Ad. Intell. Paradigms **5**(4), 299–318 (2013)
9. Prusty, M.R., Chakraborty, J., Seetha, H., Jayanthi, T., Velusamy, K.: Fuzzy logic based transient identification system for operator guidance using prototype fast breeder reactor operator training simulator. In: Proceedings of IEEE International Advance Computing Conference (IACC), pp. 1259–1264 (2014)
10. Mishra, S., Bhenede, C.N., Panigrahi, B.K.: Detection and classification of power quality disturbances using S-transform and probabilistic neural network. IEEE Trans. Power Deliv. **23**(1), 280–287 (2008)
11. Panigrahi, B.K., Pandi, V.R.: Optimal feature selection for classification of power quality disturbances using wavelet packet based fuzzy k-nearest neighbor algorithm. IET Proc. Gen. Trans. Distrib. **3**(3), 296–306 (2009)
12. Saini, I., Singh, D., Khosla, A.: QRS detection using K-nearest neighbor algorithm (KNN) and evaluation on standard ECG databases. J. Adv. Res. **4**, 331–344 (2013)
13. Yazdani, A., Ebrahimi, T., Hoffmann, U.: Classification of EEG signals using Dempster Shafer theory and a k-nearest neighbor classifier. In: Proceedings of the 4th International IEEE EMBS Conference on neural engineering, Antalya, Turkey, pp. 327–330 (2009)
14. Vapnik, V.: The Nature of Statistical Learning Theory, 2nd edn. Springer, New York (1999)
15. Roobaert, D.: DirectSVM: a fast and simple support vector machine perceptron. In: Proceedings of the 2000 IEEE Signal Processing Society Workshop, pp. 356–365 (2000)
16. Ahmed, S.S., Rao, B.P.C., Jayakumar, T.: Radial basis functions for multidimensional learning with an application to nondestructive sizing of defects. In: IEEE Symposium on Foundations of Computational Intelligence (FOCI), pp. 38–43 (2013)
17. Chen, F., Tang, B., Song, T., Li, L.: Multi-fault diagnosis study on roller bearing based on multi-kernel support vector machine with chaotic particle swarm optimization. Measurement **47**, 576–590 (2014)
18. Pan, X., Lee, B., Zhang, C.: A comparison of neural network backpropagation algorithms for electricity load forecasting. In: IEEE International Workshop on Intelligent Energy Systems (IWIES), pp. 22–27 (2013)
19. Design Document on PFBR Simulator - PFBR/08610/DN/1000/Rev A (2003)

Evaluating Internet Information Search Channels Using Hybrid MCDM Technique

Gaurav Khatwani[1]([✉]), Oshin Anand[1], and Arpan Kumar kar[2]

[1] IIM Rohtak, MDU Campus, Rohtak 124001, Haryana, India
g_khatwani@yahoo.co.in, tish.oshin@gmail.com
[2] Department of Management Studies, IIT Delhi, IV Floor,
Vishwakarma Bhavan, Hauz Khas, New Delhi 110016, India
arpan_kar@yahoo.co.in

Abstract. The evolution of technology has fragmented the market which has resulted in media proliferation. The frequent emergence of various media channels have enabled marketers and agencies to devise alternative methods to engage with consumers. The major challenge for marketers is to be informed about consumer preferences by identifying where the online consumers prefer to search pre-purchase information about the products to maximize the benefits of marketing. This study highlights methodology for group decision support for selecting an appropriate marketing channel using multiple criteria decision making (MCDM) based on context specific requirements. Firstly the influencing factors of consumer information search have been identified through literature review. Further we have used hybrid MCDM technique for ranking different alternatives. The fuzzy analytical hierarchy process (AHP) for group decision making has been used to identify relative importance of consumer search factors and TOPSIS has been used to evaluate different marketing channels. The approach is illustrated through case study.

Keywords: Fuzzy decision support systems · Multi criteria decision making · Analytical hierarchy process · TOPSIS · Information search channels

1 Introduction

Pre-purchase search is vital step in consumer decision making process specifically for high involvement products and services. There has been extensive effort by researchers in investigating consumer information search behavior [6, 35, 36]. Media plays important role in marketing process. Large number of audiences can be reached through media to deliver informations [5, 24] and advertise products [16]. The most important challenge is the fragmentation of audiences from the prospect of media buying process [22, 25, 39, 40]. The diversity offered by the internet aids consumers in searching information, evaluating and purchasing products. Some of the problems faced by marketers in the world of disruptive innovation are increased advertisement cost, media fragmentation, rapid development in information technologies and available of alternative media preferences among people.

© Springer International Publishing Switzerland 2015
B.K. Panigrahi et al. (Eds.): SEMCCO 2014, LNCS 8947, pp. 123–133, 2015.
DOI: 10.1007/978-3-319-20294-5_11

The model for pre-purchase information search created by [12] observed that individuals searching may be from internal information/long-term memory and external information. If the individual does not finds suitable information from past experience to make decision than he/she will switch to external information. We have extended the study [12] to define external information search channels from the e-commerce consumer perspective (a) personal (advice from friends or relatives using social media channels), (b) marketer-dominated (brochure on emails, online advertisements, or media), (c) neutral (discussion forums, information blogs intended for public viewing), and (d) experiential sources (online demo of products through review websites). In our study we will evaluate these 4 channels based on criteria (1) information quantity, (2) design, (3) access and transmission speed, (4) user friendliness of search structure, (5) update pace and (6) perceived time [33, 42]. The study will highlight importance of information search channels based on preferences of consumers and evaluate different information search channels using hybrid multi criteria decision making technique. In first step we find out relative importance of information search factors using fuzzy AHP and further we assess each information search channel using TOPSIS.

2 Literature Review

The literature review has been organized into three subcategories as consumer information search factors, analyzing customer needs using group decision theories and group decision using hybrid MCDM technique.

2.1 Consumer Information Search Factors

The range for available alternate sources, of product and service purchase, is wide for consumers today. Consumers must believe that the channel offers better choices than alternatives for continued usage. The consumers perceive internet as powerful search tool for information search which drives interest of marketers towards understanding consumer's use of internet and their choice of channel for information search. The studies related to online behavior have argued that search process should be a part of consumer models. The interaction model [28] adopts the [42] framework which explains that search process terminates when marginal cost of search exceeds benefits. Search cost comprises of perceived time, travel and access to media. Search benefits incorporate extent and duration of search and nature of search sources.

Previous studies on online consumer behavior have focused on online modes of product purchase [1, 13, 26, 27, 41] or information search [29, 34] but it does not examine the preferences of consumer information search channels. It is difficult to demarcate factors of information search from the factors that influence product purchase. In our study we have tried to extract the factors that influence the consumer for information search through internet. Previous studies showed that user satisfaction with the website is influenced by information quantity, design, access and transmission speed, user-friendliness of search structure, update pace and perceived time [33, 42].

2.2   Analyzing Customer Needs Using Group Decision Theories

Previous studies have validated that judicious evaluation of customer needs results in successful product development [23]. The increasing importance of customer has resulted in development of customer-related marketing approaches. It is essential to prioritize customer preference with respect to customer requirements [17]. It can be achieved by measuring relative importance of customer requirements. The fuzzy AHP has been used to prioritize customer requirements in quality function development [30]. There has been an attempt to determine weights of customer requirements using theories of group decision making by aggregating the preferences of individual decision makers [21]. Conjoint analysis can be used to prioritize customer requirements by pairwise comparison [19]. It was studied that customer requirement is inherent with vagueness and impreciseness which can be removed by converting crisp priorities into fuzzy numbers [9]. The AHP has been widely used in determining relative importance of customer needs due to its strength in multi criteria qualitative decision making [37]. The studies have also generated weights of customer requirements on nine point scale [3]. The customer requirements for concurrent design can be prioritized using AHP [15]. The comparison of real alternatives can be achieved by indirect elicitation of customer preference by adopting AHP form multi-attribute utility theory perspective [31].

2.3   Group Decision Making Using Hybrid MCDM Technique

Peeping into the yester years, there has been an extensive usage of MCDM techniques in vivid areas. Hybrid approaches have also been adopted in several capacities. Specifically a lot of work has been done in the supplier selection problems of varied dimensions and in diversified zones. There has been a complex attempt with the unification of decision tools like fuzzy DEMATEL, fuzzy ANP and fuzzy TOPSIS for comparatively intricate expanses like selection of green suppliers in adherence to the green supply chain [8]. Other aggregations like ANP, TOPSIS, NGT [20] fuzzy set operations with VIKOR [38] have been used to decide on alternatives (basically in the area of supplier choices). The practice is prevalent and therefore has been reviewed. Further classifications have been done to segregate the work to identify various techniques' (26) from three perspectives: (1) MCDM techniques, (2) Mathematical programming (MP) techniques, and (3) Artificial intelligence (AI) techniques [10]. Although the techniques highlighted by the review falls into three different categories but does not notify the vivid usage of MCDM in this area.

This work uses fuzzy AHP – TOPSIS as the hybrid methodology. There have been frequent comparisons on the result of the two techniques in fuzzy environment along with wide amalgamation of the two to solve decision criteria problems [14]. Diverse areas have used this technique for their decision making. Hazardous waste management, project planning and selection, plant location, software selection and health care industries are some expanses where there has been recent usage of this methodology [4, 7, 11, 18, 32]. The reason behind the vivid usage is the systematic way in which both of them complement each other. For the calculation of weights, TOPSIS limits itself to at least and utmost one criterion that needs to be minimized, but AHP is not constraint to any such things. Therefore calculation of priority weights can be done using AHP which further bettered using the fuzzy approach whereby ameliorating the scale and defining three different values with respect to each criterion. When it comes to the calculation complexity TOPSIS ranks higher than AHP due the matrix computation involved in its procedure. This can be easily foregone using the later as the technique which utilizes the weights as the input and evaluate different options, finally ranking them.

3   Research Gap and Contribution

The literature review, ascertain the factors that influence customers for information search on internet. Further, we found that how group decision making theories can be used to estimate consumer preferences, besides depicting the usage of hybrid MCDM techniques in it. Prior works also highlights the advantage of using combination of fuzzy AHP and TOPSIS for ranking different alternatives. Former study hardly contributes to analyze consumer preferences related to information search on internet using group decision theories. The technique used would help organizations to select appropriate channel for marketing based on consumer preferences and allocate resources appropriately, further evaluating and ranking four different information search channels based on six factors.

4   Computational Method

Factor prioritization is done by notifying dialectal judgments, and respective mapping to quantifiable fuzzy judgments. AHP and fuzzy linguistic judgments obtain crisp priorities, whose consolidation and aggregated geometric mean method (GMM) for prioritization estimate the trade-off for different dimensions.

Let $K = (k_1,...,k_n)$ be set of n users having a relative importance of λ_i such that $\lambda = (\lambda_1,.....\lambda_n)$ is the weight vector of the individual user who prioritize one dimension over other. The individual preferences are converted to fuzzy judgments using triangular functions. Comparative fuzzy judgments $A = (a_{ij})_{m \times m}$ would be coded as illustrated in Table 1.

Table 1. Scale for conversion of linguistic preferences

Definition	Fuzzy sets for the fuzzy AHP
Equal importance	{(1,0.25), (1,0.50), (3,0.25)}
Moderate importance	{(1,0.25), (3,0.50), (5,0.25)}
Strong importance	{(3,0.25), (5,0.50), (7,0.25)}
Very strong importance	{(5,0.25), (7,0.50), (9,0.25)}
Extreme high importance	{(7,0.25), (9,0.50), (9,0.25)}

$\tilde{a}_i = \tilde{a}_{i1}, \tilde{a}_{i2}, \tilde{a}_{i3}$ and $\tilde{a}_j = \tilde{a}_{j1}, \tilde{a}_{j2}, \tilde{a}_{j3}$ as illustrated:

$$\tilde{a}_i = (\tilde{a}_{i1}, \tilde{a}_{i2}, \tilde{a}_{i3}) \psi (\tilde{a}_{j1}, \tilde{a}_{j2}, \tilde{a}_{j3}) = ((\tilde{a}_{i1} \psi \tilde{a}_{j1}), (\tilde{a}_{i2} \psi \tilde{a}_{j2}), (\tilde{a}_{i3} \psi \tilde{a}_{j3})) \tag{1}$$

where ψ is hypothetical operator.

The individual priorities can be obtained by solving the following system:

$$\min \sum\nolimits_{i=1}^{n} \sum\nolimits_{j>i}^{n} \left(\ln \tilde{a}_{ij} - (\ln \tilde{p}_i - \ln \tilde{p}_j)^2 \right) \text{s.t. } \tilde{a}_{ij} \geq 0; \tilde{a}_{ij} \times \tilde{a}_{ij} = 1; \tilde{p}_i \geq 0, \sum \tilde{p}_i = 1 \tag{2}$$

The individual priority vector can be obtained by [2]

$$\tilde{p}_i = \frac{\sqrt[1/n]{\prod_{j=1}^{n} \tilde{a}_{ij}}}{\sum_{i=1}^{n} \sqrt[1/n]{\prod_{j=1}^{n} \tilde{a}_{ij}}} \tag{3}$$

where $\tilde{p}_i$ is the priority of decision criteria i such that $\tilde{P}_i = \{\tilde{p}_1, \tilde{p}_2 \ldots \ldots \tilde{p}_5\}$ for user i. In consequent steps consistencies of these priorities needs to be evaluated prior computing aggregation rules. The geometry consistency index (GCI) is used to estimate consistency of individual priorities.

$$\text{GCI}(A^{d_i}) = \frac{2}{(n-1)(n-2)} \times \sum\nolimits_{j>i}^{n} (\log|\tilde{a}_{ij}| - (\log|\tilde{p}_i| - \log|\tilde{p}_j|)^2) \tag{4}$$

The consistency criteria are defined as follows; $\text{GCI}(B^{d_i}) \leq \overline{\text{GCI}}_n$ for $n \geq 4$, GCI is 0.35. In order to achieve the decision vector, there's a prerequisite of the collective group preference, which can be accomplished through aggregated individual priorities. The aggregated priorities are obtained by: $\tilde{p}^{(c)} = \{\tilde{p}_1^{(c)}, \tilde{p}_2^{(c)} \ldots \tilde{p}_i^{(c)}\}$ where $\tilde{p}_i^{(c)}$ is obtained by the aggregation of priorities.

$$\tilde{p}_i^{(c)} = \frac{\prod_1^n (p_i^{(k)})^{\alpha_i}}{\sum_1^r \prod_1^n (p_i^{(k)})^{\alpha_i}} \tag{5}$$

The relative importance of evaluation criteria and criterion specific performance of five solutions have been evaluated using aggregated priorities. The collective priority vector $\tilde{P}^{(c)}$ and the fuzzy priority of groups can be derived respectively from GMM technique and aggregation where $\alpha = (\alpha_1, \alpha_2, \ldots \alpha_n)$ is the priority of experts. Finally fuzzy weights are converted into crisp priorities:

$$|\tilde{p}_i| = [(p_{i,1} \times 0.25) + (p_{i,2} \times 0.5) + (p_{i,3} \times 0.25)] \tag{6}$$

The normalized decision matrix can be calculated by using following method:

$$r_{ij} = \frac{x_{ij}}{(\sum_i x_{ij}^2)^{\frac{1}{2}}} \quad \text{for } i = 1,\ldots m; \ j = 1\ldots n \tag{7}$$

The weighted normalized decision matrix is obtained by multiplying each column by its associated weights

$$v_{ij} = p_i \times r_{ij} \tag{8}$$

Further we calculate ideal solution B^* and negative ideal solution B':

$$B^* = \{v_1^*,\ldots v_n^*\}, \quad \text{where } v_j^* = \{\max_i(v_{ij}) \text{if } j \in J; \min_i(v_{ij}) \text{if } j \in J'\} \tag{9}$$

$$B' = \{v_1',\ldots v_n'\}, \quad \text{where } v_j' = \{\min_i(v_{ij}) \text{if } j \in J; \max_i(v_{ij}) \text{if } j \in J'\} \tag{10}$$

The separation from ideal alternative is obtained in following way:

$$S_i^* = \left[\sum_j (v_j^* - v_{ij})^2\right]^{\frac{1}{2}}; \quad i = 1,\ldots m \tag{11}$$

Similarly, the separation from the negative ideal alternative is:

$$S_i' = \left[\sum_j (v_j' - v_{ij})^2\right]^{\frac{1}{2}}; \quad i = 1,\ldots m \tag{12}$$

The relative closeness to the ideal solution C_i^* is:

$$C_i^* = \frac{S_i'}{S_i^* + S_i'}; \quad 0 < C_i^* < 1 \tag{13}$$

The corresponding rank of the alternatives can be calculated using the values from previous step.

5 Case Study

The study identifies the criteria, important for internet search channel selection, concluding with decision on channel choice based on six defined criteria. As per existing literature [33, 42] there are six factors that influence consumers for information search on internet (1) information quantity, (2) design, (3) access and transmission speed, (4) user friendliness of search structure, (5) update pace and (6) perceived time.

Table 2. Individual and aggregated priorities for the six evaluating criteria

	Information content	Design	Access and transmission speed	User friendliness of search structure	Update pace	Perceived time
User 1	0.0763	0.1657	0.2195	0.2105	0.0890	0.2390
User 2	0.4377	0.2530	0.1438	0.1055	0.0388	0.0211
User 3	0.1843	0.0425	0.2480	0.1142	0.2213	0.1897
User 4	0.4084	0.0288	0.2229	0.1524	0.0970	0.0904
User 5	0.2369	0.1091	0.3098	0.1812	0.0629	0.1002
Aggregated scores	0.2608	0.1026	0.2558	0.1700	0.0989	0.1120

Subsequently, six factors for evaluating information search channels were prioritized using fuzzy extension of AHP for group decision making. Table 2 highlights the individual priorities of five decision makers, as well as aggregated priorities, for six factors for evaluating information search channels.

Five users were asked to rate different information search channel on the scale of 1 to 5. Table 3 indicates modes of rating by 5 different users for 4 different channels based on six criteria of information search channels.

Table 4 indicates values of normalized decision matrix calculated using ratings in Table 3.

Table 3. Associated weights of columns and mode values of rating

	Information content	Design	Access and transmission speed	User friendliness of search structure	Update pace	Perceived time
Weights	0.2608	0.1026	0.2558	0.1700	0.0989	0.1120
Personal channels	4	2	3	2	4	3
Market dominated	3	4	4	4	4	4
Neutral	2	4	3	2	3	2
Experiential sources	3	4	4	4	3	3

Table 4. The normalized decision matrix for the responses received from individual users

	Weights of different criteria					
Information search channels	0.2608	0.1026	0.2558	0.1700	0.0989	0.1120
Personal channels	0.6489	0.2774	0.4243	0.3162	0.5657	0.4867
Market dominated	0.4867	0.5547	0.5657	0.6325	0.5657	0.6489
Neutral	0.3244	0.5547	0.4243	0.3162	0.4243	0.3244
Experiential sources	0.4867	0.5547	0.5657	0.6325	0.4243	0.4867

Table 5. The weighted normalized decision matrix

Information search channels						
Personal channels	0.1692	0.0285	0.1085	0.0537	0.0559	0.0545
Market dominated	0.1269	0.0569	0.1447	0.1075	0.0559	0.0726
Neutral	0.0846	0.0569	0.1085	0.0537	0.0419	0.0363
Experiential sources	0.1269	0.0569	0.1447	0.1075	0.0419	0.0545

Table 6. Separation from ideal and negative ideal solution

Information search channels							S_i^*	S_i'
Personal channels	0.1692	0.0285	0.1085	0.0537	0.0559	0.0545	0.0731	0.0877
Market dominated	0.1269	0.0569	0.1447	0.1075	0.0559	0.0726	0.0558	0.0836
Neutral	0.0846	0.0569	0.1085	0.0537	0.0419	0.0363	0.1075	0.0461
Experiential sources	0.1269	0.0569	0.1447	0.1075	0.0419	0.0545	0.0481	0.0844

Table 7. The relative closeness ideal solution for four different channels

Information search channels	S_i^*	S_i'	C_i^*
Personal channels	0.0731	0.0877	0.5454
Market dominated	0.0558	0.0836	0.6000
Neutral	0.1075	0.0461	0.3003
Experiential sources	0.0481	0.0844	0.6370

Table 5 indicates weighted normalized decision matrix calculated by multiplying each column by its associated weights.

Table 6 indicates values of ideal and negative ideal solution calculated using Eqs. (11) and (12).

Table 7 indicates relative closeness to ideal solution for four different channels.

6   Results

Based on case specific requirements, it was found that experiential sources have the highest suitability score of (0.6370) for the specific context, considering information content highest weighted criteria. This was followed by marketed dominated, personal channels and neutral sources with score of 0.6000, 0.5454 and 0.3003 respectively. Higher score indicates closeness to ideal solution and adherence to context specific requirements.

7   Conclusion

The discourse discusses an approach to select information search channels using hybrid MCDM technique from the multi user perspective. The vitality of the study is for firms who market the product and services online, thereby help deciding them on channel selection and enable effective marketing of their product. The study limits itself to a specific context and does not count product diversification as a judgmental parameter, making it a limitation of the findings. However this can be addressed by taking aggregated performance score of judgments of much larger sample. Further, the implications of consensus achievement and other consumer characteristics like demographics, internet usage skills, and knowledge level on information search channels can also be explored in such studies.

References

1. Alba, J., Lynch, J., Weitz, B., Janiszewski, C., Lutz, R., Sawyer, A., Wood, S.: Interactive home shopping: consumer, retailer, and manufacturer incentives to participate in electronic marketplaces. J. Mark. **61**, 38–53 (1997)
2. Aguaron, J., Moreno-Jiménez, J.M.: The geometric consistency index: approximated thresholds. Eur. J. Oper. Res. **147**(1), 137–145 (2003)
3. Armacost, R.L., Componation, P.J., Mullens, M.A., Swart, W.W.: An AHP framework for prioritizing customer requirements in QFD: an industrialized housing application. IIE Trans. **26**(4), 72–79 (1994)
4. Ballı, S., Korukoğlu, S.: Operating system selection using fuzzy AHP and TOPSIS methods. Math. Comput. Appl. **14**(2), 119–130 (2009)
5. Baron, R., Sissors, J.: Advertising Media Planning. McGraw Hill Professional, New York (2010)
6. Beatty, S.E., Smith, S.M.: External search effort: an investigation across several product categories. J. Consum. Res. **25**, 83–95 (1987)
7. Büyüközkan, G., Çifçi, G.: A combined fuzzy AHP and fuzzy TOPSIS based strategic analysis of electronic service quality in healthcare industry. Expert Syst. Appl. **39**(3), 2341–2354 (2012)
8. Büyüközkan, G., Çifçi, G.: A novel hybrid MCDM approach based on fuzzy DEMATEL, fuzzy ANP and fuzzy TOPSIS to evaluate green suppliers. Expert Syst. Appl. **39**(3), 3000–3011 (2012)
9. Chan, L.K., Kao, H.P., Wu, M.L.: Rating the importance of customer needs in quality function deployment by fuzzy and entropy methods. Int. J. Prod. Res. **37**(11), 2499–2518 (1999)
10. Chai, J., Liu, J.N., Ngai, E.W.: Application of decision-making techniques in supplier selection: a systematic review of literature. Expert Syst. Appl. **40**(10), 3872–3885 (2013)
11. Choudhary, D., Shankar, R.: An STEEP-fuzzy AHP-TOPSIS framework for evaluation and selection of thermal power plant location: a case study from India. Energy **42**(1), 510–521 (2012)
12. Crotts, J.C.: Consumer decision making and pre-purchase information search. In: Mansfeld, Y., Pizam, A. (eds.) Consumer Behavior in Travel and Tourism. Routledge publication, London (1999)
13. Degeratu, A.M., Rangaswamy, A., Wu, J.: Consumer choice behavior in online and traditional supermarkets: the effects of brand name, price, and other search attributes. Int. J. Res. Mark. **17**(1), 55–78 (2000)
14. Ertuğrul, İ., Karakaşoğlu, N.: Comparison of fuzzy AHP and fuzzy TOPSIS methods for facility location selection. Int. J. Adv. Manuf. Technol. **39**(7–8), 783–795 (2008)

15. Fukuda, S., Matsuura, Y.: Prioritizing the customer's requirements by AHP for concurrent design. In: ASME Design Engineering Division Publications DE, vol. 52, pp. 13–19. ASME, New York (1993)
16. Gallucci, P.: There are no absolutes in media planning: a challenge to the currently fashionable view that effective frequency is provided by a single exposure to an advertisement. Admap **32**, 39–43 (1997)
17. Griffin, A., Hauser, J.R.: The voice of the customer. Mark. Sci. **12**(1), 1–27 (1993)
18. Gumus, A.T.: Evaluation of hazardous waste transportation firms by using a two step fuzzy-AHP and TOPSIS methodology. Expert Syst. Appl. **36**(2), 4067–4074 (2009)
19. Gustafsson, A., Gustafsson, N.: Exceeding customer expectations. In: Proceedings of the Sixth Symposium on Quality Function Deployment, pp. 52–57, June 1994)
20. Hadi-Vencheh, A., Mokhtarian, M.N.: Erratum to "a hybrid MCDM model for strategic vendor selection". Math. Comput. Model. **50**(7), 1252 (2009)
21. Ho, E.S.S.A., Lai, Y.J., Chang, S.I.: An integrated group decision-making approach to quality function deployment. IIE Trans. **31**(6), 553–567 (1999)
22. Jarvis, T., McElroy, B.: Can optimisers provide a lifeline for media? Admap **39**(2; ISSU 447), 32–36 (2004)
23. Kärkkäinen, H., Elfvengren, K.: Role of careful customer need assessment in product innovation management—empirical analysis. Int. J. Prod. Econ. **80**(1), 85–103 (2002)
24. Katz, H.: The Media Handbook: A Complete Guide to Advertising Media Selection, Planning, Research, and Buying. Routledge, London (2014)
25. Kelley, L.D., Jugenheimer, D.W.: Advertising Media Planning. ME Sharpe, New York (2008)
26. Kim, H., Kwon, S.: An exploratory research on lifestyles and purchase decision making of internet users. Korean Manag. Rev. **28**(2), 353–372 (1999)
27. Kim, S.Y., Park, S.Y.: Influencing factors of purchase intention through e-commerce. J. Consum. Stud. **10**(3), 45–66 (1999)
28. Klein, L.R.: Evaluating the potential of interactive media through a new lens: search versus experience goods. J. Bus. Res. **41**(3), 195–203 (1998)
29. Kozinets, R.V.: E-tribalized marketing?: The strategic implications of virtual communities of consumption. Eur. Manag. J. **17**(3), 252–264 (1999)
30. Kwong, C.K., Bai, H.: Determining the importance weights for the customer requirements in QFD using a fuzzy AHP with an extent analysis approach. IIE Trans. **35**(7), 619–626 (2003)
31. Larichev, O.I., Moshkovich, H.M.: ZAPROS-LM—a method and system for ordering multiattribute alternatives. Eur. J. Oper. Res. **82**(3), 503–521 (1995)
32. Mahmoodzadeh, S., Shahrabi, J., Pariazar, M., Zaeri, M.S.: Project selection by using fuzzy AHP and TOPSIS technique. World Acad. Sci. Eng. Technol. **30**, 333–338 (2007)
33. Moon, B.J.: Consumer adoption of the internet as an information search and product purchase channel: some research hypotheses. Int. J. Internet Mark. Advertising **1**(1), 104–118 (2004)
34. Moore, W.L., Lehmann, D.R.: Individual differences in search behavior for a nondurable. J. Consum. Res. **7**, 296–307 (1980)
35. Moore, R., Punj, G.: Consumer information search: a comparison of web-based and traditional decision environments. In: Proceedings of AMA Marketing Winter Marketing Educators' Conference on Theory and Practice, Feb 1999
36. Punj, G.N., Staelin, R.: A model of consumer information search behavior for new automobiles. J. Consum. Res. **9**, 366–380 (1983)
37. Saaty, T.L.: The Analytical Hierarchy Process. RWS Publications, Pittsburgh (1990)
38. Sanayei, A., Farid Mousavi, S., Yazdankhah, A.: Group decision making process for supplier selection with VIKOR under fuzzy environment. Expert Syst. Appl. **37**(1), 24–30 (2010)

39. Saunders, J.: Drowning in choice: the revolution in communications planning. Market Leader **24**, 34–39 (2004)
40. Soberman, D.: The complexity of media planning today. J. Brand Manag. **12**(6), 420–429 (2005)
41. Sohn, Y.S., Ahn, K.H.: Theoretical and empirical research on the impacts of consumer knowledge on adoption of e-commerce market. Korean Mark. Rev. **14**(1), 75–91 (1999)
42. Stigler, G. J. (1961). The economics of information. J. Polit. Econ., 213–225

A Hybrid Artificial Bee Colony Algorithm for the Terminal Assignment Problem

Jayalakshmi Banda and Alok Singh$^{(\boxtimes)}$

School of Computer and Information Sciences,
University of Hyderabad, Hyderabad 500046, India
bjayalakshmi@uohyd.ac.in, alokcs@uohyd.ernet.in

Abstract. The terminal assignment (TA) problem is an important problem in the design of telecommunication networks. The problem consists in determining the best links for connecting a given set of terminals to a given set of concentrators so that a given cost function is optimized. In this paper, we have proposed an artificial bee colony algorithm based approach for solving the TA problem. In comparison with the best methods available in the literature, the proposed approach obtained better quality solutions in shorter time.

Keywords: Artificial bee colony algorithm · Heuristic · Swarm intelligence · Terminal assignment problem · Telecommunication networks

1 Introduction

Due to rapid growth of internet, many new problems arose in the field of telecommunication network design and management. Terminal assignment (TA) problem is one such problem. In large centralized computer networks, a central computers serves numerous terminals or workstations. In such cases, concentrators are used to increase the efficiency of the network. Instead of connecting the terminals directly to the central computers, the terminals are connected to the concentrators and concentrators are connected to the central computer. The terminals and concentrators have fixed and known locations. The capacity requirements of each terminal is known. This requirement may vary from terminal to terminal. The maximum capacity of each concentrator and the costs of connecting each terminal to different concentrators are also known. The objective of the TA problem is to connect a given set of N terminals to a given set of M concentrators in such a way that the total cost of the network thus formed is minimum according to a given objective function. The assignment of the terminals to the concentrators is done under following two constraints: First, each terminal must be connected to one and only one concentrator, second, the sumtotal of capacities of the terminals connected to a concentrator must not exceed the maximum capacity of that concentrator [7,9].

TA problem is solved in the literature with two different objectives: First, with the objective of minimizing the sumtotal of link costs alone and second

B.K. Panigrahi et al. (Eds.): SEMCCO 2014, LNCS 8947, pp. 134–144, 2015.
DOI: 10.1007/978-3-319-20294-5_12

with an objective which give consideration to equitable distribution of loads among concentrators in addition to link costs. Here, we have considered the latter objective. TA problem is proved $\mathcal{NP}$-Hard under the first objective [19]. The problem can be solved in polynomial time in the special case where all terminals have the same capacity requirements and all concentrators have the same maximum capacity. The TA problem is also $\mathcal{NP}$-Hard under the second objective as first objective can be considered as a special case of the second objective where no consideration is given to load on different concentrators. The problem is harder to solve under second objective because we can not compute the individual cost of assigning a terminal to a concentrator a priori, i.e., before the complete solution is constructed.

TA problem is also closely related to a number of classical combinatorial optimization problems in different fields. Bin packing problem, task assignment problem, problem of assigning cells to switches in mobile communication networks are few examples [8].

Many different approaches have been proposed in the literature to solve the TA problem. Abuali et al. [9] proposed a greedy heuristic and a greedy genetic algorithm for a restricted version of the problem where all concentrators have the same maximum capacity. Khuri and Chiu [7] proposed another greedy heuristic and two penalty based genetic algorithms. Both Abuali et al. [9] and Khuri and Chiu [7] considered the first objective as mentioned above. Salcedo-sanz and Yao [8] considered for the first time the second objective where a hybrid Hopfield network based genetic algorithm is presented. Xu et al. [4] presented a tabu serach based approach for TA problem. Bernardino et al. designed a local search genetic algorithm (LSGA) [5], a tabu search (TS) [3], a hybrid differential evolution algorithm (HDE) [16], a bees algorithm [15], an improved hybrid differential evolution algorithm with a multiple strategy (MHDE) [6] and a discrete differential evolution algorithm (DDE) [11] for solving the TA problem with second objective. The DDE algorithm is based on discrete differential evolution model proposed by Pan et al. [17]. DDE algorithm provides the better results in comparison to LSGA, TS and MHDE [11].

In this paper, we have proposed an artificial bee colony algorithm based approach for solving the TA problem. The artificial bee colony (ABC) algorithm is a recently developed swarm intelligence technique proposed by Karaboga [1]. ABC algorithm is inspired by intelligent foraging behaviour of honey bee swarm. ABC algorithm has already been applied successfully to solve numerous discrete optimization problems [12]. This has motivated us to develop an ABC algorithm for the TA problem. We have compared our ABC approach with 4 best approaches from the literature, viz. DDE, MHDE, TS and LSGA. In comparison to these approaches, our approach not only obtains solution of better quality, but is also faster.

The remaining part of this paper is organized as follows: In Sect. 2, we formally define the TA problem. Section 3 provides an overview of ABC algorithm. Section 4 describes our ABC approach for the TA problem. Section 5 reports the computational results and compares our approach with other state-of-the-art approaches available in the literature. Finally, Sect. 6 contains some concluding remarks and directions for future research.

2   TA Problem

This section defines the TA problem formally. Given a set of terminals $T = \{T_1, T_2, \ldots, T_N\}$, a set of concentrators $C = \{C_1, C_2, \ldots, C_M\}$, a set of weights or capacities $W = \{W_1, W_2, \ldots, W_N\}$ associated with each terminal and capacities of concentrators $X = \{X_1, X_2, \ldots, X_M\}$. The capacity of terminals are such that $W_i < \min\{X_1, X_2, \ldots, X_M\} \; \forall \; T_i \in T$. The TA problem seeks an assignment of terminals to concentrators without violating the capacity constraint of concentrators such that the considered objective function is optimized. Hence, any feasible solution must satisfy the following two constraints:

$$\sum_{j=1}^{M} z_{ij} = 1 \quad \forall T_i \in T \tag{1}$$

$$\sum_{i=1}^{N} W_i z_{ij} \leq X_j \quad \forall C_j \in C \tag{2}$$

where binary variables z_{ij} indicate whether terminal T_i is assigned to concentrator C_j $(z_{ij} = 1)$ or not $(z_{ij} = 0)$. The Eq. 1 states that each terminal can be assigned to one and only one concentrator whereas Eq. 2 states that capacity constraint of no concentrator should be violated.

We have considered the same objective function for TA problem as used in [11]. This objective function considers the two factors:

 – The total number of terminals assigned to each concentrator
 – The distance between the terminals and their assigned concentrators

The objective is to minimize the Eq. 5. Equations 3 and 4 define terms needed for defining the objective function.

$$Total_{C_j} = \sum_{i=1}^{N} z_{ij} \quad \forall C_j \in C \tag{3}$$

$$Bal_{C_j} = \begin{cases} 10 & if \; (Total_{C_j} = round(\frac{N}{M}) + 1) \\ 20 \times |\; (round(\frac{N}{M}) + 1 - Total_{C_j}) | & otherwise \end{cases} \quad \forall C_j \in C \tag{4}$$

$$objective \; function \; value = 0.9 \times \sum_{j=1}^{M} Bal_{C_j} + 0.1 \times \sum_{i=1}^{N} \sum_{j=1}^{M} D_{ij} z_{ij} \tag{5}$$

where D_{ij} is the distance between terminal T_i and concentrator C_j.

3   Overview of ABC Algorithm

The artificial bee colony (ABC) algorithm introduced by Dervis Karaboga in 2005 [1] is a population based meta-heuristic algorithm based on the foraging behavior of the real honey bees. In a bee colony, there are three types of bees: employed, onlooker and scout. Employed bees exploit the food sources. These bees bring loads of nectar to the hive and share the information about the food sources exploited by them with the onlooker bees which wait in the hive for this information to be shared. The onlooker bees tend to select a food source with a probability that depends on the quality of that food source with respect to other food sources. Once an onlooker bee selects a food source, it becomes employed. Scout bees search for new food sources in the vicinity of hive and as soon as they find a new food source they become employed. An employed bee whose food source becomes empty will turn either into a scout or an onlooker. Therefore, employed and onlooker bees are responsible for exploitation, whereas exploration is left for scout bees.

Inspired by this foraging behaviour, Karaboga developed ABC algorithm. This algorithm was initially developed for optimization in continuous domain only [1,12–14]. Later, it was extended to solve discrete optimization problems [2,10,18]. For a recent survey on ABC algorithm and its applications, interested readers may refer to [12]. Some recent applications of ABC algorithm can be found in [20–22].

In ABC algorithm, the food sources represent the possible solutions to the problem under consideration and their nectar content indicates the fitness of the solutions represented. The ABC algorithm also divides the colony of artificial bees into same three types with similar function. However, unlike real bees, a one-to-one correspondence is maintained between the food sources and employed bees by associating each employed bee with one and only one food source. Usually but not always, the number of onlooker bees is taken to be equal to number of employed bees. An employed bee whose food source becomes empty will turn only into a scout but never an onlooker. Such a scout is immediately made employed by generating a food source randomly and associating this scout with this newly generated food source. The ABC algorithm consists of an iterative search process. The algorithm is initialized by associating each employee bee with a randomly generated food sources (solutions). Then the algorithm repeats through the cycles of the employed bee and onlooker bee phases. In the employed bee phase, each employed bee determines a food source in the vicinity of its current food source and evaluates its nectar amount (fitness). If the nectar amount of the new food source is better than the current one then the employee bee moves to the new food source leaving the old one, otherwise it remains at the old one. When all the employee bees finish this process, they share the nectar information of the food sources with the onlookers, then the onlooker bee phase starts.

In the onlooker bee phase, onlookers select the food sources with a probability that depends on the nectar content of the food sources. Higher the nectar content of a food source, higher will be the chances of its selection. As a result of this selection policy, good quality food sources attract more onlookers in comparison to worse ones. After all onlookers select the food sources, they determine the food sources in the vicinity of their selected food sources in a way similar to that of employee bees. Among all the new food sources determined in the vicinity of a food source i by the onlookers associated with food source i and the food source i, the best quality food source is determined. This best food source will be selected as the new location for food source i in the next iteration. The onlooker bee phase ends when all food sources are updated in the aforementioned manner and the next iteration of the ABC algorithm starts. The algorithm stops when the termination condition is satisfied. If the solution associated with a food source does not improve over some specific number of iterations say $limit$ then that food source is considered as empty and is discarded by its associated employed bee. Then that employee bee becomes scout. A new food source is generated for this scout so as to make it again employed. This new food source is usually generated in the same manner as an initial solution.

In the employed bee phase every solution is given a fair chance to improve itself, whereas in the onlooker bee phase, good quality solution are given more chance to improve themselves in comparison to poor quality solutions. This is justified considering the fact that in the vicinity of good quality solutions, chances of finding even better solutions are higher. However, if a solution is locally optimal then no better solution exists in its vicinity and any attempt to improve it through employed or onlooker bee phases will fail. Here, the concept of scout bees plays its part by replacing the locally optimal solution with a new solution. In a robust search process the balance between the exploration and exploitation must be maintained. In the ABC algorithm, this balance depends on the parameter $limit$. Smaller value of $limit$ favors exploration over exploitation whereas reverse is true for a higher value of $limit$. Therefore, the value of $limit$ should be chosen with utmost care.

4   ABC Approach for the TA Problem

In this section, we present our ABC approach for TA problem. Subsequent subsections describe salient features of our proposed approach.

4.1   Solution Encoding

To encode a solution, we have used the terminal based representation proposed in the literature [11]. The value represented by position i specifies the concentrator to which the terminal i is assigned. Figure 1 explains this representation with the help of an example where there are 10 terminals and 3 concentrators. In this figure, terminals 1, 3 and 6 are assigned to concentrator 1, terminals 2, 4, 7 and 9 are assigned to concentrator 2, terminals 5, 8 and 10 are assigned to concentrator 3.

1	2	1	2	3	1	2	3	2	3

Fig. 1. Solution representation

4.2   Initial Solution Generation

Each initial solution is obtained by using a method which is partially greedy and partially random. In this method, with probability p_{asn}, the terminals are greedily assigned to the nearest available concentrator . Here, the availability refers to the capacity of the concentrator to serve the terminal capacity requirement. If the capacity is not satisfied then the terminal is assigned to the next nearest concentrator, and this process is repeated until an available concentrator is found or none exits. With probability $1 - p_{asn}$, terminals will be assigned to the available concentrators randomly. The algorithm iterates through this process until all the terminals are assigned. The terminal to be assigned next is selected randomly.

In case no available concentrator exists for a terminal then the solution is infeasible. This solution is discarded and we start afresh in a bid to generate a feasible solution. If we are not able to generate a feasible solution even after three attempts then the last infeasible solution is included in the population, but its fitness is penalised using a penalty term as explained in Sect. 4.5. In this infeasible solution, terminals which can not be assigned to any available concentrator are assigned to some randomly chosen concentrator.

4.3   Generation of Neighboring Solution

To generate a solution S_i' in the neighborhood or vicinity of a solution S_i, each terminal in S_i is reassigned with probability p_{rand} using a greedy approach. In the greedy approach the terminals are assigned to the nearest available concentrators. S_i is replaced with the neighboring solution S_i' if the fitness of S_i' is better than S_i. In case the neighboring solution is infeasible then we discard the solution. This can happen only when original solution is infeasible.

The pseudo code for generating a neighboring solution S_i' in the vicinity of a solution S_i is as follows:

4.4   Selecting a Food Source for an Onlooker Bee

Instead of using the commonly used roulette wheel selection method, we have used the binary tournament selection method for selecting a food source for an onlooker bee. In the binary tournament selection two food sources are selected randomly, and, the better of the two food sources are selected with the probability p_{onl} and worse of the two with the probability $1 - p_{onl}$.

Algorithm 1. generate_neighboring_solution(S_i)

---

for each terminal $T_j \in T$ **do**
   p = generate a random number between 0 and 1
   if $p <= p_{rand}$ **then**
      Assign T_j to the nearest available concentrator in S_i'
   else
      Assign T_j to the same concentrator in S_i' as in S_i
   end if
end for
return S_i'

4.5 Fitness of a Solution

To evaluate the fitness of a solution, we have used the same fitness function as used in [11]. This fitness function is a modification of the objective function given in Sect. 2. The fitness function adds a penalty term called *penalization* to the objective function for infeasible solutions. The *penalization* is computed as follows:

$$penalisation = \begin{cases} 0 & if \ (solution \ is \ feasible) \\ 500 \end{cases} \tag{6}$$

$$fitness = objective \ function \ value \ + \ penalisation. \tag{7}$$

This fitness needs to be minimized.

4.6 Other Features

We have used different number of employee and onlooker bees unlike the usual practice of using the same number of employed and onlooker bees. If a solution correlated with an employed bee does not improve for *limit* number of iterations then this employed bee becomes scout. There is no limit on the number of scouts in an iteration. The number of scouts in a particular iteration depends on how many employed bee solutions got improved *limit* iterations prior to current iteration.

5 Experimental Results

Our ABC approach has been implemented in C and executed on a Intel Core 2 Duo (E8400) system with 2 GB RAM running at 3.0 GHz under Fedora 12 release. In all our computational experiments, the number of employed bees (n_e) is taken to be 50 and the number of onlooker bees (n_o) is taken to be 100. We have used p_{rand}=0.2, p_{asn} =0.85, p_{onl}=0.85, *limit*=500 in all our experiments. Our ABC approach terminates after 1500 iterations. All these parameter values are chosen empirically, after executing the algorithm multiple times. In order to

Table 1. Solution quality of various approaches

prob	LSGA			TS			MHDE			DDE			ABC		
	BestF	AvgF	StdD	BestF	AvgF	StdD	BestF	AvgF	StdD	BestF	AvgF	StdD	BestF	AvgF	StdD
1	65.63	65.63	0.00	65.63	65.63	0.00	65.63	65.63	0.00	65.63	65.63	0.00	**65.63**	**65.63**	0.00
2	134.65	134.65	0.00	134.65	134.65	0.00	134.65	134.65	0.00	134.65	134.65	0.00	**133.41**	**133.41**	0.00
3	270.26	270.69	0.23	270.26	270.76	0.30	270.26	270.75	0.15	270.26	270.47	0.22	279.94	281.17	0.66
4	286.89	286.99	0.13	286.89	287.93	0.75	286.89	287.17	0.14	286.89	286.89	0.00	**286.61**	**286.65**	0.09
5	335.09	335.99	0.60	335.09	335.99	0.59	335.09	336.55	0.39	335.09	335.26	0.17	**335.07**	336.24	0.32
6	371.12	371.68	0.24	371.12	372.44	0.45	371.12	373.19	0.42	371.12	371.38	0.22	374.55	378.44	1.38
7	401.21	402.41	0.50	401.29	403.25	0.73	401.21	403.61	0.33	401.21	401.62	0.28	**399.85**	**400.59**	0.39
8	563.19	564.94	0.52	563.34	564.5	0.54	563.19	572.04	0.76	563.19	564.07	0.38	596.65	601.85	2.53
9	642.83	646.52	0.84	642.86	644.18	0.48	642.83	648.46	0.48	642.83	643.96	0.46	687.52	690.71	1.65

test the performance of our approach, we have used the 9 benchmark instances available in the literature [11]. On each instance, we have executed our approach 40 independent times. We compare the results of our approach with those of LSGA [5], TS [3], MHDE [6] and DDE [11]. Results of these four approaches are taken from [11].

Table 1 compares the different approaches in terms of best &average solution quality and standard deviation of solution values on each of the 9 benchmark instances. In this table, result of our approaches are shown in bold whenever they are as good as or better than previous 4 approaches. From this table, it can be clearly seen that performance of our approach is more-or-less comparable to these 4 state-of-the-art approaches. Our approach obtain new best solution values for 4 instances.

Table 2 reports the time taken by various approaches to reach the best solution. As the four previous approaches were executed on an Intel Core Duo (T2300) based system which is different from the system used to execute our ABC approach, therefore times can not be compared precisely. However, a rough comparison can always be made. Even after compensating for difference in

Table 2. Time taken to reach the best solution by various algorithm

prob	LSGA	TS	MHDE	DDE	ABC
1	<1s	<1s	<1s	<1s	<1s
2	<1s	<1s	<1s	<1s	<1s
3	<1s	<1s	<1s	<1s	<1s
4	<1s	<1s	<1s	<1s	<1s
5	<1s	<1s	<1s	<1s	<1s
6	1s	<1s	<1s	<1s	<1s
7	1s	1s	2s	<1s	<1s
8	7s	1s	10s	2s	<1s
9	7s	2s	15s	3s	<1s

Table 3. Influence of parameter settings on solution quality

Parameter	Value	Problem 4		Problem 5	
		BestF	AvgF	BestF	AvgF
n_e	25	286.61	286.87	335.07	336.19
	50	**286.61**	**286.65**	**335.07**	**336.23**
	75	286.61	286.65	335.07	336.13
	100	286.61	286.62	335.07	336.12
n_o	50	286.61	286.67	335.69	336.44
	75	286.61	286.68	335.69	336.41
	100	**286.61**	**286.65**	**335.07**	**336.23**
	125	286.61	286.69	335.56	336.20
p_{asn}	0.75	286.61	286.79	335.71	336.29
	0.8	286.61	286.76	335.07	336.19
	0.85	**286.61**	**286.65**	**335.07**	**336.23**
	0.9	286.61	286.67	335.07	336.31
	0.95	286.61	286.68	335.07	336.27
p_{onl}	0.75	286.61	286.68	335.07	336.25
	0.8	286.60	286.67	335.07	336.21
	0.85	**286.61**	**286.65**	**335.07**	**336.23**
	0.9	286.61	286.70	335.69	336.30
	0.95	286.61	286.66	335.07	336.11
p_{rand}	0.1	286.61	286.71	335.84	336.44
	0.15	286.61	286.74	335.69	336.33
	0.2	**286.61**	**286.65**	**335.07**	**336.23**
	0.25	286.61	286.69	335.07	336.16
	0.3	286.61	286.77	335.69	336.32
$limit$	300	286.61	286.68	335.52	336.12
	400	286.61	286.62	335.19	336.16
	500	**286.61**	**286.65**	**335.07**	**336.23**
	600	286.61	286.72	335.07	336.20

processing speed, we can safely say that our approach is faster on large instances. Our approach requires less than 1 s to reach the best solution on all 9 instances.

To investigate the influence of parameter settings on solution quality, we have taken two different instances, viz. Problem 4 and 5. We have varied all the parameters one by one while keeping all other parameters unchanged. In doing so all other parameters were set to their values reported at the start of this section. The results are reported in Table 3. Values in bold in this table show the results with original parameter values which are used in all the experiments involving our approach. From this table it can be seen that values chosen by us provide either the best results or results which are very close to best results. In those cases where we have not got the best results with chosen parameter values, the parameter values chosen have provided best results on some other instances not included in this table.

6 Conclusions

In this paper, we have proposed an ABC algorithm based approach for the TA problem and compared it with the best methods proposed in the literature. The results shows the performance of the ABC algorithm is comparable with other methods. ABC algorithm provides good quality solutions in lesser execution times for majority of the instances.

As a future work, we plan to improve the performance of our ABC approach by hybridizing it with some local search procedure. We intend to investigate the performance of our ABC algorithm under different solution encoding schemes. Approaches similar to our ABC approach can be developed for other $\mathcal{NP}$-Hard assignment problems.

References

1. Karaboga, D., Basturk, K.: On the performance of artificial bee colony (ABC) algorithm. Appl. Soft Comput. **8**, 687–697 (2008)
2. Singh, A.: An artificial bee colony algorithm for the leaf constrained minimum spanning tree problem. Appl. Soft Comput. **9**, 625–631 (2009)
3. Bernardino, E., Bernardino, A., Sanchez- Perez, J., Vega-Rodriguez, M., Gomez-Pulido, J.: Tabu search vs hybrid genetic algorithm to solve the terminal assignment problem. In: International Conference on Applied Computing, pp. 404–409 (2008)
4. Xu, Y., Salcedo-Sanz, S., Yao, X.: Non-standard cost terminal assignment problems using tabu search approach. IEEE Conf. Evol. Comput. **2**, 2302–2306 (2004)
5. Bernardino, E., Bernardino, A., Sanchez-Perez, J., Vega-Rodriguez, M., Gomez-Pulido, J.: Solving the terminal assignment problem using a local search genetic algorithm. In: International Symposium on Distributed Computing and Artificial Intelligence, pp. 225–234, Springer, Heidelberg (2008)
6. Bernardino, E., Bernardino, A., Sanchez-Perez, J., Vega-Rodriguez, M., Gomez-Pulido, J.: A hybrid differential evolution algorithm with a multiple strategy for solving the terminal assignment problem. In: 6th Hellenic Conference on Artificial Intelligence. Springer, Heidelberg (2010)
7. Khuri, S., Chiu, T.: Heuristic algorithms for the terminal assignment problem. In: Proceedings of the ACM Symposium on Applied Computing, pp. 247–251 (1997)
8. Salcedo-Sanz, S., Yao, X.: A hybrid Hopfield network genetic algorithm approach for the terminal assignment problem. IEEE Trans. Syst. Man Cybern. **34**(6), 2343–2353 (2004)
9. Abuali, F., Schoenefeld, D., Wainwright, R.: Terminal assignment in a communications network using genetic algorithms. In: Proceedings of the 22nd Annual ACM Computer Science Conference, pp. 74–81. ACM press, Newyork (1994)

10. Singh, A., Sunder, S.: An artificial bee colony algorithm for the minimum routing cost spanning tree problem. Soft Comput. **15**, 2489–2499 (2011)
11. Bernardino, E.M., Bernardino, A.M., Sánchez-Pérez, J.M., Gómez-Pulido, J.A., Vega-Rodríguez, M.A.: Discrete differential evolution algorithm for solving the terminal assignment problem. In: Schaefer, R., Cotta, C., Kołodziej, J., Rudolph, G. (eds.) PPSN XI. LNCS, vol. 6239, pp. 229–239. Springer, Heidelberg (2010)
12. Karaboga, D., Gorkemli, B., Ozturk, C., Karaboga, N.: A comprehensive survey: artificial bee colony (ABC) algorithm and applications. Artif. Intell. Rev. **42**, 21–57 (2014)
13. Karaboga, D., Basturk, B.: A powerful and efficient algorithm for numerical function optimization: artificial bee colony (ABC) algorithm. J. Global Optim. **39**, 459–471 (2007)
14. Karaboga, D., Basturk, B.: Artificial bee colony (ABC) optimization algorithm for solving constrained optimization problems. In: Melin, P., Castillo, O., Aguilar, L.T., Kacprzyk, J., Pedrycz, W. (eds.) IFSA 2007. LNCS (LNAI), vol. 4529, pp. 789–798. Springer, Heidelberg (2007)
15. Bernardino, E.M., Bernardino, A.M., Sánchez-Pérez, J.M., Gómez-Pulido, J.A., Vega-Rodríguez, M.A.: Using the bees algorithm to assign terminals to concentrators. In: García-Pedrajas, N., Herrera, F., Fyfe, C., Benítez, J.M., Ali, M. (eds.) IEA/AIE 2010, Part II. LNCS, vol. 6097, pp. 267–276. Springer, Heidelberg (2010)
16. Bernardino, E.M., Bernardino, A.M., Sánchez-Pérez, J.M., Gómez-Pulido, J.A., Vega-Rodríguez, M.A.: A Hybrid differential evolution algorithm for solving the terminal assignment problem. In: Omatu, S., Rocha, M.P., Bravo, J., Fernández, F., Corchado, E., Bustillo, A., Corchado, J.M. (eds.) IWANN 2009, Part II. LNCS, vol. 5518, pp. 179–186. Springer, Heidelberg (2009)
17. Pan, Q.-K., Tasgetiren, M. F., Liang, Y.C.: A discrete differential evolution algorithm for the permutation flowshop scheduling problem. In: Proceedings of the 9th Annual Conference on Genetic and Evolutionary Computation, pp. 126–133 (2007)
18. Pan, Q.-K., Tasgetiren, M.F., Suganthan, P.N., Chen, A.H.-L.: A discrete artificial bee colony algorithm for the total flowtime minimization in permutation flow shops. Inf. Sci. **181**, 3459–3475 (2011)
19. Kershenbaum, A.: Telecommunications Network Design Algorithms. McGraw-Hill, New York (1993)
20. Bose, D., Kundu, S., Biswas, S., Das, S.: Circular antenna array design using novel perturbation based artificial bee colony algorithm. In: Panigrahi, B.K., Das, S., Suganthan, P.N., Nanda, P.K. (eds.) SEMCCO 2012. LNCS, vol. 7677, pp. 459–466. Springer, Heidelberg (2012)
21. Biswas, S., Kundu, S., Bose, D., Das, S., Suganthan, P.N., Panigrahi, B.K.: Migrating forager population in a multi-population artificial bee colony algorithm with modified perturbation schemes. In: 2013 IEEE Symposium on Swarm Intelligence (SIS 2013), pp. 248–255 (2013)
22. Bose, D., Biswas, S., Vasilakos, A.V., Laha, S.: Optimal filter design using an improved artificial bee colony algorithm. Inf. Sci. **281**, 443–461 (2014)

Image Restoration with Fuzzy Coefficient Driven Anisotropic Diffusion

V.B. Surya Prasath[1]([✉]) and R. Delhibabu[2,3]

[1] University of Missouri-Columbia, Columbia, MO 65211, USA
prasaths@missouri.edu
http://web.missouri.edu/ prasaths
[2] Knowledge-Based System Group,
Higher Institute of Information Technology and Information Systems, Kazan Federal University, Kazan, Russia
[3] Department of CSE, SSN Engineering College, Chennai 603110, India
delhibabur@ssn.edu.in

Abstract. Nonlinear anisotropic diffusion is widely used in image processing and computer vision for various problems. One of the basic and important problem is that of restoring noisy images and diffusion filters are an important class of denoising methods. In this work, we proposed a fuzzy diffusion coefficient which takes into account local pixel variability for better denoising and selective smoothing of edges. By using smoothed gradients along with the fuzzy diffusion coefficient function we obtain edge preserving restoration of noisy images. Experimental results on standard test images and real medical data illustrate that the proposed fuzzy diffusion improves over traditional filters in terms of structural similarity and signal to noise ratio.

Keywords: Image restoration · Fuzzy edge detection · Diffusion coefficient · Anisotropic · Denoising

1 Introduction

Selective smoothing and restoration of noisy images is a basic problem in image processing domain. One of the important class of techniques is based on anisotropic partial differential equations (PDEs) and the last two decades has seen tremendous progress in theoretical as well as numerical methods. Perona and Malik [1] made a seminal contribution by proposing a nonlinear diffusion coefficient driven PDE. Since then there have plethora of adaptations of anisotropic diffusion to various computer vision tasks, see [2] for a review. Though, the anisotropic diffusion PDE based models work well in noise removal, there exists some drawbacks in terms of artifacts in restoration results. Due to the use of noisy gradient computations resultant images can have staircasing or blocking artifacts and various remedies have been proposed in the past. For example, by modifying diffusion coefficient to handle higher noise [3], multi scale objects [4], edge preservation [5] has been considered.

© Springer International Publishing Switzerland 2015
B.K. Panigrahi et al. (Eds.): SEMCCO 2014, LNCS 8947, pp. 145–155, 2015.
DOI: 10.1007/978-3-319-20294-5_13

One of the important ingredient for obtaining good denoising is the design of the diffusion coefficient which traditionally depends on the absolute value of the gradient image. Catté et al. [6] used Gaussian smoothed gradient image to avoid ill-posedness associated with anisotropic diffusion but is known to dislocate edge locations and looses small scale edges. On the other hand multi-scale or local variance based measures [4,5] provide better location but can be stymied by noise along edges. Edge detection is challenging under high noise levels and traditional edge detectors [7] usually obtain multiple false positive edge pixels. Fuzzy techniques, in contrast, are very useful in obtaining meaningful decisions when ambiguities are present. Thus, it is worthwhile to investigate edge detection approaches from the fuzzy image processing literature [8,9] along with the powerful anisotropic diffusion flows [10]. One of the advantages of utilizing a fuzzy edge indicator is the robustness with which they can work under noise. Moreover, due to simultaneous denoising and enhancement associated with anisotropic diffusion flows [11] we can tune the diffusion coefficient to obtain better results. In this paper, we propose to use a fuzzy edge indicator function, which is computed using a local window based decision rule system, within diffusion coefficient of the Perona and Malik [1] PDE. Our approach is compared against with and without spatial regularization [6] and is proven to obtain better results in terms of signal to noise ratio and structural similarity.

In this work, we use a fuzzy membership function derived from fuzzy inference [8] which provides a measure of edginess in each neighborhood of pixels. The combination of gradient image along with such fuzzy edge indicator function provides a well-defined road map thereby guiding anisotropic diffusion along edges and not across it. We provide comparison with related diffusion PDEs and our fuzzy diffusion coefficient obtains better results in terms of noise removal and edge preservation.

Rest of the paper is organized as follows. Section 2 introduces the anisotropic diffusion PDE along with our proposed fuzzy coefficient. Section 3 illustrates the advantages of our method in comparison with related diffusion models. Finally, Sect. 4 concludes the paper.

2   Anisotropic Diffusion for Image Restoration

The Perona-Malik (PM) PDE for image restoration is the time dependent evolution of the following form:

$$
\begin{cases}
\dfrac{\partial u(x,t)}{\partial t} = \nabla \cdot \left(\mathcal{C}(|\nabla u(x,t)|^2)\nabla u(x,t) \right) & x \in \Omega, \\
u(x,0) = u_0(x) & x \in \Omega, \\
\dfrac{\partial u(x,t)}{\partial n} = 0 & x \in \partial\Omega,
\end{cases}
\tag{1}
$$

where $u_0 : \Omega \subset \mathbb{R}^2 \to \mathbb{R}$ is the given noisy gray-scale image, $x = (x_1, x_2) \in \Omega$ pixel co-ordinates on $2D$ image domain Ω. The function $\mathcal{C}(|\nabla u(x,t)|^2)$ in (1) is the diffusion coefficient which tunes the amount of smoothing according to magnitude of the gradient image. Perona and Malik [1] proposed the following decreasing functions:

$$\mathcal{C}_1(|\nabla u(x,t)|^2) = \frac{1}{1 + \dfrac{|\nabla u(x,t)|^2}{K^2}}, \tag{2}$$

$$\mathcal{C}_2(|\nabla u(x,t)|^2) = \exp\left(-\frac{|\nabla u(x,t)|^2}{K^2}\right), \tag{3}$$

where $K > 0$ is known as the contrast parameter and defines the regions for forward and backward diffusion flows [12]. This unique aspect, though provides image smoothing and enhancement simultaneously, makes the PDE (1) mathematically ill-posed.

Various adaptations have been considered to avoid the instability of ill-posedness [4–6,13,14]. The artificial temporal variable t enables us to obtain $\{u(x,t)\}_{t=0}^{T}$ a set of images depending upon the terminal time T. This one parameter (scale) family creates a semi-group and is known as the scale-space starting with the input noisy image u_0. Moreover, if the diffusion coefficient is constant $(\mathcal{C}(|\nabla u(x,t|)^2 \equiv 1)$ then Eq. (1) reduces the heat equation which has isotropically smoothed solutions.

In one of the Classical work, Catté et al. [6] removed the ill-posedness of the PM PDE (1) by making a spatial regularization in the diffusion coefficient argument,

$$\mathcal{C} = \mathcal{C}(|G_\rho \star \nabla u(x,t)|^2) \tag{4}$$

where G_ρ is the Gaussian function,

$$G_\rho = (\rho\sqrt{2\pi})^{-1} \exp\left(-|\mathbf{x}|^2/2\rho^2\right), \tag{5}$$

with ρ the standard deviation of the function, and $\star$ denotes the $2D$ convolution operation. Unfortunately, such spatial regularization by isotropic Gaussian is against the original anisotropic property of PM PDE (1). Moreover, the Gaussian smoothing of the gradient image shifts the true edge locations (see Fig. 2(c) for example), looses small scale edges, and can be detrimental to selective smoothing under anisotropic diffusion.

2.1   Fuzzy Diffusion Coefficient

To avoid the spatial regularization and localization issue of edges we utilize a fuzzy edge indicator function within the diffusion coefficient. We first outline the fuzzy edge indicator function to be used here. Following [8] we use the fuzzy inference ruled by else-action (FIRE) operator with noise protection. Figure 1(a) shows the antecedent fuzzy sets of the noise protected operator and Fig. 1(b) the rule based operator on a 3×3 neighborhood of a pixel. This example has a group of 8 THEN-rules (having the same consequent set, black pixel in Fig. 1(b)) and one ELSE-rule, we refer to [8] for more details.

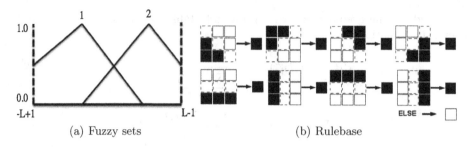

| (a) Fuzzy sets | (b) Rulebase |

Fig. 1. Fuzzy edge indicator function formulation. (a) Antecedent fuzzy sets for the noise-protected operator (b) Rulebase (size 3×3).

We use a generalized edge indicator function based on FIRE operator as follows:

$$F(u(x)) = 1 - \frac{1}{1 + \dfrac{\sum_{y \in \mathcal{N}_x^r} |u(x) - u(y)|}{\triangle}} \qquad (6)$$

where $\mathcal{N}_x^r$ is a local neighborhood of size $r \times r$ centered at the pixel $x \in \Omega$, and $\triangle = |\mathcal{N}_x^r|$ total number of pixels in the neighborhood. We do not use a thresholding step utilized by [8] as our aim here is not edge detection rather a road-map for the subsequent diffusion filter to act upon. Note other categorization based fuzzy edge indicators can also be used and we observed similar final restoration results [9].

We use the fuzzy edginess function (6) with gradient image to drive the diffusion flow and we propose to use,

$$\tilde{\mathcal{C}}(u(x, t-1), |\nabla u(x, t)|^2) = |\nabla u(x, t) \cdot F(u(x, t-1))| . \qquad (7)$$

Note, that we used the lagged-diffusivity method here and the fuzzy edge indicator function is computed from the previous iteration $(t - 1)$ and is used to obtain image at iteration t, see Sect. 2.2 for the diffusion paradigm driven by the coefficient. Figure 2 shows different gradient based edge indicator functions used in anisotropic diffusion filters for noisy and noise-free *Cameraman* gray-scale test image of size 512×512. As can be seen, when noise is present traditional gradient based approaches [1,6] provide edge maps which are corrupted spikes and noise oscillations in flat regions, see Fig. 2(b–c). Though the spatial regularization (Gaussian smoothing) avoids major noise in flat regions the intensity range is reduced. In contrast, our fuzzy diffusion coefficient (7) remains robust and with edges strongly preserved.

2.2 Proposed Scheme

We utilize the proposed fuzzy diffusion coefficient within the PDE formulation of (1). Thus, we use the following steps in obtaining denoising of a given image u_0:

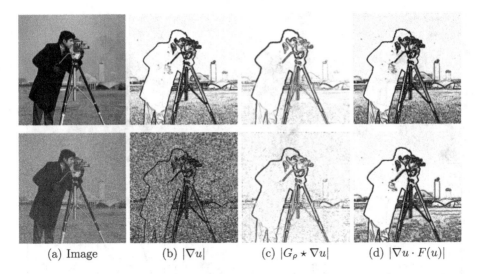

| (a) Image | (b) $|\nabla u|$ | (c) $|G_\rho \star \nabla u|$ | (d) $|\nabla u \cdot F(u)|$ |

Fig. 2. Various edge indicator functions obtained from noise-free (top row) and noisy (bottom row) *Cameraman* gray-scale image in (a). (b) Original gradient $|\nabla u|$ argument used in PM PDE (1), see Eqs. (2–3) (c) Smoothed gradient $|G_\rho \star \nabla u|$ (with $\rho = 2$), see Eq. (4) (d) $|\nabla u \cdot F(u)|$, Eq. (7). Better viewed online and zoomed in.

1. Start at time $t = 0$ with given image u_0
2. For $t = 1, 2, \ldots, T$:
   (a) Compute the fuzzy edge indicator function (6) on image $u(\cdot, t-1)$
   (c) Solve the PDE and obtain $u(x,t)$

$$
\begin{cases}
\dfrac{\partial u(x,t)}{\partial t} = \nabla \cdot \left(\tilde{\mathcal{C}}(u(x,t-1), |\nabla u(x,t)|^2) \nabla u(x,t) \right) & x \in \Omega, \\
u(x,0) = u_0(x) & x \in \Omega, \quad (8) \\
\dfrac{\partial u(x,t)}{\partial n} = 0 & x \in \partial\Omega,
\end{cases}
$$

The time-dependent PDE in (8) is solved using an additive operator splitting scheme (AOS) [15] and we use directional estimation of gradients and the finite difference scheme is proven to be stable [16].

3 Experimental Results

3.1 Setup and Parameters

We have implemented anisotropic diffusion filters considered here in MATLAB® R2012a on a Mac Laptop with 2.3 GHz Intel Core i7 with 8 GB RAM. All the images are mapped to $[0, 1]$ and the final terminal iteration T is chosen according to best results. The neighborhood size in the fuzzy indicator function (6) is chosen as $r = 3$, larger windows produce thicker edge lines and reduce structural similarity performance. The step size in the AOS finite differences based implementation of the PDE (8) chosen to be $\Delta t = 0.2$.

(a) [1]   (b) [6]   (c) Our

Fig. 3. Comparison with other anisotropic diffusion coefficient based filters. Restoration results from: (a) Perona and Malik [1], MSSIM 0.7413 (b) Catté et al. [6], MSSIM 0.7587 (c) Proposed fuzzy anisotropic diffusion method, MSSIM 0.8012. Top row: Images. Middle row: Contours. Bottom row: Crop showing details. Better viewed online and zoomed in.

3.2   Comparison Results

We compare our fuzzy diffusion coefficient based anisotropic diffusion with Perona and Malik [1] original gradient formulation, Catté et al. [6] spatial regularization. Both these schemes are discretized using the same AOS formulation as in our model, and the step size, diffusion coefficient (2) are kept the same as well.

Figure 3 shows final restoration results for the *Cameraman* image corrupted by Gaussian noise of strength $\sigma = 20$ (see Fig. 2(a) bottom). As can be seen

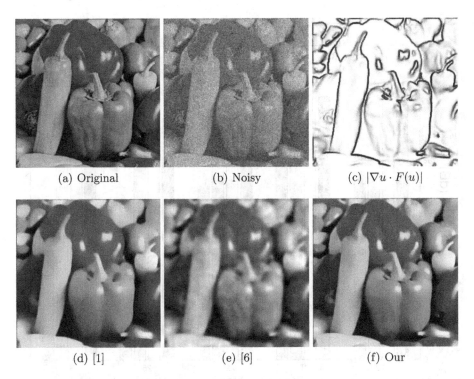

(a) Original   (b) Noisy   (c) $|\nabla u \cdot F(u)|$

(d) [1]   (e) [6]   (f) Our

Fig. 4. Comparison of different diffusion models for the noisy *Peppers* gray scale image. (a) Original image (b) Noisy image obtained by adding white additive Gaussian noise of strength ($\sigma_n = 30$), MSSIM 0.2875. Restoration results of: (c) Fuzzy diffusion coefficient from noise image $|\nabla u \cdot F(u)|$, Eq. (7) at the final iteration (d) Perona and Malik [1], MSSIM 0.7924 (e) Catté et al. [6], MSSIM 0.8015 (f) Our proposed method, MSSIM 0.8587.

from the corresponding contour maps (Fig. 3(middle row), level lines), Perona and Malik [1] result has spurious staircasing artifacts in homogeneous regions, Catte et al. [6] has spurious noise along edges, and our proposed fuzzy diffusion coefficient based result has less artifacts and better edge preservation. A closer look at the restoration results (Fig. 3(bottom row)) reveals that the Perona-Malik scheme [1] though obtains better denoising still contains spurious spikes whereas Catte et al. [6] scheme obtains blurred edges and our proposed scheme's result is devoid of such artifacts.

For quantitative comparison we use the following two metrics which indicate the quality of restored images.

1. Peak signal to noise ratio (PSNR): This is a traditional image processing metric and measured in decibels (dB) with higher values indicating better performance.

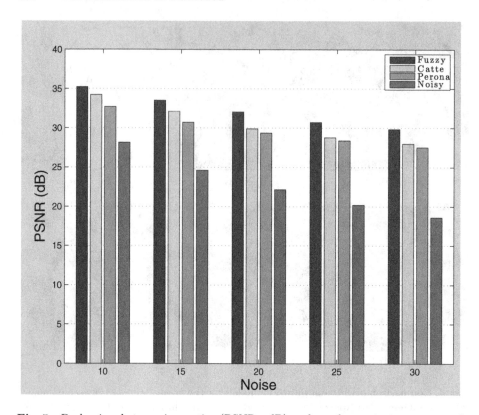

Fig. 5. Peak signal to noise ratio (PSNR, dB) values for restoring corrupted *Cameraman* image using PM PDE Eq. (1) with different diffusion coefficients for Gaussian noise levels $\sigma = 10, 15, 20, 25, 30$. `Perona` - Perona and Malik [1] original gradient, `Catte` - Catté et al. [6] spatial regularization, and `Fuzzy` - proposed fuzzy diffusion coefficients.

$$\text{PSNR}(u) = 20 * \log 10 \left(\frac{255}{\sqrt{\sum_{x \in \Omega}(u(x) - u_0(x))^2}} \right) (dB) \qquad (9)$$

2. Structural similarity (SSIM): Wang et al. [17] proposed an error metric which takes into account structural similarity between original (noise-free) and restored images[1]. The SSIM is calculated between two windows ω_1 and ω_2 of common size $N \times N$, and is given by,

$$\text{SSIM}(\omega_1, \omega_2) := \frac{(2\mu_{\omega_1}\mu_{\omega_2} + c_1)(2\sigma_{\omega_1\omega_2} + c_2)}{(\mu_{\omega_1}^2 + \mu_{\omega_2}^2 + c_1)(\sigma_{\omega_1}^2 + \sigma_{\omega_2}^2 + c_2)} \qquad (10)$$

where μ_{ω_i} the average of ω_i, $\sigma_{\omega_i}^2$ the variance of ω_i, $\sigma_{\omega_1\omega_2}$ the covariance, and c_1, c_2 stabilization parameters, see [17] for details. Mean SSIM (MSSIM) ranges between $[0, 1]$ and closer to 1 indicates better restorations.

---

[1] We use the default parameters. SSIM MATLAB code available online at https://ece.uwaterloo.ca/~z70wang/research/ssim/.

Next in Fig. 4 show denoising results on *Peppers* gray scale image corrupted by high noise level $\sigma = 30$. The final fuzzy diffusion coefficient is given in Fig. 4(c) and clearly shows that the major salient edges are kept and there are no blurring artifacts. In Figs. 3–4 our scheme's MSSIM values are the highest and confirms the visual comparison of edge preservation and strong smoothness in homogeneous (flat) regions obtained with our proposed fuzzy diffusion based scheme. Figure 5 shows the PSNR (dB) values for restoring corrupted *Cameraman* image using different diffusion coefficients. Our proposed fuzzy edge indicator based method outperforms purely gradient based diffusion methods for all the noise levels. We note that the results indicate our proposed fuzzy diffusion filter can not preserve small scale textures (see for example Fig. 3(c) background buildings) and we believe using higher order rule based fuzzy region indicators will help. This is a much harder problem as textures do not, in general, have high frequency information and classification of textures is important [18] in identifying regions where the diffusion needs to be stopped.

Finally in Fig. 6 we show a restoration result of an mammography image (size 482×403) along with fuzzy coefficient scaled to $[0, 1]$ for visualization. Figure 6(a) shows the input noise image and its contour map indicating the amount of noise

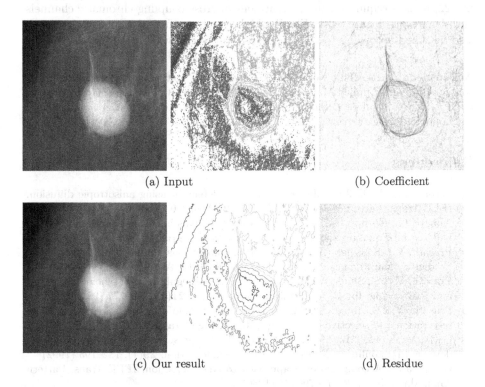

(a) Input   (b) Coefficient

(c) Our result   (d) Residue

Fig. 6. Mammography image noise removal and structure detection using our proposed method. (a) Input noisy image (b) Fuzzy edge coefficient (7) (c) Our scheme result (d) Method noise ($|u_0 - u|$).

present. By utilizing the fuzzy diffusion coefficient (7), shown in Fig. 6(b), we obtain denoising with structure preservation as seen in Fig. 6(c). We further show the residue image $|u_0 - u|$ which indicates the amount of noise removed. Moreover, it is seen that no salient structures are smoothed out with our scheme highlighting strong selective smoothing property.

4   Conclusions

In this paper, we considered a fuzzy diffusion coefficient for image selective smoothing and restoration. Traditional anisotropic diffusion filters rely on gradient image to drive the selective smoothing process and hence are highly susceptible to noise along edges. We modify the diffusion coefficient using a fuzzy rule based edge indicator function which is noise protected and provides cleaner edge maps. Experimental results are given in noisy images to highlight the advantage of the proposed method and comparison results show advantages of the fuzzy modeling with respect to diffusion filters. Other fuzzy rule based edge indicator functions are required for preserving textures and small scale details and defines our future work in this direction. Extension to color [19] and multispectral [20–22] images require a careful treatment of cross coupling chromatic channels and defines our future work. Finally, higher order diffusion [23] coefficients can also be tuned according to fuzzy edge indicators and will be studies elsewhere.

Acknowledgments. This work was done while the first author was visiting Institute for Pure and Applied Mathematics (IPAM), University of California Los Angeles (UCLA), USA. The first author thanks the IPAM institute for their great hospitality and support during the visit.

References

1. Perona, P., Malik, J.: Scale-space and edge detection using anisotropic diffusion. IEEE Trans. Pattern Anal. Mach. Intell. **12**(7), 629–639 (1990)
2. Aubert, G., Kornprobst, P.: Mathematical Problems in Image Processing: Partial Differential Equation and Calculus Of Variations. Springer, New York (2006)
3. Prasath, V.B.S., Singh, A.: Well-posed inhomogeneous nonlinear diffusion scheme for digital image denoising. J. Appl. Math. 2010, 14, Article ID 763847 (2010)
4. Prasath, V.B.S., Singh, A.: Well-posed multiscale regularization scheme for digital image denoising. Int. J. Appl. Math. Comput. Sci. **21**(4), 769–777 (2011)
5. Prasath, V.B.S., Singh, A.: An adaptive anisotropic diffusion scheme for image restoration and selective smoothing. Int. J. Image Graph. **12**(1), 18 (2012)
6. Catte, V., Lions, P.L., Morel, J.M., Coll, T.: Image selective smoothing and edge detection by nonlinear diffusion. SIAM J. Numer. Anal. **29**(1), 182–193 (1992)
7. Canny, J.F.: A computational approach to edge detection. IEEE Trans. Pattern Anal. Mach. Intell. **8**(6), 679–698 (1986)
8. Russo, F., Ramponi, G.: Edge extraction by FIRE operators. In: Proceedings of the Third IEEE Conference on Fuzzy Systems. IEEE World Congress on Computational Intelligence, vol. 1, pp. 249–253, June 1994

9. Ho, K., Ohnishi, N.: FEDGE - fuzzy edge detection by fuzzy categorization and classification of edges. In: Martin, T., Ralescu, A. (eds.) Fuzzy Logic In Artificial Intelligence Towards Intelligent Systems. Lecture Notes in Computer Science, vol. 1188, pp. 182–196. Springer, Berlin Heidelberg (1997)

10. Prasath, V.B.S., Singh, A.: Edge detectors based anisotropic diffusion for enhancement of digital images. In: Sixth Indian Conference on Computer Vision, Graphics and Image Processing (ICVGIP), Bhubaneswar, India, pp. 33–38(2008)

11. Prasath, V.B.S., Singh, A.: Controlled inverse diffusion models for image restoration and enhancement. In: First International Conference on Emerging Trends in Engineering and Technology (ICETET), Nagpur, India, pp. 90–94 (2008)

12. Prasath, V.B.S., Delhibabu, R.: Automatic contrast parameter estimation in anisotropic diffusion for image restoration. In: Ignatov, D.I., Khachay, M.Y., Panchenko, A., Konstantinova, N., Yavorsky, R.E. (eds.) Analysis of Images, Social Networks, and Texts. Communications in Computer and Information Science. Springer, New York (2014)

13. Prasath, V.B.S., Vorotnikov, D.: Weighted and well-balanced anisotropic diffusion scheme for image denoising and restoration. Nonlinear Anal.: Real World Appl. **17**, 33–46 (2013)

14. Prasath, V.B.S., Vorotnikov, D.: On a system of adaptive coupled PDEs for image restoration. J. Math. Imaging Vis. **48**(1), 35–52 (2014)

15. Weickert, J., Romeny, B.M.H., Viergever, M.A.: Efficient and reliable schemes for nonlinear diffusion filtering. IEEE Trans. Image Process. **7**(3), 398–410 (1998)

16. Prasath, V.B.S., Moreno, J.C.: Feature preserving anisotropic diffusion for image restoration. In: Fourth National Conference on Computer Vision, Pattern Recognition, Image Processing and Graphics (NCVPRIPG 2013), India, pp. 1–4, December 2013

17. Wang, Z., Bovik, A.C., Sheikh, H.R., Simoncelli, E.P.: Image quality assessment: from error visibility to structural similarity. IEEE Trans. Image Process. **13**(4), 600–612 (2004)

18. Prasath, V.B.S., Palaniappan, K., Seetharaman, G.: Multichannel texture image segmentation using weighted feature fitting based variational active contours. In: Eighth Indian Conference on Vision, Graphics and Image Processing (ICVGIP), Mumbai, India, 6pp, December 2012

19. Prasath, V.B.S., Moreno, J.C., Palaniappan, K.: Color Image Denoising By Chromatic Edges Based Vector Valued Diffusion. Technical report, ArXiv (2013)

20. Prasath, V.B.S., Singh, A.: Multispectral image denoising by well-posed anisotropic diffusion scheme with channel coupling. Int. J. Remote Sens. **31**(8), 2091–2099 (2010)

21. Prasath, V.B.S., Singh, A.: Multichannel image restoration using combined channel information and robust M-estimator approach. Int. J. Tomogr. Stat. **12**(F10), 9–22 (2010)

22. Prasath, V.B.S.: Weighted Laplacian differences based multispectral anisotropic diffusion. In: IEEE International Geoscience and Remote Sensing Symposium (IGARSS), Vancouver BC, Canada, pp. 4042–4045, July 2011

23. You, Y.L., Kaveh, M.: Fourth-order partial differential equation for noise removal. IEEE Trans. Image Process. **9**, 1723–1730 (2000)

Optimum Design of Rolling Element Bearing

S. Panda[1(✉)], T. Mohanty[3], D. Mishra[1], and B.B. Biswal[2]

[1] Department of Production Engineering, V.S.S. University of Technology,
Burla 768018, Odisha, India
{sumanta.panda,dmvssut}@gmail.com
[2] Department of Industrial Design, N.I.T., Rourkela 768024, Odisha, India
bbbiswal@gmail.com
[3] Department of Mechanical Engineering, V.S.S. University of Technology,
Burla 768018, Odisha, India
tanmayeemohanty90@gmail.com

Abstract. The primary objective of this research is to optimize the dynamic load capacity of a deep groove ball bearing. The dynamic load capacity is formulated as an objective function along with the prescribed geometric, kinematics and strength constraints. The non-linear constrained optimization problem is solved using particles swarm optimization (PSO). The algorithm incorporates the generalized method to handle mixed integer design variables and ranked based method of constraint handling. Encouraging results in terms of objective function value and CPU time are reported in this study. The optimum design result shows that the system life of an optimally designed roller element bearing is enhanced in comparisons with that of the current design without constraint violations. It is believed that the proposed algorithm can be applied to other roller element design applications.

1 Introduction

Design optimization of a mechanical system is more complicated and involves number of design variables and constraints. It is also important that the roller element bearing user and roller bearing manufacturer to work cooperatively in an early design phase to ensure that the application requirement and the bearing performance will be brought in line with each other so that best design solutions can be achieved with lowest life cycle cost for user [1]. Limited numbers of literatures are available on design optimization of roller element bearings. Changsen [2] proposed a design method using gradient based numerical optimization approach for roller element bearing. Choi and Yoon [3] used genetic algorithm (GA) for design optimization of automobile wheel bearing unit by considering the maximization of life of the unit as objective function. Chakraborthy et al. [4] designed a constraint optimization problem of ball bearing with five design variables by using GA based on the requirement of longest fatigue life. Tiwari and Rao [5] described a constrained non-linear optimization procedure based on GA for the design of roller bearing. Gupta et al. [6] proposed multi-objective optimization procedure using NSGA-II (non-dominated sorting based genetic algorithm). However, in order to achieve meaningful results in this present work ten design variables and ten realistic design constraints used by manufacturer are considered, with a ranking method

© Springer International Publishing Switzerland 2015
B.K. Panigrahi et al. (Eds.): SEMCCO 2014, LNCS 8947, pp. 156–163, 2015.
DOI: 10.1007/978-3-319-20294-5_14

approach for constraint handling. This design approach will provide confidence to the designer for the global optimization.

2 Problem Formulation for Design Optimization of Roller Bearing

On the basis of operating requirements, different objective functions for rolling element bearings may be proposed, the most important of these being the requirement of the longest fatigue life. To solve this problem for a given size of the bearing outline or *boundary dimensions* (*i.e.* bearing bore, D_3, and outside diameter, D, see Fig. 1), the *dynamic load rating* C should be maximum.

The fatigue life, L, of the bearing (in millions of revolutions) subjected to any other applied load F is given by

$$L = \left(\frac{C}{F}\right)^a \tag{1}$$

where $a = 3$ in the present case (for ball bearings).

2.1 Design Parameters

The design parameters are basically geometrical dimensions and other variables, called main parameters. These parameters are to be determined in the bearing design. The eight input parameters are

$$X = [D_b, Z, D_m, f_o, f_i, K_{Dmin}, K_{Dmax}\varepsilon, e, \zeta] \tag{2}$$

The design optimization is considered as a mixed variable optimization problem.

2.2 Objective Function

Based on the dynamic load capacity the objective function can be expressed as

$$max[C(X)] = \begin{cases} max\left[-f_c Z^{2/3} D_b^{1.8}\right] & D_b \leq 25.4\,\text{mm} \\ max\left[-3.647 f_c Z^{2/3} D_b^{1.4}\right] & D_b > 25.4\,\text{mm} \end{cases} \tag{3}$$

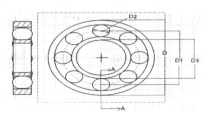

Fig. 1. Radial ball bearing geometries

$$f_c = 37.91 \left\{ 1 + \left[1.04 \left(\frac{1-\gamma}{1+\gamma} \right)^{1.72} \left(\frac{f_i(2f_o - 1)}{f_o(2f_i - 1)} \right)^{0.41} \right]^{10/3} \right\}^{-0.3} \quad x$$

$$\left[\frac{\gamma^{0.3}(1-\gamma)^{1.39}}{(1+\gamma)^{1/3}} \right] \left[\frac{2f_i}{2f_i - 1} \right]^{0.41}$$

(4)

where $\gamma = D_b \cos \alpha / D_m$ is not an independent parameter, and hence it does not appear in the vector of design parameters. Here α is the free contact angle that depends upon the type of bearing. Based on the geometrical derivation presented by Tiwari and Rao [5],

$$\phi_0 = 2\pi - 2\cos^{-1} \left[\frac{\left[U^2 + (D/2 - T - D_b)^2 - (d/2 + T)^2 \right]}{2U(D/2 - T - D_b)} \right]$$

(5)

$$2(Z - 1) \sin^{-1}(D_b/D_m) \le \phi_0$$

$$T = (D - d - 2D_b)/4; \quad U = (D - d)/2 - 3T$$

(6)

2.3   Design Constraints

In the design of rolling element bearing different constraints are proposed by researchers (Gupta et al. [6], Chakraborthy [4] and Tiwari and Rao [5]). For the convenience of the bearing assembly, number and diameter of balls should satisfy the following requirement:

$$2(Z - 1) \sin^{-1}(D_b/D_m) \le \phi_0$$

(7)

$$g_1(X) = \frac{2\pi - 2\cos^{-1} \left[\frac{[U^2 + (D/2 - T - D_b)^2 - (d/2 + T)^2]}{2U(D/2 - T - D_b)} \right]}{2\sin^{-1}(D_b/D_m)} - Z + 1 \ge 0$$

(8)

The diameter of the rolling element should be chosen from certain bounds, that is

$$K_{Dmin} \frac{D - d}{2} \le D_b \le K_{Dmax} \frac{D - d}{2}$$

(9)

where K_{Dmin} and K_{Dmax} are unknown constants From Eq. (9) the corresponding constraint conditions are given as

$$g_2(X) = 2D_b - K_{Dmin}(D - d) \geq 0 \tag{10}$$

$$g_3(X) = K_{Dmax}(D - d) - 2D_b \geq 0 \tag{11}$$

In order to guarantee the running mobility of bearings, the difference between the pitch diameter and the average diameter in a bearing should be less than a certain given value. Therefore the following two constraints are to be satisfied.

$$g_4(X) = D_m - 0.5 - e \ D + d \geq 0 \tag{12}$$

$$g_5(X) = (0.5 + e)(D + d) - D_m \geq 0 \tag{13}$$

where e is an unknown. In practice the inner ring is always subjected to more stresses than the outer ring, this necessitated the need to put a constraint on the ring thickness that it should be more than or equal to the outer ring thickness, that is

$$g_6(X) = \frac{d_i - d}{2} - \frac{D - d_o}{2} \geq 0 \tag{14}$$

where d_i and d_o are the inner and outer raceway diameters at the grooves. The thickness of bearing ring at outer raceway bottom should not be less than εD_b, where ε is an unknown constant. Therefore the constraint condition is

$$g_7(X) = 0.5(D - D_m - D_b) - \varepsilon D_b \geq 0 \tag{15}$$

The criteria of choosing possible values of ε is presented by Tiwari et al. in [5]. The width of bearing, w, gives constraint on the diameter of the ball and the constraint can be written as

$$g_8(X) = \beta w - D_b \geq 0 \tag{16}$$

Groove curvature radii of inner and outer raceways in a bearing should be more than $0.515D_b$. If it is less than $0.515D_b$, the dynamic load rating of the bearing declines. Therefore two more constraint conditions are given as

$$g_9(X) = f_i \geq 0.515 \tag{17}$$

$$g_{10}(X) = f_o \geq 0.515 \tag{18}$$

3   Constraint Handling

In the case of constrained optimisation problems, the concept of penalty function is a widely accepted approach. In order to determine the penalty term, a ranking method is used for handling design constraints in this study. In the ranking method, a fitness function $P(x)$ is constructed by adding the rank of the objective value and the rank of the sum of constraint violations as

$$P(x) = Rank[F_c(x)] + rank[\sum_{i=1}^{m} \{\max[0, g_i(x)]\}] \qquad (19)$$

where $Rank[F_c(x)]$ and $rank[\sum_{i=1}^{m} \{\max[0, g_i(x)]\}]$ denote the rank in descending order and the rank in ascending order, respectively. Thus, a design with higher load bearing capacity and less constraint violations will have a higher fitness value and have a higher chance to be selected. Moreover, the ranking method suggested is problem-independent and relieve the burden of choosing an appropriate value for r_p.

4 Particle Swarm Optimization Algorithm

Particle swarm optimization (PSO) is a population-based evolutionary algorithm originally presented by Kennedy and Eberhart [7, 8]. Within the problem space, each particle keeps track of its coordinates, which are associated with the best solution (fitness) it has found so far, pBest. Another "*best*" value tracked by the *global* version of the particle swarm optimizer is the overall best value, gBest, and its location, obtained so far by any particle in the population. The procedure for implementing the global version of PSO is given by the following steps [7, 8] (Fig. 2):

(i)   Initialize a population of particles with random positions and velocities in the n dimensional problem space.

(ii) Evaluate the fitness value of each particle.

(iii) Compare each particle's evaluated fitness with the current particle's pBest. If the current value is better than pBest, set its pBest value to the current value and the pBest location to the current location in n-dimensional space.

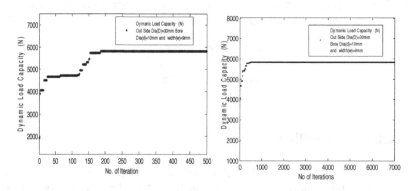

Fig. 2. Convergence characteristics of PSO

Table 1. Optimized design variables

D	d	w	D_m	D_b	Z	f_i	f_o	Φ_o	K_{Dmin}	K_{Dmax}	$\in$	e	β	C_g
30	10	9	6.20	20.05	7	0.515	0.515	3.77	0.4296	0.6482	0.3	0.0659	0.7430	5822.7
35	15	11	6.24	26.26	7	0.523	0.515	3.66	0.4371	0.6639	.0343	0.0888	0.7244	6813.5
47	20	14	8.43	35.50	8	0.515	0.515	3.61	0.4432	0.6279	0.300	0.0423	0.7453	11679.0
62	30	16	10.0	46.0	9	0.515	0.515	3.53	0.4356	0.6362	0.300	0.0577	0.7787	17484.0
80	40	18	12.5	60.9	9	0.515	0.515	3.51	0.4929	0.6628	0.300	0.0212	0.7159	26201.0
90	50	20	12.49	70	10	0.515	0.515	3.50	0.4069	0.6394	0.300	0.0656	0.7195	28159.0
110	60	22	17.04	93.70	10	0.515	0.515	3.52	0.4446	0.6961	0.331	0.0758	0.8500	49148.0
125	70	24	17.73	98.21	11	0.515	0.515	3.42	0.4333	0.6568	0.300	0.0475	0.7844	51623.0
140	80	26	18.52	121.96	11	0.515	0.515	3.50	0.4633	0.6363	0.337	0.0771	0.7276	62146.0
160	90	30	21.42	125.71	11	0.515	0.515	3.42	0.4391	0.6933	0.302	0.0715	0.8272	79015.0
170	95	32	22.75	133.59	11	0.515	0.515	3.42	0.4481	0.6499	0.300	0.0588	0.8034	88035.0

(iv) Compare the fitness evaluation with the population's overall previous best. If the current value is better than gBest, then reset gBest to the current particle's array index and value.

(v) Change the velocity and position of the particle according to:

$$v[] = v[] + c1 * rand() * (pBest[] - present[]) + \\ c2 * rand() * (gBest[] - present[]) \qquad (20)$$

$$present[] = present[] + v[] \qquad (21)$$

(vi) Loop to step (ii) until a stopping criterion is met, usually a maximum number of iterations (generations) (Table 1).

4.1 Results and Discussions

Table 2 represents the optimization results for dynamic capacity of. It can be observed that there is an improvement of dynamic capacity of bearing designed using PSO as compared to GA and catalogue. The computational time for the algorithm was 0.228 min on a Dual core- 1.8 GHz (1 GB RAM) Window 7 platform. Figure 3 shows the convergence characteristics of the algorithm. It is observed that the stable results are obtained after 183 iterations. Further it is found that increasing the nos. of iterations to very high value does not show any significant improvement in the value of objective function indicating the global optimality of the solution. In most of the reported cases the value of dynamic capacity is high.

Table 2. Comparisons of dynamic load capacity

(C_g) (PSO)	(Tiwariet al.GA) (C_d)	(Catalogue) (Cs)	$\lambda_1 = C_g/C_s$	$\lambda_2 = C_d/C_s$
5822.7	5942.36	3580	1.62	1.65
6813.5	6955.35	5870	1.16	1.18
11679.0	10890.9	9430	1.23	1.15
17484.0	16387.4	14900	1.17	1.099
26201.0	26678.4	22500	1.16	1.18
28159.0	28789.3	26900	1.04	1.07
49148.8	42695.3	40300	1.21	1.059
51623.0	51117.4	47600	1.08	1.07
62146.0	59042.9	55600	1.11	1.06
79015.0	75466.8	73900	1.06	1.02
88035.0	89244.7	83700	1.05	1.06

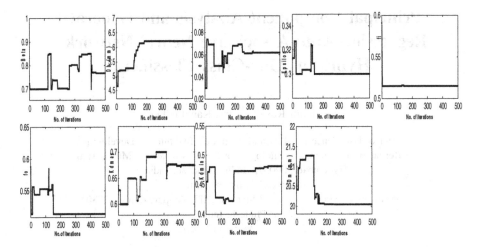

Fig. 3. Convergence characteristics of design variables

4.2   Conclusions

The PSO algorithm is used to optimize the dynamic capacity of deep groove ball bearing. The performance of the algorithm is checked with a mixed integer constrained optimization problem. The proposed PSO algorithm incorporates mixed integer variable handling and a ranked based constraint handling method. Some realistic constraints are imposed in the formulation to meet the realistic design requirement. The results indicate the superiority of the proposed PSO algorithm over other optimization algorithm.

References

1. Asimow, M.: Introduction to Engineering Design. McGraw-Hill, New York (1966)
2. Changsen, W.: Analysis of Rolling Element Bearings. Mechanical Engineering Publications Ltd., London (1991)
3. Choi, D.H., Yoon, K.C.: A design method of an automotive wheel bearing unit with discrete design variables using genetic algorithms. Trans. ASME J. Tribol. **123**(1), 181–187 (2001)
4. Chakraborthy, I., Vinay, K., Nair, S.B., Tiwari, R.: Rolling element bearing design through genetic algorithms. Eng. Optim. **35**(6), 649–659 (2003)
5. Tiwari, R., Rao, B.R.: Optimum design of rolling element bearings using genetic algorithms. Mech. Mach. Theory **42**(2), 233–250 (2007)
6. Gupta, S., Tiwari, R., Nair, B.S.: Multi-objective design optimization of rolling element bearing using genetic algorithm. Mech. Mach. Theory **42**(2), 1418–1443 (2007)
7. Kennedy, J., Eberhart R.: Particle swarm optimization. In: Proceedings of the 1995 IEEE International Conference on Neural Networks (ICNN), Perth, Australia, vol. IV, pp.1942–1948. IEEE Service Center, Piscataway (1995)
8. Kennedy, J., Eberhart R.: The particle swarm: social adaptation in information processing systems. In: Corne, D., Dorigo, M., Glover, F. (eds.) New Ideas in Optimization. McGraw-Hill, London (1999)

Principal Component Analysis and General Regression Auto Associative Neural Network Hybrid as One-Class Classifier

Vadlamani Ravi[1(✉)] and Ranabir De[2]

[1] Center of Excellence in CRM and Analytics, Institute for Development
and Research in Banking Technology, Castle Hills Road #1, Masab Tank,
Hyderabad 500057, Andhra Pradesh, India
vravi@idrbt.ac.in
[2] Departments of Mathematics and Statistics, IIT Kanpur, Kanpur 208016,
Uttar Pradesh, India
de.ranabir@gmail.com

Abstract. In this paper we develop the principal component analysis (PCA) and general regression auto associative neural network (GRAANN) based hybrid as a one-class classifier (PCA-GRAANN). We test the effectiveness of PCA-GRAANN on bankruptcy prediction datasets namely Spanish banks, Turkish banks, US banks and UK banks; UK credit dataset and the benchmark WBC dataset. When compared the results of another recently proposed hybrid, particle swarm optimization trained auto associative neural network (PSOAANN) [1], PCA-GRAANN yielded mixed results. We conclude that PCA-GRAANN can be used as a viable alternative for any one-class classifier.

Keywords: One-class classifier · Principal component analysis · General regression auto associative neural network · Credit scoring · Bankruptcy prediction

1 Introduction

Binary classification is a special case of multi-class classification. Therefore, some feed forward neural networks and logistic regression can also be employed for solving binary classification problems. However, techniques such as decision trees, support vector machine are eminently suitable for binary classification problems only. In most of the binary class classification problems one can train binary classifiers in the best possible way if there is sufficient number of samples in the positive (class of samples, where prediction is of interest) as well as the negative classes. However, in most real life problems that are binary classification problems, such as bankruptcy prediction, fraud detection, intruder detection, churn prediction, money laundering and medical diagnosis, the samples are disproportionately distributed between positive and negative classes. In such scenarios one is always interested in the positive class. But unfortunately the number of positive samples is very small in proportion to the negative class or almost missing. This phenomenon is known as data imbalance problem.

© Springer International Publishing Switzerland 2015
B.K. Panigrahi et al. (Eds.): SEMCCO 2014, LNCS 8947, pp. 164–175, 2015.
DOI: 10.1007/978-3-319-20294-5_15

When binary classifiers employed on unbalanced datasets, they predict positive class samples with very low accuracy. To overcome this difficulty of not being able to predict the positive class, some data preparation methods such as under-sampling, over-sampling etc. are mandatory. Alternatively, however, one can build one-class classifiers, which are trained on only negative class and subsequently, test them with positive class samples.

Aside from data imbalance problem, multicollinearity is another problem that plagues the multivariate datasets. Multicollinearity is a statistical phenomenon in which two or more predictor variables in a multiple regression model are highly correlated, meaning that one can be linearly predicted from the others [32]. To identify whether multicollinearity is present in the data or not, the variance inflation factor (VIF) is computed as:

$$\text{Tolerance} = 1 - R_j^2, \quad \text{VIF} = \frac{1}{\text{Tolerance}}$$

where R_j^2 is the coefficient of determination of a regression of explanatory 'j' on all the other explanators. A tolerance of less than 0.20 or 0.10 and/or a VIF of 5 or 10 and above indicates a multicollinearity problem. In this paper, we use PCA for removing multicollinearity and then feed the chosen principal components as inputs to the GRAANN and performed experiments with this one-class classifier. A good characteristic of GRAANN is that it is extremely fast in learning thereby saving a lot of time.

The remainder of the paper is organized as follows: In Sect. 2, brief description of literature review is presented. The proposed method is explained in Sect. 3. In Sect. 4, dataset description and experimental setup is presented. In Sect. 5, results and discussions are presented and finally in Sect. 6 we conclude the paper.

2 Literature Review

In the following section, we briefly review the works reported in bankruptcy prediction in banks, firms and credit scoring. Since late 1960s the bankruptcy prediction is massively researched for financial firms mainly banks [4]. Creditors, auditors, stockholders and senior management are all interested in bankruptcy prediction because it affects all of them in more or less similar manner [5]. The most efficient way of observing banks is by online examinations. These examinations are conducted within the period of every 12–18 months in banks, according to the Federal Deposit Insurance Corporation Improvement Act (1991). Six part rating system are used to identify the safety and soundness of the institution. This rating, usually known as the CAMELS rating, evaluates banks according to their basic functional areas: Capital adequacy, Asset quality, Management expertise, Earnings strength, Liquidity and Sensitivity to market risk. These ratings provide regulators with important information but Wilson and Sharda [4] reported that these CAMELS ratings decay rapidly. It is reported by Fraser [6] that banks performed better by holding relatively more securities and fewer loans.

To solve the problem of bankruptcy prediction some statistical techniques such as regression analysis, logistic regression are used. These techniques are usually used to analyze the company's financial data in order to predict the financial state of company as healthy, distressed, high probability of bankruptcy. Altman used financial ratios and multiple discriminant analysis (MDA) to predict financially distressed firms. But, the usage of statistical techniques or MDA, usually, depends on the constraint as linear separability, multivariate normality and independence of predictive variables [7–9]. But usually, most of the common financial ratios violate these assumptions. Bankruptcy prediction problem for financial firms can also be solved using various other types of classifiers. Tam proposed a backpropagation trained neural network (BPNN) for this problem and made comparison its performance with methods like as MDA, logistic regression, k-nearest neighbour (k-NN) method and ID3 [10]. He concluded that neural network performed better than other prediction techniques. Salchenberger et al. [11] find that the neural network produces fewer or equal number of classification errors for each of the forecast periods when it is compared to the logit model. This conclusion holds for total errors, type I error and type II errors. Tam and Kiang [12] observed that a neural network performed better than statistical methods and decision tree. That is why many researchers consider the neural network as a better alternative over statistical techniques for bankruptcy prediction. Atiya [13] surveyed all the prediction techniques including neural networks applied to the bankruptcy prediction problem and proposed more financial indicators, in addition to the traditions one, which he used in the design of a new neural network model. Shin et al. [14] used SVM for corporate bankruptcy prediction problem. They concluded that SVM performed better than the multi layer feed forward backpropagation (MLFF-BP) in terms of accuracy and generalization, as the training dataset size gets smaller. Canbas et al. [15] proposed a framework for constructing the integrated early warning system (IEWS) for detection of banks with serious problems. Ravikumar and Ravi [16] proposed fuzzy rule based classifier for bankruptcy prediction. They concluded that fuzzy rule based classifier outperformed the well-known technique, MLFF-BP in the case of US bank data. Ravi et al. [17] developed a semi-online training algorithm for the radial basis function neural networks (SORBF) and applied it to bankruptcy prediction in banks. Semi online RBFN without linear terms performed better than techniques such as ANFIS, SVM, MLFF-BP, RBF and Orthogonal RBF. An ensemble classifier for the bankruptcy prediction problem based on a host of intelligent techniques is proposed by Ravikumar and Ravi [18]. The ensemble classifier was developed in [19] using simple voting scheme and as part of the ensemble they employed seven classifiers such as ANFIS, SVM, RBF, SORBF1, SORBF2, Orthogonal RBF and MLFF-BP. A comprehensive review of all the statistical and intelligent techniques applied to the bankruptcy prediction problem in banks and firms was conducted by Ravikumar and Ravi [19]. Similarly, Ravi et al. [20] proposed a soft computing system for bank performance prediction. Research in credit scoring models increased rapidly in number during the past 20 years with the application of linear discriminant analysis, logistic regression (LR), decision tree, Bayes network, linear programming, backpropagation trained neural network (BPNN), support vector machines (SVM) etc. these models is the need to increase the scoring accuracy of the credit decision. Most recently, Farquad et al. [21] reviewed the existing credit scoring models and delivered a PCA-SVM hybrid for analysing the UK credit dataset. For more information, the reader is suggested to go through Farquad et al. [21].

As regards the literature on one-class classifiers, Baek and Cho [2], Pramodh and Ravi [3] and Ravi et al. [1] proposed three one-class classifiers with various auto associative neural network architectures trained by different training algorithms. All of these papers mainly concentrate to solve the bankruptcy prediction problems. Baek and Cho [2] observed that their proposed neural network outperformed a binary 2-class neural networks. Pramod and Ravi [3] developed a soft computing hybrid, wherein a global optimization meta-heuristic viz., modified great deluge algorithm (MGDA), which does point-based search, is employed to train an auto associative neural network. In Ravi et al. [1] they employed the particle swarm optimization (PSO) to train an auto associative neural network, which performs population-based search.

3 Proposed Methodology

In this paper, we propose hybrid principal component analysis and general regression auto associative neural network for one-class classification. Here, we briefly describe principal component analysis, general regression auto associative neural network and lastly the proposed hybrid as follows.

3.1 Principal Component Analysis (PCA) [22]

PCA is a traditional multivariate statistical method, mainly used for dimensionality reduction of the feature space in large data sets and it is very often used as a pre-processor to classifiers and regression techniques in data mining. It also mathematically removes the the multicollinearity present in data. It transforms linearly correlated input or predictor variables to orthogonally linearly independent input or predictor variables. The step-by-step procedure of PCA is as follows:

(i)   Let the data matrix X, comprising only predictor variables, be of order n × m, where n > m, n is the number of patterns or observations and m is the number of features. Center and scale all the features in order to standardize X. This is necessary to reduce the effect of scale and unit of measurement of predictor variables.

(ii) Then, form the matrix of squares and products of the features, namely, Z^TZ where Z is the centered and scaled version of the matrix X.

(iii) Then, the Eigen analysis of the correlation matrix of Z is carried out. The correlation matrix is obtained by dividing each entry of Z^TZ by $(n-1)$. The matrix of principal components, P, is then computed as P = Z E, where E is the matrix of order m x m, whose columns are the Eigenvectors of Z^TZ and P is the matrix of order n x m of principal components $P_1, P_2, \ldots P_m$, where P_i is an n × 1 vector, i = 1, 2,..., m.

(iv) The ratio of each of the Eigen value to the total sum of all the Eigen values indicates the proportion of variation explained by the corresponding principal component. Small Eigen values correspond to those dimensions that cause multicollinearity. A salient feature of the principal component analysis is that the Eigen values are automatically sorted in the descending order and also their corresponding Eigenvectors are rearranged accordingly. Then, the first principal component explains the maximum variance; the second principal component explains the second largest variance and so on.

For reducing the dimension of feature space by PCA, we eliminate the principal components corresponding to smaller Eigen values. For doing this, initially we pre-specify the percentage of total variation we would like to explain using the principal components. Thus, using all the principal components as new features in our subsequent analysis is equivalent to using the original features themselves, because we know that each principal component is a linear combination of the original features. In this way, the information contained in the original features is recast into a more purified form where the principal components are pair-wise orthogonal. Hence, the percentage of total variance explained is an additional parameter in this study.

3.2   General Regression Neural Network

Specht [23] first proposed GRNN. GRNN can approximate any arbitrary function from historical data. It basically performs non-parametric regression analysis. The architecture of GRNN consists of four layers namely input, pattern, summation and output layer. The input layer consists of all the input features corresponding to each data point. The pattern nodes store the input records and they are equal to input records in number. The outputs from pattern nodes are passed onto summation units. The summation unit includes a numerator summation unit and a denominator summation unit. The denominator summation unit adds up the weight values coming from each of the hidden neurons. The numerator summation unit adds up the weight values multiplied by the actual target value for each hidden neuron. The output node generates the estimated value of output by dividing the values of numerator summation unit by the denominator summation unit, and uses the result as the final estimated value.

The GRNN is a method of estimating the joint probability density function (pdf) of x and y, giving only a training set. The estimated value is the most probable value of y and is defined by

$$E(y|x)y = \hat{y}(x) = \int_{-\infty}^{+\infty} yf(x,y)dy / \int_{-\infty}^{+\infty} f(x,y)dy \tag{1}$$

The density function $f(x,y)$ can be estimated from the training set using Parzen's estimator [15].

$$f(x,y) = 1/(2\pi)^{(p+1)/2} \sigma^{(p+1)} 1/n \sum_{i=1}^{n} \exp[-(x-x^i)^T(x-x^i)/2\sigma^2]$$
$$\exp[-(y-y^i)^2/2\sigma^2] \tag{2}$$

The probability estimate $f(x,y)$ assigns a sample probability of width σ for each sample x^i and y^i, and the probability estimate is the sum of these sample probabilities [15]. Defining the scalar function D_i^2

$$D_i^2 = (x - x_i)^T (x - x_i) \tag{3}$$

and assessing the indicated integration yields the following:

$$Y(x) = \sum_{i=1}^{n} Y^i \exp(-D_i^2/2\sigma^2) / \sum_{i=1}^{n} \exp(-D_i^2/2\sigma^2) \tag{4}$$

The resulting regression (4) is directly applicable to problems involving discrete numerical data.

Unlike the multilayer perceptron (MLP), the GRNN does not require of the upfront specification of the number of hidden nodes because, it is structurally different. Further, GRNN differs from the MLP in that weights are replaced by a distribution of weights that minimizes the chance of getting entrapped in local minima.

3.3   General Regression Auto-associative Neural Networks (GRAANN)

To describe GRAANN which is proposed by Ravi and Krishna [24] in 2014, we need to briefly describe GRNN first because GRAANN is an auto-associative variant of GRNN. GRNN is extended to GRAANN in [24] by taking the input variables in the input as well as the output nodes. The process of using GRAANN is as follows:

1. Divide the dataset into two sets: a set of negative sample data and another set of positive sample data.
2. Train the GRAANN with negative sample data, using the same training algorithm of GRNN [32].
3. Lastly, use the trained GRAANN to test the positive sample data.

3.4   PCA and GRAANN Hybrid

We also proposed the hybrid PCA and GRAANN as one-class classifier. Here, we use PCAas a pre processor to take care of multicollinearity. Our proposed architecture is depicted in Fig. 1.

4   Dataset Description and Experimental Setup

In this paper, we have six classification datasets. Out of these six datasets, four are bankruptcy prediction datasets, another one is credit scoring dataset and the remaining one is benchmark WBC dataset. The banking bankruptcy datasets are Spanish, Turkish, UK and US bankruptcy. The credit scoring dataset is UK credit dataset. The remaining

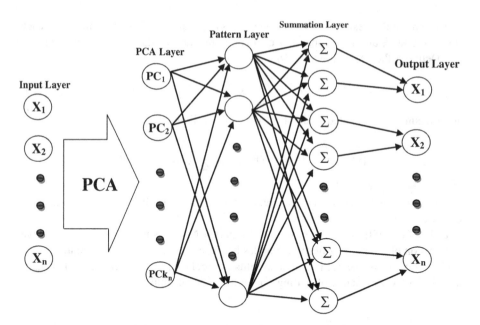

Fig. 1. Architecture of proposed PCA-GRAANN

one is benchmark Wisconsin Breast Cancer (WBC) dataset. Turkish banks' dataset is obtained from Canbas et al. [15] and it consists of 40 samples. Out of these 40 samples 22 are bankrupt and 18 are healthy. The Spanish banks' dataset is obtained from Olmeda and Fernandez [25] and it consists of 66 samples. Out of these 66 samples 37 are bankrupt and remaining 29 are healthy. The UK dataset is obtained from Rahimian et al. [26] and it consists of 60 samples. Out of these 60 samples 30 are bankrupt and remaining 30 are healthy. The US banks' data is obtained from Beynon and Peel [27] and consists of 129 samples. Out of these 129 samples 64 are bankrupt and remaining 65 are healthy. The UK credit dataset is obtained from Thomas et al. [28] and it consists of 1225 samples. Out of these 1225 samples 902 are negative samples and remaining 323 are positive samples. The benchmark dataset namely WBC is taken from UCI machine learning [29] repository and it consists of 683 samples. Out of these 683 samples 444 are malignant and remaining 239 are normal. The number of attributes and predictor variable names are shown in Table 2.

In bankruptcy datasets if a sample point represents a bankrupt bank we consider that as a positive sample data, otherwise it is a negative sample point. Also in WBC dataset if a sample point represents cancerous affected patient, that is considered positive sample, otherwise it is a negative sample.

We apply principal component analysis (PCA) to negative class samples. Then positive class data is transformed with the principal components of negative class. Here we train the network, only with the negative class data. We apply PCA on the input layer and get principal component (PC) layer. Here our idea is that the network will take the knowledge from only the negative class data. After the network is sufficiently trained, we use it for testing. For testing purpose we use only positive class data. Since it is a one-class classifier, it is expected, in the test phase, normalized root mean square error (NRMSE) would be larger compared to that of the training phase. For classifying a pattern in the test phase, relative error is computed for each of the nodes present in PC layer and output layer. We employed a threshold value for classifying the pattern as negative class or positive class. If the relative error is greater than a pre-specified threshold value for all the PC features of that pattern, then that pattern is classified to belong to positive class; otherwise, it is classified to belong to negative class. The classification rate is calculated as:

$$\text{Classification Rate} = \frac{\text{no. of patterns classified as positive}}{\text{no. of total patterns in test data}} * 100$$

5 Results and Discussions

We apply our proposed hybrid on six classification datasets viz. Turkish banks, Spanish banks, UK banks, US banks, Credit UK and WBC. Since it is a one-class classifier, the training set comprises only negative class samples (i.e. majority class), while the test set contains only positive class samples (i.e. minority class).

Then, we first apply PCA to the negative class samples. We chose the variance explained by principal components (PCs) to be at least more than 80 %. The first few PCs, which satisfy this criterion are fed as input to the GRAANN, thereby making the GRAANN learn the characteristics of the negative class. In the test phase, we selected the Eigenvectors of the selected PCs to from the input matrix for the class. We employed R statistical software [30] for implementing PCA. The dimensions of the data after applying PCA are 4, 3, 5, 4, 9 and 6 corresponding to Turkish banks, Spanish banks, UK banks, US banks, UK credit and WBC datasets respectively. We used Neuroshell [31] to implement the GRAANN. Since GRAANN is not readily available in Neuroshell we implemented multiple input multiple output (MIMO) model in GRNN and used the original input variables as output variables. In this way the GRNN transforms into GRAANN. In Neuroshell we change smoothing parameter from 0 to 1, genetic breeding pool size as 20, 50, 75, 100, 200 or 300, calibration method as genetic learning and distance metric as vanilla (Euclidean) or city block. Our threshold value used in the test phase is taken as 0.05 uniformly for all datasets.

Accuracies of the datasets are presented in Table 1. The proposed hybrid one-class classifier results are compared with that of PSOAANN [1] and GRAANN across all

Table 1. Accuracies of positive class

Datasets	GRAANN	PCA-GRAANN	PSOAANN
TURKISH	50	**94.44**	83.33
SPANISH	58.62	65.52	**93.10**
UK	56.67	**86.67**	**86.67**
US	95.38	**98.46**	**98.46**
Credit UK	80.8	67.18	**91.02**
WBC	67.36	**92.89**	91.91

Table 2. Predictor variables of the datasets

Serial number	Predictor variable name
Turkish banks' data	
1	Interest expenses/average profitable assets
2	Interest expenses/average non-profitable assets
3	(Share holders' equity + total income)/(deposits + non-deposit funds)
4	Interest income/interest expenses
5	(Share holders' equity + total income)/total assets
6	(Share holders' equity + total income)/(total assets + contingencies and commitments)
7	Networking capital/total assets
8	(Salary and employees' benefits + reserve for retirement)/no. of personnel
9	Liquid assets/(deposits + non-deposit funds)
10	Interest expenses/total expenses
11	Liquid assets/total assets
12	Standard capital ratio
Spanish banks' data	
1	Current assets/total assets
2	Current assets-cash/total assets
3	Current assets/loans
4	Reserves/loans
5	Net income/total assets
6	Net income/total equity capital
7	Net income/loans
8	Cost of sales/sales
9	Cash flow/loans
UK banks' data	
1	Sales
2	Profit before tax/capital employed (%)
3	Funds flow/total liabilities
4	(Current liabilities + long-term debit)/total assets
5	Current liabilities/total assets
6	Current assets/current liabilities
7	Current assets – stock/current liabilities
8	Current assets – current liabilities/total assets
9	LAG (number of days between account year end and the date of annual report)
10	Age
US banks' data	
1	Working capital/total assets
2	Retained earnings/total assets
3	Earnings before interest and taxes/total assets
4	Market value of equity/total assets
5	Sales/total assets

(Continued)

Table 2. (*Continued*)

Serial number	Predictor variable name
Credit UK data	
1	Year of birth
2	Number of children
3	Number of other dependents
4	Spouse's income
5	Applicant's income
6	Value of home
7	Mortgage balance outstanding
8	Outgoings on mortgage or rent
9	Outgoings on loans
10	Outgoings on hire purchase
11	Outgoings on credit cards

datasets. We notice that PCA-GRAANN outperforms the GRAANN in all datasets except Credit UK. The possible reason for its failure is that multicollinearity may not be present in this dataset since PCA as a preprocessor did not improve results. And when we compare it with PSOAANN we get better result for two datasets namely Turkish banks and WBC dataset, same for two datasets namely UK banks and US banks and worse for the remaining two namely Spanish banks and UK credit dataset. So, the proposed method yielded mixed result compared to PSOAANN. The possible reason for PSOAANN outperforming our proposed hybrid in Spanish bankruptcy and UK credit dataset, is that PCA-GRAANN consists of only one non-linear activation function namely Gaussian, whereas PSOAANN consists of two non-linear activation functions namely sigmoid in both bidden and output layers. The main advantage of our proposed hybrid is the network learns in one pass through the data thereby consuming less time than PSOAANN.

6 Conclusions

In this paper, we developed the hybrid of PCA and GRAANN as a one-class classifier. We also employed GRAANN as a one-class classifier. The performance of the proposed classifier is tested against six binary classification datasets viz. Turkish Banks, Spanish Banks, UK Banks, US Banks, Credit UK and WBC. We observed that the results yielded by the proposed classifier are mixed results when compared with the results obtained by PSOAANN. The good characteristic of our proposed classifier is that it is a one pass fast learning method and weight updation is not needed unlike PSOAANN. According to results, it can be concluded that the proposed hybrid of PCA and GRAANN as a one-class classifier is not only a simpler architecture but also sometimes achieved high accuracies. Finally, it can be also concluded that this hybrid as a one-class classifier can be used as an useful tool in classifying datasets, where the class of interest (usually the positive class) is totally missing in the training data, which is the case in many real life problems like as financial fraud detection, churn prediction, default prediction etc.

References

1. Ravi, V., Nekuri, N., Das, M.: Particle swarm optimization trained auto associative neural networks used as single class classifier. In: Panigrahi, B.K., Das, S., Suganthan, P.N., Nanda, P.K. (eds.) SEMCCO 2012. LNCS, vol. 7677, pp. 577–584. Springer, Heidelberg (2012)
2. Baek, J., Cho, S.: Bankruptcy prediction for credit risk using an auto associative neural network in Korean firms. In: The Proceedings of the CIFEr, Hong Kong (2003)
3. Pramod, C., Ravi, V.: Modified great deluge algorithm based auto-associative neural network for bankruptcy prediction. Int. J. Comput. Intell. Res. 3(4), 363–370 (2003)
4. Wilson, R.L., Sharda, R.: Bankruptcy prediction using neural networks. Decis. Support Syst. 11, 545–557 (1994)
5. Cole, R., Gunther, J.: A CAMEL rating's shelf life. In: Federal Reserve Bank of Dallas Review, 13–20 Dec 1995
6. Fraser, D.: The determinants of bank profits : an analysis of extremes. Fin. Rev. 11, 69–87 (1976)
7. Karels, G.V., Prakash, A.J.: Multivariate normality and forecasting for business bankruptcy. J. Bus. Fin. Acc. 14, 573–593 (1987)
8. Odom, M., Sharda, R.: A neural network for bankruptcy prediction. In: Proceedings of the IJCNN International Conference on Neural Networks, San Diego (1990)
9. Ohlson, J.A.: Financial rations and the probabilistic prediction of bankruptcy. J. Account. Res. 18, 109–131 (1980)
10. Tam, K.Y.: Neural network models and the prediction of bank bankruptcy. OMEGA 19, 429–445 (1991)
11. Salchenberger, L., Mine, C., Lash, N.: Neural networks : a tool for predicting thrift failures. Decis. Sci. 23, 899–916 (1992)
12. Tam, K.Y., Kiang, M.: Predicting bank failures : a neural network approach. Decis. Sci. 23, 926–947 (1992)
13. Atiya, A.F.: Bankruptcy prediction for credit risk using neural networks : a survey and new results. IEEE Trans. Neural Netw. 12, 929–935 (2001)
14. Shin, K.S., Lee, T.S., Kim, H.J.: An application of support vector machines in bankruptcy prediction model. Expert Syst. Appl. 28, 127–135 (2005)
15. Canbas, S., Caubak, A., Kilic, S.B.: Prediction of commercial bank failure via multivariate statistical analysis of financial structures : the Turkish case. Eur. J. Oper. Res. 166, 528–546 (2005)
16. Ravikumar, P., Ravi, V.: Bankruptcy prediction in banks by fuzzy rule based classifier. In: The Proceedings of 1st IEEE International Conference on Digital and Information Management, Bangalore (2006)
17. Ravi, V., Ravi Kumar, P., Ravi Srinivas, E., Kasabov, N.K.: A semi-online training algorithm for the radial basis function neural networks: applications to bankruptcy prediction in banks. In: Ravi, V. (ed.) Advances in Banking Technology and Management: Impact of ICT and CRM. Idea Group Inc., Calgary (2007)

18. Ravikumar, P., Ravi, V.: Bankruptcy prediction in banks by an ensemble classifier. In: The Proceedings of IEEE International Conference on Industrial Technology, Mumbai (2006)
19. Ravi Kumar, P., Ravi, V.: Bankruptcy prediction in banks and firms via statistical and intelligent techniques–a review. Eur. J. Oper. Res. **180**, 1–28 (2006). doi:10.1016/j.ejor.2006.08.043
20. Ravi, V., Kurniawan, H., Thai, P.N.K., Ravikumar, P.: Soft computing system for bank performance prediction. Appl. Soft Comput. J. **8**, 305–315 (2007)
21. Farquad, M.A.H., Ravi, V., Sriramjee, Praveen, G.: Credit scoring using PCA-SVM hybrid model. In: Das, V.V., Stephen, J., Chaba, Y. (eds.) CNC 2011. CCIS, vol. 142, pp. 249–253. Springer, Heidelberg (2011)
22. Rawlings, J.O.: Applied Regression Analysis: A Research Tool. Wadsworth and Brooks/Cole Statistics and Probability Series. Wadsworth Inc., Belmont (1988)
23. Specht, D.F.: A general regression neural network. IEEE Trans. Neural Netw. **2**(6), 568–576 (1991)
24. Ravi, V., Krishna, M.: A new online data imputation method based on general regression auto associative neural network. Neurocomputing **138**, 106–113 (2014)
25. Olmeda, I., Fernandez, E.: Hybrid classifiers for financial multicriteria decision making : the case of bankruptcy prediction. Comput. Econ. **10**, 317–335 (1997)
26. Rahimian, E., Singh, S., Thammachote, T., Virmani, R.: Bankruptcy prediction by Neural Network, In: Trippi, R., Turban, E. (eds.) Neural Networks in Finance and Investing. Irwin Professional publishing, Burr Ridge (1996)
27. Beynon, M.J., Peel, M.J.: Variable precision rough set theory and data discretization: an application to corporate failure prediction. Omega **29**, 561–576 (2001)
28. Thomas, L.C., Edelman, D.B., Crook, J.N.: Credit Scoring and Its Applications. SIAM, Philadelphia (2002)
29. UCI machine learning repository: http://www.ics.uci.edu/~mlearn/
30. R statistical software: http://www.r-project.org/
31. Neuroshell 2.0 software: http://www.neuroshell.com/
32. Wikipedia page of multicollinearity: http://en.wikipedia.org/wiki/Multicollinearity

Text Classification Using Ensemble Features Selection and Data Mining Techniques

B. Shravankumar[1,2] and Vadlamani Ravi[1(✉)]

[1] Centre of Excellence in CRM and Analytics, Institute for Development
and Research in Banking Technology, Castle Hills Road no 1, Masab Tank,
Hyderabad 500 057, Andhra Pradesh, India
{shravan.springer, rav_padma}@yahoo.com
[2] SCIS, University of Hyderabad, Hyderabad 500 046, Andhra Pradesh, India

Abstract. Text categorization is a task of text mining/analytics which involves extracting useful information from unstructured resources followed by categorizing these documents. In this paper, we classify the TechTC dataset collected from various Web directories. We employed feature selection methods such as Gini index, chi-square, t-statistic, correlation which drastically reduced the model building time. Various neural network models such as probabilistic neural network, group method of data handling, multi layer perceptron yielded higher accuracies compared to other techniques applied in literature.

Keywords: Text mining · Document classification · Feature selection · Classification models

1 Introduction

Real world is replete with textual information and hence text mining [20, 21] is believed to have a commercial potential higher than that of data mining. In fact, a recent study indicated that 80 % of a company's information is contained in text documents. Text mining, however, is also a much more complex task (than data mining) as it involves dealing with text data that are inherently unstructured and sometimes fuzzy. Text mining is a multidisciplinary field, involving information retrieval, text analysis, information extraction, clustering, categorization, visualization, database technology, machine learning, and data mining [35]. Text mining have several applications like Document classification [1], clustering, Email classification [36], phishing email detection [3], cyber fraud detection, malware detection [4], Phishing Websites detection [5], Plagiarism detection [31] and social network analysis [26, 34], Association rules extraction [27], Intelligence Analysis [32], Customer Relationship Management [33].

2 Literature Review

The process of Text mining mainly involves two phases. First phase is the Text preprocessing phase that transforms free-form text documents into an intermediate form i.e. each text document is represented as a vector of words, it is typically done in the popular vector representation for information retrieval [29] and the second phase is

© Springer International Publishing Switzerland 2015
B.K. Panigrahi et al. (Eds.): SEMCCO 2014, LNCS 8947, pp. 176–186, 2015.
DOI: 10.1007/978-3-319-20294-5_16

the knowledge distillation phase that deduces patterns or knowledge from the intermediate form [37]. The intermediate forms are of varying degrees of complexity are suitable for different mining purposes.

There are various text mining products and applications [22] adopted depending on the various text refining and knowledge distillation functions as well as the flavor of intermediate form adopted. Based on the constraints of the needed application, we choose the appropriate representation [38].

Let D be the domain of document database and d_j represent the ith document in the database. Let $c = (c_1, c_2, ..., c_n)$ be the set of predefined classes. Text classification can be defined as the task of assigning a Boolean value to each pair (d_j, c_i) of document database D. Classification of documents is accomplished on the basis of previous knowledge. Different constraints must be enforced on the text classification task of which a special case is binary classification [19] where each document belongs to either class 0 or 1. Binary classification problems occur in a variety of applications like spam filtering, churn prediction, bankruptcy prediction, phishing mail and website detection, intrusion detection etc.

The focal point of text mining is feature selection because the number of tokens or features is very large in any text corpus. The number of potential words often exceeds the number of documents by orders of magnitude. Feature selection is necessary to make large problems computationally efficient-conserving computation, storage and network resources for the training phase and for every future use of the classifier. Further, well-chosen features can improve classification accuracy substantially and reduce the amount of training data needed to obtain a desired level of performance. Effective feature selection is essential [23] to make the learning task efficient and more accurate.

Various statistical and machine learning techniques have been applied to text categorization [28]. Support Vector Machines (SVM) are used for the purpose text categorization primarily by Joachims [30].

3 Proposed Methodology

Text preprocessing primarily concerns conversion of unstructured data into structured data and involves tokenization, stop words removal, stemming (porter). After completion of the preprocessing step, each unique word forms a token or a feature in the data. Based on these features, we what is known as document-term matrix. There are different ways of constructing this matrix. One can simply consider the presence or absence of features in a given document and represent them by 1 and 0 respectively in the matrix. Other ways include presenting their frequencies of occurrences, their tf-idf values and so on. In this paper, we extract features from a set of unstructured text documents, perform feature selection and then invoke classifiers in that order on document term matrix. The overview of proposed method is depicted in Fig. 1.

In this study, we generated the Boolean Vector Matrix also called as Binary Document Term Matrix. Each row represents a document and each column represents a distinct word or feature. An entry of '1' in the column denotes the presence of the word in the document and '0' denotes its absence. There are various text mining tools available and we used open source tool Rapid Miner [7] for Text Preprocessing as well as classification and KNIME [8], Neuroshell [9] for classification.

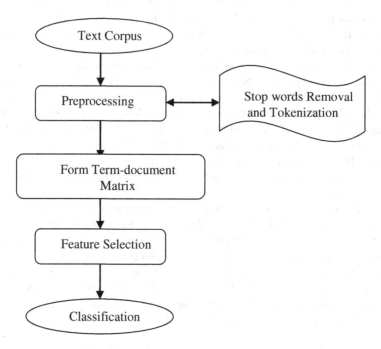

Fig. 1. Text document classification process

3.1 Feature Selection Methods

Feature selection serves two main purposes. First, it makes training and the process of applying a classifier more efficient by decreasing the size of the effective vocabulary. Second, feature selection often increases classification accuracy by eliminating noisy features [25].

In this study, we have used the following feature selection methods: (i) t-statistic (ii) Gini Index (iii) Chi-square (iv) Correlation

3.1.1 t-Statistic

Using this method, we computed t-statistic [18] values for each feature as follows:

$$t = \frac{|\mu_1 - \mu_2|}{\sqrt{\frac{\sigma_1^2}{n_1} + \frac{\sigma_2^2}{n_2}}}$$

where μ_1 and μ_2 represent the mean values of a feature for two different classes, σ_1 and σ_2 represent the corresponding standard deviations for each class and n_1 and n_2 represent number of samples in each class.

Accordingly, t values are computed for each feature. The features which have higher t-statistic value have more discriminative power compared to other features. Therefore, we can sort the features in the descending order of the t-statistic value and select as many features as we want from the top.

3.1.2 Gini Index

It is a measure of impurity of an Example Set [16]. The higher the weight of an attribute, the more relevant it is considered. Gini Index is an impurity based criterion that measures the divergence between probability distributions of the target attribute's values. It has been used in various works such as Breiman [24].

$$\text{Gini Index} = 1 - \sum p_i^2$$

3.1.3 Chi-square

The chi-squared distribution [17] has numerous applications in inferential statistics, for instance in chi-squared tests and in estimating variances. It estimates the mean of a normally distributed population and of estimating the slope of a regression line. The chi-squared distribution with k degrees of freedom is the distribution of a sum of the squares of k independent standard normal random variables.

$$\chi^2(f_i) = \sum_{i \in \{0,1\}} \sum_{j \in \{0,1\}} \frac{(v_{ij} - e_{ij})^2}{e_{ij}}$$

where

$$e_{ij} = \frac{\sum_{l \in \{0,1\}} v_{il} \sum_{l \in \{0,1\}} v_{lj}}{n}$$

Here v_{ij} indicates value of the number of examples from class c_i having feature value f_j, the number of examples from class c_1 is n_1 and that from class c_0 is n_0 and total number of examples is n.

3.1.4 Correlation

It calculates the weight of attributes with respect to the label attribute by using correlation. The higher the weight of an attribute, the more relevant it is considered. A correlation is a number between -1 and $+1$ that measures the degree of association between two attributes [43]. A positive value for the correlation implies a positive association and negative value for the correlation implies a negative or inverse association. It is calculated as follows.

$$Correl(x, y) = \frac{1}{n-1} \sum_{i=1}^{n} \frac{(x_i - \bar{x}_i)}{\sigma_{x_i}} * \frac{(y_i - \bar{y}_i)}{\sigma_{y_i}}$$

where x and y are two attributes, with means $\bar{x}_i, \bar{y}_i$ and $\sigma_{x_i}, \sigma_{y_i}$ are standard deviations of x, y respectively.

3.2   Overview of Techniques Used

3.2.1   Support Vector Machine (SVM)

It is the one of the most effective types of learners for text classification [11]. It builds a classifier that maximizes the margin (i.e., the minimum distance between the hyper plane that represents the classifier and the vectors that represent the documents). Different functions for measuring this distance (kernels) can be plugged in and out; when nonlinear kernels are used, this corresponds to mapping the original vector space into a higher dimensional vector space in which the separation between the examples belonging to different categories may be accounted more easily.

3.2.2   Decision Tree (DT)

One of the supervised learning technique [10] used for classification task. In this root node is the decision variable where as the leaf node is the class variable. We chose the root node based on Information gain or Gini index value.

3.2.3   Multi Layer Perceptron (MLP)

A popular common neural network model is Multi Layer Perceptron, It is a feed forward artificial neural network model that maps sets of input data onto a set of appropriate outputs. it consists a input, hidden, and output layer in its model. The hidden layer provides a means of explaining the nonlinearity in a dataset. Before any data has been run through the network, the weights connecting the nodes are initialized randomly. MLP uses a standard back propagation algorithm in their feed forward network. MLP trains its nodes with a desired response [12]. They learn how to transform input data into a desired response, so they are widely used for pattern classification and prediction. They have been shown to approximate the performance of accurate predictions in difficult problems.

3.2.4   Group Method of Data Handling (GMDH)

GMDH, a family of inductive algorithms for mathematical modeling of multi-parametric datasets that features fully automatic structural and parametric optimization of models [13]. GMDH can find relations in data to build a polynomial equation so that it can be used as a classifier and is different from commonly used deductive modeling. A GMDH model with multiple inputs and one output is a subset of components of the base function, as in

$$Y(x_1, x_2, \ldots, x_n) = a_0 + \sum_{i=1}^{n} a_i * f_i$$

where, f_i are elementary functions dependent on different sets of inputs, a_i are the coefficients and m is the number of the base function components. GMDH algorithm considers various component subsets of the base function called partial models and the coefficients of these models are estimated by the least squares method. The number of partial model components is gradually increased to find a model structure with optimal complexity indicated by the minimum value of an external criterion. This process is called self-organization of models [14].

3.2.5 Probabilistic Neural Network (PNN)

A probabilistic neural network (PNN) is a feed forward neural network, which was derived from the Bayesian network and a statistical algorithm called Kernel Fisher discriminate analysis. It was introduced by Specht in 1991 [15]. In a PNN, the operations are organized into a multilayered feed forward network with four layers. Input layer, Hidden layer, Pattern layer/Summation layer, Output layer.

3.2.6 K-nearest Neighbor (KNN)

K-Nearest Neighbor (KNN) classification [39], finds a group of k objects in the training set that are closest to the test object. To classify an unlabeled object, the distance of this object to the labeled objects is computed, its k-nearest neighbors are identified, and the class labels of these nearest neighbors are then used to determine the class label of the object. Given a training set D and a test object $z = (x', y')$, the algorithm computes the distance (or similarity) between z and all the training objects$(x, y) \in D$ to determine its nearest-neighbor list, D_z. (x is the data of a training object, while y is its class. Likewise, x' is the data of the test object and y' is its class.) Once the nearest-neighbor list is obtained, the test object is classified based on the majority class of its nearest neighbors.

$$\text{Majority Voting} \, y' = \arg mavx \sum_{(x_i, y_i) \in D_z} I(v = y_i)$$

where v is a class label, y_i is the class label for the ith nearest neighbors, and $I(.)$ is an indicator function that returns the value 1 if its argument is true and 0 otherwise.

3.2.7 Naive Bayes (NB)

It is one of the important classification methods also called simple Bayes [40]. It is a very old techniques and too popular to be described here. Interested readers are referred to [40, 41].

3.2.8 Repeated Incremental Pruning to Produce Error
Reduction (RIPPER)

Repeated Incremental Pruning to Produce Error Reduction (RIPPER), proposed by William [42] is a propositional rule learner, It builds a rule set using sequential covering algorithm. First it finds the best rule that covers the current set of positive examples and then eliminates both positive and negative examples covered by the rule. Each time a rule is added to the rule set, it computes the new description length and stops adding new rules when the new description length is 'd' bits longer than the smallest description length obtained so far.

4 Experimental Setup

4.1 Dataset Description

We obtained the dataset from TechTC Repository [6] available in public domain. These are acquired as part of the Open Directory Project. The TechTC Collection contains 100 labeled datasets i.e. each set contains positive and negative categories. We combined all negative documents as one group and reaming all others as one group.

4.2 Experimental Procedure

There are various text mining tools available we used open source tool RapidMiner [7] for Text Preprocessing and KNIME [8], Neuroshell [9], RapidMiner for classification. In order to apply data mining techniques we computed the binary document term matrix with Rapid Miner, an open source tool. We employed KNIME for the classification purpose involving DT, SVM, and KNN, RapidMiner for RIPPER, NB while we employed Neuroshell for GMDH and PNN, MLP. Using Rapid Miner we generate the 13725 unique features. For finding out the ensemble of features, we applied four feature selection methods such as t-statistic, Correlation, Gini index and Chi-square. Then we considered top 0.5 % features (for comparative study) with Binary Document Term Matrix and performed classification task. We repeated the same procedure for top 0.1 % features also. Throughout the paper, we performed 10 Fold Cross Validation (10 FCV) for all the classifiers and reported the average accuracies in Table 2. The Accuracy is computed as follows:

$$Accuracy = \frac{TP + TN}{TP + FN + TN + FP}$$

where TP = True Positive, TN = True Negative, FP = False positive, FN = False Negative.

5 Results and Discussions

The Features extracted by the text preprocessing stage of text mining process are having high dimensionality. To reduce the model building time and speeding up the evaluation process, we condense the number of features obtained by identifying the most discriminative features using various feature selection methods. In all these feature selection strategies we considered top 0.1 % features (i.e., top-15 features) as well as top 0.5 % features (i.e., top-69 features) and conducted various experiments.

It was quite interesting to observe that all the top-15 as well as top-69 features obtained by various features selection strategies were all identical. This shows all the features obtained by the feature selection process are very reliable in identifying the appropriate class and showcases the trustworthiness of these feature selection strategies.

The results obtained through Neural Network Models and RIPPER are good compared to other various models. We obtained higher levels of accuracy with these models in this binary classification task of collating various website data. The top-15 (corresponding to the 0.1 % of the features) and top-69 (corresponding to the 0.5 % of the features) features obtained by t-statistic, correlation, Gini-index and chi-square feature selection strategies turned out to be identical are presented in Table 1. The

Table 1. Feature subset selection of various feature selection methods.

Top 0.1 % features				
Behavior	Freshman	Riser	Evict	Enrol
Jordan	Digest	Saskatchewan	Bacon	Damp
Spike	Uplift	Spinner	Fulton	Shame
Top 0.5 % features				
Behavior	Shame	Ditch	Fellow	Sander
Freshman	Matthew	Bulgaria	Sorbet	Abel
Riser	Government	Oneida	Rondo	Infract
Evict	Toilet	Tequila	Spar	Alhambra
Enroll	Pill	Undertake	Punch	Coarse
Jordan	Veteran	Berg	Damn	Hyphen
Digest	Compress	Pitt	Midwestern	Newsprint
Saskatchewan	Bouncer	Sixteen	Squeal	Tonsil
Bacon	Rede	Reject	Tart	Princeton
Damp	Robertson	Gradual	Thriller	Plow
Spike	Heirloom	Polio	Tenderloin	Wick
Uplift	Wheeler	Bylaw	Laptop	Cello
Spinner	Eucharist	Former	Warn	Detour
Fulton	Symptom	Panther	Junk	

Table 2. Average accuracy of models using top 0.5 % and top 0.1 % of the original features

Method	Gabrilovich et al. [2] (with 0.5 % features)	Our result (with 0.5 % features)	Our Result (with 0.1 % features)
KNN	82.7	80.5	72.56
DT	84.3	81.5	79.2
SVM	85.3	76	82.5
MLP	NA	88*	87*
GMDH	NA	94.5*	93*
PNN	NA	91*	92*
RIPPER	NA	87*	85.5*
NB	NA	80	79

*Best accuracy in three NN architectures and RIPPER

Table 3. Statistical significance between various models

Models	t-test value (0.5 % features)	t-test value (0.1 % features)
GMDH - MLP	2.276	1.819
MLP - PNN	0.871	1.539
GMDH - PNN	1.291	0.397
RIPPER - MLP	0.212	0.621
RIPPER - GMDH	2.812	2.628
PNN - RIPPER	1.301	2.361

Table 4. Statistical significance of models on feature subset selection

Models	t-test value
MLP - MLP	0.31625
GMDH - GMDH	0.61667
PNN - PNN	0.57988
RIPPER - RIPPER	0.49319

Table 2 presents the accuracies of different models such as KNN, DT, SVM, RIPPER, NB, MLP, GMDH, PNN. Out of all the approaches, GMDH produced highest accuracy of 94.5 % with top- 69 features followed by GMDH and PNN with top-15 features.

In order to validate the worthiness of the results obtained by various models, we have performed t-test between various models and are presented in Table 3. It can be observed that all t-test values between various models are below 2.83, which is t-test value at 1 % level of significance and 18 degrees of freedom $(10 + 10 - 2 = 18)$. Furthermore, we have performed t-test across various models between Top 0.1 % and Top 0.5 % feature subset sizes. It can be clearly observed from Table 4 that all the t-test values are below the acceptable value of 2.83 and hence these values once again statistically prove our models.

6 Conclusion

We proposed a method involving four feature selection methods viz., t-statistic, correlation, Gini index and Chi-Square followed by KNN/DT/SVM/RIPPER/ NB/MLP/GMDH/PNN for text document classification. We built the models with 0.5 % and 0.1 % features. Based on the t-test values between datasets with 0.5 % features and 0.1 % features, we can observe that there is not much statistical difference between these results. Therefore, we conclude the results obtained by 0.1 % features should be recommended for further analysis, because of the less number of features. Further, since PNN is found not to be statistically significantly different from other NN models, thereby forcing us to recommend it owing to its fast learning.

References

1. Chinta, P.M., Murty, M.N.: Discriminative feature analysis and selection for document classification. In: Huang, T., Zeng, Z., Li, C., Leung, C.S. (eds.) ICONIP 2012, Part I. LNCS, vol. 7663, pp. 366–374. Springer, Heidelberg (2012)
2. Gabrilovich, E., Markovitch, S.: Text categorization with many redundant features: using aggressive feature selection to make SVMs competitive with C4.5. In: The 21st International Conference on Machine Learning (ICML), pp. 321–328, Banff, Alberta, Canada (2004)
3. Pandey, M., Ravi, V.: Detecting phishing emails using text and data mining. In: The Proceedings of International Conference on Computational Intelligence and Computing Research (ICCIC, 2012), pp. 249–254, Coimbatore, India (2012)
4. Sundarkumar, G.G., Ravi, V.: Malware detection by text and data mining. In: The Proceedings of International Conference on Computational Intelligence and Computing Research (ICCIC) (2013)
5. Pandey, M., Ravi, V.: Text and data mining to detect phishing websites and spam emails. SEMCCO 2, 559–573 (2013)
6. http://www.techtc.cs.technion.ac.il/techtc.html#plain_text
7. http://rapid-i.com
8. http://www.knime.org
9. http://www.neuroshell.com
10. Quinlan, J.R.: Simplifying decision trees. Int. J. Man Mach. Stud. 27(3), 221–234 (1987)
11. Joachims, T.: Text categorization with support vector machines: learning with many relevant features. LS8-Report 23, Universität Dortmund (LS VIII-Report) (1997)
12. Rosenblatt, F.: Principles of Neurodynamics: Perceptrons and the Theory of Brain Mechanisms. Spartan Books, Washington, D.C. (1961)
13. Ivakhnenko, A.G.: Heuristic self-organization in problems of engineering cybernetics. Automatica 6, 207–219 (1970)
14. Ivakhnenko, A.G.: Polynomial theory of complex system. IEEE Trans. Syst. Man Cybern. SMC-1(4):364–378 (1971)
15. Specht, D.F.: Probabilistic neural networks. Neural Netw. 3, 109–118 (1990)
16. Gini, C.: Variability and Mutability, 156 p. C. Cuppini, Bologna (1912)
17. Helmert, F.R.: Mathematical and Physical Theories of Higher Geodesy, vol. 1. B. G. Teubner, Leipzig (1964)
18. Pearson, E.S.: Student - A Statistical Biography of William Sealy Gosset. Oxford University Press, Oxford (1990)
19. Sebastiani, F.: Machine learning in automated text categorization. ACM Comput. Surv. 34 (1), 1–4 (2002)
20. Feldman, R., Dagan, I.: Knowledge discovery in textual databases. In: Proceedings of the First International Conference on Knowledge Discovery and Data Mining, KDD-95, pp. 112–117. Montreal, Canada, 20–21 Aug 1995
21. Fayyad, U., Piatetsky-Shapiro, G., Smyth, P., Uthurusamy, R. (eds.): From data mining to knowledge discovery: an overview. In: Advances in Knowledge Discovery and Data Mining, pp. 1–36. MIT Press, Cambridge (1996)
22. Tan, A.H.: Text mining: the state of the art and the challenges. In: Proceedings of the PAKDD-99 Workshop on Knowledge Discovery from Advanced Databases (1999)
23. Forman, G.: An extensive empirical study of feature selection metrics for text classification. J. Mach. Learn. Res. 3, 1289–1305 (2003)
24. Breiman, L.: Classification and Regression Trees. Chapman & Hall/CRC, London (1984)
25. http://nlp.stanford.edu/IR-book/html/htmledition/feature-selection-1.html

26. He, W., Zha, S., Li, L.: Social media competitive analysis and text mining: a case study in the pizza industry. Int. J. Inf. Manage. **33**(3), 464–472 (2013)
27. Holt, J.D., Chung, S.M.: Efficient of mining rules in text databases. In: Eighth International Conference on Information and Knowledge Management, CIKM-99, pp. 234–242. ACM, New York, NY, USA (1999)
28. Dumais, S., Platt, J., Heckerman, D., Sahami, M.: Inductive learning algorithms and representations for text categorization. In: Seventh International Conference on Information and Knowledge Management, CIKM-98, pp. 148–155. ACM, New York, NY, USA (1998)
29. Salton, G., McGill, M.J.: Introduction to Modern Information Retrieval. McGraw-Hill Inc., New York (1986)
30. Joachims, T.: Text Categorization with support vector machines: learning with many relevant features. In: Proceedings of 10th European Conference on Machine Learning (ECML-98), pp. 137–142 (1998)
31. Brin, S., Davis, J., Garcia-Molina, H.: Copy Detection mechanisms for digital documents. In: SIGMOD'95, Proceedings of the International conference on Management of data, pp. 398–409 (1995)
32. Mena, J.: Investigative Data Mining for Security and Criminal Detection. Elsevier Science, Burlington (2003)
33. Zanasi, A.: Text Mining and Its Applications to Intelligence. CRM and Knowledge Management, WIT Press, Southampton, Boston (2007)
34. Aggarwal, C.C., Wang, H.: Text Mining in Social Networks, Social Network Data Analytics, pp. 353–378. Springer, New York (2011)
35. Feldman, R., Sanger, J.: The Text Mining Handbook: Advanced Approaches in Analyzing Unstructured Data. Cambridge Press, Cambridge (2007)
36. Klimt, B., Yang, Y.: The Enron corpus: a new dataset for email classification research. ECML **2004**, 217–226 (2004)
37. Manning, C.D., Raghavan, P., Schutze, H.: An Introduction to Information Retrieval. Cambridge University Press, Cambridge (2008)
38. Salton, G., Buckley, C.: Term-weighting approaches in text retrieval. Inf. Process. Manage. **24**(5), 513–523 (1988)
39. Steinbach, M., Kumar, V.: Introduction to data mining. Pearson Addison-Wesley, Boston (2006)
40. Domingos, P., Pazzani, M.: On the optimality of the simple Bayesian classifier under zero-one loss. Mach. Learn. **29**, 103–130 (1997)
41. Wu, X., Kumar, V., Ross Quinlan, J., Ghosh, J.: Top 10 algorithms in data mining. Knowl. Inf. Syst. **14**, 1–37 (2008)
42. Cohen, W.W.: Fast effective rule induction. In: Proceedings of the Twelfth International Conference on Machine Learning, vol. 12 (1995)
43. Kenney, D.A.: Correlation and Causality. Wiley (1979)

Solving University Examination Timetabling Problem Using Intelligent Water Drops Algorithm

Bashar A. Aldeeb[1]($\boxtimes$), Norita Md Norwawi[1], Mohammed A. Al-Betar[2], and Mohd Zalisham Bin Jali[1]

[1] Faculty of Science and Technology, Universiti Sains Islam Malaysia,
71800 Nilai, Negeri Sembilan, Malaysia
bashar_deeb@hotmail.com
[2] Department of Information Technology, Al-Huson University College,
Al-Balqa Applied University, P.O. Box 50, Al-Huson, Irbid, Jordan

Abstract. This research article aims at proposing Intelligent Water Drops (IWD) algorithm to solve the university examination timetabling problems (UETP). IWD is a recent metaheuristic population-based algorithm belonging to swarm intelligent category which simulate river system. Examination timetabling is a combinatorial optimization problem that is concerned with allocating exams to timeslots efficiently. As an initial study, the IWD Algorithm is tailored to solve uncapacitated examination timetabling problem by using carter 1996 dataset and is able to produce acceptable results, though they were not better than the the results that already reported in the literature. Some examination timetabling heuristic methods such as Saturation degree concepts have been embedded in IWD to ensure the feasibility, while the IWD operators have been trigged to iteratively improve the results...

Keywords: Uncapacitated examination timetabling problem · Scheduling · Intelligent water drops algorithm

1 Introduction

Usually, construction of examination timetable follows a manually based repetition process applied in high schools, colleges and universities throughout the world which do not meet the standards of the students and lecturers. As the process requires an intricate detail with extensive efforts, the construction of a timetable can be an extremely complex task for the managers and administrators. Hence, resolving the examination timetabling issues lead to a quality based timetable that give a significant impact on the quality of the associated institutions [10].

Examination timetabling problem is defined as an allocating of exams into a restricted number of timeslots, while satisfying the maximum number of stipulations which contrast greatly across institutions. The problems of examination

© Springer International Publishing Switzerland 2015
B.K. Panigrahi et al. (Eds.): SEMCCO 2014, LNCS 8947, pp. 187–200, 2015.
DOI: 10.1007/978-3-319-20294-5_17

timetabling therefore vary in their size, complexity and constraints [12]. From the timetabling literature, two classes of constraints exists namely hard constraints and soft constraints [9,10].

Hard constraints are those which under no circumstance can they be violated. For example:

- In one timeslot, Two exams can't be planned once a number of common students are sitting for the exam.
- The number of students sitting for the exams should not surpass that of available seats.

Soft constraints are not the fundamentals rather to be reasonably fulfilled. It is usual not to find a viable solution that compliments them differently from one institution to another regarding its, importance and types. Soft constraints conflict with each other now and again, for instance:

- It is better to split clashing Exams throughout the examination session in dodging successive exams timeslots or two exams on the same day.
- The earliest possible scheduling of Exams esteemed to have majority of the students, should be done to permit adequate time for marking.
- Fulfilling the priority of exams is necessary.

A feasible timetable is defined as a solution to examination timetabling which does not discredit the hard constraint. There is a level of difficulty in determining issues concerning timetabling, where there might be need to set aside a percentage of the soft constraints as it is almost impossible not to ruin these constraints in producing results. Subsequently, they are precluded from the objective function [6].

The problem of examination timetabling may be capacitated or Uncapacitated. the problem of Uncapacitated examination timetabling doesn't consider room capacities whereas the problem of capacitated examination timetabling must contain Hard constraint such that the student number distributed to a particular room during a scheduled time period does not exceed the capacity of the room [11]. This paper emphasizes the problem of Uncapacitated Examination timetabling.

The central research of Uncapacitated Examination timetabling Problem was primarily introduced by Carter (1996) by incorporating a number of graph coloring heuristic techniques to Uncapacitated Examination timetabling Problem [9]. different studies fusing graph coloring heuristic methods for Uncapacitated Examination timetabling Problem are additionally included [3,8].

Numerous meta-heuristic approaches have been created to solve UETP , grouped into two major types, single-based approaches (e.g., great deluge, simulated annealing, tabu search and variable neighborhood search) and population-based approaches (e.g., ant colony optimization, memetic algorithms and genetic algorithms) [12]. The papers [7,9,14] have carried out surveys on several algorithmic methodologies adapted to answer timetabling problems until the end of 1990s, took over by other survey papers that [12]. Various researchers have demonstrated enthusiasm on single-based approaches resulting from approaches' capacity to use the search space within a minimal duration, despite the limitations these approaches are reported with such as being not difficult to get caught up in local optima [12].

In light of the algorithms, population-based approaches can be grouped into either Swarm Intelligence or Evolutionary Algorithms [1] relying upon the nature of the phenomenon modeled by the algorithm. The original Evolutionary Algorithms have been sought for timetabling issues can be obtained in the subsequent literature [5]. Dependence on the agreeable conduct of self organized frameworks in securing meta-heuristics that copy such a framework's critical thinking is identifiable to Swarm Intelligence [5]. In 2007, Shah (2007) investigated making calculations that model the regular phenomena of a swarm of water drops with the dirt onto the stream bunk of the river [15].

In this paper, the main aim is to investigate the applicability of IWDs algorithm for examination timetabling as an initial exploration of this method in scheduling domain. Albeit the results were not extended, the state-of-the-art methods, potential enhancement can be assumed in the future research to twist the IWD operators, therefore delivering more fruitful results.

2   Intelligent Water Drops in Nature

Water drops are watched to flow naturally in rivers creating massive moving swarms in which the water drops create the path of the movement. The environment significantly influences thishis phenomena that results in the water drops paths being changed slowly and continuously as the case for the future. It is in rivers that massive moving swarms formed by the following water drops are naturally spotted. An example is that of the hard soils environment resisting more than the soft soils. Thus, the the natural river phenomenon occurrence is depend on the frequent rivalry of the water drops in a swarm and the resistance of its surrounding water drops environment [16].

The majority of the rivers watched take after a wound way with different turns which regularly direct the water drops to its destination, normally a lake or ocean. The imagination of this nature is exemplified from the pull that we experience towards earth's gravity as is the case with a water drop flowing in a river. The water drops do not face any obstacle in its paths, therefore having an influence from its environment, it is forced to drift to its surrounding matters through a straight line by means of the shortest path leading to the center of the earth [17].

Velocity is the major characteristic to the flow of water drop. By expecting that each water drop conveys a proportion of soil, it is transferred starting with one spot then onto the next for the most part from the quick path to the slow path. A deeper indent is created as the removed soils are washed out from the fast path, which attracts more water to be formed in that area. This causes the soil removed to be carried by the water drops being piled in the slower beds of the river. Such a presumption fuses the natural water drop flow from one destination in the river to the next while considering three significant changes throughout the transition:

- Increased velocity of the water drop.
- Increased soil of the water drop.
- Decreased soil of the river's bed between the two points.

All through the course of its journey, an IWD gathers the Soil in environment and draws it out from the way interfacing its two focuses. There is a non linear inverse relationship between the amount of the Soil added to the IWD to the inverse of the time required for the IWD to flow from its current point to the other. As per the laws of physical science for direct movement, the time interim is ascertained as corresponding to the speed of the IWD and contrarily relative to the separation between the two points. Moreover, the segment of the environment that uses more IWDs will have fewersoil. It could be found that the soil is the hotspot for the information acquired as nature's domain and water drops are both interrelated to the soil [18].

Additionally, in view of the study carried out by Shah [17], that an IWD needs a tool to choose the path of its next point. Because of this nature, the IWD naturally prefers the paths with less soil rather than more soil. This path selection characteristic is used by imposing a uniform random distribution on the soils of the available paths bringing about the likelihood of the following path to be picked in a conversely proportional way to the soils of the available paths. in this manner, recognising the paths with less soil has an increased chance to be chosen by the IWD [18].

3 Problem Description

3.1 Problem Definition

The Uncapacitated Examination timetabling Problem variation in this study is emphasized on allotting a set of exams, each taken by a set of students, to a set of timeslots with determined hard (H1) and soft constraint (S1). The hard and soft constraints are shown in Table 1.

Table 1. The uncapacitated examination timetabling problem Constraints

Constraint Type	Description
Soft constraint	S_1 Conflicting exams whereby students cannot sit for two exams at the same timeslot.
Hard constraint	H_1 Exams spread out whereby the exams taken by the same student should be spread out across a timetable.

In Uncapacitated Examination timetabling Problem, the aim is to minimize the proximity cost function of soft constraint violation in a feasible timetable. The proximity cost function divides the penalty of soft constraint violations by the total number of students. The next section will describe this function formally [2].

3.2 Problem Formulation

Table 2 shows the notation for Uncapacitated Examination timetabling Problem formulation. A timetable solution is represented by a vector $x = (x_i)_M$, where x_i is timeslot assigned to exam i, where $i = \{1, 2, ..., M\}$). The proximity cost function for The Uncapacitated Examination timetabling Problem is formulated in Eq. 1

$$\min f(x) = \frac{\sum_{i=1}^{M-1} \sum_{j=i+1}^{M} c_{i,j} \times prox_{i,j}}{N} \qquad (1)$$

where $c_{i,j}$ element contains the total number of students sharing exam i and exam j, $prox_{i,j}$ element contains the penalty value made based on the distance between exam i and exam j. This provides the quality of a solution in terms of how well the exams are spread. Note that the Hard constraint $H1$ must be satisfied in the timetable such that:

$$x_i \neq x_j, \forall x_i \in \mathbf{x} \wedge C_{i,j} \geq 1$$

The value of the proximity cost function $f(x)$ is referred as the Penalty Value (PV) of a feasible timetable.

Table 2. The notations used in the UUETP formulations

Symbols	Definition
P	The total number of timeslots.
N	The total number of students.
M	The total number of exams.
T	Set of timeslots $T = \{1, 2, ..., P\}$.
S	Set of students $S = \{1, 2, ..., N\}$.
E	Set of exams $E = \{1, 2, ..., M\}$.
x	A timetable solution is given by $x = (x_i)_M$, where $i = \{1, 2, ..., M\}$.
x_i	The timeslot of exam i.
$prox_{i,j}$	Proximity coefficient matrix element: whether the timetable x is penalized based on the distance between time-period of exam i in time-period of exam j. where $$prox_{i,j} = \begin{cases} 2^{5-|x_i-x_j|} & if 1 \leq |x_i - x_j| \leq 5 \\ 0 & otherwise. \end{cases}$$
$u_{i,j}$	Student exam matrix element: whether student S_i is sitting for exam j $$u_{i,j} = \begin{cases} 1 & if x_i = x_j \\ 0 & otherwise. \end{cases}$$
$c_{i,j}$	Conflict matrix element: total number of students sharing exam i and exam j. $c_{i,j} = \sum_{k=1}^{N} u_{k,i} \times u_{k,j}$ $\forall_{i,j} \in E$

4 Intelligent Water Drops Algorithm (IWDA) for UUETP

The IWD algorithm shows in Algorithm 1 and the Fig. 1 for UUETP is presented using a graph $G = (V, E)$ where V is the total number of exams (nodes) to be scheduled, and E represents the adjacent exams between each two conflicted exams, Note that the conventional examination timetabling can be represented as a graph coloring model. In graph coloring, the examination timetabling solution is represented as a graph of V nodes and the edge between the adjacent nodes represent the existence of sharing resource between the two exams [19]. For example, Fig. 1 shows a timetabling solution of 5 exams.

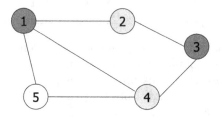

Fig. 1. Example of graph G

Exams 1 and 2 colored differently and connected using edge; this means that these two exams have sharing students. In this example the examination timetabling solution is as follows: $x = (1, 2, 1, 2, 3)$ which means that the exam 1 is scheduled in timeslot 1, exam 2 scheduled in timeslot 2 and exam 3 in timeslot 1. In IWD, each node is exam, and the graph refers to a complete and feasible solution in examination timetabling.

The following variables are used in determining the workflow of the algorithm:

1. Number of IWD, which equal to the number of timetabling solutions.
2. Initial Soil placed on the edges of the graph.
3. Initial velocity that is prevalent for each water drop (timetabling solution).
4. Maximum number of iterations.

Using this presentation via the graph, each IWD initiates its movement on the nodes of the graph along the edges (neighboring exams) between these nodes and constructing its solution. A complete iteration of the algorithm based upon the completion of all IWDs solution. The iteration best solution T^{IBest} established at the end of all iterations, and it is applied to update the global best solution T^{TBest}. The quantity of soil on the iteration best solution edges T^{IBest} is updated in regards to the quality of the solution. This is followed by a new iteration with new IWDs but with the same soil on the edges of the graph. When the variable $iter_{max}$ equal to the maximum number of iterations or T^{TBest} reaches the expected quality, the algorithm must stop.

In this IWD algorithm, the two types of parameters used are Static Parameters and Dynamic Parameters. Static parameters are the unchanged parameters during the search using IWD algorithm such as the maximum number of iterations $iter_{max}$, number of solutions and soil and velocity parameters whereas Dynamic parameters are interchangeable and they are reinitialized after each iteration of the IWD algorithm such as local best solution T^{IBest}, global best solution T^{TBest}, velocity, soil.

Algorithm 1. The main steps for IWD algorithm

1: Initialization of static parameters.
2: **while** The condition of algorithm termination is not met **do**
3:       Initialization of dynamic parameters.
4:       Spread the IWDs randomly on the nodes of the graph.
5:       Update the list of visited node $V_n(IWD)$.
6:       **while** The condition of construction termination is not met **do**
7:            **for** $n = 1$ to IWD **do**
8:                 $i =$ the current node for drop n
9:                 $j =$ selected next node, which does not violate problem constrains.
10:                move drop n from node i to node j.
11:                update the following parameters.
12:                (a) Velocity of drop n
13:                (b) Soil value of drop n
14:                (c) Soil value of edge $e(i, j)$
15:           **end for**
16:      **end while**
17:      choose the best solution in the iteration population T^{IBest}.
18:      update the soil value of all edges T^{IBest}.
19:      update the global best solution T^{TBest}.
20:      **if** value of $T^{TBest} > T^{IBest}$ **then**
21:           $T^{TBest} = T^{IBest}$.
22:      **end if**
23: **end while**
24: Stops with the global best solution.

4.1 Intelligent Water Drops: Procedures

The IWD algorithm is specified in the following steps:

Step 1 Initialization of static parameters.

The graph (V, E) of UETP is given to the algorithm. The value of global-best solution T^{TBest} is Initially set to the worst fitness value: $q(T^{TBest}) = -\infty$. In UETP the T^{TBest} refers to the best timetabling solution in the population which possesses the minimum penalty. The user specifies The maximum number of iterations $Iter_{max}$. The iteration counter $Iter_{count}$ is set to zero.

The number of water drops (number of timetabling solutions) is set to a positive integer value [18]. Certainly suggested to set the water drop equal the number of nodes N_n of the graph (for example, if the number of exams is 100, the IWDs algorithm suggested to set the initial population size to 100). However, in timetabling, the numbers of exams are normally large and to set the number of solution equal to number of exams might be affect the performance.

[18] stated that for Soil updating, $a_{soil} = 1$, $b_{soil} = 0.01$, and $c_{soil} = 1$. for velocity updating, the parameters are $a_{vel} = 1$, $b_{vel} = 0.01$ and $c_{vel} = 1$. The local soil updating parameter ρ_s, which is a small positive number less than one, is set as $\rho_s = 0.9$. The global soil updating parameter ρ_{IWDs}, which is

chosen from $[0, 1]$, is set as $\rho_{IWDs} = 0.9$. Furthermore, the initial soil on each path (edge) is denoted by the constant *InitialSoil* such as the Soil of the path between every two nodes i and j that is set by $IWDsoil(i, j) = InitialSoil$. The initial velocity of each IWD is set to *InitialVel*. Both parameters *InitialSoil* and *InitialVel* are users selected and they should be tuned experimentally for the application [18].

Step 2 Initialization of dynamic parameters.

Each IWD (timetabling solution) has a visited node list $V_n(IWD)$, which is primarily empty. The value of $V_n(IWD)$ in UETP denotes the list of exams that has readily been assigned with thier feasible timeslots: $V_n(IWD) = \{\ \}$. Each IWD's velocity is set to *InitialVel*.

All IWDs are set to have zero amount of soil.

Step 3 Spread the IWDs randomly on the nodes of the graph as their first visited nodes.

Step 4 Update the visited node list of each IWD to include the nodes just visited.

Step 5 Repeat Steps 1 to 4 for those IWDs with partial solutions.

1. For the IWD (i.e., timetabling solution) residing in node i (*exam i have been assigned with a feasible timeslot*), choose the next exam (node j), which does not violate any hard constraints (i.e., the chosen timeslot of the exam j respect the hard constraint) and it is not in the visited node list $V_n(IWD)$ of the IWD, applying the following probability $\rho_i^{IWD}(j)$:

$$\rho_i^{IWD}(j) = \frac{f(IWDsoil(i, j))}{\sum_{k \notin V_n(IWD)} f(IWDsoil(i, k))} \tag{2}$$

So that
$$f(IWDsoil(i, j)) = \frac{1}{\varepsilon_s + g(IWDsoil(i,j))} \text{ and}$$

$$g(Sarray) = \begin{cases} Sarray & if(Q \geq 0) \\ Sarray - \min_{l \notin V_n(IWD)}(Sarray) & otherwise \end{cases}$$

Where

$$Sarray = IWDsoil(i, j)$$
$$Q = \min_{l \notin V_n(IWD)}(IWDsoil(i, l)).$$

Then, Add the newly visited node j to the list $V_n(IWD)$.

It is worthy noting that the next exam (i.e., exam j) has been chosen using the saturation degree (SD) principle in UETP. In SD, the exam of the least number of available timeslots must be timetabled first [4].

2. For each IWD (timetabling solution) moving from node i to node j, update its velocity $velocity^{IWD}(t)$ by:

$$velocity^{IWD}(t + 1) = velocity^{IWD}(t) + \frac{a_{vel}}{(b_{vel} + c_{vel} * IWDsoil^2(i, j))} \tag{3}$$

where $velocity^{IWD}(t + 1)$ is the updated velocity of the IWD.

3. For each solution moving on the path from node i to j, compute the Soil $\Delta IWDSoil(i, j)$ that the IWD loads from the path by:

$$\Delta IWDSoil(i, j) = \frac{a_{vel}}{b_{soil} + c_{soil} * time^2(i, j; velocity^{IWD}(t + 1))} \quad (4)$$

Such that
$$time^2(i, j; velocity^{IWD}(t + 1)) = \frac{HUD(j)}{velocity^{IWD}(t+1)}$$
Where the heuristic undesirability $HUD(j)$ is defined appropriately for the given problem. In UETP, the HUD is calculated as follows: $if(EvaluateArray[DropIndex]! = -1)returnEvaluateArray[DropIndex]; else return0$; Where $EvaluateArray$ is a one dimensional array where we were assigned by -1 as an initial value, then the objective function was assigned for all solutions.

4. Update the soil $IWDSoil(i, j)$ of the path from node i to j traversed by that IWD and also update the soil that the IWD carries $IWDSoil^{IWD}$ by:

$$IWDsoil(i, j) = (1 - \rho_s) * IWDsoil(i, j) - \rho_s * \Delta IWDsoil(i, j)$$
$$IWDsoil^{IWD} = IWDsoil^{IWD} - \Delta IWDsoil(i, j) \quad (5)$$

Step 6 Find the iteration-best solution T^{IBest} from all the solutions T^{IWD} found by the IWDs using:

$$T^{IBest} = \arg \max_{\forall T^{IWD}} q(T^{IWD}) \quad (6)$$

Step 7 Update the soils on the paths that form the current iteration-best solution T^{IBest} by:

$$IWDsoil(i, j) = (1 + \rho_{IWD}) * IWDsoil(i, j) - \rho_{IWDs} * \frac{1}{V_{TBest} - 1}$$
$$* IWDsoil_{TBest}^{IWD}, \qquad \forall(i, j) \in T^{TBest} \quad (7)$$

Update the global best solution T^{TBest} by the current iteration-best solution T^{IBest} using:

$$T^{TBest} = \begin{cases} T^{IBest} & if \ f(T^{IBest}) \leq f(T^{TBest}) \\ T^{TBest} & otherwise \end{cases} \quad (8)$$

In UETP, the global best solution T^{TBest} is the solution that possesses the lowest penalty on all iteration while the local best solution is the best solution in each iteration, which means that we will find the global best solution T^{TBest} from all the solutions T^{IWD} found by the IWDs (solutions) by making a comparison of the value of local best solution T^{IBest} by the value of global best solution T^{TBest} then we will assign the value of local best solution T^{IBest} to the T^{TBest} if it was better than the old value for global best solution T^{TBest}.

Step 8 Increment the iteration number by Eq. 9 before moving to the next step:

$$Iter_{count} = Iter_{count} + 1, \tag{9}$$

It was found that the IWD has displayed to have the property of convergence in value [16], enabling it to find the optimal solution if the number of iterations are adequately large.

Step 9 The algorithm stops here with the global best solution T^{TBest}.

5 Experiments and Results

A number of points of reference for the problems have been made publicly available to test and compare exam timetabling techniques. Of these, the most widely used are those given by Carter [9] for the uncapacitated exam timetabling problem. Carter's dataset comprises 12 datasets which varies in size (number of exams, timeslots and students) and complexity. In this research we implemented IWDs algorithm to all 12 datasets. The objective function adds a penalty for a timetable whenever a student must sit two examinations within a timeslots of each other as in Eq. 1.

IWDs algorithm is programmed in Microsoft Visual C++ version 6.0 under Windows 8. The experiments presented here run on two computers with different CPU and RAM capability over 5 days. Note that the total number of experiments is 120 (12 datasets 10 runs).

IWDs algorithm required setting some static and dynamic parameters to solve the UETP. The following show the parameters that used in the experiments:

- The number of iteration $Iter_{max}$ equal to 10,000.
- The number of solutions Drops equal to 10.
- Initial soil $InitSoil$ equal to 100.
- Initial velocity $InitVel$.
- Local best solution T^{IBest} and Global best solution T^{TBest} equal to 100000.

It is also worth noting that these parameters have been decided based on an intensive trial and error cases. The results of IWD have been recorded in Table 4. These results display the best and worst penalty value of ten different runs for each Carter dataset.

The proposed Intelligent Water Drops (IWD) Algorithm is compared with with 23 comparative methods (See Table 3). These methods used Carter datasets [9], The comparative methods are categorized based on the number of solution iterated upon as Local Search-based Metaheuristic Methods, Population-based Metaheuristic Methods, Heuristic Methods and Hyper-Heuristic Methods .

The numbers in the table refer to the Penalty Value (PV) calculated using Eq. 1. The indicator (-) shows where the method did not guarantee a feasible timetable (e.g., a hard constraint was not met) or the method did not test the corresponding dataset. The numbers in bold show the best solution obtained

Table 3. Results of Approaches that applied on UUETP

Datasets	IWDA	heuristic and hyper-heuristic approaches									local based Metaheuristic-based search approaches										pop-based App			Memetic App
		See [6]	See [30]	See [20]	See [21]	See [22]	See [12]	See [13]	See [11]	See [3]	See [23]	See [24]	See [25]	See [26]	See [27]	See [28]	See [29]	See [8]	See [31]	See [6]	See [32]	See [33]	See [34]	See [2]
CAR-S-91	7.15	7.1	5	5.19	5.37	5.36	5.11	5.16	4.97	5.29	6.6	6.2	5.7	-	4.65	5.4	5.1	4.8	4.5	4.6	5.2	5.4	5.2	4.99
CAR-F-92	6.1	6.2	4.3	4.51	4.67	4.93	4.32	4.16	4.84	4.54	6	5.2	-	38.9	4.1	4.4	4.3	4.2	3.93	4	4.4	4.2	4.3	4.29
EAR-F-83	46.32	36.4	36.2	36.64	40.18	37.92	35.56	35.86	36.86	37.02	29.3	45.7	39.4	11.2	37.05	34.8	35.1	35.4	33.7	32.8	34.9	34.2	36.8	34.42
HEC-S-92	11.6	10.8	11.6	11.6	11.86	12.25	11.62	11.94	11.85	11.78	9.2	12.4	10.9	16.5	11.54	10.8	10.6	10.8	10.83	10	10.3	10.4	11.1	10.40
KFU-S-93	19.97	14	15	15.34	15.84	15.2	15.18	14.79	14.62	15.8	13.8	18	-	13.2	13.9	14.1	13.5	13.7	13.82	13	13.5	14.3	14.5	13.5
LSE-F-91	14.54	10.5	11	11.35	-	11.33	11.32	11.15	11.14	12.09	9.6	15.5	12.6	-	10.82	14.7	10.5	10.4	10.35	10	10.2	11.3	11.3	0.48
RYE-S-93	13.2	7.3	-	10.05	-	-	-	-	9.65	10.38	6.8	-	-	-	-	-	-	8.9	8.53	-	8.7	8.8	9.8	8.79
STA-F-83	159.43	161.9	161.5	160.8	157.4	158.19	158.88	159	158.33	160.42	158.2	160.8	157.4	168.3	168.73	-	157.3	159.1	158.35	159.9	159.2	158.03	157.3	157.04
TRE-S-92	10.2	9.6	8.4	8.47	8.39	8.92	8.52	8.6	8.48	8.67	9.4	10	-	9.3	8.35	8.7	8.4	8.3	7.92	7.9	8.4	8.6	8.6	8.16
UTA-S-92	5.08	3.5	3.4	3.52	-	3.88	3.21	3.59	3.4	3.57	3.5	4.2	4.1	-	3.2	-	3.5	3.4	3.14	3.2	3.6	3.5	3.5	3.43
UTE-S-92	31.97	25.8	27.4	27.55	27.6	28.01	28	28.3	28.88	28.07	24.4	27.8	-	29	25.83	25.4	25.1	25.7	25.39	24.8	26	25.3	26.4	25.09
YOR-F-83	44.54	41.7	40.8	39.79	-	41.37	40.71	41.81	40.74	39.8	36.2	41	39.7	38.9	37.28	37.5	37.4	36.7	36.35	37.28	36.2	36.4	39.4	35.86

Table 4. Results of applying IWDA on UUETP

Datasets key	Literature review results		Results of IWDs algorithm	
	Best	Worst	Best	Average
CAR-S-91	4.5	7.1	7.15	7.65
CAR-F-92	3.93	6.2	6.1	6.25
EAR-F-83	29.3	45.7	46.32	46.98
HEC-S-92	9.2	12.25	11.6	11.79
KFU-S-93	13	18	19.97	19.97
LSE-F-91	9.6	15.5	14.54	14.84
RYE-S-93	6.8	10.38	13.2	13.27
STA-F-83	157.04	168.73	159.43	160.34
TRE-S-92	7.9	10	10.2	10.45
UTA-S-92	3.14	4.2	5.08	5.11
UTE-S-92	24.4	29	31.97	32.31
YOR-F-83	35.86	41.81	44.54	44.54

for that Carter dataset (lowest is best). The numbers in italic fonts indicate that a different dataset version was used. Note that the results obtained by the proposed method are recorded in column 1 of the comparative table.

In the IWDs Algorithm, the results unable to supersede those produced by heuristic, hyper-heuristic, local-search based, population-search based and memetic methods in 23 out of 12 Carter datasets shown in Table 3. It is due to this matter the heuristic and hyper-heuristic methods have not met the standard results obtained by the Metaheuristic -based methods in terms of solution quality. Nevertheless, this study can be considered as an initial exploration to show the validity of using IWD in the scheduling domain despite the incompetent result. In the mean time, this study provides numerous possibilities of future improvements with high potential of being successful in the future.

Table 3 compares the results produced by IWDs algorithm with the best reported solution taken from the literature review. Table 4 shows that the results of the implementation of IWDs algorithm being initially reasonable and acceptable with no modification on the algorithm. An improvement on this method will hopefully provide high quality results and will expectably compete with the results of the other techniques that used to solve university exam timetabling problem.

6   Conclusion and Future Works

In this study, the IWD have been adapted for examination timetabling. The adaptation is initially conducted within IWD operators where the Saturation degree concepts have been incorporated. The researchers tried to implement the original IWD operators in this study to reveal its strengths and weaknesses in dealing with examination timetabling domain. Based on the initial results obtained by IWD, it is found that the algorithm is capable of solving university examination timetabling problem. Although the results produced in this research are presently not at par with the previously reported literature, an improvement using local search-based algorithm is required (and is presently in progress) to enhance its performance possibly superseding the methods used previously.

References

1. Al-Betar, M.A., Khader, A.T.: A harmony search algorithm for university course timetabling. Ann. Oper. Res. **194**, 3–31 (2012)
2. Al-Betar, M.A., Khader, A.T., Doush, I.A.: Memetic techniques for examination timetabling. Ann. Oper. Res. **218**, 23–50 (2013)
3. Asmuni, H., Burke, E.K., Garibaldi, J.M., McCollum, B., Parkes, A.J.: An investigation of fuzzy multiple heuristic orderings in the construction of university examination timetables. Comput. Oper. Res. **36**, 981–1001 (2009)
4. Brlaz, D.: New methods to color the vertices of a graph. Commun. ACM **22**, 251–256 (1979)
5. Burke, E.K., Elliman, D.G., Weare, R.F.: A genetic algorithm based university timetabling system. In: East-West Conference on Computer Technologies in Education, vol. 1, Crimea, Ukraine, pp. 35–40 (1994)
6. Burke, E.K., Eckersley, A.J., McCollum, B., Petrovic, S., Qu, R.: Hybrid variable neighbourhood approaches to university exam timetabling. Eur. J. Oper. Res. **206**, 46–53 (2010)
7. Burke, E.K., Newall, J.P., Weare, R.F.: A memetic algorithm for university exam timetabling. In: Burke, E.K., Ross, P. (eds.) PATAT 1995. LNCS, vol. 1153. Springer, Heidelberg (1996)
8. Burke, E., Bykov, Y., Newall, J., Petrovic, S.: A time-predefined local search approach to exam timetabling problems. IIE Trans. **36**, 509–528 (2004)
9. Carter, M.W., Gilbert, L., Sau, Y.L.: Examination timetabling: algorithmic strategies and applications. Oper. Res. Soc. **47**, 373–383 (1996)
10. Djannaty, F., Mirzaei, A.R.: Enhancing max-min ant system for examination timetabling problem. Int. J. Soft Comput. **3**, 230–238 (2008)
11. Pillay, N., Banzhaf, W.: A study of heuristic combinations for hyper-heuristic systems for the uncapacitated examination timetabling problem. Eur. J. Oper. Res. **197**, 482–491 (2009)
12. Qu, R.B.E., Burke, E.K., McCollum, B., Merlot, L.T.G., Lee, S.Y.: A survey of search methodologies and automated system development for examination timetabling. J. Sched. **12**, 55–89 (2009)
13. Qu, R., Burke, E.K., McCollum, B.: Adaptive automated construction of hybrid heuristics for exam timetabling and graph colouring problems. Eur. J. Oper. Res. **198**, 392–404 (2009)
14. Schaerf, A.: A survey of automated timetabling. Artif. Intell. Rev. **13**, 87–127 (1999)
15. Shah, H.H.: Problem solving by intelligent water drops. In: Evolutionary Computation, CEC 2007, IEEE Congress, pp. 3226–3231. IEEE, Singapore (2007)
16. Shah, H.H.: Intelligent water drops algorithm: a new optimization method for solving the multiple knapsack problem. Int. J. Intell. Comput. Cybernet. **1**, 193–212 (2008)

17. Shah, H.H.: The intelligent water drops algorithm: a nature-inspired swarm-based optimization algorithm. Int. J. Bio Inspired Comput. **1**, 71–79 (2009)
18. Shah, H.H.: An approach to continuous optimization by the intelligent water drops algorithm. Procedia Soc. Behav. Sci. **32**, 224–229 (2012)
19. Welsh, D.J., Powell, M.B.: An upper bound for the chromatic number of a graph and its application to timetabling problems. Comput. J. **10**, 85–86 (1967)
20. Asmuni, H., Burke, E.K., Garibaldi, J.M., McCollum, B.: Fuzzy multiple heuristic orderings for examination timetabling. In: Burke, E.K., Trick, M.A. (eds.) PATAT 2004. LNCS, vol. 3616, pp. 334–353. Springer, Heidelberg (2005)
21. Kendall, G., Hussin, N.M.: An investigation of a tabu-search-based hyperheuristic for examination timetabling. In: Kendall, G., Burke, E.K., Petrovic, S., Gendreau, M. (eds.) Multidisciplinary Scheduling: Theory and Applications, pp. 309–328. Springer, Heidelberg (2005)
22. Burke, E.K., McCollum, B., Meisels, A., Petrovic, S., Qu, R.: A graph-based hyperheuristic for educational timetabling problems. Eur. J. Oper. Res. **176**, 177–192 (2007)
23. Caramia, M., Dell'Olmo, P.F.: Novel local-search-based approaches to university examination timetabling. Inf. J. Comput. **20**, 86–99 (2008)
24. Di Gaspero, L., Schaerf, A.: Multi-neighbourhood local search with application to course timetabling. In: Burke, E.K., De Causmaecker, P. (eds.) PATAT 2002. LNCS, vol. 2740, pp. 262–275. Springer, Heidelberg (2003)
25. Gaspero, L.D.: Recolour, shake and kick: a recipe for the examination timetabling problem. In: Proceedings of the Fourth International Conference on the Practice and Theory of Automated Timetabling, Gent, Belgium, pp. 404–407 (2002)
26. Paquete, L., Stutzle, T.: Empirical analysis of tabu search for the lexicographic optimization of the examination timetabling problem. In: Proceedings of the 4th International Conference on Practice and Theory of Automated Timetabling, pp. 413–420 (2003)
27. Burke, E.K., Newall, J.P.: A multistage evolutionary algorithm for the timetable problem. Evol. Comput. **3**, 63–74 (1999)
28. Casey, S., Thompson, J.: GRASPing the examination scheduling problem. In: Burke, E.K., De Causmaecker, P. (eds.) PATAT 2002. LNCS, vol. 2740, pp. 232–244. Springer, Heidelberg (2003)
29. Merlot, L.T.G., Boland, N., Hughes, B.D., Stuckey, P.J.: A hybrid algorithm for the examination timetabling problem. In: Burke, E.K., De Causmaecker, P. (eds.) PATAT 2002. LNCS, vol. 2740, pp. 207–231. Springer, Heidelberg (2003)
30. Burke, E.K., Newall, J.P.: Solving examination timetabling problems through adaption of heuristic orderings. Ann. Oper. Res. **129**, 107–134 (2004)
31. Yang, Y., Petrovic, S.: A novel similarity measure for heuristic selection in examination timetabling. In: Burke, E.K., Trick, M.A. (eds.) PATAT 2004. LNCS, vol. 3616, pp. 247–269. Springer, Heidelberg (2005)
32. Abdullah, S., Ahmadi, S., Burke, E.K., Dror, M., McCollum, B.: A tabu-based large neighbourhood search methodology for the capacitated examination timetabling problem. Oper. Res. Soc. **58**, 1494–1502 (2007)
33. Côté, P., Wong, T., Sabourin, R.: A hybrid multi-objective evolutionary algorithm for the uncapacitated exam proximity problem. In: Burke, E.K., Trick, M.A. (eds.) PATAT 2004. LNCS, vol. 3616, pp. 294–312. Springer, Heidelberg (2005)
34. Eley, M.: Ant algorithms for the exam timetabling problem. In: Burke, E.K., Rudová, H. (eds.) PATAT 2007. LNCS, vol. 3867. Springer, Heidelberg (2007)

A Novel Hybrid Algorithm for Discovering Motifs from Financial Time Series

Dadabada Pradeepkumar[1,2], Maneesh Bhunwal[3],
and Vadlamani Ravi[1(✉)]

[1] Center of Excellence in CRM and Analytics, Institute for Development
and Research in Banking Technology, Hyderabad 500057, India
dpradeepphd@gmail.com, rav_padma@yahoo.com
[2] SCIS, University of Hyderabad, Hyderabad 500046, India
dpradeepphd@gmail.com
[3] Integrated M.SC in Mathematics and Computing, Department of Mathematics,
Indian Institute of Technology, Kharagpur, India
maneesh.bhunwal@gmail.com

Abstract. Time series motifs are pairs of individual subsequences, which are very similar to each other within the time series. In this paper, we propose an efficient and novel hybrid algorithm by taking best out of two popular algorithms namely MK algorithm and EP-C algorithm that exist in literature. We demonstrate the efficiency of our approach in terms of time elapsed and distance obtained between the subsequences through experiments conducted on financial time series datasets viz., foreign exchange rates, Gold price and Crude oil price in terms of US dollars.

Keywords: Motif discovery · Financial time series · Hybrid algorithm · MK algorithm · EP-C algorithm

1 Introduction

A time series is a collection of observations recorded chronologically. It can be seen as a combination of two parts: characteristic information and noise. Characteristic information is the reliable part and finding it is an important task. Time series motif is one of the formats of the reliable part. It is the frequently appearing pattern or sets of similar subsequences without overlapping each other in a time series [1, 2].

The motif discovery plays a key role in various time series data mining tasks such as forecasting, anomaly detection, clustering and classification, summarization and indexing and association rule mining. It is an interesting research problem in diverse fields such as Bioinformatics, Robotics, Meteorology, Speech recognition, Music analysis and Medicine [11].

This paper proposes a novel hybrid algorithm by combining the two popular motif discovery algorithms: MK (Mueen-Keogh) algorithm [3], EP-C (Extreme Points-Clustering) Algorithm [4]. The process of clustering in EP-C algorithm makes it

© Springer International Publishing Switzerland 2015
B.K. Panigrahi et al. (Eds.): SEMCCO 2014, LNCS 8947, pp. 201–211, 2015.
DOI: 10.1007/978-3-319-20294-5_18

slow and MK algorithm consumes a lot of space. The proposed algorithm overcomes these two disadvantages.

The rest of the paper is organized as follows. In Sect. 2, we briefly discuss existing motif discovery algorithms, definitions used and background work. Section 3 describes proposed method. Section 4 presents the discussion of the results. Finally, concluding remarks are presented in Sect. 5.

2 Related Work, Definitions and Background

2.1 Related Work

Several algorithms are proposed for discovering motifs from time series. Lin *et al.* [2] proposed k-motif algorithm, which is sensitive to the parameter w, the length of pattern to be discovered. When the pattern is unknown, the value of w is very difficult to estimate. To solve this problem, Tang *et al.* [9] proposed an approach that does not require an exact w value to be determined in advance, and, moreover, it can be used to identify motifs with different lengths by running it only once.

Tompa *et al.* [8] proposed an algorithm that uses random projections to reduce the search space. The algorithm chooses k positions as type of mask. The mask is then superimposed at all positions. This way, each substring is mapped to a string (of size k) by reading the symbols through the mask which becomes the projection. Chiu *et al.* [7] proposed a probabilistic method of discovering motifs. This algorithm leverages the work in Tompa *et al.* [8] by first creating a discrete representation of time series. The algorithm discretizes the time series using Piecewise Aggregate Approximation (PAA), extracts subsequences using a sliding window and uses a collision matrix as a base structure whose rows and columns are the Symbolic Aggregate Approximations (SAX) representation of each time series subsequence. This procedure is slow in the case of large time series data.

Pawan *et al.* [6] proposed an approach to discover variable length time series motif without considering sliding window length parameter. Wilson *et al.* [10] proposed the Motif Tracking Algorithm (MTA) that is a novel IS approach to identify repeating patterns in time series data by taking advantage of the associative learning properties exhibited by the natural immune system.

2.2 Definitions

All definitions we use in this work will be stated in this section.

Definition 1: A *Time Series* is an ordered sequence $T = (y_1, y_2, ..., y_n)$, of n real valued numbers.

Definition 2: A *Subsequence* of T is a smaller sequence that starts at position p_1 and ends at position p_2.

Definition 3: A *Distance Measure D (S₁, S2)* measures the distance between two subsequences. $D(S_1, S2) < \delta$, a threshold value, helps to obtain non-trivial matches that, in turn, have no overlaps.

Definition 4: A *Time series Motif* is a pair of the most similar subsequences in Time series T.

Definition 5: *Significant Extreme Points:* A Time series $T = (y_1, y_2, ..., y_n)$ has a *significant minimum* at position p with $1 < p < n$, if $(y_i, ..., y_j)$ with $1 \leq i < j \leq n$ in T exists, such that y_p is the minimum of all points of this subsequence and $y_i \geq R \times y_p$, $y_j \geq R \times y_p$ with *compression rate* $R \geq 1$. A *significant maximum* is existent at position p with $1 < p < n$, if $(y_i, ..., y_j)$ with $1 \leq i < j \leq n$ in T exists, such that y_p is the maximum of all points of this subsequence and $y_i \leq R \times y_p$, $y_j \leq R \times y_p$ with *compression rate* $R \geq 1$.

2.3   Background

The following two algorithms form background to the current work. Gruber *et al.* [4, 5] proposed the EP-C algorithm for finding time series motif. In this algorithm, first a temporarily ordered sequence of motif candidates is extracted using significant extreme points. Afterwards, similar motif candidates are grouped by means of a clustering method in order to find the most significant motif of the time series. The detailed algorithm is depicted in Fig. 1.

EP-C Algorithm

1. Extract all extreme points of the time series T. The result of this step is a sequence of extreme points EP= (ep₁,ep₂,...,epₗ)
2. Compute all the motif candidates iteratively. A motif candidate MCᵢ(T), i=1,2,...,l-2 is the subsequence of T that is bounded by extreme points epᵢ and epᵢ₊₂. Motif candidates are the subsequences that may have different lengths. To enable the computation of distances between them, we can bring them to user-defined MAX_MOTIF_LENGTH by using spline interpolation.
3. Apply K-means or hierarchical agglomerative clustering algorithm to cluster the motif candidates. The most significant motif is represented by the cluster with highest number of motif candidates.

Fig. 1. Extreme points-clustering (EP-C) algorithm

Mueen *et al.* [3] proposed an exact motif discovery algorithm, called MK Algorithm. This works as follows. First store all the subsequences. Then, select a random subsequence from it, called ref. Calculate the distance of every subsequence from *ref.* Let i and j be two subsequences. Now using triangular inequality we can say that distance between i and j is lower bounded by difference of distance *(i, ref)* and *(j, ref)*. If this is more than *best_ so_ far* distance then we need not to go for exact distance.

```
Procedure [L1, L2]=MK_Motif (D,R)
1    best-so-far = INF
2    for i=1 to R
3      refᵢ=a randomly chosen time series Dr from D
4      for j=1 to m
5        Dist ᵢⱼ=d(refᵢ,Dj)
6        if Distᵢⱼ < best-so-far
7            best-so-far= Distᵢⱼ , L₁=r, L₂=j
8      Sᵢ=standard_deviation(Distᵢ)
9    find an ordering Z of the indices to the reference time series
     in ref such that S_{Z(i)} ≥ S_{Z(i+1)}
10   find an ordering I of the indices to the time series in
     D such that Dist_{Z(1),I(j)}≤ Dist_{Z(1),I(j+1)}
11   offset=0, abandon=false
12   while abandon=false
13     offset=offset+1, abandon=true
14     for j=1 to m
15       reject=false
16       for i=1 to R
17       lower_bound=|Dist_{Z(i),I(j)} - Dist_{Z(i),I(j+offset)}|
18         if lower_bound > best-so-far
19           reject=true, break
20         else if i = 1
21             abandon=false
22       if reject=false
23         if d(D_{I(j)},D_{I(j+offset)})<best-so-far
24           best-so-far=d(D_{I(j)},D_{I(j+offset)})
25           L₁=I(j),L₂=I(j+offset)
```

Fig. 2. Mueen-Keogh (MK) algorithm

Like this we take multiple reference points and find the pair with minimum distance. The detailed algorithm is depicted in Fig. 2.

3 Proposed Motif Discovery Algorithm

The proposed algorithm is a three-step process. In the first step, all significant extreme points are extracted. Based on extracted significant points, motif candidates of different lengths are obtained. In the second step, the Homothety procedure is applied to convert all the subsequences to the same length. In the final step, MK Algorithm is applied on this two-dimensional array of motif candidates in order to obtain motif pair. The detailed description is depicted in Figs. 3, 4, 5 and 6.

Proposed Algorithm

---

1. **STEP 1:** $SIG = SIGNIFICANT\_POINT(input)$
2. // SIG is vector containing significant points and *input* is a time series
3. $data$ = FILL ($input$, SIG)
4. // data is 2D array containing motif candidates.
5. **STEP 2:** HOMETHETY($data$, $motif\_length$)
6. // convert all the subsequence to same length i.e. $motif\_length$, a user defined motif length
7. **STEP 3:** $(L_1,\ L2)$=MK_motif ($data$, R)
8. // L1, L2 are motif subsequences.

Fig. 3. Proposed motif discovery algorithm

Procedure FILL

FILL ($input$, SIG)
//Fills the possible motif candidates in a 2-Dimensional array
1. **For** i=1 to length(SIG)-2
2.   data(i)=*time series* (SIG(i) to SIG(i+2))
3. // each *time series* is a vector so that *data* is now 2-D array

Fig. 4. Procedure FILL to create two-dimensional array or motif candidates

---

Procedure HOMOTHETY

HOMOTHETY($data$, $motif\_length$)
// Convert all subsequences to $motif\_length$ and *total* is the number of subsequences
1. **for** i I =1 to *total*
2. X_length=length($data(i)$)
3. X_center=$X\_length/2$
4. $index$=0
5. $ratio$= $newLength\ /\ X\_length$
6.   **for** $x = (-(newLength/2))+X\_center$ to $(newLength/2)+X\_center$
7. $x = (x-X\_center)/ratio +X\_center$
8. $round\_x$= round(x)
9. $y =(x-round\_x)*data(i,round\_x+1)+(round\_x+1-x)*data(i,\ round\_x)$
10. $tempData(index) = y$
11. $index=index+1$;
12.   if($index = newLength$) **break**
13.   **end**
14. **end**
15. $data(i) = tempData$ // copy *tempData* in $data(i)$

Fig. 5. Procedure HOMOTHETY to convert every subsequence to $motif\_length$

Procedure SIGNIFICANT_POINT

SIGNIFICANT_POINT (T)

// *T is one dimensional array containing time series*

// *we store output of FIND-FIRST-TWO and FIND-MIN, FIND-MAX*

// *in a 1-D array and return the array. These are the significant points*

1. i = call FIND-FIRST-TWO
2. **if** $i < n$ and $T(i) > T(1)$ **then** i = call FIND-MIN(i)
3. **while** $i < n$ **do**
4. i = call FIND-MAX(i)
5. i = call FIND-MIN(i)
6. **return** T;
7.
8. Procedure FIND-FIRST-TWO
9. *//Finding the first and second significant extreme points*
10. $i_{Min} = 1, i_{Max} = 1, i = 2$
11. **while** $i < n$ and $T(i) / T(i_{Min}) < R$ and $T(i_{Max}) / T(i) < R$ **do**
12.   **if** $T(i) < T(i_{Min})$ **then** $i_{Min} = i$
13.   **if** $T(i) > T(i_{Max})$ **then** $i_{Max} = i$
14.   **if** $i_{Min} < i_{Max}$ **then**
15.   Print $(T(i_{Min}), i_{Min})$, Print $(T(i_{Max}), i_{Max})$
16.   **else**
17.   Print $(T(i_{Max}), i_{Max})$, Print$(T(i_{Min}), i_{Min})$
18. **return** i
19.
20. Procedure FIND-MIN(i)
21. *//Finding the first significant minimum after the ith point*
22. $i_{Min} = i$
23. **while** $i < n$ and $T(i)/T(i_{Min}) < R$ **do**
24.   **if** $T(i) < T(i_{Min})$ **then** $i_{Min} = i$
25. $i = i + 1$
26.   Print $(T(i_{Min}), i_{Min})$
27. **return** i
28.
29. Procedure FIND-MAX(i)
30. *//Finding the first significant maximum after the ith point*
31. $i_{Max} = i$
32. **while** $i < n$ and $T(i_{Max}) / T(i) < R$ **do**
33.   **if** $T(i) > T(i_{Max})$ **then** $i_{Max} = i$
34. $i = i + 1$
35.   Print $(T(i_{Max}), i_{Max})$
36. **return** i

Fig. 6. Procedure for obtaining significant points

4 Results and Discussion

The foreign exchange data used in our study are obtained from US Federal Reserve System (http://www.federalreserve.gov/releases/h10/hist/). The datasets collected are of daily US dollar exchange rates with respect to three currencies- GBP, INR and EUR. The daily data of USD-GBP (6036 observations) and USD-INR (6028 observations) from 1st January 1993 to 31st December 2013 and USD-EUR (3772 observations) from 3rd January 2000 to 31st December 2013, are used as datasets. In addition to these, other financial datasets such as Gold opening price in US Dollars (7839 observations) data from 05th April 1983 to 07th April 2014 is collected from (http://www.quandl.com/LBMA/GOLD-Gold-Price-London-Fixing) and Crude Oil Price in US Dollars (7777 observations) 04th April 1983 to 4th April 2014 are collected from (http://www.quandl.com/CHRIS/CME_CL1-Crude-Oil-Futures-Continuous-Contract-1-CL1-Front-Month).

The Euclidian distance measure is used to obtain the distances between two subsequences as shown in (1):

$$Dist(X, Y) = \sqrt{\sum_{i=1}^{N} (x_i - y_i)^2} \tag{1}$$

Where X and Y are two subsequences, in turn, are vectors.

Tables 1, 2, 3, 4 and 5 present the results of proposed algorithm in terms of total execution time and the distance between the obtained subsequences. These measures are also presented for EP-C algorithm. It is clearly observed that the proposed algorithm consumes less execution time than EP-C algorithm and the subsequences that are obtained by proposed algorithm are very much closer than those obtained by EP-C algorithm as measured by distance. In these tables, R, compression rate, is a user-defined parameter. The Figs. 7, 8, 9, 10 and 11 present the obtained best motifs using the proposed motif discovery algorithm.

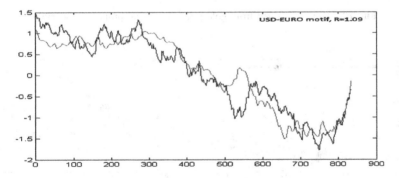

Fig. 7. Motifs obtained from USD-EUR data using proposed algorithm

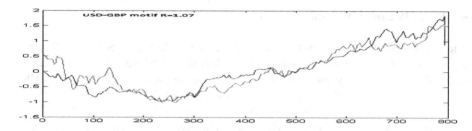

Fig. 8. Motifs obtained from USD-GBP data using proposed algorithm

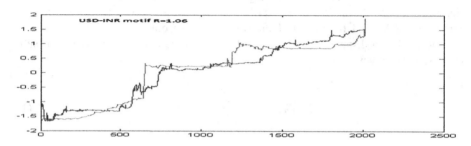

Fig. 9. Motifs obtained from USD-INR data using proposed algorithm

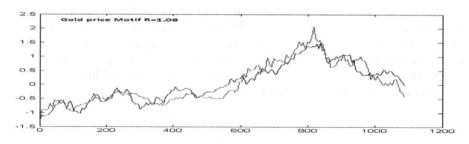

Fig. 10. Motifs obtained from gold price data using proposed algorithm

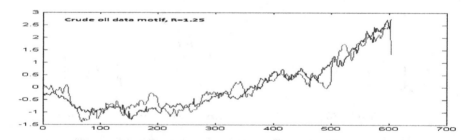

Fig. 11. Motifs obtained from crude oil price data using proposed algorithm

Table 1. Results of proposed algorithm of USD-GBP data

R value	Time elapsed		Distance between subsequences	
	EP-C algorithm	Proposed algorithm	EP-C algorithm	Proposed algorithm
1.1	3.344	**0.09**	21.67	**19.04**
1.09	2.56	**0.09**	22.37	**15.02**
1.08	3.23	**0.105**	14.19	**10.36**
1.07	2.77	**0.08**	8.54	**8.13**
1.06	3.78	**0.11**	12.72	**6.31**
1.05	4.96	**0.12**	4.65	**3.19**

Table 2. Results of proposed algorithm of USD-EUR data

R value	Time elapsed		Distance between subsequences	
	EP-C algorithm	Proposed algorithm	EP-C algorithm	Proposed algorithm
1.1	1.298	**0.05**	15.65	**15.53**
1.09	1.217	**0.06**	13.12	**13.25**
1.08	2.1	**0.07**	11.46	**10.49**
1.07	2.14	**0.08**	11.46	**10.49**
1.06	2.84	**0.08**	13.95	**9.41**
1.05	2.83	**0.09**	8.55	**8.29**

Table 3. Results of proposed algorithm of USD-INR data

R value	Time elapsed		Distance between subsequences	
	EP-C algorithm	Proposed algorithm	EP-C algorithm	Proposed algorithm
1.08	2.55	**0.08**	29.59	**25.14**
1.07	2.58	**0.09**	23.22	**16.09**
1.06	4.44	**0.11**	18.32	**14.21**
1.05	4.25	**0.1**	15.71	**10.40**
1.03	4.564	**0.01**	10.68	**5.86**

Table 4. Result of proposed algorithm of GOLD price data

R value	Time elapsed		Distance between subsequences	
	EP-C algorithm	Proposed algorithm	EP-C algorithm	Proposed algorithm
1.1	5.19	**0.14**	14.84	**9.49**
1.09	5.7	**0.14**	12.43	**9.49**
1.08	7.05	**0.016**	12.43	**8.71**
1.07	7.31	**0.2**	11.15	**6.68**
1.06	4.83	**0.13**	8.08	**4.94**

Table 5. Result of proposed algorithm of CRUDE OIL price data

	Time elapsed		Distance between subsequences	
R value	EP-C algorithm	Proposed algorithm	EP-C algorithm	Proposed algorithm
1.5	3.57	**0.13**	20.12	**19.6925**
1.3	4.31	**0.14**	15.54	**13.76**
1.25	3.32	**0.9**	13.40	**9.88**
1.2	4.11	**0.11**	12.58	**8.69**
1.15	3.43	**0.10**	13.17	**7.26**

5 Conclusion

This paper proposed a novel hybrid algorithm for discovering motifs from financial time series. It took the best out of the two popular motif discovery algorithms such as MK Algorithm and EP-C Algorithm. It overcame the difficulties of both algorithms. After experimentation on five financial datasets, it is concluded that the proposed hybrid model discovered motifs better than these two algorithms in literature. The discovered motifs can be used in making accurate predictions.

References

1. Jiang, Y.-F., Li, C.-P., Han, J.-H.: Stock temporal prediction based on time series motifs. In: Proceedings of Eighth International conference on Machine Learning and Cybernetics (2009)
2. Lin, J., Keogh, E., Lonardi, S., Patel, P.: Finding motifs in time series: In: Proceedings of 8th ACM SIGKDD International Conference on Knowledge Discovery and Data Mining, Edmonton, Alberta, Canada (2002)
3. Mueen, A., Keogh, E., Zhu, Q., Cash, S., Westover, B.: Exact Discovery of Time Series Motif. In: Proceedings of 2009 SIAM International Conference on Data Mining, pp. 1–12 (2009)
4. Gruber, C., Coduro, M., Sick, B., Signature verification with dynamic RBF network and time series motifs. In: Proceedings of 10th International Workshop on Frontiers in Hand Writing Recognition (2006)
5. Truong, C.D., Anh, D.T.: Time series prediction using motif information. In: Sombattheera, C., Loi, N.K., Wankar, R., Quan, T. (eds.) MIWAI 2012. LNCS, vol. 7694, pp. 110–121. Springer, Heidelberg (2012)
6. Nunthanid, P., Niennattrakul, V., Ratanamahatana, C.A.: Discovery of variable length time series motif. In: Proceedings of 8th Electrical Engineering/Electronics, Computer, Telecommunications and Information Technology (ECTI), pp. 472–475 (2011)
7. Chiu, B., Keogh, E., Lonardi, S.: Probabilistic discovery of time series motifs. In: Proceedings of 9th International Conference on Knowledge Discovery and Data Mining (KDD 2003), pp. 493–498 (2003)
8. Tompa, M., Buhler, J.: Finding motifs using random projections. In: Proceedings of the 5th International Conference on Computational Molecular Biology, pp. 67–74 (2001)

9. Tang, H., Liao, S.S.: Discovering original motifs with different lengths from time series. Knowl. Based Syst. **21**, 666–671 (2008)
10. Wilson, W., Birkin, P., Aickelin, U.: The motif tracking algorithm. Int. J. Autom. Comput. **04**(1), 100–106 (2007)
11. Fuchs, E., Gruber, T., Nitschke, J., Sick, B.: On-line motif detection in time series with SwiftMotif. Pattern Recogn. **42**, 3015–3031 (2009)

A Novel ELM K-Means Algorithm for Clustering

Abobakr Khalil Alshamiri, Bapi Raju Surampudi, and Alok Singh[✉]

School of Computer and Information Sciences, University of Hyderabad,
Hyderabad 500046, India
abobakr2030@yahoo.com, {bapics,alokcs}@uohyd.ernet.in

Abstract. Extreme learning machine (ELM) as a new technology has
shown its good generalization performance in regression and classification applications. Clustering analysis is an important tool to explore
the structure of data and has been employed in many disciplines and
applications. In this work, we propose a method that efficiently performs
clustering in a high-dimensional space. The method builds on ELM projection into a high-dimensional feature space and the K-means algorithm
for unsupervised clustering. The proposed ELM K-means algorithm is
tested on twelve benchmark data sets. The experimental results indicate
that ELM K-means algorithm can efficiently be used for multivariate
data clustering.

Keywords: Clustering · Extreme learning machine · K-means algorithm

1   Introduction

Clustering is the method that discovers natural grouping(s) of a set of patterns,
points, or objects. The goal of data clustering, also known as cluster analysis, is to partition a dataset into clusters (also called groups) of similar objects
on the basis of a *similarity* (or *dissimilarity*) measure, thereby minimizing the
similarities between objects belonging to different clusters and maximizing the
similarities between objects belonging to the same cluster, i.e., the objects within
a group are more similar to each other (high intra-cluster similarity) than objects
belonging to different groups (low inter-cluster similarity) [1–3]. There are several
similarity (or *dissimilarity*) measures and the choice of an appropriate measure
depends on the data under analysis and the purpose of the analysis. Clustering has been successfully applied in a large variety of applications, for example, image segmentation, object and character recognition, document retrieval,
remote sensing, data compression, etc.

Clustering techniques can be broadly classified into two categories based on
the structure of abstraction, viz. hierarchical clustering and partitional clustering [2,3]. Hierarchical clustering techniques group data objects with a sequence
of partitions, either from singleton clusters towards a cluster containing all individuals or vice versa. The result is a hierarchical structure of partitions known
as *dendrogram* in which each partition is nested within the partition at the

© Springer International Publishing Switzerland 2015
B.K. Panigrahi et al. (Eds.): SEMCCO 2014, LNCS 8947, pp. 212–222, 2015.
DOI: 10.1007/978-3-319-20294-5_19

next level in the hierarchy. Hierarchical methods can be either agglomerative or divisive. Agglomerative algorithms place each pattern in its own cluster at the outset and then successively merge (or *agglomerate*) pairs of clusters until all clusters have been merged into a single cluster that contains all patterns or the desired objective is obtained. Divisive algorithms begin with all patterns placed in one cluster and then proceed by splitting a cluster into smaller clusters recursively until individual patterns are reached or a stopping criterion is met [4,5]. In contrast to hierarchical clustering, partitional clustering assigns a set of patterns into specified or estimated number of clusters with no hierarchical structure. One of the important problems in partitional clustering is to find a partition of the given data, with a specified number of clusters, that minimizes (or maximizes) some criterion function. The sum of squared error function is one of the most widely used criteria. K-means is one of the simplest and the most well known algorithms of the partitional methods [6].

K-means algorithm is distance-based because the similarity of the patterns is computed by Euclidean distance or Cosine distance. Distance-based clustering algorithms are effective for data with an ellipsoidal or hyper-spherical distribution. If the separation boundaries between clusters are nonlinear, the algorithms will fail. One of the approaches to solving this problem is to nonlinearly transform the input data into a high-dimensional feature space (i.e., kernel mapping) and then perform the clustering within this feature space [7].

Kernel function implicitly defines a non-linear transformation that increases the separability of the data by mapping them from their original input space to a high-dimensional space called *feature space.*

Suppose we are given a data set $\aleph = \{(\mathbf{x}_i) \mid \mathbf{x}_i \in \mathbf{R}^d, i = 1, \ldots, N\}$, and a mapping function ϕ that maps the data $\mathbf{x}_i$ from the input space R^d to a new feature space F. The kernel function is defined as the dot product in the feature space:

$$K(\mathbf{x}_i, \mathbf{x}_j) = \phi(\mathbf{x}_i) \cdot \phi(\mathbf{x}_j) \tag{1}$$

Some commonly used kernel functions are given below:

- Polynomial of degree p:

$$K(\mathbf{x}_i, \mathbf{x}_j) = (\mathbf{x}_i \cdot \mathbf{x}_j + 1)^p, \qquad p \in N. \tag{2}$$

- Gaussian:

$$K(\mathbf{x}_i, \mathbf{x}_j) = \exp\left(-\frac{\|\mathbf{x}_i - \mathbf{x}_j\|^2}{2\sigma^2}\right), \ \sigma \in R. \tag{3}$$

- Neural:

$$K(\mathbf{x}_i, \mathbf{x}_j) = \tanh(a\mathbf{x}_i \cdot \mathbf{x}_j + b), \ a, b \in R. \tag{4}$$

Kernel-based clustering algorithms exploit the notion that performing a nonlinear transformation of a set of nonlinearly separable patterns into a higher-dimensional feature space increases the possibility to separate these patterns linearly. The linear partitioning in this feature space corresponds to a nonlinear partitioning in the input space. Consequently, kernel-based clustering methods may achieve better generalization performance by working in this feature space. Various kernel-based clustering methods have been proposed in the literature. Girolami [8] proposed a kernel method for clustering in feature space. The method also provides estimation of the possible number of clusters using the kernel matrix. Scholkopf et al. [9] proposed kernel K-means method where the standard K-means algorithm was presented in the feature space by employing the kernel trick. The main drawbacks of the kernel K-means clustering method are the local minima and scalability as it requires computing the full kernel matrix whose size is quadratic in the number of data points. To overcome the local minima problem, Tzortzis and Likas [10] proposed the global kernel K-means algorithm, which optimizes the clustering error in the feature space by locating near-optimal solutions. A solution to large scale kernel clustering is presented in [11,12]. Camastra and Verri [13] proposed a kernel method for clustering inspired by the classical K-means algorithm and based on one-class Support Vector Machine (SVM) description of a data set. Ant-based clustering algorithm integrated with the kernel method was proposed in [7]. The integration of kernels with K-means, fuzzy K-means, SOM, Neural gas, and one-class SVM has been shown to be effective in improving the quality of clustering [3].

In this paper, we have incorporated the extreme learning machine (ELM) method into K-means algorithm and proposed a novel K-means clustering with the ELM feature space (ELM K-means). The ELM method is used to project the data into a high-dimensional feature space and the K-means algorithm, using the Euclidean distance in the feature space as a measure of the similarity between the objects, performs the clustering within this feature space.

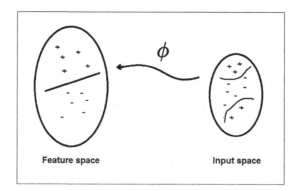

Fig. 1. Mapping from input space to feature space. The mapping function ϕ maps the data from their original input space to a high-dimensional feature space where the data are expected to be more separable.

The remainder of this paper is organized as follows: Sect. 2 describes the basics of the Extreme Learning Machine (ELM). Section 3 introduces K-means algorithm. In Sect. 4, we present the proposed ELM K-means algorithm. Experiments and results are presented and discussed in Sect. 5. Finally, Sect. 6 concludes this paper.

2   Extreme Learning Machine

ELM is a new learning algorithm, proposed by Huang et al. [14–16], for single-hidden layer feedforward neural networks (SLFNs), which randomly generates hidden nodes and analytically determines the output weights of SLFNs. Unlike the traditional slow gradient-based learning algorithms (such as backpropagation algorithms (BP)) for SLFNs, which require all parameters (weights and biases) of all the layers of the feedforward networks to be tuned, ELM randomly chooses the input weights and the hidden layer biases and analytically determines the output weights of SLFNs. Input weights are the weights of the connections between input neurons and hidden neurons and output weights are the weights of the connections between hidden neurons and output neurons. In theory, ELM algorithm tends to produce good generalization performance at extremely low computational cost. ELM has been extensively used for solving classification and regression problems. For formally defining the ELM, we will follow the same notational convention as used in [15]. For instance, we are given a set of training examples $\aleph = \{(\mathbf{x}_i, \mathbf{t}_i) \mid \mathbf{x}_i \in \mathbf{R}^d, \mathbf{t}_i \in \mathbf{R}^m, i = 1, \ldots, N\}$, standard SLFNs with L hidden neurons and activation function $g(x)$, then the output of SLFNs can be represented as [15]:

$$\sum_{i=1}^{L} \beta_i g(\mathbf{w}_i \cdot \mathbf{x}_j + b_i) = \mathbf{y}_j, \quad j = 1, \ldots, N. \tag{5}$$

where $\beta_i = [\beta_{i1}, \ldots, \beta_{im}]^T$ is the weight vector connecting the ith hidden node and the output nodes, $\mathbf{w}_i = [w_{i1}, \ldots, w_{id}]^T$ is the weight vector connecting the ith hidden node and the input nodes, and b_i is the bias of the ith hidden node. $\mathbf{w}_i \cdot \mathbf{x}_j$ is the inner product of $\mathbf{w}_i$ and $\mathbf{x}_j$. With that standard SLFNs the parameters $\beta_i, i = 1, \ldots, L$ can be estimated such that

$$\sum_{i=1}^{L} \beta_i g(\mathbf{w}_i \cdot \mathbf{x}_j + b_i) = \mathbf{t}_j, \quad j = 1, \ldots, N. \tag{6}$$

Equation (6) can be written as in [15]:

$$\mathbf{H}\beta = \mathbf{T} \tag{7}$$

where

$$\mathbf{H} = \begin{bmatrix} g(\mathbf{w}_1 \cdot \mathbf{x}_1 + b_1) & \cdots & g(\mathbf{w}_L \cdot \mathbf{x}_1 + b_L) \\ \vdots & \cdots & \vdots \\ g(\mathbf{w}_1 \cdot \mathbf{x}_N + b_1) & \cdots & g(\mathbf{w}_L \cdot \mathbf{x}_N + b_L) \end{bmatrix}_{N \times L} \tag{8}$$

$$\beta = \begin{bmatrix} \beta_1^T \\ \vdots \\ \beta_L^T \end{bmatrix}_{L \times m} \quad \text{and} \quad \mathbf{T} = \begin{bmatrix} \mathbf{t}_1^T \\ \vdots \\ \mathbf{t}_N^T \end{bmatrix}_{N \times m} \tag{9}$$

where $\mathbf{H}$ is called the hidden layer output matrix of the neural network [17].

The ELM algorithm consists of three steps and can be summarized as follows [18]:

ELM Algorithm: Given a data set $\aleph = \{(\mathbf{x}_i, \mathbf{t}_i) \mid \mathbf{x}_i \in \mathbf{R}^d, \mathbf{t}_i \in \mathbf{R}^m, i = 1, \ldots, N\}$, activation function $g(x)$, and hidden node number L.

1. Randomly generate input weight $\mathbf{w}_i$ and bias b_i, $i = 1, \ldots, L$.
2. Compute the hidden layer output matrix $\mathbf{H}$.
3. Calculate the output weight $\beta : \beta = \mathbf{H}^\dagger \mathbf{T}$, where $\mathbf{H}^\dagger$ is the Moore-Penrose generalized inverse [19] of the hidden layer output matrix $\mathbf{H}$ and $\mathbf{T} = [\mathbf{t}_i, \ldots, \mathbf{t}_N]^T$.

In ELM theory, the number of neurons in the hidden layer of the ELM should be large enough to achieve good generalization performance. A detailed discussion on hidden nodes selection in particular and ELM in general can be found in [15, 18].

3   K-Means Algorithm

K-means is an unsupervised learning algorithm that, based on some optimization measures, partitions the data set into a given number of clusters. The clustering problem, which K-means algorithm is designed to solve, can be stated as follows: Given a representation of N patterns, find K clusters based on a measure of similarity such that the patterns within a cluster are more similar to each other (high intra-cluster similarity) than patterns belonging to different clusters (low inter-cluster similarity).

Let $X = \{\mathbf{x}_i, i = 1, \ldots, N\}$ be the set of N patterns to be clustered into a set of K clusters, $C = \{c_k, k = 1, \ldots, K\}$. Typically $K \ll N$ and each pattern is a vector of dimension d ($\mathbf{x}_i \in R^d$). K-means algorithm finds a partition such that the squared Euclidean distance between the center of a cluster and the patterns in the cluster is minimized. Let μ_k be the mean of cluster c_k and it is defined as:

$$\mu_k = \frac{1}{N_k} \sum_{\mathbf{x}_i \in c_k} \mathbf{x}_i \tag{10}$$

N_k is the number of patterns in cluster c_k.

The squared error between μ_k and the patterns in cluster c_k is defined as in [20]:

$$J(c_k) = \sum_{\mathbf{x}_i \in c_k} \| \mathbf{x}_i - \mu_k \|^2 \tag{11}$$

The main objective of K-means algorithm is to minimize the sum of the squared error over all K clusters,

$$J(C) = \sum_{k=1}^{K} \sum_{\mathbf{x}_i \in c_k} \| \mathbf{x}_i - \mu_k \|^2 \tag{12}$$

K-means is an iterative algorithm. It starts by initializing the centers randomly. In every iteration, each pattern is assigned to its closest cluster, based on the distance between the pattern and the cluster center. The cluster centers in the next iteration are determined by computing the mean value of the patterns for each cluster. The algorithm terminates when there is no reassignment of any pattern from one cluster to another. The main steps of K-means algorithm are as follows:

1. Initialize K cluster centers.
2. Assign each pattern to its closest cluster.
3. Compute new cluster centers using (10).
4. Repeat steps 2 and 3 until there is no change for each cluster.

4   Proposed ELM K-Means Algorithm

This section describes the proposed approach which combines both the ELM and K-means algorithms. ELM performs a nonlinear transformation of the input data into a high-dimensional feature space. This transformation increases the separability of the input data in the high-dimensional feature space. The incorporation of ELM enables the K-means algorithm to explore the inherent data structure in the new space. In ELM, the hidden layer maps the data from the input space R^d to the high-dimensional feature space R^L ($L \gg d$) where the data clustering is performed. This idea of ELM mapping is similar to the idea behind the use of kernels, i.e., linearly non-separable features in the input space often become linearly separable after they are mapped to a high-dimensional feature space (see Fig. 1).

Given two data points $\mathbf{x}$ and $\mathbf{z}$ and an ELM with L neurons defining a mapping ϕ from the input space R^d to the feature space F

$$\phi \colon R^d \to F.$$

The Euclidean distance between $\mathbf{x}$ and $\mathbf{z}$ in the input space is

$$d(\mathbf{x}, \mathbf{z}) = \sqrt{\| \mathbf{x} - \mathbf{z} \|^2} \tag{13}$$

After the points $\mathbf{x}$ and $\mathbf{z}$ are mapped into the feature space, the Euclidean distance between $\phi(\mathbf{x})$ and $\phi(\mathbf{z})$ in the feature space becomes [7]:

$$d_F(\mathbf{x}, \mathbf{z}) = \sqrt{\| \phi(\mathbf{x}) - \phi(\mathbf{z}) \|^2}$$
$$= \sqrt{\phi(\mathbf{x}) \cdot \phi(\mathbf{x}) - 2\phi(\mathbf{x}) \cdot \phi(\mathbf{z}) + \phi(\mathbf{z}) \cdot \phi(\mathbf{z})}$$

$$\tag{14}$$

Equation (13) can be replaced by Eq. (14) as the similarity measure in the clustering algorithms working in a high-dimensional feature space. Based on this principle, the proposed ELM K-means algorithm can be visualized as mapping the data into a high-dimensional feature space and then performing clustering in the feature space.

The ELM K-means algorithm consists of three steps and can be summarized as follows:

ELM K-means Algorithm: Given a data set $\aleph = \{(\mathbf{x}_i) \mid \mathbf{x}_i \in \mathbf{R}^d, i = 1, \ldots, N\}$, activation function $g(x)$, and hidden node number L.

1. Assign arbitrary input weight $\mathbf{w}_i$ and bias b_i, $i = 1, \ldots, L$.
2. Compute the hidden layer output matrix $\mathbf{H}$.
3. Apply K-means algorithm on the hidden layer output matrix $\mathbf{H}$.

where $\mathbf{H} = [h(\mathbf{x}_i), \ldots, h(\mathbf{x}_N)]^T$ and $h(\mathbf{x}) = [g(\mathbf{w}_1, b_1, \mathbf{x}), \ldots, g(\mathbf{w}_L, b_L, \mathbf{x})]$ is the output vector of the hidden layer with respect to the input $\mathbf{x}$. $h(\mathbf{x})$ actually projects the data from the d-dimensional input space into the L-dimensional hidden layer feature space $\mathbf{H}$ in which the clustering is performed.

5   Experimental Study

In this paper, twelve benchmark data sets are used to evaluate the performance of the proposed ELM K-means algorithm. These data sets, except USPST data set, can be downloaded from the UCI Machine Learning Repository at http://www.ics.uci.edu/~mlearn/MLRepository.html. The data sets and their characteristics, viz. the number of patterns, the number of features and the number of classes are given in alphabetical order in Table 1.

5.1   Data Sets

The data sets considered in this work can be described briefly as follows. Balance data set was generated to model psychological experimental results. Each pattern is classified as having the balance scale tip to the right, tip to the left, or remain exactly in the middle. The data set includes 4 features, 3 classes and there are 625 patterns. Cancer-Diagnostic and Cancer-Original data sets are based on the "breast cancer Wisconsin - Diagnostic" and "breast cancer Wisconsin - Original" data sets, respectively. Both data sets classify a tumor as either benign or malignant. Cancer-Diagnostic data set contains 569 patterns, 30 features. Cancer-Original data sat contains 699 patterns. After removing the 16 database patterns with missing values, the database consists of 683 patterns, 9 features. Cardiotocography data set consists of measurements of fetal heart rate (FHR) and uterine contraction (UC) features on cardiotocograms classified by expert obstetricians. Classification was both with respect to a morphologic pattern (ten classes; 1 to 10) and to a fetal state (three classes; normal, suspect and pathologic). Therefore the dataset can be used either for 10-class (Cardiotocography-10) or 3-class

Table 1. Data sets characteristics

Data sets	Patterns	Features	Classes
Balance	625	4	3
Cancer-Diagnostic	569	30	2
Cancer-Original	683	9	2
Cardiotocography-3	2126	21	3
Cardiotocography-10	2126	21	10
CNAE	1080	856	9
Dermatology	358	34	6
Glass	214	9	6
Iris	150	4	3
LIBRAS	360	90	15
Spam	1534	57	2
USPST	2007	256	10

(Cardiotocography-3) experiments. The data set consists of 2126 21-dimensional patterns. CNAE data set contains 1080 documents of free text business descriptions of Brazilian companies categorized into a subset of 9 categories. The original texts were pre-processed so that each document can be represented as a vector, where the weight of each word is its frequency in the document. This data set is highly sparse (99.22 % of the matrix is filled with zeros). Dermatology data set aims to determine the type of Eryhemato-Squamous Disease. The data set contains 366 patterns. After the removal of the 8 data set patterns with missing values, the data set consists of 358 34-dimensional patterns belonging to six different classes. Glass data set contains 214 patterns, 9 features and 6 glass types. The glass types are float processed building windows, non-float processed building windows, vehicle windows, containers, tableware and head lamps. The Fisher Iris data [21] is one of the most popular data sets to test the performance of novel methods in pattern recognition and machine learning. There are three classes in this data set (Setosa, Versicolor and Virginica), each having 50 patterns with four features (sepal length, sepal width, petal length and petal width). One of the classes (viz. Setosa) is linearly separable from the other two, while the remaining two are not linearly separable (see Fig. 2, in which only two features are used). LIBRAS data set is based on the Libras Movement data set. The data set contains 15 classes of 24 patterns each. Each class references to a hand movement type in LIBRAS (Portuguese name 'Língua BRAsileira de Sinais', oficial brazilian signal language). The Spam data set consists of 1,534 patterns from two different classes, spam and not-spam. Each pattern is represented by a 57-dimensional feature vector. The USPST data set is a subset (the testing set) of the well-known handwritten digit recognition data set USPS. The data set includes 256 features, 10 classes and there are 2007 patterns.

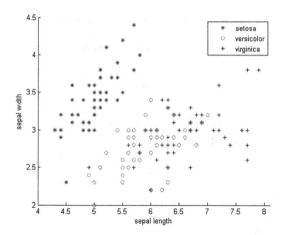

Fig. 2. Iris data set. There are three classes, Setosa class is linearly separable from the other two classes. Versicolor and Virginica classes are not linearly separable.

5.2   Results and Discussion

For each data set, we report the Average of Correctly Clustered patterns (ACC) which is defined as

$$ACC = \frac{\sum_{i=1}^{\# \text{ of runs}} \# \text{ of correctly clustered patterns}}{\# \text{ of runs}} \tag{15}$$

We also report the Percentage of Average Correct Clustering (PACC) which is the average of correctly clustered patterns (ACC) percentaged to the size of the data set.

$$PACC = 100 \times \frac{ACC}{\text{size of data set}} \tag{16}$$

The PACC values are shown in parenthesis in Table 2. The proposed ELM K-means algorithm is tested on 12 benchmark data sets and its performance is compared with the K-means algorithm. We used the Sigmoid function for non-linear mapping and the number of hidden neurons were set to 1000 for all the data sets. The input weights and biases were randomly generated from a uniform distribution over $[-1, 1]$. We ran both K-means and ELM K-means algorithms 20 independent times. The average performance, in terms of correctly clustered patterns, of these algorithms are reported in Table 2. From the results, it is obvious that the proposed ELM K-means outperformed K-means consistently on all data sets, which demonstrate the advantages of performing clustering in the ELM high-dimensional feature space. The results are also in line with the concept that the data which are not linearly separable in the input space often become linearly separable in the high-dimensional space which enables the clustering algorithm to achieve significantly better performance than that in the input space. As far as the time complexity of the proposed algorithm is concerned, it is definitely more

Table 2. Average performance, in terms of correctly clustered patterns, of the K-means and the ELM K-means algorithms

Data sets	K-means	ELM K-means
Balance	419.3 ± 24 (67.09 %)	434.2 ± 16.84 (69.47 %)
Cancer-Diagnostic	528 ± 0 (92.79 %)	536 ± 0 (94.2 %)
Cancer-Original	656 ± 0 (96.05 %)	659 ± 0 (96.49 %)
Cardiotocography-3	1655 ± 0 (77.85 %)	1666.9 ± 16.64 (78.41 %)
Cardiotocography-10	984.35 ± 35.73 (46.3 %)	1022.35 ± 45.88 (48.09 %)
CNAE	527.6 ± 55.13 (48.85 %)	602.25 ± 56.95 (55.76 %)
Dermatology	296.2 ± 20.54 (82.74 %)	304.15 ± 22.78 (84.96 %)
Glass	122.5 ± 3.8 (57.24 %)	126.15 ± 8.7 (58.95 %)
Iris	128.9 ± 12.46 (85.93 %)	129.9 ± 22.51 (86.6 %)
LIBRAS	168.1 ± 7.5 (46.69 %)	176.3 ± 6.89 (48.97 %)
Spam	1097.85 ± 155.77 (71.57 %)	1101.65 ± 158.08 (71.82 %)
USPST	1365.45 ± 46.09 (68.03 %)	1425.4 ± 76.51 (71.02 %)

in comparison to traditional K-means clustering algorithm due to higher number of dimensions involved. Moreover, there is an additional cost involving one-time computation of the hidden layer output matrix **H** of the ELM algorithm.

6 Conclusion

In this paper, extreme learning machine, which is a new and simple technique, is used with K-means algorithm (ELM K-means) for unsupervised clustering of twelve benchmark data sets. The results of the experiments demonstrate that the integration of ELM method with K-means algorithm improves the quality of clustering.

As a future work, we intend to incorporate the ELM method with some metaheuristic techniques and compare the performance of the resulting method with the ELM K-means algorithm.

References

1. Han, J., Kamber, M.: Data Mining: Concepts and Techniques. Academic Press, San Diego (2001)
2. Jain, A.K., Murty, M.N., Flynn, P.J.: Data clustering: a review. ACM Comput. Surv. 31(3), 264–323 (1999)
3. Filippone, M., Camastra, F., Masulli, F., Rovetta, S.: A survey of kernel and spectral methods for clustering. Pattern Recognit. 41, 176–190 (2008)
4. Jain, A.K., Dubes, R.C.: Algorithms for Clustering Data. Prentice-Hall, Englewood Cliffs (1989)

5. Xu, R., Wunsch II, D.: Survey of clustering algorithms. IEEE Trans. Neural Networks **16**(3), 645–678 (2005)
6. Ng, M.K.: A note on constrained K-means algorithms. Pattern Recognit. **33**, 515–519 (2000)
7. Zhang, L., Cao, Q.: A novel ant-based clustering algorithm using the kernel method. Inf. Sci. **181**, 4658–4672 (2011)
8. Girolami, M.: Mercer kernel based clustering in feature space. IEEE Trans. Neural Networks **13**(3), 780–784 (2002)
9. Scholkopf, B., Smola, A., Muller, K.R.: Nonlinear component analysis as a kernel eigenvalue problem. Neural Comput. **10**(5), 1299–1319 (1998)
10. Tzortzis, G.F., Likas, A.C.: The global kernel K-means algorithm for clustering in feature space. IEEE Trans. Neural Networks **20**(7), 1181–1194 (2009)
11. Zhang, R., Rudnicky, A.I.: A large scale clustering scheme for kernel K-means. In: Proceedings of 16th International Conference on Pattern Recognition (ICPR), Quebec, Canada, vol. 4, pp. 289–292 (2002)
12. Chitta, R., Jin, R., Havens, T.C., Jain, A.K.: Approximate kernel k-means: solution to large scale kernel clustering. In: Proceedings of 17th ACM SIGKDD International Conference on Knowledge Discovery and Data Mining (KDD), New York, USA, pp. 895–903 (2011)
13. Camastra, F., Verri, A.: A novel kernel method for clustering. IEEE Trans. Pattern Anal. Mach. Intell. **27**(5), 801–805 (2005)
14. Huang, G.B., Zhu, Q.Y., Siew, C.K.: Extreme learning machine: a new learning scheme of feedforward neural networks. In: Proceedings of International Joint Conference on Neural Networks (IJCNN), Budapest, Hungary, vol. 2, pp. 985–990 (2004)
15. Huang, G.B., Zhu, Q.Y., Siew, C.K.: Extreme learning machine: theory and applications. Neurocomputing **70**, 489–501 (2006)
16. Huang, G.B., Chen, L., Siew, C.K.: Universal approximation using incremental constructive feedforward networks with random hidden nodes. IEEE Trans. Neural Networks **17**(4), 879–892 (2006)
17. Huang, G.B.: Learning capability and storage capacity of two-hidden-layer feedforward networks. IEEE Trans. Neural Networks **14**(2), 274–281 (2003)
18. Lan, Y., Soh, Y.C., Huang, G.B.: Constructive hidden nodes selection of extreme learning machine for regression. Neurocomputing **73**, 3191–3199 (2010)
19. Serre, D.: Matrices: Theory and Applications. Springer-Verlag Inc., New York (2002)
20. Jain, A.K.: Data clustering: 50 years beyond K-means. Pattern Recognit. **31**, 651–666 (2010)
21. Fisher, R.A.: The use of multiple measurements in taxonomic problems. Ann. Eugen. **7**, 179–188 (1936)

Software Effort Estimation Using Functional Link Neural Networks Tuned with Active Learning and Optimized with Particle Swarm Optimization

Tirimula Rao Benala[1(✉)], Rajib Mall[2], Satchidananda Dehuri[3], and Pala Swetha[1]

[1] Department of Information Technology,
Jawaharlal Nehru Technological University Kakinada,
University College of Engineering, Vizianagaram 535003, India
{b.tirimula,palaswetha}@gmail.com
[2] Department of Computer Science and Engineering,
Indian Institute of Technology Kharagpur, Kharagpur, India
rajib@cse.iitkgp.ernet.in
[3] Department of Information and Communication Technology,
Fakir Mohan University, Vyasa Vihar, Balasore 756019, Odisha, India
satchi.lapa@gmail.com

Abstract. This paper puts forward a new learning model based on the collaborative effort of active learning and particle swarm optimization (PSO) in functional link artificial neural networks (FLANNs) to estimate software effort. The active learning uses quick algorithm to detect the essential content of the datasets by which the dataset is reduced and are processed through PSO optimized FLANN. The PSO uses the inertia weight, which is an important parameter in PSO that significantly affects the convergence and exploration-exploitation in the search space while training FLANN. The Chebyshev polynomial has been used for mapping the original feature space from lower to higher dimensional functional space. The method has been evaluated exhaustively on different test suits of PROMISE repository to study the performance. The computational results show that the active learning along with PSO optimized FLANN greatly improves the performance of the model and its variants for software development effort estimation.

Keywords: Software effort estimation · PSO · Active learning and FLANN

1 Introduction

Software effort estimation is the process of prediction of effort, cost, schedule, and staffing levels for successful project management [10, 11]. Accurate software cost estimation is highly required for the effective software project management. It significantly affects management activities such as resource allocation and creating

© Springer International Publishing Switzerland 2015
B.K. Panigrahi et al. (Eds.): SEMCCO 2014, LNCS 8947, pp. 223–238, 2015.
DOI: 10.1007/978-3-319-20294-5_20

reasonable schedule. The major contributing factor for accurate estimation is effort. This has led researchers to conduct extensive research on software effort estimation methods. Recently, it is boosted to many of the researchers of computational intelligence field to design an intelligent semi-automatic estimator for the aforesaid task [14]. In continuation, this paper investigates the control parameters of FLANN for software effort estimation. The beauty of this approach is that it does not do minimal approximation about the function to be evaluated for effort prediction. Basing on the structure of the dataset the model function parameters are calibrated. The Active Learning algorithm employs tuning of training dataset to characterize the essential content of software effort estimation data; i.e., the least number of features and instances are required to capture the information within software effort estimation data [Active learning]. This work is an improvement and fine tuned of our earlier work PSO-FLANN [11].

FLANN proposed by Pao, is a type of neural network consisting of one input layer and an output layer for forming arbitrarily complex decision regions to guide real world applications. FLANN has been widely used in many application areas of pattern recognition [12], data mining [13], time series forecasting [15], etc. A good survey of FLANN and its variants can be obtained in [13]. FLANN generates output (effort) by expanding the inputs (cost drivers) by nonlinear orthogonal functions like Chebyshev polynomial and then processing the final output layer. Each input neuron corresponds to a component of an input vector. The output layer consists of one output neuron that computes the software development effort as a linear weighted sum of the outputs of the input layer [9, 10]. The non-normal characteristics of the datasets always lead FLANN to low prediction accuracy and high computational complexity. To alleviate these drawbacks the proposed technique has been formulated to exploit the best features of PSO and FLANN. It is named as ACTIVE-FLANN-PSO (a. k. a FAS).

Functional link neural networks and cost estimation fundamentals are briefly reviewed in Sect. 2. The active learning and particle swarm optimization are described in Sects. 3 and 4. Our approach is presented in Sect. 5. In Sect. 6, numerical examples from Cocomo81 (Coco81), Nasa93, Maxwell dataset is used to evaluate the performance. Section 7 concludes this paper.

2 Background

In this section background of this work is discussed. Software cost estimation and FLANN architecture are described in Sects. 2.1 and 2.2, respectively.

2.1 Software Effort Estimation

Software effort estimation (SEE) is one of the important steps in software project management. It can be defined as the task of estimating the total effort required to develop a software system [6]. SEE is incorporated by a set of attributes (also known as, cost drivers) representing a software project to predict (or estimate) the cost, in terms of person-months, in turn to predict the required time to develop the software system [2, 7]. SEE assist the project managers to take strategic decisions such as bidding on a new project, managing development, maintenance or customization of the software, planning, and allocation of resource. Software effort estimation has been the process of building regression models. However, regression models may lead to underestimation and overestimation. The underestimation of software effort drops the software product quality as some of the software development life cycle activities are skipped to avoid cost over runs and to meet the deadline. The overestimation leads to wastage of resources and loss of new projects as most of the resources are engaged without any effective output [1]. According to Oliveira [2, 7], the major bottlenecks for software projects are the schedule and effort (cost) to finish it; the ever changing dynamics of project scope make the process of cost estimation complex. Due to the typical characteristics of each project, the accurate measurement of the cost and development time of software can be determined only after the project is completed [3, 7]. However, it is necessary to perform estimations before the project begins. There are various techniques and methods which can be employed to estimate software development effort, cost, and time. This paper introduces an innovative technique aimed to predict (estimate) the software development effort based on Active Learning, PSO, and FLANN.

2.2 Architecture of FLANN

A typical FLANN structure is illustrated in Fig. 1. FLANN is a typical two layer network with an implicit hidden layer. The original input space is mapped into n-dimensional feature space (n is a user defined parameter, varies across the domains) by functional expansion such that the feature space becomes linearly separable in higher space. The Chebyshev polynomial functional expansion is better suited as basis function in software cost estimation as it produces low error estimates [11, 19]. The output of the basis function is multiplied by random weights chosen in the range [−0.5, 0.5] and the summation of all such multiplications is feed to sigmoid function to predict the development effort of 'n' Person-Months [9, 10]. The learning process involves updating the weights of FLANN in order to minimize a given cost function. The weight vector is evolved by PSO, which has unique characteristics like the rapid convergence of global solutions and less number of parameters to be optimized.

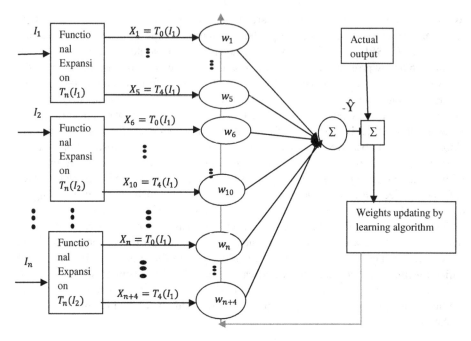

Fig. 1. FLANN architecture

3 Active Learning

Active learning is a special case of semi-supervised machine learning. To characterize the essential content of Software effort estimation data points i.e., the minimum number of features and instances required to capture the information within SEE data. If the essential content is very small then the contained information must be very succinct and the value-added complex learning schemes must be minimal [4].

In active learning, some heuristic (in our case, each row's popularity value) is used to sort instances from most interesting to least interesting. The data is then explored according to that sort order. Learning can terminate early, if the results from all the N instances are not better than from a subset of M instances, where M < N [Active learning].

QUICK is an active learning method that assists in reducing the complexity of data interpretation by identifying the essential content of SEE data sets [4]. QUICK works as follows:

- Group rows and columns by their similarity,
- Discard redundant columns (synonyms) that are too similar,
- Discard outlier rows (outliers) that are too distant, and
- In the remaining data, generate an estimate from the nearest example.

Let us assume that the TrainDataset is the training dataset after sampling the datasets into training and
test datasets,

Algorithm-1: Quick(TrainDataset[1 ... N − 1, 1 ... M])

Repeat until Pop(j) ≤ 1 are exhausted orMRE < 0.1 or

   If the Δ best(Error)~ worst(Error)of last n instances in Active Pool is very small

   %% Active Pool is nothing but our obtained reduced size of the Normalized Training Dataset%%

        Step 1: Start

        Step 2: Synonym Pruning

           Step 2.1: $D[1 ... N − 1, 1 ... M] = TrainDataset[1 ... N − 1, 1 ... M]$%
calculate distance matrix for the transposed training dataset. %

                Step 2.2: DM $[1 ... M, 1 ... M]$ = EuclideanDistance (D', D) % Assign a
rank based on nearest neighbor elements %

                Step 2.3:Enn$[1 ... M, 1 ... M]$ = rank

                    Ex: IfDM$[i, j]$ = 3, it means j is the ith third nearest neighbor

                Step 2.4: Calculate E$(k)[1 ... M, 1 ... M]$

                    if E$[1 ... M, 1 ... M]$ ≤ k E$[1 ... M, 1 ... M]$ = 1

                    else E$[1 ... M, 1 ... M]$ = 0

                Step 2.5: Calculate Popularity index Pop$[1,1 ... M]$

                    Pop$[1,1 ... M]$ = SUM(E$(K)[1 ... M, 1 ... M]$)

                    K=Sum of popularity index whose value is not equal to zero

                Step 2.6:SPD$[1 ... N − 1, 1 ... M − k]$ =

                    TrainDataset$(1 ... N − 1, Index(Pop[1,1 ... M] == 0))$

%select those features whose popularity index value is Zero%

        Step 3: Synonym Pruning Ends

        Step 4: Outlier Pruning starts

                Step 4.1:DM$[1 ... N − 1, 1 ... N − 1]$ = EucledianDistance(SPD, SPD)

%Assign a rank based on nearest neighbor elements%

                Step 4.2: Enn$(1 ... M, 1 ... M)$ = rank

                Step 4.3: Calculate E$(k)[1 ... M, 1 ... M]$

                  if E$[1 ... M, 1 ... M]$ ≤ k E$[1 ... M, 1 ... M]$ = 1

                  else E$[1 ... M, 1 ... M]$ = 0

                Step 4.4: Calculate Popularity index Pop$[1,1 ... M]$

                  Pop$[1,1 ... M]$ = SUM(E$(k)[1 ... M, 1 ... M]$)

                  n=Sum of popularity index whose value is not equal to zero

                Step 4.5:OPD$[1 ... N − n, 1 ... M − k]$ = SPD$(1 ... N − 1, 1 ... M − k)$

        Step 5: Outlier Pruning Ends

4   Particle Swarm Optimization

Particle swarm optimization is a nature inspired algorithm, invented by Kennedy and
Eberhart [21], for dealing with problems in which the best solution can be represented as a
point or surface in an n-dimensional space. Hypothesis are plotted in this space and
seeded with an initial velocity, as well as a communication channel between the particles.
Particles then move through the solution space, and are evaluated according to some
fitness criterion after watch time step. Over time, particles are accelerated towards those
particles within their communication grouping which have better fitness values [11].

    In the particle swarm optimization algorithm, particle swarm consists of "m" particles,
and the position of each particle represents for the potential solution in D-dimensional
space. The particles change its condition according to the following three principles:

(1) To keep its inertia(ω),
(2) To change the condition according to its most optimist position,
(3) To change the condition to the swarm's most optimist position.

The speed and position of each particle changes according to the following equations,

$$v_{id}^{k+1} = \omega v_{id}^k + c_1 r_1^k \left(pbest_{id}^k - x_{id}^k\right) + c_2 r_2^k \left(gbest_{id}^k - x_{id}^k\right)$$
$$x_{id}^{k+1} = x_{id}^k + v_{id}^{k+1}$$

Algorithm-2: $PSO(Y, \hat{Y}, c_1, c_2, r_1 r_2, velocity, position, \omega, pbest, gbest)$

Step 1: Calculate PSOError=sqrt$\left((Y - \hat{Y})^2\right)$

%Find the minimum Fitness or error %

Step 2: from 1...kk

Step 3: $Fitness(kk) = minimum\left(Fitness(1 ... kk)\right) \& MinWtnum = kk$

Step 4: End

Step 5: pbest=wts(MinWtnum)

 Step 6: gbest=minimum(pbest)

%%Update weights wts$[1 ... 10, 1 ... M \times 5]$(position) and changeWeights

changewts$[1 ... kk, 1 ... M \times 5]$(velocity)%%

Step 7: $changewts[1 ... kk, 1 ... kk] = iw \times changewts[1 ... kk, 1 ... M \times 5] + C_1 \times$
$r_1 \times \left(pbest - wts(1 ... kk, 1 ... kk)\right) + C_2 \times r_2 \times \left(gbest - wts(1 ... kk, 1 ... kk)\right)$

Step 8: $wts(1..kk, 1 ... kk) = wts(1 ... kk, 1 ... kk) + changewts(1 ... kk, 1 ... kk)$

$wt1s(1..kk, 1 ... kk) = wts(1 ... kk, 1 ... kk) + changewts(1 ... kk, 1 ... kk)$

%% Updating Inertia of Weights%%

Step 9: $iw = \lambda \times iw + (1 - \lambda) \times$ Variance

> *Step 1: $\lambda = 0.95$*

> *Step 2: $Variance = \sqrt{F}$*

> *% Finding Variance%*

>> *$F1 = absolute\left(FitFunn(1 ... kk) - Average\left(FitFunn(1 ... kk)\right)\right)$*

>> *$F2 = max(F1)$*

>> *if $F2 < 1$*

>>> *$F3 = -1$*

>> *else*

>>> *$F3 = -absolute(max(F2))$*
>>> *$F = sum((F1/F3)^2)$*

> *%Finding variance Ends%*

> *Step 3: End*

Step 10: End

% updated weights are send again for training dataset%

5 ACTIVE-FLANN-PSO Algorithm

In this section, we first present the methodology for software cost estimation, next algorithm, and finally performance evaluation metrics.

5.1 Methodology

ACTIVE-FLANN-PSO (a. k. a FAS) is a typical two layer feed forward neural network consisting of an input layer and output layer with an implicit hidden layer. The nodes between input layer and output layer are connected without weight vector and the nodes between hidden layer and output layer are assigned with weight vector. Unlike FLANN, the weight vector is evolved by PSO learning algorithm. There are M input nodes and N data points in every dataset. Our Active learning algorithm computes the Euclidean distance between rows (instances or data points) and columns (features depend on the cost drivers of a particular dataset) of SEE data, then prunes synonyms (similar features) and outliers (distant instances). This reduced size training dataset is processed by FLANN. The input nodes of the reduced size train dataset are expanded by a basis function to m number of nodes, where m is functionally expanded nodes. In software cost estimation domain Chebyshev polynomial basis function is the most effective function for functional expansion [9, 10, 19]. The basis function maps the input space to higher dimension.

5.2   Algorithm-3

Let us assume, D is the dataset, ND is the normalized Dataset. TrainDataset and TestDataset are the training and testing parts respectively, P is the data point of reduced size, L and H are lower and higher dimensions respectively, and TC is the termination criteria, O is the output layer, W is the weighted sum, E is the error, current best fitness value is CF. Fitness value is F, GB represents global best, PV is the particle velocity.

Step 1: For each Dataset $D[1 \dots N, 1 \dots M]$
  Step 1.1: $ND[1 \dots N, 1 \dots M] = Normalization(D[1 \dots N, 1 \dots M])$
Step 2: Divide ND 2/3rd parts into TrainDataset and 1/3rd part into TestDataset.
Step 3: For each TrainDataset
  Step 3.1: Apply Quick(TrainDataset[1 \dots N − 1, 1 \dots M])
Step 4: For each P
  Step 4.1: Map from L to H.
Step 5: For each particle initialize with small values from [-1, -1].
Step 6: While(!TC)
      {
      Apply PSO$(Y, \hat{Y}, c_1, c_2, r_1 r_2, velocity, position, \omega, pbest, gbest)$
      {
              For each swarm
                {
                For each particle in the swarm
                  {
                  For each sample in the training sample
                    {
                    Calculate W, and send it as input to O.
                    Calculate E.
                    }
                  Assign E to F.
                      If (F is better than CF)
                        {
                        Assign F to CF
                        }
                  Assign CF to GB
                  }
                For each particle
                  {
                  Call Reduced () and Find PV.
                  Update Particle Position
                  }
                }
      }
      }

The overall architechture of the FAS model with training and testing process is shown in Fig. 2.

5.3   Performance Evaluation Metrics

Five evaluation criteria were used to assess the degree of accuracy to which the estimated effort matches actual effort. These evaluation criteria have been chosen as they are widely accepted benchmark metrics for performance evaluation in the software cost estimation literature. They are as follows: Mean Magnitude of Relative Error (MMRE), Median Magnitude of relative error (MdMRE), and PRED (0.25) [5, 8, 20], Standardized Accuracy (SA) and Delta [17].

Testing Procedure including Training:

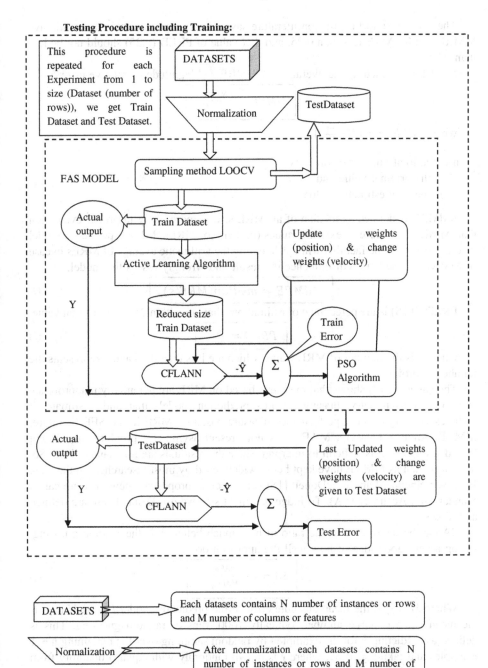

Fig. 2. Overall proposed methodology

The software effort estimation literature says a good prediction model should have MMRE and MdMRE less than 0.25, and that value of PRED (0.25) should not be less than 0.75.

MMRE is defined as the average of all MRE's (Magnitude of relative errors).

$$MMRE = \frac{\Sigma MRE}{n},$$ (1)

where, $MRE = mod\left(\frac{C_i - C_i'}{C_i}\right)$,

n is the total number of projects,
C_i is the original value and
C_i' is the new estimated value.

MdMRE is defined as median of all MRE's. It is more likely in proper evaluation than MMRE as in case of extreme values (outliers) of MREs, MMRE predicts a model incorrectly due to the fact that while calculating the arithmetic average of MREs in case of MMRE the outliers will influence the result and wrongly assess the model.

$$MdMRE = median(MRE's),$$ (2)

PRED (0.25) is the percentage of estimations that are within 25 % of original value.

$$PRED = \frac{k}{n},$$ (3)

where k is the number of MRE values which are less than 0.25 and n represents the number of projects.

The paper [5, 17] shows that measures based on MRE are potentially inappropriate due to their asymmetry, biasing towards prediction models that under-estimate. It includes the very popular performance measure based on MRE in the SEE literature: MMRE. Another measure, MAE, does not present asymmetry problems and is not biased. However, it is difficult to interpret, since the residuals are not standardized. So, measures such as MMRE have kept being widely used by most researchers in the area. However, Shepperd and MacDonell [18] very recently proposed a new measure called Standardized Accuracy (SA). To judge the effect size we use Delta. These are defined as follows:

SA can be interpreted as the ratio of how much better P_i is the random guessing, giving a very good idea of how well the approach does.

$$SA = 1 - \frac{MAE_{P_i}}{\overline{MAE_{P_0}}},$$ (4)

Where MAE_{P_i} is the mean absolute error of the prediction model P_i and $\overline{MAE_{P_0}}$ is the mean value of large number, typically 1000, runs of random guessing. This is defined as predicting $\hat{y}$ for the example t by random sampling over the remaining n − 1 examples and taking $\hat{y}_t = y_r$, where r is drawn randomly with equal probability from $1 \ldots n \bigwedge r \neq t$.

To judge the effect size, he following measure is suggested:

$$\Delta = \frac{MAE_{P_i} - \overline{MAE_{P_0}}}{s_{P_0}},$$ (5)

Where s_{P_0} is the sample standard deviation of the random guessing strategy. The values of Δ can be interpreted in terms of the categories proposed by Cohen [16] of small (≈ 0.2), medium (≈ 0.5) and large (≈ 0.8).

6 Experiments, and Results

In this section, studies were carried out on three PROMISE repository datasets, namely, Cocomo81 (Coc81), Nasa93, Maxwell [7] to investigate the performance of our method. These datasets are available at promisedata.googlecode.com.

6.1 Dataset Preparation

Before the experiments, all input variables (a. k. a features) are normalized using min-max normalization in order to eliminate the possibility of unequal influences. The three datasets shown in Table 1 are subjected to Leave-one-out cross-validation; in each iteration all the data points except for the single observation are used for training and the model is tested on that single observation. Table 1 provides main features of the data sets, including the number of features, size, the skewness, minimum, mean and maximum of effort and size in KLOCS.

Table 1. Descriptive statistics for public datasets [22]

Dataset	Nasa93	Maxwell	Coc81
Features	17	27	17
Size	93	62	63
Units	Months	Hours	Months
Minimum	8	583	6
Effort			
Median	252	5189.5	98
Mean	624	8223.2	683
Maximum effort	8211	63694	11400
Skew	4.2	3.26	4.4

6.2 Cost Estimation Models

This study explored the feasibility of using different models based on FLANN. The functional expansion, namely, Chebyshev polynomial based FLANN (C-FLANN) model is included in our experiments. Hereafter, C-FLANN will be annotated as FLANN. The proposed models using Particle Swarm Optimization and Active Learning is:FAS. For a comprehensive evaluation of the proposed models, for comparison, other popular estimation models including, Functional Link Artificial Neural Networks (FLANN) [9, 10], PSO-FLANN, and Artificial Neural Networks (ANN), are also included in the experiments.

Table 2. Nasa93 dataset

Method	MMRE		MdMRE		PRED (0.25)		SA		DELTA	
	Training	Testing	Training	Testing	Training	Testing	Training	Testing	Training	Testing
PSO-FLANN	0.0012	9.8824e-07	4.2531e-04	1.1360e-04	1	0.0108	0.9999	1	0	1.3140
FAS	0.0022	0.0049	6.3687e-04	9.0165e-04	1	1	0.9918	0.9694	0	3.5012
FLANN	0.0013	0.0021	7.8309e-04	7.9131e-04	1	1	0.9999	0.9999	0	0.0761
ANN	0.0022	0.0053	0.0018	0.0045	1	1	0.9999	0.9998	0	0.8594

Table 3. Maxwell dataset

Method	MMRE		MdMRE		PRED (0.25)		SA		DELTA	
	Training	Testing	Training	Testing	Training	Testing	Training	Testing	Training	Testing
PSO-FLANN	5.8207e-05	2.3489e-07	3.2986e-05	2.3190e-05	1	0.0161	0.9999	1	0	3.7282
FAS	8.0178e-05	1.4138e-04	3.8868e-05	4.7363e-05	1	1	0.9928	0.9752	0	3.4267
FLANN	6.6870e-05	3.4855e-06	5.3921e-05	1.9447e-06	1	1	0.9999	0.9999	0	0.2741
ANN	8.1571e-05	5.7393e-06	7.4071e-05	5.3091e-06	1	1	0.9999	0.9998	0	1.0522

Table 4. Coc81 dataset

Method	MMRE		MdMRE		PRED (0.25)		SA		DELTA	
	Training	Testing	Training	Testing	Training	Testing	Training	Testing	Training	Testing
PSO-FLANN	0.0023	1.3378e-06	9.0977e-04	1.0478e-04	1	0.0159	0.9999	1	0	2.4339
FAS	0.0034	0.0049	0.0011	7.8331e-04	1	1	0.9953	0.9840	0	3.4247
FLANN	0.0022	0.0041	6.4478e-04	4.8037e-04	1	1	1.0000	0.9999	0	0.3207
ANN	0.0050	0.0158	0.0047	0.0121	1	1	0.9998	0.9998	0	1.1774

6.3   Experimental Procedure

For the purpose of validation, we adopt Leave-one-out cross validation to evaluate the generalization error of the methods. In this scheme for each dataset of n data points and given m candidate models, each model is trained with n-1 data points and then it is tested on the sample that was left out. This process is repeated n times until every data point in the dataset have been used as cross-validation instance. Then the average training error and testing error across all three trails are computed. The advantage of this scheme is that it does not matter how the data is split since each data point is assigned in a test set, a training set and a validation set respectively once. At first, the performances of PSO-FLANN, FLANN, FAS, and ANN are investigated. The best variants on training set are selected as the candidates for comparison. Next, the optimizations of parameters of the machine learning methods are performed on the training dataset by searching through their solution space. Thirdly, the training and testing results of the best variants of all estimation methods are summarized and compared. The experimental results and the analysis are presented in the next section [20].

6.4   Experimental Results

Tables 2, 3 and 4 present a summary of all the methods applied on three PROMISE repository datasets given in Table 1. The second column, third column and fourth column in each table shows the performance of various methods with respect to performance metrics MMRE, MdMRE and PRED (0.25) respectively. Similarly, the fourth and fifth column represents SA and DELTA respectively.With these values it can be interpreted that the testing results in the proposed methods outperform the testing results of FLANN, ANN. The FAS model has comparable results with PSO-FLANN in terms of MMRE. MdMRE and PRED (0.25) and performs well in terms of DELTA in NASA93 and Coc81compared to PSO-FLANN.

Our experiments suggest that a hybrid combination of ACTIVE-FLANN-PSO (FAS) improves the accuracy very effectively when compared to FLANN, ANN and has comparable results with respect to PSO-FLANN.

7   Conclusion and Future Work

Software cost estimation by hybrid system using Active learning, PSO and FLANN-an improvement of PSO-FLANN, has been presented in this work. We have evaluated the performance of FAS. The experimental results show that our method gives improved performance as compared to conventional FLANN, ANN and outperforms the competitive techniques such as PSO-FLANN with respect to performance measure DELTA. As a future note, our best effort towards the development of a good effort estimation technique will be based on meta-heuristic techniques like artificial bee colony (ABC) algorithm, and stochastic technique like differential evaluation (DE), and simulated annealing.

References

1. Bakr, A., Turhan, B., Bener, A.: A comparative study of estimating software development effort intervals. Softw. Qual. J. **19**, 537–552 (2010)
2. de Araujo, R.A., Oliveria, A.L.I., Soares, S.: A shift-invariant morphological system for software development cost estimation. Expert Syst. Appl. **38**, 4162–4168 (2011)
3. Braga, P.L., Oliveria, A.L.I., Ribeiro, G.H.T., Meria, S.R.L.: Software effort estimation using machine learning techniques with robust confidence intervals. In: Proceedings of IEEE International Conference on Tools with Artificial Intelligence (ICTAI), pp. 181–185 (2007)
4. Kocaguneli, E., Menzies, T., Keung, J., Cok, D., Madachy, R.: Active learning and effort estimation: Finding the essential content of software effort estimation data. IEEE Trans. Softw. Eng. **39**(8), 1040–1053 (2013)
5. Foss, T., Stenrud, E., Kitchenham, B., Myrtveit, I.: A Simulation study of the model evaluation criterion MMRE. IEEE Trans. Softw. Eng. **29**(11), 985–995 (2003)
6. Keung, J.W.: Theoretical maximum prediction accuracy for analogy-based software cost estimation. In: Proceedings of 15th Asia-Pacific Software Engineering Conference, pp. 495–502 (2008)
7. Menzies, T., Caglayan, B., Kocaguneli, E., Krall, J., Peters, F., Turhan, B.: The PROMISE Repository of Empirical Software Engineering Data. Department of Computer Science, West Virginia Universit (2012). http://promisedata.googlecode.com
8. Stensrud, E., Foss, T., Kitchenham, B.A., Myrtveit, I.: An empirical validation of the relationship between the magnitude of relative error and project size. In: Proceedings of the IEEE 8th Metrics Symposium, pp. 3–12 (2002)
9. Tirimula Rao, B., Sameet, B., Kiran Swathi, G., Vikram Gupta, K., Raviteja, Ch., Sumana, S.: A novel neural network approach for software cost estimation using functional link artificial neural networks. Int. J. Comput. Sci. Netw. Secur. (IJCSNS) **9**(6), 126–131 (2009)
10. Tirimula Rao, B., Dehuri, S., Mall, R.: Functional link artificial neural networks for software cost estimation. Int. J. Appl. Evol. Comput. (IJAEC) **3**(2), 62–82 (2012)
11. Tirimula Rao, B., Chinnababu, K., Mall, R., Dehuri, S.: Particle swarm optimized functional link artificial neural networks (PSO-FLANN) n software cost estimation. In: Proceedings of the International Conference on Frontiers of Intelligent Computing: Theory and Applications (FICTA), Advances in Intelligent Systems and Computing, vol. 199, pp. 59–66 (2013)
12. Dehuri, S., Cho, S.-B.: Evolutionarily optimized features in functional link neural network for classification. Expert Syst. Appl. **37**(6), 4379–4391 (2010)
13. Dehrui, S., Cho, S.-B.: A comprehensive survey on functional link neural networks and an adaptive PSO-BP learning for CFLNN. Neural Comput. Appl. **19**(2), 187–205 (2010)
14. Tirimula Rao, B., Dehuri, S., Mall, R.: Computational intelligence in software cost estimation: an emerging paradigm. ACM SIGSOFT Softw. Eng. Notes **37**(3), 1–7 (2012)
18. Chakravarty, S., Dash, P.L., Pandi, V.R., Panigrahi, B.K.: An evolutionary functional link neural fuzzy model for financial time series forecasting. Int. J. Appl. Evol. Comput. **2**(3), 27–38 (2011)
16. Cohen, J.: Quantitative methods in psychology: a power primer. Psychol. Bull. **112**(1), 155–159 (1992)
17. Minku, Leondro L., Yao, Xin: Ensembles and locality: insight on improving software effort estimation. Inf. Softw. Technol. **55**(8), 1512–1528 (2013)
18. Shepperd, M., MacDonell, S.: Evaluating prediction systems in software project estimation. Inf. Softw. Technol. **54**(8), 820–827 (2012)
19. Abutheraa, M.A., Lester, D.: Computable function representations using effective Chebyshev polynomial. Int. J. Math. Comput. Phys. Quantum Eng. **1**(7), 294–300 (2007)

20. Tirimula Rao B., Mall, R., Dehuri, S., ChinnaBabu, K.: Software effort prediction using unsupervised learning (clustering) and functional link artificial neural networks. In: Proceedings of the IEEE World Congress on Information and Communication Technologies, India, pp. 115–120 (2012)
21. Kennedy, J., Eberhart, R.C.: Particle swarm optimization. In: Proceedings of the IEEE International Conference on Neural Networks, Perth, Australia, pp. 1942–1948 (1995)

Fraud Detection in Financial Statements Using Evolutionary Computation Based Rule Miners

Ganghishetti Pradeep[1,2], Vadlamani Ravi[1(✉)], Kaushik Nandan[3],
B.L. Deekshatulu[1], Indranil Bose[4], and A. Aditya[1]

[1] Center of Excellence in CRM and Analytics,
Institute for Development and Research in Banking Technology,
Castle Hills Road #1 Masab Tank, Hyderabad 500057
Andhra Pradesh, India
{pradeepghyd,padmarav,adityaachanta2}@gmail.com,
bldeekshatulu@idrbta.c.in
[2] SCIS, University of Hyderabad, Hyderabad 500046
Andhra Pradesh, India
[3] Indian Institute of Technology, Patna 800013, Bihar, India
kaushalta@gmail.com
[4] IIM Calcutta, Kolkata 700104, West Bengal, India
bose@iimcal.ac.in

Abstract. In this paper, we propose new rule based classifiers based on Firefly (FF) and Threshold Accepting (TA) Algorithms viz., Improved Firefly Miner, Threshold Accepting Miner, Hybridized Firefly-Threshold Accepting (FFTA) based Miner for classifying a company as fraudulent or non fraudulent with respect to their financial statements. We apply t-statistic based feature selection and investigate its impact on the results. FFTA and TA miners turned to be statistically similar. Both algorithms outperformed standard decision tree both in terms of sensitivity and the length of rules.

Keywords: Firefly algorithm · Threshold accepting algorithm · Evolutionary computing rule miner and financial statement fraud detection

1 Introduction

There has been a huge increase in the number of frauds over the past decade or so. The Lehman Brothers Scandal [1, 2] in 2008 in the US and Satyam Scandal [3] in 2009 in India are among the worst accounting scandals to have occurred in the recent times. In 2007, Lehman Brothers was ranked at the top in the "Most Admired Securities Firm" [1] by Fortune Magazine. Just a year after, the company had gone bankrupt and it was found out that it had hidden $50 billion in loans disguised as sales. It was a serious case of an accounting fraud. The Satyam Computer Services scandal was a corporate scandal that surfaced in India in 2009 where the Chairman confessed that the company's accounts had been falsified. The Global corporate community was shocked when the chairman confessed that he had manipulated the accounts by US$1.47-Billion [3]. These frauds could have been avoided had proper audits taken place. While we have auditors for the

© Springer International Publishing Switzerland 2015
B.K. Panigrahi et al. (Eds.): SEMCCO 2014, LNCS 8947, pp. 239–250, 2015.
DOI: 10.1007/978-3-319-20294-5_21

job, due to the number of cases they have to deal with as well as with the huge amount of data present, it is practically not possible for them to be always accurate. Here the Data Mining techniques come to our rescue. In this paper, we take recourse to employing Evolutionary Computational algorithms in order to generate 'if-then' rules that classify the companies into fraudulent or not. Rule based outputs are of interest to us because they are transparent and yield us knowledge in the human comprehensible form. With proper rule based outputs, we can analyze which variables are more important in determining frauds and take appropriate measures well in advance.

2 Literature Review

There has been a minor research in the field of financial statement fraud detection using data mining techniques. The techniques to have been used include case based reasoning, decision tree methods, text mining, logistic regression, neural networks etc.

According to Kirkos et al. [4], some estimates stated that fraud cost US business more than $400 billion annually. Spathis et al. [5] compared multi-criteria decision aids with statistical techniques such as logit and discriminant analysis in detecting fraudulent financial statements. A novel financial kernel for the detection of management fraud is developed using support vector machines on financial data by Cecchini et al. [6]. Huang et al. [7] developed an innovative fraud detection mechanism on the basis of Zipf's Law. Kirkos et al. [4] used the ID3 decision tree and Bayesian belief network to detect financial statement fraud. Sohl and Venkatachalam [8] used back-propagation NN for the purpose. Cerullo and Cerullo [9] explained the nature of fraud and financial statement fraud along with the characteristics of NN and their applications. Calderon and Cheh [10] examined the efficacy of NN as a potential enabler of business risk based auditing. Koskivaara [11, 12] investigated the impact of various pre processing models on the forecast capability of NN when auditing financial accounts. Busta and Weinberg [13] used six designs of NN by taking different subsets of 34 variables to distinguish between 'normal' and 'manipulated' financial data. They examined the digit distribution of the numbers in the underlying financial data based on Benford's law. This law demonstrated that the digits of naturally occurring numbers are distributed on a predictable and specific pattern. Feroz et al. [14] observed that the relative success of the NN models was due to their ability to 'learn' what were important. Brooks [15] also applied various NN models to detect financial statement fraud with great success. Fanning and Cogger [16] used NN (AutoNet) for detecting management fraud on the important publicly available predictors of fraudulent financial statements. Ramamoorti et al. [17] compared the performance of the multilayer perceptron with a Delphi study. Zhang et al. [18] conducted a review of the papers that reported the use of NN in forecasting during 1988–98.

Aamodt and Plaza [19] and Kotsiantis et al. [20] used case based reasoning to identify the fraudulent companies. Further, Deshmukh and Talluru [21] employed a 15 rules-based fuzzy reasoning system to assess the risk of management fraud. Pacheco et al. [22] developed a hybrid system consisting of NN and a fuzzy expert system for the purpose. Further, Magnusson et al. [23] used text mining and demonstrated that the language of quarterly reports provided an indication of the change in the company's financial status. Variable selection was used in a rule-based system by eliminating variables that were either redundant or possessed little predictive information [24].

Many researchers proposed rule extraction algorithms based on global optimization techniques such as Genetic Algorithms (GA), Particle Swarm Optimization (PSO), Ant Colony optimization (ACO) and Differential Evolution (DE). Firstly, Mahfoud and Mani [25] used GA and extracted rules to predict the performance of individual stocks. Shin and Lee [26] extracted rules from GA for predicting bankruptcy of firms. Then, Parpinelli et al. [27] proposed Ant-Miner, which uses ACO for extracting classification rules. Later, Kim and Han [28] used GA in discovering the rules for predicting bankruptcy of firms. Sousa et al. [29] proposed Constricted PSO (CPSO) for rule mining. Thereafter, Liu et al. [30] proposed PSO based rule extraction method, where they proposed fitness function different from [29]. Ji et al. [31] improved the Ant-miner proposed in [27]. Later, Zhao et al. [32] proposed Fuzzy-PSO, where the binary PSO generates fuzzy rules. Then, Holden and Freitas [33] hybridized PSO and ACO for discovering classification rules. Most recently, Su et al. [34] employed DE for rule extraction. Ravisankar et al. [35] used Classification and Regression Trees (C&RT) along with other techniques for determining fraud companies in the same Chinese Bank dataset. Naveen et al. [36] proposed Rule Extraction using firefly optimization and its applications to Banking. However, it failed when confronted with more than 10 dimensions of the feature space.

3   Proposed Methodology

3.1   Rule Encoding

We introduced a new rule encoding scheme as opposed to Naveen et al. [36], where each dimension of the firefly i.e. a financial attribute is represented by 3 bits. So, according to the number of attributes that we started with, i.e. 10, 18 or 35, we have 30 bits, 54 bits or 105 bits respectively allotted for rules. Here, the first bit gives us the benchmark value of the attribute. The second bit depicts us whether the attribute is less than or greater than the benchmark in the first bit. This is simply done using a random number between 0 and 1. If the number is less than 0.5, it denoted less than sign; else, it denotes greater than sign. And the last bit indicates whether to include this attribute in the rule or not. It is implemented using 0 and 1, where 0 represents that the attribute should not be included in the rule and 1 indicates otherwise (Table 1).

where D is the number of financial attributes which is 10, 18, 35 in our case. Suppose a rule is represented as in Table 1, the corresponding rule would be

If Attribute 1 < 0.87 and Attribute 3 > 0.57 then belong to a particular class.

3.2   Improved Firefly Miner (FF-miner)

Naveen et al. [36] proposed the FF miner for rule extraction using firefly optimization for application to banking. When we tried to execute the existing FF miner on our

Table 1. Rule encoding scheme

Dimension 1			Dimension 2			Dimension 3			....			Dimension D		
0.87	0.3	1	0.45	0.4	0	0.54	0.7	1	..	..	..	0.67	0.78	0

dataset, it ran into an infinite loop. So we modified the existing FF miner. We modified the way the position of the firefly is updated. To ensure the global solution space coverage, we incorporate *gbest* and *pbest* concepts from PSO [37] and update the position of the firefly accordingly. Also to reduce the rule length, we introduce a new rule encoding scheme which has been explained in Sect. 3.1. The previous encoding scheme followed by Naveen et al. [36] consisted of only first 2 bits as opposed 3 bits in our case. This new encoding scheme serves the purpose of producing variable rules as opposed to fixed maximum length rules in our previous case. This encoding scheme has been very effective in smooth functioning of our rule miners.

Existing update formula of x_i

$$x_i(t + 1) = x_i(t) + \beta_0 e^{-\gamma r^2} \left(x_i - x_j\right) + \alpha(\text{rand}() - 0.5) \tag{1}$$

Modified update formula of x_i

$$x_i(t + 1) = x_i(t) + \beta_0 e^{-\gamma r^2} \left(x_i - x_j\right) + c \times (gbest_i - x_i(t)) \tag{2}$$

Where t is the iteration number.

Firefly Algorithm [39, 40]
    1. Initialize the population of fireflies i.e., rules in our case
    2. For each of the iterations
    3. Calculate fitness for each of the firefly using equation (5)
    4. For each firefly i in the population
    5.   For each firefly j in the population
    6.   If fitness(i)<fitness(j)
    7.   Calculate Euclidean distance between firefly i and j
    8.   For each dimension in the firefly
    9.   Calculate beta using following equation.
    10.

$$\beta = \beta_0 e^{-\gamma r^2} \tag{3}$$

    11.   Update firefly position using following equation.
    12.

$$x_i(t + 1) = x_i(t) + \beta \left(x_i(t) - x_j(t)\right) + \alpha(rand() - 0.5) \tag{4}$$

    13.   End For
    14.   End If
    15.   End For
    16. End For

Pseudocode of FF miner

> For each fold of the dataset
> For run=1 to no_of_runs
> > Load Training, Testing and Validation datasets
> > Identify the total number of classes as n
> > For each class of n classes(here n=two, fraud and non fraud)
> > > Reload Training Records
> > > Count the no of records satisfying the class as tr_class_count
> > > Repeat
> > > > Apply **Firefly Algorithm** given above to generate a rule
> > > > Mark and count Training Records which covered by the rule as rule_cover_count
> > > Until rule_cover_count>=90% of (tr_class_count)
> > Reload Training Records
> > Sort The rules Based on Fitness

Compute Accuracy, Sensitivity & Specificity for training, test and validation data.

A particular firefly moves towards a brighter firefly keeping in mind that intensity also decreases with increase in distance. These form the essence of the overall firefly algorithm. Finally, we obtain the optimal value of the fitness function after some iterations, which gives us the optimal set of rules in our case. Equation 3 indicates attractiveness that varies with distance, while Eq. 4 indicates position update formula. Here, t, β_0 and γ are iteration number, attractiveness constant and light absorption coefficient respectively.

3.3 TA Miner

In the TA miner, we apply the Threshold Acceptance Algorithm [38] for the Fraud Detection Problem. TA being a local search method helped us find the local optimal solutions around different points. The parameters of TA such as thresh, threshtol, delta, acc are also identified after trial and error.

TA algorithm:

```
1. initialize candidate solution/rule
2. for each of the global iterations
3.              for each of the inner iterations
4.                      Generate new candidate solution
5.                      calculate delta which is the difference of fitness between
                        current and  previous candidate solution
6.                      if delta<thresh
7.                              Make the candidate solution as the new solution
8.                      if thresh<threshtol
9.                              calculate delta2 which is the difference of fitness between
                                old and new solution
10.                             if ABS(delta2)<acc
11.                                     break;
12.     thresh=thresh*(1-eps);
13.     Replace Solution in the population with the candidate solution
```

Pseudo code of TA miner

For each fold of the dataset

For run=1 to no_of_runs

Load Training, Testing and Validation datasets

Identify the total number of classes as n

For each class of n classes(here n=two, fraud and non fraud)

Reload Training Records

Count the number of training records satisfying satisfying the class as tr_class_count

Repeat

Apply **TA algorithm** given above to generate rule

Mark and count Training Records which covered by the rule asrule_cover_count

Until rule_cover_count>=90%of(tr_class_count)

Reload Training Records

Sort The rules Based on Fitness

Calculate Accuracy, Sensitivity &Specificity for training, test and validation data.

3.4   FFTA Miner

We propose a hybrid of the Firefly Algorithm and TA as general purpose rule miner and apply it for Fraud Detection. For each run, the algorithm runs at least as many times as the number of classes in the dataset. First of all, the dataset we have is divided into Training, Testing and Validation datasets. The total number of classes is identified from the dataset. Now for each class, the training records are loaded and we count the number of training records satisfying a particular class as tr_class_count. The Firefly – TA Algorithm (FFTA) is next applied to get the rules. This process is repeated until the number of classes covered by the rules is greater than 90 % of the tr_class_count. These rules are applied on Training, Testing and Validation Datasets. In the FFTA algorithm, we invoke the TA to replace the weakest firefly every 95 % of the iterations. The TA algorithm replaces the weakest firefly with the best solution in the neighborhood of the weakest firefly. The incorporation of TA in the algorithm thus ensured faster convergence. The pseudo code is as follows

FF-TA algorithm:

[1-3] lines of FF algorithm

If(rand<prob_ta)

Call TA

[4-16] lines of FF algorithm

FFTA Miner Pseudo Code

For each fold of the dataset
For run=1 to no_of_runs
        Load Training, Testing and Validation datasets
        Identify the total number of classes as n
        For each class of n classes (here two fraud and non fraud)
            Reload Training Records
            Count the no. of records satisfying the class as tr_class_count
            Repeat
                    Apply **FF-TA algorithm** given above to get a rule
                    Mark and count Training Records which covered by the
                    rule as rule_cover_count
            Until rule_cover_count>=90% of (tr_class_count)
        Reload Training Records
        Sort The rules Based on Fitness
        Compute Accuracy, Sensitivity, and Specificity.

The different parameters in the Firefly Algorithm such as β_0, γ, α etc. are determined by trial and error method. Similarly the parameters in the Threshold Acceptance such as thresh, threshtol, delta, acc are also identified in the overall TA algorithm.

$$\text{Fitness Function} = \text{Sensitivity} * \text{Specificity} \qquad (5)$$

$$\text{Where Sensitivity} = \frac{\text{Number of True Positives}}{\text{Number of True Positives} + \text{Number of False Negatives}}$$

$$\text{Specificity} = \frac{\text{Number of True Negatives}}{\text{Number of True Negatives} + \text{Number of False Positives}}$$

True Positives = # Fraudulent Companies correctly identified
True Negatives = # Non-fraudulent Companies correctly identified
False Negatives = # Fraudulent Companies wrongly identified as non- fraudulent
False Positives = # Non-fraudulent Companies wrongly identified as fraudulent

4   Dataset Description and Experiment Methodology

The dataset taken from [35], consists of 35 financial variables of 202 Chinese companies of which 101 are fraudulent and 101 are not. First, the dataset is divided into 80 % and 20 % groups and the latter one is designated as validation set. Then, 10-fold cross validation is performed on the 80 % dataset and we tested the obtained model in every fold on the validation set. Owing to the evolutionary nature of the Firefly and TA Algorithms, the results varied slightly, whenever the random seed is changed. Therefore, each miner is run 20 times for every fold and then the average results are computed and tabulated. Thus, we have 20*10 i.e. 200 runs for each algorithm. Following Ravisankar et al. [35], we performed the analysis with the top 18 and the top 10 features obtained through the t-statistic based feature selection method. Thus, the 3 algorithms (FF, FFTA and TA) were run on the dataset with 35, 18 and 10 features.

5   Results and Discussion

The best, worst, average sensitivities of the 10 folds have been presented in Table 2 for the miners viz., FF, FFTA and TA. These are compared in different cases i.e., 35 features, Top-18, Top-10 obtained features. First, when compared with the results of decision trees [42] reported in [35], both TA and FFTA yielded superior sensitivity and rule length also turned to be smaller for them.

Table 2. Comparison of fitness values and sensitivity within braces

No of features	Improved FF miner			TA miner			FF-TA miner		
	Best	Worst	Average	Best	Worst	Average	Best	Worst	Average
35	5294 (100)	1381.25 (25)	4468.94 (65.05)	5833 (100)	1666.5 (33.33)	5370.29 (75.13)	5526 (100)	2500 (50)	**5603.86** (79.05)
18	6429 (100)	1765.16 (33.33)	4775.71 (70.20)	5385 (100)	1623.84 (33.33)	5367.40 (74.88)	5122 (100)	1444.19 (33.33)	**5703.17** (79.52)
10	6333 (100)	1299.9 (30)	5191.18 (72.19)	6296 (100)	2432 (50)	5582.51 (**79.05**)	5833 (100)	3428.8 (66.67)	**5751.74** (79.40)

From the results, we can observe that hybridized FFTA miner produced highest sensitivity compared to individual FF and TA miners in all 3 cases i.e., with 35, 18 and 10 features. However, TA miner closely followed FFTA miner. But, in case of Top-10 features, TA miner with sensitivity 79.05 % is very much closer to that of FFTA miner which produced 79.40 %. In all the cases, FF miner was found to be inferior compared to other two algorithms. Finally, we conclude that FFTA with 10 features produced best results in terms of sensitivity and fitness value. Further, only FFTA miner could yield more than 79 % sensitivity in all cases. A t-test (see Table 3) was performed at 5 % level of significance to find if the difference between FFTA and TA is statistically significant. It turned out that the two methods are statistically similar for 10 features and different for 18 and 35 features. We didn't compare FF miner with FFTA miner as their sensitivities differ by greater amounts. Furthermore, FFTA miner yielded higher fitness values compared to FF miner and TA miner, thereby indicating that it also produced less false positives. Therefore, the hybrid FFTA miner has turned to be the holistic winner among the three miners. This is a significant outcome of the study. Also, since FFTA miner produced superior results, we performed statistical t-tests with respect to sensitivity across three cases i.e., with 35, 18, 10 features within FFTA miner and found that they are all statistically insignificant. Consequently, we recommend FFTA miner with 10 features as the best case for this dataset.

Table 3. t-test values of FFTA miner versus TA miner with 35, 18 and 10 features

35 features	7.09
18 features	8.35
10 features	0.43

The rules obtained by FFTA, FF and TA miners for the case of 10 features, which obtained a maximum of 100 % sensitivity, are presented in Tables 4, 5 and 6 respectively. We found that FFTA miner obtained just 2 rules, while the rest produced 3 rules each. Further, we found that the variable *Net_profit/Total_assets* appeared in almost all the rules produced by all the three miners. Therefore, we can conclude that this variable is the most significant variable in this study. This variable is followed by *Gross Profit*, which was picked by FFTA and FF miners but not TA miner. The optimal parameter combinations chosen for the FF, TA and FFTA algorithm are presented in Tables 7, 8 and 9.

Table 4. Rules of FFTA miner in its best run of 100 % sensitivity

Rule-1:
If(Inventory/Total_assets>0.44 & Gross_profit/Total_assets>0.96 & Net_profit/Total_assets>0.95& Inventory/Current_liabilities>0.40) Then Fraud
Rule-2:
If(Gross_profit<0.28 & Net_profit<0.36 & Net_profit/Total_assets<0.95 & Inventory/Current_liabilities>0.49) Then Non- Fraud

Table 5. Rules of FF miner in its best run of 100 % sensitivity

Rule-1:
If(Gross_profit>0.99 & Net_profit>0.99 & Primary_business_income>1.0 & Net_profit/Total_assets<0.95) Then Fraud
Rule-2:
If(Gross_profit>0.99 & Net_profit>0.99 & Net_profit/Total_assets>0.95& Net_profit/Primary_business_income>1.0 & Primary_business_income/Fixed_assets >1.0) Then Fraud
Rule-3:
If(Gross_profit<0.52 & Net_profit<0.50 & Net_profit/Primary_business_income <0.44) Then Non – Fraud

Table 6. Rules of TA miner in its best run of 100 % sensitivity

Rule-1:
If(Inventory/Total_assets>0.67 & Net_profit/Total_assets>0.95 & Inventory/Current_liabilities>0.14) Then Fraud
Rule-2:
If(Gross_profit/Total_assets>0.97 & Net_profit/Total_assets<0.95 & Primary_business_income/Fixed_assets>0.87) Then Fraud
Rule-3:
If(Net_profit/Total_assets<0.95) Then Non- Fraud

Table 7. Parameters for FF

Features	n	β_0	Υ	Δ	α	MaxIterations	Prob_rule_length
35	35	1	2.5	1	0.5	100	0.05
18	35	1	2.5	1	0.5	100	0.175
10	35	1	2.5	1	0.5	100	0.197

Table 8. Parameters for TA miner

Features	Eps	Acc	ThreshTol	Thresh	MaxInerIteration (A)	MaxOuterIterations (B)	Prob_rule_length (C)
35	0.001	0.5	0.001	0.1	250	25	0.05
18	0.001	0.5	0.001	0.1	250	25	0.175
10	0.001	0.5	0.001	0.1	250	25	0.197

Table 9. Parameters for FFTA miner

Features	N	β_0	Υ	Δ	α	MaxIterations	Prob_TA	
35	35	0.5–2.5	0.5–2.5	1	0.5	25–200	0.95	Parameters of TA from Table 8 are selected here too
18	35	0.5–2.5	0.5–2.5	1	0.5	25–200	0.95	
10	35	0.5–2.5	0.5–2.5	1	0.5	25–200	0.95	

Observing that the sensitivities yielded by all the three algorithms are no very high, we tried to find the reason behind it and performed Principal Component Analysis (PCA) visualization using NeuCom [41]. It was found out that most of the 202 companies are concentrated along a line, thereby making them difficult to discriminate. Most probably, the same behavior could be observed in the original input space also. This might be the reason why the rule mining algorithms failed to yield sensitivity of 90 % and above.

6 Conclusion

We proposes hybrid FFTA miner for financial fraud detection. It yielded far superior results compared to the traditional decision trees in terms of sensitivity with less number of rules. Further, TA and FFTA miners are not statistically significantly different, as evidenced by t-test. But since TA miner is comparatively less complex than the hybrid FFTA miner, it's preferable to apply the former for this dataset, when 10 variables are considered. But, with more variables, FFTA miner is stable and superior.

References

1. http://www.accounting-degree.org/scandals/. Accessed 10 June 2014
2. http://en.wikipedia.org/wiki/Accounting_scandals. Accessed 10 June 2014
3. http://en.wikipedia.org/wiki/Satyam_scandal. Accessed 10 June 2014
4. Kirkos, E., Spathis, C., Manolopoulos, Y.: Data mining techniques for the detection of fraudulent financial statement. Expert Syst. Appl. **32**, 995–1003 (2007)
5. Spathis, C., Doumpos, M., Zopounidis, C.: Detecting falsified financial statements: a comparative study using multi criteria analysis and multivariate statistical techniques. Eur. Acc. Rev. **11**(3), 509–535 (2002)
6. Cecchini, M., Aytug, H., Koehler, G.J., Pathak, P.: Detecting management fraud in public companies. http://warrington.ufl.edu/isom/docs/papers/DetectingManagementFraudInPublic Companies.pdf
7. Huang, S.-M., Yen, D.C., Yang, L.-W., Hua, J.-S.: An investigation of Zipf's Law for fraud detection. Decis. Support Syst. **46**(1), 70–83 (2008)
8. Sohl, J.E., Venkatachalam, A.R.: A neural network approach to forecasting model selection. Inf. Manage. **29**(6), 297–303 (1995)
9. Cerullo, M.J., Cerullo, V.: Using neural networks to predict financial reporting fraud: part 1. Comput. Fraud Secur. **5**, 14–17 (1999)
10. Calderon, T.G., Cheh, J.J.: A roadmap for future neural networks research in auditing and risk assessment. Int. J. Acc. Inf. Syst. **3**(4), 203–236 (2002)
11. Koskivaara, E.: Different pre-processing models for financial accounts when using neural networks for auditing. In: Proceedings of the 8th European Conference on Information Systems, vol. 1, pp. 326–3328. Vienna, Austria (2000)
12. Koskivaara, E.: Artificial neural networks in auditing: state of the art. ICFAI J. Audit Pract. **1** (4), 12–33 (2004)
13. Busta, B., Weinberg, R.: Using Benford's law and neural networks as a review procedure. Manage. Auditing J. **13**(6), 356–366 (1998)
14. Feroz, E.H., Kwon, T.M., Pastena, V., Park, K.J.: The efficacy of red flags in predicting the SEC's targets: an artificial neural networks approach. Int. J. Intell. Syst. Acc. Finan. Manage. **9**(3), 145–157 (2000)
15. Brooks, R.C.: Neural networks: a new technology. CPA J. http://www.nysscpa.org/cpajournal/old/15328449.htm1994
16. Fanning, K.M., Cogger, K.O.: Neural network detection of management fraud using published financial data. Int. J. Intell. Syst. Acc. Finan. Manage. **7**(1), 21–41 (1998)
17. Ramamoorti, S., Bailey Jr., A.D., Traver, R.O.: Risk assessment in internal auditing: a neural network approach. Int. J. Intell. Syst. Acc. Finan. Manage. **8**(3), 159–180 (1999)
18. Zhang, G., Patuwo, B.E., Hu, M.Y.: Forecasting with artificial neural networks: the state of the art. Int. J. Forecast. **14**(1), 35–62 (1998)
19. Aamodt, A., Plaza, E.: Case-based reasoning: foundational issues, methodological variations, and system approaches. Artif. Intell. Commun. **7**(1), 39–59 (1994)
20. Kotsiantis, S., Koumanakos, E., Tzelepis, D., Tampakas, V.: Forecasting fraudulent financial statements using data mining. Int. J. Comput. Intell. **3**(2), 104–110 (2006)
21. Deshmukh, L.Talluru: A rule-based fuzzy reasoning system for assessing the risk of management fraud. Int. J. Intell. Syst. Acc. Finan. Manage. **7**(4), 223–241 (1998)
22. Pacheco, R., Martins, A., Barcia, R.M., Khator, S.: A hybrid intelligent system applied to financial statement analysis. In: Proceedings of the 5th IEEE Conference on Fuzzy Systems, vol. 2, pp. 1007–10128. New Orleans, USA (1996)

23. Magnusson, C., Arppe, A., Eklund, T., Back, B., Vanharanta, H., Visa, A.: The language of quarterly reports as an indicator of change in the company's financial status. Inf. Manage. **42** (4), 561–574 (2005)
24. Kim, Y.: Toward a successful CRM: variable selection, sampling, and ensemble. Decis. Support Syst. **41**(2), 542–553 (2006)
25. Mahfoud, S., Mani, G.: Financial forecasting using genetic algorithms. Appl. Artif. Intell. **10**, 543–565 (1996)
26. Shin, K.-S., Lee, Y.-J.: A genetic algorithm application in bankruptcy prediction modeling. Expert Syst. Appl. **23**(3), 321–328 (2002)
27. Parpinelli, R.S., Lopes, H.S., Frietas, A.A.: Data mining with an ant colony optimization algorithm. IEEE Trans. Evol. Comput. **6**(4), 321–332 (2002)
28. Kim, M.-J., Han, I.: The discovery of experts' decision rules from qualitative bankruptcy data using genetic algorithms. Expert Syst. Appl. **25**, 637–646 (2003)
29. Sousa, T., Neves, A., Silva, A.: A particle swarm data miner. In: 11th Portuguese Conference on Artificial Intelligence, Workshop on Artificial Life and Evolutionary Algorithms, pp. 43–53 (2003)
30. Liu, Y., Qin, Z., Shi, Z., Chen, J.: Rule discovery with particle swarm optimization. In: Chi, C.-H., Lam, K.-Y. (eds.) AWCC 2004. LNCS, vol. 3309, pp. 291–296. Springer, Heidelberg (2004)
31. Ji, J., Zhang, N., Liu, C., Zhong, N.: An ant colony optimization algorithm for learning classification rules. In: Proceedings of IEEE/WIC, pp. 1034–1037 (2006)
32. Zhao, X., Zeng, J., Gao, Y., Yang, Y.: Particle swarm algorithm for classification rules generation. In: Proceedings of the Intelligent Systems Design and Applications, IEEE, pp. 957–962 (2006)
33. Holden, N., Frietas, A.A.: A hybrid PSO/ACO algorithm for classification. In: Proceedings of Genetic and Evolutionary Computation conference, pp. 2745–2750 (2007)
34. Su, H., Yang, Y., Zha, L.: Classification rule discovery with DE/QDE algorithm. Expert Syst. Appl. **37**(2), 1216–1222 (2010)
35. Ravisankar, P., Ravi, V., Raghava Rao, G., Bose, I.: Detection of financial statement fraud and feature selection using data mining techniques. Dec. Support Syst. **50**, 491–500 (2010)
36. Naveen, N., Ravi, V., Raghavendra Rao, C., Sarath, K.N.V.D.: Rule extraction using firefly optimization: application to banking. In: IEEM (2012)
37. Kennedy, J., Eberhart, R.: Particle swarm optimization. In: Proceedings of IEEE International Conference on Neural Networks (Perth, Australia), IEEE Service Center, Piscataway, NJ (1995)
38. Dueck, G., Scheuer, T.: Threshold accepting: a general purpose optimization algorithm appearing superior to simulated annealing. J. Comput. Phys. **90**, 161–175 (1990)
39. Yang, X.-S.: Firefly algorithms for multimodal optimization. In: Watanabe, O., Zeugmann, T. (eds.) SAGA 2009. LNCS, vol. 5792, pp. 169–178. Springer, Heidelberg (2009)
40. Yang, X.-S.: Firefly algorithm, stochastic test functions and design optimization. Int. J. Bio-Inspired Comput. **2**(2), 78–84 (2010)
41. Neucom. http://www.aut.ac.nz/research/research-institutes/kedri/research-centres/centre-for-data-mining-and-decision-support-systems/neucom-project-homepage#download
42. Quinlan, J.R.: Induction of decision trees. Mach. Learn. **1**, 81–106 (1986)

An Imperative Assessment of Fuzzy Based 11-Level DSTATCOM Operating Under IPD Modulation Scheme

D. Mohan Reddy[1,2]([⊠]) and T. Gowri Manohar[1]

[1] Department of EEE, SV University, Tirupati, Andra Pradesh, India
{usmohanus, gowrimanohart}@gmail.com
[2] Navodaya Institute of Technology, Raichur 584103, Karnataka, India
usmohanus@gmail.com

Abstract. To speculate and pursue the dynamic analysis of FACTS devices to achieving the enhanced power quality features with respect to system disturbances. This paper categorizes a ameliorate control methodology to improve appearance of distributed compensator by using intelligence Instantaneous Real-Reactive Power (IRP) theory. So as to make source currents to be more sinusoidal and afford an essential harmonic minimization method is evolved with the aid of the classical PI controller. This concept confronts the design of fuzzy logic based DSTATCOM for control over the hybrid In-Phase Deposition (IPD) modulation scheme fed 11-level Cascaded Multi-level Converter (CMC) engaged compensation scheme. Attaining the computer simulations, in that appeared performance of robust control action for intended intelligence based DSTATCOM accomplishes the non-adaptive control actions with respect to expressed dynamic response, humble steady state error as well as acquired good stability factor with the appreciated dynamic response of advanced compensation under Matlab/Simulink environment.

Keywords: Distributed static compensator (DSTATCOM) · Fuzzy controller · Power quality · Hybrid IPD modulation scheme · Total harmonic distortion (THD)

1 Introduction

Attendance of power switching devices like rectifier loads, uninterruptable supply systems, variable speed drives, SMPS and arc furnaces, so on in accumulate with linear type loads which may attract the harmonic distortions, exchanging reactive power from a main source. It may affect the power system dynamics such as deficient power factor, huge harmonic distortions in source current, unbalanced source currents, formation of effective neutral currents. Classical alleviated PQ methods use static capacitors, passive resonant type filters (PRF) interfaced to shunt combination to load, but those are non-effective for variable load conditions [1]. For comprehensive mitigation of such

© Springer International Publishing Switzerland 2015
B.K. Panigrahi et al. (Eds.): SEMCCO 2014, LNCS 8947, pp. 251–263, 2015.
DOI: 10.1007/978-3-319-20294-5_22

problems prefer an advanced shunt active devices are projected for compensation of stated power quality features [2]. A distributive active static compensation acts as shunt device to be interfaced at Point of Common Coupling (PCC) at distribution level side, it supports to reactive/active power exchanging and suppression of harmonized currents coming from high power semiconductor switching apparatus under the operating principle of direct in-phase computing and are committed into linear balanced type resistive load. Likewise, have so many numbers of active compensators in that shunt connected CMC based 11-level distributed compensator with the hybrid IPD modulation scheme is taking over to achieve favourable advantages to maintain ideal power quality features at PCC [3, 4]. Extreme enforced MLI configurations are merely utilized in many applications which may synthesize staircase outcome voltage is attained by the addition of several input DC sources and attained allied to sinusoidal outcome voltage response by several voltage levels operated under fundamental and high switching frequencies.

Exploit for the contemplation of the PI controller for the automation of industrial sector is completely elaborated as well as awkward in practice due to abundant and adverse objectives are to be adopted. It is extensively felt that PI values for non-linearized plants are highly arduous to find out the analytical arrangement of closed loop stability and compel high performance [5]. Overdue the complexity and the need of accurate plant model, so many evaluations on PI control it tends to be more difficult for religious engineers to merely understand and capably application to real-time systems. Modern research concerned with tuning the action of PI gains by the importance of intelligence control schemes such as Fuzzy controller [11]. Fuzzy controllers have been appealing a great deal in so as to achieve an optimal performance level in [12]. The theory of fuzzy sets makes an imperative role in dealing with the uncertainty when constituting decisions in the practical power control industry. This paper projects the utilization of hybrid IPD modulation scheme with concerned distributed compensator for enhancing the PQ problems, moreover implementation of proposed fuzzy based 11-level CMC DSTATCOM device is an ample opportunity and generation of reference currents by using instantaneous real-reactive symmetrical theory to handle over the shunt compensation [6, 7], it may administer the good transient response, low steady state error, high stability factor, low harmonized values, and fulfilment of robust action under any load disturbances and parametric variations. Computer simulations are acquitted with intelligent based 11-level compensator is validated by the dynamic performance of proposed system using Matlab/Simulink SIM-power system environmental tool.

2   Proposed Intelligent Based DSTATCOM

This nature of power semiconductor apparatus acquires harmonized currents at PCC and it may comprises of infinite odd extent as well as fundamental frequency components, distorted currents may cause the crucial problems, due to this reason need shunt/parallel device amend the ideal power quality features. Provision of FACTS technology has been advocated due o heavy knowledge and acute control of the power system network.

Employment of multilevel DSTATCOM for high power applications and it is power electronic artifice placed in between a source and non-linear load not only supports the reactive power exchanging but also minimize the harmonics coming from the diode bridge DC load and may improve power factor and operated as high reliability with high stability [8]. As Fig. 1 depicts the CMC based 11-level DSTATCOM is interfaced as resemble at (PCC) point of common coupling with the help of interfacing inductors, energy supplied by this DSTATCOM is accomplished with high range of dc link capacitor, the voltage value controlled by fuzzy controller as well as incorporated with proposed real time instantaneous strategy, here preferred hybrid IPD modulation scheme is used and it is shown in Fig. 2, to validate the performance and applications to distribution networks.

This proposed hybrid modulation scheme is the formation of secular formation of both level shift PWM and phase shift PWM to form in-phase deposition (IPD) technique to trounce the switching action of the level shift PWM scheme and to minimize the unequal output voltage imbalanced phase condition produced by CMC [9]. This optimal scheme consists of $(q - 1)$ carriers; it should require equal switching frequency and difference of peak magnitudes which are vertically disposed. Where V_{mref} constitutes the sine peak reference amplitude, V_{ccr} constitutes the magnitude of carrier signal, MI_{amp} constitutes the modulation index and $\emptyset_{sh}$ constitutes the phase disposing angle and is defined as:

$$MI_{amp} = \frac{V_{mref}}{V_{ccr(q-1)}} \tag{1}$$

$$\emptyset_{sh} = \frac{360^{\circ}}{4(q - 1)} \tag{2}$$

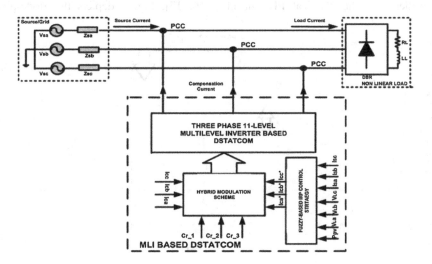

Fig. 1. Structure of proposed fuzzy based three phase CMC based 11-level DSTATCOM

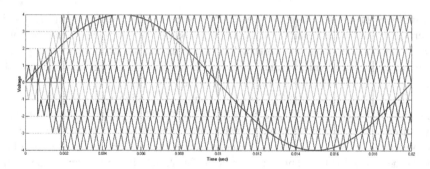

Fig. 2. Hybrid multi carrier modulation scheme

The intended switching strategy as shown below figure, it is preferred for this expansion of Fourier series analysis of output voltage by using hybrid switching strategy as depicted in Eq. (3).

$$V(\omega t) = \left(\frac{10Vdc}{\pi}\right) \sum [\cos(n\theta_1) + \cos(n\theta_2) + \cdots + \cos(n\theta_s)] \sin(n\omega t) \qquad (3)$$

3 Formulation of Fuzzy Interfaced IRP Theory

The contradict approach of this intended 11-level CMC DSTATCOM adverts to the two major sections. One of the sections is instantaneous symmetrical reference current estimation value and second section goes on propagating the switching pulses using IPD method is a primary intention for compensation of harmonics and reactive power control at PCC. So as to categorize the valuable characteristics of proposed Fuzzy controller over the classical PI controller [16, 17], Fig. 3 depicts the Bode-plot

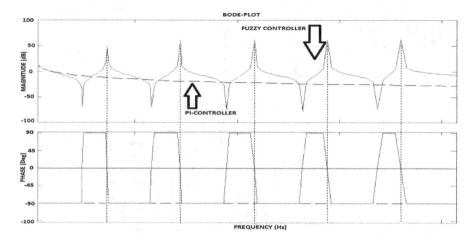

Fig. 3. Bode plot representation of classical PI controller and proposed fuzzy controller

representation for the classical PI controller and proposed controller, at low frequencies, both the gains of PI controller and proposed controller have high value and more comparable, at high frequencies the gains of PI controller drastically reduces while the proposed intelligence controller generates superior gains for ensuring zero steady-state error values for compensating the harmonized currents [10, 11].

Calculation of instantaneous reference currents using parks transformation methodology for generating reference currents are accosted by evaluating the proposed symmetrical theory as depicted in Fig. 4. The main intention of this problem is to implement a robust compensation scheme, such as DC link voltage level mainly hangs on IPD modulated signal used for switching, so as to regulate the DC link value precisely to optimal value irrespective of system disturbances and tracing of perfect gain values using the intelligence based device, the rules operating under mamdani fuzzy device and membership functions described in [12–17]. Differentiation of reactive and active component into two things like as, AC and DC parts as followed in Eqs. (4) and (5). For accomplishing the DC component with the help of high-pass filter, to eradicate the uneven demand signals.

$$p = \bar{p} + \tilde{p} \tag{4}$$

$$q = \bar{q} + \tilde{q} \tag{5}$$

According to the proposed power theory, the accomplished active (P) component is highlighted by DC component of the instantaneous symmetrical nature of αβ reference current, it is depicted as (6) follows.

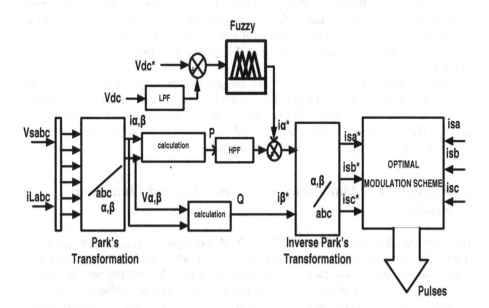

Fig. 4. Block diagram of fundamental reference current calculator by using instantaneous P-Q theory

$$i_{\alpha\beta}^* = \frac{1}{v_\alpha^2 + v_\beta^2} \begin{bmatrix} v_\alpha & v_\beta \\ v_\beta & -v_\alpha \end{bmatrix} \begin{bmatrix} p \\ q \end{bmatrix} \tag{6}$$

Moreover, generation of accurate reference currents for 11-level CMC static compensator might be Furthermore accurate reference current component for CMC based 11-level static compensator might be confederate as in Eq. (7).

$$i_{abc}^* = \sqrt{2/3} \begin{bmatrix} 1 & 0 \\ -1/2 & \sqrt{3/2} \\ -1/2 & -\sqrt{3/2} \end{bmatrix} i_{\alpha\beta}^* \tag{7}$$

As earlier stated, this control logic aims to maintain dc-link voltage of shunt compensator through a advanced Fuzzy controller, whose outcome is active reference current in fundamental reference-frame as depicts below Eq. (8).

$$i_a^* = \frac{\sum Z_{iout}(Z_i)}{\sum out\ (Z_i)} * (V_{dc}^* - V_{dc}) \tag{8}$$

where V_{dc}^* constitutes the reference voltage value and V_{dc} constitutes the measured actual value of the shunt compensator, I constitutes the 1, 2,...n and are the sampled values of aggregated membership functions respectively, which evaluate the duty commitment of a PWM scheme for control over the DC link voltage.

The intelligent based power systems are expected to play a very important role in distributed static applications in the near future [1]. Zadeh. L. A is the first presenter in the area of fuzzy set theory in 1965. Since then, a decisive language was implemented to be described using the formal methods. Fuzzy set theory has been widely used in the area of control design, a simple fuzzy control area is built up by a group of membership functions and rules on human knowledge of the system behaviour as depicted in Fig. 5 and Table 1.

Implementation of the fuzzy controller can provide optimal large signal and small signal dynamic performance at equal time, which is not attainable with the linear nature of control technique. However, fuzzy logic controller has been high potentiality to enhance the robustness of the DSTATCOM applications for improving the power quality concerns and attain high stability margin.

4 Evaluation of Matlab/Simulink Modeling and Simulation Results

The proposed CMC based 11-level DSTATCOM is designed to eradicate the harmonic current distortions entail from the power electronic loads to improve the voltage regulation, source side power factor and maximization of PCC stability and simulation results are presented by using hybrid modulation schemes is contemplate with the help of Matlab/Simulink modelling environment and Fast Fourier analysis also presented in

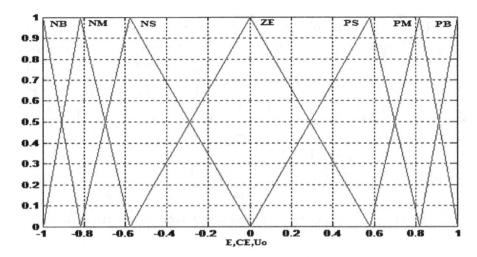

Fig. 5. Input and output membership-functions for this error (E), change in error (CE), output (Uo)

Table 1. Rules for this input-output membership functions

Change in error	Error	PB	PM	PS	ZE	NS	NM	NB
NB		ZE	NS	NM	NB	NB	NB	NB
NM		PS	ZE	NS	NM	NB	NB	NB
NS		PM	PS	ZE	NS	NM	NB	NB
ZE		PB	PM	PS	ZE	NS	NM	NB
PS		PB	PB	PM	PS	ZE	NS	NM
PM		PB	PB	PB	PM	PS	ZE	NS
PB		PB	PB	PB	PB	PM	PS	ZE

terms of total harmonic distortions (THD), and compared with the harmonic standards concerned by IEEE/IEC international standards.

As below mentioned Fig. 6 accords the source side voltage, source side current, load side current, without any presence of CMC based DSTATCOM with improved dynamic behavior in that source current is always equal to load current with minor differences in magnitude value in this condition, due to the non-linear device source currents goes to distorts and suppression of source currents using harmonic compensation methodology using shunt compensation scheme.

As below mentioned Fig. 7 shows the source side voltage, source side current, load side current, with the presence of classical PI Controlled 11-level CMC based DSTATCOM behavior gets source currents goes to pure sinusoidal but operating under high peak overshoots, due to non-linear gain values, get some high peak-overshoot and high steady state error at starting condition, because of un-perfect tuning of gain values under system disturbances for minimizing this problem may go intelligence controller.

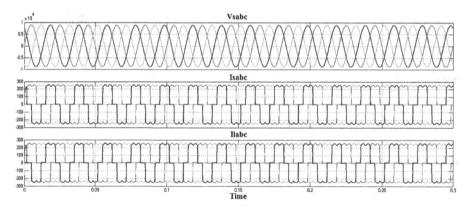

Fig. 6. (a) source voltage (Vsabc), (b) source current (Isabc), (c) load current (Ilabc)

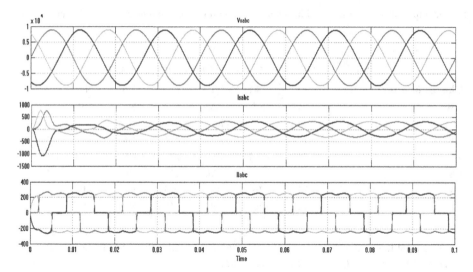

Fig. 7. (a) Source side voltage (Vsabc), (b) source side current (Isabc), (c) load side current (Ilabc)

As above Fig. 8 shows the source side voltage, source side current, load side current, utilization of Fuzzy controlled 11-level CMC based DSTATCOM behavior, due to perfect estimation of gain values by using fuzzy mamdani structure it may dampen the high peak-overshoots and low steady state error at starting condition and system operated in high stability condition with perfect harmonic compensation in source currents, then source currents goes on pure sinusoidal under non-linear load conditions and maintain the ideal power quality features.

Figure 9 shows the 11-Level Output Voltage of CMC based DSTATCOM using Hybrid IPD Modulation Scheme applications to Proposed Distributed Compensation

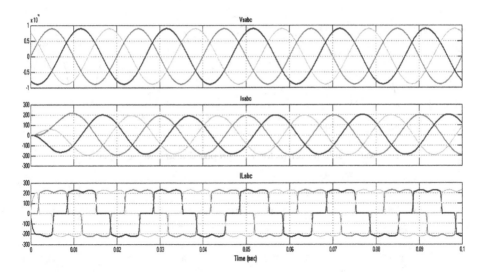

Fig. 8. (a) Source side voltage (Vsabc), (b) source side current (Isabc), (c) load side current (Ilabc)

Scheme, gets stair case output voltage it may reduces the load side filter value and within a affordable size and cost of the filter.

Figure 10 shows the Source side Power Factor with Proposed Distributed Compensator, both voltage and current will be in phase maintained as unity power factor at PCC level.

Figure 11 DC Link Voltage of proposed intelligence based 11-level CMC Distributed compensator, maintain constant DC link voltage by using fuzzy regulator, gets low steady state error value and low peak overshoots and low settling time when any disturbances coming from load, finally operated under high stability with a high reliability.

Figure 12 shows the Compensation Currents of Proposed 11-level CMC operating under Fuzzy controller, compensation currents at PCC supported by compensator

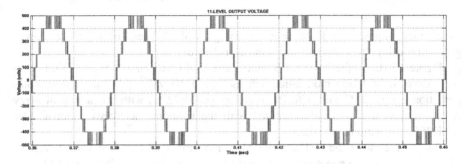

Fig. 9. 11-Level output voltage

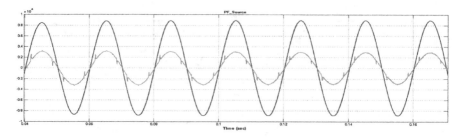

Fig. 10. Source side power factor with proposed distributed compensator

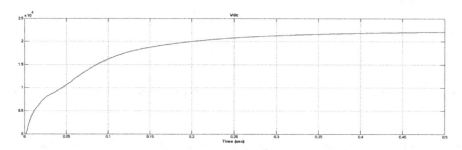

Fig. 11. DC link voltage

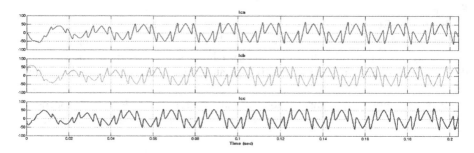

Fig. 12. Compensation currents of proposed 11-level CMC operating under fuzzy controller

which may imposed by in-phase methodology with the help of reference current generation using the instantaneous symmetrical theory.

Figure 13 shows the THD for Source Current of CMC based DSTATCOM operating under hybrid IPD modulation scheme, the THD value goes on without compensation get 28.28 % and with PI controller gets 1.72 %, with interaction of fuzzy controller gets 0.97 %, and compared with the harmonic standards concerned by IEEE/IEC international standards.

As Table 2 shows the FFT analysis of source current, PCC voltages, load currents without compensation and proposed PI and Fuzzy Controllers fed CMC based 11-level

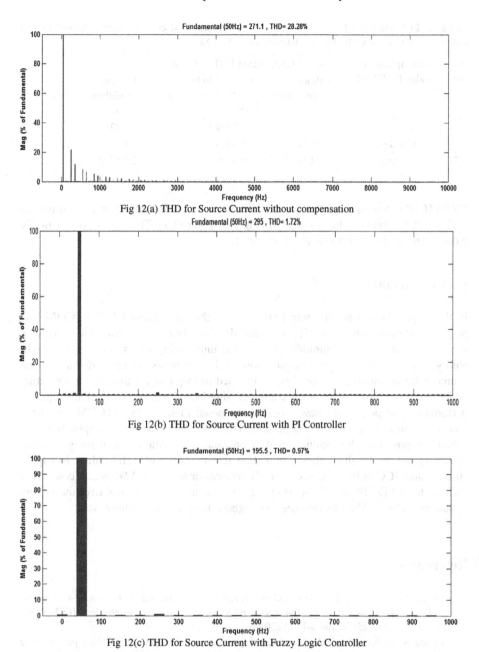

Fig 12(a) THD for Source Current without compensation

Fig 12(b) THD for Source Current with PI Controller

Fig 12(c) THD for Source Current with Fuzzy Logic Controller

Fig. 13. THD for source current (a) THD for source current without compensation (b) THD for source current with PI controller (c) THD for source current with fuzzy logic controller

Table 2. FFT analysis of source current, PCC voltages, load currents with proposed PI and Fuzzy controllers fed CMC based 11-level DSTATCOM

Sl. no	Description of value (THD %)	11-level CMC based DSTATCOM		
		Without compensation	Optimal hybrid modulation scheme (PI)	Optimal hybrid modulation scheme (Fuzzy)
01	Source current	28.28 %	1.72 %	0.97 %
02	PCC voltage	2.35 %	2.38 %	2.26 %
03	Load current	29.54 %	29.54 %	29.54 %

DSTATCOM, this optimal fuzzy controller have better features in source current as well as PCC voltage, due to this intelligence controllers THD goes to drastically reduces and maintain with in IEEE standards.

5 Conclusion

In this paper, an advanced control strategy for the three phased DSTATCOM was proposed operating under intelligence controller. This Fuzzy logic controller have very valuable features like as admirable adaptation, universality and simplicity, high reliability, good steady state performance, low peak overshoots, robust performance and source voltage and current would be maintained as in-phase condition even operating under non-linear condition. This computer simulations results verified the optimal performances of proposed a new way of CMC based 11-level DSTATCOM is updated compensation scheme for very large scale industrial and commercial applications for enhancing power quality features with a premeditated control circuit for generation switching pulses. In all of these simulation results, factor of THD values in supply currents and PCC voltages was drastically reduces or less than 2 %, which constitutes with-in the IEEE-519 and IEC-61000-3-2 standard limits and control over the system dynamics under sudden disturbances throughout the distribution network.

References

1. Yepas, A.G., Freijedo, F.D., Doval-Gandoy, J., Lopez, O., Malvar, J., Femandez-Comesana, P.: Effects of discretization methods on the performance of resonant controllers. IEEE Trans. Power Electron. **25**(7), 1692–1712 (2010)
2. Yepas, A.G., Freijedo, F.D., Doval-Gandoy, J., Lopez, O., Malvar, J.: High performance digital resonant controllers implemented with two integrators. IEEE Trans. Power Electron. **26**(2), 1692–1712 (2011)
3. Hu, H., Shi, W., Lu, Y., Xing, Y.: Design considerations for DSP controlled 400 Hz shunt active power filter in aircraft power system. IEEE Trans. Ind. Electron. **59**(9), 3624–3634 (2012)
4. Chen, Z., Luo, Y., Chen, M.: Control and performance of cascaded shunt active power filter for aircraft electric power system. IEEE Trans. Ind. Electron. **59**(9), 3614–3623 (2012)

5. Vazquez, S., Lukic, S.M., Galvan, E., Franquelo, L.G., Carrasco, J.M.: Energy storage systems for transport and grid applications. IEEE Trans. Ind. Electron. **57**(12), 3881–3895 (2010)
6. Tareila, C., Sotoodeh, P., Miller, R.D.: Design and control of a single phase DSTATCOM inverter for wind applications. In: PEMWA 2012, Denver, Co (2012)
7. Davies, M., Dommaschk, M., Dorn, J., Lang, J., Retzmann, D., Soerangr, D.: HVDC Plus Basic and Principle of Operation. Siemens AG Energy Sector, Erlandgen (2009)
8. Gemmell, B., Dorn, J., Retzmann, D., Soerangr, D.: Prospects of multilevel VSC technologies for power transmission. In: IEEE Transmission and Distribution Conference and Exposition, pp. 1–16. Siemens USA, Siemens Germany (2008)
9. Kouro, S., Malinowski, M., Gopakumar, K., Pou, J., Franquelo, L.G., Bin, Wu, Rodriguez, J., Pérez, M.A., Leon, J.I.: Recent advances and industrial applications of multilevel converters. IEEE Trans. Ind. Electron. **57**(8), 2553–2580 (2010)
10. Tareila, C., Sotoodeh, P., Miller, R.D.: Design and control of a single phase D-STATCOM inverter for wind application. In: Power Electronics and Machines in Wind Application PEMWA 2012, Denver, Co (2012)
11. Sabna, S., Prasad, D., Shivakumar, R.: Power system stability enhancement by neuro fuzzy logic based SVC for multi machine system. IJEAT **1**(4), 207–211 (2012). ISSN: 2249-8958
12. Karpagam, N., Devaraj, D.: Fuzzy logic control of static var compensator for power system oscillations damping. Int. J. Electr. Electron. Eng. **28**, 625–631 (2009)
13. Soto, D., Green, T.C.: A comparison of high power converter topologies for the implementation of FACTS controllers. IEEE Trans. Ind. Electron. **49**(5), 1072–1080 (2002)
14. Ainsworth, J.D., Davies, M., Fitz, P.J., Owe, K.E., Trainer, D.R.: Static var compensator (STATCOM) based on single phase chain circuit converters. IEE Proc. Gen. Transm. Distrib. **145**(4), 381–386 (1998)
15. Sun, Y., Ma, L.Y., Xiong, L.S.: A novel balancing method for DC voltage of cascaded multilevel STATCOM. In: Proceedings Asia-Pacfic Power and Energy Engineering Conference, pp. 1–5. Shanghai (2012)
16. Skoczowski, S., Domek, S., Pietrusewicz, K., Plater, B.: A method for improving the robustness of PID control. IEEE Trans. Ind. Electron. **52**(6), 1669–1676 (2005)
17. Kim, K., Schaefer, R.C.: Tuning a PID controller for a digital excitation control system. IEEE Trans. Ind. Appl. **41**(2), 485–492 (2005)

Real Coded Genetic Algorithm
for Development of Optimal G-K Clustering
Algorithm

C. Devi Arockia Vanitha[1]([⊠]), D. Devaraj[2], and M. Venkatesulu[3]

[1] Department of Computer Science, The S.F.R. College for Women,
Sivakasi 626123, India
vanima_c@yahoo.co.in
[2] Department of Electrical and Electronics Engineering,
Kalasalingam University, Krishnankoil 626126, India
deva230@yahoo.com
[3] Department of Computer Applications, Kalasalingam University,
Krishnankoil 626126, India
venkatesulu_m2000@yahoo.com

Abstract. Clustering has been used as a popular technique for identifying a natural grouping or meaningful partition of a given data set by using a distance or similarity function. This paper proposes a novel real coded Genetic algorithm (GA) for the development of optimal Gustafson Kessel (GK) clustering algorithm. In this work, the objective function of the GK algorithm is optimized using real coded genetic algorithm. The cluster centers are represented as real numbers and real-parameter genetic operators are applied to obtain the optimal cluster centers that minimize the intra-cluster distance. The performance of the proposed approach is demonstrated through three gene expression data sets. Xie-Beni index is used to arrive at the best possible number of clusters. The proposed method has produced the objective function value which is less than the value obtained using K-Means, Fuzzy C-Means and GK algorithms. Statistical analysis of the test results shows the superiority of the proposed algorithm over the existing methods.

Keywords: Clustering · Gene expression · Genetic algorithm (GA) · Gustafson Kessel (GK) algorithm · Xie-Beni index

1 Introduction

Gene Expression data is a real-valued expression matrix in which rows represent genes and columns represent conditions or samples. Each entry in the matrix is a measure of the expression level of a particular gene under a specific condition. A microarray experiment typically assesses a large number of DNA sequences under multiple conditions. These conditions may be a time series during a biological process or a collection of different tissue samples. Cluster analysis [6] is the process of classifying objects into groups based on specified features. The data points within a group are more similar to each other than the points in different groups. Computational approaches to identify

© Springer International Publishing Switzerland 2015
B.K. Panigrahi et al. (Eds.): SEMCCO 2014, LNCS 8947, pp. 264–274, 2015.
DOI: 10.1007/978-3-319-20294-5_23

gene clusters are aimed at identifying specific cluster types, such as those that correspond to metabolic pathways or those that represent sets of co-expressed genes [9, 11, 12].

The k-means algorithm is a simple iterative clustering algorithm that partitions a dataset into k clusters. The limitations of the k-means algorithm include the sensitivity of k-means to initialization and determining the value of k. Fang-Xiang et al. have proposed a genetic K-means clustering algorithm, called GKMCA, for clustering gene expression datasets [9]. Kalyani et al. have proposed the hybridization of K-Means with Particle Swarm optimization to explore better clustering performances [14]. Chandrasekar et al. have proposed a K-Means algorithm hybridized with Cluster Centre Initialization Algorithm (CCIA) is proposed for clustering Gene Expression Data [3].

Fuzzy c-means (FCM) clustering is a useful tool for analyzing gene expression data and extracting biological knowledge from gene expression data. FCM can get trapped in local minima when started with poor initialization and limited to clusters contained in linear subspaces of the data space because they use a fixed distance norm. Hence, several researchers formulated the entire clustering task of FCM explicitly as an optimization task and solved it using Genetic Algorithm, Differential evolution and Particle Swarm Optimization [16]. To detect clusters of different shapes in a dataset, recently Gustafson Kessel (GK) algorithm is proposed in [4, 13]. The GK method becomes computationally inefficient when applied to high dimensional data. To improve computational efficiency of GK, global optimization technique, namely, GA [5, 7, 8] is employed to GK algorithm. Genetic algorithms are essentially search algorithms based on the mechanics of natural selection and natural genetics. The entire clustering task of GK clustering method is formulated as an optimization problem and solved using GA. The primary objectives of the GA-GK algorithm are (1) to remove the noise and to filter the low expression genes in the gene expression data, (2) to obtain the optimal cluster centers with maximum intra-cluster distance, (3) to perform statistical analysis for verifying the biological relevance of the clustered genes and (4) to choose the cluster with large number of up-regulated genes for identifying the most significant genes.

This paper is organized as follows. Section 2 deals with working principle of Gustafson-Kessel algorithm. Section 3 describes overall design of GA-GK system. Section 4 provides the details of the Genetic operators used in this work. Section 5 addresses the issues for GA implementation. Section 6 provides the description about the data sets, experiment conducted, results and discussions. Section 7 concludes the work.

2 Gustafson-Kessel Algorithm

The Gustafson–Kessel [2, 4] algorithm is the fuzzy generalization of the Adaptive distance dynamic clusters algorithm, which searches for ellipsoidal clusters. It is relatively insensitive to the initialization of the partition matrix. It is based on iterative optimization of an objective functional of the c-means type [1]:

$$J(Z; U, V, \{A_i\}) = \sum_{i=1}^{K} \sum_{k=1}^{N} (\mu_{ik})^m D_{ikA_i}^2 \tag{1}$$

Here, $U = [\mu_{ik}] \in [0, 1]^{KXN}$ is a fuzzy partition matrix of the data $Z \in R^{n \times N}$, $V = [v_1, v_2, \ldots, v_K]$, $v_i \in R^n$ is a K-tuple of cluster prototypes and $m \in [1, \infty]$ is a scalar parameter which determines the fuzziness of the resulting clusters. N is the number of clusters, n is the number of samples and m is the weighting exponent. The distance norm D_{ikAi} can account for clusters of different geometrical shapes in one data set:

$$D_{ikA_i}^2 = (z_k - v_i)^T A_i (z_k - v_i) \tag{2}$$

The metric of each cluster is defined by a local norm-inducing matrix Ai, which is used as one of the optimization variables in the functional (1). This allows the distance norm to adapt to the local topological structure of the data. The matrices A_i are used as optimization variables in the c-means functional. Let $\mathbf{A_i}$ denote a c-tuple of the norm inducing matrices: $A_i = (A_1, A_2, \ldots, A_c)$. The objective function cannot be directly minimized with respect to A_i, since it is linear in A_i. To obtain a feasible solution, A_i must be constrained in some way. The usual way of accomplishing this is to constrain the determinant of A_i

$$|A_i| = \rho_i, \rho_i > 0, \forall i \tag{3}$$

Allowing the matrix A_i to vary with its determinant fixed corresponds to optimizing the cluster's shape while its volume remains constant. By using the Lagrange multiplier method, the following expression for A_i is obtained:

$$A_i = [\rho_i \det(F_i)]^{1/n} F_i^{-1} \tag{4}$$

where F_i is the *fuzzy covariance matrix* of the ith cluster defined by:

$$F_i = \frac{\sum_{k=1}^{N} (\mu_{ik})^m (z_k - v_i)(z_k - v_i)^T}{\sum_{k=1}^{N} (\mu_{ik})^m} \tag{5}$$

The substitution of Eqs. (3) and (4) into (2) gives a squared Mahalanobis distance norm, where the covariance is weighted by the membership degrees in U. The minimization of the GK objective functional is achieved by using the alternating optimization method proposed by Babuska et al. [2].

3   Problem Formulation

The purpose of the GA-GK algorithm in clustering is to obtain the optimal objective function value which groups the similar objects efficiently. This goal is achieved by proper adjustment of cluster centers and membership matrix. The initial population and cluster centers are randomly generated and membership matrix is computed using GK algorithm. Then, the fitness function is calculated for each individual in the population. An individual with the maximum fitness value is chosen to inject into the new population. The new cluster centers are generated by applying the real-coded genetic operators on the new population. The process will be repeated until there is no convergence in the results obtained. The task of optimal clustering using GK algorithm is formulated as a non-linear optimization problem as follows:

$$minimize\ J(Z; U, V, \{A_i\}) = \sum_{i=1}^{K} \sum_{k=1}^{N} (\mu_{ik})^m D_{ikA_i}^2 \qquad (6)$$

Where, $A_i = (A_1, A_2, ..., A_c)$ is a c-tuple of the norm-inducing matrices,

$$U = [\mu_{ik}] = \begin{bmatrix} \mu_{11} & \mu_{12} & \cdots & \mu_{1n} \\ \mu_{21} & \mu_{22} & \cdots & \mu_{2n} \\ \vdots & \vdots & \vdots & \vdots \\ \mu_{c1} & \mu_{c2} & \cdots & \mu_{cn} \end{bmatrix}$$

is a fuzzy partition matrix of X satisfying the following constraints,

$$\mu_{ik} \in [0,1], \quad 1 \leq i \leq c, \quad 1 \leq k \leq n,$$

$$\sum_{i=1}^{c} \mu_{ik} = 1, \quad 1 \leq k \leq n,$$

$$0 < \sum_{k=1}^{n} \mu_{ik} = 1 < n, \quad 1 \leq i \leq c \quad \text{and} \quad m \in [1, \infty)$$

is a weighting exponent that controls the membership degree μ_{ik} of each data point x_k to the cluster C_i. The choice of appropriate m value is of importance because the final clusters may vary depending on the m value selected. As $m \rightarrow 1$, J_1 produces a hard partition where $\mu_{ik} \in \{0, 1\}$. As m approaches infinity, J_∞ produces a maximum fuzzy partition where $\mu_{ik} = 1/c$. To determine the optimal number of clusters the Xie-Beni cluster validity measure [18] is used and is given by

$$V_{XB} = \frac{\sum_{k=1}^{n} \sum_{i=1}^{cc} (\mu_{ik})^2 x_k - v_i^2}{n \{ \min v_i - v_j^2 \}} \qquad (7)$$

The number of clusters corresponding to the minimum value of the Xie-Beni index indicates the best possible number of clusters. In this work, Xie-Beni index is used to quantify the separation and compactness of the clusters.

4 Real-Coded Genetic Algorithm

In the proposed GA-GK approach [7, 10], the optimization variables are represented as floating point numbers. This type of representation increase the efficiency of GA as there is no need to convert the solution variables to binary type. The details of the genetic operators applied in this work are presented below:

(i)   Selection is a method that favours the selection of best individuals from the population according to their fitness; the higher the fitness, the more chance an individual has to be selected for the next generation. In this work, Tournament selection is used.

(ii) The crossover operator is responsible for the global search property of the GA. Crossover basically combines substructures of two parent chromosomes to produce new structures, with the selected probability typically in the range of 0.6–1.0. In the proposed approach each individual in the population consists of real variables. The blend crossover operator (BLX-α) [7], is employed for real variables.

(iii) The mutation operator is used to inject new genetic material into the population. Mutation randomly alters a variable with a small probability. A variable is selected from an individual randomly and then it is set to a uniform random number between variable's lower and upper limit.

5 GA Implementation

When designing a clustering algorithm using GAs, the following issues are to be addressed: *Solution Representation, Formation of Fitness Function and Application of Genetic Operators.*

5.1 Solution Representation

The initial population is randomly generated based on the number of genes selected and number of input features. Each individual in the population represents a candidate solution. In the GA-GK Clustering problem, the elements of the solution consist of cluster centers. These variables are represented as floating point numbers. The cluster centers are formulated based on the number of clusters and number of input features. With the above representation, a typical chromosome for a cluster center in the GA-GK problem will look like the following:

$$\underbrace{1.5143}_{\text{inf}1} \quad \underbrace{2.4720}_{\text{inf }2} \quad \underbrace{2.3334}_{\text{inf}3} \quad \underbrace{7.2601}_{\text{inf}4} \quad \cdots \quad \underbrace{6.3321}_{\text{inf \_n}}$$

The use of floating point numbers to represent the solutions eases the difficulties associated with the binary-coded GA for real variables.

5.2   Fitness Function

In the GK clustering problem, the objective function is to minimize the distance between data and center. Evaluation of the individuals in the population is done by computing the objective function value for the clustering problem. The fitness value of the individual is calculated using the resultant value of the objective function. During GA run, it searches for a solution with maximum fitness function value. Hence, the minimization objective function is transformed to fitness function (f) to be maximized as, $f = \frac{K}{F}$ Where, K is a constant. This is to amplify ($1/f$), the value of which is usually small; so that the fitness value of the chromosome will be in a wider range.

6   Simulation Results

This section presents the description of the simulation carried out on three gene expression datasets to demonstrate the effectiveness of the proposed real coded genetic algorithm for the development of optimal Gustafson Kessel clustering algorithm. Table 1 gives the details of datasets and their characteristics.

Table 1. Details of gene expression datasets

Dataset	# Genes	# Samples
Yeast diauxic shift	6400	7
Yeast cell cycle	384	17
Rat CNS	112	9

Yeast Diauxic Shift data set consists of expression levels of 6400 genes measured at 7 time-points during diauxic shift. It is the fungus that is used to bake bread and ferment wine from grapes. This dataset is available at www.yeastgenome.org. To reduce the number of expression profiles, Yeast Diauxic Shift data is filtered to remove the genes that do not expressed or do not change. The empty spots on the microarray data is considered as noise and removed. Missing values are imputed. The genes with small variance over time are also filtered out.

Yeast Cell Cycle [17] data set consists of expression levels of approximately 6000 genes over two cell cycles (17 time-points). Based on the "Functional Categories of Genes", all the genes that were assigned a "phase" were extracted. The subset consists of 384 genes whose expression levels peak at different time points corresponding to the five phases of cell cycle.

Rat CNS (Central Nervous System) [17] data set consists of 112 genes measured across 9 time-points. This has been obtained by reverse transcription-coupled PCR to examine the expression levels of a set of 112 genes during rat central nervous system development over 9 time-points. This dataset is available at http://faculty.washington.edu/kayee/cluster.

The cluster centers are the solution vectors and they are evolved using real-coded Genetic Algorithm. The membership matrix is updated using the newly generated cluster centers. The objective function of GK is calculated for the new cluster centers. The same process is repeated until there is no convergence in the resultant objective function value. The validity measure is calculated for each run, and number of clusters which minimizes the measure is chosen as the "correct" number of cluster in the data. In the experimental results, the number of clusters is fixed as 3 to show the efficiency of the GA-GK algorithm. The GA-GK algorithm was run with different values of GA control parameters and the optimal clustering results were obtained with the following setting for Yeast Cell Cycle:

| Population size: | 30 | Crossover probability: | 0.8 |
| Mutation probability: | 0.05 | Tournament size: | 2 |

The convergence behavior of GA for the above setting is shown in Fig. 1.

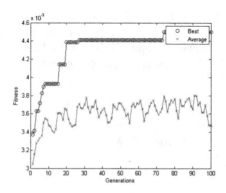

Fig. 1. Convergence characteristics (yeast diauxic shift)

Table 2. Performance comparison of proposed GA-GK approach with other algorithms

Performance parameter	Yeast cell cycle			
	K-means	FCM	GK	GA-GK
Function evaluations	101	100	7	100
Objective function value	3281.80	619.5	567.37	192.30
Xie-Beni index	–	0.5209	0.5399	1.0186

From Table 2, it is found the genetic algorithm based GK approach is more efficient in obtaining optimal clustering results than GK algorithm. The objective function value J_m of GA based GK algorithm is minimum than the other approaches and GA-GK outperformed GK approach. The Clustering results were assessed using z-score validation measure given in [13]. The standard z-score indicates how many standard deviations a measured expression value is above or below the mean. The higher the absolute value of the z-score indicates the significance of change in expression and genes are clustered with biological relevance. Table 3 gives the z-score of all approaches.

Table 3. Summary of statistical comparison of GA-GK with other approaches

Dataset	Genes/Conditions	Method	z-score
Yeast diauxic shift	6400/7	K-means	−1.7 to 2.2
		FCM	−1.9 to 1.9
		GK	−1.6 to 2.2
		GA-GK	**−2.1 to 4.2**
Yeast cell cycle	384/17	K-means	−2.2 to 1.5
		FCM	−2.1 to 1.0
		GK	−2.3 to 2.2
		GA-GK	**−3.9 to 5.8**
Rat CNS	112/9	K-means	−0.8 to 5.3
		FCM	−1.8 to 1.4
		GK	−2.4 to 5.8
		GA-GK	**−4.2 to 3.10**

For Yeast Cell Cycle dataset, the z-scores of GK ranged from −2.3 to 2.2 and showed better performance than K-means and FCM. Compared to K-means, FCM and GK algorithms, GA-GK provided better clustering performance with a range of −3.9 to 5.8. The summary of the results obtained using K-means, FCM, GK and GA-GK clustering algorithms on the three gene expression data sets are given in Tables 4, 5, 6 and 7 respectively.

Table 4. Performance of K-Means for all datasets

Dataset	Objective function value	# Function evaluations
Yeast diauxic shift	1608.8	126
Yeast cell cycle	3281.80	101
RatCNS	618.36	90

Table 5. Performance of FCM for all datasets

Dataset	Objective function value	Xie-Beni index	# Function evaluations
Yeast diauxic shift	357.70	0.3790	27
Yeast cell cycle	619.50	0.5209	20
Rat CNS	311.62	0.7641	28

Table 6. Performance of GK for all datasets

Dataset	Objective function value	Xie-Beni index	# Function evaluations
Yeast diauxic shift	1498.4	1.0697	24
Yeast cell cycle	567.37	0.5399	7
RatCNS	597.43	4.8715	112

Table 7. Performance of GAGK for all datasets

Dataset	Objective function value			Xie-Beni index	# Generations
	Min	Max	Avg		
Yeast diauxic shift	215.5	454.54	335.02	2.1703	100
Yeast cell cycle	192.30	312.50	252.40	1.0186	
Rat CNS	93.45	126.58	110.01	4.1535	

Gene Ontology Analysis: Gene Ontology (GO) is a major bioinformatics initiative to unify the representation of gene and gene product attributes across all species. The biological significance of genes selected and samples classified by the proposed method is investigated using GO based biological semantics [15]. GO terms over the functions of genes in three orthogonal taxonomies: Molecular Function (MF), Biological Process (BP) and Cellular Component (CC). Annotation is the process of assigning GO terms to gene products. Table 8 gives the GO-based most significant genes that are up-regulated with their expression values in the Yeast Diauxic Shift data.

Table 8. Most significant genes in yeast diauxic shift

Gene ID	GO term	Process name	P-value
YALO51W	GO:0005488	The selective, non-covalent, often stoichiometric, interaction of a molecule with one or more specific sites on another molecule	0.0001
YALO54C	GO:0008106	Catalysis of the reaction	0.0002
PNCA	GO:0004033	Catalysis of the reaction	0.0016
YHR007C	GO:0005372	Enables the directed movement of water (H_2O) from one side of a membrane to the other	0.0016
YALO56W	GO:0015144	Catalysis of the transfer of carbohydrate from one side of the membrane to the other	0.0016
E.COLI#40	GO:0022838	Catalysis of energy-independent facilitated diffusion, mediated by passage of a specific solute through a transmembrane aqueous pore or channel	0.0016
GENOMIC 0.25X	GO:0004032	Catalysis of the reaction	0.0033
YAL008W	GO:0050236	Catalysis of the reaction	0.0033
POLYDA	GO:0005275	Catalysis of the transfer of amines, including polyamines, from one side of the membrane to the other.	0.0176
SS DNA	GO:0005342	Catalysis of the transfer of organic acids, any acidic compound containing carbon in covalent linkage, from one side of the membrane to the other	0.0176

The P-value associated to each term is computed using the hyper geometric probability density function. The most significant GO items are arranged by ordering P-value. A biograph object is a data structure containing generic interconnected data used to implement a directed graph. Nodes represent proteins, or genes, and edges represent interactions or dependences between the nodes. In Fig. 2, red indicates an increase in mRNA and green indicates a decrease in abundance in the experimental sample with respect to the control.

The most significant genes that are up-regulated with their expression values in the Yeast Diauxic Shift are identified by clustering the yeast values using Genetic based Gustafson-Kessel algorithm. Figure 2 shows the Directed Acyclic graph (DAG) and ancestor chart [14] view of the genes selected by the proposed approach. It is observed that the GO terms 8106, 4033, 4032 and 50230 are the most significant genes involved in catalysis of the reaction process.

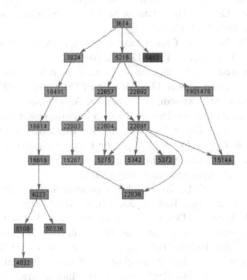

Fig. 2. DAG of the GO analysis for yeast diauxic shift (Color figure online)

7 Conclusions

Clustering is a useful technique for analysis of large dimensional data, and a variety of clustering methods have been used in biological research. The bottleneck of conventional clustering methods is to impose a fixed shape on the clusters even if the clusters in many real-life datasets may differ in shape. The Gustafson Kessel algorithm addresses the limitations of Fuzzy C-Means and other conventional clustering methods using an adaptive distance norm. The proposed method formulates GK as a non-linear optimization problem and determines the distance between data and cluster centers with continuous variables. The value of the objective function J_m is minimized by tuning with Real-Coded Genetic Algorithm. The effectiveness of the proposed GA based method for GK clustering is demonstrated using three gene expression datasets with promising results. Further, through Gene Ontology analysis, it is confirmed that the genes identified using the proposed GA-GK clustering approach have biological significance.

References

1. Babuska, R.: Fuzzy Modeling for Control. Kluwer Academic Publishers, Norwell (1999)
2. Babuska, R., Van der Veen, P.J., Kaymak, U.: Improved covariance estimation for Gustafson-Kessel clustering. In: IEEE (2002)
3. Chandrasekhar, T., Thangavel, K., Elayaraja, E.: Effective Clustering Algorithms for Gene Expression Data. Int. J. Comput. Appl. (0975 – 9997), 32(4), (2011)
4. Kim, D.W., Lee, K.H., Lee, D.: Detecting clusters of different geometrical shapes in microarray gene expression data. Bioinformatics 21(9), 1927–1934 (2005)
5. Goldberg, David E.: Genetic Algorithms in Search, Optimization and Machine Learning. Pearson Education, New York (2011)
6. Jiang, D., Tang, C., Zhang, A.: Cluster analysis for gene expression data: a survey. IEEE Trans. Knowl. Data Eng. 16(11), 1370–1386 (2004)
7. Devaraj, D.: Improved genetic algorithm for multi-objective reactive power dispatch problem. Eur. Trans. Electr. Power 17(6), 569–581 (2007). doi:10.1002/etep.146
8. Falehi, A.D., Rostami, M., Doroudi, A., Ashrafian, A.: Optimization and coordination of SVC-based supplementary controllers and PSSs to improve power system stability using a genetic algorithm. Turk. J. Electr. Eng. Comput. Sci. 20(5), 639–654 (2012)
9. Wu, F.X., Zhang, W.J., Kusalik, A.J.: A genetic k-means clustering algorithm applied to gene expression data. In: Xiang, Y., Chaib-draa, B. (eds.) Canadian AI 2003. LNCS (LNAI), vol. 2671, pp. 520–526. Springer, Heidelberg (2003)
10. Ganesh Kumar, P., Devaraj, D.: Improved genetic algorithm for optimal design of fuzzy classifier. Int. J. Comput. Appl. Technol. 35(234), 97–103 (2009)
11. Ganesh Kumar, P., Rani, C., Devaraj, D., Aruldoss Albert Victoire, T.: Hybrid ant bee algorithm for fuzzy expert system based sample classification, IEEE/ACM Trans. Comput. Biol. Bioinf. (2013). doi. 10.1109/TCBB.2014.2307325. ISSN 1545-5963
12. Yi, G., Sze, S.H., Thon, M.R.: Identifying clusters of functionally related genes in genomes. Bioinformatics 23(9), 1053–1060 (2007). doi:10.1093/bioinformatics/btl673
13. Gibbons, F., Roth, F.: Judging the quality of gene expression-based clustering methods using gene annotation. Genome Res. 12, 1574–1591 (2002)
14. Manda, K., Hanuman, A.S., Satapathy, S.C., Chaganti, V., Babu, A.V.: A software tool for data clustering using particle swarm optimization. In: Panigrahi, B.K., Das, S., Suganthan, P. N., Dash, S.S. (eds.) SEMCCO 2010. LNCS, vol. 6466, pp. 278–285. Springer, Heidelberg (2010)
15. Piyushkumar, M.A., Rajapakse, J.C.: SVM-RFE with MRMR filter for gene selection. IEEE Transa. Nanobiosci. 9(1), 31–37 (2010)
16. Ravi, V., Aggarwal, N., Chauhan, N.: Differential evolution based fuzzy clustering. In: Panigrahi, B.K., Das, S., Suganthan, P.N., Dash, S.S. (eds.) SEMCCO 2010. LNCS, vol. 6466, pp. 38–45. Springer, Heidelberg (2010)
17. Sarmah, R.: Gene expression data clustering using a fuzzy link based approach. Int. J. Comput. Inf. Syst. Ind. Manage. Appl. 5, 532–541 (2013)
18. Xie, X.L., Beni, G.: A Validity Measure for Fuzzy Clustering. IEEE Trans. Pattern Anal. Mach. Intell. 13(9), 941–947 (1991)

On-line Economic Dispatch of Distributed Generation Using Artificial Neural Networks

M. Arumuga Babu[1]([⊠]), R. Mahalakshmi[2], S. Kannan[3],
M. Karuppasamypandiyan[4], and A. Bhuvanesh[5]

[1] Department of EEE, Tejaa Shakthi Institute of Technology for Women,
Coimbatore, India
arumuga1978@gmail.com
[2] Department of EEE, Sri Krishna College of Technology, Coimbatore, India
[3] Department of EEE, Ramco Institute of Technology, Rajapalayam, India
[4] Department of EEE, University College of Engineering, BIT Campus,
Trichy, India
[5] Department of EEE, Mepco Schlenk Engineering College, Sivakasi, India

Abstract. In recent years, distributed generators (DG) are most widely installed in distribution system to meet the increasing demand and especially to reduce the losses. According to demand, dispatch of generator should be modified for economic operation. The Economic Dispatch (ED) of DGs are usually solved by conventional methods such as Lambda iteration method, Dynamic Programming etc., or any optimization technique such as Genetic algorithm (GA), Evolutionary Programming (EP) etc., This off-line methods of solving ED problem require comparatively large computation time and are not suitable for on-line applications. Therefore, it is important to estimate Real Power dispatch values within a short period. This paper presents an On-line ED of various non-renewable DGs for various demands using Artificial Neural Networks namely Back Propagation Neural Network (BPNN) and Radial Basis Function Neural Network (RBFNN). The input pattern for Neural Networks (NN) is demand and output is corresponding optimal real power dispatch. The input and output patterns for NN is obtained using evolutionary programming method. In this work two diesel engines and two fuel cells are used as DG. This case study has been illustrated in a distribution system having two types of four numbers of DGs. The test result shows that the proposed method is better for real time ED.

Keywords: Back propagation neural network · Distributed generators · Economic dispatch · Evolutionary programming · Radial basis function neural network

1 Introduction

According to the definition of CIGRE, Distributed Generation (DG) is defined as the generating plant with a capacity of less than 100 MW, usually connected to the distribution networks that are neither centrally planned nor dispatched [1]. One of the drawbacks of using non-renewable DG in distribution system is its fuel cost. Hence, to reduce this fuel cost the DGs should be optimally dispatched.

© Springer International Publishing Switzerland 2015
B.K. Panigrahi et al. (Eds.): SEMCCO 2014, LNCS 8947, pp. 275–283, 2015.
DOI: 10.1007/978-3-319-20294-5_24

Economic dispatch (ED) is one of the most important optimization problems in power system operation and planning. ED economically dispatch the generators according to demand while satisfying physical and operational constraints. Classical methods such as Lambda iteration, Base point Participation factor, Gradient method, Newton's method and Lagrange multiplier method can solve ED problem under the assumption that the incremental cost curves of the generating units are monotonically increasing piecewise-linear functions. However, in reality, the cost curves of generating units are non-convex. Classical based techniques fail to address these types of problems satisfactorily and lead to sub optimal solutions producing huge revenue loss over time. Dynamic programming (DP) can solve ED problem with inherently nonlinear and discontinuous cost curves. But it suffers from the curse of dimensionality or local optimality [2].

ED problems are also solved by many optimization algorithms namely Genetic algorithm (GA) [3, 4], Evolutionary Programming (EP) [5], Particle Swarm Optimization (PSO) [6], Artificial Immune system (AIS) [7], Differential Evolution Algorithm (DE) [8] Biogeography-based optimization (BBO) [9], Simulated Annealing (SA) [10] etc., The main drawbacks of these optimization algorithms are time consuming because for every demand the programs needs to be run to get optimal result. Hence, it is not suitable for on-line application.

This paper presents an online ED of four non-renewable DGs using Neural Network (NN). Two Types of NN has been developed for On-Line Estimation of ED namely Back Propagation Neural Network (BPNN) and Radial Basis Neural Network (RBFNN). The case study has been implemented on a four DGs test system.

2   Problem Formulation

The ED of DGs may be formulated as non-linear optimization problem. Two types of DGs are considered here. They are diesel engines and two fuel stacks. The objective function in a diesel engine consists of the fuel cost function similar to the cost function used for conventional generating plants. The operating cost of fuel cell system takes the fuel costs and includes the efficiency of fuel cell. The constraints include power generation capacity limits.

The objective function is:

$$minF_T = F_{diesel} + F_{fuelcell} \tag{1}$$

where, F_{diesel} is Fuel cost of diesel generator, $F_{Fuel\text{-}cell}$ is Fuel cost Fuel-cell
Subject to,

$$P_D = \sum_{i=1}^{n} P_{Gi} \tag{2}$$

$$P_G^{min} \leq P_G \leq P_G^{max} \tag{3}$$

where, P_D is Demand, P_G is Real power generation of DGs,n is number of DG's and P_G^{min}, P_G^{max} is Minimum and maximum capacity of DGs.

2.1 Diesel Generator

The objective function in a diesel engine consists of the fuel cost function similar to the cost function used for conventional thermal generating plants.

$$F_{diesel} = \sum_{i=1}^{n} \left(a_i * P_{diesel,i}^2 + b_i * P_{diesel,i} + c_i \right) \qquad (4)$$

where F_{diesel} is the diesel generator fuel cost; n is the number of diesel generator; $P_{diesel,i}$ is the diesel generation output in kW of unit i. a_i, b_i, c_i are fuel cost coefficient of ith generator.

2.2 Fuel Cell Plant

The operating cost of fuel cell system takes the fuel costs and includes the efficiency of fuel cell. When fuel is transferred into power, the cost function considers the efficiency of fuel cell. The generation cost of fuel cell is as follows:

$$F_{fuelcell} = \sum_{i=1}^{n} b_i \left(\frac{P_{FC,i}}{n_{FC,i}} \right) \qquad (5)$$

where $F_{fuelcell}$ is the fuel cell generation cost; b_i is the natural gas cost in \$/kg; $P_{FC,i}$ is fuel cell generation of the ith plant; $n_{FC,i}$ is fuel cell efficiency of unit i.

3 Review of Neural Networks

In this work BPA based ANN and RBF based ANN is used to solve the present problem.

3.1 BPA Based ANN

A multilayer feed forward network trained by back propagation is the most popular and versatile form of neural network for pattern mapping or function approximation problem. The structure of a BPA based multilayer feed forward network is shown in Fig. 1.

The ANN utilized here contains three layers. These are input, hidden, and output layers. During the training phase, the training data is fed into the input layer. The data is propagated to the hidden layer and then to the output layer. This is called the forward pass of the Back Propagation Algorithm. In the forward pass, each node in hidden layer gets input from all the nodes of input layer, which are multiplied with appropriate weights and then summed. The output of the hidden node is the non- linear transformation of the resulting sum. Similarly each node in output layer gets input from all the nodes of hidden layer, which are multiplied with appropriate weights and then summed. The output of this node is the non-linear transformation of the resulting sum.

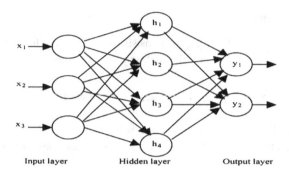

Fig. 1. Structure of BPA based neural network

3.2   RBF Based ANN

RBF networks are feed-forward networks trained using a supervised training algorithm. They are typically configured with a single hidden layer of units whose activation function is selected from a class of functions called basis functions.

Radial Basis Function Neural Network is the three layers feed forward neural network. Figure 2 shows the schematic diagram of a RBF neural network. In RBFNN the input neurons are directly fed to input layer. Then, the output of the input layer is fed to hidden layer without adding any weight. The transfer function of hidden nodes is same as that of multivariate Gaussian density function,

$$\emptyset_j(x) = \exp\left(-\frac{x - u_j^2}{2\sigma_j^2}\right) \tag{6}$$

Where x is the input vector u_j,σ_j are the center and the spread of the corresponding Gaussian function. $\| \, . \, \|$ denotes the Euclidean distance between x and u_j. Then, the connections in the second layer is weighted and the output nodes are linear summation units [11].

The value of the k_{th} output node y_k is given by,

$$y_k(x) = \sum_{j=1}^{h} w_{kj}\emptyset_j(x) + w_{k0} \tag{7}$$

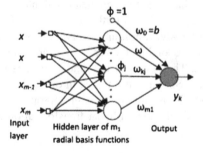

Fig. 2. Structure of RBF neural network

where w_{kj} is the connection weight between the k_{th} output node and j_{th} hidden node and w_{k0} is the bias term.

The training algorithm for RBF neural network is summarized as below.

- Determine the unit centres u_j by the K-means clustering algorithm.
- Determine the unit width σ_j using a heuristic approach that ensures the smoothness and continuity of the fitted function. The width of any hidden node is taken as the maximum Euclidean distance between the identified centres.
- Compute weights of the second layer connections are determined by linear regression using a least-squares objective function.

4   Development of Neural Network for on-Line Power Dispatch of DGs

Many optimization techniques are proposed to solve ED problem [3–10]. However, these methods are needed to solve every time when the system load changes so these methods are not suitable for the on-line power dispatch.

4.1   Training Data Development

The generation of the appropriate training data is an important step in the development of ANN models. For the ANN to accurately predict the output, the training data should represent the complete range of operating conditions of the system under consideration. For model development, a large number of training data is generated through off-line power system simulation. The schematic diagram of proposed approach is given in Fig. 3.

The procedure for generating training data to develop the neural network is as follows:

- First, a range of situations is generated by randomly varying the real power demand between 100 kW to 950 kW.

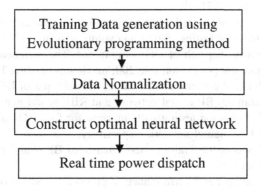

Fig. 3. Schematic diagram of the proposed approach

- For each demand compute real power dispatch of DGs using evolutionary algorithm.

4.2 Data Normalization

During training of the neural network, higher valued input variables may tend to suppress the influence of smaller ones. Also, if the raw data is directly applied to the network, there is a risk of the simulated neurons reaching the saturated conditions. If the neurons get saturated, then the changes in the input value will produce a very small change or no change in the output value. This affects the network training to a great extent. To avoid this, the raw data is normalized before the actual application to the neural network. One way to normalize the data x is by using the expression.

$$x_n = \frac{(x - x_{min})}{(x_{max} - x_{min})} + starting\ value \qquad (8)$$

Where x_n is the normalized value, x_{min} and x_{max} are the minimum and maximum values of the variable.

4.3 Network Development

The input after normalization is presented to the ANN networks for training. After training, the networks are evaluated through a different set of input–output data. Once the networks are trained and tested, they are ready for estimating the real power dispatch of DGs.

5 Simulation Results

The proposed NN is implemented on four DGs system under various power demands. Two diesels and two fuel cells are used as DGs. The fuel cost coefficient, generation capacity for diesel, fuel cell and fuel cell efficiency is presented in Table 1. The demand is varied between 100 kW to 950 kW. The simulation studies were carried out by developing program on MATLAB 13.

In the ANN model a sum of 250 input-output pairs are generated in which 200 used for training and 50 used for testing. Based on evolutionary algorithm for each demand the optimum real power dispatch of DGs is obtained. The parameters used for evolutionary programming are population size 200; maximum iteration 100; beta = 0.025.

Table 2 shows the real power dispatch values of four types of DGs obtained using evolutionary programming, BP neural network and RBF neural network.

Figures 4 and 5 shows the testing patterns error for four DGs obtained using BP neural network and RBF neural network respectively.

Figures 6 and 7 shows the Training performance of BP neural network and RBF neural network respectively.

The parameters settings and performance of proposed neural network is presented in Table 3.

Table 1. Parameters of DGs

DG type	Fuel cost coefficient for diesel/natural gas cost for fuel cell			Generation capacity (kW)		Cell efficiency
	c($/hr)	b($/kWh)/($/Kg)	a($/(kW)^2 h)	P_{min}	P_{max}	
Diesel1	0.4333	0.2333	0.0074	25	400	——
Diesel2	0.2731	0.1453	0.0042	15	350	——
Fuel cell1	0	0.05	0	0	100	90 %
Fuel cell2	0	0.05	0	0	150	95 %

Table 2. Dispatch for different load levels in test system

Methods	Demand (kW)	Dispatch of DGs (kW)			
		$P_{Diesel1}$	$P_{Diesel2}$	$P_{Fuel\ Cell1}$	$P_{Fuel\ Cell2}$
EP	810.9502	212.8403	348.4443	99.9234	149.7422
BPNN		212.5039	349.4207	99.9524	149.7422
RBFNN		212.9961	347.3780	99.3582	149.1423
EP	914.5509	317.3113	347.5691	99.9182	149.9298
BPNN		315.1947	349.4319	99.9595	149.7411
RBFNN		316.6144	348.5779	99.9176	149.7411
EP	727.4762	168.2298	309.2145	99.9453	149.8229
BPNN		167.4437	310.0856	99.9801	149.9667
RBFNN		168.5832	309.9683	99.9127	149.5437

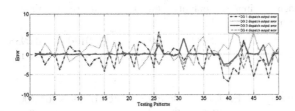

Fig. 4. Error plot for testing patterns of BPNN

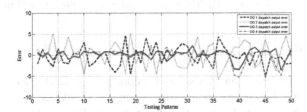

Fig. 5. Error plot for testing patterns of RBFNN

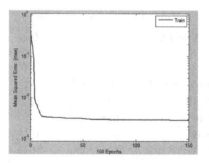

Fig. 6. Training performance of BPNN

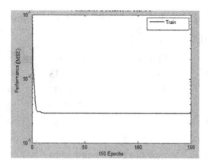

Fig. 7. Training performance of RBFNN

Table 3. Performance of the network

Neural network type	No. of hidden neurons	No. of inputs	No. of outputs	Training time (s)	Training error (mse)	Testing time (s)	Testing error (mse)
BPNN	6	1	4	69	0.00170	0.0936	0.0641
RBFNN	——	1	4	1.62	0.00028	0.046	0.0021

The time taken by the EP for calculating dispatch of DGs for 200 different loading condition is approximately 3854 s. This time may reduce to 69 s when BPNN is chosen. Further the time may reduce to 1.62 s when RBFNN is chosen also from Table 3 it is inferred that the RBFNN testing error is comparatively lower than BP neural network error. Hence, RBFNN is more suitable for on-line ED of DGs.

6 Conclusion

This paper has presented an ANN-based estimation of Real power dispatch of non-renewable DGs for on-line applications. Computer simulation was carried out on the 4 DGs System. Test results show that the proposed BPA based approach and RBF based approach provides accurate estimation of real power dispatch of DGs. In comparison with BPNN, the RBFNN accurately predict power dispatch of DGs. Hence RBFNN is more suitable for on line ED of DGs in distribution system.

References

1. CIGRE: Impact of increasing contribution of dispersed generation on the power system. Working Group 37.23, (1999)
2. Basu, M., Chowdhury, A.: Cuckoo search algorithm for economic dispatch. Energy **60**, 99–108 (2013)
3. Walter, D.C., Sheble, G.B.: Genetic algorithm solution of economic dispatch with Valve point loading. IEEE Trans. Power Syst. **8**, 1325–1332 (1993)
4. Cheng, P.H., Chang, H.C.: Large scale economic dispatch by genetic algorithm. IEEE Trans. Power Syst. **10**(4), 1919–1926 (1995)
5. Yang, H.T., Yang, P.C., Huang, C.L.: Evolutionary programming based economic dispatch for units with non-smooth fuel cost functions. IEEE Trans. Power Syst. **11**, 112–118 (1996)
6. Gaing, Z.-L.: Particle swarm optimization to solving the economic dispatch considering the generator constraints. IEEE Trans. Power Syst. **18**(3), 1187–1195 (2003)
7. Panigrahi, B.K., Yadav, S.R., Agrawal, S., Tiwari, M.K.: A clonal algorithm to solve economic load dispatch. Electr. Power Syst. Res. **77**(10), 1381–1389 (2007)
8. Wang, S.K., Chiou, J.P., Liu, C.W.: Non-smooth/non-convex economic dispatch by a novel hybrid differential evolution algorithm. IET Gener. Transm. Distrib. **1**(5), 793–803 (2007)
9. Bhattacharya, A., Chattopadhyay, P.K.: Biogeography-based optimization for different economic load dispatch problems. IEEE Trans. Power Syst. **25**(2), 1064–1077 (2010)
10. Wong, K.P., Fung, C.C.: Simulated annealing based economic dispatch algorithm. IEE Proc. Gener. Transmission and Distribution **140**(6), 509–515 (1993)
11. Devaraj, D., Yegnanrayana, B., Ramar, K.: Radial basis function networks for fast contingency ranking. Electr. Power Energy Systems **24**, 387–395 (2002)

Separation of Real Time Heart Sound Signal from Lung Sound Signal Using Neural Network

K. Sathesh[1(✉)] and N.J.R. Muniraj[2]

[1] Department of ECE, Tejaa Sakthi Institute of Technology for Women,
Coimbatore, India
sathesh_kce@yahoo.com
[2] Tejaa Sakthi Institute of Technology for Women, Coimbatore, India
njrmuniraj@yahoo.com

Abstract. While recording lung sounds, an incessant noise source takes place owing to heart sounds. This noise source severely contaminates the breath sound signal and interferes in the analysis of lung sounds. This paper presents a technique for separation of heart sound signal (HSS) from lung sound signal (LSS) using neural network (NN) with real time recorded sound signal. Here two signals are used in neural network noise separation scheme. The two signals are raw signal and reference heart signal. The raw signal is given as input signal to neural network and reference heart signal is used as target signal. The proposed system is applied and the results show the error rate of the desired sound signal (DSS), signal to noise ratio (SNR) and execution time.

Keywords: Heart sound signal · Lung sound signal · Neural network

1 Introduction

Heart sounds interfere with lung sounds in a manner that obstructs the potential of respiratory sound analysis in terms of analysis of respiratory disease. Lung sounds are created by vortical and turbulent flow [1] within lung airways during inspiration and expiration of air [2]. Lung sounds recorded on the chest wall represent not only produced sound in lung airways but also the effects of thoracic tissues and sound sensor characteristics on sound conveyed from the lungs to a data acquisition system [3].

Lung sounds show a power spectral density that is broadband with power decreasing as frequency increases [4]. The logarithm of amplitude and the logarithm of frequency are almost linearly related in healthy subjects [4] provided that the signals do not have adventitious sounds. As the flow in lung airways increases, sound intensity increases and several mathematical relations between lung sounds and airflow have been suggested [5, 6]. It is important to note that inspiratory and expiratory lung sounds be unlike in terms of both amplitude and frequency range. At comparable flows, inspiratory lung sounds will have more intensity than expiratory sounds [7, 8].

© Springer International Publishing Switzerland 2015
B.K. Panigrahi et al. (Eds.): SEMCCO 2014, LNCS 8947, pp. 284–291, 2015.
DOI: 10.1007/978-3-319-20294-5_25

Heart sounds are created by the flow of blood into and out of the heart and by the movement of structures involved in the control of this flow [9]. The first heart sound results when blood is pumped from the heart to the rest of the body, during the latter half of the cardiac cycle, and it is comprised of sounds resulting from the rise and release of pressure within the left ventricle along with the increase in ascending aortic pressure [9]. After blood leaves the ventricles, the simultaneous closing of the semi-lunar valves, which connect the ventricles with the aorta and pulmonary arteries, causes the second heart sound [10].

The electrocardiogram signifies the depolarization and repolarization of heart muscles during each cardiac cycle [10]. Depolarization of ventricular muscles during ventricular contraction results in three signals known as the Q, R, and S-waves of the electrocardiogram [10]. The first heart sound immediately follows the QRS complex. In health, the last 30–40 % of the interval between successive R-wave peaks contains a period that is void of first and second heart sounds.

Characteristics of heart sound signals have been assessed in terms of both intensity and frequency [11]. Though peak frequencies of heart sounds have been shown to be much lower than those of lung sounds [11], comparisons between lung sound recordings acquired over the anterior right upper lobe containing and excluding heart sounds [12] show that PSD in both cases is maximal below 150 Hz.

1.1 Literature Review

Separating the two signals, breath and cardiac sounds and several methods are used to solve the problem in terms of reduced interferences in a desired output signal. The adaptive algorithm is used to find the real signal recorded in both breath and cardiac sounds in a human and also in a stationary background noise [13].

During the real time sound signal recording the source of interference is unavoidable but the separation of two sound signal is very challenging task because the output heart sound signal is very useful to find the diseases for the respiratory specialists and cardiologists [14]. The blind source extraction is introduced to separate the heart sound and lung sound signal from the recorded input signal using the cyclic correlation matrix but in this technique a certain range of frequency reduces the interference [15].

Observing the heart sound signal from the chest wall of a human always have some interference in a recorded signal but the empirical mode decomposition method is used to decrease the interference of the desired output signal. The EMD method is used for both time and frequency domain analysis to give the desired output sound signal [16]. The variable gain amplifier is used for pre-processing compression stage in adaptive filter function. The least mean square algorithm helps to eliminate the heart sound interferences in adaptive filter algorithm [17]. To eliminate the interferences we use the reference signal when performing adaptive filtering. Adaptive line enhancer (ALE) with normalized least mean square (NLMS) algorithm which is used to obtain the desired sound signal from real time sound signal and the linear predictive FIR filter are used to detect the other sound signals and the interferences is presented in [18].

This paper presents a technique for separation of heart sound signal (HSS) from lung sound signal (LSS) using neural network (NN) with real time recorded sound signal obtained using digital stethoscope and its details are given in Appendix. The results show the error rate of the desired sound signal (DSS), signal to noise ratio (SNR) and execution time are computed with different hidden layers of neural network.

2   Implementation of NN to Separate HSS from LSS

The proposed approach is based on back propagation based neural network. The idea is to separate heart sound signal from raw signal (heart and lung) recorded from different age groups of male and female using stethoscope.

The proposed block diagram of neural network noise cancellation scheme is shown in Fig. 1.

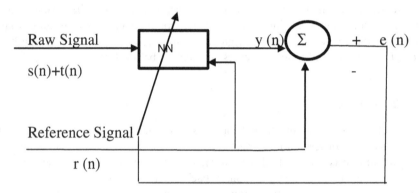

Fig. 1. Block diagram of proposed approach

where s(n) is lung sound signal, t(n) is heart sound signal, r(n) is heart sound reference signal, y(n) is neural network output and e(n) is error signal. There are 2 signals used in neural network noise separation scheme. They are raw signal and reference heart signal. The raw signal is given as input signal to neural network and reference heart signal is used as target signal.

Neural network used here contains three layers. These are input, hidden, and output layers. During the training phase, the training data is fed into the input layer. The data is propagated to the hidden layer and then to the output layer. This is called the forward pass of the back propagation algorithm. In the forward pass, each node in hidden layer gets input from all the nodes of input layer, which are multiplied with appropriate weights and then summed. The output of the hidden node is the non-linear transformation of the resulting sum. Similarly each node in output layer gets input from all the nodes of hidden layer, which are multiplied with appropriate weights and then summed. The output of this node is the non-linear transformation of the resulting sum.

This is mathematically represented as,

$$out_i = f(net_i) = f\left[\sum_{j=1}^{n} w_{ij}\, out_j + b_i\right] \tag{1}$$

where out_i is the output of the ith neuron in the layer under consideration. out_j is the output of the jth neuron in the preceding layer. w_{ij} are the connection weights between the ith neuron and the jth inputs and b_i is a constant called bias.

The output values of the output layer are compared with the target output values. The target output values are those that we attempt to teach our network. The error between actual output values and target output values are calculated and propagated back toward hidden layer. This is called the backward pass of the back propagation algorithm. The error is used to update the connection strengths between nodes, i.e. weight matrices between input-hidden layers and hidden-output layers are updated.

Mathematically it is written as,

$$W_{ij}(k + 1) = W_{ij} + \Delta W_{ij} \tag{2}$$

where is the weight from hidden unit i to output unit j at time k and ΔW_{ij} is the weight adjustment into the input layer. The feed forward of the testing data is similar to the feed forward of the training data.

3   Results and Discussion

The diagnosing the lung sound through auscultation is subjective and is mainly depends on the hearing ability and skill of physician. But, the proposed approach is an attempt to make a model for adaptively filtering heart sound signal from lung sound signal. The real time heart and lung sound signals are obtained from different age groups of male and female. The entire architecture design are simulated using MATLAB.

The Fig. 2 shows the real time recorded sound signal. It contains both heart and lung sound signal with the sources of interferences.

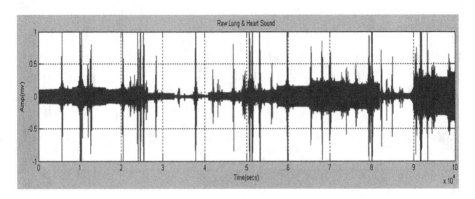

Fig. 2. Real time recorded sound signal

The proposed neural network is trained by Levenberg-Marquardt back propagation algorithm. The input signal to the neural network is heart sound signal corrupted by lung sound signal. The reference heart signal is set as target. The output of the neural network is lung sound recovered heart sound signal.

The simulation study is carried out for different hidden layer of neural network. For evaluating performance of the developed model the following parameters are evaluated. They are,

(i) Mean square error (MSE)
(ii) Signal to noise ratio (SNR)

The Table 1 shows performance analysis of neural network with different hidden layer. It shows number of hidden neurons used for developing proposed neural network approach, number of epochs taken by neural network to reach the error goal. It also shows MSE, SNR and training time of neural network.

Table 1. Analysis of NN for separation of HSS from LSS

Number of hidden layer	Number of epochs	MSE	SNR	Training timing
2	71	0.000998	148.8431	0:00:50
3	81	0.000998	148.8335	0:01:30
4	5	0.000761	195.0225	0:00:06
5	6	0.000983	151.0808	0:00:09
6	5	0.000816	182.0747	0:00:20
7	95	0.000999	148.6035	0:02:10
8	3	0.000964	154.0428	0:00:06
9	4	0.000802	185.1771	0:00:07
10	5	0.000907	163.7277	0:00:10

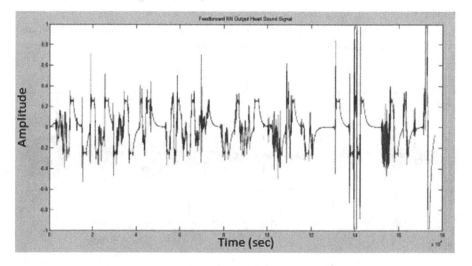

Fig. 3. Neural network output for hidden layer four

From this table it is inferred that neural network with 4 hidden nodes achieve good reasonable performance in terms of SNR and MSE.

The Fig. 3 shows neural network output for hidden layer four. (i.e.) heart sound signal extracted from lung sound signal.

The error signal of neural network output is shown in Fig. 4 for hidden layer four.

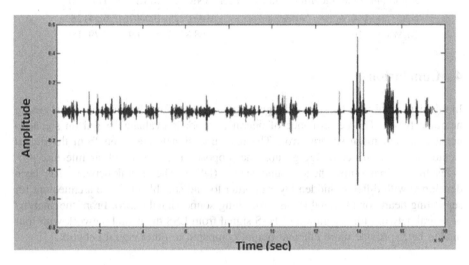

Fig. 4. The error signal of neural network output

The convergence characteristics of 4 hidden layer neural network is shown in Fig. 5. The error goal is achieved at 5th Epochs.

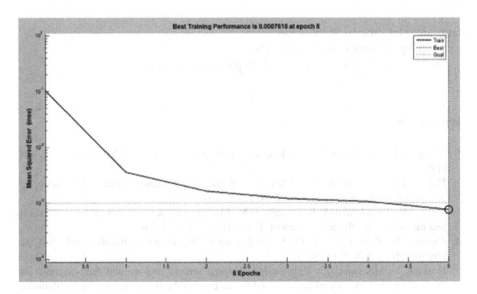

Fig. 5. Convergence characteristics of 4 hidden layers of neural network

The results from the analysis of NN for separation of HSS from LSS is compared with the results of normalized least mean square (NLMS) method and given in Table 2.

Table 2. Comparison between NN and NLMS for separation of HSS from LSS

Algorithm	Filter order/no of hidden layer	SNR	MSE	Time (s)
NN	4	195.0225	0.000761	6.54128
NLMS	16	68.8313	5.7709	2.798186

4 Conclusion

In this paper real time heart sound signals are extracted from lung sound signals using neural network. The performance of neural network is evaluated based on signal to noise ratio and mean square error. The real time signals are taken from the digital stethoscope from different age group. The proposed neural network architecture provides the desired output heart sound signal (HSS). The neural network has been developed with different hidden layer in order to find suitable effective architecture for separating heart sound signal (HSS) from lung sound signal (LSS). From the analysis of neural network for separation of HSS signal from LSS the neural network with four hidden layer provide more efficient output compared to other neural network.

Appendix

Digital Stethoscope Details

Hardware used - digital stethoscope
    Sampling frequency used - 44.1 kHz
    Open source software used -Thinklabs phonocardiography.

References

1. Blake, W.K.: Mechanics of Flow-Induced Sound and Vibration. Academic Press, Orlando (1986)
2. Hardin, J.C., Patterson Jr., J.L.: Monitoring the state of the human airways by analysis of respiratory sound. Acta Astronaut. 6(9), 1137–1151 (1979)
3. Vovk, I.V., Grinchenko, V.T., Oleinik, V.N.: Modeling the acoustic properties of the chest and measuring breath sounds. Acoust. Phys. 41(5), 667–676 (1995)
4. Gavriely, N., Palti, Y., Alroy, G.: Spectral characteristics of normal breath sounds. J. Appl. Physiol. 50(2), 307–314 (1981)
5. Hossain, I., Moussavi, Z.: Relationship between airflow and normal lung sounds. In: Proceedings of 24th Annual International Conference of the IEEE Engineering in Medicine Biology Society, EMBC 2002, pp. 1120–1122, Oct 2002

6. Gavriely, N., Cugell, D.W.: Airflow effects on amplitude and spectral content of normal breath sounds. J. Appl. Physiol. **80**(1), 5–13 (1996)
7. Manecke Jr., G.R., Dilger, J.P., Kutner, L.J., Poppers, P.J.: Auscultation revisited: the waveform and spectral characteristics of breath sounds during general anesthesia. Int. J. Clin. Monit. Comput. **14**(4), 231–240 (1997)
8. Gavriely, N., Nissan, M., Rubin, A.H., Cugell, D.W.: Spectral characteristics of chest wall breath sounds in normal subjects. Thorax **50**(12), 1292–1300 (1995)
9. Luisada, A.A.: The areas of auscultation and the two main heart sounds. Med. Times **92**, 8–11 (1964)
10. Sherwood, L.: Human Physiology: From Cells to Systems, 4th edn. Brooks/Cole, Pacific Grove (2001)
11. Arnott, P.J., Pfeiffer, G.W., Tavel, M.E.: Spectral analysis of heart sounds: relationships between some physical characteristics and frequency spectra of first and second heart sounds in normals and hypertensives. J. Biomed. Eng. **6**(2), 121–128 (1984)
12. Gnitecki, J., Moussavi, Z., Pasterkamp, H.: Recursive least squares adaptive noise cancellation filtering for heart sound reduction in lung sounds recordings. In: Proceedings of 25th Annual International Conference of the IEEE Engineering in Medicine Biology Society, EMBC 2003, pp. 2416–2419, Sept 2003
13. Rudnitski, A.G.: Two-channel processing of signals for the separation of breath and cardiac sounds. Acoust. Phys. **47**(3), 353–360 (2001)
14. Pourazad, M.T., Moussavi, Z., Farahmand, F., Ward, R.K.: Heart sounds separation from lung sounds using independent component analysis. In: Proceedings of the 2005 IEEE Engineering in Medicine and Biology 27th Annual Conference
15. Ghaderi, F., Sanei, S., Makkiabadi'r, B., Abolghasemi, V., McWhirter, J.G.: Heart and lung sound separation using periodic source extraction method. IEEE Trans., 1–6 (2009)
16. Mondal, A., Bhattacharya, P.S., Saha, G.: Reduction of heart sound interference from lung sound signals using empirical mode decomposition technique. J. Med. Eng. Technol. **35**, 344–353 (2011)
17. Guangbin, L., Shaoqin, C., Jingming, Z., Jinzhi, C., Shengju, W.: The development of a portable breath sound analysis system. In: Proceedings of 14th Annual Conference of IEEE EMBS, pp. 2582–2583 (1992)
18. Sathesh, K., Muniraj, N.J.R.: Real time heart and lung sound separation using adaptive line enhancer with NLMS. J. Theor. Appl. Inf. Technol. **65**(2), 559–562 (2014)

Optimal Placement and Sizing of Multi-type Facts Devices Using PSO and HSA

N. Karuppiah[1(✉)], V. Malathi[2], and G. Selvalakshmi[3]

[1] EEE Department, Latha Mathavan Engineering College, Madurai
TamilNadu, India
natarajankaruppiah@gmail.com
[2] EEE Department, Anna University Regional Office, Madurai
TamilNadu, India
vmeee@autmdu.ac.in
[3] Latha Mathavan InfoTech, Madurai, TamilNadu, India
selva2891@gmail.com

Abstract. Voltage stability is an important issue in power system operation. Flexible AC transmission systems, so-called FACTS devices, help to improve voltage stability and minimize real power losses. The effectiveness of FACTS devices depend on their proper location and rating. This paper presents a method, based on line flow sensitivity factors such as bus voltage stability index and line voltage stability index, to find suitable locations of multi-type FACTS devices. Also this paper proposes an application of particle swarm optimization (PSO) and harmony search algorithm (HSA) in optimizing the rating of FACTS devices. The proposed approaches are evaluated with three different objective functions namely, minimization of real power loss, improvement of voltage profile and enhancement of voltage stability. The performance of proposed methods is analyzed on IEEE 14 bus system by implementing FACTS devices such as static var compensator (SVC), thyristor controlled series capacitor (TCSC) and unified power flow controller (UPFC).The analysis shows that there is a reduction in real power loss and improvement in voltage stability and voltage profile of the system after employing FACTS devices. It also shows that both real power loss and bus voltage stability index (BVSI) have been reduced more with FACTS ratings obtained from PSO than with that from HSA.

Keywords: Voltage stability · SVC · TCSC · UPFC · PSO · HSA

1 Introduction

Modern power system is a complex nonlinear interconnected network. It consists of interconnected transmission lines, generating plants, transformers and a variety of loads. With the increase in power demand, it is more essential to improve the voltage profile of the system. Also voltage stability is a problem in power systems which are overloaded, faulted or have a shortage of reactive power. When a bulk power transmission network operates near to its voltage stability limit, it becomes complicated to control its reactive power demand. Thus enhancement of voltage stability is a major concern in power system.

B.K. Panigrahi et al. (Eds.): SEMCCO 2014, LNCS 8947, pp. 292–303, 2015.
DOI: 10.1007/978-3-319-20294-5_26

Voltage stability is defined as *the ability of a power system to maintain steady voltages at all buses in the system under normal operating conditions, and after being subjected to a disturbance.* Voltage instability occurs mainly due to the happening of sag in reactive power at various locations in an interconnected power system. Instability results as a form of a progressive fall or rise of voltages at some buses. A possible outcome of voltage instability is loss of load in an area, or tripping of transmission lines and other elements by their protective systems leading to cascading outages [1].

During the last decade, a number of control devices under the term FACTS technology have been proposed and implemented. Application of FACTS devices in modern power systems leads to better performance of the system. FACTS devices enhances system parameters like voltage stability, voltage regulation, power system loadability and enhancement of damping. There are various forms of FACTS devices, some are connected in series with line and the others are connected in shunt or a combination of series and shunt [2]. The FACTS technology is not a single high power controller but rather a group of controllers which can be applied individually or in coordination with other to control one or more of the inter related system parameters like impedance, voltage, current, and phase angle.

In this paper, multi type of FACTS devices such as static VAR compensator (SVC), thyristor controlled series capacitor (TCSC) and unified power flow controller (UPFC) are discussed. The performance of power system can be enhanced to a greater extent with these devices, only when they are located at proper location with optimal rating. Several methods have been adopted to determine optimal location and rating of FACTS devices.

In earlier days, some authors have used analytical methods like linear programming (LP) [3] and mixed integer linear programming (MILP) [4] to optimize the location of FACTS devices in order to obtain system need. Now-a-days, different AI techniques such as genetic algorithm (GA) [5–7], tabu search (TS), simulated annealing (SA), hybrid TS/SA [8], hybrid TS/PSO [9] and particle swarm optimization (PSO) [10] are used to find optimal location and sizing of FACTS devices. In paper [11–13] various parameters like real power flow performance index, Line flow sensitivity index and locational marginal price (LMP) were taken as the criteria to determine optimal location of multiple FACTS devices.

This paper, proposes a method for finding the optimal location and rating of multi type FACTS devices using sensitivity analysis and optimization algorithm in order to minimize the real power loss, to improve voltage profile and to enhance voltage stability. The voltage stability of the system is analyzed using voltage stability index approach. Based on the sensitivity indices, weak load bus and weak transmission line which needs significant reactive power support are identified. To find the optimal sizing optimization algorithms like harmony search algorithm (HSA) and particle swarm optimization (PSO) are used. Both PSO and HSA are known to effectively solve large scale nonlinear optimization problems. Harmony search algorithm works based on action of orchestra music to find the best harmony among various instruments whereas PSO algorithm resembles the flocking behavior of birds. The proposed approaches have been tested on IEEE 14-bus system and the results are presented. The test results show that the sizing of the FACTS devices identified by PSO gives better enhancement of voltage stability and minimization of losses than that of HSA.

2 Stability Indices

In power system, the stability level of all load buses and all lines can be identified with the help of the stability indices. In this paper bus voltage stability index (BVSI) and line voltage stability index (LVSI) are used to find the weakest load bus and transmission line respectively.

Line Voltage Stability Index (LVSI): LVSI represents the stability index for each line connected between two buses in an interconnected transmission system. Based on these indices, voltage stability levels can be predicted. When the stability index L_{mn} less than 1, the system is stable and when this index exceeds the value 1, the corresponding line loses its stability and voltage collapse occurs. LVSI can be calculated as,

$$L_{mn} = \frac{4X_n Q_n}{(V_m \sin(\theta_{mn} - \delta_m))^2} \tag{1}$$

where,
V_m - sending end voltage
Q_n - reactive power at receiving end
X_n - Reactance at receiving end
θ_{mn} - Impedance angle
δ_m - Angle difference between the supply voltage and the receiving end voltage

Bus Voltage Stability Index (BVSI): For a given load condition BVSIs are determined for all load buses. If this index value is moving towards zero, then the system is considered as stable and also improves system security. When this index value moves away from zero, the stability of system relatively decreases and the system is considered as unstable. The voltage stability index for load buses is to be computed as

$$L_j = \left| 1 - \sum_{i=1}^{g} F_{ji} \frac{V_i}{V_j} \right| \tag{2}$$

where,

$j = g+1....N$, total number of buses
g- No of generators connected in the system.
V_i – voltage of the ith generator bus
V_j – voltage of the bus j for which L_j has to be calculated

The values of F_{ji} can be obtained from Y bus matrix.

$$F_{ji} = [Y_{LL}]^{-1}[Y_{LG}] \tag{3}$$

where, Y_{LL} and Y_{LG} are corresponding partitioned portions of the Y-bus matrix.

3 Problem Formulation

The objective function of this paper is to find the optimal rating of FACTS devices which minimizes real power loss, improves voltage profile and enhances voltage stability is given by,

$$minf = \sum_{l=1}^{n} P_L^l + \sum_{i=1}^{n-g} V_{D_i} + \sum_{j=1}^{n-g} L_j \qquad (4)$$

where

P_L^l - Real power in a line l

V_{D_i} - Voltage deviation of load bus i, which is given by, $V_{D_i} = (1 - V_i)^2$

$\qquad \qquad \qquad \qquad \qquad \qquad \qquad \qquad \qquad \qquad \qquad \qquad (5)$

V_i - Voltage at bus i

L_j - Bus Voltage Stability Index (BVSI) of load bus j

3.1 Real Power and Bus Voltage Constraints

$$J = \prod_{LINE} OVL_{LINE} * \prod_{BUS} VS_{BUS} \qquad (6)$$

J is the factor indicating violation of line flow limits and bus voltage limits, where OVL denotes line overload factor for a line and VS denotes voltage stability index for a bus.

$$OVL = \begin{cases} 1; & if\, P_{pq} \leq P_{pq}^{max} \\ e^{\left(\mu \left| 1 - \frac{P_{pq}}{P_{pq}^{max}} \right| \right)}; & if\, P_{pq} > P_{pq}^{max} \end{cases} \qquad (7)$$

$$VS = \begin{cases} 1; & if\, 0.9 \leq V_b \leq 1.1 \\ e^{(\lambda |1 - V_b|)}; & Otherwise \end{cases} \qquad (8)$$

where,

P_{pq} - Real power flow between buses p and q

P_{pq}^{max} - Thermal limit for the line between buses p and q

V_b - Voltage at bus b

λ and μ - Positive constants both equal to 0.1

3.2 FACTS Device's Constraints

$$-0.8X_L \leq X_{TCSC} \leq 0.2X_L p.u \qquad (9)$$

$$-0.9 \leq B_{SVC} \leq 0.9 p.u \qquad (10)$$

(9) and (10) for UPFC
    where,

X_{TCSC} - Reactance added to the line by TCSC
X_L - Reactance of the line where TCSC is located
B_{SVC} - Susceptance added to the bus by SVC

4 Harmony Search Algorithm

Harmony search algorithm is a meta-heuristic optimization algorithm which works based on the act of orchestra music to find the best harmony among various components which are involved in the process to find optimal solution. In orchestra music, musical instruments can be played with some distinct musical notes based on player's experience or based on random improvisation processes. Similar to that optimal design variables for HSA are to be obtained with certain distinct values based on some computational intelligence and random processes. HSA can consider both discontinuous functions and continuous functions because it doesn't need differential gradients and initial value setting for the variables and it is also free from divergence and can escape from local optima. HS algorithm will always looks for vector that can reduce the cost function or objective function. The major steps involved in the HS algorithm are described as follows [14, 15]:

(1) Initialization of objective function
(2) Initialization of the harmony memory
(3) Improvisation a new harmony from the HM set
(4) Updating harmony memory
(5) Checking stopping criterion.

The parameters used in harmony search algorithm are given in Table 1.

Table 1. HSA parameters

Parameter	Value
Harmony memory size (HMS)	100
Number of improvisation (NI)	2000
Harmony memory considering rate (HMCR)	0.95
Maximum pitch adjustment rate (PAR max)	0.9
Minimum pitch adjustment rate (PAR min)	0.2
Bandwidth (bw)	0.2

4.1 Pseudo Code for Harmony Search Algorithm

```
Specify the algorithm parameters (HMS, NI, HMCR, PARmax, PARmin, bw, Li, Ui)
Initialize the harmony memory xi randomly
Set iter=1
for k=1: HMS
                  Run Newton Raphson power flow by connecting FACTS devices in optimal location and evaluate the
         fitness value using equation (4) fi from load flow results.
end
for iter =1: NI
         for t =1: HMS
                  if probability < HMCR
```
$$x_i^t \in \{x_1^t, x_2^t, x_3^t \dots x_{HMS}^t\}$$
$$PAR(iter) = PAR_{min} + \frac{PAR_{max} - PAR_{min}}{NI} \times iter$$
```
                  if probability<PAR(iter)
```
$$x_i^t = x_i^t \pm bw$$
```
                  end
         else
```
$$x_i^t \in [L_i, U_i]$$
```
         end
         With new harmony xi calculate the fitness value fi^t
      if fi^t < fi
```
$$f_i = f_i^t; \; x_i = x_i^t$$
```
         end
      end
end
```

5   Particle Swarm Optimization

Particle swarm optimization (PSO) is a kind of optimization algorithm used to obtain the optimal solution by simulating the schooling behavior of fishes or flocking behavior of birds. Initially a flock of birds, in which each bird called as a particle is made to fly over the searching space. These particles will fly with certain velocity to find the best global position (G_{best}) after some iteration. For each and every iteration, current position and velocity of all particle gets changed according to its current position P_{best} and the current global position G_{best}. Thus all the particles will move towards the global solution at the end of maximum iteration [16].

Velocity of each particle can be modified by the following equation

$$V_i^{k+1} = w \times v + c_1 \times rand_1 \times \left(P_{best_i} - s_i^k\right) + c_2 \times rand_2 \times \left(G_{best_i} - s_i^k\right) \quad (11)$$

where,

V_i^{k+1} - Velocity of ith particle at iteration k + 1

w - Weight function, which is given by, $w = w_{max} - \dfrac{w_{max} - w_{min}}{iter_{max}} iter$

w_{max} - Initial inertia weight

w_{min} - Final inertia weight

$iter_{max}$ - Maximum iteration number   (12)

$iter$ - Current iteration number

c_1, c_2 - Weight coefficient

$rand_1, rand_2$ - Random number between 0 and 5

P_{best_i} - Best position of particle i upto current iteration

G_{best_i} - Best overall position found by the particle upto current iteration

Now the new position can be obtained using,

$$s_i^{k+1} = s_i^k + V_i^{k+1} \tag{13}$$

5.1   PSO Algorithm to Find Optimal Rating of FACTS Devices

Step 1   : Read bus data, line data and FACTS devices (SVC, TCSC and UPFC) data
Step 2   : Specify PSO parameters and maximum number of iterations
Step 3   : The initial population of particles are generated with random position and velocity
Step 4   : Run Newton Raphson power flow by connecting FACTS devices in optimal location
Step 5   : Evaluate the fitness value using Eq. (4) for each particle from load flow results
Step 6   : Save the minimum value of fitness as P_{best} and its corresponding particles as G_{best}
Step 7   : Set iteration count equal to 1
Step 8   : Particle positions and velocities are updated using (11) and (13) respectively
Step 9   : Again for each particle the fitness function is calculated and if it is higher than the individual P_{best} then it is the current P_{best} and store the current position
Step 10   : The particle with the minimum P_{best} value among all particles is chosen as the overall G_{best} value
Step 11   : If the maximum number of iteration is reached, then the position of global best particles corresponding to optimal solution will be the optimal location of FACTS device. Otherwise increase the iteration count and go to step 9

The parameters of PSO used in this paper are given in Table 2.

Table 2. PSO parameters

Parameter	Value
No. of particles	30
No. of iterations	250
C1	1
C2	3
Initial inertia weight	0.9
Final inertia weight	0.8

6 Results and Discussions

The performances of proposed methods were analyzed by employing various combinations of FACTS devices in IEEE- 14 bus system using MATLAB and their results were presented.

6.1 Base Case Results

The IEEE-14 bus system was used as a test system. The IEEE 14 bus system consists of 5 generator buses, 9 load buses and 20 transmission lines. The load flow is performed on the test system using Newton Raphson load flow analysis since it is faster, reliable, gives more accurate results, requires less number of iterations and does not depend on size of system [17]. From the load flow results, LVSI and BVSI were determined for all lines and load buses using Eqs. (3) and (4) respectively to find the stability level of system.

6.2 Determination of Optimal Location of FACTS Devices Using Stability Indices

The transmission lines and load buses were ranked according to LVSI and BVSI. The lines and load buses that occupy the top ranks were taken as optimal location of FACTS devices. The candidate locations of SVC are found based on BVSI and those for TCSC and UPFC are found based on LVSI. It can be observed from Table 1 that for IEEE-14 bus system, the lines 5–6, 4–7, 7–8, 4–9 and 1–2 having the highest value of LVSI, are taken as the most suitable locations for TCSC and UPFC. Thus the five optimal locations of SVC, TCSC and UPFC for IEEE-14 bus are given in Table 3.

Table 3. Five possible locations of TCSC and UPFC

Rank	IEEE-14 bus system			
	Branch no	From bus	To bus	LVSI
1	10	5	6	0.2658
2	8	4	7	0.1458
3	14	7	8	0.1430
4	9	4	9	0.0880
5	1	1	2	0.0715

6.3 Determination of Optimal Sizing of FACTS Devices Using HSA and PSO

After finding optimal location of various FACTS devices, optimal capacity of FACTS devices have been obtained using HSA and PSO which is explained in Sects. 4 and 5, by placing various combinations of SVC, TCSC and UPFC at their suitable locations in IEEE-14 bus system. The optimal capacities of FACTS devices obtained from HSA and PSO and their effects on system parameters like total real power loss and total bus voltage stability index (BVSI) are given for IEEE-14 bus in Table 4. Let the first

Table 4. Optimal capacity of multi type FACTS devices and their effects in IEEE-14 bus system

No of FACTS devices	Type of FACTS device	Count	HSA				PSO			
			Location	Rating (p.u)	Active power loss reduction (MW)	Total BVSI reduction	Location	Rating (p.u)	Active power loss reduction (MW)	Total BVSI reduction
3	TCSC	1	Branch-10	-0.0197	7.4286	1.4523	Branch-10	-0.2255	7.8849	1.7736
	SVC	1	Bus-12	-0.5871			Bus-12	-0.5459		
	UPFC	1	Branch-10	-0.7576			Branch-10	-0.6980		
				-0.8349				-0.8978		
4	TCSC	2	Branch-10	-0.3019	7.0988	1.0893	Branch-10	-0.0121	7.8292	1.4445
			Branch-8	-0.3126			Branch-8	-0.4806		
	SVC	1	Bus-12	-0.4870			Bus-12	-0.5493		
	UPFC	1	Branch-10	-0.7144			Branch-10	-0.3900		
				-0.7787				-0.8986		
4	TCSC	1	Branch-10	-0.0146	9.7462	1.4243	Branch-10	-0.1555	10.0585	1.7965
	SVC	1	Bus-12	-0.0916			Bus-12	0.0590		
	UPFC	2	Branch-10	-0.2066			Branch-10	-0.6985		
				-0.7148				-0.7942		
			Branch-8	-0.2438			Branch-8	-0.6403		
				-0.7449				-0.8984		
4	SVC	2	Bus-12	-0.5863	9.7363	1.4951	Bus-12	-0.3007	9.8813	1.594
			Bus-13	0.5761			Bus-13	0.0856		
	UPFC	2	Branch-10	-0.6188			Branch-10	-0.5268		
				-0.8436				-0.4907		
			Branch-8	-0.7027			Branch-8	-0.5101		
				-0.8817				-0.8954		
4	TCSC	2	Branch-10	-0.7206	6.8713	1.4482	Branch-10	-0.7984	7.0317	1.4746
			Branch-8	-0.0799			Branch-8	-0.3025		
	SVC	2	Bus-12	-0.7372			Bus-12	-0.8700		
			Bus-13	-0.5821			Bus-13	-0.5070		

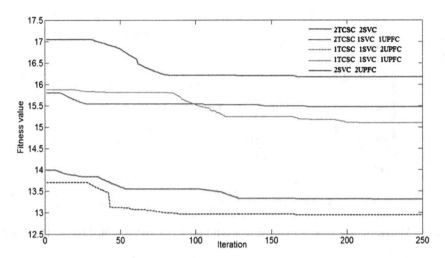

Fig. 1. Fitness curves for multi-type FACTS devices in IEEE-14 bus system

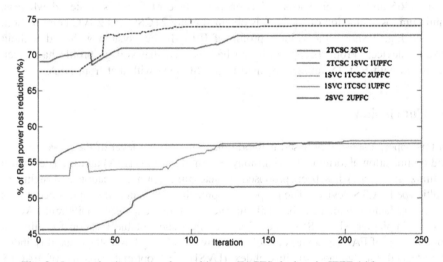

Fig. 2. Loss reduction curves for multi-type FACTS devices in IEEE-14 bus system

combination of FACTS devices be 1TCSC, 1SVC and 1UPFC. While finding the optimal rating of these devices using HSA, real power loss reduction percentage is obtained as 54.65 % and that of BVSI is 14.21 %, whereas in PSO both loss and BVSI gets reduced even more i.e. loss reduction percentage is 58 % and for BVSI it is 17.36 %.

The effects of various combinations of FACTS devices on fitness value and real power loss in IEEE-14 bus system are observed from PSO algorithm and are shown in Figs. 1 and 2 respectively. From Figs. 1 and 2 it can be observed that, in IEEE-14 bus system, by having a combination of 1TCSC, 1SVC and 2UPFC, minimum fitness value

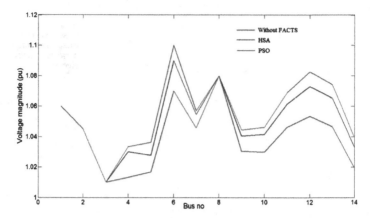

Fig. 3. Voltage profile improvement curve for IEEE-14 bus system with 1TCSC, 1SVC and 2UPFC

of 12.9466 and maximum loss reduction percentage of 73.99 is achieved whereas, minimum loss reduction of 51.73 % is obtained using 2TCSC and 2SVC combination.

The Fig. 3 shows the voltage profile of IEEE-14 bus system with and without FACTS devices. From the figure, it can be observed that voltage profile have been improved with FACTS ratings obtained from PSO than with that from HSA.

7 Conclusion

In this paper, a sensitivity based method related to stability level of the power system and optimization algorithms like harmony search algorithm (HSA) and particle swarm optimization (PSO) has been proposed to determine optimal location and sizing of multi-type FACTS devices. The proposed approach is efficient and simple since it uses sensitivity factors, which can be easily updated for future expansion. Different FACTS devices implemented are SVC, TCSC and UPFC. The suitable location for different combination of FACTS devices are obtained by calculating bus voltage stability index (BVSI) and line voltage stability index (LVSI). The optimal capacity of FACTS devices for minimizing real power loss, improving voltage profile and enhancing voltage stability are found using HSA and PSO algorithm. Simulations are done using MATLAB software and the results are presented for test system namely IEEE-14. The analysis shows that there is a reduction in real power loss and improvement in voltage stability and voltage profile of the system after employing FACTS devices. It also shows that both real power loss and total BVSI have been reduced more with FACTS ratings obtained from PSO than with that from HSA.

References

1. Kundur, P.: Power System Stability and Control. McGraw-Hill, New York (1994)
2. Mathur, Mohan, Varma, Rajiv K.: Thyristor-Based Facts Controllers for Electrical Transmission Systems. Wiley, New York (2002)
3. Abdelsalam, H.A., Aly, G.E.M., Abdelkrim, M., Shebl, K.M.: Optimal location of the unified power flow controller in electrical power system. In: IEEE Proceedings on Large Engineering Systems Conference on Power Engineering, pp. 41–46, July 2004
4. Chang, R.W., Saha, T.K.: Maximizing power system loadability by optimal allocation of SVC using mixed integer linear programming. In: IEEE Power and Energy Society General Meeting, pp. 1–7, 25–29 July 2010
5. Ghahremani, E., Kamwa, I.: Optimal placement of multiple-type FACTS devices to maximize power system loadability using a generic graphical user interface. IEEE Trans. Power Syst. 28(2), 764–778 (2013)
6. Cai, L.J., Erlich, I., Stamtsis, G.: Optimal choice and allocation of FACTS devices in deregulated electricity market using GA. In: Proceedings of 2004 IEEE Power Systems Conference and Exposition, vol. 1, pp. 201–207, 10–13 Oct 2004
7. Gerbex, S., Cherkaoui, R., Germond, A.J.: Optimal location of multi-type FACTS devices by means of genetic algorithm. IEEE Trans. Power Syst. 16, 537–544 (2001)
8. Bhasaputra, P., Ongsakul, W.: Optimal power flow with multi-type of FACTS devices by hybrid TS/SA approach. In: IEEE Proceedings on International Conference on Industrial Technology, vol. 1, pp. 285–290, Dec 2002
9. Majumdar, S., Chakraborty, A.K., Chattopadhyay, P.K.: Active power loss minimization with FACTS devices using SA/PSO techniques. In: International Conference on Power System, pp. 1–5, Dec 2009
10. Azadani, E.N., Hosseinian, S.H., Janati, M., Hasanpor, P.: Optimal placement of multiple STATCOM. In: Proceedings of 2008 IEEE International Middle-East Conference Power System, pp. 523–528, 12–15 Mar 2008
11. Acharya, N., Mithulananthan, N.: Locating series FACTS devices for congestion management in deregulated electricity markets. ELSEVIER Electr. Power Syst. Res. 77, 352–360 (2006)
12. Jumaat, S.A, Musirin, I., Othman, M.M., Mokhlis, H.: Optimal placement and sizing of multiple FACTS devices installation. In: IEEE International Conference on Power and Energy, pp. 145–150, Dec 2012
13. Rahimzadeh, S., Tavakoli Bina, M.: Looking for optimal number and placement of FACTS devices to manage the transmission congestion. ELSEVIER Energy Convers. Manag. 52(1), 437–446 (2010)
14. Yang, X.S.: Harmony search as a metaheuristic algorithm. In: Geem, Z.W. (ed.) Studies in Computational Intelligence, vol. 191, pp. 1–14. Springer, Berlin (2009)
15. Verma, A., Panigrahi, B.K., Bijwe, P.R.: Harmony search algorithm for transmission network expansion planning. IET Gener. Transm. Distrib. 4(6), 663–673 (2010)
16. Saravanan, M., et al.: Application of PSO technique for optimal location of FACTS devices considering system loadability and cost of installation. In: Power Engineering Conference, vol. 2, pp. 716–721, 29 Nov–2 Dec 2005
17. Saadat, H.: Power System Analysis. Tata McGraw-Hill, New York (2002)

Optimal Loss Reduction and Reconfiguration of Distribution System with Distributed Generation Using Harmony Search Algorithm

S. Muthubalaji[1(⌂)] and V. Malathi[2]

[1] EEE Department, Latha Mathavan Engineering College, Madurai, Tamilnadu,
India
muthusal5@gmail.com
[2] EEE Department, Anna University Regional Office, Madurai, Tamilnadu, India
vmeee@autmdu.ac.in

Abstract. Recently, to enhance the power system performance, integration of
DGs at distribution level and the rearrangement of feeders in distribution network is done. This paper presents a harmony search algorithm approach for the
reconfiguration of radial distribution system with distributed generation (DG).
The DG placement problem and reconfiguration problem is formulated as a
non-linear optimization problem with the objective of loss minimization and
voltage profile improvement. Particle swarm optimization (PSO) algorithm is
used to find the optimal location and sizing of multiple DGs. To find the optimal
set of feeders to be opened, harmony search algorithm (HSA) is proposed. The
proposed approaches are tested on IEEE 33 bus radial distribution system using
MATLAB and the results are presented.

Keywords: DG · Reconfiguration · PSO · HSA

1 Introduction

In general, distribution system consists of group of interconnected radial circuits. The
efficient operation of distribution systems can only be achieved by modifying the
open/closed status of sectionalizing-switches (normal closed) and tie switches (normal
open) of the distribution systems. Reconfiguration is done especially for three purposes: 1. for loss reduction, 2. for load balancing, and 3. for service restoration [1].

Several methods have been proposed for solving the distribution system reconfiguration (DSR) problem. In [2], a heuristic approach is used to find the new radial
configuration by finding the global minimum of losses. In [3], by optimal distribution
system configuration, the lowest current is determined by the optimal power flow
method. Other techniques like quadratic programming [4] and network partitioning
techniques [5], a heuristic nonlinear constructive method [6] are used in earlier stages.
These methods find admirable solutions for the medium size systems and not suitable
for large systems [7]. In recent years, new heuristic optimization algorithms like genetic
algorithm (GA) [8–11], evolutionary algorithms (EA) [12–16], non-dominated sorting
genetic algorithms (NSGA) [17], matroid theory [18], other meta-heuristics techniques

© Springer International Publishing Switzerland 2015
B.K. Panigrahi et al. (Eds.): SEMCCO 2014, LNCS 8947, pp. 304–315, 2015.
DOI: 10.1007/978-3-319-20294-5_27

like plant growth [19], particle swarm optimization (PSO) [20], tabu search [21] and ant colony search [22, 23] have been proposed for DSR problem. They are aimed to deal with large system with fast execution time [12].

Recently, DSR problem with distributed generation (DG) and capacitor allocation [24, 25] receives much attention. Distributed generation is a small-scale power generation that is directly connected to the distribution system or to the customer side of the meter. The benefits of DG are given in [26, 27]. The power system performance can be enhanced to a greater extent only when the DGs are installed at proper location with proper capacity. Similar to DSR problem, several techniques and optimization algorithm, real coded genetic algorithm (RCGA) [28], evolutionary algorithm (EA) [29] have been proposed to optimize the location and sizing of distributed generation.

This paper, proposes a method to reconfigure the distributed system with DG. An optimization algorithm, particle swarm optimization (PSO) is used to find the optimal location and sizing of DG and harmony search algorithm (HSA) is used to find the switches to be opened in distributed system in order to minimize the real power loss and to improve voltage profile. PSO is known to effectively solve large scale nonlinear optimization problems and it resembles the flocking behavior of birds whereas HSA works based on the act of orchestra music to find the best harmony among various components. The proposed approaches have been tested on IEEE 33-bus radial distribution system and the results are presented. In this work, simulation is done using MATLAB for four cases: (1) for base case, (2) for reconfiguration of distributed system without DG (3) for optimizing location and sizing of multiple DGs and (4) for reconfiguration of distributed system with multiple DGs. The test results show that the reconfigured network of radial distribution system with DG gives better improvement in voltage profile and minimization of losses than other cases.

2 DG Placement

2.1 Problem Formulation

Problem formulation is nothing but the formulation objective function. The objective function for DG placement is to find the optimal location and sizing of DGs which minimizes real power loss and improves voltage profile of the network. It is mathematically formulated as,

$$\min \quad f1 = \sum_{l=1}^{n} P_L^l \tag{1}$$

$$\min \quad f2 = \sum_{i=1}^{n-g} V_{D_i} \tag{2}$$

where, P_L^l - Real power in a line l. V_{D_i} - Voltage deviation of load bus i, which is given by,

$$V_{D_i} = (1 - V_i)^2 \tag{3}$$

where, V_i - Voltage at bus i.

2.2   Real Power and Bus Voltage Constraints

Real power limit of distribution feeders for the network should not be exceeded.

$$P_{pq} \leq P_{pq}^{max} \tag{4}$$

where,

P_{pq} - Actual real power flow of the feeder between buses p and q
P_{pq}^{max} - Maximum thermal limit for the feeder between buses p and q

Voltage magnitude at each bus must lie within their permissible ranges and it is given by,where,

$$V_b^{min} \leq V_b \leq V_b^{max} \tag{5}$$

V_b - Voltage at bus b
V_b^{max} - Maximum voltage at bus b
V_b^{min} - Minimum voltage at bus b

2.3   DG Rating Constraints

The ratings of DG units must be constrained between its maximum and the minimum levels as given as follows,

$$P_{DG,i}^{min} \leq P_{DG,i} \leq P_{DG,i}^{max} \tag{6}$$

$P_{DG,i}$ - DG capacity at bus i
$P_{DG,i}^{max}$ - Maximum DG capacity that can be placed at bus i
$P_{DG,i}^{min}$ - Minimum DG capacity that can be placed at bus i

3   Optimization Algorithm for DG Placement

3.1   Particle Swarm Optimization (PSO)

Particle swarm optimization (PSO) is a kind of population based optimization algorithm. This algorithm resembles the schooling behavior of fishes or flocking behavior of birds. Initially a group of particles are made to fly over the searching space with certain velocity. Among these particles, a certain particle called P_{best} will find the best global optimal solution (G_{best}). Then for each and every iteration, current position and velocity of all particles gets changed according to its current position P_{best}. Thus at the end of maximum iteration all the particles will move towards the global solution [20].

Velocity of each particle can be modified by the following equation

$$V_i^{k+1} = w \times v + c_1 \times rand_1 \times \left(P_{best_i} - s_i^k\right) + c_2 \times rand_2 \times \left(G_{best_i} - s_i^k\right) \quad (7)$$

where,

V_i^{k+1} - Velocity of particle t at iterations
w - Weight function which is given by,

$$w = w_{max} - \frac{w_{max} - w_{min}}{iter_{max}} iter \quad (8)$$

w_{max} - Initial inertia weight
w_{min} - Final inertia weight
$iter_{max}$ -Maximum iteration number
$iter$ -Current iteration number
c_1, c_2 - Weight coefficient
$rand_1, rand_2$ - Random number between 0 and 5
s_i^k - Current position of particle i at iteration k
P_{best_i} - Best position of particle i upto current iteration
G_{best_i} - Best overall position found by the particle upto current iteration

Now the new position can be obtained using,

$$s_i^{k+1} = s_i^k + V_i^{k+1} \quad (9)$$

The parameters of PSO used in this paper are given in Table 1.

Table 1. PSO parameters

Parameter	Value
No. of particles	30
No. of iterations	100
C1	1
C2	3
Initial inertia weight	0.9
Final inertia weight	0.8

4   Reconfiguration of Distribution System

4.1   Problem Formulation

Reconfiguration of feeders in distribution system should be done such that it to minimize the real power loss and to improve the voltage profile of the network. It can be mathematically written as,

$$\min \quad f1 = \sum_{l=1}^{n} P_L^l \tag{10}$$

$$\min \quad f2 = \sum_{i=1}^{n-g} V_{D_i} \tag{11}$$

where,

P_L^l - Real power in a line l
V_{D_i} - Voltage deviation of load bus i.

It is given as,

$$V_{D_i} = (1 - V_i)^2 \tag{12}$$

where,

V_i - Voltage at bus i

4.2   Real Power and Bus Voltage Constraints

Real power limit of distribution feeders for the network should not be exceeded.

$$P_{pq} \leq P_{pq}^{max} \tag{13}$$

where,

P_{pq} - Actual real power flow of the feeder between buses p and q
P_{pq}^{max} - Maximum thermal limit for the feeder between buses p and q

Voltage magnitude at each bus must lie within their permissible ranges and it is given by, where,

$$V_b^{min} \leq V_b \leq V_b^{max} \tag{14}$$

V_b - Voltage at bus b
V_b^{max} - Maximum voltage at bus b
V_b^{min} - Minimum voltage at bus b

4.3   Radiality Constraints

Under this constraint the radial structure of network should not be affected and all the nodes should be energized.

5 Optimization Algorithm for Reconfiguration

5.1   Harmony Search Algorithm (HSA)

Harmony search algorithm is a meta-heuristic optimization algorithm which works based on the act of orchestra music to find the best harmony among various components which are involved in the process to find optimal solution. In orchestra music, musical instruments can be played with some distinct musical notes based on player's experience or based on random improvisation processes. Similar to that optimal design variables for HSA are to be obtained with certain distinct values based on some computational intelligence and random processes. HSA can consider both discontinuous functions and continuous functions because it doesn't need differential gradients and initial value setting for the variables and it is also free from divergence and can escape from local optima. HS algorithm will always looks for vector that can reduce the cost function or objective function. The major steps involved in the HS algorithm are described as follows [30, 31]:

(1) *Initialization of objective function:* In this step, objective function, f(x), lower and upper bounds of objective variables, $[L_i, U_i]$ are defined. Also the parameters of HAS like harmony memory size (HMS); harmony memory considering rate (HMCR); pitch adjusting rate (PAR); number of decision variables (N); number of improvisations (NI) and the stopping criterion are specified.

(2) *Initialization of the harmony memory:* Initial random harmony vector upto HMS are generated and the fitness function is evaluated using Eq. (6) for each value in harmony vector to form harmony memory matrix (HM).

$$HM = \begin{bmatrix} f(x_1) \\ f(x_2) \\ . \\ . \\ \vdots \\ f(x_{HMS-1}) \\ f(x_{HMS}) \end{bmatrix} \qquad (15)$$

(3) *Improvisation a new harmony from the HM set:* To generate a new harmony vector which is $x' = x'_2, x'_3, \ldots x'_{HMS-1}, x'_{HMS}$ three rules are used. They are random selection, memory consideration and pitch adjustment. In random selection when harmony search finds the value for new harmony, it will randomly pick any value from the total value range with a probability of (1-HMCR). Memory consideration operator selects the values of new harmony based on solutions stored in HM with probability HMCR.

$$x_i' \leftarrow \begin{cases} x_i'\{x_1', x_2', x_3', \ldots x_{HMS}'\} & with\ probability\ HMCR \\ x_i' \in [L_i, U_i] & with\ probability\ 1 - HMCR \end{cases} \tag{16}$$

After picking the value x_i' from HM using above memory consideration process, it can be adjusted to its neighboring values by adding some amount to that value by considering the probability of PAR.

$$x_i' \leftarrow \begin{cases} Yes\ with\ probability\ PAR \\ No\ with\ probability\ 1 - PAR \end{cases} \tag{17}$$

If the decision of pitch adjustment is yes, then x_i' is replaced as follows,

$$x_i' = x_i' \pm bw \tag{18}$$

where, bw is the arbitrary distance bandwidth for a given variable.

(4) **Updating HM:** If the new harmony vector x' is better than the worst harmony in the HM, from the viewpoint of the objective function value, then the worst harmony is replaced with new harmony is entered in the HM and the existing worst harmony is omitted from the HM.

(5) **Checking stopping criterion:** Steps (3) and (4) are repeated until maximum number of improvisation is met.

The parameters used in harmony search algorithm are given in Table 2.

Table 2. HSA parameters

Parameter	Value
Harmony memory size	50
Harmony memory considering rate (HMCR)	0.95
Pitch adjustment rate (PAR)	0.9
Band width	0.2
Number of improvisations	1000

6 Results and Discussions

The performances of proposed methods are tested on IEEE- 33 bus radial distribution system using MATLAB. The single line diagram of test system is shown in Fig. 1. The test system consists of 33 buses, 32 sectionalizing switches and 5 tie line switches. In this network, sectionalizing switches which are normally closed are numbered from 1 to 32 and tie-switches which are normally opened are numbered from 33 to 37. Simulation is carried by considering four cases.

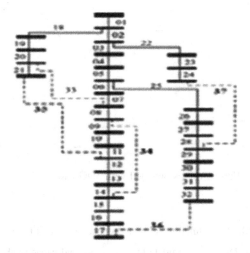

Fig. 1. Single line diagram of IEEE 33 bus radial distribution system

6.1   Case I: Base Case

In this paper, forward and backward sweep algorithm is used for load flow analysis since it is reliable and gives accurate results for distribution system [32]. First the load flow is performed on test system without connecting tie line switches and without any DG for different load levels (light, normal and heavy load levels). From the load flow results, the total real power loss and voltage deviation are obtained as 210.0594 KW and 1.1328 respectively for normal load level i.e. 100 % loading.

6.2   Case II: Reconfigured Network Without DG

Without installing any DG in the test system, harmony search algorithm (HSA), which is explained in Sect. 5, is used to reconfigure the feeders of test system. From the results of HSA, it is observed that the sectionalizing switches 7, 12, 8, 15, 23 are to be in open conditions whereas others should be in closed condition so as to improve the power system performance. By having the obtained reconfigured network the real power loss is minimized to a value of 134.9314 KW and the voltage deviation is also reduced to 0.0378 for normal load level.

6.3   Case III: Test System Without Reconfiguration with Multiple DGs

In this work, DGs which are capable of injecting real power alone are used to enhance the power system performance. The optimal locations and ratings of multiple DGs are obtained using particle swarm optimization (PSO) algorithm as given in Sect. 3 and the obtained results are given in Table 3. The fitness curve obtained for both 3 DG and 2 DG using PSO is shown in Fig. 2. Then the load flow is performed by installing DGs at their optimal locations with optimal ratings. In this case, after installing 2 DGs, for the

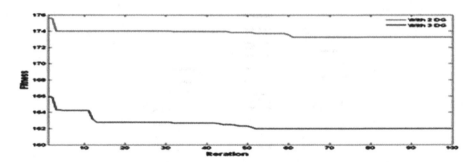

Fig. 2. Fitness curves obtained with 3DG and 2DG using PSO

Table 3. Optimal location and capacity of multiple DGS

No.of DGs	Candidate buses	Optimal capacity (KW)
2	18	136.42
	14	143.29
3	14	126.52
	18	128.12
	16	133.02

Table 4. Effects of multiple DGS on system performance for normal (100 %) load level

S. No	No. of DGs	Real power loss (KW)	% of loss reduction	Voltage deviation	% reduction of voltage deviation
1	-	210.0594	-	0.1328	-
2	2	172.9186	17.68	0.0996	25.00
3	3	161.8729	22.93	0.0884	33.43

normal load level the real power loss and the voltage deviation are reduced to 172.9186 and 0.0996 respectively. The effects of multiple DGs on system performance are shown in Table 4.

6.4   Case IV: Reconfigured Network with Multiple DGs

In this case, reconfiguration is done using HSA for the test system after installing DGs at their proper location and the results shows that the sectionalizing switches 7, 12, 9, 15, 22 are to be in open conditions and others should be in closed condition. The effects of this reconfiguration on system with DGs are obtained and it shows that both real power loss and voltage deviation gets minimized more than that of other 3 cases.

The graph showing the voltage profile for all the four cases is shown in Fig. 3. From this figure it can be observed that by having the reconfigured network with DG, the voltage profile have been improved more. The Table 5 gives the comparison of results obtained for all the four cases and the Table 6 shows the comparison of results obtained using various algorithms for normal loading conditions.

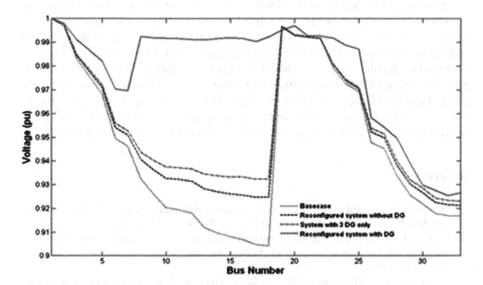

Fig. 3. Voltage profile of the IEEE-33 bus radial distribution system

Table 5. Comparison between four cases for different loading conditions

S. No	Case	No. of DGs	Switches opened	Light load (50 %)		Normal load (100 %)		Heavy load (150 %)	
				Real power loss (KW)	Voltage deviation	Real power loss (KW)	Voltage deviation	Real power loss (KW)	Voltage deviation
1	I	-	33,34,35,36,37	48.6965	0.0307	210.0594	0.1328	515.5726	0.3273
2	II	-	7,12,8,15,23	31.6955	0.0089	134.9314	0.0378	325.6698	0.2911
3	III	2	33,34,35,36,37	40.5090	0.0233	172.9186	0.0996	418.6146	0.2417
4	III	3	33,34,35,36,37	38.0460	0.0208	161.8729	0.0884	390.2218	0.2130
5	IV	2	7,12,9,15,22	17.6688	0.0088	75.1647	0.0374	181.2680	0.0899
6	IV	3	7,12,9,15,22	17.6715	0.0088	75.1056	0.0373	181.2426	0.0897

Table 6. Comparison of results between various algorithms for normal loading conditions

S.No	Algorithm used	Switched opened	Real power loss (KW)
1	NSGA without DG [17]	7,9,14.32.37	139.5
2	HACO without DG [23]	7,9,14.32.37	139.5
3	Proposed HSA without DG	7,12,8,15,23	134.9
4	Proposed HSA with 3 DGs	7,12,9,15,22	75.1

7 Conclusion

In this paper, an optimization method to reconfigure the distributed system with DG is proposed. The DG placement problem and reconfiguration problem is formulated as a non-linear optimization problem with the objective of loss minimization and voltage profile improvement. The optimal location and sizing of multiple DGs were optimized using particle swarm optimization (PSO). For reconfiguration, the optimal switches to be opened in distributed system were found using harmony search algorithm (HSA). The proposed approaches have been tested on IEEE 33-bus radial distribution system and the simulations were carried out for four cases: (1) for base case, (2) for reconfiguration of distributed system without DG (3) for optimizing location and sizing of multiple DGs and (4) for reconfiguration of distributed system with multiple DGs. Test results have shown that the feeder reconfiguration problem can be efficiently solved with HSA and the reconfigured network of radial distribution system with DG gives better improvement in voltage profile and minimization of losses than other cases.

References

1. Baran, M.E., Wu, F.F.: Network reconfiguration in distribution systems for loss reduction and load balancing. IEEE Trans. Power Deliv. **4**(2), 1401–1407 (1989)
2. Merlin, A., Back, H.:, Search for minimum-loss operational spanning tree configuration for urban power distribution systems. In: Fifth power system conference (PSCC), pp. 1–18. Cambridge (1975)
3. Shirmohammadi, D., Hong, H.W.: Reconfiguration of electric distribution networks for resistive line losses. IEEE Trans. Power Deliv. **4**(2), 1492–1498 (1989)
4. Glamocamin, V.: Optimal loss reduction of distribution networks. IEEE Trans. Power Syst. **5**(3), 774–781 (1990)
5. Sarfi, R., Salama, M., Chikhani, Y.: Distribution system reconfiguration for loss reduction: an algorithm based on network partitioning theory. IEEE Trans. Power Syst. **11**(1), 504–510 (1996)
6. McDermott, T., Drezga, I., Broadwater, R.: A heuristic nonlinear constructive method for distribution system reconfiguration. IEEE Trans. Power Syst. **14**(2), 478–483 (1999)
7. Carreno, E.M., Romero, R., Padilha-Feltrin, A.: An efficient codification to solve distribution network reconfiguration for loss reduction problem. IEEE Trans. Power Syst. **23**(4), 1542–1551 (2008)
8. Nara, K., Shiose, A., Kitagawa, M., Ishibara, T.: Implementation of genetic algorithm for distribution systems loss minimum reconfiguration. IEEE Trans. Power Syst. **7**(3), 1044–1051 (1992)
9. Lin, W.M., Cheng, F.S., Say, M.T.: Distribution feeder reconfiguration with refined genetic algorithm. Gener. Trans. Distrib. **147**(6), 349–354 (2000)
10. Zhu, J.Z.: Optimal reconfiguration of electrical distribution network using the refined genetic algorithm. Electr. Power Syst. Res. **62**, 37–42 (2002)
11. Mendoza, J., Lopez, R., Morales, D., Lopez, E., Dessante, P., Moraga, R.: Minimal loss reconfiguration using genetic algorithms with restricted population and addressed operators: real application. IEEE Trans. Power Syst. **21**(2), 948–954 (2006)
12. Gomez, F., Carneiro, S., Pereira, J.L.R., Vinagre, M., Garcia, P., Araujo, L.: A new heuristic reconfiguration algorithm for large distribution systems. IEEE Trans. Power Syst. **20**(3), 1373–1378 (2005)

13. Schmidt, H.P., Ida, N., Kagan, N., Guaraldo, J.C.: Fast reconfiguration of distribution systems considering loss minimization. IEEE Trans. Power Syst. **20**(3), 1311–1319 (2005)
14. Gomez, F., Carneiro, S., Pereira, J.L.R., Vinagre, M., Garcia, P., Araujo, L.: A new distribution system reconfiguration algorithm approach using optimum power flow and sensitivity analysis for loss reduction. IEEE Trans. Power Syst. **21**(4), 1616–1623 (2006)
15. Lopez, E., Opazo, H., Garcia, L., Bastard, P.: On line reconfiguration considering variability demand: application to real systems. IEEE Trans. Power Syst. **19**(1), 549–556 (2004)
16. Gonzalez, A., Echavarren, F.M., Rouco, L., Gomez, T., Cabetas, J.: Reconfiguration of large scale distribution networks for planning studies. Int. J. Elect. Power Energy Syst. **37**(1), 86–94 (2012)
17. Chandramohan, S., Atturulu, N., Kumudini, R.P., Ventakesh, B.: Operating cost minimization of a radial distribution system in a deregulated electricity market through reconfiguration using NSGA method. Int. J. Electr. Power Energy Syst. **32**(2), 126–132 (2010)
18. Enacheanu, B., Raison, B., Caire, R., Devaux, O., Bienia, W., Hadjsaid, N.: Radial network reconfiguration using genetic algorithm based on the matroid theory. IEEE Trans. Power Syst. **23**(1), 186–195 (2008)
19. Wang, C., Zhong, H.: Optimization of network configuration in large distribution system using plant growth simulation algorithm. IEEE Trans. Power Syst. **23**(1), 119–126 (2008)
20. Sivanagaraju, S., Viswanatha, J., Sangameswara, P.: Discrete particle swarm optimization to network reconfiguration for loss reduction and load balancing. Electr. Power Compon. Syst. **36**(5), 513–524 (2008)
21. Abdelaziz, A.Y., Mohammed, F.M., Mekhamer, S.F., Badr, M.A.L.: Distribution system reconfiguration using a modified tabu search. Electr. Power Syst. Res. **80**(8), 943–953 (2010)
22. Su, C.T., Chang, C.F., Chiou, J.P.: Distribution network reconfiguration for loss reduction by ant colony search algorithm. Elect Power Syst Res. **75**(2–3), 190–199 (2005)
23. Abdelaziz, A.Y., Osama, R.A., El-Khodary, S.M.: Reconfiguration of distribution systems for loss reduction using the hypercube ant colony optimization algorithm. IET Gen. Trans. Dist. **6**(2), 176–187 (2012)
24. Lucia, C., Borges, T., Ferreira, V.: Multistage expansion planning for active distribution networks under demand and distributed generation. Int. J. Electr. Power Energy Syst. **36**(1), 107–116 (2012)
25. Szuvovivski, I., Fernandes, T.S.P., Aoki, A.R.: Simultaneous allocation of capacitors and voltage regulators at distribution networks using genetic algorithms and optimal power flow. Int. J. Elect. Power Energy Syst. **40**(1), 62–69 (2012)
26. Daly, P.A., Morrison, J.: Understanding the potential benefits of distributed generation on power delivery systems. In: Rural Electric Power Conference, pp. 211–213 (2001)
27. Chiradeja, P., Ramakumar, R.: An approach to quantify the technical benefits of distributed generation. IEEE Trans. Energy Convers. **19**(4), 764–773 (2004)
28. Balaraman, S., Kamaraj, N.: Congestion management in deregulated power system using real coded genetic algorithm. Int. J. Electr. Power Syst. **2**(11), 6681–6690 (2010)
29. Celli, G., Ghaini, E., Mocci, S., Pilo, F.: A multi objective evolutionary algorithm for the sizing and sitting of distributed generation. IEEE Trans. Power Syst. **20**(2), 750–757 (2005)
30. Yang, X.-S.: Harmony search as a metaheuristic algorithm. In: Geem, Z.W. (ed.) Theory and Applications. SCI, vol. 191, pp. 1–14. Springer, Heidelberg (2009)
31. Verma, A., Panigrahi, B.K., Bijwe, P.R.: Harmony search algorithm for transmission network expansion planning. IET Gener. Transm. Distrib. **4**(6), 663–673 (2010)
32. Chang, G.W., Chu, S.Y., Wang, H.L.: An improved backward/forward sweep load flow algorithm for radial distribution systems. IEEE Trans. Power Syst. **22**(2), 882–884 (2007)

In silico Design of High Strength Aluminium Alloy Using Multi-objective GA

Swati Dey[1], Subhas Ganguly[1], and Shubhabrata Datta[2(✉)]

[1] Indian Institute of Engineering Science and Technology, Shibpur,
Howrah 711103, India
[2] B U Institute of Engineering, Bankura 722146, India
sdatta.me@buie.ac.in

Abstract. Multi-objective optimization is employed using genetic algorithm, for designing novel age-hardenable aluminium alloy with improved properties. Data on the mechanical properties of age-hardenable aluminium alloys is considered together for modeling the mechanical properties using artificial neural network. The models are used as objective functions to get the optimized combination of input parameters for the objectives, viz. high strength and ductility. The significance analyses of the variables on the ANN models gave a primary insight on the role of the variables. The Pareto solutions emerged from the GA based multi-objective optimization is found suitable for effective design of aluminium alloys with tailored properties. An in depth study of the role of the variables in the non-dominated solutions clearly describes the guideline for developing an alloy with improved mechanical properties.

Keywords: Alloy design · Multi-objective optimization · Genetic algorithm · Artificial neural network · Age-hardenable aluminium alloy

1 Introduction

Widely used metallic material, aluminium is a light weight metal. When combined with alloying elements, its strength can be substantially improved. Aluminium alloys which respond to heat treatment are the age-hardenable or precipitation hardened alloys. Al-Cu (2XXX), Al-Mg-Si (6XXX) and Al-Zn-Mg (7XXX) series alloys are the age-hardenable alloys. Precipitation hardening involves three stages, solutionizing, quenching and ageing. During solutionizing at high temperature, the second phase dissolves and forms super saturated solid solution upon quenching. The second phase comes out as precipitates on the matrix with time at room or elevated temperatures, known as ageing [1]. With proper alloying and heat treatment, hardness in such precipitation hardened alloy can be increased to nearly 40 times as compared to pure Al alloys. Therefore it is one of the most important strengthening mechanisms in aluminium [2]. In different series of Al alloys the composition of the intermetallic precipitates are different due to presence of different alloying elements. The objective of the present work is to design new Al alloys, having improved properties, crossing the barrier of these series and utilizing the effect of all the alloying elements used for precipitation, i.e. making the alloy age-hardenable.

© Springer International Publishing Switzerland 2015
B.K. Panigrahi et al. (Eds.): SEMCCO 2014, LNCS 8947, pp. 316–327, 2015.
DOI: 10.1007/978-3-319-20294-5_28

Searching a combination of composition and processing to achieve the above objective, experimental endeavors of trial-and-error, the method previously adopted, is tedious, time consuming and expensive. Computational approaches for designing the alloys makes the development process easier [3]. Here computational intelligence techniques come into picture as it has the ability to handle problems non-linear, complex systems as in cases of metals and alloys [4]. Genetic algorithm (GA) [5, 6] has been successfully employed for designing novel materials [7–10]. In this work multi-objective GA [11, 12] is used to search for solutions, i.e. composition and process parameters, to achieve higher strength with adequate ductility, which are conflicting in nature. In absence of any adequate physical models correlating the strength and ductility of the alloys with their composition and processing, the objective functions for the above optimization is developed using artificial neural network (ANN) [13, 14]. ANN has emerged as a tool suitable for application in various fields of materials research [15–20].

Here GA based multi-objective optimization using ANN models as objective functions produces a set of non-dominated solutions known as Pareto frontier, which provides the direction for designing the alloy with requisite properties. The Pareto solutions are thoroughly analyzed to extract useful information for the above deign. The ANN models are also used for extracting knowledge about the system through significance analyses. The solutions provided by the multi-objective optimization along with prior knowledge of the system as well as the extracted knowledge leads to the final decision making for the optimum solution(s).

2 Database

In this work, a database of age hardenable Al alloys is created through collection from a standard source [21], toward development of ANN predictive models for the properties, which can be used as objective functions for the onward optimization studies. Around 300 numbers of data is collected from the three series, i.e. 2XXX, 6XXX and 7XXX, of Al alloys consisting of the chemical composition, processing parameters, viz. amount of cold deformation, ageing time and temperature, and testing temperature as inputs and the tensile properties, viz. yield strength (YS), ultimate tensile strength (UTS) and %elongation (ductility), as outputs. Table 1 gives the list of input and output variables, the symbols used for them, the minimum, maximum, mean and the standard deviation values of the variables.

For ANN the inputs and outputs are normalized within the range of −1 to 1 using the following conversion operation

$$x_N = \frac{2(x - x_{min})}{x_{max} - x_{min}} - 1 \qquad (1)$$

where x_N is the normalized value of a variable x, x_{max} and x_{min} are the maximum and minimum values of x respectively.

Table 1. List of input and output variables with their minimum, maximum, mean and standard deviation values

Variables	Symbol used	Min	Max	Mean	Standard deviation
Silicon (wt%)	Si	0.1	1.4	0.488	0.247
Iron (wt%)	Fe	0.12	1.1	0.545	0.238
Copper (wt%)	Cu	0.1	6.3	2.377	2.103
Manganese (wt%)	Mn	0	0.8	0.293	0.235
Magnesium (wt%)	Mg	0	2.8	1.207	0.832
Chromium (wt%)	Cr	0	0.4	0.117	0.093
Nickel (wt%)	Ni	0	2	0.131	0.456
Zinc (wt%)	Zn	0.05	6.8	1.433	2.411
Zirconium (wt%)	Zr	0	0.18	0.017	0.051
Titanium (wt%)	Ti	0	0.2	0.117	0.063
Testing Temperature (°C)	T_{test}	−269	371	86.398	166.601
Solutionizing Temp (°C)	T_{soln}	468	565	510.108	23.014
Ageing Temperature (°C)	T_{age}	24	240	139.741	60.816
Ageing Time (hours)	t_{age}	1	72	32.251	27.335
Cold work	Cw	0	1	0.216	0.412
Yield Strength (MPa)	YS	10	745	244.641	176.825
Tensile Strength (MPa)	UTS	16	876	296.622	201.588
%Elongation	%El	5	125	31.494	27.711

3 Computational Procedures

3.1 Multi-objective Optimization Using Genetic Algorithm

Genetic algorithm is influenced by the principles of natural selection and natural genetics. In genetic algorithm a single set of parameter string or chromosome is treated as the genetic material of an individual solution. Initially a large population of candidate solutions is created with random parameter values. These solutions are essentially bred with each other for several simulated generations under the principle of survival of the fittest. When there are multiple objectives, the genetic search is performed following the theory of Pareto-optimality [11]. For single objective situation, we search for unique global optimum solution. But when more than one conflicting objective functions comes in the scenario then the aim becomes different. Here we try to find a set of solutions that provides the best possible compromises between the objectives, which is known as the Pareto set. The very definition the Pareto-optimality necessitate that no other solution could exist in the feasible range that is at least as good as some member of the Pareto set, in terms of all the objectives, and strictly better in terms of at least one. In the present context, no feasible solution is possible to exist having at least the same strength as some member of the Pareto set, and at the same time showing a better ductility. Conversely, it is also not possible to have any feasible solution that has at least the same ductility as any member of the Pareto set, but possesses a higher strength. Amongst them, if one member of the Pareto set shows a better ductility compared to another, it would necessarily have an inferior strength. The converse remains true as well. The Pareto set thus offers a number of equivalent optimum solutions, out of which a decision maker can easily pick and choose the most suitable ones. Further details are available elsewhere.

3.2 Developing Objective Functions Using ANN

The ANN used in the present work is a feed forward multi-layered perceptron network trained with scale conjugate gradient backpropagation algorithm. At each hidden unit (h_i), the weighted combination of the normalized inputs $\left(x_j^N\right)$ is operated on by a hyperbolic tangent transfer function as shown in Eq. (2), which ensures that each input contributes to every hidden unit.

$$h_i = \tanh\left(\sum_j w_{ij}^{(1)} x_j^N + \theta_i^{(1)}\right) \tag{2}$$

The output neuron then calculates a linear weighted sum of the outputs of the hidden units, as given in Eq. (3):

$$y = \sum_i w_i^{(2)} h_i + \theta^{(2)} \tag{3}$$

In the above equations, $y =$ output, $x_j^N =$ normalized inputs $h_i =$ Output from hidden units, $w_{ij}, w_i =$ weights and $\theta =$ bias. It is thus possible to obtain different outputs by changing the weights, w_{ij}. The optimum values of these weights are determined by "training" the network on a set of normalized input–output data. The network is trained by adjusting the weights $\left(w_{ij}\right)$ so as to minimize an error function, which is basically a regularized sum of square errors. This ultimately leads to an optimal description of the input–output relationship.

3.3 Problem Formulation

There are three objective functions in this work, i.e. maximization of YS, UTS and % El. As strength and ductility generally vary inversely, maximization of YS and UTS along with %El are conflicting objectives. To find the solution to the model system taken into account for Al alloys, as described in earlier section, a multi-objective genetic algorithm, NSGA-II [22], is utilized to determine the optimal values of strength and ductility after making necessary additions and modifications in the code. Following Eqs. (1) and (2) the trained networks attempted to maximize two objectives, one each for strength and ductility, expressed in the general form:

$$max \left[\sum_1^j W_j \left\{ \tanh \left(\sum w_{ji} x_i + b_j \right) \right\} + b \right]$$

$$\text{subject to} \quad x_i^{LB} \leq x_i \leq x_i^{UB}$$

where, w_{ij} is the input to the hidden layer weight matrix, W_j denotes hidden layer weight vector, b_j and b represent the input to hidden layer and hidden layer to output bias value for the trained network. x_i is the parameters for which the maximization search is attempted, however x_i^{LB} and x_i^{UB} are the variable bounds defining the search space for the optimization.

4   Results and Discussion

Two ANN models are developed for the purpose of developing the objective function. The first one is done considering all the compositional and process variables as the inputs and YS and UTS as the outputs. The second one is done considering %El as the output. The ANN used in this case are multi-layered perceptron with single hidden layer and trained with scaled conjugate gradient algorithm using MATLAB. The number of hidden nodes is varied to find the architecture of the ANN model with best prediction capability. For the first model, the number of hidden nodes is 7 and for the second model, the number of hidden nodes is 17. The scatter plots comparing the target and achieved outputs for UTS and %elongation are shown below in Fig. 1(a and b) respectively.

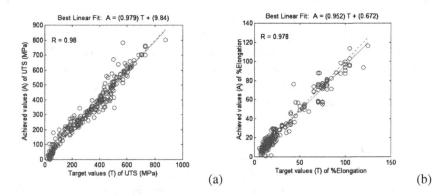

Fig. 1. Scatter plot for (a) UTS and (b) %elongation

It is difficult to identify influences of the input variables on the output of a system, particularly in case of ANN models, due the complex hidden relationships generated. Sensitivity analysis provides way to automatically identify all relevant parameters from a set of potential parameters. The sensitivity analysis is done on a trained neural network model. There are several methods for analyzing the sensitivity of the input variables. In this work the connection-weight approach, described elsewhere [23] is adopted. This approach uses input-hidden and hidden-output connection weights to calculate the variable importance. Figure 2 presents the results of sensitivity analysis of trained ANN models for YS, UTS and %elongation.

The above analyses show that some of the alloying elements, viz. Cu, Mg and Mn, are significant for improving the strength of the alloys. The solutionizing temperature is also significant. But the most significant variable is found to be testing temperature, which have a detrimental effect on the strength, as expected. The data consisted of the testing temperature from −269 °C to 371 °C. Within this wide range the strength of any Al alloy vary significantly. This resulted in high sensitivity of the variable as depicted in Fig. 2. To avoid such an effect of this particular variable, it is decided to consider the optimum solution search space taking three temperature regimes:

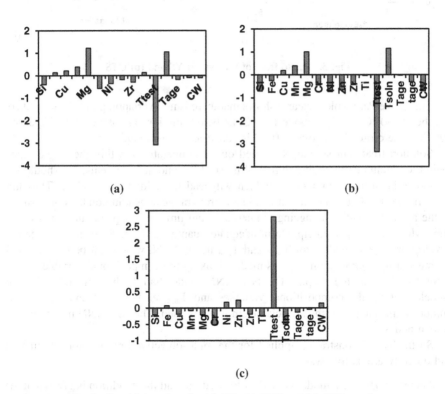

Fig. 2. Sensitivity plots for (a) YS, (b) UTS and (c) %Elongation

- Low temperature (−100 °C)
- Room temperature (25 °C)
- High temperature (150 °C)

As mentioned earlier, the ageing treatment of Al alloys is done either at room temperature (natural ageing) or at elevated temperature (artificial ageing). So it is decided that the T_{age} should be either below 30 °C or above 100 °C, to make the suggested heat treatment specific. A primary optimization study separately at both the temperatures is made. The Pareto fronts for both ageing temperatures regimes are shown in Fig. 3.

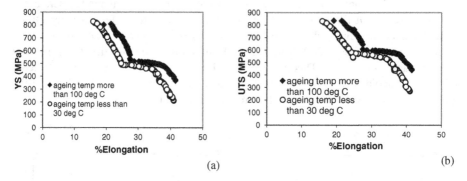

Fig. 3. Pareto front of %El vs (a) YS and (b) UTS

The above Pareto plots clearly shows that there is no overlapping in the two plots of T_{age} below 30 °C and T_{age} above 100 °C, i.e better solutions are obtained at T_{age} above 100 °C. Therefore T_{age} above 100 °C is added as a constraint.

Solution treatment should be carried out at temperatures within the single phase region to obtain complete dissolution of most of the alloying elements, but should not be above the solidus temperature, which will lead to melting of the alloy. Thus this temperature should be maintained within a narrow range depending on the composition of the alloy. Secondly the ageing temperature and time also depends upon alloy systems where the proper precipitate in adequate quantity is formed. So it is decided to develop predictive models for T_{soln} and T_{age} using ANN, which can be used as constraints during optimization. T_{soln} is modeled taking the compositional variables as the input and T_{soln} as the output. The best ANN model had 15 hidden nodes. T_{age} is modeled taking the compositional variables and T_{soln} as the input and T_{age} as the output. In this case only the artificial ageing data is used. The best ANN model had 19 hidden nodes.

So finally the constraints applied for the multi-objective optimization of strength and ductility are as follows.

- Ageing temperature model is used as a constraint and the condition is given that the T_{age} chosen by GA should fall between −25 °C and +25 °C of the T_{age} calculated from the model. This is done to make the solutions within a range of temperature suitable for the alloy system. It can be represented as:

$$\left(\frac{T_{age}}{T_{age(ANNmodel)} - 25}\right) - 1 \geq 0 \quad \text{and} \quad 1 - \left(\frac{T_{age}}{T_{age(ANNmodel)} + 25}\right) \geq 0$$

- Similarly, solutionizing temperature model is again used as a constraint and the condition is given that the T_{soln} chosen by GA should fall between -25 °C and $+25$ °C of the T_{soln} calculated from the model. It can be expressed as

$$\left(\frac{T_{so\ln}}{T_{so\ln(ANNmodel)} - 25}\right) - 1 \geq 0 \quad \text{and} \quad 1 - \left(\frac{T_{so\ln}}{T_{so\ln(ANNmodel)} + 25}\right) \geq 0$$

- The sum of the compositional parameters, i.e. weight percent of alloying elements, is kept at 10 wt% as a constraint. Higher alloy content decreases the toughness of the alloy. Written as

$$1 - \left(\frac{Si + Fe + Cu + Mn + Mg + Cr + Ni + Zn + Zr + Ti}{10}\right) \geq 0$$

- As mentioned previously, three temperatures are used for the test temperatures, for which optimization is done separately.

For all cases GA is done several times by changing various GA parameters, like the number of generations and the population size. Each time the Pareto front is plotted. This task is done to see that we reach the optimized solution and are not stuck in the sub-optimal region, using the optimum combination of generation and population on the different temperature ranges. Figure 4 shows the Pareto plots obtained for optimum combination of input and output parameters for low, room and high temperature ranges.

Table 2 gives and the range of input and output variables considering all the Pareto solutions obtained after optimization in the different temperature zones. The initial range, i.e. the range of data used for training the ANN models and also used as the upper and lower boundary of the variables during the optimization, is described in the parentheses.

For low temperature, the solutions generated from the above optimization show that the variation in the YS is mainly due to small variation in Cu, Mn, Mg and Zn. The other variables almost remained constant. For most of the solutions, Si is fixed at 0.1 (the minimum value in the search space), Fe is fixed at 1.09 (very near to the maximum value in the search space), Cr, Ni and Zr is nearly 0 and Ti is fixed at 0.06. For room temperature, the non-dominated solutions generated show that the variation in strength is due to variation in Fe, Cu, Mn, Mg, Ni, Zn, Zr and Ti. The other variables almost remained constant. For most of the solutions, Si is fixed at 0.1 (the minimum value in the search space), Cr is nearly 0. For high temperature, the above optimization show that the variation in the YS is mainly due to variation in Fe, Mn, Mg and Ni. The values of other compositional variables are almost remained constant. For most of the solutions, Si and Cu is fixed at close to 0.1 (the minimum value in the search space), Cr is nearly 0, Zn at approximately 5, Zr and Ti at 0.

Among the significant variables those which have shown variation in the Pareto solutions to a certain extent are plotted in a fashion to get the role of those variables within the non-dominated solutions. The solutions in the Pareto frontier are sorted in the order of increasing strength (YS) and decreasing ductility (%El). Then the above variables are plotted in that order. These figures are generated for the room temperature and high temperature cases, as there are no significant variables in the compositional variables in case of low temperature, as evident from Table 2.

The non-dominated solutions generated from the above optimization show that the variation in YS is mainly due to variation in Fe, Cu, Mn, Mg, Ni, Zn, Zr and Ti, in case of room temperature. The other variables almost remained constant. For most of the solutions, Si was fixed at 0.1 (the minimum value in the search space), Cr was nearly 0. The variation of Cu, Mg Ni and Zn with YS is shown in the Fig. 5. The variations of the alloying elements are found to show some interesting trends.

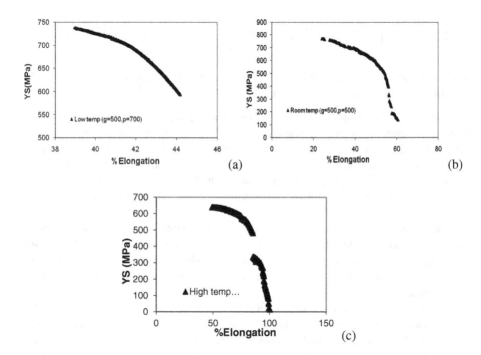

Fig. 4. Pareto fronts showing the optimized combination of generation, and population size for (a) low temperature, (b) room temperature and (c) high temperature

The condition is different in case of solutions suitable for high temperature applications. The non-dominated solutions generated from the above optimization show that the variation in the YS is mainly due to variation in Fe, Mn, Mg and Ni. The values of other compositional variables are almost remained constant. For most of the solutions, Si and Cu was fixed at close to 0.1 (the minimum value in the search space), Cr was nearly 0, Zn at approximately 5, Zr and Ti at 0. The variation of Mg and Ni with YS is shown in the Fig. 6. These results clearly depict that the performance of the alloy depend on different alloying additions at different temperature regime. This finding also clearly generates some interesting possibilities of experimental explorations.

Table 2. Variables with the range obtained in the three temperature regime

Variable name with initial range	Low temp (g = 500, p = 700)	Room temp (g = 500, p = 500)	High temp (g = 500, p = 500)
Si (0.1–1.4)	0.1–0.10009	0.1–0.10067	0.1–0.100874
Fe (0.12–1.1)	1.09–1.1	0.7351–1.099	0.32–0.9099
Cu (0.1–6.3)	0.1–0.75	0.101–2.857	0.100004–0.1068
Mn (0–0.8)	0.086–0.231	0.00002–0.586	0.1375–0.786
Mg (0–2.8)	2.58–2.79	0.354–2.799	0.085–2.799
Cr (0–0.4)	0–0.0001	0–0.000179	0–0.000297
Ni (0–2)	0–0.00019	0.076–1.371	0.126–1.577
Zn (0.05–6.8)	0.05–0.264	2.236–5.2027	4.684–5.7339
Zr (0–0.18)	0–0.000015	0.031–0.1405	0–0.000043
Ti (0–0.2)	0.061–0.06762	0–0.0708	0–0.000075
Solutn Temp (468–565)	492–515	468–527	470–510
Ageing Temp (24–240)	120–133	100–143	100–105
Ageing Time (1–72)	71.99–72	1–15	1–14
Cold Work (0–1)	0–0.000249	0.0205–0.599	0.000011–0.6131
YS(10–745)	593–738	139–771	14–639
UTS(16–876)	717–865	140–900	14–793
%El (5–125)	39–44	23–60	49–100

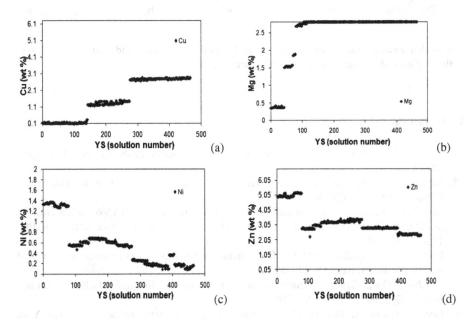

Fig. 5. Variation of (a) Cu, (b) Mg, (c) Ni and (d) Zn with YS plotted in ascending order for room temperature

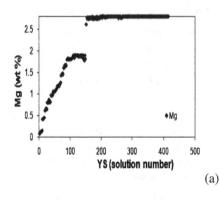
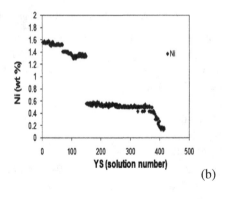

(a)

(b)

Fig. 6. Variation of (a) Mg and (b) Ni with YS plotted in ascending order for high temperature

5 Conclusions

  i. Multi-objective optimization using genetic algorithm can be utilized successfully for designing new alloys with improved performance.
 ii. ANN models can be used effectively as the objective functions for highly non-linear systems, like aluminium alloys, where no physical model exists.
iii. Analyses of Pareto frontier lead to certain trends within the solutions, which provide significant clue for the alloy design, if added with the prior knowledge of the system.
 iv. The finding points to some new areas, which need to be experimentally studied.

Acknowledgement. Swati Dey acknowledges Council of Scientific and Industrial Research, India for financial support to carry out this research work.

References

1. Polmear, I.J.: Light Alloys-from Traditional Alloys to Nanocrystals. Elsevier, Burlington (2006)
2. Raghavan, V.: Physical Metallurgy, Principles and Practice. Prentice-Hall of India Private Limited, New Delhi (2004)
3. Sheikh, H., Serajzadeh, S.: Estimation of flow stress behavior of AA5083 using artificial neural networks with regard to dynamic strain ageing effect. J. Mater. Process. Technol. **196**, 115–119 (2008)
4. Datta, S., Chattopadhyay, P.P.: Soft computing techniques in advancement of structural metals. Int. Mater. Rev. **58**, 475–504 (2013)
5. Goldberg, D.E.: Genetic Algorithms in Search, Optimization and Machine Learning. Pearson-Education, New Delhi (2002)
6. Gen, M., Cheng, R.: Genetic Algorithms and Engineering Optimization. Wiley, New York (2000)

7. Chakraborti, N.: Genetic algorithms in materials design and processing. Int. Mater. Rev. **49**, 246–260 (2004)

8. Das, P., Mukherjee, S., Ganguly, S., Bhattacharyay, B.K., Datta, S.: Genetic algorithm based optimization for multi-physical properties of HSLA steel through hybridization of NN and desirability function. Comput. Mater. Sci. **45**, 104–110 (2009)

9. Ganguly, S., Datta, S., Chakraborti, N.: Genetic algorithm based search on the role of variables in the work hardening process of multiphase steels. Comput. Mater. Sci. **45**, 158–166 (2009)

10. Mohanty, I., Bhattacharjee, D., Datta, S.: Designing cold rolled IF steel sheets with optimized tensile properties using ANN and GA. Comput. Mater. Sci. **50**, 2331–2337 (2011)

11. Deb, K.: Multiobjective Optimization Using Evolutionary Algorithms. Wiley, Chichester (2001)

12. Miettinen, K.: Nonlinear Multiobjective Optimization. Kluwer Academic Publishers, Boston (1999)

13. Haykin, S.: Neural Networks: A Comprehensive Foundation. McMillan, New York (1994)

14. Nigrin, A.: Neural Networks for Pattern Recognition. The MIT Press, Cambridge (1993)

15. Song, R.G., Zhang, Q.Z.: Heat treatment technique optimization for 7175 aluminium alloy by artificial neural network and genetic algorithm. J. Mater. Process. Technol. **117**, 84–88 (2001)

16. Song, R.G., Zhang, Q.Z., Tseng, M.K., Zhang, B.J.: The application of artificial neural networks to the investigation of aging dynamics in 7175 aluminium alloys. Mater. Sci. Eng. C **3**, 39–41 (1995)

17. Durmus, H.K., Ozkaya, E., Meric, C.: The use of neural networks for the prediction of wear loss and surface roughness of AA 6351 aluminium alloy. Mater. Des. **27**, 156–159 (2006)

18. Kundu, M., Ganguly, S., Datta, S., Chattopadhyay, P.P.: Simulating time temperature transformation diagram of steel using artificial neural network. Mater. Manuf. Processes **24**, 169–173 (2009)

19. Mohanty, I., Datta, S., Bhattacharjee, D.: Composition-processing-property correlation of cold rolled IF steel sheets using neural network. Mater. Manuf. Processes **24**, 100–105 (2009)

20. Datta, S., Sil, J., Banerjee, M.K.: Petri neural network model for the effect of controlled thermomechanical process parameters on the mechanical properties of HSLA steel. ISIJ Int. **39**, 786–791 (1999)

21. ASM Handbook: Volume 2: Properties and Selection: Nonferrous Alloys and Special-Purpose Materials. ASM International Handbook Committee (1990)

22. Deb, K., Pratap, A., Agarwal, S., Meyarivan, T.: A fast and elitist multi-objective genetic algorithm: NSGA-II. IEEE Trans. Evol. Comput. **6**, 182–197 (2002)

23. Olden, J.D., Joy, M.K., Russell, G.: An accurate comparison of methods for quantifying variable importance in artificial neural networks using simulated data. Ecol. Model. **178**, 389–397 (2004)

Augmented Current Controller with SHC Technique for Grid Current Compensation in the Distribution System

S. Rajalingam[1(✉)] and V. Malathi[2]

[1] Electrical Engineering Department, K. L. N. College of Engineering,
Madurai, India
rajalingamklnce@gmail.com
[2] Electrical Engineering Department, Anna University Regional Center,
Madurai, India
vmeee@autmdu.ac.in

Abstract. Recently renewable sources are becoming a focal point of the forthcoming century, both politically & economically. Use of renewable energy source to a large scale is a cost problem. These problems are overruled by distributing generation which is based on the divide & conquer method. As a token of this most the industries & houses implement solar power for their own use. This is a good sign for the effective implementation of this paper. This paper presents a novel control technique using the selective harmonic compensation on four leg inverter with which the distribution grid is interconnected with the domestic houses. In spite of several controllers, the proposed augmented controller has its own reliability & quick response which relies on DSP based filtering. The selective harmonic compensation technique is most suitable for balanced network condition and in the case where rating power of active filter is maintained. This augmented based control technique with SHC is demonstrated extensively with MATLAB/Simulink simulation studies.

Keywords: Current controller · Distributed generation · Distribution system · Grid interconnection · Power quality · Renewable energy

1 Introduction

The power electronic enhanced grid connected system allows us to get an uninterruptable power supply. Any excess energy that is produced is fed back into the grid. When there is scarce renewable energy, electricity from the grid supplies the needs, eliminating the expense of electricity. The power providers allow net metering [1], an arrangement where excess electricity generated by a grid connected system turns back the electricity meter as it fed back into the grid. It is necessary to know about this interconnection to electric grid, which includes (i) Equipment required for the connection to the grid (ii) State and community codes (iii) Requirements from power provider.

© Springer International Publishing Switzerland 2015
B.K. Panigrahi et al. (Eds.): SEMCCO 2014, LNCS 8947, pp. 328–338, 2015.
DOI: 10.1007/978-3-319-20294-5_29

It is necessary to have some additional equipment called balance of the system in order to safely transmit electricity to the loads. As per the power providers the system must include safety and power quality components [2]. These components include switches to disconnect the system from the grid in the event of a power surge or power failure and power conditioning unit to ensure that the power exactly matches the voltage and frequency of the electricity flowing through the grid. The Institute of Electrical and Electronics Engineers (IEEE) have written a standard IEEE 1547-2003 which provides technical requirements and tests for grid connected operation. Moreover the Underwriters Laboratories (UL) have developed UL1741 to certify inverters, converters, charge controllers and output controllers for power producing stand-alone and grid connected system [3]. UL1741 verifies that inverter complies with IEEE 1547 for grid connected applications.

One of the most important objectives of the electric utility is to supply sinusoidal voltage with constant magnitude [4]. Maintaining this sinusoidal supply voltage is not easy because the distribution side, balanced load, unbalanced load, linear load, non-linear load has their own effects on the distribution lines which make the deviation from sinusoidal voltage [5]. Another important objective of the electric utility is to supply uninterruptible green energy to the distribution side customers. This can be accomplished by interconnecting renewable energy sources such as solar and wind. One of the most common problems while connecting this power from solar, wind to the grid is on the interfacing unit [6]. Since the interfacing unit undergoes power electronic components it generates harmonics and deteriorates the quality of power with Grid current deterioration and load current unbalance.

Conventional solutions such as active filters, passive filters for reducing harmonic problems are ineffective [7, 8]. In addition, IEC 61000 and IEEE 519 have become restricted. In this paper hybrid filtering (SHC) & augmented current control techniques are incorporated to overcome this mitigation problem.

This paper is arranged as follows. Section 2 describes the system under consideration. Section 3 describes the controller for grid interfacing inverter. Section 4 presents the Simulation study, Sect. 5 concludes the paper.

2 System Description

Consider the system having renewable energy source such as solar power, Small wind power in the distribution side of the consumer. The generated power is utilized and stored in the battery of the receivers in the distribution system. This can be modified with micro inverter. This excess power can be fed to the grid with the help of the grid interfacing unit. The distribution side consumer utilizes the power from electric utility as well as from their own renewable energy source generation. Thus the consumers possess bidirectional power flow and bidirectional metering. The solar can be directly fed to the battery whereas the power generated from wind must undergo power conditioned before connecting to the battery and grid as shown in Fig. 1.

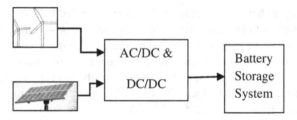

Fig. 1. RES at distribution system

2.1 Hybrid Filters with OHC Technique

The selective harmonic compensation (hereafter referred to as SHC) aims to provide in the harmonic reference current only several selected harmonic orders. The bandwidth of the compensated harmonic current is therefore limited to the selected harmonic orders. This selectivity can be implicitly provided through the selected algorithm as in Fig. 2 (i.e. Only several harmonic orders are compensated by design) or by user's choice (the user enables or disables what harmonic orders are to be compensated). This can be done in both, stationary abc-frame or synchronous dq-frame: In stationary abc-frame, by using band-pass filters or Fourier based filters tuned to output the selected harmonic orders. In synchronous fundamental dq-frames by using again band-pass filters to isolate specific harmonic orders, alias the selected harmonics, but shifted to different frequencies into the deck-frame [9].

In synchronous harmonic dq-frames by using a low pass filter to detect the DC-component, alias the selected frequency [10]. Thus, as per the detection, the harmonic compensation signal is generated using DSP toolbox.

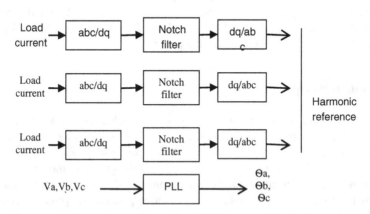

Fig. 2. Illustration of a generation of harmonic reference current using selective harmonic compensation method (SHC)

Figure 3 gives an example of SHC that uses three band pass filters to output only the 5th, 7th and 11th harmonic currents. The rest of the harmonics are not included in the reference current, therefore, they are not compensated.

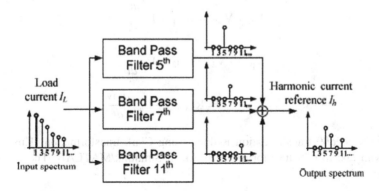

Fig. 3. Generation of harmonic current reference from load current (SHC)

2.2 Mathematical Model

The mathematical model relies on the one line diagram of the distribution system as shown in the Fig. 4. The voltage and the current reference have to be generated for generating the pulses for the interfacing unit.

Let I_1 be the current in grid with resistance R_1 and I_2 be the load side current with the resistance $R_L I_L$. I_{INV} is the current in the inverter. V_s are the source voltage. All meets at PCC. This model undergoes abc to dq transformation which generates reference current and voltage as per distribution line. The generated current is utilized for OHC and the voltage for augmented controller, which ultimately generates pulses for the interfacing unit. The transformation is further demonstrated in Clarks transformation which is utilized for the mathematical modeling of systems.

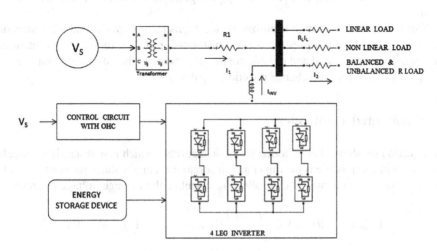

Fig. 4. Schematic block diagram of proposed system

At the point of common coupling,

$$i_1 = i_{inv} + i_2 \tag{1}$$

$$V_1 - V_{pcc} = i_1 R_1 + L_1 \frac{di1}{dt} \tag{2}$$

$$V_{pcc} - V_2 = R_2 i_2 + L_2 \frac{di2}{dt} \tag{3}$$

$$V_{pcc} - V_{inv} = R_{inv} i_{inv} + L_{inv} \frac{dinv}{dt} \tag{4}$$

The abc to αβ0 transformation is done using Clark transformation. This is done easily with abc to αβ0 transformation block in Simulink/MATLAB. The theoretical model is

$$\begin{bmatrix} V0 \\ V\alpha \\ V\beta \end{bmatrix} = \sqrt{\frac{2}{3}} \begin{bmatrix} \frac{1}{\sqrt{2}} & \frac{1}{\sqrt{2}} & \frac{1}{\sqrt{2}} \\ 1 & \frac{-1}{2} & \frac{-1}{2} \\ 0 & \frac{\sqrt{3}}{2} & \frac{-\sqrt{3}}{2} \end{bmatrix} \begin{bmatrix} V1a \\ V1b \\ V1c \end{bmatrix} \tag{5}$$

$$\begin{bmatrix} i0 \\ i\alpha \\ i\beta \end{bmatrix} = \sqrt{\frac{2}{3}} \begin{bmatrix} \frac{1}{\sqrt{2}} & \frac{1}{\sqrt{2}} & \frac{1}{\sqrt{2}} \\ 1 & \frac{-1}{2} & \frac{-1}{2} \\ 0 & \frac{\sqrt{3}}{2} & \frac{-\sqrt{3}}{2} \end{bmatrix} \begin{bmatrix} i2a \\ i2b \\ i2c \end{bmatrix} \tag{6}$$

The zero sequence power is represented as additional power in the system.

$$P_z = V_z i_z \tag{7}$$

Thus $[V0 \quad V\alpha \quad V\beta]$ and $[i0 \quad i\alpha \quad i\beta]$ are given to the controller for the control activity.

This Clarks transformation is utilized by the augmented controller and it transfers α, β to d and q and finally it uses the parks transformation of d, q to abc transformation. This incorporates the rapid and reliable control of power and the interfacing unit. It also incorporates the rapid disturbance rejection capability.

3 Augmented Controller

The equation set shown below forms the basic algorithm which is in discretized model. The output of this module is the direct and quadrature average voltage references which are used together with two PI controllers, to calculate the average voltage references.

$$U_{Md}(t_k) = Ri_d(t_k) + \left[\frac{L}{T} - \frac{R}{2}\right] \{i_d(t_k) - i_d(t_k - 1)\} - \omega L i_q(t_k) \tag{8}$$

$$U_{Mq}(t_k) = Ri_q(t_k) + \left[\frac{L}{T} - \frac{R}{2}\right]\{i_q(t_k) - i_q(t_k - 1)\} - \omega Li_d(t_k) + u(t_k) \qquad (9)$$

Deviations between the load parameters used in the controller and those actually present are compensated by the two PI controllers [11]. The dynamics which need to be handled by these PI controllers are rather limited because they relate to parameter changes due to physical environment. Hence the gains can be chosen relatively low. The discrete model uses four additional terms $Ri_d(t_k)$, $Ri_q(t_k)$, $\{i_d(t_k) - i_d(t_k-1)\} - \omega Li_q(t_k)$, $\{i_q(t_k) - i_q(t_k-1)\} - \omega Li_d(t_k) + u(t_k)$. Of which the latter two are current difference type equations.

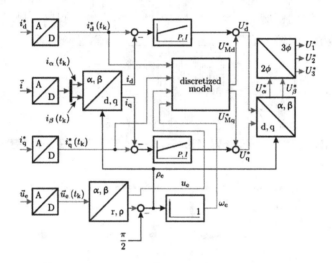

Fig. 5. Structure of augmented controller

Thus the input signals are discretized and transformed from α, β to d, q and finally resolving the pulses for interfacing unit using parks transformation (Fig. 5).

4   Simulation Results and Discussions

In order to verify the proposed control approach, an extensive simulation study is carried out using MATLAB/Simulink. The quality of power is maintained despite of highly unbalanced nonlinear load at point of common coupling. An unbalanced 3 phase 4 wire non linear load which is unbalanced and with harmonics have to be compensated. The augmented current controller and the SHC play a part in its compensation. Initially the grid interfacing unit is not connected. At t = 0.6 s the grid interfacing unit along with SHC and augmented current controller is connected. At this stage the profile of load current changes from unbalanced non linear to balanced sinusoidal current as shown in Fig. 6. Moreover, it can be noticed that the unbalanced load current gets

balanced. As the interfacing unit also supplies the load neutral current, the neutral
current gets to be compensated after t = 0.6 s as shown in Fig. 7.

The harmonics generated before compensation, i.e., at t = 0.3 s is listed in Table 1.
And the compensated harmonics level is also listed in Table 1. The Notch filter plays a
vital role in the compensation (SHC). The harmonics are calculated using FFT analysis
as shown in Figs. 8 and 9. The THD is calculated at t = 0.05 s, 0.1 s, 0.15 s, 0.2 s,

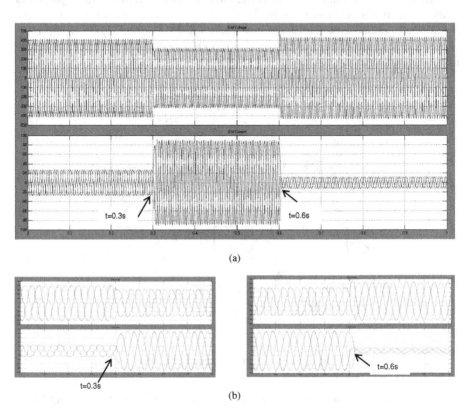

(a)

(b)

Fig. 6. Simulation results of (a) grid voltage and current (b) magnified representation of grid
voltage & current

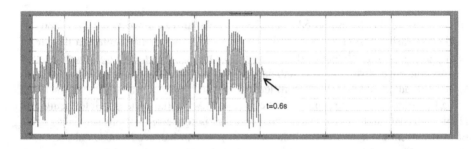

Fig. 7. Simulation result of neutral current to reach zero after t = 0.6 s

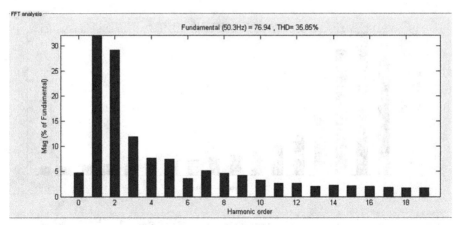

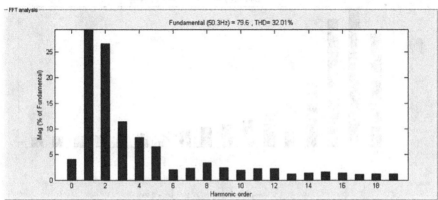

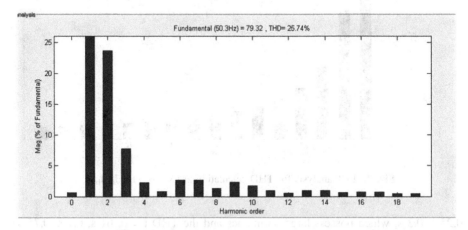

Fig. 8. FFT analysis for THD calculation at t = 3 s for I_a, I_b, I_c

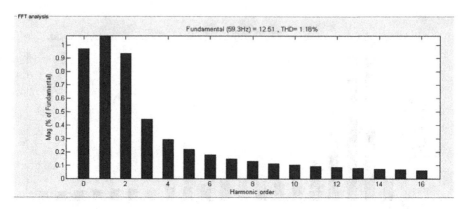

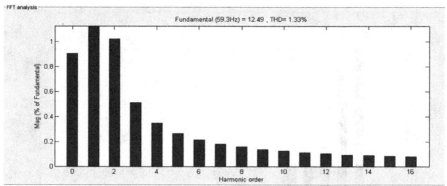

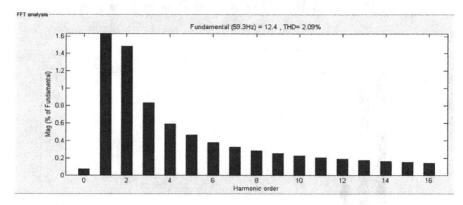

Fig. 9. FFT analysis for THD calculation at t = .61 s for I_a, I_b, I_c

0.25 s, 0.3 s, which possess large harmonics and the THD t = 0. 61 s, 0.7 s, 0.75 s, 0.8 s, 0.85 s, 0.9, 0.95 s possess harmonics within the specified limit [12, 13, 14].

Thus, from the above results, it is portrayed that the interfacing unit can be effectively controlled using SHC and augmented controller, hence compensating the current unbalance and current harmonics. This enables the grid to supply sinusoidal and balanced power.

Table 1. Total harmonic distortion of grid current before and after compensation

Phase	Before compensation			After compensation using SHC		
	A phase	B phase	C phase	A phase	B phase	C phase
THD	35.85	32.01	25.74	1.18	1.33	2.09

5 Conclusion

This paper has presented a novel control strategy based on SHC and augmented current controller in order to maintain the quality of power at the coupling point and to bring down the THD for the distribution system. It has been shown that the interfacing unit is effectively utilized for maintaining the quality of power. Extensive use of MATLAB/Simulink simulation validates the proposed controller.

Moreover the load neutral current is prevented from flowing into the grid. With this technique each consumer acts as a power conditioner and generator. The rapid disturbance rejection capability and power controlling capability with high performance and reliable operation makes the controller superior than the other conventional controller. Finally, reducing the current harmonic whose THD lies well within the prescribed standard limit of Standard IEEE 519.

References

1. Erol-Kantarci, M.: Wireless sensor networks for cost efficient residential energy management in the smart grid. IEEE Trans. Smart Grid 2, 314–325 (2011)
2. Laden Kezunovic, M.: Smart fault locations for smart grids. IEEE Trans. Smart Grid 2, 11–22 (2011)
3. Bose, B.K.: Modern Power Electronics Evolution Technology and Applications. Jaico Publishing house, Mumbai (2003)
4. Chandra, A., Singh, M., Khadkikar, V.: Grid interconnection of renewable energy sources at the distribution level, with power quality improvement features. IEEE Trans. Power Deliv. 26, 307–315 (2011)
5. Abbas, W., Saqib, M.A.: Effect of nonlinear load distributions on total harmonic distortion in power systems. In: IEEE Conference Publication ICEE 2007, pp. 1–6, April 2007
6. Su, S.-Y., Lu, C.-N., Chang, R.-F., Gutiérrez-Alcaraz, G.: Distributed generation interconnection planning: a wind power case study. IEEE Trans. Smart Grid 2, 181–189 (2011)
7. Blaabjerg, F., Teodorescue, R., Liserre, M., Timbus, A.V.: Overview of control and grid synchronization for distributed power generation systems. IEEE Trans. Ind. Electron. 53, 1398–1409 (2006)
8. Serban, E., Serban, H.: A control strategy for a distributed power generation microgrid application with voltage and current controlled source converter. IEEE Trans. Power Electron. 25, 2981–2991 (2010)
9. Grossmann, U., Ellinger, T., Berger, G., Petzoldt, J., Mall, H.G., Frako, G.: Active filter control in the stationary reference frame using lowpass to bandpass transformation. In: Proceedings of PCIM 2003, pp. 81–86 (2003)

10. Aredes, M., Monteiro, L.F.C.: A control strategy for shunt active filter. In: Proceedings of HQPC 2002, vol. 2, pp. 472–477 (2002)
11. Tanrioven, M., Alam, M.S.: Modelling control and power quality evaluation of a PEM fuel cell based power supply system for residential use. IEEE Trans. Ind. Appl. **42**, 1582–1589 (2006)
12. IEEE Std 519 – 1992: IEEE recommended practices and requirements for harmonic control in electric power systems. In: Institute of Electrical & Electronics Engineers, Inc. (1993)
13. IEEE 519 Working Groups. http://grouper.ieee.org/groups/519. Accessed 15 March 2004
14. Carnovale, D.J., Dionise, T.J., Blooming, T.M.: Price and performance considerations for Harmonic Solutions. In: Power System, World, Power Quality 2003 Conference, Long Beach

Recent Developments of Neural Networks in Biodiesel Applications

R.A. Mat Noor[✉]

Section of Chemical Engineering Technology, Universiti Kuala Lumpur –
Malaysian Institute of Chemical and Bioengineering Technology, Lot 1988,
Bandar Vendor Taboh Naning, 78000 Alor Gajah, Melaka, Malaysia
rabiatuladawiah@unikl.edu.my

Abstract. Neural networks have been applied in countless applications for so many years. From engineering, financing, administration, business, medicine; neural networks have been explored and employed especially in predicting and modeling a system or process. In recent years, biodiesel has become the major topic in science and engineering researches. In parallel with this current trend in science and engineering, neural network practitioners have taken one step further to advance into this field. This work focuses on the application of neural network in the field of biodiesel.

Keywords: Biodiesel · Biodiesel quality · Neural networks · Modeling · Renewable energy

1 Introduction

Many researches and observations on fossil fuels have resulted to the conclusion that these valuable energy resources have gradually depleted with the increase of human populations [1]. The continuous consternation towards fossil fuels has spawn researches that aim to provide alternatives to our sole dependence on fossil fuels. Biofuels derive from bio-wastes, plants or microorganisms have becomes the major success story behind these endeavors. The variance of biofuel's raw materials and different methods of producing it have contributed to quality difference amongst biofuels.

Quality of a fuel is inevitably important in order to maintain and somewhat improve the performance of engines. In the world of renewable energy, almost every renewable resource that is possible to give high yield and conversion of biodiesel has been used in biodiesel production. Such circumstances somehow have contributed to the dispute in the biodiesel quality. This phenomenon has lead to the involvement of prediction tool such as neural network to predict the biofuel quality (e.g. [2–5]).

2 The Prediction Tool - Neural Networks

Neural network is one of the most prominent predicting and modeling tools [6]. It has been utilized in myriad processes and systems since decades ago. Many factors have contributed to the success of the neural network implementations [7, 8]. In particular,

B.K. Panigrahi et al. (Eds.): SEMCCO 2014, LNCS 8947, pp. 339–350, 2015.
DOI: 10.1007/978-3-319-20294-5_30

neural network is a non-linear model, which is very useful in modeling nonlinear systems that cannot be successfully modeled by linear models. The second factor is that neural network is easy to use and develop and they basically learn by examples [9, 10]. The neural network users gather representative data, and then invoke a training algorithm to automatically learn the structure of the data [11, 12].

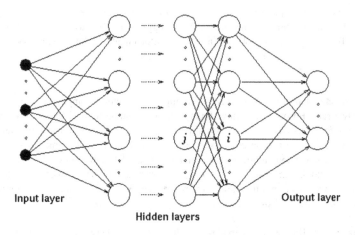

Fig. 1. A simplified neural network

Because of the tremendous capability of neural networks, currently there are many applications of neural network in industry and business and they are applied in pattern recognition such as automated recognition of hand-written text, finger print identification and moving target on a static background [13]. Neural networks have also been used in speech production where a neural network model is connected to a speech synthesizer [14]. Real time control is also a major application of neural networks with neural network models having been applied in the monitoring and control of complex plants such as chemical plants [15, 16]. Neural network has been employed in business where neural network model have played a role in predicting the stock market trend in certain period of time [17, 18]. Another area of applications of neural network models is signal processing and other typical applications such as noise suppression, filtering and digital signal processing technology [19]. These broad applications of neural networks can be a substantiation of the superiority of neural network. Figure 1 shows typical feedforward neural network architecture.

Modeling is the major application of neural network due to their ability to get trained using data records for the particular system of interest; the major problem of developing a realistic system model is obviated. Neural network applications in non-linear system has spread like wildfire due to it possess the ability to learn nonlinear relationships with limited prior knowledge about the process structure. This is possibly the area in which they show the greatest promise. Multivariable system also has taken the benefit of neural networks, which by their very nature have many inputs and many outputs and so can be readily applied to multivariable systems. The structure of neural networks is highly parallel in nature. This is likely to give rise to three benefits, very fast parallel processing, fault tolerance and robustness. Such a circumstance has brought neural network into parallel structure modeling. The great promise held out by these unique features is the main reasons for the enormous interest, which is currently being shown in this field [20].

3 Modeling of Biodiesel Processes Using Neural Networks

The growing demand of freight transportation and passenger cars has led to the growing demand on fuels. Such a circumstance has caused air pollution; green house gas emissions and fuel supply concerns. Extensive research has been conducted on alternative fuels biodiesel, which has shown to generate lower emissions. However, engine power and emissions generated from biodiesel are still not well understood that entail more and comprehensive research works to be done. Neural networks have become the premier candidate as the modeling tool. Various works have displayed the superiority of neural networks in capturing and modeling complicated and unknown processes or systems. The ability of neural networks has sparked the thought of utilizing neural networks as the modeling tool in predicting the unknown variables in biodiesel processes. Unknown parameters such as fuel consumption, unburned hydrocarbon and fuel consumption are very useful in order to analyze and deduce the quality and characteristics of biodiesel. Neural networks modeling have been applied to various mixture of biodiesel – biodiesel derived from rapeseed soapstock, biodiesel derived from vegetable oil and biodiesel blends. Next section reviews on previous works that have been utilizing neural networks as the modeling tool.

4 Biodiesel Process Modeling Using Feedforward Neural Networks

Feedforward neural networks can be considered as the most eminent neural network architecture. They are the prominent choice amongst other neural networks based on their simple architecture and excellent performance in various applications. Recently, there is a upsurge in neural network applications in biodiesel processes. Majority of the applications and research utilize feedforward neural network as the prediction and modeling tool. As early as 2005, Durán and co-workers employed feedforward neural network in their work. Their works focused on predicting the amount of particulate matter composition in the air due to engine combustion using biodiesel. Biodiesel derived from waste cooking oil were utilized in their research [21]. Yuste and Dorado on the hand conducted research on modeling of biodiesel yield using feedforward neural network in 2006. In their work, biodiesel derived from waste olive oil were used [22].

Baroutian and co-workers on the other hand worked on the prediction of another important parameter in biodiesel processes i.e. biodiesel density. In their work, they utilized biodiesel derived from vegetable oil [23]. In 2009, neural network models used for prediction starting to exhibit some progress in terms of models' outputs. Previously, neural network model were merely utilized to predict one variable only. Ghobadian and co-workers [24] used neural networks to predict several parameters on engines that are ran by biodiesel. Exhaust emission, specific fuel consumption, torques and brake powers were amongst the predicted parameters for their work. In their work, biodiesel derived form waste cooking oil were used.

Another work on biodiesel processes in 2009 was carried out by Ying and his co-workers. Their work were conducted using biodiesel derived from rapeseed soapstock. In their work, neural networks were used to model the most important biodiesel reaction. The biodiesel reaction also known as the transesterification which involves the reaction between lipids and alcohols to produce biodiesel and side product, glycerol. Ying and co-workers predicted important parameters in biodiesel reaction such as methanol substrate molar, enzyme amount, water content and reaction temperature for the biodiesel reaction [25]. Canakci and co-workers [26] on the other hand worked on the modeling of engine that was operated using biodiesel derived from waste vegetable oil. Their neural network model predicted parameters such as fuel flow rates, maximum injection pressure, emissions of carbon monoxide (CO), NOx and unburned hydrocarbon (UHC), engine load, maximum cylinder gas pressure and thermal efficiency.

The progress of neural network applications in biodiesel processes has gone further with the variation of biodiesel that has been tested and modeled in 2010. Oguz and co-workers conducted research on biodiesel by using mixture of diesel fuel, biodiesel, B20 (biodiesel blending) and bioethanol. Previously, most research carried out by using biodiesel derived from particular sources such as cooking oil, vegetable oil, olive oil and rapeseed soapstock. They developed neural networks modeling to model parameters when engine is run by biodiesel. Parameters such as fuel consumption, specific fuel consumption, engine power and moment were modeled in their work [27].

More works have focused on blended biodiesel – e.g. ethanol-gasoline blended fuels. Kiani Deh Kiani and co-workers [28] developed neural network model for assessing engine performance based ethanol-gasoline blended fuels. Engine brake power, engine output torque and exhaust emission were amongst output parameters that were predicted using multilayer perceptron (MLP). In the same year, Baroutian and his colleagues [29] worked on biodiesel that was derived from vegetable oil. In their work, neural network model was created to model the methanol recovery process, which as a matter of fact is a continuous distillation process. They investigated and predicted the distillation heating temperature, permeate flow rate and reactant ratio.

In 2011, another neural network model was developed to predict parameters based on engine that was run by biodiesel. Shivakumar and co-workers predicted engine parameters such as brake thermal efficiency, brake specific energy consumption and exhaust gas temperature. They applied the neural network model using biodiesel derived from waste cooking oil [30]. Another work in 2011 had seen a group of researchers carried out research on multiple neural networks models in order to compare between numerous neural network models with different network architectures. Several types of models i.e. neural networks and mathematical models were applied in their work namely multiple linear regression (MLR), principal component regression (PCR), partial least square regression (PLS) and feedforward neural network. Their work focused on predicting biodiesel density, kinematic viscosity, methanol and water contents. Biodiesel derived from vegetable oil were used in their work.

Research on biodiesel blends, for instance, B25, B50 and B75 were conducted in 2012. Sharon and co-workers [31] utilized biodiesel blends in their work namely B25, B50 and B75. Their research focused on predicting brake specific consumption, brake thermal efficiency, NOx, hydrocarbon (HC), CO and smoke density of the biodiesel blend. One of the most extensive yet intelligible works on neural networks in biodiesel was done by Ismail and his co-workers (Ismail et al. [31]) which focused on a substantial number of analysis and predictions namely carbon monoxide (CO) emission, carbon dioxide (CO_2) emission, nitrogen monoxide (NO) emission, unburned hydrocarbon (UHC), maximum pressure, location of maximum pressure, maximum heat release, location of maximum heat release rate and cumulative HRR.

In the year of 2013, several researchers have also attempted to utilize neural network as the prediction tool in their work. Chakraborty and Sahu [37] predicted the conversion of free fatty acids (FFA) and triglycerides in biodiesel production using neural network. They also made a comparison by using Response Surface Methodology (RSM). Based on the results, neural networks had shown superiority in the prediction of FFA and triglycerides conversion in biodiesel production.

Moradi and hi-co-workers did another work on the prediction of biodiesel yield in 2013 that comprised of prediction and study using neural networks was focused on biodiesel that was derived from soybean oil [2]. In the same year, Piloto-Rodriguez and his colleagues made use of neural network to predict cetane number of biodiesel. In order to prove the supremacy of neural networks as a prediction tool, multiple linear regression (MLR) was also applied in their work and the prediction results were then compared. Vinay Kumar and friends [38] did a study on brake specific fuel consumption, brake thermal efficiency, CO, HC and NOx emissions using feedforward neural network. Their study was specifically focused on biodiesel fueled Lanthanum Zirconate coated direct injection diesel engine. The study intended to focus on the thermal barrier coating (TBC) on engine components. They claimed that this particular field is a serious area especially the one that involves low grade fuel such as biodiesel. The biodiesel was derived Pongamia Pinnata oil through transesterification process.

A more recent work on modeling of biodiesel processes using feedforward neural networks was carried out by Meng and his co-workers [40]. They studied biodiesel kinematic viscosity at a specific temperature – 313 K. According to their work, kinematic viscosity of biodiesel at 313 K should satisfy the range specified by the international biodiesel standards. In their study, an artificial neural network (ANN) method was developed to model experimental data of 105 biodiesel samples collected from the literature. Neural network prediction results were compared with other methods such as Knothe–Steidley method and the Ramírez-Verduzco method.

Based on their work, both the Knothe–Steidley method and the Ramírez-Verduzco method tend to under-predict the kinematic viscosities.

In 2014, more works and researches diverts from modeling and development of neural network model for assessing biodiesel quality to the development of neural network model to represent and capture the optimization of biodiesel process itself. The work of Badday and his co-workers [32] shows the attempt of optimizing ultrasound-assisted transesterification of crude Jatropha oil in the production of biodiesel that was catalyzed by heteropolyacid catalyst. Neural network model was utilized to predict response in reaction. The models were also optimized to identify the suitable network topology and training method.

In this work, number of hidden neurons in the hidden layer as well as the training algorithm was optimized to highlight the most effective network architecture and training procedure that would lead to the best predicted results. The number of neurons was optimized between 3 and 20 neurons in the hidden layer applying three different training algorithms for each catalyst. Levenberg–Marquardt backpropagation, scaled conjugate gradient backpropagation, and resilient backpropagation algorithms were chosen for training the designed networks. The results rendered by neural network models were also compared to the results of the response surface methodology (RSM). Based on the results of their work, Levenberg-Marquardt backpropagation techniques delivered the best prediction which shows the most agreement with the results from RSM.

Betiku and his co-workers [33] used similar method i.e. neural network model and RSM to optimize biodiesel production process of non-edible neem seed oil. Both RSM and neural network model gave optimized process parameters such as temperature, methanol-oil ratio, reaction time and process yield. Based on their report, neural network model presented a better optimization results with the temperature of 48.15°C, KOH of 1.01 %, methanol-oil ratio of 0.200, time of 42.9 min with actual NOB (neem oil biodiesel) yield of 98.7 %.

Genetic algorithm is one of the optimization methods that is frequently paired with neural networks to form a very powerful prediction and optimization tool. Ahmad Hafiidz and his team used the combination of neural network-geneic algorithm to optimize important parameters in biodiesel processes. Based on optimization processes, it was found that 83.4 % yield and conversion of oleic acid to methyl oleate can be achieved using molar ratio methanol–oleic acid of 22:1, catalyst loading of 0.003 mol and reaction time at 3.6 h. The research also introduced a revolutionary esterification reaction using magnetic ionic liquid,1-butyl-3-methylimidazolium tetrachloroferrate ([BMIM][FeCl4]) which can be recycled and proved to be able to lower activation energy for the esterification reaction [34].

Progress and development of neural networks in the field of biodiesel processes can be summarize in the following Table 1.

Table 1. Recent works on biodiesel processes using neural networks

No.	Authors (Year)	Types of neural networks	Predicted parameters	Biodiesel type	Additional remarks
1	Ying et al. [24]	Feedforward NN	Methanol substrate molar	Biodiesel derived from rapeseed soapstock	
			Enzyme amount		
			Water content		
			Reaction temperature		
2	Ghobadian et al. [5]	Multilayer perceptron (MLP)	Exhaust emission	Biodiesel derived waste cooking oil	
			Specific fuel consumption		
			Torques		
			Brake power		
3	Oguz et al. [26]	Feedforward NN	Fuel consumption	Mixture of diesel fuel, biodiesel, B20, bioethanol-diesel	
			Specific fuel consumption		
			Power		
			Moment		
4	Baroutian et al. [28]	Feedforward NN	Heating temperature permeate flow rate		Methanol recovery (continuous distillation)
			Reactant ratio		
5	Ismail et al. [31]	Feedforward NN	Carbon monoxide (CO)		
			Carbon dioxide (CO$_2$)		
			Nitrogen monoxide (NO)		
			Unburned hydrocarbon (UHC)		
			Maximum pressure		
			Location of maximum pressure		
			Maximum heat release		
			Location of maximum		
			heat release rate		
			Cumulative HRR		
6	Ramadhas et al. [4]	Feedforward NN	Cetane number	Biodiesel derived from vegetable oil	
		Radial basis			
		Generalized regression			
		Recurrent			
7	Durán et al. [21]	feedforward NN	Particulate matter composition	Biodiesel derived waste cooking oil	
8	Sharon et al. [30]	feedforward NN	Brake specific consumption	Biodiesel blends:	
			Brake thermal efficiency	B25	
			Nox	B50	
			HC	B75	
			CO		
			Smoke density		

(*Continued*)

Table 1. (*Continued*)

No.	Authors (Year)	Types of neural networks	Predicted parameters	Biodiesel type	Additional remarks
9	Shivakumar et al. [29]	feedforward NN	Brake thermal efficiency Brake specific energy consumption Exhaust gas temperature	Biodiesel derived waste cooking oil	
10	Baroutian et al. [23]	Feedforward NN	Biodiesel density	Biodiesel derived from vegetable oil	
11	Balabin et al. [35]	Comparison: Multiple linear regression (MLR) Principal component regression (PCR) Partial least squares regression (PLS) ANN	Biodiesel density Kinematic viscosity Methanol Water contents	Biodiesel derived from vegetable oil	
12	Canakci et al. [25]	Feedforward NN	Flow rates Maximum injection pressure Emissions (CO, NOx, UHC) Engine load Maximum cylinder gas pressure Thermal efficiency	Biodiesel derived from waste vegetable oil	
13	Kiani Deh Kiani et al. [27]	Multilayer perceptron (MLP)	Engine brake power Output torque Exhaust emission	Ethanol-gasoline blended fuels	
14	Yuste and Dorado [22]	Feedforward NN	Biodiesel yield	Biodiesel derived from waste olive oil	
15	Mudgal et al. [36]	Feedforward NN	Emission (NOx, HC, CO, CO_2, PM10)		
16	Chakraborty and Sahu [37]	Feedforward NN	Conversion of FFA and triglycerides	Biodiesel	Comparison with ANN and RSM
17	Vinay Kumar et al. [38]	Feedforward NN	The brake specific fuel consumption, brake thermal efficiency, CO, HC and NOx emissions	Biodiesel derived Pongamia Pinnata oil	Performance of biodiesel Fueled Lanthanum Zirconate Coated Direct Injection Diesel Engine

(Continued)

Table 1. (*Continued*)

No.	Authors (Year)	Types of neural networks	Predicted parameters	Biodiesel type	Additional remarks
18	Piloto-Rodriguez et al. [39]	Feedforward NN	Cetane number	Biodiesel	Comparison of ANN and
19	Moradi et al. [2]	Feedforward NN	Biodiesel yield	Biodiesel derived from soy bean oil	
20	Meng et al. [40]	Feedforward NN	Kinematic viscosity of biodiesel at 313 K	Biodiesel	Comparison with the Knothe–Steidley method and the Ramírez-Verduzco method
21	Badday et al. [32]	Feedforward NN	Reaction response	Biodiesel derived from Jatropha oil	
22	Betiku et al. [33]	Feedforward NN	Reaction temperature	Biodiesel derived from non-edible neem seed oil	
			Methanol-oil ratio		
			Reaction time		
			Catalyst loading		
			Reaction yield		
23	Fauzi et al. [34]	Feedforward NN-Genetic algorithm	Methanol-oil ratio	Magnetic ionic liquid esterification of oleic acid	
			Reaction time		
			Catalyst loading		
			Reaction yield and conversion		

5 Conclusion

This review address itself into the works and research on neural networks in the field of biodiesel in recent years. Neural network have been known as a vigorous prediction tool, which is applied in numerous applications. Fossil fuel on the other hand is a very crucial daily life component and is declining in terms of the resources. Biodiesel has emerged as an alternative fuel that is derived from renewable resources and offers a great deal of opportunities in the future. Nevertheless, biodiesel quality and process parameters undoubtedly have to be taken into account if the renewable fuel is really substituting the fossil fuel. A complicated process such as the production of biodiesel has to be monitored and controlled thoroughly in order to produce high quality bio-diesel. In the review, biodiesel quality such as biodiesel density, kinematic viscosity, gas emissions, cetane number, etc. has become one of the most conducted studies amongst the reviewed articles. Biodiesel yield, methanol ratio, conversion of FFA and triglycerides are amongst the most favored process parameters that were studied in recent years. Most of the studies focused on biodiesel that is derived from vegetable oils and some of the works were conducted on biodiesel blends. Amongst the reviewed articles, several studies have attempted to provide evidence on the superiority of neural network by comparing the model with the rivals such as MLR, PCS and other latest methods. According to the review, neural network indeed can provide a reliable and robust prediction in almost any system including intricate process and system like biodiesel production.

References

1. Hoel, M., Kverndokk, S.: Depletion of fossil fuels and the impacts of global warming. J. Resour. Energy Econ. **18**, 115–136 (1996)
2. Moradi, G.R., Dehghani, S., Khosravian, F., Arjmandzadeh, A.: The optimized operational conditions for biodiesel production from soybean oil and application of artificial neural networks for estimation of the biodiesel yield. J. Renew. Energy **50**, 915–920 (2013)
3. Calabro, V., Curcio, S., Saraceno, A., Ricca, E., DE Paola, M.G., Iorio, G.: Biodiesel production from waste oils by enzymatic transesterification: process optimization with hybrid neural model. J. Biotechnol. **150**, 371 (2010)
4. Ramadhas, A.S., Jayaraj, S., Muraleedharan, C., Padmakumari, K.: Artificial neural networks used for the prediction of the cetane number of biodiesel. J. Renew. Energy **31**, 2524–2533 (2006)
5. Ghobadian, B., Rahimi, H., Nikbakht, A.M., Najafi, G., Yusaf, T.F.: Diesel engine performance and exhaust emission analysis using waste cooking biodiesel fuel with an artificial neural network. J. Renew. Energy **34**, 976–982 (2009)
6. Mat Noor, R.A., Ahmad, Z., Mat Don, M., Uzir, M.H.: Modelling and control of different types of polymerization processes using neural networks technique: a review. Can. J. Chem. Eng. **88**, 1065–1084 (2010)
7. Haykin, S.: Neural Networks. Macmillan College Publication Company, London (1994)
8. Hinton, G.E.: How neural networks learn from experience. Sci. Am. **267**, 144–151 (1992)
9. Zhang, J.: Improved online fault diagnosis through information fusion in multiple neural networks. Comput. Chem. Eng. **30**, 558–571 (2006)
10. Zhang, J.: Batch-to-batch optimal control of a batch polymerisation process based on stacked neural network models. Chem. Eng. Sci. **63**, 1273–1281 (2008)
11. English, E.M.: Stacked generalisation and simulated evolution. Biosystem **39**, 3–18 (1996)
12. Chen, L., Narendra, K.S.: Intelligent control using multiple neural networks and multiple models. Automatica **37**, 1245–1255 (2001)
13. Seong-Whan, L.: Off-line recognition of totally unconstrained handwritten numerals using multilayer cluster neural networks. IEEE Trans. Pattern Anal. Mach. Intell. **18**, 648–652 (1996)
14. Baig, A.R., Séguier, R., Vaucher, G.: A spatio-temporal neural network applied to visual speech recognition. In: Proceedings of International Conference on Artificial Neural Networks, pp. 797–802 (1999)
15. Zhang, J., Morris, A.J., Martin, E.B.: Long-term prediction models based on mixed order locally recurrent neural networks. Comput. Chem. Eng. **22**(7–8), 1051–1063 (1998)
16. Jazayeri-Rad, H.: The nonlinear model-predictive control of a chemical plant using multiple neural networks. Neural Comput. Appl. **13**, 2–15 (2004)
17. Fletcher, D., Goss, E.: Forecasting with neural networks: an application using bankruptcy data. Inf. Manag. **24**, 159–167 (1993)
18. Desai, V.S., Bharati, R.: The efficiency of neural networks in predicting returns on stock and bond indices. Decis. Sci. **29**, 405–425 (1998)
19. Larsson, L., Krol, S., Lagemann, K.: NeNEB-an application adjustable single chips neural networks processor for mobile real time image processing. In: International Workshop on Neural Networks Identification, Control, Robotics, and Signal/Image Processing, pp. 154–163 (1996)
20. Gomm, J.B., Page, G.F., Williams, D.: Introduction to neural networks. In: Page, G.F., Gomm, J.B., Williams, D. (eds.) Application of Neural Networks to Modeling and Control, pp. 1–7. Chapman & Hall, London (1993)

21. Durán, A., Lapuerta, M., Rodríguez-Fernández, J.: Neural networks estimation of diesel particulate matter composition from transesterified waste oils blends. Fuel **84**, 2080–2085 (2005)
22. Yuste, A.J., Dorado, M.P.: A neural network approach to simulate biodiesel production from waste olive oil. Energy Fuels **20**, 399–402 (2006)
23. Baroutian, S., Aroua, M.K., Abdul Raman, A.A., Nik Sulaiman, N.M.: Prediction of palm oil-based methyl ester biodiesel density using artificial neural networks. J. Appl. Sci. **8**, 1938–1943 (2008)
24. Ying, Y., Shao, P., Jiang, S., Sun, P.: Artificial neural network analysis of immobilized lipase synthesis of biodiesel from rapeseed soapstock. In: Li, D., Chunjiang, Z. (eds.) Computer and Computing Technologies in Agriculture II, Volume 2. IFIP International Federation for Information Processing, vol. 294, pp. 1239–1249. Springer, Boston (2009)
25. Canakci, M., Ozsezen, A.N., Arcaklioglu, E., Erdil, A.: Prediction of performance and exhaust emissions of a diesel engine fueled with biodiesel produced from waste frying palm oil. Expert Syst. Appl. **36**, 9268–9280 (2009)
26. Oğuz, H., Sarıtas, I., Baydan, H.E.: Prediction of diesel engine performance using biofuels with artificial neural network. Expert Syst. Appl. **37**, 6579–6586 (2010)
27. Kiani Deh Kiani, M., Ghobadian, B., Tavakoli, T., Nikbakht, A.M., Najafi, G.: Application of artificial neural networks for the prediction of performance and exhaust emissions in SI engine using ethanol- gasoline blends. Energy **35**, 65–69 (2010)
28. Baroutian, S., Aroua, M.K., Abdul Raman, A.A., Nik Sulaiman, N.M.: Methanol recovery during transesterification of palm oil in a TiO2/Al2O3 membrane reactor: experimental study and neural network modeling. Sep. Purif. Technol. **76**, 58–63 (2010)
29. Pai, P.S., Rao, B.S.: Artificial neural network based prediction of performance and emission characteristics of a variable compression ratio CI engine using WCO as a biodiesel at different injection timings. Appl. Energy **88**, 2344–2354 (2011)
30. Sharon, H., Jayaprakash, R., Karthigai Selvan, M., Soban Kumar, D.R., Sundaresan, A., Karuppasamy, K.: Biodiesel production and prediction of engine performance using SIMULINK model of trained neural network. Fuel **99**, 197–203 (2012)
31. Ismail, H.M., Ng, H.K., Queck, C.W., Gan, S.: Artificial neural networks modelling of engine-out responses for a light-duty diesel engine fuelled with biodiesel blends. Appl. Energy **92**, 769–777 (2012)
32. Badday, A.S., Abdullah, A.Z., Lee, K.-T.: Artificial neural network approach for modeling of ultrasound-assisted transesterification process of crude Jatropha oil catalyzed by heteropolyacid based catalyst. Chem. Eng. Process. Process Intensification **75**, 31–37 (2014)
33. Betiku, E., Omilakin, O.R., Ajala, S.O., Okeleye, A.A., Taiwo, A.E., Solomon, B.O.: Mathematical modeling and process parameters optimization studies by artificial neural network and response surface methodology: a case of non-edible neem (Azadirachta indica) seed oil biodiesel synthesis. Energy **72**, 266–273 (2014)
34. Fauzi, A.H.M., Amin, N.A.S., Mat, R.: Esterification of oleic acid to biodiesel using magnetic ionic liquid: multi-objective optimization and kinetic study. Appl. Energy **114**, 809–818 (2014)
35. Balabin, R.M., Lomakina, E.I., Safieva, R.Z.: Neural network (ANN) approach to biodiesel analysis: analysis of biodiesel density, kinematic viscosity, methanol and water contents using near infrared (NIR) spectroscopy. Fuel **90**, 2007–2015 (2011)
36. Mudgal, A., Gopalakrishnan, K., Hallmark, S.: Prediction of emissions from biodiesel fueled transit buses using artificial neural networks. Int. J. Traffic. Trans. Eng. **1**, 115–131 (2011)
37. Chakraborty, R., Sahu, H.: Intensification of biodiesel production from waste goat tallow using infrared radiation: process evaluation through response surface methodology and artificial neural network. App. Energy **114**, 827–836 (2013)

38. Vinay Kumar, D., Ravi Kumar, P., Santosha Kumari, M.: Prediction of performance and emissions of a biodiesel fueled Lanthanum Zirconate coated direct injection diesel engine using artificial neural networks. Procedia Eng. **64**, 993–1002 (2013)
39. Piloto-Rodriguez, R., Errasti, M., Sánchez Borroto, Y., Sierens, R., Verhelst, S.: Prediction of cetane number and ignition delay of biodiesel Using artificial neural networks. Energy Procedia **57**, 877–885 (2013)
40. Meng, X., Jia, M., Wang, T.: Neural network prediction of biodiesel kinematic viscosity at 313 K. Fuel **121**, 133–140 (2014)

Bilevel Optimization Using Bacteria Foraging Optimization Algorithm

Gautam Mahapatra[1,2(✉)], Soumya Banerjee[1],
and Ponnuthurai Nagaratnam Suganthan[3]

[1] Department of Computer Science and Engineering,
Birla Institute of Technology, Jharkand, Deoghar, India
mahapatragautam@yahoo.com, dr.soumyabanerjee@ieee.org
[2] Department of Computer Science, Asutosh College, Kolkata, India
[3] School of Electrical and Electronic Engineering,
Nanyang Technological University, Singapore 639798, Singapore
epnsugan@ntu.edu.sg

Abstract. Bilevel programming problems involve two optimization problems where the constraint region of the first level problem is implicitly determined by another optimization problem. There are number of different algorithms developed based on classical deterministic optimization methods for Bilevel Optimizations Problems (BLOP), but these are very much problem specific, non-robust and computation intensive when number of decision variables increase, while not applicable for multi-modal problems. Evolutionary Algorithms are inherently parallel, capable of local as well as global search, random, and robust techniques and can used to solve these BLOPs. In this paper, Bilevel Bacteria Foraging Optimization Algorithm (BiBFOA) is proposed for solving BLOP based on the foraging technique of common bacteria. Experimental results demonstrate the validity of the BFOA-based algorithm for solution of BLOPs.

Keywords: Bilevel optimization problem (BLOP) · Bacteria foraging optimization algorithm (BFOA) · Bibfoa · Chemotaxis · Elimination -dispersion

1 Introduction

Many complex real life systems can be formulated as multi-levels nested type optimization problems (MLOP) and according to Hansen et al. [1] these are all strongly NP-Hard type problems and Vicente et al. [2] showed that reducing them to single level or common type optimization problems is also NP-Hard type complex tasks. These types of multi-level problems are different from the common optimization problems, as they contain a nested optimization task within the constraints of another optimization problem. Bilevel optimization problem (BLOP) is the simplest possible instance of this class of problems, where only two levels of nesting are possible. The outer optimization problem is referred as the upper level task called as Leader and the inner optimization problem is refer to as the lower level task called as Follower. The nested structure of the overall problem requires that a solution to the upper level problem may be feasible only if it is an optimal solution to the lower level problem. Here is an example of such

© Springer International Publishing Switzerland 2015
B.K. Panigrahi et al. (Eds.): SEMCCO 2014, LNCS 8947, pp. 351–362, 2015.
DOI: 10.1007/978-3-319-20294-5_31

bilevel optimization problem: According to Zhang et al. [3] in present day auction-based day-ahead electricity market, each Generator Company (GC) tries to maximize its own profit by strategic bidding and for this purpose they submits a set of hourly generation prices and available capacities for the following days, based on these information and hourly-load forecast, each Market Operator (MO) will allocate generation output and try to minimize its total electricity purchase fare. The decision of any of them will influence the other. This is a typical bilevel decision making problem. Generally there are multi-Leaders (i.e. GCs) and only one Follower (i.e. MO). Other real world applications available in literatures are motivating the researchers and algorithm designers to study different form of bilevel modeling and finding the proper solution techniques.

This kind of optimization problems are generally very difficult to solve, because of non-convex and polyhedral nature of the feasible search space generated from the complex interaction between the Leader and Follower in problem space. Based on classical optimization techniques different algorithms are available in literatures for BLOPs But, all these deterministic classical approaches are providing problem specific solution methods and these are mostly relying on knowledge of the search space, non-robust in nature, and computationally expensive, especially when number of decision variables and modality of Leader and/or Follower increase in real life problems.

Now a day to solve different complex, multimodal and NP-Hard type problems various meta-heuristic optimization algorithms are very much popular. Researchers and professionals are using these techniques in various real life problems and for this reason many such methods already proposed to solve different complex real life problems modeled as a BLOP. Different form of Evolutionary Algorithm (EA), Particle Swarm Optimization (PSO), Simulated Annealing (SA) and its hybridization are studied by the researchers like Sinha et al. [4, 5], Deb et al. [6], Wang et al. [7] and Calvete et al. [8]. Both single and multi-objective forms of BLOPs are also available in literatures.

In 2002, Prof. K.M. Passino [9] proposed a new nature inspired optimization technique called BFOA mimicking the food foraging, evolutionary reproduction and environmental elimination-dispersal behaviors of common Escherichia Coli (E.Coli). This bio-inspired optimization technique is a relatively new member in the swarm intelligence. Mahapatra et al. [10] showed a number of improvements and models for bacteria foraging systems with applications in the engineering and other optimization fields. To prove the effectiveness of this algorithm some good references for theoretical analysis are Li et al. [11], Das et al. [12] and Dasgupta et al. [13]. In this paper a new algorithm called BiBFOA for BLOPs is developed, in which the BFOA by Mahapatra et al. [10] with Stretching Technology introduced by Parsopoulos et al. [14] are used for Leader and Follower optimization processes in a nested form. The experimental results demonstrate the effectiveness of BiBFOA for solving BLOPs.

2 Bilevel Optimization Problem

The general form of the bilevel optimization problem (BLOP) as defined by J.F. Bard [15] and S. Dempe [16] is:

$$\max_{X} F(X, Y)$$

$$\text{Subject to } G(X, Y) \leq 0$$

$$\max_{Y} f(X, Y)$$

$$\text{Subject to } g(X, Y) \leq 0$$

where $F, f : R^{n_1} \times R^{n_2} \rightarrow R$ are called the objective functions of the Leader and the Follower, respectively, $G : R^{n_1} \times R^{n_2} \rightarrow R^p$ and $g : R^{n_1} \times R^{n_2} \rightarrow R^q$ are constraints of the Leader and the follower, respectively; and $X \in R^{n_1}$, and $Y \in R^{n_2}$ are respectively n_1 and n_2-dimensional decision vectors for the two level problems. A vector $V^{\#} = (X^{\#}, Y^{\#})$ is a feasible solution if it satisfies all upper and lower level constraints i.e. $G(X^{\#}, Y^{\#}) \leq 0$ and $g(X^{\#}, Y^{\#}) \leq 0$, and vector $Y^{\#}$ is optimal solution for lower level objective function f () or Follower for the given upper level solution vector $X^{\#}$ with upper level objective function $F()$ or Leader. Within the total feasible polyhedral space we have to find the optimal vector $V^{*} = (X^{*}, Y^{*})$ which gives optimal values for both Leader and Follower. In BLOPs, the Leader who controls over X, makes decision first within its own polyhedral feasible search space and fixes X before the Follower selects Y within its own polyhedral feasible search space, and finds an optimal solution $V^{*} = (X^{*}, Y^{*})$ in overlapped feasible space. Here is a numeric example:

Example. Linear Leader and Linear Follower

General form of this category of BLOP will be as follows:
Leader : $\max_{X} F(X, Y) = aX + bY + k_1$, where Y solves :

$$\text{Follower} : \max_{Y} f(X, Y) = cX + dY + k_2,$$

s.t. $AX + BY \leq r, a \in R^{n_1}, b \in R^{n_2}, c \in R^{n_1}, d \in R^{n_2}, k_1, k_2 \in R, r \in R^m,$

$$A = \left(a_{ij}\right)_{m \times n_1}, B = \left(b_{ij}\right)_{m \times n_2}$$

A numerical example:

$$X = \begin{bmatrix} x_1 \\ x_2 \end{bmatrix}, X \in R^{n_1}, Y = \begin{bmatrix} y_1 \\ y_2 \end{bmatrix}, Y \in R^{n_2}, R = [0.0, 1.0], n_1 = 2, n_2 = 2,$$

$$a = [1.0, 1.0], b = [3.0, -1.0], c = [0.0], d = [1.0, 1.0], k_1 = k_2 = 0.0,$$

$$s.t. \; AX + BY \leq r, A = \begin{bmatrix} 1.0 \\ 0.0 \end{bmatrix}, B = \begin{bmatrix} 1.0 & -1.0 \\ 1.0 & 1.0 \end{bmatrix}, r = \begin{bmatrix} 1.0 \\ 1.0 \end{bmatrix}, X \geq 0, Y \geq 0$$

2.1 Challenges in Solving the BLOP Problem

BLOP is an NP-hard type problem, even in the case when all the objective and constraint functions are linear. For this reason algorithm designers have to develop efficient algorithms. Some significant challenges can be noted: (i) Order in which decisions are to be taken, (ii) No guarantee of solution, (iii) No guarantee of Pareto optimality for multi-objective type BLOPs, (iv) inherent non-convexity and non-differentiability of the complex polyhedral search space, (v) multi-modality nature of Leader and Follower functions, (vi) how to guarantee convergence to the efficient set and, at the same time, maintain the spread of outcomes, (vii) how to develop the algorithms to solve different category of problems with proper constraints handling capabilities.

3 Bacteria Foraging Optimization Algorithm (BFOA)

According to K.M. Passino [9] BFOA is a non-gradient, bio-inspired, self-organizing and recently developed efficient meta-heuristics type optimization technique. It is mimicry of the surviving technique of common E.Coli bacteria inside the very complex intestine system of human body with the help of foraging, evolutionary reproduction, environmental interaction dependent birth-death based elimination and dispersion. In complex problem domains, BFOA searches optimum living fuels i.e. energy intake per unit time, which is considered as the fitness, and it is collected by the bacterium using foraging behaviors called as chemotaxis. Due to limited life span they survive through evolution based reproduction by the fittest bacterium and to provide variation in the bacteria society. To globalize the search space and to avoid trapped into a local solutions, the natural calamities dependent birth-death based elimination-dispersal technique is used. Also, inter-communication based social swarming is considered for faster solution searches.

3.1 Chemotaxis

The random moving patterns of the bacteria in the presence of chemical attractants and repellants are called chemotaxis. For E.Coli, this process was simulated by two different moving modes 'tumble' and 'run or move or swim'. The bacterium alternates between these modes until divided into two. In tumble, bacterium randomly searches a direction of moving. In swim, it moves a number of small fixed length steps ($C(i)$) in the selected tumble direction ($\varnothing(i)$) or better nutrient collection. Mathematically, this can be expressed as:

$\theta^i(j + 1, k, l) = \theta^i(j, k, l) + C(i)\varnothing(i)$, $\forall i = 1, 2, ..., S$, where S is size of the colony; j, k and l are respectively the Chemotaxis, reproduction and elimination-dispersal step indices respectively and

$\theta^i(j + 1, k, l) \in D_1 \times D_2 \times \ldots \times D_N$, in short it is represented by θ^i be solution vector for i^{th} bacterium; $D_i, \forall i = 1, 2, \ldots, N$ are domains of $\mathbb{R}^N$ search space.

If $J(\theta^i(j,\ k,\ l))$ be the cost or fitness function then bacterium uses run if J $(\theta^i(j+1,\ k,\ l))$ is better than $J\big(\theta^i(j,k,l)\big)$. Otherwise, it enters into the next tumbling step.

For tumble $\emptyset^i(m) = \dfrac{\Delta(m)}{\sqrt{\Delta^T(m)\Delta(m)}}, \forall m = 1, 2, \ldots, N$, where $\Delta(m)$ is a random number in $[0,\ 1]$ and $\emptyset(i) = \{\emptyset^i(m)\}_{m=1}^{N}$.

3.2 Reproduction

As bacteria are not immortal and like to grow population for better social structure they use rule of evolution. When appropriate conditions appear, individual will reproduce after a certain number of chemotaxis steps. For this purpose, health of the bacteria, which is sum of fitness in each chemotaxis including initialization step is considered $J_{health}^i = \sum\limits_{j=1}^{N_c} J\big(\theta^i(j,k,l)\big)$. To maintain fixed population, bacterium with better health captures the position of bacterium with poor health. For this purpose, individual reproduces one of it identical clone.

3.3 Elimination-Dispersal

In the evolutionary process, elimination and dispersal events occur such that bacteria in a region are eliminated or a group is dispersed from the current location and may reappear in other regions due to environmental changes or some natural calamities. They have the effect of possibly destroying the chemotactic progresses. But, they also have the effect of assisting the chemotaxis, since dispersal may place bacteria near good food sources. From evolutionary point of view, elimination and dispersal were used to guarantee diversity of the individuals and to strengthen the global optimization process. In BFOA, bacteria are eliminated with a probability P_{ed}. To keep population size constant, if a bacterium is eliminated, simply disperse one new bacterium to a random location of the search space.

3.4 Swarming

Passino experimented on an interesting group behavior of the E.Coli bacteria. Subsequently, he was successful presenting this swarming behavior using a mathematical model. He observed that when a group of E.Coli bacteria is placed in the center of a semisolid agar with a single nutrient chemo-effecter, they move out from the center in a traveling ring of cells by moving up the nutrient gradient created by consumption of the nutrient by the group. This cell-to-cell signaling attractant and a replant based network group can be modeled:

$$J_{cc}^i\left(\theta_{best}^i(j,k,l),\theta_{best}\right) = Penalty(i)$$

$$= \sum_{i=1}^{S}(-d_{attract}e^{-w_{attract}\sum_{j=1}^{N}\left(\theta_{best}^{'j}-\theta_{best}^{ij}\right)^2}$$

$$+ \sum_{i=1}^{S}(-h_{repellant}e^{-w_{repellant}\sum_{j=1}^{N}\left(\theta_{best}^{'j}-\theta_{best}^{ij}\right)^2})$$

where $J_{cc}^i(\theta_{best}^i, \theta_{best})$ is the cell-to-cell cost or penalty $(Penalty(i))$ for i^{th} bacteria in the colony; $\theta_{best}^{'j}$ is the jth component of the current N-dimensional the global best solution vector $\theta_{best}^{'}$ and θ_{best}^{ij} is the jth component of N-dimensional the best solution vector attended by the ith bacterium in the colony. Other parameters are attractant and repellant dependent constants; $d_{attract}$ - the depth of the attractant released by the bacterial cell and $w_{attract}$ - the measure of the width of the attractant signal. Generally $h_{repellant}$ is the height of the repellant effect and $w_{repellant}$ is a measure of the width of the repellant.

3.5   Pseudo Code of BFOA

To implement the BFOA with all colony related parameters settings and steps for bacterium position updating due to move, swim, swarming and elimination-dispersal operations the algorithm presented in Fig. 1 can be used. Here for a particular optimization problem objective function $J(\theta)$ with other constraints is evaluated.

4   The BiBFOA Algorithm

The BiBFOA is a sequential nested optimization algorithm developed to encourage limited asymmetric cooperation between the two players. In this algorithm, we first sample the Leader's controlling variable X to find the N_l number Leader's candidate solutions $(S_l = [X, F()])$. With these candidates Leader's decisions, we use BFOA together with Stretching Technology proposed by Parsopoulos et al. [14] to obtain the Follower's response for every Leader's decision. Here, BFOA is called as sub-function with parameters like number of Followers bacteria, current Leader decision, and Follower's objective function as fitness along with Follower's constraints and iteration number. By this process a pool of candidate solutions $(S = [X, F(), Y, f()]$ for both Leaders and Followers is generated. From this set of solutions, we update the current best solution $(S^{\#})$. Once a solution is reached for all Leaders, we use the Stretching Technology to avoid the Leaders getting trapped in local optima. We repeat these steps for a pre-defined number of Leader's loop counter. We get the optimal decision vector $V^{\#} = (X^{\#}, Y^{\#})$ and corresponding optimal solution values for Leader and Follower $F^{\#} = F(X^{\#}, Y^{\#})$ and $f^{\#} = f(X^{\#}, Y^{\#})$, respectively. All together, the optimal solution is $S^{\#} = [X^{\#}, F^{\#}, Y^{\#}, f^{\#}]$. In Fig. 2 the proposed BiBFOA is presented.

Algorithm BFOA
(* S-Size of colony or population, N_c - Number of Chemotaxis Steps, N_s-Number of Swimming Steps, N_{re}- Number of reproduction steps, N_{ed}-Number of elimination and dispersal steps, P_{ed}-Probability of elimination and dispersal, C_i- Constant step size for Chemotaxis, $d_{attract}$ & $w_{attract}$- Chemotactic Attraction parameters for swarming, $h_{repellant}$ & $w_{repellant}$ - Chemotactic Repulsion parameters for swarming, N-Dimension of solution vector or problem or number of optimizing parameters, h^i - is the health of the ith bacterium, $J(\theta)$ - is the objective or fitness function*)

Step 1: [Initialization of Parameters]
1.1 $read\ S, N_c, N_s, N_{re}, N_{ed}, P_{ed}, C_i, d_{attract}, w_{attract}, h_{repellant}, w_{repellant}$
1.2 $for\ i = 1\ to\ S\ do$
    begin
        Randomly generate a $N-$ dimensional position vector $\theta^i \in D_1 \times D_2 \times \ldots \times D_N$.
        Calculate fitness value:$J^i = J(\theta^i)$.
        Initialize the ith bacterium with $J^i_{best} = J^i$, $\theta^i_{best} = \theta^i$ and $h^i = 0$
    end
1.3 Find the initial global best solution vector $\theta_{best} = \theta^i$ and fitness $J_{best} = J^i$ from current bacteria colony
1.4 Initialize Elimination-dispersal loop index $l = 1$
Step 2: [Perform all eliminations and dispersals]
repeat Step 3 thru Step 10 while $l \leq N_{ed}$
Step 3: [Perform all reproductions]
$k = 1$
repeat Step 4 thru Step 8 while $k \leq N_{re}$
Step 4: [Perform all chemotaxis steps]
$j = 1$
repeat Step 5 thru Step 7 while $j \leq N_c$
Step 5: [For each bacterium in the colony do the chemotaxis]
for $i = 1$ to S do
    begin
      5.1 Tumble
      Generate a random number $\Delta(m)$ in $[0,1]$
$$\emptyset^i(m) = \frac{\Delta(m)}{\sqrt{\Delta^T(m)\Delta(m)}}, \forall m = 1,2,\ldots,N$$
      $\emptyset(i) = \{\emptyset^i(m)\}_{m=1}^N$
      5.2 Move
$$\theta^i(j+1,k,l) = \theta^i(j,k,l) + C(i)\emptyset(i$$
      5.3 Compute fitness
$$J^i = J(\theta^i(j+1,k,l))$$
      $if(J^i$ is better than $J_{best})$ then
          set $J_{best} = J^i$
          $\theta_{best} = \theta^i(j+1,k,l)$
    end if
      $if(J^i$ is better than $J^i_{best})$ then
          set $J^i_{best} = J^i$
          $\theta^i_{best} = \theta^i(j+1,k,l)$
          $h^i = h^i + J^i$
    end if
      5.4 Swim
      $p = 0$

Fig. 1. *(continued)*

$$while \left(p \le N_s \wedge \left(J^i \text{ is better than } J^i_{best}\right)\right) do$$

$$\quad begin$$

$$\qquad \theta^i(j+1,k,l) = \theta^i(j,k,l) + C(i)\phi(i)$$

$$\qquad J^i = J(\theta^i(j+1,k,l))$$

$$\qquad if(J^i \text{ is better than } J_{best}) \text{ then}$$

$$\qquad\qquad set\, J_{best} = J^i$$

$$\qquad\qquad \theta_{best} = \theta^i(j+1,k,l)$$

$$\qquad end\, if$$

$$\qquad if(J^i \text{ is better than } J^i_{best}) \text{ then}$$

$$\qquad\qquad set\, J^i_{best} = J^i$$

$$\qquad\qquad \theta^i_{best} = \theta^i(j+1,k,l)$$

$$\qquad\qquad h^i = h^i + J^i, p = p+1$$

$$\qquad end\, if$$

$$\quad end$$

$$end$$

Step 6: [Update the chemotaxis step counter]

$$\quad j = j+1$$

Step 7: [Reproduction]

    7.1 Arrange bacteria in descending order of health

        Sort(Colony)

    7.2 Reproduce

        Replace all $S/2$ number of relatively unhealthy bacteria appearing at the bottom half of the sorted list by a copy of bacteria with better health appearing at the top of the list.

Step 8: [Update reproduction Counter]

$$\quad k = k+1$$

Step 9: [Perform eliminate and dispersal of bacteria colony]

    For each bacterium $i = 1\ to\ S$ in the colony with probability P_{ed}, eliminate and disperse. For this purpose, generate a random probability (r) and check whether it is greater or equal to the given elimination probability P_{ed} or not. If successful then eliminate the bacterium and place it at a random position in the search space $\theta^i \in D_1 \times D_2 \times \dots \times D_N$. Compute fitness value $J^i = J(\theta^i)$ and then initialize the ith bacterium with $J^i_{best} = J^i$, $\theta^i_{best} = \theta^i$ and $h^i = 0$. If necessary, also update the global best $\theta_{best} = \theta^i$ and fitness $J_{best} = J^i$.

Step 10: [Update eliminate – dispersal counter]

$$\quad l = l+1$$

Step 11: [Finished]

    Return solution vector θ_{best} and fitness J_{best}.

Fig. 1. Pseudo-code for BFOA

In this algorithm *BFOA()* is used as function along with other two functions *Stretch ()* and *Best()* respectively for the Stretching and updating the current global best solution.

5   Experimental Results

The above algorithm is implemented using Microsoft Visual C#.net 2010 and applied for solving the following two problems:

Algorithm BiBFOA
Step 1: [Generate N_l random leaders]
$S_L = S^\# = \emptyset$
$for\ l = 1\ to\ N_l\ do$
$begin$
   $while(true)do$
      $begin$
         $X_l = X^L + rand * (X^U - X^L)$
         $if(G(X_l) \le 0)\ then$
            $break$
         $end\ if$
         $S_L = S_L \cup [X_l, F()]$
      end
end
Step 2: [Process all the Leader's iterations]
$k_l = 0$
$repeat\ Step\ 3\ thru\ Step\ 6\ while\ k_l \le M^L$
Step 3: [Evaluate Follower's response for each Leader using BFOA with Stretching Technology]
$for\ l = 1\ to\ N_l\ do$
    $S = S \cup BFOA(N_f, l, S_L, f, g, M^F)$
Step 4: [Update the best solution]
$S^\# = Best(S, S^\#)$
Step 5: [Use Stretching Technology for Leader to avoid getting tapped in local optima]
$S_L' = \emptyset$
$for\ l = 1\ to\ N_l\ do$
    $S_L' = S_L' \cup Stretch(X_l, F, G)$
$S_L = S_L'$
Step 6: [Update the Leaders iteration counter]
$k_l = k_l + 1$
Step 7: [Output the solution]
$write\ S^\#$

Fig. 2. Pseudo-code for BiBFOA

Experiment I. For demonstration of the effectiveness, efficiency and comparison of the proposed BiBFOA, we selected the BLOP that used by Wang et al. [7], where Leader and Follower are respectively linear and quadratic as follows:

$$Leader : \max_{X} F(X, Y) = aX + bY$$

$$Follower : \max_{X} f(X, Y) = cX + dY + (X^T, Y^T)Q_1(X^T, Y^T)^T$$

$$where\ X = \begin{bmatrix} x_1 \\ x_2 \end{bmatrix}, X \in R^{n_1}, Y = \begin{bmatrix} y_1 \\ y_2 \end{bmatrix}, Y \in R^{n_2}, R = [0, 1], n_1 = 2, n_2 = 2,$$

$$a = [1,1], b = [3,-1], c = [0,0], d = [5,8], Q_1 = \begin{bmatrix} 1 & 3 & 2 & 0 \\ 3 & 1 & 4 & -2 \\ 2 & 4 & -2 & 1 \\ 0 & -2 & 1 & 5 \end{bmatrix}$$

$$s.t.\ AX + BY \le r, A = \begin{bmatrix} 1 & 1 \\ -1 & 1 \\ 3 & 0 \\ 0 & 0 \end{bmatrix}, B = \begin{bmatrix} 1 & 1 \\ 0 & 0 \\ 0 & -4 \\ 1 & 1 \end{bmatrix}, r = \begin{bmatrix} 12 \\ 2 \\ 5 \\ 4 \end{bmatrix}, X \ge 0, Y \ge 0$$

Our proposed BiBFOA executed for 25 independent runs with different algorithm related parameters, the best solution presented in following Table 1.

Table 1. Results for experiment I

Algorithm	$S^{\#} = [X^{\#}, F^{\#}, Y^{\#}, f^{\#}]$
BiBFOA	$[\begin{bmatrix} 6.3098 \\ 1.6787 \end{bmatrix}, 20.0016, \begin{bmatrix} 4.0001 \\ 0.0000 \end{bmatrix}, 230.0003]$
GA by Wang et al [7]	$[\begin{bmatrix} 6.3086 \\ 1.7012 \end{bmatrix}, 20.0013, \begin{bmatrix} 4.0001 \\ 0.0000 \end{bmatrix}, 230.0400]$
Exact Solution by Rishuang et al [17]	$[\begin{bmatrix} 6.3125 \\ 1.6875 \end{bmatrix}, 20.0000, \begin{bmatrix} 4.0000 \\ 0.0000 \end{bmatrix}, 229.6097]$

Experiment II. In 2014, Sinha et al. [5] developed a test suite of twelve benchmark test BLOPs with different levels of difficulties. The general form of these test problem functions and the first member (SMD1) of this suite are as follows:

$$Leader: \underset{X}{min}\ F(X,Y) = F_1(X_1) + F_2(Y_1) + F_3(X_2, Y_2)$$

$$Follower: \underset{Y}{min}\ f(X,Y) = f_1(X_1, X_2) + f_2(Y_1) + f_3(X_2, Y_2)$$

where $X = (X_1, X_2)$ and $Y = (Y_1, Y_2)$

SMD1:

$$F_1 = \sum_{i=1}^{p}(x_1^i)^2, F_2 = \sum_{i=1}^{q}(y_1^i)^2, F_3 = \sum_{i=1}^{r}(x_2^i)^2 +$$

$$\sum_{i=1}^{r}(x_2^i - \tan y_2^i)^2 f_1 = \sum_{i=1}^{p}(x_1^i)^2, f_2 = \sum_{i=1}^{q}(y_1^i)^2, f_3 = \sum_{i=1}^{r}(x_2^i - \tan y_2^i)^2$$

where $X_1 = \{x_1^i\}_{i=1}^{p} = [-5, 10]^p, X_2 = \{x_2^i\}_{i=1}^{r} = [-5, 10]^r, Y_1 = \{y_1^i\}_{i=1}^{q} = [-5, 10]^q$ and $Y_2 = \{y_2^i\}_{i=1}^{r} = [-\frac{\pi}{2}, \frac{\pi}{2}]^r$

Our experimental results for this SMD1 with $n_1 = 5$ and $n_2 = 8$ and 15 independent executions with best solutions are presented in Table 2. This is demonstrating the effectiveness of the BiBFOA and also a comparison with the BLEAQ technique proposed by Sinha et al. [5].

Table 2. Results for experiment II

Algorithm	
BiBFOA	$X^\# = [-0.0015, 0.0001, -0.0012, -0.0082, -0.0012]$
	$F^\# = -1.3223E - 005$
	$Y^\# = [0.0000, 0.0000, -0.0000, 0.0002, -0.0000, 0.0000, -0.0072, -0.0004]$
	$f^\# = 1.3303E - 005$
BLEAQ by Sinha et al. [5]	$X^\# = [0.0025, -0.0089, -0.0072, -0.0102, -0.0014]$
	$F^\# = -2.4229e - 004$
	$Y^\# = [0.0000, -0.0000, 0.0000, -0.0000, -0.0000, 0.0000, -0.0102, -0.0014]$
	$f^\# = -1.3703e - 004$
Exact Solution by Sinha et al. [5]	$X^\# = [0.0000, 0.0000, 0.0000, 0.0000, 0.0000], F^\# = 0.0000$
	$Y^\# = [0.0000, 0.0000, 0.0000, 0.0000, 0.0000, 0.0000, 0.0000, 0.0000]$
	$f^\# = 0.0000$

6   Conclusion and Future Work

This paper has explained how the robust and efficient bacteria foraging based optimization technique can be used to solve complex BLOPs. Application of the proposed BiBFOA technique for solving bilevel problems, demonstrated the effectiveness of the algorithm.

There are scopes for future development of BiBFOA for real world BLOPs, where the problems are multi-objective, multi-modal in nature and requiring sophisticated constraint handlings and other strategies for inherent challenges in BLOP. To evaluate the performance of the proposed algorithm, we will use the twelve single objective test problems suite developed by Sinha et al. [5]. Adaptive chemotaxis for exploring and exploitation of solution, crossover based reproduction for better evolution and efficient ensemble based elimination-dispersal based mutation for the development of BFOA will be investigated for the development of enhanced BiBFOA. Stretching Technology may be improved along with efficient boundary handling.

Acknowledgement. The authors wish to acknowledge the support of the Post Graduate Teaching and Research Council of Asutosh College.

References

1. Hansen, P., Jaumard, B., Savard, G.: New branch-and-bound rules for linear bilevel programming. SIAM J. Sci. Stat. Comput. **13**(5), 1194–1217 (1992)

2. Vicente, L., Savard, G., Júdice, J.: Descent approaches for quadratic bilevel programming. J. Optim. Theory Appl. **81**(2), 379–399 (1994)
3. Zhang, G., Zhang, G., Gao, Y., Lu, J.: A bilevel optimization model and a PSO-based algorithm in day-ahead electricity markets. In: Proceeds of the 2009 IEEE International Conference on Systems, Man and Cybernetics (SMC 2009), pp. 611–616, Texas, USA, October 2009
4. Sinha, A., Malo, P., Deb, K.: Efficient Evolutionary Algorithm for Single-Objective Bilevel Optimization. CoRR (2013). abs/1303.3901
5. Sinha, A., Malo, P., Deb, K.: Test problem construction for single-objective bilevel optimization. Evol. Comput. **22**(3), 439–477 (2014)
6. Deb, K., Sinha, A.: An efficient and accurate solution methodology for bilevel multi-objective programming problems using a hybrid evolutionary-local-search algorithm. Evol. Comput. **18**(3), 403–449 (2010)
7. Wang, G., Wan, Z., Wang, X., Lv, Y.: Genetic algorithm based on simplex method for solving linear-quadratic bilevel programming problem. Comput. Math Appl. **56**(10), 2550–2555 (2008)
8. Calvete, H.I., Gale, C., Mateo, P.M.: A new approach for solving linear bilevel problems using genetic algorithms. Eur. J. Oper. Res. **188**(1), 14–28 (2008)
9. Passino, K.M.: Biomimicry of bacterial foraging for distributed optimization and control. IEEE Control Syst. Mag. **22**(3), 52–67 (2002)
10. Mahapatra, G., Banerjee, S.: A study of bacterial foraging optimization algorithm and its applications to solve simultaneous equations. Int. J. Comput. Appl. **72**(5), 1–6 (2013)
11. Li, J., Dang, J., Bu, F., Wang, J.: Analysis and improvement of the bacterial foraging optimization algorithm. J. Comput. Sci. Eng. **8**(1), 1–10 (2014)
12. Das, S., Biswas, A., Dasgupta, S., Abraham, A.: Bacterial foraging optimization algorithm: theoretical foundations, analysis, and applications. In: Abraham, A., Hassanien, A.-E., Siarry, P., Engelbrecht, A. (eds.) Foundations of Computational Intelligence Volume 3. SCI, vol. 203, pp. 23–55. Springer, Heidelberg (2009)
13. Dasgupta, S., Das, S., Abraham, A., Biswas, A.: Adaptive computational chemotaxis in bacterial foraging optimization: an analysis. Evol. Comput. IEEE Trans. **13**(4), 919–941 (2009)
14. Parsopoulos, K.E., Vrahatis, M.N.: Recent approaches to global optimization problems through particle swarm optimization. Nat. Comput. **1**(2–3), 235–306 (2002)
15. Bard, J.F.: Practical Bilevel Optimization. Norwell, Kluwer, MA (1998)
16. Dempe, S.: Foundations of Bilevel Programming. Springer, Heidelberg (2002)

Damage Detection of Fixed-Fixed Beam: A Fuzzy Neuro Hybrid System Based Approach

Deepak K. Agarwalla[✉], Amiya K. Dash,
Sambit K. Bhuyan, and P.S.K. Nayak

Department of Mechanical Engineering, Institute of Technical Education
and Research, Siksha 'O' Anusandhan University, Bhubaneswar, Odisha, India
deepakagarwalla@soauniversity.ac.in

Abstract. Integration of Neural Networks (NN) and Fuzzy Logic (FL) have brought researchers from various scientific and engineering domains for the need of developing adaptive intelligent systems to address real time applications. The integration of NN and FL can be classified broadly into three categories namely concurrent model, cooperative model and fully fused model. In the present analysis, fuzzy logic and neural network have been adopted to form a damage identification tool for structural health monitoring for fixed-fixed beam made of steel. The proposed methodology utilizes the modal characteristics of the fixed-fixed beam structure using numerical modeling techniques and anticipates the position and severities of the damage present in the system. The robustness of the proposed technique has been realized by conducting experiments on the steel fixed-fixed beam with different damage characteristics.

Keywords: Neural networks · Fuzzy logic · Fixed-fixed beam · Damage experiment

Nomenclature

a_1	= depth of damage
A	= cross-sectional area of the beam
$A_{i\ (i\ =\ 1\ to\ 18)}$	= unknown coefficients of matrix A
B	= width of the beam
C_{11}	= Axial compliance
$C_{12} = C_{21}$	= Coupled axial and bending compliance
C_{22}	= Bending compliance
$\overline{C}_{11}$	= Dimensionless form of C11
$\overline{C}_{12} = \overline{C}_{21}$	= Dimensionless form of C12 = C21
$\overline{C}_{22}$	= Dimensionless form of C22
$\bar{C}_{12}$	= Axial compliance for damage position
$\bar{C}_{12} = \bar{C}_{21}$	= Coupled axial and bending compliance for damage position
$\bar{C}_{22}$	= Bending compliance for damage position
E	= young's modulus of elasticity of the beam material
$F_{i\ (i\ =\ 1,\ 2)}$	= experimentally determined function
i, j	= variables

© Springer International Publishing Switzerland 2015
B.K. Panigrahi et al. (Eds.): SEMCCO 2014, LNCS 8947, pp. 363–372, 2015.
DOI: 10.1007/978-3-319-20294-5_32

J	= strain-energy release rate
$K_{1,i\ (i=1,2)}$	= stress intensity factors for P_i loads
K_{ij}	= local flexibility matrix elements
$K'n$	= Stiffness matrix for damage position
L	= length of the beam
L_1	= location (length) of the damage from fixed end
$P_{i\ (i=1,2)}$	= axial force (i = 1), bending moment (i = 2)
$u_{i\ (i=1,2)}$	= normal functions (longitudinal) $u_i(x)$
x	= co-ordinate of the beam
y	= co-ordinate of the beam
$y_{i\ (i=1,2)}$	= normal functions (transverse) $y_i(x)$
W	= depth of the beam
ω	= natural circular frequency
β_1	= relative damage location (L_1/L)
ρ	= mass-density of the beam

1 Introduction

Most of the structural failures encountered are caused by material fatigue and presence of damages in structures. Therefore, damages of any form are to be diagnosed as earliest as possible to maintain the integrity of the structures. In spite of the existence so many traditional methods, but presence of any damage can't be ensured without diagnosing the entire structure. Fuzzy-Neuro hybrid computing technique is a potential tool for solving problems with complexity. If the parameters representing a system can be expressed in terms linguistic rules, a fuzzy inference system can be build up. A neural network can be built, if data required for training from simulations are available. From the analysis of NN and FL it is observed that drawbacks of the two methods are complementary and therefore it is desirable to build an integrated system combining the two techniques. The learning capability is an advantage for NN, while the formation of linguistic rule base is an advantage for fuzzy logic. Hence, the hybrid fuzzy-neuro technique can be used for identifying cracks present in a structural system using vibration data. Meesad and Yen have proposed an innovative neuro fuzzy for pattern classification application, specially for vibration monitoring. To handle imprecise information they have incorporated a fuzzy set into the network design. The neuro fuzzy classifier proposed has been equipped with a one pass, on-line and incremental learning algorithm. They have classified the neuro fuzzy network on the basis of fisher's Iris data. The neuro fuzzy network has been achieved 97.33 % correct classification. But after they have used the west-land data set which consists of vibration data collected from a US Navy CH-46E helicopter for better classification. By using various torque levels they have achieved 100 % correct classification. Far et al. have experimented on model based fault detection and isolation of a U-tube steam generator in a nuclear power plant. They have used two types of Neuro Fuzzy networks. They have considered Takagi-Sugeno (TS) fuzzy model for residual generation and Mamdani model for residual evaluation. They have used locally linear neuro fuzzy (LLNF) model which has been trained by the locally linear model tree (LOLIMOT) algorithm. From the experiment they have concluded that a qualitative description of faults has been extracted from the fuzzy rules obtained from the Mamdani. Zhu et al. have came up with an integrated approach for structural damage identification Wavelet neuro fuzzy model. With the wavelet transform (WT) algorithm filtering random noise (ANFIS) has been found to model the structural behavior properly and interval modeling technique to quantify damage index accurately. Finally they have concluded from the results and some other signal processing methods that the proposed method can be used to identify both the time and location when the structural damage occurs unexpectedly. Nguyen et al. have presented a new beam damage locating (BDL) method based on an algorithm. The algorithm has made by the combination of an adaptive fuzzy neural structure (AFNS) and an average quantity solution to wavelet transform coefficient (AQWTC) of beam vibration signal. AFNS has been used for remembering undamaged beam dynamic properties and AQWTC has been used for signal analysis. The experiment has done by divide the beam into two elements. From the experiment they have concluded that the effectiveness of the approach which combined fuzzy neural structure and wavelet transform method has been demonstrated. Ayoubi and Isermann have described about knowledge based fault detection and diagnosis from the analytic and heuristic symptom generation to diagnostic reasoning. They have investigated on undetermined parameters just as membership functions, relevance weights of antecedents and priority factor of rules. Finally they have came up with an application of the neuro fuzzy system to the on-line monitoring of air pressure in vehicle wheels. Subbaraj and Kannapiran have discussed on the design and development of Adaptive Neuro Fuzzy Inference System (ANFIS) based fault detection and diagnosis of pneumatic valve used in cooled water spray system in cement industry. The performance of the developed ANFIS model has been compared with Multilayer Feed Forward Neural Network (MLFFNN) trained by the back propagation algorithm. From the simulation result they have found that ANFIS performed better than ANN. Chen et al. have researched on fault detection and diagnosis methods for railway track circuits using neuro fuzzy systems. Fault detection and diagnosis system has been combined the benefits of both fuzzy logic and neural networks. They have shown in the experiment that the proposed method correctly detects and diagnosis the most commonly occurring track circuit failures in a laboratory test rig of one type of audio frequency joint less track circuit. Chen et al. have researched on fault detection and diagnosis methods for railway track circuits. The neuro fuzzy system method has the potential to detect and diagnose the most commonly occurring track circuit failures. They have shown its ability to detect and locate a fault when it occurs, and to predict incipient failures. Zio and Gola have investigated a neuro fuzzy technique for fault diagnosis and its application to rotating machinery. The fault diagnostic problem has been tackled with a neuro fuzzy approach to pattern classification. From the experiment they have verified the efficiency of the approach with respect to a literature problem and then applied to a case of motor bearing fault classification. Salahshoor et al. have conducted preliminary set of conceptual and experimental studies to realize fault categorization scheme. They have configured a proper selection of four measured variables to feed each ANFIS classifier with the most influential diagnostic information system, facilitating the training and testing phases. They have carried out to illustrate the successful diagnostic performances of the proposed FDD system against 12 major faults. Salahshoor et al. have presented a new FDD scheme for condition machinery of an industrial steam turbine using a data fusion. Fusion of a support vector machine (SVM) classifier, integrated into a common framework has been utilized to enhance the fault detection and diagnostic tasks. From this study they have found that the resulting fusion based scheme outperforms the individual SVM and ANFIS systems to detect and diagnose incipient steam turbine faults. Sadeghian and Fatehi have experimented on identification, prediction and detection of the process fault in a cement rotary kiln by locally linear neuro fuzzy technique. The model has been trained by LOLIMOT algorithm based on the tree structure algorithm. Then they have done their experiment by taking 3 models. At the end they have detected faults in validation data. Jiang et al. have proposed a novel two stage structural damage detection approach using fuzzy neural networks (FNNs) and data fusion techniques for structural health monitoring and damage detection. The final fusion decision has been made by filtering the resulting the result with superior reliability. Final they have shown that the identification accuracy can be boosted with the proposed approach instead of FNN models alone. Palmero et al. have introduced a system for detection and classification in AC motors by a neuro fuzzy ART-based system. The system has been tested on an AC motor in which 15 nondestructive fault types generated. They have found that the system has been extracted by a fuzzy rule set with an acceptable degree of interpret ability and without in-coherency, among the extracted rules. Korbicz and Kowal have researched on the problems and tackled to solve the problem of robust fault detection using Takagi-Sugeno neuro fuzzy (N-F) models. They have used the threshold technique to deal with the problems. The proposed algorithms have been applied to fault detection in a valve. They have shown the results of effectiveness of the method experimentally. From the above mentioned literature review, it has been observed that damage diagnosis of structures using hybrid artificial intelligence (AI) technique has not been used extensively. In the current analysis, the fuzzy-neuro hybrid system has served as the back bone of damage diagnostic tool.

2   Numerical Modeling

Figure 1 illustrate fixed-fixed beam, subjected to axial load (P_1) and bending moment (P_2), which effectuate combining effect in terms of longitudinal and transverse motion of the beam respectively. The beams contain damage in transverse direction of depth 'a_1' having width 'B' and thickness 'W'. The existence of damage in the beam structure modifies the localized flexibility square matrix of two dimensions.

At the damaged portion, strain energy release rate can be explained as [16];

$$J = \frac{1}{E'}(K_{I1} + K_{I2})^2, \text{ Where } \frac{1}{E'} = \frac{1 - \nu^2}{E} \text{ (for plane strain condition)};$$

$$= \frac{1}{E} \text{ (for plane stress condition)}$$

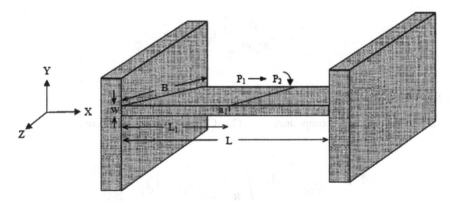

Fig. 1. Fixed- fixed beam with axial and bending load

The K_{11}, K_{12} are Stress intensity factors for 1st mode of vibration for load P_1 and P_2 respectively. The values of stress intensity factors from the referred article [16] are;

$$\frac{P_1}{WB}\sqrt{\pi a}(F_1(\frac{a}{W})) = K_{11}, \quad \frac{6P_2}{W^2B}\sqrt{\pi a}(F_2(\frac{a}{W})) = K_{12}$$

The expressions for F_1 and F_2 are as follows,

$$\left.\begin{array}{l} F_1(\frac{a}{W}) = (\frac{2W}{\pi a}\tan(\frac{\pi a}{2W}))^{0.5}\left\{\dfrac{0.752 + 2.02\,(a/W) + 0.37\,(1-\sin(a\pi/2W))^3}{\cos(a\pi/2W)}\right\} \\[4mm] F_2(\frac{a}{W}) = (\frac{2W}{\pi a}\tan(\frac{\pi a}{2W}))^{0.5}\left\{\dfrac{0.923 + 0.199\,(1-\sin(a\pi/2W))^4}{\cos(a\pi/2W)}\right\} \end{array}\right\}$$

According to Castigliano's theorem (Taking the assumption, strain energy due to the damage as U_t) the extra extension along the force P_i is;

$$\frac{\partial U_t}{\partial P_i} = u_i$$

The form of strain energy will have, $U_t = \int\limits_0^{a_1} J\,da = \int\limits_0^{a_1} \frac{\partial U_t}{\partial a}\,da$

Where $J = \frac{\partial U_t}{\partial a}$ the strain energy density function. Hence, from equations mentioned above, we can have

$$\frac{\partial}{\partial P_i}\left[\int\limits_0^{a_1} J(a)\,da\right] = u_i$$

C_{ij} the flexibility influence co-efficient by definition is

$$\frac{\partial u_i}{\partial P_j} = \frac{\partial^2}{\partial P_j \partial P_i} \int_0^{a_1} J(a)\, da = C_{ij}$$

and can be expressed as, $\dfrac{WB}{E'} \dfrac{\partial^2}{\partial P_j \partial P_i} \int_0^{\xi_1} (K_{12} + K_{11})^2\, d\xi = C_{ij}$

Using Eq. (3.8) the compliance C_{11}, C_{22}, C_{12} (= C_{21}) are as follows;

$$C_{11} = \frac{BW}{E'} \int_0^{\xi_1} \frac{\pi a}{B^2 W^2}\, 2(F_1(\xi))^2\, d\xi$$

$$= \frac{2\pi}{BE'} \int_0^{\xi_1} \xi (F_1(\xi))^2\, d\xi$$

$$C_{22} = \frac{72\pi}{E'BW^2} \int_0^{\xi_1} \xi F_2(\xi) F_2(\xi)\, d\xi$$

The dimensionless form of the influence co-efficient will be;

$$\overline{C_{11}} = C_{11} \frac{BE'}{2\pi}\; \overline{C_{12}} = C_{12} \frac{E'BW}{12\pi} = \overline{C_{21}}\,;\, \overline{C_{22}} = C_{22} \frac{E'BW^2}{72\pi}$$

The inversion of compliance matrix will lead to the formation of local stiffness matrix and can be written as;

$$K = \begin{bmatrix} C_{11} & C_{12} \\ C_{21} & C_{22} \end{bmatrix}^{-1} = \begin{bmatrix} K_{11} & K_{12} \\ K_{21} & K_{22} \end{bmatrix}$$

The stiffness matrix for the damage position can be obtained as follows:

$$K' = \begin{bmatrix} k'_{11} & k'_{12} \\ k'_{21} & k'_{22} \end{bmatrix} = \begin{bmatrix} C'_{11} & C'_{12} \\ C'_{21} & C'_{22} \end{bmatrix}^{-1}$$

The stiffness matrix obtained from the above analysis has been used to estimate the modal parameters of the fixed-fixed beam and subsequently used as the input to the fuzzy-neuro hybrid system for damage detection. The material properties of steel such as Young's modulus (200 GPa), density (7850 m^3/Kg) and Poisson's ratio (0.30) have been introduced to solve the stiffness matrix.

3   Fuzzy-Neuro Hybrid Controller for Damage Detection

This section introduces a hybrid intelligent method for prediction of damage positions and their severities in a fixed-fixed beam structure having a transverse damage using inverse analysis. As the presence of damage alters the dynamic behavior of the beam, the first three relative natural frequencies and first three average relative mode shape differences of the damaged and intact beam for different damage positions and severities are calculated using numerical. The calculated modal frequencies, mode shapes, relative damage positions (RDP) and relative damage severities (RDS) are used to design the fuzzy neural controller. The measured vibration signatures are used as inputs to the fuzzy segment of the hybrid controller and initial relative damage position and severity are the output parameters. The first three relative natural frequencies, first three average relative mode shape difference and the output from the fuzzy controller are used as inputs to the neural part of the hybrid controller and final damage position and severity are the output parameters. The measured vibration signatures are used to formulate series of fuzzy rules and training patterns for the fuzzy and neural controller. Out of numerous damage characteristics such as RDP and RDS, only ten damage scenarios are shown in the Table 1. Finally, the validation of the proposed method is carried out dynamically by means of experimental results from the developed experimental setup with same damage characteristics to that of the proposed model. The fuzzy segment of the hybrid controller for damage detection has been developed using Gaussian membership function. The Gaussian membership function based hybrid controller is shown in Fig. 2. The results obtained from the proposed technique have been presented in Table 1.

$$RDS = \frac{\text{Depth of the damage in the beam}}{\text{Thickness of the beam}}$$

$$RDP = \frac{\text{Position of the damage from one fixed end}}{\text{Length of the beam}}$$

Table 1. Comparison of results obtained from gaussian fuzzy-neuro controller and experimental analysis

Relative first natural frequency "FNF"	Relative second natural frequency "SNF"	Relative third natural frequency "TNF"	Average relative first mode shape difference "FMD"	Average relative second mode shape difference "SMD"	Average relative third mode shape difference "TMD"	Gaussian Fuzzy-neuro result		Experimental result	
						RDS	RDP	RDS	RDP
0.9979	0.9985	0.9993	0.0087	0.0036	0 0041	0.460	0.122	0.465	0.123
0.9962	0.9989	0.9991	0.0036	0.9729	0.2263	0.413	0.121	0.423	0.127
0.9936	0.9976	0.9987	0.0138	0.014	0.0832	0.167	0.373	0.167	0.378
0.9976	0.9991	0.9988	0.0014	0.0041	0.0812	0.335	0.125	0.342	0.127
0.997S	0.9983	0.9878	0.0036	0.0319	0.0141	0.174	0.243	0.171	0.250
0.9987	0.9972	0.9981	0.2936	0.3428	0.2623	0.223	0.270	0.130	0.280
0.9S49	0.9982	0.9869	0.0134	0.0211	0.0119	0.414	0.373	0.421	0.372
0.99S9	0.9973	0.9974	0.0017	0.0025	0.0079	0.467	0.248	0.482	0.270
0.9977	0.9847	0.9881	0.00 "9	0.0077	0.0291	0.337	0.374	0.341	0.378
0.99SS	0.9974	0.9991	0.0057	0.0013	0.0155	0.423	0.283	0.419	0.290

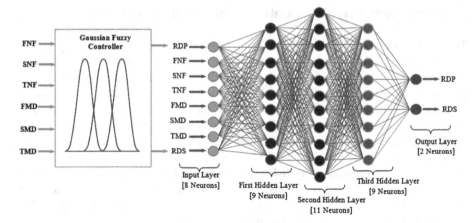

Fig. 2. Fuzzy-neuro hybrid controller for damage detection

4   Experimental Set-up

Different Experiments have been conducted using the experimental set up (Fig. 3) for measuring the vibration signatures (natural frequencies and amplitude of vibration) of the fixed-fixed beams specimens made from steel with dimension 1000 mm × 50 mm × 8 mm. The damaged and undamaged beams have been subjected to vibration with 1st, 2nd and 3rd mode of vibration by utilizing an exciter and a function generator. The dynamic characteristics of the beams have been recorded by placing the accelerometer along the length of the beams. The output obtained from the accelerometer in terms of natural frequencies and mode shapes are monitored on the vibration indicator.

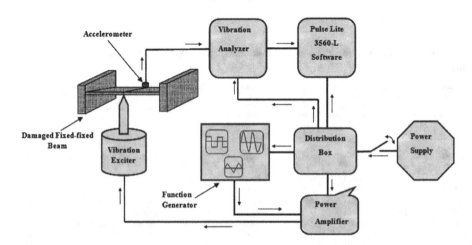

Fig. 3. Schematic diagram experimental setup with fixed-fixed beam

5 Results and Discussion

The results obtained from the fuzzy-neuro controller and the experimental analyses have been presented in Table 1.

The first three columns and the next three columns of the Table 1 depict the first three relative natural frequencies and first three average relative mode shape differences respectively. The fuzzy-neuro hybrid controller for the damage detection is illustrated by Fig. 2. The RDS and RDP values obtained from fuzzy-neuro hybrid controller are very close to the values obtained from experimental analysis. The percentages of deviations in the RDS and RDP are 2.8 % and 3.2 % respectively.

6 Conclusions

The damage diagnostic tool i.e. Fuzzy-Neuro Hybrid Controller with Gaussian membership function developed for the steel fixed-fixed beam has been found to be a significant tool for inherent damage detection. The results found from this controller have been validated by the experimental results with remarkable convergence. This damage detection technique can be used for various mechanical beam structures with different boundary conditions. However, the damage detection tool can also be used effectively for beams of different material.

References

1. Meesad, P., Yen, G.G.: Pattern classification by a neurofuzzy network: application to vibration monitoring. ISA Trans. 39(3), 293–308 (2000)
2. Lucas, C., Far, R.R., Davilu, H., Palade, V.: Model-based fault detection and isolation of a steam generator using neuro-fuzzy networks. Neurocomputing 72(13–15), 2939–2951 (2009)
3. Zhu, F., Deng, Z., Zhang, J.: An integrated approach for structural damage identification using wavelet neuro-fuzzy model. Expert Syst. Appl. 40(18), 7415–7427 (2013)
4. Nguyen, S.D., Ngo, K.N., Tran, Q.T., Choi, S.B.: A new method for beam-damage-diagnosis using adaptive fuzzy neural structure and wavelet analysis. Mech. Syst. Signal Process. 39(1–2), 181–194 (2013)
5. Ayoub, M., Isermann, R.: Neuro-fuzzy systems for diagnosis. Fuzzy Sets Syst. 89(3), 289–307 (1997)
6. Subbaraj, P., Kannapiran, B.: Fault detection and diagnosis of pneumatic valve using adaptive neuro-fuzzy inference system approach. Appl. Soft Comput. 19, 362–371 (2014)
7. Chen, J., Roberts, C., Weston, P.: Fault detection and diagnosis for railway track circuits using neuro-fuzzy systems. Control Eng. Pract. 16(5), 585–596 (2008)
8. Chen, J., Robertsx, C., Weston, P.: Neuro-fuzzy fault detection and diagnosis for railway track circuits. In: Fault Detection, Supervision and Safety of Technical Processes 2006, vol. 2, pp. 1366-1371 (2007)
9. Zio, E., Gola, G.: A neuro-fuzzy technique for fault diagnosis and its application to rotating machinery. Reliab. Eng. Syst. Saf. 94(1), 78–88 (2009)

10. Salahshoor, K., Khoshro, M.S., Kordestani, M.: Fault detection and diagnosis of an industrial steam turbine using a distributed configuration of adaptive neuro-fuzzy inference systems. Simul. Model. Pract. Theory **19**(5), 1280–1293 (2011)
11. Salahshoor, K., Kordestani, M., Khoshro, M.S.: Fault detection and diagnosis of an industrial steam turbine using fusion Of SVM (support vector machine) and ANFIS (adaptive neuro-fuzzy inference system) classifiers. Energy **35**(12), 5472–5482 (2010)
12. Sadeghian, M., Fatehi, A.: Identification prediction and detection of the process fault in a cement rotary kiln by locally linear neuro-fuzzy technique. J. Process Control **21**(2), 302–308 (2011)
13. Jiang, S.F., Zhang, C.M., Zhang, S.: Two-stage structural damage detection using fuzzy neural networks and data fusion techniques. Expert Syst. Appl. **38**(1), 511–519 (2011)
14. Palmero, G.I.S., Santamaria, J.J., de la Torre, E.J.M., Gonzalez, J.R.P.: Fault detection and fuzzy rule extraction in ac motors by a neuro-fuzzy art-based system. Eng. Appl. Artif. Intell. **18**(7), 867–874 (2005)
15. Korbicz, J., Kowal, M.: Neuro-fuzzy networks and their application to fault detection of dynamical systems. Eng. Appl. Artif. Intell. **20**(5), 609–617 (2007)
16. Tada, H., Paris, P.C., Irwin, G.R.: The Stress Analysis of Cracks Hand Book. Del Research Corp, Hellertown, Pennsylvania (1973)

Neuro Fuzzy Load Frequency Control
in a Competitive Electricity Market
Using BFOA Tuned SMES and TCPS

M. Bhavani[1](✉), K. Selvi[2], and L. Sindhumathi[2]

[1] Department of Electrical and Electronics Engineering, Anna University
Regional Office Madurai, Madurai, Tamilnadu, India
mbeee@autmdu.ac.in
[2] Department of Electrical and Electronics Engineering,
Thiagarajar College of Engineering, Madurai, Tamilnadu, India
kseee@tce.edu, sndhmathi@gmail.com

Abstract. This paper addresses the design of Load frequency control in a competitive electricity market with a practical viewpoint. The restructure of vertically integrated power system into unbundled power system components as led to the emergence of new companies for Generation, transmission and Distribution of power. The conventional two-area power system is modified to study the effects of the bilateral contracts of companies on the system dynamics. Load frequency control is used to minimize the frequency oscillations and tie line power deviations. To stabilize the frequency oscillations Superconducting Magnetic Energy Storage device (SMES) is connected at the terminal side of a area and Thyristor Controlled Phase Shifter (TCPS) connected in series with the tie line. The parameters of SMES and TCPS were optimized using Bacterial Foraging Optimization Algorithm (BFOA). This paper uses Artificial Neuro Fuzzy Inference System (ANFIS) control and the results are compared with the conventional integral controller.

Keywords: Frequency regulation · SMES · TCPS · ANFIS

1 Introduction

Load frequency control plays very prime role in the satisfactory operation of Generators that are running parallel. Whenever there is a change in demand or supply power system operation is getting affected and therefore it must always be controlled in order to maintain the frequency to its nominal value and control the un-contracted power flow through the tie-lines that are connecting the areas. In this paper all hydro restructured power system has been considered and it is evident that the load frequency control had been never possible after step load change in all hydropower system. To overcome this, the concept of power electronic devices [1] was utilized in this paper. Thyristor controlled phase shifter (TCPS) and Superconducting Magnetic Energy Storage (SMES) Device are the power electronic devices that were connected in series with tie-lines and at the end of each area respectively. The parameters of these devices are tuned using Bacterial Foraging Optimization Algorithm [2]. Many types of

© Springer International Publishing Switzerland 2015
B.K. Panigrahi et al. (Eds.): SEMCCO 2014, LNCS 8947, pp. 373–385, 2015.
DOI: 10.1007/978-3-319-20294-5_33

controllers have been tested in two area restructured power system to regain stability of the system after some disturbance. Different types of controller such as integral controller, PI controller, PID controller have been applied to this problem and from the results it is concluded that integral controller's results are more favorable compared to other controllers. Hence in this paper integral controller is employed initially and an ANFIS controller [3] is designed with the data of Integral controller and the results were found to be desirable compared to the performance of integral controller.

In the restructured electricity market the power system will be divided into different companies for business purpose such as Generation Companies (GENCOs), Distribution Companies (DISCOs), Transmission Companies (TRANCOs) and system operator (SO). SO is responsible for stable operation of power system and it also has to provide number of ancillary services. One of its services is the frequency regulation. SO is responsible for the contracts between GENCOs and DISCOs. DISCOs may contract individually with GENCOs based on their contracts or through different types of transactions such as Pool-co based transaction, bilateral transaction and the combination of above two. In this paper we have considered both Pool-co based transactions and bilateral transaction contracts separately based on hydro generating units.

The main objective of the present work is:

- To develop simulink model of two areas hydro-hydro restructured power system.
- To develop the model of SMES and TCPS.
- To optimize the parameters of SMES and TCPS through Bacterial Foraging Optimization Algorithm (BFOA).
- To replace integral controller with Neuro-Fuzzy Controller and compare their performance in damping frequency oscillations.
- To compare the performance of SMES-TCPS co-ordination and SMES-SMES co-ordination in maintaining the system stability.

2 Implementation of LFC in a Competitive Electricity Market

The system consists of two area hydro power system. Both area 1 and 2 comprises of two GENCOs and two DISCOs respectively. System parameters are mentioned in Appendix. The simulink diagram of the sample system is shown in Fig. 1. Based on different contract GENCOs will supply power to DISCOs. In order to check the stability of system after a small disturbance, a step change (ΔP_D) of 10 % is introduced in area 1(ΔP_D). It is also assumed violation of contract between GENCOs and DISCOs about 5.0 % step change (ΔP_L).

The contract between GENCOs and DISCOs [4] is easily visualized through DISCO Participation Matrix (DPM) with contract participation factor as shown below.

$$\text{DPM} = \begin{pmatrix} cpf_{11} & \cdots & cpf_{1m} \\ \vdots & \ddots & \vdots \\ cpf_{n1} & \cdots & cpf_{nm} \end{pmatrix} \tag{1}$$

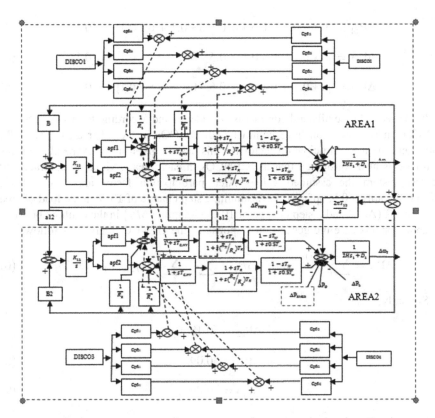

Fig. 1. Simulink model for two area hydro-hydro restructured power system with SMES and TCPS

2.1   Case Studies Carried Out

The system is investigated for two different cases such as pool-co based contract, and bilateral contract. In the first case since it is pool-co based contract the GENCOs in area 1 will have contract only with the DISCOs within that area and similarly GENCOs in area 2 will have contract only with the DISCOs in that area. In the second case bilateral contract violation in contract is considered.

For a two area power system, the contracted power delivered by i^{th} GENCO is given by $\Delta P_{gi} = \sum_{j=1}^{DISCOS=4} cpf_{ij}\Delta P_{Lj}$. The step change of 10 % in the load of area 1 and area 2 with the cpf values as given in the Appendix for the poolco based contract results in the power generation response in each GENCO as below:

$$\Delta P_{g1} = [0.5 * \Delta P_d + 0.5 * \Delta P_d + 0 * \Delta P_d + 0 * \Delta P_d] = [0.1] \qquad (2)$$

Similarly,

$$\Delta P_{g2} = [0.5 * 0.1 + 0.5 * 0.1 + 0 * 0.1 + 0 * 0.1] = [0.1] \tag{3}$$

$$\Delta P_{g3} = [0 * 0.1 + 0 * 0.1 + 0.5 * 0.1 + 0.5 * 0.1] = [0.1] \tag{4}$$

$$\Delta P_{g4} = [0 * 0.1 + 0 * 0.1 + 0.5 * 0.1 + 0.5 * 0.1] = [0.1] \tag{5}$$

In the second case bilateral contract is considered and according to this contract the GENCOs in one area can have contract with DISCOs in the other area. The DPM matrix and the area participation factor for this case is given in the Appendix. In this contract it is also considered that the GENCOs in each area is violating contract. For the test system the assumed values Area participation factor are $apf_1 = 0.75$, $apf_2 = 0.25$, $apf_3 = 0.5$, $apf_4 = 0.5$. Assuming a step change of 10 % in the load of area 1 and area 2 (ΔP_D) and a step change of 10 % violation (ΔP_L) in the contract between the areas for this case the generation response of the GENCO is given as follows,

$$\Delta P_{g1} = \sum_{j=1}^{DISCO=4} cpf_{1j} * \Delta P_D + \sum_{i=1}^{2} \sum_{j=1}^{2} apf_{ij} \Delta P_L = [0.23] \tag{6}$$

Similarly,

$$\Delta P_{g2} = [0.18] \tag{7}$$

$$\Delta P_{g3} = [0.09] \tag{8}$$

$$\Delta P_{g4} = [0.09] \tag{9}$$

From the Fig. 2 it is found that frequency oscillation is uncontrolled and system never gets stabled. So that, to bring the system stable we are connecting TCPS and SMES in the way mentioned earlier.

3   Mathematical Modeling of Power Electronic Components

3.1   Modeling of TCPS

Any signal such as the area frequency deviation Δf or area control of the system is given as input signal to TCPS. By controlling the phase shifter angle $\Delta\emptyset(s)$ of the

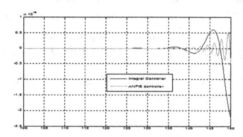

Fig. 2. Area frequency response of both the areas under uncontrolled case with 10 % step change in demand

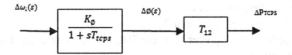

Fig. 3. Transfer function model of TCPS

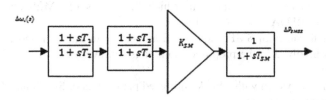

Fig. 4. Transfer function model of SMES

TCPS, tie-line power flow is controlled. TCPS is connected in series with the tie-line (Fig. 3). Detailed mo-deling of TCPS is given in [5].

Where,

$K_\emptyset$ is the gain of the TCPS controller

T_{tcps} is the time constant of TCPS controller

3.2   Modeling of SMES

In this work change in frequency is given as input signal to the SMES and this power electronic device acts as a frequency stabilizer. It will be connected at the end of each area (Fig. 4). Detailed modeling SMES is given in [5].

K_{SM} is the gain of the controlled loop

T_{SM} is the converter time delay

T_1, T_2, T_3, T_4 is to provide phase lead characteristics to compensate for phase lag between input and output signal.

4   Problem Formulation

4.1   Objective Function

The objective function is to re-establish the frequency regulation, that is to bring the frequency to its nominal value and to minimize tie-line power flow oscillations is defined as Figure of Demerit (FDM)

$$\text{FDM} = \sum \left[\Delta F_1^2 + \Delta F_2^2 + \Delta P_{\text{tie}}^2 \right] \Delta T \tag{10}$$

ΔF_1 is change in frequency in area 1

ΔF_2 is change in frequency in area 2

ΔP_{tie} is change in tie line power flow oscillations between control areas.

ΔT is the time interval.

The above objective function is minimized with the help of Bacterial Foraging based optimization Technique. The AGC system with integral controller and power electronic components is simulated in which the values of SMES and TCPS are optimized using BFOA as shown in Fig. 5.

The optimal values of SMES and TCPS are shown in Tables 1 and 2.

The steps involved in the proposed work is as follows:

Step 1:   Start.

Step 2:   Run the system with BFOA optimized parameters of SMES and TCPS using integral controller.

Step 3:   Give the area control error and change in area control error from the system with integral controller as input to ANFIS editor.

Step 4:   After training and testing the data, update system using ANFIS output.

Step 5:   Stop.

4.2   Bacterial Foraging Optimization Technique

The survival of species in the evolutionary processes depends upon their food searching behaviour. The law of evolution support those species with good food searching ability and eliminates that with poor one. The foraging stratergy of E.coli bacteria is inspired by

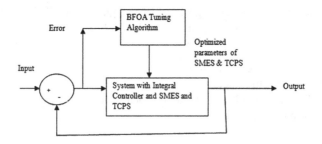

Fig. 5. Optimization of parameters using BFOA

Table 1. Optimized parameters of SMES using BFOA

Parameters	T_1	T_2	T_3	T_4	K_{sm}	T_{sm}
Values	0.1449	0.083	0.690	0.111	0.0277	0.0868

Table 2. Optimized parameters of TCPS using BFOA

Parameters	K_{TCPS}	T_{TCPS}
Values	0.1164	0.0864

Passino and thus developed BFOA which is now widely accepted as global optimization algorithm. The foraging of E.coli bacteria can explained in four different stages as chemotaxis, swarming, reproduction and elimination and dispersal [1]

The parameters initialized for run are: number of chemotactic steps (N_c), number of reproduction steps (N_{re}), number of elimiation and dispersal steps (N_{ed}), dispersal probability (P_{ed}), number of bacteria (N) & swim length (N_s). An E.coli can move in different ways: a run shows movement in a particular directions whereas a 'tumble' denotes change in direction. A tumble is represented by:

$$\theta^i(j+1,k,l) = \theta^i(j,k,l) + \varphi(j) \tag{11}$$

Where $\theta(j,k,l)$ represents ith bacterium in jth chemo-tactic, kth reproductive, lth elimination-dispersal step $v(i)$ gives the step length and $\varphi(j)$ is a unit length random direction. At the end of specified chemo-tactic steps, the bacterium is evaluated and sorted in descending order of fitness. In the process of reproduction, the first half of the bacterium is retained and duplicated while the other half is eliminated. Finally bacteria are dispersed as per elimination and dispersal probability which helps in fastening the process of optimization.

In case of BFO technique each bacterium is assigned with a set of variable to be optimized and is assigned with random values within the universe of discourse defined through upper and lower limits between which the optimal value is likely to fall. In the proposed method of optimizing the parameters of SMES and TCPS, each bacterium is allowed to take all possible values within the range and the Figure of Demerit as given by Eq. (10) is minimized. The steps involved are as given below:

Step – 1 Initialization

1. Number of parameter (P) to be optimized.
2. Number of bacterial (S) to be used for searching the total region.
3. Swimming length (N_s), after which the tumbling of bacteria will be undertaken in a chemotactic loop.
4. N_c: the number of iteration to be undertaken in a chemotactic loop ($N_c > N_s$).
5. N_{re}: the maximum number of reproduction to be undertaken.
6. N_{ed}: the maximum number of elimination and dispersal events to be imposed over bacteria.
7. P_{ed}: the probability with which the elimination and dispersal events will continue.

In this work, the initialized variables are P = 9, S = 20, N_c = 10, N_s = 4, N_{re} = 10, N_{ed} = 2, P_{ed} = 0.25.

Step – 2 Iterative algorithms for optimization:

This section involved the bacterial population chemotaxis, Swarming, reproduction, elimination and dispersal (initially $j = k = l = 0$) for the algorithm updating θ^i automatically results in updating of parameter 'P'.

1. Elimination dispersal loop: $l = l + 1$.
2. Reproduction loop: $k = k + 1$.
3. Chemotaxis loop: $j = j + 1$.

   a. For i = 1,2…S, calculate cost for each bacterium i.

   b. For i = 1,2…S, take the tumbling/swimming direction.

   c. Go to next bacterium *(i + 1)* if *i ≠ S*, go to step-b to process next bacterium.

4. If *j < Nc*, go to step 3, In this case, chemotaxis is continued since the life of the bacteria is not over.

5. If k < Nre go to step 2, as the number of reproduction steps have not been reached.

6. Elimination and dispersal: for I = 1,2…S with probability Ped, eliminates and disperse each bacterium to a random location on the optimization domain.

4.3   Neuro Fuzzy Controller

Fuzzy Logic control is accepted world-wide and Fuzzy Logic is an excellent alternative to conventional controller. Because of the complexity of the power system conventional controller not able to provide satisfactory solutions so that Neuro-Fuzzy controller is used in place of conventional controller. We may use fuzzy logic controller but the major problem in the fuzzy logic controller is constructing rule base is tedious and time consuming. So we will use neural network to construct rules. ANFIS consists of five functional block, a rule base that comprise of number of fuzzy if-then rules, a database to define the membership function of fuzzy sets in fuzzy rules, a decision making for the inference operation, a fuzzification to transform crisp input to linguistic values and finally a de-fuzzification unit to convert the fuzzy output to crisp values. The hybrid Neuro-fuzzy controller uses rules or learning algorithm that is obtained by training and testing the input values obtained from integral controller i.e., the rules for the fuzzy logic controller is developed by neural network. In this paper there are two inputs to the ANFIS and they are Area Control Error (ACE) and change in Area Control Error (ΔACE) and output to ANFIS is change in frequency in either area. First these data must be trained and tested. Now ANFIS develop rules according to the trained data. This paper considers the ANFIS structure with first order sugeno model with 25 rules (Fig. 6). Triangular membership function is used for fuzzification. Structure of ANFIS controller is shown in Fig. 7.

4.4   Steps to Design a Neuro Fuzzy Controller

1. Draw simulink model with integral controller and send area control error, change in area control error and change in frequency to workspace after running the simulink.

Fuzzy Logic Controller

Fig. 6. Block diagram of fuzzy Logic controller that is replaced instead of integral controller

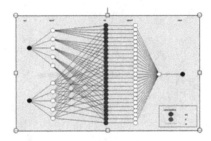

Fig. 7. Structure of ANFIS controller

2. Use anfisedit command to create FIS file.
3. Data that are sent to workspace from simulink model with integral controller gives the training data to ANFIS controller.
4. Generate FIS with triangular membership function and load the data up to particular number of epochs. In this paper data is trained up to 50 epochs.
5. Finally test the data by loading the same data or half of the data that are used for training.
6. Then export the rules to the fuzzy controller that has been replaced instead of integral controller in simulink model.

The architecture and learning algorithm of the adaptive network is given detail in [5]. Main idea of using ANFIS controller is to find out whether it works well along with the SMES and TCPS. The following figure shows the training data and training errors over 50 epochs. From the Fig. 8 it is clear that ANFIS has fitted very well to the data. It is confirmed in the Fig. 9 which shows the result between training data and ANFIS output. From the Figs. 10 and 11 it is evident very well that ANFIS can control the input signal.

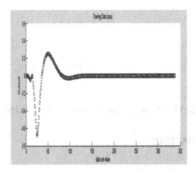

Fig. 8. Training ANFIS controller

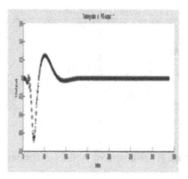

Fig. 9. Training data versus ANFIS output

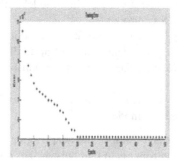

Fig. 10. Training error over 50 epochs

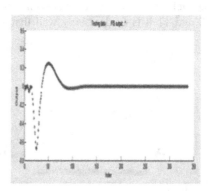

Fig. 11. Testing data versus ANFIS output

5 Results and Discussions

5.1 Case 1: Pool Co Based Contract

In the test system with the parameters of SMES and TCPS tuned using BFOA for a 10 % step load change (ΔP_d), Change in frequency in the two area and tie-line power changes are shown in Figs. 12, 13 and 14. From the result we could find that the oscillations through Neuro-Fuzzy control are reduced to a great extent and overshoot and under-shoot is being effectively reduced when compared to the Integral controller and from Fig. 17 there is no power flow through tie-line since it is a poolco-based contract. In the figure caption a denotes SMES-TCPS with Integral Controller, b denotes SMES – TCPS coordination with ANFIS controller, c denotes SMES-SMES coordination with Integral controller and d denotes SMES-SMES coordination with ANFIS controller.

5.2   Case 2: Bilateral Contract

It has been explained about the concept of bilateral contract and the test system resulted as below for step change in load and also for the violation of contract. In the bilateral contract case, the Disco participation matrix will have non zero participation factor. In this case the scheduled generation values of the GENCOs will be affected by the area participation factor (apf) as given by Eq. (6). For the test system the assumed values of this parameter are $apf_1 = 0.75$, $apf_2 = 0.25$, $apf_3 = 0.5$, $apf_4 = 0.5$. The settling time of

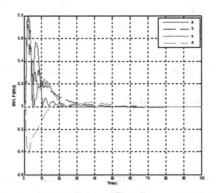

Fig. 12. Case 1- frequency deviations in area 1

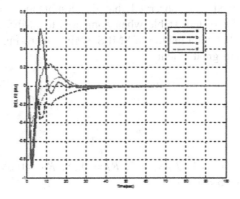

Fig. 13. Case 1 frequency deviations in area 2

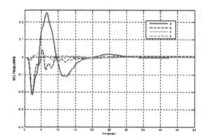

Fig. 14. Case 1- tie line power flows deviations

Table 3. Case 2, settling time of frequency and tie-line power deviations

Parameters	Settling time (seconds)			
	SMES-TCPS coordination		SMES-SMES coordination	
	Integral	ANFIS	Integral	ANFIS
ΔF_1	20	18	18	12
ΔF_2	20	16	18	11
ΔP_{tie12}	50	40	20	18

the frequency deviations in area 1 and area 2 and tie line power deviations for bilateral contract case is shown in Table 3. From the results obtained the neuro fuzzy control is again being effective in bilateral contract too.

6 Conclusions

This paper has investigated the performance of SMES and TCPS in two area hydro-hydro power system under open market scenario. The performance of SMES and TCPS were analyzed for different cases such as Poolco-Based Contract, bilateral contract through two control methods integral control and Neuro-Fuzzy control and from the results obtained it is observed that the combination of SMES-SMES is effective in bringing the system stable when compared to SMES-TCPS combination and also we conclude that combination of SMES-SMES Neuro-Fuzzy control, reduces the objective function to great extent.

Appendix

$$T_{G,Hy}(s) = 0.2, \ T_W(s) = 1, \ T_R(s) = 5, \ R_T = 0.38, \ R_P = 0.05, \ R_1 = 0.4, \ R_2 = 0.4166, \ K_i = 0.09$$

References

1. Singla, H., Kumar, A.: LQR based load frequency control with SMES in deregulated environment. IEEE Trans. Power Syst., ISSN: 978-4673-2272, November 2012
2. Ali, E.S., Abd-Elazim, S.M.: Bacterial foraging optimization algorithm based load frequency controller for interconnected power system. Electr. Power Energy Syst. **33**, 633–638 (2011)
3. Ogbonnal, B., Ndubisi, S.N.: Neural network based load frequency control for restructured power industry. Niger. J. Technol. (NIJOTECH). **31**(1), 40–47 (2012)
4. Sadeh, J., Rakshani, E.: Multi area load frequency control on deregulated power system using optimal output feedback method. IEEE Trans. Power Syst., 978-1-4244-1744-5/08
5. Bhatt, P., Ghoshal, S.P., Roy, R.: Automatic generation control of two area interconnected hydro-hydro restructured power system with TCPS and SMES. ACEEE Int. J. Electr. Power Eng. **1**(2), July 2010

A Fuzzy Entropy Based Multi-Level Image Thresholding Using Differential Evolution

S. Sarkar[1]([⊠]), S. Paul[3], R. Burman[3], S. Das[2], and S.S. Chaudhuri[3]

[1] Department of Electronics and Communication Engineering,
RCC Institute of Information Technology, Kolkata 700015, India
sarkar.soham@gmail.com
[2] Electronics and Communication Sciences Unit,
Indian Statistical Institute, Kolkata 700108, India
swagatamdas19@yahoo.co.in
[3] Department of Electronics and Telecommunication Engineering,
Jadavpur University, Kolkata 700032, India
shelism@rediffmail.com

Abstract. This paper presents a multi-level image thresholding approach based on fuzzy partition of the image histogram and entropy theory. Here a fuzzy entropy based approach is adopted in context to the multi-level image segmentation scenario. This entropy measure is then optimized to obtain the thresholds of the image. In order to solve the optimization problem, a meta-heuristic, Differential Evolution (DE) is used, which leads to a faster and accurate convergence towards the optima. The performance of DE is also measured with respect to some popular global optimization techniques like Particle Swarm Optimization (PSO) and Genetic Algorithms (GAs). The outcomes are compared with Shannon entropy, both visually and statistically in order to establish the perceptible difference in image.

Keywords: Multilevel image segmentation · Fuzzy entropy · Differential evolution · CWSSIM · MSSIM · FSIM · GSM

1 Introduction

Image thresholding, the technique to discriminate objects from its background at pixel level is one of the most important tasks of image analysis. Automatic separation between objects and background remains the most difficult and intriguing domain in the field of image processing and pattern recognition. Scientific literature presents several image segmentation processes, such as gray level thresholding, interactive pixel classification, neural network based approaches, edge detection, and fuzzy based segmentation etc. Comprehensive surveys on such techniques can be found in [1–7].

Gray level global thresholding has been a popular segmentation method. There are many techniques available for this purpose e.g. entropy based global thresholding Kapur *et al.* [8]; Sahoo *et al.* [9]; Pal [10]; Li [11]; Rosin [12]. Further, techniques like Shannon entropy, Renyi's entropy and Tsallis entropy provide the scope for investigating the process of efficient separation of the image between objects and background.

© Springer International Publishing Switzerland 2015
B.K. Panigrahi et al. (Eds.): SEMCCO 2014, LNCS 8947, pp. 386–395, 2015.
DOI: 10.1007/978-3-319-20294-5_34

Image segmentation, done via multilevel thresholding, splits the image into different classes by selecting multiple threshold points. Otsu [13] developed a non-parametric multi-level image segmentation algorithm which was later modified by Kapur *et al.* [8].A majority of the proposed methods for thresholding are histogram dependent and as there are no clear boundary between regions, these histogram based segmented leads to some ambiguity. Luca and Termini [14] tried a modification to solve this problem and introduced a fuzzy partition technique for image segmentation. Bloch examined the applications of fuzzy spatial relationship in image processing and image interpretation area [15]. Although application of fuzzy partition technique in multi-level thresholding scenario remained unattended. Notably, in 2001 Zhao *et al.* [16] first applied a multi-level approach by defining three membership functions for 3-level thresholding i.e. dark, medium and bright. Based on this paper, in 2003 Tao *et al.* [17] proposed a 3-level fuzzy entropy based image segmentation technique, where 3 different membership functions, Z-function, F-function and S-function, were used. The threshold values were obtained by maximizing the total entropy by applying a popular global optimization technique, GA [18]. Both Zhao and Tao show the betterment of results by means of visual comparison, but lacks statistical evaluations. Another important reason of using metaheuristics is to minimize the computational time and complexity of the algorithm as much as possible [16].

To pursue with the present research interest a fuzzy-entropy based multi-level image segmentation process, boosted by Differential Evolution (DE) is proposed in this paper. DE is arguably one of the most powerful real parameter optimizers of current interest [19, 20]. It has been shown that DE can outperform GA and PSO when it is used for multi-level thresholding based image segmentation problems [21, 22]. Extensive simulations have been undertaken to demonstrate the efficiency and robustness of this DE based scheme in comparison with other popular global optimization techniques like GA and PSO in terms of computational time, mean objective value and standard deviation. Results are tested against Shannon's entropy. Both visual and statistical comparison of the segmented images, are provided. Statistical comparison is done via state of art Image Quality Assessment (IQA) metrics.

This paper has been organized as the following: - In Sect. 2 a brief introduction to fuzzy entropy and multi-level fuzzy entropy based on probability partition and its mathematical formulations are presented. Following this Differential Evolution is being discussed in Sect. 3. In Sect. 4, the test findings of our proposed method are presented along with their statistical analysis. Finally, Sect. 5 concludes the paper unearthing future avenues of research.

2   Concept of Multi-Level Fuzzy Entropy

2.1   Multi- Level Shannon Entropy

Let $P = (p_1, p_2, p_3, \ldots, p_n) \in \Delta_n$, where $\Delta_n = \{ (p_1, p_{2,}, \ldots, p_n) | p_i \geq 0, i = 1, 2, \ldots, n, n \geq 2, \sum_{i=1}^{n} p_i = 1 \}$ is a set of discrete finite n-ary probability distributions. Then entropy of the total image can be defined as:

$$H(P) = -\sum_{i=1}^{n} p_i \, log_2 \, p_i, \qquad (1)$$

I denote a 8 bit gray level digital image of dimension $M \times N$. P is the normalized histogram for image with $L = 255$ gray levels. Now, if there are $n - 1$ thresholds (t), partitioning the normalized histogram into n classes, then the entropy for each class may be computed as,

$$H_1(t) = -\sum_{i=0}^{t_1} \frac{p_i}{P_1} \ln \frac{p_i}{P_1},$$

$$H_2(t) = -\sum_{i=t_1+1}^{t_2} \frac{p_i}{P_2} \ln \frac{p_i}{P_2},$$

$$H_n(t) = -\sum_{i=t_{n-1}+1}^{L-1} \frac{p_i}{P_n} \ln \frac{p_i}{P_n}.$$

where,

$$P_1(t) = \sum_{i=0}^{t_1} p_i, P_2(t) = \sum_{i=t_1+1}^{t_2} p_i, \ldots, P_n(t) = \sum_{i=t_{n-1}+1}^{L-1} p_i.$$

where For ease of computation two dummy thresholds $t_0 = 0$, $t_n = L - 1$ are introduced with $t_0 < t_1 < \ldots < t_{n-1} < t_n$. Then the optimum threshold value can be found by

$$\varphi(t_1, t_2, \ldots, t_n) = Arg\,max([H_1(t) + H_2(t) + \ldots + H_n(t)]). \qquad (2)$$

2.2 Multi-Level Fuzzy Entropy

A classical set A can be defined as a collection of element that can either belong to or not belongs to set A. Whereas as according to fuzzy set, which is a generalization of classical set, an element can partially belongs to a set A. A can be defined as

$$A = \{(x, \mu_A(x)) | x \in X\}, \qquad (3)$$

where, $0 \leq \mu_A(x) \leq 1$ and $\mu_A(x)$ is called the membership function, which measures the closeness of x to A.

For simplicity trapezoidal membership function is used in this paper to estimate the membership of n segmented regions, $\mu_1, \mu_2, \ldots, \mu_n$ by using $2 \times (n-1)$ unknown fuzzy parameters, namely $a_1, c_1 \ldots a_{n-1}, c_{n-1}$ where $0 \leq a_1 \leq c_1 \leq \ldots \leq a_{n-1} \leq c_{n-1} \leq L\text{-}1$ (Fig. 1.). Then the following membership function can be derived for n level thresholding

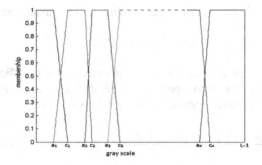

Fig. 1. Fuzzy membership function for n − level thresholding

$$\mu_1(k) = \begin{cases} 1 & k \leq a_1 \\ \frac{k-c_1}{a_1-c_1} & a_1 \leq k \leq c_1 \\ 0 & k > c_1 \end{cases} \tag{4a}$$

$$\vdots$$

$$\mu_{n-1}(k) = \begin{cases} 0 & k \leq a_{n-2} \\ \frac{k-a_{n-2}}{c_{n-2}-a_{n-2}} & a_{n-2} < k \leq c_{n-2} \\ 1 & c_{n-2} < k \leq a_{n-2} \\ \frac{k-c_{n-1}}{a_{n-1}-c_{n-1}} & a_{n-1} < k \leq c_{n-1} \\ 0 & k > c_{n-1} \end{cases} \tag{4b}$$

$$\mu_n(k) = \begin{cases} 1 & k \leq a_{n-1} \\ \frac{k-a_n}{c_n-a_n} & a_{n-1} < k \leq c_{n-1} \\ 1 & k > c_{n-1} \end{cases} \tag{4c}$$

The maximum fuzzy entropy for each segment of n −level segments can be defined by

$$\begin{aligned} H_1 &= -\sum_{i=0}^{L-1} \frac{p_i * \mu_1(i)}{P_1} * \ln\left(\frac{p_i * \mu_1(i)}{P_1}\right), \\ H_2 &= -\sum_{i=0}^{L-1} \frac{p_i * \mu_2(i)}{P_2} * \ln\left(\frac{p_i * \mu_2(i)}{P_2}\right), \\ &\vdots \\ H_n &= -\sum_{i=0}^{L-1} \frac{p_i * \mu_n(i)}{P_n} * \ln\left(\frac{p_i * \mu_n(i)}{P_n}\right). \end{aligned} \tag{5}$$

Where,

$$P_1 = \sum_{i=0}^{L-1} p_i * \mu_1(i), P_2 = \sum_{i=0}^{L-1} p_i * \mu_2(i), \ldots, P_n = \sum_{i=0}^{L-1} p_i * \mu_n(i)$$

The optimum value of parameters can be obtained by maximizing the total entropy

$$\varphi(a_1, c_1, \ldots, a_{n-1}, c_{n-1}) = Arg\, max([H_1(t) + H_2(t) + \ldots + H_n(t)]). \qquad (6)$$

A global optimization technique is needed to optimize Eq. (6) efficiently and also to reduce the time complexity of the proposed method. The $(n-1)$ no of threshold values can obtained using the fuzzy parameters in the following way:

$$t_1 = \frac{(a_1 + c_1)}{2}, t_2 = \frac{(a_2 + c_2)}{2}, \ldots, t_{n-1} = \frac{(a_{n-1} + c_{n-1})}{2}. \qquad (7)$$

3   Differential Evolution (DE)

DE, a population-based global optimization algorithm, was proposed by Storn in 1997. The ith individual (parameter vector) of the population at generation (time) t is a D-dimensional vector containing a set of D optimization parameters:

$$\overrightarrow{Z_i}(t) = [Z_{i,1}(t), Z_{i,2}(t), \ldots \ldots, Z_{i,D}(t)] \qquad (8)$$

In each generation to change the population members $\overrightarrow{Z_i}(t)$ (say), a *donor* vector $\overrightarrow{Y_i}(t)$ is created. It is the method of creating this donor vector that distinguishes the various DE schemes. In one of the earliest variants of DE, now called DE/rand/1 scheme, to create a donor vector $\overrightarrow{Y_i}(t)$ for each ith member, three other parameter vectors (say the r_1, r_2 and r_3-th vectors such that $r_1, r_2, r_3 \in [1, NP]$ and $r_1 \neq r_2 \neq r_3$) are chosen at random from the current population. The donor vector $\overrightarrow{Y_i}(t)$ is then obtained multiplying a scalar number F with the difference of any two of the three. The process for the jth component of the ith vector may be expressed as,

$$\overrightarrow{Y_{i,j}}(t) = Z_{r1,j}(t) + F.\left(Z_{r2,j}(t) - Z_{r3,j}(t)\right) \qquad (9)$$

A 'binomial' crossover operation takes place to increase the potential diversity of the population. The binomial crossover is performed on each of the D variables whenever a randomly picked number between 0 and 1 is within the Cr value. In this case the number of parameters inherited from the mutant has a (nearly) binomial distribution. Thus for each target vector $\overrightarrow{Z_i}(t)$, a trial vector $\overrightarrow{R_i}(t)$ is created in the following fashion:

$$\begin{aligned} R_{i,j}(t) &= Y_{i,j}(t) \ if \ r \ and_j(0, 1) \le Cr \ or \ j = rn(i) \\ &= Z_{i,j}(t) \ otherwise \end{aligned} \qquad (10)$$

For $j = 1, 2\ldots D$ and $rand_j(0, 1) \in [0, 1]$ is the jth evaluation of a uniform random number generator. $rn(i) \in [1, 2, \ldots \ldots, D]$ is a randomly chosen index to ensure that $\overrightarrow{R_i}(t)$ gets at least one component from $\overrightarrow{Z_i}(t)$. Finally 'selection' is performed in order to determine which one between the target vector and trial vector will survive in the

Fig. 2. Original Images (1) Clock, (2) Egg, (3) Window, (4) Billboard, (5) Orange, (6) Coin, (7) Airbus, (8) Cactus.

next generation i.e. at time $t = t + 1$. If the trial vector yields a better value of the fitness function, it replaces its target vector in the next generation; otherwise the parent is retained in the population:

$$\left. \begin{array}{l} \vec{Z_I}(t+1) = \vec{R_I}(t) \; if f\left(\vec{R_I}(t)\right) > f\left(\vec{Z_I}(t)\right) \\ = \vec{Z_I}(t) \; if f\left(\vec{R_I}(t)\right) \leq f\left(\vec{Z_I}(t)\right) \end{array} \right\} \quad (11)$$

where $f(.)$ is the function to be maximized.

Table 1. Comparison of computational time (t), mean objective value (f_m) and standard deviation (f_{std}) between DE, PSO and GA

Im		2 - level			3 – level			4 - level		
		DE	PSO	GA	DE	PSO	GA	DE	PSO	GA
1	t	**0.832**	1.265	1.890	**1.842**	2.670	3.211	**3.197**	4.097	6.178
	f_m	**13.677**	13.663	13.659	**17.328**	17.278	17.283	**20.554**	20.422	20.503
	f_{std}	**0**	0.015	0.014	**0**	17.278	17.283	**0**	20.422	20.503
2	t	**0.803**	1.199	1.708	**1.774**	2.612	3.068	**3.103**	4.050	5.972
	f_m	**12.920**	12.896	12.904	**16.461**	16.382	16.362	**19.435**	19.279	19.368
	f_{std}	**0**	0.014	0.063	**0**	0.023	0.0303	**0.003**	0.0554	0.0352
3	t	**0.877**	1.234	1.839	**1.980**	2.692	3.076	**3.234**	4.076	6.315
	f_m	**12.292**	12.281	12.266	**16.242**	16.150	16.195	**19.664**	19.474	19.594
	f_{std}	**0**	0.005	0.024	**0**	0.047	0.0343	**0.003**	0.0616	0.0412
4	t	**0.868**	1.222	1.834	**1.874**	2.711	3.271	**3.298**	4.100	6.437
	f_m	**13.172**	13.150	13.162	**17.115**	17.060	17.004	**20.449**	20.315	20.409
	f_{std}	**0**	0.021	0.072	**0**	0.015	0.0776	**0**	0.0388	0.0139
5	t	**0.828**	1.200	1.773	**1.821**	2.617	3.236	**3.209**	4.161	6.053
	f_m	**13.325**	13.303	13.313	**16.819**	16.772	16.752	**20.025**	19.806	19.880
	f_{std}	**0**	0.013	0.070	**0**	0.029	0.0381	**0**	0.0456	0.0690
6	t	**0.838**	1.186	1.823	**1.919**	2.894	3.347	**3.287**	4.171	6.431
	f_m	**13.325**	13.303	13.313	**16.819**	16.772	16.752	**20.025**	19.806	19.880
	f_{std}	**0**	0.027	0.014	**0**	0.021	0.0828	**0**	0.0545	0.0339
7	t	**0.892**	1.304	1.899	**1.957**	2.677	3.001	**3.401**	3.963	6.340
	f_m	**14.013**	13.997	13.989	**17.895**	17.842	17.859	**21.326**	21.125	21.282
	f_{std}	**0**	0.008	0.011	**0**	0.049	0.0172	**0**	0.0820	0.0151
8	t	**0.857**	1.281	1.830	**1.862**	2.739	3.077	**3.332**	4.019	6.207
	f_m	**13.693**	13.676	13.667	**17.601**	17.579	17.546	**21.101**	20.935	21.051
	f_{std}	**0**	0.010	0.013	**0**	0.009	0.0410	**0**	0.0574	0.0372

4   Experimental Results

The simulations are performed with MATLAB R2012a in a workstation with Intel® Core™ i3 2.9 GHz processor. Segmented images $f_s(x, y)$ were formed as gray scale images by using the equation and the achieved threshold values as described in [22]. Matlab codes implementing the algorithm presented in this paper may be downloaded from [23].

The DE\rand\1\bin scheme is used to compute the threshold levels efficiently. The parametric set up of DE, GA and PSO have been adopted using the guidelines provided in the respective literatures. Results of the metaheuristics algorithms have been provided as the mean of 50 independent runs where each run was continued till the exhaustion of $D \times 1000$ number of Fitness Evaluations (FEs), D denoting the search space dimensionality. Note that for a n levels segmentation problem the dimensionality of the search space is $D = 2*(n\text{-}1)$ as no. of unknown fuzzy parameters are 2.

The effectiveness of the fuzzy based approach is established by comparing the results with Shannon entropy in terms of both visual and statistical analysis. Performance of proposed method is tested with the help of two well-known image quality assessment matrices like Feature similarity (FSIM) index [24], Complex Wavelet Structural Similarity Index Measurement (CW-SSIM) [25].

Table 2. Threshold values obtained by DE for 2–4 level thresholding

Image	Lv	SE	FE	Parameter Values for FE
1	2	91, 157	68 182	6 129 130 234
	3	67 113 159	57 115 178	6 107 108 121 122 234
	4	67 113 158 189	53 114 151 205	6 100 101 126 127 175 175 234
2	2	88 136	65 150	19 111 112 188
	3	65 103 140	67 117 160	19 115 116 118 119 201
	4	65 96 126 155	52 104 130 171	19 84 85 123 124 136 136 206
3	2	148 223	111 227	6 216 217 236
	3	92 155 222	70 162 211	3 137 138 186 187 235
	4	65 108 157 222	57 115 164 221	3 110 111 118 119 209 209 233
4	2	65 139	53 181	1 105 106 255
	3	38 89 141	57 115 186	1 113 114 116 117 255
	4	38 86 135 195	38 90 130 205	1 75 76 104 105 154 154 255
5	2	53 114	46 142	12 79 80 204
	3	53 108 155	56 107 163	12 100 101 113 114 211
	4	52 85 118 159	40 85 113 164	12 68 69 101 102 123 123 205
6	2	122 186	75 199	9 141 142 255
	3	86 138 196	70 139 198	2 137 138 140 141 255
	4	77 123 165 209	54 127 161 215	2 106 107 146 147 175 175 255
7	2	124 189	57 184	1 112 113 254
	3	66 126 189	54 132 206	1 106 107 157 158 254
	4	44 86 131 189	37 91 135 208	1 73 74 108 109 161 161 254
8	2	90 174	80 207	1 158 159 255
	3	72 142 178	67 144 205	1 132 133 154 155 255
	4	50 97 143 178	42 104 141 206	1 83 84 124 125 157 157 255

Table 3. Comparison of segmented images by Shannon entropy and fuzzy entropy

Image	Shannon Entropy			Fuzzy Entropy		
	2 - level	3 - level	4 - level	2 - level	3 - level	4 - level
1						
2						
3						
4						
5						
6						
7						
8						

For testing and analysis, 8 grayscale images are used. The original images are shown in Fig. 2. The performance of DE in terms of computational time (t), mean objective value (f_m) and standard deviation (f_{std}) of objective values (Table 1). DE proves that it is not only faster but also solves the optimization problem better than GA and PSO. The obtained threshold values and fuzzy parameters of SE and FE for 2nd, 3rd and 4th level thresholding are displayed in Table 2. Table 3 exhibits qualitative comparison between SE and FE using DE for the test images by reforming the segmented image as mentioned in [22]. FE reveals better segmentation in comparison with SE for most of the test images. This finding is also established by examining the outcomes SE and FE by deploying IQA matrices FSIM (Table 4) and CW-SSIM (Table 5). In significantly majority cases FE gives better results than SE.

Table 4. Results of IQA matrices FSIM using DE

Image	2 – level		3 – level		4 – level	
	SE	FE	SE	FE	SE	FE
1	0.5654	**0.5675**	0.6768	**0.6953**	0.7192	**0.7295**
2	0.7869	**0.7962**	0.8057	**0.8216**	0.8268	**0.8278**
3	0.7405	**0.7608**	0.7698	**0.7769**	0.8007	**0.8062**
4	0.6884	**0.7672**	0.7354	**0.8315**	0.8686	**0.8693**
5	0.6814	**0.6909**	0.7118	**0.7217**	0.7174	**0.7238**
6	0.6728	**0.7167**	0.7667	**0.7892**	0.8087	**0.8186**
7	0.5721	**0.6733**	0.7189	**0.7411**	0.7828	**0.7847**
8	0.6254	**0.6382**	0.6848	**0.7180**	0.7387	**0.7592**

Table 5. Results of IQA matrices CW-SSIM using DE

Image	2 – level		3 – level		4 – level	
	SE	FE	SE	FE	SE	FE
1	0.7624	**0.8260**	0.8788	**0.9314**	0.9316	**0.9565**
2	0.4896	**0.6504**	0.6220	**0.6951**	0.7300	**0.7439**
3	0.9073	**0.9658**	0.9708	**0.9841**	0.9877	**0.9925**
4	0.9262	**0.9715**	0.9259	**0.9798**	0.9834	**0.9859**
5	0.5630	**0.6811**	0.8195	**0.8512**	0.8226	**0.8435**
6	0.8162	**0.9202**	0.9260	**0.9646**	0.9386	**0.9544**
7	0.8024	**0.8660**	0.9295	**0.9363**	0.9048	**0.9383**
8	0.9069	**0.9360**	0.9425	**0.9552**	0.9480	**0.9500**

5 Conclusion

It can be concluded from the above discussion that Fuzzy entropy based thresholding methods for multi-level segmentation performs significantly better than Shannon based approaches. Fuzzy entropy based thresholding techniques delivers satisfactory results in case of visual comparison. These claims are doubtlessly established via state-of-art image quality assessments metrics FSIM and CW-SSIM. Undoubtedly, DE adds speed and accuracy to this algorithm. However, a better self adaptive DE or other upgraded variants of DE could be used to attain better performance. In addition, several other membership functions could be tested for better separation of the segmented regions. More image performance metrics could be used in future to prove the competence of segmentation algorithms. Lastly and most importantly, 2-D histogram based approach could be implemented in order to get improved outcomes.

References

1. Riseman, E.M., Arbib, M.A.: Survey: computational techniques in the visual segmentation of static scenes. Comput. Vis. Graph. Image Process. **6**, 221–276 (1977)

2. Weszka, J.S.: A survey of threshold selection techniques. CGIP **7**(2), 259–265 (1978)
3. Fu, K.S., Mui, J.K.: A survey on image segmentation. Pattern Recogn. **13**, 3–16 (1981)
4. Haralharick, R.M., Shapiro, L.G.: Survey: image segmentation techniques. CVGIP **29**, 100–132 (1985)
5. Borisenko, V.I., Zlatotol, A.A., Muchnik, I.B.: Image segmentation (state of the art survey). Automat. Remote Control. **48**, 837–879 (1987)
6. Sahoo, P.K., Soltani, S., Wong, A.K.C., Chen, Y.C.: A survey of thresholding techniques. CVGIP **41**, 233–260 (1988)
7. Pal, N.R., Pal, S.K.: A review on image segmentation. Pattern Recogn. **26**(9), 1277–1294 (1993)
8. Kapur, J.N., Sahoo, P.K., Wong, A.K.C.: A new method for gray-level picture thresholding using the entropy of the histogram. Comput. Vis. Graph. Image Process. **29**, 273–285 (1985)
9. Wong, A.K.C., Sahoo, P.K.: A gray-level threshold selection method based on maximum entropy principle. IEEE Trans. Syst. Man Cybernet. **19**(4), 866–871 (1989)
10. Pal, N.R.: On minimum cross entropy thresholding. Pattern Recogn. **29**(4), 575–580 (1996)
11. Li, C.H., Lee, C.K.: Minimum cross entropy thresholding. Pattern Recogn. **26**, 617–625 (1993)
12. Rosin, P.L.: Unimodal thresholding. Pattern Recogn. **34**, 2083–2096 (2001)
13. Otsu, N.: A threshold selection method for grey level histograms. IEEE Trans. Syst. Man Cybernet. SMC **9**(1), 62–66 (1979)
14. Luca, A.D., Termini, S.: Definition of a non probabilistic entropy in the setting of fuzzy sets theory. Inf. contr. **20**, 301–315 (1972)
15. Bloch, I.: Fuzzy spatial relationships for image processing and interpretation: a review. Image Vis. Comput. **23**(2), 89–110 (2005)
16. Zhao, M.S., Fu, A.M.N., Yan, H.: A technique of three level thresholding based on probability partition and fuzzy 3-partition. IEEE Trans. Fuzzy Syst. **9**(3), 469–479 (2001)
17. Tao, W.B., Tian, J.W., Liu, J.: Image segmentation by three-level thresholding based on maximum fuzzy entropy and genetic algorithm. Pattern Recogn. Lett. **24**, 3069–3078 (2003)
18. Cao, L., Bao, P., Shi, Z.: The strongest schema learning GA and its application to multi-level thresholding. Image Vis. Comput. **26**, 716–724 (2008)
19. Storn, R., Price, K.: Differential evolution - a simple and efficient heuristic for global optimization over continuous spaces. J. Glob. Optim. **11**, 341–359 (1997)
20. Das, S., Suganthan, P.N.: Differential evolution - a survey of the state-of-the-art. IEEE Trans. Evol. Comput. **15**(1), 4–31 (2011)
21. Sarkar, S., Patra, G.R., Das, S.: A differential evolution based approach for multilevel image segmentation using minimum cross entropy thresholding. In: Panigrahi, B.K., Suganthan, P.N., Das, S., Satapathy, S.C. (eds.) SEMCCO 2011, Part I. LNCS, vol. 7076, pp. 51–58. Springer, Heidelberg (2011)
22. Sarkar, S., Das, S., Chaudhuri, S.S.: Multilevel image thresholding based on tsallis entropy and differential evolution. In: Panigrahi, B.K., Das, S., Suganthan, P.N., Nanda, P.K. (eds.) SEMCCO 2012. LNCS, vol. 7677, pp. 17–24. Springer, Heidelberg (2012)
23. File Exchange - Matlab Central. http://www.mathworks.in/matlabcentral/fileexchange/48055-a-fuzzy-entropy-based-multi-level-image-thresholding-using-differential-evolution
24. Zhang, L., Zhang, L., Mou, X., Zhang, D.: FSIM: A feature similarity index for image quality assessment. IEEE Trans. Image Process. **20**(8), 2378–2386 (2011)
25. Sampat, M.P., Wang, Z., Gupta, S., Bovik, A.C., Markey, M.K.: Complex wavelet structural similarity: Anew image similarity index. IEEE Trans. Image Process. **18**(11), 2385–2401 (2009)

A Novel Method of Relieving Transmission Congestion by Optimal Rescheduling with Multiple DGs Using PSO

K. Muthulakshmi[1(✉)] and C.K. Babulal[2]

[1] Department of Electrical and Electronics Engineering, Kamaraj College of Engineering and Technology, Virudhunagar 626 001, TamilNadu, India
muthusashi@gmail.com
[2] Department of Electrical and Electronics Engineering, Thiagarajar College of Engineering, Madurai 625 015, TamilNadu, India
ckbeee@tce.edu

Abstract. Congestion management is one of the most important issues for secure and reliable system operations in deregulated electricity market. Rescheduling the real power output of generators in the system is the most practiced technique for congestion management. In this research, multiple distributed generators are connected optimally along with above said conventional method to alleviate congestion. Particle Swarm Optimization (PSO) is used to determine the optimal generation levels and for finding the optimal sizes of multiple DGs, both PSO and GA are used to alleviate transmission congestion. Numerical results on modified IEEE 30 bus system is experimented for illustration. The complete experimental outcomes demonstrate that the PSO is one among the demanding optimization methods for this proposed problem than GA.

Keywords: Congestion management · Generation re-dispatch · Optimal rescheduling · Distributed Generation · Particle Swarm Optimization (PSO)

Nomenclature

DG	- Distributed Generation
LFSF	- Line Flow Sensitivity Factor
FACTS	- Flexible AC Transmission Systems
RED	- Relative Electrical Distance
FABF	- Fuzzy Adaptive Bacterial Foraging
TCSC	- Thyristor Controlled Series Compensation
PI	- Real power flow performance index
ΔP_l	- Change in real power injection at l^{th} node
ΔQ_l	- Change in reactive power injection at l^{th} node
ΔS_{ij}	- Change in line flow between node i and j
S_{ij}	- Line flow between node i and j
P_l	- Real power injection at l^{th} node
Q_l	- Reactive power injection at l^{th} node
P_g	- Power generated from generators in MW
P_d	- Power demand in MW

© Springer International Publishing Switzerland 2015
B.K. Panigrahi et al. (Eds.): SEMCCO 2014, LNCS 8947, pp. 396–408, 2015.
DOI: 10.1007/978-3-319-20294-5_35

ng   - Total number of generators available in the system
nl   - Total number of lines available in the system

1 Introduction

Transmission line congestion is one among the major key issues in deregulated power industry. Congestion occurs whenever one or more constraints of the system get violated. These violations of constraints can either be exceeding physical limits like thermal or voltage limits or specified limits which are assigned to ensure system security and reliability [1].

The system returns to its secure state, if transmission congestion is relieved. Mainly two types of techniques are used to relieve congestion as listed below.

Cost free methods

Non-cost free methods

A direct method of alleviating line overloads is developed by determining a generation rescheduling and load shedding pattern [2]. Relative electrical distance is used to optimize generator rescheduling to relieve congestion [3]. This concept is reliable, but the process of finding relative location of load nodes with respect to generator nodes is tedious. FABF based congestion management by optimal rescheduling based on the generator sensitivity to the congested line is proposed [4]. PSO based algorithm is suggested for minimizing active and reactive power rescheduling cost of generators to alleviate congestion [5]. But, both literatures have only considered some specific congested lines without considering N-1 contingency.

PSO based method is proposed for finding the optimal generation rescheduling to alleviate transmission line congestion [6]. Even though this methodology claims for its simplicity, the line connected with slack generator does not fully get alleviated from line congestion. PSO is used to minimize the rescheduling cost of active power [7]. However, the effect of rescheduling of reactive power output of generators and voltage stability constraints are ignored. The effective implementation of adaptive bacterial foraging – Nelder–Mead algorithm is demonstrated for managing the congestion during bilateral and multilateral transactions [8]. For relieving transmission congestion and for better utilization of existing grid infrastructure, placement of series FACTS device, i.e., TCSC is used [9]. This method failed to address proper location, appropriate size and cost.

Restructuring of electricity market provides the way for the increased usage of Distributed Generation (DG) with renewable energy resources. The DG, it refers to the small scale electric power generators dispersed within distribution network either located on customer side or an isolated site. It is expected that the penetration level of DGs will cover 25 % of the total demand in the next 10 years worldwide [10].

Installing DG units in distribution network may result some positive impact such as, improvement of voltage profile, power quality and reduction in total system losses [11]. Analytical methods are presented to determine the optimal location of DG in radial and networked systems with the objective of minimizing the network losses [12]. A simple, but conventional iterative search technique is combined with Newton – Raphson load-flow for finding the optimal placement of DG [13–15]. An equivalent current injection based loss sensitivity factor is used to determine the optimal locations and sizes of DGs [16]. The GA based approach is presented to establish the optimal placement and sizing of multiple DG units with the objectives of loss reduction and voltage profile improvement in distribution systems [17]. A sensitivity based method is proposed to allocate DGs simultaneously for congestion relief and voltage security [18].

Hence, this paper identifies that there is a research opening in alleviating trans-mission congestion with the help of multiple DGs along with real power rescheduling of generators. This paper employs Line Flow Sensitivity Factor (LFSF) to determine the optimal location of DG units in modified IEEE 30 bus test system.

This remaining portion of this paper is structured as follows. In Sect. 2, the pro-posed methodology is explained with the calculation of performance index (PI), con-tingency selection based on PI, optimal location for DGs based on LFSF and optimal capacity of DGs using PSO and GA. Section 3 gives a brief description about PSO. In Sect. 4, the problem formulation to alleviate congestion is discussed. Section 5 briefs about simulation results and discussions. Section 6 illustrates some of the imperative conclusions of this work.

2 Methodology

The power system operator should apply a corrective measure in order to relieve transmission congestion. For doing so, N-1 contingency measure is strictly followed by the power system operator. This kind of measure certainly leaves some important solutions against system security threat. Contingency ranking has been carried out using apparent power flow performance index.

2.1 Performance Index

Previous studies [5–7] have utilized real power flow performance index for identifying the most severe contingency cases for rescheduling of generator's real power output in order to relieve transmission congestion. This paper utilizes the static considerations based on the apparent power performance index (PI).

The severity of the system loading under normal and contingency cases can be described by an apparent power performance index and it is given by equation Eq. (1).

$$PI = \sum_{i=1}^{nl} \left(\frac{Sflow_i}{S_i^{max}} \right)^2 \tag{1}$$

The PI value is comparatively smaller, when all lines are within their thermal limits and it reaches higher value when overloads occur in the system. Hence, PI is a reliable index of severity of line overloads for a given state of power system.

2.2   Contingency Selection

Contingency analysis is carried out to assess the impact of severe contingencies and to alert the system operators about these critical contingencies. By doing so, the system operator can judge the relative severity of each contingency and decide the types of preventive actions to mitigate the potential problems. The most common limit violations include transmission line, transformer overloads and inadequate voltage levels at system buses.

As various probable outages create a contingency set, out of which some cases may lead to congestion problems or bus voltage limit violations. Such critical contingencies should be quickly identified for applying the corrective measures. The N-1 contingency criterion is taken into account for this work. This contingency selection identifies the most critical contingencies among them and ranks them in order of their apparent power performance index (PI) value in a descending order. The process of identifying these critical contingencies is referred to as contingency selection.

2.3   Finding the Optimal Locations for DG Units

Sensitivity of the power flow on congested lines is different with respect to the generator and the load buses in the system. A Line Flow Sensitivity Factor (LFSF) with active and reactive power injection to remove congestion from the overloaded lines can be calculated by change in power flow in a transmission line 'k' which is connected between bus 'i' and bus 'j' and this can be written as,

$$\Delta S_{ij} = \frac{\partial S_{ij}}{\partial P_l} \Delta P_l + \frac{\partial S_{ij}}{\partial Q_l} \Delta Q_l \qquad (2)$$

Equation (2) can be rewritten as,

$$\Delta S_{ij} = \frac{\partial S_{ij}}{\partial P_l} \Delta P_l \qquad (3)$$

By neglecting P-V coupling, Eq. (3) can be written as,

$$[LFSF]^{l_o} = \left(\frac{\partial |S_{ij}|}{\partial \delta_i}\right)\left(\frac{\partial \delta_i}{\partial P_l}\right) + \left(\frac{\partial |S_{ij}|}{\partial \delta_j}\right)\left(\frac{\partial \delta_j}{\partial P_l}\right) \qquad (4)$$

$$|S_{ij}| = (T_{ij})^{1/2} \qquad (5)$$

$$T_{ij} = V_i^4 Y_{ij}^2 + V_i^2 V_j^2 Y_{ij}^2 - 2V_i^3 V_j Y_{ij}^2 \cos \delta_{ij} + 2V_i^3 V_j Y_{ij} B_{sh} \sin(\theta_{ij} + \delta_{ij}) - 2V_i^4 Y_{ij} B_{sh} \sin \theta_{ij} + V_i^4 B_{sh}^2 \qquad (6)$$

$$\frac{\partial |S_{ij}|}{\partial \delta_i} = T_{ij}^{1/2} * (V_i^3 V_j Y_{ij} \sin \theta_{ij} + V_i^3 V_j Y_{ij} B_{sh}) \qquad (7)$$

$$\frac{\partial |S_{ij}|}{\partial \delta_j} = -\frac{\partial |S_{ij}|}{\partial \delta_i} \tag{8}$$

Then, this research calculates LFSFs values of all the load buses for all contingencies of the most critical outage. Then the calculated LFSF values are ranked. The load buses have larger negative LFSF values are selected for DGs allocation since they are the most influential on congested line. Now, the location for DG placement for relieving congestion is achieved. Therefore, it is important to calculate the DG size at these locations.

2.4 Calculation of the Optimal Sizes of DG Units

The optimal sizes of DGs are determined by PSO and GA. The objective used in these optimization techniques is minimization of real power losses. The objective function is defined as,

$$Minf = \sum_j P_{Lj} \tag{9}$$

Subjected to,
The voltage magnitude and angle must be kept within standard limits at each bus

$$V_i^{min} \le V_i \le V_i^{max} \tag{10}$$

$$\delta_i^{min} \le \delta_i \le \delta_i^{max} \tag{11}$$

Thermal limit of transmission lines for the network must not be exceeded

$$|S_{ij}| \le |S_{ij}^{max}| \tag{12}$$

3 Particle Swarm Optimization

Particle Swarm Optimization (PSO) is a population based stochastic optimization technique developed by Kennedy and Eberhart [19]. The method is derived from simulation of a simplified social model of swarms such as fish schooling and bird flocking. It is strong in solving complex problems with nonlinear and non-differentiable in nature.

Each individual in the swarm flies in the search space with a own velocity which is dynamically adjustable according to its own flying experience (velocity, inertia, gravity) and its coordinates in the problem space. This is very vital in getting the best solution (fitness). This value is known as pbest. Another finest value that is arrived by the global version of the particle swarm optimizer is the overall greatest value and its location obtained so far by any particle in the population called as gbest. The selected parameters are tabulated in Table 1. The fitness function is evaluated by using the corresponding equations. The computational steps are given as follows.

Step 1: Randomly generates an initial population (array) of particles with random positions and velocities. Set the iteration counter k = 0.

Step 2: For each particle, the objective value is calculated. Otherwise, that particle is infeasible.

Step 3: For each particle, compare its objective value with the individual best. If the objective value is lower than Pbest, set this value as the current Pbest, and record the corresponding particle position.

Step 4: Select the particle associated with the minimum individual best Pbest of all particles and set the value of this Pbest as the current overall best Gbest.

Step 5: Maximum fitness and average fitness values are calculated. Error is calculated using the equation as Error = (maximum fitness - average fitness).

Step 6: If this error is less than a specified tolerance then go to step 9.

Step 7: Update the velocity and position of particle. New fitness values are calculated for the new positions of all the particles. If the new fitness value for any particle is better than previous Pbest value then Pbest value for that particle is set to present fitness value. Similarly, Gbest value is identified from the latest Pbest values.

Step 8: The iteration count is incremented and if iteration count is not reached maximum then go to step 2.

Step 9: Global best particle gives the optimal sizing of DGs in candidate locations.

4   Problem Formulation to Alleviate Congestion

The objective function of proposed method is to minimize the apparent power performance index (PI) by finding an optimal profile of active power generation without and with multiple DG units if needed while satisfying network constraints.

The objective function of the proposed problem is defined as,

$$\text{Fitness Function: Min } PI = \sum_{i=1}^{nl} \left(\frac{Sflow_i}{S_i^{max}} \right)^2 \tag{13}$$

Table 1. The parameter selection for PSO

Social Factor C1	Cognitive Factor C2	Minimum Inertia Weight Factor Wmin	Maximum Inertia Weight Factor Wmax	Number of Particles	Maximum number of Iterations
2	2	0.4	0.9	20	100

Subjected to:

$$V_i^{min} \leq V_i \leq V_i^{max} \tag{14}$$

$$\delta_i^{min} \leq \delta_i \leq \delta_i^{max} \tag{15}$$

$$\Delta P_g^{min} \leq \Delta P_g \leq \Delta P_g^{max} \tag{16}$$

5   Results and Discussion

Simulation tests are carried out on modified IEEE 30 bus system [20] and its single line diagram is shown in Fig. 1. The necessary codes are developed in MATPOWER 4.1 package [20] with Intel i5 processor and 4 GB RAM.

Initially, base case load flow is performed by N-R load flow analysis with MATPOWER 4.1 to determine the limit violation. If the limit is violated congestion occurs. From base case load flow analysis it is found that no line gets congested. Next N-1 contingency analysis is carried out to find critical outage and results are arranged in descending manner based on their respective Performance Index (PI) as shown in Table 2. From Table 2, the outage of lines such as 4–12, 28–27, 1–2, 2–5 and 1–3 have resulted in overloading on other lines.

It can be observed from Table 2 the outage of line 4–12 is known as the most critical contingency case. With the above listed severe outage cases, several cases are created and considered as follows.

Case A: Outage of line 4–12
Case B: Increase of all load buses by 20 % plus outage of line 4–12
Case C: Increase of all load buses by 30 % plus outage of line 4–12
Case D: Outage of line 28–27

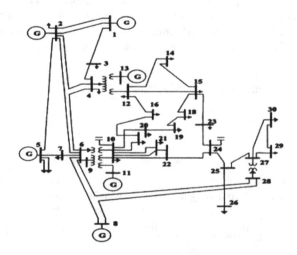

Fig. 1. Single line diagram for IEEE 30-bus system

Table 2. Contingency Ranking based on PI

Sl. No.	Line outage	PI
1	4–12	13.8480
2	28–27	12.4848
3	1–2	12.4080
4	2–5	10.1581
5	1–3	9.5250

Case E: Outage of lines 4–12 and 28–27
Case F: Increase of all load buses by 20 % plus outage of line 28–27

Thus, to relieve this transmission congestion suitable control actions must be taken. In this work, corrective action for relieving congestion is taken at the load buses by placing the DGs at suitable locations. To find the suitable location of DGs, LFSF (explained in Sect. 2.3) values are calculated for each of the overloaded lines for the most critical contingency. Only five suitable locations for each of the overloaded lines are shown in Table 3. Among these five values the buses which have most negative LFSF values are selected as the optimal locations for placing DGs.

It can be observed that bus-22 and bus-23 have the highest negative values and thus, they are selected as the most suitable locations for DGs placement with respect to the overloaded lines 1–3, 3–4 and 4–6, respectively. Then the optimal sizes of DGs are determined by PSO and GA. The results are presented in Table 4.

From Table 4, the optimal DG capacities at the buses 22 and 23 are 36.7206 MW and 17.7379 MW, respectively in PSO and 35.8059 MW and 17.4451 MW in GA.

Table 3. Five possible locations of DGs based on LFSF

Sl. No.	Line 1-3		Line 3-4		Line 4-6	
	Bus No.	LFSF	Bus No.	LFSF	Bus No.	LFSF
1	22	-0.3698	22	-0.1817	23	-0.3965
2	23	-0.3120	23	-0.1486	22	-0.3689
3	9	-0.3052	7	-0.1185	29	-0.2428
4	7	-0.2746	15	-0.1035	19	-0.2393
5	3	-0.2720	21	-0.0918	21	-0.2392

Table 4. Optimal capacity of DGs using PSO and GA

Bus No.	Optimal DG capacity in MW using PSO	Optimal DG capacity in MW using GA
22	36.7206	35.8059
23	17.7379	17.4451

5.1 Cases with Rescheduling as Corrective Action

The overloaded lines are identified without a corrective action for all listed cases. But the cases A, B, and C are capable of being relieved with rescheduling process alone. It is observed that 2 lines get congested for case A, 7 lines for case B and totally 9 lines for case C. For a secure system, the power flow in transmission lines should not exceed their permissible limit. Hence suitable corrective action should be carried out to alleviate the above said overloads.

The main scope of this proposed method is to relieve overloads in the congested lines by optimal rescheduling of generators using PSO. Initially rescheduling alone is adopted to relieve congestion and if it is not sufficient DGs are added along with rescheduling process. But fortunately, all the congested lines get alleviated in all the above 3 cases by optimal rescheduling of generators alone, without a DG placement. The comparative results for all these 3 cases are presented in Table 5.

5.2 Cases with Rescheduling Plus Multiple DGs as Corrective Action

The cases D, E, and F are coming under this category. The overloaded lines are identified without corrective action for the above listed cases. It is observed that 3 lines get congested for case D, 7 lines for case E and 6 lines for case F. Actually generator rescheduling process is applied first to relieve congestion. But, the rescheduling process

Table 5. Results for the cases require rescheduling alone

Case	Congested line	Line limit in MVA	Line flow without corrective action	Line flow after Rescheduling in PSO	% Violation
Case A	4–12	130	134.72	130	Alleviated
	16–17	16	17.93	8.31	Alleviated
Case B	1–2	130	181.16	130	Alleviated
	2–6	65	66.97	44.48	Alleviated
	4–6	90	111.62	74.03	Alleviated
	6–10	32	34.45	21.14	Alleviated
	9–10	65	65.05	56.69	Alleviated
	16–17	16	21.98	8.78	Alleviated
	10–17	32	32.67	19.92	Alleviated
Case C	1–2	130	205.15	130	Alleviated
	2–6	65	73.77	45.72	Alleviated
	4–6	90	123.62	74.90	Alleviated
	6–8	32	34.95	8.80	Alleviated
	6–10	32	37.66	20.30	Alleviated
	9–10	65	70.91	59.43	Alleviated
	16–17	16	24.09	6.57	Alleviated
	10–17	32	35.56	18.70	Alleviated
	25–27	16	16.27	7.79	Alleviated

Table 6. Results for the cases require rescheduling plus DGs

Case	Congested line	Line limit in MVA	Line flow without corrective action	Line flow after rescheduling	Status/Line flow after rescheduling plus DGs by GA	% Violation	Status/Line flow after rescheduling plus DGs by PSO	% Violation
Case D	1–2	130	131.71	130.00	Alleviated	Alleviated	Alleviated	Alleviated
	22–24	16	20.81	17.50	16.53	3.31	16.00	Alleviated
	24–25	16	19.48	19.40	19.39	21.19	19.34	20.88
Case E	1–2	130	13676	130.00	Alleviated	Alleviated	Alleviated	Alleviated
	6–9	65	65.26	29.30	Alleviated	Alleviated	Alleviated	Alleviated
	6–10	32	38.78	17.11	Alleviated	Alleviated	Alleviated	Alleviated
	16–17	16	22.20	10.20	Alleviated	Alleviated	Alleviated	Alleviated
	10–21	32	33.67	26.54	Alleviated	Alleviated	Alleviated	Alleviated
	22–24	16	31.66	19.08	16.80	5. 00	16.00	Alleviated
	24–25	16	19.57	19.54	19.40	21.25	19.31	20.69
Case F	1–2	130	177.77	130.00	Alleviated	Alleviated	Alleviated	Alleviated
	10–21	32	33.91	33.25	18.94	Alleviated	18.24	Alleviated
	15–23	16	16.05	16.99	9.97	Alleviated	9.65	Alleviated
	22–24	16	26.11	24.99	20.90	30.63	20.88	30.50
	24–25	16	24.58	24.52	24.52	53.25	24.23	51.44
	25–27	16	17.52	17.50	17.84	11.50	17.39	8.69

Table 7. Comparison of results for all the cases

Cases	Total numbers of congested lines			
	Without corrective action	After rescheduling by PSO	After rescheduling plus DGs by GA	After rescheduling plus DGs by PSO
Case A	2	Nil	NA	NA
Case B	7	Nil	NA	NA
Case C	9	Nil	NA	NA
Case D	3	2	2	1
Case E	7	2	2	1
Case F	6	5	3	3

is unable to relieve congestion. Hence, the multiple DGs which sizes are calculated by GA and PSO are located one by one in the corresponding optimal places and the results are observed. The comparative results for all these 3 cases are presented in Table 6.

From Table 6, it is observed that the total numbers of congested lines after the rescheduling process in all these 3 cases are getting reduced from 3 to 2 in case D, 7 to 2 in case E and 6 to 5 in case F. In order to alleviate all the congested lines in all the 3 cases, multiple DGs which sizes are calculated by GA are placed in optimal locations along with rescheduling process. Even though, the total numbers of congested lines in case D and case E remain same, but the percentage violation gets reduced. The number of congested lines in case F gets reduced from 5 to 3. But, when the DGs values which are calculated by PSO are applied, the number of congested lines further gets reduced from 2 to 1 for both case D and case E. This value gets reduced from 5 to 3 for case F with reduced percentage violation. Hence, the DGs values which are calculated by PSO are more effective than the DGs values which are calculated by GA.

The results obtained without corrective action, after rescheduling and after rescheduling plus DGs by GA and PSO in all the cases are compared and given in Table 7. It is clearly apparent that the total numbers of congested lines are getting reduced if additional control actions are combined together and applied simultaneously than to apply a single control action at a time.

6 Conclusion

Thus the transmission congestion due to simultaneous outages of lines and sudden increase of loads are relieved by the combined approach of real power rescheduling of generators and installation of multiple DGs in optimal locations. The value of real power rescheduling is effectively determined by PSO and the optimal capacities of multiple DGs are effectively determined with the help of GA and PSO. This method of congestion relief by PSO is computationally efficient than GA and simple as it utilizes the apparent power performance index (PI). This proposed method is tested with 6 different line outage and load variation cases. The total numbers of congested lines are fully relived by the application of rescheduling process alone in case A, B and C. The case D, E and F are requiring an additional control action as installation of multiple DGs in optimal locations along with rescheduling process.

Even though this approach claims for its simplicity, still there are few congested lines in some of the critical cases even after the installation of multiple DGs along with rescheduling process. To overcome this bottleneck a modern approaches like demand side management and FACTS device may be added to relieve the congestion completely.

References

1. Tuan, L.A., Bhattacharya, K., Daalder, J.: Transmission congestion management in bilateral markets: an interruptible load auction solution. Electr. Power Syst. Res. **74**, 379–389 (2005)
2. Xu D, Girgis AA: Optimal load shedding strategy in power systems with distributed generation. Proc. of IEEE Power Engineering Society winter meeting, pp.788–793, (2001)
3. Kaushik, K.P., Nilesh, K.P.: Generation rescheduling for congestion management using relative electrical distance. J. Inf., Knowl. Res. Electr. Eng. **2**(2), 271–276 (2012)
4. Venkaiah, C., Vinod Kumar, D.M.: Fuzzy adaptive bacterial foraging congestion management using sensitivity based optimal active power re-scheduling of generators. Appl. Soft Comput. **11**, 4921–4930 (2011)
5. Pandya, K.S., Joshi, S.K.: Sensitivity and Particle Swarm Optimization based congestion management. Electr. Power Compon. Syst. **41**(4), 465–484 (2013)
6. Muthulakshmi, K., Babulal, C.K.: Relieving transmission congestion by optimal rescheduling of generators using PSO. Appl. Mech. Mater. **626**, 213–218 (2014)
7. Dutta, S., Singh, S.P.: Optimal rescheduling of generators for congestion management based on particle swarm optimization. IEEE Trans. Power Syst. **23**(4), 1560–1568 (2008)
8. Panigrahi, B.K., Ravikumar Pandi, V.: Congestion management using adaptive bacterial foraging algorithm. Energy Convers. Manage. **50**, 1202–1209 (2009)
9. Acharya, N., Mithulananthan, N.: Locating series FACTS devices for congestion management in deregulated electricity markets. Electr. Power Syst. Res. **77**(3), 352–360 (2007)
10. A report: Distributed generation in liberalized electric markets. International Energy Agency, pp. 57–60 (2002)
11. El-Khattam, W., Hegazy, Y.G., Salama, M.M.A.: An integrated distributed generation optimization model for distribution system planning. IEEE Trans. Power Syst. **20**(2), 1158–1165 (2005)
12. Wang, C.S., Nehrir, M.H.: Analytical approaches for optimal placement of distributed generation sources in power systems. IEEE Trans. Power Syst. **19**(4), 2068–2076 (2004)
13. Keane, A., O'Malley, M.: Optimal allocation of embedded generation on distribution networks. IEEE Trans. Power Syst. **20**(3), 1640–1646 (2005)
14. Singh, R.K., Goswami, S.K.: Optimum siting and sizing of distributed generations in radial and networked systems. Electr. Power Compo. Sys. **37**(2), 127–145 (2009)
15. Ghosh, S., Ghoshal, S.P., Ghosh, S.: Optimal sizing and placement of distributed generation in a network system. Int. J. Elec. Power **32**(8), 849–856 (2010)
16. Gözel, T., Hocaoglu, M.H.: An analytical method for the sizing and siting of distributed generators in radial systems. Electr. Power Syst. Res. **79**(6), 912–918 (2009)

17. Sasiraja, R.M., Suresh kumar, V., Sudha, S.: A heuristic approach for optimal location and sizing of multiple DGs in radial distribution system. Appl. Mech. Mater. **626**, 227–233 (2014)
18. Singh, A.K., Parida, S.K.: Congestion management with distributed generation and its impact on electricity market. Int. J. Elec. Power **48**, 39–47 (2013)
19. Kennedy, J., Eberhart, R.: Particle swarm optimization. In: Proceedings of IEEE International Conference Neural Networks, pp. 1942–1948, Australia (1995)
20. Carlos, R.D.Z., Murillo-Sanchez, E.: MATPOWER; a MATLAB power system simulation package. Version 4.1.0. http://www.pserc.cornell.edu/matpower

Sentiment Detection in Online Content: A WordNet Based Approach

Soumi Dutta[1]([✉]), Moumita Roy[1], Asit Kumar Das[2], and Saptarshi Ghosh[2]

[1] Institute of Engineering and Management, Kolkata 700091, India
soumi.it@gmail.com
[2] Indian Institute of Engineering Science and Technology, Shibpur,
Howrah 711103, India

Abstract. Online Social Networks (OSN), such as Facebook, Twitter, Youtube and so on, are important sources of online content today. These platforms are used by millions of people world-wide, to share information and express their sentiment and opinion on various social issues. Sentiment analysis of online content – automatically inferring whether a particular textual content reflects a positive (e.g., happy) or negative (e.g., sad) sentiment of the person who posted the content – is an important research problem today, and has several potential applications such as analysing public opinion on various products or social issues. In this paper, we propose a simple but effective methodology of inferring the sentiment of textual content posted in online social media. Our approach is based on first identifying the positive / negative polarity of terms, i.e., whether a certain term (e.g., a word) is normally used in a positive or negative context, and then to infer the sentiment of a given text based on the polarity of the terms present in the text. A key challenge in this approach is that in online social media, different users use different words while expressing similar opinion. To address this, we use the well-known lexical database *WordNet* to identify groups of words which are synonymous to each other. We apply our proposed methodology on a large publicly available dataset containing content from six different online social media, which has been labeled as positive / negative by human annotators, and find that our methodology achieves better performance than several approaches developed earlier.

Keywords: Online social network · Sentiment analysis · WordNet

1 Introduction

Online Social Networks (OSNs), such as Facebook, Twitter, and Youtube, are presently used by hundreds of millions of users, not only to communicate with friends, but also to post content on various topics of interest. The users in these social networking sites generate huge amounts of content every day (which is known as 'user-generated content'), and this content is increasingly being used for a variety of data mining applications, ranging from content search [18], to opinion mining [10,21].

© Springer International Publishing Switzerland 2015
B.K. Panigrahi et al. (Eds.): SEMCCO 2014, LNCS 8947, pp. 409–420, 2015.
DOI: 10.1007/978-3-319-20294-5_36

One of the important research problems in mining of user-generated content in OSNs is *sentiment analysis* or *opinion mining*. In its simplest form, this involves detecting whether a piece of text reflects positive sentiment (e.g., happiness, enjoyment) or negative sentiment (e.g., sadness or anger or fear) of the user who posted / wrote the text. For instance, the text "absolutely awesome" indicates positive sentiment, while the text "i feel really sick" indicates negative sentiment. More complex variants of the problem include graded sentiment analysis, i.e., attempting to infer the degree of positive or negative sentiment; for instance, "i feel really sick" indicates much more negative sentiment than "i feel sick". However, in this study, we limit our attention to binary sentiment detection, i.e., simply inferring whether a piece of text reflects positive or negative sentiment.

Sentiment analysis involves use of data mining and natural language processing techniques for inferring the mood or opinion of users from the text they write. Sentiment analysis of text generated in online social media has many important applications. For instance, in marketing, it helps in judging the success of an advertisement campaign or new product launch (e.g., Samsung launching a new version of the Galaxy phone), such as determining whether a product or service is being liked by the general population. Again, sentiment analysis on tweets posted in the Twitter social network has been used to predict the majority decision in elections [21], and to judge the general mood of people during important socio-economic events [2].

Sentiment analysis has been studied for several years, and a large number of algorithms have been proposed for sentiment detection from English text [11] (see Sect. 2 for related work). It should be noted that sentiment analysis is a challenging problem due to several reasons. First, different people have different ways of expressing sentiment, which makes it difficult to design a common methodology for all users. Second, most traditional text processing algorithms rely on the fact that small differences between two pieces of text do not change the meaning significantly. However, in sentiment analysis, the text "Bob is good" is very different (in fact, has opposite polarity) from "Bob is not good".

Over and above the fact that sentiment analysis is a challenging problem, there are several additional challenges in sentiment analysis of content posted in online social media. The content posted in such media is usually very small, e.g., a tweet in the Twitter social network can be at most 140 characters in length. It is especially challenging to detect the sentiment of a user based on such little information, because of the lack of context. More importantly, while posting text in online social media, users frequently use informal, grammatically incorrect language. They also use conversational slang words, acronyms (e.g., 'LOL' for 'Laugh Out Loud' or 'OMG' for 'Oh My God'), and so on, to indicate their sentiment. As a result, algorithms designed for formal English text often do not give accurate results for text in online social media [10]. Also note that people often mix positive and negative sentiments in the same text. In normal text (such as books or newspaper articles), positive and negative comments are usually contained in separated sentences, which is somewhat manageable by analyzing one sentence at a time. However, in the more informal medium like online social media or blogs, users often combine different opinions in the same sentence, such as "The Indian team played very well, but were plagued by bad umpiring decisions"; though this is easy for a human to understand, it is more difficult for a machine to judge the sentiment.

In this paper, we propose a simple but effective methodology to infer the sentiment of text posted in online social media (details in Sect. 3). We take a lexical approach, where we first attempt to infer *sentiment scores* for specific tokens or words. The sentiment scores of a word basically indicate the likelihood of the word being used to convey a positive or negative sentiment. For instance, the word "impressive" is much more likely to be used in a positive sense than a negative sense; on the contrary, the word "ugly" is predominantly used in a negative sense. Then, we infer the sentiment of a given piece of text by using the sentiment scores of the terms contained in the text. One of the principal difficulties in this approach is that in online social media, different users have widely varying styles of writing text, and they use very different words to indicate similar sentiment. To address this, we use the well-known WordNet lexical directory [22] to identify groups of words which are synonymous to each other, and then treat all synonymous words (tokens) uniformly.

We applied our proposed methodology over six publicly available datasets [19] containing textual messages from six different online social media – Youtube, Twitter, MySpace, Runners World, BBC and Digg (detail in Sect. 4). We also compared the performance of our approach with that of several state-of-the-art sentiment detection approaches. Our evaluation (details in Sect. 5) shows that though our proposed method is very simple, it achieves similar or better accuracy than most of the state-of-the-art approaches.

2 Related Work

A lot of recent research has focused on inferring the sentiment opinions of users from content generated in online social networks [10,21]. Broadly, there are two different types of approaches for sentiment detection [9] – (i) machine-learning-based approaches, and (ii) lexical-based approaches. We discuss some such studies in this section. The reader is referred to [9,12] for a detailed survey and comparison among different sentiment detection approaches.

Machine learning based methods are developed based on supervised classification, where sentiment detection is modeled as a binary classification problem (i.e., positive or negative). For instance, Go *et al.* [8] proposed to use different *n*-gram based features in conjugation with part-of-speech tags to train supervised classifiers (e.g., Naive Bayes, SVM, Maximum Entropy) for sentiment detection. The primary difficulty faced by the machine learning approaches is that they need labeled data to train the classifiers, and such labeled data is difficult to obtain for online social media. A popular approach used to automatically generate labeled data is to rely on *emoticons* (such as ':-)' and ':-(') which are frequently used by people to indicate their sentiment while posting content to online social media [4]. For instance, [15] used emoticons to form the training set for classifiers, i.e., the data was lebeled 'positive' if it contained happy emoticons, and 'negative' if it contained sad or angry emoticons. On the other hand, lexical approaches make use of a predefined list of words (usually called a *'token list'*), where each word (token) has a specific sentiment score [3]. Different lexical-based approaches have been proposed in literature, such as Linguistic Inquiry and Word Count [17], SASA [16], SentiStrength [20], and so on.

Though sentiment analysis of English text has been well studied [11], sentiment inference algorithms trained on proper English text (e.g., lexical approaches which use standard English token lists) do not work as well when applied to online content [10] because online content frequent contains abbreviations and users do not use proper spellings or grammar. In fact, machine learning based approaches have been found to be more suitable for sentiment analysis of online content than the lexical approaches [1,17]. To address the difficulties in using standard English token lists, recent lexical approaches [10] attempt to construct their own token-lists which are specific to the content posted in online social media. The present study follows a similar approach, as detailed in later sections.

3   Proposed Methodology

In this section, we discuss the proposed methodology in detail. We consider that the input to the methodology will be a set of text messages, and the output will be a binary polarity (positive / negative) for each message.

Pre-processing: In most online social sites, textual messages contain URLs, punctuation marks, user-names, numbers, special characters (except emoticons), whitespaces, and so on. These are not important for sentiment analysis, hence we first tokenize the messages and filter out these tokens (if any) from the messages. We also filter out a standard set of English stop-words (e.g., 'a', 'the').

Inferring Sentiment Scores of Tokens: We take a lexical approach for sentiment detection. We first construct a *token list* which associates two sentiment scores with each token (word). The sentiment scores for a token t indicates the number of times t is used in a positive sense, and the number of times t is used in a negative sense. Prior research on sentiment detection has already produced such token lists for English language text [3]. But it has been seen that token lists meant for normal English text do *not* work well with content posted in online social networks [10]. Hence, we create a token-list specific to the input set of text messages.

To construct the token list, we need a set of clearly positive and negative messages (because we want to count the number of times a certain token is used in a positive / negative message). We initially derive a set of clearly positive and negative messages, by considering only messages that contain positive or negative emoticons. Note that prior research on sentiment analysis has shown the utility of emoticons, which frequently match the true sentiment of the writer [4].

Table 1. A sample token list, showing the number of times a certain token has been used in a positive / negative message.

Words (tokens)	Positive count	Negative count
awesome	6	2
impressive	10	1
bad	2	10
frightful	8	3
amazing	30	7
great	7	1
mischievousness	4	14
awful	2	1

Users of online social media use a variety of emoticons to express their sentiment. Example of positive emoticons are ':)', ':]', ':o)', ':o]', ':-]', and so on, and examples of negative emoticons are 'D:', 'D=','D-:', ':(', ':[', and so on. We considered a large set of positive and negative emoticons, as listed in [5–7], and then identified all the messages which contain any of these emoticons. Then we consider any message which contains only positive emoticon(s) as positive, and any message which contains only negative emoticons as negative. We found a few messages containing both types of emoticons – for such messages, we consider them to be positive if they contain more positive emoticons than negative ones (and negative if they contain more negative emoticons).[1] For instance, the message *"@planetjedward hey! going to see you in dundrum on friday :) i was talking to ur mam(my teacher) today :) NO SCHOOL because im going to you :)x ..... but I feel horrible :("* contains three positive emoticons and one negative emoticon, hence this message was considered as positive.

Then, for each token which occurred in at least one message containing an emoticon, we count the number of positive messages and the number of negative messages in which the token appears. Thus we get a token list containing two sentiment scores for each token. Table 1 shows a small illustrative token list, and the sentiment scores for some example words. For instance, the token 'impressive' has been used in 10 positive messages, as compared with only 1 negative message – this intuitively indicates that if the token 'impressive' is present in a message, then the message is much more likely to be positive.

Using WordNet to Normalize Sentiment Scores: A feature of textual content in online social media is that the content is generated by a wide diversity of users, and these users use different styles of writing. For instance, different users may use different words (having similar meaning) to express similar sentiment. In linguistics, different words having similar meaning are known as *synonyms*.

---

[1] Messages having equal number of positive and negative emoticons are ignored.

Hence, we attempted to normalize the sentiment scores across words which are synonyms of each other.

To identify synonyms, we use the WordNet dictionary [22], which is a large lexical database of English. In WordNet, nouns, verbs, adjectives and adverbs are grouped into sets of cognitive synonyms called *synsets*, each of which expresses a distinct concept [22]. For instance, the words 'shut' and 'close' are synonymous, and are contained in the same synset; similarly, the words 'car' and 'automobile' are grouped together in some other synset (see [22] for details).

We use WordNet as follows. For each token in the token list (created as described above), we check if the token list also contains synonyms of that word. If the token list contains multiple words which are synonyms of each other, then we normalize the positive and negative counts for those words (synonyms), by considering the mean values for the counts.

We explain our methodology through an example. As shown in Table 1 'awesome' is the first word. We find from WordNet that the word 'awesome' is contained in a synset which contains the following words (synonyms) – {awesome, dread, fearsome, frightening, terrible, frightful, amazing, horrific, dreaded, awed, fearful, nasty, abominable, unspeakable, horrendous, awful, awe-inspiring, atrocious, tremendous, astonishing, awing, dreadful, direful, dire, painful}. We find that the two synonyms – 'awesome' and 'frightful' – are both present in the token list in Table 1. So, we normalize the positive and negative counts of both these words, to the mean (average) value of their positive and negative counts. Hence, in the normalized token list, for both these words, the positive count will be $(6+8)/2 = 7$ and the negative count will be $(2+3)/2 = 2$ (considering integer part only). Similarly, the words 'impressive', 'amazing' and 'awful' are synonyms according to WordNet. Hence, the positive and negative counts for these words are normalized to their mean positive count and mean negative count. Table 2 shows the normalized version of the token list in Table 1, where the positive count and negative counts have been normalized for groups of synonyms.

Table 2. Normalized token list, for the original token list shown in Table 1. In this version, words which are synonymous among themselves (as identified using WordNet) have the same positive and negative counts.

Words (tokens)	Positive count	Negative count	Polarity	Sentiment score
awesome	7	2	Positive	+5
impressive	14	3	Positive	+11
bad	3	12	Negative	−9
frightful	7	2	Positive	+5
amazing	14	3	Positive	+11
great	7	1	Positive	+6
mischievousness	3	12	Negative	−9
awful	14	3	Positive	+11

Finally, in the normalized token list, if a certain token t has a higher (or equal) positive count than the negative count, we consider that token to be positive; otherwise the token is taken to be negative, as shown in Table 2 (4th column). We can also consider a sentiment score for each token, which is simply the difference between the positive and negative counts for the token (see Table 2, last column) – this score is greater than 0 for positive tokens, and less than 0 for negative ones.

Inferring Sentiment of a Text Message: As stated above, we computed a token list, where every token has a positive / negative polarity. Now, given a text message, we identify the positive and negative tokens contained in the message, and add the sentiment scores for the tokens. If the total sentiment score (for the tokens in this message) comes out to be greater than zero, we judge the message to be positive; on the other hand, if the total sentiment score comes out to be less than zero, the message is judged to be negative.

4   Dataset

To judge the performance of sentiment analysis schemes, we use a set of six datasets that were publicly made available by the SentiStrength research [19]. These consist of six sets of messages collected from different online social media sites – MySpace, Twitter, Digg, BBC forum, Runners World forum, and YouTube. The advantage of using these datasets is two-fold. First, the messages have been pre-annotated by human annotators as positive or negative, which can be used as *ground truth* for sentiment analysis task. Second, a recent study [9] applied several sentiment detection approaches over this dataset; hence, we can directly compare the performance of our approach with that of several others.

In the datasets, each message is labeled by human annotators, and has two scores – a 'mean positive' score, and a 'mean negative' score. These two scores represent two weighted metrics for positive and negative polarity of the message. Each score is between 1 and 5, where 5 means that the message is highly positive or highly negative, and 1 means weakly positive or negative.

In this work, we focus on binary polarity only, i.e., we attempt to label a given text as positive or negative. Hence, we considered a single polarity value for each message. For a particular message, if the mean positive score is greater or equal to the mean negative score, then we consider the polarity of this message to be positive, and negative otherwise. Table 3 shows some examples of messages from the Youtube and Twitter datasets. Also shown are the mean positive and mean negative scores (as originally given in the dataset), and the binary polarity (5 indicates positive, and 0 indicates negative) computed by us for each message. Finally, Table 4 summarizes the number of messages in the six datasets, along with the number of messages having positive and negative polarity.

5   Evaluation of the Approach

In this section, we evaluate the performance of the proposed approach, and compare its performance with some prior approaches.

Table 3. Examples of messages in the dataset [19] – comments in Youtube, and tweets posted in Twitter. Also shown are the mean positive and mean negative scores given in the dataset, and the binary positive / negative polarity computed by us.

mean pos	mean neg	Text	Polarity
Comments posted in Youtube			
1	2	Not a lot of "removing" going on here... bucket teeth removal maybe	0
2	2	I love looking at old gravestones	5
1	3	if that was supposed to rhyme, it didn't	0
5	1	Absolutely awesome!! Impressive	5
1	2	Yeah, because a minute and a half definitely equals 30 sec	0
Tweets posted in Twitter			
1	3	if my mom went on for the love of ray J or any reality show i'd bee pissed	0
3	1	@Mrhilton1985 Welcome to Twitter xx	5
1	3	@BarCough it's enough to make you sick, eh? there's nothing sacred anymore	0
2	1	@kjbmusic oh yeah... however, I'd still like to be in the midst of it all though... u know	5
2	1	I need a nice tea-drinking pic for our Tea Club Membership page - anyone got one theyd be happy for me to use?	5

Table 4. Labeled data sets

Dataset	Youtube	Twitter	MySpace	Runners	BBC	Digg
Positive messages	1699	1846	845	830	367	415
Negative messages	1708	2396	196	216	633	662
Total messages	3407	4241	1041	1046	1000	1077

Metrics for Comparison: To measure the performance of various sentiment detection approaches, we follow the standard methodology [9] of representing results in the form of a confusion matrix, and then compute *precision, recall, accuracy,* and *F-measure.* Table 5 shows an example of a confusion matrix, where 'True' means the ground truth polarity of a message, and 'Predicted' means the polarity predicted by a particular sentiment detection methodology. For the 'positive' class, the precision (P) is $P = a/(a+c)$, while the recall is $R = a/(a+b)$. The *accuracy* (A) is the proportion of the total number of items that are correctly

Table 5. Example of confusion matrix.

		Predicted	
		postive	negative
True	**positive**	a	b
	negative	c	d

Table 6. Average prediction performance of different methodologies, for all labeled datasets. The best scores are marked in boldface.

Metric	PANAS-t	SASA	Sentic-Net	Senti-WordNet	Happiness Index	Senti-Strength	LIWC	Proposed
Recall	0.614	0.648	0.562	0.601	0.571	0.767	0.153	**0.809**
Precision	0.741	0.667	0.934	0.786	0.945	0.78	**0.846**	0.845
Accuracy	0.677	0.649	0.59	0.643	0.639	**0.815**	0.675	0.790
F-measure	0.632	0.627	0.658	0.646	0.665	0.765	0.689	**0.779**

Table 7. F-measure for the various sentiment detection methods, for each of the six individual datasets. For each dataset, the best score is indicated in boldface.

Method	Twitter	MySpace	YouTube	BBC	Digg	Runners World	Average
PANAS-t	0.643	**0.958**	0.737	0.296	0.476	0.689	0.63
SASA	0.75	0.71	0.754	0.346	0.502	0.744	0.63
SenticNet	0.757	0.884	0.81	0.251	0.424	0.826	0.66
SentiWordNet	0.721	0.837	0.789	0.284	0.456	0.789	0.65
SentiStrength	0.843	0.915	**0.894**	**0.532**	0.632	0.778	0.77
Happiness Index	0.774	0.925	0.821	0.246	0.393	0.832	0.67
LIWC	0.69	0.862	0.731	0.377	0.585	**0.895**	0.69
Proposed	**0.875**	0.937	0.892	0.331	**0.757**	0.887	**0.78**

classified, i.e., $A = (a+d)/(a+b+c+d)$. Finally, the F-measure is the harmonic mean of precision and recall: $F = \frac{2PR}{P+R}$. The F-measure is especially important as it summarizes both precision and recall.

Results of Comparison with Other Approaches: We applied our proposed methodology (described in Sect. 3) on the dataset described in Sect. 4. As stated earlier, the recent study [9] reported the performance of a number of sentiment detection approaches on the same dataset, and we compare the performance of the proposed methodology with these prior approaches.[2] Table 6 compares the performance of the proposed method with that of seven other methods (whose results are obtained from [9]). It is evident that the proposed methodology, in spite of being very simple, performs favourably to the prior approaches. Especially, the proposed approach has the highest F-measure among all the approaches.

Since the F-measure summarizes both precision and recall, it is the most important metric of performance. Hence, we evaluate the F-measure for each individual dataset. The results are given in Table 7, along with the average F-measure over all six datasets. Again, it is seen that the overall F-measure for the proposed method is better than that for the other methods (though SentiStrength [19] performs almost equally well).

---

[2] Note that the study [9] studied one more approach (apart from the ones shown in Table 6), where the polarity of a text is directly given based on the emoticons contained in the text. Since less than 10 % of the text messages in this dataset (as well as in online social media in general) contain emoticons [9,13], this approach can be used for only 10 % of the messages (as also observed in [9]). Hence, we do not consider this approach for comparison.

Table 8. Prediction performance, averaged over all six labeled datasets

Method	Maximum entropy classifier (%)	Python textBlob (%)	Proposed method(%)
Youtube	52.65 %	**84.12 %**	81.42 %
Twitter	50.45 %	**82.88 %**	78.21 %
MySpace	49.84 %	87.99 %	**88.37 %**
Runners World	50.84 %	**82.50 %**	80.01 %
BBC	51.46 %	29.00 %	**71.80 %**
Digg	53.34 %	48.28 %	**79.85 %**
Average	51.43 %	69.13 %	**79.94 %**

Table 9. Examples of messages from Twitter and BBC, which were mis-classified by the proposed approach, along with their true polarity.

Text	True Polarity
Tweets posted in Twitter	
@Ludakit I've been served. Thanks for the splash of cold water	Positive
Out for drinks with the guys!	Positive
I have some of the weirdest cravings	Negative
cant find my wallet.. eeek	Negative
Comments posted in BBC	
It's time to take the gloves off and come out swinging	Positive
Brings a whole new meaning to 7up!	Positive
lol. Is that all you can come up with?	Negative
And do you think you have some logic? or goerge?	Negative

Finally, we compared the performance of the proposed approach with two other methodologies:

(i) *A machine learning approach:* We trained a standard Maximum Entropy classifier with the dataset, using distinct words contained in the messages as the features, and then applied the classifier on the same dataset.

(ii) *A natural language processing (NLP) approach:* Python TextBlob [14] is a standard library for NLP-based tasks, including sentiment analysis. We use this library to predict the sentiment of all messages in the dataset.

Table 8 shows the percentage of messages whose polarity was predicted correctly by the three methodologies (averaged over all six datasets). It is evident that the proposed methodology performs better than these state-of-the-art methods.

Error Analysis of the Proposed Methodology: In this final section, we perform a brief error analysis of the proposed approach by attempting to explain for what types of text messages the approach generally fails to infer sentiment correctly. Table 9 shows some examples of text messages from two of the datasets – Twitter and BBC – which were *mis-classified* by the proposed approach (i.e., the proposed approach inferred the sentiment as opposite to the true polarity shown in Table 9). We find that the misclassified messages are generally of two types, as described below.[3]

---

[3] Error analysis on the other datasets also yielded similar observations (omitted for brevity).

First, some of these messages do *not* contain any strong sentiment bearing words; the positive / negative sentiment is brought about by the whole message instead of few specific words. Examples include "Brings a whole new meaning to 7up!" and "Out for drinks with the guys!". For such messages, the token-based approach, at times, fails due to absence of any strongly positive or negative token.

Second, some of the other mis-classified messages contain one or more strongly positive / negative tokens, but the entire message has a polarity that is opposite to that of the few individual tokens. For instance, the message "lol. Is that all you can come up with?" contains the strongly positive token 'lol' (abbreviated form of 'laugh out loud'), but the polarity of the message as a whole is negative. The proposed method might end up mis-classifying such messages due to the presence of the strongly positive / negative token(s).

6 Conclusion

This work presents a simple but effective methodology for sentiment detection of textual content posted in various online social media. We adopt a lexical approach, based on creating a token list specific to the input set of text messages. The key step is to use the WordNet dictionary to unify the treatment for groups of words (tokens) that are synonymous with each other. This step helps to achieve consistent performance in the face of different words being used by different users (and in different social media). Detailed evaluation over a human annotated dataset shows that the proposed approach gives competitive or better performance than several state-of-the-art techniques for sentiment detection.

It can be noted that though the proposed approach gives competitive or better performance than several state-of-the-art methods, the best F-measures achieved by any of the methods is around 0.8. This highlights the fact that detecting sentiment of online text is inherently a very challenging problem, probably due to the wide variety of writing styles of users of online media. Thus, there is sufficient scope for improving the classification performance. Potential methods of improving performance include developing more accurate lexical databases specifically for online media (instead of relying on databases like Wordnet which are originally meant for formal English text), applying normalization techniques (e.g., Min-Max normalization) on the sentiment scores of tokens, and so on. We plan to try some of these approaches as future work.

Acknowledgement. The authors thank the anonymous reviewers for their constructive suggestions, and the authors of [9] for sharing the annotated datasets.

References

1. Bermingham, A., Smeaton, A.F.: Classifying sentiment in microblogs: is brevity an advantage? In: Proceedings of the ACM Conference on Information and Knowledge Management, pp. 1833–1836 (2010)

2. Bollen, J., Pepe, A., Mao, H.: Modeling public mood and emotion: twitter sentiment and socio-economic phenomena. CoRR abs/0911.1583 (2009)
3. Bradley, M.M., Lang, P.J.: Affective norms for english words (ANEW): instruction manual and affective ratings. Technical report C-1, Center for Research in Psychophysiology, University of Florida (1999)
4. Derks, D., Bos, A.E., von Grumbkow, J.: Emoticons and social interaction on the internet: the importance of social context. Comput. Hum. Behav. **23**(1), 842–849 (2007)
5. List of text emoticons: The ultimate resource. http://www.cool-smileys.com/text-emoticons
6. Msn messenger emoticons. http://www.messenger.msn.com/Resource/Emoticons.aspx
7. Yahoo messenger emoticons. http://www.messenger.yahoo.com/features/emoticons
8. Go, A., Bhayani, R., Huang, L.: Twitter sentiment classification using distant supervision. Technical report, Stanford University (2009)
9. Gonçalves, P., Araújo, M., Benevenuto, F., Cha, M.: Comparing and combining sentiment analysis methods. In: Proceeding of the ACM Conference on Online Social Networks (COSN), pp. 27–38 (2013)
10. Hannak, A., Anderson, E., Barrett, L.F., Lehmann, S., Mislove, A., Riedewald, M.: Tweetin' in the rain: exploring societal-scale effects of weather on mood. In: Proceedings of the AAAI Conference on Weblogs and Social Media (ICWSM), June 2012
11. Liu, B.: Web Data Mining: Exploring Hyperlinks Contents and Usage Data. Springer, Heidelberg (2006)
12. Pang, B., Lee, L.: Opinion mining and sentiment analysis. Found. Trends Inf. Retrieval **2**(1–2), 1–135 (2008)
13. Park, J., Barash, V., Fink, C., Cha, M.: Emoticon style: interpreting differences in emoticons across cultures. In: Proceedings of the AAAI Conference on Weblogs and Social Media (ICWSM) (2013)
14. TextBlob: Simplified Text Processing. http://textblob.readthedocs.org/en/dev/
15. Read, J.: Using emoticons to reduce dependency in machine learning techniques for sentiment classification. In: Proceedings of the ACL Student Research Workshop (2005)
16. Sarigiannidis, P.G., Papadimitriou, G.I., Pomportsis, A.S.: Sasa: a synthesis scheduling algorithm with prediction and sorting features. In: Proceedings of the IEEE Symposium on Computers and Communications, pp. 628–633 (2006)
17. Tausczik, Y.R., Pennebaker, J.W.: The psychological meaning of words: LIWC and computerized text analysis methods. J. Lang. Soc. Psychol. **29**(1), 24–54 (2010)
18. Teevan, J., Ramage, D., Morris, M.R.: #twittersearch: a comparison of microblog search and web search. In: Proceedings of the ACM Conference on Web Search and Data Mining (WSDM), pp. 35–44 (2011)
19. Thelwall, M.: Heart and Soul: Sentiment Strength Detection in the Social Web with SentiStrength. http://sentistrength.wlv.ac.uk/
20. Thelwall, M., Buckley, K., Paltoglou, G.: Sentiment strength detection for the social web. J. Am. Soc. Inf. Sci. Technol. **63**(1), 163–173 (2012). http://dx.doi.org/10.1002/asi.21662
21. Tumasjan, A., Sprenger, T., Sandner, P., Welpe, I.: Predicting elections with twitter: What 140 characters reveal about political sentiment. In: Proceeding of the AAAI Conference on Weblogs and Social Media (ICWSM), pp. 178–185 (2010)
22. Wordnet - a lexical database for English. http://wordnet.princeton.edu/

A Neighbourhood Based Hybrid Genetic Search Model for Feature Selection

Sunanda Das[1], Arka Ghosh[2(✉)], and Asit Kumar Das[3]

[1] Neotia Institute of Technology, Management and Science,
Jhinga, Diamond Harbour, South 24 Pargana 743368, India
Sunanda_srkr@yahoo.co.in
[2] Purabi Das School of Information Technology, Indian Institute of Engineering
Science and Technology, Shibpur, Howrah-03, India
arka.besu@gmx.com
[3] Department of Computer Science and Technology,
Indian Institute of Engineering Science and Technology, Shibpur,
Howrah-03, India
akdas@cs.becs.ac.in

Abstract. The paper presents a hybrid genetic search model (HGSM) with novel neighbourhood based uniform local search to select the subset of salient features removing redundant information from the universe of discourse. The method uses least square regression error as the fitness function for selecting the most feasible set of features from a large number of feature set. Proposed work is validated using our simulated character dataset and some real world datasets available in UCI Machine learning repository and performance comparison of proposed method with some other state of art feature selection methods are provided.

Keywords: Local search · Genetic algorithm · Data mining · Feature selection · Least square regression error

1 Introduction

Feature selection is an important prior task of Knowledge Discovery in Data Mining (KDD) to remove the spurious features from the original feature set. This method ultimately provides better performance of clustering and classification analysis in the field of pattern recognition. Feature selection algorithms [1–3] are basically of two types, namely, filter and wrapper approach. Filtering technique measures the importance of each feature based on the dataset itself, whereas wrapper methods invoke the learning algorithm to find the best quality features within the feature set. But both the methods involve combinatorial searches through the entire feature space. Generally, feature subset selection algorithm performs two measures:

(a) Firstly, the algorithm measures the quality of the feature subset. In this measurement, relevance of each feature is individually taken into account and at the same time size of the feature subset is tried to be reduced for achieving better performance of the subsequent data mining algorithms.

© Springer International Publishing Switzerland 2015
B.K. Panigrahi et al. (Eds.): SEMCCO 2014, LNCS 8947, pp. 421–431, 2015.
DOI: 10.1007/978-3-319-20294-5_37

(b) The algorithm deploys a searching strategy to obtain a globally best feature subset based on the defined measurements. For a dataset with large features, finding of best feature subset among all features by exhaustive searching is computationally infeasible.

So, feature selection [4] is basically a search process where feature space is being searched to select the optimal subset of features that can fully characterise the feature set. There are various optimized searching techniques [5] such as, Ant colony based search [6], Tabu search [7], and simulated annealing [8] which are used frequently for feature subset selection.

Recently, various feature selection methods are introduced by the researchers based on variety of evolutionary strategies [9, 10]. Rough set based feature selection method is discussed in [11]. Feature selection for structure activity and structure property correlation based on particle swarm optimization is given in [12]. Binary particle swarm optimization based feature selection for gene expression data is presented in [13]. Two phase feature selection for most discriminator feature set based on particle swarm optimization is presented in [14]. Several wrapper feature selection strategies based on evolutionary methods are given in [15, 16].

Memetic algorithms [17] represent one of the recent growing areas of research in evolutionary computation. The algorithms are quite popular for successful search in a large search space where traditional exhaustive search methods are not well suited. Genetic algorithm (GA) [18] which has great potential for finding the best approximate solution to the optimization problem is very much popular in the evolutionary optimization community. Though GA works well in an exponential search space it provides local optimal solution caused by premature convergence. To overcome this problem several hybridization of genetic algorithm are proposed in [19, 20].

Though Genetic algorithms are weak to do fine grained local search, its hybridization with local search [21] sometimes enhance the overall performance of the system. In GA, local search is applied to all newly created offspring so that each of them has the possibility of finding the best local optimum. To overcome such premature convergence of GA, hybridization of genetic algorithm with local search methods is proposed in [22] to achieve more effective optimization for local and global optimum. Hybrid model of genetic algorithm with local search is proposed in [23] for linguistic data summary from creep data. It incorporates two new operations namely cleaning operator and proposition improvement operator to maintain sustained diversity among the population. H. Ishibuchi and T. Murata [24] propose a multi-objective genetic algorithm integrating local search for finding a set of solutions of a flow shop scheduling problem. In [25], a multi-objective time dependent route planning problem is solved integrating NSGA-II [19] with local search.

In this paper, standard genetic algorithm is further extended to scrutinized search of the fitness space to achieve the global optima. As local search algorithms are well appreciated for their ability to find the local optima, the paper proposes a novel neighbourhood based hybridization of local search strategy with standard genetic algorithm. The method uses least square regression error [26] as the fitness function and binary representation of chromosome as population member. Steady state selection, single point crossover and jumping gene mutation [27] scheme are applied. For each chromosome a certain circular neighbourhood of predefined radius (in terms of hamming distance [28] between binary strings) is used.

The paper is organized into four sections. Section 2 describes the detailed methodology of the proposed hybrid genetic search model (HGSM). Section 3 demonstrates the experimental results and compares it with some other state of arts feature selection algorithms using our simulated character dataset and some real world datasets to evaluate the performance and effectiveness of the proposed method. Finally, Sect. 4 draws the conclusion and future enhancement of the work.

2   Hybrid Genetic Search Model (HGSM) Construction

First phase of our algorithm deals with selecting relevant features using Genetic algorithm, a stochastic parallel search procedure developed for problems with a large number of features. Our algorithm defined a chromosome as a string of bits whose size corresponds to the number of features. A 1 or 0 in i^{th} position of the string depicts presence or absence of the corresponding feature. Binary chromosome population of predefined population size is initialized randomly.

2.1   The Genetic Operators

Genetic Algorithm has few parameters to tune for improving the performance of the optimization problem. These operators are responsible for selection of parent chromosomes, crossover of the parents to obtain a new offspring, and mutation of the offspring to preserve the diversity among the population over generations. The selection technique determines which chromosomes are chosen for the next population. The selection process reduces the search space by removing the chromosomes with poor fitness value, where as the crossover and mutation techniques explore the search space for finding globally optimal solutions.

In the proposed work a steady state selection technique is opted and mutation probability is set to 0.1. The population size is set experimentally in between 100 to 1000. As the operators have both constructive and destructive effect, they must be adapted to the problem.

Selection: The most commonly used parent chromosomes selection techniques are proportionate reproduction, ranking selection, tournament selection, and steady state. In this paper, a steady state selection mechanism is implemented, where each population member (i.e., chromosome) is equal probable to get into mating pool.

Crossover: Every pair of parents is made sure to take part in the crossover operation to produce offspring. Single point crossover [18] scheme is utilized here to generate offspring. The offspring is kept, only if they fit better than its any parent in the population.

Mutation: Mutation plays a vital role in preserving diversity among the population over generations. Single bit mutation is very much popular in GA but it lacks diversity in population as the first bit of binary string generally does not change. To overcome the demerit, jumping gene mutation methodology [27] is used in the paper for mutating the genes. Jumping genes are a set of genes which can jump dynamically within the chromosome. These genes have a great potential for maintaining diversity throughout the entire population, crucial for evolutionary searching algorithm.

Let, a chromosome in population is $(a_1, a_2, \ldots, a_n)$. Jumping genes of length q $(q < <n)$ say, $(b_1, b_2, \ldots, b_q)$ is selected randomly and the starting position in the chromosome is chosen randomly to replace by the jumping gene. Let k is the starting position, so after mutation the muted chromosome is $(a_1, a_2, \ldots, a_{k-1}, b_1, b_2, \ldots, b_q, a_{k+q}, \ldots, a_n)$.

2.2   Local Search Strategy

In a particular generation, proximity of a population member with respect to other members of the same population is computed using the following scheme. Let, D is the snapshot of current population with four population members {1 1 0 1}, {1 0 0 1}, {1 1 1 1}, and {1 0 0 0}. Proximity of first member {1 1 0 1}, using all other population members is computed using the standard hamming distance and their mean is taken, in this example mean is 1. So with {1 1 0 1} as schema, specified number of neighbours is generated each with hamming distance 1. If any of newly created neighbours is already present in current population then it is discarded and another neighbour is created in its place. Now search is performed among these neighbours and original member {1 1 0 1} is replaced by a neighbour of better fitness than it. Similarly, neighbours of all the members are generated and population members are modified by local search strategy. In this way, fine grained search is performed.

2.3   Fitness Function

Choice of fitness function plays important role in success of any evolutionary algorithm. Proposed method uses least square regression error as the search criteria. Least square regression error [26] is a measure of linear dependency between features. If x_1 is set of conditional attribute and x_2 is set of decision attribute for any particular dataset, then objective is to find such x_1 which will have minimum least square regression error predicting x_2 from the linear model $x_2 = a + bx_1$, a and b are regression coefficient obtained by minimizing the mean square error, using proposed HGSM.

The workflow diagram of the methodology is described in Fig. 1.

3   Experimental Results

Experimental results presented here demonstrate the effectiveness of proposed feature selection technique. Experiments carried out on simulated character dataset "All_47" and some real world machine learning data set publicly available at http://archive.ics.uci.edu/ml/.

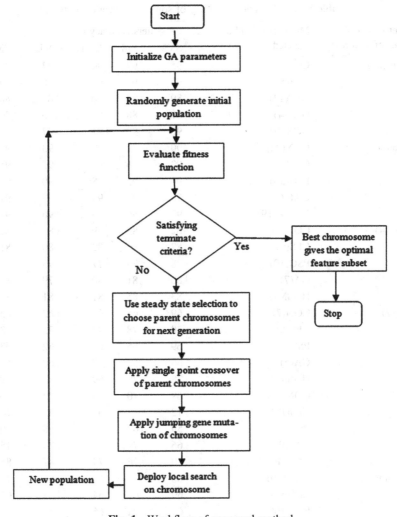

Fig. 1. Workflow of proposed method

K-fold (here, K = 10) cross validation technique is applied on the data set to generate training and test set. The training set is used for forming optimal feature set and test set is used for computing classification accuracy to measure the effectiveness of the method. Some existing feature selection methods like Consistency Subset Selection (CON) [29], Correlated Feature Selection (CFS) [30], Particle swarm optimization based feature selection (PSO) [31], Genetic Algorithm based feature selection, and the proposed method (HGSM) for feature selection is applied on the datasets and classification accuracies on reduced datasets are measured by various classifiers available at WEKA [32] tool, as listed in Table 1. CON, CFS, and PSO, GA based method are available at WEKA tool and proposed HGSM method is implemented by us.

Table 1. Classification accuracy of some important datasets

Dataset (Total number of features)	Methods (Number of selected features)	Classifiers accuracy (%)				
		SVM	J48	VOTE	MLP	SMO
Anneal (21)	CON(11)	95	97	90	97	95
	CFS(8)	96	96	90	96	94
	PSO(12)	89	83	80	87	88
	GA(14)	89	88	81	86	89
	HGSM(8)	96	97	91	97	95
Dermatology (35)	CON(22)	90	91	89	93	90
	CFS(17)	92	96	92	95	95
	PSO(23)	90	93	88	90	93
	GA(16)	88	91	93	89	91
	HGSM(19)	97	96	95	96	97
Heart (14)	CON(7)	82	83	79	80	82
	CFS(9)	82	80	82	80	81
	PSO(10)	78	79	77	75	77
	GA(7)	80	81	80	79	82
	HGSM(8)	83	85	81	81	83
Liver (7)	CON(7)	69	65	64	62	63
	CFS(6)	78	78	70	72	73
	PSO(7)	69	65	67	62	63
	GA(5)	66	59	57	60	61
	HGSM(6)	78	79	69	71	79
All_47 (48)	CON(20)	69	70	70	72	70
	CFS(19)	72	71	68	73	70
	PSO(32)	59	62	65	68	69
	GA(19)	66	74	71	74	75
	HGSM(17)	80	76	79	87	85
Arrhythmia (279)	CON(50)	66	78	69	66	71
	CFS(55)	69	65	64	62	63
	PSO(100)	63	74	66	71	75
	GA(50)	69	78	71	74	78
	HGSM(61)	89	90	89	93	96
Multiple Features (649)	CON(150)	79	78	77	69	70
	CFS(146)	78	75	70	72	73
	PSO(200)	68	62	63	68	66
	GA(189)	63	74	58	63	61
	HGSM(120)	90	92	89	93	90

From Table 1, it is observed that, for Anneal, Dermatology and simulated all_47 datasets, the proposed method HGSM provides superior results compare to the others in terms of both attribute reduction and accuracy and at the same time for Heart and Liver datasets it provides competitive results. Executing system consists of 8

CORE CPU running at 4 GHz clock frequency, 8 GB RAM operating on 1.6 GHz. In time of classification accuracy calculation, some statistical measurements like Recall (True Positive Rate), Fall-out, Specificity (False Positive Rate) and F1-score are calculated using (1), (2), (3) and (4), respectively.

$$Recall = \frac{TP}{P} = \frac{TP}{TP + FN} \tag{1}$$

$$Fall\_out = \frac{FP}{N} = \frac{FP}{FP + TN} \tag{2}$$

$$Specificity = \frac{TN}{N} = \frac{TN}{FP + TN} = 1 - Fall\_out \tag{3}$$

$$F1\_score = \frac{2 \times TP}{2 \times TP + FP + FN} \tag{4}$$

Where, TP is the positive object classified as positive, FP is the positive object classified as negative, TN is the negative object classified as negative and FN is the negative object classified as positive. The calculated various statistical measurements are shown in Table 2 to Table 6 for various classifiers. It is observed that proposed

Table 2. Statistical measure for Anneal dataset

Statistical measure	CON	CFS	PSO	GA	HGSM
Recall	0.84	0.85	0.89	0.84	0.85
Fall_out	0.22	0.23	0.32	0.33	0.23
Specificity	0.78	0.76	0.68	0.69	0.78
F1_score	0.83	0.94	0.79	0.88	0.94

Table 3. Statistical measure for Dermatology dataset

Statistical measure	CON	CFS	PSO	GA	HGSM
Recall	0.93	0.97	0.92	0.92	0.98
Fall_out	0.19	0.29	0.18	0.18	0.16
Specificity	0.81	0.71	0.82	0.82	0.84
F1_score	0.91	0.94	0.89	0.96	0.93

Table 4. Statistical measure for Heart dataset

Statistical measure	CON	CFS	PSO	GA	HGSM
Recall	0.93	0.93	0.97	0.93	0.94
Fall_out	0.06	0.06	0.42	0.14	0.02
Specificity	0.94	0.94	0.58	0.96	0.98
F1_score	0.83	0.83	0.78	0.82	0.87

Table 5. Statistical measure for Liver dataset

Statistical measure	CON	CFS	PSO	GA	HGSM
Recall	0.86	0.85	0.84	0.80	0.85
Fall_out	0.63	0.88	0.61	0.75	0.89
Specificity	0.35	0.12	0.39	0.25	0.10
F1_score	0.79	0.84	0.77	0.75	0.87

Table 6. Statistical measure for All_47 dataset

Statistical measure	CON	CFS	PSO	GA	HGSM
Recall	0.87	0.75	0.52	0.85	0.86
Fall_out	0.89	0.33	0.40	0.22	0.37
Specificity	0.10	0.67	0.59	0.39	0.63
F1_score	0.81	0.86	0.79	0.86	0.89

Table 7. Statistical measure for Arrhythmia dataset

Statistical measure	CON	CFS	PSO	GA	HGSM
Recall	0.84	0.87	0.84	0.56	0.86
Fall_out	0.62	0.82	0.56	0.69	0.90
Specificity	0.45	0.22	0.93	0.34	0.11
F1_score	0.87	0.86	0.89	0.90	0.91

Table 8. Statistical measure for Multiple Feature dataset

Statistical measure	CON	CFS	PSO	GA	HGSM
Recall	0.78	0.84	0.83	0.66	0.89
Fall_out	0.59	0.81	0.52	0.69	0.96
Specificity	0.32	0.28	0.89	0.32	0.14
F1_score	0.91	0.88	0.76	0.79	0.93

Table 9. Comparisons of F1_Score obtained by various methods

Dataset	CON	CFS	PSO	GA	HGSM
Anneal	0.83	0.94	0.79	0.88	0.94
Dermatology	0.91	0.94	0.89	0.96	0.93
Heart	0.83	0.83	0.78	0.82	0.87
Liver	0.79	0.84	0.77	0.75	0.87
All_47	0.81	0.86	0.79	0.86	0.89
Arrhythmia	0.87	0.86	0.89	0.90	0.91
Multiple Feature	0.91	0.88	0.76	0.79	0.93
Average	0.85	0.88	0.81	0.85	0.91

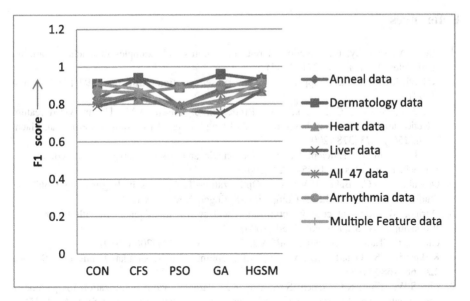

Fig. 2. Graphical representation of F1_score for various feature reduction scheme

method HGSM, in spite of very simple, performs consistent results compare to prior methods.

Separately, the F1_score of all five methods are listed in Table 9 for all seven datasets and also the average F1_score is computed. From the table, it is observed that average score is comparatively higher for the proposed method which implies the statistical significance of the proposed method. The result is also graphically shown by Fig. 2, where, each of the seven dataset is represented using separate color and along X-axis and Y-axis feature reduction methods and F1_score are plotted respectively. For each dataset represented by a specific color, we can visualize easily that the proposed method provides higher F1_score compare to almost all other feature reduction schemes (Tables 3, 4, 5, 7, 8).

4 Conclusion and Future Work

Systematic and unbiased approach to classification is of great importance in data mining. Therefore, automated discovery of this small and good feature subset is highly desirable. In the paper, a novel local search based genetic algorithm approach has been proposed to select informative feature sub set, which classify the dataset effectively and efficiently. The method uses fitness functions based on the concepts of least square regression error. Jumping gene mutation also overcomes the lack of diversity of population that may arise in case of single bit mutation. The only demerit of the method is that we have set the population size within the range 100 to 1000 experimentally. As the method guaranteed that any one member of the final population gives the reduced dimension of the system, in future we will try to minimize the population size and construct a classifier for each reduced dataset and try to ensemble them [33].

References

1. Blum, A., Langley, P.: Selection of relevant features and examples in machine learning. Artif. Intell. **97**(12), 245–271 (1997)
2. Kohavi, R., John, G.: Wrappers for feature subset selection. Artif. Intell. **97**(12), 273–324 (1997)
3. Dy, J.G., Brodley, C.E., Kak, A.L., Broderick, S., Aisen, A.M.: Unsupervised feature selection applied to content-based retrieval of lung images. IEEE Trans. Pattern Anal. Mach. Intell. **25**(3), 373–378 (2003)
4. Yu, L., Huan, L.: Efficient feature selection via analysis of relevance and redundancy. J. Mach. Learn. Res. **5**, 1205–1224 (2004)
5. Onwubolu, G.C., Babu, B.V.: New Optimization Techniques in Engineering Goldberg. Studies in fuzziness and Soft Computing. Springer, New York (2004)
6. Dorigo, M., ed.: Ant colony optimization and swarm intelligence. In: 5th International Workshop, ANTS 2006, vol. 4150 (2006)
7. Glover, F.: Tabu search-part I. ORSA J. Comput. **1**(3), 190–206 (1989)
8. Kirkpatrick, S., Gelatt, C.D., Vecchi, M.P.: Optimization by simulated annealing. Science **220**, 661–680 (1983)
9. Lin, S.W., Ying, K.C., Chen, S.C., Lee, Z.J.: Particle swarm optimization for parameter determination and feature selection of support vector machines. Expert Syst. Appl. **35**(4), 1817–1824 (2008)
10. Ramadan, R.M., Abdel-Kader, R.F.: Face recognition using particle swarm optimization-based selected features. Int. J. Signal Process. Image Process. Pattern Recogn. **2**(2), 51–65 (2009)
11. Wang, X., Yang, J., Teng, X., Xia, W., Jensen, R.: Feature selection based on rough sets and particle swarm optimization. Pattern Recogn. Lett. **28**(4), 459–471 (2007)
12. Agrafiotis, D.K., Cedeno, W.: Feature selection for structure-activity correlation using binary particle swarms. J. Med. Chem. **45**(5), 1098–1107 (2002)
13. Chuang, L.Y., Chang, H.W., Tu, C.J., Yang, C.H.: Improved binary PSO for feature selection using gene expression data. Comput. Biol. Chem. **32**(1), 29–38 (2008)
14. Huang, C.L., Dun, J.F.: A distributed PSO–SVM hybrid system with feature selection and parameter optimization. Appl. Soft Comput. **8**(4), 1381–1391 (2008)
15. Xiao, X., Dow, E.R., Eberhart, R., Miled, Z.B., Oppelt, R.J.: Gene clustering using self-organizing maps and particle swarm optimization. In: Parallel and Distributed Processing Symposium, vol. 10. IEEE (2003)
16. Pedrycz, W., Park, B.-J., Pizzi, N.J.: Identifying core sets of discriminatory features using particle swarm optimization. Expert Syst. Appl. **36**(3), 4610–4616 (2009)
17. Knowles, J.D., Corne, D.W.: M-PAES: A memetic algorithm for multiobjective optimization. Evolutionary Computation. In: Proceedings of the 2000 Congress, vol. 1. IEEE (2000)
18. Goldberg, D.E., Holland, J.H.: Genetic algorithms and machine learning. Mach. Learn. **3**(2), 95–99 (1988)
19. Deb, K., et al.: A fast and elitist multiobjective genetic algorithm: NSGA-II. IEEE Trans. Evol. Comput. **6**(2), 182–197 (2002)
20. Coello, C.A.C., Lamont, G.B., van Veldhuisen, D.A.: Evolutionary Algorithms for Solving Multi-objective Problems. Springer, Berlin (2007)
21. Aarts, E.H.L., Lenstra, J.K. (eds.): Local Search in Combinatorial Optimization. Princeton University Press, Princeton (2003)

22. Kim, K.W., Yun, Y.S., Yoon, J.M., Gen, M., Yamazaki, G.: Hybrid genetic algorithm with adaptive abilities for resource constrained multiple project scheduling. Comput. Ind. **56**(2), 143–160 (2005)
23. Diaz, C.A.D., Muro, A.G., Pérez, R.B., Morales, E.V.: A hybrid model of genetic algorithm with local search to discover linguistic data summaries from creep data. Expert Syst. Appl. **41**, 2035–2042 (2014)
24. Ishibuchi, H., Murata, T.: A multi-objective genetic local search algorithm and its application to flowshop scheduling. IEEE Trans. Syst. Man Cybern. **28**(3), 392–403 (1998)
25. Sharma, S., Mathew, T.V.: Multiobjective network design for emission and travel-time trade-off for a sustainable large urban transportation network. Environ. Plann. B Plann. Des. **38**(3), 520–538 (2011)
26. Ramsey, J.B.: Tests for specification errors in classical linear least square regression analysis. J. Royal Stat. Soc. Ser. B (Methodol.) **31**, 350–371 (1969)
27. Pati, S.K., Das, A.K., Ghosh, A.: Gene selection using multi-objective genetic algorithm integrating cellular automata and rough set theory. In: Panigrahi, B.K., Suganthan, P.N., Das, S., Dash, S.S. (eds.) SEMCCO 2013, Part II. LNCS, vol. 8298, pp. 144–155. Springer, Heidelberg (2013)
28. Norton, G.H., Salagean, A.: On the hamming distance of linear codes over a finite chain ring. IEEE Trans. Inf. Theory **46**(3), 1060–1067 (2000)
29. Dash, M., Liu, H.: Consistency-based search in feature selection. Artif. Intell. **151**(1), 155–176 (2003)
30. Hall, M.A.: Correlation-based feature selection for machine learning. Diss. The University of Waikato (1999)
31. Kennedy, J.: Particle swarm optimization. In: Sammut, C., Webb, G.I. (eds.) Encyclopedia of Machine Learning, pp. 760–766. Springer, US, London (2010)
32. Hall, M., et al.: The WEKA data mining software: an update. ACM SIGKDD Explor. Newsl. **11**(1), 10–18 (2009)
33. Albukhanajer, W.A., Jin, Y., Briffa, J.A.: Neural network ensembles for image identification using pareto-optimal features. In: IEEE Congress on Evolutionary Computation CEC (2014)

An Automated Semantically Enabled Fuzzy Based SLA in Cloud Computing Environment Using Multi-agent System

Manoranjan Parhi[✉], Binod Kumar Pattanayak,
and Manas Ranjan Patra

[1] Department of Computer Science and Engineering, Institute of Technical
Education and Research, Siksha 'O' Anusandhan University,
Khandgiri, Bhubaneswar, OR, India
mrparhi@gmail.com, bkp_iter@yahoo.co.in
[2] Department of Computer Science, Berhampur University, Berhampur 760007,
Odisha, India
mrpatra12@gmail.com

Abstract. In order to make reservations for cloud services, consumers and providers need to work on Service Level Agreements (SLAs) to achieve negotiation. Since cloud computing represents a category of distributed system, negotiation should be established between service providers and consumers in a faster and reliable manner. Automated Negotiation is such a process that is closely associated with Multi-agent Systems. We propose A Negotiation system using fuzzy ontology is addressed by us in this research work where the cloud service specification and consumer requirements with vagueness are stored on cloud ontology. Here, each party needs to choose its own agent in order for negotiation. Agents have both consumer's and provider's details and their hard and soft preferences for a particular service. Agents need to negotiate on the basis of a set of Quality of Service (QoS) parameters like duration, availability, price etc. as required by the user. On completion of the negotiation process, user receives a feedback from the agent regarding the probability of negotiation. This negotiation framework is dynamic and efficient in nature.

Keywords: Service level agreement (SLA) · Multi-agent system · Fuzzy ontology · Quality of service (QoS)

1 Introduction

Cloud computing represents a form of distributed system with a dynamic environment that is more reliable and customized. It mostly uses explicitly visualized resources that are very often scalable [1]. It continues to evolve in order for optimal collaboration among service providers using novel negotiation mechanisms thereby allowing relatively efficient services to customers. As various consumers tend to use personalized cloud services, Service Level Agreements (SLAs) emerge as a key aspect in cloud and utility computing. Such SLAs facilitate collaborative decision making among cloud service consumers and service providers in order for resolution of their mutually contradicting goals. Cloud services must conform to the QoS parameters like availability

B.K. Panigrahi et al. (Eds.): SEMCCO 2014, LNCS 8947, pp. 432–444, 2015.
DOI: 10.1007/978-3-319-20294-5_38

cost and at the same time, must generate profit. Cloud service providers as well as requesters need to support a cost-benefit model that facilitates the negotiation mechanism and the process of decision making. In the recent years, extensive research has been conducted in the area of Service Level Agreement (SLA) in accordance with Service Oriented Architecture (SOA), Grid Computing and Cloud Computing. Researches in these areas have mainly focused on three aspects of SLAM namely, SLA language specification [2], SLA negotiation techniques [3], and SLA monitoring approaches [2, 4]. An efficient approach to cloud computing is necessary in order to enable the cloud service providers and consumers to reach an agreement between them. However, a set of challenges that the service providers and consumers need to overcome before arriving to an agreement, during service composition in particular, where the consumer needs to negotiate with several cloud service providers. As consumers and providers are independent bodies, some mechanisms are necessary to resolve different hard and soft preferences with vagueness when they establish a SLA among them.

Here, the cloud virtual machine represents the target of the process of negotiation and negotiation parameters include both functional and quality of service (QoS) with uncertainty values. Here, we have proposed a novel semantically enabled multi-agent based framework for effective cloud service negotiation which can handle the fuzzy values associated with the SLA. The rest of the paper is organized as follows. Section 2 describes the background of our research work. Section 3 explains our proposed multi-agent based framework for cloud service negotiation using fuzzy ontology. We have discussed a case study on IaaS cloud service negotiation in Sect. 4. Section 5 outlines the implementation details of the case study with experimental evaluation and finally Sect. 6 concludes the paper with probable extension in future.

2 Background

2.1 Cloud Computing

In this research paper, we adopt the definition of cloud computing as suggested by The National Institute of Standards and Technology (NIST) [5] that says:

> "Cloud computing is a model for enabling convenient, on-demand network access to a shared pool of configurable computing resources (e.g., networks, servers, storage, applications, and services) that can be rapidly provisioned and released with minimal management effort or service provider interaction."

A large set of benefits that are achievable from a cloud service are fast deployment, pay-for-use, lower costs, scalability, rapid provisioning, rapid elasticity, ubiquitous network access, greater resiliency, hypervisor protection against network attacks, low-cost disaster recovery and data storage solutions, on-demand security controls, real time detection of system tampering and rapid re-constitution of services. Business organizations, mostly of medium and small profiles, are often attracted towards cloud services due to its attractive features listed above. The business model that is employed by a cloud computing environment is service-driven. Service-driven strategy refers to a fact that platform level or even hardware resources are made available to consumers by a cloud service provider in the form of a service on demand, that is, as and when requested for. There are three categories of services offered by cloud service providers: software as a service (SaaS), platform as a service (PaaS), and infrastructure as a service (IaaS).

1. *Software as a Service*: When an application is made available to a requester in an on demand basis over the global Internet, this is referred to as Saas. Examples of SaaS providers include Salesforce.com, Rackspace, gmail etc.
2. *Platform as a Service*: When platform level resources such as operating system support or software development frameworks are made available to a requester on demand, then it is referred to as PaasS. Examples of PaaS providers include Google App Engine, Microsoft Windows Azure and Force.com.
3. *Infrastructure as a Service*: When infrastructural resources in the form of virtual machines (VM) are provided to the requester over the Internet, it is referred to as IaaS. Examples of IaaS providers include Amazon EC2, GoGrid and Flexiscale.

2.2 Multi-agent System

An agent can be regarded as a computational entity which operates on behalf of other entity/entities in order to perform a task or achieve a specified goal. Self-contained software programs incorporating the domain knowledge with processing capabilities of a specific degree of independence in order to execute actions required to achieve a set of given goals, form an Agent System. A Multi-agent represents a system comprising of a set of agents which can eventually interact among each other. MAS incur few advantages as compared to isolated agents, such as reliability and robustness, modularity and scalability, adaptively, concurrency and parallelism, and dynamism etc. [6]. A large spectrum of design strategies have been proposed in order to facilitate the process of development of MAS. JADE (Java Agent Development Environment) is most popular platform today for developing Multi-agent System. Agent technology is mostly preferred in order for developing relatively complex and distributed applications. Of late, Agent-based Cloud computing [7, 8] as a novel paradigm, is capable of providing agent-based solutions based on the design and development of software agents in order to improve Cloud resources, service management, discovery, SLA negotiation, and service composition.

2.3 Ontology

The method of knowledge representation which is used in the Semantic Web [9] refers to the ontology that justifies the right meaning of it and subsequently facilitates the search for contents and information, and at the same time, improves the crawling procedure. Several definitions of ontology can be extracted from the current literature. As quoted by Thomas R. Gruber [10] "An ontology is a formal and explicit specification of a shared conceptualization". The hierarchical relationship among different concepts of cloud is incorporated in Cloud Ontology [11, 12]. For example, IaaS, PaaS and SaaS form the three children node of the cloud concept "CloudSystem". Similarity

Reasoning can be performed in consultation with Cloud ontology. Ontology can be expressed in terms of Web Ontology Language-Description Logic (OWL-DL).

2.4 Fuzzy Description Logic

Description Logic (DL) is the consequence of logical reconstruction of the so-called frame based knowledge representation language with an intention to provide a simple, precise and well established declarative semantics in order to achieve the meaning of the most popular features of the structured representation of the knowledge. Fuzzy DLs [13, 14] represent an extension to conventional DLs in order to deal with fuzzy vague or imprecise concepts.

3 Proposed System

The detailed architecture of the proposed negotiation system is depicted in Fig. 1. The various agents used in the proposed framework are detailed below.

3.1 Provider Agent

This agent can be used by the service provider for registering a new service or up gradation of an existing service. It can communicate directly with the cloud service provider and keep track of the popularity of the cloud service as per the user's feedback. In addition, provider agent is capable of updating dynamically the functionality of the cloud service from time to time.

3.2 Consumer Agent

A user friendly graphical user interface is provided by the Consumer Agent that facilitates the process of query for a cloud service. The Consumer Agent is capable of interacting with other agents like Discovery Agent in the platform through Agent Communication Language (ACL) based on Simple Protocol and RDF Query Language (SPARQL) and Web Ontology Language (OWL) DL. It reveals that the Consumer Agent is aware of the target of query request and the semantics of communication context with each other.

3.3 Discovery Agent

Discovery agent performs the task of discovery of the requested cloud services from the Semantic Service Registry with reference to the information provided by service consumer. The semantic description of cloud service providers along with their attributes are made available through service ontology. Hence, Discovery Agents can reason about the ontology thereby making the discovery of cloud services dynamic and automatic.

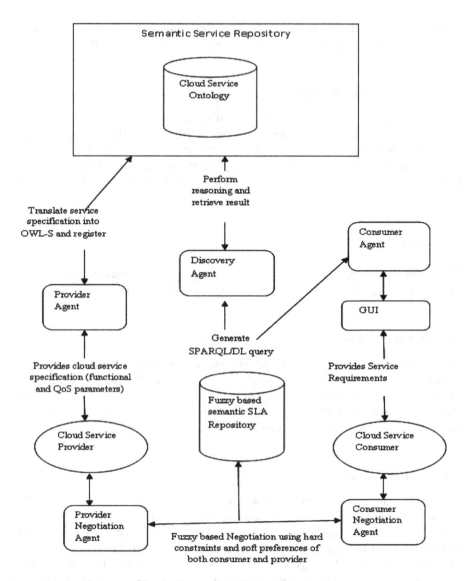

Fig. 1. Proposed negotiation framework

3.4   Consumer Negotiation Agent

After discovery of suitable cloud service provider the consumer starts the negotiation process with the provider through the consumer negotiation agent. The requester's hard constraints and soft preferences relating hardware specification like CPU, persistent storage, memory and QoS parameters like price, availability etc. are stored in the fuzzy based semantic SLA repository.

3.5 Provider Negotiation Agent

Provider Negotiation Agent starts the negotiation process after receiving the request from consumer by supplying the both hard and soft service specification of the provider which are stored in SLA repository.

Finally both negotiation agents use the fuzzy reasoner which can process the information stored in SLA repository to find the probability of negotiation among them.

4 A Case Study

We address a case study relating to fuzzy based matchmaking between an IaaS cloud service provider and a cloud service consumer. Assume that an IaaS cloud service provider like Amazon EC2 provides a Virtual Machine (VM) instance of specific configuration. A cloud service consumer is looking for a VM instance with specific requirements. Both the provider as well as the consumer has preferences (restrictions). Our aim is to find out the best service level agreement (negotiation).

4.1 Cloud Service Provider's Preferences

Soft Preferences

P1: Preferably the price of the cloud service instances is more than 0.5$ per hour but he can go down to 0.3 $ per hour to a lesser degree of satisfaction if the service usage term is at least 2 years.

P2: He provides either 32-bit or 64-bit processor architecture with at least 1 CPU and at most 4 CPUs and maximum 6 ECUs.

P3: The memory capacity is less equal to 10 GB and the persistent storage capacity is not more than 800 GB but he can go up to 900 GB to a lesser degree of satisfaction

P4: The availability of the service should be at most 99.95 % but he may go up to 100 % with lesser degree of satisfaction.

Hard Constraints

He does not want to offer the service at less than 0.3$ per hour at any circumstances.

4.2 Cloud Service Consumer's Preferences

Soft Preferences

C1: Preferably the price of the cloud service instance is no more than 0.2 $ per hour but he can go up to 0.4$ per hour to a lesser degree of satisfaction.

C2:   He wants 64 bits processor architecture with at least 4 CPU and within 5 to 10 ECU for 2 years.

C3:   The memory capacity should be between 5 GB to 15 GB and the persistence storage capacity should be at least 100 GB and not more than 1000 GB.

C4:   The availability of the service should be at least 99.99 % but he may go down to 99 %.

Hard Constraints

He doesn't want to pay more than 0.5$ per hour at any circumstances.

We have created a fuzzy based cloud ontology and it's OntoGraph as shown in Fig. 2 using protégé semantic editor with the FuzzyOWL2 plug-in for representing both cloud service provider's and consumer's soft and hard preferences. The detail of implementation is explained in the next section.

5 Implementation

We implement a prototype of the said case study in order for demonstration of the process of cloud service negotiation based on fuzzy ontology, using the proposed by us framework. The prototyping for agent creation in this framework uses the Jena semantic web library [15] and the JADE 3.4 agent system [16]. Here, interconnection of agents with cloud OWL knowledge model is allowed using Jena semantic web library. A fuzzy based cloud service ontology based on the OWL ontology is the cloud knowledge model that is presented by us in this approach [17, 18] and depicted in Fig. 2 We model it using the Protégé Ontology editor [19]. Provider agent, Consumer

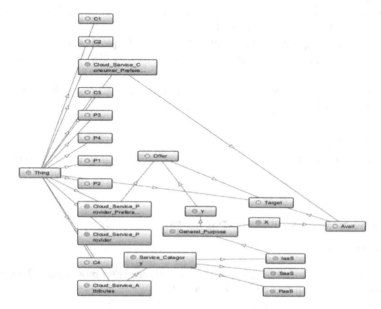

Fig. 2. Fuzzy based cloud ontology

agent, Discovery Agent and Negotiation Agent use Agent Communication Language (ACL) message in order to communicate with each other based on SPARQL and OWL DL. We have tested 2 scenarios taking different weighting factors of the soft preferences of cloud service consumers (Figs. 4 and 6) with constant weighting factor of the soft preference of the cloud service provider (Fig. 3). The experiment reveals that the probability of negotiation value of scenario-I (Fig. 5) is better than that of Scenario-II (Fig. 7).

5.1   Scenario-I

5.2   Scenario-II

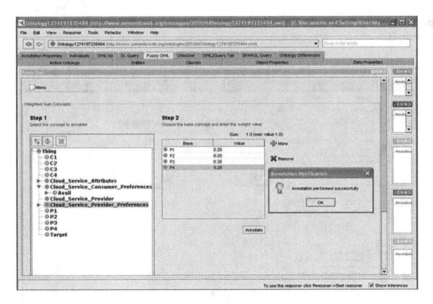

Fig. 3. Setting the weight value of the soft preferences of the cloud service provider

Here, we have shown a sample of implementation details how to encode the previous cloud service preferences and constraints. A concept named Avail collects all the consumer's preferences together in such a way that the higher is the maximal degree of satisfiability of Avail, the more the consumer is satisfied.

We have encoded the Cloud service consumer's soft preference using fuzzy DL in the following manner.

Avail = CloudServiceConsumerRequirements U CloudServiceConsumer Preferences

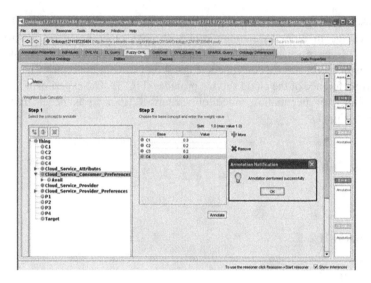

Fig. 4. - Setting the weight value of the soft preferences of the Cloud Service Consumer (Scenario-I)

Fig. 5. Probability of Negotiation (Scenario-I)

CloudServiceConsumerRequirements = X U hasPrice some leq 0.5$ per hour, where X is the cloud instance requested by the consumer.

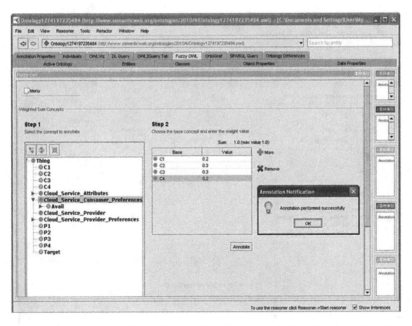

Fig. 6. Setting the weight value of the soft preferences of the Cloud Service Consumer (Scenario-II)

CloudServiceConsumerPreferences are encoded with Manchester OWL Fuzzy 2 syntax using protégé.

> *C1 = hasPrice some ls0.2_0.4DollarperHour*
> *C2 = (hasCPU some geq 4) and (hasECU some rs5_10) and (hasProcessorAr-chitecture value 64) and (hasTerm value 2)*
> *C3 = (hasMemoryCapacity some rs5_15 GB) and (hasPersistentStorageCapacity some rs100_1000 GB)*
> *C4 = hasAvailability some rs99.99_99*

where, ls0.2_0.4DollarperHour, rs5_10, rs5_15 GB, rs100_1000 GB, rs99.99_99 are defined fuzzy data types with annotation properties. For instance, ls0.2-0.4Dollarper-Hour has the following annotation property.

> *<fuzzyOwl2 fuzzyType = "datatype">*
> *<Datatype type ="leftshoulder" a = "0.2" b = "0.4"/>*
> *</fuzzyOwl2>*

Here ls and rs are the acronyms for left shoulder and right shoulder membership functions respectively. CloudServiceConsumerPreferences is a weighted sum concept, and thus, we add the following annotation property using fuzzyOWL2 API in protégé.

> *<fuzzyOwl2 fuzzyType = concept">*
> *<Concept type = "weightedSum">*
> *<Concept type = "weighted" value = "0.3" base = "C3"/>*

Fig. 7. Probability of negotiation (Scenario-II)

<Concept type = "weighted" value = "0.3" base = "C2"/>
<Concept type = "weighted" value = "0.2" base = "C1"/>
<Concept type = "weighted" value = "0.2" base = "C4"/>
</Concept>
</fuzzyOwl2>

Similar to the consumer case, the concept named Offer collects all the cloud service provider's preferences together in such a way that the higher is the maximal degree of satisfiability of Offer, the more the provider is satisfied. Due to space limitation we could not present the encoding of cloud providers preferences and constraints.

The best negotiation among the cloud service consumer and the provider is determined by the maximal degree of satisfiability of the conjunction Avail U Offer under Lukasiewicz fuzzy logic and fuzzy DL reasoner. By conducting several experiments, we have obtained an optimal match (the degree is 0.59) of negotiation on a price of 0.3 $ per hour, with 99.95 % availability tested in scenario-I.

6   Conclusion and Future Work

In this paper, we have addressed the challenges pertaining to SLA in Cloud computing environments. In addition, we proposed a Multi-agent based semantically enabled fuzzy based negotiation model in order to tackle these challenges. QoS parameters such as price, availability are taken into consideration in the process of negotiation with an aim to increase the efficiency of our strategy while filling the gap between decision making and bargaining. Our future work is to make our negotiation framework more flexible, faster and secure to support multiple cloud participants.

References

1. Zhang, Q., Cheng, L.: Cloud computing: state-of-the-art and research challenges. J. Internet Serv. Appl. -Springer 1(1), 7–18 (2010)
2. Dastjerdi, A.V., Tabatabaei, S.G.H., Buyya, R.: A dependency-aware ontology-based approach for deploying service level agreement monitoring services in cloud. Softw. Pract. Experience 42(4), 501–518 (2012)
3. Zulkernime, F.H., Martin, P.: An adaptive and intelligent SLA negotiation system for Web servcies. IEEE Trans. Serv. Comput. 4(1), 31–43 (2011)
4. Emeakaroha, V.C., Brandic, I., Maurer, M., Dustdar, S.: Low level metrics to high level SLAs-LoM2HiS framework: bridging the gap between monitored metrics and SLA parameters in cloud environments. In: Proceedings of International Conference on High Performance Computing and Simulation (HPCS), IEEE, Caen, France, June 28 –July 2, 2010
5. The NIST Definition of Cloud Computing. http://www.nist.gov/itl/cloud/upload/cloud-def-v15.pdf
6. Chang, Y.S., Yang, C.T., Luo, Y.C.: An ontology based agent generation for information retrieval on cloud environment. J. Universal. Comput. Sci. 17(8), 1135–1160 (2011)
7. Sim, K.M.: Agent-Based Cloud Computing. IEEE Trans. Serv. Comput. 5(4), 564–577 (2012)
8. Talia, D.: Clouds meet agents: toward intelligent cloud service. J. Internet Comput.-IEEE 16 (2), 78–81 (2012). 1089-7801
9. Semantic Web. http://www.w3.org/standards/semanticweb/
10. Gruber, Thomas R.: Towards principles for the design of ontologies used for knowledge sharing. Int. J. Hum.-Comput. Stu. 43(5–6), 907–928 (1995)
11. Youseff, L., Butrico, M., Silva, D.D.: Toward a unified ontology of cloud computing. In: Proceedings of IEEE Grid Computing Environments Workshop, pp 1–10, Austin, TX, November 2008
12. Hoefer, C.N., Karagiannis, G.: Taxonomy of cloud computing services. In: Proceedings of IEEE GLOBECOM Workshop on Enabling the Future Service Oriented Internet, pp. 1345–1350, Miami, FL, December 2010
13. Zimmermann, H.J.: Fuzzy Set Theory-and It's Applications, 4th edn. Kluwer Academic Publishers, Boston (2001)
14. Zhao, D.X.: Research of Semantic Service Discovery Based on Fuzzy Logic. Tianjin University, Tianjin (2008)
15. HP Labs and Open Source Community: Jena Semantic Web Library (2006). http://www.sf.net/

16. Telecom Italia: JADE (Java Agent DEvelopment Framework) Website (2004). http://jade. cselt.it/
17. W3C: Web Ontology Language (OWL) (2006). http://www.w3.org/TR/owl-features/
18. Höfer, C.N., Karagiannis, G.: Cloud computing services: taxonomy and comparison. J. Internet Serv. Appl. **2**, 81–94 (2011)
19. Stanford University: Prot´eg´e Ontology Editor (2006). http://protege.stanford.edu/

A New Hybrid Clustering Approach Based on Heuristic Kalman Algorithm

Arjun Pakrashi[✉]

Novell Software Development,
Bagmane Tech Park, C.V. Raman Nagar, Byrasandra,
Bangalore 560093, India
parjun@novell.com, phoxis@gmail.com

Abstract. Clustering is an important methodology for data mining and data analysis. K-Means is a simple and fast algorithm for clustering data. However the performance of K-means is highly sensitive on the initial seed of the algorithm. Heuristic Kalman Algorithm (HKA) is a population based stochastic optimization technique which is an effective method for searching a near-optimal solution of a function. Although HKA has good global search characteristics, it is shown that when directly applied on clustering it performs poorly. This paper proposes a new approach KHKA, which combines the benefits of the global nature of HKA and the fast convergence of K-means. KHKA was implemented and benchmarked on synthetic and real datasets from UCI Machine Learning Repository. The results were compared with other population based, stochastic algorithms. Results show that KHKA is a promising algorithm and was able to perform better than the compared algorithms with respect to the used datasets.

1 Introduction

Cluster analysis is an essential tool for data-mining, data analysis, statistics, biology, medicine, computer-vision and several other fields. Many cluster analysis algorithms exist. K-Means is one of the widely used clustering algorithm. Despite its simplicity and fast execution, being a greedy gradient based search in nature, its solution is dependent on the initial seed selected, and is prone to converge into a local optima near the point where the algorithm started. It is also shown that K-Means might fail to converge to a local minima under certain conditions [1]. The problem of clustering data is NP-Complete [2]. Therefore no optimal solution can be found in polynomial time. The class of the problem being NP-Complete and clustering being an important tool in various fields, has encouraged many researchers to investigate various approaches for clustering which includes, heuristics combined with different local and global optimization methods, population based methods, which can provide near-optimal solution in a feasible execution time. This motivates the study for this paper which attempts to construct an approach for data clustering to provide near optimal clustering results.

© Springer International Publishing Switzerland 2015
B.K. Panigrahi et al. (Eds.): SEMCCO 2014, LNCS 8947, pp. 445–455, 2015.
DOI: 10.1007/978-3-319-20294-5_39

This paper proposes a new hybrid clustering approach based on K-Means clustering algorithm and the Heuristic Kalman Algorithm (HKA) [3], which as per the knowledge of the author was not previously explored in cluster analysis domain. The performance of the proposed approach is tested with respect to several synthetic and real datasets obtained from the UCI Machine Learning repository.

The rest of the paper is structured as follows. Section 2 presents the HKA algorithm briefly and mentions some background information. In Sect. 3 we present the proposed algorithm KHKA. Section 4 shows and discusses the experimentation details and the interpretations of the results. Section 5 concludes the paper.

2   Background

2.1   Clustering

A cluster is a collection of data objects that are similar to one another within the same cluster and are dissimilar to the objects in other clusters. The process of grouping a set of physical or abstract objects into classes of similar objects is called clustering [4].

Let there be a set of n points in a d-dimensional space $X = \{x_1, x_2, \ldots, x_n\}$, where x_i is a vector of dimension d. The set of points X is to be partitioned into K clusters represented by $C = \{c_1, c_2, \ldots, c_K\}$ and corresponding cluster centroids $Z = \{z_1, z_2, \ldots, z_K\}$. Each c_i for $1 \leq i \leq K$ is a set of points in cluster i, and z_i is the cluster centroid representing the cluster c_i. where z_i is computed as follows.

$$z_i = \frac{1}{card(c_i)} \sum_{x_j \in c_i} x_j \tag{1}$$

where $1 \leq i \leq K$, and $card(.)$ is the cardinality of the set . . All points belonging to c_i is closer to the cluster centroid z_i than any other cluster centroid z_j where $i \neq j$. The task of crisp clustering requires all clusters should be non-empty $\forall_{1 \leq i \leq K}(c_i \neq \varnothing)$ with no common elements $c_i \cap c_j = \varnothing$ where $1 \leq i \leq K$, $1 \leq j \leq K$ and $i \neq j$ and $\cup_{i=1}^{K} c_i = X$.

Clustering algorithms optimizes an objective function. The objective function is selected in a way that the inter-cluster similarity is maximized and intra-cluster similarity is minimized. There are different metrics that can be optimized, within which a popular metric is sum of the Euclidean distances of the data-points x_i from the representative cluster centers z_j.

$$J(Z) = \sum_{z_j \in Z} \sum_{x_i \in X} \mu_{ij} \|x_i - z_j\| \tag{2}$$

where $\|.\|$ is the magnitude of the vector . in Euclidean space, and μ_{ij} is the cluster assignment matrix with $1 \leq i \leq n$ and $1 \leq j \leq K$, is defined as

$$\mu_{ij} = \begin{cases} 1 & if \ x_i \in c_j \\ 0 & otherwise \end{cases}$$

In case of fuzzy clustering μ_{ij} can be a real number in $[0,1]$ indicating fuzzy set membership of x_i, but this paper only considers crisp clustering. The objective is to optimize a cluster objective function, which in this case is (2), with respect to the cluster centers Z, with a fixed dataset X, and find the cluster assignments μ.

K-Means is one of the most widely used clustering algorithm even though it was first proposed in 1955 [5]. The execution and convergence of K-means is very fast, but the solution which K-means produces is dependent on the initial seed selected, and is prone to converge into a local optima near to the point where the algorithm started. A detailed study of K-Means algorithm can be found in [6].

2.2 HKA

The Heuristic Kalman Algorithm (HKA) was first presented in [3]. It is an iterative, population based, non-convex, meta-heuristic based optimization method using Kalman filtering framework. The main idea of HKA is to generate a new point in the search space through experiments, which is hopefully closer to the optimum than the previously generated point. A random number generator with a probability density function $f(q)$ with mean $m^{(k)}$ and variance-co-variance matrix $\sum^{(k)}$ is used to produce N vectors at every k^{th} iteration. The generated N points are used to get an estimate of the optimum as well as the confidence on it by a measurement process. The measurement of the optimum, the error in the measurement and the prior estimate is incorporated using the Kalman filter framework to compute the posterior optimal estimate and posterior error variance-co-variance estimate. The estimated optimum and the error variance-co-variance is used with the random number generator in the next iteration as the mean and variance-co-variance respectively. Thus the algorithm modifies the mean and the variance-co-variance matrix of the random number generator and continues the experimentation and estimation process until the global minimum is reached.

Let the objective function to optimize be $J(q)$. At k^{th} iteration a set of N points $q(k) = \{q_1^{(k)}, q_2^{(k)}, ..., q_N^{(k)}\}$ is generated from the probability density function $f(q)$ with mean $m^{(k)}$ and variance-co-variance matrix $\sum^{(k)}$. It is assumed that $J(q_1^{(k)}) < J(q_2^{(k)}) < ... < J(q_N^{(k)})$. Here each $q_i^{(k)}$ is the ith vector at k^{th} iteration representing a point in the search space.

The measurement $\xi^{(k)}$ is done by taking the mean of the best N_{best} vectors of the generated N vectors.

$$\xi^{(k)} = \frac{1}{N_{best}} \sum_{i=1}^{N_{best}} q_i^{(k)} \qquad (3)$$

This measurement $\xi^{(k)}$ is considered to have some unknown disturbance $v^{(k)}$, acting on the measurement process, centered on the optimum solution $q^{(opt)}$. The components of $v^{(k)}$ are assumed to be independent and follow a centered Gaussian distribution.

$V^{(k)}$ is used to measure the ignorance about $q^{(opt)}$ and is given by

$$
V^{(k)} = \frac{1}{N_{best}} \times \begin{bmatrix} \sum_{i=1}^{N_{best}} (q_{i,1}^{(k)} - \xi_1^{(k)})^2 & & 0 \\ & \ddots & \\ 0 & & \sum_{i=1}^{N_{best}} (q_{i,n_q}^{(k)} - \xi_{n_q}^{(k)})^2 \end{bmatrix} \tag{4}
$$

where $q_{i,j}^{(k)}$ is the jth component of the ith vector at k^{th} iteration and n_q is the number of dimensions of the vector $q^{(k)}$. The components of $v^{(k)}$ is taken to be independent, therefore the off diagonal elements of $V^{(k)}$ are zero.

The posterior estimate $\hat{q}^{(k)+}$ is computed as

$$
\hat{q}^{(k)+} = \hat{q}^{(k)-} + L^{(k)}(\xi^{(k)} - \hat{q}^{(k)-}) \tag{5}
$$

$$
L^{(k)} = P^{(k)-}(P^{(k)-} + V^{(k)})^{-1} \tag{6}
$$

$$
P^{(k)+} = (I - L^{(k)})P^{(k)-} \tag{7}
$$

where $L^{(k)}$ is the Kalman gain and $P^{(k)-}$ is the prior estimation error variance-co-variance matrix, $P^{(k)+}$ is the posterior estimation error variance-co-variance matrix and I is identity matrix. To control the decrease of the posterior estimation error variance-co-variance matrix resulting in a premature convergence, a slowdown factor is proposed by the authors in [3].

The algorithm starts with an initial mean and standard deviation for the random number generator. Next it computes $\xi^{(k)}$ using (3) and $V^{(k)}$ using (4). Then it uses (6) and (5) to compute $\hat{q}^{(k)+}$, and (7) to compute $P^{(k)+}$. A slowdown process is applied to control the rapid decrease of the variance. The estimated $\hat{q}^{(k)+}$ and $P^{(k)+}$ are assigned as the mean and variance of the random number generator in the next iteration. This continues until a stopping condition is met. The authors in [3] have proposed stopping condition as, either a maximum number of iteration is met, or the generated points by the random number generator is contained within a hyper-sphere in the search space with a predefined radius ρ.

3　Proposed Algorithm: KHKA

The proposed algorithm in this paper, KHKA, is a two stage algorithm based on HKA [3] and K-means. The clustering objective function used is the sum of Euclidean distances given in (2). The first stage employs HKA algorithm along with weighted K-Means as an operator on the generated points. This stage overcomes the drawback of running pure HKA, and shows that the first stage converges quickly due to the K-Means operator. The second stage uses the result from the first stage and further refines it employing HKA.

The set of cluster centroids of a particular solution is represented as one single vector. If there are K clusters in d dimension then a solution is represented using a vector q of length $(K \times d)$ consisting of the K cluster centroids appended one after the other, $q = [z_1, z_2, \ldots, z_K]$. Where $[.]$ is the concatenation of the comma separated vectors. Number of clusters K has to be pre-specified. Experiments show that HKA alone is not able to perform well with respect to the optimization objective $J(q)$ when compared to other algorithms.

The idea of the first stage is to make fast convergence as well as preserve global search by improving the measurement step of HKA. An attempt to achieve this is made by applying weighted K-Means operator on each of the N randomly generated vectors $q(k) = \{q_1^{(k)}, q_2^{(k)}, \ldots, q_N^{(k)}\}$, at k^{th} iteration . The K-Means operator means one single step of K-Means which consists of the cluster centroid re-computation step. The K-Means operator is applied on each of the vector representing a set of cluster centroids and get $q'(k) = \{q'^{(k)}_1, q'^{(k)}_2, \ldots, q'^{(k)}_N\}$. Where each q'_i is generated by applying (1) on each z_j encoded in q_i then re-encoding the result into q'_i. Next the set of generated samples of the vectors $q(k)$ is replaced as in (8). For a fixed dataset, a d-dimensional surface can be imagined for an objective function $J(q)$ plotted with respect the components of q. A single step in K-Means perform a steepest descent on the error surface. The weighted K-Means operator is used to control the magnitude of the step towards the steepest descent. After the weighted K-Means operator is applied to the vectors, the best N_{best} of the vectors is considered for the measurement process.

$$q_i^{(k)} = q_i^{(k)} + w(q'^{(k)}_i - q_i^{(k)}) \tag{8}$$

Where for all $q_i^{(k)} \in q(k)$ and for all $q'^{(k)}_i \in q'(k)$. The term w is the weight which controls the step towards the gradient and helps to control the effect of the K-Means operator. All experiments assume w to be an increasing function of the number of iterations as in (9).

$$w = w_{min} + (w_{max} - w_{min}) \times \left(\frac{k}{T}\right)^r \tag{9}$$

The values w_{min} and w_{max} defines the bound of on w where $0 \leq w_{min} \leq w \leq w_{max} \leq 1$. The equation (9) increases the value of w in the $[w_{min}, w_{max}]$ interval. Where T is the maximum allowed iteration and k is the current iteration with $1 \leq k \leq T$. This results in $w = w_{min}$ in the first iteration and gradually increases with iteration and reach w_{max} at the last iteration. Thus the effect of K-Means operator is weak at the beginning and as the process progresses, the effect strengthens. This process preserves global nature in the initial phase and gradually switch to quicker convergence by giving more weight to the gradient information gradient information as iteration progresses. The value r is used to change the influence of the K-Means step by making the increase super-linear or sub-linear. The value of $r = 0.8$ was set for all experiments, which makes a slightly super-linear growth of the value of w. The K-Means operator is the **Step 3** of Algorithm 1. The rest of the first stage works as in the HKA algorithm.

The second stage is similar to the first stage except it does not employ the weighted K-Means operator in **Step 3** of Algorithm 1, and uses the population generated by the Gaussian random number generator in **Step 2**, directly in the measurement process in **Step 4**. The initialization of the mean of the Gaussian generator is done using the result of the first stage. The initial standard deviation of the second stage is kept lower than the first stage to search a relatively smaller area centered on the result from the previous stage, which might have converged into a local minima or stopped at a sub-optimal point.

The maximum number of iteration the algorithm is $maxiter$. The combination of the first and the second stage is done as follows. The first stage is iterated much less number of times than the second stage. All experiments spent 25 % of $maxiter$ in the first stage and 75 % of $maxiter$ in the second stage. It is shown that executing the second stage after the first stage produces much better results than only running the first stage.

The slowdown factor from [3] was slightly modified for both the stages, which performs slowdown per dimension. This modification of the slowdown factor has improvements over the original slowdown factor. $S^{(k)+}$ is the posterior standard deviation and $S^{(k)-}$ is the prior standard deviation at k^{th} iteration are defined as in (10) and (11).

$$S^{(k)+} = S^{(k)-} + diag(\boldsymbol{a}^{(k)})(W^{(k)} - S^{(k)-}) \tag{10}$$

$$\begin{cases} a_i^{(k)} = \frac{\alpha V_{i,i}^{(k)}}{V_{i,i}^{(k)} + P_{i,i}^{(k)+}} & 1 \leq i \leq (K \times d) \\ S^{(k)-} = \sqrt{P^{(k)-}} \\ W^{(k)} = \sqrt{P^{(k)+}} \end{cases} \tag{11}$$

$\boldsymbol{a}^{(k)}$ is a vector where each $a_i^{(k)}$ is the slowdown factor for each dimension $1 \leq i \leq (K \times d)$ at iteration k. $diag(.)$ represents diagonal matrix formed using the vector . as the main diagonal.

The initial mean $\boldsymbol{m}^{(0)}$ for the first stage is taken to be the midpoint of the hyper-cube bound by the min and max values $\bar{\boldsymbol{x}}$ of the data-points per dimension and then concatenating this K times.

$$\boldsymbol{m}^{(0)} = cat(\bar{\boldsymbol{x}}, K) \; ; \; \bar{x}_j = \frac{max_{\boldsymbol{X}}(X_j) + min_{\boldsymbol{X}}(X_j)}{2} \; 1 \leq j \leq d \tag{12}$$

where $cat(v, c)$ is the concatenation of vector v , c times. $max_{\boldsymbol{X}}(X_j)$ (and $min_{\boldsymbol{X}}(X_j)$) is the max (and min) value of the jth dimension in the dataset over all data points in the dataset $\boldsymbol{X}$.

The initial variance-covariance $\sum^{(0)}$ of the first stage is taken as

$$\sum^{(0)} = \begin{bmatrix} (\sigma_1^{(0)})^2 & & 0 \\ & \ddots & \\ 0 & & (\sigma_{(K \times d)}^{(0)})^2 \end{bmatrix} \tag{13}$$

where the standard deviation is computed as in (14) where a is a constant set differently in the two stages.

$$\boldsymbol{\sigma}^{(0)} = cat(\tilde{\boldsymbol{x}}, K) \; ; \; \tilde{x}_j = \frac{max_{\boldsymbol{X}}(X_j) - min_{\boldsymbol{X}}(X_j)}{a} \; 1 \leq j \leq d \tag{14}$$

For the first stage the value of $a = 6$ and for the second stage the value of $a = 36$ is set. Setting $a = 6$ in the first stage covers $\mu \pm 3\sigma$ of the search space, which covers 99 % of the search space. The initialization of the mean of the second stage of the algorithm is done with the solution returned from the first stage. The standard deviation initialization of the second stage is set to cover a smaller area centered on the solution returned by the previous stage. For all the experiments the standard deviation is computed using (13), (14) with $a = 6$ in first stage and $a = 36$ in the second stage. The steps of the proposed algorithm is shown in Algorithm 1.

Algorithm 1. KHKA

- **Step 1,** Select N,N_{best},α, w_{min}, w_{max}, T, $k = 0$. Initialize mean $m^{(0)}$ using (12), variance-covariance matrix $\sum^{(0)}$ using (13), (14). Set $q^{(opt)} = m^{(0)}$ and $stage = 1$
- **Step 2,** Randomly generate N number of $(K \times d)$-dimensional vectors $q(k) = \{q_1^{(k)}, q_2^{(k)}, ..., q_N^{(k)}\}$ from Gaussian distribution $\mathcal{N}(m^{(k)}, \sum^{(k)})$, where K is the number of clusters, d is the dimensionality of the dataset.
- **Step 3,** If $stage = 2$, skip to **Step 4** , else if $stage = 1$, then perform weighted K-means operation on $q(k)$ by equation (8) and (9).
- **Step 4,** Compute the measurement point $\xi^{(k)}$ using equation (4) and the variance $V^{(k)}$ using (4).
- **Step 5,** Compute posterior estimation of the optimum $\hat{q}^{(k)+}$ using (5), (6) and (7). Use slowdown process to adjust the posterior standard deviation using (10) and (11) .
- **Step 6,** If $J\left(\hat{q}^{(k)+}\right) < J\left(q^{(opt)}\right)$ then $q^{(opt)} = \hat{q}^{(k)+}$
- **Step 7,** Update variables for next iteration:
  - Next iteration prior estimate is current iteration's posterior estimate: $\hat{q}^{(k+1)-} = \hat{q}^{(k)+}$
  - Next iteration prior standard deviation is current iteration's adjusted posterior standard deviation $S^{(k+1)-} = S^{(k)+}$ and $P^{(k+1)-} = (S^{(k)+})^2$
  - Next iteration mean is the posterior estimation $m^{(k+1)} = \hat{q}^{(k)+}$
  - Next iteration variance-covariance matrix is the variance computed adjusted posterior standard deviation $\sum^{(k+1)} = (S^{(k)+})^2$
  - $k = k + 1$
- **Step 8,**
  - **(a)** Case $stage = 1$: If $k \geq T * 0.25$, or the N_{best} generated points are inside a $(K \times d)$-dimensional hypersphere with a prefixed radius ρ, then goto **Step 9,** else go to **Step 2**
  - **(b)** Case $stage = 2$: If $k \geq T$, or the N_{best} generated points are inside a $(K \times d)$-dimensional hypersphere with a prefixed radius ρ then **terminate** . Else and goto **Step 2**
- **Step 9,** Re-initialize $m^{(0)} = q^{(opt)}$ for the second stage. Re-initialize the variance-covariance matrix using (13), (14) and for the second stage. Set $step = 2$ and goto **Step 2.**

---

4 Experiment

Several synthetic and real datasets having varying number of clusters, datapoints and dimensionality was used for testing. The real datasets were fetched from the UCI Machine Learning Repository [7]. A list of the datasets used in the experiment and their properties are shown below and in Table 1.

- Artset1: This is a synthetic dataset with 4 clusters. A total of 600 patterns were drawn from four independent bi-variate normal distributions, where classes were distributed according to $N_2 = \left(\mu = \begin{pmatrix} m_i \\ 0 \end{pmatrix}, \Sigma = \begin{bmatrix} 0.5 & 0.05 \\ 0.05 & 0.5 \end{bmatrix} \right)$ with $i = 1, 2, 3, 4$ and $m_1 = -3$, $m_2 = 0$, $m_3 = 3$, $m_4 = 6$.
- Artset2: This is a synthetic dataset with 5 clusters. Each feature of the classes were distributed according to: Class 1 - Uniform(85, 100), Class 2 - Uniform(70, 85), Class 3 - Uniform(55, 70) Class 4 - Uniform(40, 55), Class 5 - Uniform(25, 40).

Table 1. Datasets

	Artset1	Artset2	R15	Iris	Wine	Vowel [8]	Glass	Cancer	CMC
d	2	3	2	4	13	3	9	9	10
K	4	5	15	3	3	6	6	2	3
n	600	250	600	150	178	871	214	683	1473
Type	Synthetic	Synthetic	Synthetic	Real	Real	Real	Real	Real	Real

To compare the performance of the proposed algorithm and the improvement the datasets mentioned in Table 1 are used with the algorithms K-Means [6], KGA [9], PSO [10]. For comparison purpose a direct application of HKA on clustering and application of only the first stage of KHKA is also shown. These algorithms were implemented in C++ with Armadillo library [11]. Also the GSA-KM method proposed in [12] was compared with the results of KHKA. The experiment results are presented in Table 3.

The K-Means algorithm was initialized with K points selected randomly from the dataset. It was allowed to run until either the difference in error of two subsequent iteration values is 0 or the number of iterations has reached 100. For KGA the parameters used, the selection, crossover and mutation operators, were as specified in [9]. Ranking was performed inversely proportional to the cost function in (2). For KHKA the Gaussian random number generator was used, as in HKA. The value of r in (9) was set to 0.8. The population for PSO was selected to be a function of the number of clusters and the dimensionality of the dataset. The parameters set for KHKA, KGA and PSO are shown in Table 2. Direct application of HKA was benchmarked with a different set of parameters which acquired the best possible result in the experiment $N = 40$, $N_{best} = 10$, $maxiter = 500$, $\alpha = 0.3$. Column indicated by "HKA" shows results when HKA is initialized with the midpoint of the search space, and column "HKA R" shows

Table 2. Parameter configurations

KHKA	KGA	PSO
$N = 20$, $N_{best} = 8$	Population = 50	Population = $10 * K * d$
$maxiter = 250$	Max Gen = 1000	$c1 = 2.0$
$alpha = 0.12$	$p_c = 0.8$	$c2 = 2.0$
$[w_{min}, w_{max}] = [0.4, 1.0]$	$p_m = 0.001$	$[\omega_{min}, \omega_{max}] = [0.5, 1.0]$
$r = 0.8$		$maxiter = 500$

results when HKA is initialized with random points. Results using only the first stage of KHKA is labeled as KHKA S1. The parameters for KHKA S1 is kept identical as the full KHKA algorithm. Results of GSA-KM [12] algorithm is compared by quoting the applicable values as is from the original paper. This algorithm was not implemented. For dataset for which values of GSA-KM was not available is shown ass a '-' in the table.

All implementations were iterated upto maximum number of iterations. The performance is compared with respect to the mean, minimum, and maximum values of the objective function by executing each algorithm 50 times over each dataset.

The Table 3 cover two aspects. Values for KHKA, PSO and KGA shows that the proposed method performs better than the other methods for the specified datasets. Values for KHKA, KHKA S1 shows that the KHKA S1 performs better in most of the cases than other algorithms, but the entire algorithm KHKA has improvement than KHKA S1. Also the HKA and HKA R shows that direct application of HKA is not enough to form good clusters.

The tables show that KHKA performs very well compared to K-Means, KGA and PSO algorithm in every case. Although KHKA was able to converge to a much better minimum value but had a relatively higher standard deviation in the case of the Glass dataset. For Artset1, Artset2, Iris, KHKA was able to converge to the minimum value every time. In the case of Wisconsin Breast Cancer dataset, although KHKA was able to outperform KGA, PSO and K-Means, but the GSA-KM values shows that it was able to reach to better values. Although KHKA had better cost than GSA-KM with respect to other datasets for which GSA-KM was benchmarked in [12]. Also it is clear from the table that KHKA is significantly better with respect to a direct application of HKA.

The performance is not compared with respect to the number of function evaluations, one observation can be made. For KHKA number of function evaluations are $(N + 1) * maxiter$, for KGA $population * maxgen$ and for PSO it is $10 * K * d * maxiter$. In this experiment KHKA was able to achieve a better value in much lesser number of function evaluations when compared to KGA and PSO. The number of function evaluations were much less for K-Means, but the results were inferior compared to KHKA as well as the other algorithms. Also because of lesser number of function evaluations the execution time taken by KHKA in the experiments are lesser than all algorithms, except K-Means.

Table 3. Benchmark results

		KHKA	KHKA S1	KGA	PSO	HKA	HKA R	K-Means	GSA-KM*
Artset1	Min	**542.718**	542.748	543.007	**542.718**	**542.718**	**542.718**	543.468	-
	Mean	**542.718**	542.8387	543.057	542.7181	**542.718**	**542.718**	627.2139	-
	Max	**542.718**	542.915	543.057	542.721	**542.718**	**542.718**	911.150	-
	Std	0	0.0385	0.0232	0.0006	0	0	151.0401	-
	Time	‾0.3511	‾0.5105	‾2.4936	‾2.3991	‾1.1589	‾1.1714	‾0.0021	-
Artset2	Min	**1779.84**	1780.28	1781.85	1779.86	1903.18	1909.93	1782.10	-
	Mean	**1779.84**	1780.6566	1782.1410	1783.9744	2043.4422	2060.7004	2091.9194	-
	Max	**1779.84**	1781.01	1785.0000	1906.1800	2184.1	2222.74	2488.9500	-
	Std	0	0.1367	0.4866	18.0382	68.2349	79.7513	329.4488	-
	Time	‾0.228	‾0.3195	‾1.7812	‾2.9057	‾0.8213	‾0.867	‾0.0019	-
R15	Min	**229.406**	230.064	230.804	230.902	1039.02	878.024	230.732	-
	Mean	**230.2576**	230.9952	255.0196	265.6949	1121.6792	1050.4184	361.5763	-
	Max	**263.422**	266.063	275.700	322.591	1178.67	1183.83	593.071	-
	Std	**4.8855**	5.0105	14.2166	24.8161	34.7077	68.2724	85.8351	-
	Time	‾1.1324	‾1.6856	‾4.2379	‾60.4222	‾5.5839	‾5.6877	‾0.0040	-
Iris	Min	**96.6555**	96.8043	96.9539	**96.6555**	96.6816	**96.6555**	97.3259	96.689
	Mean	**96.6555**	96.884	97.0341	97.1877	98.1446	97.4314	101.3199	96.679
	Max	**96.6555**	96.99	97.1085	97.9017	105.641	104.805	123.85	96.705
	Std	0	0.0398	0.0295	0.6066	1.5291	1.2342	9.2456	0.0076
	Time	‾0.1081	‾0.1512	‾0.8637	‾0.9004	‾0.397	‾0.4176	‾0.0018	-
Wine	Min	**16292.50**	16299.50	16310.50	16299.30	16363.50	16368.40	16555.70	16 294.25
	Mean	**16293.052**	16312.70	16314.549	16351.078	16463.62	16474.6	16794.1373	16 294.31
	Max	**16294.60**	16338.90	16319.30	16521.80	16577.80	16670.30	18437.00	16 294.64
	Std	0.4177	9.3930	1.8799	53.63310	56.8451	60.2871	601.013	0.0406
	Time	‾0.2875	‾0.3508	‾1.2934	‾6.9399	‾0.7581	‾0.7728	‾0.0024	-
Glass	Min	**210.63**	212.231	212.971	211.081	240.076	243.928	215.678	211.47
	Mean	**213.0358**	216.3685	213.1174	214.7187	251.9302	251.7523	227.9223	214.22
	Max	215.33	235.753	**213.404**	221.526	280.382	276.23	257.057	216.08
	Std	1.2294	5.4101	0.0847	2.2753	8.1065	5.8474	14.0588	1.1371
	Time	‾0.3891	‾0.6312	‾1.7888	‾17.7495	‾1.3456	‾1.4033	‾0.0038	-
Vowel	Min	**148967**	149216	149382	148969	161303	161240	149443	-
	Mean	**149038.98**	149257.9	150962.6667	151061.42	167395.14	167246.8431	152733.1765	-
	Max	**149068**	149313	154966	160531	175325	174796	161048	-
	Std	36.4157	23.0558	1749.2301	2726.5037	2720.6321	3309.8858	3276.5285	-
	Time	‾0.8075	‾1.2073	‾3.3264	‾11.9873	‾2.6872	‾2.7685	‾0.0052	-
Cancer	Min	2971.05	2978.84	2982.6	3095.17	3007.93	2985.59	2991.98	**2965.14**
	Mean	2971.079	2981.9758	2982.8763	3613.0536	3077.8026	3088.3953	2991.98	**2965.21**
	Max	2972.1	2984.44	2982.92	4568.68	3167.68	3284.1	2991.98	**2965.30**
	Std	0.1463	1.0024	0.0700	298.088	35.3954	86.5166	0	0.0670
	Time	‾0.5378	‾0.7606	‾2.5589	‾7.5144	‾1.7858	‾1.7723	‾0.0025	-
CMC	Min	**5694**	5698.59	5700.83	5721.32	5787.65	5792.01	5703.44	5697.03
	Mean	**5694.4298**	5699.8898	5701.3684	5877.8995	5855.913	5869.8688	5704.202	5697.36
	Max	**5694.99**	5700.70	5701.60	6062.77	5937.17	5960.18	5705.27	5697.87
	Std	0.2527	0.3923	0.1655	82.7648	37.5873	39.9526	0.8901	0.2717
	Time	‾1.4339	‾2.0565	‾7.3681	‾34.1704	‾8.3787	‾4.9501	‾0.0082	-

Although in every case the mean value for KHKA was lower than the minimum value for K-Means. Therefore executing K-Means multiple times from different seeds within the same execution time duration as of KHKA, and taking the best solution in these cases does not lead to a better solution than KHKA.

5 Conclusion

The objective of this work was to propose a hybrid clustering algorithm to find near optimal clusters. The proposed algorithm is based on HKA and K-Means which combines the global nature of HKA and the fast convergence of K-Means. The experiments show that KHKA was able to get superior mean, minimum and maximum values of the objective function for the datasets mentioned in Table 1. Also it is shown that KHKA performs significantly better than direct application of HKA. Datasets having different dimensionality and number of clusters were used. For each case for a specific setup KHKA was able generate better solutions than the compared algorithms in almost all cases. This shows that KHKA is a promising algorithm and should be investigated for possible improvements and its response on different types of larger datasets.

Acknowledgments. The author would like to thank Dr. Vikram Pakrashi, University College Cork, Ireland, for the valuable suggestions, discussions and constant support throughout the entire period of research.

References

1. Selim, S.Z., Ismail, M.A.: K-means-type algorithms: a generalized convergence theorem and characterization of local optimality. IEEE Trans. Pattern Anal. Mach. Intell. **PAMI–6**, 81–87 (1984)
2. Sung, C., Jin, H.: A tabu-search-based heuristic for clustering. Pattern Recogn. **33**, 849–858 (2000)
3. Toscano, R., Lyonnet, P.: A new heuristic approach for non-convex optimization problems. Inf. Sci. **180**, 1955–1966 (2010). Special Issue on Intelligent Distributed Information Systems
4. Han, J., Kamber, M., Pei, J.: Data Mining: Concepts and Techniques, 3rd edn. Morgan Kaufmann Publishers Inc., San Francisco, CA, USA (2011)
5. Jain, A.K.: Data clustering: 50 years beyond k-means. Pattern Recogn. Lett. **31**(8), 651–666 (2010). Award winning papers from the 19th International Conference on Pattern Recognition (ICPR)
6. Bishop, C.M.: Pattern Recognition and Machine Learning (Information Science and Statistics). Springer-Verlag New York Inc, Secaucus, NJ, USA (2006)
7. Bache, K., Lichman, M.: UCI machine learning repository (2013)
8. Pal, S.K., Dutta Majumder, D.: Fuzzy sets and decision making approaches in vowel and speaker recognition. IEEE Trans. Syst. Man Cybern. **7**, 625–629 (1977)
9. Maulik, U., Bandyopadhyay, S.: Genetic algorithm-based clustering technique. Pattern Recogn. **33**, 1455–1465 (2000)
10. Chen, C.Y., Ye, F.: Particle swarm optimization algorithm and its application to clustering analysis. In: IEEE International Conference on Networking, Sensing and Control, 2004, vol. 2, pp. 789–794 (2004)
11. Sanderson, C.: Armadillo: an open source C++ linear algebra library for fast prototyping and computationally intensive experiments. Technical report, NICTA, Australia (2010)
12. Hatamlou, A., Abdullah, S., Nezamabadi-pour, H.: A combined approach for clustering based on k-means and gravitational search algorithms. Swarm Evol. Comput. **6**, 47–52 (2012)

Multi-objective Generation Scheduling Using Modified Non-dominated Sorting Genetic Algorithm- II

S. Dhanalakshmi[1(✉)], S. Kannan[2], S. Baskar[3], and K. Mahadevan[4]

[1] Velammal College of Engineering and Technology, Viraganoor,
Madurai, India
dhanaml26@gmail.com
[2] Ramco Institute of Technology, Rajapalayam, India
kannaneeeps@gmail.com
[3] Thiagarajar College of Engineering, Madurai, Tamilnadu, India
sbeee@tce.edu
[4] PSNA College of Engineering and Technology, Dindugal, India
mahadevand@rediffmail.com

Abstract. This paper presents a Modified Non-dominated Sorting Genetic Algorithm-II (MNSGA-II) solution to Multi-objective Generation Scheduling (MOGS) problem. The MOGS problem involves the decisions with regards to the unit start-up, shut down times and the assignment of the load demands to the committed generating units, considering conflicting objectives such as minimization of system operational cost and minimization of emission release. Through an intelligent encoding scheme, hard constraints such as minimum up/down time constraints are automatically satisfied. For maintaining good diversity in the performance of NSGA-II, the concepts of Dynamic Crowding Distance (DCD) is implemented in NSGA-II algorithm and given the name as MNSGA-II. In order to prove the capability of the proposed approach 10 units, 24-hour test system is considered. The performance of the MNSGA-II are compared with NSGA-II and validated with reference Pareto front generated by conventional weighted sum method using Real Coded Genetic Algorithm (RGA). Numerical results demonstrate the ability of the proposed approach, to generate well distributed pareto front solutions for MOGS problem.

Keywords: Dynamic crowding distance · Emission · Generation scheduling · Multi-objective optimization · Non-dominated sorting genetic Algorithm-II · Real coded genetic algorithm unit commitment

1 Introduction

Generation Scheduling (GS) is used to schedule the generators, in a power system, such that the total system production cost over the given time period is minimized while meeting various plant and system constraints such as the loading levels, the amount of spinning reserve for each unit and satisfying minimum up-time and down-time constraints. GS problem is a nonlinear, mixed integer combinatorial optimization

© Springer International Publishing Switzerland 2015
B.K. Panigrahi et al. (Eds.): SEMCCO 2014, LNCS 8947, pp. 456–470, 2015.
DOI: 10.1007/978-3-319-20294-5_40

problem. The global optimal solution can be obtained by complete enumeration, which is not practicable to large power systems due to its excessive computation time [1, pp. 131–160].

A number of methods have been used previously for solving the above problem and each method has its own difficulties. The various traditional methods used for this problem are Priority List based method, Branch and Bound, Dynamic Programming and Lagrangian Relaxation [2, 3]. In the Priority List method an exhaustive enumeration of all unit combinations are performed at each load level. Hence, it is hard to handle when the dimension of the problem is huge, whereas in the case of Branch-and-Bound method, finding the optimal solution is time consuming, because it can only be obtained by successive elimination of a set of inappropriate solutions [4]. Based on the "Principle of Optimality", Dynamic Programming was suggested for GS problem. But the main drawback of this was that it could not take into account the coupling time constraints and also time dependent start-up costs [5]. Lagrangian Relaxation method is superior to Dynamic Programming due to its higher solution quality and faster computational time [6] but there is no guarantee in getting an optimal solution. In addition, it is very difficult to handle the minimum up and down time constraints unless some heuristic method was used.

Recently, Evolutionary Algorithms(EAs) are having widespread application because of its two important aspects like very simple, function independent and they are not limited by the properties of the function such as continuity, existence of derivates, unimodality etc. Genetic Algorithm (GA) [7–10], Evolutionary Programming (EP) [11], Simulated Annealing (SA) [12], Tabu Search (TS) [13], Fuzzy Logic/expert systems [14–16], and Artificial Neural Networks (ANN) [17] were applied to solve this problem. But the results obtained by these methods required a considerable amount of computational time especially for a large system size. Hence recently, the traditional methods are integrated with these methods to solve this problem more effectively. These hybrid methods are claimed to accommodate more complicated constraints and also claimed to have better quality solutions even though the system under consideration is very large [18–20].

Due to the increasing environmental pollution caused by the fossil-fuelled electric power plants, the U.S. Clean Air Act amendments of 1990 have forced the utilities to reduce the emissions from such power plants [21]. Hence, it is essential to consider the emission as another objective and GS problem becomes Multi-objective Generation Scheduling (MOGS), which is a multi-objective optimization problem (MOOP) due to conflicting nature of operating cost and emission release.

In general, for solving MOOP, Weighted sum method provides a set of Pareto-optimal solutions by varying the weights, which requires multiple runs [22]. Further, the main disadvantage of this method is that it can't be used to find good distribution of pareto-solutions, for non-convex problems [23]. To overcome this, the ε-constraint method of Multi-objective optimization was used. It is based on reformulating the MOOP by keeping one of the most preferred objectives and restricting the rest of the objectives with some user-specified value ε [24]. These values are adjusted to generate the entire Pareto optimal solution. It is obvious that the solution will depends upon the chosen ε value and this method will consume more time. Currently, the ability of Evolutionary Multi-objective Algorithms (EMOAs) to find Pareto-optimal solutions is an attractive tool to solve these type of problems with multiple and conflicting objectives [25]. Evolutionary multi-objective search using Multi-Objective Genetic Algorithm towards preferred regions of the pareto front has been discussed for power system generation scheduling problem [26, 27].

Among these algorithms, NSGA-II algorithm is very popular and used to solve various power system multi-objective optimization problems, but still NSGA-II algorithm suffers in maintaining diversity among the solutions in the Pareto front. Hence in addition to NSGA-II, this paper makes use of diversity maintenance strategy which is based on Dynamic Crowding Distance (DCD) [27].

The objective of this paper is to solve the MOGS problem as a true multi-objective optimization problem and by using NSGA-II algorithm with DCD. To validate the performance of NSGA-II and MNSGA-II, conventional weighted sum method using RGA is used. In addition, in order to deal hard constraints of MOGS problem effectively intelligent coding [28, 29] is employed in this paper.

The organization of this paper is as follows. Section 2 addresses the MOGS problem formulation. Section 3 deals with basic introduction of MNSGA-II. The MNSGA-II implementation to the MOGS problem and intelligent coding scheme are described in Sect. 4. Section 5 provides test results and finally Sect. 6 concludes.

2 Multi-objective Generation Scheduling (MOGS)

The objective of MOGS problem is to minimize the operating cost and emission release over the scheduled time period, subjected to generator operational and spinning reserve constraints. MOGS problem is formulated as follows:

2.1 Objectives

2.1.1 Operating Cost
The total operating cost can be mathematically represented as in Eq. (1).

$$f_1 = \sum_{i=1}^{N}\sum_{t=1}^{T}\left[F_i(P_i^t) + ST_{i,t}(1 - U_{i,t-1})\right]U_{i,t} + (1 - U_{i,t})SD_{i,t} \quad \$/hr \quad (1)$$

where, $F_i(P_i^t)$ is represented as,

$$F_i(P_i^t) = \sum_{i=1}^{N} a_i + b_iP_i + c_iP_i^2 \quad (2)$$

where, N is the number of generators, T is the number of time periods, a_i, b_i and c_i are fuel cost coefficients of the ith generator; and P_i^t is the real power output of the ith generator at t^{th} hour and $U_{i,t}$ is the ith unit status at t^{th} hour.

2.1.2   Emission

The total emission of atmospheric pollutants, caused by the operation of fossil-fueled thermal power generation can be expressed in terms of (mg/Nm^3) as

$$f_2 = \sum_{i=1}^{N} \sum_{t=1}^{T} (\alpha_i + \beta_i P_i + \gamma_i P_i^2) \tag{3}$$

2.2   Constraints

2.2.1   Generation Capacity Constraint

For stable operation, real power outputs of each generator must be restricted by lower and upper limits as follows:

$$P_{i,\min} U_{i,t} \leq P_{i,t} \leq P_{i,\max} U_{i,t} \tag{4}$$

2.2.2   Power Balance Constraint

By neglecting losses, the total electric power generation must cover the total power demand $P^t{}_{demand}$. Hence,

$$\sum_{i=1}^{N} P_{i,t} U_{i,t} = P^t_{demand} \tag{5}$$

2.2.3   Spinning Reserve Constraint

$$P^t_{demand} + R_t = \sum_{i=1}^{N} P_{i,\max} U_{i,t} \tag{6}$$

2.2.4   Minimum up/Down Time Constraints

Minimum Up time

$$U_{i,t} = 1; \quad \sum_{j=ts}^{t-1} U_{i,j} < MUT_i , \quad for\, i = 1, \ldots\ldots N, \ t = t_s + 1, \ldots\ldots T \tag{7}$$

Minimum Down time

$$U_{i,t} = 0; \quad \sum_{j=td}^{t-1} (1 - U_{i,j}) < MDT_i , \quad for\, i = 1, \ldots\ldots N, \ t = t_d + 1, \ldots\ldots T \tag{8}$$

3 Modified Non-dominated Sorting Genetic Algorithm – II (MNSGA – II)

3.1 Introduction

Before describing the non-dominated sorting genetic algorithm-II (NSGA-II), it is necessary to discuss some terminologies related to it. They are termed as non-dominated sorting, crowding distance, elitism and crowded-tournament operator. The first step of an NSGA-II is to sort the population according to non-domination levels. In order to find solutions of the first non-dominated front in a population, each solution can be compared with every other solution in the population, to find if it is dominated. To find the individuals in the next non-dominated front, the first front solutions are discarded temporarily and the same procedure is repeated until all population members are classified.

To get an estimate of the density of solutions surrounding a particular solution in the population, an average distance of the two solutions on either side of the solution along each of the objectives is calculated. This quantity serves as an estimate of the perimeter of the cuboids formed by using the nearest neighbors as the vertices. This is termed as crowding distance. The overall crowding distance value is calculated as the sum of individual distance values corresponding to each objective. Each objective function is normalized before calculating the crowding distance. In NSGA-II once, the non-dominated sorting is over, the new population is filled by solutions of different non-dominated fronts, one at a time. First the best non-dominated front is filled and continues with solutions of the second non-dominated front and so on. All fronts which could not be accommodated are simply deleted. One important thing to be noted is, when the last allowed front is being considered, there may exists more solutions in the last front than the remaining slots in the new population. The crowded-tournament operator guides the selection process at the various stages of the algorithm toward a uniformly spread-out pareto-optimal front. Every population has two attributes: non-domination rank and crowding distance. Between two different populations with differing ranks, the population with better rank is preferred. If both populations belong to the same front, then the population with larger crowding distance is preferred.

3.2 MNSGA – II

In MOEAs, the horizontal diversity of Pareto-front is very important. The horizontal diversity is often realized by removing excess individuals in the non-dominated set (NDS) when the number of non-dominated solutions exceeds population size. NSGA-II uses Crowding Distance (CD) measure as given in (9) to remove excess individuals. The individuals having lower value of CD are preferred over individuals with higher value of CD in removal process.

$$CD_i = \frac{1}{r} \sum_{k=1}^{r} |f_{i+1}^k - f_{i-1}^k| \tag{9}$$

where, r is the number of objectives, f_{i+1}^k is the kth objective of the $i+1^{th}$ individual and f_{i-1}^k is the kth objective of the $i-1^{th}$ individual after sorting the population according to crowding distance. The major drawback of crowding distance is lack of uniform diversity in obtained non-dominated solutions as illustrated in Fig. 1.

In Fig. 1, if normal crowding distance method is adopted then the individuals C, D, and E are deleted from NDS, since they have small cd values. Because of that, some parts of paretofront are too crowded and some parts are with sparseness. Also, cd of B is small, because one side of the rectangle is short, while another side is long. However, the cd of F is large because the length of one side almost equal to another side. If one individual must be removed between the individuals B and F, because of small cd value, individual B will be removed and F will be retained in NDS. But, in order to get good horizontal diversity the individual B should be maintained, because the individual B helps to maintain uniform spread. To overcome this problem, dynamic crowding distance (DCD) method is recently suggested [28, 29].

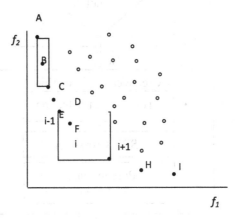

Fig. 1. Crowding distance of individuals

In this approach, one individual with lowest DCD value every time is removed and recalculates DCD for the remaining individuals. The individuals DCD are calculated as follows:

$$DCD_i = \frac{CD_i}{\log\left(\frac{1}{V_i}\right)} \tag{10}$$

Where CD_i is calculated by Eq. (9), V_i is based on Eq. (11),

$$V_i = \frac{1}{r}\sum_{k=1}^{r}\left(\left|f_{i+1}^k - f_{i-1}^k\right| - CD_i\right)^2 \tag{11}$$

V_i is the variance of CDs of individuals which are neighbors of the ith individual. V_i can give information about the difference variations of CD in different objectives. In Fig. 1, the individual B has larger value of V_i than the individual F and DCD of B is larger than F. Therefore, the individuals similar to B in the NDS will have more chance to retain.

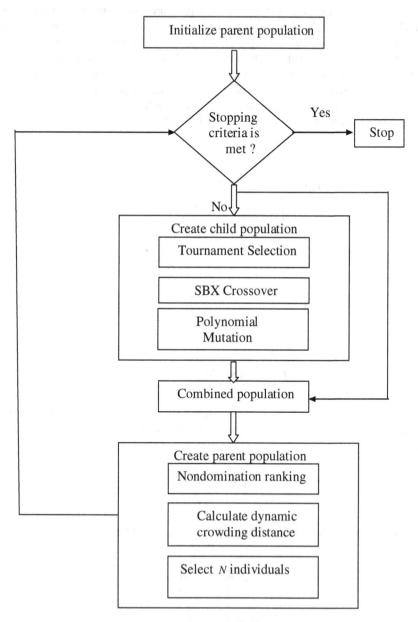

Fig. 2. Computational flow of MNSGA_II

3.3   Computational Flow

The computational flow chart of MNSGA_II is shown in Fig. 2.

4   Implementation of MOGS Problem

In the case of NSGA-II and MNSGA-II the population is generated using real numbers. In fitness function calculation, this real number vector is first rounded to the nearest integer number and then converted to a binary vector of 10 bits. Using intelligent coding scheme [30, 31] this binary vector is converted to a UC schedule without up/down constraint violations.

4.1   Penalty Parameter-Less Constraint-Handling Scheme

In this paper, a constraint-handling method which does not require any penalty parameter is used for handling other than minimum up/down time constraints. In this scheme, all feasible solutions have zero constraint violation and all infeasible solutions are evaluated according to their constraint violation alone. In penalty parameter-less scheme, the fitness function is calculated using (12) [32].

$$
F(x) = \left\{ \begin{array}{ll} f(x) & if \ g_j(x) \geq 0 \ \forall \ j = 1, 2, \ldots \ldots \ldots .m \\ f_{max} + \sum_{j=1}^{m} (g_j(x)) & otherwise \end{array} \right\} \tag{12}
$$

The advantage of this scheme when compared with the usual penalty parameter based scheme are the tedious process of choosing a suitable penalty parameter can be avoided and no need to evaluate the objective function value for constraint violation, which reduces the computation time. Thus, intelligent coding and penalty parameter-less constraint handling schemes are applied to the MOGS problem to effectively handle the hard and soft constraints.

5   Test Results

The implementation of NSGA-II and MNSGA-II algorithms are carried out using MATLAB Version 7.4 on a Pentium dual core processor desktop computer operating at 2 GHz with 1 GB RAM. The population size is selected as 120. Crossover probability (P_c) and mutation probability (P_m) are fixed at 0.9 and 0.1 respectively. Crossover index (η_c) and mutation index (η_m) are selected as 4 and 18 respectively. The maximum numbers of iterations is fixed at 500 and maximum function evaluations are fixed at 100000. The effectiveness of the algorithm has been tested on a 10 unit 24 h test system. To determine the optimal dispatch for a UC schedule, Quadratic Programming technique is used [33].

5.1   Test System Description

The 10 unit test systems operating cost and emission release function are used in this paper to demonstrate the performance of the proposed method. The demand of the system was divided into 24 intervals. The detailed fuel cost coefficients, emission coefficients, the lower power limits/upper power limits and minimum up/down time are taken from [26].

5.2   Generation of Reference Pareto Front

To compare the performance of MNSGA-II and NSGA-II multiple run generated reference pareto-front is used which is obtained using Real Coded Genetic Algorithm (RGA) with weighted sum approach [23]. The MOGS problem is treated as single objective optimization problem by linear combination of normalized objectives as follows.

$$\text{Minimize } C = w\, f_{1\_norm} + (1 - w)\, f_{2\_norm} \tag{13}$$

where, C is the combined objective function, f_{1_norm} and f_{2_norm} are the normalized objectives of f_1 and f_2. To generate 25 non-dominated solutions the algorithm is applied 25 times with varying weighting (w) factors as a uniform random number varying between 0 and 1.

5.3   Results and Discussion

The NSGA-II and MNSGA-II are applied to the MOGS problem with and without intelligent coding. Without intelligent coding, NSGA-II and MNSGA-II algorithms are not able to produce even feasible solutions. Whereas with intelligent coding, the NSGA-II and MNSGA-II algorithms have been applied ten times with different initial population, to show the effectiveness of the algorithm. The best results obtained in 10 trails are reported in Tables 1 to 4. From the Tables 1, 2, 3 and 4, it is clear that, all the hard constraints like minimum up/down time and demand constraint are satisfied.

Table 1 gives the hourly dispatch (U1-U10) for best total operating cost and the corresponding total emission release using NSGA-II. From Table 1, it is observed that the best total operating cost is 778470 \$/hr and the corresponding total emission release is 874750 mg/Nm^3, using NSGA-II. Similarly Table 2 represents the best total emission release is 700010 mg/Nm^3, and the corresponding total operating cost is 810040 \$/hr using NSGA-II.

Table 3 gives the hourly dispatch (U1-U10) for best total operating cost and the corresponding total emission release using MNSGA-II. From Table 3, it is observed that the best total operating cost is 764240 \$/hr and the corresponding total emission release is 783240 mg/Nm^3, using MNSGA-II. Similarly Table 4 represents the best total emission release is 585830 mg/Nm^3, and the corresponding total operating cost is 789870 \$/hr using MNSGA-II.

Table 1. Hourly dispatch, best total operating cost ($) and corresponding total emission release (mg/Nm³) using NSGA-II

Hour	Hourly dispatch (MW)										Best total operating cost ($)	Corresponding total emission release (mg/Nm³)
	U1	U2	U3	U4	U5	U6	U7	U8	U9	U10		
1	54	72	90	108	135	172.13	445.15	94.72	288	0	778470	874750
2	54	72	90	108	135	158	403.10	63.91	288	0		
3	54	72	90	108	135	146.14	367.81	38.05	288	0		
4	54	72	90	108	135	143.06	358.62	31.32	288	0		
5	52	72	90	108	135	0	435.99	88.01	288	0		
6	54	72	90	108	135	0	445.32	94.85	288	26.84		
7	0	72	90	108	135	0	468	134.10	288	76.90		
8	54	72	90	108	135	0	445	94.85	288	26.84		
9	54	72	90	108	0	0	468	125.32	288	65.68		
10	54	0	90	108	0	0	468	135	288	99		
11	54	0	90	108	0	0	468	124.44	288	64.56		
12	54	0	90	108	0	0	468	117.85	288	56.15		
13	54	72	90	108	0	0	435.94	87.98	288	18.08		
14	54	72	90	108	0	0	429.94	83.58	288	12.48		
15	54	72	90	108	0	0	424.69	79.73	288	7.57		
16	54	72	90	108	0	0	450.93	0	288	32.07		
17	54	72	90	108	0	0	435.93	0	288	18.07		
18	54	72	90	108	0	0	420.94	0	288	4.06		
19	54	72	90	108	0	0	381	0	288	0		
20	54	72	90	108	0	0	366	0	288	0		
21	54	0	90	108	0	0	377.70	45.30	288	0		
22	54	72	90	108	0	0	370.20	39.80	288	0		
23	54	72	90	108	0	0	404.25	64.75	288	0		
24	54	72	90	108	135	0	468	135	288	109		

Table 2. Hourly dispatch, best total emission release (mg/Nm³) and corresponding total operating cost ($) using NSGA-II

Hour	Hourly dispatch (MW)										Best total emission release (mg/Nm³)	Corresponding total operating cost ($)
	U1	U2	U3	U4	U5	U6	U7	U8	U9	U10		
1	54	0	90	0	0	244	468	135	288	180	700010	810040
2	54	0	90	0	0	208.68	468	135	288	128.32		
3	54	0	90	0	0	189.82	468	133.31	288	75.87		
4	54	0	90	0	0	186.63	468	126.36	288	67.01		
5	54	0	90	0	0	185.12	468	123.07	288	62.81		
6	54	0	0	108	0	189.32	468	132.21	288	74.47		
7	0	0	0	108	0	218.21	468	135	288	154.79		
8	0	0	0	108	0	202.86	468	135	288	112.14		
9	0	0	0	108	0	191.49	468	135	288	80.51		
10	0	0	90	108	0	0	468	135	288	153		
11	0	72	90	108	0	0	468	116.53	288	54.47		
12	54	72	90	108	0	0	446.44	95.67	288	27.89		
13	54	72	90	108	0	0	435.94	87.98	288	18.08		
14	54	0	90	108	0	0	456.94	103.36	288	37.69		
15	54	0	90	108	0	0	451.69	99.52	288	32.79		
16	0	0	90	108	0	0	468	0	288	141		
17	0	0	90	108	0	0	468	0	288	112		
18	0	0	90	108	0	0	468	0	288	83		
19	0	0	90	108	0	0	422.82	78.36	288	5.82		
20	0	0	0	108	0	0	450.94	98.97	288	32.09		
21	0	0	0	108	0	0	460.81	106.19	288	0		
22	0	0	90	108	0	0	442.92	93.08	288	0		
23	54	0	90	108	0	0	445.80	95.20	288	0		
24	54	0	90	108	0	203.13	468	135	288	112.87		

Table 3. Hourly dispatch, best total operating cost ($) and corresponding total emission release (mg/Nm³) using MNSGA-II

Hour	Hourly dispatch (MW)										Best total operating cost ($)	Corresponding total emission release (mg/Nm³)
	U1	U2	U3	U4	U5	U6	U7	U8	U9	U10		
1	54	72	90	108	135	172.13	445.15	94.72	288	0	764240	783240
2	54	72	90	108	135	158	403.10	63.91	288	0		
3	54	72	90	108	135	146.14	367.81	38.05	288	0		
4	54	72	90	108	135	143.06	358.62	31.32	288	0		
5	0	72	90	108	135	150.36	380.38	47.26	288	0		
6	54	72	90	108	135	159.48	407.52	0	288	0		
7	54	72	90	108	135	174.07	450.93	0	288	0		
8	54	72	90	108	135	159.48	407.52	0	288	0		
9	54	72	90	108	135	148.67	375.33	0	288	0		
10	54	72	90	108	135	141.38	353.62	0	288	0		
11	54	72	90	108	135	131.86	325.31	0	280.83	0		
12	54	72	90	108	135	198.90	0	135	288	101.1		
13	54	0	90	108	135	210.53	0	135	288	133.47		
14	54	72	90	108	135	188.48	0	130.38	288	72.14		
15	54	72	90	108	135	186.13	0	125.26	288	65.61		
16	0	72	90	108	135	190.32	0	134.41	288	77.27		
17	0	72	90	108	135	185.46	0	123.80	288	63.74		
18	0	72	90	108	135	180.59	0	113.19	288	50.22		
19	0	72	90	108	135	182.55	0	117.45	288	0		
20	54	72	90	0	0	0	407.13	66.87	288	0		
21	54	72	90	0	0	0	459	0	288	0		
22	54	72	90	108	0	0	410	0	288	0		
23	54	72	90	108	0	0	443.69	0	288	25.31		
24	54	72	90	108	0	219.79	468	0	288	159.21		

Table 4. Hourly dispatch, total best emission release (mg/Nm³) and corresponding total operating cost ($) using MNSGA-II

Hour	Hourly dispatch (MW)										Total best emission release (mg/Nm³)	Corresponding total operating cost ($)
	U1	U2	U3	U4	U5	U6	U7	U8	U9	U10		
1	54	0	90	108	135	177.20	460.24	105.78	288	40.78	**585830**	**789870**
2	54	0	90	108	135	180.12	467.98	0	288	48.90		
3	54	0	90	108	135	169.17	436.36	0	288	18.47		
4	54	0	0	108	135	179.69	467.61	0	288	47.70		
5	0	0	0	108	135	191.49	468	0	288	80.51		
6	0	0	0	108	135	202.86	468	0	288	112.14		
7	0	0	0	108	135	238	468	135	288	0		
8	0	0	0	108	135	187.26	468	127.74	288	0		
9	0	0	90	108	0	187.89	468	129.11	288	0		
10	0	0	90	108	0	179.27	466.42	110.31	288	0		
11	0	0	90	108	0	171.96	444.67	94.37	288	0		
12	0	72	90	108	135	213.18	0	135	288	140.82		
13	0	72	90	108	135	205.77	0	135	288	120.23		
14	0	72	90	108	135	201.54	0	135	288	108.46		
15	0	0	90	108	135	216.88	0	135	288	151.12		
16	54	0	90	108	135	194.93	0	135	288	90.07		
17	54	0	90	108	135	188.48	0	130.38	288	72.14		
18	54	0	90	108	135	183.61	0	119.77	288	58.61		
19	0	0	90	108	0	217.94	0	135	288	154.06		
20	0	0	90	0	0	0	468	132	288	0		
21	0	0	90	0	0	0	468	117	288	0		
22	0	0	90	108	0	0	442.92	93.08	288	0		
23	0	0	90	108	0	0	468	127	288	0		
24	54	0	90	108	0	203.13	468	135	288	112.87		

NSGA-II and MNSGA-II produces the pareto-optimal solutions in a single simulation run. Figure 3 illustrates the best pareto front obtained using NSGA-II and MNSGA-II. The comparison with respect to reference Pareto front is also presented in the same figure. When compared to NSGA-II, the pareto front obtained in MNSGA-II is much better in terms of non-domination level. Also the solution obtained using NSGA-II and MNSGA-II are well distributed, whereas solution obtained by RGA are poorly distributed and is having less number of non-dominated solutions

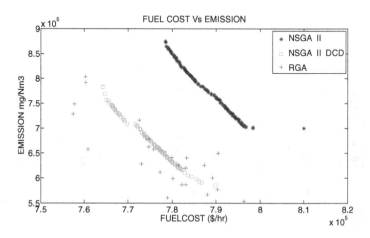

Fig. 3. Pareto optimal solutions for the 10 unit 24 h test system using NSGA-II, MNSGA-II and RGA

6 Conclusion

Multi-objective generation scheduling problem is considered with objectives of minimization of total operating cost and total emission release using modified NSGA-II algorithm. Intelligent coding scheme is employed to effectively satisfy minimum up/down time constraints. To demonstrate the effectiveness of MNSGA-II and intelligent coding scheme, 10 units 24-hour test system is taken. The reference Pareto front is generated using weighted sum method with RGA. The results obtained shows that the MNSGA-II is an effective tool for handling MOGS problem to generate a pareto front in a single simulation with the best computational time. Results also show that, pareto front obtained using MNSGA-II is well distributed with more number of non-dominated solutions as compared to the obtained pareto front by reference and the NSGA-II.

References

1. Wood, A.J., Wollenberg, B.F.: Power Generation, Operation and Control, 2nd edn. Wiley, New York (1996)
2. Yamin, H.Y.: Review on methods of generation scheduling in electric power systems. J. Electr. Power Syst. Res. **69**, 227–248 (2004)
3. Padhy, N.P.: Unit commitment – a bibliographical survey. IEEE Trans. Power Syst. **19**, 1196–1205 (2004)
4. Lee, F.N.: Short-term unit commitment – a new method. IEEE Trans. Power Syst. **3**, 691–698 (1988)
5. Pang, C.K., Sheble, G.B., Albuyeh, F.: Evaluation of dynamic programming based methods and multiple area representation for thermal unit commitment. IEEE Trans. Power Apparatus syst. **100**, 1212–1218 (1981)
6. Virmani, S., Imhof, K., Mukherjee, S.: Implementation of lagrangian based unit commitment problem. IEEE Trans. Power Syst. **10**, 772–777 (1995)
7. Kazarlis, S.A., Bakirtzis, A.G., Petridis, J.: A genetic algorithm solution to the unit commitment problem. IEEE Trans. Power Syst. **11**, 83–92 (1996)
8. Orero, S.O., Irving, M.R.: A genetic algorithm for generation scheduling in power systems. Int. J. Electr. power Energy syst. **18**, 19–26 (1996)
9. Swarup, K.S., Yamashiro, S.: Unit commitment solution methodology using genetic algorithm. IEEE Trans. Power Syst. **17**, 87–91 (2002)
10. Dasgupta, D., Mcgregor, D.R.: Thermal unit commitment using genetic algorithms. IEE Proc. Gen Trans. Dist. **141**, 459–465 (1994)
11. Juste, K.A., Kita, H., Tanaka, E., et al.: An evolutionary programming solution to the unit commitment problem. IEEE Trans. Power Syst. **14**, 1452–1459 (1999)
12. Mantawy, A.H., Abdel-Magid, Y.L., Selim, S.Z.: A simulated annealing algorithm for unit commitment. IEEE Trans. Power Syst. **13**, 197–204 (1998)
13. Mantawy, A.H., Abdel-Magid, Y.L., Selim, S.Z.: Unit commitment by tabu search. Proc. Inst. Elect. Eng. Gen. Trans. Dist. **145**, 56–64 (1998)
14. Saneifard, S., Prasad, N.R., Smolleck, H.: A fuzzy logic approach to unit commitment. IEEE Trans. Power Syst. **12**, 988–995 (1997)
15. Ouyang, Z., Shahidehpour, S.M.: Heuristic muti-area unit commitment with economic dispatch. IEE Proc. **138**, 242–252 (1991)
16. Tong, S.K., Shahidehpour, S.M., Ouyang, Z.: A heuristic short-term unit commitment. IEEE Trans. Power Syst. **6**, 1210–1216 (1991)
17. Wang, C., Shahidehpour, S.M.: Effects of ramp-rate limits on unit commitment and economic dispatch. IEEE Trans. Power Syst. **8**, 1341–1350 (1993)
18. Ongsakul, W., Petcharaks, N.: Unit commitment by enhanced adaptive lagrangian relaxation. IEEE Tran. Power Syst. **19**, 620–628 (2004)
19. Cheng, C.P., Liu, C.W., Liu, C.C.: Unit commitment by lagrangian relaxation and genetic algorithms. IEEE Trans. power Syst. **15**, 707–714 (2002)
20. Mahadevan, K., Kannan, P.S.: Lagrangian relaxation based particle swarm optimization for unit commitment problem. J. Power Energy Syst. **27**(4), 320–329 (2007)
21. Bharathi, R., Kumar, M.J., Sunitha, D., Premalatha, S.: Optimization of combined economic and emission dispatch problem – a comparative study. In: Proceedings of Eighth International Power Engineering Conference, pp. 134–139 (2007)
22. Dhillon, J.S., Parti, S.C., Kothari, D.P.: Stochastic economic emission dispatch. Electr. Power Syst. Res. **26**, 197 (1993)

23. Deb, K.: Optimization using evolutionary algorithms, 2nd edn, pp. 171–280. Wiley, New York (2001)
24. Yokoyama, R., Bae, S.H., Morita, T., Sasaki, H.: Generation dispatch based on probability security criteria. IEEE Trans. Power Syst. **3**, 317–324 (1988)
25. Abido, M.A.: Evolutionary algorithms for electric power dispatch problem. IEEE Trans. Evol. Comput. **10**(3), 315–329 (2006). doi:10.1109/tevc.2005.857073
26. Zio, E., Baraldi, P., Pedroni, N.: Optimal power system generation scheduling by multi-objective genetic algorithms with preferences. Reliab. Eng. Syst. Saf. **94**, 432–444 (2009)
27. Li, Y.F., Pedroni, N., Zio, E.: A memetic evolutionary multi-objective optimization method for environmental power unit commitment. IEEE Trans. Power Syst. **28**(3), 2660–2669 (2013)
28. Luo, B., Zheng, J., Xie, J., Wu, J.: Dynamic crowding distance - A new diversity maintenance strategy for MOEAs. In: 4th International Conference on Natural Computation (ICNC 2008), vol. 1, pp. 580–585 (2008)
29. Dhanalakshmi, S., Kannan, S., Mahadevan, K., Baskar, S.: Application of modified NSGA-II algorithm to combined economic and emission dispatch problem. Int. J. Electr. Power Energy Syst. **33**(4), 992–1002 (2011)
30. Baskar, S., Subbaraj, P., Chidambaram, P.: Application of genetic algorithms to unit commitment problem. IE(I) J. **81**, 195–201 (2001)
31. Dhanalakshmi, S., Kannan, S., Baskar, S., Mahadevan, K.: Intelligent genetic algorithm for generation scheduling under deregulated environment. In: Panigrahi, B.K., Suganthan, P.N., Das, S., Satapathy, S.C. (eds.) SEMCCO 2011, Part I. LNCS, vol. 7076, pp. 282–289. Springer, Heidelberg (2011)
32. Manoharan, P.S., Kannan, P.S., Baskar, S., Iruthayarajan, M.W.: Penalty parameter-less constraint handling scheme based evolutionary algorithm solutions to economic dispatch. IET Gener. Transm. Distrib. **2**, 478–490 (2008)
33. Danaraj, R.M.S., Gajendran, F.: Quadratic programming solution to emission and economic dispatch problems. IE (I) J. **86**, 129–132 (2005)

Design of Linear Phase FIR High Pass Filter Using PSO with Gaussian Mutation

Archana Sarangi[1], Rasmita Lenka[1],
and Shubhendu Kumar Sarangi[2(✉)]

[1] Department of Electronics and Communication Engineering,
ITER, SOA University, Bhubaneswar, India
{archanasarangi24,rasmitaalenka91}@gmail.com
[2] Department of Electronics and Instrumentation Engineering,
ITER, SOA University, Bhubaneswar, India
shubhendul977@gmail.com

Abstract. In this paper, a new optimization technique i.e. particle swarm optimization with Gaussian mutation (PSOGM) is used for the design of digital FIR High Pass filter and this technique is used to optimize filter coefficients. PSO with GM, the much improved version of particle swarm optimization algorithm (PSO), is a population based global search algorithm which finds near optimal solution in terms of a set of filter coefficients. Effectiveness of this algorithm is justified with a comparative study with real coded genetic algorithm (GA) and particle swarm optimization algorithm.

Keywords: FIR filter · HP filter · GA · PSO · PSOGM

1 Introduction

A digital filter is a mathematical algorithm implemented in hardware or software that operates on a digital input signal to produce a digital output signal. In signal processing, the basic function of a filter is signal separation and signal restoration. Signal separation is required when a signal is interfered with other signals or noise. Signal restoration is required when a signal is distorted in some way. Both of these problems can be solved by using both analog and digital filters.

Digital filters are classified into two types i.e. finite impulse response (FIR) filters and infinite impulse response (IIR) filters depending on the impulse response. A finite impulse response (FIR) filter is a type of digital filter whose impulse response is of finite duration i.e. it has a finite number of non-zero terms. The FIR filters can be classified into four categories they are low pass filter, high pass filter, band pass filter, and band stop filter. There are various optimization techniques are available which are used for filter design. Mathematically, the main objective of optimization is to minimize or maximize the objective function which having certain constrains.

Genetic Algorithm (GA) is one of the important technique in evolutionary computation research. Genetic Algorithm uses operators inspired by natural genetic variation and natural selection. Another example of evolutionary algorithm is Particle Swarm Optimization (PSO) which was developed by Eberhart and Kennedy in 1995,

© Springer International Publishing Switzerland 2015
B.K. Panigrahi et al. (Eds.): SEMCCO 2014, LNCS 8947, pp. 471–479, 2015.
DOI: 10.1007/978-3-319-20294-5_41

and it's basic concept was originally inspired by social behaviour of animals like, birds flocking or fish schooling.

2 Filter Design

The main advantages of FIR filter over IIR filter is that, it can provide exactly linear-phase frequency responses and always stable. Since, the design procedures of FIR linear phase filters can be reduced to real-valued approximation problems as the phase response of linear-phase filters is known. In this case, the coefficients have to be optimized with respect to the magnitude response only.

An FIR filter has a system function of the form given in the following:

$$H(z) = h(0) + h(1)z^{-1} + \ldots\ldots\ldots\ldots + h(N)z^{-N} \tag{2.1}$$

$$H(z) = \sum_{n=0}^{N} h(n)z^{-n} \tag{2.2}$$

Where, $h(n)$ is called impulse response.

The difference equation representation is,

$$y(n) = h(0)x(n) + h(1)x(n-1) + \ldots\ldots\ldots\ldots\ldots + h(N)x(n-N) \tag{2.3}$$

Where, N is the filter order and the length of the filter (which is equal to number of coefficients) is $(N + 1)$. $h(n)$ is filter's impulse response. The values of h(n) will determine the type of the filter, e.g., low pass, high pass, band pass etc. The values of h (n) are to be determined in the design process. This paper presents the even order FIR HP filter design with h(n) as positive even symmetric. Because the h(n) coefficients are symmetrical, the dimension of the problem is halved. Thus, $(N/2 + 1)$ number of h (n) coefficients are actually optimized, which are finally concatenated to find the required $(N + 1)$ number of filter coefficients. The length of $h(n)$ is $N + 1$; that is, the number of coefficients. In each iteration these solutions are updated [4].

The frequency response of the FIR digital filter can be calculated as,

$$H\left(e^{jw_k}\right) = \sum_{n=0}^{N} h(n)e^{-jw_k n} \tag{2.4}$$

Where $w_k = 2\pi k/N$. $H(e^{jwk})$ is the Fourier transform complex vector.

The frequency is sampled in $[0, \pi]$ with N points; the positions of the particles in this D dimensional search space represent the coefficients of the transfer function. In each iteration of evolutionary optimization, these particles find new positions, which are the new sets of coefficients.

An error fitness function given by (2.5) is the approximate error used in Parks–McClellan algorithm for filter design (Parks and McClellan, 1972).

$$E(\omega) = G(\omega)\left[H_d\left(e^{j\omega}\right) - H_i\left(e^{j\omega}\right)\right] \tag{2.5}$$

Where, $H_d(e^{jw})$ is the frequency response of the desired HP filter. $H_i(e^{jw})$ is the frequency response of the approximate filter. $G(w)$ is the weighting function used to provide different weights for the approximate errors in different frequency bands [5].

For ideal HP filter, $H_i(e^{jw})$ is given as,

$$H_i\left(e^{jw}\right) = 0 \quad \text{for } 0 \le \omega \le \omega_c$$
$$= 1 \quad \text{otherwise}$$

Where, ω_c is the cut-off frequency.

$$H_d(\omega) = [H_d(\omega_1), H_d(\omega_2)\ldots\ldots\ldots\ldots.H_d(\omega_k)]^T$$

and

$$H_i(\omega) = [H_i(\omega_1), H_i(\omega_2)\ldots\ldots\ldots\ldots\ldots.H_i(\omega_k)]^T$$

The error to be minimized is defined as:

$$J = \max_{\omega \le \omega_p}\left(|E(\omega)| - \delta_P\right) + \max_{\omega \ge \omega_s}\left(|E(\omega)| - \delta_S\right) \tag{2.6}$$

Where, δ_p and δ_s are the ripples in the pass band and stop bands. w_p and w_s are pass band and stop band normalized edge frequencies. Equation (2.6) represents the error fitness function to be minimized using the evolutionary algorithms.

3 Evolutionary Techniques

3.1 Genetic Algorithm

The genetic algorithm (GA) is an optimization and search technique based on the principles of genetics and natural selection. An objective function or fitness function is assigned to each solution and is compared with the average fitness of the whole population in order to give a measure of relative fitness. Basically four operators are used in GA such as initialization, selection, crossover and mutation [5].

3.2 Particle Swarm Optimisation

Particle swarm optimization (PSO) is an algorithm capable of optimizing nonlinear and multidimensional problems which usually reaches good solutions efficiently while requiring minimal parameterization. The algorithm and its concept of "Particle swarm optimization" (PSO) were introduced by James Kennedy and Russel Eberhart in 1995 [2].

In PSO, each particle represents a possible solution to the optimization problem. During an iteration of the pso, each particle accelerates independently in the direction of its own personal best solution found so far as well as the direction of the global best solution discovered so far by any other particle. Therefore, if a particle finds a promising new solution, all other particles will move closer to it, exploring the solution space more thoroughly. These particles are initialized with a random distribution within the solution space. As the iterations proceed, all particles tend to fly towards better and better positions over the searching process until the swarm move to close to an optimum of the fitness function [1].

Mathematically, velocities of the particle vectors are modified according to the following equation;

$$V_i^{(k+1)} = w * V_i^k + C_1 * rand_1 * \left(pbest_i^k - S_i^k\right) + C_2 * rand_2 * \left(gbest^k - S_i^k\right) \quad (3.1)$$

Where,

V_i^{k+1} is particle's new velocity for the next iteration. V_i^k is velocity of particle i at kth iteration.
w is an inertia factor. C_1 and C_2 are acceleration constant for the cognitive and social component.
$rand_1$ and $rand_2$ are two random numbers generated in the range of [0,1].
$Pbest_i^k$ is the previous best position of the ith particle at kth iteration.
$gbest^k$ is the global best position of swarm.
C_1*rand_1 is a uniformly distributed random number from 0 to C_1 and a measure of how much a particle trusts its neighbourhood best velocity.
C_2*rand_2 is a uniformly distributed random number from 0 to C_2 and a measure of how much a particle trusts the global velocity.

Treating each iteration as a unit time step, a position update equation can be stated

$$S_i^{k+1} = S_i^k + V_i^{k+1} \quad (3.2)$$

Where,

S_i^{k+1} is particle's new position i.e. moved position.
S_i^k is velocity of particle i at kth iteration. V_i^{k+1} is particle's new velocity for the next iteration.

3.3   PSO with Gaussian Mutation Algorithm

Particle Swarm Optimization with Gaussian Mutation combining the idea of the particle swarm with concepts from Evolutionary Algorithms. This method combines the traditional velocity and position update rules with the ideas of Gaussian Mutation. PSO with Gaussian mutation is an extended version of PSO, which employs a mutation mechanism used in the real-valued GA. We empirically show that PSO with Gaussian Mutation achieves better performance than PSO and real-valued GA for filter design.

We integrate a mutation often used for GA into PSO. However, we should not follow the process by which every individual of the simple PSO moves to another position inside the search area with a predetermined probability without being affected by other individuals, but leave a certain ambiguity in the transition to the next generation due to Gaussian mutation [10].

This technique employs the following equation:

$$\text{mut}(S) = S * (1 + \text{gaussian}(\sigma)) \tag{3.3}$$

Where σ is set to be 0.1 times the length of the search space in one dimension. S is a numerical value which an each object has. The individuals are selected at the predetermined probability and their positions are determined at the probability under the Gaussian distribution.

3.4   Steps for FIR High Pass Filter Design Using GA, PSO, PSO with GM

STEP 1: Initialize the parameters like population (swarm size) of the particles POPSIZE = 120, iteration cycles = 500, filter order N = 20, crossover = two point, fixing values of C_1, C_2 = 2.05, number of samples = 128, δ_p = 0.1, δ_s = 0.01, w_p = 0.45, w_s = 0.40
STEP 2: Apply window technique for filter design. Generate initial particles of filter coefficients (N/2 +1).
STEP 3: Apply GA algorithm or PSO algorithm or PSO with GM algorithm for filter design. Calculate the fitness values of each particle of the total population.
STEP 4: Compare the fitness of each particle with each pbest and gbest. If the current solution is better than its pbest and gbest then replace its pbest and gbest by the current solution.
STEP 5: Update the velocity and position of each particle as per Eqs. (3.1) and (3.2). After updating the position apply Gaussian mutation as per Eq. (3.3).
STEP 6: Repeat steps 2–5 until the maximum iteration cycles or the convergence of minimum error fitness values are met.

4   Result Analysis

This section presents the simulation study for the design of FIR HP filter. The filter order (N) is taken as 20 which results in the number of coefficients as 21. The sampling frequency is taken to be fs = 1 Hz. The number of frequency samples is 128. Each algorithm is run for fifty times to obtain its best results.

The parameters of the filter to be designed using GA, PSO and PSO with GM are: pass band ripple δ_p = 0.1, stop band ripple δ_s = 0.01, pass band (normalized) edge frequency (w_p) = 0.45; stop band (normalized) edge frequency (w_s) = 0.40; transition width = 0.1.

Table 1 shows the best chosen parameters used for GA, PSO, and PSO with GM.

The best optimized coefficients for the designed FIR HP filter with the order of 20 have been calculated by GA, PSO and PSO with GM and are given in Table 2.

Table 1. Control Parameters for GA, PSO, PSO with GM

PARAMETERS	GA	PSO	PSO With GM
Population size	120	120	120
Iteration cycle	500	500	500
Crossover rate	0.8	–	–
Crossover	Two-point	–	–
Mutation rate	0.001	–	0.1 times the length of the search space
Selection probability	1/3	–	–
d/p (dimension search)	20	20	20
C_1 (cognitive component)	–	2.05	2.05
C_2 (social component)	–	2.05	2.05
w (inertia factor)	–	0.9	0.9

Table 2. Optimised coefficients for FIR High Pass Filter in 20th Order

h(n)	GA	PSO	PSO With GM
h(1) = h(21)	0.0191	-0.1042	-0.1257
h(2) = h(20)	0.0992	0.0700	0.0373
h (3) = h(19)	0.0268	-0.0807	-0.0171
h(4) = h(18)	-0.0240	0.0519	0.0094
h(5) = h(17)	0.0162	-0.0796	0.0120
h(6) = h(16)	-0.0129	0.0747	-0.0145
h(7) = h(15)	0.0014	-0.0230	-0.0674
h(8) = h(14)	-0.0066	0.0332	0.0194
h(9) = h(13)	-0.0047	-0.0143	-0.0265
h(10) = h(12)	0.0186	0.0064	0.0097
h(11)	0.5758	0.5758	0.5758

Table 3. Comparison of the parameters in order 20 for different algorithms

ALGORITHM	EXECUTION TIME PER 100 CYCLES(s)
GA	40.316725
PSO	0.930378
PSO WITH GM	10.142514

Tables 3–4 summarize the results of different performance parameters obtained using GA, PSO and PSO with GM algorithms for HP filters of order 20.

Table 4 shows the comparison of the maximum stop band attenuation and transition width achieved by FIR HP filter using GA, PSO, PSO with GM algorithms. Among these all algorithms PSO with GM achieve highest stop band attenuation i.e. 25.03 dB

Table 4. Comparison of the parameters in order 20 for different algorithms

Algorithms	Maximum stop band attenuation (dB)	Maximum pass band ripple (normalized)	Maximum stop band ripple (normalized)	Transition width
GA	-24.15	0.105	0.062	0.115
PSO	-24.58	0.120	0.059	0.118
PSO WITH GM	-25.03	0.160	0.056	0.120

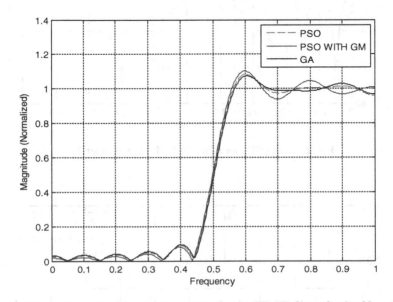

Fig. 1. Normalized frequency response for the FIR HP filter of order 20

as compared to that of GA and PSO. We can also see that for almost same level of transition width, PSO with GM produces minimum stop band ripple (normalised) among all algorithms.

Figure 1 show the normalized frequency responses of the FIR HP filter of order 20. Figure 2 show the magnitude (dB) plots for the FIR HP filters of order20.

In order to compare the algorithms in terms of error fitness values, Fig. 3 shows the convergences of error fitness values obtained by GA, PSO and PSO with GM. The convergence profiles are shown for the HP filter of order 20. PSO with GM converges to much lower error fitness value as compared to GA and PSO which yield suboptimal higher error fitness values. GA converges to the minimum error fitness value of 0.2; PSO converges to the minimum error fitness value of 0.16; whereas, PSO with GM converges to the minimum error fitness value of 0.14. For all types of filters, PSO with GM converges to the least minimum error fitness values in finding the optimum filter coefficients.

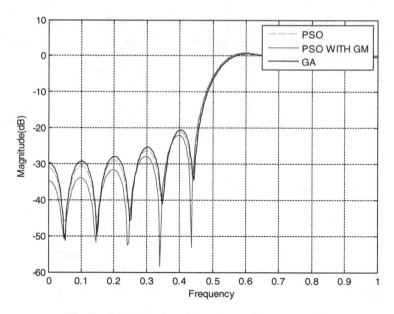

Fig. 2. Gain (dB) plot of the FIR HP filter of order 20

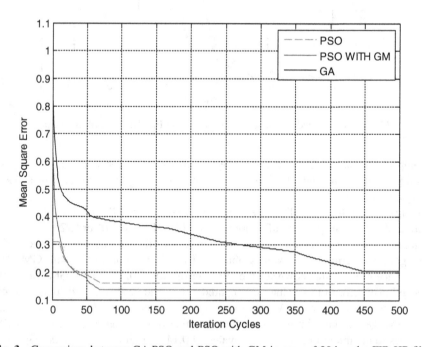

Fig. 3. Comparison between GA,PSO and PSO with GM in case of 20th order FIR HP filter

5 Conclusion

From the simulation results, it is clearly understood that with almost same level of the transition width, the PSO with GM algorithm produces the highest stop band attenuation (dB) and the lowest stop band ripple at the cost of very small increase in the pass band ripple compared to genetic algorithm and particle swarm optimization algorithm. From this it is evident that the PSO with GM may be used as a good optimizer for the solution of obtaining the optimal filter coefficients in a practical digital filter design problem in digital signal processing systems.

References

1. Mandal, S., Ghoshal, S.P., Kar, R., Mandal, D.: Novel particle swarm optimization for low pass FIR filter design. WSEAS Trans. Sign. Process. **3**, 111–120 (2012)
2. Kennedy, J., Eberhart, R.: Particle swarm optimization. In: Proceeding of the fourth IEEE International Conferences on Neural Network, pp. 1942–1948. IEEE service center (1995)
3. Kennedy, J., Eberhart, R.: A discrete binary version of the particle swarm algorithm. In: Proceedings of the IEEE International Conference on Systems, Man and Cybernetics, pp. 4104–4108. IEEE press (1997)
4. Mandal, S., Ghoshal, S.P., Kar, R., Mandal, D.: Design of optimal linear phase FIR high pass filter using craziness based particle swarm optimization technique. J. King Saud Univ. Comput. Inf. Sci. **24**, 83–92 (2012). Elsevier
5. Ababneh, J.I., Bataineh, M.H.: Linear phase FIR filter design using particle swarm optimization and genetic algorithms. J. King Saud Univ. Digit. Signal Process. **18**(4), 657–668 (2008). Elsevier
6. Eberhart, R., Shi, Y.: Comparison between genetic algorithms and particle swarm optimization. In: Proceedings of the 7th Annual Conference on Evolutionary Computation, San Diego (2000)
7. Ashutosh, P., Kasambe, P.V.: Performance evaluation of evolutionary algorithms for digital filter design. Int. J. Sci. Eng. Technol. **2**(5), 398–403 (2013)
8. SubhiAbbood, R., Faleh, H.: Design of finite impulse response filter based on genetic algorithm. Diyala J. Eng. Sci. **06**(03), 28–39 (2013)
9. Li, K., Liu, Y.: The FIR window function design based on evolutionary algorithm. In: International Conference on Mechatronic Science, Electric Engineering and Computer, Jilin, China, 19–22 August 2011
10. Higashi, N., Iba, H.: Particle Swarm Optimization with Gaussian Mutation. IEEE (2003)
11. Salivahanan, S., Gnanapriya, C.: Digital Signal Processing, 2nd edn. Mc Graw Hill Publication, New Delhi (2009)

A Binary Bat Approach for Identification of Fatigue Condition from sEMG Signals

Navaneethakrishna Makaram[✉] and Ramakrishnan Swaminathan

Non Invasive Imaging and Diagnostics Lab, Department of Applied Mechanics,
Indian Institute of Technology Madras, Chennai, India
kmakaram@yahoo.com, sramki@iitm.ac.in

Abstract. In this work, an attempt has been made to investigate the effectiveness of binary bat algorithm as a feature selection method to classify sEMG signals under fatigue and nonfatigue conditions. The sEMG signals are recorded from the biceps brachii muscle of 50 healthy volunteers. The signals are preprocessed and then multiscale Renyi entropy based feature are extracted. The binary bat algorithm is used for feature selection and the effectiveness is compared with information gain based ranker. The performance of the feature selection algorithms are validated by performing classification using Naïve Bayes, and least square support vector machines. The results show a decreasing trend in the multiscale Renyi entropy with increase in scale. Additionally, higher entropy values where observed in fatigue condition. The classification results showed that a maximum accuracy of 86.66 % is obtained with least square SVM and binary bat algorithm. It appears that, this technique is useful in identifying muscle fatigue in varied clinical conditions.

Keywords: sEMG · Fatigue · Muscle · Binary bat algorithm · Information gain · LSSVM · Naïve Bayes

1 Introduction

Muscle fatigue is a condition in which the muscle is unable to exert and maintain the force [1]. It can be caused due to various factors such as sustained or intense contraction or due to abnormal conditions like Parkinson disease [2], Guillain–Barré syndrome, Pompe disease [3] and immobilization [4]. Fatigue studies are applied in fields such as ergonomics, sports medicine [5], functional electrical stimulation, [6], myoelectric control [7] and analysis of neuromuscular conditions [4].

There are several ways to analyze muscle fatigue such as biopsy, imaging and isometric tests [2]. The most commonly used method is electromyography (EMG). EMG is a technique that is used to analyze the electrical activity manifested by the skeletal muscle [1]. There are two ways of acquiring EMG signals, namely needle EMG (nEMG) and surface EMG (sEMG) [8]. sEMG is generally used for fatigue studies due to its simplicity and non invasiveness [9].

sEMG being a complex stochastic signal, the analysis involves extraction of prominent features. There are several feature extraction methods in time and frequency domain. Time domain features such as root mean square value, average rectified value,

© Springer International Publishing Switzerland 2015
B.K. Panigrahi et al. (Eds.): SEMCCO 2014, LNCS 8947, pp. 480–489, 2015.
DOI: 10.1007/978-3-319-20294-5_42

integrated EMG [10, 11], multiple time window features [1] and spectral features such as mean frequency, median frequency and peak frequency [12] are used for the analysis. Some of the commonly used features are Dimitrov spectral index [12], zero crossing, slope sign change [13] and instantaneous median frequency [14].

In recent literature, multiple time window features with feature selection using information gain and genetic algorithm is used to classify fatigue during isometric contraction exercise [1]. Apart from this several nature inspired feature selection techniques such as ant colony optimization, genetic algorithm and particle swarm optimization (PSO) techniques are used to improve the classifier performance [15, 16]. Classification algorithms such as k-nearest neighbour [17], genetic programming [18], C-means algorithm and Linde–Buzo–Gray algorithm are reported for the classification of fatigue [19].

Binary Bat Algorithm (BBA) is a nature inspired computing algorithm which has major advantages over several heuristic algorithms like PSO and simulated annealing. It is capable of avoiding local minima and has a fast convergence rate [20].

In this work, sEMG signal from the biceps brachii muscle is acquired during dynamic contraction exercise. The signals are preprocessed and multiscale renyi entropy is extracted. The BBA is used for feature selection. The performance of the BBA is compared with the information gain based feature selection using the classification.

2 Methods

2.1 Signal Acquisition

Fifty healthy adult controls (average age of 25, average height 1.75 m, and average weight of 60 kg) are considered for the study. The subjects are asked to rest for a period of 12 h before the start of the experiment. Informed consent is taken from each subject. The skin over the biceps brachii is prepared and Ag – AgCl surface electrodes are placed over the bulk of the muscle. The electrodes are connected in a bipolar configuration with the Biopac signal acquisition system. The subjects are made to stand on an insulated platform during the entire period of the experiment. Repeated flexion and extension exercise is performed and the sEMG signals are recorded at a sampling rate of 10 kHz. The acquired signal is preprocessed offline using a 20–400 Hz band pass filter and a 50 Hz notch filter for the removal of external noises [1].

2.2 Feature Extraction

The signal is divided into six equal segments for time normalization. In this study the first (nonfatigue) and the last (fatigue) segment are used. Multiscale Renyi entropy is extracted from the segmented signal as follows.

Multiscale Renyi entropy. The computation of this feature involves two steps namely the construction of the coarse gain time series at different scales and computation of the renyi entropy values at each scale.

The coarse gain time series is constructed as shown below

$$y_j^{t_s} = \frac{1}{t_s} \sum_{i=(j-1)t_s+1}^{jt_s} x_i \tag{1}$$

where, $y_j^{t_s}$ is the associated time series at scale t_s, x is the original time series, $j = 1,2,...$ N/t_s and t_s ranges between 1 and 10 representing the ten different scales [21].

Renyi entropy is a modification of the Shannon's entropy. Renyi's

$$R_q = \frac{1}{1 - q} log_2 \left(\sum_{i=1}^{n} p_i^q \right) \tag{2}$$

where $q > 0$ and p_i is the sample probability. Here q is set to 2. A binless entropy estimation method is used to improve the computation speed [22, 23].

2.3   Feature Selection

Binary Bat algorithm. Bat Algorithm (BA) is a new powerful nature inspired metaheuristic optimization algorithm developed by Xin She Yang (2010). The (BA) is based on the echolocation capability of the micro bats.

The BA has been developed with the following assumptions: (i) All the bats make use of their echolocation ability to measure distance and they are able to differentiate between their prey and background in some magical way. (ii) Bats fly arbitrarily with velocity v_i at position x_i with fixed frequency f, varying wavelength λ and loudness A_0 to detect their targets. Bats automatically adjust their wavelength (frequency) of the pulses emitted by them and also adjust the rate of emission of the pulses depending on vicinity of the target. (iii) The loudness is assumed to vary from a very large positive value A_0 to minimum constant value Amin.

The Binary Bat algorithm (BBA) is a modification of BA. It associates each bat to a set of binary coordinates that represents the existence of a feature in the final feature set. This is done by using a sigmoid function considering the velocity v_i.

$$S(v_i^j) = \frac{1}{1 + \exp(-v_i^j)} \tag{3}$$

$$x_i^j = \begin{cases} 1 \text{ if } S(v_i^j) > \sigma \\ 0 * otherwise \end{cases} \tag{4}$$

$$\sigma \sim (0, 1) \qquad (5)$$

Here x_i^j is the feature.

The fitness function is the classifier model and the fitness value is the accuracy of classification. The classifier model used for this study is k nearest neighbors with k = 5.

The algorithm for feature selection using BBA is explained by Nakamura et al. (2012) [24].

Information gain. Information gain (IG) is a technique where the change in entropy is used as a parameter to find the relevance of the feature. It gives the amount of separation provided by the feature between the classes. The IG values of all features are calculated and the features are ranked in descending order of IG values [25].

2.4   Classification

Naïve Bayes. It is a classification algorithm based on the Bayes rule. The training data of each class is modeled using a Gaussian distribution with a diagonal covariance matrix. The test data is fed into the model and the model which gives the maximum probability is selected as the class [26].

Least square Support Vector Machine(LSSVM). Support vector machines (SVMs) are powerful tool used for data classification.SVM maps input data into a higher dimensional space by using a kernel trick such that the data becomes linearly separable. There are several optimization techniques used for determining the support vectors for defining the hyperplane separating the class. Some of the common optimization techniques are sequential minimal optimization (SMO), quadratic programming and least square. In the least square technique the support vector with non zero values are used for defining the hyperplane.
In this study a LSSVM with quadratic kernel is used for classification [27].

3   Results and Discussion

Figure 1 shows the variation of the sEMG signal during the course of the experiment. No distinct variation is seen between the initial and final segment of the whole signal. The first and last zones corresponding to nonfatigue and fatigue are shown in Figs. 2 and 3. Close examination of the signal shows minor variations in the signal amplitude.

The variation of multiscale Renyi entropy is shown in Fig. 4. It is observed that the entropy value during fatigue is higher. Additionally there is a decreasing trend observed as the time scale increases. Similar results are observed in most of the subjects.

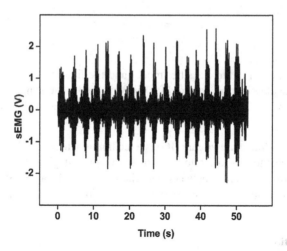

Fig. 1. Representative sEMG signal during dynamic contraction

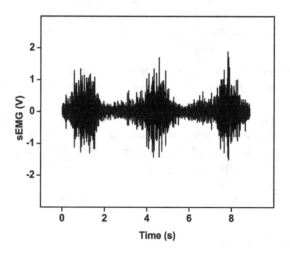

Fig. 2. Nonfatigue zone of the representative sEMG signal

3.1 Feature Selection

Renyi entropy features are extracted at ten different scales. Most of the features exhibited considerable separation between the two zones. The feature selection methods are employed in order to reduce the complexity of over fitting in classifier models.

The results of information gain are depicted in Fig. 5. The fitness value ranged between 0.1 and 0.182. It is seen that the highest fitness value is observed in the time scale 9 followed by time scale 2, 4 and 7. The features selected by IG are those with fitness values greater than 70 % of highest fitness value.

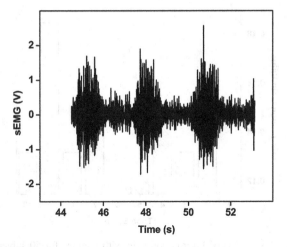

Fig. 3. Fatigue zone of the representative sEMG signal

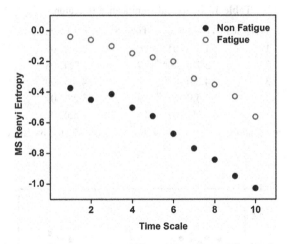

Fig. 4. Representative multiscale Renyi entropy at different timescales

The BBA selected 4 features from the feature set based on the accuracy achieved by the wrapper classifier model, as shown in Table 1. It is observed that the wrapper function of BBA gave an accuracy of 80 %.

3.2 Statistical Analysis

The most prominent feature with maximum p-value and that is selected by both BBA and IG is shown in Fig. 6. It is observed that the entropy value is higher in the case of fatigue. It may be due to the signal becoming more stationary in the zone. There is

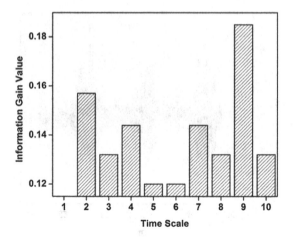

Fig. 5. Variation of Information gain with features for 50 subjects

Table 1. Statistical significance of features

Time Scale	p - value	Time Scale	p - value
1	1.93E-05	6	2.60E-07
2	5.70E-06^{a,b}	7	3.25E-08^a
3	4.23E-07^a	8	4.68E-09^{a,b}
4	3.53E-07^{a,b}	9	3.28E-09^{a,b}
5	1.29E-07	10	2.55E-09^a

a – features selected by IG, b – features selected by BBA

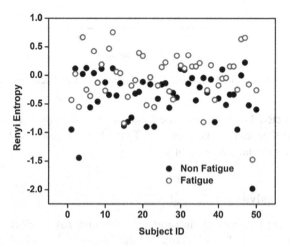

Fig. 6. Scatter plot of renyi entropy at time scale 9

considerable separation between the two classes and this can also be observed in the p-values.

As BBA selects the features based on the amount of separation between two classes and also uses the combined effect of features for selection. In addition to that, the selection of the wrapper function also plays a major role in feature selection.

3.3   Classification

The performance of the classification algorithms is shown in Table 2. The BBA - SVM gave a maximum accuracy of 86.66 % and also gave a sensitivity of 93.94 % and 80 %. The other combination of feature selection and classifier techniques such as IG-SVM performed relatively well giving an accuracy of 73.14 %. But the sensitivity and specificity of the classifiers are low compared to the BBA selected features. It is also observed that IG selected features at time scale 3, 7 and 10 along with other features selected by BBA. This improper selection of features may have resulted in poor performance of classification.

Table 2. Classifier performance

Classifier	Accuracy	Sensitivity	Specificity
BAT - SVM	86.66	93.33	80.00
BAT - NB	72.97	77.52	68.43
IG - SVM	73.14	73.07	73.21
IG - NB	67.39	60.83	73.95

4   Conclusions

The main objective of this work is to explore the application of BBA for feature selection in the classification of muscle fatigue using sEMG signals. The signals are recorded from the biceps brachii muscle of 50 healthy volunteers during dynamic contraction exercise. Multiscale Renyi entropy based features are extracted at 10 time scales. The features are further subjected to two feature selection methods namely, IG and BBA. The dominant features are selected and are used for classification with algorithms such as Naïve Bayes and least square SVM. A distinct variation between the Multiscale Renyi entropy values are observed between fatigue and nonfatigue conditions. The classification results show that that the LSSVM with a quadratic kernel gave a classification accuracy of 86.66 % with the features selected by BBA. The IG selected features performed poorly due to improper feature selection. In addition IG requires manual intervention for selecting features based on fitness value. It appears that, nature inspired binary bat algorithm along with Multiscale Renyi entropy is effective in classifying sEMG signals in fatigue and nonfatigue condition. This method can be further extended in the identifcation of muscle fatigue in varied clinical conditions.

References

1. Venugopal, G., Navaneethakrishna, M., Ramakrishnan, S.: Extraction and analysis of multiple time window features associated with muscle fatigue conditions using sEMG signals. Expert Syst. Appl. **41**, 2652–2659 (2014)
2. Falup-Pecurariu, C.: Fatigue assessment of Parkinson's disease patient in clinic: specific versus holistic. J. Neural Transm. **120**, 577–581 (2013)
3. de Vries, J.M., Hagemans, M.L.C., Bussmann, J.B.J., van der Ploeg, A.T., van Doorn, P.A.: Fatigue in neuromuscular disorders: focus on Guillain-Barré syndrome and Pompe disease. Cell. Mol. Life Sci. **67**, 701–713 (2010)
4. Greig, C.A., Jones, D.A.: Muscle physiology. Surgery **28**, 55–59 (2010)
5. Ma, L., Chablat, D., Bennis, F., Zhang, W., Hu, B., Guillaume, F.: A novel approach for determining fatigue resistances of different muscle groups in static cases. Int. J. Ind. Ergon. **41**, 10–18 (2011)
6. Thrasher, A., Graham, G.M., Popovic, M.R.: Reducing muscle fatigue due to functional electrical stimulation using random modulation of stimulation parameters. Artif. Organs **29**, 453–458 (2005)
7. Song, J.-H., Jung, J.-W., Lee, S.-W., Bien, Z.: Robust EMG pattern recognition to muscular fatigue effect for powered wheelchair control. J. Intell. Fuzzy Syst. **20**, 3–12 (2009)
8. Fuglsang-Frederiksen, A.: The role of different EMG methods in evaluating myopathy. Clin. Neurophysiol. **117**, 1173–1189 (2006)
9. Knaflitz, M., Molinari, F.: Assessment of muscle fatigue during biking. IEEE Trans. Neural Syst. Rehabil. Eng. **11**, 17–23 (2003)
10. Soylu, A.R., Arpinar-Avsar, P.: Detection of surface electromyography recording time interval without muscle fatigue effect for biceps brachii muscle during maximum voluntary contraction. J. Electromyogr. Kinesiol. **20**, 773–776 (2010)
11. Kumar, D.K., Arjunan, S.P., Naik, G.R.: Measuring increase in synchronization to identify muscle endurance limit. IEEE Trans. Neural Syst. Rehabil. Eng. **19**, 578–587 (2011)
12. Dimitrov, G.V., Arabadzhiev, T.I., Mileva, K.N., Bowtell, J.L., Crichton, N., Dimitrova, N.A.: Muscle fatigue during dynamic contractions assessed by new spectral indices. Med. Sci. Sport. Exerc. **38**, 1971–1979 (2006)
13. Rogers, D.R., MacIsaac, D.T.: EMG-based muscle fatigue assessment during dynamic contractions using principal component analysis. J. Electromyogr. Kinesiol. **21**, 811–818 (2011)
14. Pereira, G.R., de Oliveira, L.F., Nadal, J.: Isometric fatigue patterns in time and time-frequency domains of triceps surae muscle in different knee positions. J. Electromyogr. Kinesiol. **21**, 572–578 (2011)
15. Huang, H., Xie, H.-B., Guo, J.-Y., Chen, H.-J.: Ant colony optimization-based feature selection method for surface electromyography signals classification. Comput. Biol. Med. **42**, 30–38 (2012)
16. Subasi, A.: Classification of EMG signals using PSO optimized SVM for diagnosis of neuromuscular disorders. Comput. Biol. Med. **43**, 576–586 (2013)
17. Mallor, F., Leon, T., Gaston, M., Izquierdo, M.: Changes in power curve shapes as an indicator of fatigue during dynamic contractions. J. Biomech. **43**, 1627–1631 (2010)
18. Al-Mulla, M.R., Sepulveda, F., Colley, M., Kattan, A.: Classification of localized muscle fatigue with genetic programming on sEMG during isometric contraction. In: Conference on Proceedings of IEEE Engineering in Medicine and Biology Society EMBC, pp. 2633–2638 (2009)

19. Mirna, A., Rafic, Y., Mohamad, K., Herman, A.: Classification of the car seats by detecting the muscular fatigue in the EMG signal. Int. J. Comput. Cogn. **3**, 48–54 (2005)
20. Mirjalili, S., Mirjalili, S.M., Yang, X.-S.: Binary bat algorithm. Neural Comput. Appl. **25**, 663–681 (2005)
21. Costa, M., Goldberger, A.L., Peng, C.-K.: Multiscale entropy analysis of complex physiologic time series. Phys. Rev. Lett. **89**, 068102 (2002)
22. Loo, C.K., Samraj, A., Lee, G.C.: Evaluation of methods for estimating fractal dimension in motor imagery-based brain computer interface. Discret. Dyn. Nat. Soc. **2011**, 1–8 (2011)
23. Szabó, Z.: Information theoretical estimators toolbox. J. Mach. Learn. Res. **15**, 283–287 (2014)
24. Nakamura, R.Y.M., Pereira, L.A.M., Costa, K.A., Rodrigues, D., Papa, J.P., Yang, X.-S.: BBA: A Binary bat algorithm for feature selection. In: 2012 25th SIBGRAPI Conference on Graphics, Patterns and Images, pp. 291–297. IEEE (2012)
25. Shang, C., Barnes, D.: Combining support vector machines and information gain ranking for classification of mars McMurdo panorama images. In: 2010 IEEE International Conference on Image Processing, pp. 1061–1064. IEEE (2010)
26. Duda, R.O., Hart, P.E., Stork, D.G.: Pattern Classification. Wiley, New York (2001)
27. Suykens, J.A.K., Vandewalle, J.: Least squares support vector machine classifiers. Neural Process. Lett. **9**, 293–300 (1999)

Machine Learning Approach for Emotional Speech Classification

Mihir Narayan Mohanty[1(✉)] and Aurobinda Routray[2]

[1] ITER, Siksha 'O' Anusandhan University, Bhuaneswar 751030, Odisha, India
mihirmohanty@soauniversity.ac.in
[2] Department of Electrical Engineering, IIT, Kharagpur, WB, India

Abstract. Recognition of Emotion from speech is an extremely challenging task in current research. Using the reduced dimension method for feature extraction, Singular Value Decomposition (SVD) has proposed. Classification using Support Vector Machines (SVM) with SVD features shows an excellent result, which is the novelty of this work. The proposed features are evaluated for the task of emotion classification using simulation method. SVM has been designed as the classifier for classifying the unseen emotions in speech. It is shown that the classifier with such features outperforms the methods substantially. Using such features for classification outperforms the accuracy level approximately 90 % that leads towards automatic recognition.

Keywords: Emotional speech · Feature extraction · SVD · Classification · SVM

1 Introduction

Analysis of speech can help to improve speech synthesis, speaker recognition and emotion recognition. Emotion recognition using speech can find its use for variety of applications including messaging, security, and speech controllers etc. Automatic emotion recognition, based on speech is a new challenge for the researchers. That motivates to work on emotion classification using speech to test the method proposed in this piece of work. A number of approaches aiming at automatic recognition of emotion out of speech utterances have been presented over the last decade [1–4].

Even when human emotions are difficult to characterize and categorize, the effort increased in recent years due to the wide variety of applications. Emotion recognition solutions depend on which emotion is wanted to be recognized by a machine and for specific purpose.

In general there are six basic emotional states: *neutral, happiness, fear, sadness, anger and disgust (or surprise)*. In this work, we focus on three emotional states: *neutral, happiness, and anger.* Human speech includes much more information than verbal text only. Automatic recognition of emotion in speech attempts to build classifiers for recognizing unseen emotion in speech.

© Springer International Publishing Switzerland 2015
B.K. Panigrahi et al. (Eds.): SEMCCO 2014, LNCS 8947, pp. 490–501, 2015.
DOI: 10.1007/978-3-319-20294-5_43

The importance of automatically recognizing emotions in human speech has grown day by day. Increasing role of spoken language interfaces in the field of human machine interaction makes the human machine interface more efficient. Speech emotion recognition aims to automatically identify the emotional state of a human being from his or her voice. It is based on a deep analysis of speech signal, extracting some speech features that contain emotional information from the speaker's voice, and taking appropriate pattern recognition/classification methods to identify emotional states [5–16].

2 Proposed Method of Classification

Classifying data is a common task in machine learning, but classification of non-stationary signals is a difficult task. The choice for an appropriate classification paradigm is dictated by a number of factors. During the last decade, however, a new tool appeared in the field of machine learning that has proved to be able to cope with hard classification problems in several fields of application: the Support Vector Machines (SVMs). The SVMs are effective discriminative classifiers with several outstanding characteristics, namely: their solution is that with maximum margin; they are capable to deal with samples of a very higher dimensionality; and their convergence to the minimum of the associated cost function is guaranteed. These characteristics have made SVMs very popular and successful [17–23].

The problem of a high dimensional feature set is usually better addressed by feature selection for actual classification. Popular classifiers for emotion recognition such as Linear Discriminant Classifiers (LDCs) and k-Nearest Neighbour (kNN) classifiers have been used in literature [6–8, 12, 13]. However, they suffer from number of features that leads to regions of the feature space where data is very sparse [24]. An extension of LDCs is Support Vector Machines. Although SVM each not necessarily the best classifier, but it provides good generalization properties. Classification accuracies of Decision Trees such as RF, Artificial Neural Networks (ANN) and Support Vector Machine were found to be similar. ANN required by far the highest calculation times, whereas the training and testing of RF took usually longer than both SVM types. Artificial Neural Network has many disadvantages, such as complex optimization, low robustness and much training time. Random Forest in contrast is easy to use, since only one variable needs to be set by the user. However, its classification accuracies can not satisfy the machine-learning methods whereas its robustness was among the best [14–16].

All measures, namely classification accuracy, robustness, calculation complexity and usability, Support Vector Machine with Kernel emerged as the best solution for the classification.

3 Support Vector Classification

Support Vector Machine is a powerful and efficient classifier capable of dealing with high dimensional input features with theoretical bounds on the generalization error. Classifiers based on SVM have a few parameters requiring tuning. These are simple to implement and are trained through optimization of a convex quadratic cost function, which ensures a global and unique solution. Moreover, the trained SVM is defined only by the most informative training data (support vectors) and hence is sparse compared to the training data. Only a few extreme vectors from each class are required to fit the separating hyper plane in the feature (transformed) space [21].

Let T_N be set of N labeled data points in an M-dimensional hyperspace:

$$T_N = [(\mathbf{x_1}, d_1), \cdots, (\mathbf{x_N}, d_N)] \in (\mathbf{X} \times \mathbf{D})^N$$

where, $\mathbf{x_i} \in \mathbf{X}$, where $\mathbf{X}$ is the input space and $d_i \in \mathbf{D}$ where $\mathbf{D} = \{-1, +1\}$ is the label space. The problem is formulated to design a function ψ such that

$$\Psi : \mathbf{X} \to \mathbf{D} \quad \text{predicts } d \text{ from the input } \mathbf{x}.$$

Under normal circumstances $\mathbf{X}$ cannot be partitioned by a linear decision boundary. However, '$\mathbf{X}$' can be transformed into an equal or higher dimensional feature space for making it linearly separable (Cover's Theorem) [21–23]. Now the problem of finding a *nonlinear* decision boundary in $\mathbf{X}$ has been transformed into a problem of finding the optimal *hyperplane* for separating the two classes.

The hyperplane in this transformed domain (called the feature space, Fig. 3) can be parameterized by $(\mathbf{w}, b)$ pair as:

$$\sum_{j=1}^{P} w_j \phi_j(\mathbf{x}) + b = 0 \tag{1}$$

The mapping $\phi(\cdot)$ need not be computed explicitly; instead, an inner product Kernel [9] of the form

$$\langle \phi(\mathbf{x_i}), \phi(\mathbf{x_j}) \rangle = K(\mathbf{x_i}, \mathbf{x_j}) \tag{2}$$

It can be used for finding the optimal hyperplanes. Frobenius norm regularization for ease of optimization (this does not affect the spectral property of the regularization function). In [18], authors proposed using Extreme Learning Machine hidden layer to form a kernel to be used in SVM classification. When computationally easy and theoretically derived function is available, there is no reason of the use of a heuristical one.

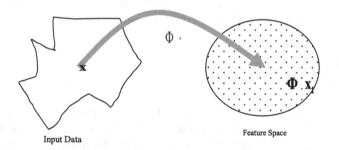

Input Data

Feature Space

Fig. 1. Transformation of pattern space to a convex feature space

As shown in Fig. 1, **Φ** maps input space to a similar or higher dimensional space where classification is linear. The decision function can be written in the feature space as

$$y(\mathbf{x}) = \sum_{i=1}^{N} \alpha_i d_i K(\mathbf{x_i}, \mathbf{x}) + b \qquad (3)$$

where, $K(\mathbf{x_i}, \mathbf{x})$ represents the Kernel.

The final classification can be obtained through,

$$\text{if } y(\mathbf{x})* > *0*\mathbf{x} \text{ is in class 1}$$
$$y(\mathbf{x})* < 0*\mathbf{x} \text{ is in class 2}$$

Such classifiers have been generated using supervised machine learning algorithms. The output of this supervised training is a machine capable of distinguishing between different emotion classes it has been trained with.

Figure 2 shows the basic system for classification. It presents regarding both training and testing stages.

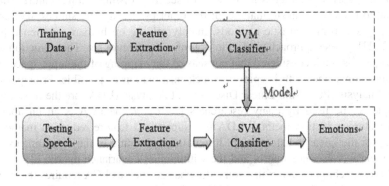

Fig. 2. Speech emotion classification system both training and testing

To select suitable [19, 20] features which are carrying information about emotions from speech signal is an important step. SVD has been considered as an efficient method of feature extraction. The singular values of auto-correlation matrix are calculated and a matrix is formed using singular values for different segments. It is explained in following section. However, estimation of auto-correlation matrix and singular value decomposition is a computationally intensive task. Moreover, in absence of enough number of samples, its estimation may not be accurate. Hence, we estimate the auto-correlation sequence using the SVD method for finding the singular values. These values were evaluated as features of the signal. The feature extraction method is depicted in following section.

Based on this basic system from Fig. 2, the proposed system block diagram for classification is shown in Fig. 3.

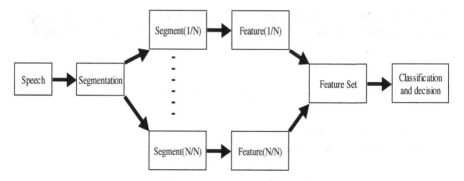

Fig. 3. The proposed emotion classification system

4 Feature Extraction

Feature extraction is used to obtain the most relevant information from the original data to be able to represent the data compactly and efficiently. The goal of the feature extractor is to characterize an object to be recognized by measurements whose values are very similar for objects in the same category, and very different for objects in different categories. This leads to the idea of seeking, distinguishing features that are invariant to irrelevant transformations of the input [3, 4]. In early studies, the features were designed using heuristic methods, mainly relying on human experience [9–14, 5–8, 22, 23]. These approaches have to optimize the feature set. The reduction of the feature space is often considered that consists of the mapping of the input space onto a less dimensional one, with keeping as much information as possible. Principal Component Analysis (PCA) and Linear Discriminant Analysis (LDA) are the most popular techniques to be used by many researchers [9–16]. While PCA is an unsupervised [5–11] feature reduction method, LDA is a supervised feature reduction method that searches for the linear transformation. It maximises the ratio of the determinants of the between-class covariance matrix and the within-class covariance matrix.

All these techniques have also some drawbacks, such as PCA requires the guess of the dimensionality of the target space, which is not always possible; LDA demands at least some degree of Gaussian distribution and linear separability of the input space. Both methods are, however, not very appropriate for feature set, as the original features are not retained after the transformation. So as an alternative method Singular Value Decomposition (SVD) has been used [11].

4.1 Mathematical Representation of SVD

Let X be a m × n matrix. The equation of the singular value decomposition of X is the following:

$$X = USV^T \tag{4}$$

where U is a m $\times$ m matrix, S is a m $\times$ n diagonal matrix, and V^T is also n $\times$ n matrix. The columns of U form an orthogonal basis, i.e.

$$u_i.u_j = \begin{cases} 0 & \text{if } i \neq j \\ 1 & \text{if } i = j \end{cases} \text{ where } u_i \text{ is a column of U}$$

Similarly, the rows of V form an orthogonal basis. S is diagonal matrix with the diagonal elements as the singular values of the matrix X.

For a symmetric matrix X,

U = V

Therefore, $X = USU^T$

$$X = [\vec{u}_1 \ \vec{u}_2 \ \vec{u}_3 \dots \vec{u}_m] \begin{bmatrix} \sigma_1 & 0 & 0 & \dots & 0 \\ 0 & \sigma_2 & 0 & \dots & 0 \\ \dots & \dots & \dots & \dots & \dots \\ 0 & 0 & & & \sigma_m \end{bmatrix} [\vec{v}_1 \ \vec{v}_2 \ \vec{v}_3 \dots \vec{v}_n]^T \quad (5)$$

Feature extraction techniques are determined based on the nature of the data to be classified. It is based on partitioning speech into small intervals known as frames. Auto-correlation of a signal gives a number of useful information about the signal. However, the accuracy of estimation depends on the number of samples p taken. We intend to find the optimal number of samples so as to minimize the computations involved in finding the auto-correlation while still being able to detect the properties of the signal with significant accuracy.

4.2   Auto-correlation Sequence Estimation

A vector $x_k = [x_0, x_1, \dots, x_n] \in \Re^{n+1}$ is a finite auto-correlation sequence if there exists a vector $y = [y_0, y_1, \dots, y_n] \in \Re^{n+1}$ such that

$$x_k = \sum_{i=0}^{n-k} y_i y_{i+k}, \ k = 0, \dots, n \quad (6)$$

$\mathbb{C}_{n+1}$ is the set of finite auto-correlation sequences in $\Re^{n+1}$. In other words, $x \in \mathbb{C}_{n+1}$ if and only if x satisfies the above equation for some $y \in \Re^{n+1}$.

4.3   Linear Matrix Inequality Characterization

In this characterization, it has been described that, $\mathbb{C}_{n+1}$ as the image of the cone of positive semidefinite matrices in $\Re^{(n+1) \times (n+1)}$ under a linear transformation.

Equation (6) can also be written as

$$x_k = y^T E^k y = \text{Tr } E^k y y^T, \ k = 0, \dots, n \quad (7)$$

where the matrix E is the unit-shift matrix, and is defined as

$$
E = \begin{bmatrix}
000\ldots000 \\
100\ldots000 \\
010\ldots000 \\
\vdots\vdots\vdots\ddots\vdots\vdots\vdots \\
000\ldots000 \\
000\ldots100 \\
000\ldots010
\end{bmatrix}
\tag{8}
$$

In Eq. (7), E^k denotes the k th power of E, i.e. E^0 is the identity matrix. Multiplying a vector y with E^k corresponds to shifting the components of y over k positions:

$$
E^k y = [0,\ldots,0,y_0,y_1,\ldots,y_{n-k}]
$$

In (7), we represent $\mathbb{C}_{n+1}$ as the image of a non-convex set (the set of positive semi-definite rank-one matrices yy^T) under a linear transformation. It can be shown that $x \in \mathbb{C}_{n+1}$ if and only if

$$
x_k = \text{Tr } E^k Y^T, \quad k = 0,\ldots,n
\tag{9}
$$

for some $Y = Y^T$.

It can also be shown that Y satisfies Eq. (9) if and only if there exists a $P = P^T \in \mathfrak{R}^{n+1}$ such that $Y = \begin{bmatrix} P & \tilde{x} \\ \tilde{x}^T & x_0 \end{bmatrix} - \begin{bmatrix} 0 & 0 \\ 0 & P \end{bmatrix}$ where $\tilde{x} = x_n\, x_{n-1}\ldots x_1]^T$. We therefore obtain the following equivalent LMI characterization for $\mathbb{C}_{n+1}$: $x \in \mathbb{C}_{n+1}$ if and only if there exists a $P = P^T \in \mathfrak{R}^{n \times n}$ such that

$$
\begin{bmatrix} P & \tilde{x} \\ \tilde{x}^T & x_0 \end{bmatrix} - \begin{bmatrix} 0 & 0 \\ 0 & P \end{bmatrix} \succeq 0
\tag{10}
$$

This is a linear matrix inequality in the variable $P = P^T$ and x.

To measure or estimate the first n + 1 auto-correlation coefficients of a stationary signal w(t), $\hat{r}_k$, has to be estimated satisfying

$$
\hat{r}_k \approx Ew(t)w(t + k)
\tag{11}
$$

The coefficients $\hat{r}_k$ can be obtained by taking an average of sampled values of w(t)w(t + k). Moreover, even if the values $\hat{r}_k$ are exact, they only represent a finite part of an underlying auto-correlation sequence Ew(t)w(t + k) of unknown and possibly infinite length. So we do not expect the sequence $\hat{r}_0,\ldots,\hat{r}_n$ to be finite auto-correlation sequence, and as a result, the estimated power spectral density $\hat{r}_0 + 2\sum_{k=1}^{n} \hat{r}_k \cos k\omega$ might not be non-negative. One approach to solve this problem is to approximate $\hat{r}$ by the closest finite auto-correlation sequence. To solve the problem

$$\text{minimize } ||x - \hat{r}||^2$$
$$\text{subject to } x \succeq 0. \tag{12}$$

5   Result

Data was collected by simulating the speaker under test conditions for getting speech signals corresponding to neutral, happy and angry situations. The recording of posed emotions in 10 neutral sentences – speech utterances was done for only 22 speakers for now (male/female, different ages, accents), using 3 emotional states (angry, neutral, happiness) and 4 background conditions (home, quiet, public place, office) using a recording device. 22 data sets were used for training and rest data for testing in each

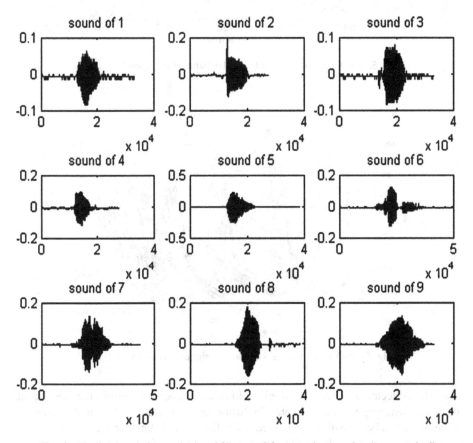

Fig. 4. Figure showing speech signal in neutral for counting number "one to nine"

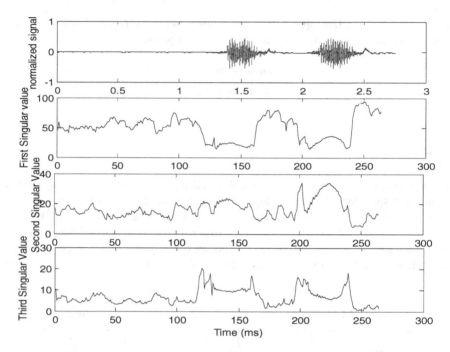

Fig. 5. First, second and third singular values for a speech "ha-ha"

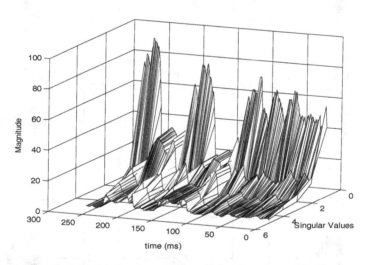

Fig. 6. 3-D plot showing variation of singular values with time.

case. The collected data seeds were given to other listeners to identify the emotion of speaker by listening to recorded data. Confusion matrix was formed using the response of the listener. The classifier was trained using the method stated above and the results were obtained. Figure 4 shows the speech samples of counting numbers from 'one' to

Table 1. Confusion matrix of listening sets

	Neutral	Happy	Angry
Neutral	20	1	1
Happy	0	21	1
Angry	0	0	22

Table 2. Performance matrix of classification result

	Neutral	Happy	Angry
Neutral	17	4	1
Happy	3	19	0
Angry	0	4	18

Table 3. Performance of the classifier

	Neutral	Happy	Angry
Neutral	88.87 %	10.03 %	1.02 %
Happy	9.08 %	90.81 %	0 %
Angry	0	9.42 %	89.76 %

Overall performance: 89.81 %

'nine'. It has been recorded with neutral condition of the subject. Figures 5 and 6 shows the singular values for the speech sample 'ha-ha'. Some of the values have been shown in Fig. 5 as well as its corresponding 3-D figure is represented in Fig. 6. The tables listed the performance result along with the confusion matrix. It has been represented in Table 1 through Table 3. Table 1 shows the confusion matrices of the listening seeds where as Table 2 shows the performance matrices of classification result for 22 speakers. Finally Table 3 shows the performance of the proposed classifier for 22 speakers with 3 emotions.

6 Conclusion

The results of classification were very encouraging. Its usage with Support Vector Machine helps in classifying such signals which are otherwise very difficult to classify. Moreover, the training data was sparse i.e. the hyper-place of the SVM was defined by a few points (support vector) which made the classification fast and less computationally intensive. It was also found that the basic emotions of speech can be perceived with good accuracy using such features. Speech Emotion Recognition has a promising future and its accuracy depends upon the features extracted, type of classification algorithm used and the correct of emotional speech database. This study aims to provide a simple guide to the researcher for those carried out their research study in the speech emotion recognition systems. More work is needed to improve the system so that it can be better used in real-time speech emotion recognition. However, since the results were obtained for a small data, strong conclusions cannot be drawn.

References

1. Schuller, B., Batliner, A., Steidl, S., Seppi, D.: Recognising realistic emotions and affect in speech: State of the art and lessons learnt from the first challenge. Speech Communication 53(9–10), 1062–1087 (2011)
2. Bosh, L.: Emotions: what is possible in the ASR framework. In: ISCA Workshop on Speech and Emotion, Belfast (2000)
3. Lambrou, T., Kudumakis, P., Speller, R., Sandler, M., Linney, A.: Classification of audio signals using statistical features on time and wavelet transform domains. In: ASSP 1998, vol. 6, pp. 3621–3624, 12–15 May 1998
4. Ververidis, D., Kotropoulos, C.: Emotional speech recognition: Resources, features, and methods. Speech Commun. 48, 1162–1181 (2006)
5. Lee, C., Mower, E., Busso, C., Lee, S., Narayanan, S.: Emotion recognition using a hierarchical binary decision tree approach. In: Proceedings of the Interspeech, Brighton, pp. 320–323 (2009)
6. Kwon, O.-W., Chan, K., Hao, J., Lee, T.-W.: Emotion recognition by speech signals. In: Proceedings of the Interspeech, pp. 125–128 (2003)
7. Lee, C.M., Narayanan, S.S.: Toward detecting emotions in spoken dialogs. IEEE Trans. Speech Audio Process. 13(2), 293–303 (2005)
8. Batliner, A., Fischer, K., Huber, R., Spilker, J., Nöth, E.: Desperately seeking emotions: actors, wizards, and human beings. In: Proceedings of the ISCA Workshop on Speech and Emotion, Newcastle, Northern Ireland, pp. 195–200 (2000)
9. Ayadi, M.M.H.E., Kamel, M.S., Karray, F.: Speech emotion recognition using gaussian mixture vector autoregressive models. In: Proceedings of the ICASSP, Honolulu, HY, pp. 957–960 (2007)
10. Steidl, S., Schuller, B., Batliner, A., Seppi, D.: The hinterland of emotions: facing the open-microphone challenge. In: Proceedings of the ACII, Amsterdam, Netherlands, pp. 690–697 (2009)
11. Kharat, G.U., Dudul, S.V.: Human emotion recognition system using optimally designed SVM with different facial feature extraction techniques. WSEAS Trans. Comput. 7(6), 650–659 (2008)
12. Litman, D., Forbes, K.: Recognizing emotions from student speech in tutoring dialogues. In: Proceedings of the ASRU, Virgin Island, USA, pp. 25–30 (2003)
13. Shami, M., Verhelst, W.: Automatic classification of expressiveness in speech: a multi-corpus study. In: Müller, C. (ed.) Speaker Classifcation II. LNCS (LNAI), vol. 4441, pp. 43–56. Springer, Heidelberg (2007)
14. Chuang, Z.-J., Wu, C.-H.: Emotion recognition using acoustic features and textual content. In: Proceedings of the ICME, Taipei, Taiwan, pp. 53–56 (2004)
15. McGilloway, S., Cowie, R., Doulas-Cowie, E., Gielen, S., Westerdijk, M., Stroeve, S.: Approaching automatic recognition of emotion from voice: a rough benchmark. In: Proceedings of the ISCA Workshop on Speech and Emotion, Newcastle, Northern Ireland, pp. 207–212 (2000)
16. Morrison, D., Wang, R., Xu, W., Silva, L.C.D.: Incremental learning for spoken affect classification and its application in call centres. Int. J. Intell. Systems Technol. Appl. 2, 242–254 (2007)
17. Mohanty, M.N., Routray, A., Pradhan, A.K., Kabisatpathy, P.: Power quality disturbances classification usingsupport vector machines with optimized time-frequency kernels. Int. J. Power Electron. 4(2), 181–196 (2012)

18. Frénay, B., Verleysen, M.: Using SVMs with randomised feature spaces: an extreme learning approach. In: Proceedings of ESANN, pp. 315–320 (2010)
19. Groutage, D., Bennink, D.: A new matrix decomposition based on optimum transformation of the singular value decomposition basis sets yields principal features of time-frequency distributions. In: Proceedings of the Tenth IEEE Workshop on Statistical Signal and Array Processing, August 2000)
20. Mohanty, M.N., Routray, A.: Estimation of autocorrelation space for classification of bio-medical signals. In: Panigrahi, B.K., Das, S., Suganthan, P.N., Nanda, P.K. (eds.) SEMCCO 2012. LNCS, vol. 7677, pp. 697–704. Springer, Heidelberg (2012)
21. Haykins, S.: Neural Networks, 2nd edn. Prentice Hall, New Jersey (1999)
22. Jolliffe, I.T.: Principal Component Analysis. Springer, Berlin (2002)
23. Fukunaga, K.: Introduction to Statistical Pattern Recognition. Academic Press, New York (1990)
24. Bellman, R.: Adaptive Control Processes. Princeton University Press, Princeton (1961)

Application of Cascaded Correlation Neural Network for Financial Performance Prediction and Analysis of BSNL

N. Albert Singh[1(✉)] and T. Naryanan[2]

[1] MS University, Tirunelveli, TN, India
mailalbertsingh@yahoo.co.in
[2] Government Arts College, Karaikudi, TN, India
ravinarayanant@yahoo.co.in

Abstract. In this paper Cascaded Correlation Neural network is used to integrate fundamental and technical analysis for financial performance prediction in Public Sector Enterprise Bharat Sanchar Nigam Limited (BSNL). The analysis is made based on the financial statement variables and macroeconomic variables. Experiments have eight years' financial data and macroeconomic data of Bharat Sanchar Nigam Limited had taken for analysis. The analytical and technical analysis in comparison with trend analysis results show that financial statement variables and macroeconomic variables together generate significant prediction of the future performance of the enterprise and accordingly effective decision can be made to improve the effectiveness of the PSU-BSNL.

Keywords: Cascaded correlation neural network · Financial analysis · Ratio analysis · PSU

1 Introduction

The financial position and performance of a company or corporate information's are provided by the financial statements of that enterprise. The business activities of a corporate include planning, financing, investing and operating activities. The financial statements provide detailed information's, achievements and transactions in the business activities. The strategy, purpose and the modalities for business activities are defined by the planning activity and also it assist decision makers in achieving their efforts and also identify the expected opportunities and pitfalls. The financial activities take care of the acquisition and management of financial resources and also it pay for its ventures and manage the business plans. In the investing activities of a company the selling of the products and services and also the maintenance of investments in manpower, equipments, land, buildings, and inventories are done. With regard to the operating activities of a company the process of production, marketing, research, promotion, etc., and also effective management of manpower were done. The operating activities perform necessary financing and investment in all the business activities.

The prime sources of information to the stakeholders of a company or a corporate were provided by the financial statements. The stakeholders include the managers,

© Springer International Publishing Switzerland 2015
B.K. Panigrahi et al. (Eds.): SEMCCO 2014, LNCS 8947, pp. 502–513, 2015.
DOI: 10.1007/978-3-319-20294-5_44

creditors, investors, etc.,. The stakeholders of a company with the analysis of financial statements of an enterprise asses the financial strength and weakness of the enterprise and also the indication about the enterprise in the future. The future conditions and performance of a company, corporate or an enterprise can be well estimated by the financial statement analysis.

Financial analysis requires depth knowledge about the accounting practices, the way of operations of an enterprise and also the business activities involved. The financial statements give a complex and factual insights of the various activities involved in an enterprise. The future of the company's best possible estimate and the predictions from the financial statements is based on the experience and also the expertise of the analyst and the analysis provides information in discovering the problems related to the performance of the enterprise. The analysis of financial statements also subject to constraints such as personal views, environmental factors, physical factors, mental fatigue, etc., of the analyst.

The financial statements disclose periodically the operation of an enterprise. If the financial statements are not properly published the stakeholders will not get information about the financial position of the company also if some information's are hided it will not give the actual status of the company with the real financial information's. In the recent past Public Sector Undertakings are leading to series of financial crisis. Business failure predictions by means of financial statement analysis are need of this hour to make an effective human decision making and also failure prediction in financial decisions.

The Literature survey and studies shows in the financial performance analysis lots of works were carried out which focuses mainly in the relationship between financial measures such as financial performance ratios of the companies. Models and classifiers based on regression analysis model, factor analysis, ANOVA models are constructed to analyze and they explain the performance of companies. The process of collecting, analyzing and applying to financial and non-financial integral information is termed as business valuation.

A detailed comparative financial statement analysis, common-size financial statement analysis, and ratio analysis was done in [1–3]. The financial statement analysis was conducted by an enterprise for reviewing the changes, trends, etc., based on the past years performance in individual categories.

The ratios are usually classified according to their functions based on profitability, liquidity, leverage and efficiency. Duft [4] analyze the ratios and the performance of a company based on their functions. Feng and Wang [5] performed an analysis on financial ratios for an airlines company. Wang and Lee [6] analyze the financial ratios of different companies by means of clustering method and similar components are formed in same cluster. Lahtinen and Toppinen [7] analyzed the financial ratios based on regression analysis for large and medium sized companies financial performance and examine the effects of cost and value added components.

An empirical analysis of financial data was done by Chan [8] and performed various evaluations with the financial statements. Credit card frauds, money laundering, etc., are detected by means of statistical methods from the financial statements by

Bolton and Hand [9]. Zhang and Zhou [10] made a detailed survey on data mining based financial analysis in bankruptcy predictions and fraud detection. Phua et al. [11] survey a fraud detection research which includes subscriptions fraud, credit transaction fraud, insurance fraud, etc., Insurance fraud and financial statement fraud are dealt by Yue and Derrig [12, 13]. Various approaches including intelligent techniques [27–29] are dealt detailed in the literature [21–26] and performance analysis in prediction of financial parameters are done.

Bharat Sanchar Nigam Limited (BSNL) is a Public Sector Undertaking (PSU) Company providing Telecom Services to the Indian Nation. BSNL is fully owned by Government of India and was formed in 2000 [14]. With respect to and based on Telecom policy 1999. BSNL starts functioning as a PSU from 1st October 2000 and take over the business of Department of Telecom Services and also the Department of Telecom Operations. The Company's registered corporate office is functioning in New Delhi, India and with limited liability by shares under the Companies Act 1956.

Based on the accrual method of accounting and the accepted accounting principles in India and also in accordance with the Companies Act, 1956 all the financial statements of BSNL was prepared. The primary segment consists of 'Basic', 'Cellular' and 'Broad Band' services provided.

Financial ratios are playing major role in financial decisions and also in predicting business failures which offers the investors an early warning sign. Financial ratio models or classifiers are commonly developed and they act as tools for forecasting the business and also they act as fiscal indicators. The statistical forecasting of business aids investors and stakeholders to measure the fiscal condition and the operation of the enterprise in the future. The financial data's pertaining to the previous years provides quantitative information in predicting and evaluating the future financial position of the enterprise.

In recent years Neural Networks are playing a major role in prediction problems solving. In this paper a detailed financial analysis of the Public Sector Undertaking (PSU) in India BSNL was analyzed based on its past and present performance and prediction using Cascaded Correlation Neural Network (CCNN). The Ratio analysis is done in analyzing the performance and the CCNN analysis is done in predicting the future of the PSU.

2 Methodology

The financial prediction of the PSU BSNL was done using Cascaded Correlation Neural Network as shown in Fig. 1. The CCNN was designed with two inputs the financial year and the parameter previous year value and the next financial year value will be predicted as the output. The CCNN learns from the training data using the quick prop algorithm as detailed by Fahlman, and Lebiere in [15, 16]. The CCNN network learns with a supervised learning structure and the model was created finally with the given training pattern.

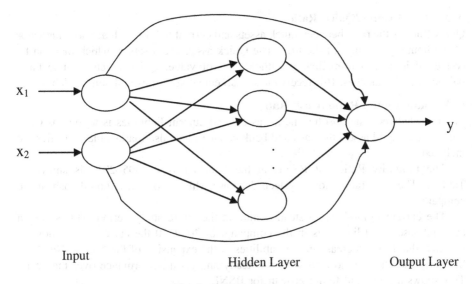

Fig. 1. CCNN architecture

3 Financial Analysis of BSNL

Financial data's obtained from financial statements are analyzed by using various techniques. The prime objective of financial data analysis is to provide the information and also the analytical component in a simplified manner.

The various analysis used for financial performance analysis are Ratio Analysis, Regression Analysis, Trend Analysis [18–20] intelligent approaches, etc., These analyses provide and interpret the financial data in terms of the operation and finance of the firm in a meaningful form.

A. Ratio Analysis/Liquidity Ratios
The liquidity ratio estimates the ability of an enterprise to meet the short term obligations. In other ords it is the capacity of the firm to pay the current liabilities in due time. It reflects the short term financial solvency of a firm. A proper balance should be maintained between liquidity and lack of liquidity.

The liquidity of the firm are explained by the following ratios

a. Current Ratio
b. Acid Test Ratio /Quick Ratio
c. Absolute Liquid Ratio /Cash Ratio

a. Current Ratio
The current ratio is the ratio between current assets and current liabilities. It measures the short term solvency of the firm. The current assets include the cash and bank balances, securities, inventory and debtors. The current liabilities include sundry creditors, short term loans, Income Tax liability, expenses and liabilities payable to the stakeholders.

b. Acid Test Ratio /Quick Ratio

Quick Ratio is the ratio between quick assets and current liabilities. It acts as a indicator of the liquidity position of the firm. The Quick assets are assets in which that can be converted into cash immediately without loss of value. Quick assets include bank balances, cash balances, Bill receivables, marketable securities and sundry debtors.

c. Absolute Liquid Ratio /Cash Ratio

The ratio between the absolute liquid assets and current liabilities is termed as Cash ratio. In the liquid assets the cash and bank balances and also marketable securities are included.

The Liquidity Ratios of BSNL in the financial year 2005–2013 is shown in Table 1. The cash ratio shows a steep decrease which shows low liquid cash in the company.

The current ratio shows a steady value in the entire study period. This shows a constant assets and liabilities in the company. In 2009–10 the current ratio shows a decrease due to the increase in the liabilities in the expansion of the Mobile Network. Similarly the Quick ratio also shows a steady and good performance over the years. This shows a good and future growth for BSNL.

However the cash ratio giving the ratio of liquid assets to the liabilities is decreasing year by year. This shows that the liquid cash available in the PSU is decreasing at a huge rate. This should be taken care and monitored by the company to have a good performance in the future for the PSU. The firm should have a strong short as well as long term financial position so that it leads to a strong working capital turnover thereby cause an increase in assets.

The turnover reflects a comfortable position upto 2008–09 and since then higher debt is witnessed. A continuous watch on the critical ratios is essential henceforth. The operating profit is declining from year 2009 and this can be attributed to the significant increase in the expenditure especially in the remuneration and operating expenses.

The financial performance of BSNL for financial year ending from 2005 to 2013 is shown in Fig. 2. The pie chart shows a decline in the revenue and increase in expenditure in various segments over the years. The return on the assets included should be monitored to improve the revenue segment.

Table 1. Liquidity ratios of BSNL

Financial year	Current ratio	Quick ratio	Cash ratio
2005–06	5.1018	4.9724	1.4154
2006–07	5.2371	5.1259	1.7158
2007–08	4.9199	4.7827	1.7285
2008–09	4.5603	4.3822	1.4858
2009–10	2.7899	2.6852	0.6275
2010–11	5.5977	5.3958	0.1279
2011–12	5.4618	5.2665	0.1023
2012–13	4.8696	4.6755	0.0597

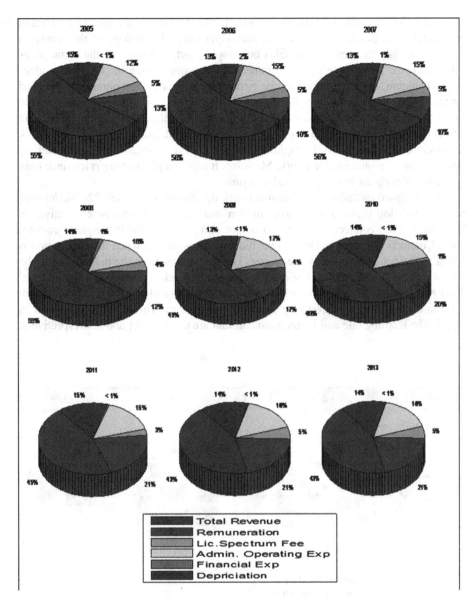

Fig. 2. Performance of BSNL in financial year 2005–2013 source: yearly financial reports of BSNL [14]

4 CCNN Based Prediction

Cascaded Correlation Neural Network (CCNN) was developed by Fahlman and Libiere in the year 1990 [15, 16]. Cascade correlation neural networks are "self organizing" networks and are similar to traditional networks in that the neuron is the most basic unit. Training the neurons however is novel. The CCNN is a supervised learning architecture that builds a near-minimal multilayer network topology in the course of training. Initially the network contains only inputs, output units, and the connections between them. This single layer of connections is trained using the Quickprop algorithm (Fahlman, 1988) to minimize the error. Cascade-correlation eliminates the need for the user to guess in advance the network's size, depth, and topology. A reasonably small (though not minimal) network is built automatically. The main drawback in artificial neural network is the rate of convergence and the manual fixation of network architecture (hidden units) throughout training. These problems are addressed by cascaded correlation neural network. Moreover it uses simple training rules since only one layer of weights is being trained at a time.

The designed cascaded correlation network posses one input unit, 220 hidden unit neurons with log sigmoid activation function and output unit with purelin activation function that are connected directly to output unit with adjustable weighted connections. Connection from input unit to the hidden unit is trained when the hidden unit is added to the net and then they are frozen. The connection from the hidden unit to the output unit is also adjustable. The designed neural network is trained with the financial datas pertaining to the years for which the data is existing. (i.e. Year from 2005 to till date) and trained using Levenberg Marquardt algorithm. The network as shown in Fig. 3. The learning rate and momentum constant are taken as 0.1 and 0.9 respectively.

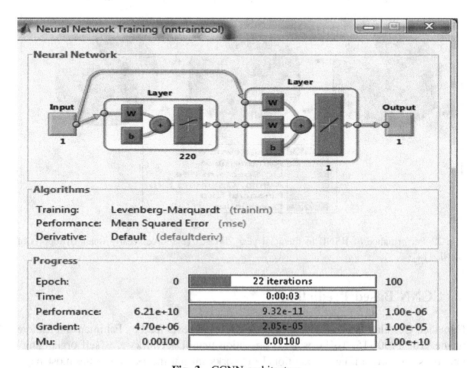

Fig. 3. CCNN architecture

Table 2. Various segment revenue analysis

Financial year	Land line revenue (Rs. in Lakhs)	% Change in land line revenue	Mobile revenue (Rs. in Lakhs)	% Change in mobile revenue	Broadband revenue (Rs. in Lakhs)	% Change in broadband revenue	Leased line revenue (Rs. in Lakhs)	% Change in leased line revenue
2005–06	2.0421*10^6	–	6.4337*10^5	–	0.1624*10^5	–	0.5315*10^5	–
2006–07	1.6605*10^6	-18.68	9.2646*10^5	44.001	0.5138*10^5	216.31	0.5126*10^5	-3.5446
2007–08	1.2668*10^6	-23.70	1.053*10^6	13.659	0.9159*10^5	78.258	0.7573*10^5	47.718
2008–09	1.0185*10^6	-19.6	1.0203*10^6	-3.1104	1.689*10^5	84.46	1.0006*10^5	32.129
2009–10	8.2677*10^5	-18.82	9.7608*10^5	-4.3299	2.4854*10^5	47.104	1.0643*10^5	6.3629
2010–11	6.8387*10^5	-17.28	8.8031*10^5	-9.811	3.3084*10^5	33.11	1.8267*10^5	71.632
2011–12	5.653*10^5	-17.33	9.7414*10^5	10.658	3.5689*10^5	7.8755	1.8038*10^5	-1.2564
2012–13	4.9472*10^5	-12.48	1.0121*10^6	3.892	3.9748*10^5	11.372	1.7967*10^5	-0.3886
2013–14	4.4249*10^5	-10.55	1.1635*10^6	14.968	5.4151*10^5	36.235	2.4741*10^5	37.699
2014–15	4.0042*10^5	-9.505	1.3172*10^6	13.205	9.0798*10^5	67.678	2.4732*10^5	-0.0352
2015–16	3.5911*10^5	-10.31	1.4684*10^6	11.484	1.8009*10^6	98.34	2.7205*10^5	9.998
2016–17	3.0726*10^5	-14.43	1.479*10^6	0.7179	3.4332*10^6	90.638	2.9942*10^5	10.061
2017–18	2.3309*10^5	-24.14	1.3412*10^6	-9.3141	6.682*10^6	94.63	3.2382*10^5	8.1498

Table 3. Revenue and expenditure prediction analysis

Financial Year	Total revenue (Rs. in Lakhs)	% Change in revenue	Remuneration (Rs. in Lakhs)	% Change in remuneration	Operating expenses (Rs. in Lakhs)	% Change in operating expenses
2005–06	4.0177*10^6	11.3231	0.7420*10^6	−11.5857	1.0497*10^6	30.3644
2006–07	3.9715*10^6	−1.1486	0.730897*10^6	−1.5047	1.0916*10^6	3.9954
2007–08	3.8047*10^6	−4.2006	0.880891*10^6	20.5219	1.1110*10^6	1.7762
2008–09	3.2812*10^6	−13.7591	1.136323*10^6	28.9970	1.1378*10^6	2.4103
2009–10	3.2045*10^6	−2.3361	1.345504*10^6	18.4086	1.0199*10^6	−10.3614
2010–11	2.9688*10^6	−7.3577	1.379095*10^6	2.4965	1.0120*10^6	−0.7738
2011–12	2.7934*10^6	−5.9086	1.340604*10^6	−2.7910	1.0294*10^6	1.7172
2012–13	2.7128*10^6	−2.8840	1.3758*10^6	2.6240	1.0402*10^6	1.0534
2013–14	2.9555*10^6	8.9466	1.6179*10^6	17.596	1.2742*10^6	22.487
2014–15	3.2822*10^6	11.056	2.3694*10^6	46.453	1.405*10^6	10.27
2015–16	3.7742*10^6	14.989	3.9763*10^6	67.816	1.6587*10^6	18.059
2016–17	4.5772*10^6	21.276	6.868*10^6	72.725	2.2524*10^6	35.788
2017–18	5.7806*10^6	26.29	1.1553*10^7	68.21	2.8655*10^6	27.221

The prediction of the system was done from year 2014 to 2018(.i.e. prediction for another 5 years).

The Financial performance of BSNL and future prediction using CCNN is given in Tables 2 and 3. The Table 2 shows the revenue performance of BSNL in various important segments and services. In the Table 2 the percentage changes were calculated from 2005–06 to 2017–2018 in predicting the future.

The revenue in Landline segment shows a negative trend year by year since the trend move towards wireless segments.

The mobile revenue is showing a positive growth steadily and in the future prediction in the year 2017–18 and a negative trend is expected due to the customers moving towards data services than voice communication services.

The Broadband segment shows a steep increase in revenue and in the upcoming years it will yield major revenue and leads to a good company position. Similarly the leased line segment also contribute a major revenue of the BSNL in the future since the customers are moving towards high demand for data communication services with the full-fledged implementation of grid and cloud computing applications.

Table 3 shows the Total Revenue at present and that predicted upto 2017–18 using CCNN. Also the expenditure done in the present and that predicted to be upto 2017–18 in major sections of Operating and Admin expenses and the remuneration to the working staff is Tabulated. Also in the Table 3 the percentage changes were calculated from 2005–06 to 2017–2018 in predicting the future.

The highest percentage increase in the remuneration expenditure at present was in 2008–09 and due to the pay revision of II PRC. In the future prediction the highest percentage in remuneration expenditure will be in 2016–17 of 72 % due to expected III PRC revision.

The highest percentage increase in the operating and administration expenditure at present was in 2005–06. After this period there is a effective control and it lead to less expenditure in this section. In the future prediction the highest percentage in operating and administration expenditure expenditure will be in 2017–18 of expected due to III PRC revision and its inflation.

The performance of the cascaded neural network based financial prediction model designed was compared with Trend analysis approach [17] and the proposed CCNN predicts the future more accurately when compared with the conventional trend analysis approach. The training performance of the CCNN is shown in Fig. 3 and it shows good training with less mean square error.

5   Conclusion

In this paper the financial performance of the Public Sector Undertaking BSNL was analyzed by Ratio analysis and Cascaded Correlation Neural Network in future prediction of BSNL. The liquidity ratios termed current ratio shows the short term solvency of the PSU is in good position. The cash ratio shows an indication of the bad condition of liquidity of the company. The CCNN based prediction analysis shows a good improvement in the revenue in data communication related segments in the upcoming years and the operating expenses made to be less to make the company more profitable.

References

1. Yalcin, N., Bayrakdaroglu, A., Kahraman, C.: Application of fuzzy multi-criteria decision making methods for financial performance evaluation of Turkish manufacturing industries. Expert Syst. Appl. **39**, 350–364 (2012)
2. Chen, J.-H.: Developing SFNN models to predict financial distress of construction companies. Expert Syst. Appl. **39**, 823–827 (2012)
3. Chen, M.-Y.: Predicting corporate financial distress based on integration of decision tree classification and logistic regression. Expert Syst. Appl. **38**, 11261–11272 (2011)
4. Duft, K. D.: Financial ratio analysis: An aid to agribusiness management (2007). http://classes.ses.wsu.edu/EconS452/section-Duft/docs/FinRatio1.pdf
5. Feng, C.M., Wang, R.T.: Performance evaluation for airlines including the consideration of financial ratios. J. Air Transp. Manage. **6**(3), 133–142 (2000)
6. Wang, Y.J., Lee, H.S.: A clustering method to identify representative financial ratios. Inf. Sci. **178**(4), 1087–1097 (2008)
7. Lahtinen, K., Toppinen, A.: Financial performance in Finnish large- and medium-sized sawmills: the effects of value-added creation and cost-efficiency seeking. J. Forest Econ. **14**(4), 289–305 (2008)
8. Chen, K.H., Shimerda, T.A.: An empirical analysis of useful financial ratios. Financ. Manage. **10**(1), 51–60 (1981)
9. Bolton, R.J., Hand, D.J.: Statistical fraud detection: a review. Stat. Sci. **17**(3), 235–255 (2002)
10. Zhang, D., Zhou, L.: Discovering golden nuggets: data mining in financial application. IEEE Trans. Syst. Man Cybern. **34**(4), 513–522 (2004)
11. Phua, C., Lee, V., Smith, K., Gayler, R.: A comprehensive survey of data mining-based fraud detection research. Artificial Intelligence Review, pp. 1–14 (2005)
12. Yue, X. Wu, Y. Wang, Y. Li, C. Chu, A review of data mining-based financial fraud detection research. In: International Conference on Wireless Communications, Networking and Mobile Computing, pp. 5519–5522 (2007)
13. Derrig, R.A.: Insurance fraud. J. Risk Insur. **69**(3), 271–287 (2002)
14. www.bsnl.co.in
15. Fahlman, S.E., Lebiere, C.: The cascade-correlation learning architecture. In: Touretzky, D.S. (ed.) Advances in Neural Information Processing Systems, vol. 2, pp. 524–532. Morgan Kaufmann, CA (1990)
16. Fahlman, S.E.: Faster-learning variations on back-propagation: an empirical study. In: Proceedings of the 1988 Connectionist Models summer School, pp. 38–51. Morgan Kaufmann (1988)
17. Albert Singh, N., Narayanan, T.: Analysis of financial statements for financial performance prediction of PSU-BSNL. In: Proceedings of the IEEE International Conference on Emerging Trends in Science, Engineering, Business and Disaster Management, pp: 589–595 (2014)
18. Bernstein, L., Wild, J.: Financial Statement Analysis: Theory, Application, and Interpretation. Irwin McGraw Hill, Boston (1998)
19. Ross, S., Westerfleld, R., Jaffe, J.: Corporate Finance, 6th edn. McGraw-Hill, New York (2002)
20. White, G.I., Sondhi, A.C., Fried, D.: The Analysis and Use of Financial Statements. John Wiley and Sons Inc, New York (2003)
21. Glancy, F.H., Yadav, S.B.: A computational model for financial reporting fraud detection. Decis. Support Syst. **50**, 595–601 (2011)

22. Ngai, E.W.T., Hu, Y., Wong, Y.H., Chen, Y., Sun, X.: The application of data mining techniques in financial fraud detection: a classification framework and an academic review of literature. Decis. Support Syst. **50**(3), 559–569 (2011)
23. Shue, L.-Y., Chen, C.-W., Shiue, W.: The development of an ontology-based expert system for corporate financial rating. Expert Syst. Appl. **36**, 2130–2142 (2009)
24. Seng, J.-L., Lai, J.T.: An intelligent information segmentation approach to extract financial data for business valuation. Expert Syst. Appl. **37**, 6515–6530 (2010)
25. Chen, W.-S., Yin-Kuan, D.: Using neural networks and data mining techniques for the financial distress prediction model. Expert Syst. Appl. **36**, 4075–4086 (2009)
26. Halkos, G.E., Tzeremes, N.G.: Industry performance evaluation with the use of financial ratios: an application of bootstrapped DEA. Expert Syst. Appl. Int. J. **39**(5), 5872–5880 (2012)
27. Sudheer, Ch., Maheswaran, R., Panigrahi, B.K., Mathur, S.: A hybrid SVM-PSO model for forecasting monthly streamflow. Neural Comput. Appl. **24**(6), 1381–1389 (2014)
28. Shrivastava, N.A., Panigrahi, B.K.: A hybrid wavelet-ELM based short term price forecasting for electricity markets. Int. J. Electr. Power Energy Systems **55**, 41–50 (2014)
29. Ch, S., Anand, N., Panigrahi, B.K., Mathur, S.: Streamflow forecasting by SVM with quantum behaved particle swarm optimization. Neurocomputing **101**(4), 18–23 (2013)

Application of Support Vector Machine Classifier for Computer Aided Diagnosis of Brain Tumor from MRI

V. Amsaveni[1], N. Albert Singh[2(✉)], and J. Dheeba[3]

[1] Electronics and Instrumentation Engineering, Noorul Islam University,
Kumaracoil, TN, India
amsa.kumar@ymail.com
[2] Sub Divisional Engineer, BSNL, Nagercoil, TN, India
mailalbertsingh@yahoo.co.in
[3] Noorul Islam University, Kumaracoil, TN, India
deeps_3u4@yahoo.com

Abstract. In this paper a computerized scheme for automatic detection of tumors in brain is examined. Diagnosis of these lesions at the early stage is a very difficult task in normal brain images. The algorithm incorporates steps for preprocessing, feature extraction and classification using brain tumor detection. This paper proposes a supervised machine learning algorithm for detection of tumor. A feature extraction methodology is used to extract the Gabor texture features of the abnormal brain tissues and normal brain tissues prior to classification. Then support vector machine classifier is applied at the end to determine whether the given input data is tumor or non tumor. The detection performance is evaluated using Receiver Operating Characteristic curves. The result shows significantly improves the classification accuracy.

Keywords: Magnetic resonance imaging · Support vector machine · Computer aided detection

1 Introduction

Brain has a very complex structure and is considered the kernel part of the body. Nature has tightly safeguarded the brain inside a skull that hinders the study of its function as well as makes the diagnosis of its diseases more intricate. Brain tumors either include tumors in the central spinal cord or inside the cranium [1]. Automatic defects detection in MRI is quite useful in several diagnostic and MRI are two imaging modalities that help researchers and medical practitioners to study the brain by looking at it non-invasively.

Magnetic Resonance Imaging (MRI) is non invasive procedure and can be used safely for brain imaging as often as necessary [2]. MRI images are used to produce accurate and detailed pictures of organs from different angles to diagnose any abnormalities. There are two types of MRI, high field for producing high quality images and low field MRI for low accuracy in diagnosis. MRI images allow the physician to visualize even hair line cracks and tears in injuries to ligaments, muscles and other soft

© Springer International Publishing Switzerland 2015
B.K. Panigrahi et al. (Eds.): SEMCCO 2014, LNCS 8947, pp. 514–522, 2015.
DOI: 10.1007/978-3-319-20294-5_45

tissues. Magnetic resonance imaging (MRI) is excellent for showing abnormalities of the brain images.

Computer-aided detection or diagnosis (CAD) system effectively detects and diagnoses the cancer in their early stages. CAD systems can play a key role in the early detection of cancers and helps to reduce the death rate with cancers. Hence CAD systems and related techniques have attracted the attention of both researchers and radiologists [3, 10].

In [4] Pan Lin et al. developed an efficient automatic framework for Segmentation of Brain Images. Abhishek Raj et al. [5] have demonstrated an improved method for computer aided detection of brain tumor. They used de-noising in wavelet domain followed by enhancement using a non-linear enhancement function. The brain tumor was detected by employing large sized structuring elements along with thresholding. Yan Zhu et al. [6] evaluated a computer aided diagnosis systems for detecting malignant texture in biological study using Hopfield Neural Network.

In Sharma et al. [7] has provided an efficient algorithm for detecting the edges of brain tumor. The first step starts with the acquisition of MRI scan of brain and then digital imaging techniques are applied for getting the exact location and size of tumor. The brain images consist the region containing tumor has more intensity. Tirpude et al. [8] has provided an accurate detection of the boundary of the tumor, along with correct visual location of the tumor with the help of a bounding circle. This study has also provided a diagnosis decision whether the tumor is present or absent along with the exact size of the tumor. Dheeba et al. [9] has the methods of automatic detection of breast cancer from mammogram images using Support Vector Machine (SVM) in different stages of Computer Aided Detection System. SVM based evolutionary approaches are discussed in detail for various applications in [16, 17].

The major objective of this paper is to take texture features from the MRI to discriminate between tumor and the normal tissue in the brain image. The proposed SVM was proved as a better classification algorithm for various applications as evident from the literature survey [9, 16, 17] referred. In the first stage, the original image is preprocessed and features are extracted from the image using Gabor features. In the second stage, the extracted features are compared by means of their ability in detecting tumor using Support Vector Machine Classifier (SVM).

2 Proposed Work

The objective of proposed system is used to detect tumor from brain images. It involves preprocessing, feature extraction and classification using support vector machine. The overall diagram of proposed system is shown in Fig. 1.

2.1 Preprocessing

The purpose is basically to remove the noise to improve the image quality and also removal of the image background. The histogram of the input image is equalized to enhance the images. The image is de-noised using a median filter.

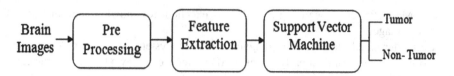

Brain Images → Pre Processing → Feature Extraction → Support Vector Machine → Tumor / Non-Tumor

Fig. 1. Proposed CAD system for brain tumor detection

2.2 Feature Extraction

The extracted features are distinguished as either cancerous or not using their texture properties. For the efficient feature extraction, we employ the Gabor approach of texture analysis. The most vital properties are related to the intensity variations.

The Gabor wavelet is a sinusoidal plane wave with a specific frequency and orientation, modulated by a Gaussian envelope [11]. It is able to characterize the spatial frequency structure in the image while preserving information of spatial relations and this is suitable for extracting the orientation dependent frequency contents of patterns. Also, the use of Gabor filters in extracting texture features is motivated by many factors [11] like spatial frequency structure, frequency properties of image in different orientations, etc.,. The statistics of these micro features in a given region are usually used to characterize the underlying texture information.

The work involves extraction of the important features for image recognition. The features extracted give the property of the texture, and are stored in it. These features are compared with the features of sample images for classification. A two dimensional Gabor function g(x, y) and its Fourier transform G (u, v) can be written in Eqs. (1) and (2) respectively.

$$g(x,y) = \left(\frac{1}{2\pi\sigma_x\sigma_y}\right) \exp\left[-\frac{1}{2}\left(\frac{x^2}{\sigma_x^2} + \frac{y^2}{\sigma_y^2}\right) + 2\pi jWx\right] \tag{1}$$

$$G(u,v) = \exp\left[-\frac{1}{2}\left(\frac{(u-W)^2}{\sigma_u^2} + \frac{v^2}{\sigma_v^2}\right)\right] \tag{2}$$

Here, $\sigma_u = 1/2\pi\sigma_x$ and $\sigma_v = 1/2\pi\sigma_y$. This transform detects the edges more accurately from the images. Its efficiency is high when compared to other transforms. It splits the image into its corresponding low frequency and high frequency components. Let g(x, y) be the mother Gabor wavelet, then the filter dictionary can be obtained by appreciate iterations of g(x, y) through the generating function as,

$$g_{mn}(x,y) = a^{-m}G(x',y'), a \geq 1, m, n = \text{Integer} \tag{3}$$

$$
\begin{aligned}
x' &= a^{-m}(x \cos\theta + y \sin\theta) \\
y' &= a^{-m}(-x \sin\theta + y \cos\theta)
\end{aligned} \tag{4}
$$

Here, $\theta = n\pi/k$. Let k be the total number of iterations and S the number of images in the multi resolution decomposition. In a given image I(x, y), its Gabor wavelets transform is defined as,

$$W_{mn}(x, y) = \int I(x_1, y_1) g_{mn} * (x - x_1, y - y_1) dx_1 dy_1 \qquad (5)$$

Here $*$ indicates the complex conjugate. It is assumed as the local texture regions of the image. The statistical parameters like maximum, minimum and standard deviation can be calculated from the Gabor wavelets.

2.3   Support Vector Machine Based Tumor Classification

Support Vector Machines are based on the principle of structural risk minimization, which aims at minimizing the bound on the generalization error (i.e., error made by the learning machine on data unseen during training) rather than minimizing the mean square error over the data set [13]. As a result, this leads to good generalization and an SVM tends to perform well when applied to data outside the training set. SVMs gain flexibility and SVMs can be robust, even when the training sample has some bias. For two input case (x_1, x_2) the support vector representation is shown in Fig. 2. SVM has proven its efficiency over neural networks. Unlike neural networks, this model builds does not need hypothesizing number of neurons in the middle layer or defining the centre of Gaussian functions in radial basis kernel of non-linear type [12]. Best hyper plane is the one that represents the largest separation or margin between the two classes.

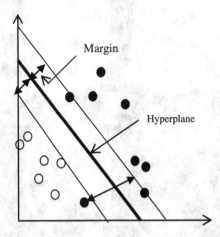

Fig. 2. Support vector machine with a hyperplane

The nonlinear SVM with a Gaussian radial basis kernel is used in the proposed classifier. The kernel function is

$$K(X_i, X_j) = e^{-\frac{\|x_i - x_j\|^2}{2\sigma^2}} \tag{6}$$

In the machine learning approach using SVM every point is mapped in space so that the data points are categorized into different categories using Gaussian radial-basis function kernel. SVM defines the similarity measure between the two classes and the support vectors is the separator. The new feature space can be calculated and it is a powerful supervised learning method.

Minimize,

$$F_{SVM} = \frac{\|w\|^2}{2} + C \sum_{i=1}^{n} E_i \tag{7}$$

where C is a constant value that controls the exchange of values between margin maximization and classification error. E is the classification error that occurs while training.

The support vectors are elements of the training set that lie exactly on or inside the decision boundaries of the classifier. The classifier uses these borderline examples to define its decision boundary between the two classes (i.e. 'Abnormal' or 'Normal'). SVM's are constructed by setting a hyper plane that separates two or more classes of data. By construction of these hyper planes, the SVM discovers the boundaries between

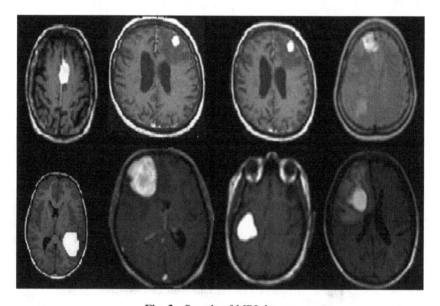

Fig. 3. Sample of MRI dataset

input classes: the elements of the input data that define these boundaries are called support vectors.

3 Results and Discussions

The data set used for study of the proposed system consists of 50 brain images collected from diagnostic centers. All the images are acquired using MRI scan machine in the dimension of 680*600. Sample dataset images are shown in Fig. 3. Preprocessing was carried out as briefed in Sect. 2 and the Gabor features are extracted for 24 orientations. A total of 2030 patterns are created with tumor positive and tumor negative examples. The proposed SVM classifier is trained with 1015 patterns (50 %) and is tested with remaining 1015 patterns (50 %) which produce result as either tumor or non tumor.

SVM uses an optimum linear separating hyper plane to separate two set of data in a feature space [14]. The cost factor C of the SVM is taken as 3.5 in the Eq. 7. This optimum hyper plane is produced by maximizing minimum margin between the two

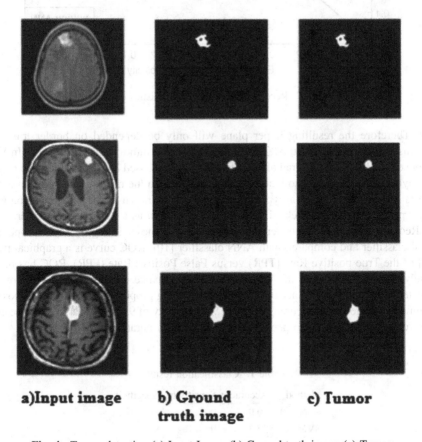

a)Input image   b) Ground   c) Tumor
truth image

Fig. 4. Tumor detection (a) Input Image (b) Ground truth image (c) Tumor

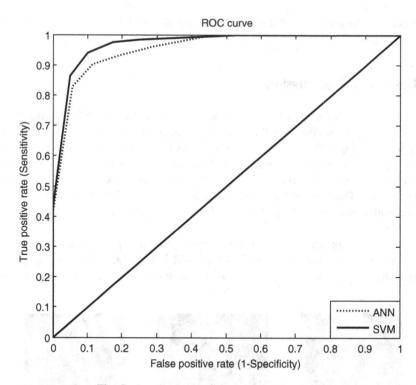

Fig. 5. Receiver operating characteristics curve

sets. Therefore the resulting hyper plane will only be depended on border training patterns called support vectors. The Fig. 4 shows the tumor detection results. In the proposed method Gaussian radial basis function kernel based SVM classifier was used. The hyper plane is chosen so that the distance from it to the nearest data point on each side is maximized. If such a hyper plane exists, it is known as the maximum margin hyper plane and the linear classifier it defines is known as a maximum classifier.

Receiver Operating Characteristic (ROC) curve is shown in Fig. 5 for the proposed SVM classifier and compared with ANN classifier [10]. ROC curve is a graphical plot [15] of the True positive Rate (TPR) versus False Positive Rate (FPR). ROC has been widely used to determine the classification performance. As a result the tumor is detected within a pixel and accuracy is improved using proposed system. The proposed scheme has achieved an accuracy of 94.33 % sensitivity of 95.21 %. Large database are required for the classifier to perform the classification parameters correctly.

Table 1. Classification results

Method	Accuracy	Sensitivity	Specificity
BPN [10]	89.9 %	90.2 %	88.6 %
SVM	94.3 %	95.0 %	92.3 %

To compare the performance of our proposed method, we used a Back Propagation Neural network (BPN) classifier [10]. Table 1 lists the classification results. To estimate the performance accuracy, sensitivity and specificity are evaluated and the proposed SVM classifier gives better performance. The significance of the performance measures are based on the receiver operating characteristics curve as dealt detail in [15].

The performance measures are as shown below.

$$Accuracy = \frac{TP + TN}{TP + TN + FN + FP} X100 \tag{7}$$

$$Sensitivity = \frac{TP}{TP + FN} X100 \tag{8}$$

$$Specificity = \frac{TN}{FP + TN} X100 \tag{9}$$

4 Conclusion

The proposed medical decision support system for tumor detection in MRI brain images using SVM as a classifier for classification of Brain images. The algorithm developed helps the radiologists in identifying whether the pixel of image is normal or abnormal. The proposed method provides a good classification accuracy of 94.33 % accuracy during testing phase. The proposed approach is computationally less intensive and yields good results. The results show that the proposed algorithm is efficient and very successful. The high detection accuracy with low false alarm rate makes it a capable radiologist's assistant.

References

1. Malich, A., Marx, C., Facius, M., et al.: Tumor detection rate of a new commercially available computer-aided detection system. Eur. Radiol. **11**, 2454–2459 (2001)
2. Hu, X., Tan, K.K., Levin, N.: Three-dimensional magnetic resonance images of the brain, application to neurosurgical planning. J. Neurosurg. **72**, 123–134 (1990)
3. Logeswari, T., Karnan, M.: An improved implementation of brain tumor detection based on soft computing. J. Canc. Res. Expe. Ontology. Med. Imag. **2**(1), 147–151 (2010)
4. Lin, P., Yang, Y., Zheng, C-X., Gu, J-W.:An efficient automatic framework for segmentation of MRI brain image. In: Proceedings of the Fourth IEEE International Conference on Computer and Information Technology(CIT 2004), pp. 237–241 (2004)
5. Raj, A., Alankrita, A.S., Bhateja, V.: Computer aided detection of brain tumor in magnetic resonance images. Int. J. Eng. Technol. **3**(5), 189–192 (2011)
6. Zhu*, Y., Yan, H.: Computerized tumor boundary detection using a hopfield neural network. IEEE Trans. Med. Imaging **16**(1), 55–67 (1997)
7. Sharma, P., Diwakar, M., Choudhary, S.: Application of edge detection for brain tumor detection. Int. J. Comput. Appl. **58**(16), 21–27 (2012)

8. Tirpude, N., Welekar, R.: Automated detection and extraction of brain tumor from MRI images. Int. J. Comput. Appl. **77**(4), 26–30 (2013)

9. Dheeba. J., Tamil Selvi, S.: Classification of malignant and benign microcalcification using SVM classifier. In: Proceedings of IEEE Conference, ICETECT 2011, pp:686–690 (2011)

10. Amsaveni, V., Albert Singh, N., Ajan Babu, V.: Back propagation neural network based brain tumor detection. In: Proceedings of International Conference on Modeling Optimization and Computing (2014)

11. Raad, V.: Design of Gabor wavelets for analysis of texture features in cervical imaging. In: Proceedings of IEEE 25th Annual International Conference, vol. 1, p. 806, Sep. 17–21 (2003)

12. Huang, Y.L., Chen, D.R.: Support vector machines in sonography: application to decision making in the diagnosis of breast cancer. J. Clin. Imag. **29**(3), 179–184 (2005)

13. Sivanandam, S.N., Deepa, S.N.: Introduction to Neural Networks using MATLAB 6.0. Tata McGraw-Hill Publishing Company Limited, Noida (2006). ISBN 0-07-059112-1

14. Huang, C., Davis, L.S., Townshed, J.R.G.: An assessment of support vector machines for land cover classification. Int. J. Remote Sens. **23**(4), 725–749 (2002)

15. Obuchowski, Nancy A.: Receiver operating characteristics curves and their use in radiology. Radiology **229**, 3–8 (2003)

16. Agrawal, S., Panda, R., Bhuyan, S., Panigrahi, B.K.: Tsallis entropy based optimal multilevel thresholding using cuckoo search algorithm. Swarm Evol. Comput. **11**, 16–30 (2013)

17. Sudheer, Ch., Maheswaran, R., Panigrahi, B.K., Mathur, S.: A hybrid SVM-PSO model for forecasting monthly streamflow. Neural Comput. Appl. **24**(6), 1381–1389 (2014)

Tuning a Robust Performance of Adaptive Fuzzy-PI Driven DSTATCOM for Non-linear Process Applications

G. Satyanarayana[1(✉)] and K. Lakshmi Ganesh[2]

[1] University of Hyderabad, Hyderabad, India
gallasatya.eee@gmail.com
[2] Vishnu Institute of Technology, Bhimavaram, India
klganesh201@gmail.com

Abstract. The Classical PI controllers have been imperatively preferred for the control action of the active compensators in a power distribution system. However, the performance of these controllers is affected greatly by varying parameters and uncertainties in modeling and also high stability issues. In other side fuzzy logic based PI controllers have more robust and accurate appearance. The main intention of this work is to analyze and implementation of an adaptive intelligent controller for DSTATCOM for the expedited in-phase vectorial formulation template with mamdani fuzzy structure. The in-phase de-opposition of the current wave injected by the compensator is able to enhancing power quality features at PCC level. The efficient performance of robust adaptive fuzzy algorithm for the PI gain values are to be controlled by the operation of DSTATCOM. It enforce the non-adaptive control actions in terms of expressive dynamic response, inferior steady state error and achieve good stability with the appreciate dynamic behavior of adaptive intelligent type DSTATCOM under Matlab/Simulink tool.

Keywords: Distributed compensator (DSTATCOM) · Fuzzy logic controller · Power quality · Proportional controller · Unit vector template, total harmonic distortions

1 Introduction

The conveyance of neat power has been evermore a crucial mission for imperative utilities. In olden days the simplicity of the power system network with presence of pure linearized things maintains as gentle task. By the increased usage of high power semiconductor technology in real-time appliances may become the transportation of efficient power by way of distribution system is actually big achievement as proposed in [1]. The presence of this semiconductor technology attains superior power quality concerns at the point of common coupling (PCC). Amid of all power quality issues, exchanging of the real and the reactive component from the main source requires significant attention. Power electronic based advanced compensation schemes have been implemented in order to afford the more erudition and control over the power system network compared to formal methods. With the advancement of high power

© Springer International Publishing Switzerland 2015
B.K. Panigrahi et al. (Eds.): SEMCCO 2014, LNCS 8947, pp. 523–533, 2015.
DOI: 10.1007/978-3-319-20294-5_46

semiconductor methodology applications to power distribution systems, advanced static compensation schemes for mitigation of distribution side concerns a distributed static compensation scheme (DSTATCOM). It is exploited as a shunt device which can alleviate the currents related PQ concerns with voltage and current controlled mode of operations is proposed in [2, 3]. Extensively current driven voltage source inverters (VSI) advanced multilevel inverters in [4] based active devices are preferred to engage the PCC concerns by using efficient control strategies. Classical controllers are more naturally utilized by many industries due to their simple operation, excellent function, and easy of implementing.

The procedure for evaluating and designing of the PI controller for industrial applications is exactly elaborated and it should be more complex. In practice, widely trace that gain factors for the nonlinear systems are so harsh to determination of stability for the closed loop system approach is proposed by [4]. Due to their high complication and need to importance of accurate model, so many literature survey is highlighted in [5, 6]. It may tend to more complexity for perceiving and to adequately apply for many practical applications. At Present most of research methods pertaining the exact tuning approach of (P) proportional and (I) integral gains by the way of intelligent based control schemes are proposed in [7]. Intelligent or fuzzy type PI (FPI) controllers are expected so as to acquire an appetite performance degree. This advanced FPI control actions can be found in imperative applications for this FACTS technology is studied in [8] and has more attracted to the aggravated attention of many control approaches due to model free conception. Now, the main intention of this paper is the naivety and possibility of optimal fuzzy driven PI fed DC link voltage controller is evaluated, because of which computes the losses in DSTATCOM and it is prospected for obtaining supernatural results over formal control schemes. By maintaining the as-usual membership functions for system condition is deviated, this proposed controller may effectively trace-out the exact value of K_P and K_I by designing to be adaptive component and achieves robust appearance over the variation of system parameter and disorders. The dynamic analysis of proposed concept is evaluated by using Matlab/Simulink tool and results are conferred.

2 Proposed Distributed Compensation Scheme

The eminent pollutes in distribution AC networks are especially complies due to appearance of efficient non-linear loads and more lagging loads. For this circumstance needs the utilization of electric power for various consumers to induct several optimal compensators to predicate the best quality nature of power. Moreover, DSTATCOM majorly consists of a three phase (VSC) voltage source converter based on intelligent control of semiconductor valves, with respect to source as a DC link capacitor. The reference current generation by the unit vector control strategy and this compensation device is interfaced at the point of common coupling (PCC) through interfaced filters [9].

In general, the schematic diagram of proposed fuzzy logic driven adaptive controller fed DSTATCOM as depicted in Fig. 1, interfaced to a three phase AC mains supply which have a source impedance to be feeding a three phase non-linear diode

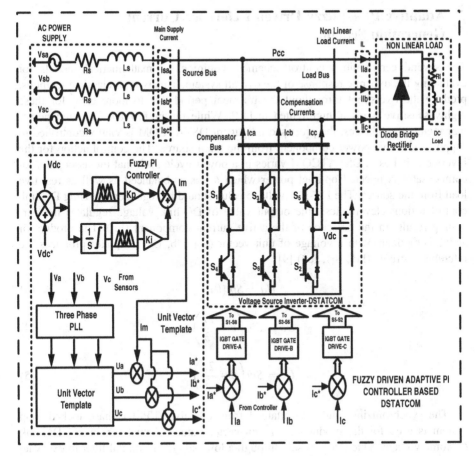

Fig. 1. Schematic diagram of proposed fuzzy driven adaptive PI controller Fed DSTATCOM topology

bridge rectifier load as proposed in [10]. Interfacing LC filters are exploited at AC side of the DSTATCOM for minimizing the ripple content present in compensation currents. The compensation currents are interposed by compensator to eradicate the harmonics/reactive power compensation with the robust compensation scheme. The optimal operation of proposed intelligent based DSTATCOM may depend mainly on the generation of reference current signals are used for generation of the switching pulses. The main approaches for such control action of the proposed controller to regulate the error value between the desired conditions. The outcome response almost depends on system performance. Here, the work of the fuzzy logic block-set is adaptively auto-tune the PI controller parameters to regulate the error in between the dc link reference value with actual DC link value [11].

3 Adaptive PI + Fuzzy Driven Reference Current Generation Scheme

The several ceremonious control schemes require exact mathematical models for evaluating the dynamic response of the overall system. This type of classical methods, produce the overshoot throughout the transient period due to more error for these highly sensitive loads is highlighted in [12]. While the performance of high power management appliances, the proposed intelligent DSTATCOM is vitally controlled to support the active power component from the main source. The control action for the inverter switches in DSTATCOM varies in a power cycle such that the association of compensator is injected optimal power which arises as balanced as well as resistive load from the source. The DC-link voltage value should be regulated by using DC link control action. Nevertheless, the output value of DC-link voltage regulates the pertaining results in the presence of the active current component (Im). The product of active component with a voltage of unit vector (Ua, Ub, Uc) templates produces the reference currents (Ia*, Ib*, Ic*) [9].

$$Ua = Sin(\theta) \tag{3}$$

$$Ub = Sin\left(\theta - \frac{2\pi}{3}\right) \tag{4}$$

$$Uc = Sin\left(\theta + \frac{2\pi}{3}\right) \tag{5}$$

The synchronizing angle (θ) attained from effective (EPLL) phase locked loop system is used for the production of unit-vector values. Actual sensing of DC-link outcome voltage value (Vdc) is sent through a low pass (LPF) digital filter to excavate the ripples coming from the outcome response. The deviation of this filtered DC-link value and constant DC-link outcome value (Vdc*) is applied to a proposed fuzzy driven adaptive PI regulator to regulate the magnitude as a constant under load variations. The processing DC link outcome error V_{dcerr} is given as:

$$V_{dcerr} = V_{dc}^* - V_{dc} \tag{6}$$

The proposed controller ventures the minimization of the error by the adjustment of the process/plant control incomes. Where Kpm_{Vdc}, Kim_{Vdc} is the proportional gain factor as well as integral gain factors, a high proportional gain which may result in a heavy change in the outcome for a prescribed change in the error value for high value of gain factors, the overall system operated under unstable region as presented in [13]. Finally, abstraction of these optimal gain values by using trail and an error procedure, but it has some demerits like never minimize the error value due to uneven gain functions, for that advanced techniques are available in real time applications such as fuzzy control action, but here proposed adaptive technique control action is used to reduce the overshoot produced by the PI component and may amend the coordinated control process stability.

$$I_m = I_m + Kpm_{Vdc}(V_{dcerr} - V_{dcerr}) + Kim_{Vdc}V_{dcerr} \qquad (7)$$

Adaptive fuzzy logic control theory is a new theme of process/plant control actions, it has gained more attention in industrial sector due to lack of highly quantitative form. No need exact mathematical model of this fuzzy logic control of any such type of plants. Consequently, it was highly applied to any plant model it should be unfamiliar. Since manipulating the specified data is based on imposed fuzzy set theory, fuzzification process is compulsory during the early stage as well as need de-fuzzification process at destiny stage. Implementation of Adaptive Fuzzy Logic Controller (AFLC) type control action may handling the optimal tuning of classical controller gain values for distributed conditioner by using mamdani type fuzzy inference system [14].The instantaneous vector values of three phase reference currents are generated with combination of unit vectorized values and optimal magnitude value as shown in Eqs. (8, 9, 10).

$$I_a^* = I_m * U_a \qquad (8)$$

$$I_b^* = I_m * U_b \qquad (9)$$

$$I_c^* = I_m * U_c \qquad (10)$$

The coming reference currents (Ia*, Ib*, Ic*) resemble with actual line currents (Ia, Ib, Ic) to achieve the reference current errors as shown in Eqs. (12, 13, 14).

$$I_{aerr} = I_a^* - I_a \qquad (12)$$

$$I_{berr} = I_b^* - I_b \qquad (13)$$

$$I_{cerr} = I_c^* - I_c \qquad (14)$$

These reference current errors are sent to (HCC) hysteresis current controller. This hysteresis current controller produces the switching signals to the gate drive circuit for each IGBT switch in converter topology. It can be express on the basis of error generation between the actual component as well as reference current component of the proposed intelligent based DSTATCOM. Implementation of this optimal control scheme is same as Fuzzy model, it provides a classical methodology for manipulating, implementing, representing a human heuristic knowledge for designing a control algorithm to the entire system is proposed in [9]. The proposed technique becomes very accurate and model free algorithm, essentially vigorous to system disturbances with the ease implementation.

There is no exact mathematical algorithm for this Fuzzy + PI algorithm; normally they are designed based on the general knowledge of the plant. It is implemented to manipulate the change in voltage of the distributed compensator using Mamdani style fuzzy inference system. The foremost term in this compensation scheme is the tracing of proportional gain factors which is more responsible to degrade overshoot, system oscillations. The operating membership functions of this robust application are, Ve*r and ΔVe*r are the input factor as well as ΔV*out is the output function are defined from the generalized domain as shown in Fig. 2.

The formation of this work is to manipulate the overshoots, oscillations, uneven settling time, and steady state error values of the overall system. The change in error and error values acts as input for this optimal intelligence system. Based on this input values attain seven multi variables such as; NS: Negative Small, NM: Negative Medium, NB: Negative Big, PS: Positive Small, PM: Positive Medium and PB: Positive Big, ZE: Zero Area as proposed in [9]. The near to optimal fuzzy rules for providing control variables can be referred as shown in Table 1, which makes the precise performance throughout the steady state and transient condition.

4   Matlab/Simulink Modeling and Simulation Results

As Table 2 specifies the design parameters for the implementation of robust performance based fuzzy driven adaptive PI controller fed distributed compensator (DSTATCOM) for power quality improving features using Matlab/Simulink platform.

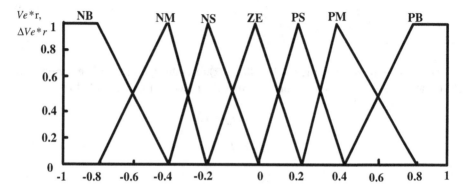

Fig. 2. Operating membership functions for input, output variables

Table 1. Operating rules for proposed Fuzzy + PI driven strategy

Ve^*r / $\Delta Ve*r$	NB	NM	NS	ZE	PS	PM	PB
NB	NB	NB	NB	NB	NM	NS	ZE
NM	NB	NB	NB	NM	NS	ZE	PS
NS	NB	NB	NM	NS	ZE	PS	PM
ZE	NB	NM	NS	ZE	PS	PM	PB
PS	NM	NS	ZE	PS	PM	PB	PB
PM	NS	ZE	PS	PM	PB	PB	PB
PB	NB	NM	NS	ZE	PS	PM	PB

Table 2. Design specifications.

Design Specifications		
	Parameters	Values
Source side	Source voltage	400 V (Ph-Ph).
	Source impedance	R = 0.1Ω, L = 0.9mH.
Voltage source inverter (VSI)	DC link capacitor	Cdc = 10000μF.
	Interfacing inductor	Rc = 0.05Ω, Lc = 10 mH.
	Ripple filter	Cr = 10 μF, Rr = 8Ω.
Load side	20KW diode bridge rectifier with LC filter at load side	L = 2mH, C = 500 μF.

As Fig. 3 shows the three phase PCC voltage, source current, load current, and compensation current respectively for PI controller fed distributed compensator (DSTATCOM), due to the uneven gain values source current attains high settling time and also more steady state error values, as well as a slow dynamic response in source currents, for this basic need to control the parameters through a optimal algorithm. As above Fig. 4 shows the three phase PCC voltage, source current, load current, compensation current DC-link voltage respectively for the robust performance of fuzzy

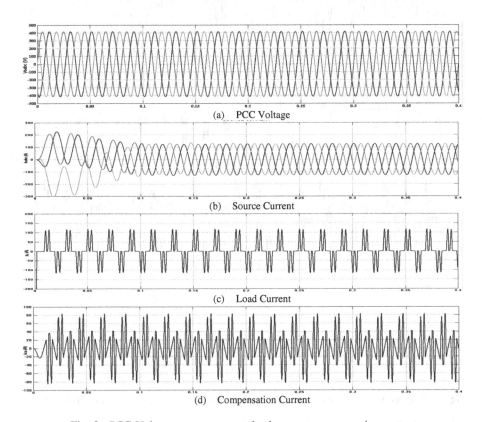

(a)   PCC Voltage

(b)   Source Current

(c)   Load Current

(d)   Compensation Current

Fig. 3. PCC Voltage, source current, load current, compensation current

driven PI controller fed distributed compensator because of near to optimal gain values source current and DC link voltage attains low settling time and also minimal steady state error, as well as fast dynamic response with more stable operation.

Figure 5 depicts the FFT analysis of the robust performance of adaptive fuzzy logic based PI control action on proposed DSTATCOM topology for measuring THD values, for only PI controller value is 2.70 %, for adaptive fuzzy method 0.14 %, it would be in IEEE standards. As Table 3 depicts the THD comparison of improved robust performance of various control concepts applied to DSTATCOM for enhancing the PQ

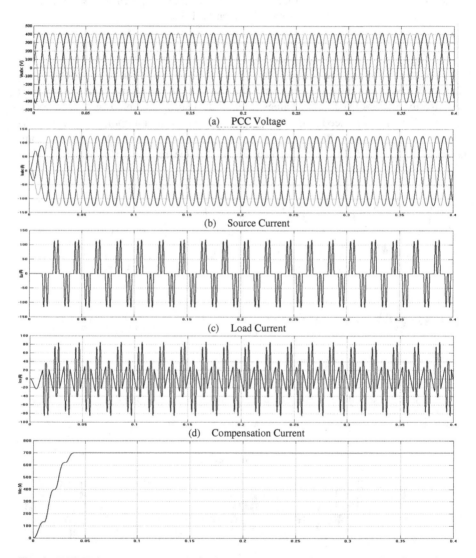

Fig. 4. PCC Voltage, source current, load current, compensation current and dc-link voltage

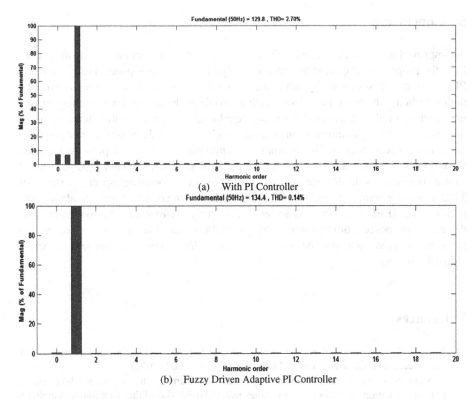

Fig. 5. FFT analysis of advanced fuzzy logic control action of proposed DSTATCOM topology with various control strategies

problems, in that proposed adaptive scheme have better features compared to formal compensation schemes. Here compared THD for various factors like source current and PCC voltage, load current. Utilization of adaptive techniques, THD drastically goes to reduce and achieve better stability factor compare to no compensation scheme and PI control scheme, Fuzzy scheme.

Table 3. THD comparison of improved robust performance of various control concepts applied to DSTATCOM for enhancing the PQ problems

Variable name	Several compensation schemes			
	No compensation scheme	PI scheme	Fuzzy scheme	Proposed adaptive scheme
PCC voltage	2.73 %	1.34 %	1.21 %	0.89 %
Source current	26.2 %	2.70 %	1.96 %	0.14 %
Load current	**26.2 %**	**25.8 %**	**25.2 %**	**25.1 %**

5 Conclusion

An improved robust appearance of adaptive fuzzy controller with interfacing the formal PI in the proposed compensation scheme is implemented in this paper. Fuzzy logic fed PI control action shows really attractive features like assimilation is very admirable, high simplicity and more prevalence. Using two fuzzy logic sets for the tuning of two gain factors of the PI controller for the regulation of power quality features using proposed distributed compensation scheme which gives stable as well as fast response under load disturbances and load variations. Simulation results are depicts the intended algorithm have more accurate for the selection of such fundamental components of source parameters with distorted currents. In all over the operating aspects, presence of THD values for source current and PCC voltage has been complied with standard limits of 5 % as per IEEE 519;1992 and achieve satisfactory performance. Moreover, realistic design of proposed compensator is to be well-considerable and to be proven the advanced adaptive control strategy is more practical for real time applications as merely industrial sectors.

References

1. Kumar, C., Mishra, M.K.: A voltage-controlled DSTATCOM for power-quality improvement. IEEE Trans. Power Deliv. **29**(3), 1499–1507 (2014)
2. Satyanarayana, G., Lakshmi Ganesh, K., Narendra Kumar, Ch., Vijaya Krishna, M.: A critical evaluation of power quality features using Hybrid Multi-Filter Conditioner topology. In: 2013 International Conference on Green Computing, Communication and Conservation of Energy (ICGCE), pp. 731–736, 12–14 December 2013
3. Prasad, K.N.V., Ranjith Kumar, G., Anil Kumar, Y.S., Satyanarayana, G.: Realization of cascaded H-bridge 5-Level multilevel inverter as Dynamic Voltage Restorer. In: 2013 International Conference on Computer Communication and Informatics (ICCCI), pp. 1–6, 4–6 January 2013
4. Prasad, K.N.V., Ranjith Kumar, G., Kiran, T.V., Satyanarayana, G.: Comparison of different topologies of cascaded H-Bridge multilevel inverter. In: 2013 International Conference on Computer Communication and Informatics (ICCCI), pp. 1–6, 4–6 January (2013)
5. Srikanthan, S., Mishra, M.K.: DC capacitor voltage equalization in neutral clamped inverters for DSTATCOM application. IEEE Trans. Ind. Electron. **57**(80), 2768–2775 (2010)
6. Singh, B., Solanki, J.: A comparison of control algorithms for DSTATCOM. IEEE Trans. Ind. Electron. **56**(7), 2738–2745 (2009)
7. Escobar, G., Stankovic, A.M., Mattavelli, P.: An adaptive controller in stationary reference frame for D-STATCOM in unbalanced operation. IEEE Trans. Ind. Electron. **51**(2), 401–409 (2004)
8. Bhattacharya, A., Chakraborty, C.: A shunt active power filter with enhanced performance using ANN-based predictive and adaptive controllers. IEEE Trans. Ind. Electron. **58**(2), 421–428 (2011)
9. Satyanarayana, G., Prasad, K.N.V., Ranjith Kumar, G., Lakshmi Ganesh, K.: Improvement of power quality by using hybrid fuzzy controlled based IPQC at various load conditions. In: 2013 International Conference on Energy Efficient Technologies for Sustainability (ICEETS), pp. 1243–1250, 10–12 April 2013

10. Nithya, S., Gour, A.S., Vakumaran, N.S., Radhakrishnan, T.K., Balasubramanian, T., Anantharaman, N.: Intelligent controller implementation in real time for a non-linear process. In: IEEE International Symposium on Industrial Electronics, pp. 2508–2513 (2008)
11. Mohagheghi, S., Venayagamoorthy, G.K., Rajagopalan, S., Harley, R.G.: Hardware implementation of a mamdani fuzzy logic controller for a static compensator in a multi-machine power system. IEEE Trans. Ind. Appl. **44**(4), 1535–1544 (2009)
12. Bhende, C.N., Mishra, S., Jain, S.K.: TS-Fuzzy-controlled active power filter for load compensation. IEEE Trans. Power Deliv. **21**(3), 1459–1465 (2006)
13. Chandra, A., Singh, B., Singh, B.N., Al-Haddad, K.: An improved control algorithm of shunt active filter for voltage regulation, harmonic elimination, pfc, balancing of non-linear loads. IEEE Trans. Power Electron. **15**(3), 495–507 (2000)
14. Ricardo, A., Christian, A., Raphaell, S.: A robust adaptive control strategy of active power filter for power factor correction, harmonic compensation, balancing of non-linear loads. IEEE Trans. Power Electron. **27**(2), 718–730 (2012)

The Effect of Swapping Vectors During Mutation in Differential Evolution

Goran Martinović[(✉)] and Dražen Bajer

Faculty of Electrical Engineering, J. J. Strossmayer University of Osijek, Kneza
Trpimira 2b, 31000 Osijek, Croatia
{goran.martinovic,drazen.bajer}@etfos.hr

Abstract. This paper considers the effect of swapping vectors during
mutation, which are used for mutant vector construction. In the clas-
sic/canonical differential evolution three mutually different vector are
picked from the population, where one represents the base vector, and
the difference of the remaining two represents the difference vector. Motivated by the fact that there is no selection pressure in selecting the base
vector, the effect of setting the best one of the selected three as the base
vector is investigated. This way, a corresponding selection pressure is
achieved and the exploration of the search space is directed more towards
better solutions. Additionally, the order of the vectors used for generating the difference vector is considered as well. The experimental analysis
conducted on a fair number of standard benchmark functions of different dimensionalities and properties indicates that the aforementioned
approach performs competitively or better compared to the canonical
differential evolution.

Keywords: Base vector · Difference vector · Differential evolution ·
Mutation · Vector swapping

1 Introduction

Differential evolution (DE) [1,2] is a simple, yet effective direct search method for
global optimization. It established itself as one of the most effective and efficient
metaheuristics for continuous optimization. DE has been successfully applied on
a multitude of different global optimization problems, for example, parameters
identification [3], data clustering [4], feature subset selection [5] and frequency
assignment [6].

Since the inception of DE until date, numerous modifications were proposed
that yield higher performance in certain situations compared to the canonical algorithm. A comprehensive overview of state-of-the-art DE variants can
be found in [7]. Although there exist rather complex DE variants that offer
high performance in solving global optimization problems, it is not a far-fetched
assumption that simple algorithm modifications pose a more tempting choice
for less experienced practitioners trying to solve their problem with DE. That

© Springer International Publishing Switzerland 2015
B.K. Panigrahi et al. (Eds.): SEMCCO 2014, LNCS 8947, pp. 534–546, 2015.
DOI: 10.1007/978-3-319-20294-5_47

being said, relatively simple modifications of the canonical DE that offer higher performance can be found in literature. Das *et al.* [8] proposed two simple DE variants incorporating mechanisms for adjusting the value of the mutation control parameter. The first, called DE with Random Scale Factor (DERSF), sets the scale factor during the creation of each mutant to a random value in the range [0.5, 1]. The second, called DE with Time Varying Scale Factor (DETVSF) linearly decreases the scale factor from a maximal to a minimal predefined value during runtime. The experimental analysis showed that DERSF and DETVSF perform better compared to the canonical DE and particle swarm optimization (PSO), and two PSO variants which adjust the inertia weight in principally the same way as in the proposed DE variants. Zhan and Zhang [9] proposed DE with Random Walk (DE-RW) which introduces a simple modification to the crossover operator. Namely, during crossover, some components of the vector may receive a random value which is in the range of the search space. The probability that a given component receives a random value is linearly decreased during runtime. The experimental analysis indicated that DE-RW, depending on the set control parameters (for mutation and crossover), may provide considerably higher performance than the canonical DE. Liu and Sun [10] incorporated the k-Nearest Neighbors algorithm into the DE for the purpose of predicting the objective function value of new solutions. This way, the number of objective function evaluations can be reduced, which in effect can reduce the execution time considerably, since the evaluation of the objective function can be computationally very demanding. The experimental analysis confirmed that the proposed approach required substantially less objective function evaluations than the canonical DE while retaining performance. Huang and Cheng [11] proposed a simple mechanism for dynamically adjusting the control parameters of DE during runtime. The mechanism employs a sine and cosine function and is tuned to provide small changes in the beginning and end of the search while providing rapid changes in between. The experimental analysis suggests a performance improvement in terms of convergence speed and optimization error. Xu *et al.* [12] introduced a simple modification to the mutation operator of DE. Namely, the second best population member is selected as the first vector for generating the difference vector. According to the authors, this should improve the convergence speed. The experimental analysis conducted on a few test functions supports that claim.

This paper considers the effect of swapping vectors, according to their quality, participating in mutation i.e. mutant generation. In the canonical DE, the base vector and the vectors composing the difference vector are selected randomly from the population. Thus, the effect on performance of setting the best one of those selected as the base vector is investigated. In addition to that, the order (in terms of quality) of vectors composing the difference vector is examined for the purpose of determining its impact on the performance. It must be noted that the idea of setting the best of the three randomly selected population members as base vector is not new and was already introduced. Unlike the approach in [13], here the scale factor is not random but is kept fixed, since the goal was to investigate the effect of vector swapping.

The rest of the paper is structured as follows. Section 2 introduces DE and the canonical algorithm, and describes the approaches for swapping the vector used for mutant generation. The setup of the conducted experimental analysis is described and obtained results are presented in Sect. 3. Finally, the paper ends with a conclusion given in Sect. 4.

2   Differential Evolution

Differential evolution is a population-based search and optimization method. Like other common evolutionary algorithms it employs crossover and mutation for creating new individuals, and selection for picking individuals for a new generation. A particularly important role in the performance of DE is played by its mutation operator which perturbs a selected individual according to a scaled difference of another two population members. The population in DE is composed of NP real-valued vectors $\boldsymbol{v}^j = (v_1^j, \ldots, v_d^j) \in \mathbb{R}^d$, $j = 1, \ldots, NP$. The mode of operation of the canonical DE, usually denoted as DE/rand/1/bin [1], (other DE variants and their descriptions can be found in e.g. [2,7]) is presented in Algorithm 1, and can be described as follows.

In each generation/iteration a new population of size NP is created by mutation and crossover of individuals i.e. vectors of the current population. The initial population is usually randomly generated inside the search space $[lb_1, ub_1] \times \cdots \times [lb_d, ub_d]$, where lb_i and ub_i for $i = 1, \ldots, d$ are the lower and upper bound for the i-th component of each vector, respectively. Mutation creates for each target vector $\boldsymbol{v}^j$ a corresponding mutant or donor

$$\boldsymbol{u}^j = \boldsymbol{v}^{r1} + F \cdot (\boldsymbol{v}^{r2} - \boldsymbol{v}^{r3}), \tag{1}$$

where $\boldsymbol{v}^{r1}$, $\boldsymbol{v}^{r2}$ and $\boldsymbol{v}^{r3}$ are randomly selected vectors from the population, such that $j \neq r1 \neq r2 \neq r3$. The base vector $\boldsymbol{v}^{r1}$ is perturbed by a difference vector which in turn represents the difference of $\boldsymbol{v}^{r2}$ and $\boldsymbol{v}^{r3}$. The scale factor $F \in [0, \infty)$ is a parameter that determines the mutation step-size. Further on, the mutant $\boldsymbol{u}^j$ and target vector $\boldsymbol{v}^j$ are crossed over in order to create a trial vector

$$t_i^j = \begin{cases} u_i^j, & \text{if } \; \mathcal{U}[0,1) \leq CR \text{ or } i = r_i \\ v_i^j, & \text{else} \end{cases}, \quad i = 1, \ldots, d, \tag{2}$$

where $\mathcal{U}[0,1)$ is uniformly distributed random variable in $[0, 1)$, the parameter $CR \in [0,1]$ represents the crossover-rate, while r_i is randomly chosen number from the set $\{1, \ldots, d\}$. After the new population of trial vectors is created, they pass into the next generation only if they are equal or better (in terms of the objective function) than the corresponding target vector.

2.1   Swapping of Vectors Used for Mutant Generation

The selection of the base vector in DE/rand/1/bin, according to (1), is performed randomly, implying that no selection pressure is exhibited. Hence, slow convergence and the need of a large number of objective function evaluations for finding

---

Algorithm 1. Canonical DE (DE/rand/1/bin) in pseudo-code

1: Initialization and parameter setting
2: **for** $t := 1 \rightarrow t_{max}$ **do**
3:     **for** $j := 1 \rightarrow NP$ **do**   *%Create trial vector population*
4:         create mutant vector u^j (Eq. (1))
5:         cross over v^j and u^j to create trial vector t^j (Eq. (2))
6:     **end for**
7:     **for** $j := 1 \rightarrow NP$ **do**   *%Select new generation*
8:         **if** $f(t^j) \leq f(v^j)$ **then**
9:             $v^j := t^j$
10:         **end if**
11:     **end for**
12: **end for**

---

a good solutions might occur as a consequence. On the other hand, increased selection pressure may enhance performance (as was suggested in e.g. [14]), but too high a selection pressure might result in premature convergence and lead the algorithm into local optima, from which it might not escape.

Selection pressure in choosing the base vector can be simply introduced into the DE/rand/1/bin strategy by setting the best of the three selected vectors as the base vector. In other words, by swapping the vectors or rearranging vector indices such that $f(v^{r1}) \leq f(v^{r2})$ and $f(v^{r1}) \leq f(v^{r3})$. This way, the exploration of the search space is directed more towards better solutions i.e. exploitation is increased, which in turn increases the convergence speed. The aforementioned, basically represents a 3-tournament selection [15] for choosing the base vector and accordingly the two worst population members may never be chosen as base vector. It should be noted that the number of possible difference vectors for a given base vector is decreased (compared to the DE/rand/1/bin strategy), but their mean is still equal to 0. Nonetheless, this decrease should not represent a problem, but for very small populations. The described approach i.e. strategy will be denoted as DE/s1/1/bin.

In the aforementioned strategy, the remaining two vectors (tournament losers) compose the difference vector, and their quality is not considered while determining v^{r2} or v^{r3}. Setting the better one as v^{r2} or v^{r3} may affect algorithm performance. Although, the expected contribution is not large since a part of the possible difference vectors will be lost (compared to DE/s1/1/bin). The strategy in which the vectors are swapped such that $f(v^{r1}) \leq f(v^{r2}) \leq f(v^{r3})$ will be denoted as DE/s2/1/bin. Furthermore, the strategy in which the vectors are swapped such that $f(v^{r1}) \leq f(v^{r3}) \leq f(v^{r2})$ will be denoted as DE/s3/1/bin.

3   Experimental Analysis

An experimental analysis was conducted on a fair number of standard benchmark functions in order to assert the strengths and weaknesses of the presented strategies. The test suite included functions of various dimensionalities and properties.

Table 1. Benchmark functions, used

Function	d	S	f^*
$f_1(\boldsymbol{x}) = \sum_{i=1}^{d} x_i^2$	30, 50	$[-100, 100]^d$	0
$f_2(\boldsymbol{x}) = \sum_{i=1}^{d} |x_i| + \prod_{i=1}^{d} |x_i|$	30, 50	$[-10, 10]^d$	0
$f_3(\boldsymbol{x}) = \sum_{i=1}^{d} \left(\sum_{j=1}^{i} x_j \right)^2$	30, 50	$[-100, 100]^d$	0
$f_4(\boldsymbol{x}) = \max_i \{ |x_i|, 1 \leq i \leq d \}$	30, 50	$[-100, 100]^d$	0
$f_5(\boldsymbol{x}) = \sum_{i=1}^{d-1} \left[100(x_{i+1} - x_i^2)^2 + (x_i - 1)^2 \right]$	30, 50	$[-30, 30]^d$	0
$f_6(\boldsymbol{x}) = \sum_{i=1}^{d} x_i^2 + \left(\sum_{i=1}^{d} 0.5 i x_i \right)^2 + \left(\sum_{i=1}^{d} 0.5 i x_i \right)^4$	30, 50	$[-5, 10]^d$	0
$f_7(\boldsymbol{x}) = \sum_{i=1}^{d} (\lfloor x_i + 0.5 \rfloor)^2$	30, 50	$[-100, 100]^d$	0
$f_8(\boldsymbol{x}) = \sum_{i=1}^{d} i x_i^4 + \mathcal{U}[0, 1)$	30, 50	$[-1.28, 1.28]^d$	0
$f_9(\boldsymbol{x}) = \sum_{i=1}^{d} -x_i \sin(\sqrt{|x_i|})$	30, 50	$[-500, 500]^d$	$-420.9687 \cdot d$
$f_{10}(\boldsymbol{x}) = \sum_{i=1}^{d} \left[x_i^2 - 10 \cos(2\pi x_i) + 10 \right]$	30, 50	$[-5.12, 5.12]^d$	0
$f_{11}(\boldsymbol{x}) = -20 \exp \left(-0.2 \sqrt{\frac{1}{d} \sum_{i=1}^{d} x_i} \right)$ $- \exp \left(\frac{1}{d} \sum_{i=1}^{d} \cos(2\pi x_i) \right) + 20 + e$	30, 50	$[-32, 32]^d$	0
$f_{12}(\boldsymbol{x}) = \frac{1}{4000} \sum_{i=1}^{d} x_i^2 - \prod_{i=1}^{d} \cos \left(\frac{x_i}{\sqrt{i}} \right)$	30, 50	$[-600, 600]^d$	0
$f_{13}(\boldsymbol{x}) = \frac{\pi}{d} \Big\{ 10 \sin(\pi y_i) + \sum_{i=1}^{d-1} (y_i - 1)^2 [1 + 10 \sin^2(\pi y_{i+1})]$ $+ (y_d - 1)^2 \Big\} + \sum_{i=1}^{d} u(x_i, 10, 100, 4)$	30, 50	$[-50, 50]^d$	0
$f_{14}(\boldsymbol{x}) = 0.1 \Big\{ \sin^2(3\pi x_i) + \sum_{i=1}^{d-1} (x_i - 1)^2 [1 + \sin^2(3\pi x_{i+1})]$ $+ (x_d - 1)[1 + \sin^2(2\pi x_d)] \Big\} + \sum_{i=1}^{d} u(x_i, 5, 100, 4)$	30, 50	$[-50, 50]^d$	0
$f_{15}(\boldsymbol{x}) = \sum_{i=1}^{d-1} \left(0.5 + \frac{\sin^2\left(\sqrt{100 x_i^2 + x_{i+1}^2} \right) - 0.5}{1 + 0.001(x_i^2 - 2 x_i x_{i+1} + x_{i+1}^2)^2} \right)$	30, 50	$[-100, 100]^d$	0
$f_{16}(\boldsymbol{x}) = \left[\frac{1}{500} + \sum_{j=1}^{25} \frac{1}{j + \sum_{i=1}^{2}(x_i - a_{ij})^6} \right]^{-1}$	2	$[-65.536, 65.536]^d$	≈ 1
$f_{17}(\boldsymbol{x}) = \sum_{i=1}^{11} \left[a_i - \frac{x_1(b_i^2 + b_i x_2)}{b_i^2 + b_i x_3 + x_4} \right]^2$	4	$[-5, 5]^d$	0.0003075
$f_{18}(\boldsymbol{x}) = 4 x_1^2 - 2.1 x_1^4 + \frac{1}{3} x_1^6 + x_1 x_2 - 4 x_2^2 + 4 x_2^4$	2	$[-5, 5]^d$	-1.0316285
$f_{19}(\boldsymbol{x}) = \left(x_2 - \frac{5.1}{4\pi^2} x_1^2 + \frac{5}{\pi} x_1 - 6 \right)^2 + 10 \left(1 - \frac{1}{8\pi} \right) \cos(x_1) + 10$	2	$[-5, 10] \times [0, 15]$	0.398
$f_{20}(\boldsymbol{x}) = \left[1 + (x_1 + x_2 + 1)^2 (19 - 14 x_1 + 3 x_1^2 - 14 x_2 + 6 x_1 x_2 \right.$ $+ 3 x_2^2) \big] \cdot \left[30 + (2 x_1 - 3 x_2)^2 (18 - 32 x_1 + 12 x_1^2 \right.$ $+ 48 x_2 - 36 x_1 x_2 + 27 x_2^2) \big]$	2	$[-2, 2]^d$	3
$f_{21}(\boldsymbol{x}) = -\sum_{i=1}^{4} c_i \exp \left[-\sum_{j=1}^{3} a_{ij}(x_j - p_{ij})^2 \right]$	3	$[0, 1]^d$	-3.86
$f_{22}(\boldsymbol{x}) = -\sum_{i=1}^{4} c_i \exp \left[-\sum_{j=1}^{6} a_{ij}(x_j - p_{ij})^2 \right]$	6	$[0, 1]^d$	-3.32
$f_{23}(\boldsymbol{x}) = -\sum_{i=1}^{5} \left[(\boldsymbol{x} - a_i)(\boldsymbol{x} - a_i)^T + c_i \right]^{-1}$	4	$[0, 10]^d$	≈ -10
$f_{24}(\boldsymbol{x}) = -\sum_{i=1}^{7} \left[(\boldsymbol{x} - a_i)(\boldsymbol{x} - a_i)^T + c_i \right]^{-1}$	4	$[0, 10]^d$	≈ -10
$f_{25}(\boldsymbol{x}) = -\sum_{i=1}^{10} \left[(\boldsymbol{x} - a_i)(\boldsymbol{x} - a_i)^T + c_i \right]^{-1}$	4	$[0, 10]^d$	≈ -10

A decent number of test functions is necessary in order to adequately assess algorithm performance, although it is not uncommon to use 10 or less functions, as was done in e.g. [10,11,16–18]. The functions used, are listed in Table 1, while more details about individual functions may be found in [19–22].

3.1   Experiment Setup

The performance of the presented strategies DE/s1, s2, s3/1/bin have been compared to each other and DE/rand/1/bin. All algorithms/strategies were implemented in the C# programming language. Values of the parameters used, were the same for all. More precisely, $NP = 10 \cdot d$, $CR = 0.9$ and $F = 0.5$, while the number of (main loop) iterations was 5000 for functions of $d \leq 30$ and 10000 for functions of $d = 50$. The population was randomly initialized inside the whole search space $\mathcal{S}$ according to Table 1. The condition for termination was the execution of the set number of iterations. For each benchmark function from Table 1 and each strategy 100 independent runs were performed.

3.2 Results and Discussion

The results obtained in the experimental analysis are reported in Tables 2, 3, 4, 5 and 6, where Avg. t_{best} denotes the mean value of the iterations in which the best solution was found, while Stat. sig. indicates if there is a statistically significant difference between DE/rand/1/bin and the corresponding strategies, where $\bigcirc$ denotes no significant difference, $\triangle$ a significant difference in favor of the corresponding strategy, and $\triangledown$ a significant difference in favor of the canonical DE. Two-tailed t-tests with confidence interval of 95 % were performed. It must be noted the values less than $1 \cdot 10^{-15}$ (1E-15) have been taken as 0. Figures 1, 2, 3, 4 and 5 show, for several chosen functions, the mean value of the objective function for the best solution throughout the iterations. The figures are based on the average of 100 independent runs.

Tables 2 and 3 present the obtained results on unimodal functions f_1–f_6, the step function f_7 and quartic function (noise) f_8 for dimensionalities $d = 30$ and $d = 50$, respectively. The results show that each of the considered strategies (DE/s1, s2, s3/1/bin) performed equally or better compared to DE/rand/1/bin. This suggests a more effective exploration of the search space. A considerable difference may be noticed on functions f_3, f_4, f_5, and f_6 for $d = 30$ i $d = 50$. Also, it can be noticed that DE/s2/1/bin performed slightly better on most of the aforementioned functions than DE/s1, s3/1/bin. The mean value of the iterations in which the best solution was found is similar for all strategies. Figures 1 and 2 suggest that each of the presented strategies exhibit an almost identical behavior in terms of the best solution. Thus, it can be concluded that the order of vectors composing the difference vector does not play a significant role.

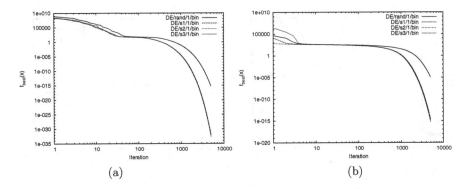

Fig. 1. Mean objective function value of the best solution throughout the iterations on (a) f_2 and (b) f_6 for $d = 30$

Table 2. Experimental results on functions f_1–f_8 for $d = 30$

Func.	Alg.	Best	Mean	Stddev	Worst	Median	Avg. t_{best}	Stat. sig.
	DE/rand/1/bin	0	0	0	0	0	4994.58	—
f_1	DE/s1/1/bin	0	0	0	0	0	4997.44	○
	DE/s2/1/bin	0	0	0	0	0	4997.14	○
	DE/s3/1/bin	0	0	0	0	0	4997.80	○
	DE/rand/1/bin	0	0	0	1.26E-15	0	4994.10	—
f_2	DE/s1/1/bin	0	0	0	0	0	4996.71	○
	DE/s2/1/bin	0	0	0	0	0	4997.01	○
	DE/s3/1/bin	0	0	0	0	0	4996.81	○
	DE/rand/1/bin	2.67E-05	1.04E-04	5.48E-05	3.15E-04	9.58E-05	4971.54	—
f_3	DE/s1/1/bin	1.04E-15	9.85E-15	8.08E-15	5.40E-14	7.77E-15	4987.82	△
	DE/s2/1/bin	0	2.73E-15	2.23E-15	1.03E-14	2.13E-15	4987.75	△
	DE/s3/1/bin	3.41E-15	1.80E-14	1.62E-14	1.02E-13	1.33E-14	4987.88	△
	DE/rand/1/bin	3.43E-07	1.01E-06	3.63E-07	2.19E-06	9.50E-07	4987.68	—
f_4	DE/s1/1/bin	0	2.28E-15	1.70E-15	1.07E-14	2.03E-15	4993.71	△
	DE/s2/1/bin	0	0	3.09E-15	2.56E-15	0	4993.96	△
	DE/s3/1/bin	0	3.49E-15	2.30E-15	1.14E-14	2.98E-15	4994.00	△
	DE/rand/1/bin	1.35E-10	6.10E-10	4.75476E-10	3.18E-09	4.91E-10	4988.25	—
f_5	DE/s1/1/bin	0	0	0	0	0	4901.81	△
	DE/s2/1/bin	0	0	0	0	0	4534.89	△
	DE/s3/1/bin	0	0	0	0	0	4995.12	△
	DE/rand/1/bin	2.95E-06	1.05E-05	5.96E-06	3.04E-05	8.93E-06	4970.30	—
f_6	DE/s1/1/bin	0	0	1.06E-15	5.74E-15	0	4985.82	△
	DE/s2/1/bin	0	0	0	0	0	4987.23	△
	DE/s3/1/bin	0	1.98E-15	2.23E-15	1.26E-14	1.52E-15	4986.66	△
	DE/rand/1/bin	0	0	0	0	0	631.27	—
f_7	DE/s1/1/bin	0	0	0	0	0	323.75	○
	DE/s2/1/bin	0	0	0	0	0	317.43	○
	DE/s3/1/bin	0	0	0	0	0	325.74	○
	DE/rand/1/bin	1.64E-03	4.44E-03	1.07E-03	7.50E-03	4.58E-03	4177.22	—
f_8	DE/s1/1/bin	7.96E-04	2.14E-03	5.94E-04	3.56E-03	2.17E-03	4205.41	△
	DE/s2/1/bin	9.25E-04	2.19E-03	5.20E-04	3.41E-03	2.12E-03	4215.97	△
	DE/s3/1/bin	8.12E-04	2.10E-03	4.94E-04	3.41E-03	2.08E-03	4134.28	△

Tables 4 and 5 present the results obtained on multimodal functions f_9–f_{15} for dimensionalities $d = 30$ and $d = 50$, respectively. According to the reported results, the presented strategies perform equally or better than DE/rand/1/bin on all, but DE/s1/1/bin on function f_9 for $d = 30$. A notable difference between DE/rand/1/bin and the considered strategies may be observed on functions f_9, f_{10} and f_{11} for $d = 30$ and $d = 50$. Observing the mean value of the iterations in which the best solution was found, suggests that the presented strategies require significantly less iterations in order to reach a final solution compared to DE/rand/1/bin. According to Figs. 3 and 4, the presented strategies exhibit an almost identical behavior, as was the case on unimodal functions (Figs. 1 and 2)

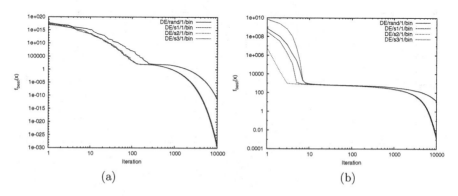

(a)   (b)

Fig. 2. Mean objective function value of the best solution throughout the iterations on (a) f_2 and (b) f_6 for $d = 50$

Table 3. Experimental results on functions f_1–f_8 for $d = 50$

Func.	Alg.	Best	Mean	Stddev	Worst	Median	Avg. t_{best}	Stat. sig.
f_1	DE/rand/1/bin	0	0	0	0	0	9987.10	—
	DE/s1/1/bin	0	0	0	0	0	9994.94	○
	DE/s2/1/bin	0	0	0	0	0	9995.15	○
	DE/s3/1/bin	0	0	0	0	0	9995.50	○
f_2	DE/rand/1/bin	0	0	0	0	0	9987.70	—
	DE/s1/1/bin	0	0	0	0	0	9994.45	○
	DE/s2/1/bin	0	0	0	0	0	9995.23	○
	DE/s3/1/bin	0	0	0	0	0	9994.83	○
f_3	DE/rand/1/bin	6.71E+01	1.23E+02	3.48E+01	2.28E+02	1.15E+02	9843.85	—
	DE/s1/1/bin	5.18E-03	1.50E-02	7.84E-03	5.46E-02	1.33E-02	9938.97	△
	DE/s2/1/bin	2.09E-03	8.13E-03	4.68E-03	3.20E-02	7.18E-03	9933.32	△
	DE/s3/1/bin	6.45E-03	2.04E-02	1.13E-02	9.32E-02	1.79E-02	9954.17	△
f_4	DE/rand/1/bin	4.49E-04	8.15E-04	2.25E-04	1.37E-03	8.02E-04	9960.32	—
	DE/s1/1/bin	3.58E-11	3.81E-08	3.53E-07	3.53E-06	1.11E-10	9981.66	△
	DE/s2/1/bin	1.43E-11	4.95E-11	3.01E-11	2.75E-10	4.34E-11	9984.31	△
	DE/s3/1/bin	4.30E-11	3.84E-02	3.84E-01	3.84E-01	1.85E-10	9847.34	○
f_5	DE/rand/1/bin	2.96E-03	9.56E-03	4.76E-03	2.59E-02	8.64E-03	9977.72	—
	DE/s1/1/bin	0	0	0	0	0	9990.97	△
	DE/s2/1/bin	0	0	0	0	0	9991.36	△
	DE/s3/1/bin	0	0	0	0	0	9990.64	△
f_6	DE/rand/1/bin	6.21	1.21E+01	2.88	1.88E+01	1.21E+01	9798.84	—
	DE/s1/1/bin	3.70E-04	1.74E-03	9.23E-04	6.50E-03	1.53E-03	9947.13	△
	DE/s2/1/bin	1.66E-04	1.01E-03	5.63E-04	3.20E-03	8.51E-04	9952.28	△
	DE/s3/1/bin	5.83E-04	2.29E-03	1.31E-03	7.38E-03	1.96E-03	9950.07	△
f_7	DE/rand/1/bin	0	0	0	0	0	1596.31	—
	DE/s1/1/bin	0	0	0	0	0	716.84	○
	DE/s2/1/bin	0	0	0	0	0	694.14	○
	DE/s3/1/bin	0	0	0	0	0	728.09	○
f_8	DE/rand/1/bin	3.68E-03	7.03E-03	1.54E-03	1.03E-02	7.05E-03	8791.18	—
	DE/s1/1/bin	1.83E-03	3.16E-03	6.61E-04	4.66E-03	3.11E-03	8560.24	△
	DE/s2/1/bin	1.33E-03	3.17E-03	6.29E-04	4.36E-03	3.17E-03	8484.47	△
	DE/s3/1/bin	1.82E-03	3.14E-03	6.08E-04	4.74E-03	3.08E-03	8653.83	△

the order of the vectors composing the difference vector seems insignificant. Based on all the aforementioned, the considered strategies perform a more efficient (in terms of iterations required to reach a final solution) and effective (in terms of solution quality) exploration of the search space.

Table 6 presents the results obtained on multimodal functions of small dimensionalities and few local minima f_{16}–f_{25}. Unlike the previous results, DE/rand/1/bin performed equally or slightly better compared to DE/s1, s2, s3/1/bin (except on f_{22}, where it performed slightly worse than DE/s2/1/bin). However, this might be due to the set control parameter values (F and CR), considering that the presented strategies performed better on significantly higher dimensional multimodal functions. Another, more likely, reason might be the population size, which is every small because of the low dimensionality of the

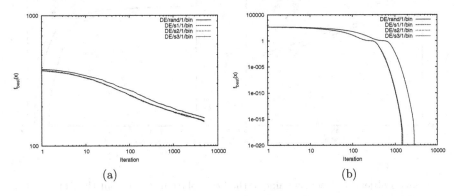

(a)   (b)

Fig. 3. Mean objective function value of the best solution throughout the iterations on (a) f_{10} and (b) f_{12} for $d = 30$

Table 4. Experimental results on functions f_9-f_{15} for $d = 30$

Func.	Alg.	Best	Mean	Stddev	Worst	Median	Avg. t_{best}	Stat. sig.
f_9	DE/rand/1/bin	-1.26E+04	-1.256949E+04	7.31E-12	-1.26E+04	-1.26E+04	4187.84	—
	DE/s1/1/bin	-1.26E+04	-1.256118E+04	3.48E+01	-1.23E+04	-1.26E+04	2004.89	▽
	DE/s2/1/bin	-1.26E+04	-1.256475E+04	2.33E+01	-1.25E+04	-1.26E+04	1721.47	○
	DE/s3/1/bin	-1.26E+04	-1.256831E+04	1.18E+01	-1.25E+04	-1.26E+04	2195.61	○
f_{10}	DE/rand/1/bin	126.55	163.60	8.98	181.89	163.63	3537.89	—
	DE/s1/1/bin	116.40	152.87	11.54	173.98	155.21	3641.37	△
	DE/s2/1/bin	116.62	154.14	11.07	175.16	155.74	3657.35	△
	DE/s3/1/bin	125.81	153.75	10.40	175.50	155.16	3456.33	△
f_{11}	DE/rand/1/bin	3.997E-15	4.494E-15	1.24E-15	7.550E-15	3.997E-15	4504.82	—
	DE/s1/1/bin	3.997E-15	3.997E-15	0	3.997E-15	3.997E-15	2554.25	△
	DE/s2/1/bin	3.997E-15	3.997E-15	0	3.997E-15	3.997E-15	2469.15	△
	DE/s3/1/bin	3.997E-15	3.997E-15	0	3.997E-15	3.997E-15	2560.16	△
f_{12}	DE/rand/1/bin	0	0	0	0	0	2731.34	—
	DE/s1/1/bin	0	0	0	0	0	1388.96	○
	DE/s2/1/bin	0	0	0	0	0	1371.70	○
	DE/s3/1/bin	0	0	0	0	0	1403.01	○
f_{13}	DE/rand/1/bin	0	0	0	0	0	4838.26	—
	DE/s1/1/bin	0	0	0	0	0	2464.38	○
	DE/s2/1/bin	0	0	0	0	0	2418.39	○
	DE/s3/1/bin	0	0	0	0	0	2477.06	○
f_{14}	DE/rand/1/bin	0	0	0	0	0	4804.84	—
	DE/s1/1/bin	0	0	0	0	0	2463.87	○
	DE/s2/1/bin	0	0	0	0	0	2416.86	○
	DE/s3/1/bin	0	0	0	0	0	2477.69	○
f_{15}	DE/rand/1/bin	2.64328	4.3589	0.8516	6.35228	4.32582	4505.68	—
	DE/s1/1/bin	1.52674	4.1618	1.0333	6.94825	4.12534	4541.26	○
	DE/s2/1/bin	1.95636	3.9728	0.8556	7.10094	4.03089	4526.19	△
	DE/s3/1/bin	2.62841	4.3034	0.8589	6.56185	4.23409	4521.33	○

functions ($NP = 10 \cdot d$). Thus, the already limited number of possible difference vectors is even more limited in the presented strategies. Also, the results
of DE/s1/1/bin, which performed slightly better than DE/s2, s3/1/bin on most
functions, suggest that the reduced number of possible difference vectors may
be the reason for lower performance. Considering the low dimensionality of the
functions, the low value of the mean of iterations in which the best solution was
found is not surprising. This is also suggested by Fig. 5. Nonetheless, it can be
noticed that this value was the lowest for DE/s2/1/bin in most cases. Figure 5
indicates that the behavior of all strategies is similar, but also that in some cases
the considered strategies may get stuck in local optima early on and from which
they may not escape.

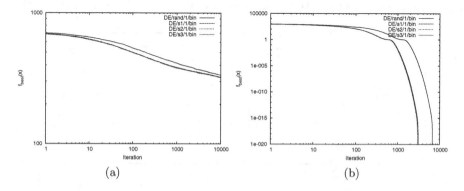

(a)   (b)

Fig. 4. Mean objective function value of the best solution throughout the iterations on
(a) f_{10} and (b) f_{12} for $d = 50$

Table 5. Experimental results on functions f_9–f_{15} for $d = 50$

Func.	Alg.	Best	Mean	Stddev	Worst	Median	Avg. t_{best}	Stat. sig.
f_9	DE/rand/1/bin	-2.094914E+04	-1.6506E+04	3.54E+03	-1.07E+04	-1.579521E+04	9788.70	—
	DE/s1/1/bin	-2.094914E+04	-2.0944E+04	2.33E+01	-2.08E+04	-2.094914E+04	6195.81	△
	DE/s2/1/bin	-2.094914E+04	-2.0936E+04	4.43E+01	-2.07E+04	-2.094914E+04	4822.56	△
	DE/s3/1/bin	-2.094914E+04	-2.0875E+04	6.59E+02	-1.44E+04	-2.094914E+04	6615.55	△
f_{10}	DE/rand/1/bin	3.01E+02	3.355E+02	1.38E+01	3.65E+02	3.3757E+02	7086.82	—
	DE/s1/1/bin	2.86E+02	3.216E+02	1.37E+01	3.47E+02	3.2380E+02	7093.09	△
	DE/s2/1/bin	2.70E+02	3.220E+02	1.46E+01	3.50E+02	3.2371E+02	7217.75	△
	DE/s3/1/bin	2.73E+02	3.203E+02	1.34E+01	3.46E+02	3.2142E+02	7325.78	△
f_{11}	DE/rand/1/bin	2.1760E-14	3.8387E-14	1.2170E-14	7.86038E-14	3.9524E-14	9979.18	—
	DE/s1/1/bin	3.9968E-15	5.9153E-15	1.7796E-15	7.54952E-15	7.54952E-15	6128.81	△
	DE/s2/1/bin	3.9968E-15	5.9508E-15	1.7764E-15	7.54952E-15	7.54952E-15	5556.65	△
	DE/s3/1/bin	3.9968E-15	5.8442E-15	1.7839E-15	7.54952E-15	7.54952E-15	5968.22	△
f_{12}	DE/rand/1/bin	0	0	0	0	0	6602.36	—
	DE/s1/1/bin	0	0	0	0	0	2975.28	○
	DE/s2/1/bin	0	0	0	0	0	2892.66	○
	DE/s3/1/bin	0	0	0	0	0	3019.28	○
f_{13}	DE/rand/1/bin	0	0	0	0	0	9987.47	—
	DE/s1/1/bin	0	0	0	0	0	5406.44	○
	DE/s2/1/bin	0	0	0	0	0	5260.40	○
	DE/s3/1/bin	0	0	0	0	0	5477.21	○
f_{14}	DE/rand/1/bin	0	0	0	0	0	9987.50	—
	DE/s1/1/bin	0	0	0	0	0	5374.45	○
	DE/s2/1/bin	0	0	0	0	0	5220.88	○
	DE/s3/1/bin	0	0	0	0	0	5442.34	○
f_{15}	DE/rand/1/bin	6.46793	1.06E+01	1.6814	1.4037E+01	10.74289	9022.93	—
	DE/s1/1/bin	6.55403	1.01E+01	1.8396	1.39E+01	9.90120	8657.10	○
	DE/s2/1/bin	4.65415	9.0893	1.5940	1.32E+01	8.96423	9038.57	△
	DE/s3/1/bin	6.23712	1.03E+01	1.5520	1.3972E+01	10.10096	8854.21	○

Table 6. Experimental results on functions f_{16}–f_{25}

Func.	Alg.	Best	Mean	Stddev	Worst	Median	Avg. t_{best}	Stat. sig.
f_{16}	DE/rand/1/bin	0.998	1.393	1.27	10.76	0.998	360.11	—
	DE/s1/1/bin	0.998	1.916	1.83	12.67	0.998	712.65	▽
	DE/s2/1/bin	0.998	1.699	1.64	10.76	0.998	311.49	○
	DE/s3/1/bin	0.998	2.611	2.60	15.51	1.992	1750.44	▽
f_{17}	DE/rand/1/bin	3.075E-04	4.57E-04	2.83E-04	1.30E-03	3.09E-04	2759.48	—
	DE/s1/1/bin	3.075E-04	7.08E-04	2.00E-03	2.04E-02	4.20E-04	3662.98	○
	DE/s2/1/bin	3.075E-04	2.43E-03	6.01E-03	2.04E-02	3.07E-04	1170.53	▽
	DE/s3/1/bin	3.075E-04	1.06E-03	2.79E-03	2.04E-02	6.20E-04	4685.45	○
f_{18}	DE/rand/1/bin	-1.031628	-1.031628	0	-1.031628	-1.031628	145.63	—
	DE/s1/1/bin	-1.031628	-1.031628	0	-1.031628	-1.031628	120.62	○
	DE/s2/1/bin	-1.031628	-1.031628	0	-1.031628	-1.031628	110.28	○
	DE/s3/1/bin	-1.031628	-1.031615	0.0001	-1.030575	-1.031628	466.94	○
f_{19}	DE/rand/1/bin	0.398	0.398	0	0.398	0.398	81.57	—
	DE/s1/1/bin	0.398	0.398	0	0.398	0.398	53.69	○
	DE/s2/1/bin	0.398	0.398	0	0.398	0.398	53.27	○
	DE/s3/1/bin	0.398	0.399	0.01	0.488	0.398	301.84	○
f_{20}	DE/rand/1/bin	3	3.00	0	3.00	3	153.60	—
	DE/s1/1/bin	3	3.00	0	3.00	3	122.44	○
	DE/s2/1/bin	3	3.00	0	3.00	3	118.93	○
	DE/s3/1/bin	3	4.14	5.39	31.44	3	158.52	○
f_{21}	DE/rand/1/bin	-3.86	-3.8628	0	-3.86	-3.86	142.84	—
	DE/s1/1/bin	-3.86	-3.8628	0	-3.86	-3.86	101.05	○
	DE/s2/1/bin	-3.86	-3.8628	0	-3.86	-3.86	100.51	○
	DE/s3/1/bin	-3.86	-3.8624	0.003	-3.84	-3.86	249.20	○
f_{22}	DE/rand/1/bin	-3.32	-3.2364	0.054	-3.203	-3.203	465.24	—
	DE/s1/1/bin	-3.32	-3.2447	0.057	-3.203	-3.203	564.12	○
	DE/s2/1/bin	-3.32	-3.2602	0.060	-3.203	-3.203	621.48	△
	DE/s3/1/bin	-3.32	-3.2349	0.053	-3.203	-3.203	640.19	○
f_{23}	DE/rand/1/bin	-10.1532	-9.8513	1.3484	-2.6829	-10.1532	290.45	—
	DE/s1/1/bin	-10.1532	-9.5710	1.6802	-2.6829	-10.1532	284.65	○
	DE/s2/1/bin	-10.1532	-8.7154	2.4862	-2.6305	-10.1532	231.54	▽
	DE/s3/1/bin	-10.1532	-9.1999	2.3285	-2.6305	-10.1532	192.63	▽
f_{24}	DE/rand/1/bin	-10.40294	-10.28	0.8493	-3.7243	-10.40294	490.40	—
	DE/s1/1/bin	-10.40294	-9.92	1.6441	-3.7243	-10.40294	413.39	○
	DE/s2/1/bin	-10.15320	-8.72	2.4862	-2.6305	-10.15320	231.54	▽
	DE/s3/1/bin	-10.40294	-9.70	2.0247	-2.7659	-10.40294	438.03	▽
f_{25}	DE/rand/1/bin	-10.53641	-10.2394	1.4646	-2.87114	-10.53641	325.97	—
	DE/s1/1/bin	-10.53641	-10.3342	1.1713	-2.42734	-10.53641	216.65	○
	DE/s2/1/bin	-10.53641	-10.1944	1.5104	-2.80663	-10.53641	202.06	○
	DE/s3/1/bin	-10.53641	-10.1346	1.5925	-2.87114	-10.53641	282.01	○

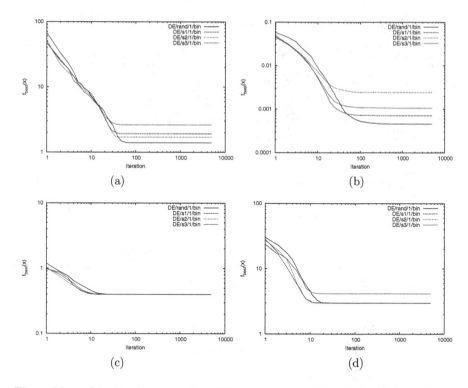

Fig. 5. Mean objective function value of the best solution throughout the iterations on (a) f_{16}, (b) f_{17}, (c) f_{19} and (d) f_{20}

Accounting the standard deviation and median of found solutions, and the difference between the worst and best as well, insight into algorithm stability may be gained. Accordingly, on most functions, each strategy proved to be stable. This implies they are able to find solutions close (in terms of the objective function) to the mean with a high probability, while also indicating that the vectors swapping did not affect algorithm stability.

4   Conclusion

The paper presented three simple strategies for DE in order to examine the effect of swapping vectors used for generating a mutant vector. Unlike the canonical DE, as base vector the best of the three randomly chosen population members is set. This way, a more effective exploitation of better solutions is achieved. The conducted experimental analysis showed that this resulted in higher performance on unimodal and multimodal functions of higher dimensionalities, while competitive performance was achieved on low dimensional multimodal functions. Additionally, it showed that the order (in terms of quality) of vectors composing the difference vector may affect performance but in a considerably lesser extent.

Based on all of the aforementioned, the described approach for selecting the base vector represents an effective and implementation-wise simple alternative to the canonical DE. In order to more completely assess the performance of the presented approaches, future work might include an extended experimental analysis on additional test functions and higher dimensional functions. Furthermore, the impact on performance of set control parameter values should be explored and also the impact of the population size, since the number of difference vectors directly depends on it.

Acknowledgments. This work was supported by research project grant No. 165-0362980-2002 from the Ministry of Science, Education and Sports of the Republic of Croatia. The authors would like to thank the anonymous reviewers for their useful comments that helped improve the paper.

References

1. Storn, R., Price, K.: Differential evolution - a simple and efficient heuristic for global optimization over continuous spaces. J. Glob. Optim. **11**, 342–359 (1997)
2. Price, K., Storn, R.M., Lampinen, J.A.: Differential Evolution: A Practical Approach to Global Optimization. Springer-Verlag New York Inc., Secaucus (2005)
3. Quaranta, G., Monti, G., Marano, G.C.: Parameters identification of Van der Pol-Duffing oscillators via particle swarm optimization and differential evolution. Mech. Syst. Signal Process. **24**, 2076–2095 (2010)
4. Martinović, G., Bajer, D.: Data clustering with differential evolution incorporating macromutations. In: Panigrahi, B.K., Suganthan, P.N., Das, S., Dash, S.S. (eds.) SEMCCO 2013, Part I. LNCS, vol. 8297, pp. 158–169. Springer, Heidelberg (2013)
5. Martinović, G., Bajer, D., Zorić, B.: A differential evolution approach to dimensionality reduction for classification needs. Int. J. Appl. Math. Comput. Sci. **24**, 111–122 (2014)
6. Salman, A.A., Ahmad, I., Omran, M.G.H., Mohammad, M.Gh.: Frequency assignment problem in satellite communications using differential evolution. Comput. Operat. Res. **37**, 2152–2163 (2010)
7. Das, S., Suganthan, P.N.: Differential evolution: a survey of the state-of-the-art. IEEE Trans. Evol. Comput. **15**, 4–31 (2011)
8. Das, S., Konar, A., Chakraborty, U.K.: Two improved differential evolution schemes for faster global search. In: 7th Annual Conference on Genetic and Evolutionary Computation, pp. 991–998. ACM, New York (2005)
9. Zhan, Z.-H., Zhang, J.: Enhance differential evolution with random walk. In: 14th International Conference on Genetic and Evolutionary Computation Conference Companion, pp. 1513–1514. ACM, New York (2012)
10. Liu, Y., Sun, F.: A fast differential evolution algorithm using k-nearest neighbour predictor. Expert Syst. Appl. **28**, 4254–4258 (2011)
11. Huang, Z., Chen, Y.: An improved differential evolution algorithm based on adaptive parameter. J. Control Sci. Eng. **2013**, 5 (2013)
12. Li, R., Xu, L., Shi, X.-W., Zhang, N., Lv, Z.-Q.: Improved differential evolution strategy for antenna array pattern synthesis problems. Prog. Electromagnet. Res. **113**, 429–441 (2011)

13. Kaelo, P., Ali, M.M.: A numerical study of some modified differential evolution algorithms. Eur. J. Op. Res. **169**, 1176–1184 (2006)
14. Neri, F., Tirronen, V.: Recent advances in differential evolution: a survey and experimental analysis. Artif. Intell. Rev. **33**, 61–106 (2010)
15. Blickle, T., Thiele, L.: A comparison of selection schemes used in evolutionary algorithms. Evol. Comput. **4**, 361–394 (1996)
16. Karaboga, D., Basturk, B.: A powerful and efficient algorithm for numerical function optimization: artificial bee colony (ABC) algorithm. J. Glob. Optim. **39**, 459–471 (2007)
17. Noman, N., Bollegala, D., Iba, H.: An adaptive differential evolution algorithm. In: 2011 IEEE Congress on Evolutionary Computation, pp. 2229–2236 (2011)
18. Bansal, J.C., Singh, P.K., Saraswat, M., Verma, A., Jadon, S.S., Abraham, A.: Inertia weight strategies in particle swarm optimization. In: Third World Congress on Nature and Biologically Inspired Computing, pp. 633–640. IEEE (2011)
19. Yao, S., Liu, Y., Lin, G.: Evolutionary programming made faster. IEEE Trans. Evol. Comput. **3**, 82–102 (1999)
20. Das, S., Abraham, A., Chakraborty, U.K., Konar, A.: Differential evolution using a neighborhood-based mutation operator. IEEE Trans. Evol. Comput. **13**, 526–553 (2009)
21. Ji, M., Klinowski, J.: Taboo evolutionary programming: a new method of global optimization. Proc. R. Soc. A **462**, 3613–3627 (2006)
22. Jamil, M., Yang, X.-S.: A literature survey of benchmark functions for global optimisation problems. Int. J. Math. Model. Numer. Optim. **4**, 150–194 (2013)

Development of Self-consistent Multi-objective Harmony Search Algorithm

Siddharth Jain[✉], Jaydev Kalivarapu, and Swarup Bag

Department of Mechanical Engineering,
Indian Institute of Technology Guwahati, Guwahati 781039, Assam, India
{j.siddharth,jaydev}@iitg.ac.in,
swarupbag@iitg.ernet.in

Abstract. This work presents the development of multi-objective harmony search (MOHS) algorithm for optimization problem using self-adaptive improved harmony search (SIHS) algorithm which is a variant of recently developed harmony search algorithm (HS) for single objective optimization. The approach used in this work is decomposing of multiple objectives into several single objective functions which are simultaneously optimized in such a way that a nearly uniform distribution of the solutions along the pareto-front is followed. The algorithm upon testing for standard test functions has shown promising results.

Keywords: Harmony Search · Multi-objective optimization · Pareto front

Abbreviations and Acronyms

BW	Band Width
DE	Differential Evolution
DV	Decision Variables
EA	Evolutionary Algorithm
GA	Genetic Algorithm
HMCR	Harmony Memory Consideration Rate
HSA	Harmony Search Algorithm
HS	Harmony search
PAR	Pitch Adjustment Rate
PF	Pareto Front
IHS	Improved Harmony Search
SIHS	Self-adaptive Improved harmony search algorithm
SPEA	Strength Pareto Evolutionary Algorithm
IHSA	Improved Harmony Search Algorithm
MOEA	Multi-Objective Evolutionary algorithm
MOGA	Multi-Objective Genetic Algorithm
MOHS	Multi-Objective Harmony Search
MOOP	Multi-Objective Optimization Problem
NOI	Number of Iterations
NPGA	Niche Pareto Genetic Algorithm
NSGA	Non-dominated Sorting Genetic Algorithm

© Springer International Publishing Switzerland 2015
B.K. Panigrahi et al. (Eds.): SEMCCO 2014, LNCS 8947, pp. 547–569, 2015.
DOI: 10.1007/978-3-319-20294-5_48

1 Introduction

Although most real world optimization problems can be formulated as single-objective but in instances of conflicting objective functions there arises the requirement of pareto-optimal front. A Multi-objective optimization problem (MOOP) consists of more than one objective function. Generally a MOOP has been solved as a single objective problem in the past and hence yielding only one result. A general multi objective problem can be summarized as below:

$$
\begin{aligned}
\text{min/max} \quad & f_m(x), m = 1, 2, \ldots M \\
\text{Subject to} \quad & g_j(x) \geq 0, j = 1, 2, \ldots J \\
& h_k(x) = 0, k = 1, 2, \ldots K \\
& x_i^l \leq x_i \leq x_i^u
\end{aligned}
\tag{1}
$$

It is possible that there are a host of conflicting objectives that are needed to be fulfilled at a particular point of time. The presence of these multiple objective problems gives rise to a set of optimal solutions that are known as Pareto-optimal solutions or a Pareto front (PF). No other point dominates (in terms of optimality) or is better than this pareto-optimal front. Generally a slight improvement of the Pareto optimal point in terms of one objective leads to deterioration of the other objective function. A Pareto front of two minimization functions f_1 and f_2 is shown in Fig. 1.

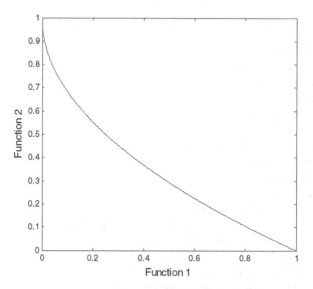

Fig. 1. Pareto Optimal Front

Evolutionary Algorithms (EAs) are nature-inspired stochastic search techniques that mimic natural evolution mechanisms. These algorithms have been a valuable tool in the field of multi-objective optimization, mostly because their population based approach and flexibility. Although several techniques have been developed for multi-objective optimization, the Non-dominated Sorting Genetic Algorithm (NSGA-II) has shown promising results. This algorithm uses pareto-dominance and crowding distance concepts to find near approximate solutions along the pareto-front.

This work implements self-adaptive improved harmony search (SIHS) algorithm for multi-objective optimization problem, a variant of recently developed Harmony Search (HS) algorithm. HS algorithm was originally developed by Geem et al. [1] in 2001. Afterwards a significant improvement has been done by several researchers. The working principles and further developments of HS algorithm are explained in the later sections.

2 Literature Review

One of the cornerstones in Multi-Objective evolutionary algorithms was the presentation of Multi Objective Genetic Algorithm (MOGA) by **Fonseca et al.** [2]. The authors used a rank-based fitness assignment method to optimize various problems. Genetic algorithm (GA) here is seen as the element of a multi-objective optimization loop which uses inputs from the decision maker (DM). It also uses the concept of sharing function to get better solutions. The ability of MOGA to solve various optimization problems is demonstrated here.

Horn et al. [3] proposed another non-elitist algorithm by the name of Niched Pareto genetic algorithm (NPGA) to find a diverse "Pareto optimal population". The algorithm is substantiated with its application on two artificial problems and one open problem in hydro systems.

Zitzler et al. [4] proposed strength pareto evolutionary algorithm (SPEA) which they further improved in another paper and called it SPEA-2 [5]. The authors also presented a comparative study of various multi-objective optimization techniques that have been developed and are fair enough to search for multiple solutions in a run.

One of the popular and classic benchmark algorithm in multi objective optimization was proposed by **Deb et al.** [6] which goes famously in the research circle by the name of NSGA-II. NSGA-II is a fast and elitist method which considerably improved the performance from NSGA and other MOEA that were present up until that moment. It was able to find a diverse Pareto optimal front in spite of a drastic reduction in the time complexity of the algorithm. Currently the authors have moved a step further and are trying to propose NSGA-III.

Zhang et al. [7] proposed a multi-objective evolutionary algorithm based on a method of decomposition (MOEA/D). This algorithm was particularly suited well for optimizing problems with 2 or more objectives in relatively less time. It first decomposes a multi-objective optimization problem into various scalar optimization sub-problems and then optimizes them simultaneously. This algorithm has lower computational complexity than multi-objective genetic local search (MOGLS) and NSGA-II [6, 7].

Ricart et al. [8] used harmony search algorithm as the base and proposed two variants of modified harmony search to test ZDT family of functions. The author concluded the competence of such an EA with respect to general HS algorithm.

Sivasubramani et al. [9] proposed a multi-objective harmony search algorithm (MOHSA) to find optimality in power flow (PF) problem. Fast elitist non-dominated sorting and crowding distances were been used to find the Pareto optimal front. It was observed that a clear and well distributed Pareto optimal solution can produce good results.

Pavelski et al. [10] investigated the efficiency of HS by adapting it along with the (NSGA-II) framework. The proposed methods were then tested against each other using a set of benchmark instances.

A multi-objective binary harmony search algorithm (MBHS) was proposed by **Wang et al.** [11]. With MBHS, they solved binary-coded multi-objective optimization problems. A modified pitch adjustment operator was used by them to improve the search capability of MBHS. They also used the concept of the non-dominated sorting based crowding distance and adopted the evaluated solution to update the harmony memory and hence maintain the diversity of algorithm. Promising result was found when the algorithm was compared with NSGA-II.

3   Background of Harmony Search Algorithm

The harmony search is a population based metaheuristic algorithm, based on the musician's process of finding a perfect state of harmony. Just in a way a musician intends to compose music with perfect harmony and reach a perfect state this algorithm endeavours to optimize the given objective function and reach the best solution available to the problem.

3.1   Analogies – Music Improvization and Optimization

For every music instrument the pitch generally determines the aesthetic quality of music, hence is analogous to the value of a decision variable which determines the fitness value. Also, in a composition process the variation in pitch changes the harmony; likewise the variation in the value of a single decision variable changes the objective function value in HS algorithm. Therefore, the pitch of the musical instrument could be considered analogous to the value of each decision variable.

Now consider an orchestra group. The final music that comes out of the orchestra is a combination of the contribution of all the fellow musicians. Similarly, the objective function value is an output of each decision variable. Therefore a musician is analogous to a decision variable. In a similar way there exists an analogy between the whole orchestra together playing different harmonies and the harmony memory.

3.2   Improvization Process

The following are the three major actions that skilled musicians undertake to improve his tune or harmony:

(a) The musician uses repetition and uses the pitch from his/her memory which is analogous to choosing any value from HS memory.
(b) The musician plays a slight variation of the pitch he/she remembers which is analogous choosing a slight variation of one value from the HS memory.
(c) The musician plays altogether a new tone which is analogous to choosing totally random value from the possible value range.

The following are the basic steps that are carried out as a part of the HS algorithm

Step 1: Defining the objective function and initializing the algorithm parameters namely, Harmony memory considering rate (HMCR), Pitch adjusting rate (PAR), Band width (BW) etc.
Step 2: Randomly initializing the harmony memory (HM).
Step 3: Improvising a new harmony from the HM with probability HMCR or generating a new harmony randomly with probability 1-HMCR.
Step 4: Updating the harmony memory (HM) based on survival of the fittest principle.
Step 5: Checking for the convergence criteria and going to step 3 if the convergence criteria is not met.

3.3   Algorithm Parameters

The harmony memory is of the form

$$X = \begin{bmatrix} x_{1,1} & \cdots & x_{1,DV} \\ \vdots & \ddots & \vdots \\ x_{HMS,1} & \cdots & x_{HMS,DV} \end{bmatrix} \tag{2}$$

where HMS represents the harmony memory size (the number of tuples in the matrix X) and DV represents the number of decision variables. The value of each decision variable is restricted by a lower bound (x_i^l) and an upper bound (x_i^u) i.e.

$$x_i^l \leq x_i \leq x_i^u \tag{3}$$

The harmony memory needs to be initialized for the first time. This initialization of the harmony memory is carried out randomly by an inbuilt function of the C language. This C function returns the value *rand* $\in [0, 1]$ and is uniformly distributed. Each decision variable is initialized by the following equation.

$$x_i = x_i^l + rand \times \left(x_i^l - x_i^u \right) \tag{4}$$

The following subsection gives a brief outline of the various parameters used in Harmony search algorithm:

3.3.1   Bandwidth

Bandwidth is the maximum amount of change permitted in pitch adjustment of a design
variable. This is one of the deciding factor of the time complexity and thus the performance of the algorithm. Larger BW value is required for the algorithm to search in a
large space, while a smaller BW value is suitable for fine-tuning of the best solution
vectors. If the BW value is maintained consistently high throughout the algorithm, close
convergence to the best harmony would never be achieved. Conversely, if the BW value
is maintained consistently low, exploration of the search space would take large number
of iterations and hence higher running time. The original proposed harmony search
algorithm uses a constant bandwidth value. But by dynamically varying the bandwidth
the results would improve significantly. So, in this algorithm (SIHS) we dynamically
vary the BW value by maintaining a higher value at initial stages, and then gradually
decrease the BW to a very low value to ensure the convergence to the solution. The
variation of bandwidth with iteration'i' follows the equation:

$$BW[i] = \frac{BW[max]}{1 + k\left(\frac{i}{NI}\right)^3} , i < pivot \tag{5}$$
$$= BW[min], i \geq pivot$$

where, $k = 50 \times \log\left(\frac{BW[max]}{100 \times BW[min]}\right)$

The dependence of dynamic bandwidth function on generation in SIHS algorithm is
shown in Fig. 2.

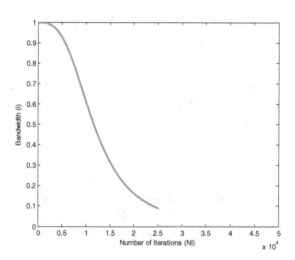

Fig. 2.   Variation of Bandwidth with number of iterations

3.3.2   Harmony Memory Consideration Rate (HMCR)

This informally can be quoted to be the acceptance rate. This ensures that the best
harmonies will be carried over to the new harmony memory. It is typically assigned a
value $\in [0, 1]$. If this rate is too low, only a few best harmonies are selected and the

function may converge too slowly. If this rate is extremely high (near 1), almost all the harmonies are repeated in the harmony memory, that is the other harmonies are not explored well [13]. This leads to potentially wrong solutions. Therefore, typically, we use $HMCR \in [0.7, 0.95]$. $HMCR$ in an opposite way also defines the amount of randomization. The probability of randomization is (1- $HMCR$).This randomization is needed to increase the diversity of the solutions. The use of randomization can drive the system further to explore various diverse solutions so as to find the global optimal point.

3.3.3 Pitch Adjustment Rate (PAR)

This gives the probability of moving from the existing to a new harmony. A very high pitch-adjusting rate (> 0.9) may cause the solution to scatter around potential optima in a random search. Thus, we usually use $PAR \in [0.4, 0.75]$ in most applications. Actual probability of pitch adjustment is a combination of both $HMCR$ and PAR and is $HMCR \times PAR$. The pitch adjustment operation essentially produces a new solution around the existing quality solution by varying the pitch slightly by a small random amount. The following equation gives the linear relation governing the operation of pitch adjustment.

$$x_{i,new} = x_{i,old} + BW \times rand \qquad (6)$$

$x_{i,new}$ is the new harmony which is now stored in the harmony memory. Here $rand$ is a random number in the range of $[-1, 1]$. This is essentially corresponds to a local search operation.

4   Development of Multi-objective Harmony Search (MOHS) Algorithm

The aim of MOHS is to find a set of solutions of two or more objectives that should have the following characteristics:

a. The set of points should be close or on the Pareto optimal front and form a set of non-dominated solutions.
b. The point should form as diverse Pareto front as possible.

A modification of the robust SISH algorithm is used to find the Pareto optimal front. The success of SIHS for single objective functions is detailed in the result and discussions section. The algorithm makes it fit for the points to reach as close as possible to the Pareto optimal front. Some constraints related to the Euclidian distance of the set have been incorporated to maintain a diverse population.

4.1   Steps in MOHS

The following are some of the steps that are carried out as a part of the MOHS algorithm

Step 1: Defining the objective functions and initialize the algorithm parameters namely, Harmony memory considering rate (HMCR), pitch adjusting rate (PAR), band width (BW), number of objective functions (N) and populations size (NPOP) etc.

Step 2: Based on the population size (NPOP) and the number of objective functions (N) assign a uniformly distributed weight matrix along N dimensions.

Step 3: For each NPOP assign the weighted objective function and formulate it into a single objective optimization problem.

Step 4: Randomly initializing the harmony memory (HM) for each member of the population (NPOP).

Step 5: Improvise the harmony and update based on the survival of the fittest principle.

Step 6: Checking for the convergence criteria and repeat if the convergence criteria is not met.

4.2   Pseudo Code of MOHS

The pseudo code in Fig. 3 illustrated governing algorithm which forms the backbone of MOHS.

The weight matrix is decided in such a way that the near uniform distribution of solutions is maintained throughout.

1	Begin
2	Define objective functions f_n (x), x=(x$_1$,x$_2$, ...,x$_{dk}$)^T
3	Define constraints
4	Define *PAR, HMCR, BW,N,NPOP*;
5	Construct Weight Matrix
6	Formulate NPOP single objective functions
7	Initialize Harmony Memory for NPOP
8	while (j < *NPOP*)
9	while (i < *N*)
10	if (*rand* < *HMCR*)
11	Choose a random Harmony from the memory
12	if (*rand* < *PAR*)
13	Use pitch adjustment formula to change memory
14	else if (*rand* > *PAR*)
15	Use memory randomly
16	end if
17	else if (*rand* > *HMCR*)
18	Generate new harmony randomly
19	end if
20	Update harmony memory
21	i = i+1
22	end while
23	j = j+1
24	end while
25	end

Fig. 3. Pseudo code for multi-objective optimization algorithm

4.3   Flowchart

(See Fig. 4)

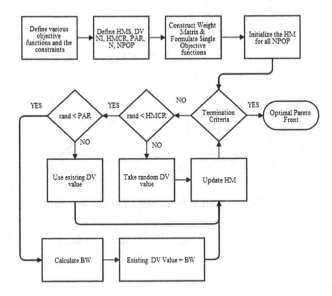

Fig. 4. Flow chart for MOHS

4.4   Objective Function Formulation

The weights are needed to be assigned at equal intervals to maintain the diversity of the population. Following equation gives the weight assignment criteria with number of objective function as N:

$$\sum_{i=1}^{n} w_i = 1 \tag{7}$$

Here all the w_i are required to be distributed uniformly about the ideal point. Figure 6 illustrates the weight distribution for 20 solutions and two objective functions (Fig. 5).

Figure 7 illustrates the weight distribution for 28 solutions and two objective functions.

A simple procedure is followed to bring the set of population points close to the lines passing through the weighted points. Consider first an ideal point z*, the coordinates of which are the minimum of all the individual objective functions. Under Ideal condition we would want our optimal point to be z*, but due to the constraints of the problem this might not always be possible. Hence we try to tend all our points in the direction of z*.

$$z^* = \min(f_1, f_2, \ldots \ldots f_n) \tag{8}$$

Figure 8 shows the point z* which clearly violates the boundary of the Pareto front and hence is unreachable. Now with dual objective of minimizing the distance from the line (d2) and minimizing the distance from z* (d1) we formulate an objective function.

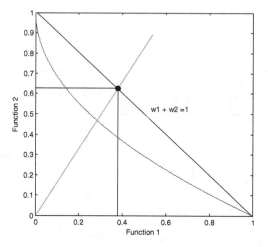

Fig. 5. Weight Assignment for N = 2

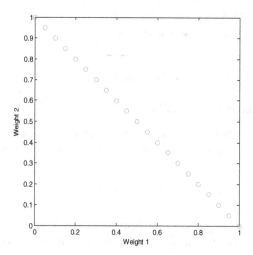

Fig. 6. Weights for N = 2 & NPOP = 21

The objective function can be formulated as given below where the first part is representative of the distance d1 and the second part is representative of a constraint to minimize distance d2.

$$\text{minf} = \sum_{i=1}^{n} (f_i - z^*)^2 + \sum_{i=1}^{n} c_i(f_{i+1}w_i - f_iw_{i+1}) \tag{9}$$

where c_i is a penalty variable generally taken between 10 to 1000 so as to force the solution to be along the corresponding line.

For two conflicting normalized objective functions having their minima both at 0, the following equation and Fig. 9 summarizes the scenario:

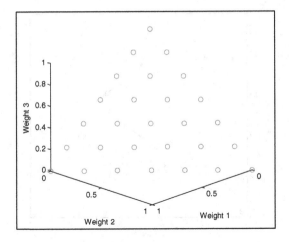

Fig. 7. Weights for N = 3 & NPOP = 28

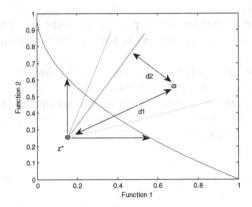

Fig. 8. Ideal Point z*, distances d1 and d2

$$\min f = f_1^2 + f_2^2 + c_1(f_2 w_1 - f_1 w_2) \tag{10}$$

In the MOHS algorithm each of the members of the NPOP is represented by and backed by a harmony memory which converges to the same line. So for the actual case the number of members generally present in the population is NPOP × HMS. For the sake of convenience we represent the population size as NPOP and do not multiply it with NPOP. A sample is shown below which tries to work with MOHS to find the Pareto front with a NPOP = 3. 30 and N = 2. Initially the population is assigned randomly to each line.

After some iterations have gone through improvisation takes place. The points begin to form a cluster along their respective lines and also begin to move near the Pareto optimal front.

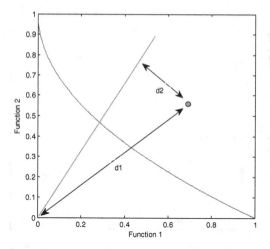

Fig. 9. Distance minimization for N = 2 and normalized functions

As the MOHS progresses further the points gain momentum and form even close clusters. The cluster so formed is now very near to the Pareto optimal front and is about to converge.

After MOHS has finished running the points finally converge and form a set of non-dominated solutions on the Pareto optimal front.

Similar methods have been replicated for N = 3 and have been tested on various objective functions. The results so found are summarized in the results and discussion section (Figs. 10, 11, 12 and 13).

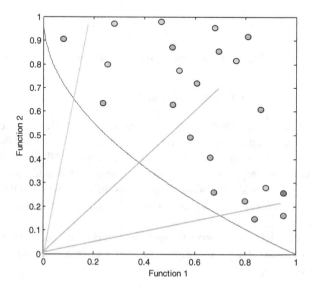

Fig. 10. Initial random population

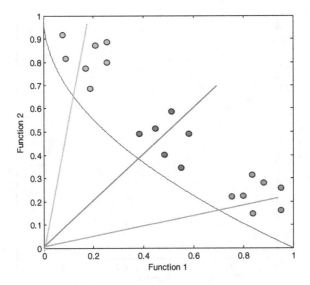

Fig. 11. Improvisation

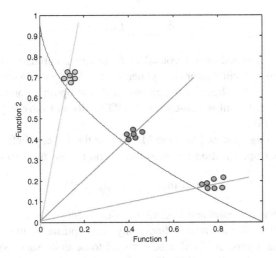

Fig. 12. Further improvement and close clustering

4.5   Proof of Concept of MOHS

MOHS method is an inspiration from the paper on a multi-objective evolutionary algorithm based on decomposition (MOEA/D) [7]. Similar to MOEA/D, MOHS decomposes the multi-objective problem into a number of single objective optimization functions and solves them simultaneously.

The weight sum approach for any algorithm requires the optimization of the following function:

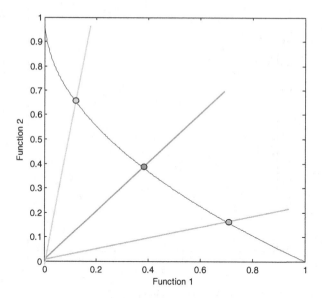

Fig. 13. Final Output

$$\min \sum_{i=1}^{n} f_i w_i \tag{11}$$

This approach as stated above considers a convex combination of the different objectives. Different weight vectors are generally used to get different set of optimal points. However, with the above approach not all Pareto optimal points can be reached especially if the Pareto front is non-concave. MOHS doesn't have any such disability related to concave PF's.

Another interesting approach to solve MOOP's is the Tchebycheff approach. In this approach, the scalar optimization problem formulation is given as follows:

$$\min f = \max_{1 \leq i \leq N} w_i (f_i - z^*) \tag{12}$$

where z^* is the reference point and is similar to that in MOHS and w_i is the weight for each optimal solution. We are able to find many such optimal solution by varying the weight vector. This approach has also been found to be quite successful in literature.

Applying various methods for MOHS we found the method applied in the objective function formulation in the section above to be the most suitable method to solve Multi-Objective optimization problems.

5   Multi-objective Optimization

5.1   Test Functions

Following are shown various test functions that have been used to test the robustness for multi-objective harmony search algorithm

5.1.1   ZDT 1

$$\min f_1(x) = x_1$$

$$\min f_2(x) = g(x)\left(1 - \sqrt{\frac{f_1(x)}{g(x)}}\right) \tag{13}$$

where $g(x) = 1 + \frac{9(\sum_{i=2}^{n} x_i)}{n-1}$ *and* $* \gtrless \leq \xi_\iota \leq \varnothing$

The Pareto front of ZDT 1 as observed is convex and satisfies the equation $f_2 = 1 - \sqrt{f_1}$. The test function is solved for n = 30.

5.1.2   ZDT 2

$$\min f_1(x) = x_1$$

$$\min f_2(x) = g(x)\left(1 - \left(\frac{f_1(x)}{g(x)}\right)^2\right) \tag{14}$$

where $g(x) = 1 + \frac{9(\sum_{i=2}^{n} x_i)}{n-1}$ *and* $0 \leq x_i \leq 1$

The Pareto front of ZDT 2 as observed is concave and satisfies the equation $f_2 = 1 - f_1^2$. The test function is solved for n = 30.

5.1.3   ZDT 3

$$\min f_1(x) = x_1$$

$$\min f_2(x) = g(x)\left(1 - \sqrt{\frac{f_1(x)}{g(x)}} - \frac{f_1(x)}{g(x)}\sin(10\pi x_1)\right) \tag{15}$$

where $g(x) = 1 + \frac{9(\sum_{i=2}^{n} x_i)}{n-1}$ *and* $0 \leq x_i \leq 1$

The Pareto front of ZDT 3 as observed is disconnected and of varying shapes and satisfies the equation $f_2 = 1 - \sqrt{f_1} - f_1 \sin(10\pi f_1)$ in for a limited domain of f_1. The test function is solved for n = 30.

5.1.4   ZDT 4

$$\min f_1(x) = x_1$$

$$\min f_2(x) = g(x)\left(1 - \sqrt{\frac{f_1(x)}{g(x)}}\right) \tag{16}$$

where $g(x) = 1 + 10(n-1) + \sum_{i=2}^{n}(x_i^2 - 10\cos(4\pi x_1))$ &$0 \leq x_1 \leq 1, -5 \leq x_i \leq 5$

The given test functions has many local Pareto fronts in the feasible range. The test function is solved for n = 10.

5.1.5   DTLZ 1

$$\min f_1(x) = (1 + g(x))x_1x_2$$
$$\min f_2(x) = (1 + g(x))x_1(1 - x_2) \qquad (17)$$
$$\min f_3(x) = (1 + g(x))(1 - x_1)$$

where $g(x) = 100(n-2) + 100\sum_{i=3}^{n}\left((x_i - 0.5)^2 - \cos(20\pi(x_i - 0.5))\right)$ &$0 \leq x_i \leq 1$

Its PF is non convex and the function value solution of the objective function satisfies $\sum_{i=1}^{3}f_i = 1$ with $f_i \geq 0$. The test function is solved for n = 10.

5.1.6   DTLZ 2

$$\min f_1(x) = (1 + g(x))\cos\left(\frac{\pi x_1}{2}\right)\cos\left(\frac{\pi x_2}{2}\right)$$
$$\min f_2(x) = (1 + g(x))\cos\left(\frac{\pi x_1}{2}\right)\sin\left(\frac{\pi x_2}{2}\right) \qquad (18)$$
$$\min f_3(x) = (1 + g(x))\sin\left(\frac{\pi x_1}{2}\right)$$

where $g(x) = \sum_{i=3}^{n}x_i^2$ &$0 \leq x_1, x_2 \leq 1$ & $-1 \leq x_i \leq 1$

Its PF is non convex and the function value solution of the objective function satisfies $\sum_{i=1}^{3}f_i^2 = 1$ with $f_i \geq 0$. The test function is solved for n = 10.

5.2   Results Tabulation and Discussion

All the parameters that have been used are the same as that used in the SIHS-II implementation of the harmony search except BW[max] = 0.5. The other parameter values are HMCR = 0.9, PAR = 0.9, HMS = 10, BW[min] = 0.0002 etc. The value of the penalty parameter ranges from 10 to 1000 depending upon the test function but 100 works well for all the test functions. The number of iterations NI have been kept fixed at a value 5000.

5.2.1   ZDT 1

Figures 14, 15 and 16 demonstrate the results on optimizing the test function ZDT 1. The solutions thereby obtained are very close to the pareto optimal front and are also uniformly distributed.

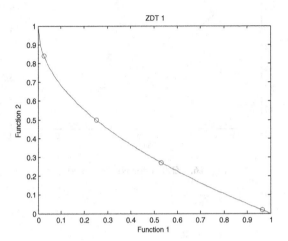

Fig. 14. ZDT 1 for NPOP = 4

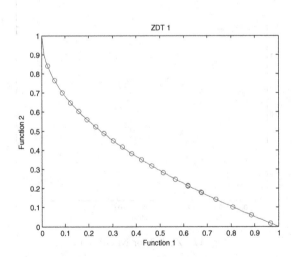

Fig. 15. ZDT 1 for NPOP = 20

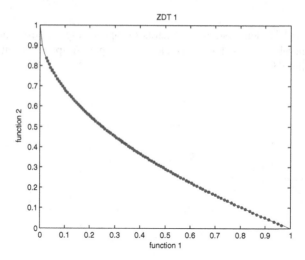

Fig. 16. ZDT 1 for NPOP = 100

5.2.2   ZDT 2
(See Fig. 17)

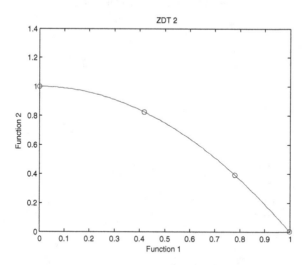

Fig. 17. ZDT 2 for NPOP = 4

5.2.3   ZDT 3
As stated before the Pareto front of ZDT 3 is discontinuous in nature. Since the algorithm does not adopt the concept of non-dominance implicitly, therefore we have to remove the non-dominated solutions explicitly from this Pareto front (Figs. 18, 19, 20 and 21).

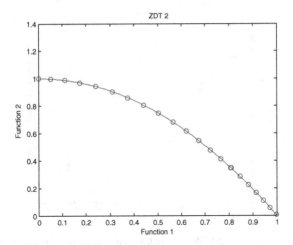

Fig. 18. ZDT 2 for NPOP = 20

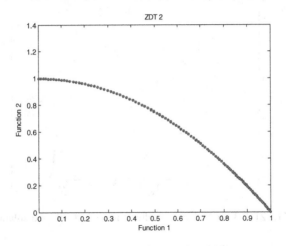

Fig. 19. ZDT 2 for NPOP = 100

5.2.4   ZDT 4

The initial front created before the removal of non-dominated solutions is shown in the Fig. 22. Figure 23 shows the front after removal of non-dominated solutions.

DTLZ 1 and DTLZ 2 are optimization problems with 3 objective functions. Upon optimization of these test functions the following graphs demonstrate the results. It can be witnessed that the solutions have been uniformly distributed along the Pareto front (Figs. 26 and 27).

5.2.5   DTLZ 1

(See Fig. 24)

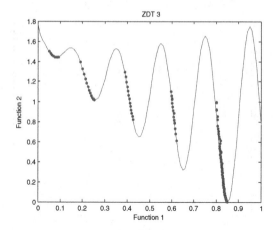

Fig. 20. ZDT 3 for NPOP = 10 before removal of dominated solutions

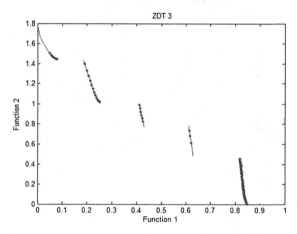

Fig. 21. ZDT 3 for NPOP = 10 after removing dominated solutions

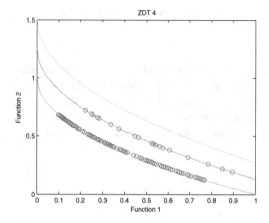

Fig. 22. ZDT 4 for NPOP = 100 before removal of dominated solutions

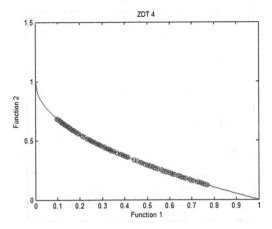

Fig. 23. ZDT 4 for NPOP = 100 after removing dominated solutions

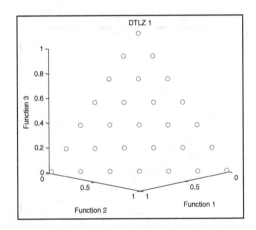

Fig. 24. DTLZ 1 for NPOP = 28

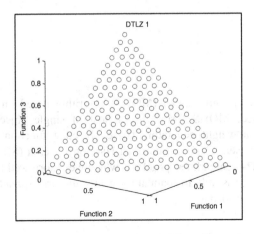

Fig. 25. DTLZ 1 for NPOP = 190

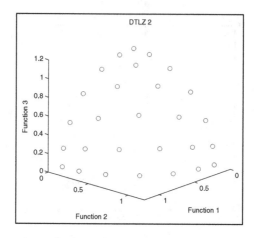

Fig. 26. DTLZ 2 for NPOP = 28

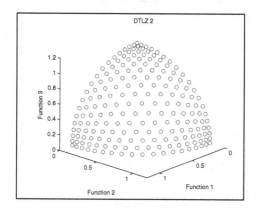

Fig. 27. DTLZ 2 for NPOP = 190

5.2.6 DTLZ 2
(See Fig. 25)

6 Conclusion

A Multi Objective Harmony Search (MOHS) algorithm based on a decomposition approach is proposed. MOHS formulates a host of single objective optimization problems by using a weight generator. These objective functions are then solved simultaneously using Self-adaptive Improved Harmony Search (SIHS) algorithm. On six different difficult benchmark test problems which were borrowed from the literature, the proposed MOHS was able to maintain a nearly uniform spread of solutions and converged on the Pareto front.

References

1. Geem, Z.W., Kim, J.H.: A new heuristic optimization algorithm: harmony search. Simulation **76**(2), 60–68 (2001)
2. Fonseca, C.M., Fleming, P.J.: Genetic algorithms for multiobjective optimization: formulation, discssions and generalization. In: Forrest, S. (ed.) Proceedings of the Fifth International Conference. Morgan Kaufmann, San Mateo (1993)
3. Horn, J., Nafpliotis, N., Goldberg, D.E.: A niched pareto genetic algorithm for multiobjective optimization. In: Proceedings of the First IEEE Conference on Evolutionary Computation, vol. 1, pp. 82–87 (1994)
4. Zitzler, E., Thiele, L.: Multiobjective evolutionary algorithms : a comparative case study and the strength pareto approach. IEEE Trans. Evol. Comput. **3**(4), 257–271 (1999)
5. Zitzler, E., Laumanns, M., Thiele, L.: SPEA2: improving the strength pareto evolutionary algorithm. TIK-Report **103**, 1–21 (2001)
6. Deb, K., Member, A., Pratap, A., Agarwal, S., Meyarivan, T.: A fast and elitist multiobjective genetic algorithm. IEEE Trans. Evol. Comput. **6**(2), 182–197 (2002)
7. Zhang, Q., Member, S., Li, H.: MOEA/D: a multiobjective evolutionary algorithm based on decomposition. IEEE Trans. Evol. Comput. **11**(6), 712–731 (2007)
8. Ricart, J., Hüttemann, G., Lima, J., Barán, B.: Multiobjective harmony search algorithm proposals. Electron. Notes Theor. Comput. Sci. **281**, 51–67 (2011)
9. Sivasubramani, S., Swarup, K.S.: Multi-objective harmony search algorithm for optimal power flow problem. Int. J. Electr. Power Energy Syst. **33**(3), 745–752 (2011)
10. Pavelski, L.M., Almeida, C.P., Goncalves, R.A.: Harmony Search for Multi-objective Optimization. In: 2012 Brazilian Symposium on Neural Networks, pp. 220–225 (2012)
11. Wang, Ling, Mao, Yunfei, Niu, Qun, Fei, Minrui: A multi-objective binary harmony search algorithm. In: Tan, Ying, Shi, Yuhui, Chai, Yi, Wang, Guoyin (eds.) ICSI 2011, Part II. LNCS, vol. 6729, pp. 74–81. Springer, Heidelberg (2011)
12. Yang, X.: Harmony search as a metaheuristic algorithm. In: Proceedings of Studies in Computational Intelligence, vol. 191, pp. 1–18 (2009)

Predicting Trends in the Twitter Social Network: A Machine Learning Approach

Anubrata Das[1]([✉]), Moumita Roy[2], Soumi Dutta[2], Saptarshi Ghosh[1], and Asit Kumar Das[1]

[1] Indian Institute of Engineering Science and Technology Shibpur,
Howrah 711103, India
anubrata.besuest@gmail.com
[2] Institute of Engineering and Management, Kolkata 700091, India

Abstract. The Twitter microblogging site is one of the most popular websites in the Web today, where millions of users post real-time messages (tweets) on different topics of their interest. The content that becomes popular in Twitter (i.e., discussed by a large number of users) on a certain day can be used for a variety of purposes, including recommendation of popular content and marketing and advertisement campaigns. In this scenario, it would be of great interest to be able to *predict what content will become popular topics of discussion in Twitter in the recent future*. This problem is very challenging due to the inherent dynamicity in the Twitter system, where topics can become hugely popular within short intervals of time. The Twitter site periodically declares a set of *trending topics*, which are the keywords (e.g., hashtags) that are at the center of discussion in the Twitter network at a given point of time. However, the exact algorithm that Twitter uses to identify the trending topics at a certain time is not known publicly. In this paper, we aim to predict the keywords (hashtags) that are likely to become trending in Twitter in the recent future. We model this prediction task as a machine learning classification problem, and analyze millions of tweets from the Twitter stream to identify features for distinguishing between trending hashtags and non-trending ones. We train classifiers on features measured over one day, and use the classifiers to distinguish between trending and non-trending hashtags on the next day. The classifiers achieve very high precision and reasonably high recall in identifying the hashtags that are likely to become trending.

Keywords: Online social network · Twitter · Trending topics · Predicting trends · Machine learning · Classification

1 Introduction

The Twitter microblogging site (https://twitter.com) is one of the most popular online social networking sites in the Web today. It is used by more than 218 million active users, who post more than 500 million tweets (short text-based

B.K. Panigrahi et al. (Eds.): SEMCCO 2014, LNCS 8947, pp. 570–581, 2015.
DOI: 10.1007/978-3-319-20294-5_49

posts of up to 140 characters) on average per day. One of the most interesting features of Twitter is its real-time nature – at any given instance of time, millions of Twitter users are exchanging views on various topics or incidents/events that are happening currently in any corner of the world. Hence the content posted in Twitter is very useful to gather real-time news on a variety of topics.

Topics that are discussed widely in Twitter during a given period of time (e.g., on a certain day) are of great interest to users. Often, these topics are related to some major events in the off-line world, such as natural calamities, global sports events, death of celebrities, and so on. Again, some of the globally popular topics of conversation in Twitter are related to Twitter-specific memes which are popular within the Twitter system only [7].

Since users in a social network are naturally interested to know what are the currently popular topics of discussion in that network, Twitter attempts to help users discover what is popular currently. For this, Twitter periodically declares a set of *Trending Topics* [11] – keywords/phrases that are being most discussed by users in Twitter at a certain point of time. For instance, during the World Cup 2014 Football tournament, the keyword (hashtag) *#GERvsBRA* was a trending topic on the day of the Germany vs. Brazil semi-final match. The trending topics are decided by Twitter using their own algorithm, which is not made publicly available (in order to prevent possible misuse by spammers [8]). However, it is understood that, to decide whether a topic is trending, Twitter takes into account not only the global popularity of the topic, but also factors like the 'freshness' of the topic (i.e., whether the topic has become the centre of discussion very recently).[1]

In this scenario, there is a lot of incentive to be able to predict in advance what topics are likely to be trending in the recent future, in a social system such as Twitter. The ability to make this prediction accurately will have important impact on several aspects of how social systems are used nowadays. For example, if advertisers know which topics are about to trend, they can prepare targeted advertisements related to those topics. Again, during a mass emergency such as a political unrest, if it can be predicted early that a rumor/false information is about to become trending (discussed by many people), steps can be taken by the corresponding authority to prevent its spread.

However, the problem of predicting popularity of information in online social media like Twitter is extremely challenging because of the supremely dynamic and unstructured nature of the data posted in such media. For instance, a new keyword can become trending in Twitter in a very short interval of time. Because of these challenges, the problem of predicting what topic will become trending (popular) in the near future has received a lot of attention from the research community on social media analysis.

---

[1] Twitter specifically says [11]: "Twitter Trends are automatically generated by an algorithm that attempts to identify topics that are being talked about more right now than they were previously. The Trends list is designed to help people discover the 'most breaking' breaking news from across the world, in real-time."

We, in this paper, attempt to address a Twitter-specific version of the problem of predicting what information is likely to become popular in the recent future. Specifically, we attempt to predict which keywords (hashtags) are likely to become 'trending' in Twitter (i.e., to be included in the set of Trending Topics declared by Twitter) on a certain day. We take a machine learning based approach – we model the trend prediction problem as a classification problem (details in Sect. 4). We study large amounts of live data collected from Twitter, to identify a set of novel features for distinguishing between trending and non-trending hashtags, and use these features to develop classifiers. We train the classifiers on trending and non-trending hashtags posted in Twitter on a certain day, and use the classifiers to classify hashtags as trending/non-trending on the next day. Our experiments show that classifiers trained on our extracted features achieve very high precision and reasonably high recall in distinguishing between trending and non-trending hashtags.

The rest of the paper is organized as follows. Section 2 gives some background information on the Twitter social media site, and discusses relevant prior work. Section 3 describes the dataset used in our study. As stated earlier, we model the Twitter trend prediction task as a classification problem – this is described in Sect. 4. Section 5 discusses the features used to develop the classifiers, and Sect. 6 states the performance of the classifiers in distinguishing between trending and non-trending hashtags. The study is concluded in Sect. 7.

2   Background and Related Work

In this section, we provide a brief background of the Twitter social network, which would help to contextualize the discussions in later sections. We also discusses some prior work on predicting the future in social media.

2.1   A Brief Background on Twitter

Twitter (https://twitter.com) allows users to communicate with each other through the real-time exchange of short messages (called 'tweets'), and to form a social network by following (subscribing to) other users. If a user u finds another user v interesting, then u can subscribe to v (in Twitter terminology, u can 'follow' v), and all tweets posted by v will be made available to u in real-time. Every user in Twitter has a user-account that has a profile page showing basic information about the user (such as the name, location of the user). We now briefly describe some terms related to Twitter, which will help readers in understanding the subsequent discussions.

Tweet: A tweet (also known as a *microblog*) is a message or status update posted by a user. Tweets are restricted to at most 140 characters, and they can contain specific keywords (called, hashtags), URLs, and so on.

Hashtags: Certain terms in a tweet can be highlighted, by using the term as a hashtag. To indicate that a term is a hashtag, it needs to be preceded with

Fig. 1. A screen-shot from Twitter, showing example tweets containing hashtags (underlined in red) (Color figure online).

Fig. 2. A screen-shot from Twitter, showing the list of Trending Topics at a certain point of time.

a # symbol. Hashtags are ideally used to indicate topics that are important at the present moment. For instance, during the Football World Cup 2014, some of the popular hashtags were #WorldCup, #Brazil2014, and so on. Figure 1 shows some examples of tweets containing hashtags.

Trending topics or 'trends': If a particular keyword (e.g., a hashtag) is being discussed in many tweets posted during a certain interval of time, that keyword can appear in the list of *Trending Topics*, which are the most talked about topics on Twitter at that point in time [11]. Twitter declares a set of trending topics periodically, (e.g., every day) – this allows users an easy way to follow tweets on these popular topics. Figure 2 shows an example of the set of trending topics declared by Twitter at a certain point of time.

Note that in this study, we consider the trending topics declared by Twitter at a granulariy of days, as detailed in later sections. Also, though Twitter declares separate trending topics for separate geographical locations (e.g., country-specific trends), we only consider the world-wide trends declared by Twitter (which comprise of the globally popular trends) as shown in Fig. 2.

2.2 Related Work

The objective of this work is to predict which keywords (e.g., hashtags) are likely to become popular or trending in Twitter in the recent future (with respect to the time when we attempt the prediction). We briefly discuss some related work on predicting the future in social media and on hashtags in Twitter.

Predicting the Future in Social Media: This problem of predicting what information is likely to become popular in the recent future has received some attention from the social media research community. For instance, Bothos *et al.* [2] attempted to predict future events using agent-based prediction markets, where the agents rely upon user-sentiments and assessments extracted from social media to make transactions. Asur *et al.* [1] attempted to use data from Twitter to forecast box-office revenues for movies, i.e., to predict which movies will become popular in the recent future. Szabo *et al.* [10] formulated a scheme to predict the popularity of content in the Digg (digg.com) and Youtube (www.youtube.com) social websites. Several studies have attempted to predict which research papers are likely to achieve large number of citations in future [3]. Again, some other studies [4,5] have attempted to predict information cascades in online social media such as Twitter and Facebook, i.e., how a particular piece of information (such as a URL or a photo) is likely to be exchanged or shared among the users. The models developed in these studies can be utilized to predict which information are likely to have large information cascades, and hence become popular in the social network.

Hashtags in Twitter: Though several researchers have studied the nature of hashtags in Twitter [12] and developed methods for classifying trending topics [7] and preventing trending topic spam [8], not much research has been done on predicting which topics (hashtags) are likely to become trending. To the best of our knowledge, there has been only one attempt to predict trending topics in Twitter. Stanislav *et al.* [9] developed a method for predicting trends using classification of time series data – the algorithm takes some recent activities of a particular topic, and then compares its pattern with those of trending topics in the past. The proposed method was found to detect trends before Twitter for 79% of the time, with 95% accuracy. The current study takes a completely different approach towards predicting trending topics, where features are extracted for particular hashtags to estimate their level of popularity, and then hashtags are classified as trending or non-trending based on these features (as detailed in subsequent sections).

3 Dataset

This section describes the dataset used for the present study. The Twitter online social network provides an API[2] to collect different forms of data, including streams of tweets posted at the website, profile details of particular users, and so on. Especially, Twitter provides a 1 % random sample of all tweets posted in

---

[2] Twitter API: https://dev.twitter.com.

Table 1. Statistics of the data set, i.e., the 1 % random sample of tweets provided by Twitter, crawled over a particular day (Day 1) and the first six hours of the next day (Day 2). We also collected the trending topics declared by Twitter for these two days.

Day	#Tweets	#Users	#Hashtags	#Trends
Day 1	4,051,506	3,145,957	237,100	67
Day 2 (first 6 h)	1,087,149	936,169	74,203	67

the Twitter website world-wide. We designed a Web-based crawler to collect the 1 % Twitter random sample, and collected the sample during a particular day, and the first six hours of the next day. We refer to these two days as Day 1 and Day 2 respectively.

Table 1 summarizes the statistics of the dataset collected over the two days. Note that though we are using only 1 % of the Twitter stream, even this amounts to millions of tweets per day, since hundreds of millions of tweets are posted in Twitter every day. Along with the number of tweets collected on each day, Table 1 also shows the number of distinct users who posted the tweets collected on each day, and the number of hashtags contained in these tweets.

Additionally, we also used the Twitter API to collect the set of trending topics (hashtags) on these two days, i.e., the set of keywords which Twitter declared as trending on these two days.[3] Table 1 also gives the number of trending hashtags collected over the two days.

4 Setting up the Trend Prediction Task as a Classification Problem

The goal of this study is to predict which hashtags are likely to become trending (popular) in Twitter in the recent future. We model this prediction problem as a machine learning classification problem, which is described in this section.

As stated in Sect. 3, we collected the 1 % random sample of tweets provided by Twitter over a particular day (referred to as Day 1), and for the first six hours of the next day (referred to as Day 2). We also collected the set of trending hashtags declared by Twitter on each of these two days; we refer to the set of trending hashtags on Day 1 as T_1, and the set of trending hashtags on Day 2 as T_2.

Since we intend to set up the trend prediction task as a classification problem, we need examples of trending hashtags as well as non-trending hashtags in order to train classifiers. For this, we extracted the hashtags from all tweets posted on Day 1 as well as Day 2. Then, we identified the *non-trending* hashtags from the tweets posted on Day 1, and randomly selected $|T_1|$ number of non-trending hashtags. In other words, we identified an equal number of non-trending hashtags as there were trending hashtags on the same day; we refer to this set of non-trending hashtags on Day 1 as N_1 ($|N_1| = |T_1|$). Similarly, we identified $|T_2|$

---

[3] The trending topics declared by Twitter can also include words or phrases apart from hashtags. However, for simplicity, this study only considers trending hashtags.

number of *non-trending* hashtags from the tweets posted on Day 2; we refer to the set of non-trending hashtags on Day 2 as N_2, where $|N_2| = |T_2|$.

We consider the set of hashtags $\{T_1 \cup N_1\}$ as the training set for classifiers. For each hashtag in this set, we compute the features described later in Sect. 5 over the tweets posted during Day 1, and use these features to train classifiers. Then, we use the set of hashtags $\{T_2 \cup N_2\}$ to test the performance of the classifiers. In other words, for each hashtag in $\{T_2 \cup N_2\}$, we compute the features over the tweets posted *during the first six hours of Day 2*, and use these features to test the classifiers.

Thus, our classifiers are trained over trending and non-trending hashtags from Day 1, and their classification performance is measured by whether they can distinguish between trending and non-trending hashtags on Day 2. Note that we attempt to classify between trending and non-trending hashtags of Day 2, based on Twitter data from only the first six hours of Day 2. This means that, effectively, we are attempting to predict, after the first six hours of Day 2, which hashtags are likely to become trending over the rest of the day (Day 2).

5   Features for Trending/Non-trending Classification

The previous section discussed how we model the problem of predicting trending topics in Twitter as a classification problem. This section describes the properties of hashtags, based on which features are extracted for training classifiers for the trending vs. non-trending classification problem.

For a given hashtag h, the set of properties considered by us are described below.

1. **Lifetime:** The lifetime of a hashtag h is the number of hours during which it was discussed in Twitter. More specifically, this is the number of hours during which the hashtag h appeared in at least one tweet posted during that hour.
2. **Tweet-count:** This is the total number of tweets containing the particular hashtag h, which were posted during the lifetime of h.
3. **User-count:** This is the total number of distinct users who posted at least one tweet containing hashtag h during the lifetime of h.
4. **Velocity:** This feature captures the *rate of change of the number of tweets* containing a particular hashtag. Let the number of tweets containing hashtag h that are posted during a particular hour k be denoted by N_k^h. Then the velocity of hashtag h during the hour k is $N_{k+1}^h - N_k^h$, i.e., the difference between the number of tweets containing h posted during hour k and the next hour. Note that velocity can be negative as well – for instance, if a hashtag is included in lesser number of tweets during hour $k + 1$ than during hour k, then its velocity during hour k will be negative.
5. **Acceleration:** This is analogous to the *rate of change of velocity* at a particular hour. This is computed in a way similar to the Velocity feature described above. Let the velocity of hashtag h during the hour k be denoted by V_k^h (computed in the way described above). Then the acceleration of h during

hour k is computed as $V_{k+1}^h - V_k^h$. Similar to velocity, acceleration can be negative as well.

The intuition behind the choice of these properties is as follows. The first three properties – lifetime, tweet-count, and user-count – help to estimate the global level of popularity of a hashtag. For instance, if many tweets were posted containing a particular hashtag (high tweet-count) by many different users (high user-count) over a long period of time (high lifetime), then this hashtag is a very popular one, and is more likely to be declared trending. The last two properties – velocity and acceleration – help to estimate how quickly a hashtag is gaining (or losing) popularity. Even if a hashtag is discussed for a relatively small time-period (low lifetime), if its popularity increase rapidly (high velocity or acceleration), then it can be declared trending during that time-period. Thus, these properties attempt to capture the dynamicity or 'freshness' in the popularity of the hashtag, which is one of the factors which Twitter takes into account while choosing trending topics [11].

To better justify the intuition behind the choice of these properties, we plot these properties for some trending and non-trending hashtags. The properties for these hashtags are computed based on the data collected during Day 1. Figure 3 shows the hourly variation (over a day) of tweet-count, velocity, and acceleration for the two trending hashtags #PeoplesChoice and #MusicFans, and two non-trending hashtags #tired and #travel. In all the figures, the x-axis is the hour of day (during Day 1), and the y-axis shows the variation of the respective properties

Figure 3(a) shows that the trending hashtags appear in much larger number of tweets than the non-trending ones. Similarly, Figs. 3(b) and (c) show that trending hashtags show appreciable *temporal variation* in the number of tweets in which they appear; in other words, the trending hashtags show peak popularity during certain time-periods (and they are most probably declared trending during these periods). On the other hand, the non-trending hashtags show very little variation over time – their velocity and acceleration are very close to zero throughout the day. Thus it is evident that the selected features should be able to distinguish between trending and non-trending hashtags in Twitter.

Finally, it can be noted from the above figures that even for trending hashtags, the velocity and acceleration do *not* remain uniformly high during all hours of a day. Different trending hashtags may see peak velocity/acceleration during different hours of the day. Hence, for a given hashtag h, we consider the *maximum values* of its velocity and acceleration over all hours of a day, as the final feature value. The rationale behind choosing the maximum values is that the hashtag was probably declared trending around the time when its velocity/acceleration was maximum, hence choosing the maximum values will help to better distinguish trending hashtags from non-trending ones.

Thus, for a given hashtag, we have a feature vector of length 5, containing (i) its lifetime, (ii) its tweet-count, (iii) its user-count, and the maximum values of its (iv) velocity, and (v) acceleration at some hour during its lifetime. These feature vectors, computed for hashtags posted on Day 1, are used to train the

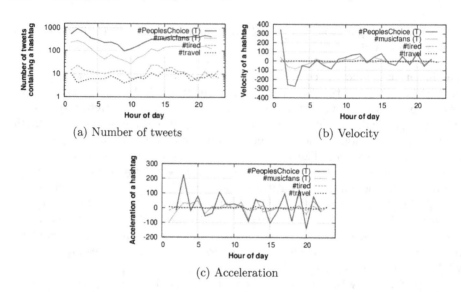

(a) Number of tweets   (b) Velocity

(c) Acceleration

Fig. 3. Variation in properties of particular hashtags during different hours in a day (as measured on Day 1): (a) number of tweets containing a hashtag, (b) velocity of a hashtag, (c) acceleration of a hashtag. Plots shown for two trending hashtags (#PeoplesChoice and #MusicFans) and two non-trending ones (#tired and #travel).

classifiers. Subsequently, similar feature vectors are computed for the hashtags posted on Day 2 (based on the tweets obtained during the first six hours of Day 2) and used to test the performance of the classifier.

6   Evaluation of Prediction Performance

In this section, we discuss the performance of classifiers trained over the features described in Sect. 5. The experimental setup in which the classifiers are used has been described in Sect. 4.

6.1   Metrics for Measuring Performance

To measure the performance of various classifiers in the trending/non-trending classification problem, we follow the standard methodology of representing results in the form of a *confusion matrix*, and then use standard metrics such as *precision*, *recall*, and *accuracy*. Table 2 shows an example of a confusion matrix, where 'True' means the ground truth for a hashtag (i.e., whether it was actually declared trending by Twitter on Day 2, or not), and 'Predicted' means the class (trending/non-trending) inferred for this hashtag by a particular classifier. Here a, b, c and d represent the number of hashtags in the different categories, e.g., a number of hashtags were actually trending (True) and were correctly classified as trending by a certain classifier (Predicted).

Table 2. Example of confusion matrix.

		Predicted	
		Trending	Non-trending
True	Trending	a	b
	Non-trending	c	d

The *precision* with respect to a certain class is the ratio of the number of items that are correctly predicted to be in that class, to the total number of items predicted in that class. From the confusion matrix in Table 2), the precision (P) for the 'trending' class is $P = a/(a + c)$; we refer to this metric as *Precision-trends*. Similarly, the *recall* (R) for a certain class is the ratio of the number of items that are correctly predicted to be in that class, to the total number of items actually belonging to that class. The recall of the 'trending' class is $R = a/(a + b)$. We refer to this metric as *Recall-trends*. The closer the precision and recall are to 1.0, the better is the classification performance. Finally, the *accuracy* of classification (A) is the proportion of the total number of items that are correctly classified, i.e., $A = (a + d)/(a + b + c + d)$.

6.2   Results

For the classification, we used a set of standard classifiers from the well-known Weka machine learning tool-kit [6]. Table 3 reports the Precision-trends, Recall-trends, (i.e., precision and recall for the hashtags in the trending class) and the accuracy metrics for the trending vs. non-trending classification using various classifiers.

It can be observed that all the classifiers achieve more than 98 % accuracy, and some, in fact, achieve more than 99 % accuracy. Also, for almost all classifiers (except for two), Precision-Trends is 1.0, which implies that all the hashtags which are classified as trending by the classifiers are actually the ones which are declared trending by Twitter.

The Recall-trends values are somewhat lower – some of the classifiers achieve recall of 0.833. This means that there are some trending topics in Twitter which the classifiers fail to identify. This is understandable, since we are attempting to perform the classification based on the data of only the first six hours of Day 2 (as detailed in Sect. 4). It is very likely that some of the hashtags which became popular later in the day (and hence were declared trending by Twitter for the day) were not so popular during the first six hours, which is why the classifiers mis-classify them.

Overall, the performance of the classifiers demonstrates the effectiveness of the features that were used to distinguished between trending and non-trending hashtags in Twitter. This also implies that the proposed classification methodology can be used at a certain point of time (e.g., after the first six hours of the day) to predict what topics (hashtags) are likely to be trending during the rest of the day, with reasonable accuracy.

Table 3. Results for the trending vs. non-trending classification, using some standard classifiers from the Weka machine learning toolkit [6].

Classifier	Accuracy	Precision-trends	Recall-trends
Multilayer perception	98.18 %	1.0	0.667
Simple logistics	98.18 %	1.0	0.667
Spegasos	98.18 %	1.0	0.667
Ibk	98.18 %	1.0	0.667
AdaBoostM1	98.18 %	0.833	0.833
Decorate	98.18 %	1.0	0.667
LogitBoost	98.18 %	0.833	0.833
Nnge	98.18 %	1.0	0.667
LMT	98.18 %	1.0	0.667
Kstar	99.09 %	1.0	0.833
RandomCommmittee	99.09 %	1.0	0.833
Adtree	99.09 %	1.0	0.833
LADTree	99.09 %	1.0	0.833
RandomForest	99.09 %	1.0	0.833
RandomTree	99.09 %	1.0	0.833

7   Conclusion

In this paper, we proposed a machine learning based technique for predicting which hashtags are likely to become trending (popular) in Twitter in the recent future. For this, we used a set of only five features which attempt to capture the extent of the popularity gained by a hashtag, and the rate at which its popularity is growing.

We found that several standard classifiers trained on these five features achieve more than 98 % precision and more than 80 % recall in classifying between trending and non-trending hashtags in Twitter on a certain day. More importantly, this classification performance was obtained based on data for only the first six hours of the day (and having trained the classifiers on the data for the previous day) – this implies that the proposed scheme can be used to predict which topics (hashtags) are likely to become popular in Twitter in the coming few hours. This result has significant importance in applications such as online advertising and social media analytics.

As future work, we intend to enhance the feature-set by considering properties of the users who post a particular hashtag (e.g., popularity of the users). Further, feature selection techniques can also be used to select the more important features for the trending/non-trending classification task in order to improve the performance (especially the recall).

Acknowledgement. The authors thank the anonymous reviewers for their constructive suggestions, and Parantapa Bhattacharya and Muhammad Bilal Zafar for their help in collecting Twitter data.

References

1. Asur, S., Huberman, B.A.: Predicting the future with social media. In: Proceedings of the IEEE/WIC/ACM International Conference on Web Intelligence and Intelligent Agent Technology, vol. 1, pp. 492–499 (2010)
2. Bothos, E., Apostolou, D., Mentzas, G.: Using social media to predict future events with agent-based markets. IEEE Intell. Syst. **25**, 50–58 (2010)
3. Chakraborty, T., Kumar, S., Goyal, P., Ganguly, N., Mukherjee, A.: Towards a stratified learning approach to predict future citation counts. In: Proceedings of ACM / IEEE Joint Conference on Digital Libraries (2014)
4. Cheng, J., Adamic, L., Dow, P.A., Kleinberg, J.M., Leskovec, J.: Can cascades be predicted? In: Proceedings of the International Conference on World Wide Web, pp. 925–936 (2014)
5. Galuba, W., Aberer, K., Chakraborty, D., Despotovic, Z., Kellerer, W.: Outtweeting the twitterers - predicting information cascades in microblogs. In: Proceedings of Workshop on Online Social Networks (2010)
6. Hall, M., Frank, E., Holmes, G., Pfahringer, B., Reutemann, P., Witten, I.H.: The WEKA data mining software: an update. SIGKDD Explor. **11**(1), 10–18 (2009)
7. Lee, K., Palsetia, D., Narayanan, R., Patwary, M.M.A., Agrawal, A., Choudhary, A.: Twitter trending topic classification. In: Proceedings of the IEEE International Conference on Data Mining Workshops, pp. 251–258 (2011)
8. Martinez-Romo, J., Araujo, L.: Detecting malicious tweets in trending topics using a statistical analysis of language. Expert Syst. Appl. **40**(8), 2992–3000 (2013)
9. Nikolov, S.: Trend or no trend : a novel nonparametric method for classifying time series. Master's thesis, Massachusetts Institute of Technology, USA (2012)
10. Szabo, G., Huberman, B.A.: Predicting the popularity of online content. Commun. ACM **53**(8), 80–88 (2010)
11. Twitter Blog: Trend or not trend. https://blog.twitter.com/2010/trend-or-not-trend
12. Yang, J., Leskovec, J.: Patterns of temporal variation in online media. In: Proceedings of ACM International Conference on Web Search and Data Mining, pp. 177–186 (2011)

Optimizing the Efficiency of Straight and U-Shaped Robotic Assembly Lines

J. Mukund Nilakantan and S.G. Ponnambalam[(✉)]

Advanced Engineering Platform & School of Engineering, Monash University
Malaysia, 46150 Bandar Sunway, Malaysia
{mukund.janardhanan, sgponnambalam}@monash.edu

Abstract. In an industrial production line, efficiency is considered to be a crucial factor. Efficient production line results in increased production and efficient utilization of all available resources. This research describes a type of robotic assembly line balancing problem, in which the assembly tasks are to be allocated to workstations, and each workstation needs to be allotted with a robot which performs these tasks in minimum time with an objective of maximizing line efficiency, Smoothness Index and cycle time are calculated for the efficient assembly line. In this paper, a differential evolution approach is proposed to solve straight and U- shaped robotic assembly line. Performance of the algorithm is tested on the benchmark datasets for both the problems and the results are reported.

Keywords: Differential evolution · Cycle time · Smoothness index · Line efficiency · Assembly line balancing

1 Introduction

In a manufacturing sector assembly is one of the most important process. Different parts which are designed and manufactured individually are to be assembled together to make a final product. The assembly process is of great economic importance in the manufacturing sector, hence substantial amount of work is done for improving the efficiency and for designing a cost effective assembly line [1]. Assembly line could be classified into two types: straight assembly lines and U-shaped assembly line. U-shaped assembly line is introduced and modeled by Miltenburg and Wijngaard [2]. In a straight-line layout, operators must work on a continuous length of the line where as in a U type layout, operators are allowed to work across both "sides" of the line. In case of the U-shaped assembly lines entrance and exit are in the same position [3]. In U-shaped assembly lines task can be assigned to a workstation after all its predecessor or all successors are assigned to an earlier or the same workstation. This is the distinguishing feature of U-shaped assembly line balancing problems that must allow for the forward and backward assignment of tasks to workstations [4].

In the recent years robots are widely used in assembly lines and they are called robotic assembly lines. Robots used for the assembly could be programmed to perform different types of tasks and applications. Different robots are available with different capabilities and efficiencies. Hence, proper allocation of the robot for the workstation is

B.K. Panigrahi et al. (Eds.): SEMCCO 2014, LNCS 8947, pp. 582–595, 2015.
DOI: 10.1007/978-3-319-20294-5_50

an important task. [5]. The robotic assembly line balancing (RALB) problem aims at assigning tasks to the workstations and proper allocation of robot is required for improving the efficiency and productivity of the assembly line. Rubinovitz and Bukchin [6] first formulated the robotic assembly line balancing (RALB) problem with an objective of minimizing the number of workstations for a fixed cycle time. Problem aims at allocating equal amounts of tasks to the workstations while allocating the most efficient robot type from the given set of available types. Later, Rubinovitz et al. [1] presented a branch and bound method to solve the same problem. Bukchin and Tzur [7] presented a problem of a flexible assembly line with different types of equipment available. They tried to minimize the total equipment cost using branch &bound procedure to solve small and medium sized problems. A heuristic approach is proposed by Tsai and Yao [8] for a flexible robotic assembly line which produces a family of products. Kim and Park [9] proposed an integer programming formulation and a cutting plane algorithm for RALB. All the above mentioned work aims at minimizing the number of workstations and this problems falls under the category of type I robotic assembly line balancing. Levitin et al. [10] dealt with the type II of robotic assembly line balancing (RALB-II) problem where the objective of the problem is to assign tasks workstations and select best available robot in such a way that the cycle time is minimized. Gao et al. [5] presented a 0-1 integer programming problem for RALB and hybrid genetic algorithm (hGA) is proposed to find efficient solutions. Yoosefelahi et al. [11] presented a new formulation of the robotic assembly line balancing problem of type II. The algorithm aims at minimizing the cycle time, the robot setup costs and the robot costs. Three versions of multi-objective evolution strategies has been developed to solve this problem. Mukund Nilakantan and Ponnambalam [12] applied a standard PSO to solve robotic assembly line balancing problem of type II in a straight assembly line. Daoud et al. [13] proposed a set of metaheuristics to solve robotic assembly line problems of type E. The major objective is to maximize the efficiency of the line and to balance the different tasks between the robots. Since assembly line balancing problem falls under the category of NP-hard evolutionary algorithms are to be used to obtain nearer-to-optimal results. Literature survey reveals that most of the work done on RALB are for the straight robotic assembly line [5] and there has been no research done on U shaped robotic assembly line balancing problem. This research aims at proposing an algorithm to solve straight line and U-shaped robotic assembly line problem by using Differential Evolution algorithm. In this paper, the assembly tasks are to be allocated to workstations, and each workstation needs to be allotted with a robot which performs these tasks in minimum time with an objective of obtaining maximum line efficiency for a fixed number of workstations for both straight and U-shaped assembly lines. The remaining of this paper is organized as follows: Sect. 2 describes the mathematical model formulation of RALB problem addressed in this paper along with assumptions considered. Section 3 details the implementation of Differential Evolution. Section 4 presents the experimental results and discussions and it is concluded in Sect. 5.

2 Problem Definition and Mathematical Model

In an assembly line (straight and U-shaped), different assembly tasks are to be performed by each station to produce a given product. Precedence constraints are specified and it determines the order in which tasks should be executed. There will be a set of workstations and robots (workers) considered in the assembly line. In a balanced robotic assembly line, tasks needs to be assigned to the workstations and best robot needs to be allotted to the station to perform these assembly tasks. The major objective of the problem is to obtain maximum efficiency for the assembly line. In case of a robotic straight line assembly for a given workstation, the set of possible assignable tasks is decided by those tasks whose predecessors have already been assigned to workstations, whereas in case of robotic U-shaped line problem the set of assignable tasks is determined by all those tasks whose predecessors or successors have already been assigned.

The following assumptions are considered in this work [5, 10].

1. A task (operation) cannot be split among two or more workstations.
2. Time taken to perform a task depends on the robot) assigned.
3. At a time only one robot can be assigned to a workstation.
4. Number of workstations is equal to the number of robots as the aim is to improve the productivity by reducing the cycle time.
5. Any task can be processed at any station by any robot.
6. All types of robots are available without limitations. In case of the robots purchase cost is not considered.
7. Material handling, loading and unloading time, as well as set-up and tool changing time are negligible, or are included in the task time. This assumption is realistic on a single-model assembly line.
8. Assembly line is designed for a unique model of a single product

2.1 Notations and Mathematical Model

• Indices

   i, j: Index of assembly tasks
   h: Robot
   s: Workstation
   F: Set of tasks, $F = \{g \mid g = 1, 2 \ldots .n\}$.
   H: Set of available robots
   S: Set of workstations
   N_w: Number of workstations
   N_a: Number of tasks
   N_r: Number of robots (workers)
   C: Cycle time
   sq: Sequence of tasks represents feasible solution
   t_{hi}: processing time of task i by robot h

S_{max}: maximum station time,

S_k: kth workstation time.

D_i: Set of immediate predecessors of task i in the precedence network

P: A set of precedence constraints ($P = \{(x, y)|$ task x must be completed before task $y\}$

$L_a = \{$g $|$ task g is done at workstation $a\}$

LE: Line Efficiency

• Decision Variables

$$x_{shi} = \begin{cases} 1 & \textit{if task i is assigned to robot h in station s} \\ 0, & \textit{otherwise} \end{cases}$$

$$y_{sh} = \begin{cases} 1 & \textit{if robot h to workstation s} \\ 0, & \textit{otherwise} \end{cases}$$

According to the notations and the assumptions considered, an integer programming (IP) model for this problem is formulated as follows [14].

$$\max Z = LE \tag{1}$$

$$\sum_{h \in H} \sum_{s \in S} x_{shi} = 1, \forall i \in F, \tag{2}$$

$$\sum_{s \in S} y_{sh} \leq 1 \, \forall h \in H, \tag{3}$$

$$\sum_{h \in H} y_{sh} \leq 1 \, \forall s \in S, \tag{4}$$

$$\sum_{h \in H} \sum_{s \in S} s.x_{shi} \leq \sum_{h \in H} \sum_{s \in S} s.x_{shj} \, \forall i,j/i \in D_j, \tag{5}$$

$$\sum_{i \in F} t_{hi}.x_{shi} \leq C \, \forall h \in H; \forall s \in S, \tag{6}$$

$$\sum_{i \in F} x_{shi} \leq M.y_{sh} \, \forall h \in H; \forall s \in S \tag{7}$$

Here M is a sufficiently large constant which should have a value larger than $|F|.|H|.max_{i \varepsilon F, h \varepsilon H}\{t_{hi}|t_{hi} <\}$. The objective of Eq. (1) is to maximize the line efficiency while minimizing the the cycle time. Equation (2) checks task i is assigned to a single workstation s and robot h. Equations (3) and (4) ensures that every robot can be assigned to an only one workstation, and that in every station there is only one robot (worker). Equation (5) ensures the precedence constraints are not violated on the U-shaped assembly line. Equations (6) and (7) imply that every robot h assigned to station s can have more than one task, whenever given cycle time C is not overcome. Equations (6) and (7) are defined separately in order to maintain the model linearity as cycle time C and ysh are both variables. The above presented mathematical model is for the straight robotic assembly line. In case of U-shaped robotic assembly line, Eq. (5) changes to following equations.

For each task y:

$$
\begin{aligned}
&\text{if} (x, y) \in P, x \in L_a, y \in L_b, \text{then } a \leq b, \quad \text{for all } x; or \\
&\text{if} (y, z) \in P, y \in L_b, y \in L_c, \text{then } c \leq b, \quad \text{for all } z;
\end{aligned}
\tag{8}
$$

Line efficiency of a given assembly line is the direct indication of the efficiency. The line efficiency is calculated as follows.

$$
LE = \frac{\sum_{k=1}^{N_w} S_k}{N_w * C} * 100
\tag{9}
$$

3   Differential Evolution for RALB

Storn and Price [15] proposed a simple algorithm for optimization and engineering problems called Differential Evolution (DE). Different types of numerical optimization problems have been tested using DE and it could be found that DE outperforms other popular evolutionary algorithms [16, 17]. Combinatorial optimization problems with discrete decision variables such as machine layout problem [18], and flow-shop

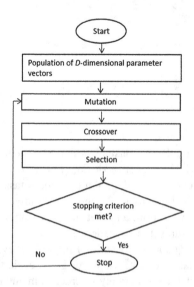

Fig. 1. Flowchat of DE

scheduling problems [19] have been tested with DE and better results are reported. Implementation of DE on RALB problem is explained in the following sections. DE starts with the initialization of a random population, composed of target vectors. A mutation process is done to the target vectors to create a new set of vectors called donor vectors. The crossover operation is then carried out between the target vectors with their corresponding donor vectors to generate trial vectors. Then selection operation is performed, where the target vectors are compared to the corresponding trial vectors based on the objective function to determine which one of the vectors would be selected for the next generation. The above mentioned three processes are repeated until the termination condition is satisfied. Figure 1 shows the flowchart of DE.

3.1 Population Initialization

Evolutionary algorithms generally starts with a randomly generated search space which evolves iteratively to find nearer to optimal solutions. Heuristic rules reported in literature for assembly line balancing problems are used to generate a set of random solutions. Fourteen heuristics are proposed in the literature to generate chromosomes for the multi-objective GA proposed to solve simple assembly line balancing (sALB) problem [20]. Remaining set of particles are randomly generated based on these vectors. In total twenty five target vectors are generated as the initial population. The vector represents a sequence of numbers (tasks) arranged in a way that it meets the precedence relationship. Table 1 shows the seven strings (target vectors) generated using the seven heuristics rules. For an example, the robot task times for 11 task 4 robot problem is presented in Table 2. The precedence diagram for the 11 task problem is presented in Fig. 2.

Table 1. Initial population generated using the heuristic rules

Rule Number	Rule	Task Sequence										
1	Maximum ranked positional weight	1	2	6	3	4	5	7	8	10	9	11
2	Minimum reverse positional weight	1	5	4	3	2	7	9	6	8	10	11
3	Minimum total number of predecessor tasks	1	2	3	4	5	6	8	10	7	9	11
4	Maximum total number of follower tasks	1	2	3	4	5	6	7	8	9	10	11
5	Maximum Task time	1	5	2	6	3	4	7	8	10	9	11
6	Minimum Task time	1	4	3	2	5	7	9	6	8	10	11
7	Random task assignment	1	2	3	6	5	4	7	8	10	9	11

3.2 Mutation

A population of donor vectors is created by perturbing the population of target vectors. Perturbation is performed by adding the difference between two randomly selected target vectors to a third target vector which is given in the Eq. 10.

Table 2. Performance time for 11 tasks by 4 robots

Tasks	Robot 1	Robot 2	Robot 3	Robot 4	Average Time (τ)
1	81	37	51	49	54.5
2	109	101	90	42	85.5
3	65	80	38	52	58.75
4	51	41	91	40	55.75
5	92	36	33	25	46.5
6	77	65	83	71	74
7	51	51	40	49	47.75
8	50	42	34	44	42.5
9	43	76	41	33	48.25
10	45	46	41	77	52.25
11	76	38	83	87	71

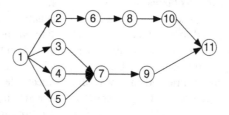

Fig. 2. Precedence graph of 11task problem

$$y_{ig} = x_{r1,g} + F(x_{r2,G} - x_{r3,G}), where \quad i = 1, \ldots 5 \tag{10}$$

F is known as the mutation scale factor. For an example let us consider three vectors:

$x_{r1,G} = \{1,2,6,3,4,5,7,8,10,9,11\}, x_{r2,G} = \{1,2,3,4,5,6,7,8,9,10,11\}$ and $x_{r3,G} = \{1,2,3,6,5,4,7,8,10,9,11\}$

$y_{ig} = \{1,2,6,3,4,5,7,8,10,9,11\} + F*\{1,2,3,4,5,6,7,8,9,10,11\}-\{1,2,3,6,5,4,7,8,10,9,11\}$

The pairs of transpositions to get $x_{r3,G}$ from $x_{r2,G}$ are identified. Then apply the mutation factor, the number of pairs are selected and these pairs are used to transposition the values in $x_{r1,g}$ with F = 0.5, y_{ig} is generated as explained below.

$y_{ig} = \{1,2,6,3,4,5,7,8,10,19,11\} + 0.5*(3,5)(8,9) = \{1,2,6,3,4,5,7,8,10,9,11\} + (8,9) = \{1,2,6,3,4,5,7,8,9,10,11\}$

3.3   Crossover

Trial vectors are generated by using OX operator (Order crossover) proposed by Davis [21]. OX Operators works as follows:

- Select a subsection of task sequence from target vector at random.
- Produce a proto-trail vectors by copying the substring of task sequence into the corresponding positions.
- Delete the tasks that are already in the substring from the donor vector. The resulted sequence of tasks contains tasks that the proto-trial vector needs.
- Place the tasks into the unfixed positions of the proto-trial from left to right according to the order of the sequence in the donor vector.

An example explaining this method is given in Fig. 3.

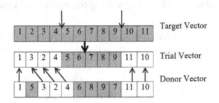

Fig. 3. Illustration of the OX operator

Crossover is done for selected vectors from the population. The selection of the number of vectors is based on the crossover (C_R) rate. A reordering procedure is also done to make the vectors feasible if the created vector does not meet the precedence constraints [10].

3.4 Selection

Each target vector competes with the corresponding trial vector to be carried on to the next generation/iteration. The vector with the better function value is copied to the next generation. In this research selection is based on the efficiency of the assembly line which is the objective function evaluated.

$$x_{i,G+1} = \begin{cases} z_{i,G} \; if f\left(z_{i,G}\right) > f\left(x_{i,G}\right) \\ x_{i,G} otherwise \end{cases} \tag{11}$$

The proposed method is terminated if the iteration approaches a predefined criteria, usually a sufficiently good fitness or in this case, a predefined maximum number of iterations (generations) is used.

3.5 Objective Function Evaluation

The objective function evaluated for this research for straight and U-shaped type of assembly line is Line Efficiency (LE). The following section explains how the objective function is evaluated.

3.6 Straight and U-Shaped Robotic Assembly Line

A consecutive heuristic procedure is used to assign the tasks and robots to the work-stations [10]. This heuristic method is used to minimize the cycle time of a straight robotic assembly line. Procedure starts with considering an initial cycle time for the assembly line, C_0. The aim of this procedure is to assign tasks and robots consecutively to the workstations in an efficient manner. The procedure attempts to allocate assembly tasks to a workstation using robots that allow the assignment of maximum number of tasks to be performed at each work station. If it is not possible to allocate all the tasks to workstations for the given initial C_0, C_0 is incremented by 'one' until all the tasks are assigned to all workstations. The stepwise procedure of consecutive heuristic is explained below.

Step 1. Initial value of C_0 is the mean of the minimum performance time of robots (workers) for the tasks. Initial assembly line time

$$C_0 = \left\lceil \sum_{j=1}^{N_a} \min_{1 \leq i \leq N_r} c_{i,j}/N_w \right\rceil \tag{11}$$

Step 2. First station is opened and the tasks according to the sequence is allocated and checked if any of the robots can perform the tasks within C_0. Tasks are added to the same workstation until at least one robot can perform the allotted tasks within C_0.

Step 3. Next station is opened if the previous station is filled. Repeat the check of C_0

Step 4. If all task are not possible to assigned to the given number of workstations, increment C_0 by 'one' and repeat step 2 to 3 until all tasks are allotted to the given number of workstations.

Step 5. Assign robots to the workstations based on the minimum robot (worker) performance time.

Step 6. Based on the workstation time and cycle time, the line efficiency is calculated for the given vector.

Figure 4 shows the example of on how the allocation is done for the given sequence. And efficiency is calculated.

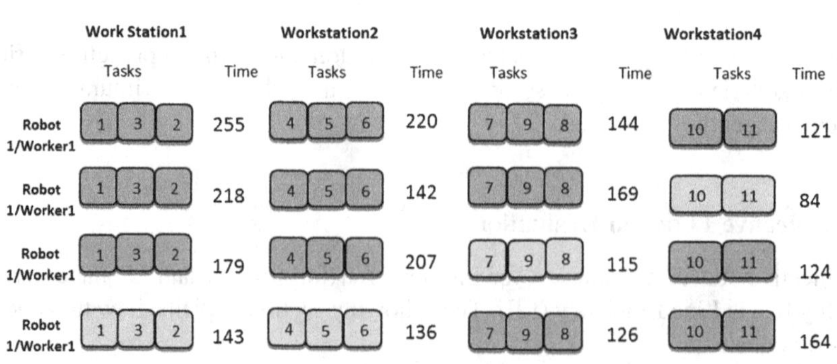

Fig. 4. Task and robot allocation for a straight robotic assembly line

Straight line robotic assembly line's efficiency is calculated as follows

$$LE = \frac{\sum\limits_{k=1}^{N_w} S_k}{N_w * C} * 100 = (143 + 136 + 115 + 84)/(4 * 143) * 100 = 83.56\%$$

Here number of workstation is 4 and cycle time is found to be 143. Smoothness index is an index which indicates the relative smoothness of a given assembly line. A smoothness index of 0 indicates that assembly line is perfectly balanced. Smoothness index for both the assembly lines are evaluated for the final best result obtained using DE. Smoothness index is evaluated as follows.

$$SI = \sqrt{\frac{\sum\limits_{k=1}^{m} (S_{max} - S_k)^2}{m}} \tag{12}$$

Smoothness Index of the straight robotic assembly line is found to be 14.4. Task and robot allocation in a U-shaped assembly line is done using the same procedure except for the task allocation, the tasks are selected from both the sides of the sequence and constraints are checked. Fig shows the tasks allocated for U-shaped robotic assembly line for the same sequence used for straight robotic assembly line.

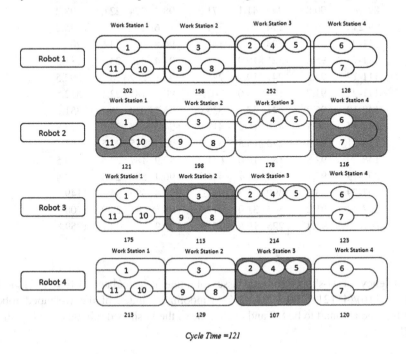

Fig. 5. Task and robot allocation for a U-shaped robotic assembly line

Table 3. Experimental Results obtained using DE for Straight and U-shaped Robotic assembly line

Task and Robot	Straight Line RALB				U-shaped RALB			
	LE (%)	c	SI	CPU time	LE	c	SI	CPU time
25-3	97.3	503	18.6	6.5	99.1	500	6.02	8.5
25-4	88.6	329	40.4	7.2	91.5	318	33.5	9.1
25-6	88.2	208	29.3	7.8	96.9	183	7.3	9.7
25-9	84.5	114	23.3	8.4	88.9	109	15.8	10.2
35-4	98.0	347	9.6	12.6	98.6	345	3.6	14.5
35-5	93.0	335	31.9	18.2	97.4	334	11.8	16.8
35-7	92.0	219	21.7	22.1	94.8	215	13.5	18.4
35-12	82.3	115	24.5	34.2	87.3	106	17.8	28.5
53-5	92.1	485	45.2	18.2	97.3	459	16.7	28.8
53-7	93.4	304	26.0	21.2	93.8	286	21.8	36.0
53-10	91.4	234	24.3	27.8	93.7	220	16.4	50.2
53-14	82.2	161	32.0	38.8	90.0	148	18.3	50.9
70-7	95.0	447	29.2	42.3	97.4	427	12.2	52.1
70-10	93.8	272	21	53.7	94.0	266	22	56.6
70-14	87.6	211	29.6	65.3	92.8	199	18.0	62.2
70-19	87.5	144	23.5	82.3	89.2	140	17.9	87.4
89-8	82.3	486	35.6	46.6	84	475	19.9	93.1
89-12	94.3	317	22.6	58.1	96	315	16.4	93.6
89-16	90.8	247	41.1	71.3	98.2	224	22.03	98.2
89-21	88.2	174	23.1	91.2	88.6	172	25	195.2
111-9	97.8	523	16.9	161.2	96.8	520	23.6	206.1
111-13	95.6	321	19.9	231.1	94.4	319	23.5	281.3
111-17	93.2	247	19.7	248.6	93.8	242	18.3	292.5
111-22	91.7	183	18.0	302.1	90.1	181	22.1	312.5
148-10	96.2	641	32.2	335.6	96.7	629	26.3	351.2
148-14	96.4	420	18.2	417.9	94.0	418	32.2	443.8
148-21	94.5	273	15.5	542.3	92.7	275	22.5	583.5
148-29	92.8	189	18.0	611.2	89.9	187	22.5	663.5
297-19	97.1	594	20.7	946.3	96.4	589	24.5	1137.4
297-29	93.3	399	31.3	963.3	93.4	390	34.2	1149.7
297-38	91.2	305	31.0	1012.5	93.6	291	22.9	1208.7
297-50	92.4	225	19.8	1105.3	90.9	222	22.7	1259.8

Efficiency of U-shaped robotic assembly line is calculated. LE = (121 + 115 + 107 + 116)/(4*121)*100 = 94.83 %. Smoothness index of the U-shaped robotic assembly line is found to be 8.0 and cycle time of the U-shaped robotic assembly line is 121 (Fig. 5).

4 Results and Discussions

In order to test the proposed DE algorithm a set of benchmark instances available in the literature are considered. A total of 32 test problems ranging from 25 to 297 tasks are available in the literature [22]. Series of test was conducted to select the parameters used in the algorithm. Table 3 reports the results obtained for both the types of the assembly lines. Solutions reported are the average of 10 runs. The parameter settings of DE algorithm is described as follows: The population size is set to 25 and number of generations as 30. Mutation factor is set to 0.5 for all the 32 problems and C_R rate is fixed to 0.7. Better solution is given importance and not on the computational time. For the RALB problem addressed here, the selection of available robots helps to reduce the cycle time and in turn increases the productivity of the assembly line. Table 3 shows the problems evaluated. 25-3, 25-4...297-38,297-50 shows the different task size problems with different robot types. Line efficiency, Smoothness Index, Cycle Time and CPU time in seconds are obtained for straight robotic assembly line and U-shaped robotic assembly line. In this research smoothness index ('SI') is evaluated after finding out the best possible allocation for the tasks and robots for 32 problems in both the assembly line types. The cycle time ('c') of the assembly lines reported here is for the best results obtained while evaluating the objective of maximizing the line efficiency. Computational time is high for U-shaped robotic assembly line problem may be due to increased solution search space. Line efficiency and smoothness index for the small sized problems is better for U-shaped assembly line when compared to that of the straight robotic assembly line. The cycle time of the U-shaped robotic assembly line is also lower than the straight robotic assembly line. In case of large sized problems (from 111 task problem) straight robotic assembly line reports better line efficiency and smoothness index. But the cycle time is still lower for U-shaped robotic assembly line. In conclusion, U-shaped robotic assembly line performs better in case of cycle time but line efficiency is higher for straight robotic assembly line for large sized datasets.The computational time to reach the reported results of the 32 representative RALB problems are also reported. The computational time taken for producing the results od U-shaped robotic assembly line takes higher time due to large space area compared to the straight robotic assembly line.

5 Conclusion

In this paper, straight and U-shaped Robotic Assembly Line Balancing (RALB) problem to maximize the line efficiency are considered. Benchmark problems available in the open literature are used to evaluate the performance of the proposed DE. Smoothness index and cycle time are also calculated once a solution for maximum line efficiency has been obtained. It is observed that U-shaped robotic assembly line produces higher line efficiency compared to that of straight robotic assembly line for small sized datasets and for large sized datasets straight robotic assembly line is having higher line efficiency. When the cycle time is compared U-shaped robotic assembly line reports better solution than the straight robotic assembly line. Computational time for the DE algorithm are also reported. DE parameters are selected through a series of fine tuning and these parameters are used to find the solution reported here.

References

1. Rubinovitz, J., Bukchin, J., Lenz, E.: RALB–A heuristic algorithm for design and balancing of robotic assembly lines. CIRP Ann.-Manufact. Technol. **42**, 497–500 (1993)
2. Miltenburg, G., Wijngaard, J.: The U-line line balancing problem. Manage. Sci. **40**, 1378–1388 (1994)
3. Toklu, B., özcan, U.: A fuzzy goal programming model for the simple U-line balancing problem with multiple objectives. Eng. Optim. **40**, 191–204 (2008)
4. Kara, Y.: Line balancing and model sequencing to reduce work overload in mixed-model U-line production environments. Eng. Optim. **40**, 669–684 (2008)
5. Gao, J., Sun, L., Wang, L., Gen, M.: An efficient approach for type II robotic assembly line balancing problems. Comput. Ind. Eng. **56**, 1065–1080 (2009)
6. Rubinovitz, J., Bukchin, J.: Design and balancing of robotic assembly lines. Society of Manufacturing Engineers (1991)
7. Bukchin, J., Tzur, M.: Design of flexible assembly line to minimize equipment cost. IIE Trans. **32**, 585–598 (2000)
8. Tsai, D.-M., Yao, M.-J.: A line-balance-based capacity planning procedure for series-type robotic assembly line. Int. J. Prod. Res. **31**, 1901–1920 (1993)
9. Kim, H., Park, S.: A strong cutting plane algorithm for the robotic assembly line balancing problem. Int. J. Prod. Res. **33**, 2311–2323 (1995)
10. Levitin, G., Rubinovitz, J., Shnits, B.: A genetic algorithm for robotic assembly line balancing. Eur. J. Oper. Res. **168**, 811–825 (2006)
11. Yoosefelahi, A., Aminnayeri, M., Mosadegh, H., Ardakani, H.D.: Type II robotic assembly line balancing problem: an evolution strategies algorithm for a multi-objective model. J. Manufact. Syst. **31**, 139–151 (2012)
12. Mukund Nilakantan, J., Ponnambalam, S.G: An efficient PSO for type II robotic assembly line balancing problem. In: Automation Science and Engineering (CASE), 2012 IEEE International Conference on, pp. 600–605. IEEE (2012)
13. Daoud, S., Chehade, H., Yalaoui, F., Amodeo, L.: Solving a robotic assembly line balancing problem using efficient hybrid methods. J. Heuristics **20**, 235–259 (2014)
14. Miralles, C., Garcia-Sabater, J.P., Andres, C., Cardos, M.: Advantages of assembly lines in sheltered work centres for disabled. A case study. Int. J. Prod. Econ. **110**, 187–197 (2007)
15. Storn, R., Price, K.: Differential evolution–a simple and efficient heuristic for global optimization over continuous spaces. J. Global Optim. **11**, 341–359 (1997)
16. Ali, M.M., Törn, A.: Population set-based global optimization algorithms: some modifications and numerical studies. Comput. Oper. Res. **31**, 1703–1725 (2004)
17. Kaelo, P., Ali, M.: A numerical study of some modified differential evolution algorithms. Eur. J. Oper. Res. **169**, 1176–1184 (2006)
18. Nearchou, A.C.: Meta-heuristics from nature for the loop layout design problem. Int. J. Prod. Econ. **101**, 312–328 (2006)
19. Nearchou, A.C., Omirou, S.L.: Differential evolution for sequencing and scheduling optimization. J. Heuristics **12**, 395–411 (2006)

20. Ponnambalam, S.G., Aravindan, P., Naidu, G.M.: A multi-objective genetic algorithm for solving assembly line balancing problem. Int. J. Adv. Manufact. Technol. **16**, 341–352 (2000)
21. Davis, L.: Applying adaptive algorithms to epistatic domains. In: IJCAI, pp. 162–164 (1985)
22. Scholl, A.: Data of assembly line balancing problems. Darmstadt Technical University, Department of Business Administration, Economics and Law, Institute for Business Studies (BWL) (1995)

Trajectory Planning and Obstacle Avoidance Control of Redundant Robots Using Differential Evolution and Particle Swarm Optimization Algorithms

Sujan Warnakulasooriya[1] and S.G. Ponnambalam[2(✉)]

[1] MAS Unichela Pvt. Ltd., no. 124, Horana Road, Panadura, Srilanka
sujanmw@gmail.com
[2] Advanced Engineering Platform and School of Engineering,
Monash University Malaysia, 46150 Bandar Sunway, Malaysia
sgponnambalam@monash.edu

Abstract. The problem of trajectory planning and obstacle avoidance in redundant robots is addressed in this paper. Four variants of Particle Swarm Optimization (PSO) and a Differential Evolution (DE) algorithm are proposed to solve this problem. Simulation experiments on a 5 degree-of-freedom (DOF) robot manipulator in an environment with static obstacles are conducted. The manipulator is required to move from a start position to a goal position with minimum error while avoiding collision with the obstacles in the workspace. The performance of the proposed algorithms is compared with the results reported in the literature and the comparative results are presented. It is observed that qPSO-C performs better in free space and PSO-C performs better in environment with obstacles in terms of minimizing error average convergence time. The performance of DE improves when the number of obstacles increases.

Keywords: Trajectory planning · Obstacle avoidance · Redundant robot · Differential evolution · Particle swarm optimization

1 Introduction

Robot manipulators are extensively used in repetitive tasks which require excellent accuracy and precision. These robot manipulators may have several degrees of freedom while it may also require avoiding collisions with obstacles which may exist in the surrounding environment. There are two common approaches for controlling such robot manipulators: forward kinematics and inverse kinematics. Forward kinematics approach can be better realized in joint space where the changes in joint angle values would immediately affect end-effector position. In contrary, inverse kinematics can be viewed as Cartesian space mapping problem where exact joint angle values are required to be computed according to the input of desired end-effector position. Thus heuristic approach may offer rich dividends in tackling this issue. Kim and Lee [1] proposed a hybrid algorithm with fuzzy logic and the procedure does not require solving the inverse kinematics of manipulators. Behesti and Tehrani [2] also used fuzzy

© Springer International Publishing Switzerland 2015
B.K. Panigrahi et al. (Eds.): SEMCCO 2014, LNCS 8947, pp. 596–605, 2015.
DOI: 10.1007/978-3-319-20294-5_51

logic concept and obstacle avoidance. Nearchou [3] proposed a genetic algorithm to determine the solution set of joint angles. Secară and Vlădăreanu [4] presented a strategy for obstacles avoidance of a redundant manipulator based on an iterative genetic algorithm. The objective of the strategy is to simultaneously minimize the end-effector location error and the manipulator total joint displacement while the collision with the obstacles is avoided. Zhang and Wang [5] developed a recurrent neural network and applied for kinematic control of redundant manipulators with obstacle avoidance capability. Differential Evolution [6] has also been used in robot manipulator problems [7, 8]. Particle Swarm Optimization which uses a swarm, moving in a continuously adjusting velocity towards the global best caught the eye of many researchers [9–11] as a possible route in achieving suitable algorithm for trajectory planning and obstacle avoidance. When enhancing the performance of the algorithm, issues such as avoiding singularities [12] and including a feedback using image processing was also addressed in [13, 14]. Goh and Ponnambalam [15] tested the performance of four variants of PSO for obstacle avoidance control of redundant robots.

The aim of this paper is to further improve the performance of the variants proposed by Goh and Ponnambalam [15] and also to propose a differential evolution algorithm. The paper is organized as follows. Section 2 presents the problem statement. Sections 3 and 4 present the implementation details of PSO and DE respectively. Section 5 details the parameter fine tuning for PSO and DE. Results and discussion are presented in Sect. 6. Conclusion is presented in Sect. 7.

2 Problem Statement

The objective of this paper is to propose DE and PSO to find Collision-free configuration of a 5-DOF planar redundant robot manipulator that allows the robot end effecter to travel from an initial position to the desired goal point with minimal error (greatest accuracy). The obstacles are static and presented as polygon in which closed loop of straight lines is formed. The performance of the proposed DE and the variants of PSO are evaluated.

2.1 Kinematics of a Robot Manipulator

A standard method introduced by Denavit and Hartenberg (D-H) [16] is useful to define joint matrices and link matrices to standardize the coordinate frames for spatial linkages. In the D-H convention, coordinate frames are attached to the joints between two links such that one transformation is associated with the joint and the second is associated with the link. This concept will allow the user to define the entire robot kinematics with a strict but yet simple representation. With respect to the robot manipulator, the corresponding D-H table is presented in Table 1. When the D-H table is available, devising the corresponding transformation matrix is a simple task. Take one row at a time and substitute appropriately those values to the standard transformation matrix which is given in Fig. 1.

Table 1. Denavit-Hartenberg table

i	a_{i-1}	a_{i-1}	d_i	θ_i
1	0	0	0	θ_1
2	0	l_1	0	θ_2
3	0	l_2	0	θ_3
4	0	l_3	0	θ_4
5	0	l_4	0	θ_5

$$
{}^{i-1}_{i}T = \begin{bmatrix}
c\theta_i & -s\theta_i & 0 & a_{i-1} \\
s\theta_i c\alpha_{i-1} & c\theta_i c\alpha_{i-1} & -s\alpha_{i-1} & -s\alpha_{i-1}d_i \\
s\theta_i s\alpha_{i-1} & c\theta_i s\alpha_{i-1} & c\alpha_{i-1} & c\alpha_{i-1}d_i \\
0 & 0 & 0 & 1
\end{bmatrix}
$$

Fig. 1. The standard transformation matrix

$$
\begin{bmatrix} x \\ y \\ 0 \\ 1 \end{bmatrix} = \begin{bmatrix} c\theta_1 & -s\theta_1 & 0 & 0 \\ s\theta_1 & c\theta_1 & 0 & 0 \\ 0 & 0 & 1 & 0 \\ 0 & 0 & 0 & 1 \end{bmatrix} \begin{bmatrix} c\theta_2 & -s\theta_2 & 0 & l_1 \\ s\theta_2 & c\theta_2 & 0 & 0 \\ 0 & 0 & 1 & 0 \\ 0 & 0 & 0 & 1 \end{bmatrix} \begin{bmatrix} c\theta_3 & -s\theta_3 & 0 & l_2 \\ s\theta_3 & c\theta_3 & 0 & 0 \\ 0 & 0 & 1 & 0 \\ 0 & 0 & 0 & 1 \end{bmatrix} \begin{bmatrix} c\theta_4 & -s\theta_4 & 0 & l_3 \\ s\theta_4 & c\theta_4 & 0 & 0 \\ 0 & 0 & 1 & 0 \\ 0 & 0 & 0 & 1 \end{bmatrix} \begin{bmatrix} c\theta_5 & -s\theta_5 & 0 & l_4 \\ s\theta_5 & c\theta_5 & 0 & 0 \\ 0 & 0 & 1 & 0 \\ 0 & 0 & 0 & 1 \end{bmatrix} \begin{bmatrix} l_5 \\ 0 \\ 0 \\ 1 \end{bmatrix}
$$

Fig. 2. Transformation matrices to obtain end effecter position

Using the above transformation matrix if all the link lengths and joint angles are known, by doing the matrix multiplication as shown in Fig. 2, position of the end effecter could be calculated.

3 Objective Function and Constraint

The main objective of this paper is to minimize the positional error between the end-effector and goal point. Also, the secondary objective is to satisfy the constraint of collision-free positioning of the robot manipulator. Considering the ability for robot to avoid collision with obstacle in workspace during movement to goal point, an additional weight called 'collision' is added to the error equation. Considering the ability for robot to avoid collision with obstacle in workspace during movement to goal point, this is included in the objective function with the property shown in Eq. (1).

$$
collision = \begin{cases} 1, & \text{if collision - free movement} \\ 0, & \text{otherwise} \end{cases} \tag{1}
$$

Simple logic is used to check if any of the links are colliding with any boundary of an obstacle. The process is carried out by iteratively selecting each link and by testing if the coordinates of the link cut through the area belongs to the obstacle. If it cuts through, then an additional weight is added to the error function which will result the specific joint angle combination to be disregarded during the search process.

The objective function is to minimize the error and to avoid collision. The objective function is shown in Eq. (2).

$$error = \sqrt{(Target_X - Current_X)^2 + (Target_Y - Current_Y)^2} + Collution \qquad (2)$$

Where $Target_x$ and $Cuurent_x$ are the x-cordinastes of the goal position and the current position, and $Target_y$ and $Cuurent_y$ are the y-cordinastes of the goal position and the current position of the manipulator.

Singularities of the kinematic mapping, which determines the position of the end–effecter in terms of the manipulator's joint variables, may impede control algorithms, lead to large joint velocities, forces and torques and reduce instantaneous mobility. However they can also enable fine control, and the singularities exhibited by trajectories of the points in the end–effecter can be used to mechanical advantage.

Strictly speaking singularity can be simply defined as two links working as one link, which results the manipulator to have a lesser degree of freedom. Avoiding singularities is a necessity in a robotic manipulator.

Joint angle values are checked after each iteration and if the joint angle lie between −2.5 and 2.5°, it is randomly set to a different value to avoid singularities.

4 Differential Evolution

Differential Evolution [6] is a metaheuristic search algorithm tries to optimize the candidate solution space by iteratively making modifications to the existing solution. Even though the most optimum answer is not guaranteed, it is possible to obtain a solution with an acceptable error margin.

4.1 Generation of Initial Solution

Initial solution space generated is common to both PSO and DE algorithms. User can define the number of solution in a sample space but number of members in one solution is fixed as the numbers of joint angles which is fixed as five. Keeping practical aspects such as maximum and minimum servo angle, solution space should be randomly generated to accommodate the range of the servo motor.

Given below are sample strings (target vectors) with angles generated randomly within a specified range.

$$\begin{bmatrix} 65.74 & 12.77 & -51.69 & 24.44 & 76.73 \end{bmatrix}$$
$$\begin{bmatrix} 15.13 & -76.71 & -64.62 & 35.47 & 64.00 \end{bmatrix}$$

$$\begin{bmatrix} -60.85 & 41.96 & 71.60 & -45.14 & -14.49 \end{bmatrix}$$

The three main steps in DE are Mutation, Crossover and Selection and the implementation details are explained below.

4.1.1 Mutation

Mutation operation is applied to every individual in the population. Equation (1) is used to do mutation.

$$M_a = I_{r1} + MF * (I_{r2} - I_{r3}) \tag{1}$$

Where, M_a is the donor vector, MF is the mutation factor and I_{r1}, I_{r12} and I_{r3} are randomly selected target vectors.

4.1.2 Crossover

Crossover operation is performed taking one joint angle at a time in to consideration. A random number is generated and if it is larger than the crossover factor, corresponding crossover vector point will be replaced by the donor vector point. Otherwise crossover vector point will use the value of the target vector point. Equations (2), (3) and (4) are used for crossover.

$$K = rand \rightarrow \in [0, 1] \tag{2}$$

$$K \geq CF, C_{a,b} = M_{a,b} \tag{3}$$

$$K < CF, C_{a,b} = I_{a,b} \tag{4}$$

Where, K is the random number, $M_{a,b}$ is the donor vector, $I_{a,b}$ is the target vector, CF is the crossover factor and $C_{a,b}$ is the trail Vector Point.

4.1.3 Selection

The selection operator of DE adopts a one-to-one competition between the target vector and the trial vector. If the objective function value of the trial vector is less than or equal to that of the target vector, then the trial vector will survive into the next generation, otherwise, the target vector will enter the next generation.

5 Particle Swarm Optimization

Particle Swarm Optimization [17] is an optimization method which uses an existing candidate solution iteratively to achieve the solution with the required quality. In PSO existing solution will move in the search space according to a simple mathematical formula over the particles position and velocity, up until it finds the optimal solution. In addition each particle will remember the best solution achieved (personnel best) and exchange information with other particles to determine the best solution (global best). Particles will move into a new position by adjusting its velocity in every generation. Thus the new position will be the sum of previous position and the current velocity.

In a standard PSO there are only two equations governing the performance. The first equation will update the velocity while second equation will update the position.

$$V_{id} = wV_{id} + C_1 r_1 (P_{ib} - X_{id}) + C_2 r_2 (P_{gb} - X_{id}) \qquad (5)$$

$$X_{id} = X_{id} + V_{id} \qquad (6)$$

V_{id} is the current/new velocity while X_{id} is the current/new position. w is the current velocity factor and r_1 and r_2 are random numbers distributed uniformly in [0, 1]. P_{ib} is the personnel best solution achieved by the selected particle whereas Pgb is the global best solution achieved by the whole Swarm. C_1 and C_2 are weights for personnel best and global best.

5.1 Variants of PSO

The four variants used by Chyan and Ponnambalam [14] are used in this paper. By conducting various experiments the performance of these four variants are improved. The performance improvement is by adopting suitable weights and by employing mechanisms to escape from local optima, if it happens. Reader can refer [14] for details of the four variants namely, namely PSO-C, PSO-W, qPSO-C and qPSO-W.

6 Parameter Fine Tuning for DE and PSO

Fine tuning parameters are an essential aspect as it aids immensely to enhance the performance of the respective algorithm. However deciding on what is the best parameter takes ample lot of time as many experiments have to be conducted. Nevertheless when an algorithm is fine-tuned perfectly, boost in performance can be quite rewarding. After conducting sensitivity analysis on the parameters, it is found that the mutation factor of 0.7 and the crossover factor of 0.5 perform better for DE algorithm implemented in this paper.

A rigorous analysis on the parameters for PSO-c and PSO-W variants is conducted and the parameters used in the paper are provided in table below. It is found that with these parameters and a local search approach implemented in the PSO variants, which is explained in Sect. 6.1 could obtain better results than the results reported in [14]. For the better understanding the parameter used in [14] and the optimal parameters found in this paper after the analysis conducted are presented in Table 2.

Table 2. Details of parameter fine tuning

Variant	Parameters	Parameters used in [15]		Parameter's used in this paper	
		Range tested	Optimal parameter	Range tested	Optimal parameter linearly decreasing from 0.9 to 0.4
All PSO variants	w	0.9 to 0.4	Linearly decreasing from 0.9 to 0.4 for first 100 iterations	0.9 to 0.4	Linearly decreasing from 0.9 to 0.4 for first 100 iterations
PSO-W	C_1	0.1 to 3	0.7	0.4 to 1.7	0.4
	C_2	0.1 to 3	1.0	0.4 to 1.7	0.6
PSO-C	C_1	2 to 6	5.8	2 to 4	2.4
	C_2	2 to 6	2.8	2 to 4	3.2
DE	Mutation factor	n/a	n/a	0.1 to 1.0	0.7
	Cross over factor	n/a	n/a	0.1 to 1.0	0.5

6.1   Strategies to Escape from Local Optima

One of the main issues of the metaheuristic search algorithms is that they converge too fast at times and due to this it may get stuck in local optima. Getting stuck in local optima may significantly reduce the performances of these algorithms. Identification of entrapment in local optima could be identified by a counter, where the counter is incremented by one when the quality of the solution is not improved. When this counter reaches a certain fixed value it could be concluded that the search process stuck in a local optima. If the solution gets stuck in local optima, it is difficult to move out from the local optima. To avoid this situation, an Iterated Local Search approach is adopted in this paper. The approach is to regenerate the solution space after a user defined number of counts when the process stuck in local optima. Another approach followed is the elite preserve strategy. Five best solutions in the previous generation is also randomly injected into the next generation. The PSO variants perform better with the optimal parameters and the strategies adopted in this paper. The other parameter values required for the variants are the same as in [15].

7   Experimental Conditions

The experimental conditions of the simulations conducted are detailed in this section.
The initial position of the manipulator is at X = Y = 0. The target position is X = Y = 22. The termination condition for all the algorithms is 500. Maximum error margin is set to 0.1. The population size is 60. The maximum loop count to start regeneration is set 50. Experiments are conducted with no obstacle, one obstacle and

two obstacles in the environment. The obstacles are in the shape of rectangle with different positions.

The X-Y coordinates of the vertices of the obstacles are given below.

Obstacle-1 = [(−10, 8), (−10, 16), (11, 16), (11, 8), (−10, 8]

Obstacle-2 = [(28, 15), (28, 35), (38, 35), (38 15), (28, 15)]

8 Results and Discussion

The results of the experiments conducted in three scenarios are presented in this section. Each experiment is conducted ten time and the average values are reported. The measures used to evaluate the algorithms are average error, average converging time (in Sec) and average loop count. Table 3 shows the performance results of the algorithms in the environment with no obstacles.

In the above table performances of each of the algorithms is analyzed. A main criterion of concern is if algorithm can produce a result with an acceptable error margin. As it is illustrated from the above table all the algorithms will converge within the given margin. So in order to compare the algorithms, secondary criterions such as Converging Time and Loop Count should be taken in to consideration. Considering the loop count it is revealed from the above results that qPSO-C is the best algorithm closely followed by PSO-C for free space.

Table 4 shows the performance results of the algorithms in the environment with one obstacle.

It is evident from the results in Table 4 that all the algorithms converge within the acceptable error margin and thus secondary evaluation criterions should be considered. Above results for one obstacle space reveals a significant change with the results from the free space condition with PSO-C performs better over other algorithms.

Table 5 shows the performance results of the algorithms in the environment with two obstacles. Still PSO-C performs better over other algorithms. It is also observed that the performance of DE is improving as the number of obstacles increase.

Table 3. Performance of the algorithms in free space (no obstacles)

Free space	DE	PSO_C	PSO_W	qPSO_C	qPSO_W
Average error	0.0788	0.0589	0.0657	0.0790	0.0694
Average converging time (s)	0.4787	0.1724	0.3908	0.1832	0.3969
Average loop count	46.8	9.3	41.0	8.1	31.7

Table 4. Performance of the algorithms with one obstacle

One obstacle	DE	PSO_C	PSO_W	qPSO_C	qPSO_W
Average error	0.0715	0.0675	0.0742	0.0676	0.0632
Average converging time (s)	0.6028	0.1901	0.5501	0.2534	0.7313
Average loop count	42.0	7.1	35.4	8.7	48.8

Table 5. Performance results of the algorithms with two obstacles

Two obstacle	DE	PSO_C	PSO_W	qPSO_C	qPSO_W
Average error	0.0781	0.0669	0.0679	0.5080	0.0738
Average converging Time (s)	0.7093	0.2474	0.6803	0.2845	0.9858
Average loop count	37.4	7.7	35.6	8.3	46.8

9   Conclusions

Trajectory planning and obstacle avoidance problem for a robot manipulator is studied in this research. Four variants (PSO-C, PSO-W, qPSO-C and qPSO-W) of Particle Swarm Optimization (PSO) and Differential Evolution (DE) are proposed to solve this problem. Simulation experiments on a 5 degree-of-freedom (DOF) robot manipulator in an environment with static obstacles are conducted. Joint angles are used to generate the strings for DE and PSO. Mechanisms are introduced in these algorithms to escape from local optima during the search process. The performance of the four variants of PSO compared to the results reported in the literature. With the optimal parameters identified through sensitivity analysis, the four PSO variants are performing better than the earlier reported results. Performances of all five algorithms are evaluated. Since all the algorithms converge to a satisfactory error margin, convergence time and loop count are used as the parameters for comparison. Based on the results presented, it is concluded that qPSO-C is performing better in free space while PSO-C is performing better when obstacles are present. The performance of DE improves with the increase in number of obstacles. Additional experiments are to be conducted to test the performance of DE. Future work is also planned to conduct experiments in 3D real environments with feedback control to minimize the error.

References

1. Kim, S.W., Lee, J.J.: Resolved motion rate control of redundant robots using an adaptive fuzzy logic. Second IEEE International Conference on Fuzzy Systems, pp. 333–338(1993)
2. Beheshti, M.T.H., Tehrani, A.K.: Obstacle avoidance for kinematically redundant robots using an adaptive fuzzy logic algorithm. In: Proceedings of the American Control Conference, vol. 2, pp. 1371–1375 (1999)
3. Nearchou, A.C.: Solving the inverse kinematics problem of redundant robots operating in complex environments via a modified genetic algorithm. Mech. Mach. Theory 33(3), 273–292 (1998)
4. Secară, C., Vlădăreanu, L.: Iterative genetic algorithm based strategy for obstacles avoidance of a redundant manipulator. In: Proceedings of American Conference on Applied Mathematics, Stevens Point, pp. 361–366, USA (2010)
5. Zhang, Y., Wang, J.: Obstacle avoidance for kinematically redundant manipulators using a dual neural network. IEEE Trans. Syst. Man Cybern. Part B: Cybern. 34(1), 752–759 (2004)
6. Price, K., Storn, R.: Differential evolution – a simple and efficient heuristic for global optimization over continuous spaces. J. Global Optim. II, 341–359 (1997)

7. Liu, Yu., Ni, F.-l., Liu, H., Wen-fu, X.: Enhancing pose accuracy of space robot by improved differential evolution. J. Cent. South Univ. **19**, 933–943 (2012)

8. Saravanan, R., Ramabalan, S., Balamurugan, C.: Evolutionary collision-free optimal trajectory planning. Int. J. Adv. Manuf. Technol. **36**, 1234–1251 (2008)

9. Gang, H., Li, D., Yang, J.: A research on particle swarm optimization and its application in robot manipulators. In: Pacific-Asia Workshop on Computational Intelligence and Industrial Application, PACIIA, vol. 2, pp. 377–381 (2008)

10. Eberhart, R.C., Kennedy, J.: A new optimizer using particle swarm theory. In: Proceedings of the Sixth International Symposium on Micro Machine and Human Science, vol. 1, pp. 39–43 (1995)

11. Wen, X., Sheng, D., Huang, J.: A Hybrid Particle Swarm Optimization for Manipulator Inverse Kinematics Control. In: Huang, D.-S., Wunsch II, D.C., Levine, D.S., Jo, K.-H. (eds.) ICIC 2008. LNCS, vol. 5226, pp. 784–791. Springer, Heidelberg (2008)

12. Donelan, P.S.: Singularities of robot manipulators. Singul. Theory, pp. 189–217 (2007)

13. Desa, S.M., Qussay, A.S.: Image subtraction for real time moving object extraction. In: International Conference on Computer Graphics, Imaging and Visualization, CGIV 2004. Proceedings, pp. 41–45 (2004)

14. Qidwai, U., Chi-hau, C.: Digital image processing: an algorithmic approach with MATLAB. Chapman & Hall/CRC, London (2009)

15. Chyan, G.S., Ponnambalam, S.G.: Obstacle avoidance control of redundant robots using variants of particle swarm optimization. Rob. Comput.-Integr. Manuf. **28**(2), 147–153 (2012)

16. Hartenberg, R.S., Denavit, J.: A kinematic notation for lower-pair mechanisms based on matrices. ASME Journal of Applied Mechanics **22**(77), 215–221 (1995)

17. Eberhart, R.C., Kennedy, J.: A new optimizer using particle swarm theory. In: Proceedings of the sixth international symposium on micro machine and human science, vol. 1, pp. 39–43 (1995)

Meta-Cognitive Learning Neural Classifier for Alzheimer's Disease Detection

B.S. Mahanand[1]([✉]), G. Sateesh Babu[2], and S. Suresh[2]

[1] Department of Information Science and Engineering, Sri Jayachamarajendra
College of Engineering, Mysore, India
bsmahanand@sjce.ac.in
[2] School of Computer Engineering, Nanyang Technological University,
Singapore, Singapore
{sbgiduthuri,ssundaram}@ntu.edu.sg

Abstract. In this paper, we present an approach for Alzheimer's
Disease (AD) detection from Magnetic Resonance Images (MRI) using
Meta-cognitive Radial Basis Function Network (McRBFN) classifier.
The McRBFN classifier uses Voxel Based Morphometric (VBM) fea-
tures extracted from MRI and employs a sequential Projection Based
Learning (PBL) algorithm for classification. The meta-cognitive learning present in PBL-McRBFN helps in selecting proper samples to learn
based on its current knowledge and evolve the architecture automatically.
The study has been conducted using the well-known Alzheimer's Disease
Neuroimaging Initiative (ADNI) data set. We compared the performance
of the proposed classifier with reported results of existing classifiers in
the literature. The performance results clearly indicates the better performance of PBL-McRBFN classifier for AD detection.

Keywords: Alzheimer's disease · Magnetic resonance imaging · Voxel-
based morphometry · Meta-cognitive learning algorithm

1 Introduction

Alzheimer's Disease (AD) is a progressive neurodegenerative disorder that causes
memory loss, problems in learning, confusion and poor judgment [1]. AD is considered to be one of the most common causes of dementia (clinical syndrome
characterized by significant loss or decline in memory and other cognitive abilities) among elderly persons. Around $60-80\%$ of age related dementia is caused
due to AD [2]. The only way to make a definitive diagnosis of AD is from a brain
autopsy revealing the characteristics of the neurofibrillary tangles and amyloid
plaques that define AD. Early detection of AD using non-invasive imaging techniques will help in providing assistance to them and thereby one can slowdown
the progression [3,4]. Magnetic Resonance Imaging (MRI) is a powerful brain
imaging tools to understand the neural changes at both the structural and functional levels related to AD.

© Springer International Publishing Switzerland 2015
B.K. Panigrahi et al. (Eds.): SEMCCO 2014, LNCS 8947, pp. 606–617, 2015.
DOI: 10.1007/978-3-319-20294-5_52

Early detection of AD from MRI requires appropriate methods to detect, locate and quantify tissue atrophy in the brain. Primarily, the visual assessment of the degree of atrophy in the neuroanatomical structures is performed by an expert using MRI. However, this may be adequate in a normal clinical setting, but is not enough to get quantitative measures such as the fine incremental grades of atrophy and overall brain volume. Two major ways of estimating the brain volume changes from the MRI are: (i) Regions-of-Interest (ROI) approach; (ii) whole brain morphometric approach.

In the ROI approach, a volumetric analysis is performed by manually delineating specific brain regions. In practice, a priori knowledge about abnormal regions is not always available. However, in AD diagnosis, a lot of studies rely on manual tracing of hippocampus and entorhinal cortex which is laborious and time consuming [5,6].Therefore, several approaches that enable the assessment of the whole brain have been reported in the literature [7–9]. Voxel Based Morphometry (VBM) is one of the widely used, fully automated, whole brain morphometric analysis [9]. VBM is based on the Statistical Parametric Mapping (SPM) method, often employed for the investigation of tissue volume changes between the brain MRI scans of the diseased group versus the normal persons.

Machine learning algorithms for AD detection requires samples with significant information as training samples. Ideal classifier for AD detection must incorporate sample selection in training for effective learning. Recent studies on human learning [10] reveal that the learning process is effective when the learners adopt self-regulation in the learning process using the concept of meta-cognition. Briefly, meta-cognition means cognition about cognition. In a meta-cognitive framework, human-beings think about their cognitive processes, develop new strategies to improve their cognitive skills and evaluate the information contained in their memory.

Various meta-cognitive learning algorithms have been proposed and are available in the literature [11–13]. Several machine learning algorithms have been developed based on the models of human meta-cognition for real-valued neural networks [14], complex-valued neural networks [15–17] and neuro-fuzzy inference systems [18–20]. Recently proposed projection based learning in Meta-cognitive Radial Basis Function Network (PBL-McRBFN) [21] uses human meta-cognitive principles for effective learning and have been successfully used to solve biomedical problems [22–24]. PBL-McRBFN begins with zero hidden neuron and adds neuron during the learning process to obtain a compact structure. For the newly added neuron, the input/hidden layer parameters are fixed based on the current sample and the output weights are estimated by minimizing an error function given by a hinge loss function. The problem of finding the optimal weights is first formulated as a nonlinear programming problem using the principles of minimization. The projection based learning algorithm then converts the optimization problem into solving a system of linear equations and provides a solution for the optimal weights corresponding to the minimum error. Hence, in this paper we propose an efficient classification method PBL-McRBFN for AD detection.

The rest of this paper is organized as follows. Materials and methods section describes the data set, feature extraction procedure and a brief review of PBL-McRBFN classifier. In the results section, experiments on ADNI data set is presented to demonstrate the PBL-McRBFN classification accuracy on AD detection. Finally, the conclusions from this study are summarized in the conclusion section.

2   Materials and Methods

This section presents a brief description of the data used, the feature extraction process using the VBM analysis and also a brief review of the sequential learning PBL-McRBFN classifier.

2.1   Data Set

Data used in the preparation of this article were obtained from the Alzheimer's Disease Neuroimaging Initiative (ADNI) database (adni.loni.usc.edu). The ADNI was launched in 2003 by the National Institute on Aging (NIA), the National Institute of Biomedical Imaging and Bioengineering (NIBIB), the Food and Drug Administration (FDA), private pharmaceutical companies and non-profit organizations, as a USD 60 million, 5-year public-private partnership. The primary goal of ADNI has been to test whether serial Magnetic Resonance Imaging (MRI), positron emission tomography (PET), other biological markers, and clinical and neuropsychological assessment can be combined to measure the progression of mild cognitive impairment (MCI) and early Alzheimer's disease (AD). Determination of sensitive and specific markers of very early AD progression is intended to aid researchers and clinicians to develop new treatments and monitor their effectiveness, as well as lessen the time and cost of clinical trials. The Principal Investigator of this initiative is Michael W. Weiner, MD, VA Medical Center and University of California San Francisco. ADNI is the result of efforts of many co-investigators from a broad range of academic institutions and private corporations, and subjects have been recruited from over 50 sites across the U.S. and Canada. The initial goal of ADNI was to recruit 800 subjects but ADNI has been followed by ADNI-GO and ADNI-2. To date these three protocols have recruited over 1500 adults, ages 55 to 90, to participate in the research, consisting of cognitively normal older individuals, people with early or late MCI, and people with early AD. The follow up duration of each group is specified in the protocols for ADNI-1, ADNI-2 and ADNI-GO. Subjects originally recruited for ADNI-1 and ADNI-GO had the option to be followed in ADNI-2. For up-to-date information, see www.adni-info.org.

All 432 elder persons (232 normal persons and 200 AD patients) available in the ADNI data set as of February 2012 is considered in this study. Standard 1.5 T screening/baseline T1-weighted images obtained using volumetric 3D MPRAGE protocol with resolutions ranging from 0.9 mm × 0.9 mm × 1.20 mm to 1.3 mm × 1.3 mm × 1.20 mm were included from the ADNI data set. The detailed information of the MRI protocols and preprocessing steps are presented in [25]. The demographics for the 432 elderly persons used in our study is shown in Table 1.

Table 1. Demographic information of ADNI data used in our study

	Normal Persons	AD Patients
No. of persons	232	200
Percentage of Male	51.7%	51.5%
Age(mean±std)	76.01±5.00	75.65±7.70
MMSE(mean±std)	29.11±1.00	23.29±2.05
CDR 0/0.5/1/2	232/0/0/0	0/98/102/0

2.2 Feature Extraction

A feature extraction method based on the VBM is employed in this work [26]. VBM is a fast and fully automated approach to identify the regional gray matter differences between the brains of normal persons and AD patients [9]. The steps involved in our VBM analysis can be summarized as: unified segmentation, smoothing and statistical testing. The unified segmentation step is a generative modeling approach, in which tissue segmentation, bias correction and image registration are combined in a single model [27]. The segmented and registered gray matter images are then smoothed by convolving with an isotropic Gaussian kernel. Here, a 10 mm full-width at half-maximum kernel was employed. After performing the unified segmentation and smoothing steps, finally statistical tests were conducted. Statistical testing uses a general linear model which is based on the random Gaussian field theory [28]. A two-sample t-test is performed on the smoothed images of normal persons and AD patients and a multiple comparison correction method, namely, family wise error with a $P < 0.05$ has been applied.

From this unified VBM analysis, significant regions with an increase in gray matter density in the normal persons relative to the AD patients are obtained. The voxel location of significant regions are used as mask in order to extract the features from all the segmented gray matter images. The feature extraction process computes a vector with all the gray matter segmentation values for the voxel locations included in each of the VBM identified regions. The extracted features (gray matter tissue probability values) are then used as an input to the sequential PBL-McRBFN classifier.

2.3 A Brief Review of the Sequential PBL-McRBFN Classification Algorithm

The objective of the PBL-McRBFN classifier is to approximate the function $\mathbf{x}^t \in \Re^m \rightarrow \mathbf{y}^t \in \Re^n$. McRBFN architecture is same as in [29], has cognitive component and meta-cognitive component.

Cognitive Component of McRBFN. The cognitive component of McRBFN is a radial basis function network. The hidden layer employs the Gaussian activation function. Without loss of generality, we assume that the McRBFN builds

K Gaussian neurons from $t-1$ training samples. For a given input $\mathbf{x}^t$, the predicted output $\widehat{y}_j^t$ is given as

$$\widehat{y}_j^t = \sum_{k=1}^{K} w_{kj} h_k^t, \quad j = 1, \cdots, n \tag{1}$$

Where w_{kj} is the weight connecting the kth hidden neuron to the jth output neuron and h_k^t is the response of the kth hidden neuron to the input $\mathbf{x}^t$ is given by

$$h_k^t = exp\left(-\frac{\|\mathbf{x}^t - \boldsymbol{\mu}_k^l\|^2}{(\sigma_k^l)^2}\right) \tag{2}$$

Where $\boldsymbol{\mu}_k^l \in \Re^m$ is the center and $\sigma_k^l \in \Re^+$ is the width of the kth hidden neuron. Here, the superscript l represents the corresponding class of the hidden neuron. **Projection based learning algorithm** works on the principle of minimization of error function. For t consecutive samples, the error function is

$$J(\mathbf{W}) = \frac{1}{2} \sum_{i=1}^{t} \sum_{j=1}^{n} \begin{cases} 0 & \text{if } y_j^i \widehat{y}_j^i > 1 \\ \left(y_j^i - \widehat{y}_j^i\right)^2 & \text{otherwise} \end{cases} \tag{3}$$

The optimal output weights $(\mathbf{W}^* \in \Re^{K \times n})$ are estimated such that $J(\mathbf{W}^*)$ is minimum. The solution can be determined as $\mathbf{W}^* = \mathbf{A}^{-1}\mathbf{B}$. Where the projection matrix $\mathbf{A} \in \Re^{K \times K}$ and the output matrix $\mathbf{B} \in \Re^{K \times n}$ are given by

$$a_{kp} = \sum_{i=1}^{t} h_k^i h_p^i, \quad k = 1, \cdots, K; \ p = 1, \cdots, K \tag{4}$$

$$b_{pj} = \sum_{i=1}^{t} h_p^i y_j^i, \quad p = 1, \cdots, K; \ j = 1, \cdots, n \tag{5}$$

Meta-Cognitive Component of McRBFN. The meta-cognitive component contains a dynamic model of the cognitive component, the knowledge measures and the self-regulated thresholds. During the learning process, the meta-cognitive component monitors the cognitive component and updates its dynamic model of the cognitive component.

The meta-cognitive component knowledge measures are defined as shown below:

Predicted class label $(\widehat{c}^t)$: $\widehat{c}^t = arg \ \max_{j \in 1, \cdots, n} \widehat{y}_j^t$

Maximum hinge loss (E^t): The hinge loss $\left(\mathbf{e}^t = \left[e_1^t, \cdots, e_j^t, \cdots, e_n^t\right]^T\right) \in \Re^n$ is

$$e_j^t = \begin{cases} 0 & \text{if } y_j^t \widehat{y}_j^t > 1 \\ y_j^t - \widehat{y}_j^t & \text{otherwise} \end{cases} \quad j = 1, \cdots, n \tag{6}$$

The maximum absolute hinge loss (E^t) is given by

$$E^t = \max_{j \in 1, 2, \cdots, n} \left|e_j^t\right| \tag{7}$$

Confidence of Classifier $(\hat{p}(c^t|\mathbf{x}^t))$ is given as

$$\hat{p}(j|\mathbf{x}^t) = \frac{min(1, max(-1, \hat{y}_j^t)) + 1}{2}, \quad j = c^t \tag{8}$$

Class-wise Significance (ψ_c): The class-wise significance (ψ_c) is defined as

$$\psi_c = \frac{1}{K^c} \sum_{k=1}^{K^c} h\left(\mathbf{x}^t, \boldsymbol{\mu}_k^c\right) \tag{9}$$

For more details on the knowledge measures of McRBFN, one can refer to [29].

Learning Strategies. The meta-cognitive component comprises of four learning strategies using the knowledge measures and the self-regulated thresholds and directly addresses the basic principles of self-regulated human learning (i.e., *what-to-learn*, *when-to-learn* and *how-to-learn*) and selects the best strategy for the new training sample.

Sample delete strategy is given by

$$\hat{c}^t == c^t \ \textbf{AND} \ \hat{p}(c^t|\mathbf{x}^t) \geq \beta_d \tag{10}$$

Where β_d is the deletion threshold.

Neuron growth strategy is given by

$$(\hat{c}^t \neq c^t \ \textbf{OR} \ E^t \geq \beta_a) \ \textbf{AND} \ \psi_c(\mathbf{x}^t) \leq \beta_c \tag{11}$$

Where β_c is the knowledge measurement threshold and β_a is the self-adaptive addition threshold. The β_a is adapted as $\beta_a := \delta\beta_a + (1 - \delta)E^t$ and δ is the slope that controls rate of self-adaptation and is set close to 1. Based on the nearest neuron distances, the new hidden neuron center $(\boldsymbol{\mu}_{K+1}^c)$ and width (σ_{K+1}^c) parameters are determined for the different overlapping/no-overlapping conditions as in [21,29]. When a neuron is added to McRBFN, the output weights are initialized as:
The size of matrix $\mathbf{A}$ is increased from $K \times K$ to $(K+1) \times (K+1)$

$$\mathbf{A}^t = \left[\begin{array}{c|c} \mathbf{A}_{K \times K}^{t-1} + (\mathbf{h}^t)^T \mathbf{h}^t & \mathbf{a}_{K+1}^T \\ \hline \mathbf{a}_{K+1} & a_{K+1,K+1} \end{array} \right] \tag{12}$$

Where $\mathbf{h}^t = [h_1^t, h_2^t, \cdots, h_K^t]$ is a vector of the existing K hidden neurons response for new (t^{th}) training sample. Existing hidden neurons are used as pseudo-samples to calculate $\mathbf{a}_{K+1} \in \Re^{1 \times K}$ and $a_{K+1,K+1} \in \Re^+$ terms as

$$a_{K+1,p} = \sum_{i=1}^{K+1} h_{K+1}^i h_p^i, \ p = 1, \cdots, K \tag{13}$$

$$a_{K+1,K+1} = \sum_{i=1}^{K+1} h_{K+1}^i h_{K+1}^i \tag{14}$$

B matrix size is increased from $K \times n$ to $(K+1) \times n$

$$\mathbf{B}^t_{(K+1) \times n} = \begin{bmatrix} \mathbf{B}^{t-1}_{K \times n} + (\mathbf{h}^t)^T (\mathbf{y}^t)^T \\ \mathbf{b}_{K+1} \end{bmatrix} \tag{15}$$

and $\mathbf{b}_{K+1} \in \Re^{1 \times n}$ is a row vector assigned as

$$b_{K+1,j} = \sum_{i=1}^{K+1} h^i_{K+1} \tilde{y}^i_j, \; j = 1, \cdots, n \tag{16}$$

Where $\tilde{y}^i$ is the pseudo-output for the ith pseudo sample or hidden neuron $(\boldsymbol{\mu}^l_i)$ given as

$$\tilde{y}^i_j = \begin{cases} 1 & if \quad l = j \\ -1 & otherwise \end{cases} \; j = 1, \cdots, n \tag{17}$$

The $\mathbf{h}^t$ vector in Eqs. (12) and (16) contains very small values, since t^{th} sample is added as a hidden neuron which is significantly different from the existing hidden neurons. After neglecting $\mathbf{h}^t$ vector in Eqs. (12) and (16) the output weights are estimated finally as

$$\begin{bmatrix} \mathbf{W}^t_K \\ \mathbf{w}^t_{K+1} \end{bmatrix} = \begin{bmatrix} \mathbf{A}^{t-1}_{K \times K} & \mathbf{a}^T_{K+1} \\ \mathbf{a}_{K+1} & a_{K+1,K+1} \end{bmatrix}^{-1} \begin{bmatrix} \mathbf{B}^{t-1}_{K \times n} \\ \mathbf{b}_{K+1} \end{bmatrix} \tag{18}$$

where $\mathbf{W}^t_K$ is the output weight matrix for K hidden neurons, and $\mathbf{w}^t_{K+1}$ is the vector of output weights for new hidden neuron after learning from t^{th} sample.

Parameters update strategy is given by

$$c^t == \hat{c}^t \; \textbf{AND} \; E^t \geq \beta_u \tag{19}$$

Where β_u is the self-adaptive update threshold. The β_u is adapted based on the hinge loss as $\beta_u := \delta \beta_u + (1 - \delta) E^t$.

The $\mathbf{A} \in \Re^{K \times K}$ and $\mathbf{B} \in \Re^{K \times n}$ matrices updated as

$$\mathbf{A}^t = \mathbf{A}^{t-1} + (\mathbf{h}^t)^T \mathbf{h}^t; \; \mathbf{B}^t = \mathbf{B}^{t-1} + (\mathbf{h}^t)^T (\mathbf{y}^t)^T \tag{20}$$

Finally the output weights are updated as

$$\mathbf{W}^t_K = \mathbf{W}^{t-1}_K + (\mathbf{A}^t)^{-1} (\mathbf{h}^t)^T (\mathbf{e}^t)^T \tag{21}$$

where $\mathbf{e}^t$ is hinge loss for t^{th} sample as in Eq. (6).

Sample reserve strategy. If the new training sample does not satisfy either the sample deletion or the neuron growth or the cognitive component parameters update criterion, then the current sample is pushed to the rear end of data stream. Since McRBFN modifies the strategies based on the knowledge in the current sample, these samples may be used in later stage.

The training process stops when no further sample is available in the data stream or number of samples in the reserve remains same. For more details on the PBL-McRBFN classifier, one can refer to [21]. Next, we evaluate the performance of the PBL-McRBFN classifier on the well-known ADNI data set.

3   Results

In this section, we present the performance results of PBL-McRBFN classifier for AD detection using ADNI data set and also compare the performance with existing results in the literature.

The performance of the PBL-McRBFN classifier has been evaluated using the ADNI data set [25]. The complete ADNI data set consists of 232 normal persons and 200 AD patients. After verification of the unified segmentation results, 6 normal persons and 4 AD patients were excluded (due to bad segmentation) from the VBM analysis. In our study we considered 422 samples, for each sample 23797 morphometric features were obtained from the VBM analysis. In our classification study, for each of the 10 random trial experiment, 50 % samples are randomly chosen for training and the remaining used for testing. The classification performance of the PBL-McRBFN classifier using 23797 VBM features feature sets is presented in Table 2.

Table 2. Classification performance of PBL-McRBFN on the ADNI data set

Feature Type	No. of Features	K		Accuracy(%)	Sensitivity(%)	Specificity(%)
VBM	23797	64	Training	96.35±0.94	95.71±1.32	96.99±1.00
			Testing	85.27±1.02	82.03±2.34	88.49±1.77

PBL-McRBFN classification accuracy on the 23797 VBM features set is 85.27%. Next, we compare the PBL-McRBFN classification results using the ADNI data set with other reported results in the literature.

Comparison with Related Works: Here, we compare the results of the PBL-McRBFN classifier results with some recent results reported in the literature that are also based on ADNI data set for AD classification. In particular, four recent methods have been compared in Table 3. In [33], the automatic diagnostic capabilities of four structural MRI feature extraction methods (manifold based learning, hippocampal volume, cortical thickness and tensor-based morphometry) are compared using a Support Vector Machine (SVM) classifier. The best obtained result using the tensor-based morphometry is provided in Table 3. In [30], the Linear Program (LP) boosting method with a novel additional regularization have been proposed to incorporate the spatial smoothness of MRI feature space into the learning process. In [31], ten methods, which include five voxel-based methods, three cortical thickness based methods, and two hippocampus based methods are compared using a SVM classifier. The best result obtained using the voxel-wise Gray Matter (GM) features is provided in Table 3. In [32], 93 volumetric features extracted from the 93 ROI in GM density maps of MRI data have been used for classification.

From Table 3, it can be seen that among the VBM based features method, PBL-McRBFN's performance is 3% more than that of the LP boosting method

Table 3. Performance comparison with existing results on the ADNI data set

Feature Type	Algorithm	Subjects	Classification Accuracy(%)
VBM	PBL-McRBFN 50-50% train-test data Single trial	226 Normal 196 AD	**86.02**
VBM	PBL-McRBFN 50-50% train-test data 10 random trial	226 Normal 196 AD	**85.27**
VBM	PBL-McRBFN 75-25% train-test data Single trial	226 Normal 196 AD	**87.22**
VBM	PBL-McRBFN 95-5% train-test data Single trial	226 Normal 196 AD	**91.67**
VBM [30]	LP boosting leave-N-out cross-validation	94 Normal 89 AD	82.00
VBM [31]	SVM 50-50% train-test data Single trial	162 Normal 137 AD	88.58
93 ROI [32]	SVM 10-fold cross-validation	52 Normal 51 AD	86.20
Tensor-based morphometry [33]	SVM 95-5% train-test data leave-N-out cross-validation, 100 times	231 Normal 198 AD	87.00

[30] and 2% lower than that of the SVM method [31]. This may be due to the fact that the SVM method in [31] uses a lower number of subjects in the study. Comparing the performance of the PBL-McRBFN classifier using the VBM features with the method of SVM using the 93 ROI features [32] and also the method using the tensor based morphometry features [33], one can see that PBL-McRBFN's performance is similar.

4 Conclusions

This paper has presented an approach for AD detection using the Projection Based Learning Meta-cognitive Radial Basis Function Network (PBL-McRBFN) classifier. The PBL-McRBFN classifier uses VBM features extracted from MRI.

The performance of PBL-McRBFN is compared with the results reported in the literature. The results clearly indicate the better performance of the PBL-McRBFN classifier for AD detection and this approach can be used for other neurodegenerative disorders.

Acknowledgment. Data collection and sharing for this project was funded by the Alzheimer's Disease Neuroimaging Initiative (ADNI) (National Institutes of Health Grant U01 AG024904). ADNI is funded by the National Institute on Aging, the National Institute of Biomedical Imaging and Bioengineering, and through generous contributions from the following: Abbott; Alzheimer's Association; Alzheimer's Drug Discovery Foundation; Amorfix Life Sciences Ltd.; AstraZeneca; Bayer HealthCare; BioClinica, Inc.; Biogen Idec Inc.; Bristol-Myers Squibb Company; Eisai Inc.; Elan Pharmaceuticals Inc.; Eli Lilly and Company; F. Hoffmann-La Roche Ltd and its affiliated company Genentech, Inc.; GE Healthcare; Innogenetics, N.V.; IXICO Ltd.; Janssen Alzheimer Immunotherapy Research and Development, LLC.; Johnson and Johnson Pharmaceutical Research and Development LLC.; Medpace, Inc.; Merck and Co., Inc.; Meso Scale Diagnostics, LLC.; Novartis Pharmaceuticals Corporation; Pfizer Inc.; Servier; Synarc Inc.; and Takeda Pharmaceutical Company. The Canadian Institutes of Health Research is providing funds to support ADNI clinical sites in Canada. Private sector contributions are facilitated by the Foundation for the National Institutes of Health (www.fnih.org). The grantee organization is the Northern California Institute for Research and Education, and the study is coordinated by the Alzheimer's Disease Cooperative Study at the University of California, San Diego. ADNI data are disseminated by the Laboratory for Neuro Imaging at the University of California, Los Angeles. The above research was also supported by NIH grants P30 AG010129 and K01 AG030514.

References

1. Adeli, H., Ghosh-Dastidar, S., Dadmehr, N.: Alzheimer's disease and models of computation: imaging, classification, and neural models. J. Alzheimer's Dis. **7**, 187–199 (2005)
2. Barker, W.W., Luis, C.A., Kashuba, A., Luis, M., Harwood, D.G., Loewenstein, D., Waters, C., Jimison, P., Shepherd, E., Sevush, S., Graff-Radford, N., Newland, D., Todd, M., Miller, B., Gold, M., Heilman, K., Doty, L., Goodman, I., Robinson, B., Pearl, G., Dickson, D., Duara, R.: Relative frequencies of Alzheimer disease, Lewy body, vascular and frontotemporal dementia, and hippocampal sclerosis in the state of Florida brain bank. Alzheimer Dis. Assoc. Disord. **16**, 203–212 (2002)
3. Segovia, F., Górriz, J.M., Ramírez, J., Salas-González, D., Álvarez, I.: Early diagnosis of Alzheimer's disease based on partial least squares and support vector machine. Expert Syst. Appl. **40**, 677–683 (2013)
4. Charlon, Y., Fourty, N., Bourennane, W., Campo, E.: Design and evaluation of a device worn for fall detection and localization: application for the continuous monitoring of risks incurred by dependents in an alzheimer's care unit. Expert Syst. Appl. **40**, 7316–7330 (2013)
5. Jack Jr, C.R., Petersen, R.C., Xu, Y.C., ÓBrien, P.C., Smith, G.E., Ivnik, R.J., Boeve, B.F., Waring, S.C., Tangalos, E.G., Kokmen, E.: Prediction of AD with MRI-based hippocampal volume in mild cognitive impairment. Neurology **52**, 1397–1403 (1999)

6. Killiany, R.J., Hyman, B.T., Gomez-Isla, T., Moss, M.B., Kikinis, R., Jolesz, F., Tanzi, R., Jones, K., Albert, M.S.: MRI measures of entorhinal cortex vs hippocampus in preclinical AD. Neurology **58**, 1188–1196 (2002)

7. Fornito, A., Yücel, M., Wood, S.J., Adamson, C., Velakoulis, D., Saling, M.M., McGorry, P.D., Pantelis, C.: Surface-based morphometry of the anterior cingulate cortex in first episode schizophrenia. Hum. Brain Mapp. **29**, 478–489 (2008)

8. Ashburner, J., Hutton, C., Frackowiak, R.S.J., Johnsrude, I., Price, C., Friston, K.J.: Identifying global anatomical differences: deformation-based morphometry. NeuroImage **6**, 348–357 (1998)

9. Ashburner, J., Friston, K.J.: Voxel-based morphometry-the methods. NeuroImage **11**, 805–821 (2000)

10. Isaacson, R., Fujita, F.: Metacognitive knowledge monitoring and self-regulated learning: academic success and reflections on learning. J. Sch. Teach. Learn. **6**, 39–55 (2006)

11. Nelson, T.O., Narens, L.: Metamemory: a theoretical framework and new findings. Psychol. Learn. Motiv. **26**, 125–173 (1990)

12. Subramanian, K., Sundaram, S., Sundararajan, N.: A meta-cognitive neuro-fuzzy inference system (McFIS) for sequential classification problems. IEEE Trans. Fuzzy Syst. **21**, 1080–1095 (2013)

13. Sateesh Babu, G., Suresh, S., Mahanand, B.S.: Meta-cognitive q-Gaussian RBF network for binary classification: Application to mild cognitive impairment (MCI). In: The International Joint Conference on Neural Networks (IJCNN), pp. 1–8 (2013)

14. Sateesh Babu, G., Suresh, S.: Metacognitive neural network for classification problems in a sequential learning framework. Neurocomputing **81**, 86–96 (2011)

15. Suresh, S., Savitha, R., Sundararajan, N.: A sequential learning algorithm for complex valued self regulating resource allocation network- CSRAN. IEEE Trans. Neural Netw. **22**, 1061–1072 (2011)

16. Savitha, R., Suresh, S., Sundararajan, N.: Metacognitive learning in a fully complex-valued radial basis function neural network. Neural Comput. **24**, 1297–1328 (2012)

17. Savitha, R., Suresh, S., Sundararajan, N.: A meta-cognitive learning algorithm for a fully complex-valued relaxation network. Neural Netw. **32**, 209–218 (2012)

18. Subramanian, K., Suresh, S.: A meta-cognitive sequential learning algorithm for neuro-fuzzy inference system. Appl. Soft Comput. **12**, 3603–3614 (2012)

19. Subramanian, K., Savitha, R., Suresh, S.: A complex-valued neuro-fuzzy inference system and its learning mechanism. Neurocomputing **123**, 110–120 (2014)

20. Subramanian, K., Das, A.K., Suresh, S., Savitha, R.: A meta-cognitive interval type-2 fuzzy inference system and its projection based learning algorithm. Evolving Syst. **5**(4), 219–230 (2014). doi:10.1007/s12530-013-9102-9

21. Sateesh Babu, G., Suresh, S.: Meta-cognitive RBF Network and its Projection Based Learning algorithm for classification problems. Appl. Soft Comput. **13**, 654–666 (2013)

22. Sateesh Babu, G., Suresh, S., Mahanand, B.S.: Alzheimer's disease detection using a projection based learning meta-cognitive RBF network. In: The 2012 International Joint Conference on Neural Networks (IJCNN), pp. 408–415 (2012)

23. Sateesh Babu, G., Suresh, S., Uma Sangumathi, K., Kim, H.J.: A projection based learning meta-cognitive RBF network classifier for effective diagnosis of Parkinson's disease. In: Wang, J., Yen, G.G., Polycarpou, M.M. (eds.) ISNN 2012, Part II. LNCS, vol. 7368, pp. 611–620. Springer, Heidelberg (2012)

24. Sateesh Babu, G., Suresh, S.: Parkinson's disease prediction using gene expression - a projection based learning meta-cognitive neural classifier approach. Expert Syst. Appl. **40**, 1519–1529 (2013)
25. Jack, C.R., Bernstein, M.A., Fox, N.C., Thompson, P., Alexander, G., Harvey, D., Borowski, B., Britson, P.J., Jennifer, L.W., Ward, C., Dale, A.M., Felmlee, J.P., Gunter, J.L., Hill, D.L., Killiany, R., Schuff, N., Fox-Bosetti, S., Lin, C., Studholme, C., DeCarli, C.S., Gunnar, K., Ward, H.A., Metzger, G.J., Scott, K.T., Mallozzi, R., Blezek, D., Levy, J., Debbins, J.P., Fleisher, A.S., Albert, M., Green, R., Bartzokis, G., Glover, G., Mugler, J., Weiner, M.W.: The Alzheimer's disease neuroimaging initiative (ADNI): MRI methods. J. Magn. Reson. Imaging **27**, 685–691 (2008)
26. Mahanand, B.S., Suresh, S., Sundararajan, N., Kumar, M.A.: Identification of brain regions responsible for Alzheimer's disease using a self-adaptive resource allocation network. Neural Netw. **32**, 313–322 (2012)
27. Ashburner, J., Friston, K.J.: Unified segmentation. NeuroImage **26**, 839–851 (2005)
28. Friston, K.J., Holmes, A.P., Worsley, K.J., Poline, J.B., Frith, C.D., Frackowiak, R.S.J.: Statistical parametric maps in functional imaging: a general linear approach. Hum. Brain Mapp. **2**, 189–210 (1994)
29. Sateesh Babu, G., Suresh, S.: Meta-cognitive neural network for classification problems in a sequential learning framework. Neurocomputing **81**, 86–96 (2012)
30. Hinrichs, C., Singh, V., Mukherjee, L., Xu, G., Chung, M.K., Johnson, S.C.: Spatially augmented LPboosting for AD classification with evaluations on the ADNI dataset. NeuroImage **48**, 138–149 (2009)
31. Cuingnet, R., Gerardin, E., Tessieras, J., Auzias, G., Lehéricy, S., Habert, M.O., Chupin, M., Benali, H., Colliot, O.: Automatic classification of patients with Alzheimer's disease from structural MRI: a comparison of ten methods using the ADNI database. NeuroImage **56**, 766–781 (2011)
32. Zhang, D., Wang, Y., Zhou, L., Yuan, H., Shen, D.: Multimodal classification of Alzheimer's disease and mild cognitive impairment. NeuroImage **55**, 856–867 (2011)
33. Wolz, R., Julkunen, V., Koikkalainen, J., Niskanen, E., Zhang, D.P., Rueckert, D., Soininen, H., Lötjönen, J.: The Alzheimer's disease neuroimaging initiative: multi-method analysis of MRI images in early diagnostics of Alzheimer's disease. PLoS ONE **6**, e25446 (2011)

Privacy Preserving Data Mining Using General Regression Auto-Associative Neural Network: Application to Regression Problems

Vadlamani Ravi[1]([⊠]) and Amit Yadav[2]

[1] Centre of Excellence in CRM and Analytics,
Institute for Development and Research in Banking Technology,
Hyderabad 500057, Andhra Pradesh, India
rav_pdma@yahoo.com
[2] Integrated M.Sc. in Applied Mathematics, Department of Mathematics,
Indian Institute of Technology, Roorkee 247667, India
ayamit92@gmail.com

Abstract. Data mining has proved its significance in various areas like healthcare, counter-terrorism etc. But it has several times raised issues concerning privacy, legality and ethics. Thus, a need for privacy preserving data mining arose. While preserving privacy one thing that should be made sure is that the accuracy of the final predictions should not suffer drastically. This paper proposes a novel General Regression Auto- Associative Neural Network (GRAANN) for privacy preservation. Then, General Regression Neural Network (GRNN) is applied for data mining purpose, leading to GRAANN + GRNN hybrid. The hybrid is tested on five benchmark datasets. From the accuracy of the predictions made it can be concluded that GRAANN can be used as optimum technique for privacy preservation.

Keywords: Data mining · Privacy preservation · General regression auto associative neural network · SMAPE

1 Introduction

In view of the technological advancement, the ability to store data belonging to various fields such as healthcare, counter terrorism, medicine etc. has been drastically increased. Such data can prove useful while making important decisions. But the main disadvantage that data mining sometimes leads to is the violation of individual privacy [1]. Thus, privacy preserving data mining (PPDM) came into picture in which data is first perturbed and then mining is performed on the modified dataset. Research devoted much effort to offset this issue in data mining resulting in many data mining techniques, which included privacy protection mechanisms based on different approaches [2–5].

Thus, while modifying dataset it should be made sure that there is no significant decline in accuracies of the final predictions. This paper proposes a novel privacy preserving technique namely, General Regression Auto-Associative Neural Network (GRAANN). General Regression Neural Network is then invoked on the perturbed dataset for data mining purpose. The rest of the paper is organized as follows.

© Springer International Publishing Switzerland 2015
B.K. Panigrahi et al. (Eds.): SEMCCO 2014, LNCS 8947, pp. 618–624, 2015.
DOI: 10.1007/978-3-319-20294-5_53

In Sect. 2, we briefly discuss existing privacy preserving data mining techniques, definitions used and background work. Section 3 describes proposed method. Section 4 reviews the results of experiments. Finally, we have the concluding remarks in Sect. 5.

2   Related Work

Significant amount of work has been done in privacy preserving data mining [6]. The origin of privacy preserving data mining can be traced back to when Clifton and Marks [6] first suggested that how adopting a common platform for discussing privacy preservation would result in decrement of privacy violation issues.

Agarwal and Srikant [7] performed randomization of sensitive values using Gaussian and Uniform perturbations. Their algorithms rely on a Bayesian procedure for correcting perturbed distributions. Then, Verykios et al. [8] classified the existing privacy preserving algorithms into five different categories: data modification, data or rule hiding, data distribution, privacy preservation and DM algorithm. Bertino [9] classified existing PPDM algorithms through a proposed taxonomy. Ketel and Homaifar [10] proposed a geometric rotation based data perturbation. Privacy preserving classification methods prevent a miner from classifier construction which could predict sensitive data. Privacy preserving clustering techniques that distort sensitive numerical attributes, while preserving general features was proposed [11].

Another work includes hybridization of random projection and random rotation methods by Ramu and Ravi [12]. The hybrids were tested on four bankruptcy and six benchmark problems. Logistic regression, MLP and Decision tree were used for classifying with 10-fold cross-validation. Bansal [13] et al. introduced a novel algorithm for preserving privacy through neural network learning. Ravi et al. [14] proposed a novel privacy preservation technique namely particle swarm optimization trained Auto-Associative Neural Network. The work dealt with classification problems. Logistic regression and Decision tree were then applied for data mining purpose. Thus, hybrids of PSOAANN + LT and PSOAANN + DT were introduced. The hybrids were tested on four bankruptcy and five benchmark classification problems.

3   Proposed Method

The main objective of the research and the proposed method are briefly described here. Leakage of crucial information may lead to violation of individual privacy. Thus, before mining the data privacy need to be preserved. Accuracies of prediction will undoubtedly be affected due to data perturbation. Thus, the data miner has to take the important decision of maintaining the suitable balance between the amount of privacy he wants to preserve and the accuracies of prediction that he could sacrifice. Many real world problems require the application of privacy preserving data mining such as healthcare and financial data. Thus, privacy preservation of data becomes a necessity.

In this paper, we propose a novel privacy preservation technique namely General Regression Auto-Associative Neural Network (GRAANN) for regression problems, followed by General regression Neural Network (GRNN), which is invoked for data mining purpose. Five benchmark datasets are analyzed using the proposed GRA-ANN + GRNN hybrid. Thus, it's a two stage process, where, in Stage1, GRAANN is trained by taking the original data as input and keeping the same as output. Since, the predicted output cannot be exactly the same as the original output, the data gets perturbed as a result of the training process. In Stage 2, regression task is performed on the perturbed dataset using GRNN.

3.1   General Regression Neural Network

Specht [15] first proposed GRNN. GRNN can approximate any arbitrary function from historical data. It basically performs non-parametric regression analysis. The architecture of GRNN consists of four layers namely input, pattern, summation and output layer. The input layer consists of all the input features corresponding to each data point. The pattern nodes store the input records and they are equal to input records in number. The outputs from pattern nodes are passed onto summation units. The summation unit includes a numerator summation unit and a denominator summation unit. The denominator summation unit adds up the weight values coming from each of the hidden neurons. The numerator summation unit adds up the weight values multiplied by the actual target value for each hidden neuron. The output node generates the estimated value of output by dividing the values of numerator summation unit by the denominator summation unit, and uses the result as the final estimated value.

The GRNN is a method of estimating the joint probability density function (pdf) of x and y, giving only a training set. The estimated value is the most probable value of y and is defined by

$$E(y|x)y = \hat{y}(x) = \int_{-\infty}^{+\infty} yf(x,y)dy / \int_{-\infty}^{+\infty} f(x,y)dy \tag{3}$$

The density function $f(x,y)$ can be estimated from the training set using Parzen's estimator [15].

$$f(x,y) = 1/(2\pi)^{(p+1)/2}\sigma^{(p+1)}1/n\sum_{i=1}^{n}\exp[-(x-x^i)^T(x-x^i)/2\sigma^2]$$
$$\exp[-(y-y^i)^2/2\sigma^2] \tag{4}$$

The probability estimate $f(x,y)$ assigns a sample probability of width σ for each sample x^i and y^i, and the probability estimate is the sum of these sample probabilities [15]. Defining the scalar function D_i^2

$$D_i^2 = (x-x_i)^T(x-x_i) \tag{5}$$

and assessing the indicated integration yields the following:

$$Y(x) = \sum_{i=1}^{n} Y^i \exp(-D_i^2/2\sigma^2) / \sum_{i=1}^{n} \exp(-D_i^2/2\sigma^2) \tag{6}$$

The resulting regression (6) is directly applicable to problems involving descrete numerical data.

Unlike the Multilayer Perceptron (MLP), the GRNN does not require of the upfront specification of the number of hidden nodes because, it is structurally different. Further, GRNN differs from the MLP in that weights are replaced by a distribution of weights that minimizes the chance of getting entrapped in local minima.

3.2   General Regression Auto-Associative Neural Network

It is nothing but an auto associative variant of GRNN. The ability of GRNN to solve multi-input and multi-output problems enabled Ravi and Krishna [16] to extend GRNN to GRAANN by taking the input variables in the output nodes also. Figure 1 depicts the architecture of the GRAANN. In the output layer, after the training is completed, we obtain the modified or predicted input variables $(X'_1, X'_2, \ldots, X'_n)$ for the input variables $(X_1, X_2, \ldots, X_n)$. Ravi and Krishna [16] proposed GRAANN for data imputation purpose. However, any auto associative neural network is high versatile in that it can be used for various applications viz., data imputation, privacy preservation, nonlinear principal component analysis and single-class classification. However, GRAANN is employed to perform privacy preservation in the data.

The advantage of using GRAANN over other traditional methods is its unique features comprising of quick learning, simple training algorithm and being discriminative against infrequent outliers and erroneous observations. Thus, auto-association is attained leading to privacy preservation. The end result is that the original input

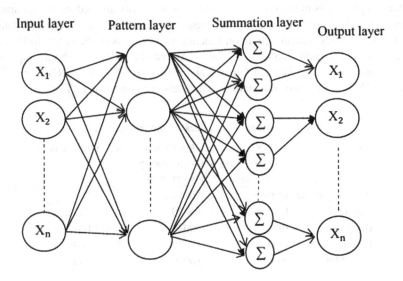

Fig. 1. Architecture of GRAANN

variables undergo a non-linear transformation yielding their perturbed version. We have also measured the amount of privacy preserved in each of the dataset by calculating symmetric mean absolute percentage error (SMAPE). SMAPE is based on percentage of relative errors. It is calculated as follows.

$$\text{SMAPE} = \frac{1}{n}\sum_{i=1}^{n} \frac{2|x_i - x_i'|}{(x_i + x_i')}.$$

Where x_i is the actual input and x_i' is the predicted input and n is the number of data points.

Since most of our datasets are multivariate. SMAPE value is calculated individually over each of the input feature and average is taken over them to be taken as unified measure of privacy preservation. Once the privacy is preserved, prediction is made using General Regression Neural Network. Then accuracy is measured by calculating the mean squared error value (MSE).

4   Results and Discussions

The GRAANN is first implemented in the software NeuroShell 2 followed by GRNN. The hybrid is tested on five regression datasets namely Boston Housing, Pollution, Body Fat, Forest Fires and Auto MPG. The mentioned datasets used in the study are obtained from the UCI Machine Learning Repository [17].

Mean Square Error (MSE) values are determined by observing the best results out of all possible combinations of the different parameters available in the NeuroShell 2. The Pool size which is a parameter for Genetic Algorithm is set at 100 for GRAANN and 300 for GRNN. Increasing the pool size increases the accuracy of predicted output. So, we chose the maximum pool size i.e. 300 in case of GRNN. But in case of GRAANN, more the accuracy of the predicted output, less the amount of privacy preserved. So, in case of GRAANN we have to keep the pool size a bit low in such a way that (i) privacy is preserved and (ii) it should not drastically reduce the accuracy of the final output obtained by making the predictions using privacy preserved data i.e. output of GRAANN. Linear activation function is used in both the cases. MSE values are determined for each dataset in 10-fold cross validation setup. The average accuracies obtained over the Tenfold Cross Validation (10- FCV) for GRNN and GRA-ANN + GRNN in the case of benchmark datasets are presented in Table 1.

Table 1. Average MSE values on the test sample data

Datasets	GRNN (Without privacy preservation)	GRAANN + GRNN (With privacy preservation)	t-Test Values
Boston Housing	0.0040	0.0117	1.755
Pollution	0.0026	0.0070	1.937
Body Fat	0.0030	0.0076	1.06
Forest Fires	0.0027	0.0029	0.069
Auto MPG	0.0036	0.0076	1.342

t-test is performed on the MSE values between privacy preserved data and the data without privacy preservation in all the five datasets and t-test values are presented in Table 1. From the t-test, it is observed that there is no statistically significant difference between the two cases at 1 % level of significance. Also, the average SMAPE value for each dataset is presented in Table 2. This SMAPE values indicate the quality of privacy preservation. Higher the SMAPE value, higher is the quality of privacy preservation.

Table 2. Average SMAPE values of privacy preserved data obtained by GRAANN.

Datasets	SMAPE percentage (Average value over all the features)
Boston Housing	47.69
Pollution	30.02
Body Fat	13.6
Forest Fires	36.69
Auto MPG	35.41

Therefore, we conclude that GRAANN-based hybrid model can be used to solve privacy preservation data mining problems in the context of regression. Also, we noticed that the proposed hybrid model did not sacrifice the accuracies of the prediction drastically, which is a significant outcome of the present study.

5 Conclusions

In this paper, we propose a new privacy preservation data mining technique namely General Regression Auto-Associative Neural Network coupled with GRNN. The efficacy of this proposed hybrid was tested on five benchmark regression datasets. SMAPE value was used to determine the quality of privacy preservation. Hence, we conclude that GRAANN + GRNN hybrid preserved privacy efficiently without sacrificing the accuracies. This is the most significant outcome of the study.

References

1. Aggarwal, C.C., Pei, J., Zhang, B.: On privacy preservation against adversarial data mining. In: Proceedings of the 12th ACM International Conference on Knowledge Discovery and Data Mining (SIGKDD), Philadelphia (2006)
2. Aggarwal, C.C., Yu, P.S.: Privacy-Preserving Data Mining: Models and Algorithms. Springer, US (2008)
3. Atzori, M., Bonchi, F., Giannotti, F., Pedreschi, D.: Anonymity preserving pattern discovery. Int. J. Very Large Data Bases (VLDBJ) 17(4), 703–727 (2008)
4. Abul, O., Bonchi, F., Nanni, M.: Never walk alone: uncertainty for anonymity in moving objects databases. In Proceedings of the 24th IEEE International Conference on Data Engineering (ICDE), pp. 376–385 (2008)

5. Ge, X., Zhu, J.: Privacy preserving data mining. In: Funatsu, K. (ed.) New Fundamental Tech-nologies in Data Mining, pp. 535–560. InTech, Rijeka (2011)
6. Clifton, C., Marks, D.: Security and privacy implications of data mining. In: Proceedings of SIGMOD Workshop on Research Issues on Data Mining and Knowledge Discovery (DMKD), pp.15–20, Canada (1996)
7. Agarwal, R., Srikant, R.: Preserving privacy in data mining. In: ACM SIGMOD International Conference on Management of Data (2000)
8. Verykios, V.S., Bertino, E., Fovino, I.N., Parasiliti, L., Saygin, Y., Theodoridis, Y.: State-of-the-art in privacy preserving data mining. SIGMOD Rec. 33(1), 50–57 (2004)
9. Bertino, E.: A framework for evaluating privacy preserving data mining algorithms. Data Min. Knowl. Discov. 11, 121–154 (2005)
10. Ketel, M., Homaifar, A.: Privacy-preserving mining by rotational data transformation. In: Proceedings of the 43rd Annual Southeast Regional Conference, vol. 1, pp. 233–236 (2005)
11. Inan, A., Levi, A., et al.: Privacy preserving clustering on horizontally partitioned data. Data Knowl. Eng. (DKE) 63(3), 646–666 (2007)
12. Ramu, K., Ravi, V.: Privacy preservation in data mining using hybrid perturbation methods: an application to bankruptcy prediction in banks. Int. J. Data Anal. Tech. Strat. 1(4), 313–331 (2009)
13. Bansal, A., Chen, T., Zhong, S.: Privacy preserving back-propagation neural network learning over arbitrarily partitioned data. J. Neuro Comput. Appl. 20, 1433–3058 (2010)
14. Ravi, V., Naveen, N., Rao, C.R.: Privacy preserving data mining using particle swarm optimization trained auto–associative neural network: an application to bankruptcy prediction in banks. Int. J. Data Min. Model. Manage. 4(1), 39–56 (2012)
15. Specht, D.F.: A general regression neural network. IEEE Trans. Neural Netw. 2(6), 568–576 (1991)
16. Ravi, V., Krishna, M.: A new online data imputation method based on general regression auto associative neural network. Neurocomput. 138, 106–113 (2014)
17. Bache, K., Lichman, M.: UCI Machine Learning Repository, University of California, School of Information and Computer Science, Irvine, CA (2013). http://archive.ics.uci.edu/ml

Opposition Based Particle Swarm Optimizer with Ring Topology

Tapas Si$^{(\boxtimes)}$ and Biplab Mandal

Department of Computer Science and Engineering,
Bankura Unnayani Institute of Engineering,
Bankura, West Bengal, India
c2.tapas@gmail.com

Abstract. Particle Swarm Optimizer is population based global search algorithm mimicking the behavior of fish–schooling, bird's flocking etc. Recently the opposition based learning scheme is incorporated in Particle Swarm Optimizer to improve its performance. Till now opposition based Particle Swarm Optimizer is implemented with *gbest* topology. This paper proposes the opposition based Particle Swarm Optimizer with *lbest* or ring topology. The proposed method is applied on 20 benchmark unconstrained functions. The obtained results are compared with other well–known opposition based Particle Swarm Optimizers with statistical analysis. The experimental results with statistical analysis show that the proposed algorithm outperforms over other algorithms for most of the functions.

Keywords: Particle swarm optimizer · Opposition based learning · Ring topology · *gbest* · *lbest* · Function optimization

1 Introduction

Particle Swarm Optimization(PSO) [1] algorithm is population based global optimization simulating the behaviour of fish schooling and bird's flocking. Each individual in PSO is known as particle. PSO with *gbest* topology in which all particles have the global best information of the swarm has quick convergence but often gets trap into local optima. PSO with *lbest* topology [3] in which all particles don't have the global best information of the swarm has slow convergence but provide better solution than *gbest* PSO. Recently, a new machine learning scheme, opposition based learning(OBL) proposed by Tizhoosh [5], has been successfully applied in *gbest* PSO which improved the performance of the PSO.

L. Han et al. [7] proposed opposition based PSO in which they applied opposition based learning strategy in population initialization, particle's position in generation (*generation jumping*) with a *jumping rate* and in global best position of the swarm (*best individual jumping*). M.G.H. Omran [9] introduced an improved OPSO (*i*OPSO) in which opposition based initialization is used and the particle with the worst fitness x_l is replaced by its opposite (*anti–particle*)

© Springer International Publishing Switzerland 2015
B.K. Panigrahi et al. (Eds.): SEMCCO 2014, LNCS 8947, pp. 625–635, 2015.
DOI: 10.1007/978-3-319-20294-5_54

in each iteration. H. Wang et al. [8] proposed a new OPSO method in which they included opposition based initialization, generation jumping with dynamic search space range and dynamic cauchy mutation operators in the *gbest* position in each generation in order to extend the search space of the best particle. H. Wang et al. [10] proposed GOPSO, in which generalized opposition-based learning (GOBL) and Cauchy mutation in *gbest* position are employed. Opposition based comprehensive learning Particle Swarm Optimization algorithm was proposed by Z. Wu [11]. M. Rashid et al. [6] use generation jumping in particles position along with velocity in PSO. M. Kaucic [12] proposed a multi-start opposition-based particle swarm optimization algorithm with adaptive velocity for bound constrained global optimization. T. Si et al. [13] proposed OpbestPSO algorithm in which opposition based initialization, opposition based learning in *pbest* position are employed. After reviewing the related literatures, it is found that the opposition based learning is incorporated in PSO with *gbest* topology. Therefore, the key objective of this paper is to use opposition based learning scheme in PSO with ring or *lbest* topology and analysis its performance.

Organization of this Paper: Particle Swarm Optimization algorithm is described in Sect. 2. Proposed method is discussed in Sect. 3. Experimental setup is given in Sect. 4. Results & discussions are given in Sect. 5. Finally a conclusion is given in Sect. 6.

2   Particle Swarm Optimizer

Particle Swarm Optimization(PSO) [1,2] algorithm is simulating the behavior of fish schooling and bird's flocking etc. and it is a population based global search algorithm. $x_{ij}(t)$ is particle's position in t time or iteration, where particle's index is $i(= 1, 2, 3, ..., NP)$ and index $j(= 1, 2, 3, ..., D)$ of the dimension D of the problem to be solved. In each dimension each particle moves in the trajectory space using velocity $v_{ij}(t)$. Each particle store their personal best position $x^{pbest}(t)$ in the memory. Global best position $x^{gbest}(t)$ of swarm is the best of all $x^{pbest}(t)$ in their memory. PSO has several types of topology such as *gbest*, *lbest* or ring, star, Von-Neumann etc [4]. In *gbest* topology, each particle has global best information of the swarm during the search. On the other hand, in *lbest* topology, particles don't have the global best information and instead, they have their neighbor's personal best information in their neighborhood. The velocity update equation in PSO with *gbest* topology is expressed as following:

$$v_i(t+1) = w \times v_i(t) + c_1 \times r_1 \times (x_i^{pbest}(t) - x_i(t)) + c_2 \times r_2 \times (x^{gbest}(t) - x_i(t)) \quad (1)$$

and the particle's position is updated by the following equation:

$$x_i(t + 1) = x_i(t) + v_i(t + 1) \quad (2)$$

where w is inertia weight in the range $(0, 1)$. c_1 is particle's personal cognizance and c_2 is social cognizance. r_1 and r_2 are uniformly distributed random number in the range $[0, 1]$. $(X_{min}, X_{max})^D$ is search region of each of the test function where X_{min} and X_{max} determines the extension in each dimension.

The velocity update equation in PSO with *lbest* topology is expressed as following:

$$v_i(t+1) = w \times v_i(t) + c_1 \times r_1 \times (x_i^{pbest}(t) - x_i(t)) + c_2 \times r_2 \times (x^{nbest}(t) - x_i(t)) \quad (3)$$

where $x^{nbest}(t)$ is the neighborhood's best of ith particle. The figures of *gbest* and *lbest* are given in Fig. 1.

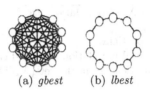

(a) *gbest*   (b) *lbest*

Fig. 1. PSO Topology

3 Proposed Method

H. R. Tizhoosh [5] introduced opposition based learning(OBL) in the year 2005. This learning scheme is based on the opposite of number. Suppose, $\mathbf{X} \in [A, B]$ a real vector, then the opposite of that vector $\mathbf{X}'$ of $\mathbf{X}$ is calculated by the following equation:

$$X' = A + B - X \quad (4)$$

For example, if $A = -5$ and $B = 5$, then the opposite of $X = -3$ will be $X' = 3$. In opposition based bio-inspired algorithm, the task is to find out a near-optimal solution $\mathbf{X}^*$ so that $f(\mathbf{X})^* < f(\mathbf{X})$ (in case of minimization). Now, according to OBL theory, if X has chance of getting a near-optimal or optimal solution, then its opposite vector X' has also a 50 % chance of getting the same solution. In the proposed algorithm named as OPSO*lbest*, opposition based initialization and generation jumping are used in PSO with ring or *lbest* topology. A static ring topology i.e. initially a ring topology is formed depending on the index of the individuals and that topology is used in all the iteration. The neighbourhood size is set to 2. The opposite of particle's position is calculated in the dynamic search space range $[A, B]$ using the following equation:

$$x_i' = (A + B) - x_i \quad (5)$$

The dynamic search space range $[A, B]$ is calculated as following:

$$A_j = min(X_{ij}), \qquad B_j = max(X_{ij}) \quad (6)$$

$i = 1, 2, ..., NP, \quad j = 1, 2, ..., D$
The particle's position is restricted in the range (X_{min}, X_{max}) using the following rule:

$X_i = min(max(X_i, X_{min}), X_{max})$
and similarly velocity is also restricted in the range (V_{min}, V_{max}) using the following rule:
$V_i = min(max(V_i, X_{min}), X_{max})$
The details description of the algorithm is given in Table 1.

Table 1. OPSO*lbest* Algorithm

Algorithm:OPSO*lbest*
1. Initialize the population X_i of population size NP
2. Initialize the velocity V_i
3. Calculate the fitness of particles
4. Calculate opposite of initial population OX_i and calculate the fitness
5. Select NP number of particles from the set $\{X, OX\}$.
6. Calculate *pbest* and *gbest*.
7. **While** termination criteria
8. **If** $rand() < P_{Gen-Jump}$
9. Calculate opposite of population OX_i and calculate the fitness
10. Select NP number of particles from the set $\{X, OX\}$.
11. Calculate *pbest* and *gbest*.
12. **Else**
13. **For** each individual
14. Perform velocity and position update for each particle using Eq. (3) and Eq. (2) respectively.
15. Calculate new fitness
16. Update *pbest* and *gbest*
17. **End For**
18. **End If**
19. **End While**

4   Experimental Setup

There are 20 different global optimization problems, including uni–modal functions ($F_1 - F_5$) and multimodal functions ($F_6 - F_{20}$) collected from CEC–2013 benchmark problems [15]. All functions are used in this work to be minimized. The description of these benchmark function can be obtained from Ref. [15].

Maximum number of function evaluations or $E = |f(X) - f(X^*)| \leq e$ where $f(X)$ is the current best and $f(X^*)$ is the global optimum of the functions. E is the best-run-error of a run of the algorithm and e is the threshold error. The parameters of OPSO*lbest* are set as following: Problem's Dimension ($D = 30$, Population Size($NP = 2 \times D = 60$, $FEs = 3,00,000$, $V_{max} = 0.5 \times (X_{max} - X_{min})$, $c_1 = c_2 = 1.49445$, $w = 0.72984$, Generation jumping probability

$(P_{Gen-Jump} = 0.3$, Threshold error $e = 1e - 03$ and total number of runs for each problem $= 30$.

The simulations are carried out in the PC having the following configuration: System:Windows 2007, CPU: P IV 2 GHz (Core 2 Duo), RAM: 2 GB, Software: Matlab 2008a.

5   Results and Discussions

In this work, PSO*lbest*, OPSO*lbest*, OpbestPSO [13] and OPSO [8] algorithms are applied on 20 unconstrained optimization problems collected from CEC-2013 benchmark problems. All the algorithms are simulated with same initial populations for same run to make a fair comparison among the algorithms. All the algorithms are simulated for 30 runs. The mean and standard deviation of best-run-errors are given in Table 2. The best results of the algorithms are marked with bold-face in the aforementioned table. The convergence graphs has been given in Figs. 2, 3 and 4. A t-test statistics [14] has been carried out between OPSO*lbest* and the best of the remaining algorithms for 30 samples and degree of freedom=58 with significance level $\alpha = 0.05$. The last column of the Table 2 indicates the significance of difference. The higher significant difference is denoted by "+" and no significant difference is denoted by "$\approx$" symbol. The proposed OPSO*lbest* algorithm outperforms over other algorithms for unimoadal function F_1 and for multimodal functions F_4-F7, $F_{10}-F_{13}$, F_{19}(a total 11 out of 20). The PSO*lbest* algorithm outperforms over other algorithms for only one unimoadal function F_2. The OpbestPSO algorithm outperforms over other algorithms for only one multimoadal function F_{15}. OPSO [8] algorithm outperforms over other algorithms for multimoadal functions F_{14}, F_{16} and F_{20}(a total 3 out of 20). There are no statistical significant difference between proposed OPSO*lbest* and the best of remaining other algorithms for multimodal functions F_3, F_8, F_{13} and F_{18} (a total 4 out of 20). Finally, the Wilcoxon signed rank test statistics [14] are carried out to measure the overall significance of differences among the algorithms and it is given in Table 4. For this test, pair-wise caparisons are made with the following null hypothesis: H_0:The pair of algorithms are equivalent. against the alternative hypothesis:H_1:The pair of algorithms are not equivalent. The null hypothesis H_0 for all three pairs are rejected for the critical value $\alpha = 0.05$ and the alternative null hypothesis H_1 is true that all the pairs in Table 4 are not equivalent. Therefore, the performance of OPSO*lbest* is significantly different from the other algorithms. All the algorithms take the complete number of FEs for all runs and for all functions.

The proposed PSO*lbest* algorithm is tested for different values of generation jumping probability to check the influence of this parameter in its performance. The means and standard deviations of best-run-errors for 30 runs with different values of generation jumping probability are given in Table 3. The Wilcoxon sign rank test has been carried out to see the statistical significance and the test results are given in Table 5 and it is seen that, for $P = \{0.2, 0.3, 0.4, 0.5\}$, there is no difference in the performances but the performances are significantly different for $P = \{0.6, 0.7\}$ (Table 5).

Table 2. Mean and standard deviation of best-run-errors

Problems	PSOlbest		OPSOlbest		OpbestPSO [13]		OPSO [8]		t-test
	Mean	Std. Dev.	Mean	Std. Dev.	Mean	Std. Dev.	Mean	Std. Dev.	
F_1	6524.89	2751.77	1225.29	736.51	11174.23	5114.03	5714.69	3930.34	+
F_2	22885671.18	11108480.48	37461378.12	29392804.56	39640488.01	14198819.35	65862868.03	31075963.05	+
F_3	20177900927	10531744881	15931338549	11962410033	31664755528	16700909572	58741618287	28635527322	≈
F_4	40968.16458	12397.12418	29614.36242	11207.72656	42473.52922	8887.012704	43476.60329	7759.275655	+
F_5	927.0715356	398.3973903	626.414891	436.1850523	1790.163171	1115.876007	2433.964728	1671.195783	+
F_6	271.9512292	121.0658395	189.3304557	97.97690362	498.2708649	257.4177692	412.2101736	372.670112	+
F_7	162.1872644	34.92978522	117.0718608	33.80212237	166.0236717	36.35249212	218.9853367	51.50718076	+
F_8	20.94585207	0.041143031	20.96020965	0.064355885	20.93528552	0.067245272	20.98119562	0.057721894	≈
F_9	32.65940347	1.988781828	30.41119095	3.707041457	33.96654468	3.101114643	32.19895148	4.473634487	≈
F_{10}	634.3432101	201.4421991	356.4695677	214.3748687	702.5191988	287.3479205	878.0117077	546.5235716	+
F_{11}	267.770344	57.35222519	205.5160729	54.86608741	316.4431246	73.19465146	282.926107	51.84289454	+
F_{12}	279.6302185	53.61508717	197.5088092	59.86636135	294.2095601	73.2680403	336.8803696	51.89374234	+
F_{13}	320.4327778	47.37349352	211.7931417	45.82347682	368.4500958	82.27093823	329.9147675	49.60878495	+
F_{14}	4976.795914	642.619909	6572.141345	658.7629942	4842.648344	628.6841658	336.1241649	55.62336816	+
F_{15}	5952.829783	452.0909134	7273.360429	610.2716689	5005.029914	819.9983698	6983.441814	847.1332072	+
F_{16}	101.6514539	0.256414432	102.5268014	0.333100488	101.6345533	0.443759729	2.758999448	0.313516154	+
F_{17}	506.1807489	71.89851823	350.2882164	34.88779591	481.3930796	62.26237772	368.9956288	97.51060563	≈
F_{18}	518.0998038	82.56976489	370.849333	32.73049358	473.9780009	70.59374572	355.1387355	70.52156078	≈
F_{19}	3570.754626	5605.351903	165.0709796	124.9754249	2109.96618	2568.406719	17052.0548	71830.17993	+
F_{20}	113.7364307	0.782325627	113.5736868	0.657513406	113.9888422	0.611580284	13.38642144	0.384969425	+

Table 3. Mean and standard deviation of best-run-errors of OPSO$lbest$ with different generation jumping probability

FUN#	$P = 0.2$		$P = 0.3$		$P = 0.4$		$P = 0.5$		$P = 0.6$		$P = 0.7$	
	Mean	Std. Dev.	Mean	Std. Dev.	Mean	Std. Dev.	Mean	Std. Dev.	Mean	Std. Dev.	Mean	Std. Dev.
F_1	1083.65	569.3459	1225.23	736.5131	344.98	379.4730	703.48	1157.8919	1241.33	1503.0810	1495.452513	1268.3340
F_2	49.94e6	23.69e6	37.46e6	29.39e6	34.62e6	32.41e6	40.24e6	28.20e6	72.63e6	69.00e6	78.41e6	49.52e6
F_3	14.77e9	11.91e9	15.93e9	11.96e9	16.34e9	15.76e9	20.56e9	13.22e9	33.94e9	16.79e9	45.31e9	17.66e9
F_4	21848.51	11345.13	29614.36	11207.73	34141.70	8995.81	44489.93	12008.37	52104.26	7100.69	66582.12	9967.22
F_5	464.31	249.89	626.41	436.19	487.24	587.13	427.27	544.80	511.46	395.27	1141.89	667.08
F_6	196.15	71.16	189.33	97.98	161.53	84.64	164.21	100.41	176.57	170.60	237.61	107.06
F_7	114.80	45.06	117.07	33.80	134.91	50.81	141.85	50.60	182.20	60.91	213.88	56.04
F_8	20.95	0.04	20.96	0.07	20.98	0.04	20.97	0.06	20.99	0.05	20.10	0.04
F_9	30.82	3.51	30.41	3.71	32.10	3.02	34.56	3.49	35.60	2.96	37.10	3.15
F_{10}	387.21	138.57	356.47	214.37	338.97	377.21	296.69	342.29	353.29	342.35	610.29	404.59
F_{11}	201.22	53.72	205.52	54.87	191.53	75.76	215.50	39.97	250.82	80.66	267.65	58.98
F_{12}	209.13	74.95	197.50	59.87	193.01	58.57	214.48	54.56	235.86	40.37	284.68	60.09
F_{13}	215.62	45.80	211.79	45.82	223.67	40.21	249.82	48.13	264.19	46.21	291.45	47.99
F_{14}	5597.57	710.26	6572.14	658.76	7098.64	598.34	7432.65	354.77	7454.33	441.97	7533.19	471.35
F_{15}	6393.44	726.79	7273.36	610.27	7494.52	353.56	7635.04	302.39	7725.43	284.64	7850.69	234.60
F_{16}	102.62	0.23	102.53	0.33	102.54	0.39	102.59	0.23	102.80	0.31	102.70	0.36
F_{17}	352.84	56.34	350.28	34.89	381.21	39.39	382.32	52.38	412.32	54.34	435.34	44.84
F_{18}	354.02	53.35	370.85	32.73	381.85	39.39	381.85	27.98	418.84	31.29	454.01	54.74
F_{19}	154.56	42.35	165.07	124.98	254.18	694.92	126.93	19.78	911.10	4215.81	1894.61	8972.41
F_{20}	113.16	0.65	113.57	0.66	113.82	0.56	113.80	0.48	114.11	0.46	114.21	0.55

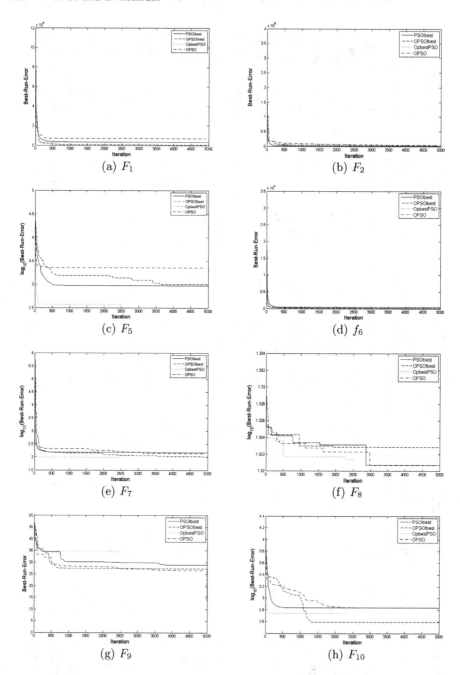

Fig. 2. Convergence graphs for functions F_1, F_2, $F_5 - F_{10}$

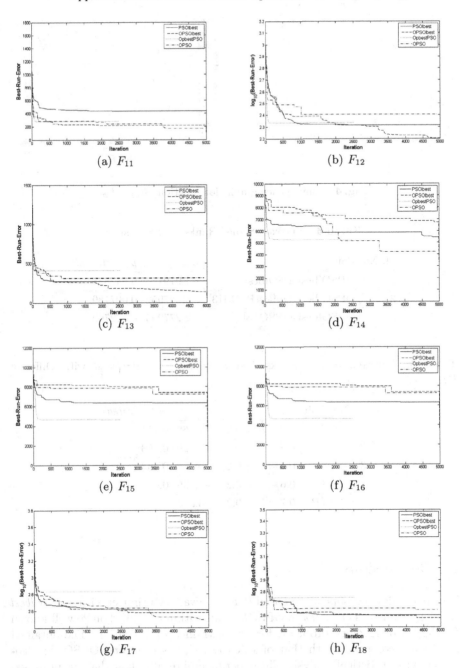

Fig. 3. Convergence graphs for functions $F_{11} - F_{18}$

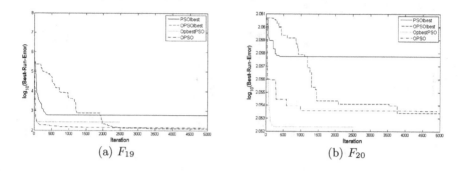

Fig. 4. Convergence graphs for functions $F_{19} - F_{20}$

Table 4. Wilcoxon Signed Ranks Test Statistics

Sl. No	Pair	Z	$p(2 - tailed)$
1	OPSOlbest-PSOlbest	-1.979	0.047858
2	OPSOlbest-OpbestPSO [13]	-2.687952	0.007189
3	OPSOlbest-OPSO [8]	-2.277293	0.022769

Table 5. Wilcoxon Signed Ranks Test Statistics for OPSO*lbest* with Different $P_{GEN-Jump}$

Sl. No	Pair	Z	$p(2 - tailed)$
1	$(P = 0.3)$-$(P = 0.2)$	-1.368	0.171
2	$(P = 0.4)$-$(P = 0.2)$	-1.120	0.263
3	$(P = 0.5)$-$(P = 0.2)$	-0.784	0.433
4	$(P = 0.6)$-$(P = 0.2)$	-3.435	0.001
5	$(P = 0.7)$-$(P = 0.2)$	-3.883	0.000

6   Conclusions

This paper devised opposition based Particle Swarm Optimizer with ring or *lbest* topology named as OPSO*lbest*. OPSO*lbest* algorithm is applied on 20 well-known CEC-2013 benchmark problems for unconstrained optimization. The obtained results are compared with that of PSO*lbest*, OpbestPSO and OPSO [8] algorithms with statistical analysis. The experimental results show that the proposed OPSO*lbest* algorithm statistically outperforms over other algorithms for most of the functions. The different neighbourhood size in OPSO*lbest* can be employed in its performance improvement. The future works of this paper are also directed towards the performance improvement by using different types of topology.

References

1. Kennedy, J., Eberhart, R.C.: Particle swarm optimization. In: IEEE International Conference on Neural Networks, Piscataway, NJ, pp. 1942–1948 (1995)
2. Shi, Y., Eberhart, R.C.: A modified particle swarm optimizer. In: Proceedings of the IEEE Congress on Evolutionary Computation (CEC 1998), Piscataway, NJ, pp. 69–73 (1998)
3. Kennedy, J., Mendes, R.: Population structure and particle swarm performance. In: IEEE Proceedings of the 2002 Congress on Evolutionary Computation (vol. 2), (CEC 2002), Honolulu, HI, pp. 1671–1676 (2002)
4. Lane, J., Engelbrecht, A., Gain, J.: Particle swarm optimization with spatially meaningful neighbours. In: IEEE Swarm Intelligence Symposium, 2008, St. Louis, MO, pp. 1–8 (2008)
5. Tizhoosh, H.R.: Opposition-based learning: a new scheme for machine intelligence. In: Proceedings of the 2005 International Conference on Computational Intelligence for Modelling, Control and Automation, and International Conference on Intelligent Agents, Web Technologies and Internet Commerce (CIMCA-IAWTIC05) (2005)
6. Rashid, M., Baig, A.R.: Improved opposition-based PSO for feedforward neural network training. In: International Conference on Information Science and Applications (ICISA), pp. 1–6. IEEE Press (2010)
7. Han, J., He, X.: A novel opposition-based particle swarm optimization for noisy problems. In: Third International Conference on Natural Computation (ICNC 2007), vol. 3, pp. 624–629 (2007)
8. Wang, H., Liu, Y.: Opposition-based particle swarm algorithm with cauchy mutation (2007)
9. Omran, M.G.H., Al-Sharhan, S.: Using opposition-based learning to improve the performance of particle swarm optimization, In: IEEE Swarm Intelligence Symposium (SIS 2008), pp. 1–6 (2008)
10. Wang, H., Wua, Z., Rahnamayan, S., Liu, Y., Ventresca, M.: Enhancing particle swarm optimization using generalized opposition-based learning. Inf. Sci. **181**, 4699–4714 (2011)
11. Wu, Z., Ni, Z., Zhang, C., Gu, L.: Opposition based comprehensive learning particle swarm optimization. In: Proceedings of 2008 3rd International Conference on Intelligent System and Knowledge Engineering, pp. 1013–1019 (2008)
12. Kaucic, M.: A multi-start opposition-based particle swarm optimization algorithm with adaptive velocity for bound constrained global optimization. J. Glob. Optim. **55**(1), 165–188 (2012). Springer Science+Business Media, LLC
13. Si, T., De, A., Bhattacharjee, A.K.: Particle Swarm Optimization with Generalized Opposition Based Learning in Particles Pbest Position. In: International Conference on Circuit, Power and Computing Technologies (ICCPCT), pp. 1662–1667 (2014)
14. Derrac, J., Garcia, S., Molina, D., Herrera, F.: A practical tutorial on the use of nonparametric statistical tests as a methodology for comparing evolutionary and swarm intelligence algorithms. Swarm Evol. Comput. **1**, 3–18 (2011)
15. Liang, J.J., Qu, B.Y., Suganthan, P.N., Hernandez-Diaz, A.G.: Problem Definitions and Evaluation Criteria for the CEC 2013 Special Session on Real-Parameter Optimization. http://www.ntu.edu.sg/home/EPNSugan/index_files/CEC2013/CEC2013.htm

Memetic Algorithm Used in Character Recognition

Rashmi Welekar[1]([envelope]) and Nileshsingh V. Thakur[2]

[1] Department of Computer Science and Engineering, Shri Ramdeobaba College
of Engineering and Management, Nagpur, Maharashtra, India
rashmi.welekar@gmail.com
[2] Department of Computer Science and Engineering, Prof Ram Meghe College
of Engineering and Management, Badnera-Amravati, Maharashtra, India
thakurnisvis@rediffmail.com

Abstract. Memetic algorithms (MAs) are basically optimization algorithms which fully exploit the problem under consideration. This paper describes the character recognition problem using traditional approach, genetic algorithm approach and memetic algorithm approach. It also describes the basic architecture of MA and elaborates the memetic algorithm based approach to character recognition. The comparison with traditional approach and genetic algorithm approach shows that MA remarkably reduces the error rate. This paper is useful for the beginners who apply nature based computing in character recognition.

Keywords: Memetic algorithms · Genetic algorithms · Minimum edit distance · Connected segments · Character recognition

1 Introduction

The Darwinian Theory is the inspiration for search and optimization techniques popularly known as Evolutionary algorithms (EAs). These evolutionary approaches incorporate the concept of natural selection. The solutions to problem areas under EAs are called as chromosomes. The chromosomes evolve themselves with application of crossover mechanism, mutation, and natural selection & are simulated through computer code. The pure EAs alone are not effective for search in complex problems. EAs along with the combination of other techniques can improve the efficiency of search. EAs combined with local search (LS) are named "memetic algorithms" (MAs) in [1, 2]. This paper describes how MA is useful in character recognition for reducing the error rate.

2 Memetic Algorithms

Memetic Algorithms. (MA) are one of the latest trends in evolutionary computation. Memetic algorithms club together any population-based approach with methods of local improvement for problem search. There are different names for MA in the literature e.g. hybrid Evolutionary algorithms, cultural algorithms, Baldwinian EAs, Lamarckian EAs, or genetic local search.

© Springer International Publishing Switzerland 2015
B.K. Panigrahi et al. (Eds.): SEMCCO 2014, LNCS 8947, pp. 636–646, 2015.
DOI: 10.1007/978-3-319-20294-5_55

The term "meme" was also put forward and defined in 1976 by Dawkins as "the basic unit of cultural transmission", and according to the English Oxford Dictionary as "an element of culture that may be considered to be passed on by non-genetic means". The term "Memetic algorithm" was coined by Moscato in his technical paper [2] in 1989. The concept is inspired from Darwinian concept of natural evolution and Dawkins' idea of a meme. His perception of MA was a form of population-based Genetic Algorithm (GA) which is hybrid with local search being introduced to refine individuals.

In the literature, the other names for MAs are hybrid genetic algorithms (GAs) (for e.g. [3–5]), genetic local searchers (for e.g. [6]), Lamarckian GAs (for e.g. [7]), and Baldwinian GAs (for e.g. [8]) etc. MAs are future generation of EAs that incorporates local search to refine individuals for example by improving their fitness by hill climbing. MAs are population-based metaheuristics. This means that the algorithm maintain a population of candidate solutions for the problem at hand. As such, the term MA has been used to describe a GA which favors local search. The elements in MA are called as memes similar to genes in GA. MA uses the newly created solutions using a Local Search method which are improvised individuals. This is made possible by exploiting the best search regions identified in the global sampling done by the EA.

Like GA, MA also generates the population randomly. Crossover and mutation operators are applied in the same way as GAs to generate offspring. The solution identified as the best, then undergoes the local search. Local search is applied to improve optimality. EAs and MAs have been applied in a number of different areas, for example protein structure formation, job scheduling in industry, operational research and optimization, automatic programming, and machine and robot learning. They have also been used in wide variety of areas to study and optimize models of economies, social systems, immune systems, ecologies, population genetics, and the interaction between evolution and learning. From an optimization point of view, MAs require orders of magnitude fewer evaluations to find optima and they identify higher quality solutions than traditional Evolutionary approaches.

The applications of MA range a wide variety of domains. Few of the recent notable implementations can be found in [16–18].

3 Outline of the Approach

Memetic Algorithms (MAs) are a powerful combination of local search with standard evolutionary algorithms. MA incorporates improvement on the basis of local-search methods, along with standard mutation and crossover operators. This paper presents a MA for Character Recognition. Character recognition problem is solved with traditional method, Genetic algorithms as well as MA. The description starts with the implementation of traditional approach.

3.1   Character Recognition Using Traditional Approach

The offline character recognition problem handled in this paper is solved using traditional approach. The steps followed are data acquisition, preprocessing, character segmentation and character recognition. The following sections discuss the idea in detail.

3.1.1   Character Encoding

Character recognition has large set of applications. They are diversified from recognition of address for sorting of mails to the use of online electronic forms. Depending on the application, the recognition system is either based on scanned image data *(off-line recognition)* or on runtime writing *(on-line recognition)* [9]. Online and offline recognition has different set of problems based on nature of data used. *On-line data* do not have segmentation problem because of spatial nature of data as they are separated by the time difference of the writing but the time based information can harden the recognition process.

On the other hand, *off-line* recognition works on scanned images which means the data is two-dimensional and overlapping characters can pose segmentation problems. With more information at hand on-line recognition becomes simpler. The work done earlier on converted or independent on-line and off-line data provide higher recognition performance for on-line data [10].

The state of the art discussion for character recognition can be found in [19–21]. In [19] Saba and Rehman have discussed the current advances and comparisons in cursive script recognition. Verma B. and Blumenstein M. in [20] have discussed Pattern Recognition Technologies and its applications. Alginahi, Y. in [21] has discussed preprocessing techniques in character recognition.

In the traditional approach discussed in this paper, experiments were performed over database collected by generating handwritten character samples. The input to the system is an image in the form of the file in standard graphic format like ".jpg". The preprocessor does the conversion of the image in the given file format into bitmap & converts the bitmap into array of bits having value 0 or 1, 0.

Once the binary image containing 1's and 0's is generated, the segmentation process is carried out. For segmentation the image is divided into columns. Based on the continuous 1's in a column a segment has been made. The set of all such segments is generated. The first step in segmentation is to find out segment in the vertical line i.e. segment set. Each segment is coded using operators and coding indicates how the segment is connected with next segment. The operators are nothing but the alphabets assigned to the segments based on their connectivity with the segments in very next column, height of a segment & position of a segment from the top of the column [11]. Following are the operators used for segment connectivity as shown in Fig. 1a.

Fig. 1. Operators used to encode a character into string

Fig. 2. Sample Image for coding

For the sample image shown in Fig. 2, the coding is described as follows:
NDNNQQQQUUUQUUUUUNNNUUNUQUQUQNQNQUQUQQQQQQQDQQ
UQQDUQUQUNUDUUQDNQQQQQQQQQ
Also the code *N* is used where no operators of type *U, D & Q* are found.

3.1.2   Recognition Method

The recognition method used is based on the concept of minimum edit distance. The similarity between two strings i.e. the source string (*s*) and the target string (*t*) [12] is calculated. The measure or distance is the number of insertions, deletions, or substitutions required to transform *s* into *t*. For example,

- If *s* is "skip" and *t* is "skop", then D(*s,t*) = 1, because one substitution (change "i" to "o") is sufficient to transform *s* into *t*.

The test string is checked against the string stored in the database. The distance against all the strings present in the database is calculated and the minimum value amongst them is identified. The handwritten samples have been taken from 6 different writers, 26 characters each. The test samples are taken from a seventh writer. Using the above approach the error rate is 15.38 % as shown in Table 1.

Table 1. Error rate using traditional approach for character recognition

Using Minimum	No. Of Samples	%Error Rate
Edit Distance	26*6	15.38 %

3.2   Character Recognition Approach Using Genetic Algorithm

The mechanism for discrimination of characters i.e. Data Collection, Preprocessing and Segmentation Coding, is same as in the above approach but for recognition genetic algorithm approach is used.

The image of the character is stored as string. This string acts as an input to the genetic algorithm which is used for recognition. Genetic algorithms are based on the concept of natural genetics and natural process of selection.

Simple GA is modified as in [15] and the algorithm consists of following steps:

1. Create a random population of *N* chromosomes.
2. Compute the fitness *f(x)* of every chromosome *x* in the current population.
3. Create a new population by iterating the following steps until the newly generated population reaches to population *N*:

   a. Copy the fittest 4 chromosome or genes to the next generation automatically (*Elitism*).
   b. With the remaining chromosomes, cross over two parent chromosomes to form two new offspring.
   c. Take the fitter offspring into the new population.

4. Copy the new population onto the previous (existing) population.
5. If the loop stopping condition is satisfied, then stop and give the result as the best solution in current population.
6. Otherwise, jump to Step 2.

3.2.1   Fitness Function

The fitness measure of a chromosome is the degree of match or similarity between the features of the test chromosome and the feature of database chromosomes. The minimum edit distance technique is used as in above case to calculate fitness of each chromosome.

3.2.2   Selection Reproduction Operator

This operator generates a competition between varying chromosomes. Actually, this operator verifies that the best chromosome will be won while the worse chromosomes are rejected. This paper uses tournament selection where two parent chromosomes are chosen at random for mating. In order to introduce new chromosomes in the population two operators been used: the elitism operator and the crossover.

3.2.3   Elitism

Elitism helps to automatically promote best or fittest n chromosomes in the next generation. This improves the overall fitness of the next generation. This approach chooses the first four fittest chromosomes to be placed directly in the next generation.

3.2.4   Crossover

The *crossover* operator is very important in a Genetic or a Memetic Algorithm and plays a great part in the behavior of the algorithm. A *crossover* operator combines two different solutions from the previous generation. This operator allows constructing new solutions from existing solutions. It creates offspring of the pairs of parents from the selection step. Chromosomes which undergo crossings mate randomly with a higher probability. A subchromosome is identified & selected in every parent and the resulting offspring is generated by concatenation of the sub-chromosomes. There are 3 types of crossover operators - uniform crossover, one-point crossover and two-point crossover. In the current experiment the one-point crossover operator is implemented. This operator takes a random cross point and swaps the sub-chromosomes of the two parents at this cross point. The resulting organisms are called as children. Figure 3 shows one-point crossover.

Parent 1:	11001l010	Parent 2: 001100l111
Offspring1:	11001l111	Offspring2: 001100l010

Fig. 3. One point crossover

The experimental results using GA are as follows: The database consists of strings of sample characters. The test image's string is compared against this database using a genetic algorithm. The error rate using genetic algorithm is shown in Table 2.

Table 2. Error rate using genetic algorithm approach for character recognition

Using Genetic	No. Of Samples	%Error Rate
Algorithm	26*6	7.69 %

The experimental results are better using genetic algorithm than traditional approach for character recognition as per the above discussion.

3.3   Character Recognition Approach Using Memetic Algorithm

The memetic algorithm implemented in this paper differs from a classical evolutionary algorithm. In this approach each child undergoes at each generation a step of local search (LS), which classifies algorithm as "memetic" [13]. Two children are generated after one point crossover. For the first time the fittest child is inserted into the next generation. From the next iteration the local search is applied. The minimum edit distance of the new child is computed and it is compared with the previous child. If it is less, then only the new child is inserted into the next generation. This technique enhances the quality of the next generation. Our ultimate solution is to find the string with minimum value of minimum edit distance. When the population has a large variety of fitness values, the local search works toward optimization and less fit child tend to be rejected.

3.3.1   A General Memetic Algorithm

A general memtic algorithm is implemented using following steps [14]:

1. Generate individuals for the initial population
2. Apply local search to improve each individual
3. Repeat
4. Select pairs of parents for crossover
5. Crossover: Produce children from each pair of parents
6. Perform mutation on each child
7. Apply local search to each child
8. Population replacement: Select children for the population in the next generation

   Until predefined number of generations are completed.

3.3.2   Sketch of the Memetic Algorithm Used in This Paper.
Memetic Algorithm

1: **input**: A problem instance **I**
2: **for** i = 1 to population size **do**
3: si ← random initial solution

4: si ← solution si after Local Search (LS)
5: **end for**
6: sort population by fitness
7: **while** termination condition not reached **do**
8: select two parents from population by tournament selection
9: s ← child solution after one point crossover
10: s ← child solution after applying Local Search (LS)
11: child solution is inserted if better than previous individual
12: sort population by fitness
13: best_sol ← best solution in the population
14: **end while**
15: **output:** The best solution best_sol achieved for **I**

In the MA used in this paper, first the population is initialized by the strings representation of the images from database and two parents are selected by tournament selection. Then local search method is applied on the new child to verify his eligibility into the next generation.

The local search procedure used is as follows:

While (stopping criteria is not reached) do
New solution ← neighbors (fittest solution);
If new solution is improved than the actual solution then
Fittest Solution ← new solution
End if, End while

The fittest solution is Best Solution. This continues until a terminating condition is reached. The population is sorted by fitness.

4 Experimental Results and Discussion

The program is coded in java on a 2.93 GHz Intel core2 Duo PC with 2 GB of RAM. The database consists of handwritten character samples collected from six different authors (subject). A sample database of 4 authors (subject) is shown in Fig. 4.

The string representation of these characters is treated as the initial population. The test images for 26 characters are taken from an independent seventh author (subject). In order to assess the efficiency of the strategy suggested for this problem, computational tests were carried out. Comparison of memetic algorithm (it is a hybrid algorithm between a genetic algorithm and a local search procedure), a genetic algorithm and traditional approach is done. Traditional approach, GA and memetic algorithm is applied. The MA shows remarkable improvement in the recognition rate by reducing error rate. Also a character misclassified by the GA is recognized by the MA.

The experimental results using MA are shown in Table 3.

Table 3. Error rate using memetic algorithm approach for character recognition

Using A Simple	No. Of Samples	%Error Rate
Memetic Algorithm	26*6	3.84 %

Fig. 4. A sample database of four authors (subject)

The comparison of the three methods used in this paper is shown Fig. 5 is as follows:

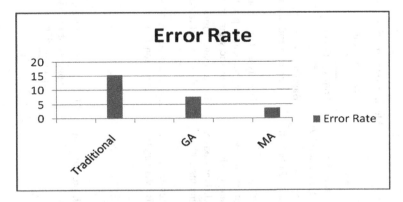

Fig. 5. Comparison of the three approaches used in character recognition

Above comparison shows that MA performs better than traditional and genetic algorithm based approach. Table 4 discusses various approaches used by various authors in the area of character recognition. Radmilo Bozinivic, Sargur Shrihari in [26]

Table 4. Comparison of proposed approach with other approaches for character recognition

Sr. No	Authors	Features identified	Feature extraction Technique	Recognition Mechanism	Recognition rate
1	Radmilo Bozinivic, Sargur Shrihari(1989)	Points,contours	Event generation. Set of 16 events are used.	Letter & Word hypothesization,	72 %
2	Andrew Senior &Anthony Robinson (1998)	Baseline estimation, dots, junctions,end points, loops	Skeletonization algorithm, connected component analysis	HMM	87 %
3	Chun ki Cheng,Xin Xu Liu,Blumenstein,V.M. Marasamy(2004)	It analyses the surrounding of segmentation point found by heuristic segmenter.	Modified direction feature, segmentation point validation	Using BP-MLP	67.54 %
4	B. gatos,I. Pratikakis,S. J. Perantonis(2006)	Word image normalization, robust hybrid feature extraction	Dividing word image into set of zones & then calculate density of character pixel in each zone.	K-NN classification algorithm	81.05 %
5	M. Blumenstein, X.Y. Liu &B. Verma(2007)	Direction feature,Modified Direction Feature	It extracts direction information from the structure of character contours.	With MLP: Lower case Upper case: With RBF: Lower case: Upper case:	70.22 % 80.33 % 71.33 % 81.58 %
6	Approach presented in this paper	Relationship between vertical segments of binary character representation	String representation of character	Memetic Algorithm	96.16 %

have extracted countours using event generation and achieved 72 % recognition rate by letter hypothization. Andrew Senior and Anthony Robinson in [22] have identified features such as dots, end points, turning points, loops and baseline estimation. The feature extraction mechanism used in [22] is skeletonization and connected component analysis, whereas HMM is used for recognition. With this approach they have achieved 87 % recognition rate. In [23] B. Gatos, Pratikakis and Perantonis have used robust feature extraction technique and with K-NN classification achieved 81.05 % recognition rate. M. Blumenstein, Verma and Liu in [24, 25] have used modified direction feature and MLP is used for recognition. They have achieved 70.22 % to 80.33 % recognition rate for lower case and upper case characters respectively. With the proposed approach in this paper character recognition rate using memetic algorithm is 96.16 %.

5 Conclusion

This paper has designed a memetic algorithm for character recognition. The memetic algorithm approach is compared with a genetic algorithm and traditional approach. Experimental results show that MA achieves higher recognition rate than GA and traditional approach. The computational experiences that have been made shown that MA obtains the best results.

References

1. Krasnogor, N., Smith, J.: A tutorial for competent memetic algorithms model taxonomy and design issues. IEEE Trans. Evol. Comput. 9(5), 474–488 (2005)
2. Moscato, P.: On evolution, search, optimization, GAs and martial arts: toward memetic algorithms California Inst. Technol. Pasadena, CA, Tech. Rep. Caltech Concurrent Comput. Prog. Rep. 826 (1989)
3. He, M.: Hybrid genetic algorithms for telecommunications network back-up routing. BT Technol. J. 18(4), 42–56 (2000)
4. Vazquez, M., Whitley, L.: A hybrid genetic algorithm for the quadratic assignment problem. In Proceedings Genetic Evolutionary Computation Conference, pp. 135–142 (2000)
5. Fleurent, C., Ferland, J.: Genetic hybrids for the quadratic assignment problem. In: DIMACS, Series in Discrete Mathematics and Theoretical Computer Science. Providence, RI: American Math. Soc. (1993)
6. Merz, P.: Memetic algorithms for combinatorial optimization problems: Fitness landscapes and effective search strategies. Ph.D. Dissertation, Parallel Syst. Res. Group, Dept. Elec. Eng. Comput. Sci., Univ. Siegen, Siegen, Germany, (2000)
7. Morris, G.M., Goodsell, D.S., Halliday, R.S., Huey, R., Hart, W.E., Belew, R.K., Olson, A. J.: Automated docking using a lamarkian genetic algorithm and an empirical binding free energy function. J. Comput. Chem. 14, 1639–1662 (1998)
8. Ku, K.W., Mak, M.W.: Empirical analysis of the factors that affect the baldwin effect. In: Eiben, A.E., Bäck, T., Schoenauer, M., Schwefel, H.-P. (eds.) PPSN 1998. LNCS, vol. 1498, pp. 481–490. Springer, Heidelberg (1998)

9. Plamondan, R., Shrihari, S.N.: Online and offline handwriting recognition: a comprehensive survey. IEEE Trans. Pattern Anal. Mach. Intell. **22**(1), 63–84 (2000)
10. Roberto, J.: Rodrigues and antonio carlos gay thome: cursive character recognition – a character segmentation method using projection profile-based technique. In: 6th International Conference on Information System, Analysis and Synthesis – ISAS (2000)
11. Latesh Malik, P.S.: Deshpande & Sandhya Bhagat: Character recognition using relationship between connected segments and neural network. Wseas Trans. Comput. **5**(1), 3 (2006)
12. Minimum Edit Distance. http://www.merriampark.com/ld.htm
13. Bazzoli, A., Tettamanzi, A.G.: A memetic algorithm for protein structure prediction in a 3D-Lattice HP model. In: Raidl, G.R., Cagnoni, S., Branke, J., Corne, D.W., Drechsler, R., Jin, Y., Johnson, C.G., Machado, P., Marchiori, E., Rothlauf, F., Smith, G.D., Squillero, G. (eds.) EvoWorkshops 2004. LNCS, vol. 3005, pp. 1–10. Springer, Heidelberg (2004)
14. Alegre, J.F., Alvarez, A., Casado, S., Pacheco, J.A.: Use of Memetic Algorithms To Solve A Stochastic Location Model, Health Resources For Diabetics In Some Provinces Of Castilla Leon. XIII Jornadas de, ASEPUMA (2005)
15. Smith, J.: Genetic Algorithms: Simulating Evolution on the Computer. Part 1 (2002)
16. Altntas, C., Asta, S., Ozcan, E., Yigit, T.: A self-generating memetic algorithm for examination timetabling. In: 10th International Conference of the Practice and Theory of Automated Timetabling, pp. 26–29 (2014)
17. Ye, T., Wang, T., Lu, Z., Hao, J.-K.: A Multi-parent Memetic Algorithm for the Linear Ordering Problem. arXiv preprint arXiv:1405.4507 (2014)
18. Martínez-Salazar, I., Molina, J., Caballero, R.: Francisco, Ángel-Bello: memetic algorithms for solving a bi-objective transportation location routing problem. In: Proceedings of the 2014 Industrial and Systems Engineering Research Conference (2014)
19. Rehman, A., Saba, T.: Off-Line cursive script recognition: current advances, comparisons and remaining problems. Artif. Intell. Rev. **37**, 261–288 (2012)
20. Verma, B., Blumenstein, M.: Pattern Recognition Technologies and Applications: Recent Advances (An Imprint of IGI Global Publications), pp. 1–16. Information Science Reference. Hershey, New York (2008)
21. Alginahi, Y.: Preprocessing techniques in character recognition, character recognition. In: Minoru M. (ed.), ISBN: 978-953-307-105-3, Techopen Publishers, pp. 1–20 (2010)
22. Senior, A.W., Robinson, A.J.: An offline cursive handwriting recognition system. IEEE Trans. Pattern Anal. Mach. Intell. **20**(3), 309–321 (1998)
23. Gatos, B., Pratikakis, S.J.: Perantonis: hybrid offline cursive handwriting word recognition. In: 18th International Conference on Pattern Recognition (ICPR 2006), pp. 998–1002 (2006)
24. Blumenstein, M., Liu, X.Y., Verma, B.: A modified direction feature for cursive character recognition. PR **40**(2), 376–388 (2007)
25. Cheng, C.K., Liu, X.X., Blumenstein, M., Marasamy, V.M.: Enhancing neural confidence based segmentation for cursive handwriting recognition. In: SEAL 04 and 2004 FIRA Robot World Congress (2004)
26. Bozinovic, R.M., Shrihari, S.N.: Offline cursive script word recognition. IEEE Trans. Pattern Anal. Mach. Intell. **11**(1), 68–83 (1989)

Hybrid Particle Swarm Optimization Algorithm and Firefly Algorithm Based Combined Economic and Emission Dispatch Including Valve Point Effect

S. Arunachalam[✉], T. AgnesBhomila, and M. Ramesh Babu

Department of E.E.E, St. Joseph's College of Engineering, Chennai, India
{mailtoarunachalam, agnesbhomila}@gmail.com,
rameshbabum@stjosephs.ac.in

Abstract. For economic and efficient operation of power system optimal scheduling of generators to minimize fuel cost of generating units and its emission is a major consideration. This paper presents a new approach to Combined Economic and Emission Dispatch (CEED) problem having conflicting economic and emission objectives using a Hybrid Particle Swarm Optimization and Firefly (HPSOFF) algorithm. The CEED problem is therefore formulated as a multi-objective optimization problem with the valve point effect using a price based penalty factor method. The effectiveness of the proposed HPSOFF algorithm is demonstrated with ten bus generator systems, and the numerical results are compared and discussed with available algorithms. The numerical results indicate that the proposed algorithm is able to provide better solution with reasonable computational time.

Keywords: Economic dispatch · Emission dispatch · Power loss · Multi objective optimization

1 Introduction

The main objective of Economic Dispatch (ED) problem is to determine the optimal combination of power outputs for all generating units, which minimizes the total fuel cost of the thermal power plants, while satisfying system load demand and operating constraints of the generators [1]. This makes the ED problem a large-scale, non-linear constrained optimization problem.

In general, the only objective of the ED problem is to minimize the total fuel cost. It is also necessary to consider related societal issues because of the scale of the electric industry and its importance to modern life. One of these issues is the environmental impact of electricity generation. The environmental issues caused by the pollutant emissions produced by fossil-fuelled electric power plants, have become a matter of concern.After the 1990 Clean Air Act amendments [2], environmental considerations have regained considerable attention in the power system industry, modern utilities have been forced to simultaneously optimize both economic and emission objectives.

© Springer International Publishing Switzerland 2015
B.K. Panigrahi et al. (Eds.): SEMCCO 2014, LNCS 8947, pp. 647–660, 2015.
DOI: 10.1007/978-3-319-20294-5_56

Economic dispatch (ED) has become a fundamental function in operation and control of power systems [1, 2]. The ED problem can be stated as determining the least cost power generation schedule from a set of online generating units to satisfy the load demand at a given point of time [3, 4]. Though the core objective of the problem is to minimize the operating cost satisfying the load demand [5], several types of physical and operational constraints make ED highly nonlinear constrained optimization problem [6, 7], especially for larger systems [8–11]. After the 1990 Clean Air Act amendments, environmental considerations have regained considerable attention in the power system industry due to the significant amount of emission and other pollutants derived from fossil fuel based power generation [12, 13]. The most important emissions are sulphur dioxide (SO_2) and nitrogen oxides (NO_x) [14]. Considering only the minimum environmental impact is not practical which results in high production cost of the system. Conversely, to operate the system with minimum cost will result in higher emission. So a combined approach is the best to achieve an optimal solution. Evolutionary computing techniques when applied to multi-objective optimization have clear edge over traditional methods. On the other hand Pareto optimization based methods are also used to solve various types of economic dispatch problem and presented in [15–18].

Multi-objective optimization problem is formulated using Combined Economic Emission Dispatch (CEED) approach which merges the cost and emission objectives into one optimization function such that equal importance is assigned to both objectives [19–23]. One such approach is to use a combination of polynomial and exponential terms. The parameters are determined by curve fitting techniques based on realistic data. The CEED problem is solved using a PSO and FFA algorithm and also using hybrid HPSOFF algorithm for a 10 bus test system. A comparison of PSO and FFA and HPSOFF algorithm is presented as case studies and the results suggest HPSOFF technique give a better result than PSO or FFA algorithm.

2 Combined Economic and Emission Dispatch (CEED)

The multi-objective CEED problem is formulated by combining the economic dispatch problem and emission dispatch problem into a single objective using price penalty factor method.

2.1 Formulation of CEED Problem

The objective of the CEED problem which has two conflicting objectives as economic and emission objective is to find the optimal schedules of the thermal generating units which minimizes the total fuel cost and emission from the thermal units subject to power balance equality constraint and bounds. The mathematical formulation of the CEED problem is given below

$$min[F_{TV}, E_T] \tag{1}$$

subject to power balance equation given in (2) and bounds given in (3)

$$\sum_{i=1}^{nb} P_i - P_D - P_L = 0 \tag{2}$$

$$P_{i,min} \leq P_i \leq P_{i,max} \tag{3}$$

where
F_{TV} Total fuel cost of Ng generating units with valve point effect

$$F_{TV} = \sum_{i=1}^{Ng} F(P_i) = \sum_{i=1}^{Ng} a_i P_i^2 + b_i P_i + c_i + d_i * \sin\left(e_i\left(P_{i,min} - P_i\right)\right)^{\$}\big/_h \tag{4}$$

E_T Total emission cost Ng generating units

$$E_T = \sum_{i=1}^{Ng} E(P_i) = \sum_{i=1}^{Ng} \alpha_i P_i^2 + \beta_i P_i + \gamma_i + \eta_i e^{\delta_i P_i} Kg\big/_h \tag{5}$$

$\alpha_i, \beta_i, \gamma_i, \eta_i, \delta_i$ Emission coefficients of thermal unit i
a_i, b_i, c_i Fuel cost coefficients of thermal unit i
e_i, f_i Coefficients to model the effect of valve point of thermal unit i
Ng Total number of thermal generating units
nb Number of buses
P_i Power generation of thermal unit i
P_D Total demand of the system
P_L Real Power transmission loss in the system
$P_{i,min}$ Minimum generation limit of thermal unit i
$P_{i,max}$ Maximum generation limit of thermal unit i
In the above formulation the transmission loss in the system is calculated using B matrix coefficients calculated from load flow solution as given in [14] and incorporated into power balance equality constraint. These loss coefficients are independent of slack bus. The transmission loss in the system is expressed using B matrix coefficients as

$$P_L = \sum_{i=1}^{nb} \sum_{j=1}^{nb} P_i B_{ij} P_j + \sum_{i=1}^{nb} B_{i0} P_i + B_{00} \tag{6}$$

The above multi objective problem can be combined into a single objective problem using price penalty factor approach. The price penalty factor approach to combine this multi objective problem in to a single objective is given in the next section.

2.2   Penalty Factor Approach

As mentioned earlier Multi-objective CEED is converted into a single objective problem using penalty factor approach. The sequential steps involved in calculating penalty factor are listed below [23]

- Evaluate the maximum cost of each generator at its maximum output.

$$F\left(P_{i,max}\right) = a_i P_{i,max}^2 + b_i P_{i,max} + c_i + e_i * \sin\left(f_i\left(P_{i,min} - P_{i,max}\right)\right)^{\$}/_h \qquad (7)$$

- Evaluate the maximum emission of each generator at its maximum output.

$$E\left(P_{i,max}\right) = \sum\nolimits_{i=1}^{Ng} \alpha_i P_{i,max}^2 + \beta_i P_{i,max} + \gamma_i + \eta_i e^{\delta_i P_{i,max}} Kg/_h \qquad (8)$$

- Divide the maximum cost of each generator by its maximum emission

$$h_i = \frac{F\left(P_{i,max}\right)}{E\left(P_{i,max}\right)} \qquad (9)$$

Arrange h_i in ascending order. Add $P_{i,max}$ of each unit one at a time starting from the smallest h_i unit until it meets the total demand P_D

At this stage, h_i associated with the last unit in the process is the price penalty factor h in $\$/_{Kg}$ for the given load.

2.3   Problem Formulation Using Price Penalty Factor Approach

The multi objective CEED is converted into single objective optimization using price penalty factor and the respective formulation is given below

$$min \sum\nolimits_{i=1}^{Ng} F_{TV}(P_i) + h \sum\nolimits_{i=1}^{Ng} E(P_i) \qquad (10)$$

subject to power balance equality constraint and bounds given below

$$\sum\nolimits_{i=1}^{nb} P_i - P_D - P_L = 0 \qquad (11)$$

$$P_{i,min} \leq P_i \leq P_{i,max} \qquad (12)$$

In (10) the $F_{TV}(P_i)$ can also be replaced by $F_T(P_i)$ if the valve point effect has to be neglected. $F_T = \sum_{i=1}^{Ng} F(P_i) = \sum_{i=1}^{Ng} a_i P_i^2 + b_i P_i + c_i$. In this paper the above formulation is solved using hybrid (HPSOFF) algorithm. A Brief algorithm of PSO and FFA is presented in the next section.

3   Particle Swarm Optimization Algorithm

PSO is one of the modern heuristic algorithms developed by Kennedy and Eberhart in 1995. The flock of birds that have no leaders will find food randomly, following one of the members of the group that has the closest position to a food source. The flock achieves the best condition simultaneously through communication among members who already have better solution. This would happen repeatedly until the best solution or food source is discovered. The control parameters of PSO algorithm are Initial Position of Particles, Maximum particle velocity, Maximum Iteration, Acceleration constant for local Best influence, Acceleration constant for global Best influence, Initial Inertia weight, Final Inertia Weight and Error gradient.

4   Firefly Algorithm

A Firefly Algorithm (FA) is a meta heuristic algorithm inspired by the flashing behavior of fireflies. This algorithm is based on the natural behavior of fireflies which is based on the bioluminescence phenomenon. The firefly algorithm has basic idealized rules that are followed while movement of one firefly to other.

- All fireflies are unisex and they will move towards more attractive and brighter ones regardless of their sex.
- The degree of attractiveness of a firefly is proportional to its brightness.
- Also the brightness may decrease as the distance from the other fire flies increases due to the fact that the air absorbs light.
- If there is not a brighter or more attractive fire fly than a particular one it will then move randomly.
- The brightness or light intensity of a fire fly is determined by the value of the objective function of a given problem.

By using the above rules it is possible to achieve the optimum value of the objective function.

5   HPSOFF Algorithm

In this paper, a hybrid PSO-FFA algorithm is proposed for solving CEED problem. The proposed PSO-FFA is a method of combining the advantages of faster computation of Particle Swarm Optimization with robustness of Firefly Algorithm (FFA) so as to increase the global search capability. The PSO algorithm starts with a set of solutions and based upon the survival of fittest principle, only the best solution moves from one phase to another. This process is repeated until the any of the convergence criteria is met. At the end of the iterations the optimal solution is the one with the minimum total cost out of the set of solutions. The time of convergence of PSO depends upon the values of the randomly set control parameters. FFA algorithm starts with an initial operating solution and every iteration improves the solution until the convergence criteria is met. The optimal solution obtained from FFA algorithm depends upon the quality of the initial solution provided. In this paper the initial solution provided to FFA is the optimal solution obtained from PSO algorithm. Since a best initial solution from PSO is given to FFA algorithm the optimal solution obtained from this Hybrid approach is better than the solution obtained from PSO or FFA algorithms.

The sequential steps involved in the proposed HPSOFF algorithm is given below

1. The cost data, emission data and valve point data of each generating unit are read and system load is also specified. The operating limits of the thermal plants are specified.
2. The penalty factor to combine the multi objective problem into a single objective problem is obtained from the algorithm given in Sect. 2.2.
3. Using this penalty factor a lossless dispatch is carried out using PSO algorithm for the formulation given by Eqs. (10) to (12).
4. With the obtained solution an AC power flow is carried out and the B-loss coefficients are obtained [22]. These coefficients are used for calculation of real power loss in the subsequent iterations.
5. The various control parameters of the PSO algorithm are initialized. Formulation given by Eqs. (10) to (12) is solved using the PSO algorithm developed in MATLAB.
6. PSO runs till its stopping criterion (the maximum number of iterations) is met,
7. In order to obtain the optimal control parameters, the steps 7 to 10 is run many times with one control parameter fixed and all other control parameters are varied. This step is repeated to find the best control parameter for PSO algorithm.
8. With the best control parameters set, the PSO algorithm is carried and the optimal solution is obtained. With this optimal schedule an AC load flow is carried out and using the solutions of AC load flow the new loss Coefficients are obtained and considered for the subsequent iteration.
9. The optimal solution of PSO is given as the starting point (Initial guess vector) to the FFA algorithm and the control parameters of FFA are set.
10. Then, the FFA algorithm starts its search process and it is run until its stopping criterion is met.
11. With this optimal solution the total fuel cost of the thermal generating units and its emission cost are calculated.

6   Case Study

This case study consists of a standard test system with 10 generating units. The complexity to the solution process has significantly increased since the valve point effect is considered. In this system with higher non-linearity, it has more local minima and thus it is difficult to attain the global solution. The load demand of this test system is 2000 MW. The fuel cost coefficients with valve point co-efficient and emission function coefficients to minimize sulphur oxides(SOx) and Nitrogen oxides(NOx) caused by thermal plant along with generator capacity limits of each generator are given in appendix Tables 5 and 6. Here the losses in the system are also considered. The B matrix of the test system is tabulated in appendix Table 7. As mentioned earlier economic and emission objectives are combined using Penalty factor approach. The penalty factor obtained from the procedure described in Sect. 2.2 is $h = 51.99\$ /kg$

For this system the optimal dispatches is obtained using PSO, FFA, and HPSOFF algorithm and are compared in the subsequent sections. The simulations are all carried

Table 1. Solution of CEED problem obtained using ABC algorithm

P1 (MW)	P2 (MW)	P3 (MW)	P4 (MW)	P5 (MW)	P6 (MW)	P7 (MW)	P8 (MW)	P9 (MW)	P10 (MW)	Fuel Cost ($/hr)	Emission (kg/hr)	Total Cost ($/hr)	TIME (sec)
54.99	78.16	79.94	75.00	159.99	239.99	269.53	287.08	409.81	423.77	111261	3934.5	320593	8.01
54.99	77.47	79.63	79.18	159.99	239.99	255.02	296.15	410.94	429.07	111272	3948.9	321069	6.01
54.99	77.77	78.91	80.04	159.99	239.95	255.02	296.15	410.94	429.07	111228	3942.1	321003	6.17
54.93	76.04	78.15	78.20	159.92	232.11	262.55	287.51	419.28	434.10	111229	3957.5	321456	6.29
54.99	**78.82**	**78.90**	**79.58**	**159.99**	**239.99**	**290.19**	**302.99**	**398.40**	**397.85**	**111263**	**3922.0**	**320069**	**5.98**
54.99	76.96	80.44	79.71	159.99	235.2	287.53	293.05	381.94	432.28	111269	3940.2	320781	6.03
54.99	76.87	78.53	78.30	159.99	228.58	271.94	286.15	418.33	428.93	111262	3954.4	321176	6.92
54.99	77.86	79.55	78.86	159.99	239.99	262.63	296.63	433.66	397.75	111265	3940.1	320914	6.90
54.99	78.25	79.61	78.98	159.99	239.99	273.23	289.12	410.62	417.44	111266	3934.1	320411	6.69
54.99	78.35	78.59	78.42	159.99	239.8	269.63	271.00	426.58	425.27	111266	3945.9	321164	6.92
54.99	78.62	79.30	78.56	159.99	239.93	281.35	273.33	435.63	400.50	111261	3939.5	320890	6.85
54.98	78.27	79.03	79.09	159.99	239.87	268.47	285.36	414.72	422.5	111262	3936.2	320672	6.55
54.99	76.88	79.25	78.11	159.99	235.57	276.54	289.88	419.86	411.10	111264	3936.3	320565	6.13
54.99	77.65	79.87	78.98	159.99	235.59	285.04	284.03	433.94	390.94	111252	3940.7	320817	6.75
54.99	78.61	78.35	78.78	160.00	239.99	266.24	284.33	420.07	421.06	111262	3935.5	320792	6.95
54.99	77.06	78.62	78.39	159.99	226.1	283.14	271.56	430.83	422.07	111263	3961.0	321447	6.90
54.99	77.43	79.20	78.46	159.99	239.99	282.47	271.92	403.9	434.05	111253	3940.0	320900	6.79
54.99	77.98	78.70	79.32	159.99	239.97	266.01	282.39	420.47	422.62	111254	3939.7	320848	6.72
54.99	78.20	79.00	79.49	159.99	238.18	264.01	291.08	422.59	414.84	111226	3939.3	320768	6.68
54.99	77.90	79.00	79.83	159.99	239.99	278.67	268.58	423.36	420.14	111224	3939.7	320876	6.32

Table 2. Optimal Schedule of CEED problem obtained using Firefly algorithm.

P1 (MW)	P2 (MW)	P3 (MW)	P4 (MW)	P5 (MW)	P6 (MW)	P7 (MW)	P8 (MW)	P9 (MW)	P10 (MW)	Fuel Cost ($/hr)	Emission (kg/hr)	Total Cost ($/hr)	TIME (sec)
30.99	60.39	99.24	83.72	122.05	206.57	240.14	309.69	458.33	449.06	114518	4172.8	331490	1.94

out using algorithms developed in MATLAB (V2009a) software installed in HP Compaq Presario V3000 Laptop with Windows XP operating system, AMD Turion processor, 1.61 GHz and 960 MB of RAM.

6.1   Solution of CEED Problem Using PSO Algorithm

Since the evolutionary algorithm is used to solve CEED, certain parameters of the algorithm have to be randomly adjusted. The control parameters of PSO algorithm are set as follows

- Initial Position:Random
- Maximum particle velocity: 1
- Maximum Iteration: 500
- Acceleration constant for local Best influence: 2
- Acceleration constant for global Best influence: 2
- Initial Inertia weight: 0.9
- Final Inertia Weight: 0.4
- Error gradient: $1e^{-6}$

The optimal particle size for this case study after testing with various values is found to be 50. With these parameters PSO algorithm is run for twenty times and the schedules are shown in Table 1.

The optimal schedules from the ABC algorithm is shown in bold in Table 1. At the end of several trial runs the best optimal fuel cost is found to be 111263 $/hr and the emission is found to be 3922 kg/hr. The transmission loss for the optimal schedule showed in bold in Table 1 is 81.704 MW. The total cost is obtained as 320069 $/hr. These results are obtained within a computation time of 5.98 s.

6.2   Solution of CEED Problem Using Firefly Method

Similar to PSO method, the parameters of FIREFLY method is set by trial and error technique and the parameters are set at

- Number of Fireflies: 40
- Maximum Iterations: 500
- Alpha: 0.5
- Beta: 0.2
- Absorption Coefficient gamma:0.1

With these parameters Firefly algorithm is run for twenty times and the optimal schedule is shown in Table 1.

At the end of several trails the best optimal fuel cost is found to be 114518 $/*hr* and the emission is found to be 4172.8 *kg/hr*. The total cost is obtained as 331490. in 1.94 s. Even though the optimal schedules obtained by the firefly algorithm is inferior to PSO algorithm it converges faster than PSO algorithm.

Table 3. Solution of CEED problem obtained using HPSOFF algorithm

P1 (MW)	P2 (MW)	P3 (MW)	P4 (MW)	P5 (MW)	P6 (MW)	P7 (MW)	P8 (MW)	P9 (MW)	P10 (MW)	Fuel Cost ($/hr)	Emission (kg/hr)	Total Cost ($/hr)	TIME (sec)
41.21	73.54	86.56	78.17	153.44	235.19	286.31	304.22	399.49	410.06	114989	3938.9	331361	14.21
37.21	68.67	83.97	82.88	160.00	238.01	291.41	299.73	403.43	397.61	115186	3929.7	319187	14.39
34.64	73.10	93.79	81.03	159.31	233.87	275.63	294.50	404.34	411.30	114893	3950.4	319541	17.07
34.83	75.90	90.64	93.99	159.69	236.69	290.20	299.56	391.14	388.14	115035	3930.5	319405	15.97
38.09	68.28	95.45	82.15	159.92	236.49	283.35	306.34	391.74	402.80	115130	3935.4	319761	15.53
34.84	69.39	91.74	78.04	159.88	231.87	293.65	301.23	391.86	409.14	114779	3938.8	315921	14.96
22.95	74.19	91.22	84.81	159.98	236.96	278.16	305.41	401.05	394.67	114484	3951.8	319402	15.62
34.80	72.15	85.80	83.13	159.99	232.12	287.73	297.28	402.29	406.36	114749	3931.1	319154	15.33
26.17	68.70	90.60	85.82	158.49	236.50	278.57	301.62	391.29	415.14	114466	3947.9	319750	16.24
33.51	77.30	84.82	90.07	159.99	235.84	285.17	305.04	399.11	388.80	114922	3937.5	319062	15.19
29.52	58.75	87.36	96.74	160.00	238.78	278.69	300.87	409.38	395.90	114949	3976.0	320664	13.32
40.17	68.78	94.26	88.55	158.21	234.33	284.58	291.06	412.82	293.97	115081	3941.3	320016	16.39
32.09	73.09	85.26	86.32	159.99	232.63	280.64	297.80	403.32	407.81	114621	3933.7	319167	16.52
35.41	70.23	79.15	89.58	158.02	235.73	278.02	296.52	419.70	399.99	114860	3945.9	319647	14.99
22.76	74.67	86.81	84.62	160.00	238.56	280.53	301.47	399.70	400.22	114437	3945.0	319157	16.30
31.72	74.94	91.85	87.82	159.99	238.24	281.59	286.65	393.01	412.73	114945	3936.5	319257	13.59
37.59	71.84	86.66	84.56	160.00	231.85	277.55	301.94	407.77	404.75	114924	3937.1	319360	16.37
36.15	**76.03**	**88.35**	**84.23**	**160.00**	**237.0**	**280.85**	**297.7**	**410.36**	**391.93**	**115012**	**3923.3**	**319038**	**16.08**
37.22	69.77	88.84	96.39	159.99	236.44	282.53	297.56	397.71	397.23	115103	3943.0	319757	15.05
35.41	68.46	89.18	88.07	151.87	238.59	294.62	294.62	295.32	396.22	114876	3953.4	319934	17.74

Table 4. Comparison of the optimal schedules obtained by PSO, FFA, HPSOFF method.and Hybrid ABC-SA method used in [29]

SCHEDULES	PSO	FFA	HPSOFF	Ref [29]
P1(MW)	54.99	30.99	36.15	55.00
P2(MW)	78.82	60.39	76.03	70.32
P3(MW)	78.90	99.24	88.35	81.18
P4(MW)	79.58	83.72	84.23	96.47
P5(MW)	159.99	122.05	160.00	159.72
P6(MW)	239.99	206.57	237.05	155.92
P7(MW)	290.19	240.14	280.85	229.31
P8(MW)	302.91	309.69	297.77	337.57
P9(MW)	398.40	458.33	410.36	431.34
P10(MW)	397.85	449.06	391.93	467.57
TOTAL COST ($/hr)	320069	331490	**319038**	330210
TIME (sec)	5.98	1.94	**16.08**	22.35

Table 5. Fuel cost coefficients of 10 generating units

UNIT	a ($/MW^2)hr	b $/(MW)hr	c $/hr	d ($/hr)	e rad/MW
1	0.12951	40.5407	1000.40	33	0.0174
2	0.10908	39.5804	950.606	25	0.0178
3	0.12511	36.5104	900.705	32	0.0162
4	0.12111	39.5104	800.705	30	0.0168
5	0.15247	38.539	756.799	30	0.0148
6	0.10587	46.1592	451.325	20	0.0163
7	0.03546	38.3055	1243.53	20	0.0152
8	0.02803	40.3965	1049.99	30	0.0128
9	0.02111	36.3278	1658.56	60	0.0136
10	0.01799	38.2704	1356.65	40	0.0141

Table 6. Emission coefficients of 10 generating units

A (lb/MW)^2 ^{h}	β (lb/MWhr)	γ lb/hr	eta lb/hr	Lambda (1/MW)	P$_{Max (MW)}$	P$_{Min (MW)}$
0.04702	-3.9864	360.0012	0.25475	0.01234	55	10
0.04652	-3.9524	350.0012	0.25473	0.01234	80	20
0.04652	-3.9023	330.0056	0.25163	0.01215	120	47
0.04652	-3.9023	330.0056	0.25163	0.01215	130	20
0.0042	0.3277	13.8593	0.2497	0.012	160	50
0.0042	0.3277	13.8593	0.2497	0.012	240	70
0.0068	-0.5455	40.2699	0.248	0.0129	300	60
0.0068	-0.5455	40.2699	0.2499	0.01203	340	70
0.0046	-0.5112	42.8955	0.2547	0.01234	470	135
0.0046	-0.5112	42.8955	0.2547	0.01234	470	150

Table 7. B Loss coefficeints of 10 generating units

0.000049	0.000014	0.000015	0.000016	0.000016	0.000016	0.000016	0.000016	0.000016	0.000016
0.000014	0.000045	0.000016	0.000016	0.000017	0.000015	0.000015	0.000016	0.000018	0.000018
0.000015	0.000016	0.000039	0.00001	0.000012	0.000012	0.000014	0.000014	0.000016	0.000016
0.000015	0.000016	0.00001	0.00004	0.000014	0.00001	0.000011	0.000012	0.000014	0.000015
0.000016	0.000017	0.000012	0.000014	0.000035	0.000011	0.000013	0.000013	0.000015	0.000016
0.000017	0.000015	0.000012	0.00001	0.000011	0.000036	0.000012	0.000012	0.000014	0.000015
0.000017	0.000015	0.000014	0.000011	0.000013	0.000012	0.000038	0.000016	0.000016	0.000018
0.000018	0.000016	0.000014	0.000012	0.000013	0.000012	0.000016	0.00004	0.000015	0.000016
0.000019	0.000018	0.000016	0.000014	0.000015	0.000014	0.000016	0.000015	0.000042	0.000019
0.00002	0.000018	0.000016	0.000015	0.000016	0.000015	0.000018	0.000016	0.000019	0.000044

6.3 Solution of CEED Problem Using HPSOFF Algorithm

In this method the best schedule obtained in PSO method is given as initial start to Firefly algorithm and the parameters of the firefly algorithm are set as Number of Fireflies: 40, Maximum Iterations:500, Alpha:0.5, Beta:0.2 and Absorption Coefficient gamma:0.1. HPSOFF algorithm is run for 20 times and the schedules obtained from the hybrid method are shown in Table 3. The optimal schedule is shown in bold in Table 3.

The transmission loss for the optimal schedule shown in bold in Table 3 is 62.602 MW. The optimal cost obtained using HPSOFF is 319038 \$/hr is better when compared to the optimal cost of 320069\$/hr obtained using PSO algorithm shown in Table 1 and the optimal cost of 331490 \$/hr obtained using firefly algorithm shown in Table 2. The comparison of the results obtained from the proposed method is shown in Table 4.

7 Conclusion

This paper has implemented a hybrid PSO and FF algorithm for solving the combined economic and emission dispatch problem including valve point effect. Results obtained from the proposed method are compared with PSO, FFA and HPSOFF. From the case studies carried out on the test systems and the results obtained indicate the proposed algorithm is able to find better optimal schedules in a reasonable computational time since it combines the advantages of faster computation of Particle Swarm Optimization with robustness of Firefly Algorithm (FFA) so as to increase the global search capability.

References

1. Wood, A.J., Wollenberg, B.F.: Power Generation, Operation and Control. Wiley, New York (1996)
2. Da-Kuo, H., Fu-li, W., M., Zhi-Zhong : Hybrid genetic algorithm for Economic Dispatch with Valve point effect, Electr. Power Syst. Res. **78**, 626–633 (2008)
3. Lu, Y., Zhou, J., Yinghaili, H.Q., Zhang, Y.: An adaptive hybrid differential evolution algorithm for dynamic economic dispatch with valve point effects. Electr. Power Syst. Res. **37**, 4842–4849 (2010)
4. Hota, P.K., Barisal, A.K., Chakrabarthi, R.: Economic Emission load dispatch through fuzzy based bacterial Foraging algorithm. Electr. Power Syst. Res. **32**, 794–803 (2010)
5. Zhang, P.X., Zhao, B., Cao, Y.J., Cheng, S.J.: A novel multi-objective genetic algorithm for economic power dispatch. In: 39th International Universities Power Engineering Conference, UPEC 2004, vol. 1, p. 422–6, 6–8 September 2004
6. Gong, D., Zhang, Y., Qi, C.: Environmental/economic power dispatch using a hybrid multi objective optimization algorithm. Int. J. Electr. Power Energy Syst. **32**(6), 607–614 (2010)
7. Han, X.S., Gooi, H.B., Kirschen, D.S.: Dynamic economic dispatch: feasible and optimal solutions. IEEE Trans. Power Syst. **16**(1), 8–22 (2001)

8. Granelli, P., Marannino, P., Montagna, M., Silvestri, A.: Fast and efficient gradient projection algorithm for dynamic generation dispatching. Proc. Inst. Elect. Eng. Gener Trans. Distrib. **136**(5), 295–302 (1989)
9. Li, F., Morgan, R., Williams, D.: Hybrid genetic approaches to ramping rate constrained dynamic economic dispatch. Elect. Power Syst. Res. **43**(2), 97–103 (1997)
10. Aruldoss, A.V.T., Ebenezer, J.A.: Deterministically guided PSO for dynamic dispatch considering valve-point effect. Elect. Power Syst. Res. **73**(3), 313–322 (2005)
11. Abido, M.A.: Environmental/economic power dispatch using multi objective evolutionary algorithms. IEEE Trans. Power Syst. **18**(4), 1529–1537 (2003)
12. El-Keib, A.A., Ma, H., Hart, J.L.: Economic dispatch in view of the clean air act of 1990. IEEE Trans. Power Syst. **9**(2), 972–978 (1994)
13. IEEE Current Operating Problems Working Group, Potential impacts of clean air regulations on system operations, IEEE Trans. Power Syst. **10**(2), 647–653 (1995)
14. Abido, M.A.: A novel multi objective evolutionary algorithm for environmental/economic power dispatch. Electr. Power Syst. Res. **65**, 71–81 (2003)
15. Panigrahi, B.K., Ravikumar, V., Pandi, S.D., Swagatam, D.: Multi objective fuzzy dominance based bacterial foraging algorithm to solve economic emission dispatch problem. Energy **35**(12), 4761–4770 (2010)
16. Pandi, V.R., Panigrahi, B.K., Hong, W.C., Sharma, R.: A multiobjective bacterial foraging algorithm to solve the environmental economic dispatch problem. Energy Sources Part B **9** (3), 236–247 (2014)
17. Agrawal, S., Panigrahi, B.K., Tiwari, M.K.: Multiobjective particle swarm algorithm with fuzzy clustering for electrical power dispatch. IEEE Trans. Evol. Comput. **12**(5), 529–541
18. Panigrahi, B.K., Pandi, V.R., Das, S.: An adaptive particle swarm optimization approach for static and dynamic economic load dispatch. Int. J. Energy Convers. Manage. **49**, 1407–1415 (2008)
19. Yokoyama, R., Bae, S.H., Morita, T., Sasaki, H.: Multi objective generation dispatch based on probability security criteria. IEEE Trans. Power Syst. **3**(1), 24–317 (1988)
20. Abido, M.A.: Multi objective particle swarm optimization for environmental/economic dispatch problem. Electr. Power Res. **79**, 1105–1113 (2009)
21. Abido, M.A.: Multi objective evolutionary algorithms for electric power dispatch problem. IEEE Trans. Evol. Comput. **10**(3), 315–319 (2006)
22. John, J., Stevenson, G.W.D. Jr.: Power system Analysis. TATA McGraw-Hill Edition
23. Arunachalam, S., Saranya, R., Sangeetha, N.: Hybrid artificial bee colony algorithm and simulated annealing algorithm for combined economic and emission dispatch including valve point effect. In: Panigrahi, B.K., Suganthan, P.N., Das, S., Dash, S.S. (eds.) SEMCCO 2013, Part I. LNCS, vol. 8297, pp. 354–365. Springer, Heidelberg (2013)

Solution of Optimal Power Flow with FACTS Devices Using Opposition-Based Gravitational Search Algorithm

Binod Shaw[1], V. Mukherjee[2(✉)], and S.P. Ghoshal[3]

[1] Department of Electrical Engineering, Asansol Engineering College, Asansol, West Bengal, India
binodshaw2000@gmail.com
[2] Department of Electrical Engineering, Indian School of Mines, Dhanbad, Jharkhand, India
vivek_agamani@yahoo.com
[3] Department of Electrical Engineering, National Institute of Technology, Durgapur, West Bengal, India
spghoshalnitdgp@gmail.com

Abstract. This paper presents the solution of optimal power flow (OPF) of power system with flexible AC transmission systems (FACTS) devices by using opposition-based gravitational search algorithm (OGSA). OPF problem with FACTS is solved by the way of minimizing an objective function which reflects cost of generation, emission and active power transmission loss. FACTS devices considered include thyristor controlled series capacitor and thyristor controlled phase shifter. The proposed approach has been examined and tested on the IEEE 57-bus test power system. The obtained results are compared with those reported in the literature. Simulation results demonstrate the superiority and accuracy of the proposed algorithm. Considering the quality of the solution obtained, the proposed algorithm seems to be effective and robust to solve the studied problem.

Keywords: Flexible ac transmission systems · Opposition-based gravitational search algorithm · Optimal power flow

Nomenclature

N_G	Number of generators
$P_{G_i}^{min}$, $P_{G_i}^{max}$	Minimum and maximum active power generation of ith generator, respectively
δ_{ij}	Phase difference of voltages between ith and jth bus
P_{Li}	Active power demand of the ith bus
Q_{Gi}, Q_{Li}	Reactive power generation and demand of the ith bus, respectively
P_{TCPS}, Q_{TCPS}	Injected active and reactive powers of TCPS at the ith bus, respectively
N_B	Number of buses
Y_{ij}	Admittance of transmission line connected between the ith and the jth bus

© Springer International Publishing Switzerland 2015
B.K. Panigrahi et al. (Eds.): SEMCCO 2014, LNCS 8947, pp. 661–673, 2015.
DOI: 10.1007/978-3-319-20294-5_57

θ_{ij}	Admittance angle of transmission line connected between the ith and the jth bus
N_{TCPS}	Number of TCPS devices
N_{TCSC}	Number of TCSC devices
$X_{TCSC_i}^{\min}, X_{TCSC_i}^{\max}$	Minimum and maximum reactance of the ith TCSC, respectively
$\phi_{TCPS_i}^{\min}, \phi_{TCPS_i}^{\max}$	Minimum and maximum phase shift angle of the ith TCPS respectively
$E(P_G)$	Total emission
$\alpha_i, \beta_i, \gamma_i, \eta_i$ and λ_i	Emission coefficients of ith generator
N_{TL}	Number of transmission lines

1 Introduction

In recent years, the fast progress in the field of power electronics and microelectronics has resulted into a new opportunity for more flexible operation of power system. These new devices have made the present transmission and distribution of electricity more reliable, controllable and efficient. Optimal power flow (OPF) is a non-linear problem and can be non-convex in some cases. Moreover, incorporation of flexible AC transmission system (FACTS) devices complicates the problem further. Such complicated problems need a well-efficient optimization technique for solving.

Traditional optimization techniques such as gradient method [1], linear programming (LP) [2, 3] and Newton's method [4] are used to solve the OPF problem of power system assuming continuous, differentiable and monotonically increasing cost function. However, these methods have failed in handling non-convex and non-linear engineering optimization problems and tended to get stuck at local optimum solutions. Since OPF incorporating FACTS devices with valve point discontinuities are highly non-linear optimization problems with non-differentiable features, stochastic search techniques such as genetic algorithm (GA) [5–11], particle swarm optimization (PSO) [12, 13], differential evolution (DE) [14] etc. have been used to solve these problems.

Literature review reveals that computational intelligence-based techniques have been applied for solving OPF problem with FACTS devices. These techniques have shown effectiveness in overcoming the disadvantages of classical algorithms.

In this paper, opposition-based gravitational search algorithm (OGSA) is applied to the OPF problem with FACTS devices. IEEE 57-bus test power system is adopted and this problem is solved with different objectives that reflect minimization of either fuel cost or that of emission or that of active transmission power loss (P_{Loss}). Results obtained are compared to other computational intelligence-based meta-heuristics surfaced in the recent state-of-the-art literature.

The rest of this paper is organized as follows. In Sect. 2, static modeling of FACTS devices is presented. In Sect. 3, mathematical modeling of OPF with FACTS problem is formulated. Proposed optimization algorithm and its application to the OPF with

FACTS problem is narrated in Sect. 4. Numerical examples and simulation results are presented in Sect. 5 to demonstrate the performance of the proposed algorithm for the OPF with FACTS problem. Section 6 focuses on the conclusion of the present work.

2 Static Model of FACTS Devices

2.1 Thyristor Controlled Series Compensator (TCSC)

The effect of TCSC on a network may be represented by a controllable reactance inserted in the related transmission line. Active power flow through the compensated transmission line can be maintained at a specified level under a wide range of operating conditions.

The power flow equations of the branch having TCSC between ith and jth bus can be derived as follows [14]:

$$P_{ij} = V_i^2 g_{ij} - V_i V_j g_{ij} \cos(\delta_i - \delta_j) - V_i V_j b_{ij} \sin(\delta_i - \delta_j) \tag{1}$$

$$Q_{ij} = -V_i^2 b_{ij} - V_i V_j g_{ij} \sin(\delta_i - \delta_j) + V_i V_j b_{ij} \cos(\delta_i - \delta_j) \tag{2}$$

$$P_{ij} = V_j^2 g_{ij} - V_i V_j g_{ij} \cos(\delta_i - \delta_j) - V_i V_j b_{ij} \sin(\delta_i - \delta_j) \tag{3}$$

$$Q_{ij} = -V_j^2 b_{ij} - V_i V_j g_{ij} \sin(\delta_i - \delta_j) + V_{ij} V_j b_{ij} \cos(\delta_i - \delta_j) \tag{4}$$

where $g_{ij} = \frac{r_{ij}}{r_{ij}^2 + (x_{ij} - X_c)^2}$, $b_{ij} = \frac{x_{ij} - X_c}{r_{ij}^2 + (x_{ij} - X_c)^2}$

2.2 Thyristor Controlled Phase Shifter (TCPS)

The static model of a TCPS connected between ith bus and jth bus, having a complex tapping ratio, $1 : a\angle\phi = [1 : a_r + sqrt(-1) \times a_i]$ and series admittance of the transformer is $(g_{ij} - sqrt(-1) \times b_{ij})$. The real and reactive power flows from the ith and the jth bus may be derived similar to TCSC and may be expressed as [14]:

$$P_{ij} = \frac{V_i^2 g_{ij}}{\cos^2 \varphi} - \frac{V_i V_j}{\cos \varphi} \left[g_{ij} \cos(\delta_i - \delta_j + \varphi) + b_{ij} \sin(\delta_i - \delta_j + \varphi) \right] \tag{5}$$

$$Q_{ij} = -\frac{V_i^2 b_{ij}}{\cos^2 \varphi} - \frac{V_i V_j}{\cos \varphi} \left[g_{ij} \sin(\delta_i - \delta_j + \varphi) - b_{ij} \cos(\delta_i - \delta_j + \varphi) \right] \tag{6}$$

$$P_{ij} = V_j^2 g_{ij} - \frac{V_i V_j}{\cos \varphi} \left[g_{ij} \cos(\delta_i - \delta_i + \varphi) - b_{ij} \sin(\delta_i - \delta_j + \varphi) \right] \tag{7}$$

$$Q_{ij} = -V_j^2 b_{ij} - \frac{V_i V_j}{\cos \varphi} \left[g_{ij} \sin(\delta_i - \delta_j + \varphi) + b_{ij} \cos(\delta_i - \delta_j + \varphi) \right] \tag{8}$$

3 Mathematical Modeling of OPF Problem with FACTS

3.1 Minimization of Fuel Cost

3.1.1 Cost Function with Quadratic Cost Function

Total fuel cost of generating units having quadratic cost function without valve point effect is given by (9) and (10) [14].

$$Min \ F_T = Min \ \sum_{i=1}^{N_G} F_i(P_i) \quad \$/h \tag{9}$$

$$F_i(P_{G_i}) = a_i + b_i P_{G_i} + c_i P_{G_i}^2 \quad \$/h \qquad i = 1,\ldots\ldots, N_G \tag{10}$$

3.1.2 Cost Function with Valve Point Effect

For more practical and accurate model of the cost function, multiple valve steam turbines are incorporated for flexible operational facilities. Total cost of generating units with valve point loading is given by (11) [14].

$$F_i(P_i) = a_i + b_i P_i + c_i P_i^2 + \left| e_i \times \sin(f_i \times (P_i^{min} - P_i)) \right| \tag{11}$$

3.2 Minimization of Emission

Mathematical formulation for this type of objective function is given as (11) and (13) [14].

$$E_i(P_{Gi}) = 10^{-2} \times \left(\alpha_i + \beta_i P_{Gi}^2 \right) + \xi_i \exp(P_{Gi} \lambda_i) \ ton/h \tag{12}$$

$$Min \ E_T = Min \ \sum_{i=1}^{N_G} E_i(P_{Gi}) \quad ton/h \tag{13}$$

3.3 Minimization of Real Power Loss

The objective of the reactive power optimization is to minimize the active power loss in the transmission network, which can be defined as in (14) [15].

$$Min \ P_{Loss} = f(\vec{X_1}, \ \vec{X_2}) = \sum_{k \in N_E} g_k(V_i^2 + V_j^2 - 2V_i V_j \cos \theta_{ij}) \tag{14}$$

3.4   Constraints of OPF Problem with FACTS

3.4.1   Equality Constraints of OPF Problem with FACTS

The constraints represent the load flow equations as in (15) [14].

$$
\begin{cases}
\displaystyle\sum_{i=1}^{N_B}(P_{Gi}-P_{Li})+\sum_{i=1}^{N_{TCPS}}P_{TCPS}=\sum_{i=1}^{N_B}\sum_{i=1}^{N_B}|V_i||V_j||Y_{ij}|\cos\left(\theta_{ij}-\delta_{ij}\right)\\[6mm]
\displaystyle\sum_{i=1}^{N_B}(Q_{Gi}-Q_{Li})+\sum_{i=1}^{N_{TCPS}}Q_{TCPS}=-\sum_{i=1}^{N_B}\sum_{i=1}^{N_B}|V_i||V_j||Y_{ij}|\sin\left(\theta_{ij}-\delta_{ij}\right)
\end{cases}
\tag{15}
$$

3.4.2   Inequality Constraints of OPF Problem with FACTS

(a) *Generator constraints*: Generator voltage, active and reactive power of the *i*th bus between their respective upper and lower limits and are as given by (16) [14].

$$
\left.\begin{array}{ll}
V_{Gi}^{\min}\leq V_i\leq V_{Gi}^{\max} & i=1,2,\cdots,N_G\\[3mm]
P_{Gi}^{\min}\leq P_i\leq P_{Gi}^{\max} & i=1,2,\cdots,N_G\\[3mm]
Q_{Gi}^{\min}\leq Q_i\leq Q_{Gi}^{\max} & i=1,2,\cdots,N_G
\end{array}\right\}
\tag{16}
$$

(b) *Transformer tap constraints*: Transformer tap settings are bounded between upper and lower limits as represented by (17) [14].

$$
T_i^{\min}\leq T_i\leq T_i^{\max}\quad i=1,2,\cdots,N_T
\tag{17}
$$

(c) *Shunt compensator constraints*: Degree of compensation is restricted by minimum and maximum limits and is given by (18) [14].

$$
Q_{Ci}^{\min}\leq Q_{Ci}\leq Q_{Ci}^{\max}\quad i=1,2,\cdots,N_C
\tag{18}
$$

(d) *Load bus constraints*: Voltage of each PQ bus must be within its lower and upper operating limits and are given by (19) [14].

$$
V_{Li}^{\min}\leq V_i\leq V_{Li}^{\max}\quad i=1,2,\cdots,N_L
\tag{19}
$$

(e) *Transmission line constraints*: Line flow through each transmission line must be within its capacity limits and, mathematically, these constraints may be expressed as in (20) [14].

$$
S_{li}\leq S_{li}^{\max}\quad i=1,2,\cdots,N_{TL}
\tag{20}
$$

(f) **TCSC reactance constraints**: TCSC reactance is restricted by their upper and lower limits as in (21) [14].

$$X_{TCSC_i}^{\min} \leq X_{TCSC} \leq X_{TCSC_i}^{\max}, \qquad i \in N_{TCSC} \tag{21}$$

(g) **TCPS phase shift constraints**: TCPS phase shifts are restricted by their upper and lower limits as in (22) [14].

$$\phi_{TCPS_i}^{\min} \leq \phi_{TCPS} \leq \phi_{TCPS_i}^{\max}, \qquad i \in N_{TCPS} \tag{22}$$

4   Proposed Optimization Algorithm and Its Application to OPF with FACTS Problems

4.1   Gravitational Search Algorithm (GSA)

Rashedi et al. proposes GSA in [16]. Based on GSA, mass of each agent is calculated after computing current population's fitness given in (23)-(24)

$$m_i\,(t) = \frac{fit_i(t) - worst(t)}{best(t) - worst(t)} \tag{23}$$

$$M_i\,(t) = \frac{m_i(t)}{\sum_1^{Np} m_i(t)} \tag{24}$$

where $worst\,(t)$ and $best\,(t)$ are defined in (25)-(26).

$$best\,(t) = \min_{j \in \{1,\dots,n\}} fit_j\,(t) \tag{25}$$

$$worst\,(t) = \max_{j \in \{1,\dots,n\}} fit_j\,(t) \tag{26}$$

Total forces applied on an agent from a set of heavier masses should be considered based on the law of gravity as stated in (27) which is followed by calculation of acceleration using the law of motion as presented in (28). Afterwards, next velocity of an agent, (as given in (29)), is calculated as a fraction of its current velocity added to its acceleration. Then, its next position may be calculated by using (30).

$$F_i^d(t) = \sum_{j \in Kbest, j \neq i}^{Np} rand_j \times G(t) \times \frac{M_i(t) \times M_j(t)}{R_{ij}(t) + \varepsilon} \times \left(x_j^d(t) - x_i^d(t) \right) \tag{27}$$

$$a_i^d\,(t) = \frac{F_i^d(t)}{M_i(t)} = \sum_{j \in Kbest, j \neq i}^{Np} rand_j \times G(t) \times \frac{M_j(t)}{R_{ij}(t) + \varepsilon} \times \left(x_j^d(t) - x_i^d(t) \right) \tag{28}$$

$$v_i^d (t+1) = rand_i \times v_i^d (t) + a_i^d (t) \tag{29}$$

$$x_i^d (t+1) = x_i^d (t)' + v_i^d (t+1) \tag{30}$$

In GSA, the gravitational constant (G) will take an initial value (G_0), and it will be reduced with time as given in (31)

$$G(t) = G_0 \times e^{-\tau\left(\frac{iter}{iter_{max}}\right)} \tag{31}$$

4.2 Opposition-Based GSA

Tizhoosh introduced the concept of *opposition-based learning* (OBL) in [17]. The steps of the proposed OGSA algorithm are enumerated in Fig. 1.

Step 1	Read the parameters of power system (line data, bus data, fuel cost co-efficient, load flow parameters, FACTS data etc) and those of OGSA ($N_p = 60$, NFFE=1000, runtime, $rNorm = 2$, $rPower$, $G_0 = 100$, $\tau = 20$, $J_r = 0.4$, ε etc) and specify the lower and upper limits of each parameter (like lower and upper limits of (a) active power generation, (b) generator bus voltage, (c) load bus voltage, (d) reactive power generation, (e) tap changing transformers, (f) shunt compensating devices, (g) reactance values of TCSC devices, (h) phase shifting angles of TCPS devices and (i) line flow through each transmission line etc.
Step 2	Population-based initialization (P_0).
Step 3	Opposition-based population initialization (OP_0).
Step 4	Select N_p fittest individuals from set of $\{P_0, OP_0\}$ as initial population P_0
Step 5	Fitness evaluation of the agents using the objective function of the problem based on the results of Newton–Raphson power flow analysis [18].
Step 6	Update $M_i (t)$ based on (23)-(24), $best(t)$ based on (25), and $worst(t)$ based on (26), and $G(t)$ based on (31) for $i = 1,2,\ldots\ldots.,N_p$.
Step 7	Calculation of the total forces in different directions by using (27).
Step 8	Calculation of acceleration by (28) and the velocity by (29).
Step 9	Updating agents' positions by (30).
Step 10	Check for the constraints of the problem.
Step 11	Opposition based generation jumping.
Step 12	Go to Step 5 until a stopping criterion is satisfied.

Fig. 1. Pseudo code of the proposed OGSA algorithm

5 Numerical Examples and Solution Results

The proposed hybrid OGSA has been applied to solve the OPF with FACTS problem of IEEE 57-bus test power system. The software has been written in MATLAB 2008a language and executed on a 2.63 GHz Pentium IV personal computer with 3 GB RAM.

5.1   IEEE-57- Bus Test System

IEEE 57-bus test system is considered for the present simulation. In this work, five lines, (18, 19), (31, 32), (34, 32), (40, 56) and (39, 57) are installed with TCSC and five lines, (4, 5), (5, 6), (26, 27), (41, 43) and (53, 54) are installed with TCPS. Here, voltage magnitude limits of generator buses and load buses are set to 0.95 p. u. $\leq V_G \leq 1.1$ p.u. and 0.93 p.u. $\leq V_L \leq 1.1$ p.u., respectively.

5.1.1   Minimization of Fuel Cost for IEEE 57-Bus Power System

The proposed OGSA method is used to solve the OPF with FACTS problem of IEEE 57-bus test power system. The optimal settings of control variables, fuel cost, emission, and CPU time as reported in [19] by adopting RCGA and DE are included in Table 1 along with those yielded by adopting the proposed OGSA method. The simulation results presented in this table show that OGSA gives the least value of fuel cost (**8240.04 $/h**) among all the other algorithms. The comparative convergence characteristic of minimum of fuel cost as obtained by the proposed OGSA, DE and RCGA is illustrated in Fig. 2. This may help us to note that the convergence profile of the proposed OGSA is faster than the comparative algorithms.

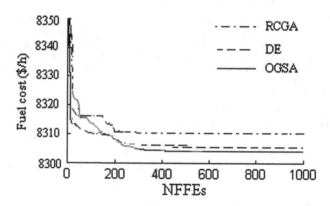

Fig. 2. Comparative convergence profile of fuel for IEEE 57-bus test power system with FACTS devices.

5.1.2   Minimization of Emission for IEEE 57-Bus Power System

While adopting emission as an objective function which requires to be minimized, the optimal settings of control variables, fuel cost, emission, and CPU time as reported in RCGA [19] and DE [19] are included in Table 2. From this table, it may be observed that the emission value yielded, by the proposed OGSA approach, is the lowest one among the compared algorithms. It is clear that OGSA algorithm has succeeded in finding the near optimal solution for the accomplishment of this objective. From the comparative RCGA, DE and the proposed OGSA based convergence profiles of emission for this test power system, as depicted in Fig. 3, it is observed the convergence profile of the proposed OGSA is faster than the comparative algorithms.

Table 1. Best control variable settings for fuel cost minimization objective of IEEE 57-bus test power system offered by different algorithms

Control variables	RCGA [19]	DE [19]	OGSA
P_{G1} (MW)	517.45	520.09	519.18
P_{G2} (MW)	0	0	0
P_{G3} (MW)	94.81	103.74	102.95
P_{G6} (MW)	0	0	0
P_{G8} (MW)	181.75	175.63	176.83
P_{G9} (MW)	0	0	0
P_{G12} (MW)	489.77	485.23	483.15
Total P_G (MW)	1283.78	1284.69	1282.11
Xc_{18-19} (p.u.)	0.0572	0.0604	0.0613
Xc_{31-32} (p.u.)	0.0832	0.0199	0.0197
Xc_{34-32} (p.u.)	0.0203	0.0015	0.0014
Xc_{40-56} (p.u.)	0.0480	0.0932	0.0929
Xc_{39-57} (p.u.)	0.0624	0.0466	0.0457
ϕ_{4-5} (°)	-0.7678	-0.6131	-0.6127
ϕ_{5-6} (°)	-0.7620	-0.6188	-0.6107
ϕ_{26-27} (°)	-0.3438	-0.4698	-0.4617
ϕ_{41-43} (°)	-0.3953	0.5099	0.5067
ϕ_{53-54} (°)	-0.4011	-0.1146	-0.1104
Cost ($/h)	8410.50	8305.00	**8240.04**
Emission (ton/h)	2.4331	2.4333	2.4223
P_{Loss}(MW)	32.98	33.89	31.31
CPU time (s)	874.9	689.9	650.9

5.1.3 Minimization of Transmission Loss (P_{Loss}) for IEEE 57-Bus Power System

The proposed OGSA is applied for P_{Loss} minimization objective of this test power system. The results reported in the literature like RCGA [19] and DE [19] are compared with OGSA-based best results and the potential benefit of the proposed OGSA as an optimizing algorithm for this specific application is presented in Table 3. The best solutions of the minimum P_{Loss} as obtained OGSA and other afore-mentioned algorithms are also presented in Table 3. The obtained minimum real power loss from the proposed approach is found to be **14.06 MW**. The value of P_{Loss} (MW) yielded by OGSA is **2.3 MW** (i.e. 14.06 %) less than the DE-based best result of 16.363 MW reported in [19]. The comparative RCGA, DE and the proposed OGSA based convergence profiles of P_{Loss} (MW) for this test power system is depicted in Fig. 4.

Table 2. Best control variable settings for emission minimization objective of IEEE 57-bus test power system offered by different algorithms

Control variables	RCGA [19]	DE [19]	OGGA
P_{G1} (MW)	341.91	298.12	297.12
P_{G2} (MW)	0	0	0
P_{G3} (MW)	91.90	83.24	82.49
P_{G6} (MW)	0	0	0
P_{G8} (MW)	419.25	413.63	414.19
P_{G9} (MW)	0	0	0
P_{G12} (MW)	418.45	474.14	474.14
Total P_G (MW)	1271.51	1269.13	1267.94
Xc_{18-19} (p.u.)	0.0830	0.0830	0.0819
Xc_{31-32} (p.u.)	0.0672	0.0672	0.0667
Xc_{34-32} (p.u.)	0.0009	0.0009	0.0008
Xc_{40-56} (p.u.)	0.0437	0.0437	0.0445
Xc_{39-57} (p.u.)	0.0772	0.0772	0.0766
ϕ_{4-5} (°)	-0.8995	-0.8995	-0.8937
ϕ_{5-6} (°)	0.4297	0.4297	0.4299
ϕ_{26-27} (°)	-0.8079	-0.8079	-0.8047
ϕ_{41-43} (°)	-0.1375	-0.1375	-0.1365
ϕ_{53-54} (°)	-1.0313	-1.0313	-1.0324
Cost ($/h)	15861.00	15903.00	15913.09
Emission(ton/h)	1.8894	1.8589	**1.8570**
P_{Loss} (MW)	20.71	18.33	17.14
CPU time (s)	878.7	694.2	690.3

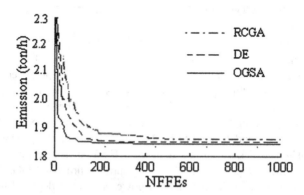

Fig. 3. Comparative convergence profile of emission for IEEE 57-bus test power system with FACTS devices.

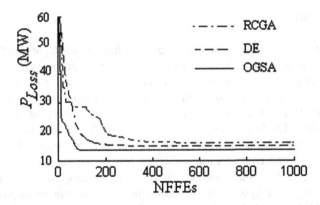

Fig. 4. Comparative convergence profile of transmission loss for IEEE 57-bus test power system with FACTS devices.

Table 3. Best control variable settings for active power transmission loss minimization objective of IEEE 57-bus test power system offered by different algorithms

Control variables	RCGA [19]	DE [19]	OGGA
P_{G1} (MW)	303.24	318.58	318.18
P_{G2} (MW)	0	0	0
P_{G3} (MW)	63.19	45.90	44.5
P_{G6} (MW)	0	0	0
P_{G8} (MW)	400.75	407.65	407.15
P_{G9} (MW)	0	0	0
P_{G12} (MW)	500.00	495.03	495.03
Total P_G (MW)	1267.18	1267.16	1264.86
Xc_{18-19} (p.u.)	0.0593	0.0100	0.0101
Xc_{31-32} (p.u.)	0.0179	0.0004	0.0003
Xc_{34-32} (p.u.)	0.0189	0.0079	0.0079
Xc_{40-56} (p.u.)	0.0641	0.0819	0.0804
Xc_{39-57} (p.u.)	0.0055	0.0841	0.0848
ϕ_{4-5} (°)	-0.6532	-0.0745	-0.0755
ϕ_{5-6} (°)	-0.0917	-0.2807	-0.2827
ϕ_{26-27} (°)	-0.7620	-0.9798	-0.9777
ϕ_{41-43} (°)	0.6933	-0.9053	-0.9054
ϕ_{53-54} (°)	0.2406	0.9798	0.9791
Cost ($/h)	15427.00	15696.00	15656.39
Emission(ton/h)	1.9068	1.9671	1.9640
P_{Loss} (MW)	16.38	16.363	**14.06**
CPU time (s)	881.3	701.7	691.2

6 Conclusion

This paper has presented opposition-based gravitational search algorithm to deal with optimal power flow problem for FACTS device equipped power system having different objectives such as minimization of fuel cost, or that of emission or that of active power transmission loss. The results obtained from the proposed approach have been compared with those obtained from real coded genetic algorithm and differential evolution on the IEEE 57-bus test power systems with TCSC and TCPS at the fixed locations. From the simulation work, it is observed that the proposed OGSA yields optimal settings of the control variables of the test power network. The simulation results also indicate the robustness and superiority of the proposed approach to solve this problem of power system. It is noticed that the concept of opposition-based learning in GSA for population initialization and also for generation jumping enhances its optimization capability in terms of its searching capability and robustness as compared to the basic GSA. The results obtained from the simulation of the present paper obviously demonstrate that the proposed OGSA yields better-quality solution in comparison to the GSA-based results previously reported in the recent-state-of-the art literature. Thus, the proposed OGSA may be recommended as a very promising algorithm for solving some more other complex engineering optimization problems for the future researchers.

References

1. Bouktir, T., Belkacemi, M., Zehar, K.: Optimal power flow using modified gradient method. In: Proceedings International Conference ICEL 2000, vol. 2, pp. 436–442. U.S.T. Oran, Algeria (2000)
2. Scott, B., Marinho, J.L.: Linear programming for power system network security applications. IEEE Trans. Power App. Syst. **98**(3), 837–845 (1979)
3. Ge, S.Y., Chung, T.S.: Optimal active power flow incorporating power flow control needs in flexible AC transmission systems. IEEE Trans. Power Syst. **14**(2), 738–744 (1999)
4. Ambriz-Perez, H., Acha, E., Fuerte-Esquivel, C.R.: Incorporation of a TCSC firing model for optimal power flow solutions using Newton's method. Int. J. Elect. Power Energy Syst. **28**(2), 77–85 (2006)
5. Lai, L.L., Ma, J.T.: Power flow control with UPFC using genetic algorithms. In: Proceedings of the International Conference on Intelligent Systems Power System, pp. 373–377 (1996)
6. Leung, H.C., Chung, T.S.: Optimal power flow with a versatile FACTS controller by genetic algorithm approach. In: Proceedings of the IEEE Power Engineering Society Winter Meeting, pp. 2806–2811 (2000)
7. Ongsakul, W., Tippayachai, J.: Parallel micro genetic algorithm based on merit order loading solutions for constrained dynamic economic dispatch. Elect. Power Syst. Res. **61**(2), 77–88 (2002)
8. Cai, L.J., Erlich, L.: Optimal choice and allocation of FACTS devices using genetic algorithms. In: Proceedings of the Twelfth Intelligent Systems Application to Power Systems, pp. 1–6 (2003)

9. Padhy, N.P., Abdel-Moamen, M.A., Kumar, B.J.: Optimal location and initial parameter settings of multiple TCSCs for reactive power planning using genetic algorithms. In: Proceedings of the IEEE Power Engineering Society General Meeting, pp. 1110–1114 (2004)

10. Ippolito, L., Cortiglia, A.L., Petrocelli, M.: Optimal allocation of FACTS devices by using multi-objective optimal power flow and genetic algorithms. Int. J. Emerg. Elect. Power Syst. 7(2) (2006) Article-1, 2006

11. Mahdad, B., Srairi, K., Bouktir, T.: Optimal power flow for large-scale power system with shunt FACTS using efficient parallel GA. Int. J. Elect. Power Energy Syst. 32(2), 507–517 (2010)

12. Saravanan, M.S., Slochanal, M.R., Venkatesh, P., Stephen, J., Abraham, P.: Application of particle swarm optimization technique for optimal location of FACTS devices considering cost of installation and system loadability. Elect. Power Syst. Res. 77(3–4), 276–283 (2007)

13. Benabid, R., Boudour, M., Abido, M.A.: Optimal location and setting of SVC and TCSC devices using non-dominated sorting particle swarm optimization. Elect. Power Syst. Res. 79(12), 1668–1677 (2009)

14. Basu, M.: Optimal power flow with FACTS devices using differential evolution. Int. J. Elect. Power Energy Syst. 30(2), 150–156 (2008)

15. Dai, C., Chen, W., Zhu, Y., Zhang, X.: Seeker optimization algorithm for optimal reactive power dispatch. IEEE Trans. Power Syst. 24(3), 1218–1231 (2009)

16. Rashedi, E., Nezamabadi-pour, H., Saryazdi, S.: GSA: a gravitational search algorithm. Inf. Sc. 179(13), 2232–2248 (2009)

17. Tizhoosh, H.R.: Opposition-based learning: a new scheme for machine intelligence. In: Proceedings of the International Conference Computational Intel, Modeling, Control and Automation, pp. 695–701 (2005)

18. Wang, X.F., Song, Y., Irving, M.: Modern power systems analysis. Springer, New York (2008)

19. Basu, M.: Multi-objective optimal power flow with FACTS devices. Energy Convers. Manage. 52(2), 903–910 (2011)

Multi Robot Path Planning for Known and Unknown Target Using Bacteria Foraging Algorithm

Sanjeev Sharma$^{(\boxtimes)}$, Chiranjib Sur, Anupam Shukla, and Ritu Tiwari

ABV- Indian Institute of Information Technology and Management,
Gwalior, India
{sanjeev.sharma1868,chiranjibsur,dranupamshukla,
tiwariritu2}@gmail.com

Abstract. This paper discusses a new method for multi robot path planning using bacteria foraging algorithm for known and unknown target. Here direction based movement is used to classify unknown and unknown target. The directional is representing by divide the area virtually by clustering based method. In which each cluster point represents the direction. When the target is known robot has idea for direction of movement to reach target. But when the target is unknown robot have no idea related to existence of target in which direction. After decide the direction robot will move according to the bacteria foraging algorithm that modified according to the robotics problem. The algorithm is tested for both simple and complex environments. Four parameters move, time, coverage and energy are calculated for comparison. The results show that proposed method work well for both known and unknown target path planning problem.

1 Introduction and Literature Review

Robotics can be used in many real life application like hazardous waste cleanup [1], search and rescue [2, 3], surveillance systems [4], planet exploration [5], monitoring in military combat environments [6], medication delivery in medical facilities [7], etc. When the complexity of work increase it is better to work with multi robot system (MRS) [8].

The use of multi robot has lots benefits as compare to single robot. First, they may be cooperative to they can complete the task faster than using single robot. Team of robot may be more faults tolerant so efficiency may be increase. The task accomplishment is reliable and optimized with faster enhancement through parallel implementation. The cost of enhancement in time and reliability is traded with energy and cost of infrastructure.

Basic need for mobile robot is movement from one place to another, finding path is known as path planning. Path planning or navigation is the elementary requirement for moving robots. There are two main issues in navigation- obstacle avoidance and goal seeking. Goal seeking is the process of navigating from start to destination and obstacle avoidance is to complete the mission without colliding with any of the obstacles [9, 10].

B.K. Panigrahi et al. (Eds.): SEMCCO 2014, LNCS 8947, pp. 674–685, 2015.
DOI: 10.1007/978-3-319-20294-5_58

Robot path planning can be treated as optimization problem [11] where the objective may be to minimize the distance or it may be other. NIA enhance and guide the robot-agent movement in the environment increasing the chances of better combination generation and divergent path selection.

Many work has been done where the path planning solve by nature inspired algorithm. Some literatures related to the work are given here.

In [12], a method is given for robot path planning using multi objective PSO. This method is given for danger source environment. Here the environment is represented by series horizontal and vertical line. Multi objective PSO used for two indices, one is length and another is degree of path. Here a self adaptive mutation operation based on the degree of path block is designed to improve the feasibility. Both feasible and infeasible solutions are saved and the global leader of particles is form them. Local leares of particles and feasible and unfeasible solution block is updated by constraineds pareto dominance. They show the effectives of their approach by simulation.

In [13], this paper proposed a new method based on chaos immune particle swarm optimization is proposed to solve the path planning problem in complex environment. Here authors combine the chaos and PSO with immune network to improve the efficiency. This method leads to fast search for path. Simulation results show that method efficiently able to find the path.

In [14], multi robot path planning is solving by using differential evaluation and Q learning. Differential evaluation is used for global search and Q learning is used for local search. Here objective function is determined according to the problem and proposed algorithm is used to minimize that to select the next position to all robots from current position. Algorithm is tested for both real and simulated environment.

Huwedi et al. [15], use the genetic algorithm to find out the optimal path for the multiple robots. They used static environment and the decouple approach. In the first path first is to find out the optimal path planning for individual robot form the start point to goal position using genetic algorithm. In the second phase strategy used to avoid the collision of each robot. This paper used information exchange strategy for the cooperation.

Rashmi at el. [16] presented the multi robot path planning using honey bee mating optimization (HBMO) algorithm. Here objective is to select the ultimate shortest path without collide with the obstacle. HBMO used here for local path for individual robots. Here for finding the better position of robot two objective functions are constructed, first one is to decide the next position of the robot, and second one to avoid the collision with obstacle and other robot. Here two metrics are used to measures the performance of algorithm, one is average total path deviation, and second one is average uncovered target distance.

Many other papers [17, 18] used genetic algorithm for the path planning of robot, the objective is to find out the shortest path that are free from collision.

The rest of the paper is organized as follows: Sect. 2 discusses the basic bacteria foraging algorithm and its modified version that we will be use in to solve the path planning problem. Section 3 discusses the directional movement according to that problem classified for known and unknown target. Over all working procedure is described by flow graph that are given in Sect. 4. Experiments and results are given in Sect. 5. Al last conclusion is given in Sect. 6.

2 Bacteria Foraging Algorithm

The Bacteria Foraging Optimization (BFO) Algorithm was first introduced by Kevin M. Passinoin the year 2002 and its mathematical formulation implies that it more suited continuous search domains. BFO consists of four stages: chemotaxis, swarming, reproduction and elimination-dispersal [19–25]:

2.1 Chemotaxis

Chemotaxis is the affinity of the bacteria to move towards favorable chemicals and away from the toxic ones.

2.2 Swarming

Swarming is the phenomenon in which the bacteria follow its natural behavior of being attracted to other bacteria under the influence of other bacteria and their fitness in the form of attraction (towards better ones) and repellent (towards worst ones) and this kind of combined effect of other fellow agents makes the swarm intelligent better known as social-influenced intelligence.

2.3 Reproduction

The bacteria cells possess the typical cell characteristics of periodical death and then reproducing new cells through the process of cell splitting like asexual reproduction procedure. In reproduction the healthy agents at the best positions of the search space splits into two to promote better search in that area. It compensates for the decrease in the number of bacteria agents.

2.4 Elimination/Dispersal

In this step the least fitted (with respect to optimization) bacteria either is eliminated from the solution pool or being shifted to some random place within the search space. The reproduction and elimination mutually compensate the variation in the number of agents.

The four steps are not sequential and are nested inside another loop and hence when one step occurs, it happens quite sometimes before getting out of the loop to the other.

Here each bacterium represents the one possible solution, which work like agent and the objective is to optimize the function.

Let j is the index of chemotaxis, k is the index of reproduction step and l is the index of elimination dispersal.

Let:

p :- dimension of the search space

S :- number of bacteria in population

Nc :- total number of chemotaxis steps

Ns :- the swimming length

Nre :- the total number of reproduction steps

Ned :- total number of reproduction step

Ped :- represent the probability of elimination dispersal probability.

C(i) :- represent the size of the step taken in tumble

1. Initialize parameters S, Nc, Ns, Nre, Ned, Ped, C(i), $d_{attractant}$, $w_{attractent}$, $h_{repellant}$, and $w_{repellant}$

   Initialize the location of the population

2. Iterative algorithm for optimization

   This section models the bacterial population chemotaxis, swarming, reproduction, elimination, and dispersal.

2.1 Elimination-dispersal loop: l = l+1

2.2 Reproduction loop k = k+1

2.3 Chemotaxis loop j = j+1

(a) For i = 1,2...S, calculate the fitness of each bacterium

(b) Calculate J = J(I, j,k l) + Jcc (θ, P(j,k,l));

(c) Let jlast = j(I,j,k,l) to save this value since we may find a better cost

(d) Generate a random direction $\varDelta(i)$, for tumble.

(e) Move the bacteria via equation ()

(f) Compute j(i,j + 1,k,l)

(g) Swim

   i. Let m = 0

   ii. While m < Ns

   M = m+1

   If Jsw(I,j + 1,k,l) < Jlast (if doing better), let Jlast = J(I,j + 1,k,l) and let

$$\theta^i(j+1,k,l) = \theta^i(j,k,l) + C(i)\frac{\varDelta(i)}{\sqrt{\varDelta^T(i)\varDelta(i)}}$$

   And use this $\theta^i(j+1,k,l)$ to compute the new j(I,j + 1,k,l)

(h) Go to the next bacterium (i + 1) if i ≠ S

3. If j < Nc, go to step 2.3.

4. Reproduction:

(a) For the given k and l, and each i = 1,2,...,S, let

$$j^i_{health} = \sum_{j=1}^{N_c+1} J(i,j,k,l)$$

Represent the health of the bacterium i. Sort bacteria and chemotactic in assending cost $j_{health}^{.i}$.

(b) The Sr bacteria with the highest jhealth values die and the remaining Sr bacteria with the best values split.
5. If k < Nre, go to step 2.2
6. Elimination- dispersal: For i = 1,2,...,S with probability Ped, eliminate and disperse each bacterium(this keep the no of population constant). If the bacteria is eliminated simply disperse another one to a random location. If l < Ned go to step 2.1, otherwise end

2.5   Modified Bacteria Foraging Algorithm

For the movement of the robots, a modified version of the BFO is used using the existing parameters of the robot environment and is given by the following equations.

$$x_k^{new} = x_k + dx*dd \tag{1}$$

$$dx = \alpha_1 . \sum \frac{(x_i - x_k)}{|x_i - x_k|} \tag{2}$$

$$dd = \beta_1 . \min|x_i - x_k| \tag{3}$$

Where x_i is any agent other than x_k that is the agent which is being considered or we can say $x_k \neq x_i$ or more precisely $i \neq k$. α_1 and β_1 are the weightage factors.

Equation (1) shows the change of position and has two components that is direction and step size given by dd and dx. Direction is given by the summation of all the other agents in the search space, while the step size is provided by distance that the agent has from the nearest agent and is given by Eq. (3). α_1 and β_1 help keeping the value of the movement step within the permissible range.

3   Directional Movement

This is a new way to use of multi robot in efficient way to explore the area to search target in unknown environment. Here the robots are scatter in environment by clustering based distribution factor (CBDF). This CBDF method divide the environment in n clusters and robots has choice to move in any direction. So when we have multi robot system we distribute robots in like so they will cover different direction. So the more chances to search the target. If Nature inspired algorithm had been alone in the algorithm the random scattering effect of the agents would have been hindered because of the random forward and backward movement based searches and hence would have been on kind of struck in local optima. But with the introduction of the Clustering Based Distribution Factor (CBDF) it has been possible for the robot agents to come out of the local optima and search for better opportunity and if possible global optima that is the required target can easily be reached. It can be given in two ways.

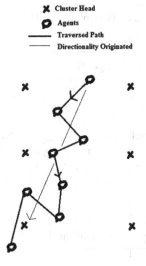

Fig. 1. Directional scattering effect

3.1   Scheme 1 - Directional Scattering Effect

The direction factor is derived out of the cluster head and normally selected randomly to explore new direction and outings. Unlike Zig-Zag Search Effect, Directional Scattering Effect concentrates on direction for quite some time and is dependent on the volume of the workspace. Figure 1 shows the diagram for directional scattering effect.

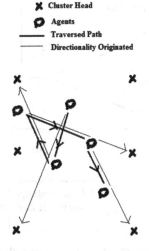

Fig. 2. Zig-Zag search effect

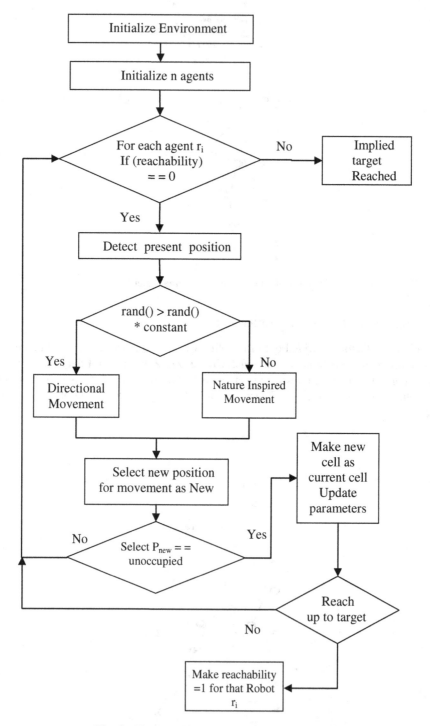

Fig. 3. Flow graph for multi robot path planning

3.2   Scheme 2 - Zig-Zag Search Effect

Zig-Zag Search Effect (ZSE) is like the Directional Scattering Effect in all respect but mostly used in local search. Here the direction changes more frequently, thus helping more hovering over the workspace. Here also the cluster heads based direction is chosen dynamically and randomly. It is showing in Fig. 2.

4   Flow Graph

Figure 3 showing the flow graph for path planning for multi robots. Here first map and agent and other variable are initialized. After that check for reachbility for any robots, because any one of robot is reach up to target. Our objective tracking or searching of goal is accomplished. Next the proposed methodology is applied for movement of the robots. As the movement of the robots progress parameters like time, coverage, energy and moves are to be calculated. Determine the fitness and repeat the process until not reach up to target.

5   Experiments and Results

5.1   Workspace Modeling and Parameters

Here we are considering two environments; one is multi obstacle environment and second is chess like environment. Both environments shown in Fig. 4(a), (b) are different in structure and density of obstacle.

Parameters set up are given in Table 1.

5.2   Path Planning Results

5.2.1   Unknown Target

Here we are showing the traverse path to reach up to target from source. For movement from one point to another we are using bacteria foraging algorithm.

(a) Multi Obstacle Environment   (b) Chess Like environment

Fig. 4.   (a) Multi obstacle environment (b) Chess like environment

Table 1. Experimental parameters

Parameters	Value
Map size	600 × 600
Sensor range	4
Target	Known/Unknown
Number of robots	5
Start point	Any point set as start

When the target is unknown robots has no idea to moving direction. So multiple robots search environment for target and the explored area during searching is mark by red color in environment. Explored map for multi obstacle and chess environment are given in Fig. 5(a), (b) respectively.

5.2.2   Unknown Target

Here we are showing the path planning simulated result for known target guided by BFO algorithm. Figure 6(a) is showing the path for multi obstacle environment and Fig. 6(b) showing the path for chess environment.

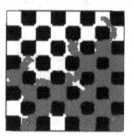

(a) Multi obstacle Environment   (b) Chess like Environment

Fig. 5. (a) Multi obstacle environment (b) Chess like environment

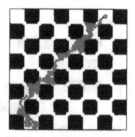

(a) Multi obstacle Environment   (b) Chess like environment

Fig. 6. (a) Multi obstacle Environment (b) Chess like environment

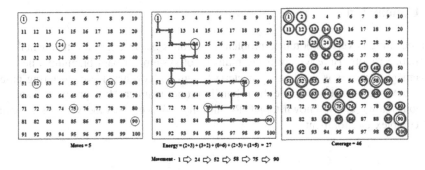

Fig. 7. Parameters calculation

5.3 Parameters Calculation

Here four parameters move, time, coverage and energy are considered for comparison purpose. Figure 7 demonstrated how parameters are calculated.

5.3.1 Move

Moves represent the number of node cover from start node to last node. If given exam start node is 1 and target node is 90. Here the covered node is 5 $(1 \rightarrow 24 \rightarrow 52 \rightarrow 58 \rightarrow 75 \rightarrow 90)$.

5.3.2 Time

Here time is simulation time that can vary according to the number of agents and other parameters.

5.3.3 Energy

Here energy is considered as number of shift in any direction (either horizontal or vertically). In given example movement from 1 to 90 the total energy consumes is 27.

5.3.4 Coverage

Coverage is an important aspect of exploration for the agents and covers all the nodes it can visualize from the nodes it has covered. The coverage area depends on the visibility or sensing range of the agents. Hence the coverage area considered of only those area from it has covered and all the nodes that are adjacent to them considering the range its sensor can cover.

Table 2 shows the calculated parameters value for both known and unknown target.

Table 2. Calculated values for parameters

	Map1		Map2	
	known target	Unknown target	Known target	Unknown target
Move	5185	27492	1007	5453
Time	10.0051	20.0097	2.5301	9.0056
Coverage	13056	82326	6023	25866
Energy	31098	164142	6253	51859

6 Conclusion

Path planning is very importance problem in robotics because it is a fundamental task for mobile robots. Here we are using multi robot system for path planning where the movement of robots is inspired by bacteria foraging algorithm. Here clustering based distributed factor that will guide the robots in proper manner. Here problem is solving for both known and unknown target. Results show that the method works for simple and complex environment.

References

1. Prassler, E., Stroulia, E., Strobel, M.: Office waste cleanup: an application for service robots. In: IEEE International Conference on Robotics and Automation, vol. **3**, pp. 1863–1868 (1997)
2. Jennings, J.S., Whelan, G., Evans, W.F.: Cooperative search and rescue with a team of mobile robots. In: 8th International Conference on Advanced Robotics, pp. 193–200 (1997)
3. Davids, A.: Urban search and rescue robots: from tragedy to technology. IEEE Intell. Syst. **17**(2), 81–83 (2002)
4. Hougen, D.F., Benjaafar, S., Bonney, J.C., Budenske, J.R., Dvorak, M., Gini, M., French, H., Krantz, D.G., Li, P.Y., Malver, F., Nelson, B., Papanikolopoulos, N., Rybski, P.E., Stoeter, S.A., Voyles, R., Yesin, K.B.: A miniature robotic system for reconnaissance and surveillance. IEEE Int. Conf. Robot. Autom. **1**, 501–507 (2000)
5. Chatila, R., Lacroix, S., Simeon, T., Herrb, M.: Planetary exploration by a mobile robot: mission teleprogramming and autonomous navigation. Auton. Robots **2**(4), 333–344 (1995)
6. Singer, P.: Military robotics and ethics: a world of killer apps. Nature **477**(7365), 399–401 (2011)
7. Dario, P., Guglielmelli, E., Allotta, B., Carrozza, M.C.: Robotics for medical applications. IEEE Robot. Autom. Mag. **3**(3), 44–56 (1996)
8. Ahmadi, M., Stone, P.: A multi-robot system for continuous area sweeping tasks. In: IEEE International Conference on Robotics and Automation, pp. 1724–1729. ICRA (2006)
9. Barraquand, J., Bruno, L., Latombe, J.-C.: Numerical potential field techniques for robot path planning. IEEE Trans. Syst. Man Cybern. **22**(2), 224–241 (1992)
10. Willms, A.R., Yang, S.X.: An efficient dynamic system for real-time robot-path planning. IEEE Trans. Syst. Man Cybern. Part B: Cybern. **36**(4), 755–766 (2006)
11. Bennewitz, M., Burgard, W., Thrun, S.: Finding and optimizing solvable priority schemes for decoupled path planning techniques for teams of mobile robots. Robot. Auton. Syst. **41** (2), 89–99 (2002)
12. Gong, D.W., Zhang, J.H., Zhang, Y.: Multi-objective particle swarm optimization for robot path planning in environment with danger sources. J. Comput. **6**(8), 1554–1561 (2011)
13. Hao, W., Qin, S.: Multi-objective path planning for space exploration robot based on chaos immune particle swarm optimization algorithm. In: Deng, H., Miao, D., Lei, J., Wang, F.L. (eds.) AICI 2011, Part II. LNCS, vol. 7003, pp. 42–52. Springer, Heidelberg (2011)
14. Rakshit, P., Banerjee, D., Konar, A., Janarthanan, R.: An adaptive memetic algorithm for multi-robot path-planning. In: Panigrahi, B.K., Das, S., Suganthan, P.N., Nanda, P.K. (eds.) SEMCCO 2012. LNCS, vol. 7677, pp. 248–258. Springer, Heidelberg (2012)

15. Ashraf, S., Budabbus, H., S.M.: Finding an optimal path planning for multiple robots using genetic algorithm. In: The 13th International Arab Conference on Information Technology, ACIT (2012)
16. Sahoo, R.R., Rakshit, P., Haidar, M.T., Swarnalipi, S., Balabantaray, B.K., Mohapatra, S.: Navigational path planning of multi-robot using honey bee mating optimization algorithm (HBMO). Int. J. Comput. Appl. **27**(11), 0975–8887 (2011)
17. Ismail, A.T., Sheta, A., Al-Weshah, M.: A mobile robot path planning using genetic algorithm in static environment. J. Comput. Sci. **4**(4), 341–344 (2008)
18. Ahmed, F., Deb, K.: Multi-objective optimal path planning using elitist non-dominated sorting genetic algorithms. Springer J. Soft Comput. **17**(7), 1283–1299 (2013)
19. Das, S., Biswas, A., Dasgupta, S., Abraham, A.: Bacterial foraging optimization algorithm: theoretical foundations, analysis, and applications. Found. Comput. Intell. **3**, 23–55 (2009)
20. Passino, K.M.: Biomimicry of bacterial foraging for distributed optimization and control. IEEE Control Syst. **22**(3), 52–67 (2002)
21. Biswas, A., Dasgupta, S., Das, S., Abraham, A.: Synergy of PSO and bacterial foraging optimization—a comparative study on numerical benchmarks. In: Corchado, E., Corchado, J.M., Abraham, A. (eds.) Innovations in Hybrid Intelligent Systems, vol. 44, pp. 255–263. Springer, Berlin (2007)
22. Shen, H., Zhu, Y., Zhou, X., Guo, H., Chang, C.: Bacterial foraging optimization algorithm with particle swarm optimization strategy for global numerical optimization. In: Proceedings of the First ACM/SIGEVO Summit on Genetic and Evolutionary Computation, pp. 497–504 (2009)
23. Tang, W.J., Wu, Q.H., Saunders, J.R.: Bacterial foraging algorithm for dynamic environments. In: IEEE Congress on Evolutionary Computation, 2006. CEC, pp. 1324 −1330 (2006)
24. Choudhury, B., Acharya, O.P., Patnaik, A.: Fault finding in antenna array using bacteria foraging optimization technique. J. Commun. Comput. **9**(3), 345–349 (2012)
25. Munoz, M.A., Halgamuge, S., Alfonso, W., Caicedo, E.F.: Simplifying the bacteria foraging optimization algorithm In: IEEE Congress on Evolutionary Computation (CEC), pp. 1–7 (2010)

Stochastic Unit Commitment Problem Incorporating Renewable Energy Power

N.M. Ramya[1]($\boxtimes$), M. Ramesh Babu[2], and S. Arunachalam[2]

[1] Department of E.E.E, Karpagam College of Engineering,
Coimbatore, Tamilnadu, India
ramyasivabalan2014@gmail.com
[2] Department of E.E.E, St. Joseph's College of Engineering,
Chennai, Tamilnadu, India
rameshbabum@stjosephs.ac.in,
mailtoarunachalam@gmail.com

Abstract. It is necessary to incorporate wind and pumped storage plants in classical unit commitment problem due to the increase in use of renewable energy sources. The cost of power generation will be reduced due to inclusion of the renewable energy resources. In this work a Weibull probability density function is used to predict the wind speed. The proposed Unit Commitment (UC) problem includes the factors account for both overestimation and underestimation of available wind power. Pumped storage hydro plants are also included in the scheduling process to balance the uncertainties in the wind power generation. Premature convergence and high computation time are the main drawbacks of the conventional PSO algorithm to solve the optimization problems. In this work a Modified PSO (MPSO) algorithm is proposed to remove the drawbacks of the conventional PSO to solve the proposed stochastic Unit Commitment problem (SUC).

Keywords: Stochastic unit commitment · Particle swarm optimization (PSO) · Reserve cost · Penalty cost

1 Introduction

Electrical power industry restructuring has created highly vibrant and competitive market that altered many aspects of the power industry [1, 2]. In this changed scenario, scarcity of energy resources, increased power generation cost, environment concern, continuous growing demand for electrical energy necessitate optimal scheduling [3–5]. In modern power system effective scheduling of available energy resources for satisfying load demand has become an important task [6]. Rapid expansion of wind mills in recent years rise the challenges to the power system operator for scheduling of all available generating units [7]. Due to the sudden changes of wind power outputs, other renewable energy sources especially pumped storage power sources are added to balance the uncertainty.

In Wind Energy Conversion Systems (WECS), the wind power output depends on wind velocity and direction [8]. There are many investigations on the prediction of wind

© Springer International Publishing Switzerland 2015
B.K. Panigrahi et al. (Eds.): SEMCCO 2014, LNCS 8947, pp. 686–696, 2015.
DOI: 10.1007/978-3-319-20294-5_59

speed to determine the wind power such as fuzzy logic [9, 10], Neural Network [11] etc. The main curiosity of this paper is to solve the scheduling problem of the available power generators.

Unit Commitment problem with the Inclusion of renewable energy sources are termed as stochastic Unit Commitment problem (SUC), due to the uncertainties in power generation from the renewable energy resources. The objective of unit commitment problem is to minimize the overall system operation cost over the scheduling time period while meeting the system power demand and other constraints. It consists of two basic problems, first is determining the on/off status of generating units in presence of start up and shut down constraints; second one is economic dispatch problem which is optimal allocation of power output to the generating units to meet the power demand plus losses [12, 13].

The SUC problem is a large scale, non linear, mixed integer combinatorial optimization problem with various constraints [14, 15]. To solve this optimization problem there are many conventional and non conventional methods are used namely Priority list, Dynamic programming, Lagrangian relaxation [16], Genetic algorithm [17], simulated annealing [18], Particle swarm optimization [19–21] and various algorithms of evolutionary computation.

This paper is organized as follows: Sect. 2 formulates the SUC problem. Section 3 describes the proposed solution method in detail. Section 4 contains the numerical results and compares with traditional PSO method results. Finally concluding remarks are discussed as well in the last section.

2 Problem Formulation

The SUC problem minimizes the Overall Cost (OC) over the scheduled time horizon under the spinning reserve and operational constraints of generating units. Mathematically, the objective equation is as follows:

Minimize

$$
OC_T = \sum_{t=1}^{T} \left\{ \sum_{i=1}^{N} \left\{ F_i(P_i(t)) + SUC_i(1 - U_i(t-1)) \right\} U_i(t) + \sum_{i=1}^{M} C_i(wg_i(t)) \right.
$$
$$
\left. + \sum_{i=1}^{M} PC_i\big(wg_{i,av}(t) - wg_i(t)\big) + \sum_{i=1}^{M} RC_i\big(wg_i(t) - wg_{i,av}(t)\big) \right\} \tag{1}
$$

T- Total scheduling time horizon

M - Number of conventional generators

N - Number of wind powered generators

S - Number of pumped storage generators

$F_i(P_i(t))$ - Fuel cost function of ith conventional generator at 't' time period.

$U_i(t)$ - On/Off status of ith conventional generator at 't' time period.

SUC_i - Start up cost of ith conventional generators.

$C_i(w_i(t))$ - Direct Cost function for the ith wind powered generator at 't' time period.

$PC_i(t)$ - Penalty Cost function for the ith wind powered generator at 't' time period.

$RC_i(t)$ - Reserve cost of ith wind powered generator at 't' time period.

$Wg_{i,av}(t)$ - Available wind power from the ith wind powered generator at 't' time period.

$wg_i(t)$ - Scheduled wind power from the ith wind powered generator at 't' time period.

The Fuel cost function of ith conventional generator represented as follows:

$$F_i(P_i(t)) = a_i P_i^2(t) + b_i P_i(t) + c_i \tag{2}$$

where a_i, b_i, c_i are the cost coefficients of ith thermal generator. The second term in the objective function is for startup cost function of the conventional generators.

In [21] proposed that the wind speed profile at a given location closely follows the weibull distribution over time. The probability distribution function for a weibull distribution is as follows:

$$f_v(v) = \left(\frac{k}{c}\right)\left(\frac{v}{c}\right)^{(k-1)} e^{-(vc)k}, 0 < v < \infty \tag{3}$$

V wind speed random variable; v wind speed; c scale factor at a given location
k shape factor at a given location.

The power output from WECS is continuous between cut in and cutout speed and discrete below cut in wind speed and above cutout wind speed. Then the wind speed weibull distribution is converted to wind power distribution.

Depending upon the ownership of the conventional and renewable energy generators, the SUC problem may take different forms. Basically, there is zero cost involved in the production of power from WECS. If the WECS is owned by utility a linear cost may be collected for initial outlay and maintenance, which is proportional to the scheduled power from WECS.

$$C_i(wg_i(t)) = d_i wg_i(t) \tag{4}$$

where d_i is the direct cost coefficient of ith WECS

In case of non utility owned WECS the cost of power is based on contraction agreements. In all our studies, the WECS is developed for most general case, it is adaptable for all situations, regardless of who owns the generating units.

The wind power output is not constant at any time; it may be greater than or lower than the assumed power at that instant. In case, if the actual power is greater than the power which is assumed, then the penalty cost is calculated for not utilizing efficiently the available power from WECS. Penalty cost function will take the following form:

$$PC_i(Wg_{i,av}(t) - wg_i(t)) = k_{p,i}(Wg_{i,av}(t) - wg_i(t))$$
$$= k_{p,i} \int_{wg_i}^{wg_{r,i}} (wg - wg_i(t)) f_w(wg) dw \tag{5}$$

where $k_{p,i}$ is the penalty cost coefficient for the ith wind powered generator.

In another situation if the available power is less than the assumed power there is an unbalance between load and power generation. The reserve unit is needed to satisfy this power balance, reasonably the reserve cost is calculated which is linearly related to the difference between assumed power and actual power available. The reserve cost function is as follows:

$$RC_i\big(wg_i(t) - Wg_{i,av}(t)\big) = k_{r,i}\big(wg_i(t) - Wg_{i,av}(t)\big)$$
$$= k_{r,i} \int_0^{wg_i} (wg_i(t) - wg)f_w(wg)dw \qquad (6)$$

where $k_{r,i}$ is the reserve cost coefficient for the ith wind powered generator.

2.1   System Constraints

2.1.1   Power Balance Constraint

$$\sum_{i=1}^{N} U_i(t) * P_i(t) + Wg_i(t) + PS_i(t) = P_L(t) \qquad (7)$$

2.2   Thermal Unit Constraints

2.2.1   Unit Generation Limits

The power output from thermal generators should be within minimum and maximum limits for economical and security reasons respectively.

$$P_{i,min}(t) \le P_i(t) \le P_{i,max}(t) \qquad (8)$$

2.2.2   Minimum up/Down Time Constraints

Once the unit is committed/recommitted there should be predefined minimum time after it can be recommitted/committed.

$$\big[T_{on,i}(t-1) - T_{on,i}\big] * [U_i(t-1) - U_i(t)] \ge 0$$
$$\big[T_{off,i}(t-1) - T_{off,i}\big] * [U_i(t) - U_i(t-1)] \ge 0 \qquad (9)$$

2.3   Wind Unit Constraints

2.3.1   Wind Unit Generation Limits

The power output from WECS units is within zero and rated wind power.

$$0 \le wg_i(t) \le wg_{r,i}(t) \qquad (10)$$

2.4   Pumped Storage Generator Constraints

2.4.1   Generation Mode

During the power generating mode the water is flowing from upper reservoir to the lower reservoir.

$$0 \le ps_i(t) \le ps_i^{max} \qquad (11)$$

2.4.2 Pumping Mode

During the pumping mode the water is pumped from lower reservoir to upper reservoir.

$$ps_i^{min}(t) \leq ps_i(t) \leq 0 \tag{12}$$

2.4.3 Reservoir Storage Limits

$$V_{i,min}(t) \leq V_i(t) \leq V_{i,max}(t) \tag{13}$$

2.4.4 Water discharge limits

$$q_{i,min}(t) \leq q_i(t) \leq q_{i,max}(t) \tag{14}$$

3 Proposed Algorithm

Particle Swarm Optimization (PSO) is a modern heuristic algorithm can be used to solve non linear and mixed integer optimization problems and it is based on the social behavior bird flocks and fish schools. The main advantages of PSO are its simplicity, robustness in controlling parameters and its computational efficiency. Many researchers proposed different modification in traditional PSO algorithm to improve the performance. At every iteration particle move towards an optimum solution, through its present velocity, particle's best solution obtained so far and global best solution obtained among all particles. In D dimensional search space the position and velocity of each particle i are represented as the vectors of $x_i = [x_{i1}, x_{i2}, \ldots x_{id}]$ and $v_i = [v_{i1}, v_{i2}, \ldots v_{id}]$ respectively in the PSO algorithm. The local best (pbest) and global best (gbest) position of particle i are $pbest_i = [pbest_{i1}, pbest_{i2}, \ldots pbest_{id}]$ and $gbest_i = [gbest_{i1}, gbest_{i2}, \ldots gbest_{id}]$ respectively. The updated velocity and position of each particle can be expressed using the current velocity and distance from pbest and gbest. To speed up the convergence the neighborhood best position also added in the velocity equation as follows:

$$V_i^{k+1} = wV_i^k + C1 * \left(pbest - x_i^k\right) + C2 * rand_2 * \left(gbest - x_i^k\right)$$
$$+ C3 * rand_3 * \left(pnei - x_i^k\right) \tag{15}$$

$$x_i^{k+1} = x_i^k + v_i^{k+1} \tag{16}$$

where $w, c1, c2, c3$ *andrand* are inertia weight, acceleration constants and random number in between 0 and 1 respectively.

The inertia weight represents the habitual behavior of the particle. The acceleration constant accelerates or pushes the particle towards best position. Large $c1, c2, c3$ value results in abrupt movement of the particles towards it target solution. Small values of these components results in a particle to roam far away from the target region. In this article, acceleration constant values are randomly generated in between 0.5 and 2.0. The "Inertia Weight Approach (IWA)" is followed to set inertia weight. The IWA formula is as follows:

$$w = w_{max} - (w_{max} - w_{min}) * \frac{iter}{iter_{max}} \quad (17)$$

Where w_{max}, w_{min} are maximum and minimum inertia weights. $iter_{max}, iter$ are maximum and current iteration respectively.

4 Simulation Results

4.1 Example Case Study to Validate the Proposed Method

The modified IEEE 30 bus system is studied in this section to solve the SUC problem considering a power demand of 850 MW in proposed method. To know the effectiveness of the proposed algorithm it is compared with traditional PSO algorithm results for the same demand. The simulation was carried out on a Intel core i3, 2.10 GHZ, 4 GB RAM processor and coding was written in Matlab software 2010 version. In the modified test system the 4th and 5th units are considered as WECS units and 6th is considered pumped storage unit. The thermal generating units data are detailed in Table 1. The WECS units data and pumped storage (PS) unit data are given well in Tables 2 and 3 respectively.

The following parameters for MPSO and PSO algorithm are well detailed below: Pop-No of population-20, Nv- No of Variables-9,Iter-No of iteration- 500. MPSO:$w_{min} = 0.4, w_{max} = 0.9 \, c1_{min} = c2_{min} = c3_{min}=0.5, c1_{max} = c2_{max} = c3_{max} = 2.$ PSO:$w = 0.9, c1 = c2 = 2.$

Table 1. Cost coefficients, minimum and maximum limits of thermal generators

Unit	a_i	b_i	c_i	$p_{i,min}$ (Mw)	$p_{i,max}$ (Mw)	MUT	MDT
1	0.00375	2	0	50	200	2	4
2	0.0075	1.75	0	20	80	2	3
3	0.0625	1	0	15	50	1	1

Table 2. WECS data

Gen.No	wg_{min} (Mw)	wg_{max} (Mw)	v_i	v_r	v_o
4	5	100	5	15	45
5	5	100	5	15	45

Table 3. Pumped storage unit data

Generator details	Mode	
	Generation	Pumping
ps_{min}(Mw)	0	30
ps_{max}(Mw)	30	0
V_{min}(acre-ft)	47.0	47.0
V_{max}(acre-ft)	50.0	50.0

Table 4. Comparison of methods after 25 trial runs

Total generation cost ($/h)	Method	
	PSO	MPSO
Minimum	230.623	229.045
Maximum	247.593	243.825
Average	239.773	236.194

Table 5. Comparison of methods for total time taken after 25 trial runs

Total time (S)	Method	
	PSO	MPSO
Minimum	275.6281	268.3173
Maximum	349.5278	342.6923
Average	312.1381	289.4388

To prove the need for modification in traditional PSO algorithm, the SUC problem was first solved by traditional method. In 25 different trial runs the traditional algorithm produced its best solution of $.233.623 for 14 times. In rest of the trials the particles locate the solution which is nearer to the optimal position. By comparing the PSO results with MPSO results for the same 25 trial runs, the solution produced by MPSO is lesser than the traditional one. The MPSO produced $229.045 for 17 times out of 25 (Tables 4 and 5).

For WECS units the coefficient for penalty and reserve cost are as follows: $k_{p1} = k_{p2} = 0; k_{r1} = k_{r2} = 1$. The solution of SUC problem is depending on the values of penalty cost, reserve cost and also c factor in the weibull distribution function.

4.2   Numerical Solutions

In this section the 24 h demand pattern is taken to validate the feasibility of the proposed algorithm. The load pattern is given in Fig. 1.

This case is simulated for 25 trial runs to demonstrate the superiority and robustness of the proposed method than the traditional method. This case is a SUC problem considering the transmission line losses. The CPU time averaged for MPSO method to solve this SUC problem is 20643.891419 s. It is 897 s (14.95 min) less than the CPU

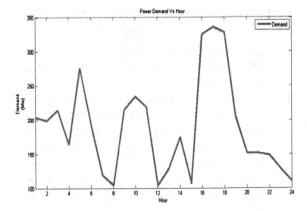

Fig. 1. Load pattern for 24 h

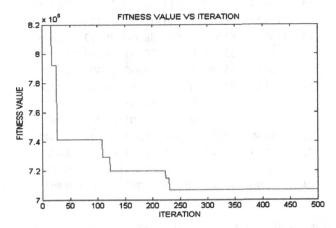

Fig. 2. Convergence characteristics of SUC problem using proposed method.

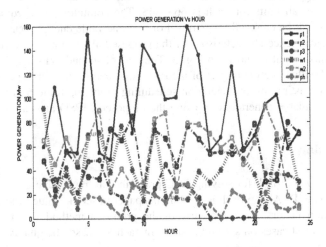

Fig. 3. Power output of generators for 24 h

Table 6. Optimum results of SUC problem for 24 h using MPSO algorithm

Hour	P1	P2	P3	W1	W2	PH
1	60.000	47.773	32.027	91.770	65.074	28.953
2	109.22	23.943	32.810	18.479	45.067	11.648
3	55.859	56.016	35.938	42.261	67.270	28.611
4	54.443	43.831	21.630	8.272	46.680	13.164
5	152.93	34.931	47.393	69.571	67.234	18.526
6	54.679	32.786	48.793	71.412	89.635	16.758
7	48.947	74.304	22.074	38.248	23.676	10.005
8	139.714	65.359	17.992	76.604	41.142	1.029
9	70.794	84.808	0	40.026	25.967	28.148
10	144.11	24.731	0	14.963	30.008	23.215
11	127.59	73.630	24.664	78.616	82.643	19.312
12	99.082	66.471	44.750	17.92	87.582	13.054
13	100.64	43.130	27.613	16.715	22.471	28.415
14	159.58	76.850	26.956	15.564	79.123	28.351
15	135.80	65.986	16.955	38.550	78.013	11.666
16	55.689	53.695	0	29.281	70.243	10.837
17	67.089	55.298	0	39.958	58.308	0
18	125.859	53.222	0	59.264	66.646	22.266
19	55.411	57.092	0	48.764	44.554	16.572
20	68.307	78.134	0	36.101	62.270	1.002
21	94.401	30.114	36.791	7.775	93.241	20.442
22	102.23	31.444	35.872	64.285	69.517	8.490
23	57.664	79.456	35.588	69.574	17.972	6.248
24	71.906	70.206	30.023	23.791	7.9013	9.887

time taken by the traditional PSO algorithm. About 2736.6 Mw power is supplied renewable energy source it effectively reduces the total operating cost. The total operating cost of all units for 24 h is 663984$. The commitment schedule and total operating cost will be changed for removal of the renewable energy sources. Figure 2 depicts the convergence characteristics of the proposed algorithm. The variation of all generating units output is shown in Fig. 3. The cost of second WECS is less than the first WECS. To illustrate the impact of incorporating renewable energy generators into the system on existing utility generation scheduling problem, Table 6 give the power output of all available generators by using the proposed MPSO algorithm.

5 Conclusion

A modified PSO approach for solving SUC problem with renewable energy resources is presented. The 'IWA' approach is used in this paper to set the value of inertia weight and acceleration factors. The feasibility of the proposed method was illustrated by conducting two test cases on six unit system. In each test case, the quality of solution, convergence and computation time of the proposed MPSO method is better than the traditional method results.

References

1. Wood, A.J., Wollenberg, B.F.: Power Generation Operation and control. John Wiley and Sons, New York (1996)
2. Wood, A.J., Wollenberg, B.F.: Power Generation, Operation and Control, 2nd edn. Wiley, New York (1996)
3. Ummels, B.C., Gibescu, M., Pelgrum, E., Kling, W.L., Brand, A.J.: Impacts of wind power on thermal generation unit commitment and dispatch. IEEE Trans. Energy Convers. 22(1), 44–51 (2007)
4. Constantinescu, E.M., Zavala, V.M., Rocklin, M., Lee, S., Anitescu, M.: A computational framework for uncertainty quantification and stochastic optimization in unit commitment with wind power generation. IEEE Trans. Power Syst. 26(1), 431–441 (2011)
5. Chen, P.-H.: Pumped storage scheduling using evolutionary particle swarm optimization. IEEE Trans. Energy Convers. 23(1), 294–301 (2008)
6. Roy, S.: Market constrained optimal planning for wind energy conversion systems over multiple installation sites. IEEE Trans. Energy Convers. 17(1), 124–129 (2002)
7. Pappala, V.S., Erlich, I., Rohrig, K., Dobschinski, J.: A stochastic model for the optimal operation of a wind-thermal power system. IEEE Trans. Power Syst. 24(2), 940–950 (2009)
8. Hetzer, J., Yu, D.C., Bhattarai, K.: An economic dispatch model incorporating wind power. IEEE Trans. Energy Convers. 23(2), 603–611 (2008)
9. Damousis, I.G., Alexiadis, M.C., Theocharis, J.B., Dokopoulos, P.S.: A fuzzy model for wind speed prediction and power generation in wind parks using spatial correlation. IEEE Trans. Energy Convers. 19(2), 352–3361 (2004)
10. Miranda, V., Hang, P.S.: Economic dispatch model with fuzzy wind constraints and attitudes of dispatchers. IEEE Trans. Power Syst. 20(4), 2143–2145 (2005)
11. Li, S., Wunsch, D.C., O'Hair, E.A., Giesselmann, M.G.: Using neural networks to estimate wind turbine power generation. IEEE Trans. Energy Convers. 16(3), 276–282 (2001)
12. Ruiz, P.A., Philbrick, C.R., Sauer, P.W.: Modelling approaches for computational cost reduction in stochastic unit commitment formulations. IEEE Trans. Power Syst. 25(1), 588–589 (2010)
13. Ozturk, U.A., Mazumdar, M., Norman, B.A.: A solution to the stochastic unit commitment using chance constrained programming. IEEE Trans. Power Syst. 19(3), 1589–1598 (2004)
14. Jiang, R., Wang, J., Guan, Y.: Robust unit commitment with wind power and pumped storage hydro. IEEE Trans. Power Syst. 27(2), 800–810 (2012)
15. Victoire, T.A.A., Jeyakumar, A.E.: Reserve constrained dynamic dispatch of units with valve-point effects. IEEE Trans. Power Syst. 20(3), 1273–1282 (2005)
16. Cheng, C.-P., Liu, C.-W., Liu, C.-C.: Unit commitment by lagrangian relaxation and genetic algorithms. IEEE Trans. Energy Convers. 15(2), 707–714 (2000)
17. Damousis, I.G., Bakirtzis, A.G., Dokopoulos, P.S.: A solution to the unit-commitment problem using integer-coded genetic algorithm. IEEE Trans. Power Syst. 19(2), 1165–1172 (2004)
18. Chen, C.L.: Simulated annealing-based optimal wind-thermal coordination scheduling. IET Gen. Trans. Distrib. 1(3), 447–455 (2007)
19. Selvakumar, A.I., Thanushkodi, K.: A new particle swarm optimization solution to nonconvex economic dispatch problems. IEEE Trans. Power Syst. 22(1), 42–51 (2007)

20. Pappala, V.S., Erlich, I.: A new approach for solving the unit commitment problem by adaptive particle swarm optimization. In: IEEE Transactions on Energy Conversion (2008)
21. Mallipeddi, R., Suganthan, P.N.: Unit commitment - a survey and comparison of conventional and nature inspired algorithms. Int. J. Bio-Inspired Comput. **6**(2), 71–90 (2014)
22. Patel, M.R.: Wind and Solar Power Systems. CRC Press, Boca Raton, FL (1999)

Nondominated Sorting Genetic Algorithm-II Based Sidelobe Suppression of Concentric Regular Hexagonal Array of Antennas

Sudipta Das[1(✉)], Durbadal Mandal[1], Rajib Kar[1],
and Sakti Prasad Ghoshal[2]

[1] Department of Electronics and Communication Engineering, National Institute
of Technology Durgapur, Durgapur 713209, India
{sudipta.sit59,durbadal.bittu,rajibkarece}@gmail.com
[2] Department of Electrical Engineering, National Institute of Technology
Durgapur, Durgapur 713209, India
spghoshalnitdgp@gmail.com

Abstract. Research in the evolutionary optimization algorithm (EA) has turned its focus towards solving real life and complex multi-objective problems (MOP). Objective of this work is to obtain good quality design parameters for uniformly excited concentric hexagonal array to achieve low sidelobe pencil beam radiation pattern and high directivity. The optimizing variables are the inter-ring gaps and inter-element gaps in each ring. The objective function vector comprises of three pattern parameters relative peak sidelobe level, peak directivity and the population of the array. Widely accepted multi-objective evolutionary algorithm, namely, Elitist Non-dominated Sorting based Genetic Algorithm (NSGA II) is utilized to achieve these solutions. Optimized design parameters are found better than un-optimized design parameters in every aspect.

1 Introduction

Antenna array designing became popular for the community of researchers in the domain of evolutionary computation, because of the complexity and the trade-off between the design parameters. For this purpose antenna design problem is sometimes considered as a complex benchmark function to test the searching ability of the evolutionary algorithms [1]. Realizing the need to solve multiple desired radiation characteristics simultaneously, some attempts have already been made to optimize antenna array geometry [2–6].

Hexagonal arrays are useful in smart array appliances [7] and thus several attempts were made to optimize hexagonal array performance [7–10].

This work aims at optimizing hexagonal array geometry to obtain low-sidelobe pencil-beam highly-directive radiation pattern with as small number of elements as possible. The novelty of this work is in the use of geometrical parameter like number of elements and pattern parameters like sidelobe and directivity directly to constitute the objective vector. For simplicity elements of the array have been assumed to be isotropic. It is seen that all the six-ring designs obtained from the first nondominated front

© Springer International Publishing Switzerland 2015
B.K. Panigrahi et al. (Eds.): SEMCCO 2014, LNCS 8947, pp. 697–705, 2015.
DOI: 10.1007/978-3-319-20294-5_60

are better in almost every design aspect than a nine-ring concentric regular hexagonal array with half-wave element inter-spacing.

The rest part of this paper is presented as in the following sections: Design equations defining the array geometry are given in Sect. 2; Objective function is described in Sect. 3; Steps of NSGA II are briefly described in Sect. 4; Obtained results are tabulated and discussed in Sect. 5 and the whole work summarizes in Sect. 6.

2 Array Design Equation

Array factor of hexagonal array can be calculated from the geometry of triangle and the generalized array factor of planar array [10]. Schematic geometry of a concentric hexagonal array lying on x-y plane is given in Fig. 1.

Array factor of a uniformly excited broadside M-ring concentric hexagonal array can be written as [10],

$$AF = 1 + \sum_{m=1}^{M} \sum_{n=1}^{N_m} \sum_{q=1}^{6} e^{jkr_{mnq}\sin\theta\cos(\phi-\phi_{mnq})} \tag{1}$$

where

N_m is the number of elements in one triangular sector on m^{th} ring;
k is wave-number;

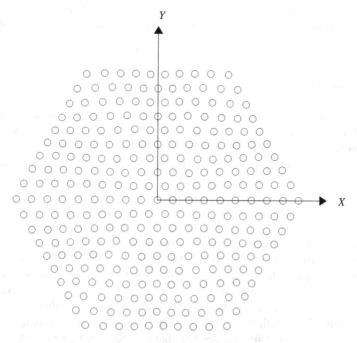

Fig. 1. Geometry of a regular concentric regular hexagonal array assumed to lie on x-y plane

$\{\theta, \phi\}$ is the angular co-ordinate of all the points in the visible region of the array, $\{\theta \in (0, \pi), \phi \in (0, 2\pi)\}$;

$\{r_{mnq}, \phi_{mnq}\}$ are the co-ordinates of lth element of nth side of mth ring in one angular sector of the array geometry. Given radius a_m and inter-element gap for a ring d_m for m^{th} ring, r_{mnq}, ϕ_{mnq} and N_m can be calculated as follows:

$$N_m = \left\lfloor \frac{a_m}{d_m} \right\rfloor$$

$$r_{mnq} = \sqrt{a_m^2 + (n-1)^2 d_m^2 - a(n-1)d_m}, \qquad n = 1, 2, 3 \ldots N_m \qquad (2)$$

$$\phi_{mnq} = \cos^{-1}\left(\frac{r_{mnq}^2 + r_{mnq-1}^2 - d_m^2}{2 l_{n-1} l_n}\right) + \frac{(q-1)\pi}{3}$$

3 The Objective Function

Goal of this work is to obtain an optimal design of concentric hexagonal array that can provide possible array designs with the lowest sidelobe pencil beam pattern and the highest directivity with the smallest number of elements on the aperture. The objective function vector or cost function vector $\left(\overrightarrow{CF}\right)$ is given as follows:

$$\overrightarrow{CF} = \{SLL, D', N\} \qquad (3)$$

In (3) SLL, D' and N refer to the peak relative sidelobe level, negative of peak directivity [11] and total number of elements on the aperture, respectively. Peak directivity D is usually positive quantity, but a minus sign is associated with it to drive the whole search towards exploring minima locations of objective hyperplane.

This work considers an 9-ring initial array geometry with $a_m = d_m = \frac{m\lambda}{2}$. Thus, for initial design $N = 271$. Since inter-relation between the parameters of $\overrightarrow{CF}$ are not yet mathematically modeled, authors opted to carry out unconstrained search.

4 Nondominated Sorting Genetic Algorithm II (NSGA–II)

After Goldberg [12] realized the basic objective to carry out successful search for acceptable solutions for MOP. Elitist non dominated sorting GA II (NSGA II) follows not only the same steps of genetic algorithm for single objective, but some additional steps to tackle multi-objective problems. This work utilizes real coded NSGA II [13] for the considered problem and the whole search procedure as applied in this work is listed step by step below

4.1. A population of 100 randomized individuals is created maintaining limits of every variable. Each population member is a string of inter-element gaps followed by another string of predefined ring-wise element separations $\{\{0, a_1, \Delta a_m\}, \{d_1, d_2, \cdots d_M\}\}$, Δ being forward difference operator. Stopping criteria (500 generations), tournament size, crossover and mutation types with individual internal parameters. For this work a simulated binary crossover [14] operator with index to control the spread factor as 2 is opted for crossover operation, and for mutation, polynomial mutation operator with external parameter to control mutation of 2 is opted.

4.2. Then non dominated sorting is carried out to record non-domination rank of every individual in the population. Until the stopping criteria satisfied the following steps are repeated;

4.3. Since the present work carries out an unconstrained search, all the solutions are considered feasible. Hence for mating selection crowded distance based tournament selection operator is called for filling the mating pool. This operator operates on a pair of solutions, and favours more potential solution (less non-domination rank calculated at step b or e) if found, otherwise (if both the solutions are at same front) it selects the solution which is from relatively less crowded region.

4.4. Solutions are combined in a successive pair-wise order to create offspring solutions, which are then individually mutated.

The old and new population are merged, and a non-domination rank is re calculated. Out of these 200 solutions worst 100 solutions based on non-domination rank are discarded. This process by default maintains the elite chromosomes from the past.

5   Results and Discussion

In this section, some of the obtained results will be tabulated and the corresponding 3D radiation patterns are shown. For comparison, pattern parameters of the initial array design are also included with those obtained by NSGA II.

Table 1 tabulates some solutions from the first non-dominated front. Figure 2 depicts the obtained pareto-optimal front. Figure 3 depicts the initial array geometry; Fig. 4 depicts the geometry of the first set from Table 1; Fig. 5 portrays the radiation pattern of the initial array and Fig. 6 portrays the radiation pattern as obtained from the geometry of the first design set of Table 1.

Table 1. Details of geometries and pattern parameters (SLL, D, and N) of initial and optimized hexagonal array

	Sl No.	Details of array geometry									SLL	D	N
Un-optimized geometry		$\frac{a_m}{\lambda}$ 0.5	1	1.5	2	2.5	3	3.5	4	4.5	-18.25	28.58	271
		$\frac{d_m}{\lambda}$ 0.5	0.5	0.5	0.5	0.5	0.5	0.5	0.5	0.5			
NSGA II optimized geometry	1	$\frac{a_m}{\lambda}$ 0.80	1.68	2.49	3.40	4.36	5.23	–	–	–	-21.56	29.56	151
		$\frac{d_m}{\lambda}$ 0.79	0.51	0.56	0.62	0.68	0.87	–	–	–			
	2	$\frac{a_m}{\lambda}$ 0.77	1.59	2.17	3.01	3.86	4.69	–	–	–	-22.06	28.45	145
		$\frac{d_m}{\lambda}$ 0.73	0.52	0.52	0.71	0.64	0.69	–	–	–			
	3	$\frac{a_m}{\lambda}$ 0.85	1.82	2.60	3.38	4.17	4.98	–	–	–	-20.01	28.81	133
		$\frac{d_m}{\lambda}$ 0.72	0.51	0.74	0.83	0.72	0.72	–	–	–			

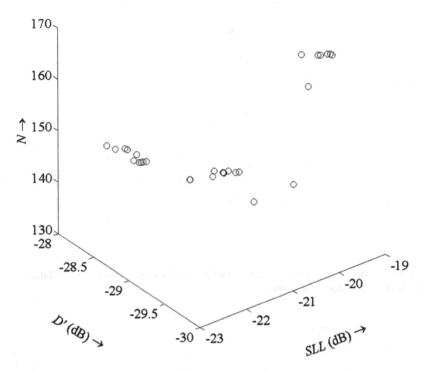

Fig. 2. Obtained pareto optimal front (PF) for concentric hexagonal array design optimization for achieving low-sidelobe and hightly directive pencil beam pattern.

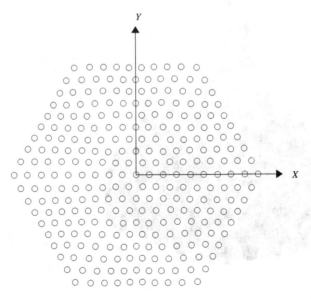

Fig. 3. Un-optimized 9-ring concentric hexagonal array geometry with $a_m/_\lambda = d_m/_\lambda = 0.5$.

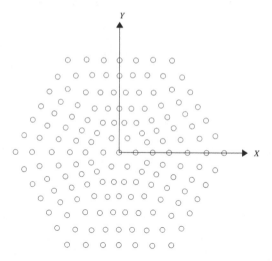

Fig. 4. Hexagonal array geometry obtained with NSGA II for optimal set of a_m, and d_m (Set 1 of NSGA-II optimized design in Table 1).

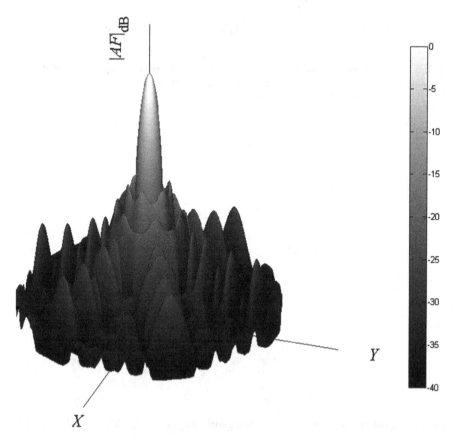

Fig. 5. Radiation pattern of un-optimized 9-ring concentric hexagonal array (Table 1).

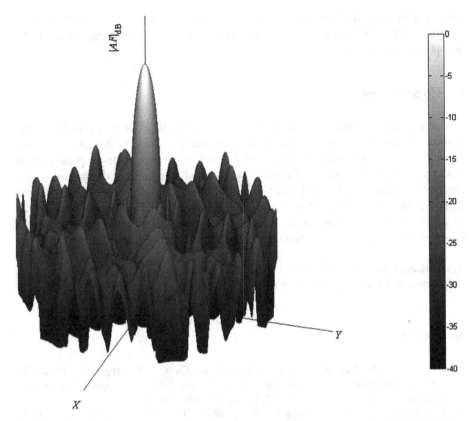

Fig. 6. Radiation pattern of the concentric hexagonal array design optimized with NSGA II (set 1 of NSGA II optimized array Table 1).

From Table 1 one can observe that for NSGA II based concentric hexagonal antenna array three design cases, obtained *SLL* values were respectively, -21.56 dB, -22.06 dB and -20.01 dB respectively, which are comparatively lower than that of the un-optimized 9-ring array (*SLL* value is -18.25 dB); The obtained *D* values of the respective array designs are 29.56 dB, 28.45 dB and 28.81 dB, the first and the third of which are higher than that of the un-optimized array (*D* value of un-optimized array is 28.58 dB). For the second set *D* value is very near to that of the un-optimized array. First, second and third sets of the NSGA II optimized arrays have respectively only 45.62 %, 43.81 % and 40.18 % elements of that of the un-optimized array. One can additionally observe that all the optimized arrays have smaller aperture span, and require lower number of rings.

Figure 2 portrays the obtained pareto front. The solutions in the actual front are crowded in some places, but this figure is obtained by keeping solutions from less crowded regions. From Figs. 3 and 4 one can easily infer that optimized array design requires relatively smaller number of elements, lower number of rings and smaller aperture span. Figures 5 and 6 portray the radiation profiles of un-optimized hexagonal array and first set of optimized hexagonal arrays respectively. One can observe the sidelobe profile of the optimized array design is much lower than that of the un-optimized array.

6 Conclusions

The mathematical relation between relative peak sidelobe level, peak directivity and the number of elements on the aperture is not proposed yet. Same is the case for almost every real life design problem, where, inter-relations between trade-off parameters is not known to the user, though there is a steady need of optimized design using such parameters. Evolutionary multi-objective optimization is useful in such cases. In this work NSGA II has been utilized to obtain hexagonal array design solutions almost all of which are found to be better in every aspect of the performance as compared to the un-optimized array design set. NSGA II is hence proved to be promising in such cases.

Acknowledgments. This work is supported by SERB, Department of Science and Technology, Government of India (project no. SB/EMEQ-319/2013).

References

1. Suganthan, P.N., Hansen, N., Liang, J.J., Deb, K., Chen, Y.-P., Auger, A., Tiwari, S.: Problem definitions and evaluation criteria for the CEC 2005 special session on real-parameter Optimization, KanGAL Report, 2005005 (2005)
2. Haupt, R.L.: Thinned arrays using genetic algorithms. IEEE Trans. Antennas Propag. **42**(7), 993–999 (1994)
3. Khodier, M.M., Christodoulou, C.G.: Linear array geometry synthesis with minimum sidelobe level and null control using particle swarm optimization. IEEE Trans. Antennas Propag. **53**(8), 2674–2679 (2005)
4. Kurup, D.G., Himdi, M., Rydberg, A.: Synthesis of uniform amplitude unequally spaced antenna arrays using the differential evolution algorithm. IEEE Trans. Antennas Propagat. **51**(9), 2210–2217 (2003)
5. Das, S., Mandal, D., Ghoshal, S.P., Kar, R.: Application of differential evolution with best of random mutation strategy on asymmetric location only synthesis of broadside circular antenna array. In: Panigrahi, B.K., Das, S., Suganthan, P.N., Nanda, P.K. (eds.) SEMCCO 2012. LNCS, vol. 7677, pp. 33–40. Springer, Heidelberg (2012)
6. Yan, K.-K., Lu, Y.: Sidelobe reduction in array-pattern synthesis using genetic algorithm. IEEE Trans. Antennas Propag. **45**(7), 1117–1122 (1997)
7. Gozasht, F., Dadashzadeh, G.R., Nikmehr, S.: A comprehensive performance study of circular and hexagonal array geometries in the LMS algorithm for smart antenna applications. Prog. Electromagnet. Res., PIER **68**, 281–296 (2007)
8. Goto, N.: Pattern synthesis of hexagonal planar arrays. IEEE Trans. Antennas Propag. **10**(8), 479–481 (1972)
9. Mahmoud, K.R., El-Adawy, M., Ibrahem, S.M.M., Bansal, R., Zainud-Deen, S.H.: A comparison between circular and hexagonal array geometries for smart antenna systems using particle swarm optimization algorithm. Prog. Electromagnet. Res., PIER **72**, 75–90 (2007)

10. Li, D.F., Gong, Z.L.: Design of hexagonal, planar arrays using genetic algorithms for performance improvement. In: The Proceedings of 2000 2nd Intemational Conference on Microwave and Millimeter Wave Technology, pp. 455–460 (2000)
11. Das, S., Mandal, D., Kar, R., Ghoshal, S.P.: A generalized closed form expression of directivity of arbitrary planar antenna arrays. IEEE Trans. Antennas Propag. 61(7), 3909–3911 (2013)
12. Goldberg, D.E.: Genetic Algorithms for Search, optimization, and Machine Learning. Addision-Wesley, Reading (1989)
13. Deb, K., Agrawal, S., Pratap, A., Meyarivan, T.: A fast and elitist multiobjective genetic algorithm: NSGA-II. IEEE Trans. Evol. Comput. 6(2), 182–197 (2002)
14. Deb, K., Agrawal, R.B.: Simulated binary crossover for continuous search space. Complex Syst. 9, 1–34 (2009)

G_{best} Guided Gravitational Search Algorithm for Economic Load Dispatch

Hari Mohan Dubey[1(✉)], B.K. Panigrahi[2], Manjaree Pandit[1],
and Mugdha Udgir[3]

[1] Department of Electrical Engineering, Madhav Institute of Technology and
Science Gwalior, Gwalior, India
harimohandubey@rediffmail.com, manjaree_p@hotmail.com
[2] Department of Electrical Engineering, Indian Institute of Technology, Delhi,
India
bkpanigrahi@ee.iitd.ac.in
[3] Department of Electrical and Electronics Engineering, Shri Vaishnav Institute
of Technology and Science, Indore, India
mugdhaudgir@gmail.com

Abstract. This article presents a nature inspired optimization algorithm to solve complex economic load dispatch problem using hybrid PSOGSA algorithm. The hybrid PSOGSA utilizes the ability of social thinking in PSO to strengthen the search ability of GSA. The performance of the algorithm is verified by implementation on three test systems having different complexity levels and dimensions; the standard 6 unit system have non smooth cost curve, the 26-unit system is modeled with cubical cost function and a large scale 110 unit system is selected for validation. Results obtained are compared with the methods available in the recent literature. The findings affirm the capability of hybrid PSOGSA in obtaining higher quality solutions efficiently over other existing methods.

1 Introduction

The main aim of economic load dispatch problem (ELD) is to find the optimal combination of generating units which minimizes total generation cost while satisfying equality and inequality constraints. ELD problem is formulated as a convex problem and input versus output characteristics curve is of monotonically increasing nature with lots of local minima [1].

Recently, evolutionary computation and different metaheuristic approaches such as Genetic Algorithm, Particle Swarm Optimization [2], Differential Evolution [3], Evolutionary Programming [4] has been successfully applied to solve ELD problem. Also other heuristic methods such as New Particle Swarm with Local Random Search (NPSO_LRS) [5], Self-Organizing Hierarchical Particle Swarm Optimization (SOH_PSO) [6], Bacterial Foraging Optimization Nelder Mead Hybrid Algorithm (ABF-NM) [7], Biogeography based optimization(BBO) [8], Hybrid Swarm

© Springer International Publishing Switzerland 2015
B.K. Panigrahi et al. (Eds.): SEMCCO 2014, LNCS 8947, pp. 706–720, 2015.
DOI: 10.1007/978-3-319-20294-5_61

Intelligence Harmony Search [9], Equal Embedded Algorithm(EEA) [10], Neighborhood search-driven accelerated biogeography based optimization (aBBOmDE) [11], θ-PSO [12] and Cuckoo Search Algorithm(CSA) [13] have been successfully applied to solve the ELD problem.

This article presents a comparative analysis of hybrid PSOGSA, Gravitational Search Algorithm (GSA) and Particle Swarm Optimization (PSO) to solve economic load dispatch problem. Hybrid PSOGSA algorithm is a population based algorithm which coordinate the exploration ability of GSA with exploitation ability of PSO. In this 'gbest' is used to attain the global optimal solution.

To demonstrate the efficiency of three algorithms three different standard test cases are considered (i) 6 unit system with ramp rate limits and prohibited operating zone (ii) a large scale 110 unit system (iii) 26 unit system with cubic cost function and without loss coefficient. The paper is organized as follows: Sect. 2 provides mathematical formulation of ELD problem with various practical constraints, a brief description of hybrid PSOGSA is presented in Sect. 3, the obtained experimental result from the simulation are compared with the recent reported methods in Sect. 4. Conclusion is drawn in Sect. 5.

2 Problem Formulation

The problem is expressed as:

$$\min f = \sum_{i=1}^{N_G} F_i(P_i) \tag{1}$$

Where

$$F_i(P_i) = a_i P_i^2 + b_i P_i + c_i \tag{2}$$

The more realistic cubic cost function is characterized as:

$$F_i(P_i) = a_i P_i^3 + b_i P_i^2 + c_i P_i + d_i \tag{3}$$

The generation cost $F_i(P_i)$ is minimized subject to the following constraints:

(1) Real Power Balance Constraints-

$$\sum_{i=1}^{N_G} P_i = P_D + P_L \tag{4}$$

$$P_L = \sum_{i=1}^{N_G} \sum_{j=1}^{N_G} P_i B_{ij} P_j \tag{5}$$

(2) Generator Capacity Constraints-

$$P_i^{min} \le P_i \le P_i^{max} \tag{6}$$

(3) Ramp Rate Constraints

When considering the ramp rate limits, the operating limits are modified as follows:

$$P_i - P_i^0 \leq UR_i \tag{7}$$

$$P_i^0 - P_i \leq DR_i \tag{8}$$

and

$$\max\left(P_i^{min}, P_i^0 - DR_i\right) \leq P_i \leq \min\left(P_i^{max}, P_i^0 + UR_i\right) \tag{9}$$

Where P_i^0 is the previous hour generation of unit i, P_i is the current output power of unit i, UR_i and DR_i are the upper and lower ramp rate limits of ith generator.

(4) Prohibited Operating Zone

Mathematically the constraints are formulated as:

$$P_i^{min} \leq P_i \leq \underline{P}^{pz} \text{and } \bar{P}^{pz} \leq P_i \leq P_i^{max} \tag{10}$$

Where $\bar{P}^{pz}$ and $\underline{P}^{pz}$ are the upper and lower limits for a given prohibited zone of ith generator.

2.1 ELD Constraints Handling

The fitness function for the ELD problem is formulated by aggregating the fuel cost function and constraint violation with a penalty function defined as:

$$FF = f + \lambda_1\left(\sum_{i=1}^{N_G} P_i - P_D - P_L\right)^2 + \lambda_r\left(\sum_{i=1}^{N_G}\left(P_i - P_r^{lim}\right)^2\right) + \lambda_p\left(\sum_{i=1}^{N_G}\left(P_p^{lim}\right)^2\right) \tag{11}$$

Where λ_1, λ_r and λ_p represents the penalty factor for power balance, ramp rate limits and prohibited operating zones. In case of inequality constraints the operating limits are modified as:

$$P_r^{lim} = \begin{cases} \max\left(P_i^{min}, P_i^0 - DR_i\right) & P_i < max(P_i^{min}, P_i^0 - DR_i) \\ \min\left(P_i^{max}, P_i^0 - UR_i\right) & > \min\left(P_i^{max}, P_i^0 - UR_i\right), \\ P_i & \text{otherwise} \end{cases} \tag{12a}$$

$$P_p^{lim} = \begin{pmatrix} \min\left(P_i - \underline{P}^{pz}, \bar{P}^{pz} - P_i\right) & \underline{P}^{pz} \leq P_i \leq \bar{P}^{pz} \\ 0 & \text{otherwise} \end{pmatrix} . \tag{12b}$$

3 Hybrid PSOGSA Algorithm

The hybrid PSOGSA algorithm was developed by [15]. Hybrid PSOGSA is an effective optimization method as it utilizes the gbest of PSO in finding the optimal solution with the local search capability of GSA. Hybrid PSOGSA uses a memory in the form of gbest so that the best solution is accessible anytime.

It is assumed that the system is having N agents. N agents are initialized randomly as:

$$X_i = \left(x_i^1, \ldots, x_i^d, \ldots, x_i^n\right), \quad i = 1, 2, \ldots\ldots N \tag{13}$$

Where x_i^d presents the position of agent i in dimension d.

The force at specific time t acting on mass i from mass j is defined as follows [14]:

$$F_{ij}^d(t) = G(t) \frac{M_i(t) \times M_j(t)}{R_{ij}(t) + \varepsilon} \left(x_j^d(t) - x_i^d(t)\right) \tag{14}$$

Where $M_i(t)$ and $M_j(t)$ are masses of agents i and j, $G(t)$ is the gravitational constant, $R_{ij}(t)$ is the Euclidean distance between the agents i and j and ε is a small constant.

$$R_{ij}(t) = \| X_i(t), X_j(t) \|_2 \tag{15}$$

Gravitational constant $G(t)$ is :

$$G(t) = G_0 e^{-\alpha \frac{t}{T}} \tag{16}$$

Where G_0 is the descending coefficient, α is user defined constant, t represents the current iteration and T is the maximum number of iterations.

The total force i^{th} agent is calculated as:

$$F_i^d(t) = \sum\nolimits_{j\in kbest, j\neq i}^N rand_j F_{ij}^d(t) \tag{17}$$

Where kbest corresponds to the set of K agents which have optimum fitness value and heavier mass.

The acceleration of agent i is calculated as:

$$ac_i^d(t) = \frac{F_i^d(t)}{M_i(t)} \tag{18}$$

The velocity of an agent is updated as-

$$v_i^d(t+1) = w.v_i^d(t) + c_1' \times rand \times ac_i^d(t) + c_2' \times rand \times \left(gbest - x_i^d(t)\right) \tag{19}$$

Where $v_i^d(t)$ represents the velocity of ith agent at iteration t in dimension d, w is the inertia weight, c_j' is the weighting factor, rand is a random number between 0 and 1,

$ac_i^d(t)$ is the acceleration of ith agent at iteration t within dimension d, gbest is the best solution found so far and x_i^d is the position of ith agent in dimension d.

The position of agent is updated as-

$$x_i^d(t+1) = x_i^d(t) + v_i^d(t+1) \tag{20}$$

The value of masses is calculated as follows:

$$m_i(t) = \frac{fit_i(t) - worst(t)}{best(t) - worst(t)} \quad i = 1, 2. ....N \tag{21}$$

$$M_i(t) = \frac{m_i(t)}{\sum_{j=1}^{N} m_j(t)} \tag{22}$$

Where $fit_i(t)$ is the fitness value of the agent i at any time t, and best(t) and worst(t) are expressed as minimum and maximum value of fitness of entire population.

3.1   Implementation of Hybrid PSOGSA for ELD Problems

The step by step procedure to solve the ELD problem using hybrid PSOGSA method is as follows:

Step I: The initial parameters such as population size, generator coefficients, ramp rate limits, maximum number of generations, control parameters of hybrid PSOGSA algorithm are selected.

Step II: The population is generated randomly between the upper and lower limits of generator and is represented by $X_i = \left(P_i^1, ...P_i^d, ...P_i^n\right), i = 1, 2, ...N$ where N is the population size and P_i^d is the position of agent i in dimension d. The power is initialized as $P_i = \left(P_i^{min} + rand(0, 1) \times \left(P_i^{max} - P_i^{min}\right)\right)$ where $i = 1, 2, ...N$ here N is the population size. The solutions generated must satisfy the constraints given by the Eqs. (6 and 9). If the generated initial population falls in the given prohibited zone of ith generator than the population is again initialized corresponding to the upper and lower limits of zones given by the Eq. (10).

Step III: The fitness value for each agent is computed using (11) such that the constraints are satisfied. The penalty factor is multiplied with the constraint violation term so that the final solution evaluated should not possess any penalty for constraint violation. The best and worst fitness value for each agent is updated and mass for each agent is calculated using the Eq. (21).

Step IV: In this the total force on each agent in random direction is calculated using the Eq. (17).

Step V: Each agent will modify its position according to the Eq. (20) and the fitness function for the new location is computed and is compared with the old location using the step III. It memorizes the solution with best fitness value and set as gbest.

Step VI: The solution is computed for a number of trials. In case the solution does not improve, the solution with the best fitness value achieved so far is considered as the optimal one. This process is repeated until the termination criterion is satisfied.

4 Simulation Result and Discussion

For all test cases the algorithms are implemented in MATLAB 7.8 and the system configuration is Intel core i3 processor with 2 GHz speed and 2 GB RAM.

4.1 Test Case I: 6 Unit System

This test system consists of six thermal generating units with non smooth cost function and loss coefficients. The entire data for six unit system is taken from [2] with demand of 1263 MW. The experimental result obtained from hybrid PSOGSA, Gravitational Search Algorithm(GSA), Particle Swarm Optimization(PSO) in terms of minimum cost are compared with Hybrid Swarm Intelligence Based Harmony Search(HHS) [9], Biogeography Based Optimization(BBO) [8], Neighborhood search driven accelerated biogeography based optimization (aBBOmDE) [11], θ-PSO [12] and Cuckoo Search Algorithm(CSA) [13] and are presented in Table 1. Figure 1 depicts the convergence characteristic for 6 unit system.

4.2 Test Case II: 110 Unit System

In this case, a large scale 110 unit system is considered. The input data for this system is adopted from [16], simulation is performed for three different demands 10000, 15000 and 20000 MW. Optimum power output for different load demands obtained by hybrid PSOGSA is presented in Table 2. The best results for cost obtained from hybrid PSOGSA, GSA and PSO are compared with Real Quantum Evolutionary Algorithm (RQEA) [17] Differential Evolution (DE) [11], Biogeography Based Optimization (BBO) [11] and Neighborhood search driven accelerated biogeography based optimization (aBBOmDE) [11] as listed in Table 5. The convergence graph for 110 unit system with a demand of 20000 MW is shown in Fig. 2.

Table 1. Result of 6 unit system with a demand of 1263 MW

Unit	aBBOmDE [11]	HHS [9]	BBO [8]	θ-PSO [12]	CSA [13]	GSA	PSO	PSOGSA
Pg1	447.3944	449.9094	447.3997	447.3555	447.4768	447.0585	447.064	447.3770
Pg2	173.4968	172.7347	173.2392	173.2577	173.2234	173.1711	173.162	173.2458
Pg3	263.2259	262.9643	263.3163	263.3848	263.3787	263.9066	263.88	263.3720
Pg4	138.8915	136.03	138.0006	139.0440	138.9524	139.0393	139.061	139.0025
Pg5	165.1239	166.967	165.4104	165.3317	165.4120	165.5636	165.639	165.3820
Pg6	87.2793	86.8778	87.07979	87.0593	87.0024	86.6100	86.6095	87.0136
Power loss	12.412	12.4834	12.446	12.4429	12.447	12.3490	12.4163	**12.39298**
O/P(MW)	1275.4121	1275.4832	1275.446	1275.433	1275.447	1275.3491	1275.416	**1275.3929**
Min cost ($/hr)	15442.673	15442.8313	15443.0963	15442.9411	15443.08	15442.6608	15442.6609	**15442.3928**

*: Results are compared with the methods reported in the literature.

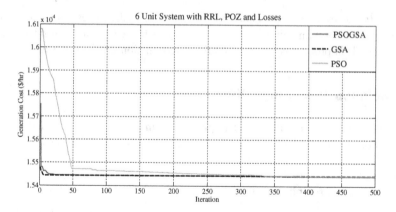

Fig. 1. Convergence characteristic for 6 unit system

4.3   Test Case III: 26 Unit System

The test system contains 26 thermal generating units with higher order cost function. The detailed data for this test system is listed in [10], for a demand of 2900 MW. Optimal generation dispatch results obtained from hybrid PSOGSA, GSA and PSO are presented in Table 3 and are compared with Equal Embedded Algorithm (EEA) [10]. Figure 3 shows the convergence characteristic of 26 unit system with cubical cost function.

4.4   Comparative Study

(1) Solution Quality. From Tables 1, 2 and 3 it is seen that the optimal cost obtained by the hybrid PSOGSA algorithm is 15442.3928$/hr for test case I, for test system II is 131936.4557$/hr, 197968.6159$/hr and 313179.6519$/hr for a demand of 10000 MW, 15000 MW and 20000 MW and for test system III, which is a cubical cost function the best cost obtained by the hybrid PSOGSA is 43436.5293$/hr. The standard deviation and average cost obtained by the PSOGSA method for repeated 20 trials is less as compared to other methods in all test cases. The statistical analysis in terms of minimum cost, maximum cost and average cost obtained by PSOGSA method for test case I, II and III is presented in Tables 4, 5 and 6. It can be seen from the Tables 4, 5 and 6 that the result obtained using PSOGSA is better as compared to all other reported methods in literature.

(2) Robustness. The behavior of heuristic search method is not judged from a single trial so it requires many trials with different initial solutions. For 20 different trials the minimum, maximum and average cost for the three test systems is presented in Tables 4, 5, and 6. The results clearly signify that PSOGSA method provides results in a consistent manner as compared to all other reported methods.

Table 2. Optimal generation dispatch of 110 unit system obtained by hybrid PSOGSA

Unit	PSOGSA			Unit	PSOGSA		
	PD = 10000 MW	PD = 15000 MW	PD = 20000 MW		PD = 10000 MW	PD = 15000 MW	PD = 20000 MW
Pg1	2.40001	2.4	12	Pg57	25.20026	25.2	96
Pg2	2.4	2.4	12	Pg58	35	35	100
Pg3	2.400007	2.4	12	Pg59	35	35	100
Pg4	2.4	2.4	12	Pg60	45.00016	45	120
Pg5	2.4	2.400046	12	Pg61	45	45	120
Pg6	4.000026	4	20	Pg62	45	45	120
Pg7	4.000014	4	20	Pg63	54.30089	184.9999	185
Pg8	4.000123	4.000001	20	Pg64	54.3	184.9999	185
Pg9	4	4	20	Pg65	54.30007	185	185
Pg10	15.2	63.53795	76	Pg66	54.3	185	185
Pg11	15.20235	61.28667	76	Pg67	70	70.00001	197
Pg12	15.2	58.55581	76	Pg68	70	70	197
Pg13	15.2	56.0274	76	Pg69	70.0001	70	197
Pg14	25	25.00001	100	Pg70	150	360	360
Pg15	25	25	100	Pg71	400	400	400
Pg16	25.00001	25	100	Pg72	400	399.9996	400
Pg17	120.3977	155	155	Pg73	60	104.012	300
Pg18	119.0395	155	155	Pg74	50	190.6651	250
Pg19	115.7254	155	155	Pg75	30	90	90
Pg20	109.9798	155	155	Pg76	50	50	50
Pg21	68.9	68.9	197	Pg77	160	160.0084	450
Pg22	68.9	68.9	197	Pg78	150	301.0637	600
Pg23	68.90001	68.9	197	Pg79	50	170.3482	200

(Continued)

Table 2. (Continued)

Unit	PSOGSA			Unit	PSOGSA		
	PD = 10000 MW	PD = 15000 MW	PD = 20000 MW		PD = 10000 MW	PD = 15000 MW	PD = 20000 MW
Pg24	306.4908	350	350	Pg80	20.00189	95.6132	120
Pg25	400	400	400	Pg81	10	10	55
Pg26	400	400	400	Pg82	12	12	40
Pg27	140.0001	500	500	Pg83	20	20	80
Pg28	140.0001	500	500	Pg84	50	200	200
Pg29	50	200	200	Pg85	80.00002	325	325
Pg30	25.00689	100	100	Pg86	279.338	440	440
Pg31	10.00001	10	50	Pg87	10	11.79598	35
Pg32	5.006725	20	20	Pg88	20	23.44483	55
Pg33	20.00024	78.81734	80	Pg89	20.00076	77.96158	100
Pg34	75.00002	250	250	Pg90	40.00139	90.06551	220
Pg35	209.3128	360	360	Pg91	30.00081	57.3638	140
Pg36	224.2491	400	400	Pg92	40.00051	97.05157	100
Pg37	10	40	40	Pg93	440	440	440
Pg38	20	70	70	Pg94	381.0324	500	500
Pg39	25.00002	100	100	Pg95	600	600	600
Pg40	20	119.9999	120	Pg96	301.2184	470.4384	700
Pg41	40.00062	154.5767	180	Pg97	3.6	3.600001	15
Pg42	50.00027	220	220	Pg98	3.600077	3.600002	15
Pg43	440	440	440	Pg99	4.4	4.4	22
Pg44	559.9977	560	560	Pg100	4.4	4.4	22
Pg45	659.9998	660	660	Pg101	10.00031	10	60
Pg46	418.0934	615.2659	700	Pg102	10	10	80

(Continued)

Table 2. (Continued)

Unit	PSOGSA		
	PD = 10000 MW	PD = 15000 MW	PD = 20000 MW
Pg47	5.4	5.400186	32
Pg48	5.4	5.4	32
Pg49	8.4	8.4	52
Pg50	8.4	8.400012	52
Pg51	8.400001	8.4	52
Pg52	12	12	60
Pg53	12.00002	12	60
Pg54	12	12	60
Pg55	12	12	60
Pg56	25.2	25.2	96

Unit	PSOGSA		
	PD = 10000 MW	PD = 15000 MW	PD = 20000 MW
Pg103	20	20.00002	100
Pg104	20.00001	20	120
Pg105	40.00018	40.00035	150
Pg106	40.00014	40	171.3655
Pg107	50	50.00008	136.7562
Pg108	30.00013	30	150
Pg109	40	40	309.8783
Pg110	20.00002	20	200
O/P (MW)	10000	15000	20000
Min cost ($/hr)	131936.4557	197968.6159	313179.6519

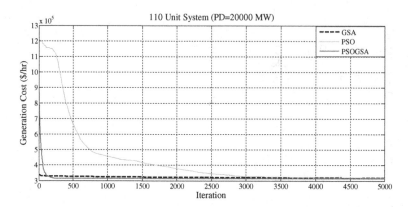

Fig. 2. Convergence graph for 110 unit system for a demand of 20000 MW

Table 3. Result of 26 unit system with a demand of 2900 MW

Unit	EEA [10]	PSO	GSA	PSOGSA
Pg1	2.4000	2.4000	2.4000	2.4000
Pg2	2.4000	2.4000	2.4000	2.4000
Pg3	2.4000	2.4000	2.4000	2.4000
Pg4	2.4000	2.4000	2.4000	2.4000
Pg5	2.4000	2.4000	2.4000	2.4000
Pg6	4.0000	4.0000	4.0000	4.0000
Pg7	4.0000	4.0000	4.0000	4.0000
Pg8	4.0000	4.0000	4.0000	4.0000
Pg9	4.0000	4.0000	4.0000	4.0000
Pg10	76.0000	76.0000	76.0000	76.0000
Pg11	76.0000	76.0000	76.0000	76.0000
Pg12	76.0000	76.0000	76.0000	76.0000
Pg13	76.0000	76.0000	76.0000	76.0000
Pg14	100.0000	100.0000	100.0000	100.0000
Pg15	100.0000	100.0000	100.0000	100.0000
Pg16	100.0000	100.0000	100.0000	100.0000
Pg17	155.0000	155.0000	155.0000	155.0000
Pg18	155.0000	155.0000	155.0000	155.0000
Pg19	155.0000	155.0000	155.0000	155.0000
Pg20	155.0000	155.0000	155.0000	155.0000
Pg21	190.9900	188.6775	197.0000	191.1919
Pg22	166.0000	167.4651	162.1558	165.9282
Pg23	141.0000	141.8573	138.8440	140.8799

(*Continued*)

Table 3. (*Continued*)

Unit	EEA [10]	PSO	GSA	PSOGSA
Pg24	350.0000	350.0000	350.0000	350.0000
Pg25	400.0000	400.0000	400.0000	400.0000
Pg26	400.0000	400.0000	400.0000	400.0000
O/P(MW)	2900	2900	2900	2900
Min cost ($/hr)	43436.5	43436.5426	43436.6409	43436.5293
Time/Iter (sec)	0.01	NR*	0.0264	0.0370

NR*: Not reported

*: Results are compared with the methods reported in the literature

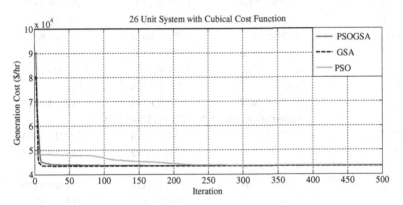

Fig. 3. Convergence characteristic for 26 unit system with cubical cost function

Table 4. Comparison of convergence result for 6 unit system

Method	Generation cost ($/hr)			S.D
	Max	Min	Avg	
NPSO-LRS [5]	15452	15450	15450.5	NR*
ABF-NM [7]	NR*	15443.8164	15446.95383	2.58223
DE [3]	15449.874	15449.766	15449.777	NR*
SOH-PSO [6]	15609.64	15446.02	15497.35	NR*
BBO [8]	15443.096	15443.096	15443.096	NR*
Hybrid SI-based HS [9]	NR*	15442.8423	15446.7142	1.8275
aBBOmDE [11]	15442.9930	15442.6733	15442.83	NR*
θ-PSO [12]	15442.9419	15442.9411	15442.9500	0.0015
CSA [13]	NR*	15443.08	NR*	NR*
GSA	**15443.7879**	**15442.6608**	**15442.77351**	**0.3381**
PSO	NR*	**15442.6609**	NR*	NR*
PSOGSA	**15442.3931**	**15442.3928**	**15442.39294**	**0.00008**

NR*: Not reported

Table 5. Comparison of best result with different methods for 110 unit system

Method	Generation cost ($/hr; PD = 10000 MW		
	Max cost	Min cost	Avg cost
RQEA [17]	131942.4931	131941.8851	131942.0439
aBBOmDE [11]	131945.3176	131935.9871	131940.7124
DE [11]	131957.3541	131940.4328	131946.6127
BBO [11]	131960.9124	131941.8621	13150.8721
GSA	132046.6016	131937.0959	132004.73017
PSO	NR*	131936.9622	NR*
PSOGSA	**131951.561**	**131936.4557**	**131942.1791**
	Generation cost ($/hr);PD = 15000 MW		
RQEA [17]	197988.2006	197988.1393	197988.1835
aBBOmDE [11]	197988.7561	197971.2192	197980.5328
DE [11]	197995.0825	197985.6327	197992.6124
BBO [11]	197999.6518	197987.6192	197995.6515
GSA	198024.7206	197970.2136	197984.7217
PSO	NR*	197970.2166	NR*
PSOGSA	**197978.3677**	**197968.6159**	**197974.1419**
	Generation cost ($/hr);PD = 20000 MW		
RQEA [17]	313211.8189	313211.5688	313211.5983
aBBOmDE [11]	313202.7612	313179.7482	313190.7643
DE [11]	313235.9721	313210.0172	313225.8713
BBO [11]	313257.8356	313211.8324	313240.8972
GSA	313772.3085	313184.2523	313380.2725
PSO	NR*	313179.7506	NR*
PSOGSA	**313181.4272**	**313179.6519**	**313180.2764**

Table 6. Comparison of convergence result for 26 unit system

Method	Generation cost ($/hr)			S.D
	Max	Min	Avg	
EEA [10]	NR*	43436.5	NR*	NR*
PSO	NR*	43436.5426	NR*	NR*
GSA	43686.86517	43436.6409	43529.86517	136.2421
PSOGSA	43436.77943	43436.5293	43436.58068	0.06834

NR*: Not reported

5 Conclusion

In this article hybrid PSOGSA, PSO and GSA were implemented to solve complex economic load dispatch problems. The hybrid PSOGSA combines features of PSO and GSA i.e. acceleration ability of GSA to accelerate the problem in search space with gbest in searching the global optimum for the problem. For practical operation of generator a non smooth cost function is modeled with ramp rate limit and prohibited operating zones. From the comparative analysis, it is concluded that the results obtained using hybrid PSOGSA provides good convergence and higher quality solutions. It can be effectively used for complex and constrained ELD problems.

References

1. Wood, A.J., Wollenberg, B.F.: Power Generation Operation and Control. Wiley, New York (1984)
2. Gaing, Z.L.: Particle swarm optimization to solving the economic dispatch considering the generator constraints. IEEE Trans. Power Syst. **18**(3), 1187–1195 (2003)
3. Nomana, N., Iba, H.: Differential evolution for economic load dispatch problems. Electr. Power Syst. Res. **78**, 1322–1331 (2008)
4. Sinha, N., Chakrabarti, R., Chattopadhyay, P.K.: Evolutionary programming techniques for economic load dispatch. IEEE Trans. Evol. Comput. **20**(1), 83–94 (2003)
5. Immanuel Selvakumar, A., Thanushkodi, K.: A new particle swarm optimization solution to nonconvex economic dispatch problems. IEEE Trans. Power Syst. **22**(1), 42–51 (2007)
6. Chaturvedi, K.T., Pandit, M., Srivastava, L.: Self-organizing hierarchical particle swarm optimization for non-convex economic dispatch. IEEE Trans. Power Syst. **23**(3), 1079–1087 (2008)
7. Panigrahi, B.K., Pandi, V.R.: Bacterial foraging optimization nelder mead hybrid algorithm for economic load dispatch. IET Gener. Transm. Distrib. **2**(4), 556–565 (2008)
8. Bhattacharya, A., Chattopadhyay, P.K.: Biogeography Based optimization for different economic load dispatch problems. IEEE Trans. Power Syst. **25**(2), 1064–1077 (2010)
9. Pandi, V.R., Panigrahi, B.K., Bansal, R.C., Das, S., Mohapatra, A.: Economic load dispatch using hybrid swarm intelligence based harmony search algorithm. Electr. Power Compon. Syst. **39**(8), 751–767 (2011)
10. Chandram, K., Subrahmanyam, N., Sydulu, M.: Equal embedded algorithm for economic load dispatch problem with transmission losses. Electr. Power Energy Syst. **33**, 500–507 (2011)
11. Lohokare, M.R., Panigrahi, B.K., Pattnaik, S.S., Devi, S., Mohapatra, A.: Neighborhood search-driven accelerated biogeography-based optimization for optimal load dispatch. IEEE Trans. Syst. Man Cybern.-Part C: Appl. Rev. **42**(5), 641–652 (2012)
12. Hosseinnezhad, V., Babaei, E.: Economic load dispatch using θ-PSO. Electr. Power Energy Syst. **49**, 160–169 (2013)
13. Basu, M., Chowdhury, A.: Cuckoo search algorithm for economic dispatch. Energy **60**, 99–108 (2013)
14. Rashedi, E., Nezamabadi-pour, H., Saryazdi, S.: GSA: a gravitational search algorithm. Inf. Sci. **179**, 2232–2248 (2009)

15. Mirjalili, S., Mohd Hashim, S.Z.: A new hybrid PSOGSA algorithm for function optimization. In: IEEE International Conference on Computer and Information and application (ICCIA 2010), pp. 374–377 (2010)

16. Orero, S.O., Irving, M.R.: Large scale unit commitment using a hybrid genetic algorithm. Electr. Power Energy Syst. **19**(1), 45–55 (1997)

17. Babu, G.S.S., Das, D.B., Patvardhan, C.: Real parameter quantum evolutionary algorithm for economic load dispatch. IET Gener. Transm. Distrib. **2**(1), 22–31 (2008)

Improved Flower Pollination Algorithm for Short Term Hydrothermal Scheduling

Hari Mohan Dubey[1(✉)], B.K. Panigrahi[2], and Manjaree Pandit[1]

[1] Department of Electrical Engineering,
Madhav Institute of Technology and Science, Gwalior, India
harimohandubey@rediffmail.com, manjaree_p@hotmail.com
[2] Department of Electrical Engineering,
Indian Institute of Technology, Delhi, India
bkpanigrahi@ee.iitd.ac.in

Abstract. This paper presents improved flower pollination algorithm (IFPA) for solution of short term hydrothermal scheduling problem. Flower pollination algorithm (FPA) is a new meta-heuristic search algorithm inspired by the pollination process of flowers. The FPA performs efficiently due to its effective control of global and local search mechanisms which allow user controlled exploration and exploitation of the search space. In IFPA the local pollination process of FPA is controlled by adding a scaling factor and an additional intensive exploitation phase is added to tune and improve the best solution. The performance of IFPA and FPA is analyzed on three different standard test cases considering smooth cost function with and without prohibited discharge zones, valve point loading effect in thermal unit with smooth cost function and constraint such as prohibited discharge zones. The simulation results are also compared with FPA and some recently reported methodologies to confirm the performance superiority of the proposed IFPA algorithm.

1 Introduction

In the present scenario, efficient hydrothermal scheduling is one of the important task in power system operation. Hydrothermal Scheduling (HTS) problem is a complex, non linear, dynamic and constrained optimization problem. The aim of integrated operation is to utilize the available energy resources in such a way that both fuel cost and emission due to use of fossil fuel is minimized. The goal of short term HTS is to determine the optimal sharing of hydro and thermal generators such that the load demands as well as various operating constraints in a scheduled horizon of time interval are satisfied. In the past few years Short term HTS has become an active research field. Traditional methods such as Dynamic Programming (DP) [1], Linear programming (LP) [2], has been applied to solve the HTS problem but these methods may not perform satisfactory due to the highly non linear characteristics of HTS problem and associated constraints.

In recent years, population based optimization approach like Genetic Algorithm (GA) [3], Evolutionary Programming (EP) [4], Particle swarm optimization (PSO) [5], improved PSO(IPSO) [6], adaptive particle swarm optimization(APSO) [7],

B.K. Panigrahi et al. (Eds.): SEMCCO 2014, LNCS 8947, pp. 721–737, 2015.
DOI: 10.1007/978-3-319-20294-5_62

Differential Evolution (DE) [8], modified differential evolution(MDE) [9], Modified hybrid differential evolution(MHDE) [10], Teaching learning based optimization (TLBO) [11] have been successfully employed to solve the HTS problem.

Even though various methodologies for optimization have been developed so far, but the complexity of the task needs development of efficient algorithms to specifically allocate the best feasible solution. In this context, the aim of this study is to present a new heuristic approach for solution of HTS problem and to provide a practical alternative over other existing methods.

Flower pollination algorithm (FPA) is a new meta-heuristic optimization technique inspired by pollination process of flowers, developed by Xin- She Yang in 2012 [12]. Pollination can be achieved by self or cross pollination through either abiotic or biotic process. From biological evolution point of view, the objective of flower pollination is survival of the fittest and optimal reproduction of plant in terms of numbers as well as fitness quality. The FPA adopted and formulated such behaviour of flowing plants for solution of constrained optimization problems.

In this paper improve flower pollination algorithm (IFPA) is proposed for solution of complex HTS problems considering practical operating constraints.

The rest of paper is organized as follows: Sect. 2 presents the problem formulation of short term hydrothermal scheduling (HTS) of power system. Section 3 describes the FPA and IFPA method and Sect. 4 presents the implementation process to solve short term HTS problem. The simulation results and conclusions are presented in Sects. 5 and 6.

2 Problem Formulation

The aim of short time HTS problem is to minimize the fuel cost of thermal generating units without violating any constraint associated with hydro and thermal plant such that all load demand over the scheduling horizon are satisfied. Figure 1 shows the schematic diagram of hydro thermal test system. As cascade nature of hydraulic system, time dependent reservoir inflows along with operating constraints of thermal and hydro plant.Which makes the problem much complex.

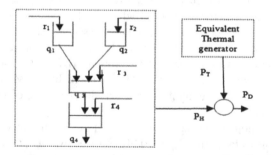

Fig. 1. Schematic diagram of hydrothermal system

2.1   Objective Function

$$Min \quad FC(P_T) = \sum_{i=1}^{n_t} \sum_{j=1}^{NH} a_i \times P_T^2{}_{i,j} + b_i \times P_{Ti,j} + c_i + \left| e_i \times \sin(f_i \times (P_{Ti}^{\min} - P_{Ti,j})) \right| \tag{1}$$

2.2   Constraints

(1) *Power balance constraints*

$$\sum_{i=1}^{n_h} P_{Hi,j} + \sum_{i=1}^{n_t} P_{Ti,j} = P_{D_j} + P_{L_j} \tag{2}$$

The hydroelectric generation is a function of water discharge rate and reservoir water head which in turn, is a function of storage. Mathematically,

$$P_{Hi,j} = c_{1,i}V_{i,j}^2 + c_{2,i}Q_{i,j}^2 + c_{3,i}V_{i,j}Q_{i,j} + c_{4,i}V_{i,j} + c_{5,i}Q_{i,j} + c_{6,i} \tag{3}$$

(2) *Generation limits constraints*

$$P_{Hi}^{\min} \leq P_{Hi,j} \leq P_{Hi}^{\max} \qquad i = 1, 2, \ldots, n_h; \qquad j = 1, 2, \ldots, NH \tag{4}$$

$$P_{Ti}^{\min} \leq P_{Ti,j} \leq P_{Ti}^{\max} \qquad i = 1, 2, \ldots, n_t; \qquad j = 1, 2, \ldots, NH \tag{5}$$

(3) *Water dynamic balance*

$$V_{i,j} = V_{i,j-1} + I_{i,j} - Q_{i,j} - S_{i,j} + \sum_{k=1}^{u_i} (Q_{k,j-D_{k,i}} + S_{k,j-D_{k,i}}) \tag{6}$$

(4) *Reservoir storage volume limit*

$$V_i^{\min} \leq V_{i,j} \leq V_i^{\max} \qquad i = 1, 2, \ldots, n_h; \qquad j = 1, 2, \ldots, NH \tag{7}$$

(5) *Discharge rates limit*

$$Q_i^{\min} \le Q_{i,j} \le Q_i^{\max} \qquad i = 1, 2, \ldots, n_h; \qquad\qquad j = 1, 2, \ldots, NH \qquad (8)$$

3 Flower Pollination Algorithm

The Flower Pollination Algorithm (FPA) is a new population based optimization technique inspired by pollination process of flowering plants in nature developed by Yang in 2012 [12].

The main purpose of a flower is reproduction through pollination. Broadly pollination process can be divided into two groups: biotic and abiotic. Pollination process of flower is related with shifting of pollen through pollinators for reproduction of flowers. Pollinators like birds, insects' bats or other living things belong to biotic pollination process. Whereas abiotic pollination is related to transfer of pollen through wind and diffusion. It does not require any pollinator.

Pollination may be realized by either cross pollination or by self pollination. In self pollination process fertilization of one flower can be achieved by its own pollen or pollen of other flowers within the same plant. When the transfer of pollen takes places over long distances with the help of pollinators, it comes under biotic, cross pollination.

Long distance pollination process is referred as global pollination whereas transfer of pollen from different flowers within the same plant is called local pollination.

In pollination over long distance, pollen jumps over larger steps and shows Levy flight behaviour, therefore Levy distribution [13] is adopted for global pollination. Flower constancy can be used an incremental step using the similarity or difference of two flowers.

On the basis of features of pollination process, flower constancy and behaviour of pollinator, there are four idealised rules for FPA as below:

Rule 1: The global pollination process is considered to take place through biotic and cross-pollination and pollinators' movement obeys levy flight behaviour.

Rule 2: The local pollination is considered to take place through abiotic and self pollination.

Rule 3: In local neighbourhood pollination can take place with pollens from the same plant or same species probabilistically depending on the similarity of the two flowers involved in pollination process.

Rule 4: A switch probability lying between 0–1 is employed to choose between local and global pollination in such a way that a higher probability is indicated for pollination in plants situated in a neighbourhood. This mimics the higher frequency of local pollination in nature.

3.1 Improved Flower Pollination Algorithm

The FPA is found to perform efficiently because the global and local search is controlled by the switching probability. The solution diversity is maintained because the pollen (solutions/population) is allowed to explore the search space during global pollination and exploitation of the solution is encouraged when local pollination is carried out. The FPA algorithm gets an edge in solving complex problems as these two processes are occurring randomly one after the other, thus maintaining solution diversity. However, it was observed that random selection of exploration and exploitation phases based on the selected value of switching probability sometimes causes the FPA to lose direction and move away from the global best solution.

In this paper a improved FPA is proposed where (i) the local pollination phase is modified by taking a scaling factor F to control the mutation occurring in flowers during pollination (ii) An additional intensive exploitation phase is added to improve the best solution. The implementation details are given in Sect. 4. The pseudo-code of IFPA is given below.

Pseudo Code: Improved Flower pollination Algorithm

Generate initial population of flower/pollen within predefined min and max limit
Evaluate fitness of each pollen and select best pollen X_{best}
Define switching probability $\rho \in [0,1]$

While (t<Iter_max)
  For i= 1 to N_p
    If $rand_1 > \rho$
      Describe step vector L of N_G dimension that follows Levy distribution
$$X_i^{new} = X_i^{old} + L(\lambda) \times (X_{best} - X_i^{old}) \quad \text{(Global pollination)}$$
    else
$$X_i^{new} = X_i^{old} + F(X_j^{old} - X_k^{old}) \quad \text{(Local pollination)} \qquad \text{where F: scaling factor}$$
    End (if)
  End (For)
  For i= 1 to N
    If $rand_2 > \rho$
$$X_i^{new} = X_{best} + [(rand_3 - rand_4) \times X_{best}] \quad \text{(Intensive Exploitation of the best flower)}$$
    End (if)
  End (For)
Evaluate new solution
  If new solution is found to be better update the population
  End (for)
  Find best solution X_{best}
End (while)

4 Implementation of Algorithm

Step 1: Randomly select the dependent variables such as water discharge rate of all plants for number of hours and generation of thermal units for all time intervals within the operating limits. The storage volume of each reservoir is computed using (6) and the generation of hydro plants using (3). After this, the thermal power generation is calculated using (1). The population of flower N_P is initialized as $X = [X_1, X_2, \ldots, X_{Np}]^T$, where each flowers X_i is formulated as:

$$X_i = \begin{bmatrix} Q^i_{1,1} & .. & Q^i_{1,j} & .. & Q^i_{1,n_h}, & P^i_{S_{1,1}} & .. & P^i_{S_{1,j}} & .. & P^i_{S_{1,n_i}} \\ & .. & & .. & & .. & & .. & & .. \\ Q^i_{k,1} & .. & Q^i_{k,j} & .. & Q^i_{k,n_h}, & P^i_{S_{k,1}} & .. & P^i_{S_{k,j}} & .. & P^i_{S_{k,n_i}} \\ & .. & & .. & & .. & & .. & & .. \\ Q^i_{NH,1} & .. & Q^i_{NH,j} & .. & Q^i_{NH,n_h}, & P^i_{S_{NH,1}} & .. & P^i_{S_{NH,j}} & .. & P^i_{S_{NH,n_i}} \end{bmatrix} \tag{9}$$

Step 2: Initialize the generation count

Step 3: The objective function is evaluated using (1). With constraints equation, various constraints violation is determined. The improved fuel cost is calculated as given below:

$$FC(P_T)^* = FC(P_T) + \sum_{k=1}^{TC} \lambda_k \times Vio_k^2 \tag{10}$$

Where λ_k is the penalty value for kth constraint, TC is the total number of constraints, and Vio_k represents the amount of violation of kth constraint.

Step 4: *Global pollination (Generation of new solution via levy flight)*
    Insect carrying pollen may travel over long distances by taking big steps and causing cross pollination. The new solution is computed on the basis of previous best flower via levy flight.
    The new solution by each flower can be calculated using global search as explained below if $rand_1 >$ switching probability. Otherwise new population member is generated through local search.

$$X_i^{new} = X_i^{old} + \Delta X_i^{new} \tag{11}$$

$$\Delta X_i^{new} = (X_i^{old} - X_{best}) \times L(\lambda) \tag{12}$$

The parameter $L(\lambda)$ is a step size which represents the strength of pollination. Levy flight distribution is used to represent this step size and λ is the distribution factor selected in the range 0.3–1.99. The Levy flight is calculated as

$$L(\lambda) = K \times \phi \times \frac{\sigma_x(\lambda)}{\sigma_y(\lambda)} \tag{13}$$

Where K is adaptive in nature, K∈ [0, 1].and,

Table 1. Hourly discharge, generation schedule and thermal generations (Case 1)

| Hour | Hydro plant | | | | Power generation (MW) | | | | Thermal O/P (MW) | Thermal generation cost ($) |
| | Discharge (× 10⁴ m³) | | | | | | | | | |
	Plant 1	Plant 2	Plant 3	Plant 4	Plant 1	Plant 2	Plant 3	Plant 4		
1	9.954	7.545	29.999	13.000	85.807	59.532	0	200.096	1024.5640	26771.092
2	10.166	6.002	29.983	13.000	86.340	50.437	0	187.754	1065.4671	27727.410
3	9.280	6.045	29.983	13.004	81.634	52.398	0	173.761	1052.205	27416.613
4	8.231	6.029	29.999	13.010	75.379	53.873	0	156.855	1003.892	26290.325
5	8.151	6.019	18.282	13.007	74.157	54.822	24.875	178.775	957.369	25214.604
6	8.146	6.004	18.272	13.000	73.717	55.2182	24.919	198.914	1057.230	27534.302
7	8.123	6.261	16.564	13.000	73.536	56.931	31.265	217.384	1270.881	32631.207
8	8.508	7.323	15.834	13.040	75.954	63.976	33.468	234.493	1592.107	40638.073
9	8.659	7.694	14.980	13.019	77.293	66.491	35.522	239.129	1821.562	46610.192
10	8.765	7.908	15.397	13.012	78.678	68.394	34.770	243.733	1894.423	48550.609
11	8.629	8.142	15.476	13.016	79.029	70.260	35.246	246.821	1798.642	46004.156
12	8.563	9.405	15.683	13.179	79.089	76.606	35.957	250.724	1867.622	47834.366
13	8.524	8.458	16.041	14.409	79.578	71.138	36.980	263.219	1779.084	45488.703
14	8.453	8.233	16.979	15.523	80.081	70.230	35.469	273.176	1741.041	44490.454
15	8.302	8.643	17.213	15.350	79.773	72.802	36.298	271.773	1669.352	42625.041
16	8.094	9.164	16.888	15.691	78.828	75.058	38.135	274.729	1603.248	40923.190
17	7.999	9.456	16.420	16.033	78.392	75.217	40.298	277.643	1658.448	42343.114
18	7.761	9.619	15.768	16.979	76.819	73.913	43.033	285.287	1660.947	42407.675
19	7.587	10.535	14.602	17.213	75.505	76.011	46.478	287.097	1754.906	44853.592
20	7.617	10.874	13.692	16.888	75.415	75.564	49.054	284.577	1795.387	45918.276
21	7.418	12.115	10.013	18.351	73.939	78.063	50.520	293.505	1743.971	44567.131
22	7.450	9.480	10.026	19.623	74.270	66.792	52.794	297.783	1628.358	41567.597
23	5.348	10.111	10.041	20.773	57.900	68.309	54.594	297.517	1371.677	35099.207
24	5.260	10.925	10.030	21.733	57.436	69.652	56.116	292.794	1114.000	28870.792

Total Cost of thermal generation ($/day): 922377.7345

Table 2. Comparison of optimal costs obtained by different algorithms (Case 1)

Method	Best fuel cost($/day)	Avg. fuel cost($/day)	Worst fuel cost($/day)	Method	Best fuel cost($/day)	Avg. fuel cost($/day)	Worst fuel cost($/day)
FEP [4]	930267.92	930897.44	931396.81	PSO [5]	928878.00	933085.00	938012.00
CEP [4]	930166.25	930373.23	930927.01	EPSO [5]	922904.00	923527.00	924808.00
IFEP [4]	930129.82	930290.13	930881.92	MDE [9]	922555.44	–	–
IPSO [6]	922553.49	–	–	TLBO [11]	922373.39	922462.24	922873.81
APSO [7]	926151.54	–	–	FPA	922387.92	922441.49	922459.99
MAPSO [7]	922421.66	922544.00	923508.00	IFPA	922377.73	922401.59	922459.99

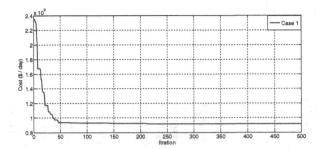

Fig. 2. Cost convergence characteristic of IFPA (case 1)

$$\phi = \frac{randn_1}{|randn_2|^{1/\lambda}} \tag{14}$$

Where $randn_1$ and $randn_2$ are normally distributed d-dimensional random numbers. The values of $\sigma_1(\lambda)$ and $\sigma_2(\lambda)$ given by

$$\sigma_1(\lambda) = \left[\Gamma(1 + \lambda) \times \sin(\pi\lambda/2)/\Gamma\left(\frac{1+\lambda}{2}\right) \times \lambda \times 2^{\left(\frac{\lambda-1}{2}\right)} \right]^{1/\lambda} \tag{15}$$

$$\sigma_2(\lambda) = 1 \tag{16}$$

$\Gamma(.)$ is the gamma distribution applicable for larger step size.

Additionally the solution is again checked for other operating constraints and repairing strategy is used as if violation occurs.

Step 5: Local pollination (*Generation of new solution by flower constancy*)

As per FPA (Rule 2 and Rule 3) local pollination can be expressed as

$$X_i^{new} = X_i^{old} + F(X_j^{old} - X_k^{old}) \tag{17}$$

Where X_j^{old} and X_k^{old} are pollen from distinct flowers of the same plant type. Mathematically if X_j^{old} and X_k^{old} selected from same population, which is equivalent to a local random walk, where F is the scaling factor to control, user defined parameter within [0, 1].

The flower pollination process takes place at both local as well as at the global level. In nature it is observed that flowers are more likely to be pollinated by local pollens from neighbouring flowers as compared to pollen coming from flowers which are situated at long distances.

Step 6: *Intensive Random Exploitation of the best flower*

To achieve the global best solution further exploitation of the best solution is carried out depending on the switching probability as shown below.

Table 3. Hourly plant discharge, generation schedule and thermal generations (Case 2)

Hour	Hydro plant Discharge (X 10⁴ m³)				Power Generation (MW)				Thermal O/P (MW)	Thermal Generation Cost ($)
	Plant 1	Plant 2	Plant 3	Plant 4	Plant 1	Plant 2	Plant 3	Plant 4		
1	9.282	8.338	29.723	13.003	82.722	63.751	0	200.118	1023.407	26744.154
2	10.379	6.373	29.999	13.001	87.436	52.372	0	187.762	1062.429	27656.147
3	9.196	6.060	29.738	13.001	81.391	51.854	0	173.740	1053.014	27435.546
4	7.578	6.357	29.740	13.000	71.675	55.402	0	156.788	1006.133	26342.383
5	9.200	6.002	19.055	13.000	80.026	53.937	21.854	178.395	955.786	25178.150
6	9.630	6.275	17.478	13.002	81.069	56.263	28.319	198.651	1045.696	27264.330
7	9.276	8.424	17.210	13.297	78.839	68.736	29.882	219.306	1253.235	32203.329
8	9.062	8.045	14.727	13.002	77.741	65.917	37.702	233.178	1585.461	40468.239
9	6.381	6.804	15.835	13.001	62.199	58.710	35.576	238.746	1844.766	47225.853
10	9.468	8.159	14.351	13.002	81.821	67.742	40.335	242.752	1887.347	48361.237
11	9.259	8.077	15.295	13.893	81.770	67.766	38.639	254.417	1787.407	45707.877
12	7.269	9.027	15.867	13.098	70.588	72.600	38.318	247.992	1880.499	48178.148
13	7.856	8.391	16.395	13.002	75.366	68.825	39.010	249.391	1797.405	45971.524
14	9.338	8.519	16.039	14.676	84.898	69.827	40.843	265.414	1739.015	44437.442
15	9.020	8.588	17.143	914.971	83.677	70.451	38.879	268.389	1668.602	42605.628
16	7.197	9.171	16.622	15.866	72.444	72.988	41.598	276.236	1606.732	41012.435
17	7.931	9.264	16.072	18.132	77.788	72.144	44.274	292.167	16436.246	41960.596
18	7.541	8.297	16.717	18.042	75.189	65.455	43.037	289.563	1666.754	42557.836
19	6.882	10.018	15.163	15.425	70.371	72.555	47.524	270.611	1778.937	45484.833
20	9.006	10.491	14.379	18.272	83.954	73.041	49.797	291.233	1781.973	45564.748
21	5.380	12.007	10.948	18.065	57.819	76.823	52.038	287.807	1765.511	45131.878
22	7.409	9.496	10.003	19.002	74.129	66.022	53.270	291.702	1634.874	41735.230
23	5.939	10.213	10.0200	20.471	63.0792	67.815	54.580	294.503	1370.021	35058.319
24	5.511	9.593	10.016	21.123	59.718	63.800	56.090	290.052	1120.338	29020.823

Total Cost of thermal generation($/day): 923306.6975

Table 4. Comparison of optimal costs obtained by different algorithms (Case 2)

Method	Best fuel cost($/day)	Avg. fuel cost($/day)	Worst fuel cost($/day)
IPSO[6]	923443.17	–	–
TLBO [11]	923041.91	923174.58	923463.16
FPA	923436.79	924060.80	9259603.29
IFPA	923306.69	923390.42	923433.79

$$X_i^{new} = X_{best} + H * \Delta X_i^{new} \tag{18}$$

Where H is a control parameter which is generated for each population based on switching probability as shown.

$$H = \begin{cases} 1 & if \quad rand_2 < \rho \\ 0 & otherwise \end{cases} \tag{19}$$

$$\Delta X_i^{new} = rand_3 + [(rand_4 - rand_5) \times (Xbest_i)] \tag{20}$$

Where $rand_2$, $rand_3$, $rand_4$ and $rand_5$ are random numbers drawn from uniform distribution between [0, 1]. These are perturbations for position of flower or pollen in $Xbest_i$.

Step 7: *Stopping criteria*

The algorithm terminates when the current generation reaches the maximum number of generations.

5 Simulation Result and Discussion

In order to verify the effectiveness and applicability of IFPA, the test system has been adopted from [3, 4], and additional data with valve point loading effect and prohibited discharge zones have been referred from [6]. It comprises of a multi-chain cascade of four hydro plants and number of thermal units represented by an equivalent thermal plant. Fuel cost function of equivalent thermal plant with valve point loading effect is given as:

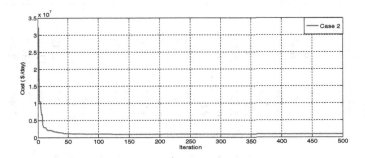

Fig. 3. Cost convergence characteristic of IFPA (case 2)

Table 5. Hourly plant discharge, generation schedule and thermal generations (case 3)

Hour	Hydro plant Discharge (X 10⁴ m³)				Power Generation (MW)				Thermal O/P (MW)	Thermal Generation Cost ($)
	Plant 1	Plant 2	Plant 3	Plant 4	Plant 1	Plant 2	Plant 3	Plant 4		
1	9.9630	8.273	29.657	13.420	85.842	63.420	0	203.298	1017.438	26605.192
2	11.7750	6.898	29.982	13.141	91.678	55.632	0	188.291	1054.398	27467.969
3	9.251	6.023	29.722	13.045	80.910	51.352	0	173.338	1054.398	27467.978
4	10.934	8.333	29.137	13.045	86.593	66.650	0	156.277	980.478	25747.882
5	7.373	6.973	13.280	13.070	68.044	58.831	41.601	178.004	943.518	24896.021
6	7.252	6.108	28.670	13.048	67.157	53.385	0	198.098	1091.358	28336.213
7	5.327	9.124	16.236	13.000	53.624	70.291	33.943	215.983	1276.157	32759.396
8	6.533	6.340	12.490	13.012	63.798	53.658	41.583	232.161	1608.797	41065.368
9	9.601	6.041	12.213	13.011	82.635	52.627	41.777	232.403	1830.556	46848.571
10	10.138	10.228	12.971	13.138	85.437	76.612	42.766	247.668	1867.514	47831.563
11	9.911	6.099	11.735	13.350	85.203	53.944	44.998	252.256	1793.596	45871.047
12	5.328	6.168	13.692	13.011	56.082	55.393	45.657	248.389	1904.476	48820.018
13	9.992	6.368	17.342	13.321	87.535	57.648	40.638	250.581	1793.596	45871.044
14	6.425	6.336	18.741	13.006	66.333	58.747	33.946	247.374	1793.596	45871.042
15	7.923	8.253	14.096	13.409	77.848	71.641	47.808	249.984	1682.717	42971.251
16	6.731	6.650	15.406	13.062	69.658	61.956	45.576	247.051	1645.757	42015.580
17	9.682	11.259	17.125	15.173	88.996	41.022	41.022	269.007	1645.757	42015.576
18	7.498	11.338	16.716	18.305	75.404	82.343	42.294	294.200	1645.757	42015.575
19	9.443	6.4590	15.105	13.748	87.275	56.026	46.697	256.403	1793.596	45871.043
20	5.068	13.198	12.911	18.766	55.323	85.616	51.140	294.321	1793.596	45871.045
21	7.231	14.292	10.095	15.765	73.198	84.497	52.624	273.042	1756.637	44898.979
22	7.301	12.496	11.742	21.268	73.815	77.258	54.762	305.366	1608.797	41065.372
23	7.914	12.381	10.784	19.707	78.328	73.563	56.048	291.982	1350.077	34566.920
24	6.394	6.352	13.901	21.203	67.313	45.113	58.828	290.426	1128.318	29209.921

Total Cost of thermal generation($/day): 925960.5803

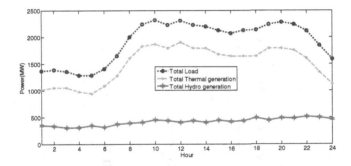

Fig. 4. Hydro generation, thermal generation and load demand (case 3)

$$FC(P_{Tj}) = 0.002P_{Tj}^2 + 19.2P_{Tj} + 5000 + \left| 700 \sin(0.085(P_{Tj}^{\min} - P_{Tj})) \right| \qquad (21)$$

The lower and upper operating limits are 500 MW and 2500 MW respectively. The schedule period of 24 h, with 1 h time intervals is considered for simulation. The problem under consideration is classified into three cases based on types of their fuel cost functions and operational constraints. The present work has been executed in Matlab 7.0 for solution of HTS problem.

The system configuration is Pentium dual core processor with 2.80 GHz and 1 GB RAM. After various runs with different values of control parameter for IFPA the optimum parameters are selected as: number of flower (Np) 50, switching probability (ρ) 0.5, multiplication factor (K) 0.1 and scaling factor (F) 0.5, whereas for FPA have number of flower (Np) 50, switching probability (ρ) 0.5.

Case 1: HTS Problem with Quadratic Cost Functions
In this, the cost function of thermal units of hydrothermal systems is quadratic without prohibited discharge zone. The simulation results in terms of optimal hydro discharge, hydro power generations along with minimum cost obtained by IFPA algorithm are summarized in Table 1. Comparison of cost is made with FPA, TLBO [11], MDE [9], MAPSO [7], PSO [5], EGA [5] and others in Table 2. The best cost reported so far is 922373.39 ($) [11] whereas IFPA capitulates better result in term of thermal generation cost 922377.7345 ($) which is better then MDE [9], PSO [5], IFEP [4] and others while satisfying all associated constraints. Convergence characteristic obtained by IFPA for this test case is shown in Fig. 2.

Case2: HTS Problem with Quadratic Cost Functions and PDZ
The optimal water discharge hydro and thermal generation and the correspond cost obtained by IFPA is shown in Table 3. The comparison of cost obtained by IFPA in terms of best fuel cost, average fuel cost and worst fuel cost are made with FPA, IPSO [6], and TLBO [11] in Table 4. For problem under consideration the optimum generation cost attained by IFPA 923306.6975 ($) where as by FPA is obtained 923436.79 ($).Cost convergence characteristic for this test case is shown in Fig. 3.

Table 6. Comparison of optimal costs obtained by different algorithms for case 3

Method	Best fuel cost($/day)	Avg. fuel cost($/day)	Worst fuel cost($/day)	Method	Best fuel cost($/day)	Avg fuel cost($/day)	Worst fuel cost($/day)
FEP [4]	935021.93	942262.75	951524.37	DE [6]	928236.94	–	–
CEP [4]	934713.18	933801.47	946795.20	NLP [6]	936709.52	–	–
IFEP [4]	933949.25	938508.87	942593.02	MDE [9]	925960.56	–	–
IPSO [6]	925978.84	–	–	TLBO [11]	924550.78	924702.43	925149.06
APSO [7]	925991.35	–	–	FPA	925961.54417	926412.93	931702.22
MAPSO [7]	924636.88	926496	927431	IFPA	925960.5803	925971.31	925978.83

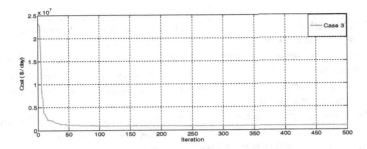

Fig. 5. Cost convergence characteristic of IFPA (case 3)

Case3: HTS Problem with Valve Point Effect and Prohibited Discharge Zone

To demonstrate the feasibility for practical system, VPL effect of thermal generator is considered in this case along with PDZ constraints of hydro plants. Out of 25 independent run, the result obtained by IFPA for 24 h schedule in terms of optimal hydro discharge, hydro and thermal power generations along with corresponding cost are listed in Table 5. Graphical representation of Hydro generation, thermal generation corresponding to load demand over 24 h is shown in Fig. 4. The statistical result in term of cost obtained by different methods available in literature as IFEP [4], IPSO [6] MAPSO [7], DE [6] MDE [9], TLBO [11], FPA and others are listed in Table 6, which depicts the superior search capability of IFPA in comparison to other method for problem under consideration except TLBO. Figure 5 shows the cost convergence obtained by proposed IFPA method for this case.

6 Conclusion

A novel Flower pollination algorithm and improved Flower pollination algorithm is implemented for solution of short term HTS problem. In the FPA algorithm the exploration and exploitation phases are controlled by a switching probability and thus premature convergence is avoided. In this paper an improved FPA is proposed where the local exploitation operation has been more effective by modification. To investigate the potential of FPA and IFPA algorithm three different cases quadratic cost function, quadratic cost function with prohibited discharge zones and quadratic cost function with prohibited discharge zones along with valve point loading effect are considered. The proposed algorithm is simple, comparatively easy to implement. Finally the outcome of simulation achieved by FPA and proposed IFPA for optimization are compared with most recently as well as best known results by any other method in terms of cost, Best fuel cost, Avg. fuel cost and Worst fuel cost.

The solutions obtained by IFPA have found to be superior solution quality and good convergence characteristics. Considering all it can be concluded that proposed approach performs better, except TLBO.

References

1. Yang, J.S., Chen, N.: Short-term hydrothermal coordination using multi-pass dynamic programming. IEEE Trans. Power Syst. **4**(3), 1050–1056 (1989)
2. Mohan, M.R., Kuppusamy, K., Khan, M.A.: Optimal short-term hydro-thermal scheduling using decomposition approach and linear programming method. Int. J. Electr. Power Energ. Syst. **14**(1), 39–44 (1992)
3. Orero, S.O., Irving, M.R.: A genetic algorithm modeling framework and solution technique for short-term optimal hydrothermal scheduling. IEEE Trans. Power Syst. **13**(2), 501–518 (1998)
4. Sinha, N., Chakrabarti, R., Chattopadhyay, P.K.: Fast evolutionary technique for short-term hydrothermal scheduling. IEEE Trans. Power Syst. **18**(1), 214–220 (2003)
5. Yuan, X., Wang, L., Yuan, Y.: Application of enhanced PSO approach to optimal scheduling of hydro system. Energ. Convers. Manag. **49**(11), 2966–2972 (2008)
6. Hota, P.K., Barisal, A.K., Chakrabarti, R.: An improved PSO technique for short-term optimal hydrothermal scheduling. Electr. Power Syst. Res. **79**(7), 1047–1053 (2009)
7. Amjady, N., Soleymanpour, H.R.: Daily hydrothermal generation scheduling by a new modified adaptive particle swarm optimization technique. Electr. Power Syst. Res. **80**(6), 723–732 (2010)
8. Mandal, K.K., Chakraborty, N.: Differential evolution technique-based short-term economic generation scheduling of hydrothermal systems. Electr. Power Syst. Res. **78**(11), 1972–1979 (2008)
9. Lakshminarasimman, L., Subramanian, S.: Short-term scheduling of hydrothermal power system with cascaded reservoirs by using modified differential evolution. IEE Proc. Gener. Transm. Distrib. **153**(6), 693–700 (2006)
10. Lakshminarasimman, L., Subramanian, S.: Modified hybrid differential evolution for short-term scheduling of hydrothermal power system with cascaded reservoirs. Energ. Convers. Manag. **49**(10), 2513–2521 (2008)
11. Roy, P.K.: Teaching learning based optimization for short-term hydrothermal scheduling problem considering valve point effect and prohibited discharge constraint. Electr. Power Energ. Syst. **53**, 10–19 (2013)

12. Yang, X.: Flower pollination algorithm for global optimization. In: Durand-Lose, J., Jonoska, N. (eds.) UCNC 2012. LNCS, vol. 7445, pp. 240–249. Springer, Heidelberg (2012)
13. Pavlyukevich, I.: Levy flight, non local search and simulated annealing. J. Comput. Phys. **226**(1), 1830–1844 (2007)

Proposal of a CBIR Framework for Retinal Images Using Fusion Edge Detection and Zernike Moments

J. Sivakamasundari$^{(\boxtimes)}$ and V. Natarajan

Department of Instrumentation Engineering, Madras Institute of Technology,
Anna University, Chennai, India
sivakamasundarijl7@gmail.com

Abstract. Automated segmentation of blood vessels in retinal images is a critical component in the detection of diabetic retinopathy (DR). In this work, an attempt has been made to develop a Content Based Image Retrieval (CBIR) framework for retinal images. Various edge detection methods such as LoG, Canny, Sobel, Prewitt and Roberts are employed on preprocessed retinal fundus images to segment blood vessels. The output images of individual methods are integrated into four combinations such as LoG-Canny, Sobel-Canny, Sobel-Prewitt and Roberts-Prewitt using D-S fusion technique. The low and high-order invariant Zernike moments are extracted from the segmented blood vessels in four combinations and are analyzed. Results show that the D-S fusion based LoG-Canny edge detection provides continuous vessel map and higher vessel width than the other three combinations. The high-order Zernike moments of this group shows significant differentiation between normal and abnormal images. The retrieval performance such as precision and recall for D-S fusion based CBIR system is found to be 93 % and 81 % respectively. This CBIR system could be useful for automated diabetic retinopathy detection in mass screening.

Keywords: Retinal blood vessels · Diabetic retinopathy · Edge detection · Content based image retrieval · Dempster-Shafer fusion · Zernike moments

1 Introduction

Retina is a unique region of eye where the blood vessels are directly observed in vivo [1]. The retinal vascular network is an important structure for diagnosis, evaluation, treatment, and clinical study of many diseases such as DR, hypertension and arteriosclerosis [2]. Globally, the number of people with DR are estimated to increase to 191.0 million and the number with vision-threatening diabetic retinopathy are projected to increase from 37.3 million to 56.3 million by 2030 [3]. DR affects the retinal microvasculature. The change in the retinal blood vessel structures such as tortuosity, bifurcation, and the variation of vessel width, helps in the early diagnosis and effective treatment of several pathologies [4].

Computer-aided automatic vessel segmentation helps in many clinical investigations especially for the analysis of a huge quantity of retinal fundus images in the

© Springer International Publishing Switzerland 2015
B.K. Panigrahi et al. (Eds.): SEMCCO 2014, LNCS 8947, pp. 738–749, 2015.
DOI: 10.1007/978-3-319-20294-5_63

screening programs [5]. Various methods for detection of blood vessels on retinal images have been reported [6]. These methods are classified into three categories namely model based, probing and edge detection methods [7]. Vessel edge information of retinal images are obtained by various edge detection methods. Gradient operators such as LoG, Sobel, Prewitt, Roberts, Canny and Kirsch templates are used for the detection of blood vessels and compared [8]. Canny and Kirsch edge based methods are used to identify the blood vessels in DR screening [9, 10].

The edge detectors such as Canny, LoG, Sobel and Prewitt are not able to identify the vessels more accurately in fundus images due to the smooth change in intensity variations [11]. Hence an integrated edge detection method has been proposed for retinal blood vessel detection. Dempster–Shafer rule integrates the strength of two different edge detection methods by means of a probability based fusion technique to improve the accuracy of vessel edge information. This fusion method combines the outputs of LoG and Canny methods to improve edge detection accuracy [7].

Zernike moments are the region-based descriptors used in the field of pattern, character recognition, image retrieval and image reconstructions. These are used as rotation-invariant features in which each moment order captures unique information without any redundancy [12]. Pattern analysis of the retinal fundus images for person identification and classification of benign and malignant masses in mammographic images have been proposed based on Zernike moments [13, 14].

CBIR in medical image retrieval applications are used to assist physicians in clinical decision-support techniques and research fields [15]. CBIR has also been used in medical image annotation and retrieval system for X-ray images [16]. Canny edge detection algorithm has been used in the medical CBIR for brain MR and retinal images [17, 18]. The Canny edge operator and Hu invariant moments have been proposed to retrieve general images [19]. Sobel and Canny edge operators with Zernike moments are used in general and trademark image retrieval systems [20, 21].

In this work, an attempt has been made to generate a vessel map with more accurate and continuous vessel edge information by combining the strength of two edge detection methods. The segmented images obtained from basic edge operations are subjected to D-S fusion technique in four combinations such as LoG-Canny, Sobel-Canny, Sobel-Prewitt and Roberts-Prewitt. The invariant Zernike moments are obtained from the output images of D-S fusion based vessel segmentation in four groups. Quantitative analyses are carried out for normal and abnormal retinal image classification. The D-S fusion based CBIR system is developed using Zernike features. Similarity matching is carried out between features of query and database images using Euclidean distance measure. Similar images are ranked and retrieved.

2 Methodology

In this work, retinal images are obtained from the publicly available image database such as DRIVE, DIARETDB1 and HRF images [22]. The framework of CBIR system for retinal image retrieval is shown in Fig. 1. It is divided into two main subsystems namely, enrolment and query subsystem. The enrolment subsystem includes, retinal image database and its corresponding feature vectors obtained from the segmented

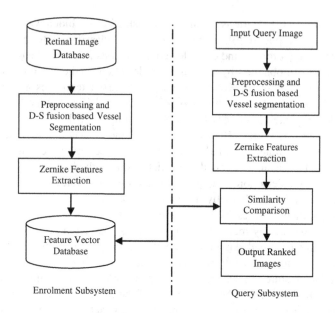

Fig. 1. CBIR framework

images stored in separate database. The user's query image is applied through the query subsystem. The features of query image also obtained. The query subsystem retrieves closely matching images from the retinal image database using similarity comparison method.

Random samples of 30 normal and 30 abnormal images are subjected to training and 55 normal and 55 abnormal images are used for testing. Green channel extraction is employed for the improvement of vessel contrast from its background. Morphological enhancement is carried out for the removal of non-uniform illumination. These images are segmented using D-S fusion based LoG-Canny method.

2.1   Retinal Blood Vessel Segmentation Methods

2.1.1   LoG Edge Detection Method

The LoG edge detection is a second derivative method. This method uses a Gaussian filter to eliminate noise and combines the Laplacian for edge detection. The Gaussian kernel is written as:

$$LoG = \nabla^2 \left(h(x,y) \right) = \left[\frac{x^2 + y^2 - 2\sigma^2}{\sigma^2} \right] e^{-\frac{(x^2+y^2)}{2\sigma^2}} \tag{1}$$

where the 2D Gaussian function is given as $h(x,y) = e^{-\frac{(x^2+y^2)}{2\sigma^2}}$ and σ is the width of the Gaussian curve that controls the degree of smoothing. The influence of noise is considerable. It generates closed contours, which are not real [7].

2.1.2   Canny Edge Detection

Canny edge detection defines the edges as zero-crossing of the second derivatives. In this method, the image is smoothed by a Gaussian filter. The gradient of the smoothed array $g(x,y)$ is used to produce the x and y partial derivatives $G_x(x, y)$ and $G_y(x, y)$. From the rectangular-to-polar conversion, the gradient magnitude array $G(x,y)$ and gradient angle array $\theta(x,y)$ are computed as:

$$G(x, y) = \sqrt{G_x^2(x, y) + G_y^2(x, y)} \qquad (2)$$

$$\theta(x, y) = \tan^{-1}\left(\frac{G_y^2(x, y)}{G_x^2(x, y)}\right) \qquad (3)$$

The gradient angle of an edge in four discrete orientations represents vertical, horizontal and the two diagonals. Edges generated using gradient contains wide ridges around local maxima. For obtaining edges the value of $G(x, y)$ is considered as less than one of its two neighbors along $\theta(x,y)$. Then the non-maximal suppressed array $N(x,y)$ is considered as zero. Upper and lower hysteresis thresholds track the edges. The false edges are reduced by false edge point reduction and edge linking.

Canny method detects edges but is more sensitive to noise. The resultant image may contain broken edges and some are located either inside or outside of the true edges. But LoG identifies more continuous edges than the Canny edge method. Therefore in this work, the D-S theory is used to combine strengths of Canny and LoG edge detection algorithms to improve the vessel edge information [7].

2.1.3   Dempster–Shafer Based Retinal Blood Vessel Detection

Depmster–Shafer theory is a mathematical theory of evidence based on belief functions and plausible reasoning. This is used to combine separate evidences of information to calculate the probability density of an event [23]. The outputs of both LoG and Canny edge detection methods are combined using D-S rule. The LoG and Canny edge methods are considered as evidences and their outputs are taken as events for D-S based fusion. Continuous retinal blood vessel map is achieved by this technique [7].

Dempster–Shafer Theory. Dempster–Shafer theory combines the multiple belief functions using their basic assignments of probability. This is merely a conjunctive operation (AND). It is represented as joint $m_{1\oplus2}(A)$ and is calculated from the aggregation of two basic probability assignments m_1 and m_2 is given by:

$$m_{1\oplus2}(A) = \frac{\sum\limits_{B\cap C=A} m_1(B)m_2(C)}{1 - K} \text{ when } A \neq \phi \qquad (4)$$

$$m_{1\oplus2}(\phi) = 0 \quad \text{and} \quad K = \sum\limits_{B\cap C=\varphi} m_1(B)m_2(C) \qquad (5)$$

where A, B and C are event sets generated by the D-S fusion, LoG and Canny edge detection methods respectively. To ignore the conflicts caused by events such as LoG and Canny methods the term $m_{1\oplus2}(\varphi)$ is defined where K represents basic probability of mass related with conflicts. It is determined by summing the products of the basic probability assignments of all sets where the intersection is null. The output images of LoG and Canny edge methods are represented by edge (E) or non-edge (N). Then the edge confidence of LoG and Canny methods is denoted as m_1 and m_2 respectively. The D-S rule is given as:

$$m(E) = \frac{m_1(E)m_2(E)}{1 - m_1(E)m_2(N) - m_1(N)m_2(E)} \tag{6}$$

where $m(E)$, $m_1(E)$ and $m_2(E)$ are edge confidence of D-S fusion, LoG and Canny methods respectively. Non-edge confidence of LoG and the Canny edge methods are $m_1(N)$ and $m_2(N)$. Non-edge confidence of D-S fusion is calculated as $m(N) = 1-m(E)$. The output confidence score of LoG and Canny edge methods are computed by:

$$m_1(E) = \frac{g(i,j)}{g_{max}} \quad and \quad m_2(E) = \frac{g(i,j)}{Threshold} \tag{7}$$

where $g(i, j)$ is the gradient magnitude of an image pixel (i, j) and g_{max} is the maximum gradient magnitude of an image. The threshold value is maximum intensity gradient value of the pixels [7].

2.2   Features Extraction

The Zernike polynomials are sequence of polynomials that are continuous and orthogonal over a unit circle [24]. The complex Zernike moments are derived from Zernike polynomials. Then the complex Zernike moments of order n with repetition m are defined as:

$$Z_{n,m} = \frac{n+1}{\pi} \sum_x \sum_y f(x,y) \cdot V_{n,m}(x,y) \tag{8}$$

$$Z_{n,m} = \frac{n+1}{\pi} \sum_r \sum_\theta f(r\cos\theta, r\sin\theta) \cdot R_{n,m}(r) \cdot \exp(jm\theta), \quad r \leq 1 \tag{9}$$

where r is the length of vector from the origin to (x, y) to the shape centroid, θ is the angle between r and x axis, n is a non-negative integer representing the order of the radial polynomial and m is a positive or negative integer satisfying the constraints $n-|m| =$ even and $|m| \leq n$ represents the repetition of the azimuthal angle. The π is a normalization factor of pixels located in the unit circle by the mapping transform, which corresponds to the area of the unit circle in the continuous domain. $R_{m,n}$ is radial polynomial and $V_{n,m}$ represents 2-D Zernike basis function. The term $R_{n,m}(r).\exp(jm\theta)$ reflects angular frequency of Zernike moments in its trigonometric harmonics.

The magnitudes of the complex Zernike moments are used as rotation invariant features. The magnitudes of the acquired Zernike moments are normalized and used as shape descriptors. Two groups such as high-order (32) and low-order (32) Zernike moments are obtained for different iterations from the segmented images. High-order Zernike moments are better descriptors of shape than the low-order [14]. In this work, Zernike features are obtained from the D-S fusion based segmented blood vessels from all combinations. The statistically significant features are used in content based retinal image retrieval system.

3 Results and Discussion

The original normal and abnormal images and their preprocessing steps are shown in Figs. 2(a–d) and 3(a–d) respectively. The grayscale of original images are shown in Figs. 2(b) and 3(b). The vessel contrast is improved against the background using green channel extraction as shown in Figs. 2(c) and 3(c). Vessel contrast is further improved and also non uniform illumination is eliminated by the morphological operations as shown in the Figs. 2(d) and 3(d). Further, undesired background is suppressed from the retinal vessels. The blood vessels are segmented by various edge detection operators

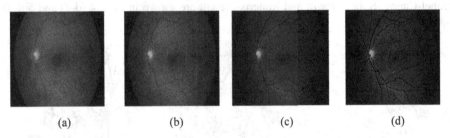

(a)   (b)   (c)   (d)

Fig. 2. Preprocessing of normal retinal image (a) original, (b) grayscale, (c) green channel and (d) morphological treated images

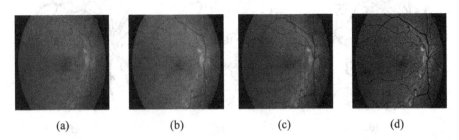

(a)   (b)   (c)   (d)

Fig. 3. Preprocessing of abnormal retinal image (a) original, (b) grayscale, (c) green channel and (d) morphological treated images

such as LoG, Canny, Sobel, Prewitt and Roberts. The integration of segmented binary output is carried out using D-S rule. The combinations of four groups are considered for D-S integration. The segmentation results of normal and DR affected images are given in Figs. 4 and 5.

From Fig. 4 (a) it is observed that the LoG operator detects continuous pixels from primary vessel edges but thin vessels are not identified much than Canny operator. The Canny edge method detects most of the primary and small blood vessels but it suffers discontinuities in the primary vessels as shown in Fig. 4(b). D-S fusion method rectifies these drawbacks and the resultant image gets continuous vessel edge map with smooth and wide vessels. It detects thin vessels also in normal images as represented in Fig. 4 (c).

The LoG and Canny edge segmentation outputs are shown in Fig. 5(a) and (b) for abnormal images. The Canny method shows discontinuities even in major vessel joints but detects more small vessels. The LoG operation detects less small vessels and shows broken edges at the thin vessel joints. But it identifies the pathological pixels and differentiates from the small vessels. From Fig. 5(c) it is observed that the D-S fusion of LoG-Canny edge detection identifies continuous vessel map of primary and small vasculatures along with disease conditions in abnormal images. The D-S integration shows significant difference between thin vessels and pathological pixels.

The resultant images of D-S fusion method in other combinations such as Sobel-Canny, Sobel-Prewitt and Roberts-Prewitt are shown in Figs. 4 (d–f) and 5(d–f)

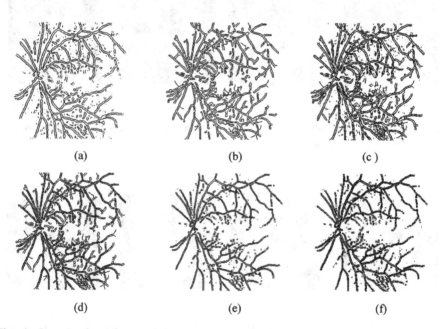

(a)   (b)   (c)

(d)   (e)   (f)

Fig. 4. Segmentation of normal images using various edge detection methods (a) LoG, (b) Canny, (c) D-S fusion of LoG-Canny, (d) D-S fusion of Sobel-Canny, (e) D-S fusion of Sobel-Prewitt and (f) D-S fusion of Roberts-Prewitt

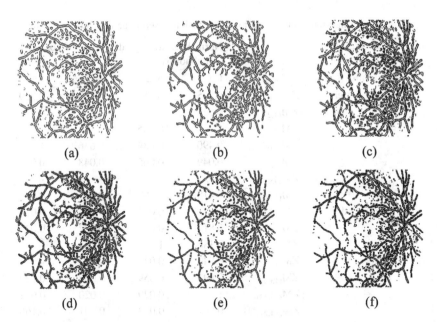

Fig. 5. Segmentation of abnormal images using various edge detection methods (a) LoG, (b) Canny, (c) D-S fusion of LoG-Canny, (d) D-S fusion of Sobel-Canny, (e) D-S fusion of Sobel-Prewitt and (f) D-S fusion of Roberts-Prewitt

for normal and DR affected images. The segmented vessels suffer with uneven thin vessel width, dark mass inside the vessels and more isolated edge pixels that appear like noise in normal images. The unconnected vessel pixels detected by these methods appears like pathological conditions in the case of abnormal images and may lead to misclassification. The results recommend that the LoG-Canny group is used for further analysis because of the continuous vessel map with significant differentiation of vessels and abnormal conditions.

Low and high-order Zernike moments are obtained from the segmented vessels for four edge combinations of D-S outputs in normal and abnormal images. Statistical significance t-test is calculated for all 64 moments. The normalized average differences between normal and abnormal images are obtained. The statistically significant moments with p-value less than 0.0001 are shown in Table 1.

It shows for 7 low-order and 12 high-order Zernike moments out of 64 moments which are highly statistically significant to improve the retrieval performance of CBIR system. The LoG-Canny group shows high normalized difference between normal and abnormal images and differentiates them distinctly than the other three combinations. It is also found that the high-order moments such as $ZM_{(10,10)}$ and $ZM_{(13,13)}$ shows highest normalized average difference of one. The normalized average difference of low-order moments $ZM_{(8,8)}$, $ZM_{(9,9)}$ and high-order moments above $ZM_{(16,0)}$ are found to be very less and may not be used for differentiation of normal and disease affected images.

Table 1. Zernike moments for various D-S fusion based edge detection methods

S.No	Zernike Moments		Normalized average difference of normal and abnormal images *			
	Group	$ZM_{(n,m)}$	L-C	S-C	S-P	R-P
1	Low-Order	$ZM_{(4,0)}$	0.205	0.553	0.503	0.719
2		$ZM_{(4,2)}$	0.722	–	–	–
3		$ZM_{(7,7)}$	1	0.035	–	–
4		$ZM_{(8,0)}$	0.490	0.684	0.636	1
5		$ZM_{(8,8)}$	0.049	0.065	0.048	0.064
6		$ZM_{(9,9)}$	0.022	–	–	–
7		$ZM_{(10,0)}$	0.418	0.607	0.461	0.611
8	High-Order	$ZM_{(10,10)}$	1	0.053	0.034	0.035
9		$ZM_{(11,11)}$	0.817	0.041	0.027	0.035
10		$ZM_{(12,0)}$	0.186	1	1	–
11		$ZM_{(12,12)}$	0.840	0.041	–	–
12		$ZM_{(13,1)}$	0.992	0.059	0.069	0.122
13		$ZM_{(13,13)}$	1	0.029	0.020	0.028
14		$ZM_{(14,2)}$	0.897	0.083	0.097	0.165
15		$ZM_{(15,15)}$	0.034	0.059	0.048	0.057
16		$ZM_{(16,0)}$	0.536	0.827	0.664	0.971
17		$ZM_{(16,4)}$	0.030	0.065	0.139	0.071
18		$ZM_{(16,16)}$	0.034	0.053	0.034	0.043
19		$ZM_{(17,17)}$	0.034	0.053	0.027	0.043

*$P < 0.0001$ Highly statistically significant
LoG-Canny (L-C), Sobel-Canny (S-C), Sobel-Prewitt (S-P) and Roberts-Prewitt (R-P)

The variation of normalized average difference between normal and DR affected images for different Zernike moments are represented in Fig. 6. Three low and seven high-order moments obtained for LoG-Canny group exhibits high range (above 0.5) of average difference than the other combinations. Hence, LoG-Canny group provides significant classification of normal and abnormal images. This variations in $ZM_{(12,0)}$ and $ZM_{(13,13)}$ are represented in Fig. 7(a) and (b) respectively. The graphical user interface (GUI) developed for D-S fusion based CBIR system. The input query image and its statistically significant Zernike moments obtained are shown in Fig. 8 (a). The retrieval of top four ranked similar images are shown in Fig. 8(b).

The performance measures of D-S fusion based CBIR system is compared with the simple Canny edge based CBIR systems [9] and are shown in Table 2. Higher precision (93 %) and recall (81 %) are achieved for D-S fusion based LoG-Canny CBIR method than the other method.

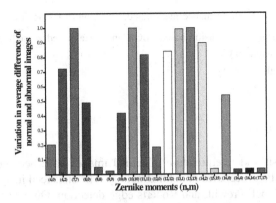

Fig. 6. Variation of normalized average difference for low and high-order Zernike moments in D-S fusion of LoG-Canny based edge detection method

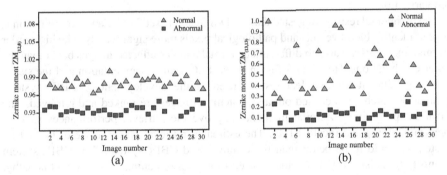

Fig. 7. Variations of high-order Zernike moments in differentiation of normal and abnormal images using D-S fusion of LoG-Canny edge detection method (a) $ZM_{(12,0)}$ and (b) $ZM_{(13,13)}$

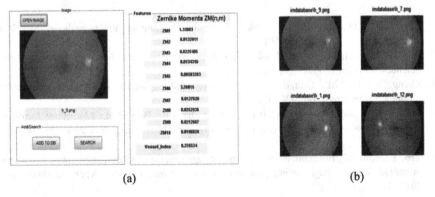

Fig. 8. GUI of CBIR system (a) normal retinal query image and its Zernike moments and (b) retrieved normal images

Table 2. Performance measures comparison of CBIR systems

Measures	D-S fusion based LoG-Canny	Canny edge method
Precision	93 %	80 %
Recall	81 %	38 %

4 Conclusions

Automated analysis and interpretation of retinal images have become necessary and important diagnostic procedures in ophthalmology. The enhanced images are subjected to LoG, Canny, Sobel, Prewitt, and Roberts edge detection. Outputs of the individual methods are subjected to the D-S fusion based method in four combinations of edge operations such as LoG-Canny, Sobel-Canny, Sobel-Prewitt and Roberts-Prewitt. The Zernike moments are extracted from the segmented vessels and quantitative analysis are carried out.

Experimental results suggested that the D-S fusion based LoG-Canny combination is able to identify blood vessels and pathological pixels more significantly. The high-order Zernike moments are able to differentiate normal and DR affected images better than the other combinations. Hence D-S fusion based LoG-Canny segmentation and the statistically significant Zernike features are used in the development of CBIR system. Similarity matching is carried out and matching images are ranked and retrieved. The invariant property of Zernike moments improve the retrieval performances such as precision (93 %) and recall (81 %). The estimated retrieval performance of this CBIR system is found to be better than the Canny based CBIR system. This CBIR system seems to be satisfactory and could be useful for mass screening of diabetic retinopathy.

References

1. Abràmoff, M.D., Garvin, M.K., Sonka, M.: Retinal imaging and image analysis. IEEE Rev. Biomed. Eng. **3**, 169–208 (2010)
2. Kanski, J.J.: Clinical Ophthalmology: A Systemic Approach, 6th edn. Elsevier Health Sciences, London (2007). 952 pages
3. Zheng, Y., He, M., Congdon, N.: The worldwide epidemic of diabetic retinopathy. Indian J. Ophthalmol. **60**, 428–431 (2012)
4. Winder, R.J., Morrow, P.J., McRitchie, I.N., Bailie, J.R., Hart, P.M.: Algorithms for digital image processing in diabetic retinopathy. Comput. Med. Imaging Graph. **33**, 608–622 (2009)
5. Yin, Y., Adel, M., Bourennane, S.: Automatic segmentation and measurement of vasculature in retinal fundus images using probabilistic formulation. Comput. Math. Methods Med. **2013**, 1–16 (2013)
6. Fraz, M.M., Remagnino, P., Hoppe, A., Uyyanonvara, B., Rudnicka, A.R., Owen, C.G., Barman, S.A.: Blood vessel segmentation methodologies in retinal images - a survey. Comput. Methods Programs Biomed. **108**, 407–433 (2012)

7. Li, X., Wee, W.G.: Retinal vessel detection and measurement for computer-aided medical diagnosis. J. Digit. Imaging **27**, 120–132 (2014)
8. Karasulu, B.: Automatic extraction of retinal blood vessels: a software implementation. Eur. Sci. J. **8**, 47–57 (2012)
9. Sivakamasundari, J., Natrajan, V.: Analysis of human retinal vasculature for content based image retrieval applications. In: Panigrahi, B.K., Suganthan, P.N., Das, S., Dash, S.S. (eds.) SEMCCO 2013, Part II. LNCS, vol. 8298, pp. 606–616. Springer, Heidelberg (2013)
10. Sivakamasundari, J., Kavitha, G., Natarajan, V. Ramakrishnan, S.: Proposal of a content based retinal image retrieval system using kirsch template based edge detection. In: IEEE Conference on Informatics, Electronics & Vision, Dhaka, Bangladesh (2014)
11. Zolfagharnasab, H., Naghsh-Nilchi, A.R.: Cauchy based matched filter for retinal vessels detection. J. Med. Sig. Sens. **4**, 1–9 (2014)
12. Goyal, A., Walia, E.: Variants of dense descriptors and Zernike moments as features for accurate shape-based image retrieval. SIViP **8**, 1–17 (2013)
13. Aich, S., Mamun, G.M.A.: An efficient supervised approach for retinal person identification using Zernike moments. Int. J. Comput. Appl. **81**, 34–37 (2013)
14. Tahmasbi, A., Saki, F., Shokouhi, S.B.: Classification of benign and malignant masses based on Zernike moments. Comput. Biol. Med. **41**, 726–735 (2011)
15. Muller, H., Michoux, N., Bandon, D., Geissbuhler, A.: A review of content based image retrieval systems in medical applications – clinical benefits and future directions. Int. J. Med. Inf. **73**, 1–23 (2004)
16. Mueen, A., Zainuddin, R., Sapiyan Baba, M.: MIARS: a medical image retrieval system. J. Med. Syst. **34**, 859–864 (2010)
17. Ramamurthy, B., Chandran, K.R.: Content based image retrieval for medical images using canny edge detection algorithm. Int. J. Comput. Appl. **17**, 32–37 (2011)
18. Sivakamasundari, J., Kavitha, G., Natarajan, V., Ramakrishnan, S.: Content based human retinal image retrieval using vascular feature extraction. In: Pan, J.-S., Chen, S.-M., Nguyen, N.T. (eds.) ACIIDS 2012, Part II. LNCS, vol. 7197, pp. 468–476. Springer, Heidelberg (2012)
19. Xiang, F., Yong, H., Dandan, S., Jiexian, Z.: An image retrieval method based on Hu invariant moment and improved annular histogram. Elektronika IR Elektrotechnika **19**, 114–118 (2013)
20. Jadhav, D., Patil, M., Patil, A., Phalak, L.: A novel three stage CBIR using varying higher-order Zernike moments and its performance analysis. Int. J. Comput. Appl. **75**, 33–38 (2013)
21. Wei, C.H., Li, Y., Chau, W.Y., Li, C.T.: Trademark image retrieval using synthetic features for describing global shape and interior structure. Pattern Recogn. **42**, 386–394 (2009)
22. Köhler, T., Budai, A., Kraus, M., Odstrcilik, J., Michelson, G., Hornegger, J.: Automatic no-reference quality assessment for retinal fundus images using vessel segmentation. In: IEEE International Symposium on Computer- Based Medical Systems, Porto, Portugal (2013)
23. Shafer, G.: Perspectives on the theory and practice of belief functions. Int. J. Approx. Reason. **4**, 323–362 (1990)
24. Lakshminarayanan, V., Fleck, A.: Zernike polynomials: a guide. J. Mod. Opt. **58**, 545–561 (2011)

Different Penalty Handling Based Economic Dispatch Using Time Varying Acceleration Coefficients

Ruchi Solanki[1(✉)], K.T. Chaturvedi[2], and N.P. Patidar[1]

[1] MANIT, Bhopal, India
ruchiabhaysolanki@gmail.com, nppatidar@yahoo.com
[2] UIT-RGPV, Bhopal, India
dr_ktc@yahoo.com

Abstract. This paper presents a novel and efficient method for solving the economic dispatch (ED) problem with non-smooth cost function by modifying the particle swarm optimization algorithm employing time varying acceleration and time varying penalty (PSO-TVAC&P) coefficients. The proposed approach is suggested to deal with equality and inequality constraints with high degree of non linearity in the ED problems. To show the efficiency and effectiveness of proposed PSO-TVAC&P algorithm, it is tested on two test systems considering ramp rate limits, prohibited zones and valve point loading effects.

1 Introduction

Economic load dispatch (ELD) is constraint driven, non-convex, non-smooth optimization problem, which distribute the total power demand among the various online connected generating units in a most economical manner while considering the different physical and operational constraints. Economic load dispatch helps in saving considerable amount involved in the operation of fossil fuel based power plants. For the last past years, different kinds of optimization techniques have been developed to solve this cumbersome optimization problem. Among those are conventional methods like lambda iteration method, base point and participation factor method, gradient search method, quadratic programming [1] etc. The implementation of these methods rely on the nature of the problem i.e. convexity and continuity of the problem and hence, approximate the problem as quadratic or piecewise quadratic monotonically increasing cost functions. [1]. The basic ELD problem takes care of only equality constraint of power balance and inequality constraint of generating capacity limit. But practical problem of ELD have a variety of nonlinearities and discontinuities due to ramp rate limit, prohibited operating zones and valve point loading effect [2, 3]. Therefore practical ELD problem is transformed into non-convex, non-smooth optimization problem, difficult to solve by classical methods.

Heuristic optimization techniques such as evolutionary programming [5, 6], tabu-search [7], artificial intelligence [8], neural network [9], genetic algorithm [2, 3, 10], particle swarm optimization [11–15] etc. have been previously adopted for ELD problem of non-convex nature. These methods are independent of convexity

© Springer International Publishing Switzerland 2015
B.K. Panigrahi et al. (Eds.): SEMCCO 2014, LNCS 8947, pp. 750–764, 2015.
DOI: 10.1007/978-3-319-20294-5_64

assumptions and also consumes less computational time. These heuristic technique not always guarantee global optimal solution but often achieve near global solution at a faster rate.

In last few years, to improve convergence characteristic and to find the global optimal solution, many researches using soft computing techniques have been reported like θ-particle swarm optimization where velocity vector is replaced with phase angle vector [29], quantum mechanics inspired PSO (HQPSO) using harmonic oscillator [19], hybrid methodology integrating bee colony optimization (BCO) with sequential quadratic programming for solving dynamic economic dispatch [17], for enlarging search space and speed up convergence, a new update velocity is used by hybridizing cultural algorithm (CA) with PSO called SCAPSO [18], Self-organizing hierarchical particle swarm optimization (SOH-PSO) is employed to reinitialize particle's velocity when population stagnates at local minima, which the particle velocities are reinitialized whenever the population stagnates at local optima during the search [22], random drift particle swarm optimization (RDPSO) is inspired from the effect of external electric field on the behaviour of free electron model in metal conductors [31].

A new strategy which based on variation of acceleration coefficients of PSO with time is proposed in this paper along with different penalties for non-convex economic dispatch problem to overcome the drawback of premature convergence and to find the global optimal solution. If a high value is assigned to cognitive component, the particle will wander excessively. On the other hand, if the value of social component is high, premature convergence will take place [13]. Hence time varying acceleration coefficients (TVAC) [28] are employed to make a proper balance between social and cognitive components during the search. This paper proposes a new modified PSO based algorithm, Integration of this approach with time varying penalty helps in exploring the search space very effectively to identity the promising solution region. Effectiveness of the PSO_TVAC&P was demonstrated on two different sized (small and large) power systems with 6 and 40 generating units.

2 Formulation of Nonconvex Economic Dispatch(NCED)

The aim of economic dispatch is to allocate load on different generating units in such a way to minimize the total generating cost. The total generation costs are usually approximated by a quadratic function. So ED problem is formulated as:

$$MinFC = \sum_{j=1}^{N_G} F_j(P_j) \tag{1}$$

where F_j is defined as:

$$F_j(P_j) = a_j P_j^2 + b_j P_j + c_j \tag{2}$$

subject to the constraints given by:

$$\sum_{j=1}^{N_G} P_j - (P_D + P_{Loss}) = 0 \tag{3}$$

$$P_{j,\min} \leq P_j \leq P_{j,\max} \qquad j = 1, 2, \ldots, NG \tag{4}$$

For a given total real load P_D the system loss P_{Loss} is a function of active power generation at each generating unit.

But the practical ED problem is not convex because of generator nonlinearities such as valve point loading effects, prohibited operating zones and ramp rate limits, which are included in the present paper.

2.1   Valve Point Loading Effect

The presence of number of valves introduce ripples due to throttling losses in the heat-rate curve of the generator and make objective function nonconvex and discontinuous with multiple minima and a rectified sinusoidal function [2] is added to cost function to model the effect of valve point loading and modified output function is given as below:

$$F_j(P_j) = a_j P_j^2 + b_j P_j + c_j + \left| g_j \times \sin(h_j \times (P_{j,\min} - P_j)) \right| \tag{5}$$

where $a_j, b_j,$ and c_j are the fuel-cost coefficients of the ith unit, and g_j and h_j are the fuel cost-coefficients of the jth unit with valve-point effects.

2.2   Generator Ramp-Rate Limits

In certain interval, the kth unit generated power, P_k may not exceed the previous hour generated power P_{K0} by certain value RR_k^{up}, the up-ramp limit and also it may not be less than previous interval by more than RR_k^{down} the down ramp rate limit of the generator.

So power generated by k th unit should lie in the range given as

$$\max\left(P_k^{\min}, P_{k0} - RR_k^{down}\right) \leq P_k \leq \min\left(P_k^{\max}, P_{k0} + RR_k^{up}\right) \tag{6}$$

2.3   Prohibited Operating Zone

Prohibited operating zones (POZs) are the range of generated power of any unit where the operation causes unwanted vibration of the turbine shaft because of the opening and closing of steam valve which might be detrimental to shaft and bearings. The cost curves of practical generators are discontinuous as whole of the unit operating range is not always available for allocation The prohibited operating zones divide the operating range of a unit between its maximum and minimum generation limits, into a number of disconnected convex sub-zones making the cost curve discontinuous. It is difficult to find exact operating zones of a generating unit either by testing or from operating records. So, unit is not operated in such zones. Mathematically the feasible operating zones of generating unit k can be expressed as:

$$\begin{cases} P_k^{min} \leq P_k \leq P_{k,1}^{low} \\ P_{k,(z-1)}^{up} \leq P_k \leq P_{k,z}^{low} \qquad z = 2,3,\ldots\ldots\ldots N \\ P_{k,N}^{up} \leq P_k \leq P_k^{max} \end{cases} \qquad (7)$$

where z represents the number of prohibited zones of unit k, $P_{k,(z-1)}^{up}$ is the upper limit of $(z-1)$th prohibited zone of kth unit. $P_{k,z}^{low}$ is the lower limit of zth prohibited zone.

3 Review of Different PSO Techniques

Since the introduction of PSO method [16], it has gained popularity among researchers and being used with several different strategies for the problem like ED and other multifaceted problem in various fields. Here, a short review of the significant developments in this field is presented.

3.1 Classical PSO

A population based optimization technique called PSO was first introduced by Kennedy and Eberhart in 1995. PSO is based on social behavior of fish school or birds flocks. In the recent years, PSO has gained attention of many researchers being simple in application and efficacy in solving problem with inexpensive computational time. In PSO, each individual in the search space called particle offers a potential solution to the mentioned problem. The status of the particle is defined by position and velocity vector related to it.

The position and velocity vector of jth particle in D-dimensional search space at nth iteration is represented as $S_{j,n} = (S_{j,n}^1, S_{j,n}^2, S_{j,n}^d, \ldots\ldots\ldots S_{j,n}^D)$ and $V_{j,n} = (V_{j,n}^1, V_{j,n}^2, \ldots V_{j,n}^d, \ldots\ldots\ldots V_{j,n}^D)$ respectively. The best solution achieved by jth particle until the current iteration (n) is given as $P_{pbest_{j,n}} = (P_{pbest_{j,n}}^1, P_{pbest_{j,n}}^2, \ldots, P_{pbest_{j,n}}^d, \ldots, P_{pbest_{j,n}}^D)$. The best $P_{pbest_{j,n}}$ among the entire particles is denoted as global best P_{gbest_n}. The particle velocity is updated by

$$V_{j,n+1}^d = \omega\, V_{j,n}^d + c_1\, R_1\left(P_{pbest_{j,n}}^d - S_{j,n}^d\right) + c_2\, R_2\left(P_{gbest_n}^d - S_{j,n}^d\right) \qquad (8)$$

$$S_{j,n+1}^d = S_{j,n}^d + V_{j,n+1}^d \qquad (9)$$

For $1 \leq j \leq N$ and $1 \leq d \leq D$. ω is the inertia weight, c_1 and c_2 are acceleration coefficients and R_1 and R_2 are the random numbers distributed uniformly on (0,1).

3.2   PSO with Time-Varying Acceleration Coefficients (PSO_TVAC)

With the advancement of research in the field of PSO, it has been observed that the tuning among various parameters of PSO plays a researchers have observed that the fine tuning of parameters of PSO, plays a very important part in achieving optimal solution of the problem precisely and efficiently [11–13]. In view of this, a novel PSO strategy has been proposed in this paper where time varying acceleration coefficients are being employed to solve the non-convex economic dispatch (NCED) problem with ramp rate, prohibited operating zone and valve point loading. In the latter stages, convergence of the algorithm to attain global optima should be motivated for finding optimum solution effectively.

The particles will roam excessively through the search space if the value of cognitive component is comparatively high with regard to social component. Conversely, premature convergence will happen, if the value of social component is comparatively high. In the majority of the studies, both the acceleration coefficients are set at 2, to make the mean of two stochastic factors in (8) equal to one. By doing so the particles would over fly only half the time of search.

In time varying acceleration coefficient (TVAC), the acceleration coefficients are set in such a manner to enhance the global search in the initial part of the optimization and motivate the particles to converge to the global optima at the end of the search. The cognitive component c_1 reduces with time as the search progresses and social component c_2 increases. At the starting a large value of c_1 and small value of c_2, allows particle to explore the whole search space instead of moving towards the particle best during early stages. A small c_1 and large c_2 value permit the particles to converge to the global optima in the later search. The acceleration coefficients are defined as [28]:

$$c_1 = \left(c_{1f} - c_{1i}\right) \frac{I}{I_{\max}} + c_{1i} \tag{10}$$

$$c_2 = \left(c_{2f} - c_{2i}\right) \frac{I}{I_{\max}} + c_{2i} \tag{11}$$

where c_{1i}, c_{1f}, c_{2i} and c_{2f} are initial and final values of cognitive and social acceleration factors respectively. I is the number of iteration and I_{max} is the maximum number of iterations.

3.3   PSO with Time-Varying Acceleration Coefficients and Penalty (PSO_TVAC&P)

Using PSO_TVAC techniques, optimum set of parameters is achieved by experimentation and solutions found near the global value. It has been found that convergence characteristics of PSO_TVAC algorithm, does not show the significant improvement in the latter part of the search. To overcome this problem, time varying penalty is introduced. Combination of these two (PSO_TVAC and time varying penalty) is found to be more effective throughout the search. When PSO_TVAC algorithm combines with time varying penalty, the combined approach converges throughout the search. At the beginning stage of the search, PSO_TVAC is more effective and for latter part of the search, when population stagnates, time varying penalty pulls it toward the global minima. Three types of time varying penalties are used, they are known as linear, square and cubic penalty. These penalties are employed in cost function, as shown in following equations

$$\psi_L = C_1(iter) \tag{12}$$

$$\psi_S = C_2(iter)^2 \tag{13}$$

$$\psi_C = C_3(iter)^3 \tag{14}$$

where C_1, C_2 and C_3 are penalty parameters.

Evaluation value of cost function is given by

$$f(P_j) = \sum_{j=1}^{N_G} F_j(P_j) + \psi \left[\sum_{j=1}^{N_G} P_j - (P_D + P_{Loss}) \right]^2 \tag{15}$$

Linear, square and cubic penalties are incorporated in cost function and then PSO_TVAC technique are applied for finding optimal solution and it is denoted by PSO_TVAC&PL, PSO_TVAC&PS and PSO_TVAC&PC respectively.

3.4 Solution of NCED Problem Using PSO_TVAC with Time Varying Penalty

The paper presents solution of NCED problem with valve point loading, prohibited operating zones and ramp rate limits, employing PSO_TVAC with time varying penalties for practical power system operation. The novel PSO technique is found to carry out very proficiently for the discontinuous and non-smooth cost functions. The implementation steps are as follows:

Step 1- Swarm initialization: The particles of the swarm for a population size of N are randomly generated between 0-1 and located between the maximum and the minimum generating capacity of the generating units. If there are Z generating units, the jth particle is represented as $N_j = (N_{j1}, N_{j2}, N_{j3} \dots \dots \dots \dots \dots N_{jz})$. The dth dimension of the jth particle is allocated a value of N_{jd} as given below to satisfy the constraint given by (3). Here, k $\in[0,1]$.

$$N_{jd} = N_{d,\min} + k(N_{d,\max} - N_{d,\min}) \tag{16}$$

Step 2- Defining the Evaluation function: The fitness of each particle in the swarm is evaluated through a fitness function called evaluation function defined later. If there is any violation of the constraint, then a penalty function is incorporated in the evaluation function to reduce the fitness value of the particle. The penalty parameters (C_1, C_2 and C_3) are to be chosen judiciously to mark a clear distinction between possible and impossible solution.

The evaluation function $f(P_j)$ is defined to minimize the non smooth cost function given by(5) for a given load demand P_D while satisfying the constraints given by (3,4) as:

$$f(P_j) = \sum_{j=1}^{N_G} F_j(C_j) + \psi \left[\sum_{j=1}^{N_G} P_j - (P_D + P_{Loss}) \right]^2 + \xi \left[\sum_{k=1}^{n_i} P_j(violation)_k \right]^2 \tag{17}$$

where ψ is the penalty parameter for not satisfying load demand and ξ represents the penalty for a unit loading falling within a prohibited operating zone.

Step-3: Particle best and global best initialization: The initial P_{pbest} values of the particles are set by the fitness values obtained in the above step and P_{gbest} is set as the best value among all the P_{pbest} values.

Step- 4: Velocity Evaluation: The velocity is updated using (12). The excessive wandering of particles, is controlled by keeping velocity between $-V_{j,\max}$ and $V_{j,\max}$ The maximum velocity limit for the jth generating unit is computed as follows:

$$V_{j,\max} = \frac{P_j^{\max} - P_j^{\min}}{T} \tag{18}$$

where T is the chosen number of intervals in the dth dimension. For all the examples used for testing by applying PSO, $V_{j,\max}$ was set between 10-15 % of the dynamic range of the variable on each dimension.

Step-7: Update the Swarm: By(9), the particle position vector is updated, then P_{pbest}, and P_{gbest} values are updated.

Step- 8: Stopping criteria: The maximum number of iterations performed is used as the stopping criteria in the paper.

4 Numerical Results and Analysis

The PSO_TVAC&P based approaches, for practical non convex ED problem is tested on two test systems. The PSO_TVAC&P is found to improve the convergence behavior of the swarm significantly for the tested functions. Performance has been compared and validated with previously published results. On compassion with some PSO variants, the PSO_TVAC&P is found to surpass other methods.

4.1 Testing Schemes

The NCED problem was solved using the PSO_TVAC with time varying penalty (PSO_TVAC&P) and its performance is compared with other soft computing techniques based algorithm which are reported in previous papers [8, 11–13, 20–27]. Different sets of parameter are tried and then optimum set of parameter is obtained. It has also been observed that linear penalty is found more effective as compared to square and cubic penalty. Optimum population size for 6and 40 unit systems have been found 50 and 200 respectively. The performance of each system has been judged out of 50 trials, each trial contains 125 iterations, using MATLAB 7.0.1 on a Pentium IV processor, 2.8 GHz. with 2 GB RAM.

4.2 Efficiency of PSO_TVAC&P on Different Standards

The convergence behavior of the PSO_TVAC&P was tested for different cases having different dimensions and varying levels of complexity to study the effectiveness of the approach in handling premature convergence. The first test system has 6-generating units [8], a total load of 1263 MW; all the units have prohibited zones and ramp rate limit constraints and power losses have been calculated using B-matrix from [8]. The best reported cost is \$15,443.24 [26] with power balance of -0.01. The second system consists of 40 units with valve point loading effects and a total load of 10500 MW [2]. The system has many local minima and the global minimum is not reported yet. The best cost reported so far is \$121423.63 [20]. The cost found in this paper using PSO_TVAC&P is lower than reported for both the systems under test.

4.3 Selection of Parameters for PSO_TVAC&P

The performance of PSO algorithm is quite sensitive to the various parameter settings. Tuning of parameters is essential in all PSO based methods [11–13]. Based on empirical studies on a number of mathematical benchmarks, the best range of variation as 2.7-0.3 for c_1, 0.3-2.7 for c_2. The author experimented on a number of ED problems by changing the range of variation for the coefficients (c_{1i} and c_{2f} between 2.7-1.8 and c_{1f} and c_{2i} from 0.5-0.3). At the end of search, time varying penalty plays a key rule to find the global minima. Linear, square and cubic penalty have been tested on two test systems. Linear penalty based PSO_TVAC (PSO_TVAC&PL) has been found superior over two other penalty based methods. The results for two systems, out of 50 different trials; are presented in Tables 1 and 2 respectively. PSO_TVAC&PL records a clear superiority over two other penalty based methods. It can be observed that in general PSO_TVAC with linear time varying penalty performs better for all combinations of parameters as compared to PSO algorithms with fixed values of c_1 and c_2. Table 1 shows that for optimal set of parameter combination, the minimum cost is lower than the previously reported minimum of US\$15,443.24 [23] with power balance of -0.01 but the best cost of \$15,442.9810/h is achieved when c_1 is varied between 2.7-0.3, c_2 between 0.3-2.4. Table 2 show that for optimal combination of acceleration coefficients with time varying linear penalty, the minimum cost achieved is less than previously

Table 1. Results of three penalty based methods with variation of parameter for 6-unit system

S.No.	c_{1i}	c_{1f}	c_{2i}	c_{2f}	PSO_TVAC&PL	PSO_TVAC&PS	PSO_TVAC&PC
1	2.7	.3	.3	2.7	15447.5743	15449.2574	15451.7785
2	**2.7**	**.3**	**.3**	**2.4**	**15442.9810**	**15448.5743**	**15449.2077**
3	2.7	.3	.3	2.1	15448.3493	15450.2792	15452.7123
4	2.7	.3	.3	1.8	15449.1295	15451.2752	15453.7291
5	2.4	.3	.3	2.7	15446.2492	15450.7391	15451.3425
6	2.4	.3	.3	2.4	15446.2794	15448.7291	15450.1992
7	2.4	.3	.3	2.1	15447.9251	15450.1994	15452.7295
8	2.4	.3	.3	1.8	15449.1523	15451.9321	15453.6234
9	1	.3	.3	2.7	15448.2134	15450.1119	15453.0214
10	1.8	.3	.3	1.8	15447.2084	15450.9092	15452.2034

Table 2. Results of three penalty based methods with variation of parameter for 40-unit system

S.No.	c_{1i}	c_{1f}	c_{2i}	c_{2f}	PSO_TVAC&PL	PSO_TVAC&PS	PSO_TVAC&PC
1	2.7	.3	.3	2.7	121436.8757	121467.7698	121486.7213
2	**2.7**	**.3**	**.3**	**2.4**	**121421.2632**	**121439.6106**	**121467.7465**
3	2.7	.3	.3	2.1	121439.2159	121469.1239	121490.4512
4	2.7	.3	.3	1.8	121442.8854	121472.4594	121494.9430
5	2.4	.3	.3	2.7	121438.0552	121468.6542	121487.2647
6	2.4	.3	.3	2.4	121437.5251	121463.2574	121485.7199
7	2.4	.3	.3	2.1	121440.6239	121469.9540	121487.9078
8	2.4	.3	.3	1.8	121442.775	121472.2213	121490.0759
9	2.1	.3	.3	2.7	121440.1808	121468.5329	121484.9724
10	1.8	.3	.3	18	121443.6052	121474.2130	121493.1352

reported best cost of \$121423.63 [20] for 40 unit systems. The least cost achieved for same system by PSO_TVAC&PL is \$121421.2632 /h.

4.4   Convergence Characteristics

The Figs. 1 and 2 show the superior convergence characteristics of PSO_TVAC&PL. PSO_TVAC&PL records the clear superiority over two other penalty based methods. The characteristics of PSO_TVAC&PL, are continuously drooping throughout the search because the TVAC provide optimal search capability by proper tuning of cognitive and social parameters during the search and time varying penalty plays a key role at later part of search.

4.5   Computational Efficiency

Tables 3 and 4 present the best cost achieved by the PSO_TVAC with different time varying penalty for the two test cases with constraint satisfaction. The PSO_TVAC&PL method is computationally efficient as time requirement is quite comparable to all PSO methods.

Table 3. Generator output for least cost (6- unit system)

Unit Power	PSO_TVAC&PL	PSO_TVAC&PS	PSO_TVAC&PC
Output	($/h)	($/h)	($/h)
P1(MW)	447.07	429.27	426.72
P2(MW)	173.18	186.44	190.40
P3(MW)	263.93	261.42	259.41
P4(MW)	139.06	131.48	139.53
P5(MW)	165.58	173.33	161.03
P6(MW)	86.62	93.67	98.18
Total power output(MW)	1275.44	1275.61	1275.27
Total loss(MW)	12.44	12.61	12.34
Total generation cost($/h)	15442.98	15448.63	15449.45
Power balance (MW)	−0.007	−0.008	−0.072
CPU Time(sec)	0.0615	0.0617	0.0620

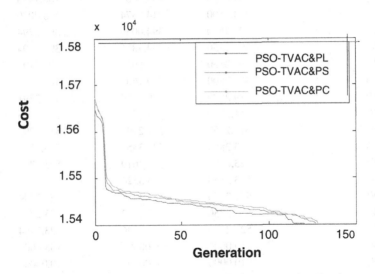

Fig. 1. Convergence characteristics of PSO_ TVAC&P strategies (6-unit system)

4.6 Comparison of Best Solutions

The best solution obtained by PSO_TVAC&PL for the six-unit system is compared with recently published results of PSO [11], NPSO_LRS [13], SA_PSO [20], SOH-PSO [22], BF-NM [23], APSO [24], ICA-PSO [26], θ-PSO [29] and IPSO-TVAC [30] in Table 5. The results show that PSO_TVAC&PL obtains the minimum cost as compared to the other methods. Results of 40-unit system are compared with EP [6], MPSO [12], NPSO-LRS [13], SA_PSO [20], SOH-PSO [22], BF-NM [23],UHGA [25], IGAMU [27], MHSA [32], RDPSO [31], TSARGA [33] and HMAPSO [4] in Table 6. For both the systems the performance of PSO_TVAC&PL is found to be superior.

Table 4. Generator output for least cost (40- unit system)

Unit Power Output	PSO_TVAC&PL ($/h)	PSO_TVAC&PS ($/h)	PSO_TVAC&PC ($/h)
P1(MW)	110.8000	110.0656	110.7998
P2(MW)	110.8000	110.8607	110.7998
P3(MW)	97.4000	97.3274	97.3974
P4(MW)	179.7300	180.0313	179.7331
P5(MW)	87.8000	88.5705	92.1446
P6(MW)	140.0000	140.0000	140.0000
P7(MW)	259.6000	259.6346	259.5997
P8(MW)	284.6000	284.6935	284.5997
P9(MW)	284.6000	284.5960	284.5997
P10(MW)	130.0000	130.0000	130.0120
P11(MW)	94.0000	168.8899	94.0000
P12(MW)	94.0000	94.0000	168.7998
P13(MW)	214.7600	214.3574	125.0000
P14(MW)	394.2850	394.0050	394.2794
P15(MW)	394.2850	394.4876	394.2794
P16(MW)	394.2850	304.5928	394.2794
P17(MW)	489.2800	489.1603	489.2799
P18(MW)	489.2800	489.3924	489.2791
P19(MW)	511.2850	511.2777	511.2793
P20(MW)	511.2850	511.2198	511.2792
P21(MW)	523.2850	523.3558	523.2794
P22(MW)	523.2850	523.3619	523.2794
P23(MW)	523.2850	523.3524	523.2794
P24(MW)	523.2850	523.3290	523.2794
P25(MW)	523.2850	523.8282	523.2794
P26(MW)	523.2850	523.3536	523.2794
P27(MW)	10.0000	10.0000	10.0000
P28(MW)	10.0000	10.0000	10.0000
P29(MW)	10.0000	10.0000	10.0000
P30(MW)	87.8000	96.4234	97.0000
P31(MW)	190.0000	190.0000	190.0000
P32(MW)	190.0000	190.0000	190.0000
P33(MW)	190.0000	190.0000	190.0000
P34(MW)	164.8000	164.7522	164.7998
P35(MW)	194.3300	200.0000	200.0000
P36(MW)	200.0000	200.0000	200.0000

(Continued)

Table 4. (*Continued*)

Unit Power Output	PSO_TVAC&PL	PSO_TVAC&PS	PSO_TVAC&PC
	($/h)	($/h)	($/h)
P37(MW)	110.0000	110.0000	109.9878
P38(MW)	110.0000	110.0000	105.7720
P39(MW)	110.0000	110.0000	110.0000
P40(MW)	511.2850	511.0863	511.2794
Total power output(MW)	10500	10500	10500
Total generation cost($/h)	121412.5810	121458.4179	121476.6502

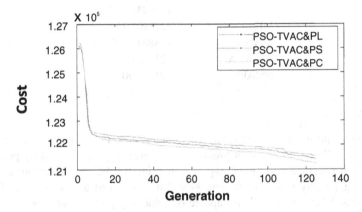

Fig. 2. Convergence characteristics of PSO_ TVAC&P strategies (40-unit system)

Table 5. Minimum cost by different methods (6-units)

Method	Minimum cost	Total Power	Power Loss	Power balance
	($/h)	(MW)	(MW)	(MW)
PSO_TVAC&PL	15442.98	1275.44	12.44	−0.007
PSO	15454	1276.01	12.9584	−0.0516
SA-PSO	15447.00	1275.7	12.733	−0.033
SOH-PSO	15446.02	1275.55	12.55	−0.008
BF-NM	15443.8164	1275.4	12.4437	−0.043
APSO	15443.5751	1275.3764	12.421628	−0.04522
NPSO-LRS	15450.5	1275.94	12.9361	−0.0039
ICA-PSO	15443.24	1275.46	12.47	−0.01
θ-PSO	15443.2717	1275.4446	12.4459	−0.0013
IPSO-TVAC	15443.063	1275.4460	12.4460	−NA

Table 6. Minimum cost by different methods (40- unit system)

Method	Minimum cost ($/h)
PSO_TVAC&PL	121412.581
IGAMU	121819.25
SA-PSO	121430.00
SOH-PSO	121501.14
BF-NM	121423.63
UHGA	121424.48
NPSO-LRS	121664.43
MPSO	122252.26
EP	122624.35
MHSA	121690.271
RDPSO	128864.4525
TSARGA	121463.07
HMAPSO	121586.90

4.7   Conclusion

The complex problem of nonconvex economic power dispatch is solved using PSO_TVAC &P. The problem of premature convergence is addressed by proper balance between the local and global exploration using TVAC, and later part of search, time varying penalty helps for finding global minima. The test results clearly demonstrated that PSO_TVAC&PL is capable of achieving global solutions. It is simple, computationally efficient and has good convergence characteristics. It has been shown through different trials that this method outperforms other reported methods in terms of solution quality, computational efficiency and convergence characteristics.

The paper presents solution of NCED problem, with valve point loading, prohibited operating zones and ramp rate limits, employing PSO_TVAC with time varying penalties to exercise proper control over the global and local exploration of the swarm during the optimization process by using TVAC and time varying penalty is used to overcome the problem of population stagnation at later stages converges it.

References

1. Wood, A.J., Wollenberg, B.F.: Power Generation, Operation And Control. Wiley, New York (1984)
2. Walter, D.C., Sheble, G.B.: Gentic algorithm solution of economic load dispatch with valve point loading. IEEE Transact. Power Syst. **8**, 1325–1332 (1993)
3. Orero, S.O., Irving, M.R.: Economic dispatch of generators with prohibited operating zones: a genetic algorithm approach. In: IEEE proceedings of the Generation, transmission and Distribution, vol. 143, No. 6, November 1996
4. Kumar, R., Sharma, D., Sadu, A.: A hybrid multi-agent based particle swarm optimization algorithm for economic power dispatch. Electr. Power Energy Syst. **33**, 115–123 (2011)

5. Sinha, N., Chakraborty, R., Chattopadhyay, P.K.: Evolutionary programming techniques for economic load dispatch. IEEE Trans. Evol. Comput. **7**(1), 83–93 (2003)

6. Swaroop, K.S., Rohit Kumar, P.: A new evolutionary computation technique for economic dispatch with security constraints. Int. J. Electr. Power Energy Syst. **28**, 273–283 (2006)

7. Lin, W.M., Cheng, F.S., Tsay, M.T.: An improved tabu search for economic dispatch with multiple minima. IEEE Trans. Power Syst. **17**(1), 108–112 (2002)

8. Lin, W.M., Cheng, F.S., Tsay, M.T.: Nonconvex economic dispatch by integrated artificial intelligence. IEEE Trans. Power Syst. **16**(2), 307–311 (2001)

9. Chaturvedi, K.T., Srivastava, V., Pandit, M.: Levenberg- Marquardt algorithm based optimal load dispatch. In: IEEE Power India Conference 2006, New Delhi 10-12th April 2006, available on ieeexplore site

10. Damousis, I.G., Bakirtzis, A.G., Dokopolous, P.S.: Network constrained economic dispatch using real-coded genetic algorithms. IEEE Transact. Power Syst. **18**(1), 198–205 (2003)

11. Gaing, Z.L.: Particle swarm optimization to solving the economic dispatch considering generator constraints. IEEE Trans. Power Syst. **18**(3), 1718–1727 (2003)

12. Park, J.B., Lee, K.S., Shin, J.R., Lee, K.Y.: A Particle swarm optimization for economic dispatch with non-smooth cost functions. IEEE Trans. Power Syst. **20**(1), 34–42 (2005)

13. Immanual Selvakumar, A., Thanushkodi, K.: A new particle swarm optimization solution to nonconvex economic dispatch problems. IEEE Trans. Power Syst. **22**(1), 42–51 (2007)

14. Aruldoss, T., Victoire, A., Jeyakumar, A.E.: Reserve constrained dynamic dispatch of units with valve point effects. IEEE Trans. Power Syst. **20**(3), 1273–1282 (2005)

15. Chaturvedi, K.C., Pandit, M., Srivastava, L.: Environmental economic load dispatch employing particle swarm optimization technique. In: Proceedings Of International Conference On Recent Advances And Applications Of Computer In Electrical Engineering, (RACE), Bikaner, India, 24-25, March 2007

16. Kennedy, J., Eberhart, R: Particle swarm optimization. In: Proceedings of the IEEE Conference on Neural Networks (ICNN 1995), vol. IV, pp.1942–1948, Perth, Australia (1995)

17. Basu, M.: Hybridization of bee colony optimization and sequential quadratic programming for dynamic economic dispatch. Electr. Power Energy Syst. **44**, 591–596 (2013)

18. Niu, Q., Wang, X., Zhou, Z.: An efficient cultural particle swarm optimization for economic load dispatch with valve-point effect. In: 2011 International Conference on Power Electronics and Engineering Application, Procedia Engineering 23, pp.828–834 (2011)

19. Chakraborty, S., Senjyu, T., Saber, A.Y., Funabashi, T.: Solving economic load dispatch problem with valve point effects using a hybrid quantum mechanics inspired particle swarm optimization. IET Gener. Transim. Distrib **5**(10), 1042–1052 (2011)

20. Kuo, C.: A novel coding scheme for practical economic dispatch by modified particle swarm approach. IEEE Trans. Power Syst. **23**(4), 1825–1835 (2008)

21. Coelho, L.D.S., Mariani, V.C.: Particle swarm approach based on quantum mechanics and harmonic oscillator potential well for economic load dispatch with valve-point effects. Energy Convers. Manage. **49**(11), 3080–3085 (2008)

22. Chaturvedi, K., Pandit, M., Srivastava, L.: Self-organizing hierarchical particle swarm optimization for nonconvex economic dispatch. IEEE Trans. Power Syst. **23**(3), 1079–1087 (2008)

23. Panigrahi, B.K., Pandi, V.R.: Bacterial foraging optimisation:Nelder-Mead hybrid algorithm for economic load dispatch. IET Gen. Transm. Distrib. **2**(4), 556–565 (2008)

24. Panigrahi, B.K., Pandi, V.R., Das, S.: Adaptive particle swarm optimization approach for static and dynamic economic load dispatch. Energy Convers. Manage. **49**(6), 1407–1415 (2008)

25. He, D.-K., Wang, F.-L., Mao, Z.-Z.: Hybrid genetic algorithm for economic dispatch with valve-point effect. Elect. Power Syst. Res. **78**(4), 626–633 (2008)
26. Vlachogiannis, J.G., Lee, K.Y.: Economic load dispatch—a comparative study on heuristic optimization techniques with an improved coordinated aggregation-based PSO. IEEE Trans. Power Syst. **24**(2), 991–1001 (2009)
27. Chiang, C.-L.: Genetic-based algorithm for power economic load dispatch. IET Gen. Transm. Distrib. **1**(2), 261–269 (2007)
28. Ratnaweera, A., Halgamuge, S.K., Watson, H.C.: Self-organizing hierarchical Particle swarm optimizer with time-varying acceleration coefficients. IEEE Trans. Evol. Comput. **8**(3), 240–255 (2004)
29. Hosseinnezhad, V., Babaei, E.: Economic dispatch using θ-PSO. Electr. Power Energy Syst. **49**, 160–169 (2013)
30. Mohammadi-Ivatloo, B., Rabiee, A., Soroudi, A., Ehsan, M.: Iteration PSO with time varying acceleration coefficients for solving non-convex economic dispatch problems. Electr. Power Energy Syst. **42**(1), 508–516 (2012)
31. Sun, J., Palade, V., Xiao-Jun, W., Fang, W., Wang, Z.: Solving the power economic dispatch problem with generator constraints by random drift particle swarm optimization. IEEE Trans. Power Syst. **10**(1), 222–232 (2014)
32. Jeddi, B., Vahidinasab, V.: A modified harmony search method for environmental/economic load dispatch of real-world power systems. Energy Convers. Manag. **78**, 661–675 (2014)
33. Khamsawang, S., Jiriwibhakorn, S.: DSPSO–TSA for economic dispatch problem with nonsmooth and noncontinuous cost functions. Energy Conser. Manag. **51**(2), 365–375 (2010)

An Efficient Method for Parameter Estimation of Software Reliability Growth Model Using Artificial Bee Colony Optimization

Rao K. Mallikharjuna[1(✉)] and Anuradha Kodali[2]

[1] Department of IT, GITAM University, Visakhapatnam, Andhra Pradesh, India
mallikharjunarao0883@gmail.com
[2] School of Computing, GRIET, Hyderabad, India
kodali.anuradha@yahoo.com

Abstract. One of the established trends of research areas and practices in software engineering that dealt with the measurement and enhancement of reliability is software reliability engineering. Stochastic software reliability models find typical usage for analysis. These are the models that perform modeling on failure process of the software and exploit other software metrics or failure data as cornerstone for parameter estimation. The ability of the models for estimating and predicting the current reliability and future failure behavior, respectively, is high. Due to any failures and faults in the system, a product becomes unreliable. The lack of understanding of nature of the software makes the measurement of software reliability as a challenging task. It is not possible to determine a best way to measure the reliability and other aspects of software. This paper proposes an efficient software reliability growth model (SRGM) in which logistic exponential TEF is exploited. This model offers increased failure rate recognition and suitable ways to resolve faults and so on. Our work estimates the SRGM parameters using optimization algorithm. Such estimation can aid in developing precise software reliability model. In order to accomplish the optimization, we use artificial bee colony (ABC) algorithm. As the parameters optimization considerably improves the quality of parameters to be used for reliability growth model, reliability growth can also be improved considerably.

Keywords: Software reliability · Logistic exponential TEF · Testing termination time · Testing coverage · Artificial bee colony · Swarm intelligence · Genetic algorithm

1 Introduction

Modern society is highly engaged with the roles of software. Software engineers and software development organizations seeks great responsibilities on maintaining quality, reliability and consumer satisfaction with the software products. Software development testing is generally considered as one of the major quality control techniques [6]. In order to calculate and predict the product quality, software reliability is found as a significant attribute [13]. Software reliability can be defined as a probability of zero-failure operation of particular software at a specific instant of time in a specific

© Springer International Publishing Switzerland 2015
B.K. Panigrahi et al. (Eds.): SEMCCO 2014, LNCS 8947, pp. 765–776, 2015.
DOI: 10.1007/978-3-319-20294-5_65

kind of environment [5]. In order to ensure the cumulative reliability of software, it is important to precisely model the software reliability and to predict the probable trends. Certain, but important metrics such as time period, MTBF, number of faults and MTTFs through SRGMS would be helpful for such circumstances [14].

Numerous research efforts have been made on methodologies to quantify software reliability, which is found as one of the highly recognized aspects of software quality [2]. Due to the direct influence of residual faults in the software system on determining failure rate, unreliability in software arises. Amount of faults, which are available in the code, can also be considered as a significant measure by the developers for planning maintenance activities [1].

Quantitative evaluation on software reliability can be done using mathematical tools such as software reliability model, which is found as very helpful. The model describes growth process of software reliability, which is obtained from the original testing phase, as arbitrary variables using software failure occurrence phenomenon or software fault detection phenomenon [15]. Major factors that include in the context of software testing are testing effort and efficacy of test cases. Existing works either make assumption of constant consumption rate of testing resources or avoiding testing effort and efficacies [5].

Analytical tractability can be guaranteed if the software faults are imagined to be fixed at once they are identified and no new faults are generated at the time of debugging. Though the fault debugging process consumes a finite time, this debugging time practically has a straight influence on the residual number of faults and thus, affects the reliability of the software application [3]. Taking the inadequacies related to the software reliability growth models, which have its application on a safety-critical software system, into account is essential as well. The expected total number of inherent software faults computed by the software reliability growth models, which are highly sensitive to time-to-failure data, is one among the major limitations of high severity [9]. Some other limitations also arise during the application of software reliability growth models to safety-critical software. But, the most severe limitation is the expected total number of inherent software faults calculated by the software reliability growth models that have larger sensitivity towards time-to-failure data [4].

The rest of the paper is organized as follows. Section 2 presents the various researches performed in relation to our suggested work. Section 3 elucidates the plan, approach and the suggested technique. Section 4 proves and details about the results of our suggested technique and finally, Sect. 5 closes our proposed method for parameter estimation of software reliability growth model.

2   Literature Review

A handful of researches have been presented in the literature to develop the software reliability growth models, while imperfect debugging and error generation are present. These studies aim to help in enhancing the software performance. A brief review of some recent researches is presented here.

Joseph et al. [18] have dealt with a simplified model that assists in evaluating the reliability of the open source software depending on the available failure data.

The methodology works by discovering a fixed number of packages initially and then, defines the failure rate in accordance to the failure data for this preset number of packages. The defined function of the failure rate aids in attaining the reliability model. Comparisons on the reliability values that have resulted from the developed model against the exact reliability values have been made as well.

Quadri et al. [11] have made consideration on the time dependent behaviors of testing effort expenditures, which were expressed by New Modified Weibull Distribution (NMWD). Software Reliability Growth Models (SRGM) that relies on the NHPP were developed and they include the (NMWD) testing-effort expenditure at the time of software testing phase. The error detection rate to the amount of testing-effort used up during the testing phase was imagined to be proportional to the present error content. Estimation of the model parameters were carried out by Least Square and Maximum Likelihood estimation techniques. The software measures were examined with the help of numerical experiments on real data that were obtained from several software projects.

Ahmad et al. [16] have proposed a paper that deals with the comparison of the predictive capability of two popular software reliability growth models (SRGM), namely, the exponential growth model and the inflection S-shaped growth models. Initially, a review on the exponential Weibull (EW) testing-effort functions and a discussion on the exponential type and inflection S-shaped type SRGM with EW testing-effort were made. Later on, the actual data applications were analyzed and the predictive capability of those two SRGM was compared graphically. The results have shown that the inflection S-shaped type SRGM offers enhanced prediction capability than the exponential type SRGM.

Prasad et al. [17] have proposed that the software reliability may be employed as a measure of the Software system's success in delivering its function in a suitable manner. Software process improvement allows software products to be produced with high degree of reliability. SPC was the application of proper statistical tools to processes in order to achieve uninterrupted enhancement in quality, reliability of software products and services and productivity in the workforce. A control mechanism that depends on time between failures observations using half logistic distribution, with Modified Maximum likelihood Estimation (MMLE) that is based on Non Homogenous Poisson Process (NHPP) have also been proposed in this paper.

Herein, Williams [7] have explained a modified approach for computing the delivery cost of a software product using an imperfect debugging phenomenon, when warranty was to be granted. The computation of optimal release time for several reliability levels can be performed by reducing the cost. Calculation of the delivery cost, the reliability of the software system and the optimal release time were done with an imperfect debugging software reliability growth model. Numerical illustration aids the optimal release policies.

The field of optimization was abundant with algorithms, which are inspired from nature based phenomena. The increasing popularity of such algorithms stems from their applications in real life situations. Bose et al. [10] have proposed a real life problem in the form of the design of circular antenna array . The design of the antenna array is based on the application of a variant of Artificial Bee Colony Algorithm using selective neighborhood called sNABC. They used a neighborhood based perturbation on the basis of Euclidean distance and fitness of individuals are used for obtaining minimum side lobe levels, maximum directivity and appropriate null control.

Swarm intelligence (SI) was briefly defined as the collective behaviour of decentralized and self-organized swarms. The well known examples for these swarms are bird flocks, fish schools and the colony of social insects such as termites, ants and bees. Although the self-organization features are required by SI are strongly and clearly seen in honey bee colonies, unfortunately the researchers have recently started to be interested in the behaviour of these swarm systems to describe intelligent approaches, especially from the beginning of 2000s. Among those, artificial bee colony (ABC) was the one which had been most widely studied on and applied to solve the real world problems, so far. Day by day the number of researchers being interested in ABC algorithm increases rapidly. Karaboga et al. [21] have presented a comprehensive survey of the advances with ABC and its applications. It was hoped that this survey would be very beneficial for the researchers studying on SI, particularly ABC algorithm.

Bosea et al. [12] have proposed a hybrid variant of a swarm-based metaheuristics called Artificial Bee Colony (ABC) algorithm and referred to as CRbABC_Dt (Collective Resource-based ABC with Decentralized tasking) and it incorporates the idea of decentralization of attraction from super-fit members along with neighborhood information and wider exploration of search space. All the components considered in the design are selected from standard series and the resulting deviation from the idealized design procedure had been investigated. Additional empirical experimentation has also been included based on the benchmarking problems proposed for the CEC 2013 Special Session & Competition on Real-Parameter Single Objective Optimization.

3 Proposed Method for Software Reliability Growth Model Extraction

3.1 Software Reliability Growth Model

For the past few years, Software reliability engineering has emerged as a most attractive research area. Numerous advancements have been made by several researchers in reliability testing for rendering improved reliability. Efficient estimation of the number of residual faults, which gives rise to software failures during the testing phase, is one among the software reliability paradigms. Improved accuracy in fault estimation enables the software to be developed or maintained with more operating efficiency. The use of software reliability growth model is to envisage the software reliability, failure rate, effort needed and similar other measures of a specific software that is being designed. It is one among the mathematical tools that help in describing the quantitative nature of any software. Plenty of software reliability growth models are available and a few of them are listed below.

- Weibull Model,
- Raleigh Model,
- Exponential Model,
- Logarithmic Poisson Model,

- Delayed S-shaped Growth Model,
- Imperfect Debugging Model,
- Inflection S-shaped Growth Model, and
- Logistic Model.

The proposed scheme makes use of logistic exponential TEF for the reliability growth model. In addition, soft computing application has been employed to classify and optimize the various parameters that are generated using the model.

3.2 Logistic Exponential TEF for the Reliability Growth Model

The logistic exponential Testing effort function for reliability growth model is one among the most frequently used models that is known for its simplicity. Usually, the fault elimination procedure in the logistic exponential TEF follows the Non homogeneous Poisson process (NHPP). A number of parameter measures are being estimated and the optimization of these parameter values can result in an improved reliability model. The various parameters involved in the proposed method are explained in the following sections.

3.2.1 Mean Value of Number of Faults

The initial step in computing the mean value of number of faults is the computation of the total number of faults that arise in the corresponding software. Immediately after calculating the total failure, the measurement of the mean of these values is made. The expression for calculating the Mean value of number of faults is given in Eq. 1.

$$m(f) = R(1 - \exp(-n*T))/(1 + \beta * \exp(-n*T)) \tag{1}$$

where,

    R is the Failure Rate
    n is the mean value of Failure
    T is the total Resources
    β is the exponential constant

3.2.2 Mean Value of Failure

During the execution of software, the number of failures that are generated within a specific time period may get changed. Computing this failure rate serves as a major parameter during the testing of software performance. The mean value of failure can be measured by using the expression shown in Eq. 2,

$$f(t) = f_i/f_n \tag{2}$$

where,

    f (t) is the mean failure
    f_i represents the number of failure interval
    f_n represents the total number of failures

3.2.3 Software Reliability Measure

The software reliability, most commonly, defines the probability of software to operate with less error or failure in the processing in specific time duration. The reliability measure is thought to be a major factor for verifying the performance of the particular software module. Moreover, Software reliability can apparently point out the quality desirable for its operation. The expression for software reliability is given in Eq. 3.

$$R_s(\phi/T_\pi, C_\pi) = \exp\left\{-\left[M_f((T_\pi + \phi), C_\pi/h) - M_f(T_\pi, C_\pi/h)\right]\right\} \tag{3}$$

where,

R_s is the software reliability measure
T_π is the testing termination time
C_π is the testing coverage
h represents the total parameter estimate
M_f is the mean number of faults detected
ϕ is the time deviation.

After calculating these parameters for SRGM model, optimization of these parameters is to be carried out. Performing optimization will help in developing an improved software growth model because it increases the software reliability and decreases the failure rate to some degree. The optimization process is capable of presenting an improved failure free software reliability growth model. The proposed method uses artificial bee colony optimization.

For designing better SRGM, we have chosen the optimization algorithm, as the parameters required for the designing can be selected in a better manner. Hence by selecting better parameters, the failure rate that are existing in SRGM model can be reduced and better reliability can be obtained by choosing the apt parameter for modeling. So we model the ABC algorithm accordingly. So we are linking the SRGM parameters with ABC for optimization.

3.3 Proposed Artificial Bee Colony for Optimization

The bees in the ABC model aims to find the best solution. While the position of a food source indicates a possible solution to the optimization problem, the nectar amount of a food source corresponds to the quality (fitness) of the associated solution [20]. Each of the employed bees share their information with the onlookers and then, visits the food source area visited by her in the past cycle using the knowledge residing in her memory about the previous food source. Once the previous food source is reached, the employed bee selects a new food source through visual information in the neighborhood of the one in her memory and evaluates the quantity of nectar in the new food source [19]. The different steps that are employed in ABC algorithm are given below,

Step 1: Initialization of population for processing
Step 2: Employed bees choose a set of food source arbitrarily to determine the nectar amount

Step 3:   Then the onlooker bees select the food sources based on the information provided by the employed bees and it depends on the nectar information distributed by the employed bees

Step 4:   Scout bees are then send to search the nectar randomly

Step 5:   Store the best solution

Step 6:   Repeat until requirements are met

3.3.1   Employee Bee Phase

The colony of artificial bees consists of three groups of bees, namely, employed bees, onlookers and scouts. A bee that remains in the dance area to decide on which food source is to be selected called an onlooker and a bee that reaches the food source visited by it previously is named an employed bee. A bee that performs random search is called a scout. First half of the colony is occupied by the employed artificial bees and the second half is occupied by the onlookers. Each food source has only one employed bee. This implies that the employed bees and the food sources around the hive are same in number.

In the initial stage, employed bees choose a set of food source positions arbitrarily and determine their nectar amounts. Then, they return to their hive and inform about the nectar amounts to the onlooker bees, which are waiting in the dancing portion of the hive. ABC initially generates an arbitrarily distributed initial population p_i, which has n solutions, where each solution represents a food source position and S_p represents population size. Each solution can be represented as h_i, *where* $1 \leq i \leq n$ is a vector with N elements that are number of optimization parameters taken into consideration. Once initialization process is done, the population of positions is subjected to iterative searching process enabled by employed bees, onlooker bees, and scout bees.

3.3.2   Onlooker Bee Phase

This phase enables onlooker bees to select the food sources based on the information provided by the employed bees followed by generating new solutions. The onlooker bee depends on the nectar information distributed by the employed bees on giving preference to the food source. The probability of selecting a food source by an onlooker bee increases, when the nectar amount of the food source increases. Hence, onlooker bees are recruited for the employed bees that have higher nectar because of the richness of the food source. The probability formulation (P_f) for onlooker bee to select a food source can be given as

$$P_f = \frac{F_c}{\sum\limits_{j=1}^{n} F_j} \tag{4}$$

where,

F_c represents fitness of the solution

F_j represents fitness value of j-th source, $1 \geq j \geq n$

n represents number of food sources that are equal to the number of employed bees.

The onlooker bee reaches the selected food source and finds a new food source from the neighborhood region based on the memory of visual information. Visual information is developed on the basis of comparison between food source positions. In the case of abandons of any food source due to its low nectar amount, scout bee is assigned to replace the abandoned food position by a new arbitrary food source position. The artificial onlooker bee performs probabilistic enhancements on the position (solution) in the memory to find new food source and evaluates the nectar amount (fitness value) of the new source (new solution).

Consider the old position and new positions as $s_{i,a}$ and $t_{i,a}$, respectively that can be defined as

$$s_{i,a} = t_{i,a} + \varphi_{i,a}(t_{i,a} - t_{j,a}), \ i \neq j \tag{5}$$

where,

$$j = \{1, 2, \ldots, n\}$$

$$a = \{1, 2, \ldots, N\}$$

$\varphi_{i,a}$ is an arbitrary integer in the range $[-1, 1]$.

From the position update equation, it can be understood that decrease in deviation between $t_{i,a}$ and $t_{j,a}$ leads to decrease in the perturbation on the position $t_{i,a}$. Hence, a dynamic reduction on step length is encouraged here, when the optimal solution from the search space is approached by the search procedure. The position updating step can be rearranged as follows

$$s_{i,a} - t_{i,a} = \varphi_{i,a}(t_{i,a} - t_{j,a}) \tag{6}$$

The time domain representation for $s_{i,a}$, which is the position update from $t_{i,a}$, can be written as follows by considering these parameters as z_{T+1} and z_T, respectively.

$$z_{T+1} - z_T = \varphi_{i,a}(t_{i,a} - t_{j,a}) \tag{7}$$

The left side $z_{T+1} - z_T$ is the discrete version of the derivative of order $\varphi = 1$. Hence we have,

$$D^{\alpha}[z_{T+1}] = \varphi_{i,a}(t_{i,a} - t_{j,a}) \tag{8}$$

3.3.3 Scout Bee Phase

The employed bee whose food source is exhausted by the employed and onlooker bees becomes a scout and it carries out random search. Simulating this process can be done by replacing the Food sources can be considered to abandon when they do not exhibit any improvement over a predefined number of cycles called limit. Despite such random search produce convergence at the initial stage, it will not work out effectively over the range of final iterations. Hence, the scout bee performs global search in the initial range of iterations, whereas it performs local search in the final range of iterations. If there is no enhancement is obtained from the best food source in the last range of iterations, it can be selected as a scout and it is eliminated from the population.

We have compared our proposed work with that of Genetic Algorithm. Genetic algorithm is normally an evaluation algorithm where different steps are followed inorder to optimize the parameters. The steps include initialization, fitness evaluation, crossover and mutation. In our proposed method we have chosen ABC over GA as genetic algorithm have some issues related to the fitness evaluation. Meanwhile ABC is more efficient in evaluation of fitness and hence it has more advantages when we consider the optimization scenario.

4   Results and Discussion

In general, SRGM is a tool to evaluate quantitative nature of software, to develop test status, to schedule status and to monitor the improvements in reliability. In order to evaluate the performance of a software system, software reliability assessment and prediction is significant. Our paper has designed an SRGM model with logistic exponential TEF. Implementation of the proposed method is done in the working platform of JAVA and the obtained results are analyzed to study the performance of the proposed methodology. Number of failures that have occurred while testing the software and the time of occurrence are tabulated in Table 1. Figure 1 illustrates the respective values, but before and after optimization.

Table 1. Number of failures at various times before and after optimization.

Time (sec)	No of failures		
	Before optimization	After optimization (ABC)	After optimization (GA)
1	0.96	0.14	0.34
5	0.97	0.34	0.51
10	0.98	0.86	0.91
20	1.32	0.86	1.25
25	1.4	0.51	0.84

The above affixed graphical illustration Fig. 1, evaluates the failures of software testing at respective instance and construes that the number of failures have been highly reduced because of optimization.

Figure 2 shows the graphical representation of no of failures extracted using ABC and GA.

The reliability values and cost of the particular software at varying instants that are determined before and after optimization is tabulated in Table 2. The reliability values obtained after optimization using both ABC and GA are illustrated in the table.

Figure 3 shows the graphical illustration of the reliability and time instants before and after optimization. It can be observed from the graph that the proposed method has produced high reliability after performing the optimization.

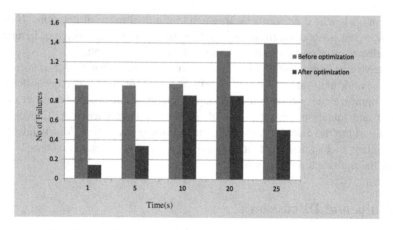

Fig. 1. Graphical representation of no of failures versus time.

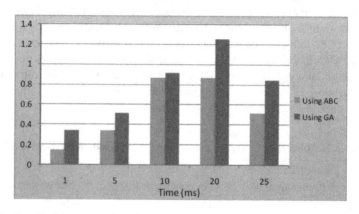

Fig. 2. Graphical representation of comparison of number of failures in ABC and GA.

Table 2. Reliability estimate for corresponding time before and after optimization.

Time	Reliability		
	Before optimization	After optimization (ABC)	After optimization (GA)
1	6.6789	0.0258	1.8541
5	1.7633	0.5985	1.2545
10	2.8765	0.3690	1.8795
20	2.6276	0.2723	2.1214
25	3.0912	0.5419	2.5245

The Fig. 4 given below shows the reliability comparision of obtained values using the GA and ABC.From the graphical representation it is clear that our proposed method with ABC is more reliable when compared with that of Genetic algorithm.

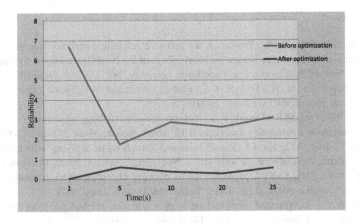

Fig. 3. Graphical representation of reliability versus time.

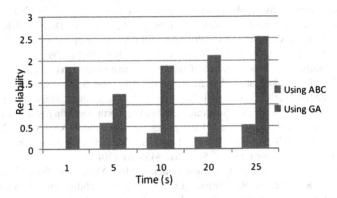

Fig. 4. Graphical representation for comparison of reliability in ABC and GA

5 Conclusion

This paper proposed an efficient software reliability growth model (SRGM) in which logistic exponential TEF is utilized for reliability growth model. This model exhibits various advantages such as improved recognition of failure rate, better solution for faults removal, etc. Further, we have utilized artificial bee colony (ABC) algorithm, which is an optimization algorithm, to assist in estimation of SRGM parameters. This would help in improving the software reliability model by improving the quality of estimated parameters and hence the reliability growth can be improved. The implementation results have demonstrated the effectiveness of the proposed method of software reliability growth modeling.

References

1. Gokhale, S.S., Lyu, M.R., Trivedi, K.S.: software reliability analysis incorporating fault detection and debugging activities. In: Proceedings of the Ninth International Symposium on Software Reliability Engineering, Paderborn, Germany, pp. 202–211, November 1998
2. Goseva-Popstojanova, K., Trivedi, K.S.: Failure correlation in software reliability models. IEEE Trans. Reliab. **49**(1), 37–48 (2000)
3. Gokhale, S.S., Lyu, M.R., Trivedi, K.S.: Incorporating fault debugging activities into software reliabilitymodels: a simulation approach. IEEE Trans. Reliab. **55**(2), 281–292 (2006)
4. Kim, M.C., Jang, S.C., Ha, J.J.: Possibilities and limitations of applying software reliability growth models to safetycritical software. J. Nucl. Eng. Technol. **39**(2), 145–148 (2007)
5. Huang, C.-Y., Kuo, S.-Y., Lyu, M.R.: An assessment of testing-effort dependent software reliability growth models. IEEE Trans. Reliab. **56**(2), 198–211 (2007)
6. Andersson, C.: A replicated empirical study of a selection method for software reliability growth models. J. Empir. Softw. Eng. **12**(2), 161–182 (2007)
7. Williams, D.R.P.: Study of the warranty cost model for software reliability with an imperfect debugging phenomenon. Turk. J. Electr. Eng. **15**(3), 369–381 (2007)
8. Utkin, L.V., Zatenko, S.I., Coolen, F.P.A.: Combining imprecise Bayesian and maximum likelihood estimation for reliability growth models. In: Proceedings of the Sixth International Symposium on Imprecise Probability: Theories and Applications, Durham, UK (2009)
9. Son, H.S., Kang, H.G., Chang, S.C.: Procedure for application of software reliability growth models to NPP PSA. J. Nucl. Eng. Technol. **41**(8), 1065–1072 (2009)
10. Bose, D., Kundu, S., Biswas, S., Das, S.: Circular antenna array design using novel perturbation based artificial bee colony algorithm. In: Panigrahi, B.K., Das, S., Suganthan, P.N., Nanda, P.K. (eds.) SEMCCO 2012. LNCS, vol. 7677, pp. 459–466. Springer, Heidelberg (2012)
11. Quadri, S.M.K., Ahmad, N.: Software reliability growth modeling with new modified weibull testing–effort and optimal release policy. Int. J. Comput. Appl. **6**(12), 1–10 (2010)
12. Bosea, D., Biswasa, S., Vasilakosb, A.V., Lahaa, S.: Optimal filter design using an improved artificial bee colony algorithm. Inf. Sci. **281**, 443–461 (2014)
13. Mir, K.A.: A software reliability growth model. J. Mod. Math. Stat. **5**(1), 13–16 (2011)
14. Quadri, S.M.K., Ahmad, N., Farooq, S.U.: Software reliability growth modeling with generalized exponential testing - effort and optimal software release policy. Glob. J. Comput. Sci. Technol. **11**(2), 27–42 (2011)
15. Inoue, S., Yamada, S.: A bivariate software reliability model with change-point and its applications. Am. J. Oper. Res. **1**(1), 1–7 (2011)
16. Ahmad, N., Quadri, S.M.K., Mohd, R.: Comparison of predictive capability of software reliability growth models with exponentiated weibull distribution. Int. J. Comput. Appl. **15**(6), 40–43 (2011)
17. Prasad, R.S., Rao, K.R.H., Kantha, R.R.L.: Software reliability measuring using modified maximum likelihood estimation and SPC. Int. J. Comput. Appl. **21**(7), 1–5 (2011)
18. Joseph, S., Shouri, P.V., Raj, J.V.P.: A simplified model for evaluating software reliability at the developmental stage. Int. J. Softw. Eng. (IJSE) **1**(5), 125–131 (2011)
19. Karaboga, D., Akay, B.: a comparative study of artificial bee colony algorithm. J. Appl. Math. Comput. **214**, 108–132 (2009)
20. Karaboga, D., Ozturk, C.: Fuzzy clustering with artificial bee colony algorithm. J. Sci. Res. Essays **5**(14), 1899–1902 (2010)
21. Karaboga, D., Gorkemli, B., Ozturk, C., Karaboga, N.A.: Comprehensive survey: artificial bee colony (ABC) algorithm and applications. Artif. Intell. Rev. **42**(1), 21–57 (2014)

Genetic Algorithm Based Placement of Radio Interferometry Antennas

Amit Kumar Mishra[✉] and Adi Lazar

University of Cape Town, Cape Town, South Africa
akmishra@ieee.org

Abstract. In this paper, we thoroughly investigate the application of naive genetic algorithm to the problem of antenna placement in radio astronomy. The cost functions were the cost of cable length and the challenge of avoiding beat frequencies in the imaging process. We showed that genetic algorithm does help us in generating better placements than those given by symmetric conventional placements procedure. This is a novel use of genetic algorithm. Hence in this study a better understanding of the cost functions and the domain outweighs the investigation into different types of evolutionary algorithms.

Keywords: Radio astronomy · Genetic algorithm

1 Introduction

Radio interferometer arrays are born out of the necessity to achieve greater resolution and accuracy in the interception and measurement of radio signals from astronomical sources. The angular resolution of a single interferometry dish can be approximated by $R = 1.22\frac{\lambda}{D}$ where λ is the wavelength of the observed frequency, and D is the diameter of the dish [1]. Therefore for increasing frequencies increasingly larger diameters are necessary to achieve minimum resolution requirements. Furthermore, due to the longer wavelengths typically observed by radio interferometers they require larger diameters than optical telescopes [2]. Placement of radio telescopes in an array is an important design challenge. However, there has been not much use of soft computing optimisation processes like genetic algorithm in this.

The novelty of the work lies in the application of multi-objective genetic algorithm (GA) to the problem of antenna placement in radio astronomical array design. As the domain is new hence we have kept this study as a preliminary one and have discussed the use of naive GA. An extension of the work will contain the application of more suitable evolutionary algorithms to this domain.

Rest of the paper is organised as follows. Section 2 describes the two objective functions that we have used. Section 3 describes the experimental setup. Section 4 gives the results and we close the paper in Sect. 5 with some conclusive remarks.

© Springer International Publishing Switzerland 2015
B.K. Panigrahi et al. (Eds.): SEMCCO 2014, LNCS 8947, pp. 777–787, 2015.
DOI: 10.1007/978-3-319-20294-5_66

2   Description of the Objective Functions

Several cost and performance criteria arise naturally out of the design of a radio telescope array's configuration. Two non-trivial criteria considered for the optimisation process in the current work are the cost of cable length, to be minimised, and the imaging performance of the array, measured by the array's ability to uniformly sample the uv plane, based on the model presented by Cohanim et al. in [3], to be maximsed.

2.1   Visibility Function: Imaging Performance of the Array

For the synthesis of a 2-D image of the sky, it is possible to expand both the baseline coordinates and the source position coordinates in the sky to two dimensions. Let u and v be the spatial frequency components of the baseline vector in the E-W and N-S directions respectively, and l and m be the coordinates of the source in the sky. The reference position, or position of the nominal source in the sky, is taken as the origin of the (l, m) sky coordinate system, and aligns with the w axis (normal to the uv plane) such that the uv plane is normal to the source direction vector $\hat{s}_0$. The (l, m) coordinates are then defined as the cosines of the u and v axes respectively [2]. These coordinates can be measured in radians due to the small angle assumptions, and the fact that the range of the observation is generally less than a few degrees [4].

Due to the convolution theorem the above convolution of the beam response and the sky intensity distribution can be transformed to a multiplication of their Fourier transforms $A_v(l, m)$, and $I_v(l, m)$ respectively. The sampling of the uv plane then corresponds to a sampling of the two dimensional spatial frequency spectrum of the Fourier transform of the sky's intensity distribution [4]. The complex visibility $V(u, v)$ and the intensity $I(l, m)$ are thus a Fourier pair and are linked by the visibility function

$$V_v(u, v) = \int \int A_v(l, m) I_v(l, m) \exp^{-j2\pi(ul+vm)} \, dl dm$$

The sky intensity distribution can then be reconstructed to some degree from the inverse Fourier transform of the observed complex visibility $V(u, v)$ [4]. This partially complete image is known as the *dirty image*, and can be improved by introduction of information based on prior knowledge into iterative deconvolution techniques, of which CLEAN is the best known [5].

Since the uv plane can only be sampled at discrete points, corresponding to the configuration of baselines in the array, it is an objective of the array design to maximise the unique baseline orientations, and hence the sampling of the uv plane. Points which are not sampled in the uv plane correlate to missing information in the Fourier domain $V(u, v)$ of the sky brightness distribution, and hence the fidelity of the reconstructed image [3,6]. In [6], Keto shows that to achieve the best sampling of the uv plane, two criteria are desired. Namely equal spatial resolution in all directions, and uniformity of the sampling in Fourier space. This achieves the highest signal-to-noise ratio, and the highest resolution simultaneously [6]. This corresponds to a uniform distribution of sampling points in the uv plane, contained within a circular boundary, whose radius is a function of wavelength λ of the maximum observable frequency.

For the purposes of maximising the uv coverage achieved by an array, Cornwell [7] suggests a process of maximising the mean distance between observation points as a strategy for decreasing redundancy during an optimisation of dish configuration. Since this is computationally expensive, Cohanim et al. [3] suggest a method of comparison of the resultant uv grid with a nominal grid, rendered once per simulation to represent the optimum uv distribution given any number of antennae.

2.2 Cable Length

The cost metric used for the contrasting objective function to the optimisation of the uv sampling is cable length, which is of course a cost to be minimised. For a given configuration of stations, an analytic solution exists to establish the minimum cable length possible to ensure interconnectivity between all stations, known as minimum spanning trees [3]. A tree is a set of straight lines connecting a set of coordinates such that [8]:

1. No closed loops occur
2. Each point is visited by at least one line
3. The tree is connected

The length of the tree is the sum of its linkages. In the single linkage algorithm, used here [3], the set of all coordinate distances are collected and the coordinates are connected into clusters starting with the shortest link and connecting progressively larger linkages, as some threshold distance d_i is continuously incremented. Clusters are connected by the two points in them which yield the shortest distance and this is iterated until all the points form one cluster, corresponding to the MST [8] (Table 1).

3 Experimental Setup

In developing the genetic algorithm, a framework for the multi-objective algorithm was expanded to include multiple variables, namely the x and y coordinates of the station placements in physical space. As a starting point the framework development was based on the model presented by Cohanim et al. in [3].

The encoding was done by representing each individual solution by a 2-dimensional array. In this case each row, holding a binary string of length L, corresponds to one station in the solution. The number of rows in each solution therefore corresponds to the number of stations under design consideration and is the same for all individuals. The number of columns corresponds to the length of the bit string encoding length, L, used here to encode the xy coordinates of a single station in a solution. Here the first $L/2$ bits are used for the x coordinate, and the second $L/2$ for the y coordinate, and these are in turn encoded in a similar manner to the x values in the previous rounds of development, using the user specified range and domain. The entire population is therefore represented by a 3-dimensional array of size $N_{stn} \times L \times M$, where N_{stn} is the number of stations under consideration, L, the number of bits used to encode each station's coordinates, and the 3rd dimension, M corresponding to the number individuals in the population.

Initialisations for each simulation include user inputs for the range $[y_0, y_f]$ and domain $[x_0, x_f]$ of the considered design space; M, the population size; N_{stn}, the number of stations; L, bit string encoding length for each station placement; *Generations*, the number of generations for the simulation; and the manner in which the population is generated (discussed next). The program then proceeds to calculate: N_{uv}, the number of uv observation points, calculated as $N_{uv} = (N_{stn}) \times (N_{stn} - 1)$; and the nominal grid generated using N_{uv}, by means of a search by enumeration.

Since a solution for a specific number of stations requires a nominal grid with a specific amount of uv observation points, as well as a uniform radial distribution and arc length along all rings, an analytic solution is difficult to find by calculation given any number of points, resulting in a constant radial density distribution and constant arc length from coordinate placements throughout the grid. Therefore, when the nominal grid needs to be generated for any given number of stations, the grid will be calculated by an algorithm that we have designed and coin as UVnominal(). A flowchart using pseudo-code for the algorithm is presented in Fig. 1. This is the benchmark with which all the following uv coverage comparisons will be made. The nominal grid is normalised to lie within a radius of 1 in the uv plane, as are all the uv sampling grids to be compared to it. It is designed to maximise the uniformity of the sampling of the uv plane. The process of comparison is as expounded as [3].

3.1   Population Generation

All but the development simulations were run with a population of $M = 500$, station number $N_{stn} = 60$, and bit string per station $L = 20$. The manner in which the population was generated was, however varied, and is discussed below.

Random Population. Initially the population was generated randomly, as this is the classic Genetic Algorithm approach. The range and domain are arbitrarily set to $[-1, 1]$ for simplicity and generality. A typical randomly generated solution is presented in Fig. 2(a), along with its corresponding uv plane coverage in Fig. 2b.

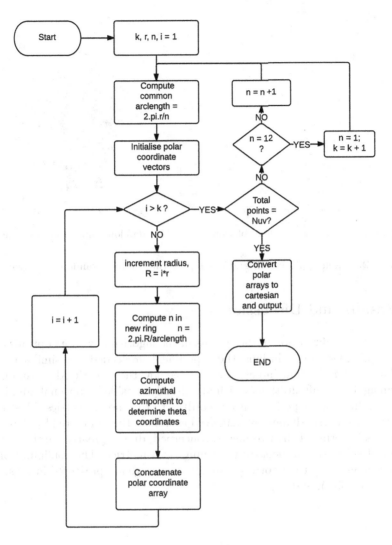

Fig. 1. Flowchart of the UVnominal() function

Table 1. Uv and Cable length for symmetric geometric seeds

Seed	uv Coverage	Cable length
Random	0.56102	8.3506
VLA	0.45198	3.4851
Equilateral triangle	0.63785	5.8928
Reuleaux triangle	0.30395	6.1728
Circle	0.56836	6.1742

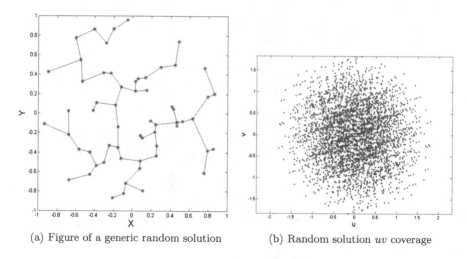

(a) Figure of a generic random solution   (b) Random solution uv coverage

Fig. 2. Antenna placement and $u - v$ performance for a random coverage

4   Results and Discussions

Following the confirmation of the success of the algorithm with its optimisations of randomly generated solutions, the experiment proceeded in a similar manner to Cohanim *et al.* [3]. The intention was to see how the Genetic Algorithm might perform against configurations which are already considered optimal, and in the process evaluate their performance according to the chosen metrics. Most other instinctive geometric shapes are perceived as inherently dominated by these configurations in terms of the two metric concerned, due to greater parallelism and number of sides, simultaneously worsening both metrics. The configurations of the seeds along with their corresponding uv coverage are presented in Figs. 3(a), (b), 4(a), (b), 5(a), and (b).

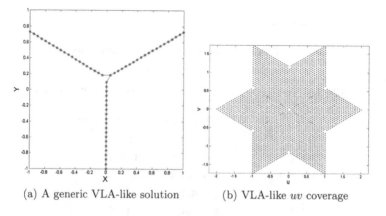

(a) A generic VLA-like solution   (b) VLA-like uv coverage

Fig. 3. Antenna placement and $u - v$ performance for a VLA-like solution

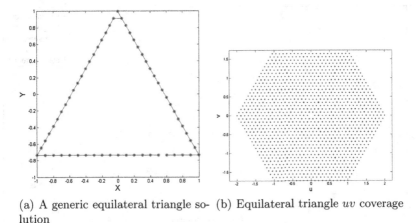

(a) A generic equilateral triangle so-   (b) Equilateral triangle uv coverage
lution

Fig. 4. Antenna placement and $u - v$ performance for a equilateral triangle solution

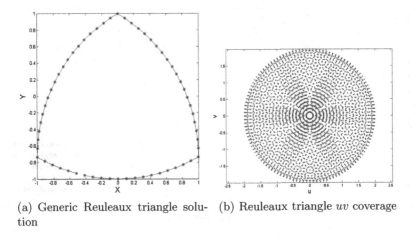

(a) Generic Reuleaux triangle solu-   (b) Reuleaux triangle uv coverage
tion

Fig. 5. Antenna placement and $u - v$ performance for a Reuleaux triangle solution

In addition to the ideal symmetric configurations, stations are also placed at random positions along the perimeter of these figures to ensure diversity. This is to prevent premature convergence due to the inevitable homogeneity of the selected population. Attempting to introduce genetic diversity is hoped to assist in exploring the design space more thoroughly. These seeds were placed altogether in the population, and the initial population can be seen without the symmetric seeds in Fig. 6. The position of the symmetric seeds in the design space can be seen in Fig. 7. Simulations were carried out on purely randomised seeded configurations, and randomised configurations with 10 % symmetric seeds.

It is interesting to note that randomisations of the triangle and circle configurations vastly improve on the metric returns. The circle appears to perform

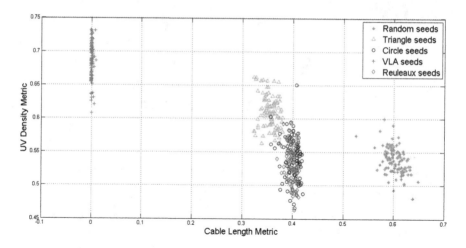

Fig. 6. Evaluative distribution of randomised seeded population at first generation

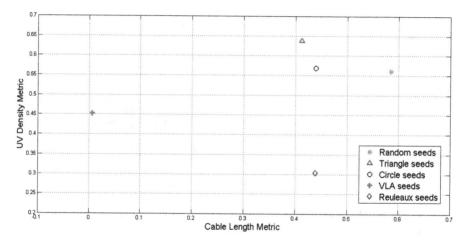

Fig. 7. Purely symmetric seeds in the design space

badly according to the evaluative metric seemingly due to the very high concentrations of sampling points in the interior and exterior rings, and relatively sparse sampling in the interior. This is due to the high rotational symmetry of the circle, which increases redundancy in the uv plane [6]. The triangle has many redundant sampling points due to the high level of equal baseline vectors in its configurations, arising from the parallelism of its station baseline configurations. As such it is deemed very poor in uv performance, but with relative returns on cable length.

It is seen from Fig. 6 that the disruption of these symmetries by perturbation of station placements around the perimeters significantly increases the uv sampling for these shapes. in the circle's case, to the point where it's randomisation is a contender for one of the best configurations for uv sampling. Thus randomisations of the station placements are deemed very important for the exploration of the design space, and the GA can be very beneficial to optimise these configurations in isolation.

4.1   Non-linear Aggregating Objective Function

The goal of the optimisation of the multi-objective problem, and hence approach to the design of its objective function can be considered with respect to two different outcomes. One, in the case of so called 'aggregating functions', concentrates convergence of a solution on a particular region of the Pareto Front. In such a case the aggregating function is some linear combination of the objective functions, a variety of methods for which exist, some to be discussed. In such an optimisation the region of the objective space which is to be optimised is controlled by the designer by allocation of weights and scaling constants of the objectives and the ideal vector (goals) for the functions. In contrast, the goal to some optimisations might be the generation of, or rather the approximation to the Pareto Front. Generating the Pareto Front, is extremely computationally expensive, and often unachievable due to the nature of the problem [9], therefore GA and other methods of stochastic search strategies are useful to find good approximations to it.

In attempting to approximate the Pareto front using the GA or any other EA, the task is two-fold; to minimise the distance between the solution population and the Pareto Front, and to maintain sufficient diversity in the population as to produce solutions along a sufficiently large portion of the Pareto Front [9]. A wide variety of techniques are available in the literature for the permutations of the objective, fitness, and selection functions which may facilitate improvements in this regard, and due to the sheer number of slight variations of each, will be discussed only as they are experimented with. Zitzler [9] addresses, the problem of fitness assignments, diversity preservation, and elitism with respect to this regard.

The graphical results from an optimisation using a randomly generated population are presented in Figs. 8, 9, and 10. The objective function here is a non linear aggregating function, in which the respective objective are combined by a multiplication with equal exponential weightings.

Figure 8 shows the progressive evaluations of the population at each generation. The initial population is shown in dark blue, and progressive plottings are colour shifted through light blue, cyan, green, yellow, orange and finally red. The very darkest red represent the solutions found at the final generation of the optimisation. Clearly a generational shift towards the Pareto front is observed.

Furthermore the rate of improvement is seen to have slowed down significantly towards the end, which is supported by Figs. 9 and 10, showing minimum and maximum cable length and uv sampling density, respectively. This suggests that little improvement could be achieved with further iterations.

Figures 9 and 10 represent the best and worst evaluations of the cable length and uv metric at each generation, respectively.

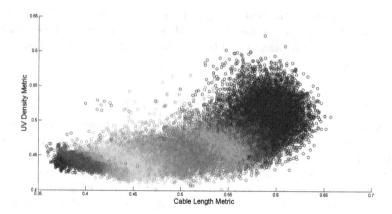

Fig. 8. A generational shift in the population towards the Pareto Front

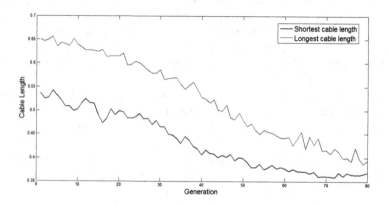

Fig. 9. Maximum and minimum cable length solution vs generation

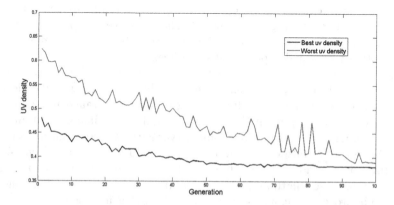

Fig. 10. Maximum and minimum *uv* density solution vs generation

5 Conclusion

In the current work we thoroughly investigated the application of naive GA to the problem of antenna placement in radio astronomy. The cost functions were the cost of cable length and the challenge of avoiding beat frequencies in the imaging process. We showed that genetic algorithm does help us in generating better placements than those given by symmetric conventional placements.

Lastly it must be repeated here that this is not a conventional use of evolutionary algorithms. Hence a better understanding of the cost functions and the domain outweigh the investigation into different types of evolutionary algorithms. Hence this work focuses more on investigating different aspects of the solution rather than investigating different kinds of algorithms. In future work we intend to apply other apt algorithms to this problem and also to consider other objective functions derived from the astronomy community (e.g. if it is possible to design an array more suitable for pulsar searching).

References

1. Gary, D.E.: Radio Astronomy. http://web.njit.edu/~gary/728. Accessed September 2013
2. Thompson, A.R., Moran, J.M., Swenson Jr., G.W.: Interferometry and synthesis in radio astronomy. Wiley, New York (2008)
3. Cohanim, B.E., Hewitt, J.N., de Weck, O.: The design of radio telescope array configurations using multiobjective optimization: imaging performance versus cable length. Astrophys. J. Suppl. Ser. **154**(2), 705–719 (2004)
4. Jin, N., Rahmat-Samii, Y.: Analysis and particle swarm optimization of correlator antenna arrays for radio astronomy applications. IEEE Trans. Antennas Propag. **56**(5), 1269–1279 (2008)
5. Gharahdaghi, A.: Geometric configuration optimization for baseline interferometry. Res. J. Recent Sci. **2**(5), 78–82 (2013)
6. Keto, E.: The shapes of cross-correlation interferometers. Astrophys. J. **475**(2), 843 (1997)
7. Cornwell, T.: A novel principle for optimization of the instantaneous fourier plane coverage of correction arrays. IEEE Trans. Antennas Propag. **36**(8), 1165–1167 (1988)
8. Gower, J.C., Ross, G.: Minimum spanning trees and single linkage cluster analysis. Appl. Stat. **18**, 54–64 (1969)
9. Zitzler, E., Laumanns, M., Bleuler, S.: A tutorial on evolutionary multiobjective optimization. In: Gandibleux, X., et al. (eds.) Metaheuristics for Multiobjective Optimisation, pp. 3–37. Springer, Heidelberg (2004)
10. Coello, C.A.C., et al.: A comprehensive survey of evolutionary-based multiobjective optimization techniques. Knowl. Inform. Syst. **1**(3), 129–156 (1999)
11. MATLAB, version 7.10.0 (R2010a). The MathWorks Inc., Natick, Massachusetts (2010)
12. Haniff, C.: An introduction to the theory of interferometry. New. Astron. Rev. **51**(8–9), 565–575 (2007). http://www.sciencedirect.com/science/article/pii/S1387647307000619

An Improved Cuckoo Search Algorithm for Parallel Machine Scheduling

Dipak Laha[✉] and Dhiren Kumar Behera

Department of Mechanical Engineering, Jadavpur University,
Kolkata 700032, India
dipaklaha_jume@yahoo.com

Abstract. This paper proposes a cuckoo search-based algorithm (CSA) to minimize makespan for identical parallel machine scheduling problems. Job permutation schedules are used to implement CSA for this problem. We present a heuristic approach based on mod function to convert a continuous position in CSA into discrete permutation schedule for obtaining a cuckoo by Levy flights. Empirical results with a large number of randomly generated benchmark problem instances demonstrate that the proposed method produces solutions that are fairly superior to that of two state-of-the-art algorithms in the literature.

Keywords: Parallel machine scheduling · Makespan · Cuckoo search algorithm · Heuristic · Permutation schedule

1 Introduction

The problem of scheduling a set of n independent jobs to a given set of m identical parallel machines with the objective of minimizing makespan has long received the attention of researchers since the seminal work of McNaughton (1959).

Apart from theoretical aspects, the research is motivated in parallel machine scheduling (PMS) area due to immense practical applications of these problems which are routinely encountered in many real-life situations such as production lines, semiconductor manufacturing, shipping docks, university, hospitals, and computer systems (Su and Lien 2009). The objective of the problem is to schedule a set of independent jobs for processing through a set of identical parallel machines in order to minimize the maximum completion time of the last job in the schedule, i.e., the makespan of the schedule. Minimization of makespan results in maximization of utilization of machines, thereby increasing the productivity and on-time delivery. A comprehensive survey of this scheduling research and applications are given by Mokotoff (2001).

Due to the NP-hard scheduling problem (Garey and Johnson 1979), computation of complete enumeration of all possible schedules is prohibitively large. Therefore, heuristic and metaheuristics approaches because of their polynomial time complexity are frequently applied to obtain near-optimal schedules, especially, for problems involving large number of jobs.

Metaheuristics such as SA (Lee, Wu and Chen 2006), HSA (Chen, Pan, Wang and Li 2011) and PSO (Kashan and Karimi 2009) have been implemented to identical parallel machine scheduling problems. Recently a new metaheuristic, cuckoo search

© Springer International Publishing Switzerland 2015
B.K. Panigrahi et al. (Eds.): SEMCCO 2014, LNCS 8947, pp. 788–800, 2015.
DOI: 10.1007/978-3-319-20294-5_67

algorithm (CSA) developed by Yang and Deb (2009) have been utilized in different engineering and management problems such as reliability optimization (Valian, Tavakoli, Mohanna and Haghi 2013; Valian and Valian 2013), video target tracking (Walia and Kapoor 2014), scheduling (Marichelvam, Prabaharan and Yang 2014; Chandrasekharan and Simon 2012; Li and Yin 2013; Peng, Wenming and Yi 2013), flexible manufacturing system (Burnwal and Deb 2013) and travelling salesman problems (Ouaarab, Ahiod and Yang 2014). Also, some theoretical aspects of the cuckoo search algorithm have been studied by Agarwa, Panda, Bhuyan and Panigrahi (2013) and Das, Dasgupta and Panigrahi (2013). It is a stochastic search optimization technique, which is inspired by the combination of the obligate brood parasite behaviour of some cuckoo species and Levy flight foraging patterns of some animals and insects.

In this paper, we present a new variant of cuckoo search algorithm to minimize makespan for the identical PMS problem. The proposed algorithm is compared with the SA of Lee et al. (2006) and PSO of Kashan and Karimi (2009).

The remainder of this paper is organized as follows: Sect. 2 presents a brief review of cuckoo search algorithm. The proposed algorithm is described in Sect. 3. A numerical illustration is provided in Sect. 4. The computational results are provided in Sect. 5. Finally conclusions are made in Sect. 6.

2   Cuckoo Search Algorithm

2.1   The Cuckoo Behavior

Some cuckoo species due to the brood parasite behavior lays their eggs in the nests of another host bird species with the purpose that the host birds hatch these as their own eggs and brood young cuckoo chicks. However, it is true that all the eggs are not hatched but a part of these are abandoned by the host birds. In order to increase the productivity of new cuckoos, the female cuckoos use various strategies, resulting in reducing the probability of some eggs being abandoned (Payne, Sorenson and Klitz 2005). Some cuckoo species have evolved with the similar appearance and behavior of host species by mimicking in the color and patterns of eggs in some chosen nests.

2.2   Levy Flights

Apart from the brood behavior of the cuckoo species, the CSA is also based on foraging pattern of some animals and insects governed by the characteristics of Levy flights (Brown, Liebovitch and Glendon 2007). Levy flights, originated by Paul Levy, a French mathematician. In nature, the foraging path followed by an animal or an insect is effectively a structured randomized walk where the next move follows immediately the current location/state as well as the transition probability to the next location, characterized by Levy flights. A Levy flight is typically a random walk with the distributed step-lengths according to a heavy-tailed probability distribution. Yang and Deb (2009) have demonstrated that CSA perform better considering the random walk based on Levy flights instead of pure random walk.

2.3   Cuckoo Search Implementation

The CSA (Yang and Deb 2009) is developed based on three important assumptions such as each cuckoo lays an egg and selects a nest randomly; The best nest with the highest quality egg is selected for the next generations and finally, the number of nests are fixed and a host bird can discover an alien egg with probability p_a$\in$ [0,1]. Based on these assumptions, the pseudo code of the CSA is given below:

1. Objective function $f(x), x = (x_1, \ldots, x_d)^T$
2. Generate initial population of n host nests $x_i (i = 1, \ldots, n)$
3. While (t < MaxGeneration) or (stop criterion) do
4. Get a cuckoo randomly by Levy flights
5. Evaluate its quality/fitness F_i
6. Choose a nest among n (say, j) randomly
7. If $(F_i > F_j)$ then
8. Replace j by the new solution
9. End if
10. A fraction (p_a) of worst nests are abandoned and new ones are built
11. Keep the best solutions (or nests with quality solutions)
12. Rank the solutions and find the current best
13. End while
14. Postprocess results and visualization

The new solution generated $x_i(t + 1)$ for say, cuckoo i using a Levy flight is given:

$$x_i(t + 1) = x_i(t) + \alpha \otimes Levy(\lambda) \tag{1}$$

where $\alpha > 0$ represents the step size and depends on the scale of the problem of interest. In many instances, $\alpha = O(1)$ can be used. The Levy flights normally as:

$$Levy u = t^{-\lambda}, 1 < \lambda \leq 3 \tag{2}$$

The above distribution obeys a power law form of step-length with a heavy tail. It has an infinite variance and infinite mean which provides opportunity for global search instead of getting stuck at local minima. In this study, we assume $\lambda = 2$ and $\alpha = 10^6 * n$, where, n denotes the number of jobs.

3   Proposed Algorithm

3.1   Improved Cuckoo Search Algorithm

We now describe the proposed SA heuristic to minimize MS in an identical PMS problem.

Inputs. A set N = {1,2,...,n} of n jobs, a set M = {1,2,...,m} of m identical parallel machines, processing time t_i for each job i $\in N$ and P = $\sum_{i=1}^{n} p_i$.

Objective function $f(x), x = (x_1, \ldots, x_d)^T$
Generate initial population of n host nests $x_i (i = 1, \ldots, n)$ (describes in Sect. 3.2)
Determine the LB on the MS given as:

$$LB = \max \left\{ \max_{1 \leq i \leq n} p_i, \sum_{i \in N} \frac{pi}{m} \right\} \tag{3}$$

1. If the current best solution is equal to LB, the procedure terminates and the best schedule is obtained.
2. While (t < MaxGeneration) or (stop criterion) do
3. Get a cuckoo randomly by Levy flights (given in Sect. 3.3)
4. Evaluate its quality/fitness F_i
5. Choose a nest among n (say, j) randomly
6. If $(F_i > F_j)$ then
7. Replace j by the new solution
8. End if
9. A fraction (p_a) of worst nests are abandoned and new ones are built by generating smart cuckoos (Sect. 3.4)
10. Keep the best solutions (or nests with quality solutions)
11. Rank the solutions and find the current best
12. End while
13. Postprocess results and visualization

3.2   Initial Population Generation

Obtain the initial schedule, S = {S1, S2,...,Sm} using the LPT algorithm (1969). We select the LPT for generating the initial solution because of its good performance in less computational times. The rest (n-1) schedules are generated randomly by interchanging any two jobs from the initial schedule.

3.3   Heuristic to Use Levy Flights in the Schedule Generation

We propose a heuristic for converting the continuous position via Levy flights in CSA into a discrete job permutation. The steps of the heuristic are given below.

1. Let the current best schedule is ρ. Consider the schedule of jobs ρ as an integer, keeping the jobs along with their relative positions in the integer unaltered in subsequent steps of the algorithm.
2. Compute Levy flights given in Eq. 2 at iteration t and obtain a nearest integer value.
3. Obtain the position value for the respective job by adding the integer obtained from step 2 with the integer from step 1 (according to Eq. 1).
4. Apply modulo (position value, n + 1) (n being number of jobs) from the last position value and carry over the quotient to the next position value. Consider this

integer as another schedule ρ'. If there are repetition of jobs in the schedule ρ', set aside the missing jobs in a set σ and go to step 5; otherwise go to step 8.

5. Set $i = 1$.
6. If job i has repetition more than once, consider first two same jobs and if the latter has been changed from the job (say, a) in ρ', replace the former by 'a', else replace the latter one by the first job from the set σ. Set $i = i + 1$ and go to step 7.
7. If $i < n$, return to step 6; otherwise, go to step 8.
8. Obtain the final feasible schedule ρ'.

3.4   Heuristic to Generate Smart Cuckoos in the Algorithm

The steps of the proposed heuristic are as follows.

1. Select a schedule ρ^1 randomly from the set of best schedules in step 12 (Sect. 3.1) and sort the machines in descending order of their completion times. Set $c = 0$.
2. If we find more than one largest machines in the schedule ρ^1, go to step 3; otherwise go to step 5.
3. Convert into single largest machine in the schedule ρ^1 as follows:
4. Select the subsets of jobs from any two largest machines, say, M_r and M_s and obtain the two jobs a and b ($a \in S_r, b \in S_s$) with $min|t_a - t_b|$. Interchange the positions of these jobs a and b to update the subset of jobs S_r and S_s. Obtain the corresponding $C(S_r)$ and $C(S_j)$ and the MS of the generated schedule ρ^1 and go to step 5.
5. If we find processing times of all the jobs in the largest machine is less than those of jobs in the remaining machines in the schedule ρ^1, return to step 1; otherwise go to step 6.
6. Set $j = 1$. Identify the largest machine as $M_1(r \in m)$ with $MS = C(S_1) = max_{1 \leq k \leq m} C(S_k)$ of the schedule ρ^1.
7. Set $j = j + 1$.
8. If $j < m$ go to step 9. Otherwise go to step 11.

Table 1. Permutation schedule representation of cuckoo x_i^t ($n = 8, t = 3$)

Steps of the heuristic (Sect. 3.3)	Job index:	1	2	3	4	5	6	7	8
S1	Initial job permutation:	2	3	6	4	5	1	7	8
S2	Levy flights value (Eq. 2):			8	8	8	8	8	8
S3	position value (rows 2 + 3):	2	3	14	12	13	9	15	16
S4	Mod (position value, $n + 1$):	2	4	6	4	5	1	7	7
S5 – S7	New revised job permutation:	2	4	6	3	5	1	8	7

Table 2. Summary of the experimental framework

Experiment	m	n	p
E_1	3, 4, 5	2 m, 3 m, 5 m	U(1,20), U(20,50)
E_2	2, 3, 4, 6, 8, 10	10, 30, 50, 100	U(100,800)
E_3	3, 5, 8, 10	3 m + 1, 3 m + 2, 4 m + 1, 4 m + 2, 5 m + 1, 5 m + 2	U(1,100), U(100,200), U (100,800)
E_4	2, 3	9, 10	U(1,20), U(20,50), U(1,100), U (50,100), U(100,200), U (100,800)

9. Considering the subsets of jobs in the largest machine (M_1) and M_j, identify the two jobs u and v ($u \in S_1, v \in S_j$) with $max\{t_u - t_v\} < (C(S_1) - C(S_j))$ for interchanging the positions of these jobs to update the subset of jobs S_1 and S_j with the corresponding $C(S_1)$ and $C(S_j)$ and determine the MS of the generated schedule ρ^j and go to step 10. Otherwise return to step 7.

10. Set $c = c + 1$ and return to step 7.

Table 3. Results for experiment E_1

m	n	p	SA (2006)		DPSO (2009)		HDPSO (2009)		Proposed algorithm	
			mean	cpu time	mean	cpu time	mean	cpu time	mean	cpu time
3	6	U(1,20)	1.059	0.06	1.059	0.89	1.059	0.92	1.070	0.01
	9		1.009	0.05	1.009	0.55	1.009	0.53	1.009	0.01
	15		1.000	0.01	1.000	0.02	1.000	0.02	1.000	0.00
	6	U(20,50)	1.057	0.07	1.057	1.17	1.057	1.23	1.049	0.01
	9		1.008	0.09	1.008	1.09	1.008	1.12	1.011	0.03
	15		1.001	0.10	1.000	0.13	1.000	0.09	1.000	0.00
4	8	U(1,20)	1.069	0.08	1.069	1.56	1.069	1.53	1.067	0.05
	12		1.004	0.04	1.002	0.13	1.002	0.13	1.007	0.01
	20		1.000	0.06	1.000	0.03	1.000	0.02	1.000	0.00
	8	U(20,50)	1.060	0.1	1.060	1.89	1.060	1.80	1.052	0.06
	12		1.011	0.18	1.009	1.42	1.009	1.50	1.009	0.03
	20		1.001	0.20	1.000	0.08	1.000	0.04	1.000	0.00
5	10	U(1,20)	1.059	0.10	1.059	1.54	1.059	1.73	1.052	0.03
	15		1.010	0.11	1.008	0.45	1.008	0.45	1.005	0.01
	25		1.000	0.10	1.000	0.03	1.000	0.03	1.000	0.00
	10	U(20,50)	1.059	0.13	1.059	2.07	1.059	2.28	1.052	0.04
	15		1.009	0.25	1.007	1.46	1.007	1.59	1.007	0.03
	25		1.001	0.30	1.000	0.24	1.000	0.04	1.000	0.00
Average			1.023	0.11	1.023	0.81	1.022	0.83	1.022	0.02

Table 4. Results for experiment E_2 using U(100,800)

m	n	SA (2006)		DPSO (2009)		HDPSO (2009)		Proposed algorithm	
		mean	cpu time	mean	cpu time	mean	cpu time	mean	cpu time
2	10	1.0009	0.15	1.0008	1.25	1.0008	1.37	1.0011	0.040
3		1.0071	0.21	1.0063	1.97	1.0063	2.17	1.0065	0.053
2	30	1.0000	0.21	1.0000	0.07	1.0000	0.06	1.0000	0.002
3		1.0002	1.53	1.000	1.77	1.0000	0.32	1.0000	0.026
4		1.0009	2.35	1.0004	3.11	1.0000	1.44	1.0001	0.064
6		1.0027	2.13	1.0019	3.48	1.0004	4.81	1.0007	0.109
8		1.0058	2.49	1.0050	3.64	1.0014	5.94	1.0025	0.0113
10		1.0109	2.08	1.0095	3.82	1.0035	6.75	1.0079	0.116
2	50	1.0000	0.25	1.0000	0.09	1.0000	0.14	1.0000	0.002
3		1.0001	4.11	1.0000	1.72	1.0000	0.18	1.0000	0.004
4		1.0004	6.83	1.0001	4.18	1.0000	0.46	1.0000	0.023
6		1.0014	7.89	1.0009	5.42	1.0000	3.07	1.0001	0.117
8		1.0027	8.94	1.0020	5.72	1.0002	6.75	1.0003	0.152
10		1.0031	7.91	1.0035	6.01	1.0005	10.17	1.0007	0.176
2	100	1.0000	0.86	1.0000	0.10	1.0000	0.92	1.0000	0.002
3		1.0000	12.19	1.0000	1.13	1.0000	0.44	1.0000	0.005
4		1.0000	16.36	1.0000	6.79	1.0000	0.36	1.0000	0.009
6		1.0002	32.10	1.0003	11.40	1.0000	0.49	1.0000	0.045
8		1.0005	38.63	1.0007	12.19	1.0000	1.25	1.0000	0.108
10		1.0000	40.01	1.0012	12.95	1.0000	3.65	1.000	0.188
Average		1.0018	9.36	1.0016	4.34	1.0006	2.53	1.0010	0.063

11. A set of c number of schedules of jobs are generated. If c is less than the abandoned worst schedules to be replaced (say, d) (for step 12, Sect. 3.1), go to step 12. Otherwise stop.

12. Select $(d - c)$ number of different schedules randomly from the set of best schedules (from step 12 in Sect. 3.1). Considering each best schedule, generate a new schedule by interchanging the positions of two jobs selected randomly from the largest machine and one of the rest machines and obtain the corresponding MS of the generated schedule and stop.

3.5 Stopping Criterion

In order to study the quality of solution of a given problem, the CSA is terminated either it satisfies the LB of the problem or a sufficiently large value of max-gen, a number that exceeds 1000 iterations.

Table 5. Results for experiment E_3 using U(1,100)

m	n	SA (2006)		DPSO (2009)		HDPSO (2009)		Proposed algorithm	
		mean	cpu time	mean	cpu time	mean	cpu time	mean	cpu time
3	10	1.0115	0.14	1.0107	1.37	1.0107	1.54	1.0102	0.037
	11	1.0045	0.14	1.0037	0.92	1.0037	1.01	1.0044	0.028
	13	1.0019	0.15	1.0005	0.37	1.0003	0.23	1.0017	0.023
	14	1.0009	0.15	1.0000	0.14	1.0000	0.06	1.0008	0.018
	16	1.0004	0.16	1.0000	0.09	1.0000	0.04	1.0003	0.012
	17	1.0005	0.14	1.0000	0.04	1.0000	0.04	1.0002	0.010
5	16	1.0096	0.39	1.0046	1.64	1.0039	1.76	1.0056	0.048
	17	1.0086	0.5	1.0036	1.55	1.0024	1.45	1.0055	0.051
	21	1.0031	0.52	1.0006	0.84	1.0000	0.28	1.0012	0.028
	22	1.0030	0.50	1.0010	0.96	1.0000	0.25	1.0013	0.032
	26	1.0020	0.60	1.0004	0.71	1.0000	0.13	1.0002	0.022
	27	1.0010	0.57	1.0003	0.63	1.0000	0.10	1.0002	0.013
8	25	1.0127	1.00	1.0094	2.97	1.0041	2.02	1.0067	0.078
	26	1.0095	0.98	1.0069	3.01	1.0016	1.68	1.0061	0.082
	33	1.0030	1.27	1.0028	2.83	1.0002	0.61	1.0013	0.048
	34	1.0033	1.46	1.0027	2.81	1.0001	0.64	1.0016	0.055
	41	1.0021	1.62	1.0012	2.54	1.0000	0.37	1.0008	0.040
	42	1.0018	1.64	1.0013	2.39	1.0000	0.29	1.0003	0.026
10	31	1.0123	1.42	1.0120	3.82	1.0050	3.41	1.0069	0.089
	32	1.0094	1.38	1.0089	3.63	1.0011	2.40	1.0065	0.092
	41	1.0039	2.15	1.0037	3.91	1.0004	1.24	1.0024	0.081
	42	1.0045	2.58	1.0040	4.31	1.0005	1.59	1.0020	0.070
	51	1.0030	3.14	1.0021	4.31	1.0000	0.53	1.0006	0.051
	52	1.0026	3.08	1.0022	4.41	1.0000	0.37	1.0006	0.042
Average		1.0047	1.07	1.0034	2.09	1.0014	0.91	1.0028	0.045

4 Numerical Illustration

We consider the following scheduling problem to illustrate the above heuristic. A set of 8 jobs available simultaneously with respective processing times 3, 5, 2, 8, 6, 10, 4, and 13 is to be processed on 3 identical parallel machines. Let the subset of jobs assigned to machines 1, 2 and 3 be $S_1 = \{2, 3, 6\}$, $S_2 = \{4, 5, 1\}$, $and\ S_3 = \{7, 8\}$ respectively and the corresponding MS = 16. In this case, the schedule of jobs is the subsets $\{S_1, S_2, S_3\}$ of the given 8 jobs. Now, we represent this as job permutation schedule: $\{2(1)-3(1)-6(1)-4(2)-5(2)-1(2)-7(3)-8(3)\}$, where first three jobs 2, 3, 6 in the schedule are assigned to machine 1 and the next three jobs 4, 5, 1 to machine 2 and the last two jobs 7, 8 to machine 3. The set of jobs in a schedule are placed in the same order as given by indexing of machines. The schedule will be changed only when jobs in two subsets

Table 6. Results for Experiment E_3 using U(100,200)

m	n	SA (2006)		DPSO (2009)		HDPSO (2009)		Proposed algorithm	
		mean	cpu time	mean	cpu time	mean	cpu time	mean	cpu time
3	10	1.0122	0.22	1.0119	2.07	1.0119	2.23	1.0123	0.051
	11	1.0137	0.28	1.0129	2.08	1.0125	2.32	1.0094	0.048
	13	1.0024	0.34	1.0011	1.56	1.0010	1.36	1.0023	0.035
	14	1.0021	0.38	1.0014	1.43	1.0007	0.75	1.0011	0.034
	16	1.0010	0.50	1.0002	0.77	1.0000	0.18	1.0002	0.017
	17	1.011	0.50	1.0002	0.89	1.0000	0.13	1.0001	0.015
5	16	1.0130	0.63	1.0097	2.62	1.0087	3.18	1.0085	0.086
	17	1.0141	0.80	1.0122	2.72	1.0096	3.35	1.0076	0.061
	21	1.0043	1.07	1.0014	2.60	1.0000	0.62	1.0006	0.038
	22	1.0042	1.22	1.0020	2.82	1.0002	0.98	1.0007	0.039
	26	1.0035	1.39	1.0007	2.51	1.0000	0.30	1.0002	0.026
	27	1.0027	1.82	1.0013	2.82	1.0000	0.35	1.0002	0.030
8	25	1.0118	1.53	1.0071	3.36	1.0030	3.79	1.0031	0.084
	26	1.0129	1.59	1.0077	3.44	1.0023	3.74	1.0033	0.087
	33	1.0060	2.94	1.0027	3.77	1.0000	0.65	1.0007	0.063
	34	1.0068	3.13	1.0032	3.97	1.0000	0.95	1.0005	0.060
	41	1.0051	4.40	1.0019	4.29	1.0000	0.72	1.0003	0.052
	42	1.0047	4.80	1.0022	4.65	1.0000	0.50	1.0002	0.044
10	31	1.0134	2.34	1.0072	3.99	1.0015	3.58	1.0023	0.088
	32	1.0137	2.76	1.0081	4.10	1.0016	4.06	1.0025	0.098
	41	1.0091	4.60	1.0036	4.85	1.0002	1.54	1.0007	0.081
	42	1.0085	4.86	1.0043	4.85	1.0000	1.03	1.0007	0.072
	51	1.0057	8.36	1.0026	5.78	1.0000	0.54	1.0004	0.071
	52	1.0065	8.05	1.0033	5.88	1.0000	0.97	1.0003	0.069
Average		1.0074	2.43	1.0045	3.24	1.0022	1.57	1.0024	0.056

interchange with each other. However, the number of jobs assigned to each machine are determined from the initial schedule and remains unaltered throughout the execution of the algorithm.

To illustrate the heuristic given in Sect. 3.3, we consider an example considering initial job permutation and the detailed implementation of this heuristic are presented in Table 1.

5   Computational Experimentation

To compare the relative performance of DPSO and HDPSO by Kashan and Karimi (2009), SA by Lee et al. (2006) and the proposed CSA, we carried out the same experimental framework as was used by Kashan and Karimi (2009) based on the

Table 7. Results for Experiment E_3 using U(100,800)

m	n	SA (2006)		DPSO (2009)		HDPSO (2009)		Proposed algorithm	
		mean	cpu time	mean	cpu time	mean	cpu time	mean	cpu time
3	10	1.0089	0.22	1.0078	2.12	1.0078	2.39	1.0081	0.050
	11	1.0056	0.28	1.0047	2.11	1.0046	2.43	1.0051	0.052
	13	1.0024	0.37	1.0013	2.20	1.0009	2.65	1.0015	0.057
	14	1.0018	0.48	1.0006	1.96	1.0005	2.15	1.0010	0.054
	16	1.0014	0.56	1.0003	2.00	1.0001	1.69	1.0005	0.053
	17	1.0014	0.63	1.0002	1.77	1.0000	1.22	1.0003	0.047
5	16	1.0102	0.56	1.0072	2.63	1.0057	3.43	1.0080	0.066
	17	1.0088	0.71	1.0047	2.70	1.0032	3.53	1.0046	0.069
	21	1.0046	1.19	1.0020	2.90	1.0006	3.71	1.0016	0.078
	22	1.0046	1.20	1.0019	2.97	1.0005	3.69	1.0014	0.084
	26	1.0035	1.76	1.0013	3.17	1.0003	3.53	1.0005	0.087
	27	1.0029	1.94	1.0012	3.16	1.0002	3.82	1.0005	0.090
8	25	1.0119	1.58	1.0087	3.26	1.0032	5.17	1.0065	0.098
	26	1.0096	1.90	1.0076	3.33	1.0026	5.32	1.0053	0.099
	33	1.0058	3.48	1.0043	3.88	1.0011	6.35	1.0016	0.126
	34	1.0064	3.50	1.0040	4.08	1.0009	6.62	1.0016	0.126
	41	1.0036	6.03	1.0026	4.76	1.0004	7.31	1.0007	0.145
	42	1.0041	6.10	1.0025	4.87	1.0004	7.56	1.0006	0.147
10	31	1.0125	2.51	1.0092	3.87	1.0032	7.03	1.0066	0.119
	32	1.0118	2.99	1.0082	3.98	1.0026	7.21	1.0049	0.123
	41	1.0059	5.84	1.0050	5.00	1.0009	8.93	1.0017	0.148
	42	1.0066	6.81	1.0051	5.09	1.0010	8.89	1.0014	0.153
	51	1.0046	9.27	1.0035	6.12	1.0004	10.44	1.0007	0.174
	52	1.0042	9.89	1.0035	6.19	1.0004	10.38	1.0007	0.181
Average		1.0059	2.90	1.0040	3.50	1.0017	5.22	1.0027	0.101

benchmark experimental framework originally proposed by Gupta and Ruiz-Torres (2001), Lee and Massey (1988) and Kedia (1971). The details of this experimental framework is given in Table 2. Fifty independent problem instances were generated for each combination of m and n. Hence, a total number of 6000 problem instances were considered. As is typically used in the different experimentations, the processing time probability distribution follows a discrete U(1,20), U(1,100), U(20,50), U(50,100), U (100,200) and U(100,800).

In order to compare their performance, we considered the metric for the performance measure: the average ratio of the MS over its LB obtained from Eq. (3) for a given problem size is defined as follows.

Table 8. Results for Experiment E_4

m	n	p	SA (2006)		DPSO (2009)		HDPSO (2009)		Proposed algorithm	
			mean	cpu time	mean	cpu time	mean	cpu time	mean	cpu time
2	9	U(1,20)	1.001	0.00	1.000	0.01	1.000	0.01	1.000	0.00
		U(20,50)	1.001	0.03	1.001	0.22	1.001	0.21	1.001	0.04
		U(1,100)	1.001	0.04	1.001	0.25	1.001	0.28	1.001	0.01
		U(50,100)	1.004	0.11	1.004	1.07	1.004	1.07	1.004	0.02
		U(100,200)	1.004	0.14	1.004	1.22	1.004	1.23	1.004	0.04
		U(100,800)	1.002	0.14	1.002	1.33	1.002	1.46	1.002	0.01
3	10	U(1,20)	1.001	0.02	1.001	0.14	1.001	0.14	1.001	0.00
		U(20,50)	1.008	0.14	1.007	1.16	1.007	1.20	1.007	0.03
		U(1,100)	1.010	0.14	1.009	1.39	1.009	1.50	1.007	0.04
		U(50,100)	1.010	0.20	1.009	1.61	1.009	1.65	1.010	0.05
		U(100,200)	1.017	0.22	1.016	2.00	1.016	2.08	1.016	0.06
		U(100,800)	1.009	0.22	1.009	1.95	1.009	2.22	1.009	0.05
Average			1.006	0.11	1.005	1.02	1.005	1.08	1.005	0.03

$$\text{mean} = \sum_i^{np} \left(MS(H_i)/LB_i \right)/np \tag{4}$$

where np is the number of problem instances for a given job and machine combination and MS(Hi) is the MS value obtained by the heuristic H for the i-th problem instance.

In order to use the original results of the SA, DPSO, and HDPSO by Kashan and Karimi (2009) in this comparative study, we did not code these algorithms and considered these computational results with the proposed CSA following same experimental framework as was done by Kashan and Karimi (2009). The proposed CSA was coded in C and run on a Pentium Dual Core, 2.80 GHZ with 3 GB RAM.

To obtain a fair comparison of the effectiveness of the proposed method with the existing algorithms, we noted the average execution time in seconds required by the proposed method for running 50 times of a particular problem size.

Table 3 displays the comparative evaluation of the proposed method and the existing methods for experimental framework E_1. The results in terms of the mean performance show that the proposed heuristic produces better results than those obtained by the existing method. It can be seen that there is no significant performance difference among SA, DPSO and HDPSO algorithms. Regarding the CPU times, the proposed method requires an average of 0.020 s whereas it is 0.11, 0.81 and 0.83 s for the SA, DPSO and HDPSO. In comparison with the Pentium 4, 2.66 GHz CPU as used by Kashan and Karimi (2009), although the proposed method was run on Pentium Dual Core, 2.80 GHz CPU, which is 2-3 times faster, it is evident that the computation time taken by the proposed method is less than that required by any of the existing algorithms.

The computational results of experimental frameworks E_2, E_3 and E_4 are given in Tables 4, 5, 6, 7 and 8 respectively. As depicted in Table 4, it reveals that the HDPSO algorithm performs the best, whereas the proposed method performs the next best among all the algorithms. There is no significant improvement of the HDPSO over the proposed method. As regard to CPU times, the proposed method is found to be fastest among these algorithms. An identical metric of the performance of the comparing algorithms carries over to the results of Tables 5, 6 and 7 as well. It is evident from the results of Table 8 that the proposed heuristic outperforms the existing algorithms.

6 Conclusions

This paper has proposed a cuckoo search algorithm for the identical parallel machine scheduling problem with the objective of minimizing the makespan. A heuristic approach based on modulus function is used to convert a continuous position in CSA into discrete permutation schedule for obtaining a cuckoo by Levy flights. Another heuristic has been presented to generate better cuckoos in the algorithm. The computational results show that the proposed algorithm produces better solutions than those by the SA and DPSO algorithms and similar performance with the HDPSO. Regarding the complexity, the proposed algorithm is found to be fastest among the algorithms.

References

Agarwal, S., Panda, R., Bhuyan, S., Panigrahi, B.K.: Tsallis entrophy based optimal multilevel threshold using cuckoo search algorithm. Swarm Evol. Comput. **11**, 16–30 (2013)

Brown, C., Liebovitch, L.S., Glendon, R.: Levy flights in Dobe Ju/hoansi foraging patterns. Hum. Ecol. **35**, 129–138 (2007)

Burnwal, S., Deb, S.: Scheduling optimization of flexible manufacturing system using cuckoo search-based approach. Int. J. Manuf. Technol. **64**, 951–959 (2013)

Chandrasekharan, K., Simon, S.P.: Multi-objective scheduling problem: Hybrid approach using fuzzy assisted cuckoo search algorithm. Swarm Evol. Comput. **5**, 1–16 (2012)

Chen, J., Pan, Q.K., Wang, L., Li, J.Q.: A hybrid harmony search algorithm for identical parallel machines scheduling. Eng. Optim. **1**, 1–16 (2011)

Das, Swagatam, Dasgupta, Preetam, Panigrahi, Bijaya Ketan: Inter-species Cuckoo Search via Different Levy Flights. In: Panigrahi, Bijaya Ketan, Suganthan, Ponnuthurai Nagaratnam, Das, Swagatam, Dash, Shubhransu Sekhar (eds.) SEMCCO 2013, Part I. LNCS, vol. 8297, pp. 515–526. Springer, Heidelberg (2013)

Garey, M.R., Johnson, J.S.: Computers and Intractability: A Guide to the Theory of NP-Completeness. Freeman, San Francisco (1979)

Peng, G., Wenming, C., Yi, W.: Parallel machine scheduling with step deteriorating jobs and setup times by a hybrid discrete cuckoo search algorithm. Arxiv.1309.1453 [math.OC] (2013)

Gupta, J.N.D., Ruiz-Torres, J.: A LISTFIT heuristic for minimizing makespan on identical parallel machines. Prod. Plan. Control **12**, 28–36 (2001)

Kedia, S.K.: A job scheduling problem with parallel processors. Unpublished report, Department of Industrial and Operations Engineering. University of Michigan, Ann Arbor, MI (1971)

Lee, C.Y., Massey, J.D.: Multiprocessor scheduling: combining LPT and MULTIFIT. Discrete Appl. Math. **20**, 233–242 (1988)

Lee, W.-C., Wu, C.-C., Chen, P.: A simulated annealing approach to makespan minimization on identical parallel machines. Int. J. Adv. Manuf. Technol. **31**, 328–333 (2006)

McNaughton, R.: Scheduling with deadlines and loss functions. Manage. Sci. **6**, 1–8 (1959)

Li, X., Yin, M.A.: Hybrid cuckoo search via Levy flights for the permutation flow shop scheduling problem. Int. J. Prod. Res. **51**, 4732–4754 (2013)

Kashan, A.H., Karimi, B.: A discrete particle swarm optimization algorithm for scheduling parallel machines. Comput. Ind. Eng. **56**, 216–223 (2009)

Marichelvam, M.K., Prabaharan, T., Yang, X.S.: Improved cuckoo search algorithm for hybrid flow shop scheduling problems to minimize makespan. Appl. Soft Comput. **19**, 93–101 (2014)

Mokotoff, E.: Parallel machine scheduling problems: a survey. Asia-Pac. J. Oper. Res. **18**, 193–242 (2001)

Ouaarab, A., Ahiod, B., Yang, X.S.: Discrete cuckoo search algorithm for the travelling salesman. Neural Comput. & Applic. **24**, 1659–1669 (2014)

Payne, R.B., Sorenson, M.D., Klitz, K.: The Cuckoos. Oxford University Press, Oxford (2005)

Su, L.H., Lien, C.Y.: Scheduling parallel machines with resource-dependent processing times. Int. J. Prod. Econ. **17**, 256–266 (2009)

Valian, E., Tavakoli, S., Mohanna, S., Haghi, A.: Improved cuckoo search for reliability optimization problems. Comput. Ind. Eng. **64**, 459–468 (2013)

Valian, E., Valian, E.: A cuckoo search algorithm by Levy flights for solving reliability redundancy allocation problems. Eng. Optim. **45**, 1273–1286 (2013)

Walia, G.S., Kapoor, R.: Intelligent video target using an evolutionary particle filter based upon improved cuckoo search **41**, 6315–6326 (2014)

Yang, X.S., Deb, S.: Cuckoo search via Levy flights. In: IEEE World Congress on Nature & Biologically Inspired Computing, NaBIC 2009, pp. 210-214 (2009)

Application of Artificial Bee Colony Optimization: Power System Voltage Stability Problems

Kiran S. Harish[✉], Sekhar Dash Subhransu, C. Subramani,
and ChandraBabu Paduchuri

Department of EEE, SRM University, Kattankulathur 603203, India
harish99kiran@gmail.com

Abstract. This paper highlights the effective usage of Artificial Bee Colony (ABC) to predict the stability of the system based on the Fast Voltage Stability Index (FVSI). The content of the paper is to compare the effectiveness of optimization techniques with the conventional method. The system stability, the point collapse and the weakest busses are identified based on the line reactive power loading in the power system network. Based on the weak bus identified either Thyristor Controlled Series Compensator (TCSC) or Unified Power Flow Controller (UPFC) will be connected to enhance the stability of the power system network. These techniques are coded with the newton raphson load flow analysis, implemented and tested with IEEE 30 bus system.

Keywords: ABC · FVSI · Voltage stability · TCSC · UPFC

1 Introduction

Voltage stability [1, 2] is a big problem with the resent development and increase in consumers. For this voltage stability problem there are many research works are still in progress to find a better solution. The stability of the system can be evaluated by the voltage profile of the line, commonly known as the Voltage Stability Analysis (VSA). To find the stability of the system equation is framed in a ratio form to find the index of the system and its corresponding voltage at the bus.

Initially the stability of the system was found by the use of PV curve and QV curve [3] by P. Kunder et al. Then slowly many other method where used to find such as L-Index [4], Modal analysis [5], Line Stability Index (Lmn) [6], Line Stability Index (LQP) [7], Bus Power Index [8], Power Transfer Stability Index (PTSI) [9], New Voltage Stability Index (NVSI) [10], Fast Voltage Stability Index (FVSI) [11, 12], Global Voltage Stability Index (GVSI) [13] and more. Each index has its own merits and demerits.

In this paper FVSI is used as a stability analyzer. The effectiveness of the indices is analyzed with the optimization techniques such as Artificial Bee Colony (ABC) algorithm [14].

The conventional load flow with Newton Rapshon method is used to get the necessary data's for the index which is given as the input data to the optimization

© Springer International Publishing Switzerland 2015
B.K. Panigrahi et al. (Eds.): SEMCCO 2014, LNCS 8947, pp. 801–808, 2015.
DOI: 10.1007/978-3-319-20294-5_68

techniques. The optimization techniques used will give the index of the system for the corresponding loading condition.

In the following Sect. 2, the indices used are elaborated. Optimization technique is explained and the way it is coded in the MATLAB editor environment is summarized in Sect. 3. The Sect. 4 deals with the possible FACTS controller that could be connected in the network. The coding result for the 62 bus Indian utility system is tabulated in Sect. 5 with the conclusion and the further scope of analysis.

2   Fast Voltage Stability Index (FVSI)

Stability Index of the system gives the distance to the collapse point of the power system or the maximum operating range of the power system. As stated in the Sect. 1 there are many ways to identify the stability index of the system of which the Fast Voltage Stability Index (FVSI).

The formation of the indices are based on a simple two bus system and then developed to be used in the actual system and not any other bus in the system. The two bus line diagram is shown in Fig. 1.

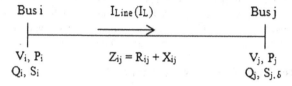

Fig. 1. Two bus system modal

Where,
V_i, V_j - Voltage at the sending and receiving end buses.
P_i, Q_i – Active and reactive power at the sending end bus.
P_j, Q_j – Active and reactive power at the receiving end bus.
δ - Angular difference between the sending and the receiving end power.

$$Z_{ij} = R_{ij} + X_{ij}$$

R_{ij} is the line resistance and
X_{ij} is the line reactance.

The system is said to be in stable operating conduction when the indices obtained is between the ranges 0.0000 to 0.9999, above which the system stability will collapses.

The FVSI index is based on the voltage and reactive power of the receiving end bus of the power system network. Based on the two bus system shown in Fig. 1, the final equation of FVSI index is found to as

$$FVSI_{ij} = \frac{4Z_{ij}^2 Q_j}{V_i^2 X_{ij}} \tag{1}$$

where Z – line impedance

Xij – line reactance
Qj – reactive power at the receiving end
Vi – sending end voltage.

The value indicated by the FVSI that is close to 1 indicates that the particular line is close to its instability point. Hence the FVSI should be maintained less than or equal to 0.9999 in order to maintain the system stability.

3 Optimization Techniques

Optimization is a process of finding the maxima and the minimum of the function concerned. It was first used by George Dantzig is 1940, initially for military application and later it is has found its way in many area. One of the popular optimization techniques is the Swarm Intelligence (SI). There are few algorithm classified in SI techniques they are Particle Swarm Optimization (PSO) algorithm, Ant Colony optimization (ACO), Artificial Bee Colony (ABC) algorithm, Differential evolution (DE), the bee algorithm, artificial immune system, grey wolf optimizer, bat algorithm, gravitational search algorithm, altruism algorithm, glowworm swarm optimization, river formation dynamics, self-propelled particles, stochastic diffusion search and multi-swarm optimization.

Off all the SI techniques most commonly used algorithms are PSO, ABC, ACO and DE. These algorithms had found its application in many fields, of all the techniques this paper uses ABC algorithm to find the stability of the power system network. Other areas where ABC algorithm used are subsisted in the following content.

Digbalay Bose et al. [14] has used ABC algorithm as a search procedure for an optimal solution for analog filter design and selection of power values. The author's used ABC as a collective resource based ABC with decentralized tasking with neighborhood information and wider exploration of search space.

Gaurav Prasad Dixit et al., [15] used ABC algorithm for multi-objective optimization problem in power system. Considering the environmental impact that grows from the emission produced by fossil-fuelled power plant, the economic dispatch that minimizes only the total fuel cost can no longer be considered as single objective. Author's uses ABC based strategy based on mathematical modeling to solve economic, emission and combined economic and emissions dispatch problems by a single equivalent objective function. Author's also state that ABC algorithm is easy to implement and capable of searching near global optimum solution at fast convergence and efficiency.

Biswas S et al. [16] has modified the ABC algorithm in order to enhance the performance. Also to maintain multiple swarm population that applies different perturbation strategies and gradually migration of the population from worse performing strategy to a better mode of perturbation. The author has used 8 different algorithms as comparative study for 25 IEEE benchmark problems.

Das S et al. [17] developed a robust search technique with ABC algorithm to exhibits elevated performance in multidimensional objective space and compared with some high competitive state-of-the-art methods.

Based on the review the Artificial Bee Colony (ABC) algorithm is utilized as an optimization technique to identify the stability of the power system network.

3.1   Artificial Bee Colony (ABC) Algorithm

Karaboga in 2005 proposed the Artificial Bee Colony Algorithm [18–22] based on the honey bee swarm behavior. In a normal bee colony the bees can be categorized into three such as the onlooker bees, scout bees and the employer bees. Based on the food sources the numbers of employer bee are selected, that are the based on the number of lines the index to be found. The onlooker bees look out for the patron of the movement of the employee bee to find the best food source, i.e., the best index value of each line is found by the employee bee and identified by the onlooker bee based on the movement patron.

$$F_{ij} = \max\left(FVSI_{ij}\right) \tag{2}$$

When the employee bee completes its tasks the entire employee bee in that food sources will become a scout bee and moves in again in that direction to find a new food source, otherwise when the best index solution for the line is obtained than the employee bee converts it-self into a scout bee and moves into the next line to find the possible best index in it. The fitness function for the ABC algorithm is given in Eq. (2).

The peso code [23–28] for the ABC algorithm is given in the following steps.

Step 01: Run the load flow analysis and form matrix format tabulation for the parameters required such as reactive power of the line, receiving end voltage and the line impedance.

Step 02: The best solution to be identified in each line is defined as 0.9999.

Step 03: The number of food sources is initialized as the number of line.

Step 04: The employee bees sent to find the best possible solution in the first line or the first food sources. i.e., the best possible solution based on receiving end voltage, reactive power and impedance of the line.

Step 05: Calculate the fitness function for the corresponding value.

Step 06: Check for the best solution is either fitness function value or the initialized value.

Step 07: Repeat step 4 to step 6 until the fitness function value becomes the best solution.

Step 08: Check for the maximum number of line reached else increase line count by 1 and go to step 4.

Step 09: Return all the line fitness function value.

Step 10: End.

4   FACTS Controller

There are many types of Flexible AC Transmission System (FACTS) controllers classified based on who it is connected to the transmission line such as shunt, series or both combined.

In this paper we will be using two controllers one in series is Thyristor Controlled Series Compensator (TCSC) and the other controller is combination of both shunt & series is Unified Power Flow Controller (UPFC).

The selection of these controllers is based on the steady state and the dynamic state stability of the controllers. For the possible problem such as voltage limits, loop flow thermal limits, short circuit level, transient stability, damping, post contingency and voltage stability. By the use these controllers a better solution can be obtained. The other advantage of these controllers is that they have the ability to improve the power factor Extra High Voltage (EHV) Transmission line.

The description of the controller is available in varies sources, so only the rating of the controller is described. As per the Siemens AG database [19, 20] the rating of the controller are found to be,

$$R_{TCSC} = rf * 0.45 - 0.25 \tag{3}$$

$$R_{UPFC} = rf * 180 \tag{4}$$

Where
rf- is the rating factor of the controller.

The rating of the controller connected in the system is taken as 1p.u, in 1st case and -1p.u, in the 2nd case the results are tabulated based on the index.

5 Test Results and Discussions

The optimization technique along with the FVSI index is coded in the MATLAB coding environment. The result discussion is based on index obtained and as well as on voltage profile of the bus. The feasible FACTS controller to be connected is identified by obtaining the indices while connecting both the controller individually. The improvement of the bus voltage for each FACTS controller is also discussed.

The test system is loaded to its critical loading of Pmax as 4,189 MW and Qmax as 1,829.9 MVAR. The indices are obtained for all the lines with and without FACTS controller. The tabulation 1 shows the results obtained by the conventional method, optimization technique, with and without FACTS controller. Only 10 line index with maximum index value are shown with its line no and connecting bus in the Table 1.

By the conventional method (NR) the critical line is found to be as line no 82 connecting bus 58 to 12, also a similar result is obtained by ABC algorithm. Hence, the FACTS controller is connected in the line no 82(58-12). The result obtained after connecting the FACTS controller by conventional method and by the optimization technique shows a remarkable increase in the loading of power system test network.

Figure 2 shows the top 20 weak busses based on conventional method. Based on the voltage profile it is found that bus no 11 has a 0.8347p.u voltage, then bus no 20 with 0.8587p.u and bus no 10 with 0.8648p.u as bus voltage. The test system shows an improvement in the voltage profile when TCSC or UPFC are connected. A better voltage margin or voltage profile can be seen when UPFC is connected to the test system.

Table 1. FVSI indices test result for 62 Bus Indian Utility System

Line no	Without		With TCSC		With UPFC	
	NR	ABC	NR	ABC	NR	ABC
82(58-12)	0.9999	0.9999	0.0754	0.0736	0.0194	0.0186
5(1-10)	0.9903	0.9896	0.0814	0.0806	0.0177	0.0173
19(12-11)	0.9373	0.9353	0.0622	0.0615	0.2367	0.2304
86(60-12)	0.8267	0.8258	0.1216	0.1292	0.0368	0.0359
30(20-23)	0.6090	0.6050	0.2520	0.2460	0.1310	0.1302
20(12-13)	0.5684	0.5648	0.058	0.051	0.2363	0.2353
18(11-16)	0.4042	0.4032	0.119	0.1206	0.0482	0.0473
23(13-17)	0.3631	0.3622	0.0103	0.0101	0.0732	0.0721
73(51-53)	0.2954	0.3845	0.0969	0.0963	0.0736	0.0721
29(17-21)	0.2668	0.2648	0.4092	0.3992	0.4083	0.3992

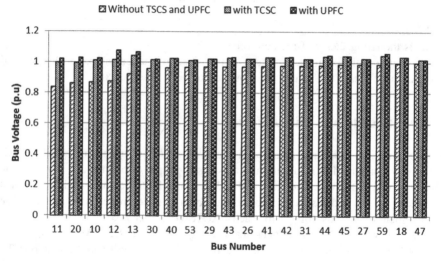

Fig. 2. Voltage profile of top 20 weak buses without FACTS controller and corresponding bus voltage with TCSC or UPFC

6　Conclusions

In this paper ABC optimization technique has been implemented effectively and weak bus has been identified. The FVSI index is used as an indicator for voltage stability. The FVSI calculation has been done with normal NR method and ABC algorithm. The ABC gave a better accurate result when compared to NR method.

The voltage stability of the system has improved with the help of TCSC and UPFC. The FACTS devices are connected separately at the weak bus determined from ABC algorithm and tested.

References

1. Ajjarapu, V.: Computational Techniques for Voltage Stability Assessment and Control, ch. 4 & 5, pp. 117–206 (2006) ISBN: 10-9780387260808
2. Subramani, C., SekharDash, S., Jagdeeshkumar, M., Bhaskar, M.A.: Stability index based voltage collapse prediction and contingency analysis. J. Electr. Eng. Technol. 4(4), 438–442 (2009)
3. Editor/Coordinator: Claudio Canizares, Voltage Stability Assessment: Concepts, Practices and Tools. IEEE/PES power System Stability Subcommittee Special Publication (2002)
4. Kessal, P., Glavitsch, H.: Estimating the voltage stability of a power system. IEEE Trans. Power Delivery 1(3), 346–354 (1986)
5. Gao, B., Morison, G.K., kundur, P.: Voltage stability evaluation using modal analysis. IEEE Trans. Power Syst. 74(4), 1529–1542 (1992)
6. Moghavemi, M., Omar, F.M.: Technique for contingency monitoring and voltage collapse prediction. IEEE Proc. Gener. Transm. Distrib. 145(6), 634–640 (1998)
7. Mohamed, S.Y.A., Jasmon, G.B.: A static voltage collapse indicator using line stability factors. J. Ind. Technol. 7(1), 73–85 (1989)
8. Kundur, P., Ajjarapu, V., Andersson, G., Bose, A., Canizarios, C., Nikos, H., Hill, D., Slankovic, A., Taylor, C., Van Cutsem, T., Vittal, V.: Defination and classification of power system. IEEE Trans. Power Syst. 19(2), 1387–1400 (2004)
9. Moghavvemi, M., Omar, F.M.: Real-time contingency evaluation and ranking technique. IEEE Proc. Gener. Transm. Distrib. 145(5), 517–524 (1998)
10. Sahu, S.K., Reddy, S.S., Jayakumar, S.V.: New Voltage Stability Index (NVSI) for Voltage Stability Analysis in Power System. Int. J. Electr. Electron. Eng. Res. 2(4), 13–20 (2012)
11. Musirin, I., Rahman, T.K.A.: Novel Fast Voltage Stability Index (FVSI) for voltage stability analysis. In: Conference on Research and Development Proceedings, pp. 265–268 (2002)
12. Subramani, C., Dash, S.S., Kumar, V., kiran, H.: Implementation of line stability index for contingency analysis and screening in power systems. J. Comput. Sci. 8(4), 585–590 (2012)
13. Sakthivel, S., Mary, D., Ezhilan, C.: Global voltage stability limit improvement by real and reactive power optimization through evolutionary programming algorithm. Int. J. Adv. Sci. Tech. Res. 1(2), 88–102 (2012)
14. Bose, D., Biswas, S., Vasilakos, A.V., Laha, S.: Optimal filter design using an improved artificial bee colony algorithm. Inf. Sci. 281, 443–461 (2014)
15. Dixit, G.P., Dubey, H.M., Pandit, M., Panigrahi, B.K.: Artificial bee colony optimization for combined economic load and emission dispatch, pp. 340–345. IET Conference Publications (583 CP) (2011)
16. Biswas, S., Kundu, S., Bose, D., Das, S., Suganthan, P.N., Panigrahi, B.K.: Migrating forager population in a multi-population artificial bee colony algorithm with modified perturbation schemes, In: IEEE Symposium on Swarm Intelligence (SIS), pp. 248–255 (2013)
17. Das, S., Biswas, S., Panigrahi, B.K., Kundu, S., Basu, D.: A spatially informative optic flow model of bee colony with saccadic flight strategy for global optimization. IEEE Trans. Cybern. 44(10), 1884–1897 (2014)
18. Trivedi, A., Srinivasan, D., Biswas, S., Reindl, T.: A hybrid of genetic algorithm and differential evolution for the unit commitment problem. IEEE Transactions on Cybernetics. (in Press)
19. Karaboga, D., Gorkemli, B., Ozturk, C., Karaboga, N.: A comprehensive survey: artificial bee colony (ABC) algorithm and applications. Artif. Intell. Rev. 42(1), 21–57 (2014)

20. Bose, D., Kundu, S., Biswas, S., Das, S.: Circular antenna array design using novel perturbation based artificial bee colony algorithm. Swarm, Evol. Memetic Comput. **7677**, 459–466 (2012)

21. Das, S., Kundu, S., Biswas, S.: Synergizing fitness learning with proximity-based food source selection in artificial bee colony algorithm for numerical optimization. Appl. Soft Comput. **13**(12), 4676–4694 (2013)

22. Gao, W.: Study on immunized ant colony optimization. In: Third International Conference on Natural Computation, vol. 4, pp. 792–796 (2007)

23. Quan, H., Shi, X.: On the analysis of the improved artifical bee colony algorithm. In: 4th International Conference on Natural Computation, vol. 7, pp. 654–658 (2008)

24. Tedorovic, D., Lucic, P., Markovic, G., Orco, M.D.: Bee colony optimization: principles and application. In: 8th Seminar on Neural Network Application in Electrical Engineering, vol. 6, pp. 151–156 (2006)

25. De, M., Goswami, S.K.: Optimal reactive power procurement with voltage stability consideration in deregulated power system. IEEE Trans. Power Syst. **29**(5), 2078–2086 (2014)

26. Gao, W.-f., Liu, S.-Y., Huang, L.-L.: A novel artificial bee colony algorithm based on modified search equation and orthogonal learning. IEEE Trans. Cybern. **43**(3), 1011–1024 (2012)

27. Harish Kiran, S., Subramani, C., Dash, S.S., Arun Bhaskar, M., Jagadeesh Kumar, M.: Particle swarm optimization algorithm to find the location of facts controller for a transmission line. In: International Conference on Process Automation, Control and Computing (PACC), pp. 1–5. IEEE (2011)

28. Moirangthem, J., Krishnanand, K.R., Subhransu, S.D., Ramas, R.: Adaptive differential evoluation for solving non-linear coordion pronlem of directional overcurrent relays. IET Gener. Transm. Distrib. **7**(4), 329–336 (2013)

Multi-objective Optimization of Economic-Emission Load Dispatch Using Cluster Based Differential Evolution

Deep Kiran[✉], B.K. Panigrahi, and A.R. Abhyankar

Department of Electrical Engineering, Indian Institute of Technology Delhi,
New Delhi 110016, India
{deepkiran,bkpanigrahi,abhyankar}@ee.iitd.ac.in

Abstract. A cluster based multi-objective differential evolution algorithm with non-domination based sorting is used to evaluate the environmental/economic dispatch (EED) problem containing the incommensurable objectives of best economic dispatch with minimum cost and least emission is presented in this paper. The environmental concerns arises due to fossil fuel fired electric generators and global warming that leads to the transformation of the classical single objective economic load dispatch problem into multi-objective environmental/economic dispatch problem. Also, an investigation of cluster based differential evolution algorithm is presented and applied on different test systems.

Keywords: Cost minimization · Emission minimization · Cluster based differential evolution algorithm · Load modeling · Multi-objective optimization

1 Introduction

In a deregulated market scenario, the operation of electrical power systems is driven by market economy. They are expected to meet the required power demand in a cost-effective manner. The objective of the traditional economic dispatch is to allocate generation levels to various generators in the system so that the load demand is met in the most economical way. The utilities in the present scenario are expected to reduce their SO_X, NO_X and CO_X emissions [1]. Therefore, apart from the objective of cost minimization, the objective of lower emission must also be taken into account.

EED is a multi-objective problem having conflicting objectives, since the minimization of cost tends to increase the emission. This leads to the requirement of trade-off analysis so as to define suitable dispatch policies for various levels of demand [2]. The novel non-dominated sorting genetic algorithm (NSGA) [3], niched pareto genetic algorithm (NPGA) [4] and strength pareto evolutionary algorithm (SPEA) [5] was successfully applied to EED problem. An elitist multi-objective evolutionary algorithm called NSGA-II was developed in [6] and applied to EED problems.

© Springer International Publishing Switzerland 2015
B.K. Panigrahi et al. (Eds.): SEMCCO 2014, LNCS 8947, pp. 809–820, 2015.
DOI: 10.1007/978-3-319-20294-5_69

Differential evolution (DE) algorithm [7] is a noticeable optimizer which can be used in a different variant of highly nonlinear and complex optimization problems [8]. In recent years, DE or hybrid DE was used for economic dispatch problem and other power systems optimization problems [9]. In [10], the economicenvironmental dispatch problem is solved using the DE technique considering emissions either as constraints or as a second objective function. To avoid disadvantages of the weighted sum method, an algorithm based on non-dominated sorting differential evolution algorithm (NSDE) for solving optimal EED problems was proposed in [11].

Clustering based DE (CbDE) is the very efficient version of DE [12]. The group of objects consists of similarity and dissimilarity with objects of other groups. Authors of [12] also explains the two different type of clustering: crisp and fuzzy. With the use k-Means clustering of DE is explained in [13,14] which shows the enhancement in DE. In [15,16], control variables are automatically adopted during the run, which avoids the complication of tuning the control parameters in the DE algorithm.

The moot question for the researchers is to adjudicate the best pareto front achieved among several runs of the different optimizers. In [17,18], a metric known as spacing is explained by demonstrating the capability of providing the equidistantly distributed points in the available pareto front. Another metric uses euclidean distance to evaluate the non-uniformity or spread of the pareto front which is known as diversity metric [19,20].

The paper is organized as follows. In Sect. 2 the objective is outlined along with the formulations followed in the system modeling. Section 3 describes the formulation of non-dominated sorting based DE algorithm. Section 4 describes the simulation strategy for implementing the solution to EED problem and the experimental results obtained. Section 5 is the conclusion.

2   EED Problem Formulation

The environmental economic dispatch being multi-objective has more than one objective against the optimization of each other. Both operational equality and inequality constraints are imposed while optimizing the two objectives, fuel cost $F(P_G)$ and emission $E(P_G)$ simultaneously, where P_G is the real power generation.

$$\text{Min.}\{F(P_G), E(P_G)\} \tag{1}$$

2.1   Fuel Cost

The primary objective of the conventional economic dispatch is the minimization of total generation cost while satisfying several constraints. It is mathematically expressed as:

$$\text{Min.}F(P_G) = \sum_{i=1}^{N_G} F_i(P_{Gi}) \tag{2}$$

where $F_i(P_{Gi})$ is the ith generator cost function and is approximated as a quadratic function of the power output from the generating units, i.e.

$$F_i(P_{Gi}) = a_i + b_i P_{Gi} + c_i P_{Gi}^2 \quad i = 1, 2, 3, ..., N_G \tag{3}$$

where a_i, b_i, c_i are the cost coefficients, N_G represents the number of generating units in the system and P_{Gi} is the power output of the ith generator. The generator cost function with non-smooth cost characteristics due to the valve point effect is given by

$$F_i(P_{Gi}) = a_i + b_i P_{Gi} + c_i P_{Gi}^2 + |e_i \sin(f_i(P_{Gi}^{min})) \tag{4}$$

where e_i, f_i are the cost coefficients related to the valve-point loading and they contribute to the non-smoothness of the cost curve.

2.2 Emission

The minimum emission dispatch is the simultaneous minimization of classical economic dispatch including emission objective which is modeled as:

$$E(P_G) = \sum_{i=1}^{N_G} \alpha_i + \beta_i P_{Gi} + \gamma_i P_{Gi}^2 + \zeta_i \exp(\lambda_i P_{Gi}) \tag{5}$$

Here, α_i, β_i, γ_i, ζ_i, λ_i are the emission coefficients of the ith generator.

2.3 Constraints

$$P_{Gi} - P_{Di} = \sum_j (V_i V_j Y_{ij} \cos(\theta_{ij} + \delta_j - \delta_i)) \tag{6}$$

$$Q_{Gi} - Q_{Di} = -\sum_j (V_i V_j Y_{ij} \sin(\theta_{ij} + \delta_j - \delta_i)) \tag{7}$$

$$\sum_{i=1}^{N_G} P_{Gi} - P_D - P_{Loss} = 0 \tag{8}$$

$$P_{Gi}^{min} \leq P_{Gi} \leq P_{Gi}^{max} \tag{9}$$

$$Q_{Gi}^{min} \leq Q_{Gi} \leq Q_{Gi}^{max} \tag{10}$$

$$V_i^{min} \leq V_i \leq V_i^{max} \tag{11}$$

where, i and j are the bus numbers, ij represents the line between bus i and j, P_G and P_D are the real power generation and demand in Mega-Watts (MW), Q_G and Q_D are the reactive power generation and demand in Mega-VArs (MVAr), V and δ are the voltage magnitude and angle in per unit and radians, Y and θ are the admittance magnitude in per unit and angle in radians respectively, superscript min and max represents the minimum and maximum limits of the quantity respectively.

2.4 Load Modeling

The enormous use of induction machines in the day-to-day appliances has raised a concern for keeping the unity voltage profile. The efficiency of those appliances excessively depends on the voltage profile. Equation below represents the real power load dependence with the voltage as an exponential function [21].

$$P_L = P_{l0}\left(\frac{V}{V_0}\right)^{np} \tag{12}$$

$$Q_L = Q_{l0}\left(\frac{V}{V_0}\right)^{nq} \tag{13}$$

where, P_L and Q_L are the real and reactive power load, V_0, P_{l0} and Q_{l0} are the nominal voltage magnitude, real and reactive power load respectively. np and nq are the voltage exponent which dependent on the type and composition of the load. These equations depicts the real time dynamics of the loads with the variation in the voltage profile of the load buses.

3   Multi-objective Optimization

The deviation in loads due to voltage dependency while minimizing the cost or emission which is not acceptable below certain limit. These functions need to be coupled which can limit the voltage reduction of the system. Emission is a function of real power which will provide a trade-off for the multi-objective optimization. This trade-off will be beneficial for the decision making in selecting the operating region of the system. The demand for robust optimization techniques is on the rise as the cumbersomeness of the real world optimization problems becoming more complex. Cluster based DE is adopted as optimization technique which emerged as a simple and efficient scheme for global optimization over continuous spaces more than a decade ago. The pareto optimal set retrieved from the non-dominated solution, an approach in [22] extract the best solution from the set. The best solution will be the collective optimal solution among the pareto optimal set.

3.1   Concept of Clustering

Clustering algorithms proposed in the literature can be divided into two main categories: crisp (or hard) clustering procedures where each data point belongs to only one cluster, and fuzzy clustering techniques where every data point belongs to every cluster with a specific degree of membership [23]. K-means clustering is employed [23] which is one of the widely used clustering techniques that partition n observations into k clusters in which each observation belongs to the cluster with the nearest mean.

Each cluster pass through different mutation operators mentioned in (14–18). The quality for each operator is different which creates chances for getting diverse variations in the solutions from each cluster. The solution from each cluster are merged for non-dominated sorting by crowding distance approach to get the pareto front.

3.2 Cluster Based Differential Evolution (CbDE)

Over the past few years, many researchers have contributed to make it a general and fast optimization method for any kind of objective function by twist and tune of the various constituents of DE, i.e., initialization, mutation, diversity enhancement and selection of DE [7] as well as by the choice of the control variables. The concept for clustering in DE is explained in the algorithm with small modification as per our problem is:

Initialization. Define upper and lower limits of each generators capacity and voltage of each bus. Randomly select initial value for real power generation, i.e. target vectors, by each generator uniformly over the entire bound region.

Clustering. The population is divided equally into five clusters (i.e. five groups). These groups will be used by different mutation operators for the next step.

Mutation. For a given parameter vector randomly select three vectors such that all the three indices are distinct. Add the weighted difference of two to the third to get the donor vector. However, there are different mutation operators available to be applied [24]:

$$\text{``DE/rand/1''} : V_{i,G} = X_{r_1,G} + F(X_{r_2,G} - X_{r_3,G}) \tag{14}$$

$$\text{``DE/best/1''} : V_{i,G} = X_{best,G} + F(X_{r_1,G} - X_{r_2,G}) \tag{15}$$

$$\text{``DE/current to best/1''} : V_{i,G} = X_{i,G} + F(X_{best,G} - X_{i,G}) + F(X_{r_1,G} - X_{r_2,G}) \tag{16}$$

$$\text{``DE/best/2''} : V_{i,G} = X_{best,G} + F(X_{r_1,G} - X_{r_2,G}) + F(X_{r_3,G} - X_{r_4,G}) \tag{17}$$

$$\text{``DE/rand/2''} : V_{i,G} = X_{r_1,G} + F(X_{r_2,G} - X_{r_3,G}) + F(X_{r_4,G} - X_{r_5,G}) \tag{18}$$

where $X_{i,G}$ is the ith target vector at G generation and associated mutant vector $V_{i,G} = \{V_{1i,G}, V_{2i,G}, ..., V_{ni,G}\}$. The indices r_1, r_2, r_3, r_4, r_5 are random and mutually different integers generated in the range of total population size. F is a factor in $[0, 2]$ for scaling differential vectors and $X_{best,G}$ is the individual vector with best fitness value in the population at generation G.

Recombination. Recombination incorporates successful solutions from the previous generation of each cluster. The trial vector is developed from the elements of the target vector and the elements of the donor vector. Elements of the donor vector enter the trial vector with probability CR. If random value is less then CR then donor vector is selected otherwise target vector is selected.

Selection. The best fitness value among target vector and trial vector are compared and is only allowed to move to next generation of each cluster.

Amalgamation. All the clusters are merged together to get a overall population set, when the stopping criterion has been reached. The optimum fitness value is the best that overall population set.

3.3 Performance Metric Analysis

The comparison is achieved by the performance metrics in terms of attainment surface, spacing and diversity.

Spacing. The two pareto fronts are analyzed on the basis of their distribution in the objective space. A metric to measure the range (distance) variance of the two Pareto fronts [17,18]. This metric is defined as:

$$S \triangleq \sqrt{\frac{1}{n-1} \sum_{i=1}^{n} (d - d_i)^2} \tag{19}$$

where, $d_i = min_j(|f_1{}^i(x) - f_1{}^j(x)|) + |f_2{}^i(x) - f_2{}^j(x)|), i, j = 1, ..., n$
d is the mean of all d_i, and n is the number of non-dominated vectors in the pareto set. A value of zero for this metric indicates all members of t he pareto front currently available are equidistantly spaced.

Diversity. This will evaluate the extent of the distribution of the two pareto under comparison by the obtained pareto optimal front over another pareto optimal front from the first to the last extreme member. Spread is commonly used to measure the diversity ability [19,20]. Spread measurement is as:

$$Spread = \frac{d_f + d_l + \sum_{i=1}^{|Q|-1}(d_i - d)}{d_f + d_l + (|Q| - 1)d} \tag{20}$$

$$d = \frac{\sum_{i=1}^{|Q|-1} d_i}{|Q| - 1} \tag{21}$$

$$d_i = \sqrt{(f_1^i - f_1^{i+1})^2 + (f_2^i - f_2^{i+1})^2} \tag{22}$$

where, assuming there are Q solutions, d_f is the Euclidean distance between the first extreme member in pareto and another pareto optimal front and d_l is the last member. The spread measurement evaluating extend of distribution using the distance between the members in obtained pareto optimal front and both extreme member of the true front. Thus, the smaller spread will show a better diversity ability and the minimum spread value will be zero.

3.4 Fitness Function

Penalty function is added to the objective function to punish the solution which is infeasible. The fitness function can be formulated as

$$Fitness\ function = \frac{1}{1 + F_{aug}} \tag{23}$$

$$F_{aug} = F + \lambda((V - V_{max})^2 + (V - V_{min})^2 + (Q - Q_{max})^2 + (Q - Q_{min})^2) \tag{24}$$

where, F_{aug} is the power system augmented operating objective, alpha is penalty multiplier, V_{max} and V_{min} is maximum and minimum voltage limit on each bus, Q_{max} and Q_{min} is maximum and minimum reactive power limit on each bus respectively.

4   Results and Discussion

The verification of the concepts are performed on three test systems. Also, the pareto fronts obtained by multi-objective optimization are examined by the performance metrics to measure their capability on spacing between each points and diversity in the solution over the complete search space. Transmission losses are considered in this system and is expressed by using the Newton-Raphson load flow method for 6 unit system and the B loss coefficients for 14 and 40 unit system.

4.1   Test Systems

There are three cases which are considered for the analysis:

1. Six unit system - (a) Without voltage dependency (b) With voltage dependency
2. Fourteen unit system - (a) Type 1 (b) Type 2
3. Forty unit system

Different strategies are applied on each case. All the simulations are performed on MATLAB.

Six Unit System. Six unit system - IEEE 30 bus system [25] is used for the verification of the results. To get the optimal solution for the fitness function, five real power generation and six generator voltages are the control variables in the system. The exponential load is modeled as $np = 1$ and $nq = 2$. Generator bus voltages has upper limit of $1.1pu$ and lower limit of $0.95pu$ and load bus voltages has upper limit of $1.05pu$ and lower limit of $0.90pu$.

Without voltage dependency. The multi-objective functions are optimized and presented in the Table 1. The minimum generation cost is obtained as $607.825\,\$/hr$ whereas for the minimization of emission has the best value obtained is $0.1942\,ton/hr$.

The wider range of the pareto front, shown in Fig. 1(a) generated between cost and emission avails the more choices for the deciding authority. The compromised solution shows the economical way-out for operating the system.

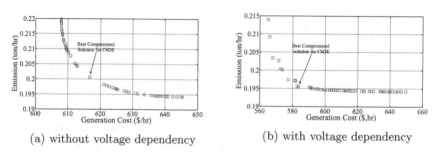

(a) without voltage dependency   (b) with voltage dependency

Fig. 1. Pareto optimal front of six unit system

With voltage dependency. The voltage dependent loads shows the reduction in the generation cost shown in Table 1. It can be observed that the maximum reduction in cost is 565 $/hr. The emission does not depend on voltage and therefore it can be seen that the loads are increased to its maximum value to reduce the emission to 0.1942 ton/hr. The minimum emission looks same as without voltage dependency case but it is not because when the cost is compared, the loads are increased to little above its nominal value to increase the cost to 649.7 $/hr.

The pareto front obtained between cost and emission, shown in Fig. 1(b), shows the extent of CbDE. The compromised solution helps in deciding the best operating region among all solutions.

Fourteen Unit System. Fourteen unit system - IEEE 118 bus system [26] is used. To get the optimal solution for the fitness function, thirteen real power generations are the control variables in the system within their specified limits.

Type 1. The multi-objective functions are optimized and presented in the Table 1. The generation cost reduces to 4306 $/hr and the emission has reduced to 4.572 ton/hr.

The pareto front generated for cost and emission is shown below in Fig. 2(a). It shows the better diversity and performance of CbDE. The compromised solution is to judge the most economical operating region for the decision making authority.

Type 2. Table 1 presents the single and multi-objective function values for cost and emission. The cost and emission minimization obtained is 20905 $/hr and 221.5 ton/hr respectively.

Cost and emission based pareto front formation which is shown in Fig. 2(b). The diverseness in the pareto front of CbDE provides the maximum deviation of operating region to decide on the best situation. The compromised solution acquaints that the system is operating at these parameters is most efficient point.

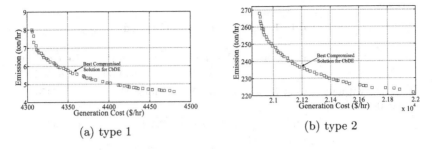

Fig. 2. Pareto optimal front of fourteen unit system

Forty Unit System. The data of forty unit system without losses is given in [27]. It is evident from the Table 1 that, for the cost minimization, the cost minimizes to 121369.1 $/hr. Whereas the emission is reduced to maximum at 188301.4 ton/hr.

Figure 3 shows the pareto front obtained for cost and emission. It is apparent that the values are maximum diverse in nature in the overall search space. The compromised solution provides the most optimal operating point among all solutions.

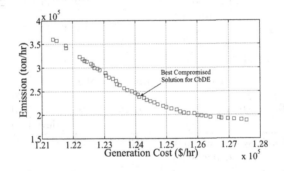

Fig. 3. Pareto optimal front of forty unit system

4.2   Performance Metric Analysis

The spacing and diversity values shown for each test system in Table 2. The values in table shows the best, mean, standard deviation and variance for each case. These values obtained are one of the best in its category with respect to the values quoted in literature earlier. The spacing metric values shows the differences in the points of each solutions obtained by each run which is spaced not so equidistantly but have wider range for the solutions in the search space. From the broader prospects, CbDE possesses the ability of precision in its solution for each run along with larger extent for the pareto fronts in the search space.

Table 1. Optimal solutions obtained

Test system	Function	Cost mini-mization	Emission min-imization	Best compro-mised
6 unit system without voltage dependency	Cost ($/hr)	**607.825**	645.3192	616.7376
	Emission (ton/hr)	0.2198	**0.1942**	0.2007
6 unit system with voltage dependency	Cost ($/hr)	**565**	649.7	583.6
	Emission (ton/hr)	0.214	**0.1942**	0.1954
14 unit system type 1	Cost ($/hr)	**4306**	4480	4355.8
	Emission (ton/hr)	8.001	**4.572**	5.596
14 unit system type 2	Cost ($/hr)	**20905**	21984	21185
	Emission (ton/hr)	268.1	**221.5**	236
40 unit system	Cost ($/hr)	**121369.1**	127561.1	124021.9
	Emission (ton/hr)	359901.4	**188301.4**	238213.3

Table 2. Performance metrics

Metric	Test system	Best	Mean	Standard deviation	Variance
Spacing	6 unit system without voltage dependency	0.3217	0.4598	0.1338	0.0179
	6 unit system with voltage dependency	0.7439	0.8588	0.1053	0.0111
	14 unit system type 1	1.2604	2.2878	0.8829	0.7795
	14 unit system type 2	6.3767	24.5796	25.0661	628.3098
	40 unit system	1449.8	1649.7	125.3	16198
Diversity	6 unit system without voltage dependency	0.5902	0.7436	0.0853	0.0073
	6 unit system with voltage dependency	0.7216	0.7781	0.0544	0.0030
	14 unit system type 1	0.648	0.7129	0.0685	0.0047
	14 unit system type 2	0.5986	0.7445	0.0735	0.0054
	40 unit system	0.5595	0.6554	0.0719	0.0052

5 Conclusion

The investigation of EED problem is performed on 6, 14 and 40 unit system. The generation cost and emission being the two contradicting objectives as one of the objective increases the other reduces and vice-versa which made a mandatory need to be applied as multi-objective problem. An illustration of cluster based differential evolution algorithm (CbDE) which has little modification over DE. CbDE is observed to give better analysis of results over the aboriginal DE among the results given in literature. The results have capability to outperform some difficult objective functions. CbDE uses the clustering phenomenon which shows the best results and wins over the diverseness among many algorithm. Each cluster is made to perform on any one mutation operator and towards the end, all the clusters are merged together to generate the overall best solution. This merger provides the diverseness and spread in the solution. This provides the win-win situation for the CbDE over other variants of DE which can also be seen in the performance metrics which justifies the diverseness and spacing in the solutions acquired.

References

1. Le, K.D., Golden, J.L., Stansberry, C., Vice, R., Wood, J., Ballance, J., Brown, G., Kamya, J.Y., Nielsen, E.K., Nakajima, H., Ookubo, M., Iyoda, I., Cauley, G.: Potential impacts of clean air regulations on system operations. IEEE Trans. Power Syst. 10(2), 647–656 (1995)
2. Zahavi, J., Eisenberg, L.: An application of the economic-environmental power dispatch. IEEE Trans. Syst. Man Cybern. 7(7), 523–530 (1977)
3. Abido, M.: A novel multiobjective evolutionary algorithm for environmental/economic power dispatch. Int. J. Electr. Power Syst. Res. 65(1), 71–81 (2003)
4. Abido, M.: A niched pareto genetic algorithm for multiobjective environmental/economic dispatch. Int. J. Electr. Power Energy Syst. 25(2), 97–105 (2003)
5. Abido, M.: Environmental/economic power dispatch using multiobjective evolutionary algorithms. IEEE Trans. Power Syst. 18(4), 1529–1537 (2003)
6. King, R.T.F.A., Rughooputh, H.C.S., Deb, K.: Evolutionary multi-objective environmental/economic dispatch: stochastic versus deterministic approaches. In: Coello Coello, C.A., Hernández Aguirre, A., Zitzler, E. (eds.) EMO 2005. LNCS, vol. 3410, pp. 677–691. Springer, Heidelberg (2005)
7. Storn, R., Price, K.: Differential evolution simple and efficient heuristic for global optimization over continuous spaces. J. Global Optim. 11(4), 341–359 (1997)
8. Vesterstrom, J., Thomsen, R.: A comparative study of differential evolution, particle swarm optimization, and evolutionary algorithms on numerical benchmark problems. In: IEEE Congress Evolutionary Computation, vol. 2, pp. 1980–1987 (2004)
9. dos Santos Coelho, L., Mariani, V.: Combining of chaotic differential evolution and quadratic programming for economic dispatch optimization with valve-point effect. IEEE Trans. Power Syst. 21(2), 989–996 (2006)
10. Perez-Guerrero, R., Cedeno-Maldonado, J.: Differential evolution based economic environmental power dispatch. In: Proceedings of the 37th Annual North American Power Symposium, pp. 191–197 (2005)

11. Sinha, N., Purkayastha, B., Purkayastha, B.: Optimal combined non-convex economic and emission load dispatch using NSDE. In: International Conference on Computational Intelligence and Multimedia Applications, vol.1, pp. 473–480 (2007)
12. Das, S., Abraham, A., Konar, A.: Automatic clustering using an improved differential evolution algorithm. IEEE Trans. Syst. Man Cybern. Part A: Syst. Hum. **38**(1), 218–237 (2008)
13. Liu, G., Li, Y., Nie, X., Zheng, H.: A novel clustering-based differential evolution with 2 multi-parent crossovers for global optimization. Int. J. Appl. Soft Comput. **12**(2), 663–681 (2012)
14. Kwedlo, W.: A clustering method combining differential evolution with the k-means algorithm. Int. Assoc. Pattern Recognit. Lett. **32**(12), 1613–1621 (2011)
15. Balamurugan, R., Subramanian, S.: Self-adaptive differential evolution based power economic dispatch of generators with valve-point effects and multiple fuel options. Int. J. Comput. Sci. Eng. **1**(1), 10–17 (2007)
16. Thitithamrongchai, C., Eua-Arporn, B.: Economic load dispatch for piecewise quadratic cost function using hybrid self-adaptive differential evolution with augmented lagrange multiplier method. In: International Conference on Power System Technology, pp. 1–8 (2006)
17. Van Veldhuizen, D., Lamont, G.: On measuring multiobjective evolutionary algorithm performance. In: Proceedings of the 2000 Congress on Evolution Computation, vol. 1, pp. 204–211 (2000)
18. Panigrahi, B., Pandi, V.R., Das, S., Das, S.: Multiobjective fuzzy dominance based bacterial foraging algorithm to solve economic emission dispatch problem. Energy **35**(12), 4761–4770 (2010)
19. Deb, K., Pratap, A., Agarwal, S., Meyarivan, T.: A fast and elitist multiobjective genetic algorithm: NSGA-II. IEEE Trans. Evol. Comput. **6**(2), 182–197 (2002)
20. Lim, K.S., Buyamin, S., Ibrahim, Z.: Convergence and diversity measurement for vector evaluated particle swarm optimization based on ZDT test problems. In: Fifth Asia Modelling Symposium (AMS), pp. 32–36 (2011)
21. Kundur, P.: Power System Stability and Control. McGraw-Hill, Inc, New York (1994)
22. Abido, M., Bakhashwain, J.: Optimal var dispatch using a multiobjective evolutionary algorithm. Int. J. Electr. Power Energy Syst. **27**(1), 13–20 (2005)
23. Jain, A.K., Murty, M.N., Flynn, P.J.: Data clustering: a review. ACM Comput. Surv. **31**(3), 264–323 (1999)
24. Qin, A.K., Suganthan, P.: Self-adaptive differential evolution algorithm for numerical optimization. In: IEEE Congress Evolutionary Computation, vol. 2. pp. 1785–1791 (2005)
25. Alsac, O., Stott, B.: Optimal load flow with steady-state security. IEEE Trans. Power Apparatus Syst. **93**(3) 745–751 (1974)
26. Guerrero, R.P.: Differential evolution based power dispatch algorithms. Master's thesis, Electrical Engineering Department, University of Puerto Rico, Mayaguez Campus (2004)
27. Basu, M.: Economic environmental dispatch using multi-objective differential evolution. Int. J. Appl. Soft Comput. **11**(2), 2845–2853 (2011)

ROBO*G* Autonomously Navigating Outdoor Robo-Guide

Kranthi Kumar Rachavarapu[✉], Irfan Feroz Gramoni Mohammed,
Chakravarthi Jada,
Harish Yenala, and Anil Kumar Vadathya

Rajiv Gandhi University of Knowledge Technologies,
Basara 504107, India
{rkkr.2100,irfan2497,chakravarthij,yharish.586,anil.rgukt}@gmail.com

Abstract. ROBO*G*: The Robo-Guide is an autonomously navigating vehicle capable of learning the navigational directions of a locality by using Artificial Neural Networks. The main task of ROBO*G* is to guide people from one location to any other location in a trained region. The prime feature of ROBO*G* is its simplicity of implementation and working. The map information is learned by Artificial Neural Network using the proposed concept of branch and node. The Multi-Layered Perceptron is trained using the standard Error Back Propagation Algorithm. Road Detection & Tracking and Destination Identification are employed to achieve autonomous navigation. All the Image Processing techniques used are computationally inexpensive. The ROBO*G* is tested successfully in the outdoor environment for autonomous navigation and due to the simplicity in implementation it can be easily trained for any region.

Keywords: Autonomous vehicle · Guiding robot · Learning strategies · Artificial Neural Networks · Image segmentation · Image Registration

1 Introduction

Autonomous vehicles are capable of navigating by sensing the environments without human intervention using various sensors equipped with them. Surrounding environments can be sensed with radar, GPS, camera or laser range finder and advanced control systems can interpret sensory information to identify appropriate navigation paths, as well as obstacles and relevant signage. Many advanced techniques are capable of fusing information from various sensors for both localization and navigation. Though the need for autonomous vehicles prevails from a long time, the demand is increasing during recent times.

Robot based guiding vehicles are special class of autonomous vehicles that can navigate between certain locations and they need to possess some intelligence to learn the path information and recognize the locations. These vehicles can be used for various tasks like guiding people to specific locations, surveillance in hazardous places like nuclear plants, carrying materials to different plants in industries, attending customers at public places etc.

© Springer International Publishing Switzerland 2015
B.K. Panigrahi et al. (Eds.): SEMCCO 2014, LNCS 8947, pp. 821–836, 2015.
DOI: 10.1007/978-3-319-20294-5_70

In recent years, very few trails are made to extend robotic technology for guiding applications in public areas. Jinny [1] is a human friendly multi-functional indoor service robot developed for real time environment. Based on its own state and condition of environments the robot can select its own motion planning algorithm. Minerva [2,3] is a robo-guide in Smithsonians National Museum and is developed for spontaneous short-term interaction suitable in tour-guide applications. The museum for Kommunikation [4] has one more Robo-guide which welcomes visitors, leading a guide tour through its appearance. Robox [5] has face tracking, motion tracking, speech recognition, speech synthesis and facial expressions capabilities. It has adopted probabilistic feature based localization and navigation. Any autonomous, particularly the guiding robots should be easily adaptive to train itself to new locations as well. All the above mentioned robotic guides are not truly adaptive with respect to change of locations. For instance the Autonomous Land Vehicle In Neural Networks (ALVINN) designed by Dean A Pomerleau [6] uses ANN and it drives autonomously at a speed of 55 miles/hr. But ALVINN is only a self driving car.

The present work ROBOG is our endeavour to propose a possible solution to all the above mentioned shortcomings. The ROBOG is specifically designed to adapt or learn particularly in prospective view. A new autonomous navigation algorithm is designed based on image processing and tested on ROBOG for practical implementation. A newly proposed Branch and Junction representation of map is used to train the Artificial Neural Networks.

This paper presents design methodology and progressive work of ROBOG. The rest of the paper is arranged as follows. Section 2 describes first generation and present generation ROBOG and their working principles. Section 3 explains map-learning using Neural Networks. Section 4 gives road tracking and its implementation followed by junction and destination identification. Finally the concluding remarks are provided in Sect. 5.

2   ROBOG

ROBOG is an autonomously navigating mobile robot created with the aim to assist people by guiding them from a specified location to a desired destination.

In our previous work [7], the Academic Block's of RGUKT-Basara, shown in Fig. 1(b), was used as a test floor and using Artificial Neural Network (ANN) the ROBOG was trained to learn the map using the proposed "Branch and Junction" concept which is explained in Sect. 3. The Academic Block model was prepared on the laboratory floor using black-tape which represents the path to be traversed and the first generation ROBOG used is shown in Fig. 1(a). ROBOG is equipped with IR sensors and Arduino Mega-2560 micro-controller, and is designed to track the path till it encounters a junction. The trained ANN will decide the steering direction based on the user's choice of destination. A complete description of work is available in [7].

This present work is a continuation of the previous work and aims at designing a mobile robot that can be used in outdoor environment as a guiding tool.

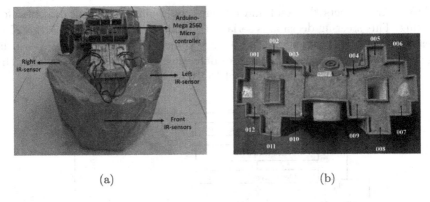

(a)   (b)

Fig. 1. (a) The first generation ROBOG (b) RGUKT-Basara academic block model

Here, the entire RGUKT-Basara campus shown in Fig. 6 is considered as the test environment. The implementation steps involved in ROBO*G* are as follows:

1. Map Learning using Artificial Neural Networks
2. Road Detection and Tracking
3. Destination Identification
4. Hardware Implementation

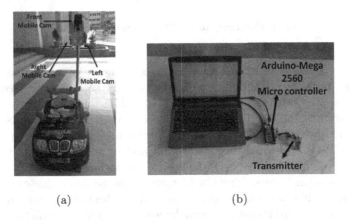

(a)   (b)

Fig. 2. (a) ROBO*G* (b) A general purpose computer equipped with arduino interfaced transmitter

The present generation ROBO*G*, shown in Fig. 2(a), is equipped with 3 cameras (Android mobile phones with IPCAM mobile application) and connected to a general purpose computer through WiFi. The first camera, aligned in the forward direction, captures images of the road and sends it to MATLAB via IPCAM application. The Road Detection and Tracking algorithm, programmed in MATLAB, detects the road and outputs the required steering direction for tracking. This steering decision is serially communicated to Arduino Mega-2560 micro-controller which controls the remote controller of the vehicle, shown in Fig. 2(b). The two side-cameras help in detecting junctions and identifying the destination. The complete work flow of ROBOG is shown in Fig. 3.

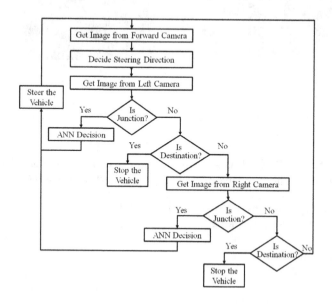

Fig. 3. Flowchart of ROBOG working principle

For every possible destination in the map, a unique numbering is assigned beforehand. Initially, the mobile robot asks the user to input the present location and required destination numbers. The mobile robot tracks the road till it encounters any intersection of roads where the Artificial Neural Network is prompted to provide a suitable steering direction based on the required destination. ROBOG executes this instruction and returns to its routine task of tracking the road. Simultaneously, the vehicle checks for the possibility of reaching the destination by matching the features of images from side-cameras with the existing models of possible destinations. If a potential destination match is found the vehicle stops its maneuvering by assuming that the vehicle has arrived at the destination.

3   Map Learning Using Artificial Neural Networks

Maps are often updated according to changes made in that particular region. The learning algorithm required should be flexible to accommodate new location information by updating existing information. This can be accomplished if the algorithm is trainable and can generalize decisions when unaccustomed situations arise. Though many other complex learning principles satisfy this criterion, ANN is a classical and simpler concept which is practically implementable and can generalize highly non-linear data.

Artificial Neural Network (ANN) is a parallel distributed processor made up of simple processing units and is used to model complex relationships between inputs and outputs. The prime strength of ANN lies in the fact that it acquires a global perspective, despite its local computations, as it exhibits a high degree of connectivity.

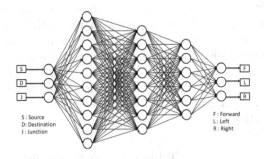

Fig. 4. ROBO*G* - Artificial neural network architecture

A single neuron called Perceptron is capable of linearly separating a set of data into two classes by providing a linear combination of applied inputs and a bias. A Multi-Layered Perceptron (MLP) is a network of one input layer, one or more hidden layers and one output layer of neurons. Every neuron in each layer of MLP is connected to all the neurons of the next layer only. Therefore the outputs of neurons from one layer form inputs for the next layer. The hidden layers enable ANN to learn complex tasks by extracting progressively more meaningful features from input patterns through higher order polynomial statistics. The signal applied to input layer propagates from one layer to other till it reaches output neuron and produces outputs. The minimization of Mean Square difference between the actual network output and the desired outputs is a necessary condition to check whether the network is learning. Often, an error-correction learning rule known as Error Back Propagation (EBP) algorithm is used to train the network. EBP provides a mathematical framework to calculate the required change in parameters in order to reduce a (error) function value. In ANN with EBP, the error produced is propagated backward through the network and is used to adjust the weights to the desired effects with the help of an error correction rule. In a statistical sense, the actual response of the network becomes closer to the desired response as the weights are updated in several propagations [8,9].

3.1   Map Representation in ANN Training

Representation of Data in a way as to be understood by intelligent systems has always been a challenge ever since the dawn of machine intelligence. Human beings perceive and learn data, patterns and processes in a remarkable way with the help of neurons in the brain. These patterns and data should be presented to intelligent systems within the reach of their capabilities.

The navigational directions i.e., the map of Rajiv Gandhi University of Knowledge Technologies (RGUKT) in aerial view and in the form of branches and nodes is shown in Fig. 6(a) and (b) respectively. Along with the intersection of paths, a 90° turn in a path is also considered as a junction since a turn is required and the path ahead cannot be detected by front-facing camera. 13 points are marked in the map and data set is collected comprising of path information (at a particular junction sequence, the direction to be navigated to reach particular destination point) from each point to every other point.

For illustrative purpose, a sample part of the map is shown in Fig. 5 and the navigational information for this map is listed in Table 1. To navigate from location 1 to location 3, at junction-1 the vehicle needs to go straight and at junction-2 right. Each row of the table is a sample of data for training. Similarly representing the whole map of RGUKT-Basara campus yielded a data-set of 946 samples for 13 locations.

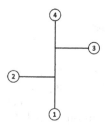

Fig. 5. Sample data

Table 1. Sample training data of ANN

SOURCE	DESTINATION	JUNCTION	FORWARD	LEFT	RIGHT
1	2	1	0	1	0
1	3	1	1	0	0
1	3	2	0	0	1
1	4	1	1	0	0
1	4	2	1	0	0

Table 2. Binarized sample training data of ANN

SOURCE	DESTINATION	JUNCTION	FORWARD	LEFT	RIGHT
1000	0100	1000	0	1	0
1000	0010	1000	1	0	0
1000	0010	0100	0	0	1
1000	0001	1000	1	0	0
1000	0001	0100	1	0	0

ANN can be trained with integer values of the three inputs but training the network with such a huge data of samples with so little variation poses a challenge and is time consuming. ANN [8,9] is capable of expertly handling binary data which limits the variation. Therefore the above presented sample data is converted into binary format as shown in Table 2. This approach makes the learning of network fast and flexible in terms of parameters used.

One advantage of this form of representation is the fact that the length of any branch between any two nodes does not play any role. It doesn't depend on vehicle capabilities and provides simple instruction of ON and OFF conditions for motors to represent Forward, Left and Right. To train the MLP, 39 inputs viz., 13 binary inputs for the initial location, 13 for the destination and 13 for the junction sequence number are given to the input layer along with the three desired outputs of steering direction. Training of network is done by taking ROBO*G* from every location in the map to all other places in all possible paths. During training, after the initial location and destination are entered, ROBO*G* navigates the road and stops when it detects a junction. It waits for the directional command fed manually by a remote and trains the network with the given inputs and the fed commands as output. When next junction is detected it increases the junction sequence number and does its routine. The MLP architecture used is a three hidden-layered structure with 100, 60 and 25 neurons in respective layers as shown in Fig. 4.

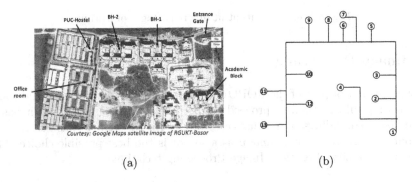

<table>
<tr><td>(a)</td><td>(b)</td></tr>
</table>

Fig. 6. (a) RGUKT-Basar aerial view (b) RGUKT map using *branch and node*

3.2 ANN Results

The convergence plot of the ANN error is shown in Fig. 7. The mean squared error is allowed to oscillate in initial iterations for faster convergence by choosing a moderate value of learning rate. The training was given for 20000 iterations. The MSE falls under the acceptable range within 10000 iterations. Figure 8 shows the three network outputs for a path from location-1 to location-13 at certain iterations. The evolution of training as the iterations are increasing can be easily observed in Fig. 8.

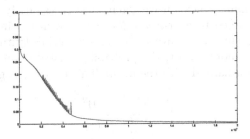

Fig. 7. Error convergence using EBP

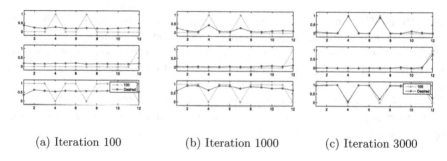

(a) Iteration 100   (b) Iteration 1000   (c) Iteration 3000

Fig. 8. Network output at different stages of learning

4   Image Processing

Though the major part of the ROBOG is representation of knowledge and learning the map information, to proceed to the practical implementation, it has to sense the surroundings and react accordingly. As the vehicle has to travel in the outdoor environments, *camera* as a sensor is the best possible choice. This creates a necessity of efficient Image Processing techniques.

4.1   Road Detection

Road Detection is an important problem in Computer Vision and has many applications in autonomous ground vehicle navigation. The primary concern is to segment the road scene from the given image. Usually, structured roads are characterized by there asphalt [10], color [11,12] or standard lane markings [13] on the edges which are easier to identify and a lot of work has been carried out using these as features. On the other hand, unstructured and dirt roads are difficult to identify and forms a better perspective for real-time cases. The present work provides a novel approach to identify the unstructured and dirt road.

The proposed method involves segmenting the road scene from given RGB image using a predefined static feature - Texture Description. Image segmentation using static features lack the generalization capacity as the features are hand-designed and are too restrictive to model the complex patterns. However these are computationally inexpensive and in most cases satisfy the requirements.

The road is assumed to a *nearly-uniform* region in the image whereas the surroundings are assumed to have a randomly varying texture. To make the uniformity measure more robust, the probability distribution is weighted with the intensity and normalized with the mean. This measure is given by

$$U = \frac{\sum_{j=1}^{L} j p(j)^2}{\sum_{j=1}^{L} j p(j)} \tag{1}$$

where L is maximum gray level intensity, $p(j)$ is the probability of occurrence of intensity j. The range of Uniformity-measure is $\frac{1}{L} \leq U \leq 1$.

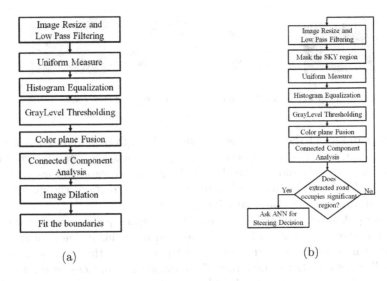

(a)   (b)

Fig. 9. (a) Road detection flow chart (b) Junction detection flow chart

Flow chart for Road Detection algorithm is given in Fig. 9. The uniformity measure is applied to a local window of 5×5 with non-overlapping blocks to reduce the time. This is applied individually to Red, Blue and Green color planes. As road is uniform in all three color planes, the common region in these three images can be a road region. This Color Plane Fusion (CPF) removes some spurious effects but not all. So for this image, best connected components are chosen, using 8-neighborhood, as road scene after dilating it with 5×5 mask to fill the gaps. As processing is on non-overlapping blocks, the edges of the extracted road will not be accurate and hence, there is a need for Boundary Fitting. The boundaries are estimated by assuming to be straight which is a valid argument in most cases but it can be generalized to any smooth curve.

Fig. 10. Step wise results for Road-Detection: Paved road

Fig. 11. Step wise results for Read Detection: Dirt path

Fig. 12. Final detected road for paved and dirt road

Figures 10 and 11 show step-wise results of Road Detection and Tracking for *Paved* road and *Dirt* road respectively. Figure 12 show the final detected road for other paved roads and dirt roads. As the proposed algorithm uses all three color planes' information along with the texture information, the performance is improved and is computationally inexpensive.

The output image is a binary image where the white pixels represent the road region. The steering direction has to be decided from this image by considering that the goal is to maintain the vehicle at the center of the road. This is done in the following way. Let m be a row of the image, D_L and D_R be the length of non-road region in the left and right side of the image in the mth row respectively as shown in Fig. 13. As the extracted road region is the approximate, consider a tolerance limit of ϵ. The pseudo code for deciding the steering direction is given below.

$$if \ \|D_L - D_R\| < \epsilon \rightarrow steer Forward$$
$$if \ \|D_L + \epsilon\| < D_R \rightarrow steer Left$$
$$if \ \|D_R + \epsilon\| < D_L \rightarrow steer Right$$

Figure 13 shows a detected case for Forward, Right and Left steering each respectively. The choice of ϵ that gave best results in our case is $N/10$ where N is the number of pixels in horizontal direction in the image.

Road Detection and Tracking based on Uniformity measure also achieves the obstacle-avoidance. This can be justified as follows. Any obstacle on the road creates non-uniform texture making itself a non-road region. As the ROBO*G* tries to steer towards the center of the road, it steers itself away from any obstacle on the road.

Fig. 13. Steering decision

4.2   Junction Identification

The aim of Junction Identification algorithm is to decide whether or not road exists in the side view of the vehicle - which creates possibility of existence of multiple paths. Whenever a junction is encountered, as multiple paths are available, the trained ANN gives suitable steering direction based on its learning history.

The flow chart of Junction Detection is given in Fig. 9(b). The process of Junction Identification is similar to that of Road Detection except with a few changes. Initially, for the given image uniform regions are extracted. After CPF, best connected components are extracted. No post processing techniques such as boundary-fit are applied. The major problem with junction detection is the existence of few spurious regions which are also uniform - like sky. Without explicitly looking into Sky-Detection problem, a few rows from the top of the image are neglected from the processing which ensures for no false decisions. If the road is present in the image then major portion of the image has to be uniform and in those cases, it is assumed that the junction is detected.

Figures 14 and 15 show cases for Junction Identification in the absence and presence of junction respectively. The threshold is taken as $M \times N/3$ where M, N represent the size of the image.

Fig. 14. Junction detection

Fig. 15. Junction detection

4.3 Road Tracking and Hardware Implementation

ROBO*G*, the mobile robot shown in Fig. 2 has Ackermann steering geometry and is remotely controlled by a wireless link of 27 MHz. It has two motors: one for thrusting the vehicle and another for steering. The steering decision, available after road-detection, is serially communicated to Arduino Mega-2560 micro-controller, via wired connection, which then activates the corresponding signal in the transmitter (shown in Fig. 2(b)). Thus the vehicle is controlled with just the images from the front camera as input. This forms a closed loop feedback system with camera as the sensor, micro-controller as controller and motors as actuators. As any practical system, the vehicle used as ROBOG is non-ideal in dynamics and therefore, to measure and restrict its imperfections, few experiments were done to find optimal conditions to ensure the flexibility and ease in implementation.

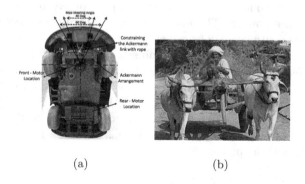

(a)   (b)

Fig. 16. (a) Bottom view of ROBOG (b) Typical indian Bullock-Cart

The range of rotation of wheels is high (more than 30° on either side) as shown in Fig. 16(a) and is not symmetric on either side. With the speed of almost one meter per second, the vehicle is capable of changing its facing angle to a large extent if the range of rotation is large. To confirm this, an experiment is done in which the vehicle is placed at the center of the road and road detection and tracking algorithm is run. The vehicle is tracking the road but the response is more oscillatory with sharp turns leading to instability. Then the vehicle is placed at different places on the road and the experiment is repeated during which the vehicle is crossing the road before suitable instruction is received. These observations can be seen in Fig. 17(a).

(a)   (b)   (c)

Fig. 17. (a) Oscillatory and road crossing (b) withoutrope (c) withrope

To show the asymmetry of range of rotation, in another experiment, the vehicle is given continuous left and right alternating instructions with a time period of 500 ms for each instruction while placing the vehicle at different places on road.

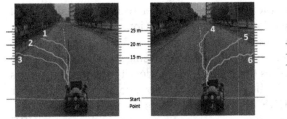

Fig. 18. Responses for various T_L and T_R **Fig. 19.** Road tracking with reduced steering angle

If the vehicle geometry were symmetrical, it should have traced a straight course with a small acceptable oscillatory behavior. But the oscillations are large and the vehicle is biased to move towards left direction and is shown in Fig. 17(b).

While conducting the experiment, *Indian Bullock-Cart* principle has been used. In the bullock cart, as shown in Fig. 16(b), two ropes tied to two oxen are used to control the rotation of the cart. Left and right ropes are pulled to turn the cart left and right side respectively. Here we delay the motion of respective wheel as analogous to pulling the rope to control the rotation of the robot.

To reduce the range of rotation a truss of the Ackermann link is tied to a stable vehicle body part to constrain its movement. The same experiment (similar to Fig. 17(b)) is repeated with the constrained range of rotation ($16°$ on either side) and the results are shown in Fig. 17(c). In these results it can be observed that the vehicle is biased to move towards right side. This is because only one rear wheel (left) of the vehicle is connected to motor as shown in Fig. 16(a) and the other one is free. The one sided thrust pushes it to right side.

This hardware bias can be compensated in the programming by varying the time period given to the transmitter to activate the turn signal for left and right instructions (hereby denoted as T_R and T_L respectively). To find the required steering angles to make the vehicle trace a straight path, different values for T_L and T_R are employed and the paths traced by the vehicle are shown in Fig. 18. From these, the optimum values of T_L and T_R, to track the path with smallest possible deviation from the center of the road, are concluded 90 msec and 125 msec respectively and can be seen in path-4 in Fig. 18.

After tuning the vehicle to these experimental results ($T_L = 90$ msec, $T_R = 125$ msec and the angle of steering to $16°$), the path traced by the robot is shown in Fig. 19 when it is placed on different locations on the road. From this we can conclude that the vehicle is maintaining its position to the center of the road irrespective of its initial location with less oscillatory behavior.

4.4   Destination Identification

Image Matching is another important problem in Computer Vision applications. Image Registration based on Normalized-Correlation methods gives good performance but they are not invariant to scale and rotation. Hence this technique has very limited application in practice. There are other techniques using Local Feature Descriptors that are invariant to lighting conditions, viewpoint, scaling, rotation, shifting and object orientation.

For Destination Identification in ROBOG, we are using Speeded Up Robust Features (SURF) [14]. This involves three steps. First, identify the interest points in the image like corners, edges, blobs, junctions etc. Next, define a feature vector around the interest points. SURF uses Harr wavelets as feature descriptors. Finally match the features using distance measure like euclidean distance. SURF is faster in implementation and it is scale and rotational invariant.

For our application, the captured image is re-sized and the Speeded Up Robust Features are estimated. Among these features, the necessary features are identified and the remaining are removed. A history of the possible destination image features is stored in memory beforehand. The present image SURF features are matched with the features of the required destination which are already estimated and stored. If the match measure is greater than threshold, the algorithm declares that the required destination is identified and stops the vehicle. If the match is not proper, the vehicle continues its navigation. The complete flow chart of Destination Identification is given in Fig. 20. A sample test case where SURF feature matching and SURF feature mismatch is shown in Fig. 21.

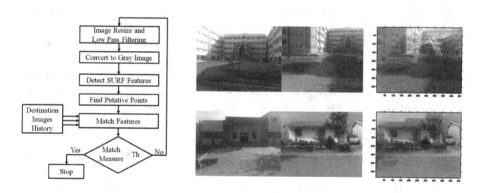

Fig. 20. Destination identification

Fig. 21. Surf features matching

A practical test case results of destination identification for 4 destination is shown in Fig. 22. In this figure, the column 2 shows the reference destination images. Column 1 shows the match percentage for each of the destinations. For maximum match, the image seen by the vehicle is shown in column-3. Here, the maximum percentage of matching is varying between 84 %–91 %. To declare as a destination, we are using a threshold of 80 % match. The spurious peak in destination-1 match percentage plot is because of the structural similarity between destination-1 and destination-2. This similarity can be observed in the reference images in column-2. However this doesn't lead to a false decision because the match percentage is less than 60 %.

All the image processing techniques are implemented in MATLAB R2012a on 2 GB RAM and AMD-TURION processor machine. The ROBO*G* is tested successfully in the outdoor environment for Road Tracking, Junction Detection and Destination Identification.

From above Sect. 3, we observe that usage of ANN makes ROBO*G* adaptive to dynamic and unmodified environment and the knowledge base is easily manageable and modifiable. From Sect. 4, we observe all image processing algorithms are less expensive and ROBO*G* is supporting perfectly which has been extensively described from the tracking & hardware implementation. The hardware system is simple and cheap. Results of all the experiments conducted show that ROBO*G* is highly reliable and user-friendly.

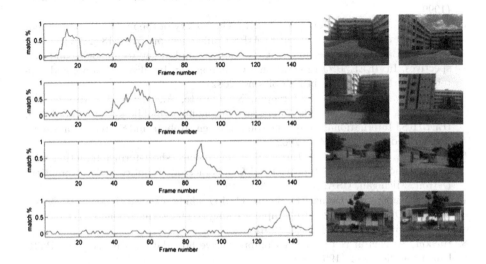

Fig. 22. Destination identification

5   Conclusions and Future Works

A Robot Guide, ROBO*G*, that can learn the navigational directions of a region using ANN is designed and developed with simple steps. A simple method is explained for the representation of map in a way to be understood by Neural Networks. The proposed approaches for Road Detection, Tracking, Junction Detection and Destination Identification are tested using the present generation ROBO*G* in the outdoor environment and the results are highly satisfactory. Since the training of ANN can be done in a simple way using the proposed representation, the ROBO*G* can easily be trained to guide for other neighborhoods. As an extension of the reported work, all the above individual tasks can be embedded and install ROBOG permanently in RGUKT. There is need for increasing the processing speed. To prove its compatibility, ease of usage and wide applicability for any locality ROBOG needs to be trained and tested for regions other than RGUKT.

References

1. Kim, G., Chung, W., Kim, K.-R., Kim, M., Han, S., Shinn, R.H.: The autonomous tour-guide robot Jinny. In: Proceedings of the 2004 IEEE/RSJ International Conference on Intelligent Robots and Systems, (IROS 2004), vol. 4, pp. 3450–3455. IEEE (2004)
2. Thrun, S., Bennewitz, M., Burgard, W., Cremers, A.B., Dellaert, F., Fox, D.: MINERVA: a second-generation museum tour-guide robot. In: IEEE International Conference on Robotics and Automation, Detroit, Michigan, USA, pp. 1999–2005 (1999)
3. Willeke, T., Kunz, C., Nourbakhsh, I.R.: The history of the mobot museum robot series: an evolutionary study. In: FLAIRS Conference, pp. 514–518 (2001)
4. Graf, B., Barth, O.: Entertainment robotics: examples, key technologies and perspectives. In: IEEE/RSJ International Conference on Intelligent Robots and Systems - Workshop Robots in Exhibitions (2002)
5. Jensen, B., Froidevaux, G., Greppin, X., Lorotte, A., Mayor, L., Meisser, M., Ramel, G., Siegwart, R.: The interactive autonomous mobile system RoboX. In: IEEE/RSJ International Conference on Intelligent Robots and Systems, Lausanne, Switzerland, pp. 1221–1227 (2002)
6. Schulte, J., Rosenberg, C., Turun, S.: Spontaneous, short-term interaction with mobile robots. In: IEEE International Conference on Robotics and Automation, Detroit, Michigan, USA, pp. 1999–2005 (1999)
7. Harish, Y., Kranthi Kumar, R., Feroz, G.M.D., Jada, C., Anil Kumar, V., Mesa, M.: ROBOG: robo guide with simple learning strategy. In: Students' Technology Symposium, pp. 224–228. IEEE (2014)
8. Haykin, S.: Neural Networks: A Comprehensive Foundation. Prentice Hall PTR, Upper Saddle River (1994)
9. Yegnanarayana, B.: Artificial Neural Networks. PHI Learning Pvt. Ltd., New Delhi (2009)
10. Alvarez, J.M.A., Lopez, A.M.: Road detection based on illuminant invariance. IEEE Trans. Intell. Transp. Syst. **12**(1), 184–193 (2011)
11. He, Y., Wang, H., Zhang, B.: Color-based road detection in urban traffic scenes. IEEE Trans. Intell. Transp. Syst. **5**(4), 309–318 (2004)
12. Rotaru, C., Graf, T., Zhang, J.: Color image segmentation in HSI space for automotive applications. J. Real-Time Image Proces. **3**(4), 311–322 (2008)
13. López, A., Serrat, J., Canero, C., Lumbreras, F., Graf, T.: Robust lane markings detection and road geometry computation. Int. J. Automot. Technol. **11**(3), 395–407 (2010)
14. Bay, H., Ess, A., Tuytelaars, T., Van Gool, L.: SURF: speeded up robust features. Comput. Vis. Image Underst. (CVIU) **110**(3), 346–359 (2008)
15. Gonzalez, R.C., Woods, R.E.: Digital image processing (2002)

Complexity Reduction Using Two Stage Tracking

Ravi Narayan Panda[1], Sasmita Kumari Padhy[2],
and Siba Prasada Panigrahi[3(✉)]

[1] Nalanda Institute of Technology, Bhubaneswar, Odisha, India
[2] National Institute of Technology, Patna, India
[3] National Institute of Technology, Yupia, Arunachal Pradesh, India
siba_panigrahy15@rediffmail.com

Abstract. The Estimation of MIMO Channels becomes a tedious task in the non-stationary environment. This is because of pilot overhead and corresponding interference. To reduce this pilot overhead, QR decomposition is proposed in the literature. However, higher the rate of the QR decomposition will result in a computationally intensive system. In this paper, we propose a two stage estimation solution to reduce the complexity as well as to eliminate the interference arising out of pilot overhead. Advantages of this paper can be seen as separation of channel impulse response and interference, elimination of the interference arising out of pilot overhead, and reduction in computational complexity.

1 Introduction

One of most popular approach in channel equalization is Decision Feedback Equalization (DFE) [1–13]. The main drawback with DFE is adjustment of its weights directly by the concerned algorithms. Alternative equalizers like RLS or Kalman filter [2–4] are computationally intensive for Multiple Input Multiple Output (MIMO) channels. To reduce the complexity associated with DFE algorithms, QR decomposition preprocessing is proposed in [16]. However, higher will be the rate of QR decomposition, the higher will be the complexity where as when this rate is lower that results in poor performance. The throughput and complexity are two implementation issues of the QR decomposition, but, the increasing complexity of QR decomposition caused by high MIMO dimension is an essential issue.

Looking at the requirement and demand for a simpler, faster system and above all less complex systems motivated the research to propose the methods based on lattice basis reduction [17], rank reduction [18], model reduction [19], peak-to-average power ratio (PAPR) reduction schemes [20], etc.

In this paper, we propose a two stage estimation process for the contaminated channel those is computationally less complex than existing proposals in the literature.

As compared to above mentioned works, advantages of this paper is faster alternative to channel inversion in a MIMO scheme. The method developed in this paper

© Springer International Publishing Switzerland 2015
B.K. Panigrahi et al. (Eds.): SEMCCO 2014, LNCS 8947, pp. 837–846, 2015.
DOI: 10.1007/978-3-319-20294-5_71

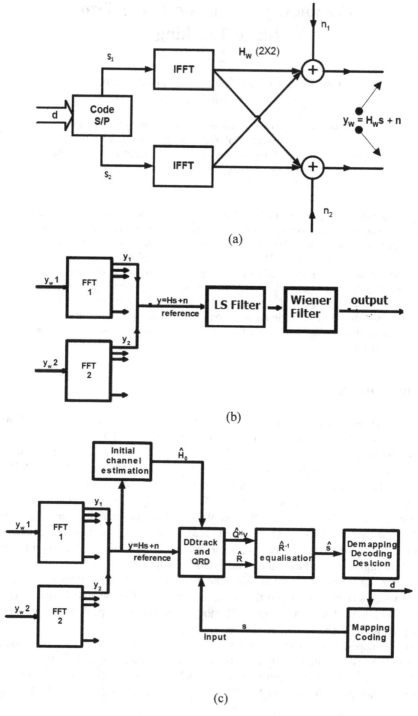

Fig. 1. (a) MIMO-OFDM transmitter (b) proposed receiver (c) QRD tracking.

can be applied to 2 X 2, 4 X 4 and even 8 X 8 MIMO systems using the architecture already developed in [21]. However, for simplicity, following sections experiments on 2 X 2 systems.

2 System Model

A simple base-band model of 2 X 2 MIMO-OFDM system is illustrated in Fig. 1. The serial data input d is encoded, then interleaved and then converted to two parallel streams of s_1 and s_2. After the IFFTs, a wideband channel H_w that corrupts the data and AWGN is added in the channel. The received signal that is wideband can be denoted by y_w. At each of the receivers, there appears an N-point FFT. This FFTs transform the wideband channel, H_w, into N groups of 2 X 2 narrowband channels, **H**. $y = \begin{bmatrix} y_1 \\ y_2 \end{bmatrix}$ being the output signal of one such group.

The system considered in this paper has similar structure for the transmitter as that of the system discussed in [16] and shown in Fig. 1 (a). The system for the receiver is different and shown in Figs. 1(b) and 1 (c) respectively for this paper and that of [16].

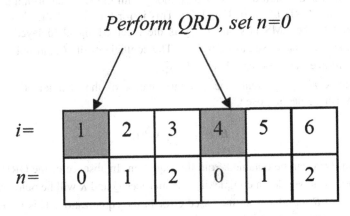

Fig. 2. An example of the indexing, QRD performed every 3rd symbol.

3 The QRD Approach

In this section, we reproduce the QRD approach of complexity reduction as suggested in [16]. This approach consists of two steps, tracking the channel matrix and tracking the upper triangular matrix respectively.

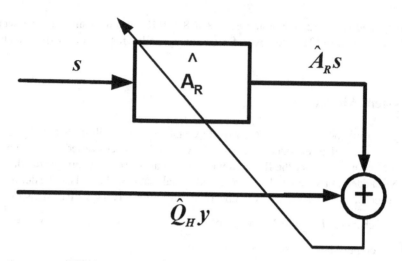

Fig. 3. LMS configuration for tracking the AR matrix.

3.1   Tracking the Channel Matrix H

A structure that is decision-directed is used along with the LMS algorithm and shown in DD track and QRD block of Fig. 1 (c). This is for tracking of the channel matrix **H**. The input to the LMS is s and the y is the received signal (delayed version of transmitted signal that is used as reference). The coefficients of $\hat{H}$ adjusted using LMS so as to minimize the error signal $\left| y - \hat{H} * s \right|$.

The matrix $\hat{H}(i)$ represents the estimate matrix of the channel at the ith time instance. It can be decomposed,

$$\hat{H}(i) = \hat{Q}(i) * \hat{R}(i) \tag{1}$$

The term $\hat{Q}^H y$ can be obtained from this equation. In absence of the QRD at every time instance, to lower down complexity, the matrices $\hat{Q}$ and $\hat{R}$ will be outdated. These outdated $\hat{Q}$ and $\hat{R}$ introduces an increased error in the equalization. This is because of the older estimates. The error matrix, $e\Gamma_{H(i)}$, is:

$$e\Gamma_{H(i)} = H_{(i)} - \hat{Q}_{i-n} * \hat{R}_{i-n} \tag{2}$$

Here $H_{(i)}$ is the actual channel matrix at the time instance, i, while $\hat{Q}_{i-n}$ and $\hat{R}_{i-n}$ are unitary and upper triangular matrices obtained n time instances earlier, from the LMS estimate $\hat{H}_{(i-n)}$. Obviously, when n = 0 (QR decomposition is performed at every time instance) $e\Gamma_{H(i)}$ will represent the tracking error of the LMS algorithm. When n = (i-1) the QR decomposition is performed only once, directly after the training sequence, and so $e\Gamma_{H(i)}$ will represent the error due to Doppler variations in the channel.

The diagrammatical representation of the indexing is shown in Fig. 2. The channel matrix $\hat{H}_{(0)}$ is obtained immediately after the initial training period, and the QR decomposition is performed to initialize the $\hat{Q}^H$ and $\hat{A}_R$ blocks. In this scenario, the LMS algorithm tracks the **AR** matrix only. The **Q** matrix is held fixed until it is updated by the next QR decomposition. At any time instance the channel matrix **H** can be presented as:

$$H_{(i)} = Q_{(i-n)} * A_{R(i)} \tag{3}$$

Here, $H_{(i)}$ is the actual channel matrix at the ith time instance, $Q_{(i-n)}$ is a unitary matrix obtained n time instances ago, and $A_{R(i)}$ is generally a non-upper triangular matrix. $A_{R(i)}$ has the upper triangular form when n = 0, immediately after a QR decomposition. As n increases $Q_{(i-n)}$ becomes more outdated, hence $A_{R(i)}$ has to change to compensate for the changing channel. As a result $A_{R(i)}$ has non-zero components introduced below the main diagonal as well as non-real components on the main diagonal.

The LMS tracking configuration is shown in Fig. 3. The key difference between this and the previous sub-section is that the reference signal for the LMS algorithm is now taken after the $\hat{Q}^H$ processing block.

If $\hat{A}_{R(i)}$ is an estimate of an upper triangular matrix $A_{R(i)}$ at the time instance i, then the error $e\Gamma_{(i)}$ due to tracking and noise can be expressed as:

$$e\Gamma_{(i)} = \hat{Q}^H_{(i-n)} * y_i - \hat{A}_{R(i)} * s_{(i)} \tag{4}$$

Substituting from Eq. (4)

$$\begin{aligned}
e\Gamma_{(i)} &= \hat{Q}^H_{(i-n)} * Q_{(i-n)} * A_{R(i)} * s_{(i)} - \hat{A}_{R(i)} * s_{(i)} + \hat{Q}^H_{(i-n)} * n_{(i)} \\
&= s_{(i)} \left[\hat{Q}^H_{(i-n)} * Q_{(i-n)} * A_{R(i)} - \hat{A}_{R(i)} \right] + \hat{Q}^H_{(i-n)} * n_{(i)}
\end{aligned} \tag{5}$$

This error signal is used to update the LMS tracking algorithm [190].

The R^{-1} equalization block of Fig. 1(c) makes the back substitution process. A modified copy of $\hat{A}_{R(i)}$ is needed. The $\hat{A}_{R(i)}$ matrix, non-upper triangular matrix, is not suitable for this block. On the main diagonal all the non-zero imaginary elements and also all the elements below the main diagonal in this correction are set to zero. So formed UTM, $\hat{R}_f$ can be used for back substitution. However, this operation of forcing to zero, generates an additional error.

The effective channel estimate, $\hat{H}_{f(i)}$ along with tracking and zero-forcing errors hence:

$$\hat{H}_{f(i)} = \hat{Q}_{(i-n)} \circ \hat{R}_{f(i)} \tag{6}$$

The new error matrix becomes:

$$e\Gamma R_{(i)} = H_{(i)} - \hat{H}_{f(i)} \tag{7}$$

Expanding (7) using Eq. (6) gives:

$$e\Gamma R_{(i)} = Q_{(i-n)} * A_{R(i)} - \hat{Q}_{(i-n)} * R_{f(i)} \tag{8}$$

When this error power increases more than a threshold, user preset, the QRD can be undertaken on $\hat{A}_{R(i)}$ in order to bring it back to a form of upper triangular matrix and to unitary matrix **Q** updation as:

$$\hat{H}_{(i)} = \hat{Q}_{(i-n)} * \hat{A}_{R(i)} = \hat{Q}_{(i-n)} * QRD\left(\hat{A}_{R(i)}\right) = \hat{Q}_{(i-n)} * Q'_{(i)} * R'_{(i)} \tag{9}$$

Here, $\hat{Q}_{(i-n)} * Q'_{(i)}$ forms a new unitary matrix and $R'_{(i)}$ is the new upper triangular matrix that updates the $\hat{A}_R$ value.

4 Proposed Two-Stage Approach

If the channel covariance matrix, $R = E[hh^H]$ is known, then the MMSE criterion for the equalizer is [22, 23]:

$$\min\left\{E\left[(h - \hat{h})^H (h - \hat{h})\right]\right\} \tag{10}$$

Where, $\hat{h} = Gr$ = MMSE estimation of CIR vector, $G = R[R + \sigma^2 Q^{-1}]^{-1}$ $(S^H S)^{-1} S^H$ = channel estimation filter, $Q = S^H S$ = correlation matrix that is pilot-dependent and main concern of this article.

This paper proposes a two stage channel estimation scheme. These two steps are discussed below.

Step-1:

Design the least square (LS) filter to eliminate the interference because of non-orthogonal pilots, subjected to a LS constraint. Let the filter is G_{LS}.

Select the G_{LS} according to [24]:

$$\min_{G_{LS}}\left\{(r - S\hat{r})^H (r - S\hat{r})\right\} = (S^H S)^{-1} S \tag{11}$$

Output of step-1:

$$\hat{r} = G_{LS}r = G_{LS}Sh + G_{LS}n \tag{12}$$

Linear processing of which gives rise to:

$$\hat{r} = h + G_{LS}n = h + \hat{n} \tag{13}$$

Where, $\hat{n}$ is zero-mean complex Gaussian noise vector.

It is clear from above equation that the output contains of two distinct parts, CIR vector and noise, clearly pointing towards elimination of other interferences.

Step-2:

Design the wiener filter for improvement in quality of the channel estimation subject to knowledge on the channel statistics. Let the filter is $\hat{G}$.

Where, $\hat{h} = \hat{G}\hat{r}$.

The wiener filter solution as provided in [15] given by:

$$\hat{G} = R\left[R + \sigma^2 Q^{-1}\right]^{-1} \tag{14}$$

Hence combined response in the two steps given by:

$$G = \hat{G}G_{LS} = R\left[R + \sigma^2 Q^{-1}\right]^{-1} Q^{-1} S^H \tag{15}$$

5 Computational Complexity Comparison

The computational complexity of proposed two stage approach depends on computation of Eq. (15). Computation of the LS filter of step 1 depends mainly on computation of the two-dimensional search in Eq. (12) and Computation of the wiener filter of step 2 once again two-dimensional search in Eq. (14).

On the other hand QRD approach of [16] requires computation of three-dimensional Eq. (9).

Hence, computational complexities encountered in the proposed approach are less than that of QRD approach.

6 Simulation Results

6.1 Scenario

In this paper, we have considered channel F 802.11n standard, the same channel considered in [14], for the purpose of ease in comparison. The channel is a low Doppler channels. Assuming stationary terminals but with moving scatterers. Simulation parameters and assumptions chosen are also the same as in [16] and outlined below:

- An OFDM symbol of period around 4µsec (3.2 µs with a cyclic prefix of 0.8 µs)
- N = number of sub-carriers = 64
- A system bandwidth of 20 MHz
- Modulation is QPSK
- Perfect hardware, perfect synchronization and no offset in frequency

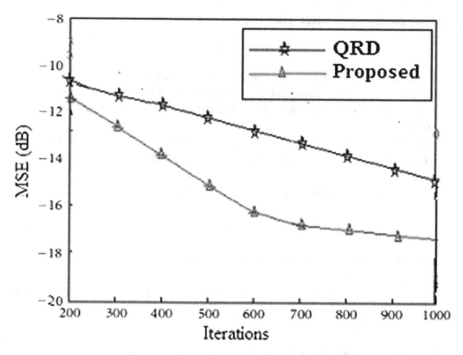

Fig. 4. MSE performance of the equalizers.

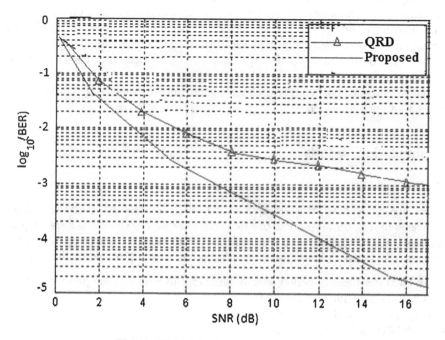

Fig. 5. BER performance of the equalizers.

For the comparisons, two parameters, Mean Square Error (MSE) & Bit Error Rate (BER), were taken as performance index.

For convergence comparison among the equalizers, i.e., evaluation of MSE under similar conditions, Signal to Noise Ratio (SNR) is kept fixed at 10 dB.

7 Results and Analysis

Figure 4 shows the error convergence at 10 dB for different equalizers. It is evident from the figure that, convergence characteristics of proposed approach is better than QRD based approach.

BER comparison among the equalizers is depicted in Fig. 5. It is seen from Fig. 5 that the proposed equalizer performs better than QRD based approach.

8 Conclusion

Estimation of MIMO Channels becomes a tedious task in the non-stationary environment. This is because of pilot overhead and corresponding interference. To reduce this pilot overhead, QR decomposition is proposed in the literature. However, higher rate of the QR decomposition becomes computationally intensive.

In this paper, we propose a two stage estimation solution to reduce the complexity as well as to eliminate the interference arising out of pilot overhead. Advantages of this paper can be seen as separation of channel impulse response and interference, elimination of the interference arising out of pilot overhead, and reduction in computational complexity.

References

1. Jiang, W., Asai, Y., Onizawa, T., Aikawa, S.: Fast algorithm for decision feedback equalization in multiple input multiple output channel. In: Vehicular Technology Conference, vol. 5, pp. 2423–2428 (2006)
2. Komninakis, C., Fraqouli, C., Sayed, A.H., Wesel, R.D.: Multi-input multi-output fading channel tracking and equalization using Kalman estimation. IEEE Trans. Sig. Process. **50**, 1065–1076 (2002)
3. Fechtel, S.A., Meyr, H.: An investigation of channel estimation and equalization techniques for moderately rapid fading HF-channels. ICC **2**, 768–772 (1991)
4. Tong, J.: An adaptive channel tracking method for MIMO-OFDM systems. In: ICCCAS, vol. 1, pp. 354–358 (2004)
5. Zia, A.: Channel identification and tracking using alternating projections. Statistical Signal Processing, pp. 430–433 (2003)
6. Schafhuber, D., Matz, G., Hlawatsch, F.: Kalman tracking of time varying channels in wireless MIMO-OFDM systems. Sign. Syst. Comput. **2**, 1261–1265 (2003)
7. Oberli, C.: Maximum likelihood tracking algorithms for MIMO-OFDM. Commun. **4**, 2468–2472 (2004)

8. Deng, K., Yin, Q., Meng, Y.: Blind symbol detection for multiple-input multiple-output systems via particle filtering. IEEE Int. Conf. Acoust. Speech Sig. Process. **3**, 1041–1044 (2005)
9. Cescato, D., Bölcskei, H.: Algorithms for interpolation-based QR decomposition in MIMO-OFDM systems. IEEE Trans. Signal Process. **59**(4), 1719–1733 (2011)
10. Po-Lin, C., Lin-Zheng, H., Li-Wei, C., Yuan-Hao, H.: Interpolation-based QR decomposition and channel estimation processor for MIMO-OFDM system. IEEE Transact. Circuits Syst. I **58**(5), 1129–1141 (2011)
11. Bouchired, S., Ibnkahla, M., Roviras, D., Castanie, F.: Equalization of satellite UMTS channels using neural network devices. In: Proceedings of IEEE, ICASSP 1999, Phoenix, May 1999
12. Lin, H., Yamashita, K.: Hybrid simplex genetic algorithm for blind equalization using RBF networks. Math. Comput. Simul. **59**, 293–304 (2002)
13. Han, S., Pedrycz, W., Changwook, H.: Nonlinear channel blind equalization using hybrid genetic algorithm with simulated annealing. Math. Comput. Model. **41**, 697–709 (2005)
14. Lucky, R.W.: Automatic equalization of digital communication. Bell Syst. Tech. J **44**, 547–588 (1965)
15. George, D.A., Bowen, R.R., Storey, J.R.: An adaptive decision feedback equalizer. IEEE Transact. Commun. Technol. (COM) **19**, 281–293 (1971)
16. Gor, L: Complexity Reduction In: Multiple Input Multiple Output Algorithms, Ph.d. thesis. Victoria University (2007)
17. Fischer, R.F.H., Windpassinger, C., Stierstorfer, C., Siegl, C., Schenk, A., Abay, U.: Lattice-reduction-aided MMSE equalization and the successive estimation of correlated data. AEU – Int. J. Electron. Commun. **65**(8), 688–693 (2011)
18. Oliver, J., Aravind, R., Prabhu, K.M.M.: A krylov: Subspace based low-rank channel estimation in OFDM systems. Sig. Process. **90**(6), 1861–1872 (2010)
19. Panda, R.N., Padhy, S.K., Prasad, S., Panigrahi, S.P.: Reduced complexity dynamic systems using approximate control moments. Circuits Syst. Sig. Process. **31**(5), 1731–1744 (2012)
20. Gao, J., Zhu, X., Nandi, A.K.: Independent component analysis for multiple-input multiple output wireless communication systems. Sig. Process. **91**(4), 607–623 (2011)
21. Huang, Z., Tsai, P.: Efficient implementation of QR decomposition for Gigabit MIMO-OFDM systems. IEEE Transact. Circuits Syst. I **58**(10), 2531–2542 (2011)
22. Widrow, B., Stearns, S.: Adaptive Signal Processing. Prentice-Hall Inc., Murray Hill (1985)
23. Li, H.Y., Fu, H.L., Guan, A.H.: Game theoretic power control algorithm in cognitive radio networks. J. Chongqing Univ. Posts Telecommun.: Nat. Sci. **22**(6), 756–760 (2010)
24. Zhao, C.S., Kwak, K.: Joint sensing time and power allocation in cooperatively cognitive networks. IEEE Commun. Lett. **14**(2), 163–165 (2010)

FFA Trained Radial Basis Function Neural Networks in Channel Equalization

Pradumna Mohapatra[1] and Siba Prasada Panigrahi[2(✉)]

[1] Orissa Engineering College, Bhubaneswar, Odisha, India
[2] National Institute of Technology, Yupia, Arunachal Pradesh, India
siba_panigrahy15@rediffmail.com

Abstract. This paper introduces one novel method for Channel Equalization. Though, use of RBFNN for Channel Equalization is mature in the literature, use of FFA trained RBFNN is the first of its kind used in this paper. In this paper, FFA is used as training algorithms for RBFNN equalizers. In contrast to methods available in the literature where the problem of channel equalization is treated as an optimisation problem, but in this paper we treat it as a classification problem. Importance of the proposed equalizer is that, as evident from simulation results, outperforms contemporary RBF based equalizers of the literature.

1 Introduction

A Channel equalizer recovers digital information from digital communication channels. The art of using ANN for wireless communication has been gaining momentum since last three decades [1–4]. As compared to FFNN, the RBFNN:

- Has a more compact structure and hence, it requires easier training procedure and less training time [5].
- Has good generalization ability and it can approximate nonlinear functions to arbitrary precision [6].

All these features qualify the RBFNN to be a more preferable choice for the problem of channel equalization. Also, RBFNN equalizers.

- Provide better stability, speed of convergence and convergence properties [7].
- Simulations performed in the literature reveals that the RBF equalizer produces superior performance as compared to other existing ANN based equalizers [8].

Hence the works on channel equalization using RBFNN became an established and an active area of academic research and development [3, 9–14].

However, RBFNN training always remains as a challenge because of existing trial-and-error methods. In order to avoid these problems, Barreto et al. [15] used GA and Feng [16] used PSO to decide the centers of hidden neurons, spread and bias parameters by minimizing the MSE of the desired outputs and actual outputs.

The main contribution of this research is the use of FFA trained RBF (FFRBF) for the problem of channel equalization. The important difference of the method used in literature and in this paper, as mentioned before, is that use of optimization algorithms

© Springer International Publishing Switzerland 2015
B.K. Panigrahi et al. (Eds.): SEMCCO 2014, LNCS 8947, pp. 847–855, 2015.
DOI: 10.1007/978-3-319-20294-5_72

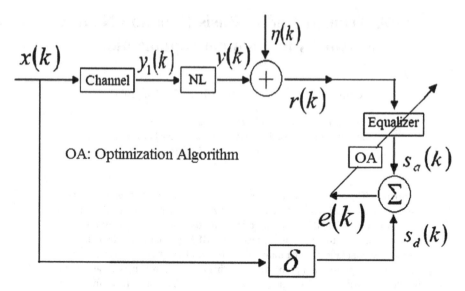

Fig. 1. Base-band model of digital communication system.

for finding optimal RBFNN while those used in literature use the traditional hit and trial methods. Importance of the proposed equalizers is proved through simulation results. It is seen from the simulation results that these equalizers outperforms RBF [8, 9] based equalizers available in the literature.

The organization of the paper is as follows: Sect. 2 discusses the problem statement. A discussion on the FFRBF equalizer is provided in Sect. 3. Performance evaluation of the proposed equalizers, through simulations, find place in Sect. 4. Finally conclusion of the paper is outlined in Sect. 5.

2   RBFNN Equalizer

Nonlinear equalization of base-band equivalent of digital communication systems is depicted in Fig. 1. For a binary transmitted sequence, which is denoted as $x(k)$ for the kth time instance, A FIR model is widely used to model a linear channel whose output, $y_1(k)$, at time instant k is written as:

$$y_1(k) = \sum_{i=0}^{N-1} h_i x(k-i) \tag{1}$$

Here, $h_i(i = 0, 1, \cdots N - 1)$ are the channel tap values and N is the length of the FIR channel. Nonlinear distortions introduced in the channel during the process of transmission, is shown by a separate block 'NL'. A popular nonlinear function is:

$$y(k) = F(y_1(k)) = y_1(k) + by_1(k)^3 \tag{2}$$

Here, b is a constant value. Hence, the output of the nonlinear channel is:

$$y(k) = \left(\sum_{i=0}^{N-1} h_i x(k-i)\right) + b\left(\sum_{i=0}^{N-1} h_i x(k-i)\right)^3 \tag{3}$$

The output of the channel $y(k)$ is corrupted by noise, $\eta(k)$, which is modelled in this paper, as an additive white Gaussian noise process with a zero mean and variance σ^2. The corrupted signal $r(k)$ is received at the receiver, i.e., input to the equalizer, is given by:

$$r(k) \cong r(k) + \eta(k) \tag{4}$$

Equalizer cancels the effects of channel distortion and noise and recovers transmitted symbol, $x(k-\delta)$, from the knowledge of the received signal samples, where 'δ' is the transmission delay associated with the channel.

The desired signal is a delayed version of transmitted signal and is denoted as $s_d(k)$ is defined by:

$$s_d(k) = x(k-\delta) \tag{5}$$

The equalization process is treated as a classification problem [2–4], where the equalizer task is to partition the input equalizer space $x(k) = [x(k), x(k-1), \cdots x(k-N+1)]^T$ into two distinct regions (for binary transmitted symbols, $x(k-\delta)$).

The optimal solution of the nonlinear classification method is the Bays solution. The decision function for the optimal Bays solution is:

$$f_{bay}(x(k)) = \sum_{j=1}^{N} \beta_j \exp\left(\frac{-\|x(k) - c_j\|}{2\sigma^2}\right) \tag{6}$$

For binary transmitted symbols:

$$\beta_j = \begin{cases} +1 & for \quad c_j \in C_d^{(+1)} \\ -1 & for \quad c_j \in C_d^{(-1)} \end{cases} \tag{7}$$

Here, $C_d^{(+1)}/C_d^{(-1)}$ is the set of channel states, c_j is binary symbol, $x(k-\delta) = +1/-1$ and σ^2 is the noise variance.

In Fig. 1, the block "Equalizer" is a RBF Neural Network. Number of layers and number of neurons in each layer (except input layer) for this RBFNN are decided by optimised values and combination of these values using optimization algorithms. In input layer, number of neuron is kept same as N, i.e., number of channel taps.

The response of the equalizer is:

$$f_{RBF}(s(k)) = \sum_{j=1}^{z} w_j \exp\left(\frac{-\|s(k) - t_j\|^2}{\alpha_j}\right)$$

$$= W^T(k)\phi(k) \tag{8}$$

Here,

$$W(k) = [w_1(k), w_2(k), \cdots w_z(k)]^T$$

$$\phi(k) = [\varphi_1(k), \varphi_2(k), \cdots \varphi_z(k)]^T$$

$$\varphi_j = \exp\left(\frac{-\|s(k) - t_j\|^2}{\alpha_j}\right) \quad \text{for} \quad j = 1, 2, \cdots z$$

Here, t_j and α_j are respectively: the vectors centers and the spreads of the neurons hidden layer (s). The vector w_j contains the weights connections.

The output of the RBFNN (8) implements the Bayesian decision function (6), if the centers of hidden layer neurons t_j are equals to the channel states c_j and the weights connections are adequately regulated.

The decision function of the RBFNN, i.e., output of equalizer, is:

$$s_d(k - \delta) = \begin{cases} +1 & f_{ANN}(x(k)) \geq 0 \\ -1 & elsewhere \end{cases} \tag{9}$$

Hence, the difference between the equalizer output (i.e., $\hat{x}(k - \delta)$) and desired signal (i.e., $x(k - \delta)$) is termed as error, $e(k)$, and used for updating the equalizer weights. Two parameters, MSE and BER ($E[e(k)].E$ being expectation operator), are popularly taken as performance index.

3 The FFA Trained RBF, FFRBF

In One of recently proposed optimization method is FFA [18, 19], In this paper we make use of FFA for training of RBFNN equalizers as discussed in following few lines.

The individuals of the fireflies include the parameters of weights (w), spread parameters (α), center vector (c) and the bias parameters (β). The mean vector c_i of the ith neuron of hidden layers is defined by $c_i = (c_{i1}, c_{i2}, \cdots, c_{im})$, therefore, the parametric vector t_i of each of fireflies with $IJ + I + MI + J$ parameters is expressed as:

$$t_i = \begin{pmatrix} w_{11}^i, w_{12}^i, \cdots, w_{IJ}^i, \alpha_1^i, \alpha_2^i, \cdots, \alpha_I^i, c_{11}^i, c_{12}^i, \\ \cdots c_{1m}^i, \cdots c_{I1}^i, c_{I2}^i, \cdots, c_{Im}^i, \beta_1^i, \cdots \beta_J^i \end{pmatrix} \tag{10}$$

As we mean in this paper, each of fireflies can represent a specific RBF network for equalization. In FF-based training algorithm, the optimum vectors t_i of firefly of specific trained RBF network can maximize the fitness function defined as:

$$f(t_i) = \frac{1}{1 + MSE} = \frac{1}{1 + \frac{1}{Q} \sum\limits_{k=1}^{Q} \|d(k) - y(k)\|^2} \tag{11}$$

Here, $d(k)$ and $y(k)$ are the desired output and actual output for training sample x_i of RBF network designed by parametric vector t_i and that of equalizer as defined earlier. The Q is the number of the training samples.

4 Simulation Results and Analysis

For performance evaluation of proposed equalizers simulations were conducted for the following two channels:

$$H_1(z) = [0.26 \quad 0.93 \quad 0.26] \tag{12}$$

$$H_2(z) = [1 \quad 1 \quad 1] \tag{13}$$

Non-linearity as discussed in Eq. (2) and noise additive white Gaussian noise process with a zero mean and unit variance is introduced. For the comparisons, two parameters, MSE & BER, were taken as performance index. For evaluation of MSE, SNR is kept fixed at 10 dB.

MSE was averaged over the simulations run for 300 iterations. For population based algorithms, number of population chosen was 50.

For the simulations parameters of FFA is taken same as [20]. These are Attractiveness = 1.0; Number of particles = 50; Light Absorption Coefficient = 2.0; Iterations = 1000.

The comparisons were made in order to evaluate performance of proposed equalizers: Proposed FFRBF equalizer with GAP-RBF [17] and MCRBF [10] equalizers.

Figures 2 and 3 shows MSE performance of the equalizers for channel (12) and (13) respectively. While evaluating MSE for channel (12) from Fig. 2, following observations were obtained.

- It was observed that, GAP-RBF, MCRBF and proposed FFRBF equalizers converges after 249, 228 and 165 iterations respectively.
- Proposed PRBF shows better convergence characteristics as compared to other equalizers

While evaluating MSE for channel (13) from Fig. 3, following observations were obtained.

- None of the equalizers converge within 300 iterations, with proposed FFRBF showing better convergence characteristics as compared to other equalizers

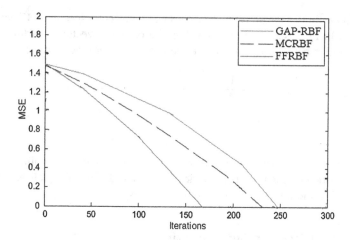

Fig. 2. MSE performance of proposed equalizers for channel (12)

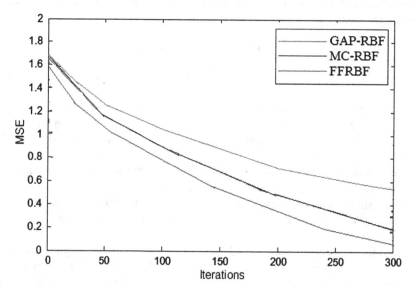

Fig. 3. MSE performance of proposed equalizers for channel (13).

Figures 4 and 5 shows BER performance of the equalizers for channel (12) and (13) respectively. While evaluating BER for channel (12) from Fig. 4, it is observed that:

- For all the values of SNR, FFRBF performs better than other equalizers

While evaluating BER for channel (13) from Fig. 5, following observations were obtained.

- For all SNR values, FFRBF outperforms other equalizers.

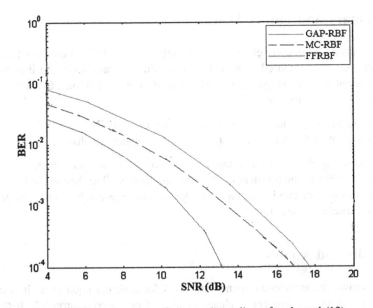

Fig. 4. BER performance of proposed equalizers for channel (12).

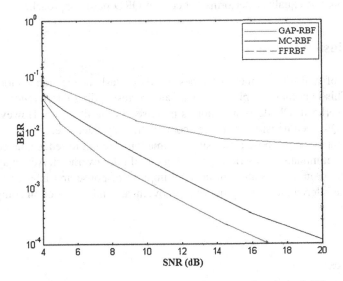

Fig. 5. BER performance of proposed equalizers for channel (13).

5 Summary and Future Work

This paper proposed one novel equalizer, namely FFRBF. FFA is used for training of RBF equalizer. As compared to RBF based equalizers available in the literature, the proposed equalizers of this paper outperform in all noise conditions. Contributions by this paper can be outlined as:

- Development of one new methods for training of RBFNN
- Development of three new, robust, stable and efficient equalizers.

This paper applied the advantages, as explained in the literature, of RBFNN training using FFA in the problem of channel equalization. The theoretical background for better performance can be seen as a pointer for future research and may be reflected in some of articles in near future..

6 Results and Analysis

Figure 4 shows the error convergence at 10 dB for different equalizers. It is evident from the figure that, convergence characteristics of proposed approach is better than QRD based approach.

BER comparison among the equalizers is depicted in Fig. 5. It is seen from Fig. 5 that the proposed equalizer performs better than QRD based approach.

7 Conclusion

Estimation of MIMO Channels becomes a tedious task in the non-stationary environment. This is because of pilot overhead and corresponding interference. To reduce this pilot overhead, QR decomposition is proposed in the literature. However, higher rate of the QR decomposition becomes computationally intensive.

In this paper, we propose a two stage estimation solution to reduce the complexity as well as to eliminate the interference arising out of pilot overhead. Advantages of this paper can be seen as separation of channel impulse response and interference, elimination of the interference arising out of pilot overhead, and reduction in computational complexity.

References

1. Seyman, M.N., Taşpınar, N.: Channel estimation based on neural network in space time block coded MIMO–OFDM system. Digit. Sig. Proc. 23(1), 275–280 (2013)
2. Ruan, X., Zhang, Y.: Blind sequence estimation of MPSK signals using dynamically driven recurrent neural networks. Neurocomput. 129, 421–427 (2014)
3. Rizaner, A.: Radial basis function network assisted single-user channel estimation by using a linear minimum mean square error detector under impulsive noise. Comput. Electr. Eng. 39 (4), 1288–1299 (2013)

4. Sahoo, H.K., Dash, P.K., Rath, N.P.: NARX model based nonlinear dynamic system identification using low complexity neural networks and robust H∞ filter. Appl. Soft Comput. **13**(7), 3324–3334 (2013)

5. Qasem, S.N., Shamsuddin, S.M., Zain, A.M.: Multi-objective hybrid evolutionary algorithms for radial basis function neural network design. Knowl.-Based Syst. **27**, 475–497 (2012)

6. Dong, X., Wang, C., Zhang, Z.: RBF neural network control system optimized by particle swarm optimization. In: 3rd IEEE International Conference on Computer Science and Information Technology, pp. 348–351Chengdu-China (2010)

7. Kahphooi, S., Zhihong, M., Wu, H.R.: Nonlinear adaptive RBF neural filter with Lyapunov adaptation algorithm and its application to nonlinear channel equalization. In: Proceedings of the Fifth International Symposium on Signal Processing and Its Applications, vol.1, pp. 151–154 (1999)

8. Chen, S., Mulgrew, B.: Grant, M.P.: A clustering technique for digital communication channel equalisation using radial basis function network. IEEE Trans. Neural Netw. **4**(4), 570–579 (1993)

9. Rajbhandari, S., Faith, J., Ghassemlooy, Z., Angelova, M.: Comparative study of classifiers to mitigate intersymbol interference in diffuse indoor optical wireless communication links. Optik – Int. J. Light Electron Opt. **124**(20), 4192–4196 (2013)

10. Zeng, X., Zhao, H., Jin, W., He, Z., Li, T.: Identification of nonlinear dynamic systems using convex combinations of multiple adaptive radius basis function networks. Measurement **46**, 628–638 (2013)

11. Yee, M.S., Yeap, B.L., Hanzo, L.: Radial basis function-assisted turbo equalization. IEEE Trans. Commun. **51**(4), 664–675 (2003)

12. Xie, N., Leung, H.: Blind equalization using a predictive radial basis function neural network. Trans. Neural Netw. **16**(3), 709–720 (2005)

13. Lee, J., Sankar, R.: Theoretical derivation of minimum mean square error of RBF based equalizer. Sig. Process. **87**, 1613–1625 (2007)

14. Li, M.N., Huang, G.B., Saratchandran, P., Sundarrajan, N.: Performance evaluation of GAP-RBF network in channel equalization. Neural Process. Lett. **22**, 223–233 (2005)

15. Barreto, A.M.S., Barbosa, H.J.C., Ebecken, N.F.F.: Growing compact RBF networks using a genetic algorithm. In: Proceedings of the VII Brazilian Symposium on Neural Networks, pp. 61–66 (2002)

16. Feng, H.M.: Self-generating RBFNs using evolutional PSO learning. Neurocomput. **70**, 241–251 (2006)

17. Mandal, A., Zafar, H., Das, S., Vasilakos, A.V.: A modified differential evolution algorithm for shaped beam linear array antenna design. Prog. Electromagnet. Res. **125**, 439–457 (2012)

18. Yang, X.S.: Nature-inspired Metaheuristic Alogirthms. Luniver Press, Frome (2008)

19. Yang, X.S.: Firefly algorithm, stochastic test functions and design optimization. Int. J. Bio-inspired Comput. **2**(2), 78–84 (2010)

20. Shafaati, M., Mojallali, H.: Modified firefly optimization for IIR system identification. Control Eng. Appl. Inf. **14**(4), 59–69 (2012)

Image Inpainting with Modified F-Transform

V.B. Surya Prasath[1](✉) and R. Delhibabu[2,3]

[1] University of Missouri-Columbia, Columbia, MO 65211, USA
prasaths@missouri.edu
http://web.missouri.edu/~prasaths
[2] Knowledge-Based System Group,
Higher Institute of Information Technology and Information Systems,
Kazan Federal University, Kazan, Russia
[3] Department of CSE, SSN Engineering College, Chennai 603110, India
delhibabur@ssn.edu.in

Abstract. Restoring damaged images is an important problem in image processing and has been studied for applications such as inpainting missing regions, art restoration. In this work, we consider a modified (fuzzy transform) F-transform for restoration of damages such as holes, scratches. By utilizing weights calculated from known image regions using local variance from patches, we modify the classical F-transform to handle the missing regions effectively with edge preservation and local smoothness. Comparison with interpolation - nearest neighbor, bilinear and modern inpainting - Navier - Stokes, fast-marching methods illustrate that by using our proposed modified F-transform we obtain better results.

Keywords: Image inpainting · Fuzzy transform · Local variance · Approximation · Interpolation

1 Introduction

Image inpainting is a relatively modern image processing problem motivated from the restoration tasks performed in damaged real-life artworks. Application areas include reconstruction, artwork restoration and intelligent filling in of missing information. Motivated by the use of manual replication of known regions interpolation methods are utilized to obtain values in missing digital image regions. Unfortunately, interpolation techniques are limited to small support and better propagation of information from known image regions is required.

In a ground-breaking work, Bertalmio et al [1] proposed an automatic variational inpainting method which relies on diffusing pixels values on the boundary of missing regions. The method proposed by Bertalmio et al [2] is based on Navier-Stokes equation and utilize the properties of diffusion [3]. Later Sapiro [4] extended the method to handle color images and videos. Criminisi et al [5] proposed exemplar-based texture synthesis method. Telea [6] utilized the fast marching method [7] to tackle the inpainting problem and obtained better restoration

© Springer International Publishing Switzerland 2015
B.K. Panigrahi et al. (Eds.): SEMCCO 2014, LNCS 8947, pp. 856–867, 2015.
DOI: 10.1007/978-3-319-20294-5_73

results when the damage is due to scratches. Unfortunately diffusion based models can have leakage due to excessive smoothing, and edges can also be blurred [8–10], see [11] for a review on variational and diffusion based schemes.

In this paper, we use a fuzzy transform based image restoration model for damaged digital images. Following the work of Perfillieva [12] we consider (fuzzy transform) F-transform with Ruspinis condition along h-uniform property. By utilizing local patches information from known image regions we obtain better information for filling in missing regions. A multi-step approach is considered following Perfilieva and Vlašánek [13] and the weights from local patches [14] are fused along with the F-transform reconstruction. Note that F-transform is different from traditional interpolation techniques and by using a generating function based partition of the image domain we obtain better inpainting results as shown by experimental results. Further, we compare our technique to traditional interpolation techniques and modern inpainting methods of [2,6]. Experimental results on scratch and text corrupted images indicate our proposed method performs better and the reconstructions are accurate.

The rest of the paper is organized as follows. Section 2 introduces the method originally proposed by Perfilieva [12] with our modification. Section 3 show applications in various damaged digital images and comparison with related schemes. Finally, Sect. 4 concludes the paper.

2   F-Transform Image Reconstruction

We recall the F-transform introduced by Perfilieva [12] in 2006 which provides a correspondence of a two dimensional discrete function with its matrix (finite set) of F-transform components.

Let $\Omega = \{(i,j) \,|\, i,j = 0,1,\ldots,N-1\}$ be the pixel locations of a given (discrete) image $u : \Omega \to \{0,1,\ldots,255\}$ of size $|\Omega| = N \times N$. A fuzzy partition with the Ruspini condition (also known as *Ruspini partition*) was introduced by [12].

Definition 1. *Let* $x_1 < x_2 < \ldots < x_n$, $n \leq 2$ *be node points in* $[a,b]$ *such that* $x_1 = a$, $x_n = b$. *The collection of fuzzy sets* $A_1, A_2, \ldots, A_n$ *satisfies a Ruspini partition on* $[a,b]$ *if they satisfy the following conditions for* $k = 1,\ldots,n$:

1. $A_k : [a,b] \to [0,1]$, $A_k(x_k) = 1$;
2. $A_k(x) = 0$ *if* $x \notin (x_{k-1}, x_{k+1})$, *with* $x_0 = a$ *and* $x_{n+1} = b$;
3. $A_k(\cdot)$ *is continuous*
4. $A_k(x)$ *strictly increases on* $[x_{k-1}, x_k]$ *for* $k = 2,\ldots,n$ *and strictly decreases on* $[x_k, x_{k=1}]$ *for* $k = 1,\ldots,n-1$;
5. $\sum_{k=1}^{n} A_k(x) = 1$, *for all* $x \in [a,b]$.

Remark 1. Note that a fuzzy set on X is usually identified with the membership function, a mapping between X to $[0,1]$. The requirement in 5 is known as the Ruspini condition and is a fuzzy partition-of-unity.

The basic functions are membership functions $A_1, \ldots, A_n$ defined on $[a, b]$. The shape of the basic functions is crucial and can be chosen according to the problem at hand. We recall the following definition which is required in what follows.

Definition 2. *A Ruspini partition of $[a, b]$ is h-uniform if its node points $x_1, \ldots, x_n$, $n \geq 3$ are h-equidistant. That is,*

$$x_k = a + h(k - 1) \quad for \quad k = 1, \ldots, n$$

where

$$h = \frac{b - a}{n - 1}$$

and it satisfies the extra conditions

6. $A_k(x_k - x) = A_k(x_k + x)$, *for all $x \in [0, h]$, $k = 2, \ldots, n - 1$*
7. $A_k(x) = A_{k-1}(x - h)$, *for all $k = 2, \ldots, n - 1$ and $x \in [x_k, x_{k+1}]$, and $A_{k+1}(x) = A_k(x - h)$, for all $k = 2, \ldots, n - 1$ and $x \in [x_k, x_{k+1}]$.*

The advantage of a h-uniform fuzzy partition of $[a, b]$ is that it can be generated by $A_0 : [-1, 1] \to [0, 1]$, an even, continuous bell shape function with $A_0(0) = 1$. That is, we can generate the basic functions A_k $(k = 1, \ldots, n)$ from A_0 as follows:

$$A_1(x) = \begin{cases} A_0\left(\frac{x - x_1}{h}\right), & x \in [x_1, x_2], \\ 0, & \text{otherwise,} \end{cases} \qquad A_n(x) = \begin{cases} A_0\left(\frac{x - x_n}{h}\right), & x \in [x_{n-1}, x_n], \\ 0, & \text{otherwise.} \end{cases}$$

and for $k = 2, \ldots, n - 1$,

$$A_k(x) = \begin{cases} A_0\left(\frac{x - x_k}{h}\right), & x \in [x_{k-1}, x_{k+1}], \\ 0, & \text{otherwise.} \end{cases}$$

For example, the function $A_0(x) = 1 - |x|$ is a generating function for h-uniform triangular partition.

Remark 2. A point $x \in [a, b]$ is covered if $A_k(x) > 0$ for a basic function A_k and h is the radius of partition.

We apply the discrete F-transform to 2-D digital images (gray-scale) for the purpose of image inpainting applications. We next briefly outline the F-transform based method for inpainting and use a multi-step approach [13] along with non-local means [15] based patch information in our modification.

2.1   Modified F-Transform for Inpainting

The discrete F-transform of an image u with respect to two sets of basic functions $\{A_1, \ldots, A_n\}$, $\{B_1, \ldots, B_m\}$ is given by,

$$U_{kl} = \frac{\sum_{j=1}^m \sum_{i=1}^n f(p_i, p_j) A_k(p_i) B_l(q_j)}{\sum_{j=1}^m \sum_{i=1}^n A_k(p_i) B_l(q_j)}, \quad k = 1, \ldots, n, \quad l = 1, \ldots, m. \quad (1)$$

The set $\{U_{kl}\}$ contains the components of the F-transform. The inverse F-transform $\hat{u} : \Omega \to [0,1]$ of the image function u with respect to two sets basic functions $\{A_1, \ldots, A_n\}$, $\{B_1, \ldots, B_m\}$ is given by,

$$\hat{u}(i,j) = \sum_{j=1}^{m} \sum_{i=1}^{n} U_{kl} A_k(i) B_l(j). \tag{2}$$

It has been proved in [12] that the inverse F-transform function $\hat{u}$ can be made to approximate the original function u with better precision and depending upon the radius h of the fuzzy partition.

For inpainting the missing pixels, we can utilize the precision control of the discrete inverse F-transform. Let us assume that the image domain is the union of known (pixel information *available* Ω^a) and unknown (pixel information *corrupted* Ω^c) regions:

$$\Omega = \Omega^c \cup \Omega^a. \tag{3}$$

We further assume that the h-uniform fuzzy partition $\{A_1, \ldots, A_n\}$, $\{B_1, \ldots, B_m\}$ of the image domain Ω satisfies the following *least support condition* which guarantees the covering of corrupted pixel by basic functions which cover at least one available pixel.

Definition 3. *For $x = (i,j) \in \Omega^c$ (corrupted pixel) there exists basis functions A_k, B_l and $\tilde{x} = (i',j') \in \Omega^a$ in the available region such that*

$$A_k(i) > 0, A_k(i') > 0, B_l(j) > 0, B_l(j') > 0$$

The following steps are then followed to obtain the pixel values of corrupted pixels using the discrete inverse F-transform based on h-uniform fuzzy partitions.

Step 1: For h_0 a small value, chose a fuzzy partition of the image domain Ω

Step 2: Compute discrete inverse F-transform Eqn. (2) $\hat{u}$ of the given image u

Step 3: For pixels in the corrupted image region Ω^c, replace the intensity values by the value of its inverse F-transform image $\hat{u}$, that is

$$u(i,j) = \begin{cases} u(i,i), & \text{if } (i,j) \in \Omega^a \\ \hat{u}(i,j), & \text{if } (i,j) \in \Omega^c. \end{cases}$$

Step 4: Repeat steps **1,2** and **3** for a bigger $\tilde{h}_i$ ($> h_{i-1}$), for $i = 1, 2, \ldots$ by overwriting the pixels in corrupted domain Ω^c until $\Omega^c = \emptyset$.

Note that the above reconstruction depends on the the generating function A_0 of the h-unifrom fuzzy partition of the image domain and we chose triangular shaped basic functions. These satisfy the Ruspini condition (see Definition 2) and are given as follows:

$$A_1(x) = \begin{cases} 1 - \dfrac{(x - x_1)}{h_1}, & x \in [x_1, x_2], \\ 0, & \text{otherwise,} \end{cases} \quad A_n(x) = \begin{cases} \dfrac{(x - x_{n-1})}{h_{n-1}}, & x \in [x_{n-1}, x_n], \\ 0, & \text{otherwise.} \end{cases} \tag{4}$$

and for $k = 2, \ldots, n - 1$, $h_k = x_{K+1} - x_k$,

$$A_k(x) = \begin{cases} \dfrac{(x - x_{k-1})}{h_{k-1}}, & x \in [x_{k-1}, x_{k+1}], \\ 1 - \dfrac{(x - x_k)}{h_k}, & x \in [x_k, x_{k+1}], \\ 0, & \text{otherwise.} \end{cases} \tag{5}$$

2.2   Weights from Local Variance of Patches

Following the success we obtained in image restoration [9,14] with adaptive weights, we propose to use local information from patches extracted from the available pixels covered by the basic functions utilized in F-transform, see Definition 3. That is, we extract a $\omega \times \omega$ sized patch $\mathcal{P}_\omega(x)$ at a pixel $x \in \Omega^a$ covered by the h-uniform fuzzy partition $\{A_1, \ldots, A_n\}, \{B_1, \ldots, B_m\}$ of the image domain Ω. Next we compute the local variance from $x \in \Omega^a$,

$$\mathcal{V}_\omega(x) = \frac{1}{|\mathcal{P}_\omega(x)|} \sum_{y \in \mathcal{P}_\omega(x)} (u(x) - m_r(x)) \tag{6}$$

where $m_r(x)$ is the mean value in the patch $\mathcal{P}_\omega(x)$. We normalize the local variance $\mathcal{V}_\omega$ by its maximum and minimum values and use it in a sigmoid function for the weights,

$$W(x) = \exp\left(-\frac{1}{\delta}\mathcal{V}_\omega(x)\right) \tag{7}$$

where $\delta > 0$ controls the extent of variance induced discontinuities (edges) in the local patch $\mathcal{P}_\omega(x)$, see Fig. 1 for an illustration of the weights as edge maps. The weights are used in the components of the F-transform (1) for their corresponding basic functions $\{A_1, \ldots, A_n\}, \{B_1, \ldots, B_m\}$. This increases the inpainting accuracy as we utilize the local variance around known pixels to unknown pixel values, experimental results indicate the addition of weights in the F-transform improves the accuracy. In what follows, we call this local variance weights based F-transform the *modified F-transform* (MFT) and compare with different interpolation, modern inpainting approaches [2,6], along with the original F-transform based inpainting method [13].

Remark 3. Note that although the weights (6) are computed from the non-corrupted pixels $x \in \Omega^a$, the patch may contain corrupted pixels in the neighborhood. We use zero in those places and compute the local variance.

(a) Original

(b) Weights

Fig. 1. Local variance based weights indicate salient edges in an image. (a) Original gray scale *Lena* image of size 512×512 used in our experiments. (b) Pixel-wise weight map shown in $[0, 1]$ for visualization.

3 Experimental Results

3.1 Setup and Parameters

We use the triangle shaped functions in (4-5) the h-uniform fuzzy partition based inpainting method, see Sect. 2.1. We start with $h = 1$ and increase by one until the criteria that the corrupted pixel region Ω^c is empty. We found that for small scratches and text superimposed on images $h = 4$ is the maximum radius and beyond which the inpainting domain Ω^c becomes empty. The patch size $\omega = 9$, see Sect. 2.2, is set for the experiments reported here and higher values for the patch sizes decrease the performance of our inpainting method since the local

 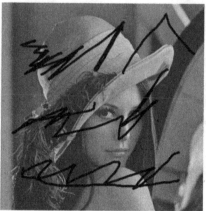

(a) 'scratch'

Lorem ipsum dolor sit amet, co auctor mauris in sapien eleifenc dum semper. Nullam ut ante eri stas in, eleifend eget dolor. Ves is tempor augue varius id. Maur uisque pharetra, metus at lacini , vitae consequat massa odio p e penatibus et magnis dis partu aecenas non quam tellus. Fusc m non, rhoncus at enim. Donec ue sit amet, luctus sed velit. Prc retium velit gravida.

(b) 'text'

Fig. 2. Test masks (left) and corrupted images (right) for 'scratch' and 'text' of size 512×512 used in our experiments.

variance is low for larger patch sizes. Since we assume the non-corrupted regions are noise free the $\delta = 1$ in (6) is set, see [14] for more details.

3.2 Comparison Results

We compare our method to the classical interpolation methods: (a) nearest neighbor and (b) bilinear interpolation. Further, the modern inpainting methods of (a) Telea's fast marching approach [6] and (b) Navier-Stokes [2] method and (c) original F-transform [13]. We test two types of damages, namely 'scratch' and 'text' superimposition, see Fig. 2 which shows the corresponding masks of the inpainting domain Ω^c which needs to be filled in using the information available from nearby image regions.

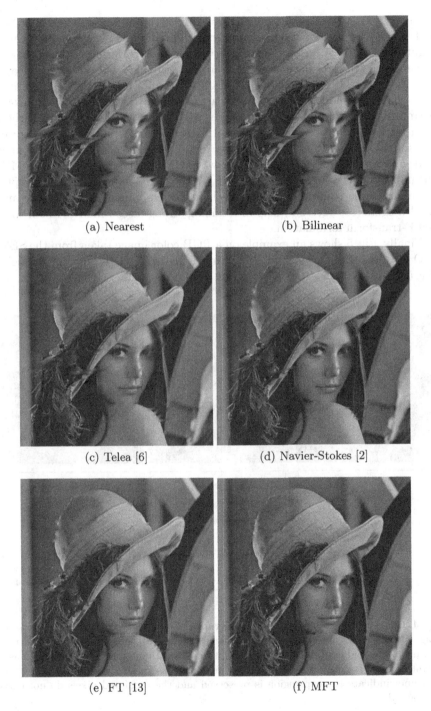

(a) Nearest

(b) Bilinear

(c) Telea [6]

(d) Navier-Stokes [2]

(e) FT [13]

(f) MFT

Fig. 3. Our modified F-transform performs well in removing the damage caused by 'scratch' on *Lena* image of size 512×512.

Figure 3 shows restorations of *Lena* image corrupted by scratches (Fig. 2(a) right image) by various schemes. Interpolations methods such as the nearest neighbor (Fig. 3(a)) and bilinear (Fig. 3(b)) methods perform poorly as they do not use localized information available in the available image regions. Telea [6] (Fig. 3(c)) and the Navier-Stokes [2] (Fig. 3(d)) perform better than traditional interpolation methods but still contain artifacts near image edges due to excessive diffusion. In comparison, our proposed MFT (Fig. 3(f) performs well without artifacts when compared to the original F-transform method (Fig. 3). Figure 4 shows a close-up of the cap region (top row) and corresponding contour maps (bottom row) for restorations results with FT [13] and our proposed MFT schemes. Similar results were observed for the 'text' superimposed corrupted image and these results indicate that the edges computed with local variance based weights (see Sect. 2.2) help in retaining strong discontinuities in our modified F-transform formulation.

Finally, Fig. 5 shows an example on a RGB color image taken from the SEM-CCO 2014 conference website[1]. We marked the mask of the inpainting region (Fig. 5(b)) and the modified F-transform (Fig. 5(c)) is run on the gray-scale ver-

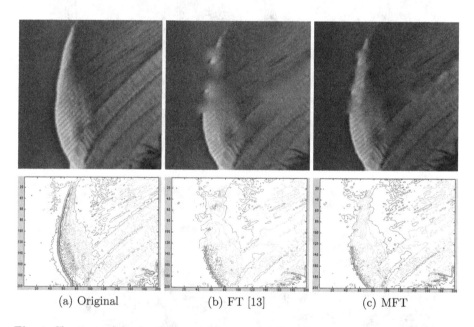

    (a) Original   (b) FT [13]   (c) MFT

Fig. 4. Close-up results for the 'scratch' corrupted *Lena* image cap region. (a) Original image (b) FT [13], and (c) Our MFT scheme results. Top row: Images Bottom row: Contour maps highlighting the level lines (isophotes). Due to the local variance based weighting edge regions are well-preserved in the reconstruction with our scheme. The level lines indicate the cap region is preserved and the inpainted pixels do not carry over outside.

---

[1] http://semcco2014.org/.

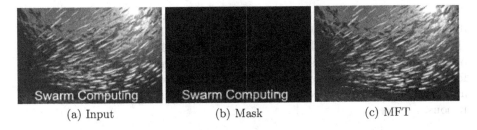

(a) Input   (b) Mask   (c) MFT

Fig. 5. Inpainting result on a RGB color image of size 183×118 taken from the semcco website. (a) Input image with 'text' superimposed on top (b) Mask has the words 'Swarm Computing' (c) Our MFT scheme inpainting result. Better viewed online and zoomed in.

Table 1. RMSE and MSSIM comparison for different schemes for the reconstruction of the *Lena* image. Corrupted images were obtained by adding 'scratch' and 'text' masks to the original image, see Fig. 2. Best results are in **boldface** and second-best underlined.

Corruption	Nearest	Bilinear	Telea [6]	Navier-Stokes [2]	FT [13]	MFT
'scratch'	7.402	6.429	6.096	<u>6.047</u>	6.173	**6.008**
	0.9853	0.9887	0.9896	<u>0.9898</u>	0.9894	**0.9910**
'text'	7.666	7.107	6.576	<u>6.367</u>	6.692	**6.323**
	0.9840	0.9862	0.9878	<u>0.9884</u>	0.9873	**0.9921**

sion of the original image. The MFT result obtains a good inpainting result overall and the small artifacts, around where the word "Swarm" was, are due to the lack of incorporation of chromatic edges information. We believe incorporating spectral information as in denoising [16], and segmentation methods [17–19] will avoid such color mix-up.

To compare the methods quantatively, we utilize the root mean squared error (RMSE) and structural similarity (SSIM) of Wang et al [20]. Note that lower RMSE (closer to 0) and higher SSIM (closer to 1) indicate better reconstructions. Table 1 shows that the RMSE and mean SSIM (MSSIM, taken over each image) values for our scheme is better than other inpainting methods for the reconstruction of different corrupted images.

4   Conclusions

Image inpainting with a modified F-transform is considered here. By using Rubpini's conditions we used the least support condition along with a weights computed from known image region local variances. Application to images damaged by text super-imposition and scratches indicate we obtain good restoration results with modified F-transform method. Comparison with other inpainting techniques such as the nearest, bilinear interpolation techniques, along with modern inpainting models of Telea's fast marching method and Navier-Stokes diffusion based scheme show we obtain improved results for different inpainting challenges. We are currently evaluating our modified F-transform method for other damages such as 'noise' and 'holes' and nonlocal patch similarity metrics for improved weights computation. Further, we plan to investigate the proposed approach on a larger collection of images with ground-truth available image regions.

Acknowledgments. This work was done while the first author was visiting Institute for Pure and Applied Mathematics (IPAM), University of California Los Angeles (UCLA), USA. The first author thanks the IPAM institute for their great hospitality and support during the visit.

References

1. Bertalmio, M., Sapiro, G., Caselles, V., Ballester, C.: Image inpainting. In: Proceedings of the 27th Annual Conference on Computer Graphics and Interactive Techniques, pp. 417–424. ACM Press/Addison-Wesley Publishing Co. (2000)
2. Bertalmio, M., Bertozzi, A.L., Sapiro, G.: Navier-stokes, fluid dynamics, and image and video inpainting. Proceedings of the IEEE Computer Society Conference on Computer Vision and Pattern Recognition (CVPR). **1**, 355–362 (2001)
3. Prasath, V.B.S., Moreno, J.C.: Feature preserving anisotropic diffusion for image restoration. In: Fourth National Conference on Computer Vision, Pattern Recognition, Image Processing and Graphics (NCVPRIPG 2013), India, pp. 1–4, December 2013
4. Sapiro, G.: Inpainting the colors. In: IEEE International Conference on Image Processing (ICIP), vol. II, pp. 698–701, September 2005
5. Criminisi, A., Pérez, P., Toyama, K.: Region filling and object removal by exemplar-based image inpainting. IEEE Trans. Image Process. **13**(9), 1200–1212 (2004)
6. Telea, A.: An image inpainting technique based on the fast marching method. J. Graph. Tools **9**(1), 23–34 (2004)
7. Sethian, J.A.: Level Set Methods: Evolving Interfaces in Geometry, Fluid Mechanics, Computer Vision and Materials Sciences. Cambridge University Press, Cambridge (1996)
8. Prasath, V.B.S., Singh, A.: Well-posed inhomogeneous nonlinear diffusion scheme for digital image denoising. J. Appl. Math. 2010, p. 14 Article ID 763847 (2010)
9. Prasath, V.B.S., Singh, A.: An adaptive anisotropic diffusion scheme for image restoration and selective smoothing. Int. J. Image Graph. **12**(1), 18 (2012)
10. Prasath, V.B.S., Vorotnikov, D.: Weighted and well-balanced anisotropic diffusion scheme for image denoising and restoration. Nonlinear Anal. Real World Appl. **17**, 33–46 (2013)
11. Aubert, G., Kornprobst, P.: Mathematical Problems in Image Processing: Partial Differential Equation and Calculus of Variations. Springer, New York (2006)
12. Perfilieva, I.: Fuzzy transforms: theory and applications. Fuzzy Sets Syst. **157**, 993–1023 (2006)
13. Perfilieva, I., Vlasanek, P.: Image reconstruction by means of F-transform. Knowledge-Based Systems, pp. 9 (2014, in press)

14. Prasath, V.B.S.: A well-posed multiscale regularization scheme for digital image denoising. Int. J. Appl. Math. Comput. Sci. **21**(4), 769–777 (2011)
15. Buades, A., Coll, B., Morel, J.M.: A review of image denoising methods, with a new one. Multiscale Model. Simul. **4**(2), 490–530 (2006)
16. Prasath, V.B.S., Singh, A.: Multispectral image denoising by well-posed anisotropic diffusion scheme with channel coupling. Int. J. Remote Sens. **31**(8), 2091–2099 (2010)
17. Prasath, V.B.S.: Color image segmentation based on vectorial multiscale diffusion with inter-scale linking. In: Chaudhury, S., Mitra, S., Murthy, C.A., Sastry, P.S., Pal, S.K. (eds.) PReMI 2009. LNCS, vol. 5909, pp. 339–344. Springer, Heidelberg (2009)
18. Prasath, V.B.S., Palaniappan, K., Seetharaman, G.: Multichannel texture image segmentation using weighted feature fitting based variational active contours. In: Eighth Indian Conference on Vision, Graphics and Image Processing (ICVGIP), Mumbai, Indi, p. 6, December 2012
19. Prasath, V.B.S., Moreno, J.C., Palaniappan, K.: Color image denoising by chromatic edges based vector valued diffusion. Technical report. ArXiv (2013)
20. Wang, Z., Bovik, A.C., Sheikh, H.R., Simoncelli, E.P.: Image quality assessment: from error visibility to structural similarity. IEEE Trans. Image Process. **13**(4), 600–612 (2004)

Improved ADALINE Based Algorithm for Power System Frequency Estimation

S. Nanda[1], S. Hasan[2]($\boxtimes$), B.K. Swain[2], and P.K. Dash[2]

[1] KIIT University Bhubaneswar, Bhubaneswar, India
[2] S'O'A University, Bhubaneswar, Bhubaneswar, India
shaziahasan@soauniversity.ac.in

Abstract. This paper intends to present an adaptive algorithm for estimating the frequency, amplitude, and phase of a sinusoid under non stationary condition present in time-varying power signals. The proposed algorithm estimates precisely the frequency variation, phase variation, and the amplitude and shows accuracy in estimation even in the presence of harmonic and inter harmonic as noise. This method uses Taylor series expansion of the signal to cope with the sudden changes. Then a modified ADALINE is used because of its low computational complexity, for which it can be implemented in real time. The performance of the proposed algorithm has been extensively tested and demonstrated.

Keywords: Taylor series expansion · ADALINE · Amplitude and phase estimation · Frequency estimation

1 Introduction

Presently, amplitude, phase and frequency estimation of sinusoidal signal parameters of a non stationery sinusoidal signal buried in noise is relevant to a wide range of applications like in digital communications, dynamical system identification, biomedical engineering, radar, monitoring, protection and control etc. and therefore this is still a very significant and promising research area. Many techniques have been developed in literature to track the parameters of a sinusoidal signal which are based on conventional signal processing techniques like, "Least mean square technique(LMS)" [1], "Recursive least square(RLS)" [2], "Kalman filter" [3], "Adaptive Notch filters" [4], "Phase-lock-loop based techniques" [5], 'Fourier algorithm" [6, 7] etc. Fourier algorithm can handle stationary sinusoidal signal however, it fails to handle signals under dynamic conditions. Because of the simplicity in structure and function- fitting ability of Neural methods [8, 9] they are used in tracking of fundamental frequency components as well as the harmonic components of a sinusoidal signal but they fail when the signal is dynamic in nature. Even the result detoriates more in case of deviation noticed in fundamental frequency and the presence of inter harmonics. A simple conventional adaptive linear element (ADALINE) can be a better choice to track all frequency components of power signals accurately. However, it lacks the capability to detect the harmonics and inter harmonics accurately.

© Springer International Publishing Switzerland 2015
B.K. Panigrahi et al. (Eds.): SEMCCO 2014, LNCS 8947, pp. 868–877, 2015.
DOI: 10.1007/978-3-319-20294-5_74

This paper presents a modified Adaline based approach using Taylor series expansion and a tuned least square algorithm for estimation and tracking of signal parameters. This approach also shows excellent performance for non stationery sinusoidal signals with dynamic variations. This method has also been tested for signals with sudden changes, under noisy conditions and also in the presence of harmonics. The paper is organized as follows; Sect. 2 presents the signal model and the analysis of the proposed method for amplitude, phase and frequency estimation. In Sect. 3 a different modified approach is presented. Section 4 covers the performance through simulations along with a comparison with other techniques. Section 5 deals with the conclusion.

2 Problem Formulation

Let us assume, a time- varying sinusoidal signal in discrete form as:

$$y(k) = a(k). \cos[k\omega(k) + \phi(k)] + g(k) \tag{1}$$

Where, $a(k), \omega(k)$ and $\phi(k)$ are "the amplitude", "angular frequency" and "phase" of the sinusoid respectively.

$\omega(k) = 2\pi f(k)$ and $f(k)$ is the fundamental frequency of the signal, while $g(k)$ is an additive white noise with unknown variance σ_g^2. Let us designate $\theta(k) = 2\pi f k + \phi(k)$. The rate of change of phase angle is equal to frequency so the signal frequency can be represented as [8]:

$$f = \frac{1}{2\pi} \frac{d}{dt}(\theta(k)) = f_0 + \frac{1}{2\pi} \frac{d}{dt}(\phi(k)) \tag{2}$$

Let us rewrite the Eq. (1) according to trigonometric function as

$$y(k) = c_p(k). \cos(2\pi f(k)) - s_q. \sin(2\pi f(k)) \tag{3}$$

Where $c_p(k) = a(k). \cos \phi(k)$ and $s_q(k) = a(k). \sin \phi(k)$.

$c_p(k)$ and $s_q(k)$ are the coefficients functions that expresses the envelope of the steadily changing sinusoid. Using Taylor series the coefficient functions can be expanded as follows-

$$c_p(k) \cong p_0 + p_1 k + p_2 k^2 + p_3 k^3 \text{ and } s_q(k) = q_0 + q_1 k + q_2 k^2 + q_3 k^3 \tag{4}$$

Where $p_0 = c_p(0)$, $p_1 = \frac{dc_p(k)}{dt}$ at k = 0, $p_2 = \frac{d^2 c_p(k)}{dt^2}$ at k = 0 and $p_3 = \frac{d^3 c_p(k)}{dt^3}$ at k = 0. $q_0 = s_q(0)$, $s_1 = \frac{ds_q(k)}{dt}$ at k = 0, $q_2 = \frac{d^2 s_q(k)}{dt^2}$ at k = 0 and $q_3 = \frac{d^3 s_q(k)}{dt^3}$ at k = 0.

Now we can obtain the amplitude and phase angle of the described given sinusoid using Eqs. (3) and (4) as follows at k = 0:

$$A_{\text{ESTIMATED}} = \sqrt{p_0^2 + q_0^2} \tag{5}$$

and

$$\phi_{\text{ESTIMATED}} = \arctan(q_0/p_0) \tag{6}$$

where

$$p_0 = a(0).\cos\phi(0), \quad q_0 = a(0).\sin\phi(0) \tag{7}$$

Similarly for estimating the frequency of the given sinusoid, consider Eq. (4) at $k = 0$ the first derivative will be

$$p_1 = \frac{d}{dt}(a(0).\cos\phi(0)) \tag{8}$$

$$q_1 = \frac{d}{dt}(a(0).\sin\phi(0)) \tag{9}$$

By substituting Eq. (7) in Eqs. (8) and (9) and by neglecting

$$\frac{d}{dt}(a(0)):$$
$$\frac{d}{dt}(\phi(0)) = \frac{p_0 q_1 - q_0 p_1}{p_0^2 + q_0^2} \tag{10}$$

Now from Eqs. (2) and (10) we get the formula for computing the frequency:

$$f = f_0. + \frac{1}{2\pi}\left(\frac{p_0 q_1 - q_0 p_1}{p_0^2 + q_0^2}\right) \tag{11}$$

Let us discuss how to estimate the coefficients of the Taylor series expansion by using a Adaline method.

In this regard, let the signal be represented as:

$$z(k) = A(k)\cos(2\pi f_0 k dt + \phi(k)) \tag{12}$$

After Taylor series expansion we can represent the signal as:

$$z(k) = (p_0 + p_1 k + p_2 k^2).\cos(2\pi f_0 k) - (q_0 + q_1 k + q_2 k^2).\sin(2\pi f_0 k) \tag{13}$$

For representing the signal in Adaline structure we arrange Eq. (12) in two vectors i.e. the weight vector w(k) and the input vector I(k).

$$w(k) = [p_0 \ p_1 \ p_2 \ q_0 \ q_1 \ q_2] \tag{14}$$

And the sampled input vector is given as:

$$I(k) = [\cos(2\pi f_0 kdt) \ kdt \cos(2\pi f_0 kdt) \ (kdt)^2 \cos(2\pi f_0 kdt) \ -\sin(2\pi f 0 kdt)$$
$$-kdt \sin(2\pi f_0 kdt) \ (kdt)^2 \sin(2\pi f_0 kdt)] \tag{15}$$

Now the Adaline structure can be represented as

$$z(k) = w(k)I^T(k) \tag{16}$$

The error signal which is used for updating the weights can be calculated as

$$e(k) = z(k) - w(k)I^T(k) \tag{17}$$

First approach used for minimizing the error is given as [1]

$$w(k+1) = w(k) + \eta \tanh(0.5 * e(k)) * I(k)/I(k) * I^T(k) \tag{18}$$

Where η is the learning parameter which determines the rate of convergence. So by using Eq. (18) the weights are updated as follows:

$$\left. \begin{aligned} p_0(k+1) &= p_0(k) + \eta \tanh(0.5 * e(k)) \cos(2\pi f_0 kdt) \ / \ \cos^2(2\pi f_0 kdt) \\ p_1(k+1) &= p_1(k) + \eta \tanh(0.5 * e(k)) \cos(2\pi f_0 kdt) \ / \ kdt \cos^2(2\pi f_0 kdt) \\ p_2(k+1) &= p_2(k) + \eta \tanh(0.5 * e(k)) \cos(2\pi f_0 kdt) \ /(kdt)^2 \cos^2(2\pi f_0 kdt) \\ q_0(k+1) &= q_0(k) + \eta \tanh(0.5 * e(k)(-\sin(2\pi f_0 kdt)) \ / \ \sin^2(2\pi f_0 kdt) \\ q_1(k+1) &= q_1(k) + \eta \tanh(0.5 * e(k)(-\sin(2\pi f_0 kdt)) \ / kdt \sin^2(2\pi f_0 kdt) \\ q_2(k+1) &= q_2(k) + \eta \tanh(0.5 * e(k))(-\sin(2\pi f_0 kdt)) \ / \ (kdt)^2 \sin^2(2\pi f_0 kdt) \end{aligned} \right\} \tag{19}$$

By using Eq. (19) the weights are updated thereby reducing the error(k) and then these weights are used for tracking amplitude, phase and frequency of the sinusoidal signal by using the Eqs. (5,6,11).

3 Modified Approach

For faster convergence and to make the learning parameter adaptive another approach [9] has also been used in this paper given as:

$$w(k+1) = \tau(k) * w(k) + \eta(k) * e(k) * I(k)/I(k) * I^T(k) \tag{20}$$

where $\tau(k) = e^{\eta(k)}$ and the learning rate η is given as

$$\eta(k) = \alpha * a\tan(\delta * abs(e(k) * e(k-1))). + \beta * \eta(k-1) \tag{21}$$

where α, δ and β are parameters which help in tuning.

Hence in this approach using Eq. (20) the weights are updated as follows:

$$\left.\begin{aligned}
p_0(k+1) &= \tau(k) * p_0(k) + \eta(k) * e(k) * \cos(2\pi f_0 kdt) \,/\, \cos^2(2\pi f_0 kdt) \\
p_2(k+1) &= \tau(k) * p_2(k) + \eta(k) * e(k) * \cos(2\pi f_0 kdt) \,/\, (kdt)^2 \cos^2(2\pi f_0 kdt) \\
p_1(k+1) &= \tau(k) * p_1(k) + \eta(k) * e(k) * \cos(2\pi f_0 kdt) \,/\, (kdt)\cos^2(2\pi f_0 kdt) \\
q_0(k+1) &= \tau(k) * q_0(k) + \eta(k) * e(k) * (-\sin(2\pi f_0 kdt)) \,/\, \sin^2(2\pi f_0 kdt) \\
q_1(k+1) &= \tau(k)q_1(k) + \eta(k) * e(k)(-\sin(2\pi f_0 kdt)) \,/\, (kdt)\sin^2(2\pi f_0 kdt) \\
q_2(k+1) &= \tau(k)q_2(k) + \eta(k) * e(k) * (-\sin(2\pi f_0 kdt)) \,/\, (kdt)^2 \sin^2(2\pi f_0 kdt)
\end{aligned}\right\} \tag{22}$$

Now these weights which are obtained from Eq. (22) can be used for estimating the amplitude,phase and frequency of the sinusoidal signal. This method shows better results in respect to noise sensitivity while estimating the parameters of a nonstationery sinusoidal signal which has been demonstrated in the succeeding sections.

4   Simulation Studies

Numerous examples have been tested to evaluate the performance of the above described approaches. The test signals represent various operating conditions like noise, damping oscillations, harmonics etc. The test signal is sampled at rate of 5 kHz for all the cases that has been considered. The results obtained by using the two approaches described in Sect. 2 are also compared with IFM method (Improved Fourier method) [10].

CASE1: Noise Rejection Ability. The test signal considered for this case is

$$y(k) = a(k).\cos[2\pi f_0 t + \phi(k)] + g(k). \tag{23}$$

which is super imposed with zero mean Gaussian noise $g(k)$. Here $a = 1.44$ p.u, f0 = 50 Hz, and $\phi(k) = 0.6$ rad.This signal is tested under 20db,30db and 40 dB noise conditions. After 100 runs the mean of the RMSE is tabulated in Table 1. The result of three approaches IFM [10], Adaline [8] and proposed method have been summarized in Table 1. From this table we can conclude that the Modified Adaline approach shows better noise rejection capabilities compared to other algorithms.

CASE II: Modulation in Amplitude and Double Step in Frequency Simultaneously. In this case the test signal considered is

$$y(k) = 1.2 + a\bmod(k).\cos[2\pi f_0 t + \phi(k)]$$
$$a\bmod(k) = 0.1 * \cos(2\pi 5t) + 0.05 * \cos(18\pi t). \tag{24}$$

Table 1. RMSE values

Property	IFM			ADALINE			MODIFIED ADALINE		
	20 dB	30 dB	40 dB	20 dB	30 dB	40 dB	20 dB	30 dB	40 dB
AMPLITUDE	.2100	.1223	.0476	.0676	.0510	.0473	.0592	.0507	.0026
FREQUENCY.	.0523	.0348	.0125	.0510	.0426	.0211	.0108	.0202	.0100
PHASE.	.0887	.0843	.0544	.0922	.0781	.0735	.0426	.0254	.0139

The amplitude of the signal is modulated using the equation given above. In this case the frequency undergoes a step up of 1 Hz after 500 samples and again undergoes a step down of 1 Hz after 200 samples and restores its original value i.e. 60 Hz. The signal is corrupted with 30 dB noise. The superior performance of the proposed algorithm can be seen from Figs. 1 and 2.

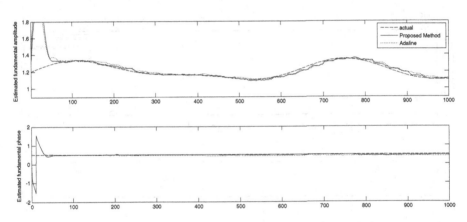

Fig. 1. Modulated fundamental amplitude and fundamental phase

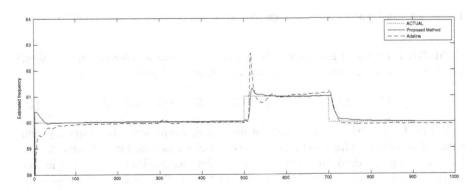

Fig. 2. Double step frequency

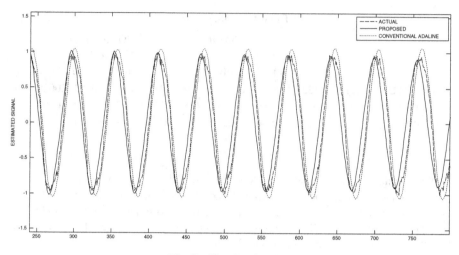

Fig. 3. Signal estimation

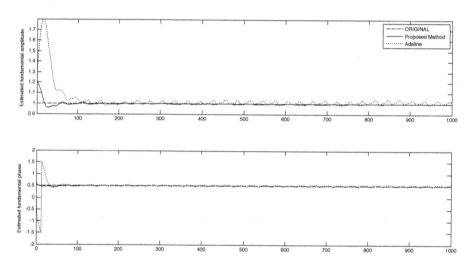

Fig. 4. Estimated fundamental amplitude ad fundamental phase in the presence of harmonics.

CASE III: Presence of Harmonics as Noise. In this case we consider the test signal which consists of different order of harmonics which is expressed as

$$y(k) = A(k) \cos(2\pi f_0 kdt + \phi(k)) + A_r(k) \cos(2\pi f_r kdt + \phi_r(k)) \tag{25}$$

Where A represents the amplitude of the signal, f represents the frequency component ϕ denotes the phase and r shows the order of harmonics. Let us assume that we have superimposed third, fifth, seventh and eleventh harmonics to our test signal and set their magnitudes to (33 %,25 %,16 % and 12 %). The corresponding results are shown in Figs. 3, 4 and 5 and the estimation error are listed in Table 2. From the results

Table 2. Estimation errors in harmonic contamination

Harmonics	Amplitude estimation error			Frequency estimation error			Phase estimation error		
	IFM	ADALINE	PROPOSED	IFM	ADALINE	PROPOSED	IFM	ADALINE	PROPOSED
3rd	.00412	.0064	.0011	.0011	.0042	.0001	.0520	.0511	.0231
5th	.00533	.0055	.0023	.0023	.0045	.0012	.0733	.0566	.0433
7th	.0065	.0075	.0041	.0030	.0043	.0026	.0745	.0632	.0559
11th	.0088	.0082	.0058	.0042	.0038	.0022	.0811	.0775	.0429

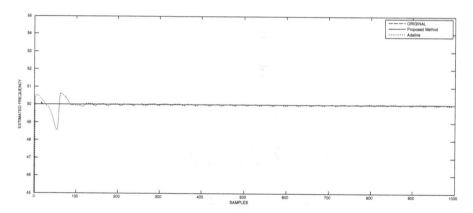

Fig. 5. Estimated fundamental frequency in the presence of harmonics

it is obvious that the proposed method performs better than the other methods even after contamination with different order harmonics. We have calculated the estimation errors by taking the mean over 0.2 s period of input signals. Moreover, the results for all the three algorithms for each harmonic contamination case are presented in Table 2 which clearly shows the superiority of the method that has been proposed.

5 Conclusion

This paper proposes an adaptive ADALINE algorithm based on Taylor series expansion of the signal for the estimation of amplitude, phase and frequency a time varying sinusoid in noise. Several case studies have been presented highlighting the noise rejection capability of the proposed algorithm, with example showing signals with sudden change in frequency, modulated signal and performance of the algorithm under different harmonic conditions. Low computational complexity of the ADALINE based algorithm makes the proposed algorithm efficient for real time implementations.

References

1. Yong-mei, S., Xiao-xia, D., Wei, Z., Yuan-yuan, K.: Novel variable step-size adaptive LMS time delay estimation algorithm with nonlinear preprocess In: 4th International Congress on Image and Signal Processing, pp. 2767–2770 (2011)
2. So, H.C.: A comparative study of three recursive least squares algorithms for single-tone frequency tracking. Signal Process. 83(9), 2059–2062 (2003)
3. Chen, C.I., Chang, G.W., Hong, R.C., Lee, H.M.: Extended real model of Kalman filter for time varying harmonics estimation. IEEE Trans. Power Deliv. 25(1), 17–26 (2010)
4. Niedzwickei, M., Kaczmarek, P.: Tracking analysis of a generalized Notch filters. IEEE Trans. Signal Process. 54(1), 304–314 (2006)
5. Karimi-Ghartemani, M., Iravani, M.R.: Measurement of harmonics /inter- harmonics of time varying frequencies. IEEE, Trans-Power Del. 20(1), 23–31 (2005)

6. Yu, C.S.: A discrete Fourier transform based adaptive mimic phasor estimator for distance relaying application. IEEE Trans. Power Deliv. **21**(4), 1836–1846 (2006)
7. Phadke, A.G., Thorp, J., Adamiak, M.: A new measurement technique for tracking voltage phasors, local system frequency and rate of change of frequency. IEEE Trans. Power App. Syst. **PAS-102**(5), 1025–1038 (1983)
8. Bose, B.K.: Neural network applications in power electronics and motor drives—an introduction and perspective. IEEE Trans. Ind. Electron. **54**(1), 14–33 (2007)
9. Bertoluzzo, M., Buja, G.S., Castellan, S., Fiorentin, P.: Neural network technique for the joint time–frequency analysis of distorted signal. IEEE Trans. Ind. Electron. **50**(6), 1109–1115 (2003)
10. Ren, J., Kezunovic, M.: An improved fourier method for power system frequency estimation. In: NorthAmerican Power Symposium (NAPS), Boston, MA, pp.1–6, 4–6 August 2011
11. Li, T.-T., Shi, M., Yi, Q.-M.: An improved variable step-size LMS algorithm. In: 7th International Conference on Wireless Communications, Networking and Mobile Computing (WiCOM), Wuhan, pp. 1–4, 23–25 September 2011

Author Index

Printed in the United States
By Bookmasters